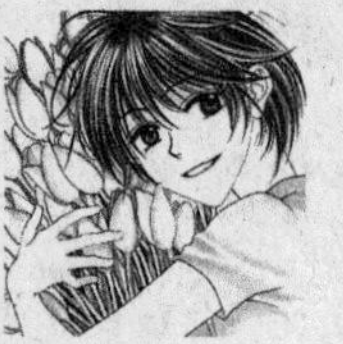

ABOUT THE AUTHOR

Hisaya Nakajo's manga series **Hanazakari no Kimitachi he** ("For You in Full Blossom," casually known as **Hana-Kimi**) has been a hit since it first appeared in 1997 in the shôjo manga magazine **Hana to Yume** ("Flowers and Dreams"). In Japan, a **Hana-Kimi** art book and several "drama CDs" have been released. Her other manga series include **Missing Piece** (2 volumes) and **Yumemiru Happa** ("The Dreaming Leaf," 1 volume).

Hisaya Nakajo's website:
www.wild-vanilla.com

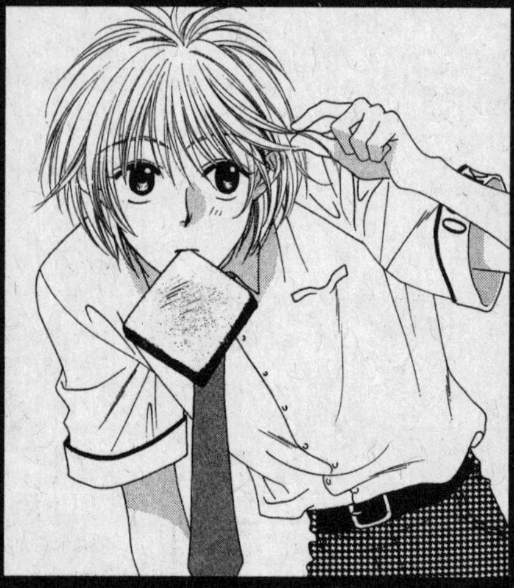

HANA-KIMI
For You in Full Blossom
3-in-1 Edition
Volume 2
A compilation of the graphic novel volumes 4-6

Story & Art by HISAYA NAKAJO

Translation ✿ **DAVID URY**
English Adaptation ✿ **GERARD JONES**
Touch-up Art & Lettering ✿ **GABE CRATE**
Additional Touch-up ✿ **WALDEN WONG** (3-in-1 Edition)
Design ✿ **IZUMI EVERS** (Graphic Novel Edition)
Design ✿ **FAWN LAU** (3-in-1 Edition)
Editor ✿ **JASON THOMPSON** (Graphic Novel Edition)
Editor ✿ **JOEL ENOS** (3-in-1 Edition)

Hanazakari no Kimitachi he by Hisaya Nakajo © Hisaya Nakajo 1996, 1997, 1998
All rights reserved. First published in Japan in 1998 by HAKUSENSHA,
Inc., Tokyo. English language translation rights arranged with
HAKUSENSHA, Inc., Tokyo.

Printed in the U.S.A.

Published by VIZ Media, LLC
P.O. Box 77010
San Francisco, CA 94107

10 9 8 7 6 5 4 3 2
3-in-1 edition first printing, May 2012
Second printing, October 2014

PARENTAL ADVISORY
HANA-KIMI is rated T+ for Older Teen and is
recommended for ages 16 and up. It may contain strong
language, sexual themes and alcohol and tobacco usage.
ratings.viz.com

www.shojobeat.com

Hana-Kimi

For You in Full Blossom

4

story and art by
HISAYA NAKAJO

CONTENTS

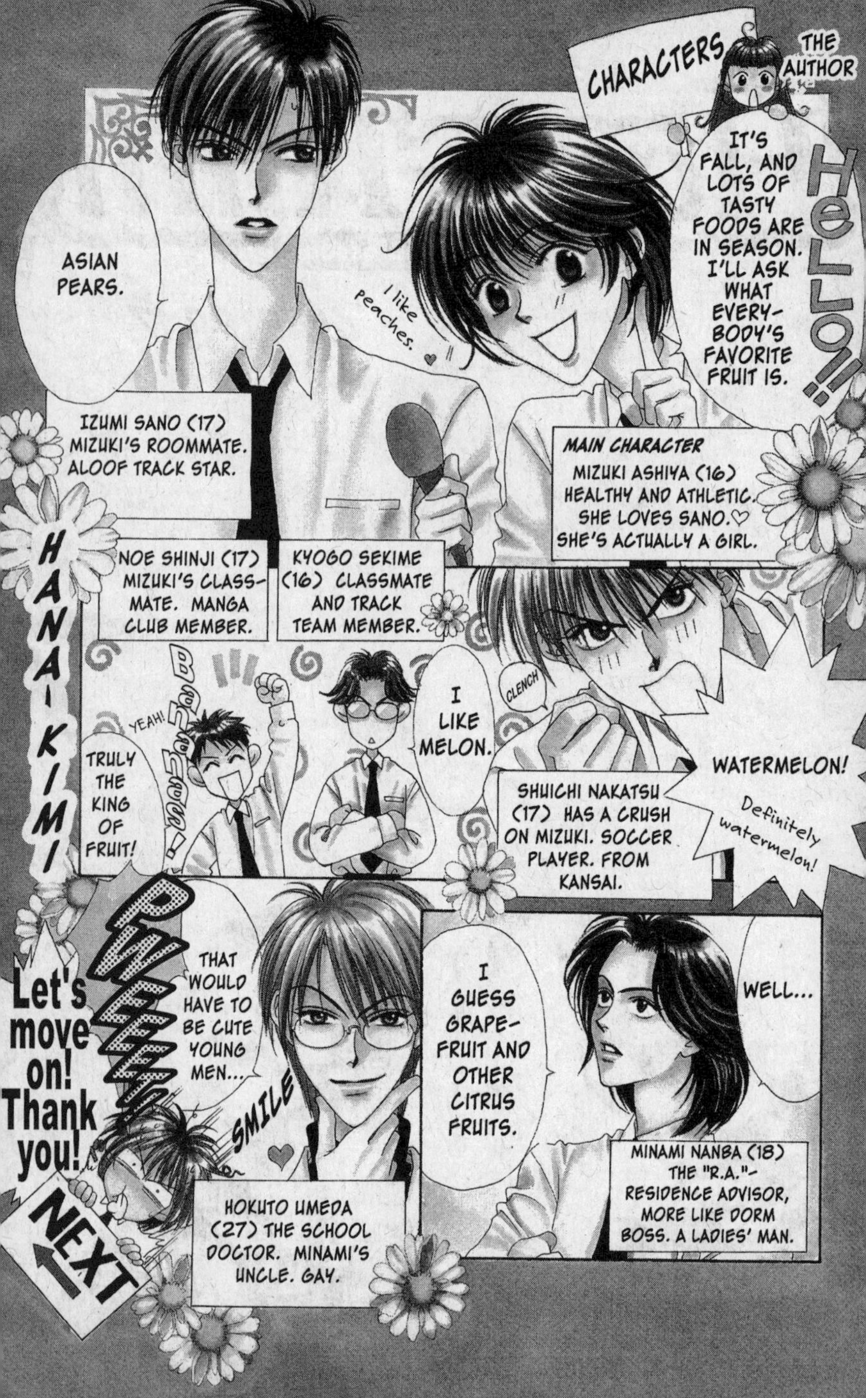

CHARACTERS
THE AUTHOR
HELLO!!
IT'S FALL, AND LOTS OF TASTY FOODS ARE IN SEASON. I'LL ASK WHAT EVERYBODY'S FAVORITE FRUIT IS.
I like peaches.
MAIN CHARACTER
MIZUKI ASHIYA (16) HEALTHY AND ATHLETIC. SHE LOVES SANO.♡ SHE'S ACTUALLY A GIRL.
ASIAN PEARS.
IZUMI SANO (17) MIZUKI'S ROOMMATE. ALOOF TRACK STAR.
KYOGO SEKIME (16) CLASSMATE AND TRACK TEAM MEMBER.
NOE SHINJI (17) MIZUKI'S CLASSMATE. MANGA CLUB MEMBER.
HANA-KIMI
CLENCH
WATERMELON!
Definitely watermelon!
SHUICHI NAKATSU (17) HAS A CRUSH ON MIZUKI. SOCCER PLAYER. FROM KANSAI.
I LIKE MELON.
YEAH!
TRULY THE KING OF FRUIT!
WELL...
I GUESS GRAPEFRUIT AND OTHER CITRUS FRUITS.
MINAMI NANBA (18) THE "R.A."- RESIDENCE ADVISOR, MORE LIKE DORM BOSS. A LADIES' MAN.
THAT WOULD HAVE TO BE CUTE YOUNG MEN...
SMILE
HOKUTO UMEDA (27) THE SCHOOL DOCTOR. MINAMI'S UNCLE. GAY.
Let's move on! Thank you!
NEXT

Hana-Kimi

For You in Full Blossom

CHAPTER 17

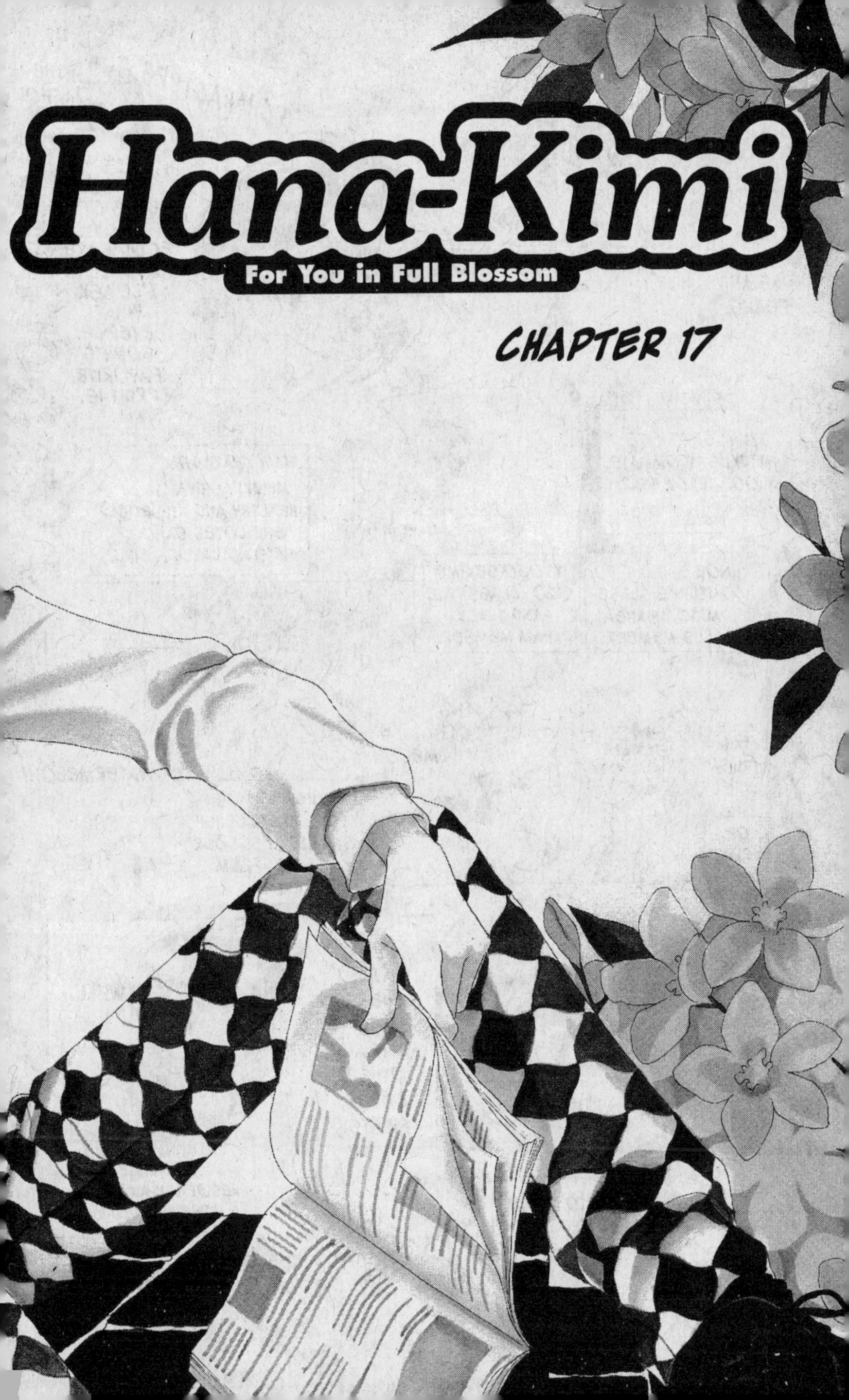

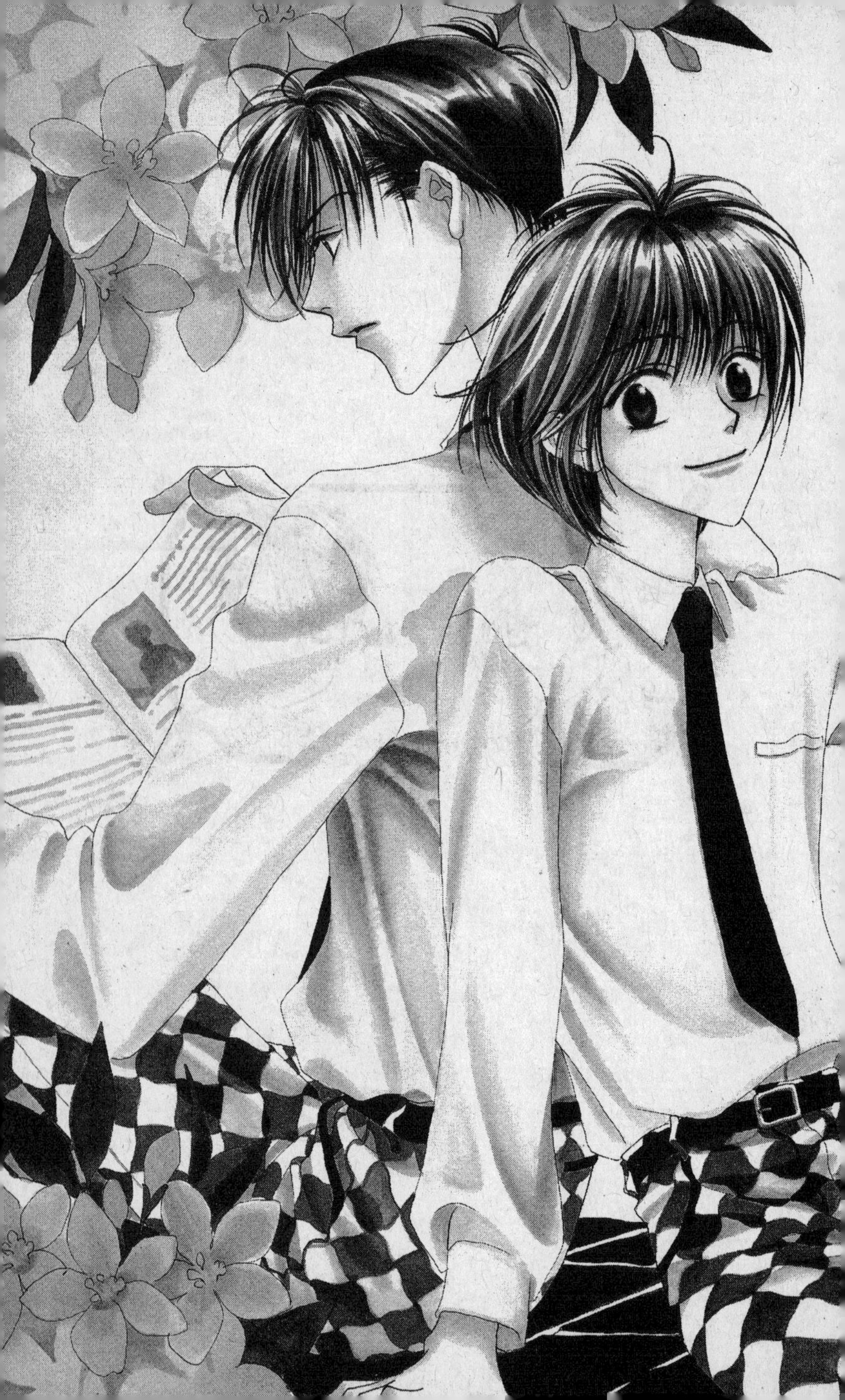

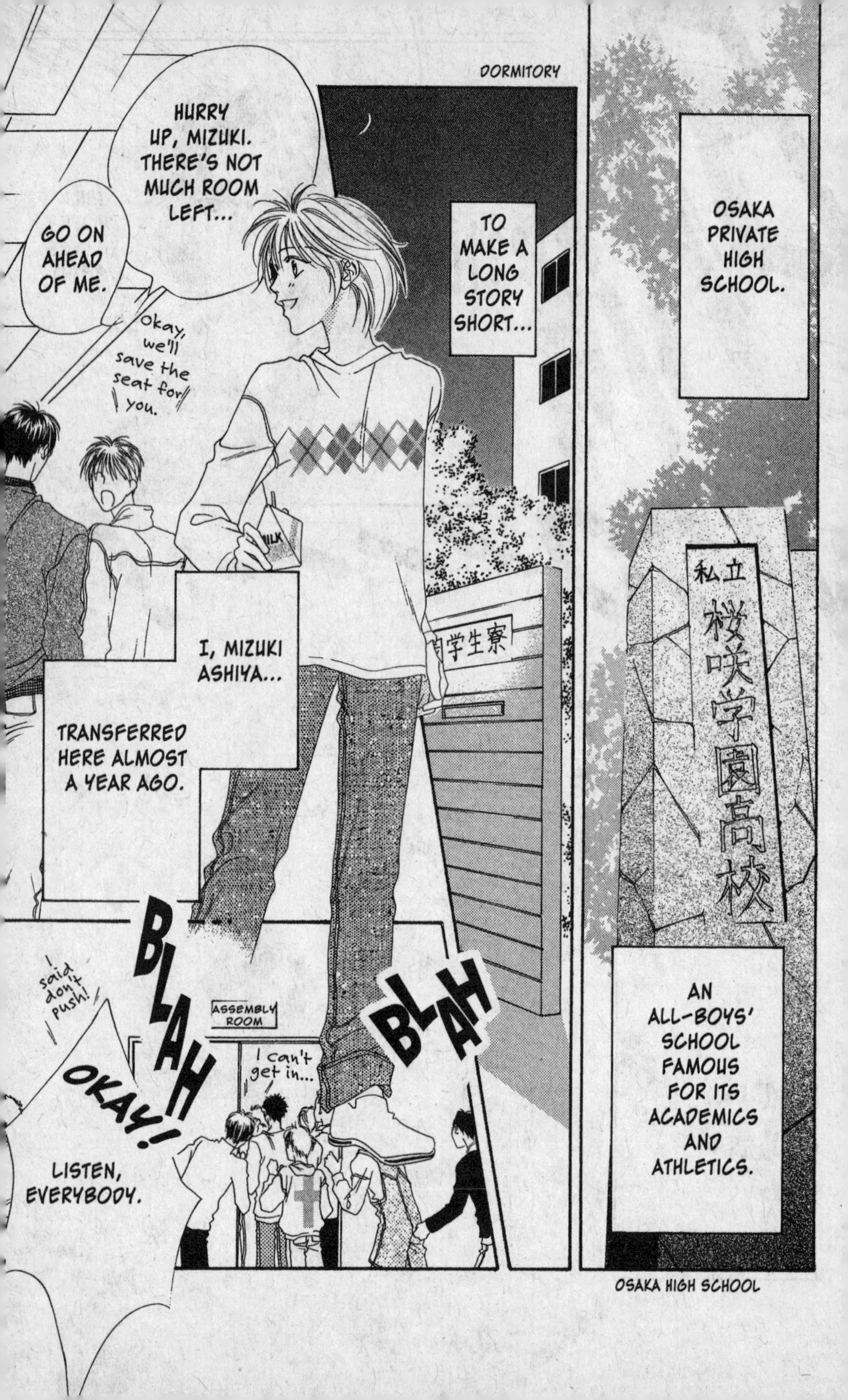
OSAKA PRIVATE HIGH SCHOOL.
私立 桜咲学園高校
AN ALL-BOYS' SCHOOL FAMOUS FOR ITS ACADEMICS AND ATHLETICS.
OSAKA HIGH SCHOOL
DORMITORY
TO MAKE A LONG STORY SHORT...
学生寮
HURRY UP, MIZUKI. THERE'S NOT MUCH ROOM LEFT...
GO ON AHEAD OF ME.
Okay, we'll save the seat for you.
I, MIZUKI ASHIYA...
TRANSFERRED HERE ALMOST A YEAR AGO.
BLAH
BLAH
I can't get in...
ASSEMBLY ROOM
I said don't push!
OKAY!
LISTEN, EVERYBODY.

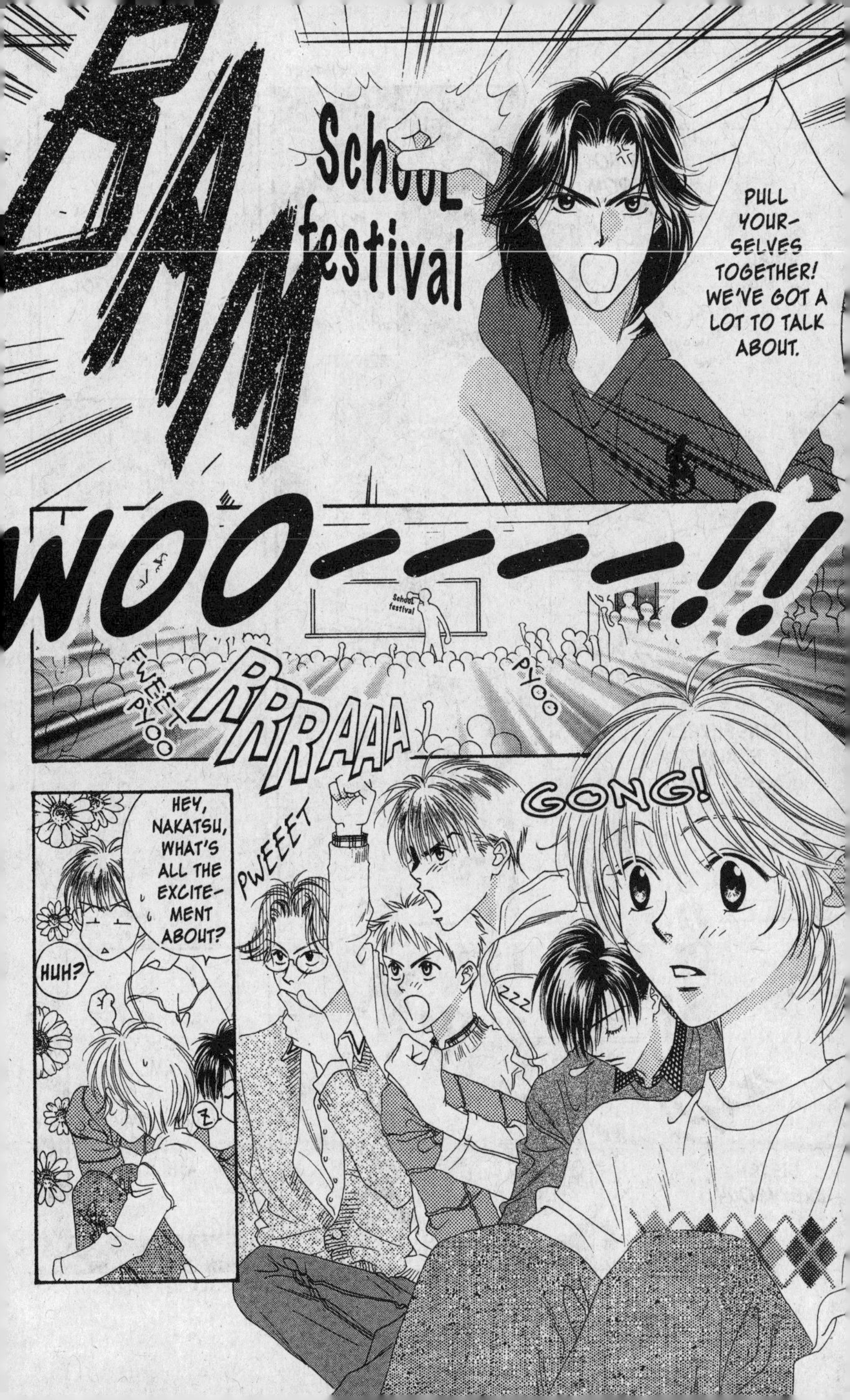
PULL YOUR-SELVES TOGETHER! WE'VE GOT A LOT TO TALK ABOUT.
School festival
BAM
WOO----!!
PYOO
RRRAAA
FWEET PYOO
School festival
GONG!
PWEEET
ZZZ
HEY, NAKATSU, WHAT'S ALL THE EXCITE-MENT ABOUT?
HUH?
Z

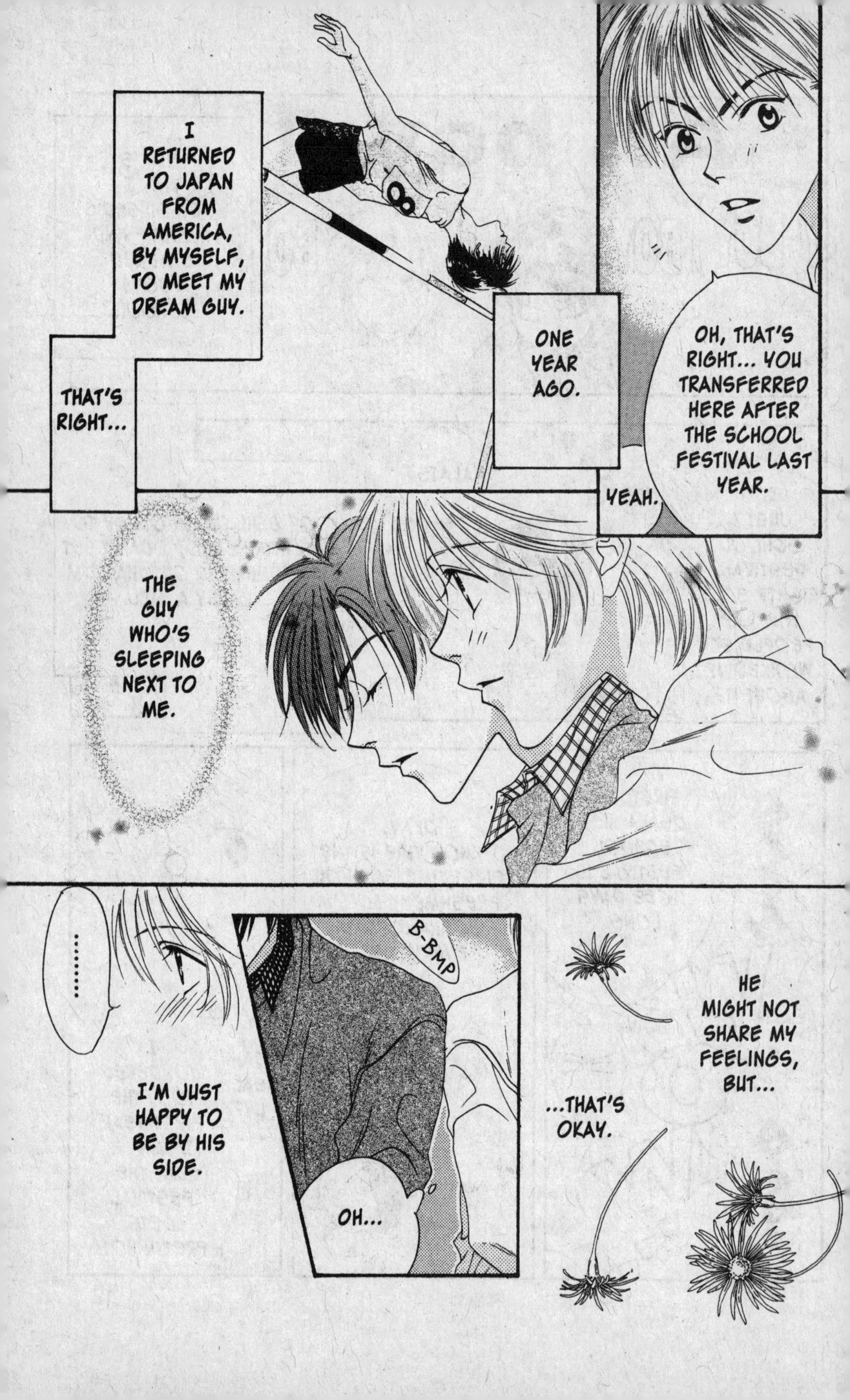
OH, THAT'S RIGHT... YOU TRANSFERRED HERE AFTER THE SCHOOL FESTIVAL LAST YEAR.
YEAH.
ONE YEAR AGO.
I RETURNED TO JAPAN FROM AMERICA, BY MYSELF, TO MEET MY DREAM GUY.
THAT'S RIGHT...
THE GUY WHO'S SLEEPING NEXT TO ME.
HE MIGHT NOT SHARE MY FEELINGS, BUT...
...THAT'S OKAY.
B-BMP
OH...
......
I'M JUST HAPPY TO BE BY HIS SIDE.

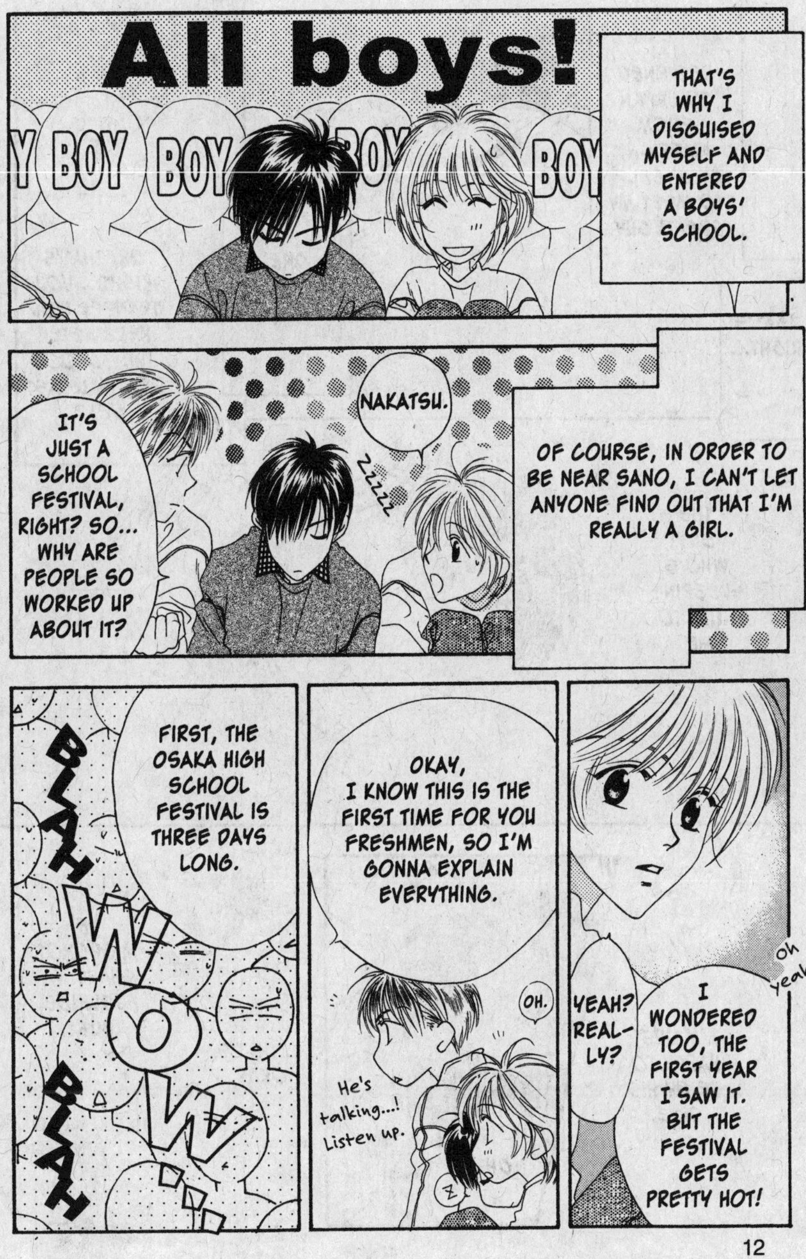
All boys!
BOY BOY BOY BOY
THAT'S WHY I DISGUISED MYSELF AND ENTERED A BOYS' SCHOOL.
OF COURSE, IN ORDER TO BE NEAR SANO, I CAN'T LET ANYONE FIND OUT THAT I'M REALLY A GIRL.
NAKATSU.
ZZZZZ
IT'S JUST A SCHOOL FESTIVAL, RIGHT? SO... WHY ARE PEOPLE SO WORKED UP ABOUT IT?
Oh yeah...
I WONDERED TOO, THE FIRST YEAR I SAW IT. BUT THE FESTIVAL GETS PRETTY HOT!
YEAH? REAL-LY?
OKAY, I KNOW THIS IS THE FIRST TIME FOR YOU FRESHMEN, SO I'M GONNA EXPLAIN EVERYTHING.
OH.
He's talking...! Listen up.
FIRST, THE OSAKA HIGH SCHOOL FESTIVAL IS THREE DAYS LONG.
BLAH
WOW
BLAH

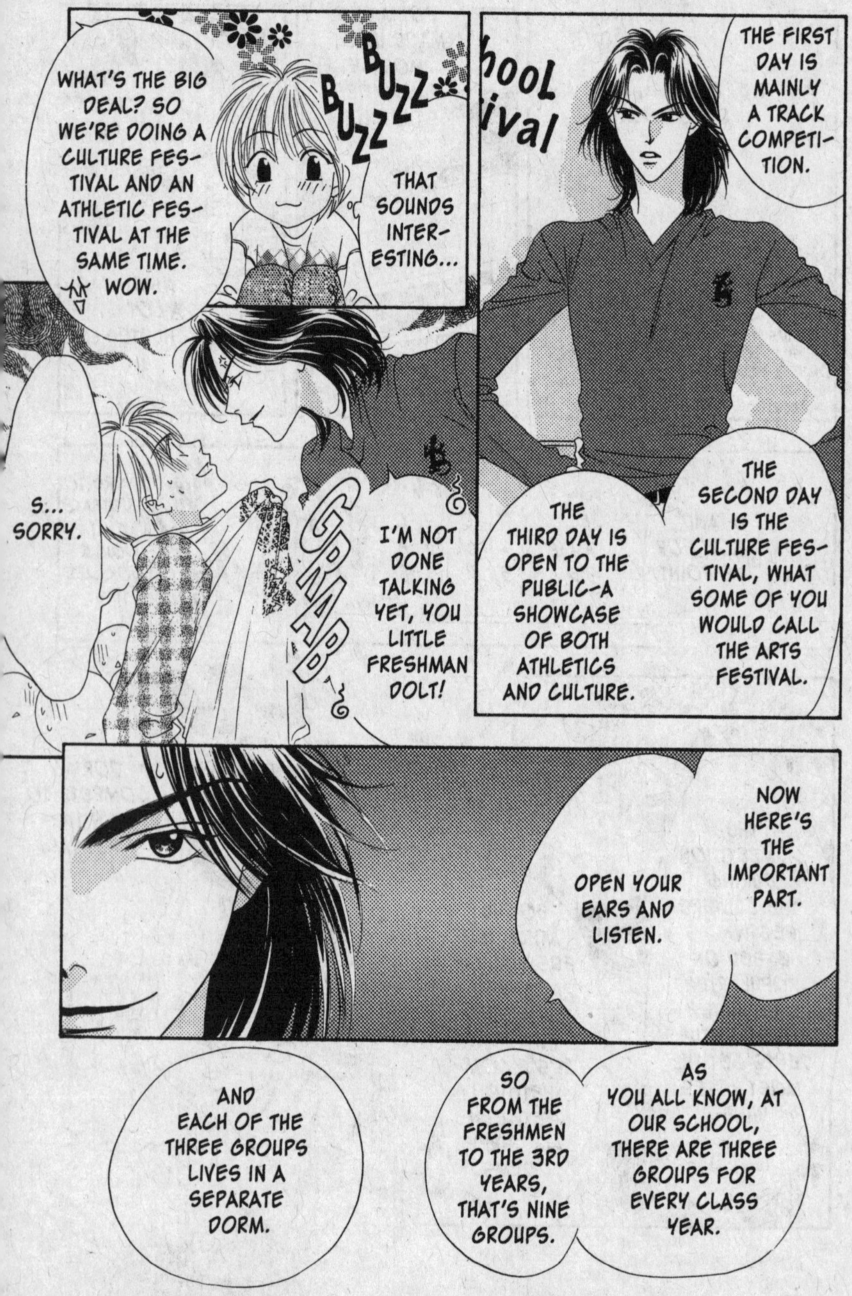
THE FIRST DAY IS MAINLY A TRACK COMPETITION.
THE SECOND DAY IS THE CULTURE FESTIVAL, WHAT SOME OF YOU WOULD CALL THE ARTS FESTIVAL.
THE THIRD DAY IS OPEN TO THE PUBLIC—A SHOWCASE OF BOTH ATHLETICS AND CULTURE.
BUZZZ BUZZZ
THAT SOUNDS INTERESTING...
WHAT'S THE BIG DEAL? SO WE'RE DOING A CULTURE FESTIVAL AND AN ATHLETIC FESTIVAL AT THE SAME TIME. WOW.
GRAB
I'M NOT DONE TALKING YET, YOU LITTLE FRESHMAN DOLT!
S... SORRY.
NOW HERE'S THE IMPORTANT PART.
OPEN YOUR EARS AND LISTEN.
AS YOU ALL KNOW, AT OUR SCHOOL, THERE ARE THREE GROUPS FOR EVERY CLASS YEAR.
SO FROM THE FRESHMEN TO THE 3RD YEARS, THAT'S NINE GROUPS.
AND EACH OF THE THREE GROUPS LIVES IN A SEPARATE DORM.

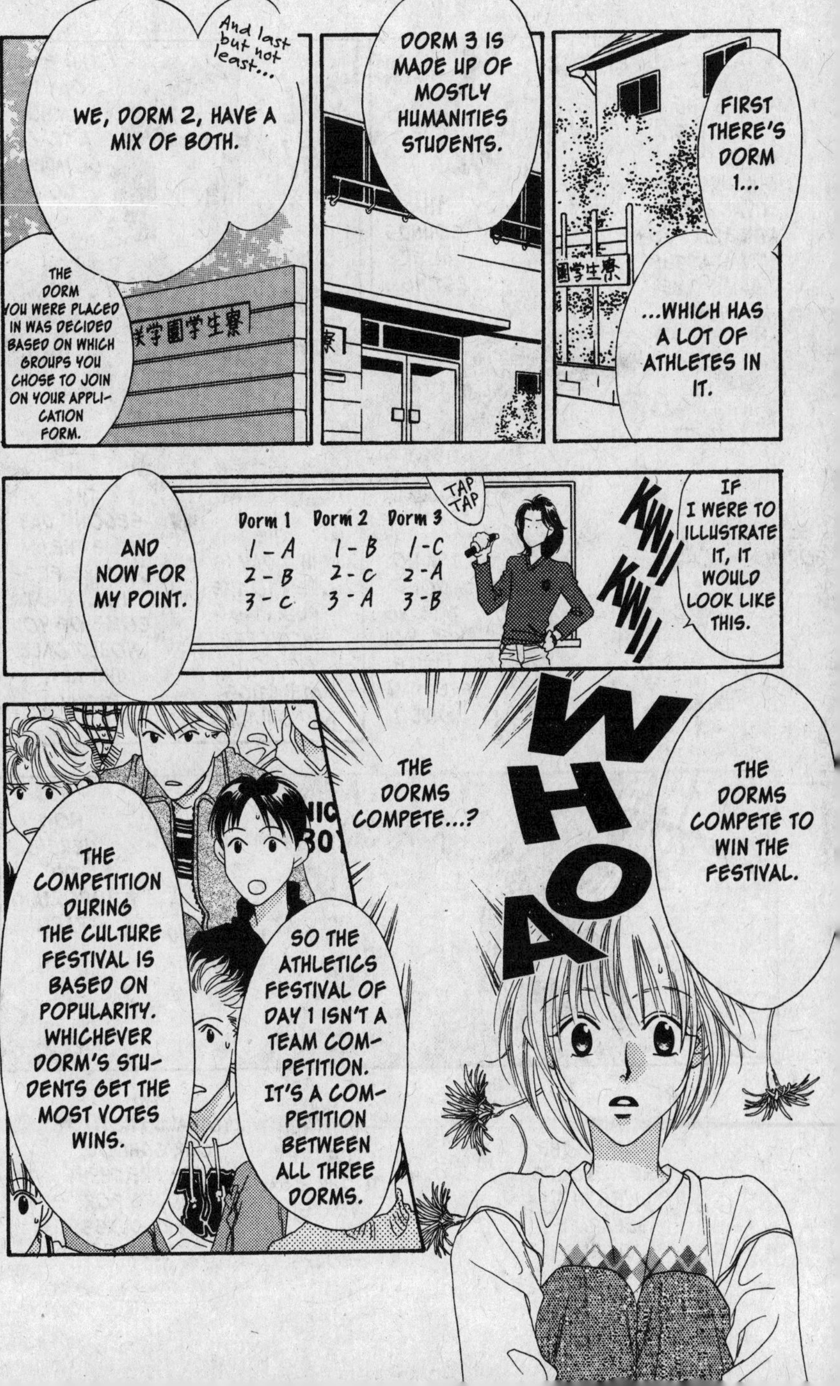
FIRST THERE'S DORM 1...
...WHICH HAS A LOT OF ATHLETES IN IT.
DORM 3 IS MADE UP OF MOSTLY HUMANITIES STUDENTS.
And last but not least...
WE, DORM 2, HAVE A MIX OF BOTH.
THE DORM YOU WERE PLACED IN WAS DECIDED BASED ON WHICH GROUPS YOU CHOSE TO JOIN ON YOUR APPLICATION FORM.
IF I WERE TO ILLUSTRATE IT, IT WOULD LOOK LIKE THIS.
KWII KWII
TAP TAP
Dorm 1 Dorm 2 Dorm 3
1-A 1-B 1-C
2-B 2-C 2-A
3-C 3-A 3-B
AND NOW FOR MY POINT.
THE DORMS COMPETE TO WIN THE FESTIVAL.
WHOA
THE DORMS COMPETE...?
SO THE ATHLETICS FESTIVAL OF DAY 1 ISN'T A TEAM COMPETITION. IT'S A COMPETITION BETWEEN ALL THREE DORMS.
THE COMPETITION DURING THE CULTURE FESTIVAL IS BASED ON POPULARITY. WHICHEVER DORM'S STUDENTS GET THE MOST VOTES WINS.

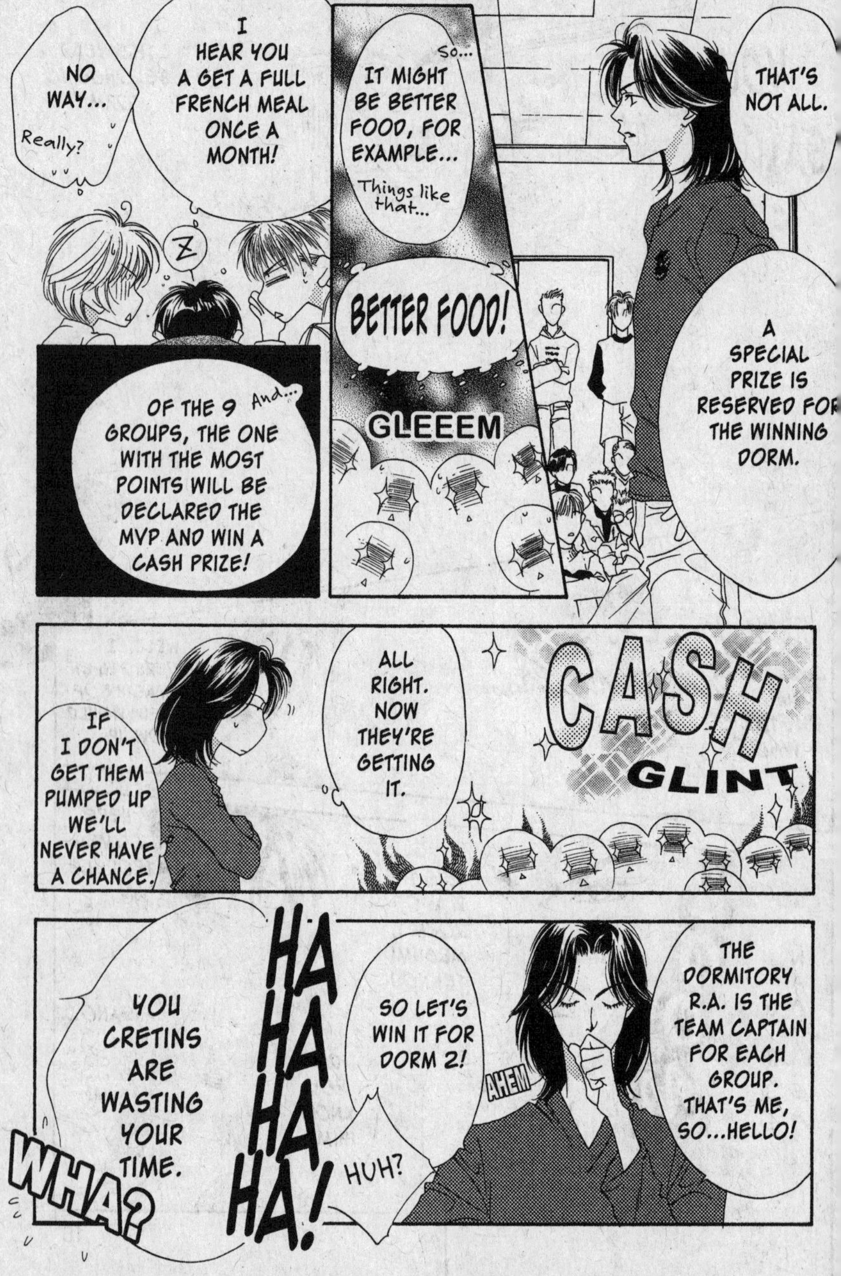
THAT'S NOT ALL.
A SPECIAL PRIZE IS RESERVED FOR THE WINNING DORM.
So...
IT MIGHT BE BETTER FOOD, FOR EXAMPLE...
Things like that...
BETTER FOOD!
GLEEEM
I HEAR YOU A GET A FULL FRENCH MEAL ONCE A MONTH!
NO WAY...
Really?
And...
OF THE 9 GROUPS, THE ONE WITH THE MOST POINTS WILL BE DECLARED THE MVP AND WIN A CASH PRIZE!
CASH
GLINT
ALL RIGHT. NOW THEY'RE GETTING IT.
IF I DON'T GET THEM PUMPED UP WE'LL NEVER HAVE A CHANCE.
THE DORMITORY R.A. IS THE TEAM CAPTAIN FOR EACH GROUP. THAT'S ME, SO...HELLO!
AHEM
SO LET'S WIN IT FOR DORM 2!
HUH?
HA HA HA HA!
YOU CRETINS ARE WASTING YOUR TIME.
WHA?

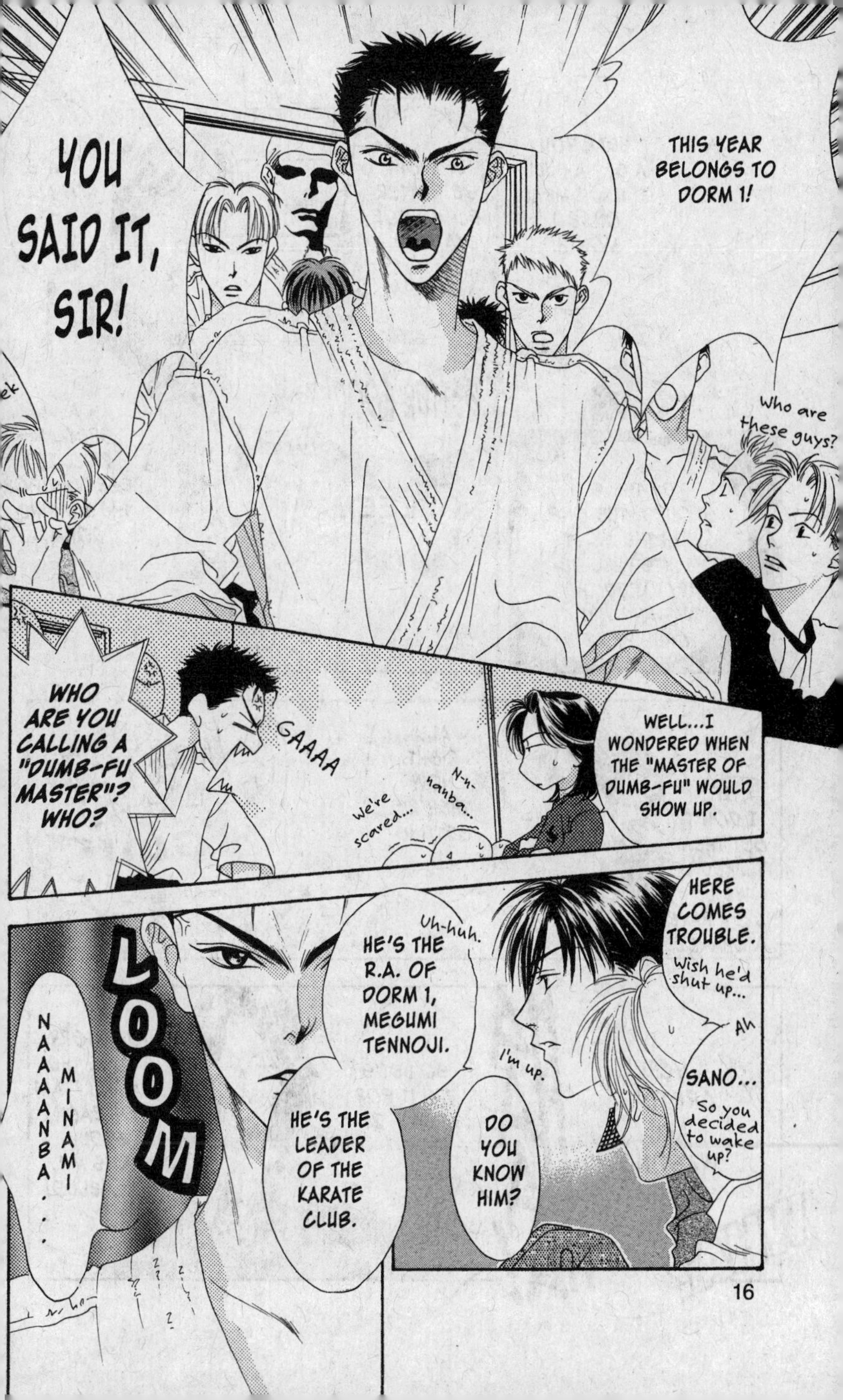
THIS YEAR BELONGS TO DORM 1!
Who are these guys?
YOU SAID IT, SIR!
WELL...I WONDERED WHEN THE "MASTER OF DUMB-FU" WOULD SHOW UP.
WHO ARE YOU CALLING A "DUMB-FU MASTER"? WHO?
GAAAA
N-n-nanba...
We're scared...
HERE COMES TROUBLE.
Wish he'd shut up...
Ah
SANO...
So you decided to wake up?
I'm up.
DO YOU KNOW HIM?
Uh-huh.
HE'S THE R.A. OF DORM 1, MEGUMI TENNOJI.
HE'S THE LEADER OF THE KARATE CLUB.
LOOM
MINAMI
NAAAANBA...

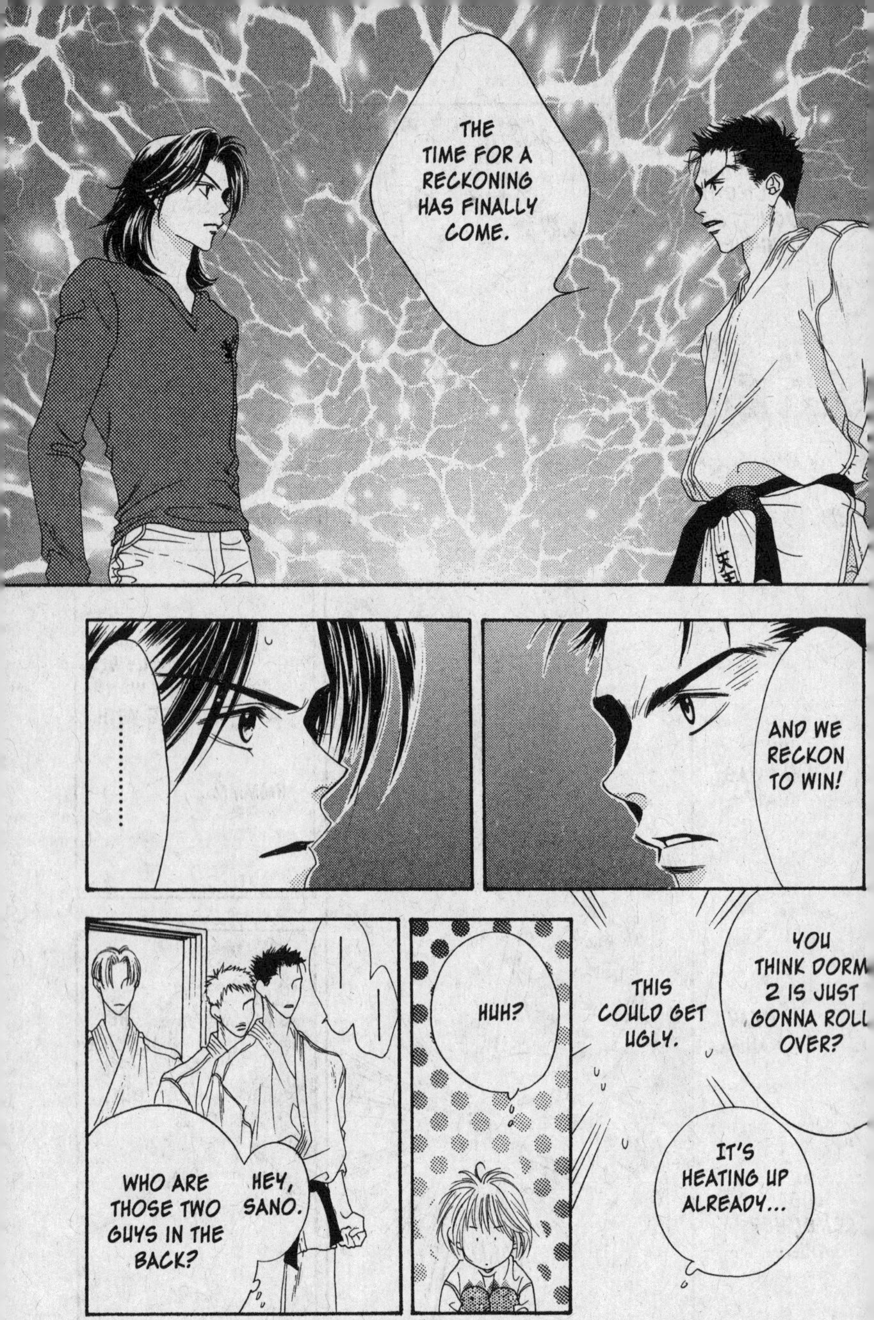
THE TIME FOR A RECKONING HAS FINALLY COME.
AND WE RECKON TO WIN!
......
YOU THINK DORM 2 IS JUST GONNA ROLL OVER?
THIS COULD GET UGLY.
IT'S HEATING UP ALREADY...
HUH?
HEY, SANO.
WHO ARE THOSE TWO GUYS IN THE BACK?

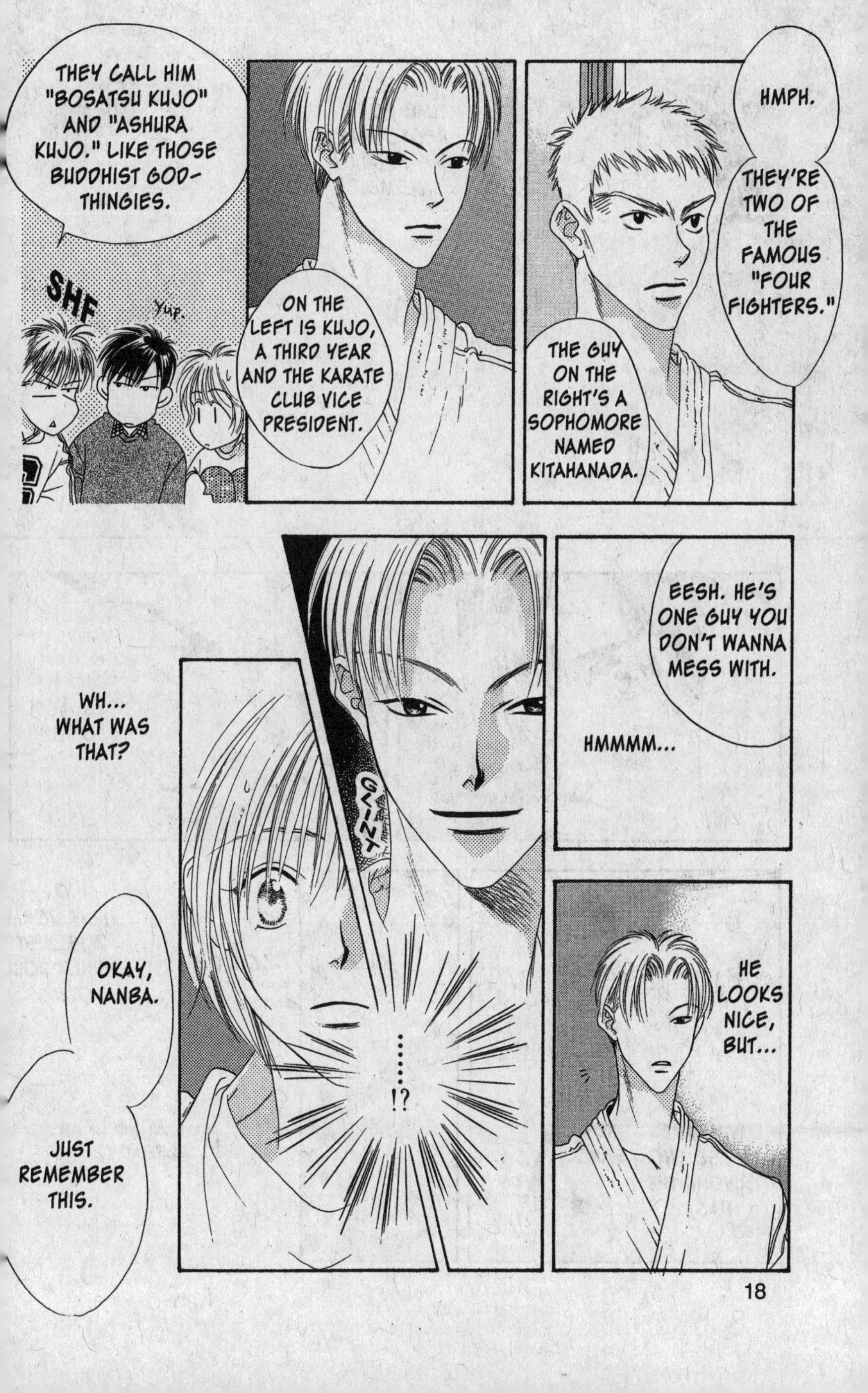
HMPH.
THEY'RE TWO OF THE FAMOUS "FOUR FIGHTERS."
THE GUY ON THE RIGHT'S A SOPHOMORE NAMED KITAHANADA.
ON THE LEFT IS KUJO, A THIRD YEAR AND THE KARATE CLUB VICE PRESIDENT.
THEY CALL HIM "BOSATSU KUJO" AND "ASHURA KUJO." LIKE THOSE BUDDHIST GOD-THINGIES.
SHF
Yup.
EESH. HE'S ONE GUY YOU DON'T WANNA MESS WITH.
HMMMM...
HE LOOKS NICE, BUT...
GLINT
......!?
WH... WHAT WAS THAT?
OKAY, NANBA.
JUST REMEMBER THIS.

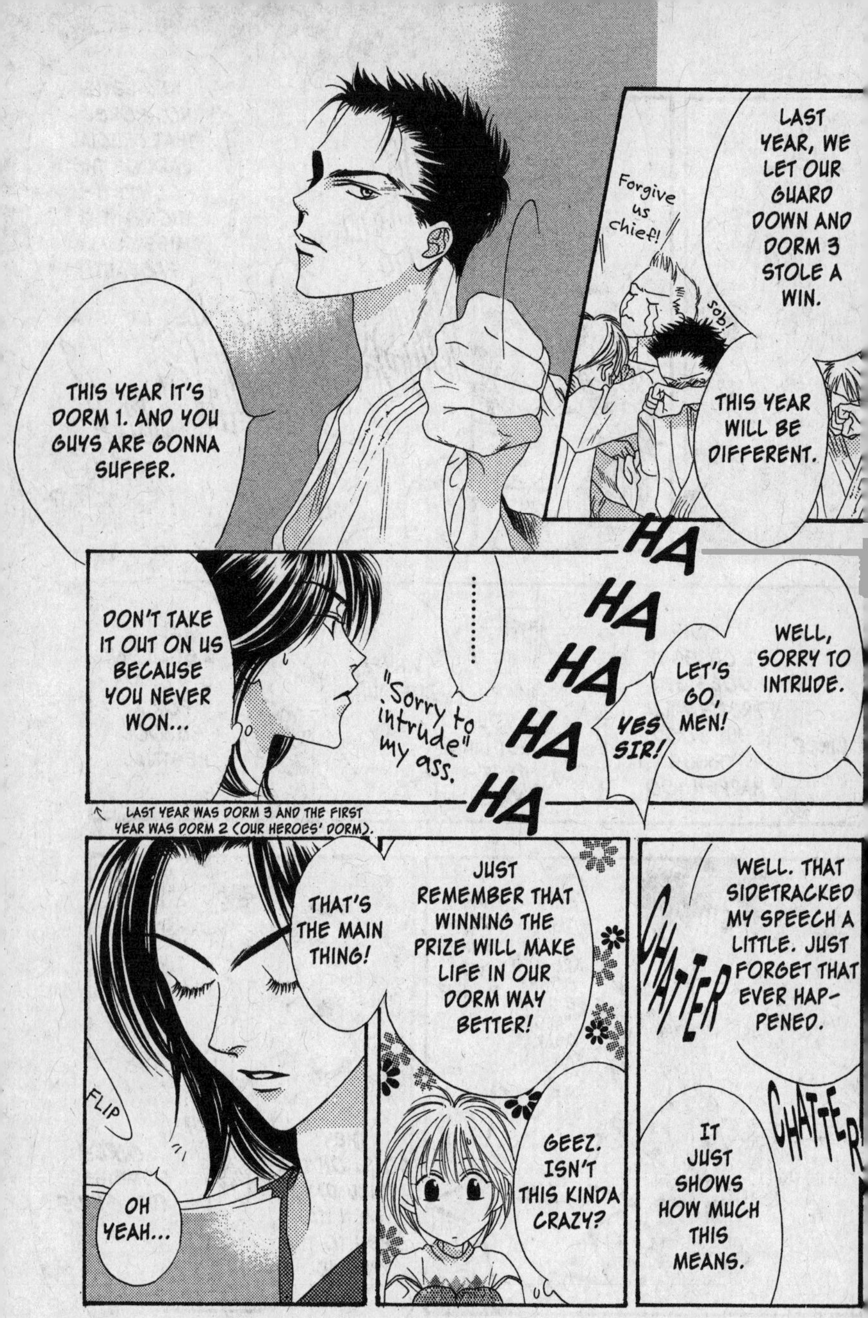
LAST YEAR, WE LET OUR GUARD DOWN AND DORM 3 STOLE A WIN.
Forgive us chief!
sob!
THIS YEAR WILL BE DIFFERENT.
THIS YEAR IT'S DORM 1. AND YOU GUYS ARE GONNA SUFFER.
WELL, SORRY TO INTRUDE.
LET'S GO, MEN!
YES SIR!
HA HA HA HA HA
"Sorry to intrude" my ass.
......
DON'T TAKE IT OUT ON US BECAUSE YOU NEVER WON...
LAST YEAR WAS DORM 3 AND THE FIRST YEAR WAS DORM 2 (OUR HEROES' DORM).
WELL. THAT SIDETRACKED MY SPEECH A LITTLE. JUST FORGET THAT EVER HAP-PENED.
CHATTER
CHATTER
IT JUST SHOWS HOW MUCH THIS MEANS.
JUST REMEMBER THAT WINNING THE PRIZE WILL MAKE LIFE IN OUR DORM WAY BETTER!
THAT'S THE MAIN THING!
GEEZ. ISN'T THIS KINDA CRAZY?
FLIP
OH YEAH...

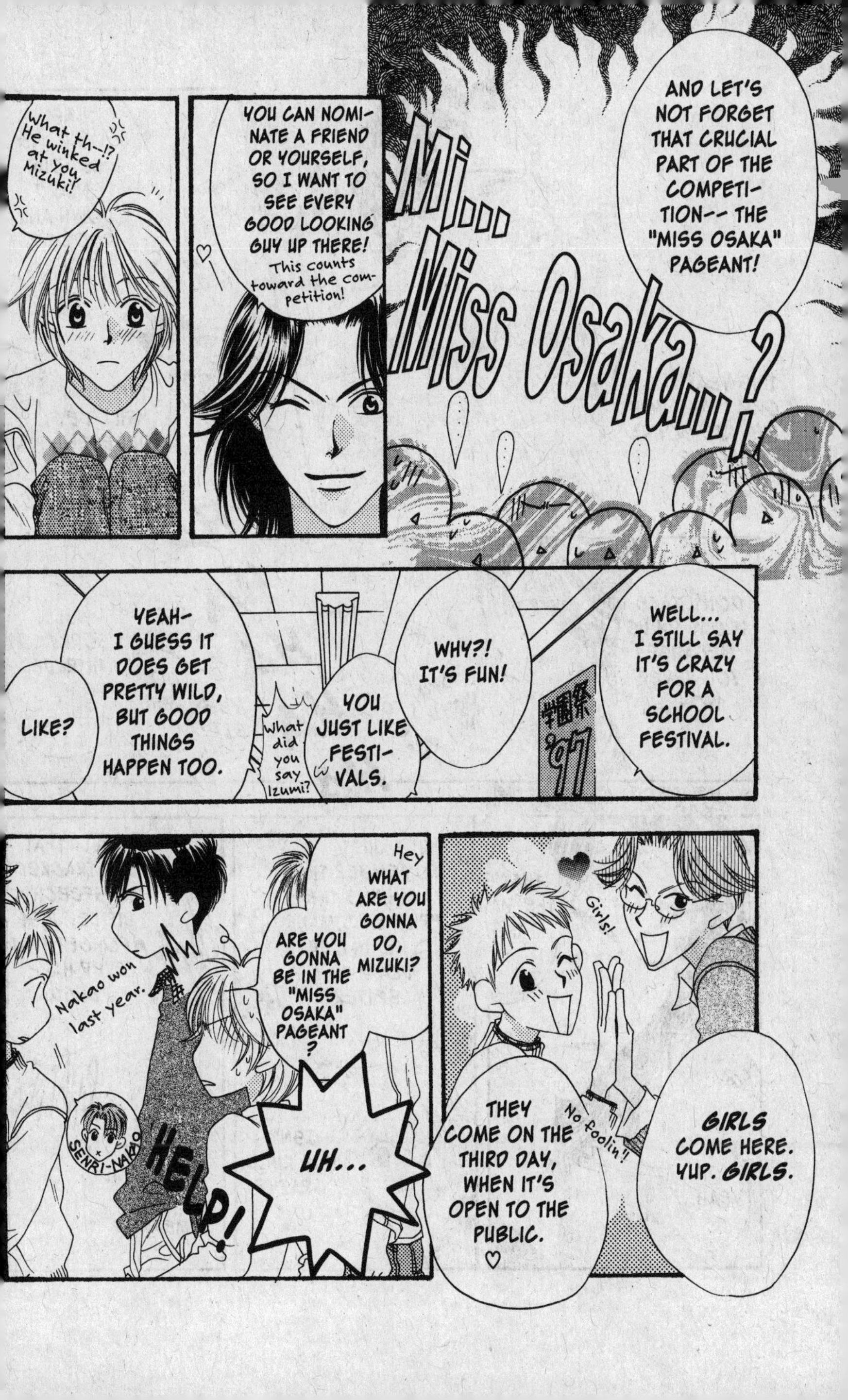
AND LET'S NOT FORGET THAT CRUCIAL PART OF THE COMPETITION-- THE "MISS OSAKA" PAGEANT!
Mi... Miss Osaka...?
YOU CAN NOMINATE A FRIEND OR YOURSELF, SO I WANT TO SEE EVERY GOOD LOOKING GUY UP THERE!
This counts toward the competition!
What th--!? He winked at you Mizuki!
WELL... I STILL SAY IT'S CRAZY FOR A SCHOOL FESTIVAL.
学園祭 '97
WHY?! IT'S FUN!
YOU JUST LIKE FESTIVALS.
What did you say Izumi?
YEAH- I GUESS IT DOES GET PRETTY WILD, BUT GOOD THINGS HAPPEN TOO.
LIKE?
Girls!
GIRLS COME HERE. YUP. GIRLS.
No foolin'!
THEY COME ON THE THIRD DAY, WHEN IT'S OPEN TO THE PUBLIC. ♡
Hey WHAT ARE YOU GONNA DO, MIZUKI?
ARE YOU GONNA BE IN THE "MISS OSAKA" PAGEANT?
UH...
HELP!
Nakao won last year.
SENRI-NAKAO

Greetings!

THIS IS THE 4TH "HANA-KIMI" BOOK!! YAY! IT'S THE SCHOOL FESTIVAL STORY I'VE ALWAYS WANTED TO WRITE. THERE ARE THREE DORMS IN OSAKA HIGH SCHOOL, BUT I REALLY WANTED TO MAKE IT FOUR DORMS. AND LISTEN TO THE NAMES I THOUGHT OF--"SEIRYU, BYAKKO, GENBU, AND SUZAKU"! (HA HA HA HA... PLEASE LAUGH.) HIMEJIMA WOULD BE IN THE SEIRYU DORM, KUJO IN THE BYAKKO DORM, TENNOJI IN THE GENBU DORM, AND NANBA IN THE SUZAKU DORM. BUT I THOUGHT THAT WOULD BE TOO MUCH, SO I STOPPED.

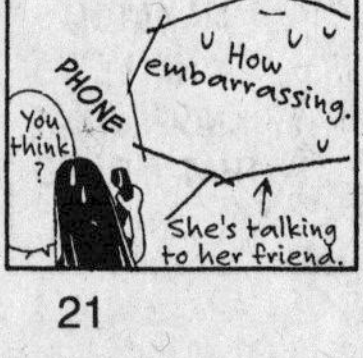
How embarrassing.
PHONE
You think?
She's talking to her friend.

THE GODS WHO WATCH OVER THE FOUR COMPASS DIRECTIONS (NORTH, SOUTH, EAST AND WEST).

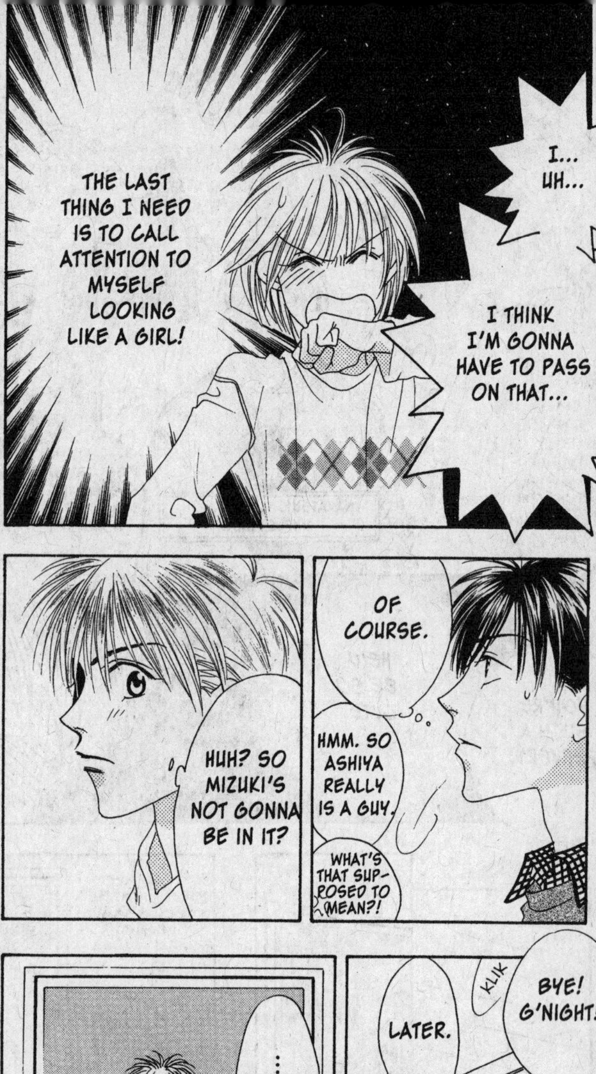
I... UH...
I THINK I'M GONNA HAVE TO PASS ON THAT...
THE LAST THING I NEED IS TO CALL ATTENTION TO MYSELF LOOKING LIKE A GIRL!
OF COURSE.
HMM. SO ASHIYA REALLY IS A GUY.
WHAT'S THAT SUPPOSED TO MEAN?!
HUH? SO MIZUKI'S NOT GONNA BE IN IT?
BYE! G'NIGHT!
KLIK
LATER.
YEAH, SEE YOU TOMORROW.
GOOD NIGHT
KLIK
205
......

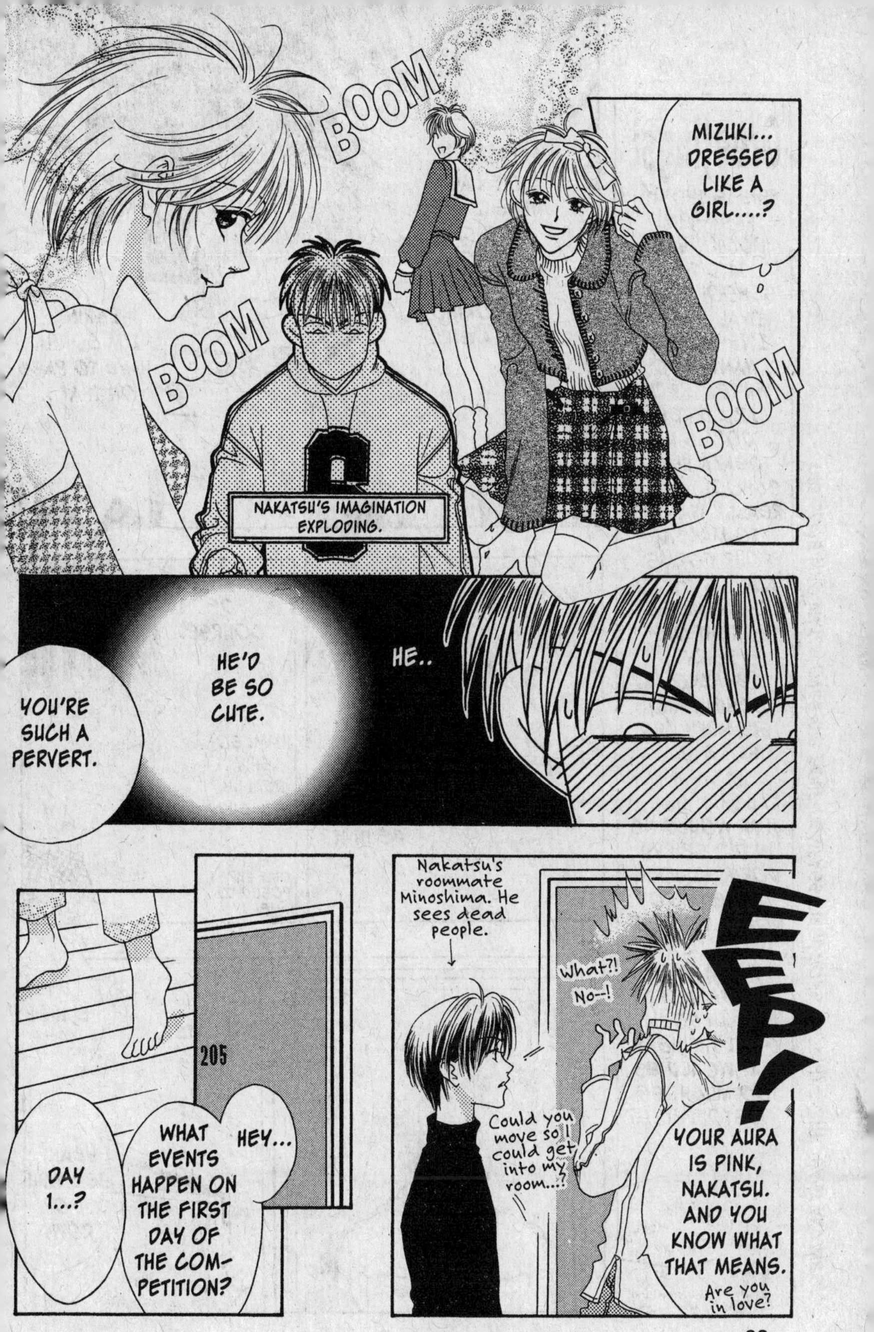
BOOM
MIZUKI... DRESSED LIKE A GIRL....?
BOOM
BOOM
NAKATSU'S IMAGINATION EXPLODING.
HE..
HE'D BE SO CUTE.
YOU'RE SUCH A PERVERT.
EEP!
What?! No--!
Nakatsu's roommate Minoshima. He sees dead people.
YOUR AURA IS PINK, NAKATSU. AND YOU KNOW WHAT THAT MEANS.
Are you in love?
Could you move so I could get into my room...?
205
HEY...
WHAT EVENTS HAPPEN ON THE FIRST DAY OF THE COM-PETITION?
DAY 1...?

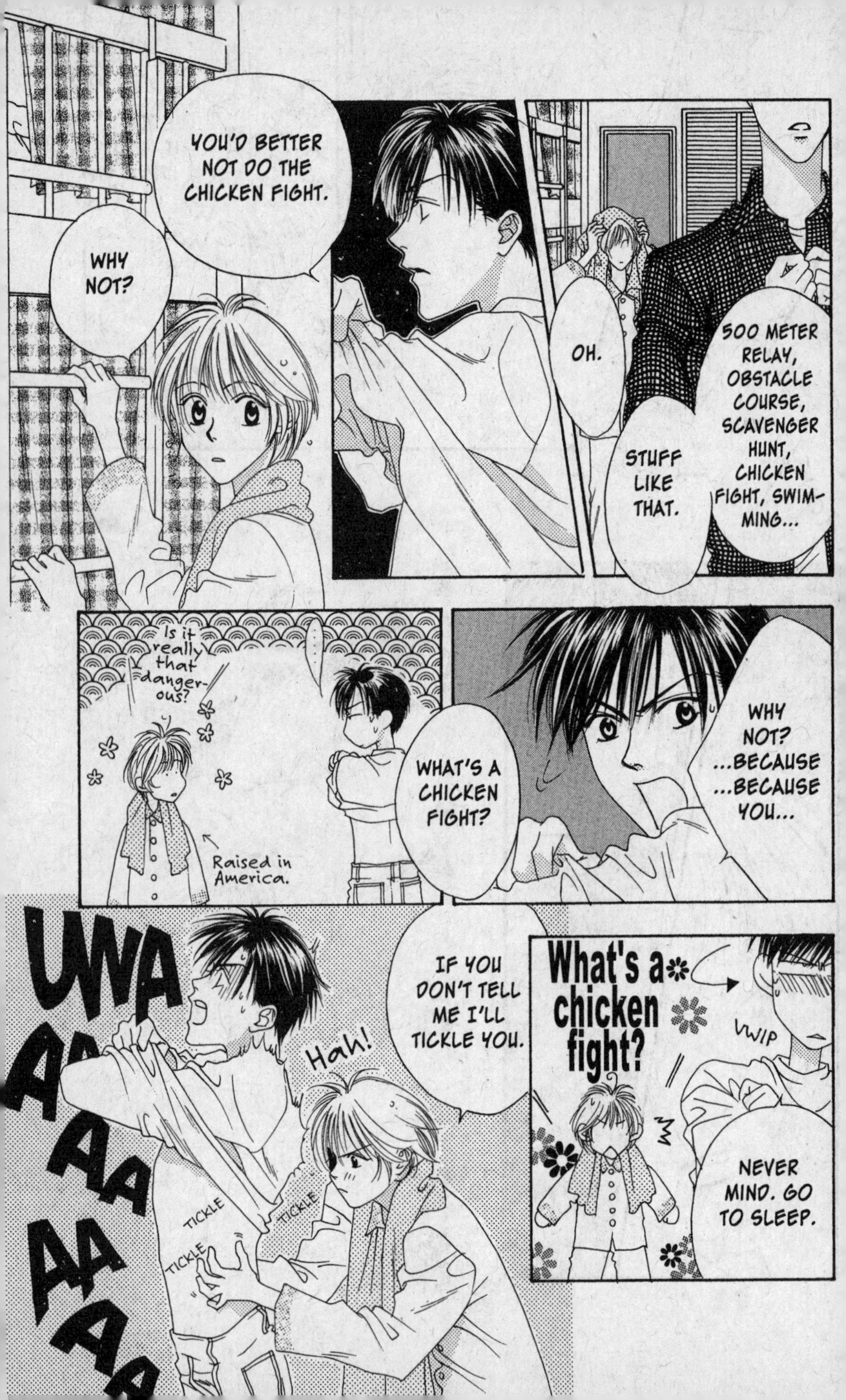
500 METER RELAY, OBSTACLE COURSE, SCAVENGER HUNT, CHICKEN FIGHT, SWIMMING...
STUFF LIKE THAT.
OH.
YOU'D BETTER NOT DO THE CHICKEN FIGHT.
WHY NOT?
WHY NOT? ...BECAUSE ...BECAUSE YOU...
WHAT'S A CHICKEN FIGHT?
Is it really that danger-ous?
Raised in America.
What's a chicken fight?
VWIP
NEVER MIND. GO TO SLEEP.
IF YOU DON'T TELL ME I'LL TICKLE YOU.
Hah!
TICKLE
TICKLE
TICKLE
UWAAAAAAAAA

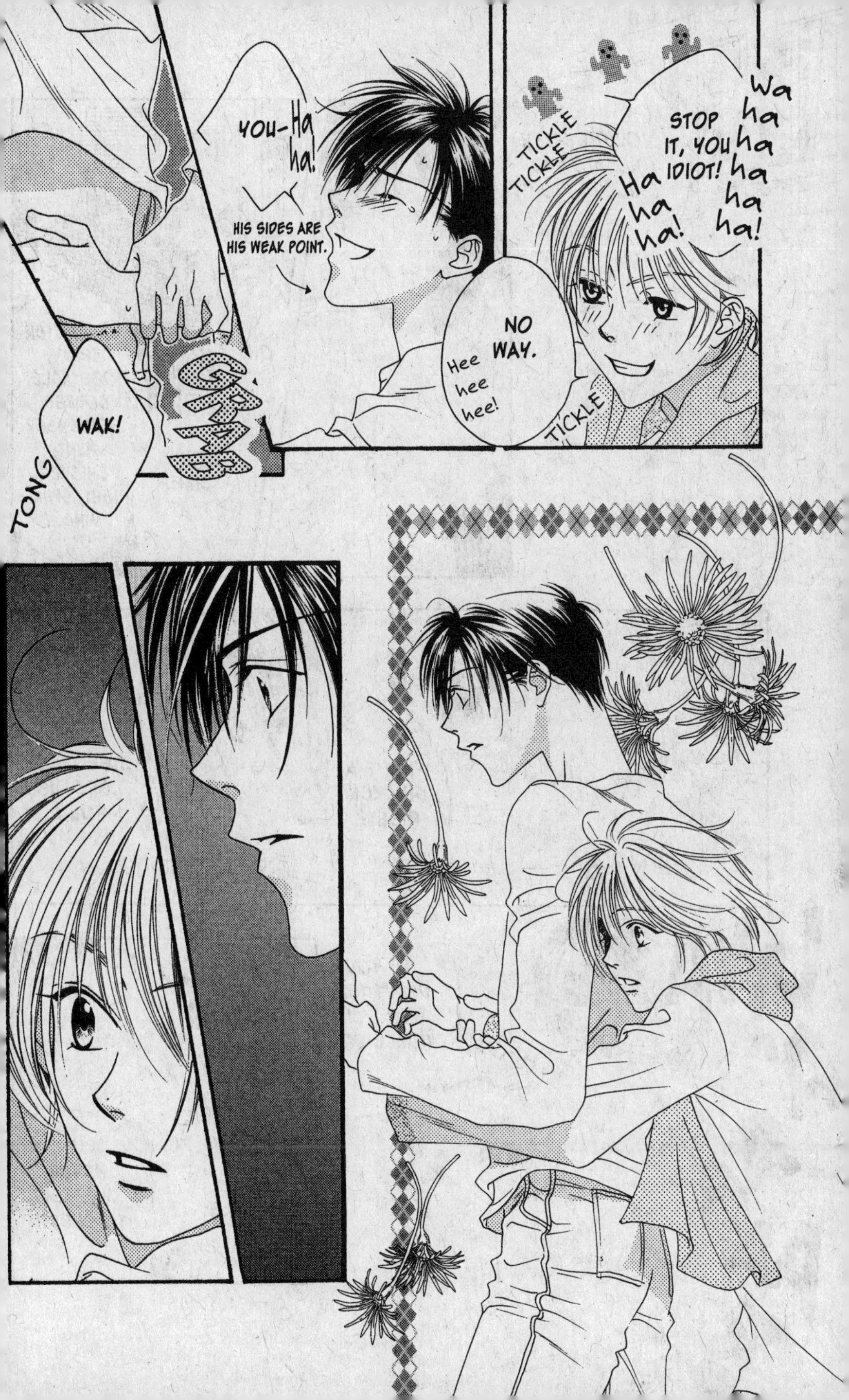
Wa ha ha ha ha ha!
STOP IT, YOU IDIOT!
Ha ha ha!
TICKLE TICKLE
NO WAY.
Hee hee hee!
TICKLE
YOU- Ha ha!
HIS SIDES ARE HIS WEAK POINT.
GRAB
WAK!
TONG

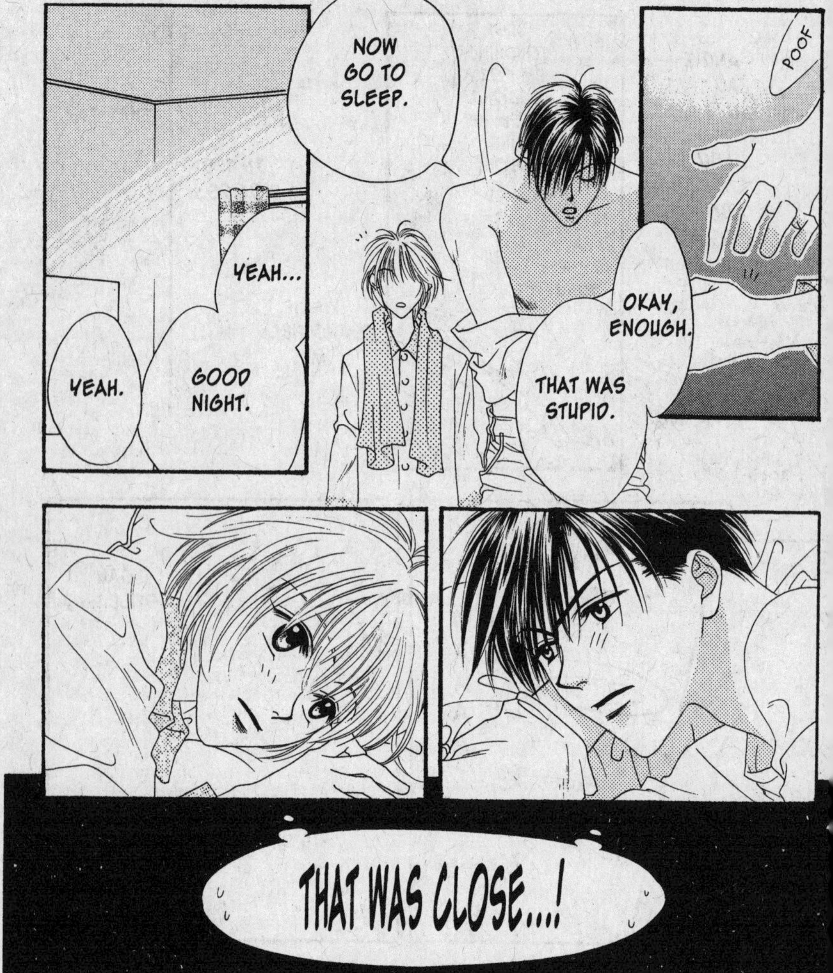
POOF
OKAY, ENOUGH.
THAT WAS STUPID.
NOW GO TO SLEEP.
YEAH...
GOOD NIGHT.
YEAH.
THAT WAS CLOSE...!
IT MADE ME THINK OF OUR SUMMER JOB.

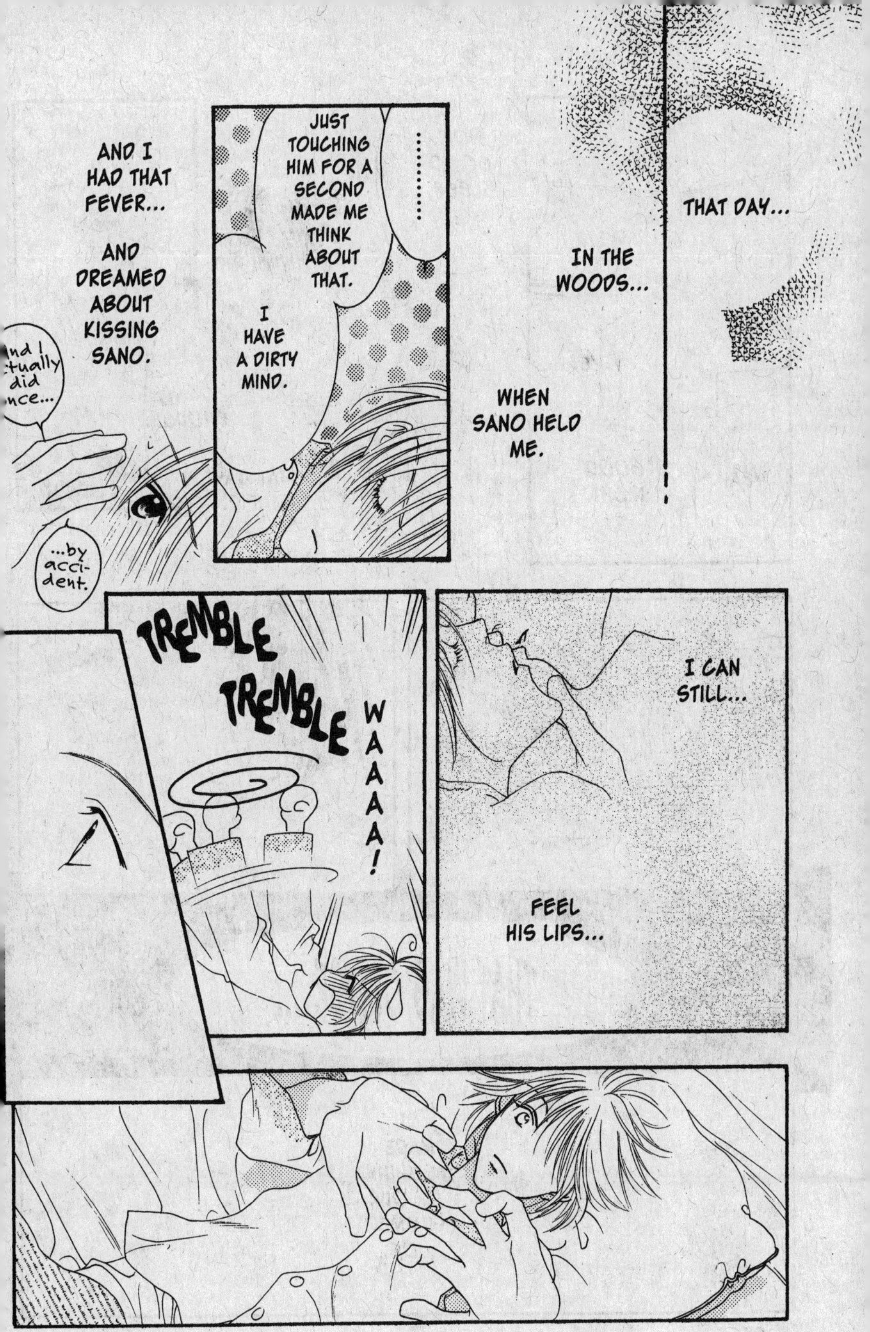
THAT DAY...
IN THE WOODS...
WHEN SANO HELD ME.
......
JUST TOUCHING HIM FOR A SECOND MADE ME THINK ABOUT THAT.
I HAVE A DIRTY MIND.
AND I HAD THAT FEVER...
AND DREAMED ABOUT KISSING SANO.
nd I ctually did nce...
...by acci-dent.
I CAN STILL...
FEEL HIS LIPS...
TREMBLE
TREMBLE
WAAAAA!

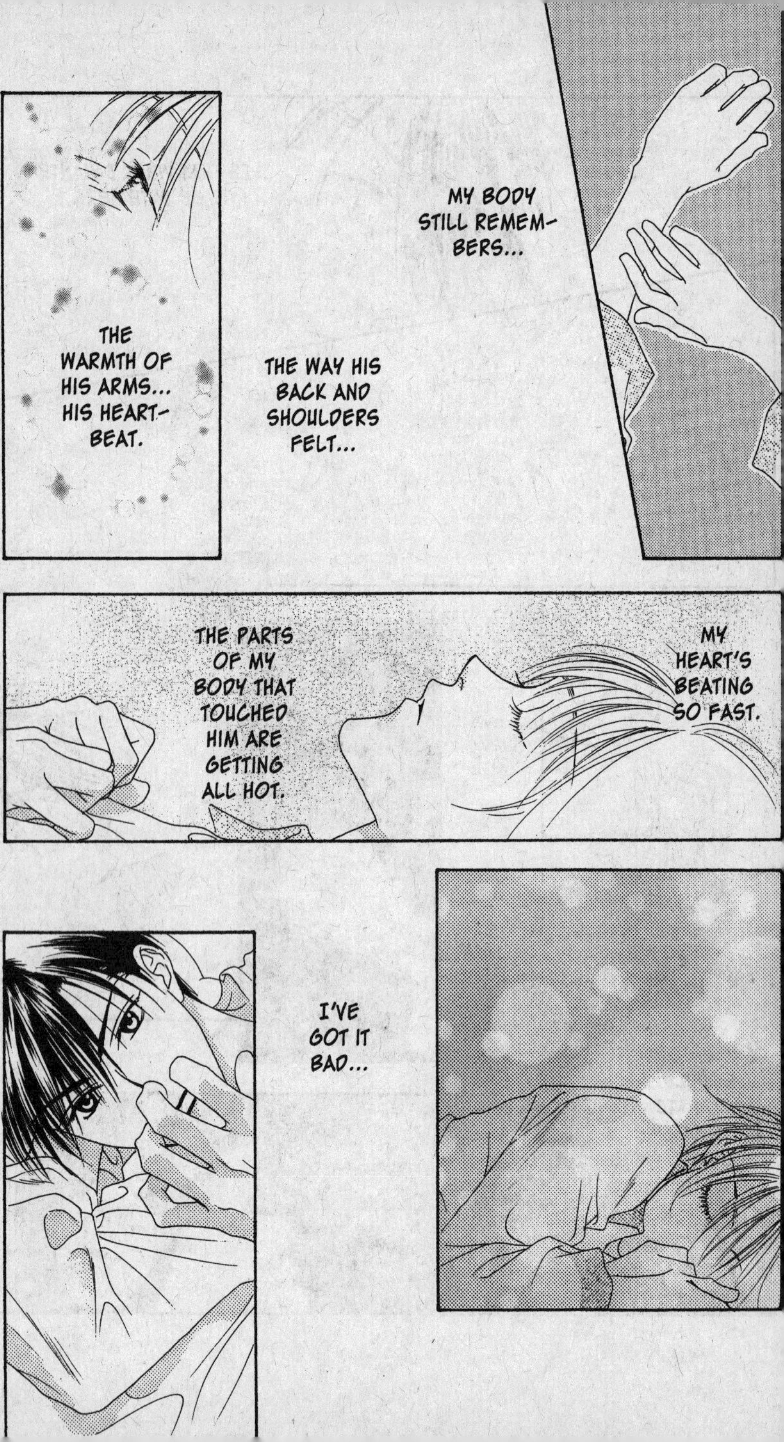
MY BODY STILL REMEMBERS...
THE WAY HIS BACK AND SHOULDERS FELT...
THE WARMTH OF HIS ARMS... HIS HEARTBEAT.
MY HEART'S BEATING SO FAST.
THE PARTS OF MY BODY THAT TOUCHED HIM ARE GETTING ALL HOT.
I'VE GOT IT BAD...

IS THAT WHAT I WANT? TO BE WITH HER...?

I...

EVERYBODY SHOULD PARTICIPATE IN AT LEAST ONE EVENT.

RRRING RRRING

Woo-hoo!

October 16th
100m relay. Obstacle course. Scavenger hunt. chicken fight. ball push. Daruma

Swimming, Dodge Ball

All right, all the events have been decided!

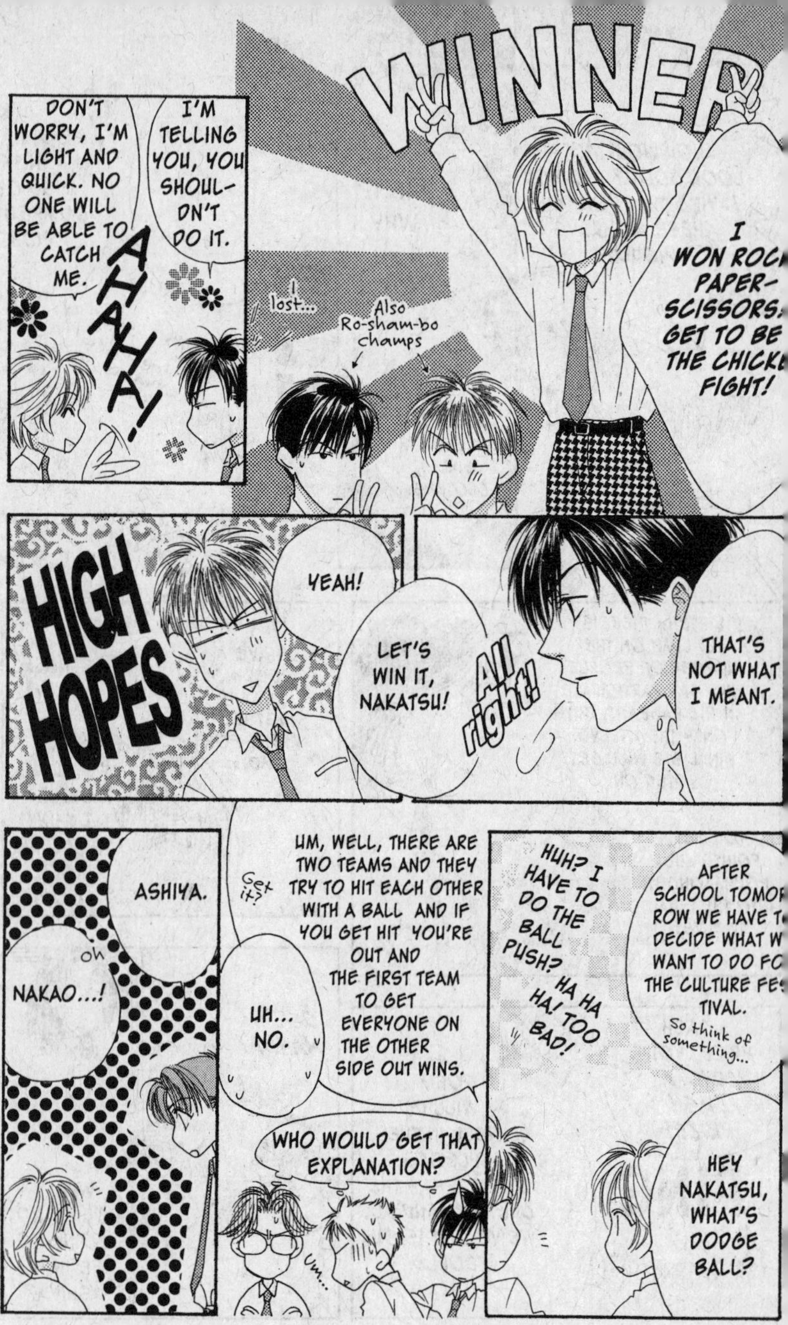

WINNER
I WON ROC PAPER-SCISSORS. GET TO BE THE CHICK FIGHT!
I lost...
Also Ro-sham-bo champs
I'M TELLING YOU, YOU SHOUL-DN'T DO IT.
DON'T WORRY, I'M LIGHT AND QUICK. NO ONE WILL BE ABLE TO CATCH ME.
AHAHA!
THAT'S NOT WHAT I MEANT.
All right!
LET'S WIN IT, NAKATSU!
YEAH!
HIGH HOPES
AFTER SCHOOL TOMOR ROW WE HAVE T DECIDE WHAT W WANT TO DO FO THE CULTURE FES TIVAL.
So think of something...
HUH? I HAVE TO DO THE BALL PUSH? HA HA HA! TOO BAD!
HEY NAKATSU, WHAT'S DODGE BALL?
UM, WELL, THERE ARE TWO TEAMS AND THEY TRY TO HIT EACH OTHER WITH A BALL AND IF YOU GET HIT YOU'RE OUT AND THE FIRST TEAM TO GET EVERYONE ON THE OTHER SIDE OUT WINS.
Get it?
UH... NO.
WHO WOULD GET THAT EXPLANATION?
Um...
ASHIYA.
oh
NAKAO...!

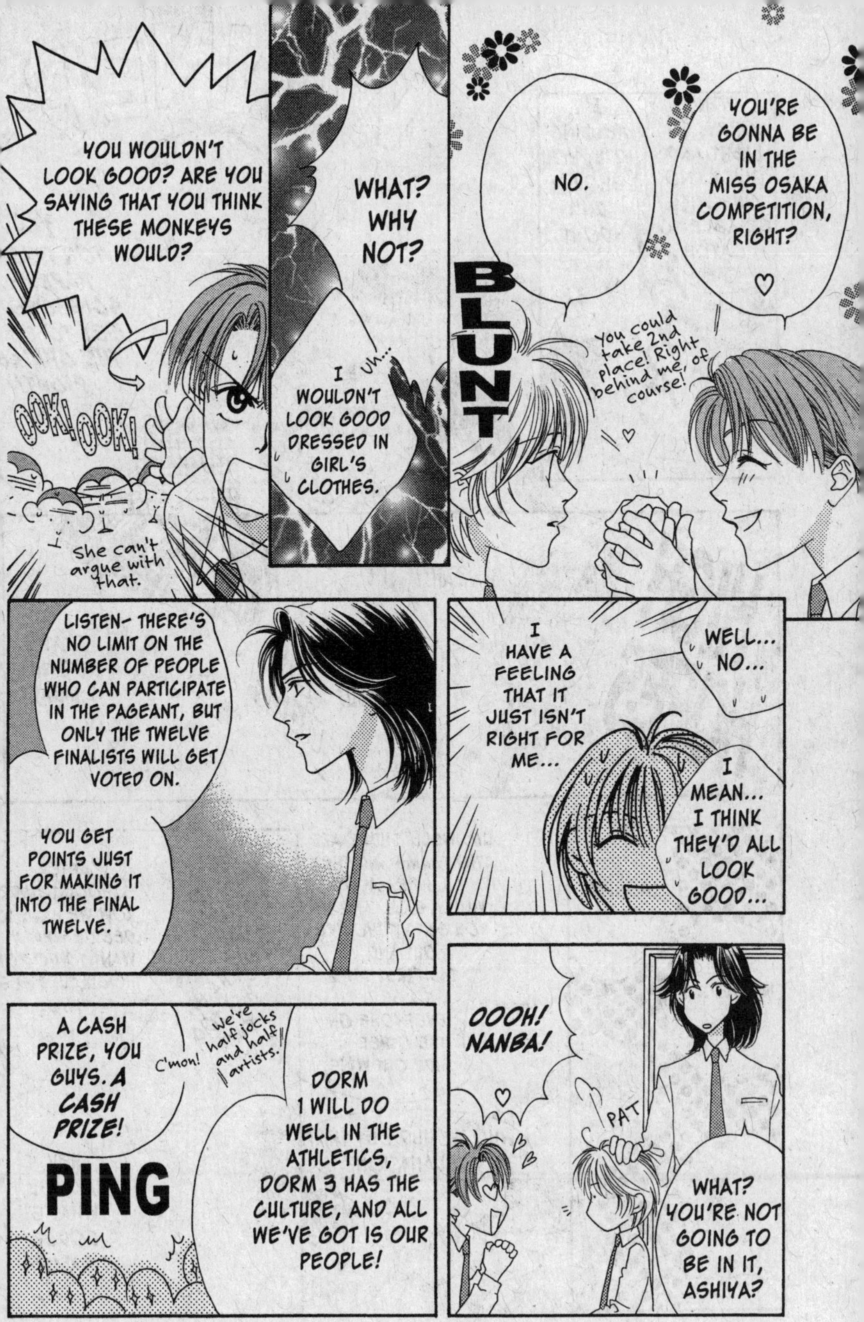

YOU'RE GONNA BE IN THE MISS OSAKA COMPETITION, RIGHT? ♡
You could take 2nd place! Right behind me, of course!
NO.
BLUNT
WHAT? WHY NOT?
Uh...
I WOULDN'T LOOK GOOD DRESSED IN GIRL'S CLOTHES.
YOU WOULDN'T LOOK GOOD? ARE YOU SAYING THAT YOU THINK THESE MONKEYS WOULD?
OOK! OOK!
She can't argue with that.
WELL... NO...
I MEAN... I THINK THEY'D ALL LOOK GOOD...
I HAVE A FEELING THAT IT JUST ISN'T RIGHT FOR ME...
LISTEN- THERE'S NO LIMIT ON THE NUMBER OF PEOPLE WHO CAN PARTICIPATE IN THE PAGEANT, BUT ONLY THE TWELVE FINALISTS WILL GET VOTED ON.
YOU GET POINTS JUST FOR MAKING IT INTO THE FINAL TWELVE.
OOOH! NANBA!
PAT
WHAT? YOU'RE NOT GOING TO BE IN IT, ASHIYA?
DORM 1 WILL DO WELL IN THE ATHLETICS, DORM 3 HAS THE CULTURE, AND ALL WE'VE GOT IS OUR PEOPLE!
We're half jocks and half artists.
C'mon!
A CASH PRIZE, YOU GUYS. A CASH PRIZE!
PING

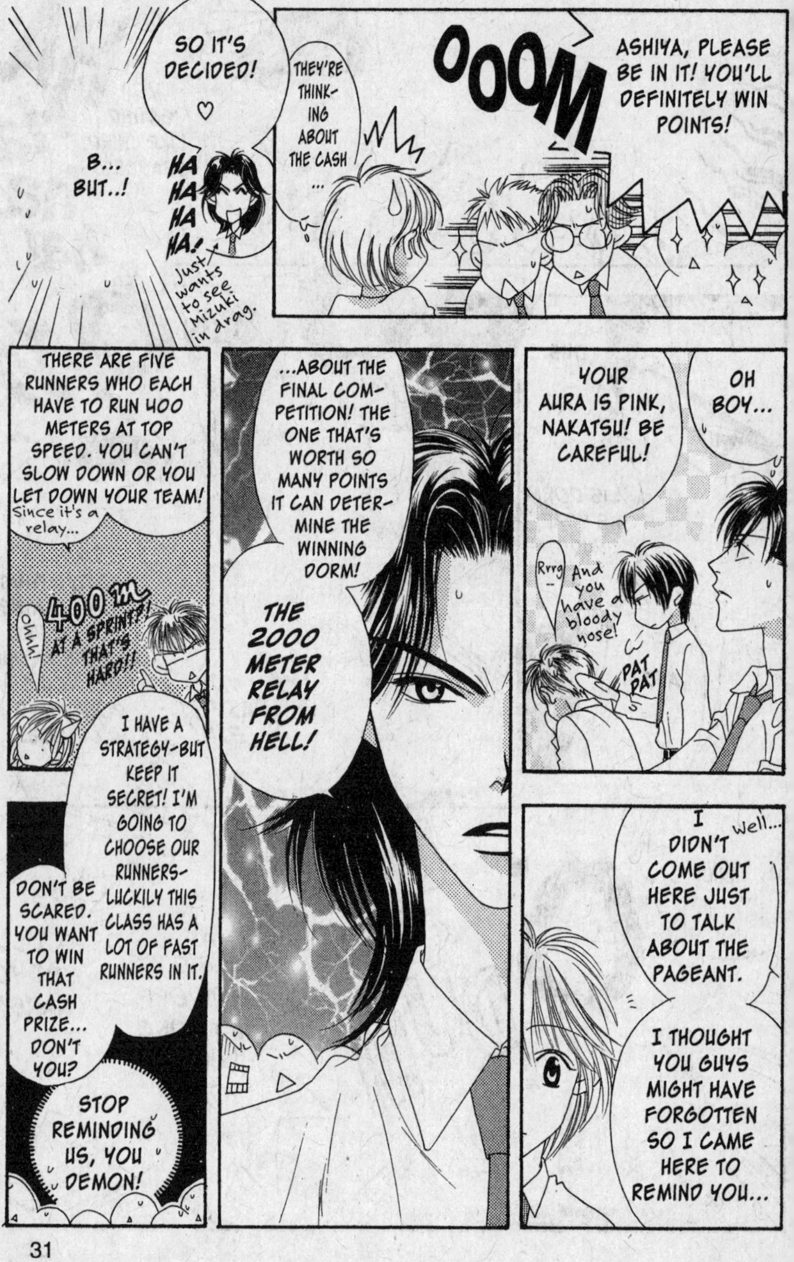

ASHIYA, PLEASE BE IN IT! YOU'LL DEFINITELY WIN POINTS!
OOOM
THEY'RE THINKING ABOUT THE CASH...
SO IT'S DECIDED! ♥
HA HA HA HA!
Just wants to see Mizuki in drag.
B... BUT..!
OH BOY...
YOUR AURA IS PINK, NAKATSU! BE CAREFUL!
And you have a bloody nose!
PAT PAT
Rrrg--
I DIDN'T COME OUT HERE JUST TO TALK ABOUT THE PAGEANT.
Well...
I THOUGHT YOU GUYS MIGHT HAVE FORGOTTEN SO I CAME HERE TO REMIND YOU...
...ABOUT THE FINAL COMPETITION! THE ONE THAT'S WORTH SO MANY POINTS IT CAN DETERMINE THE WINNING DORM!
THE 2000 METER RELAY FROM HELL!
THERE ARE FIVE RUNNERS WHO EACH HAVE TO RUN 400 METERS AT TOP SPEED. YOU CAN'T SLOW DOWN OR YOU LET DOWN YOUR TEAM!
Since it's a relay...
400m AT A SPRINT?! THAT'S HARD!!
I HAVE A STRATEGY-BUT KEEP IT SECRET! I'M GOING TO CHOOSE OUR RUNNERS-LUCKILY THIS CLASS HAS A LOT OF FAST RUNNERS IN IT.
DON'T BE SCARED. YOU WANT TO WIN THAT CASH PRIZE... DON'T YOU?
STOP REMINDING US, YOU DEMON!

SWEET AND SOUR-- NANBA'S LEADERSHIP STYLE.

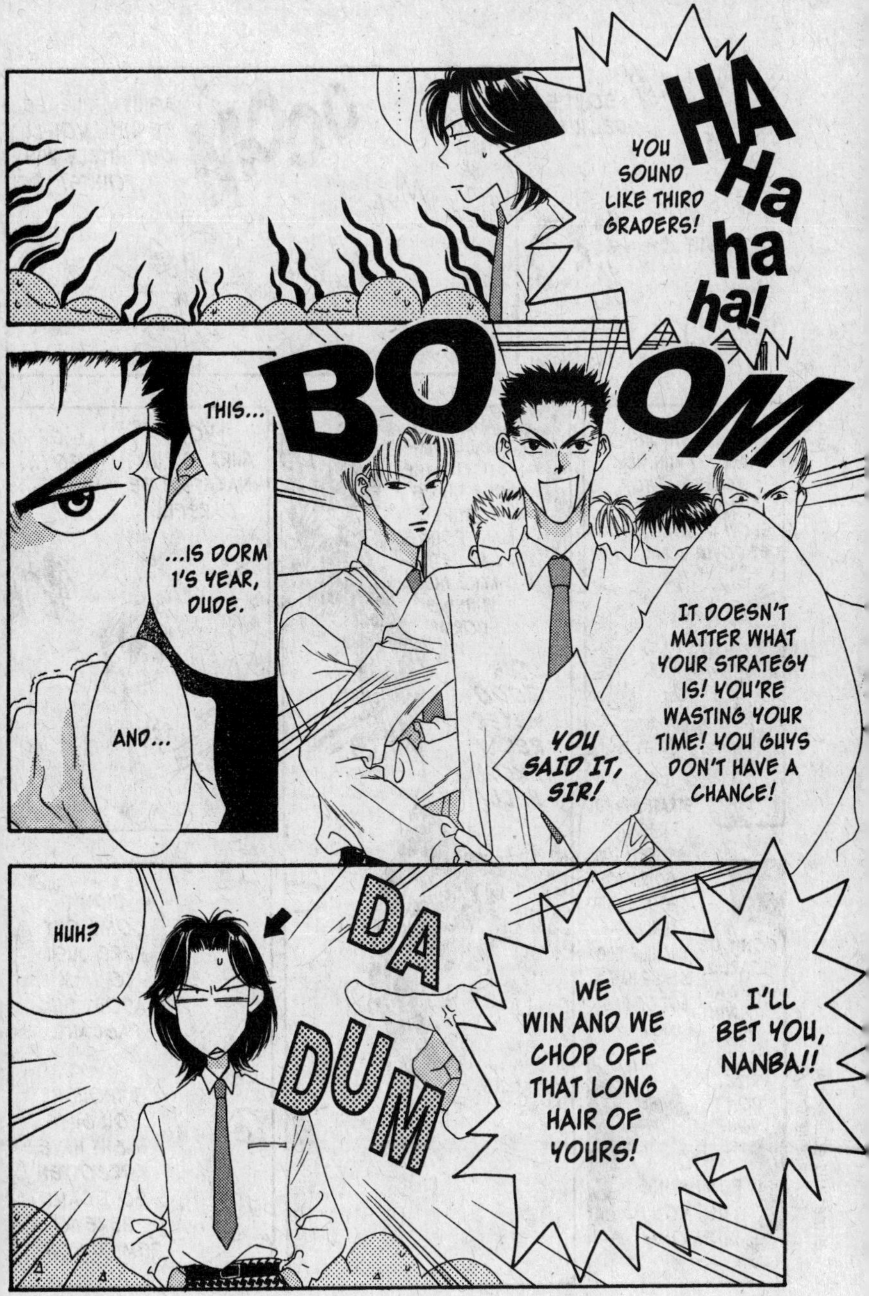
HA Ha ha ha!
YOU SOUND LIKE THIRD GRADERS!
BOOM
IT DOESN'T MATTER WHAT YOUR STRATEGY IS! YOU'RE WASTING YOUR TIME! YOU GUYS DON'T HAVE A CHANCE!
YOU SAID IT, SIR!
THIS...
...IS DORM 1'S YEAR, DUDE.
AND...
I'LL BET YOU, NANBA!!
WE WIN AND WE CHOP OFF THAT LONG HAIR OF YOURS!
DA DUM
HUH?

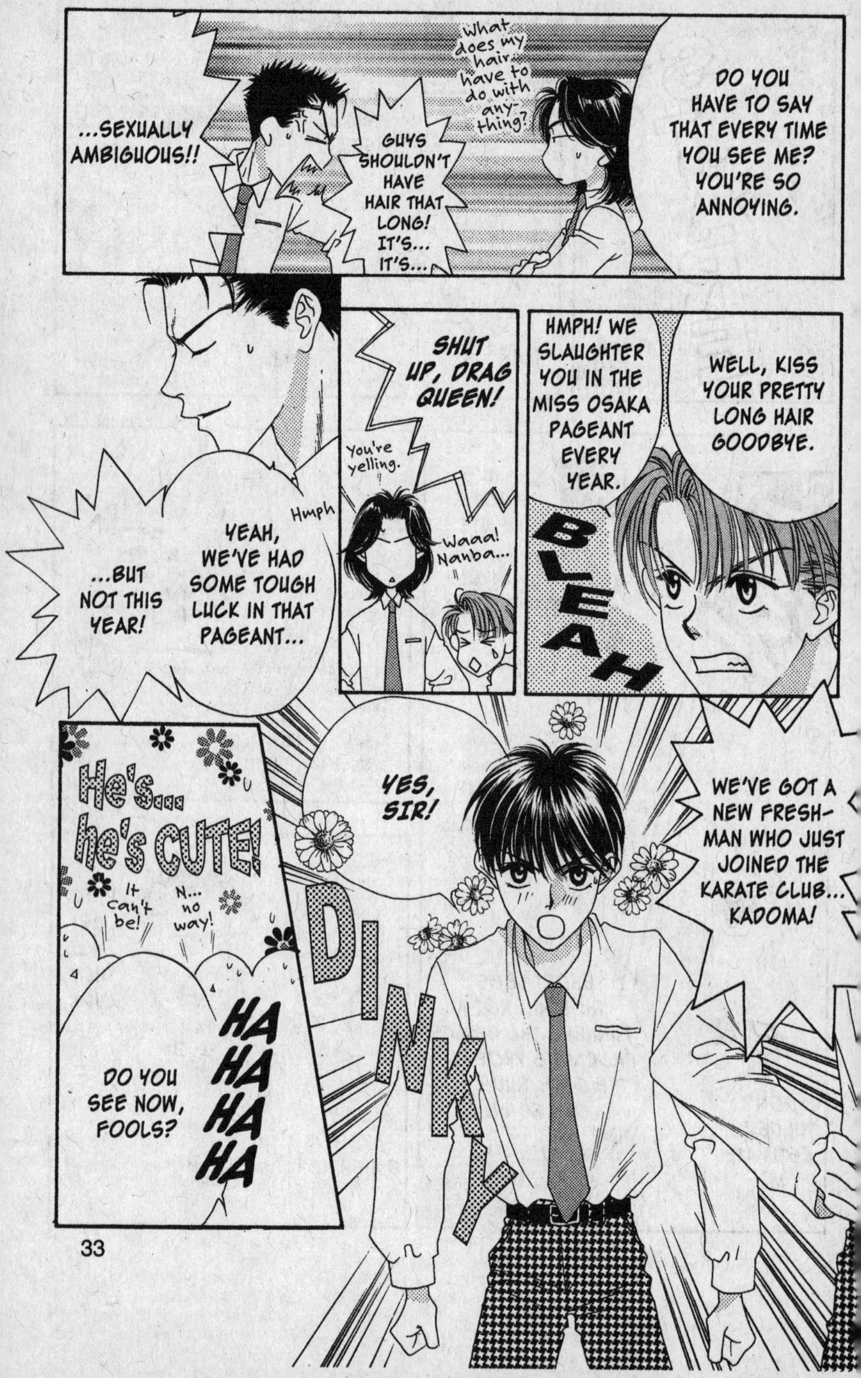
DO YOU HAVE TO SAY THAT EVERY TIME YOU SEE ME? YOU'RE SO ANNOYING.
What does my hair have to do with anything?
GUYS SHOULDN'T HAVE HAIR THAT LONG! IT'S... IT'S...
...SEXUALLY AMBIGUOUS!!
WELL, KISS YOUR PRETTY LONG HAIR GOODBYE.
HMPH! WE SLAUGHTER YOU IN THE MISS OSAKA PAGEANT EVERY YEAR.
BLEAH
SHUT UP, DRAG QUEEN!
You're yelling.
Waaa! Nanba...
Hmph
YEAH, WE'VE HAD SOME TOUGH LUCK IN THAT PAGEANT...
...BUT NOT THIS YEAR!
WE'VE GOT A NEW FRESHMAN WHO JUST JOINED THE KARATE CLUB... KADOMA!
YES, SIR!
DINK
He's... he's CUTE!
N... no way!
It can't be!
HA HA HA HA
DO YOU SEE NOW, FOOLS?

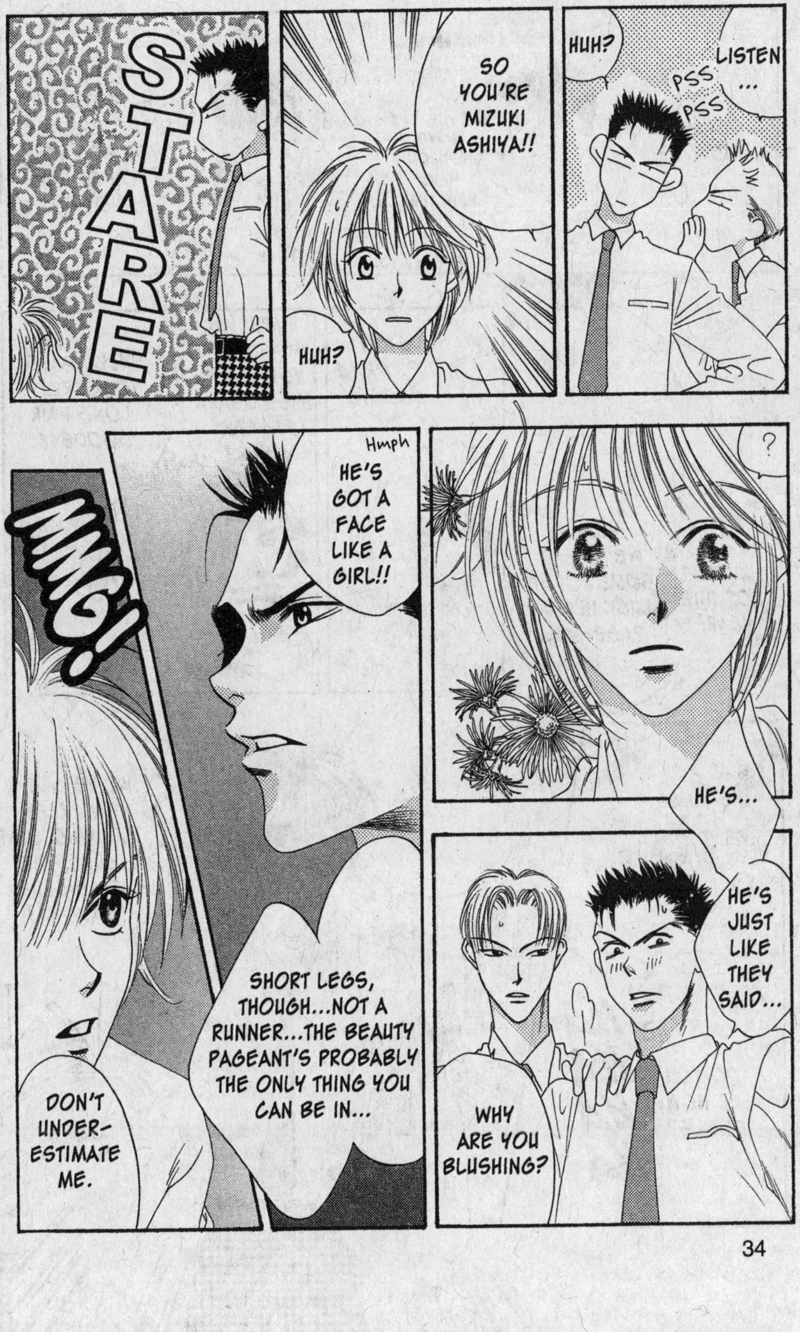

LISTEN...
PSS PSS
HUH?
SO YOU'RE MIZUKI ASHIYA!!
HUH?
STARE
?
HE'S...
HE'S JUST LIKE THEY SAID...
WHY ARE YOU BLUSHING?
Hmph
HE'S GOT A FACE LIKE A GIRL!!
MMG!
SHORT LEGS, THOUGH...NOT A RUNNER...THE BEAUTY PAGEANT'S PROBABLY THE ONLY THING YOU CAN BE IN...
DON'T UNDER-ESTIMATE ME.

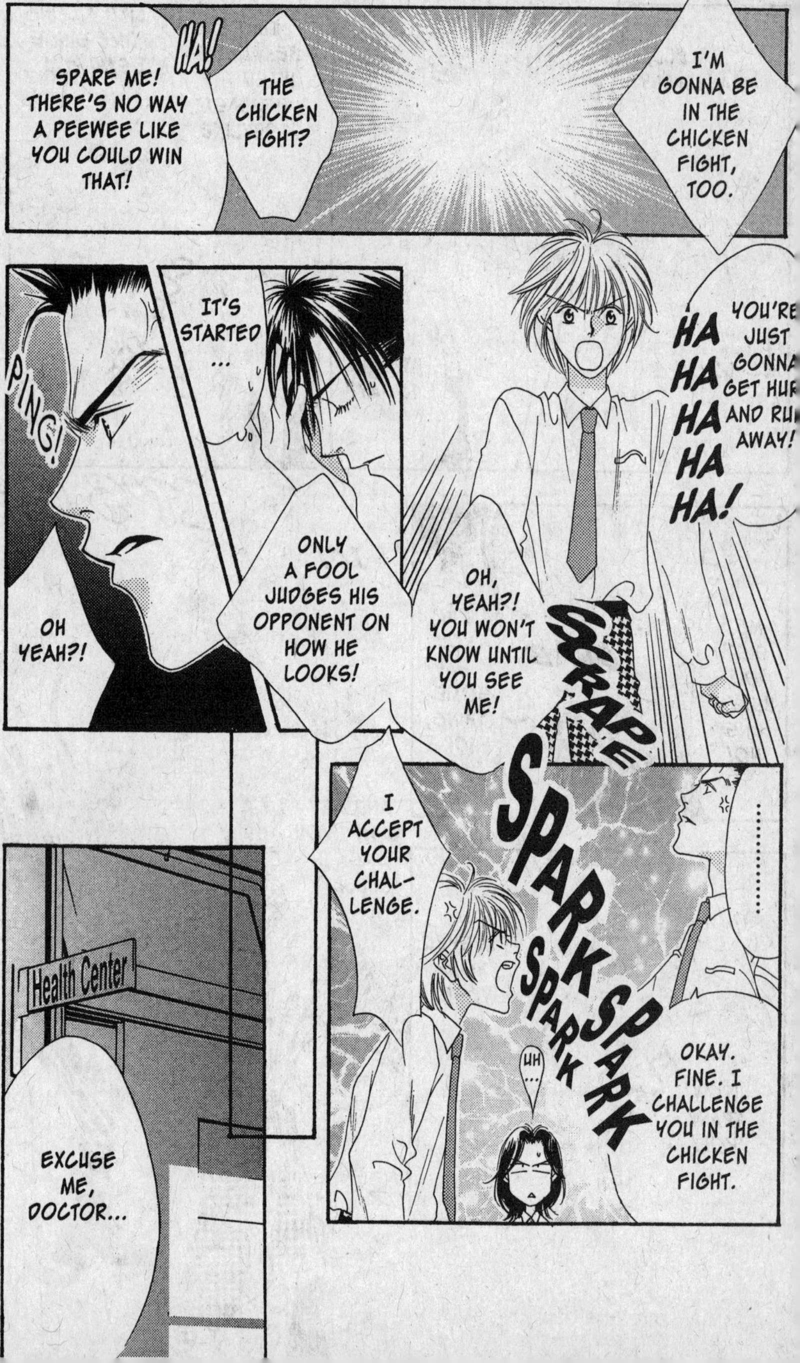
I'M GONNA BE IN THE CHICKEN FIGHT, TOO.
THE CHICKEN FIGHT?
HA!
SPARE ME! THERE'S NO WAY A PEEWEE LIKE YOU COULD WIN THAT!
YOU'RE JUST GONNA GET HUR AND RU AWAY!
HA HA HA HA HA HA!
OH, YEAH?! YOU WON'T KNOW UNTIL YOU SEE ME!
SCRAPE
IT'S STARTED...
ONLY A FOOL JUDGES HIS OPPONENT ON HOW HE LOOKS!
PING!
OH YEAH?!
......
SPARK SPARK SPARK SPARK
I ACCEPT YOUR CHAL-LENGE.
OKAY. FINE. I CHALLENGE YOU IN THE CHICKEN FIGHT.
UH...
Health Center
EXCUSE ME, DOCTOR...

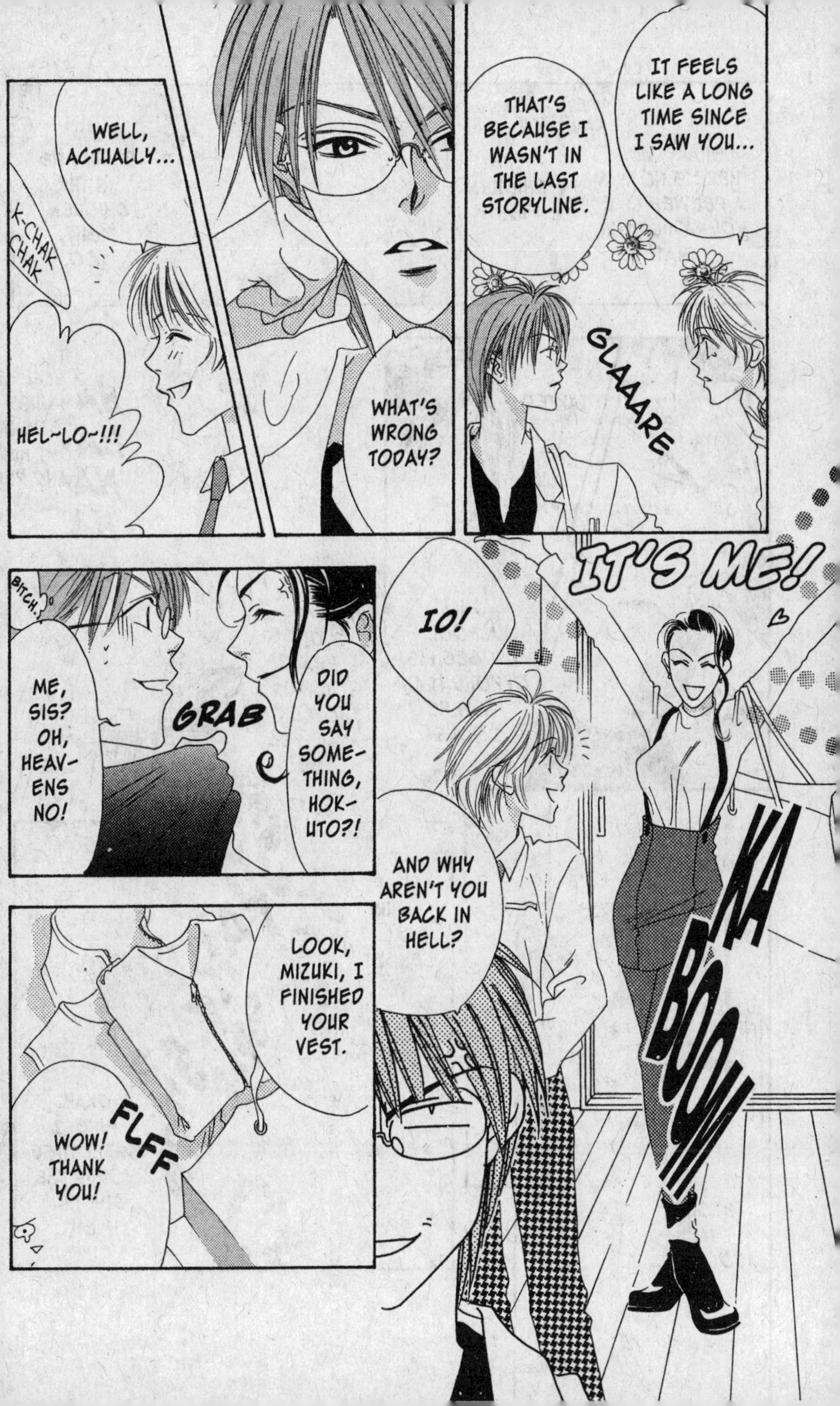
IT FEELS LIKE A LONG TIME SINCE I SAW YOU...
THAT'S BECAUSE I WASN'T IN THE LAST STORYLINE.
GLAAARE
WHAT'S WRONG TODAY?
WELL, ACTUALLY...
K-CHAK CHAK
HEL~LO~!!!
IT'S ME!
IO!
KA-BOOM
AND WHY AREN'T YOU BACK IN HELL?
DID YOU SAY SOME-THING, HOK-UTO?!
GRAB
BITCH.
ME, SIS? OH, HEAV-ENS NO!
LOOK, MIZUKI, I FINISHED YOUR VEST.
FLFF
WOW! THANK YOU!

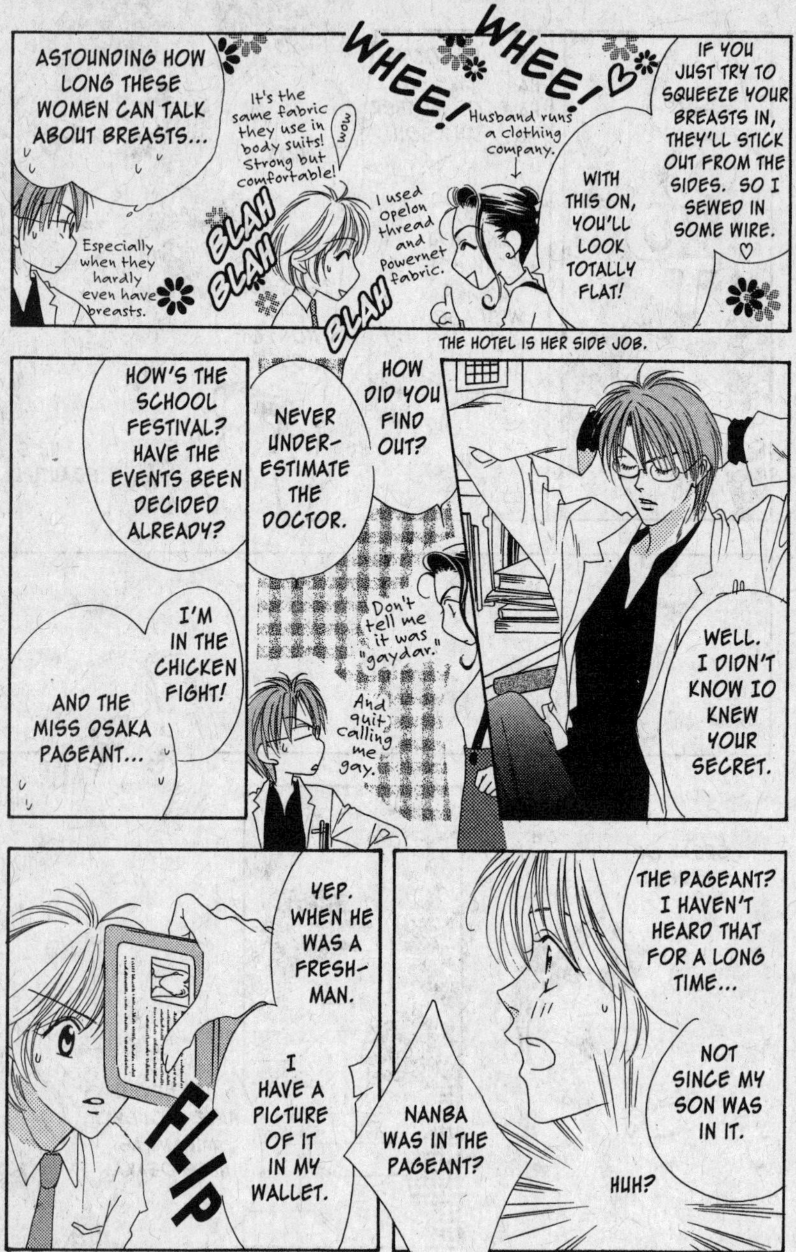
IF YOU JUST TRY TO SQUEEZE YOUR BREASTS IN, THEY'LL STICK OUT FROM THE SIDES. SO I SEWED IN SOME WIRE. ♡
WITH THIS ON, YOU'LL LOOK TOTALLY FLAT!
WHEE! WHEE! ♡
Husband runs a clothing company.
I used Opelon thread and Powernet fabric.
BLAH BLAH BLAH
It's the same fabric they use in body suits! Strong but comfortable!
WOW
ASTOUNDING HOW LONG THESE WOMEN CAN TALK ABOUT BREASTS...
Especially when they hardly even have breasts.
THE HOTEL IS HER SIDE JOB.
WELL. I DIDN'T KNOW IO KNEW YOUR SECRET.
HOW DID YOU FIND OUT?
NEVER UNDER-ESTIMATE THE DOCTOR.
Don't tell me it was "gaydar."
And quit calling me gay.
HOW'S THE SCHOOL FESTIVAL? HAVE THE EVENTS BEEN DECIDED ALREADY?
I'M IN THE CHICKEN FIGHT!
AND THE MISS OSAKA PAGEANT...
THE PAGEANT? I HAVEN'T HEARD THAT FOR A LONG TIME...
NOT SINCE MY SON WAS IN IT.
HUH?
NANBA WAS IN THE PAGEANT?
YEP. WHEN HE WAS A FRESH-MAN.
I HAVE A PICTURE OF IT IN MY WALLET.
FLIP

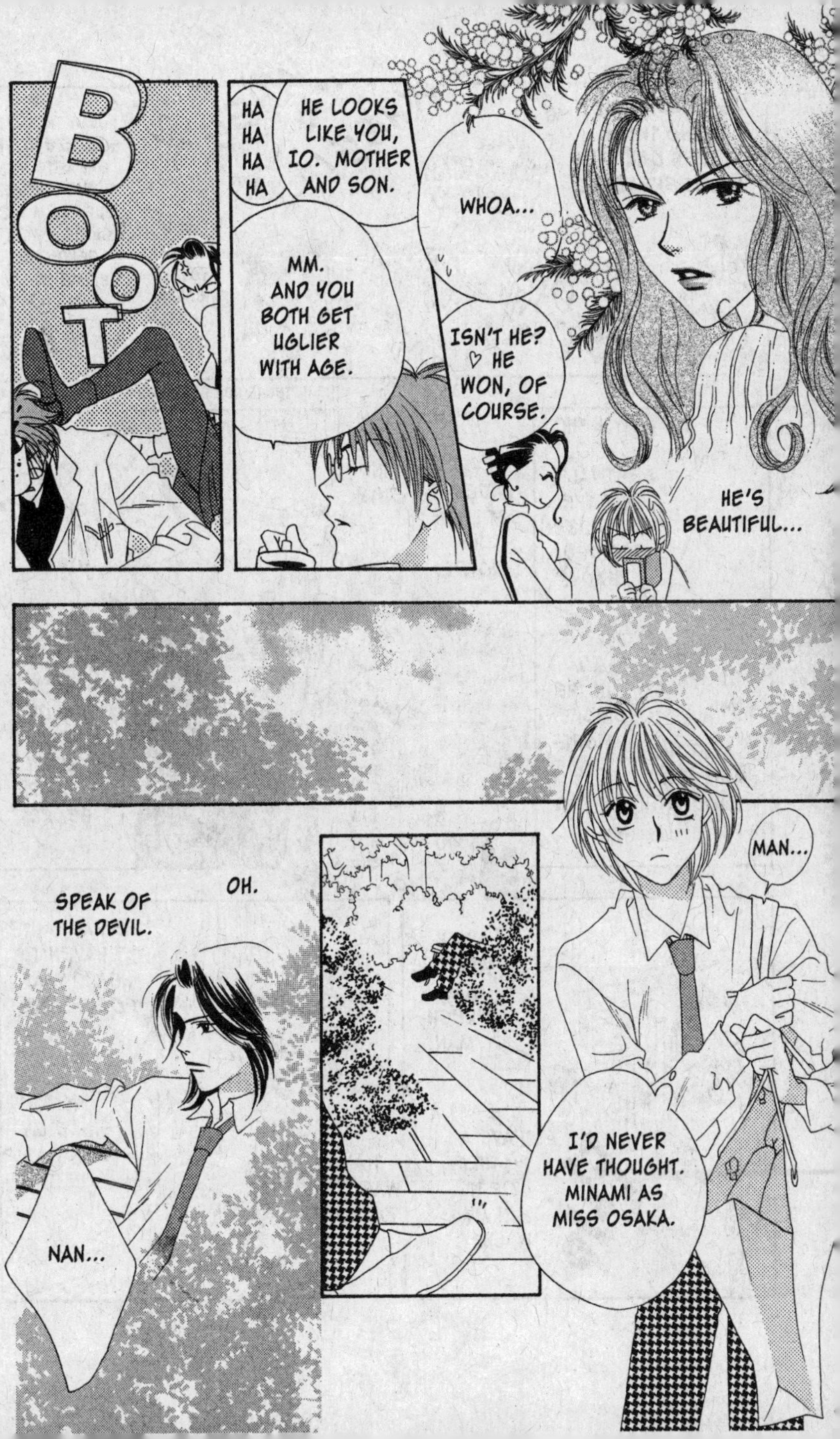
WHOA...
ISN'T HE? ♡ HE WON, OF COURSE.
HE'S BEAUTIFUL...
HE LOOKS LIKE YOU, IO. MOTHER AND SON.
HA HA HA HA
MM. AND YOU BOTH GET UGLIER WITH AGE.
BOOT
MAN...
I'D NEVER HAVE THOUGHT. MINAMI AS MISS OSAKA.
OH.
SPEAK OF THE DEVIL.
NAN...

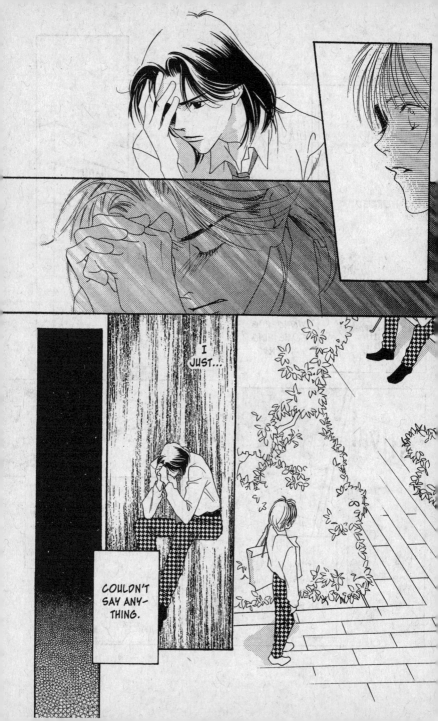

I JUST...

COULDN'T SAY ANY-
THING.

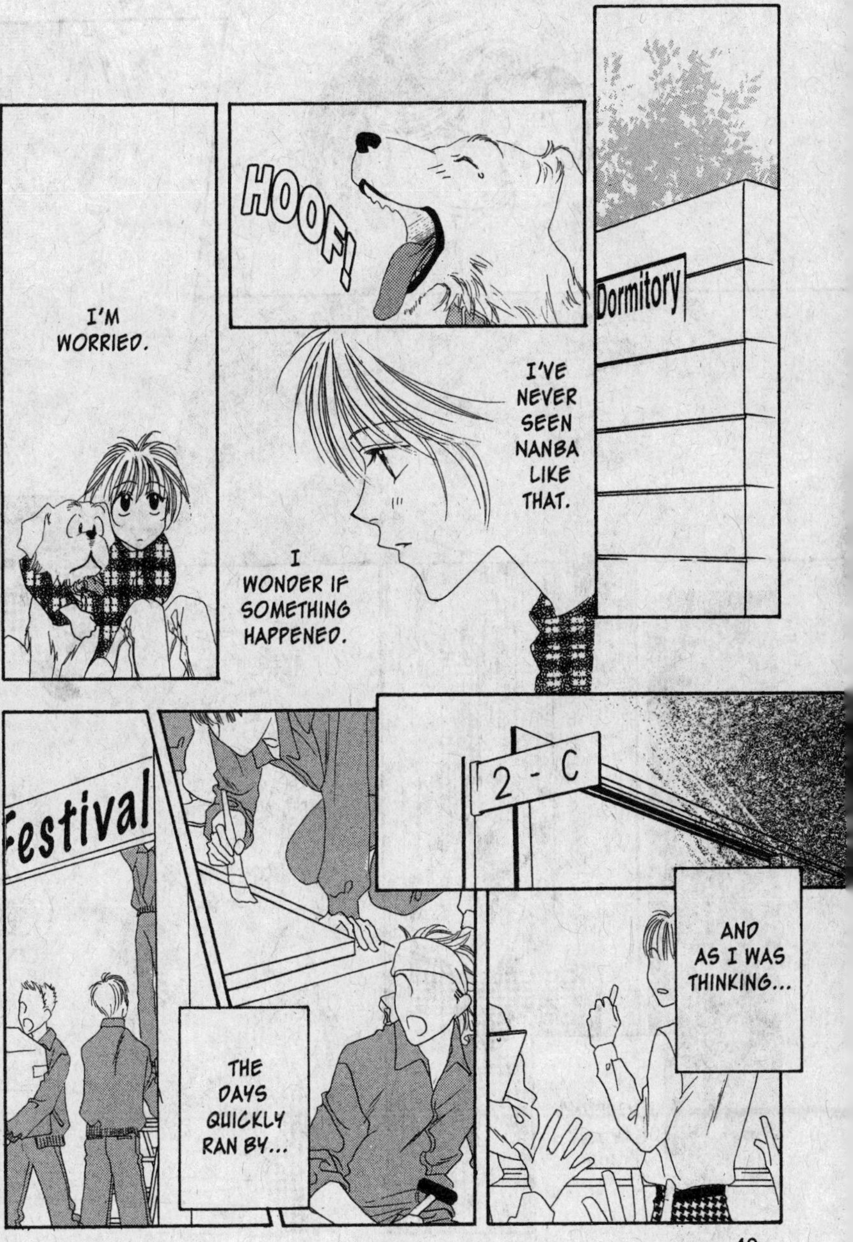
Dormitory
HOOF!
I'VE NEVER SEEN NANBA LIKE THAT.
I WONDER IF SOMETHING HAPPENED.
I'M WORRIED.
2 - C
AND AS I WAS THINKING...
THE DAYS QUICKLY RAN BY...
Festival

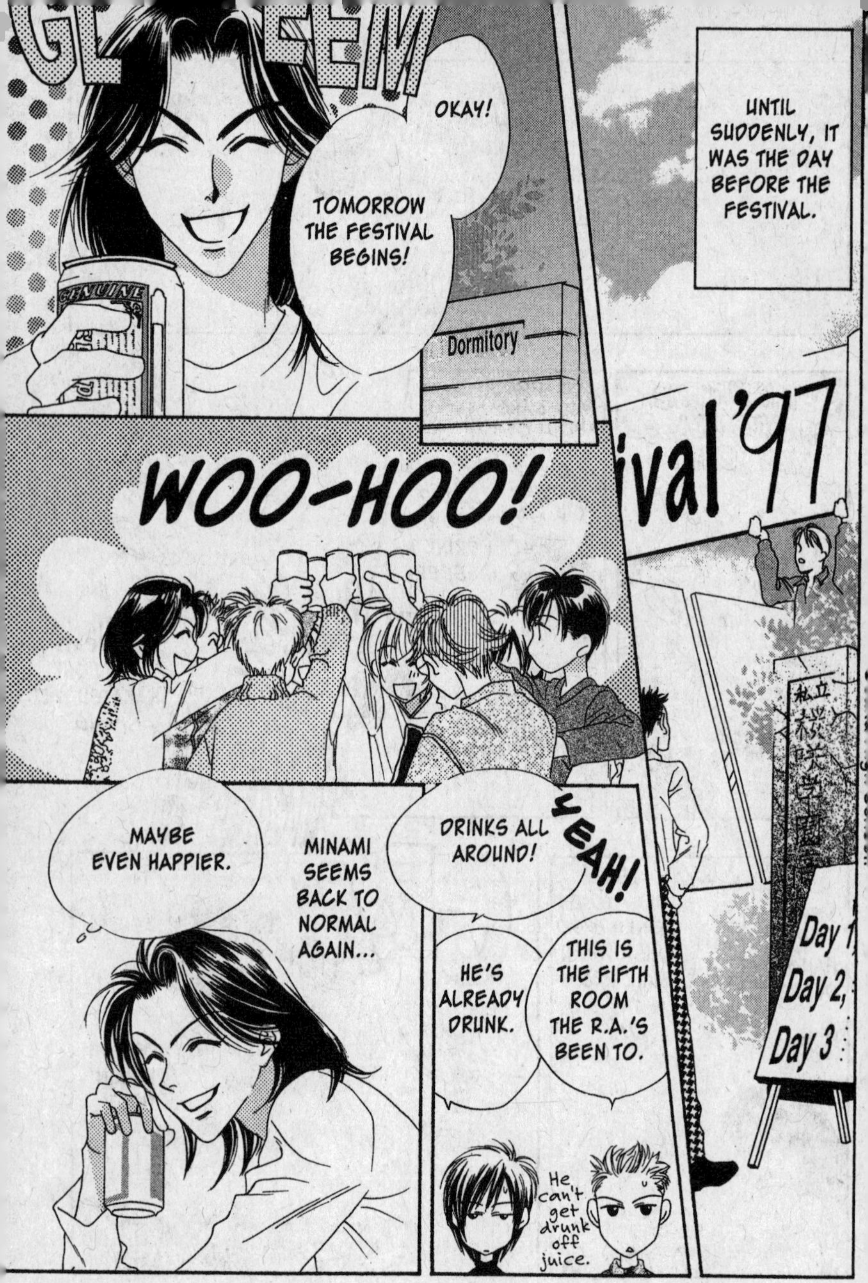
UNTIL SUDDENLY, IT WAS THE DAY BEFORE THE FESTIVAL.
ival '97
Day 1
Day 2,
Day 3
Dormitory
OKAY!
TOMORROW THE FESTIVAL BEGINS!
GENUINE
WOO-HOO!
DRINKS ALL AROUND!
YEAH!
THIS IS THE FIFTH ROOM THE R.A.'S BEEN TO.
HE'S ALREADY DRUNK.
He can't get drunk off juice.
MINAMI SEEMS BACK TO NORMAL AGAIN...
MAYBE EVEN HAPPIER.

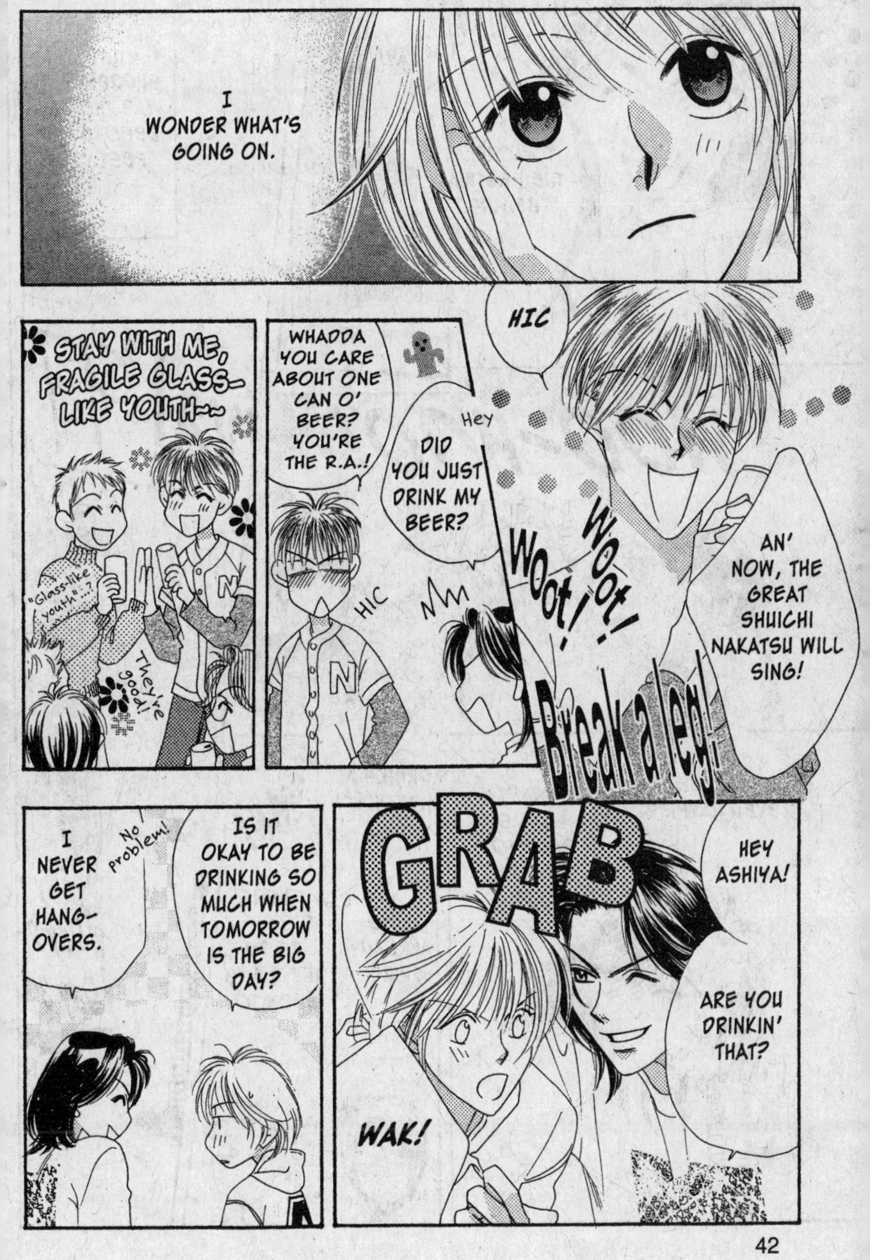
I WONDER WHAT'S GOING ON.
HIC
AN' NOW, THE GREAT SHUICHI NAKATSU WILL SING!
Woot! Woot!
Break a leg!
Hey
DID YOU JUST DRINK MY BEER?
WHADDA YOU CARE ABOUT ONE CAN O' BEER? YOU'RE THE R.A.!
HIC
STAY WITH ME, FRAGILE GLASS-LIKE YOUTH~~
"Glass-like youth"...?
They're good!
GRAB
HEY ASHIYA!
ARE YOU DRINKIN' THAT?
WAK!
IS IT OKAY TO BE DRINKING SO MUCH WHEN TOMORROW IS THE BIG DAY?
I NEVER GET HANG-OVERS.
No problem!

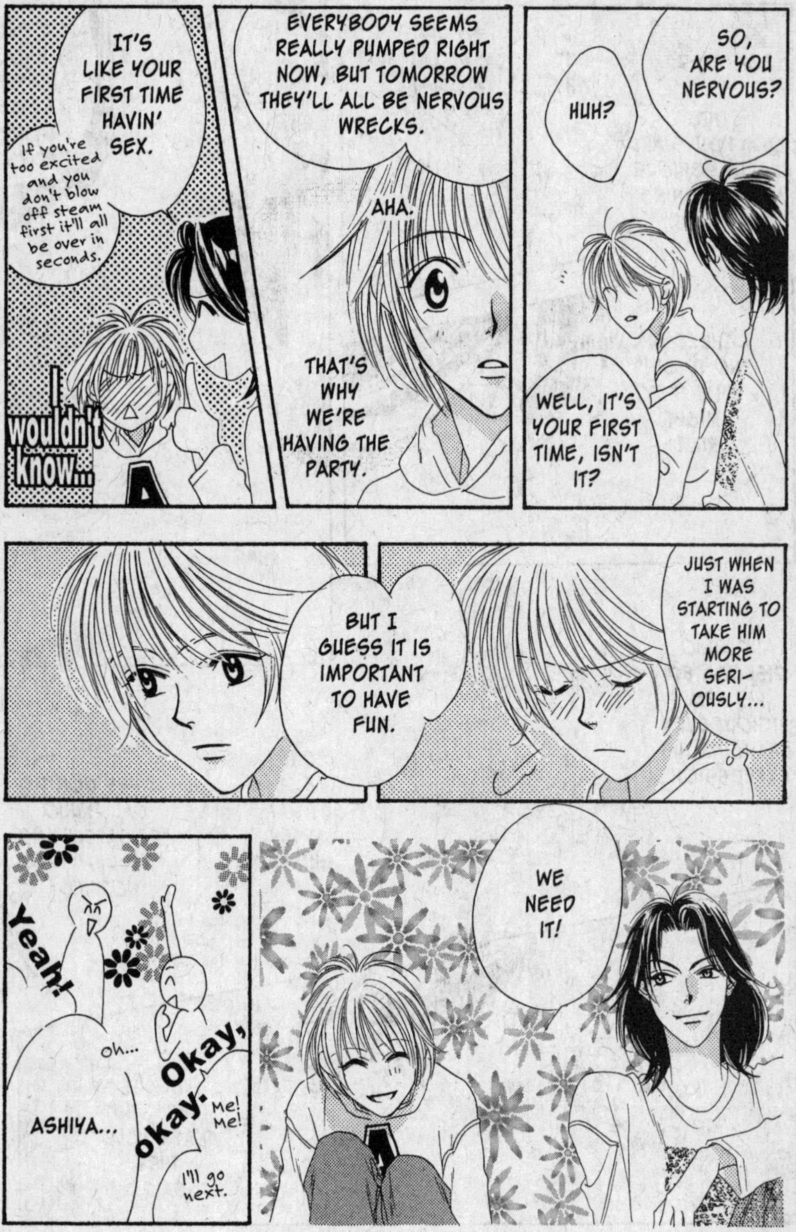
SO, ARE YOU NERVOUS?
HUH?
WELL, IT'S YOUR FIRST TIME, ISN'T IT?
EVERYBODY SEEMS REALLY PUMPED RIGHT NOW, BUT TOMORROW THEY'LL ALL BE NERVOUS WRECKS.
AHA.
THAT'S WHY WE'RE HAVING THE PARTY.
IT'S LIKE YOUR FIRST TIME HAVIN' SEX.
If you're too excited and you don't blow off steam first it'll all be over in seconds.
I wouldn't know...
JUST WHEN I WAS STARTING TO TAKE HIM MORE SERI-OUSLY...
BUT I GUESS IT IS IMPORTANT TO HAVE FUN.
WE NEED IT!
Yeah!
Okay, okay.
Me! Me!
I'll go next.
oh...
ASHIYA...

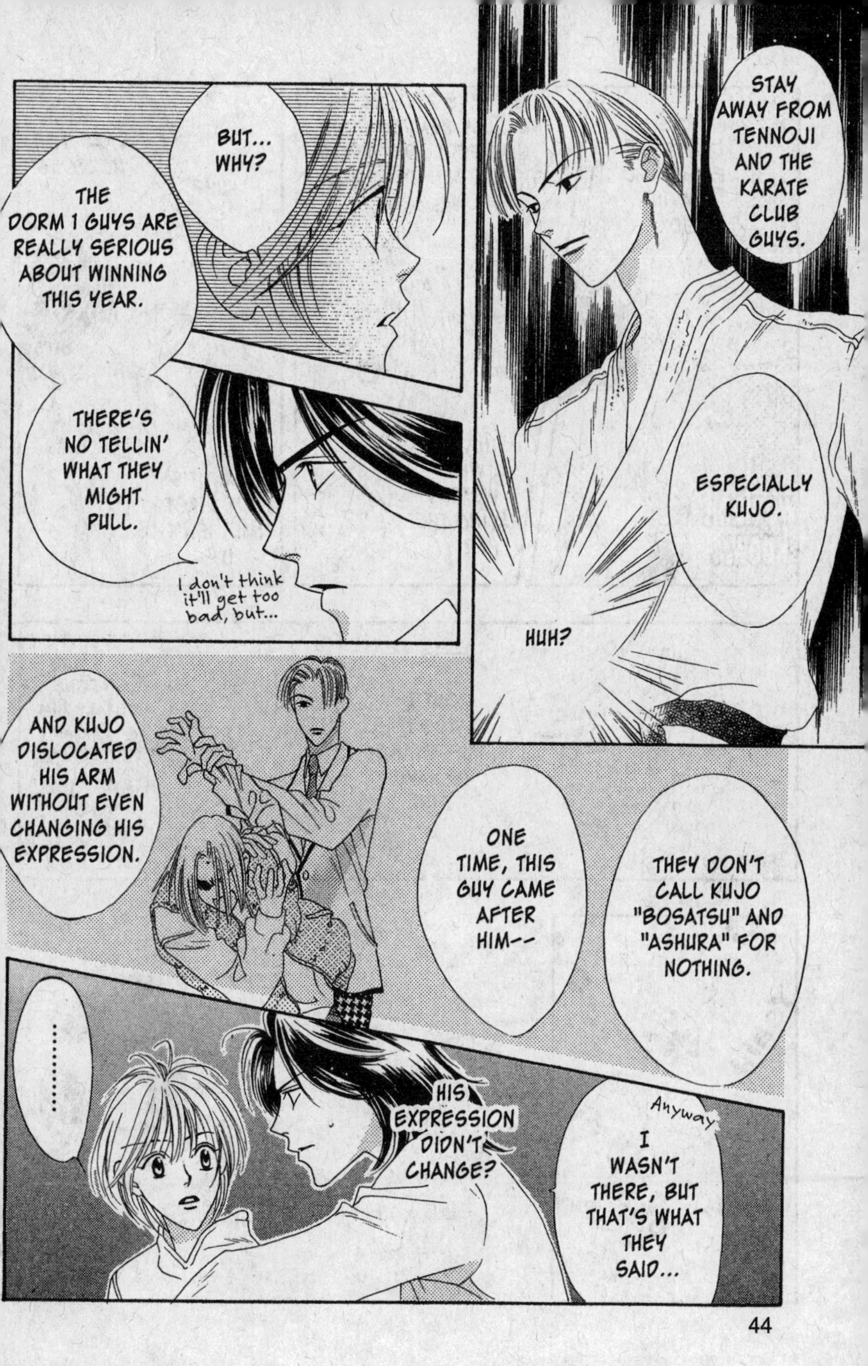
STAY AWAY FROM TENNOJI AND THE KARATE CLUB GUYS.
ESPECIALLY KUJO.
HUH?
BUT... WHY?
THE DORM 1 GUYS ARE REALLY SERIOUS ABOUT WINNING THIS YEAR.
THERE'S NO TELLIN' WHAT THEY MIGHT PULL.
I don't think it'll get too bad, but...
THEY DON'T CALL KUJO "BOSATSU" AND "ASHURA" FOR NOTHING.
ONE TIME, THIS GUY CAME AFTER HIM--
AND KUJO DISLOCATED HIS ARM WITHOUT EVEN CHANGING HIS EXPRESSION.
Anyway
I WASN'T THERE, BUT THAT'S WHAT THEY SAID...
HIS EXPRESSION DIDN'T CHANGE?
......

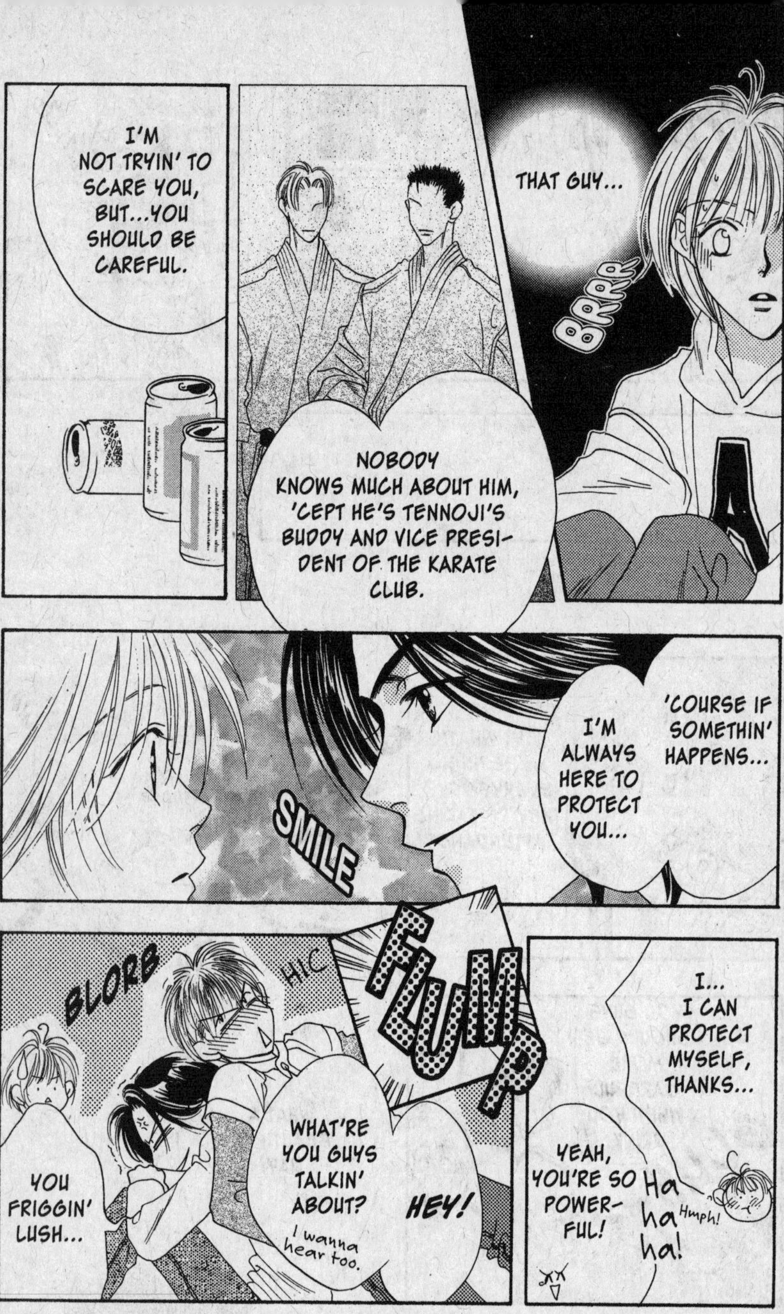
THAT GUY...
BRRR
NOBODY KNOWS MUCH ABOUT HIM, 'CEPT HE'S TENNOJI'S BUDDY AND VICE PRESIDENT OF THE KARATE CLUB.
I'M NOT TRYIN' TO SCARE YOU, BUT...YOU SHOULD BE CAREFUL.
'COURSE IF SOMETHIN' HAPPENS...
I'M ALWAYS HERE TO PROTECT YOU...
SMILE
I... I CAN PROTECT MYSELF, THANKS...
Hmph!
YEAH, YOU'RE SO POWERFUL!
Ha ha ha!
FLUMP
HEY!
WHAT'RE YOU GUYS TALKIN' ABOUT?
I wanna hear too.
HIC
BLORB
YOU FRIGGIN' LUSH...

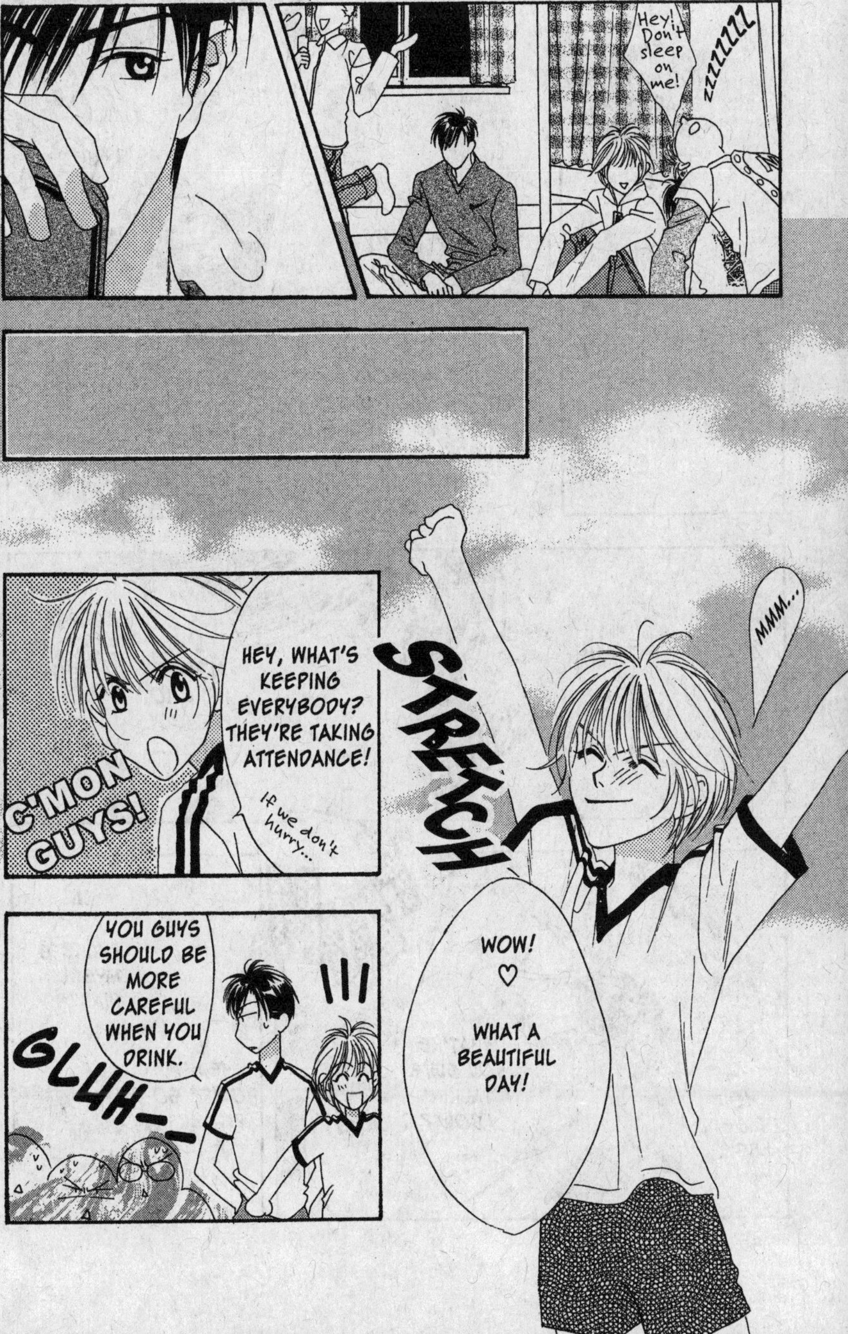
ZZZZZZZZ
Hey! Don't sleep on me!
MMM...
STRETCH
WOW! ♡ WHAT A BEAUTIFUL DAY!
HEY, WHAT'S KEEPING EVERYBODY? THEY'RE TAKING ATTENDANCE!
If we don't hurry...
C'MON GUYS!
YOU GUYS SHOULD BE MORE CAREFUL WHEN YOU DRINK.
GLUH--

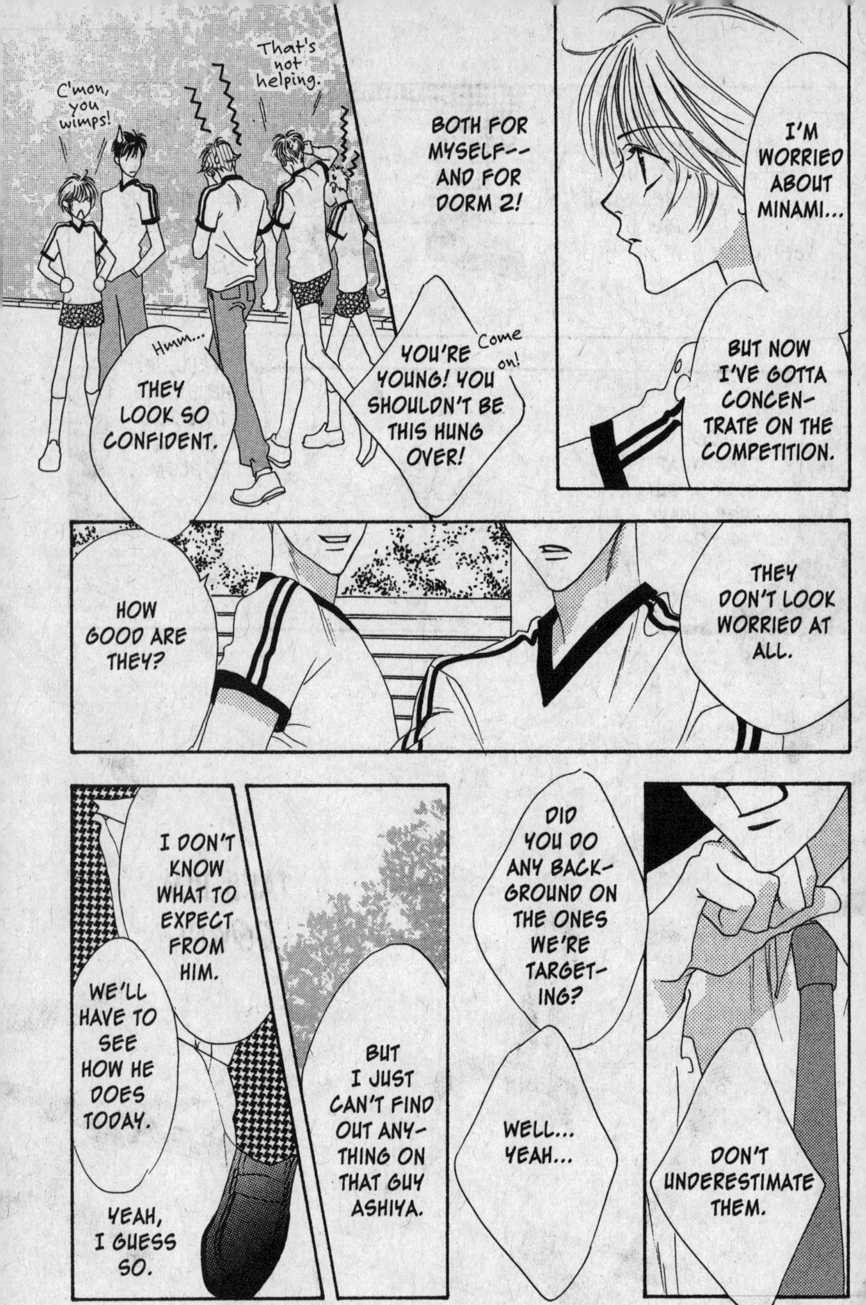
I'M WORRIED ABOUT MINAMI...
BUT NOW I'VE GOTTA CONCENTRATE ON THE COMPETITION.
BOTH FOR MYSELF-- AND FOR DORM 2!
That's not helping.
C'mon, you wimps!
YOU'RE YOUNG! YOU SHOULDN'T BE THIS HUNG OVER!
Come on!
Hmm...
THEY LOOK SO CONFIDENT.
THEY DON'T LOOK WORRIED AT ALL.
HOW GOOD ARE THEY?
DON'T UNDERESTIMATE THEM.
DID YOU DO ANY BACK-GROUND ON THE ONES WE'RE TARGET-ING?
WELL... YEAH...
BUT I JUST CAN'T FIND OUT ANY-THING ON THAT GUY ASHIYA.
I DON'T KNOW WHAT TO EXPECT FROM HIM.
WE'LL HAVE TO SEE HOW HE DOES TODAY.
YEAH, I GUESS SO.

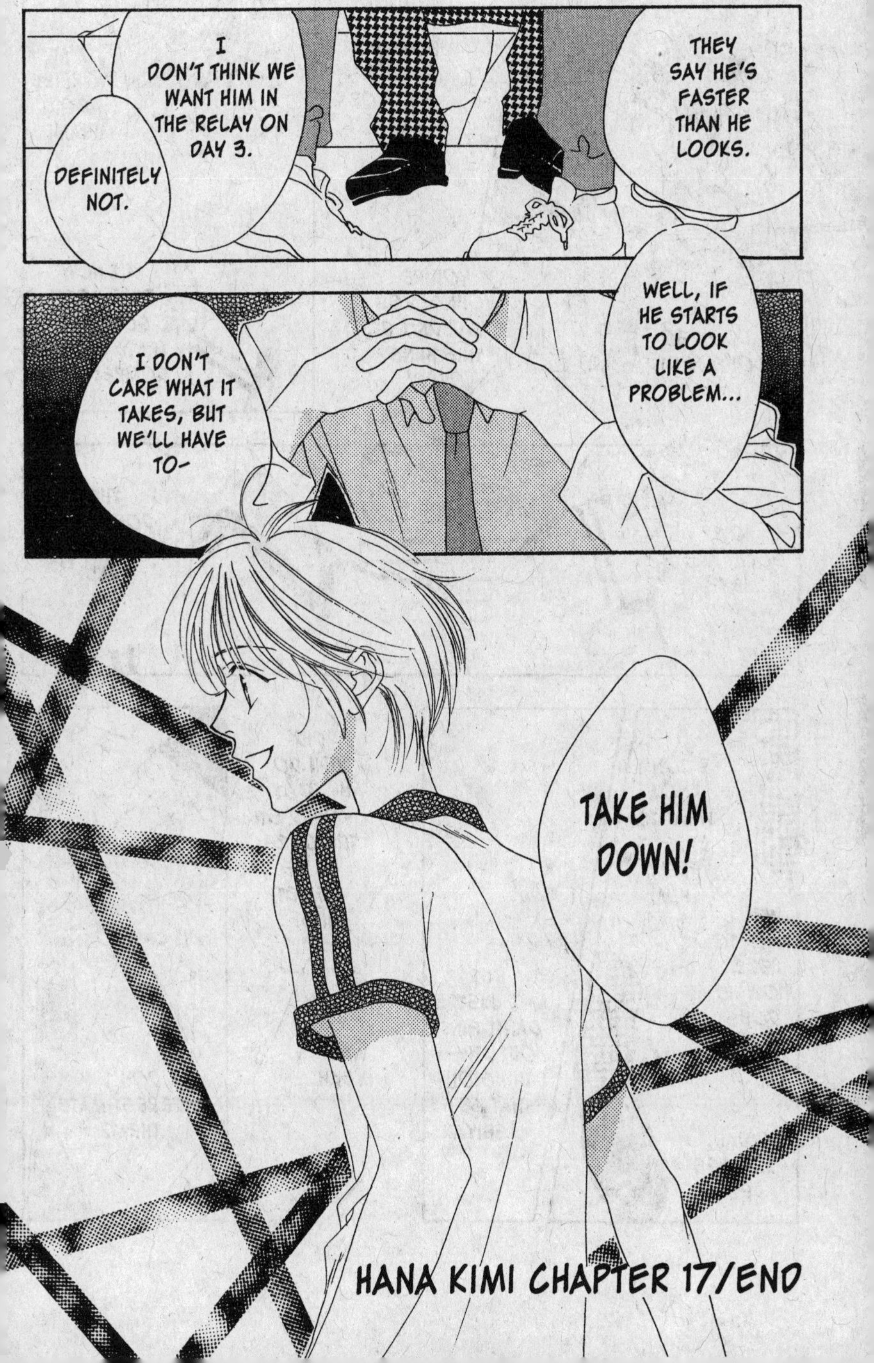
THEY SAY HE'S FASTER THAN HE LOOKS.
I DON'T THINK WE WANT HIM IN THE RELAY ON DAY 3.
DEFINITELY NOT.
WELL, IF HE STARTS TO LOOK LIKE A PROBLEM...
I DON'T CARE WHAT IT TAKES, BUT WE'LL HAVE TO-
TAKE HIM DOWN!

HANA KIMI CHAPTER 17/END

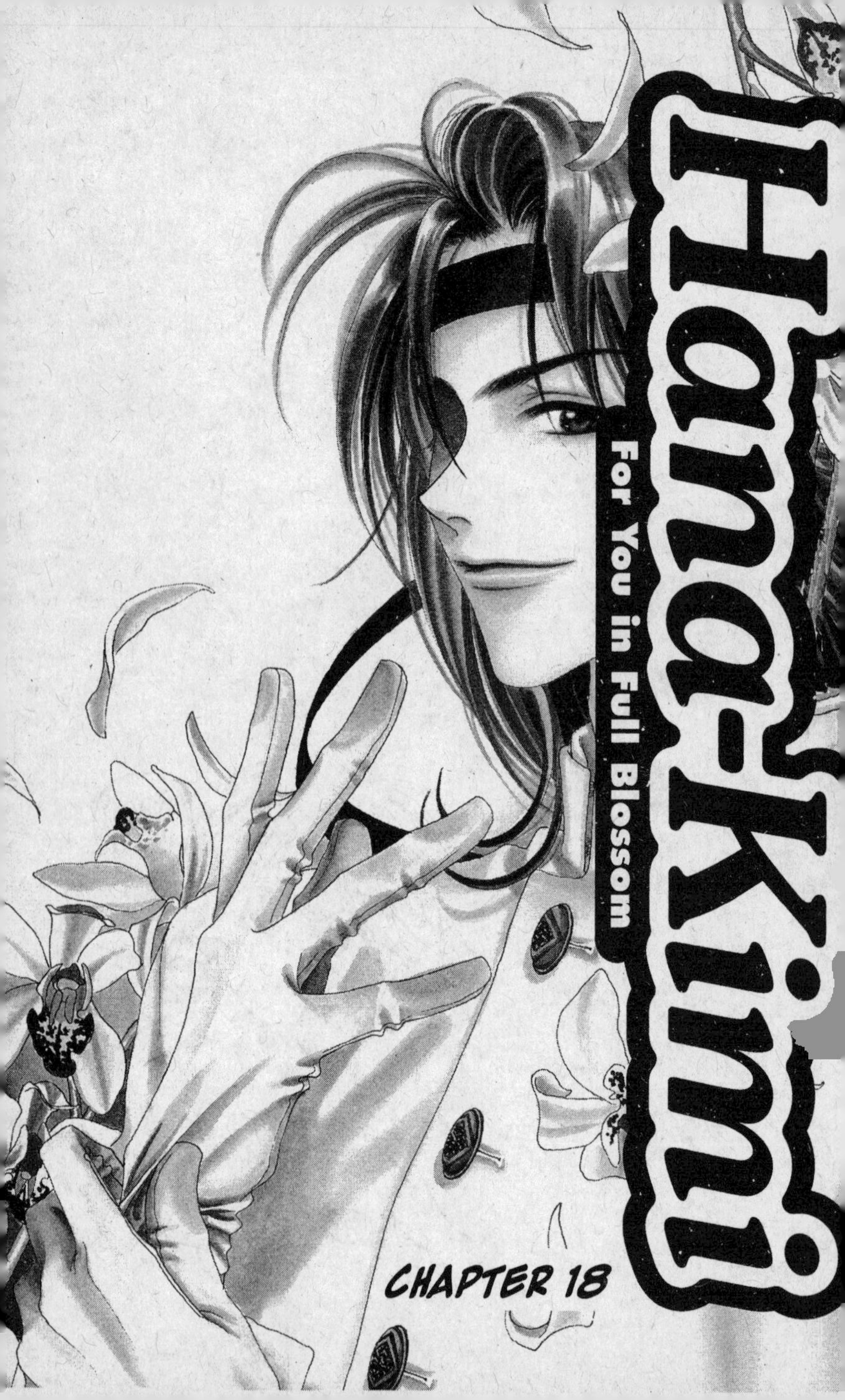
Hana-Kimi!
For You in Full Blossom
CHAPTER 18

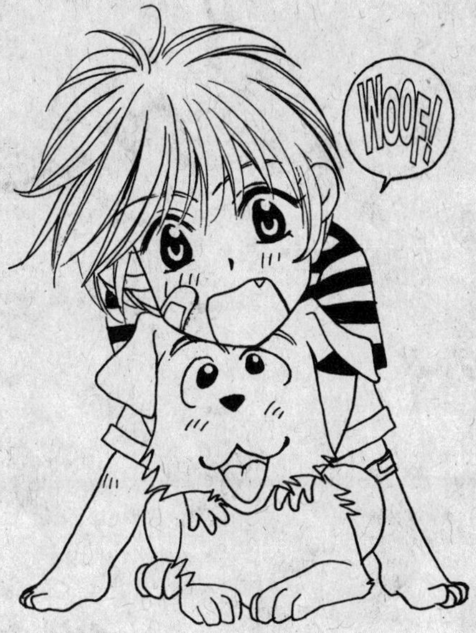
WOOF!

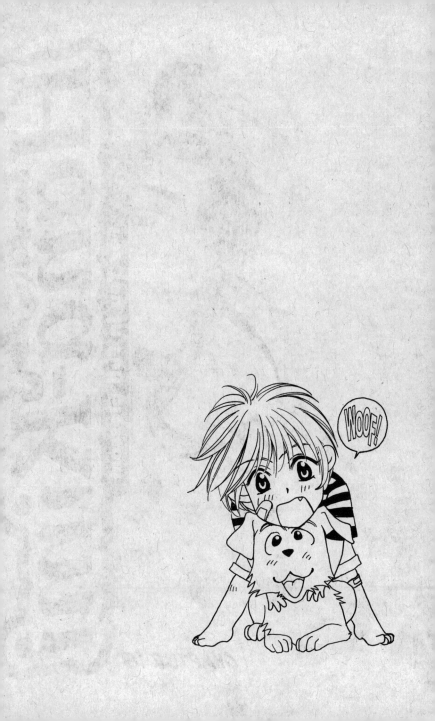

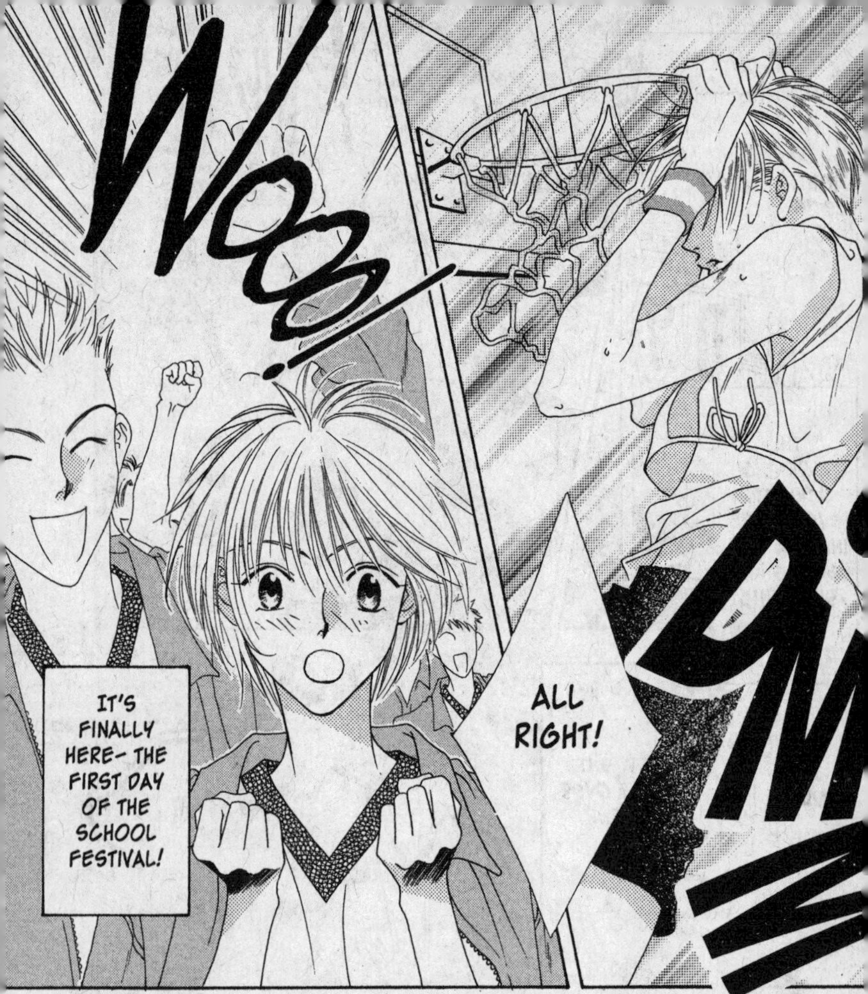
WOO!
ALL RIGHT!
IT'S FINALLY HERE- THE FIRST DAY OF THE SCHOOL FESTIVAL!

Valentine's Day

THANK YOU FOR ALL THE STUFF YOU SENT IN. CUTE STUFF, HAND MADE STUFF, EVEN HOMEMADE CHOCOLATE. MY WHOLE STAFF WAS VERY GRATEFUL. (CHOCOLATE BOOSTS MY ENERGY WHILE ON THE JOB. ESPECIALLY SINCE I DON'T USUALLY EAT SWEETS.) MOST OF THE CHOCOLATE WAS SENT TO ME. BUT SOMEONE EVEN SENT CHOCOLATE TO HIMEJIMA (SEE PAGE 59). WHAT A SURPRISE! JUST ONE PERSON. I WAS IMPRESSED BY EVERYBODY'S CAREFUL WRAPPING. AND OF COURSE, THE CHOCOLATE WAS GOOD, TOO.

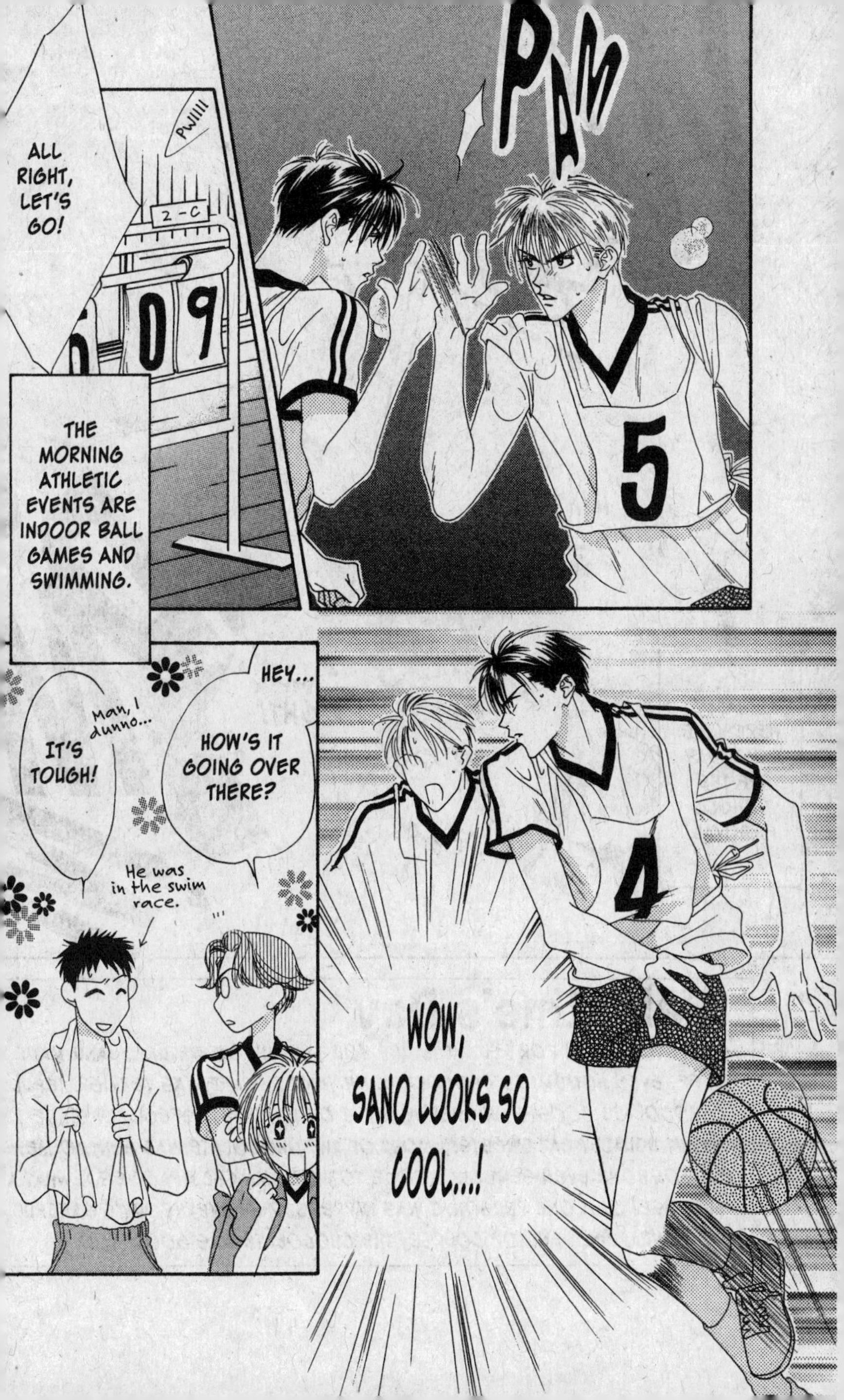
PAM
PWIIII
2-C
ALL RIGHT, LET'S GO!
THE MORNING ATHLETIC EVENTS ARE INDOOR BALL GAMES AND SWIMMING.
WOW, SANO LOOKS SO COOL...!
HEY... HOW'S IT GOING OVER THERE?
IT'S TOUGH!
Man, I dunno...
He was in the swim race.
...

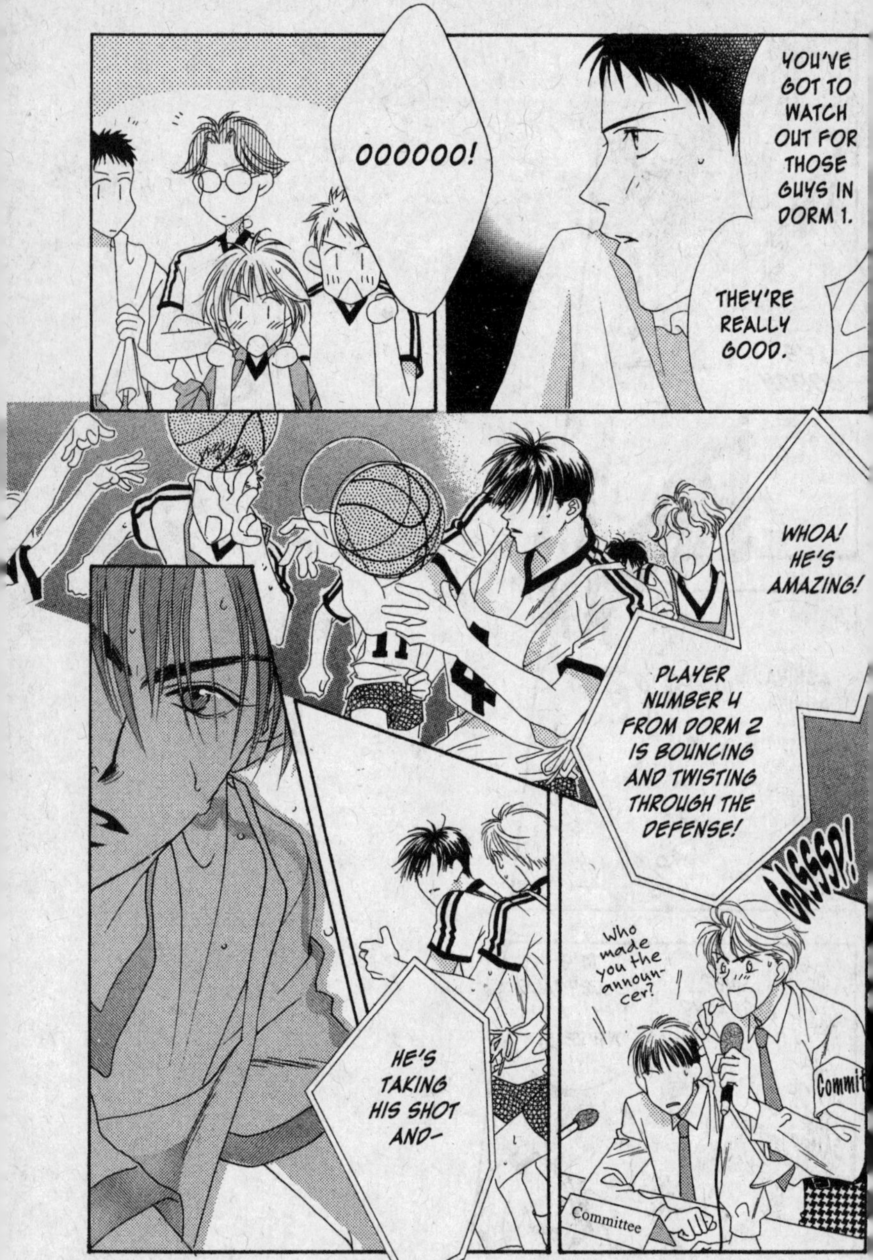
YOU'VE GOT TO WATCH OUT FOR THOSE GUYS IN DORM 1.
THEY'RE REALLY GOOD.
OOOOOO!
WHOA! HE'S AMAZING!
PLAYER NUMBER 4 FROM DORM 2 IS BOUNCING AND TWISTING THROUGH THE DEFENSE!
GASSSP!
Who made you the announcer?
Commit
Committee
HE'S TAKING HIS SHOT AND-

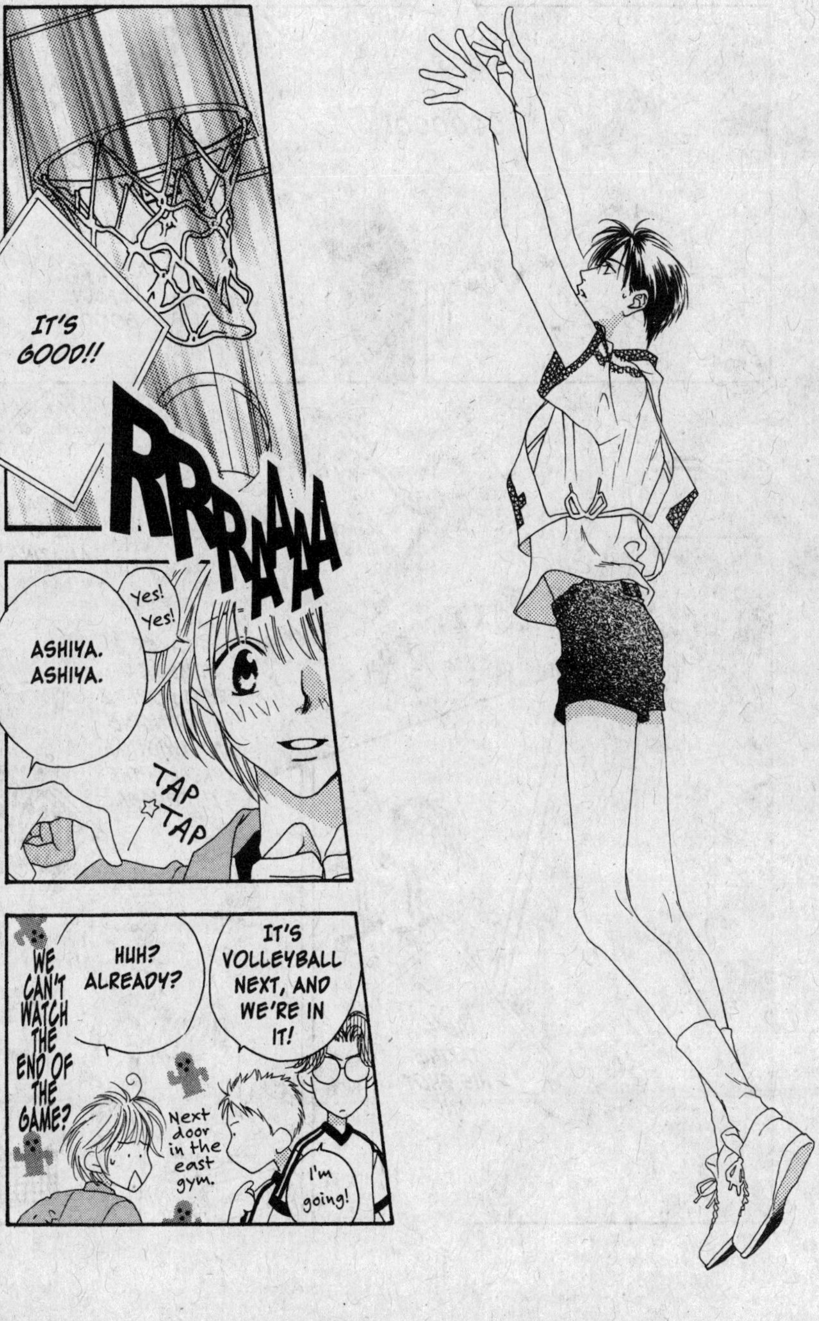
IT'S GOOD!!
RRRAAAA
Yes! Yes!
ASHIYA. ASHIYA.
TAP TAP
IT'S VOLLEYBALL NEXT, AND WE'RE IN IT!
HUH? ALREADY?
WE CAN'T WATCH THE END OF THE GAME?
I'm going!
Next door in the east gym.

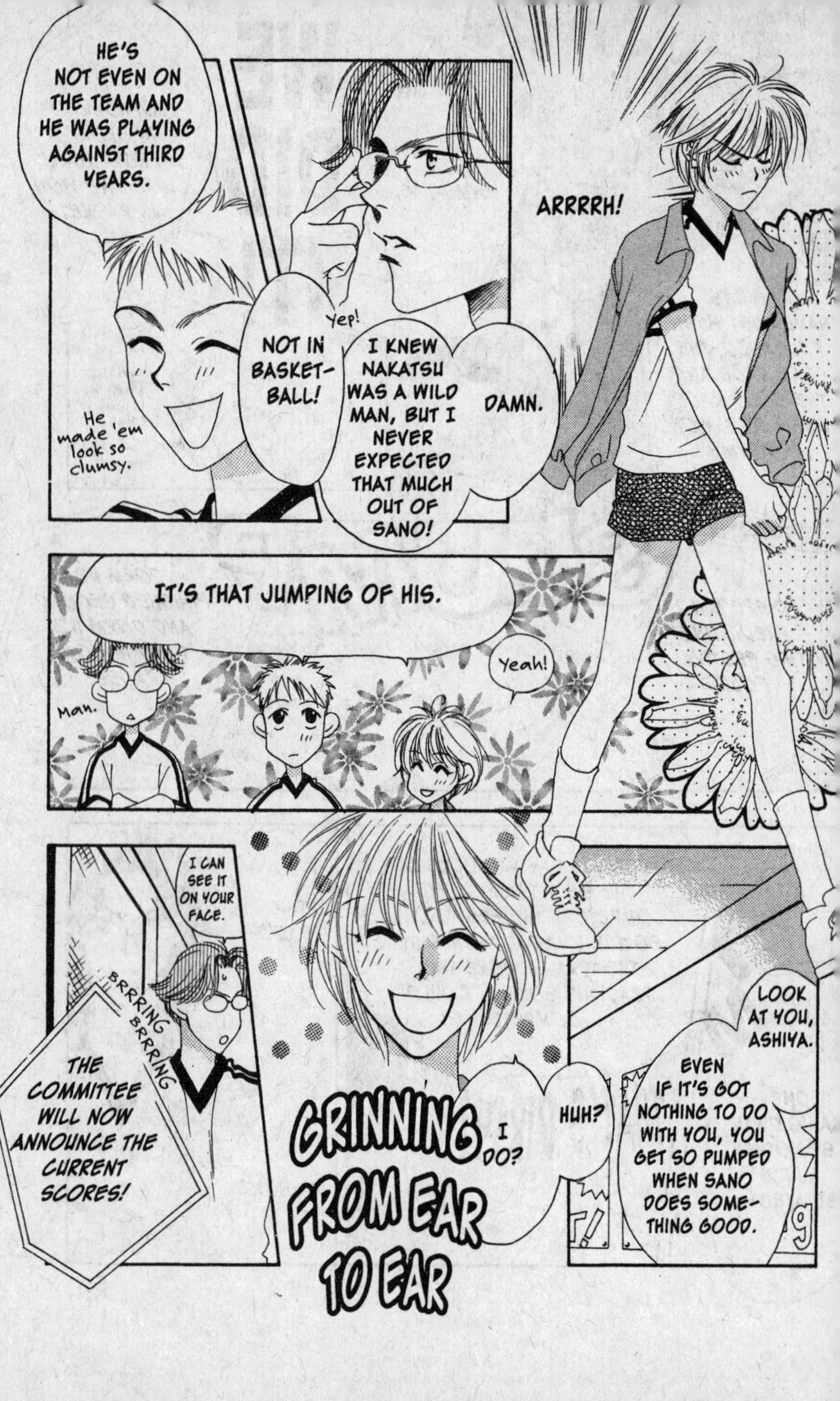
ARRRRH!
DAMN.
I KNEW NAKATSU WAS A WILD MAN, BUT I NEVER EXPECTED THAT MUCH OUT OF SANO!
Yep!
NOT IN BASKETBALL!
HE'S NOT EVEN ON THE TEAM AND HE WAS PLAYING AGAINST THIRD YEARS.
He made 'em look so clumsy.
IT'S THAT JUMPING OF HIS.
Yeah!
Man.
LOOK AT YOU, ASHIYA.
EVEN IF IT'S GOT NOTHING TO DO WITH YOU, YOU GET SO PUMPED WHEN SANO DOES SOMETHING GOOD.
HUH?
I DO?
GRINNING FROM EAR TO EAR
I CAN SEE IT ON YOUR FACE.
BRRRING BRRRING
THE COMMITTEE WILL NOW ANNOUNCE THE CURRENT SCORES!

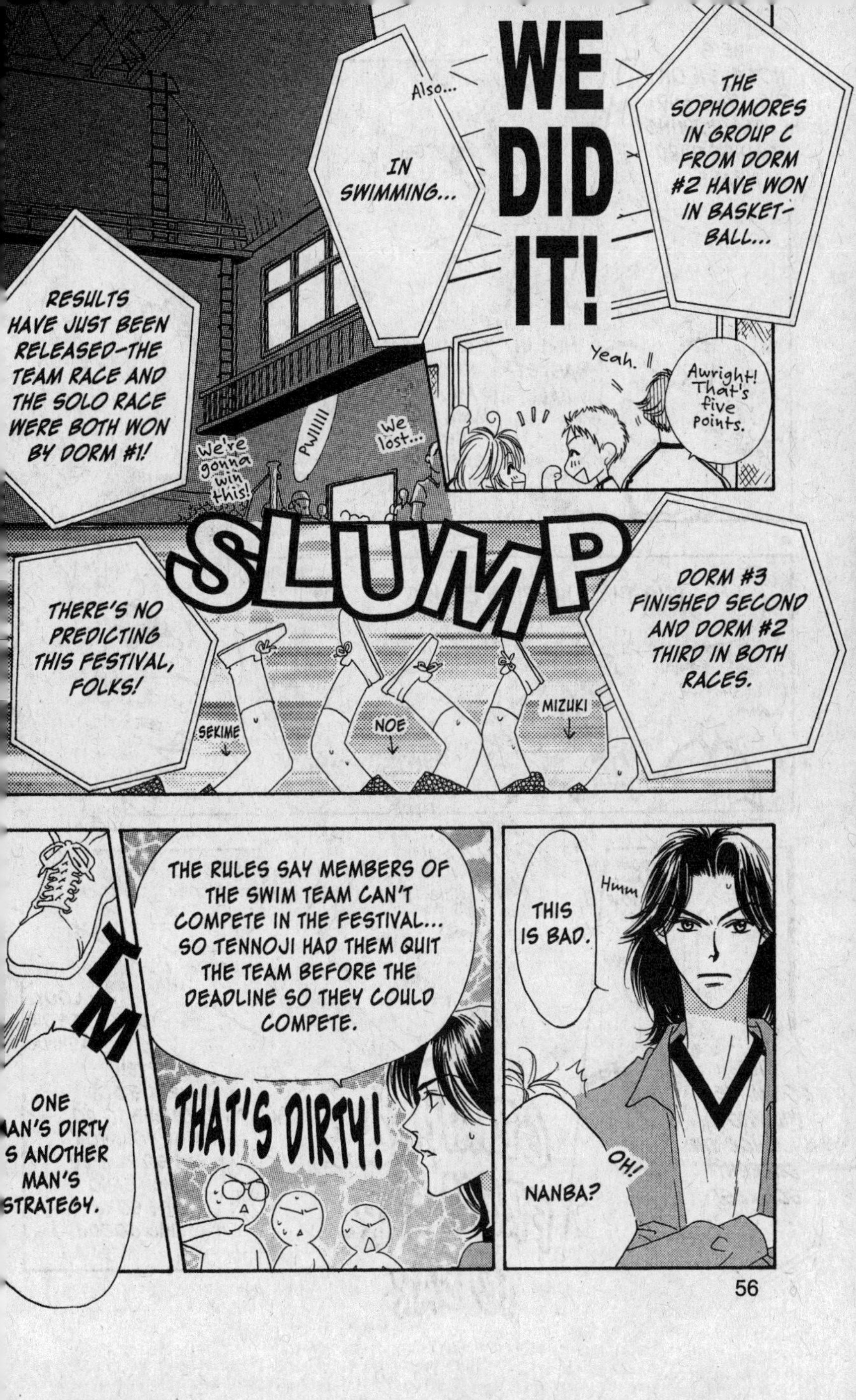
THE SOPHOMORES IN GROUP C FROM DORM #2 HAVE WON IN BASKETBALL...
WE DID IT!
Also...
IN SWIMMING...
Awright! That's five points.
Yeah.
RESULTS HAVE JUST BEEN RELEASED—THE TEAM RACE AND THE SOLO RACE WERE BOTH WON BY DORM #1!
We lost...
PWIIIII
We're gonna win this!
DORM #3 FINISHED SECOND AND DORM #2 THIRD IN BOTH RACES.
SLUMP
MIZUKI
NOE
SEKIME
THERE'S NO PREDICTING THIS FESTIVAL, FOLKS!
Hmm
THIS IS BAD.
OH!
NANBA?
THE RULES SAY MEMBERS OF THE SWIM TEAM CAN'T COMPETE IN THE FESTIVAL... SO TENNOJI HAD THEM QUIT THE TEAM BEFORE THE DEADLINE SO THEY COULD COMPETE.
THAT'S DIRTY!
TM
ONE AN'S DIRTY S ANOTHER MAN'S STRATEGY.

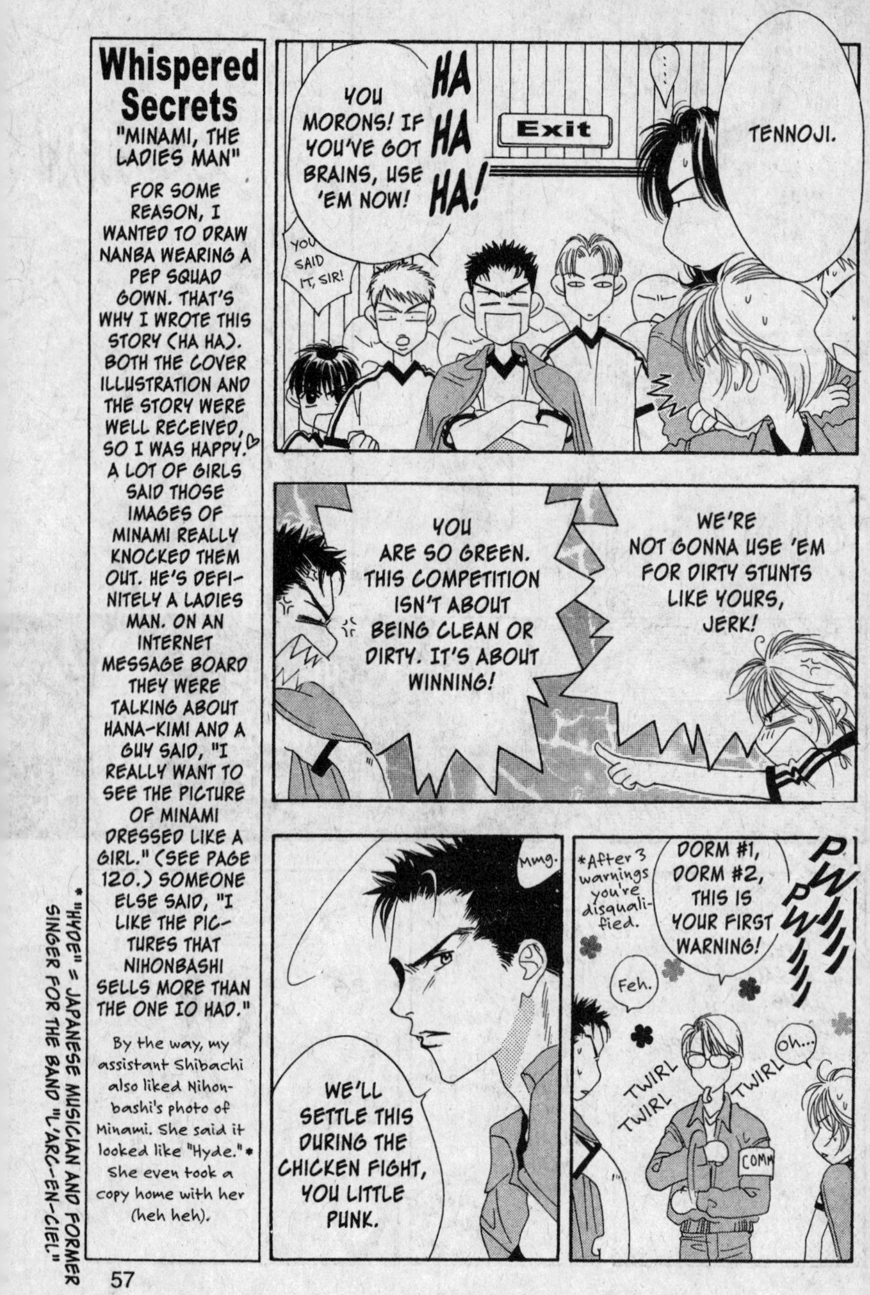
...
TENNOJI.
HA HA HA!
YOU MORONS! IF YOU'VE GOT BRAINS, USE 'EM NOW!
YOU SAID IT, SIR!
WE'RE NOT GONNA USE 'EM FOR DIRTY STUNTS LIKE YOURS, JERK!
YOU ARE SO GREEN. THIS COMPETITION ISN'T ABOUT BEING CLEAN OR DIRTY. IT'S ABOUT WINNING!
PWWW
DORM #1, DORM #2, THIS IS YOUR FIRST WARNING!
*After 3 warnings you're disqualified.
Feh.
Oh...
TWIRL TWIRL
TWIRL
COMM
Mmg.
WE'LL SETTLE THIS DURING THE CHICKEN FIGHT, YOU LITTLE PUNK.

Whispered Secrets

"MINAMI, THE LADIES MAN"

FOR SOME REASON, I WANTED TO DRAW NANBA WEARING A PEP SQUAD GOWN. THAT'S WHY I WROTE THIS STORY (HA HA). BOTH THE COVER ILLUSTRATION AND THE STORY WERE WELL RECEIVED, SO I WAS HAPPY.♡ A LOT OF GIRLS SAID THOSE IMAGES OF MINAMI REALLY KNOCKED THEM OUT. HE'S DEFINITELY A LADIES MAN. ON AN INTERNET MESSAGE BOARD THEY WERE TALKING ABOUT HANA-KIMI AND A GUY SAID, "I REALLY WANT TO SEE THE PICTURE OF MINAMI DRESSED LIKE A GIRL." (SEE PAGE 120.) SOMEONE ELSE SAID, "I LIKE THE PICTURES THAT NIHONBASHI SELLS MORE THAN THE ONE IO HAD."

By the way, my assistant Shibachi also liked Nihonbashi's photo of Minami. She said it looked like "Hyde."* She even took a copy home with her (heh heh).

* "HYDE" = JAPANESE MUSICIAN AND FORMER SINGER FOR THE BAND "L'ARC-EN-CIEL."

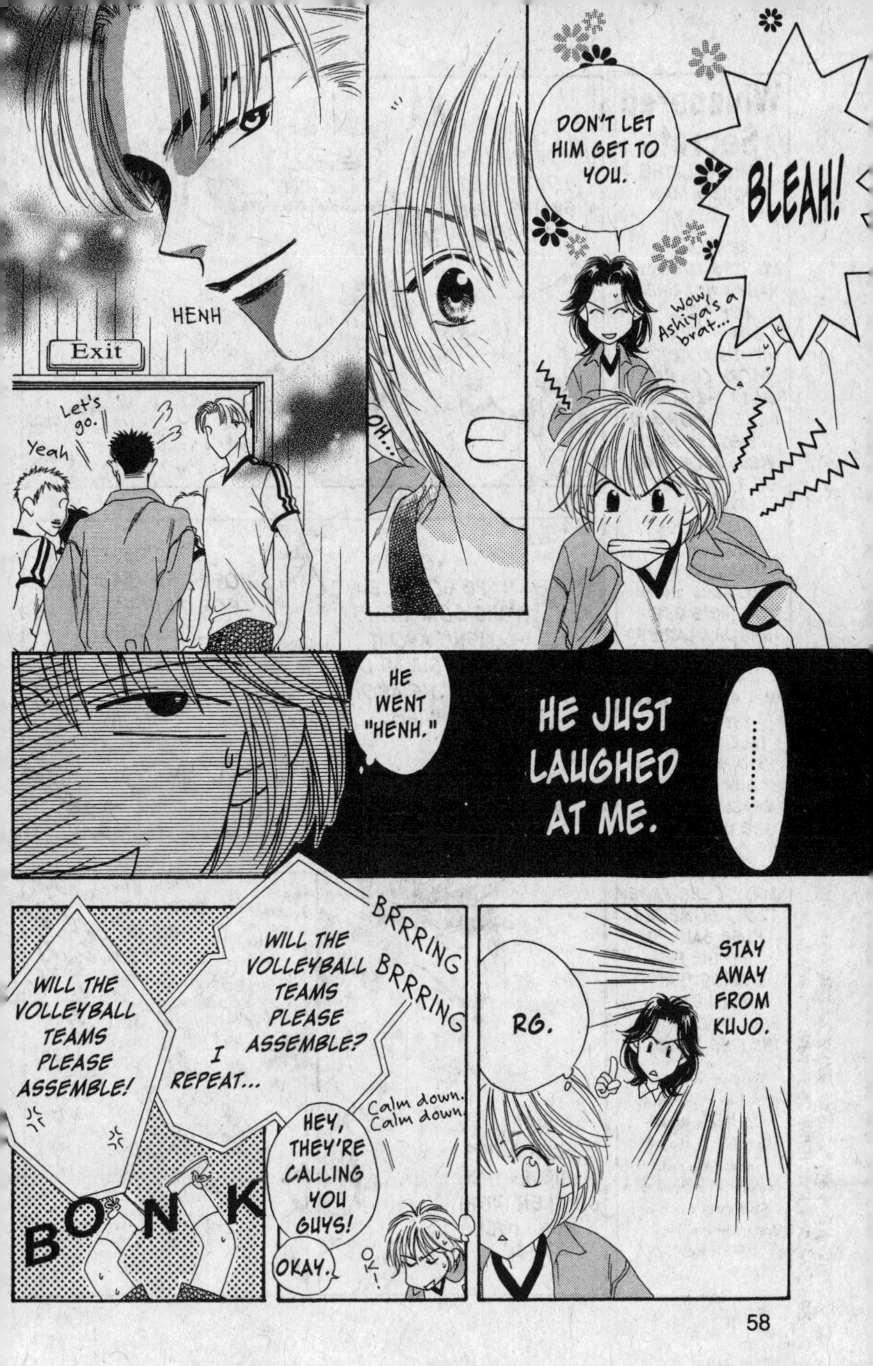
BLEAH!
DON'T LET HIM GET TO YOU.
Wow, Ashiya's a brat...
OH...
HENH
Exit
Let's go.
Yeah
......
HE JUST LAUGHED AT ME.
HE WENT "HENH."
STAY AWAY FROM KUJO.
RG.
BRRRING BRRRING
WILL THE VOLLEYBALL TEAMS PLEASE ASSEMBLE?
I REPEAT...
WILL THE VOLLEYBALL TEAMS PLEASE ASSEMBLE!
Calm down. Calm down.
HEY, THEY'RE CALLING YOU GUYS!
OKAY.
OK!
BONK

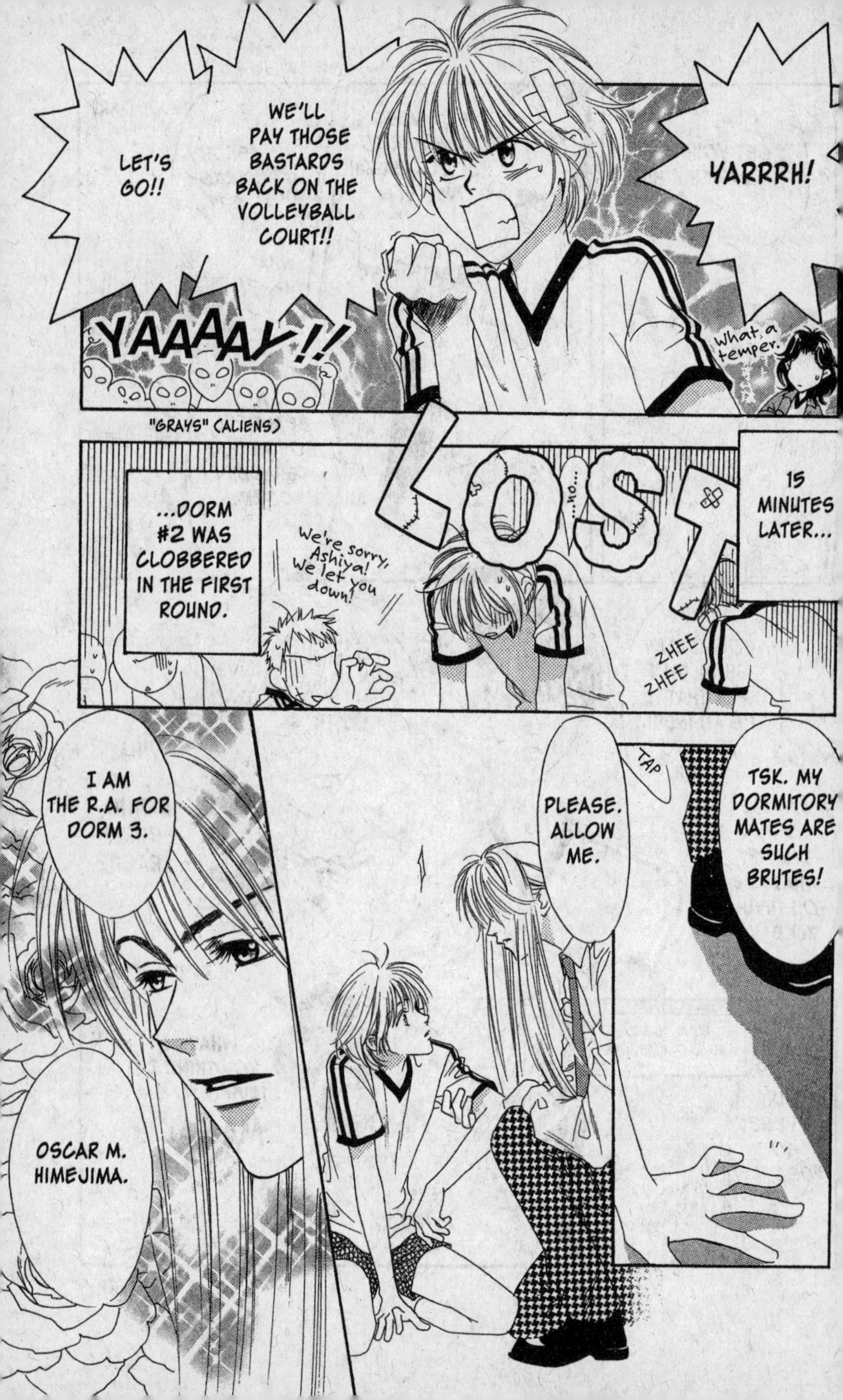
YARRRH!
What a temper.
WE'LL PAY THOSE BASTARDS BACK ON THE VOLLEYBALL COURT!!
LET'S GO!!
YAAAAY!!
"GRAYS" (ALIENS)
15 MINUTES LATER...
LOST
...no...
ZHEE ZHEE
We're sorry, Ashiya! We let you down!
...DORM #2 WAS CLOBBERED IN THE FIRST ROUND.
TSK. MY DORMITORY MATES ARE SUCH BRUTES!
TAP
PLEASE. ALLOW ME.
I AM THE R.A. FOR DORM 3.
OSCAR M. HIMEJIMA.

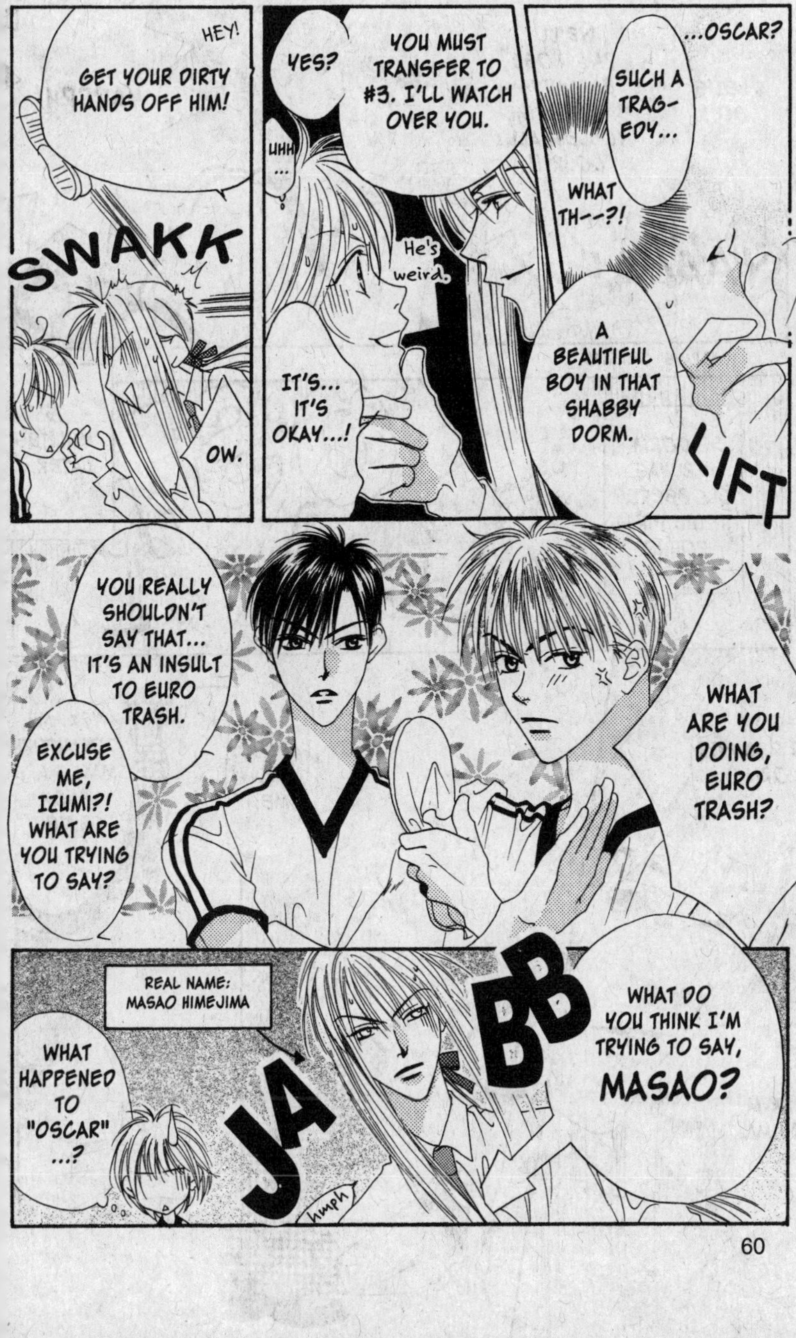
...OSCAR?
SUCH A TRAG-EDY...
WHAT TH--?!
A BEAUTIFUL BOY IN THAT SHABBY DORM.
LIFT
YES?
YOU MUST TRANSFER TO #3. I'LL WATCH OVER YOU.
UHH...
He's weird.
IT'S... IT'S OKAY...!
HEY!
GET YOUR DIRTY HANDS OFF HIM!
SWAKK
OW.
WHAT ARE YOU DOING, EURO TRASH?
YOU REALLY SHOULDN'T SAY THAT... IT'S AN INSULT TO EURO TRASH.
EXCUSE ME, IZUMI?! WHAT ARE YOU TRYING TO SAY?
WHAT DO YOU THINK I'M TRYING TO SAY, MASAO?
JABB
REAL NAME: MASAO HIMEJIMA
hmph
WHAT HAPPENED TO "OSCAR" ...?

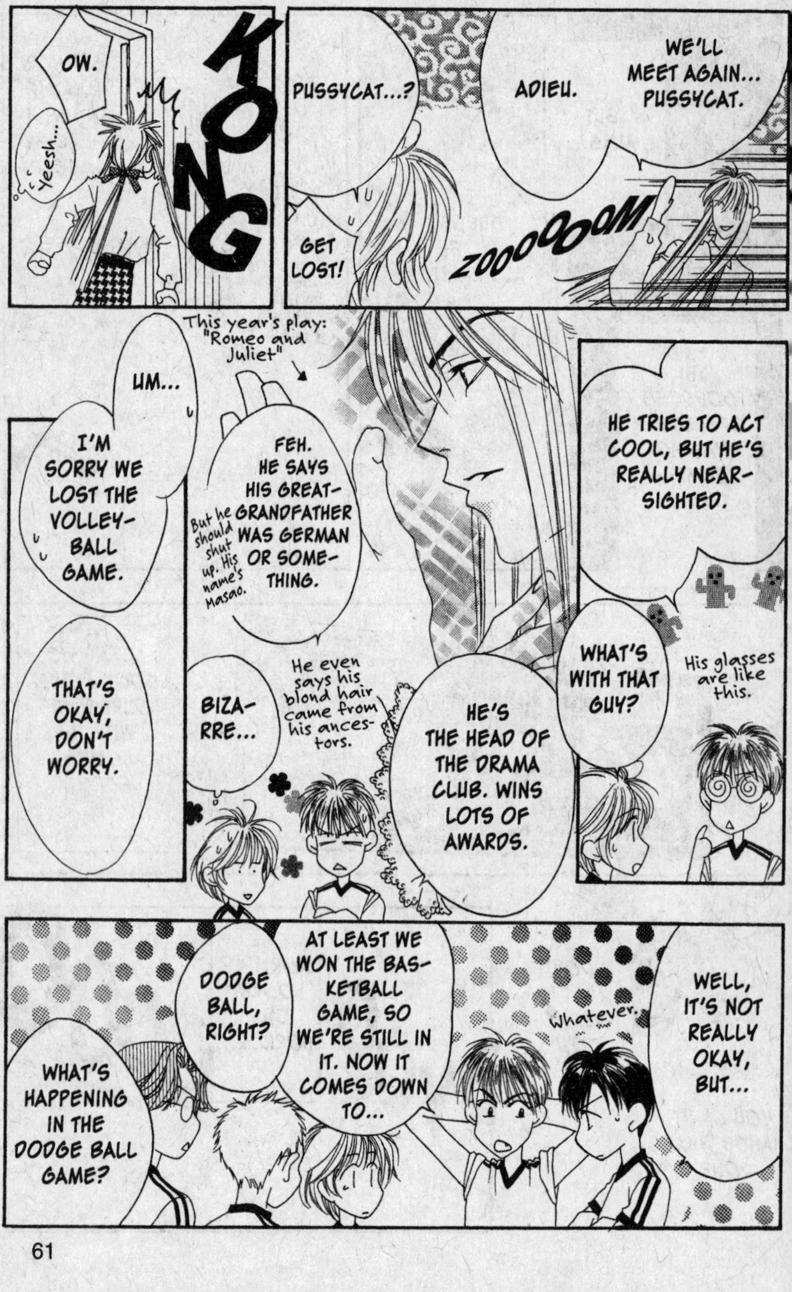
WE'LL MEET AGAIN... PUSSYCAT.
ADIEU.
PUSSYCAT...?
ZOOOOOOOM
GET LOST!
KONG
OW.
Yeesh...
HE TRIES TO ACT COOL, BUT HE'S REALLY NEAR-SIGHTED.
WHAT'S WITH THAT GUY?
His glasses are like this.
This year's play: "Romeo and Juliet"
HE'S THE HEAD OF THE DRAMA CLUB. WINS LOTS OF AWARDS.
FEH. HE SAYS HIS GREAT-GRANDFATHER WAS GERMAN OR SOMETHING.
But he should shut up. His name's Masao.
He even says his blond hair came from his ancestors.
BIZARRE...
UM...
I'M SORRY WE LOST THE VOLLEYBALL GAME.
THAT'S OKAY, DON'T WORRY.
WELL, IT'S NOT REALLY OKAY, BUT...
Whatever.
AT LEAST WE WON THE BASKETBALL GAME, SO WE'RE STILL IN IT. NOW IT COMES DOWN TO...
DODGE BALL, RIGHT?
WHAT'S HAPPENING IN THE DODGE BALL GAME?

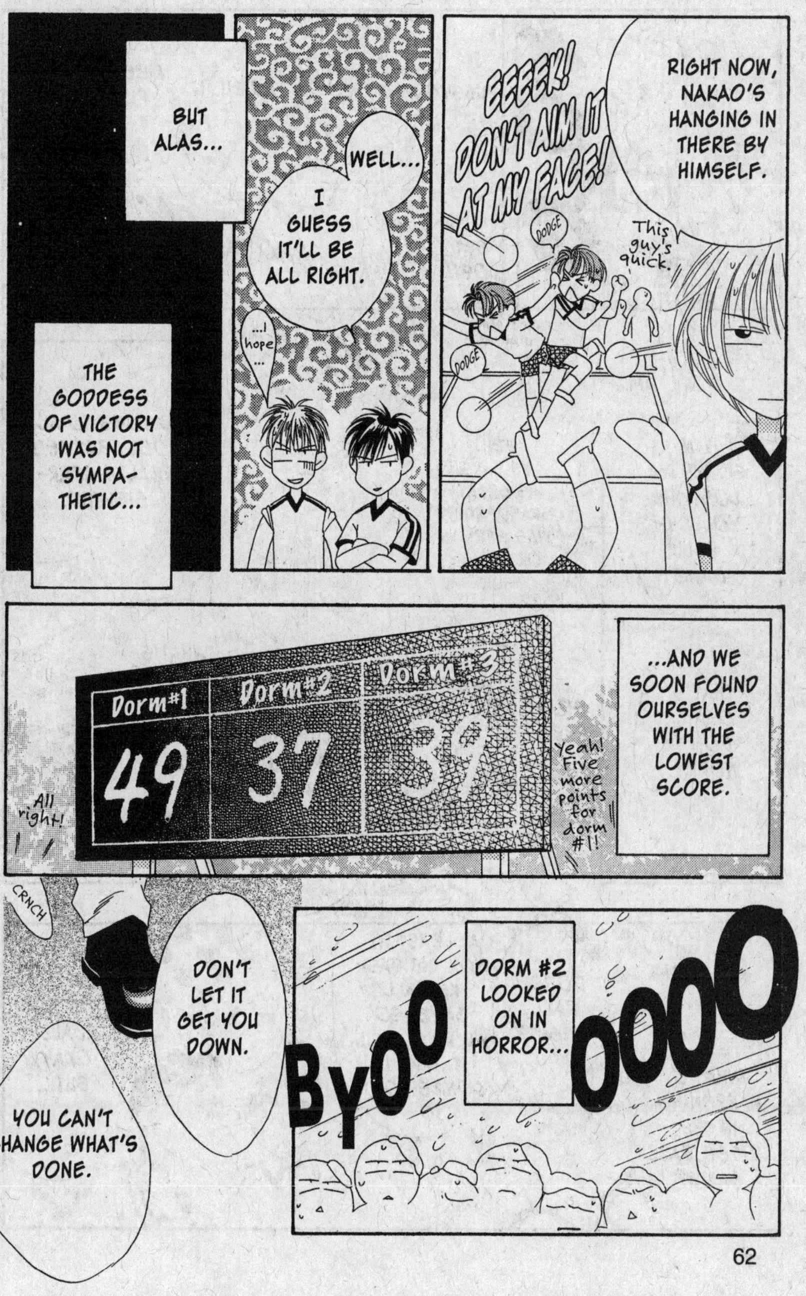
RIGHT NOW, NAKAO'S HANGING IN THERE BY HIMSELF.
EEEEK! DON'T AIM IT AT MY FACE!
DODGE
This guy's quick.
DODGE
WELL...
I GUESS IT'LL BE ALL RIGHT.
...I hope...
BUT ALAS...
THE GODDESS OF VICTORY WAS NOT SYMPA-THETIC...
...AND WE SOON FOUND OURSELVES WITH THE LOWEST SCORE.
Yeah! Five more points for dorm #1!
Dorm#1
Dorm#2
Dorm#3
49
37
39
All right!
DORM #2 LOOKED ON IN HORROR...
BYOOOOOOO
CRNCH
DON'T LET IT GET YOU DOWN.
YOU CAN'T CHANGE WHAT'S DONE.

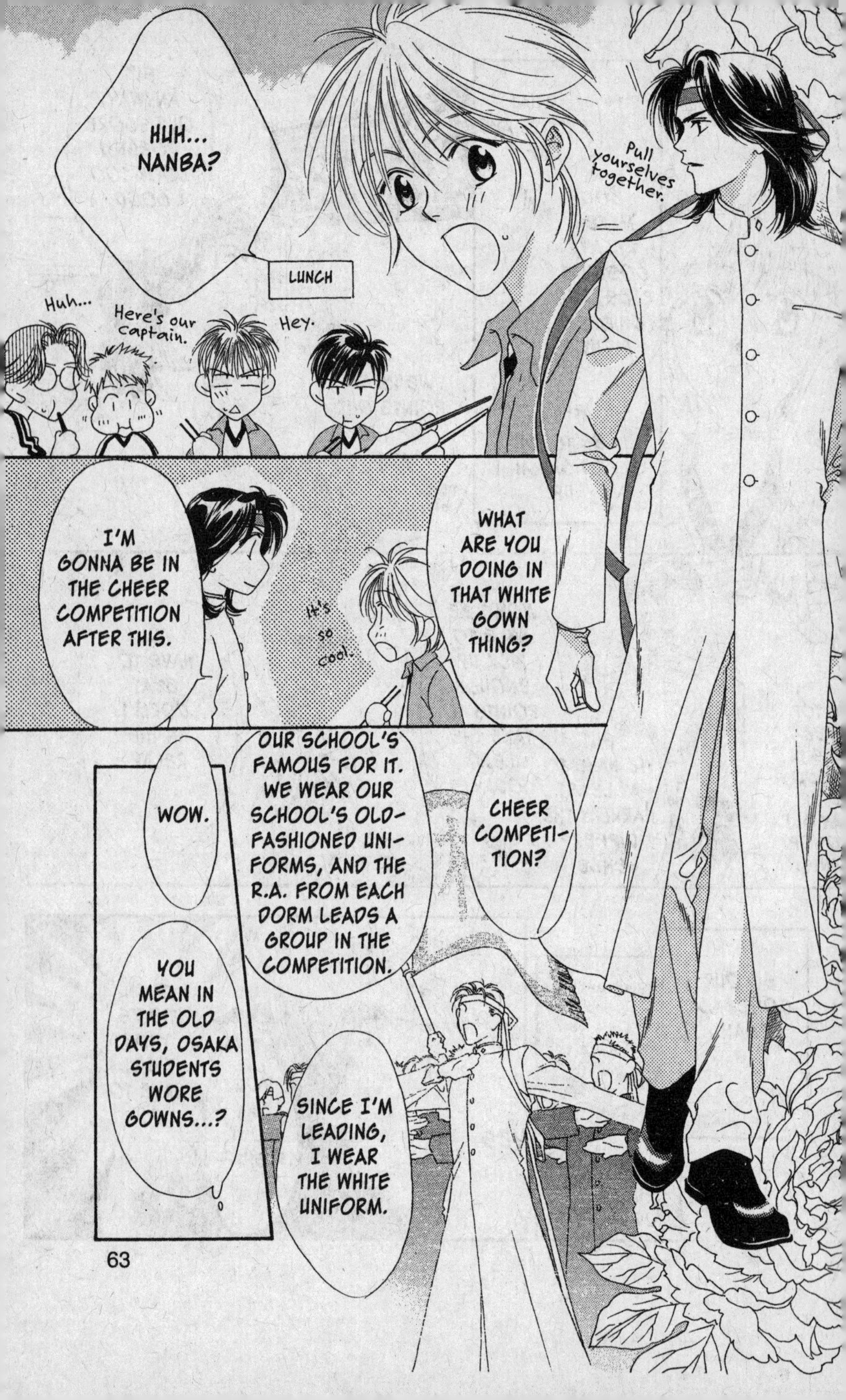
LUNCH
Pull yourselves together.
HUH... NANBA?
Hey.
Here's our captain.
Huh...
WHAT ARE YOU DOING IN THAT WHITE GOWN THING?
It's so cool.
I'M GONNA BE IN THE CHEER COMPETITION AFTER THIS.
CHEER COMPETITION?
OUR SCHOOL'S FAMOUS FOR IT. WE WEAR OUR SCHOOL'S OLD-FASHIONED UNIFORMS, AND THE R.A. FROM EACH DORM LEADS A GROUP IN THE COMPETITION.
WOW.
SINCE I'M LEADING, I WEAR THE WHITE UNIFORM.
YOU MEAN IN THE OLD DAYS, OSAKA STUDENTS WORE GOWNS...?

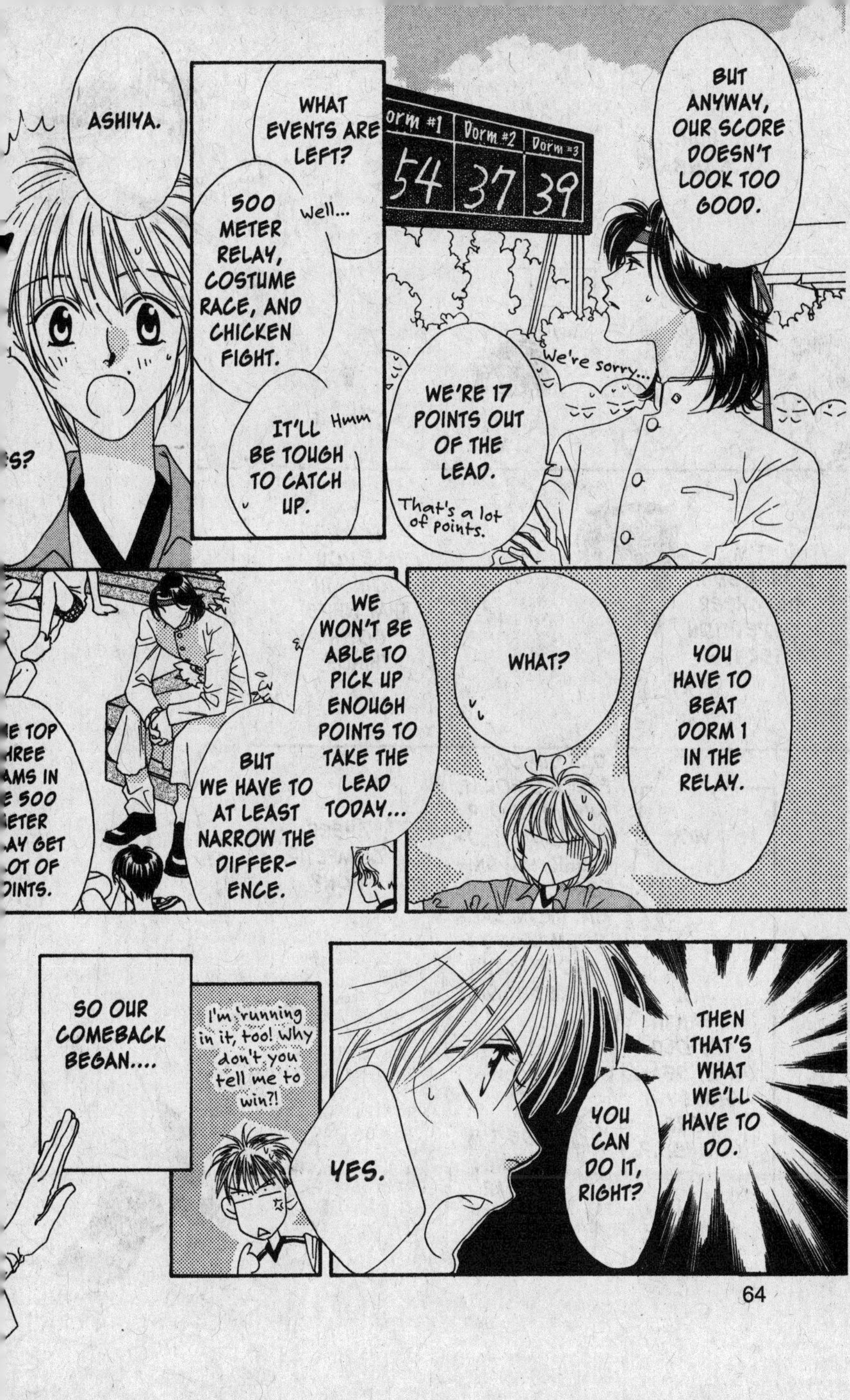
BUT ANYWAY, OUR SCORE DOESN'T LOOK TOO GOOD.
Dorm #1 Dorm #2 Dorm #3
54 37 39
We're sorry...
WE'RE 17 POINTS OUT OF THE LEAD.
That's a lot of points.
WHAT EVENTS ARE LEFT?
Well...
500 METER RELAY, COSTUME RACE, AND CHICKEN FIGHT.
Hmm
IT'LL BE TOUGH TO CATCH UP.
ASHIYA.
YOU HAVE TO BEAT DORM 1 IN THE RELAY.
WHAT?
WE WON'T BE ABLE TO PICK UP ENOUGH POINTS TO TAKE THE LEAD TODAY...
BUT WE HAVE TO AT LEAST NARROW THE DIFFERENCE.
THEN THAT'S WHAT WE'LL HAVE TO DO.
YOU CAN DO IT, RIGHT?
YES.
I'm running in it, too! Why don't you tell me to win?!
SO OUR COMEBACK BEGAN....

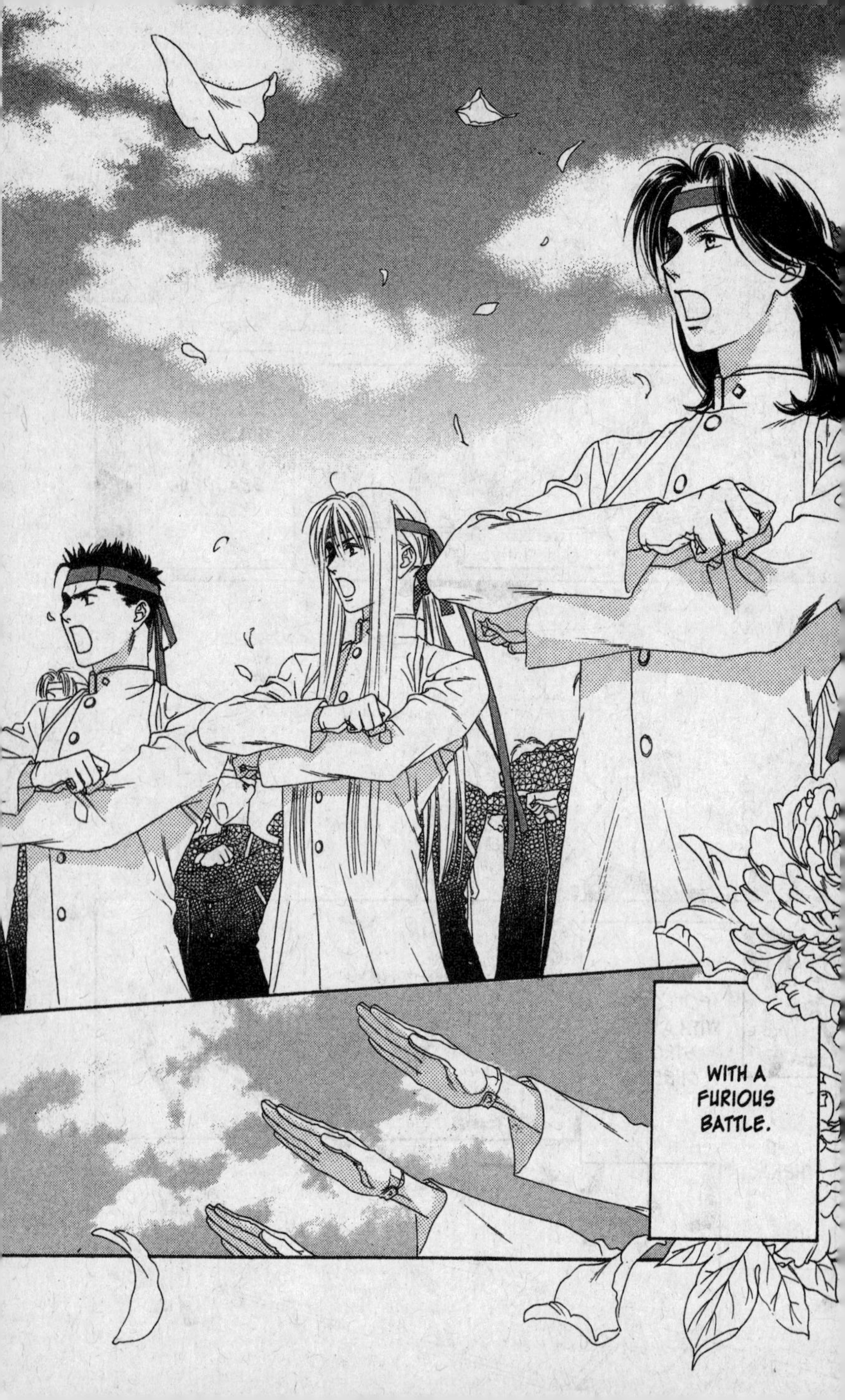
WITH A FURIOUS BATTLE.

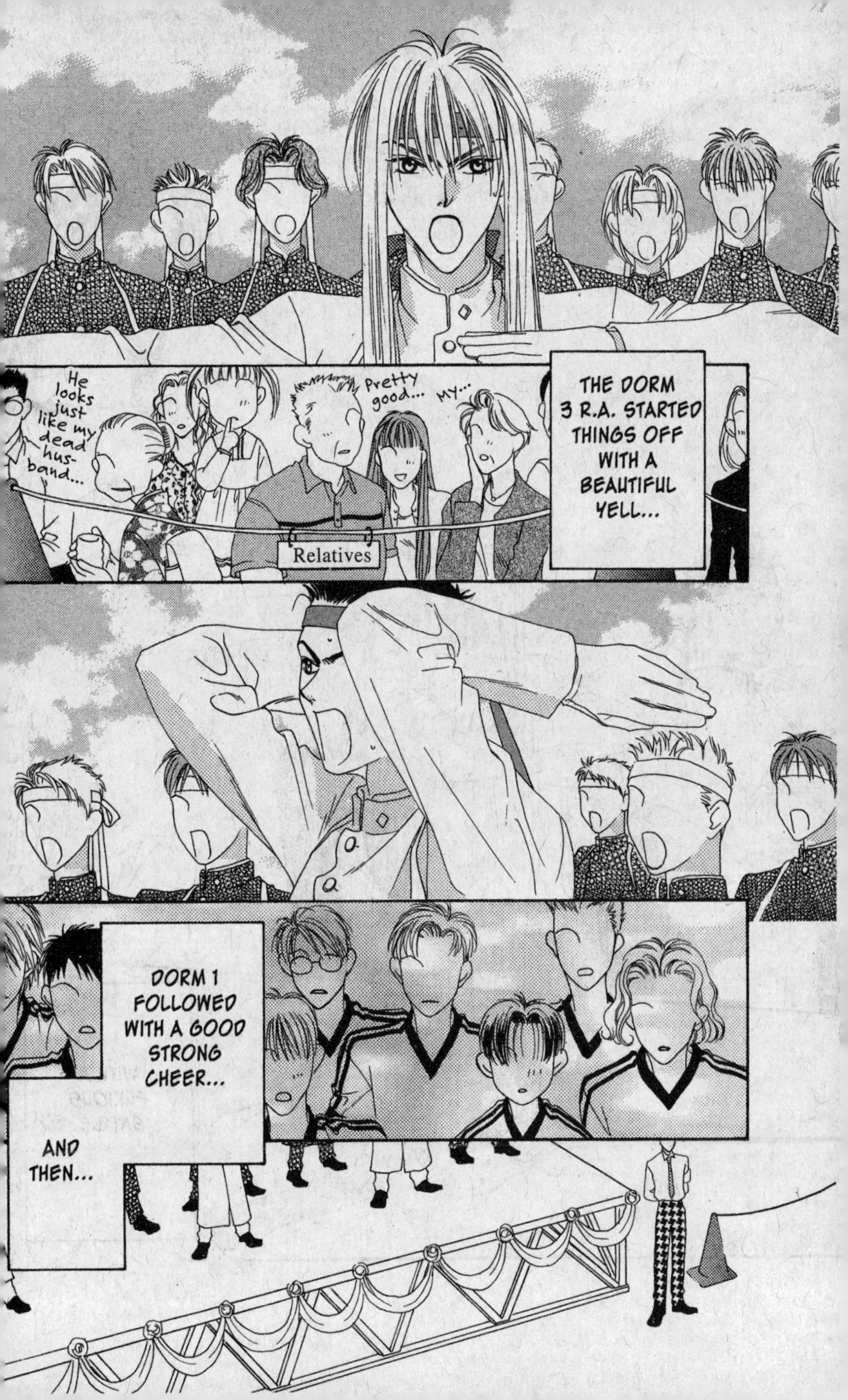
THE DORM 3 R.A. STARTED THINGS OFF WITH A BEAUTIFUL YELL...
My...
Pretty good...
He looks just like my dead hus-band...
Relatives
DORM 1 FOLLOWED WITH A GOOD STRONG CHEER...
AND THEN...

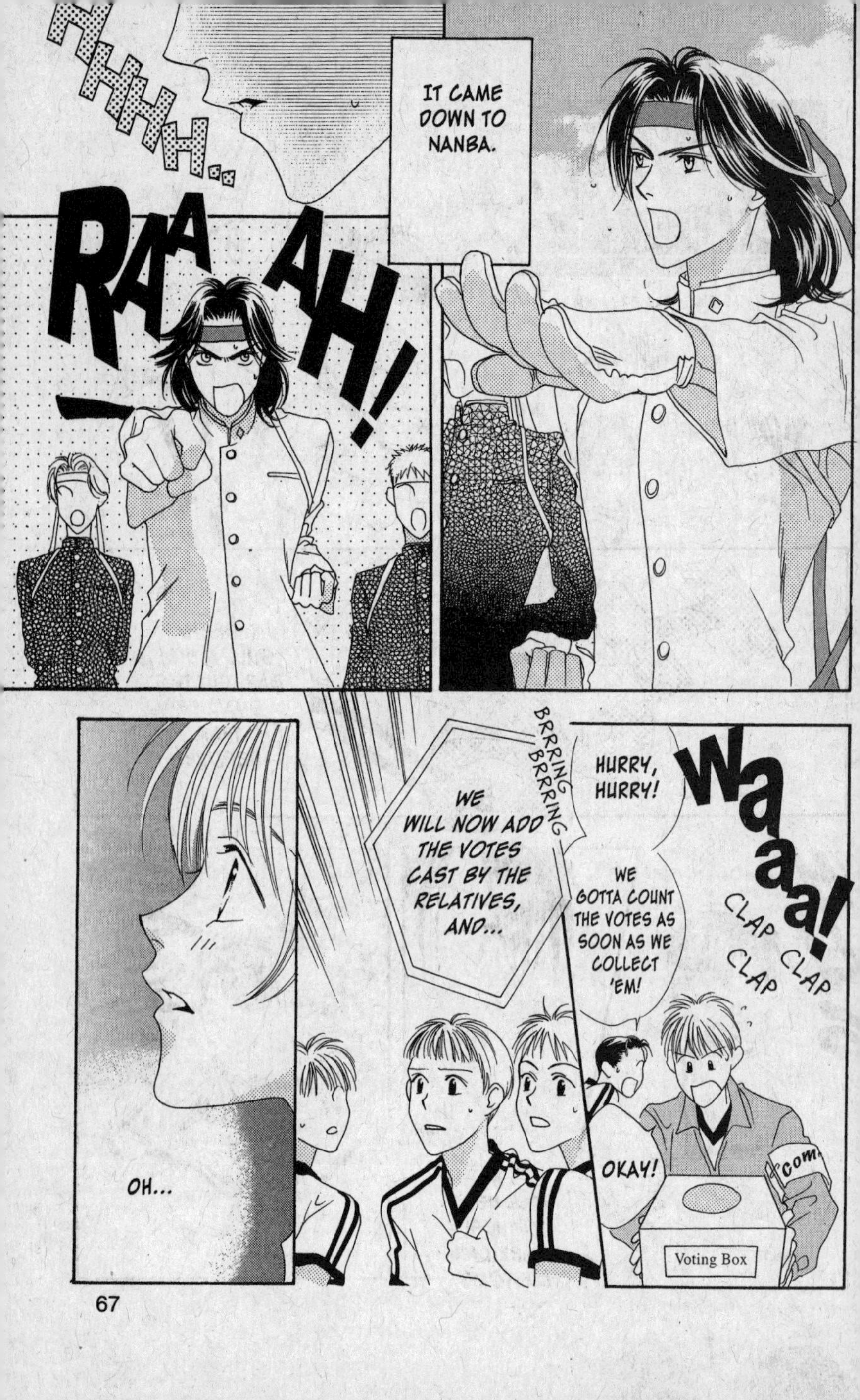
IT CAME DOWN TO NANBA.
HHHHH..
RAAAH!
WAAAA!
HURRY, HURRY!
WE GOTTA COUNT THE VOTES AS SOON AS WE COLLECT 'EM!
CLAP CLAP CLAP
OKAY!
Voting Box
BRRRING BRRRING
WE WILL NOW ADD THE VOTES CAST BY THE RELATIVES, AND...
OH...

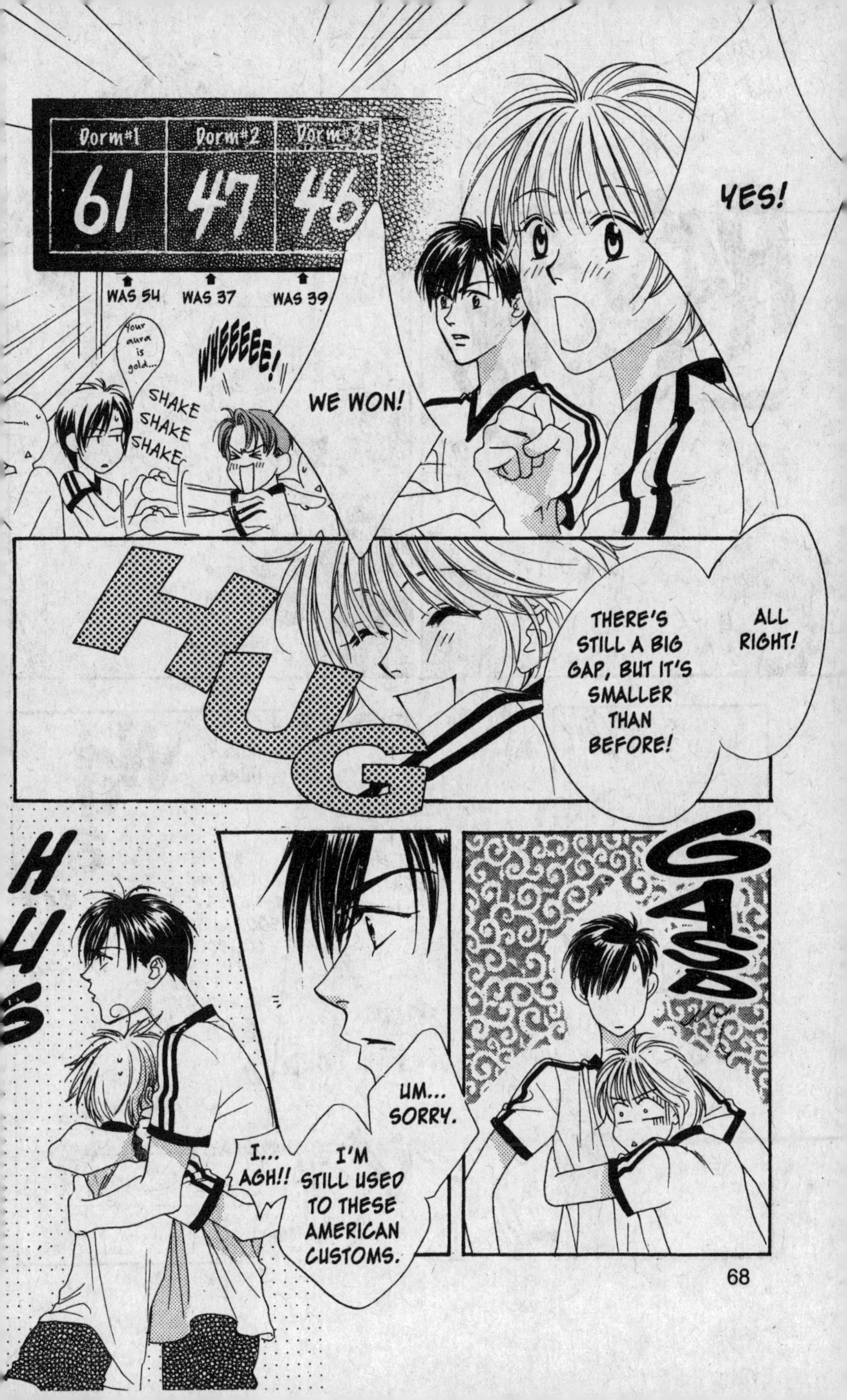
Dorm#1
Dorm#2
Dorm#3
61
47
46
WAS 54
WAS 37
WAS 39
YES!
WE WON!
WHEEEEE!
Your aura is gold...
SHAKE SHAKE SHAKE
HUG
ALL RIGHT!
THERE'S STILL A BIG GAP, BUT IT'S SMALLER THAN BEFORE!
GASP
UM... SORRY.
I'M STILL USED TO THESE AMERICAN CUSTOMS.
HUG
I... AGH!!

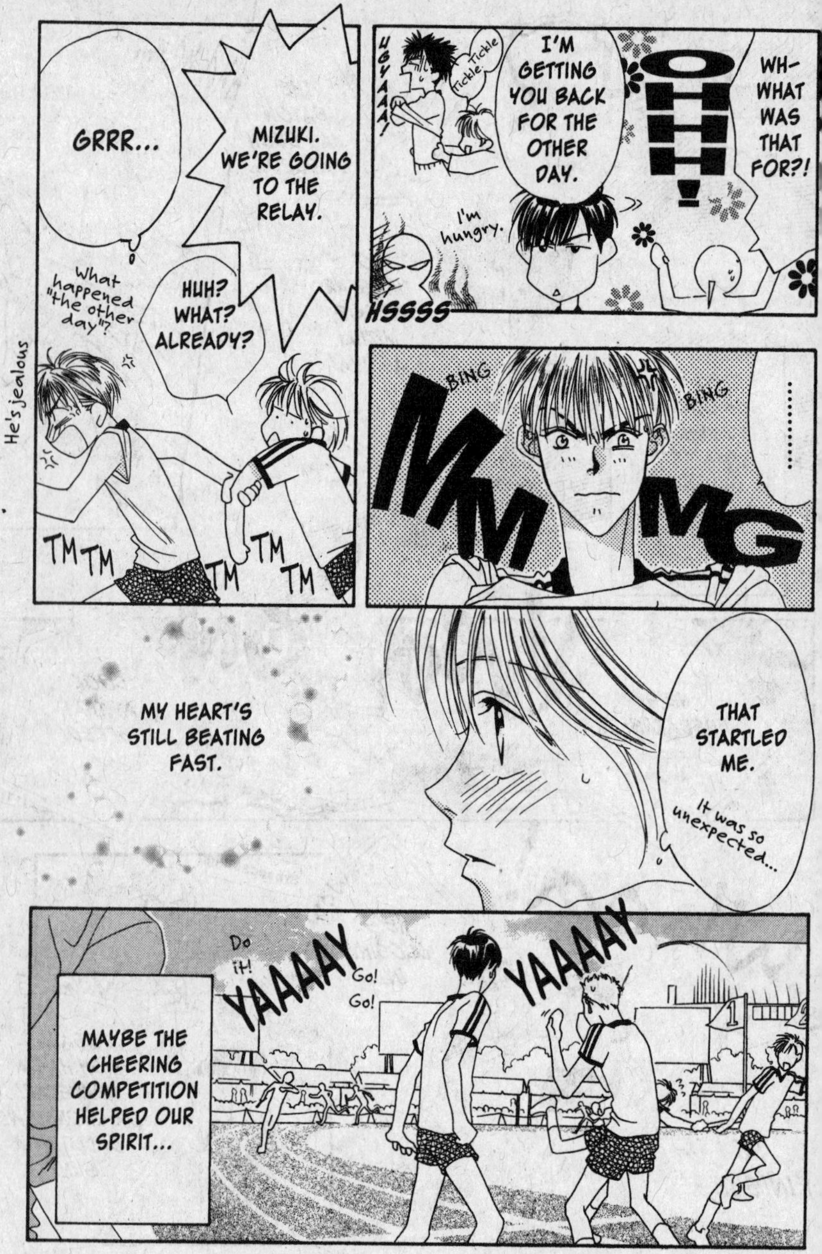
WH-WHAT WAS THAT FOR?!
OHH!
I'M GETTING YOU BACK FOR THE OTHER DAY.
Tickle Tickle
UGYAAAA!
I'm hungry.
HSSSS
......
BING
BING
MMMG
MIZUKI. WE'RE GOING TO THE RELAY.
GRRR...
HUH? WHAT? ALREADY?
What happened "the other day"?
TM TM TM TM
He's jealous
THAT STARTLED ME.
It was so unexpected...
MY HEART'S STILL BEATING FAST.
YAAAAY
Do it!
YAAAAY
Go! Go!
MAYBE THE CHEERING COMPETITION HELPED OUR SPIRIT...

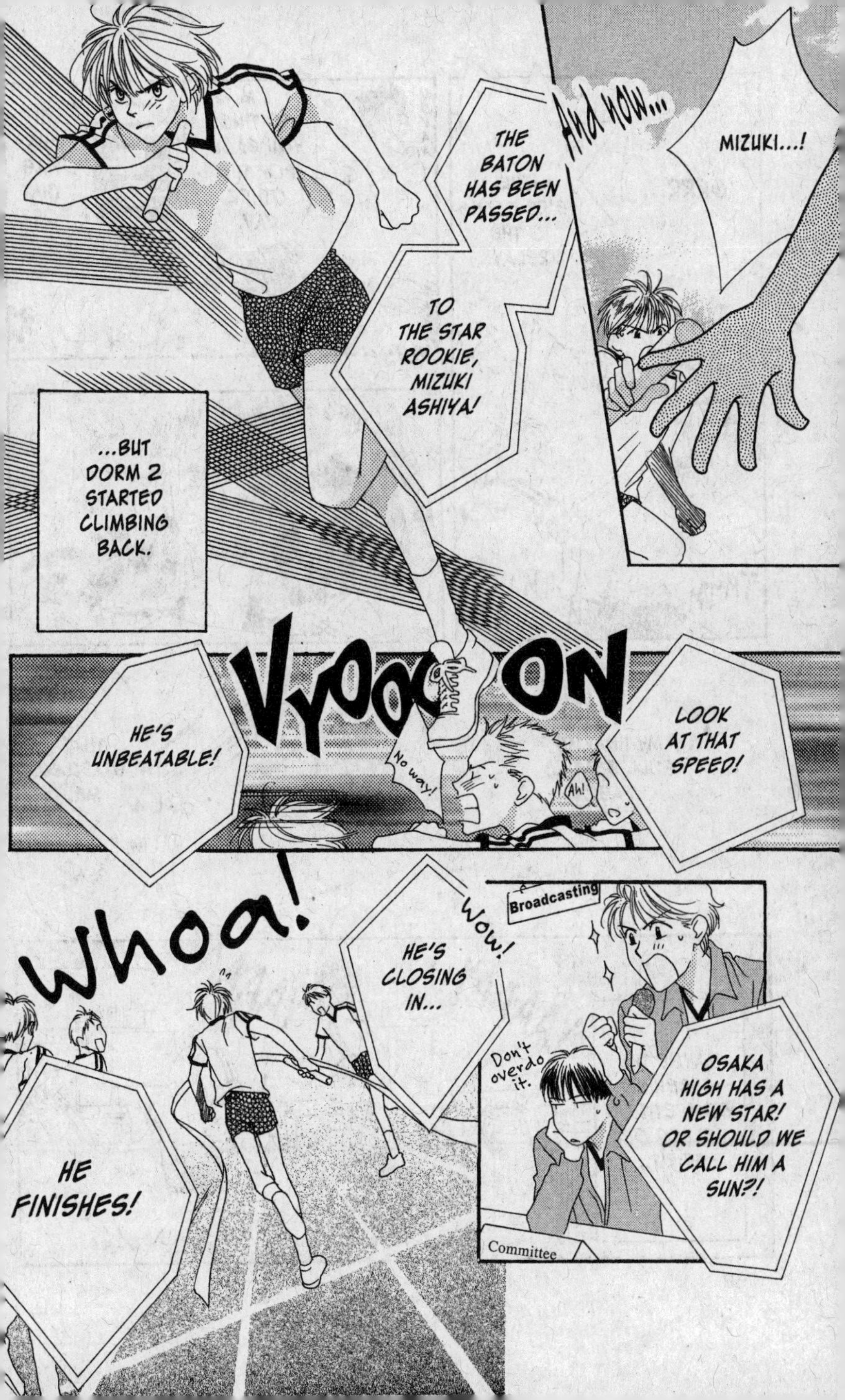
And now...
MIZUKI...!
THE BATON HAS BEEN PASSED...
TO THE STAR ROOKIE, MIZUKI ASHIYA!
...BUT DORM 2 STARTED CLIMBING BACK.
LOOK AT THAT SPEED!
Ah!
VYOOOON
No way!
HE'S UNBEATABLE!
Broadcasting
OSAKA HIGH HAS A NEW STAR! OR SHOULD WE CALL HIM A SUN?!
Don't overdo it.
Committee
Wow!
HE'S CLOSING IN...
Whoa!
HE FINISHES!

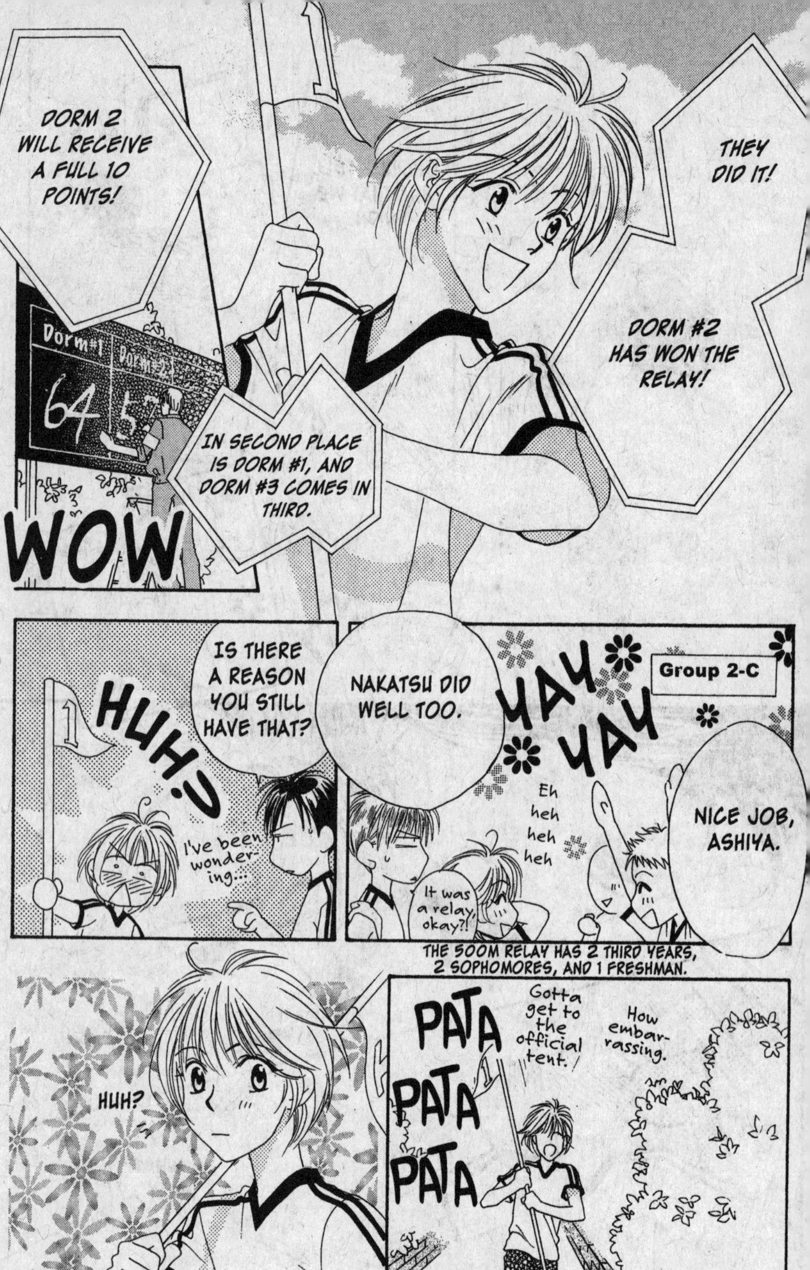
THEY DID IT!
DORM 2 WILL RECEIVE A FULL 10 POINTS!
DORM #2 HAS WON THE RELAY!
Dorm#1
Dorm#2
64
IN SECOND PLACE IS DORM #1, AND DORM #3 COMES IN THIRD.
WOW
Group 2-C
NICE JOB, ASHIYA.
YAY YAY
Eh heh heh heh
NAKATSU DID WELL TOO.
It was a relay, okay?!
IS THERE A REASON YOU STILL HAVE THAT?
HUH?
I've been wondering...
THE 500M RELAY HAS 2 THIRD YEARS, 2 SOPHOMORES, AND 1 FRESHMAN.
How embarrassing.
Gotta get to the official tent.
PATA PATA PATA
HUH?

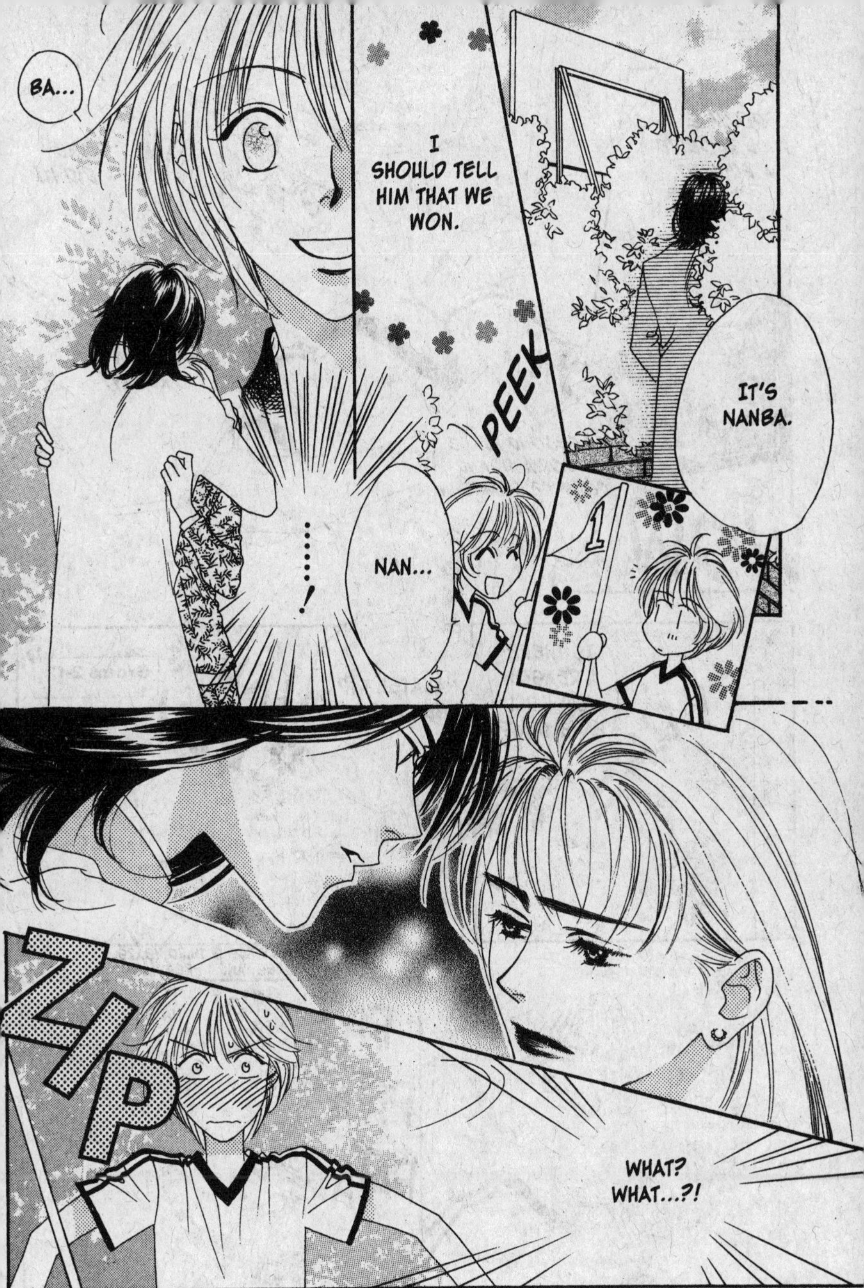
I SHOULD TELL HIM THAT WE WON.
IT'S NANBA.
PEEK
NAN...
...!
BA...
WHAT? WHAT...?!
ZIP

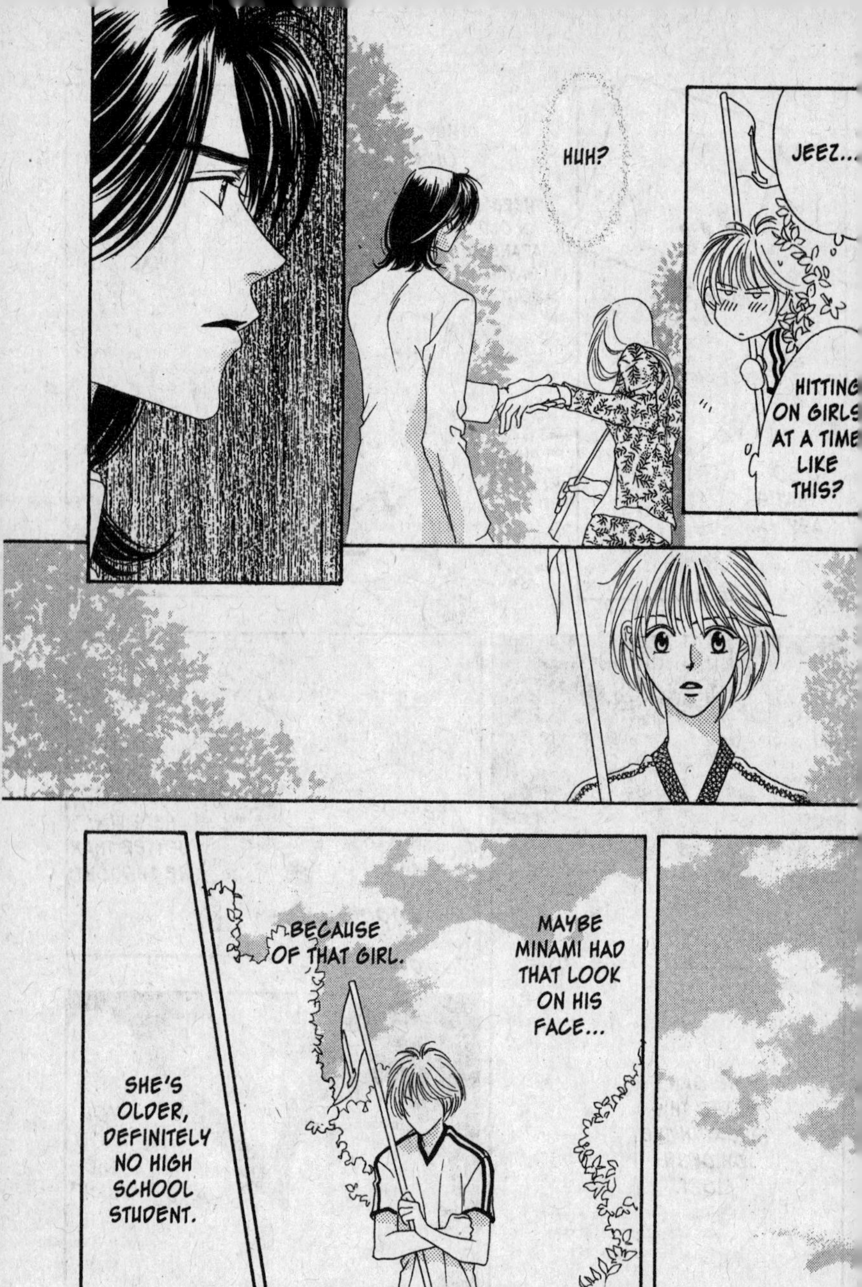
JEEZ...
HITTING ON GIRLS AT A TIME LIKE THIS?
HUH?
MAYBE MINAMI HAD THAT LOOK ON HIS FACE...
BECAUSE OF THAT GIRL.
SHE'S OLDER, DEFINITELY NO HIGH SCHOOL STUDENT.

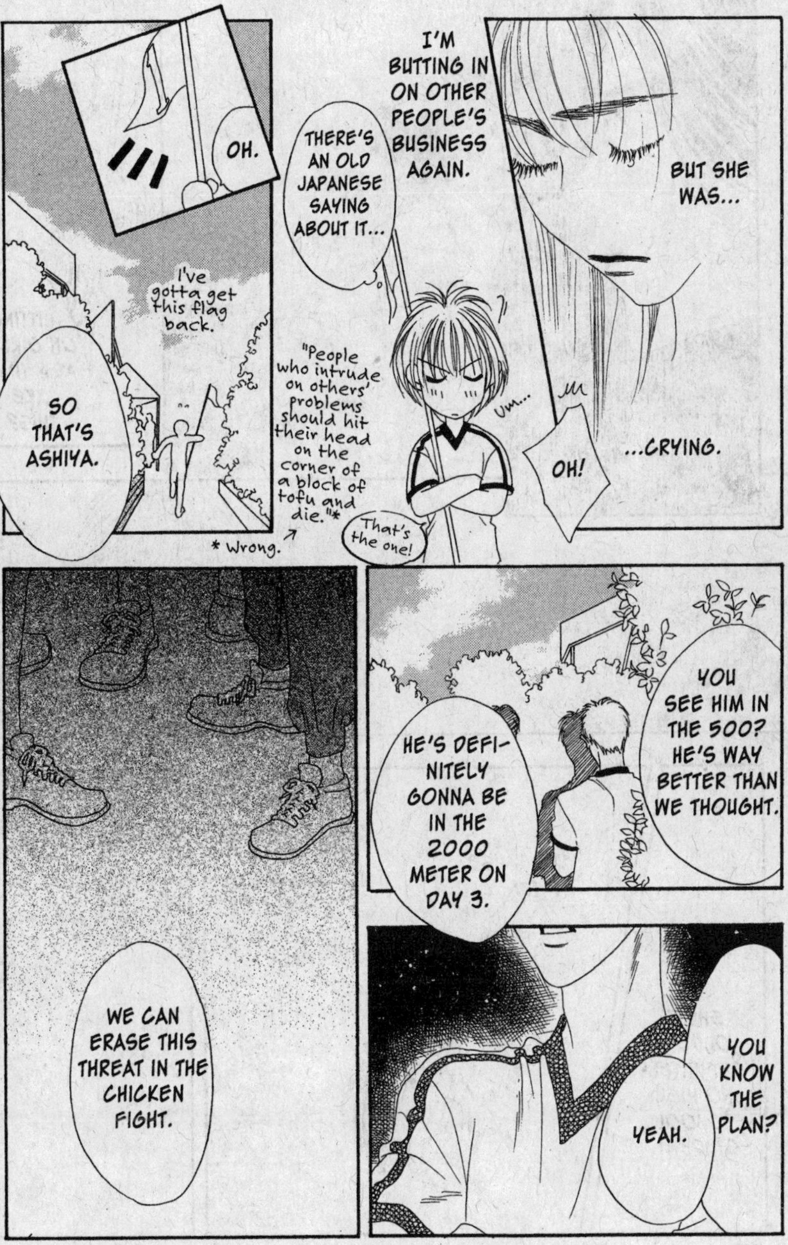
BUT SHE WAS...
...CRYING.
OH!
I'M BUTTING IN ON OTHER PEOPLE'S BUSINESS AGAIN.
THERE'S AN OLD JAPANESE SAYING ABOUT IT...
Um...
"People who intrude on others' problems should hit their head on the corner of a block of tofu and die."*
That's the one!
* Wrong.
OH.
I've gotta get this flag back.
SO THAT'S ASHIYA.
YOU SEE HIM IN THE 500? HE'S WAY BETTER THAN WE THOUGHT.
HE'S DEFI-NITELY GONNA BE IN THE 2000 METER ON DAY 3.
YOU KNOW THE PLAN?
YEAH.
WE CAN ERASE THIS THREAT IN THE CHICKEN FIGHT.

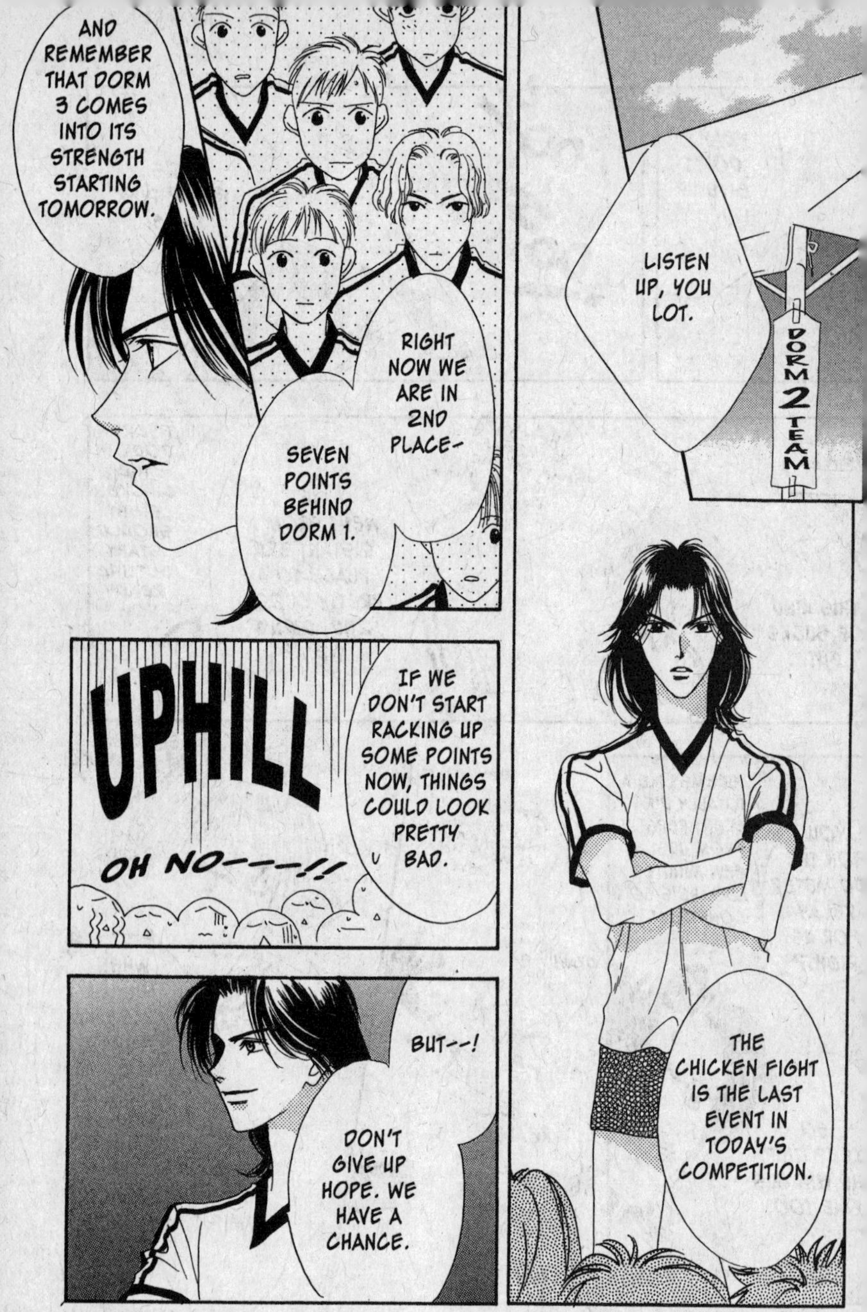
LISTEN UP, YOU LOT.
DORM 2 TEAM
THE CHICKEN FIGHT IS THE LAST EVENT IN TODAY'S COMPETITION.
RIGHT NOW WE ARE IN 2ND PLACE-
SEVEN POINTS BEHIND DORM 1.
AND REMEMBER THAT DORM 3 COMES INTO ITS STRENGTH STARTING TOMORROW.
IF WE DON'T START RACKING UP SOME POINTS NOW, THINGS COULD LOOK PRETTY BAD.
UPHILL
OH NO---!!
BUT--!
DON'T GIVE UP HOPE. WE HAVE A CHANCE.

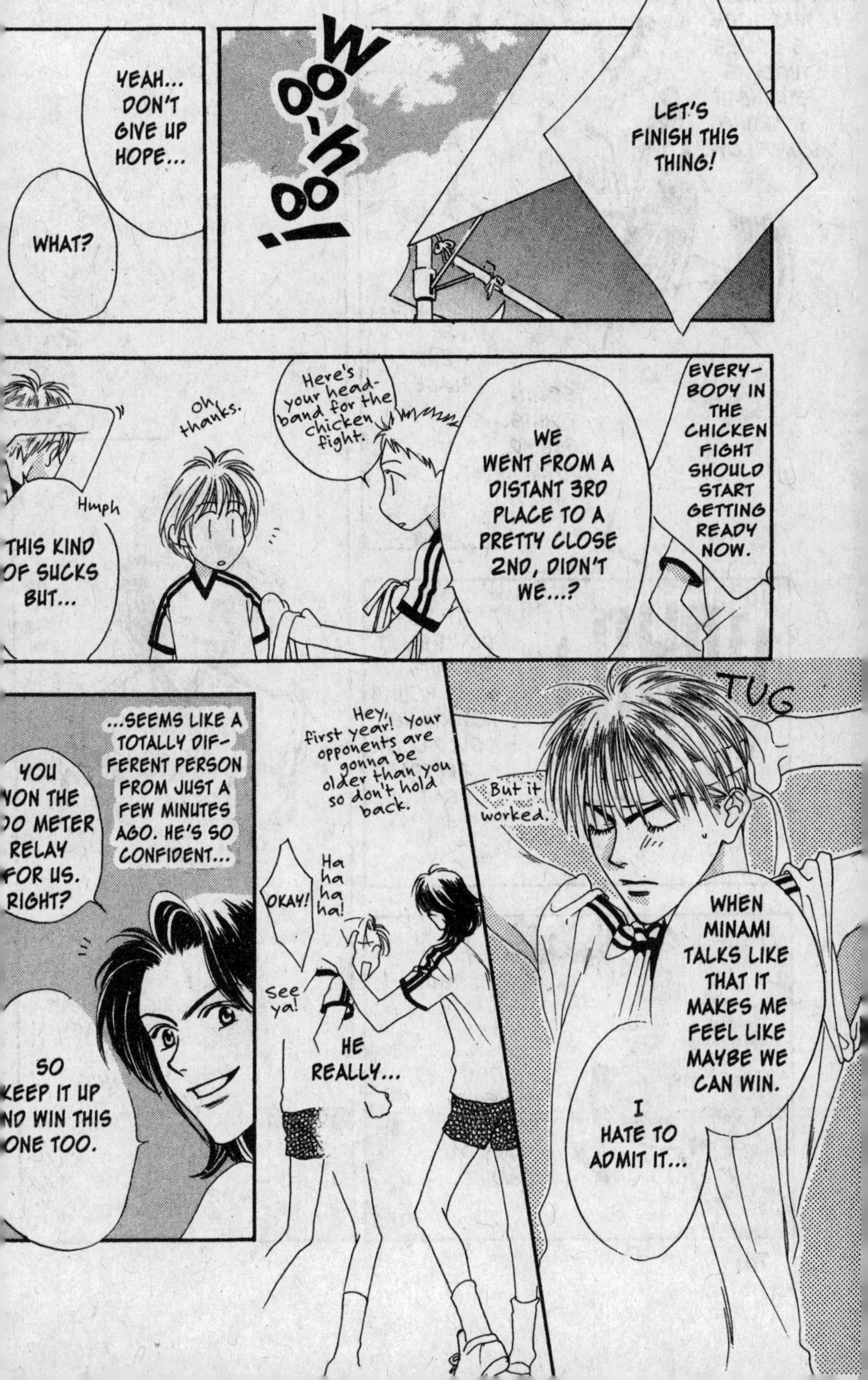
LET'S FINISH THIS THING!
WOO-HOO!
YEAH... DON'T GIVE UP HOPE...
WHAT?
EVERYBODY IN THE CHICKEN FIGHT SHOULD START GETTING READY NOW.
WE WENT FROM A DISTANT 3RD PLACE TO A PRETTY CLOSE 2ND, DIDN'T WE...?
Here's your headband for the chicken fight.
Oh thanks.
Hmph
THIS KIND OF SUCKS BUT...
TUG
But it worked.
WHEN MINAMI TALKS LIKE THAT IT MAKES ME FEEL LIKE MAYBE WE CAN WIN.
I HATE TO ADMIT IT...
Hey, first year! Your opponents are gonna be older than you so don't hold back.
Ha ha ha ha!
OKAY!
See ya!
HE REALLY...
...SEEMS LIKE A TOTALLY DIFFERENT PERSON FROM JUST A FEW MINUTES AGO. HE'S SO CONFIDENT...
YOU WON THE 00 METER RELAY FOR US. RIGHT?
SO KEEP IT UP AND WIN THIS ONE TOO.

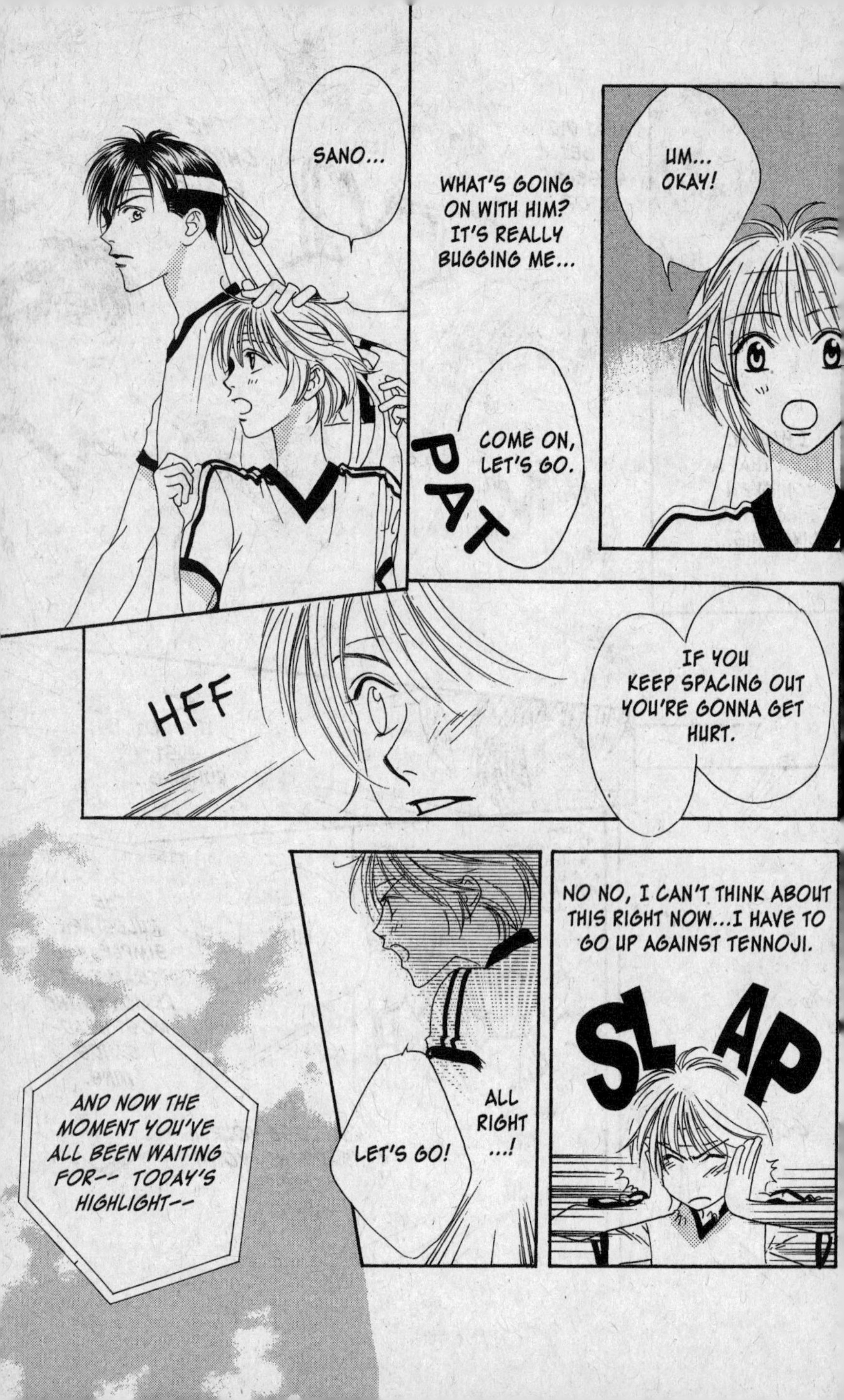
UM... OKAY!
WHAT'S GOING ON WITH HIM? IT'S REALLY BUGGING ME...
COME ON, LET'S GO.
PAT
SANO...
IF YOU KEEP SPACING OUT YOU'RE GONNA GET HURT.
HFF
NO NO, I CAN'T THINK ABOUT THIS RIGHT NOW...I HAVE TO GO UP AGAINST TENNOJI.
SLAP
ALL RIGHT ...!
LET'S GO!
AND NOW THE MOMENT YOU'VE ALL BEEN WAITING FOR-- TODAY'S HIGHLIGHT--

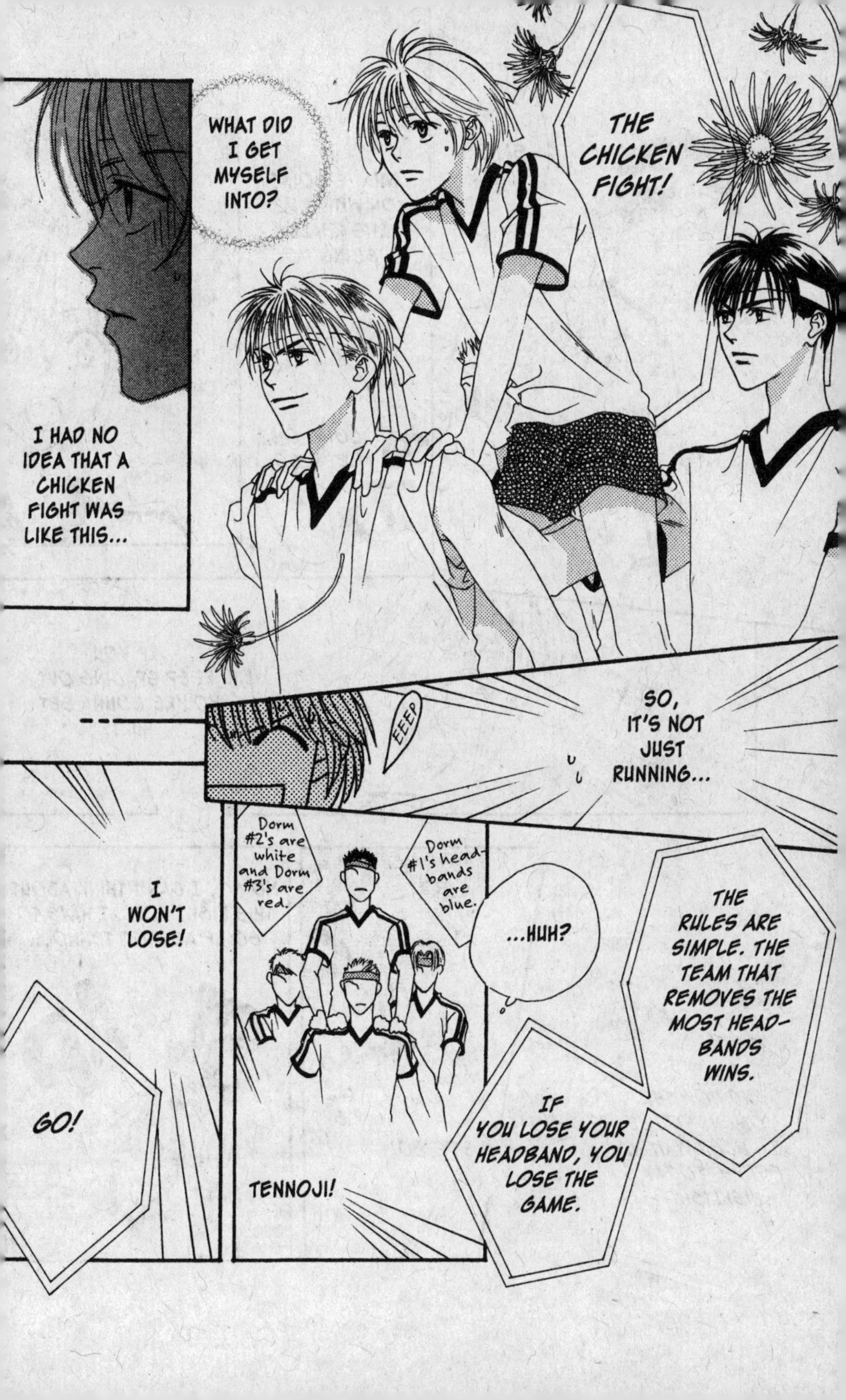
THE CHICKEN FIGHT!
WHAT DID I GET MYSELF INTO?
I HAD NO IDEA THAT A CHICKEN FIGHT WAS LIKE THIS...
SO, IT'S NOT JUST RUNNING...
EEEP

THE RULES ARE SIMPLE. THE TEAM THAT REMOVES THE MOST HEAD-BANDS WINS.
IF YOU LOSE YOUR HEADBAND, YOU LOSE THE GAME.
...HUH?
Dorm #1's head-bands are blue.
Dorm #2's are white and Dorm #3's are red.
TENNOJI!
I WON'T LOSE!
GO!

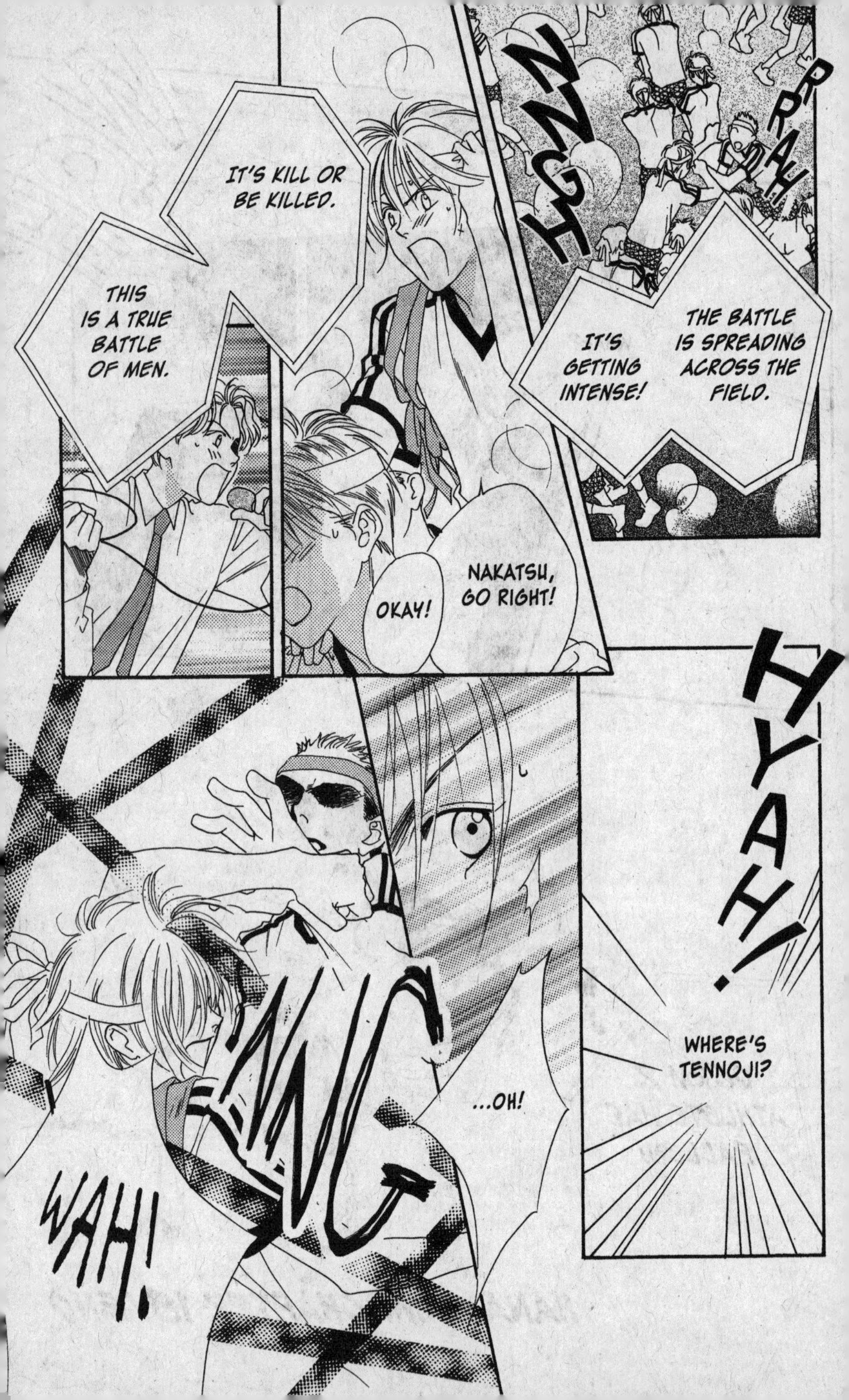

RRAH
NNGH
THE BATTLE IS SPREADING ACROSS THE FIELD.
IT'S GETTING INTENSE!
IT'S KILL OR BE KILLED.
NAKATSU, GO RIGHT!
OKAY!
THIS IS A TRUE BATTLE OF MEN.
HYAH!
WHERE'S TENNOJI?
...OH!
WAH!

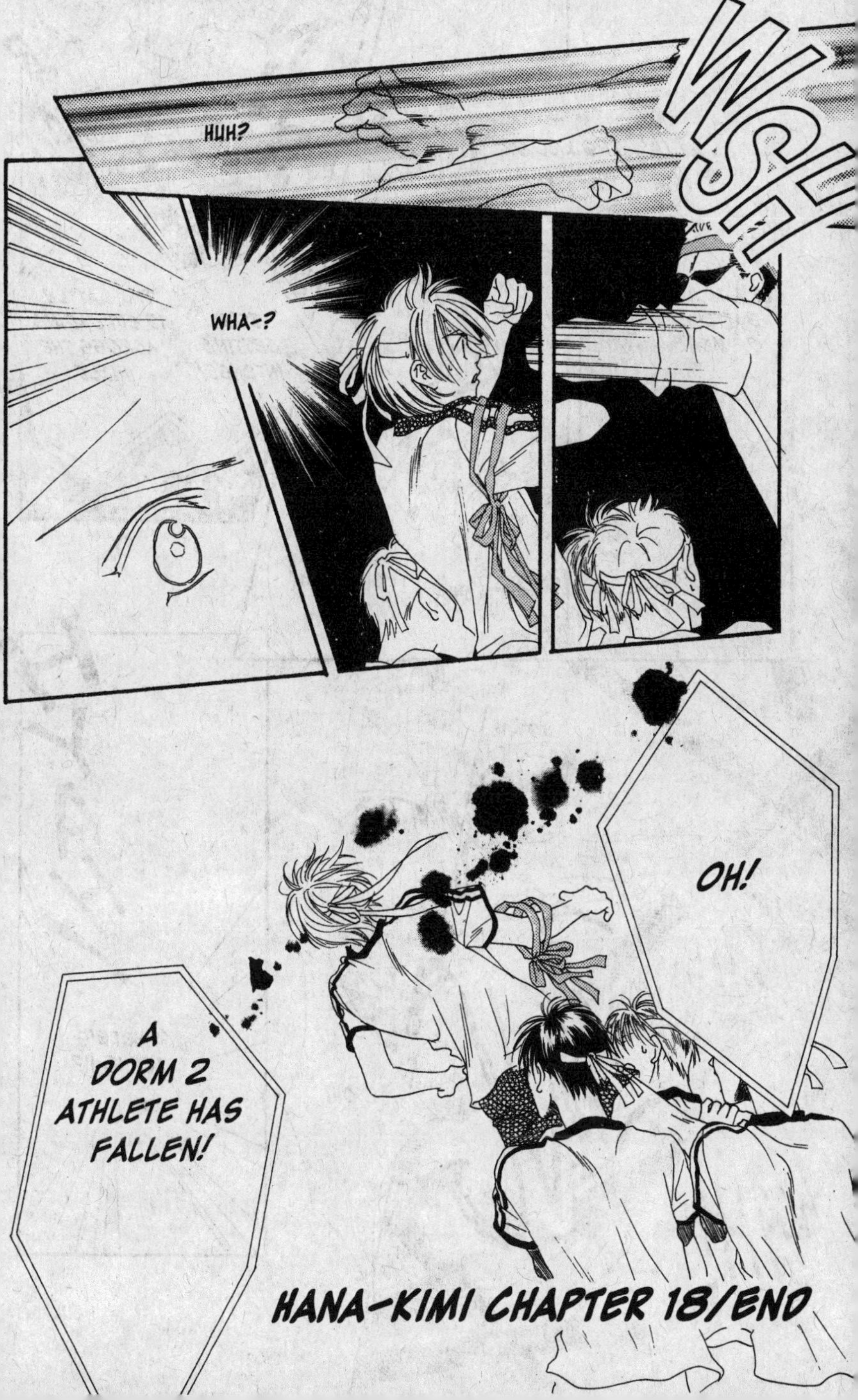
WSH
HUH?
WHA-?
OH!
A DORM 2 ATHLETE HAS FALLEN!
HANA-KIMI CHAPTER 18/END

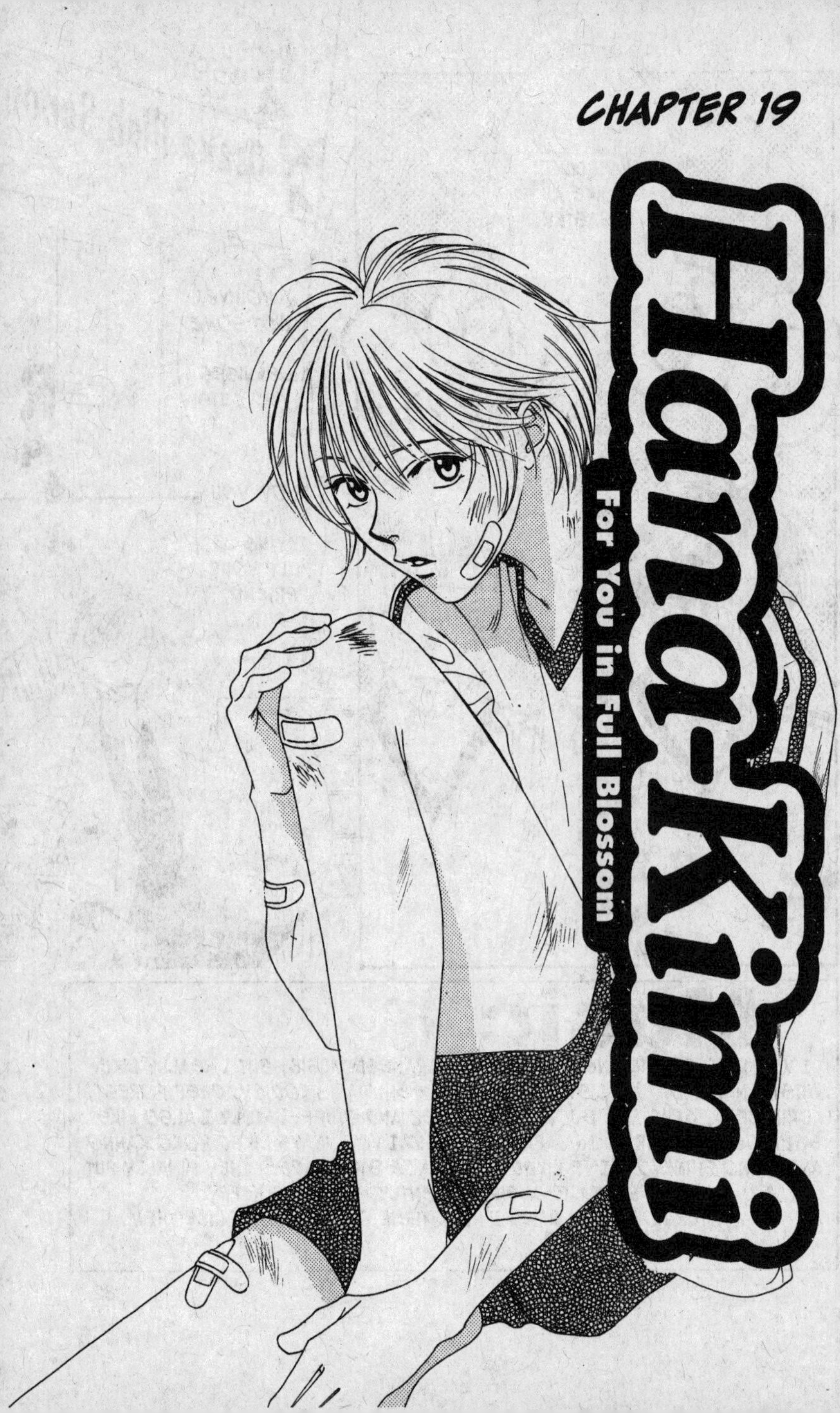
CHAPTER 19
Hana-Kimi!
For You in Full Blossom

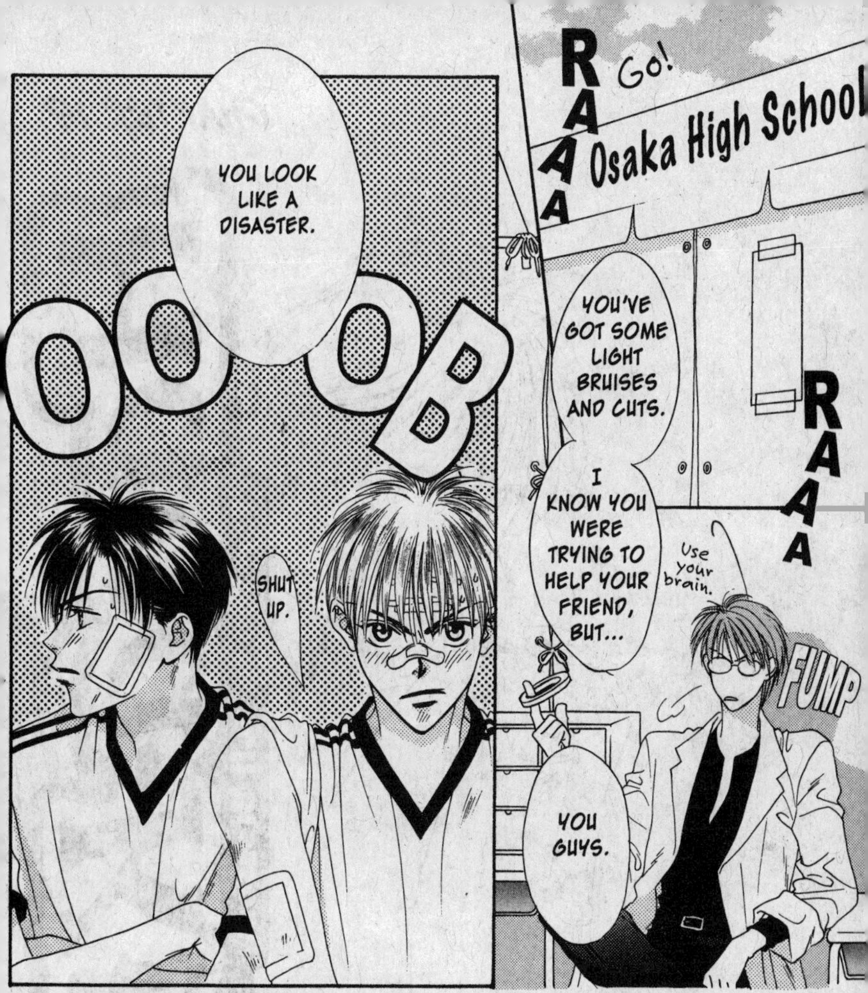
RAAA
Go!
Osaka High School
YOU'VE GOT SOME LIGHT BRUISES AND CUTS.
I KNOW YOU WERE TRYING TO HELP YOUR FRIEND, BUT...
RAAA
Use your brain.
FUMP
YOU GUYS.
YOU LOOK LIKE A DISASTER.
OOOB
SHUT UP.

Music

I'VE STARTED LISTENING TO A LOT OF JAPANESE MUSIC, BUT I REALLY LIKE WESTERN MUSIC. ♡ I LISTEN TO A LOT OF ENIGMA, PRODIGY, DEEP FOREST, ERIC CELA, OPUS III, BJORK, STONE AGE AND STUFF. LATELY I ALSO LIKE SWEETBOX AND CURVE. IN JAPANESE MUSIC I'VE ALWAYS LIKED YOKO KANNO AND AKINO SHINKYO! (I'VE LIKED THEM SINCE 8TH GRADE.) THEY FINALLY PUT OUT A "BEST OF" ALBUM RECENTLY, SO I WAS HAPPY. ♡
NO MATTER HOW MANY TIMES I HEAR THEIR SONGS I STILL LIKE THEM.

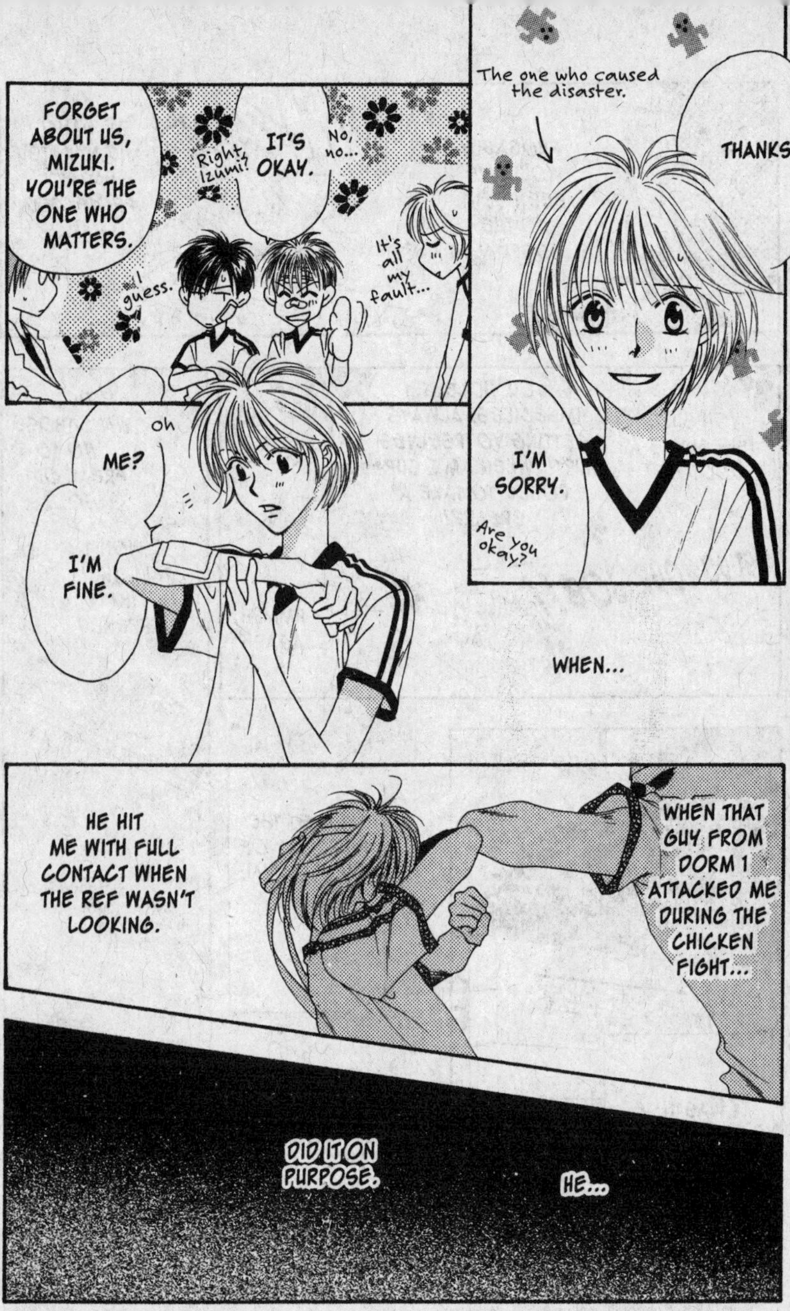
The one who caused the disaster.
THANKS.
I'M SORRY.
Are you okay?
FORGET ABOUT US, MIZUKI. YOU'RE THE ONE WHO MATTERS.
Right, Izumi?
No, no...
IT'S OKAY.
I guess.
It's all my fault...
oh
ME?
I'M FINE.
WHEN...
WHEN THAT GUY FROM DORM 1 ATTACKED ME DURING THE CHICKEN FIGHT...
HE HIT ME WITH FULL CONTACT WHEN THE REF WASN'T LOOKING.
HE...
DID IT ON PURPOSE.

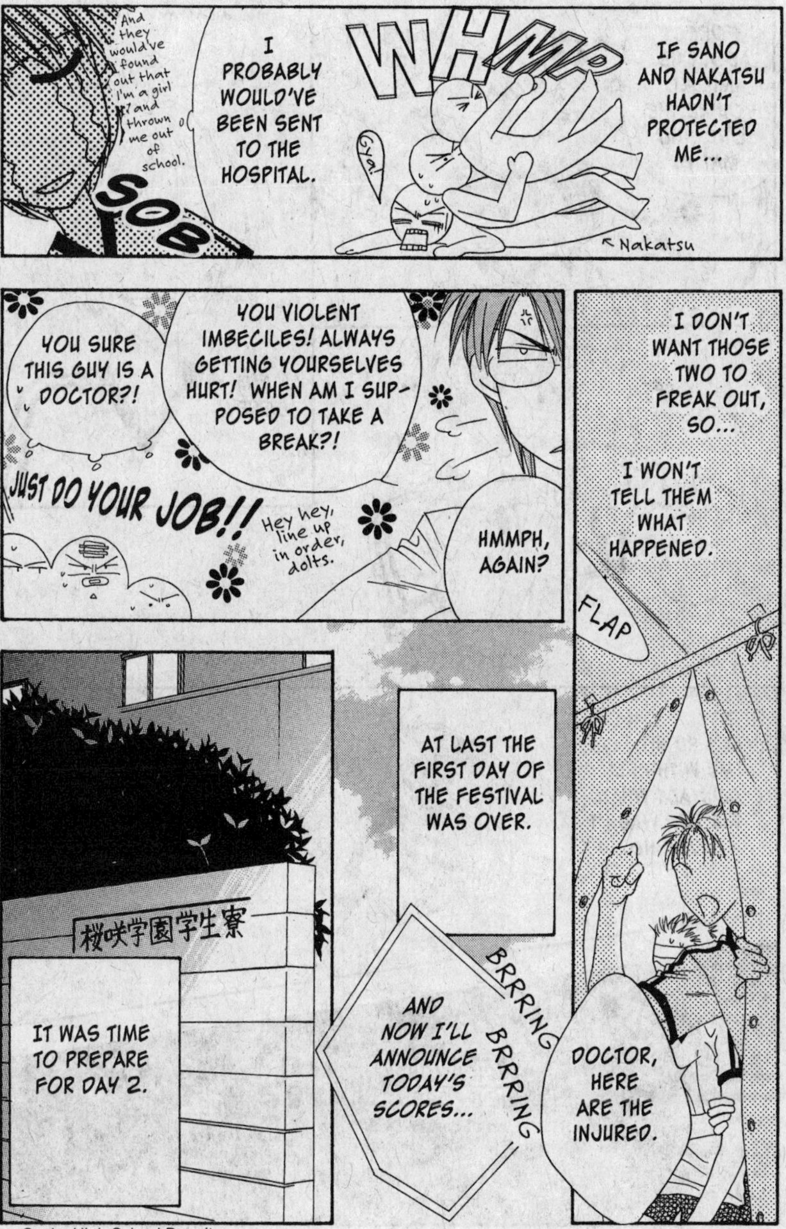
IF SANO AND NAKATSU HADN'T PROTECTED ME...
WHMP
Gya!
Nakatsu
I PROBABLY WOULD'VE BEEN SENT TO THE HOSPITAL.
And they would've found out that I'm a girl and thrown me out of school.
SOB
I DON'T WANT THOSE TWO TO FREAK OUT, SO...
I WON'T TELL THEM WHAT HAPPENED.
FLAP
DOCTOR, HERE ARE THE INJURED.
HMMPH, AGAIN?
YOU VIOLENT IMBECILES! ALWAYS GETTING YOURSELVES HURT! WHEN AM I SUPPOSED TO TAKE A BREAK?!
YOU SURE THIS GUY IS A DOCTOR?!
JUST DO YOUR JOB!!
Hey hey, line up in order, dolts.
AT LAST THE FIRST DAY OF THE FESTIVAL WAS OVER.
BRRRING BRRRING
AND NOW I'LL ANNOUNCE TODAY'S SCORES...
桜咲学園学生寮
IT WAS TIME TO PREPARE FOR DAY 2.
Osaka High School Dormitory

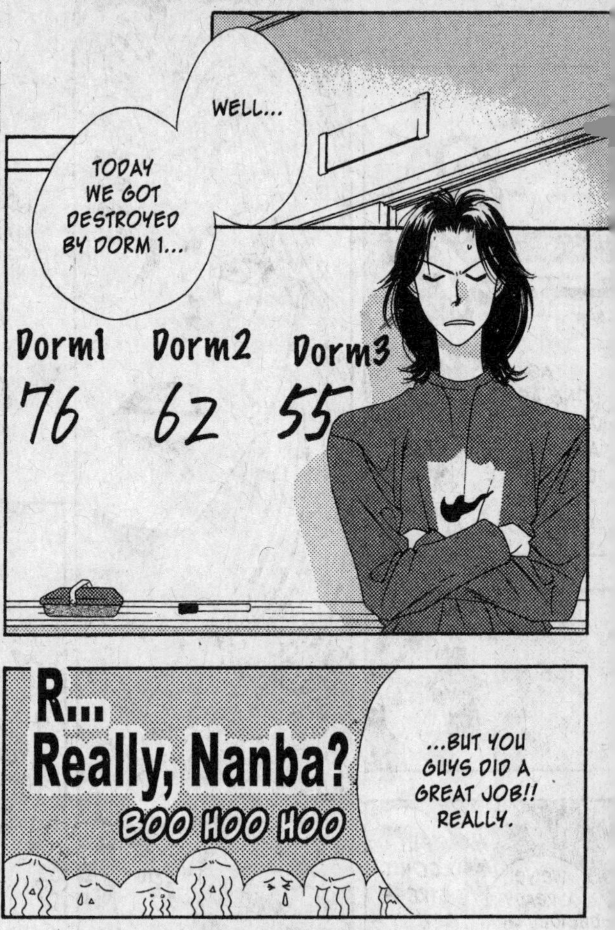
WELL...
TODAY WE GOT DESTROYED BY DORM 1...
Dorm1 Dorm2 Dorm3
76 62 55
...BUT YOU GUYS DID A GREAT JOB!! REALLY.
R... Really, Nanba?
BOO HOO HOO
WE ONLY HAVE TWO DAYS LEFT...
AND STARTING TOMORROW I THINK DORM 3 IS GONNA START TO RALLY.
SO WE'RE LEFT WITH ONLY ONE PATH...

Whispered secrets

Costumes

THIS TIME I GOT TO DRAW SOME COOL STUFF, SO IT WAS REALLY FUN! ♡ I LOVED DRAWING MIZUKI AS ALICE IN WONDERLAND AND NAKAO AS SNOW WHITE, BUT THE BEST WAS THE THREE IDIOTS DRESSED AS CHARACTERS FROM "HEIDI" ("ALPS NO SHOJO HEIDI" IN JAPANESE). I KNEW THEY WERE GONNA LOOK LIKE THAT! ♡ BUT SANO WAS DEFINITELY THE FAVORITE. APPARENTLY HE'S BEEN GETTING SEXIER AND SEXIER. WHAT DID YOU THINK? (HA-HA) I KNEW I WOULDN'T GET THE CHANCE TO DRAW THEM IN GIRLS' CLOTHES AGAIN SO I HAD FUN.

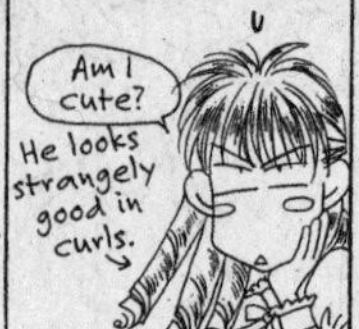
Am I cute?
He looks strangely good in curls.

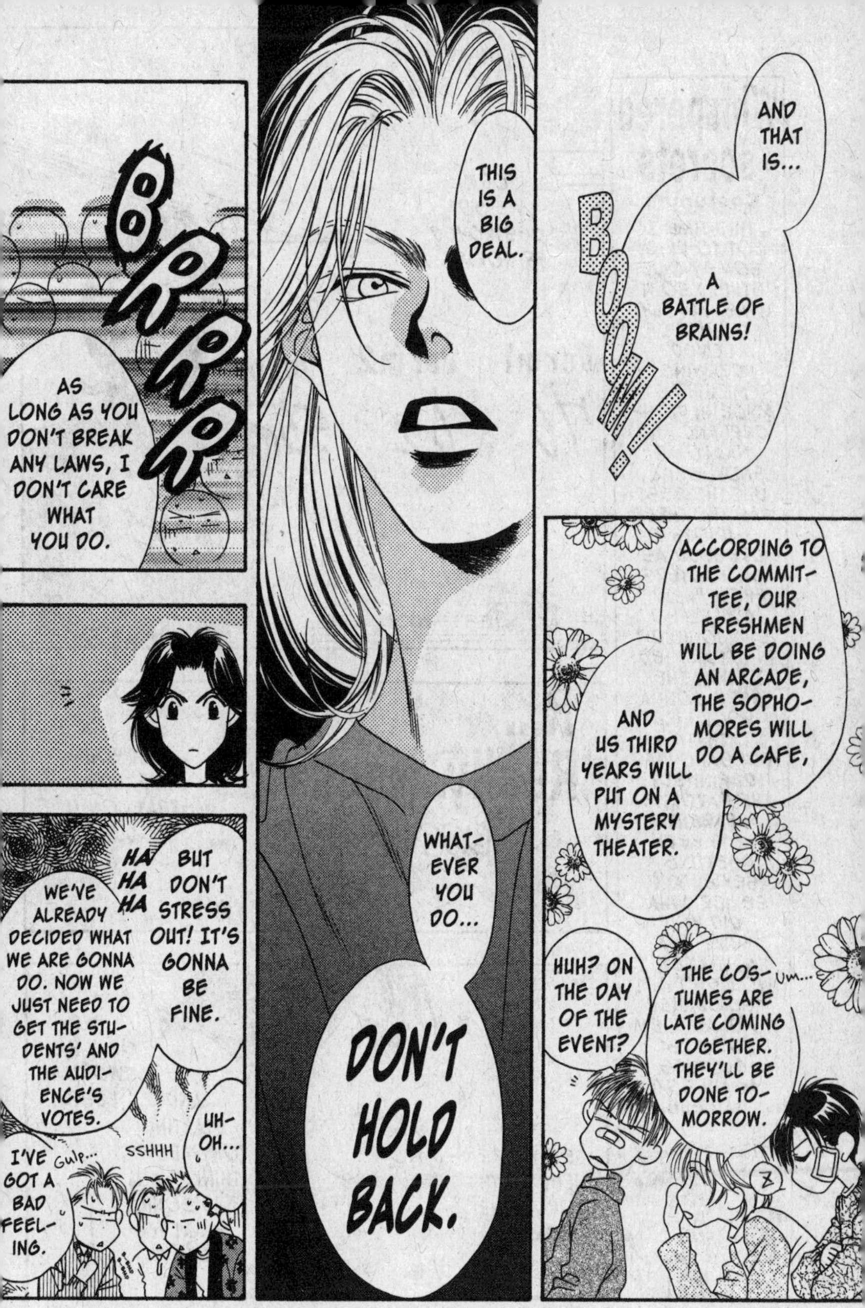
AND THAT IS...
A BATTLE OF BRAINS!
BOOM!
ACCORDING TO THE COMMITTEE, OUR FRESHMEN WILL BE DOING AN ARCADE, THE SOPHOMORES WILL DO A CAFE,
AND US THIRD YEARS WILL PUT ON A MYSTERY THEATER.
THE COSTUMES ARE LATE COMING TOGETHER. THEY'LL BE DONE TOMORROW.
Um...
HUH? ON THE DAY OF THE EVENT?
THIS IS A BIG DEAL.
WHATEVER YOU DO...
DON'T HOLD BACK.
BRRRR
AS LONG AS YOU DON'T BREAK ANY LAWS, I DON'T CARE WHAT YOU DO.
BUT DON'T STRESS OUT! IT'S GONNA BE FINE.
HA HA HA
WE'VE ALREADY DECIDED WHAT WE ARE GONNA DO. NOW WE JUST NEED TO GET THE STUDENTS' AND THE AUDIENCE'S VOTES.
UH-OH...
SSHHH
Gulp...
I'VE GOT A BAD FEELING.

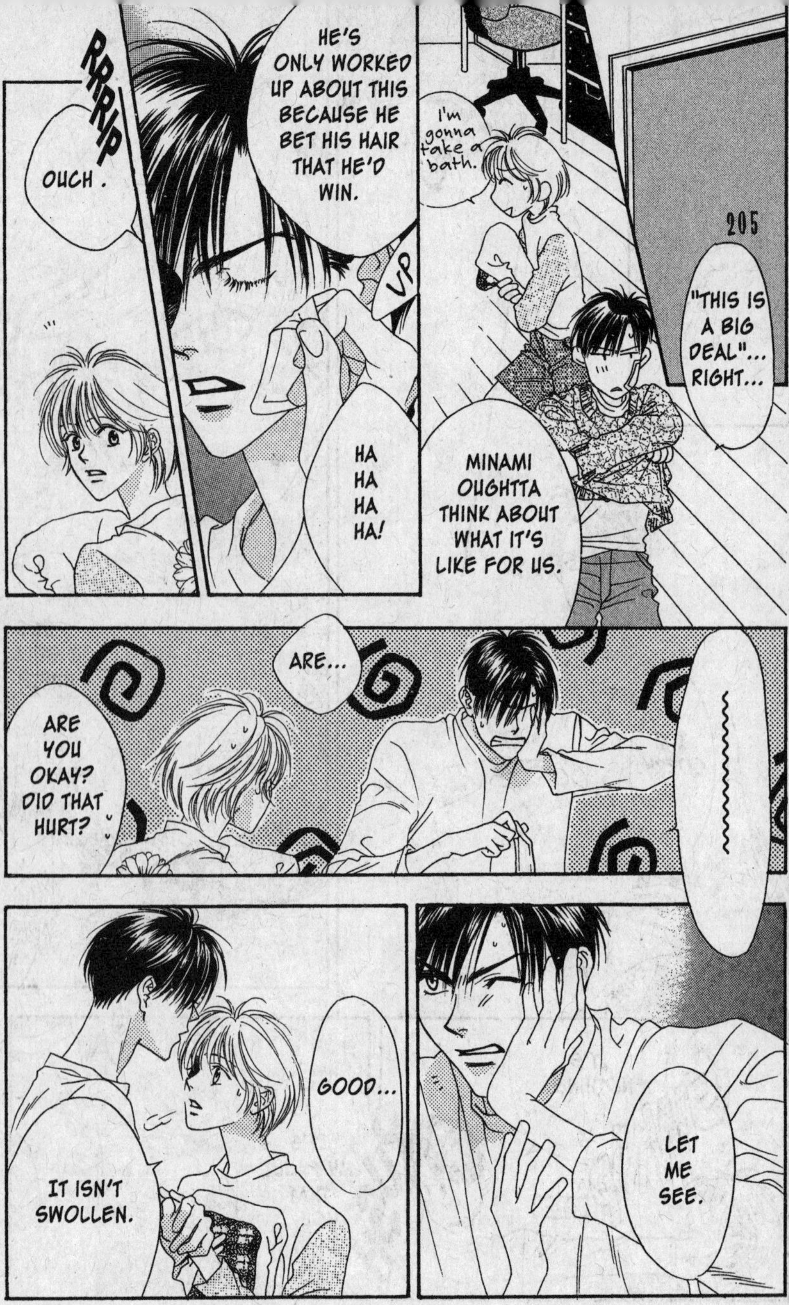
I'm gonna take a bath.
205
"THIS IS A BIG DEAL"... RIGHT...
MINAMI OUGHTTA THINK ABOUT WHAT IT'S LIKE FOR US.
HE'S ONLY WORKED UP ABOUT THIS BECAUSE HE BET HIS HAIR THAT HE'D WIN.
VP
HA HA HA HA!
RRRIP
OUCH.
...
ARE...
ARE YOU OKAY? DID THAT HURT?
LET ME SEE.
GOOD...
IT ISN'T SWOLLEN.

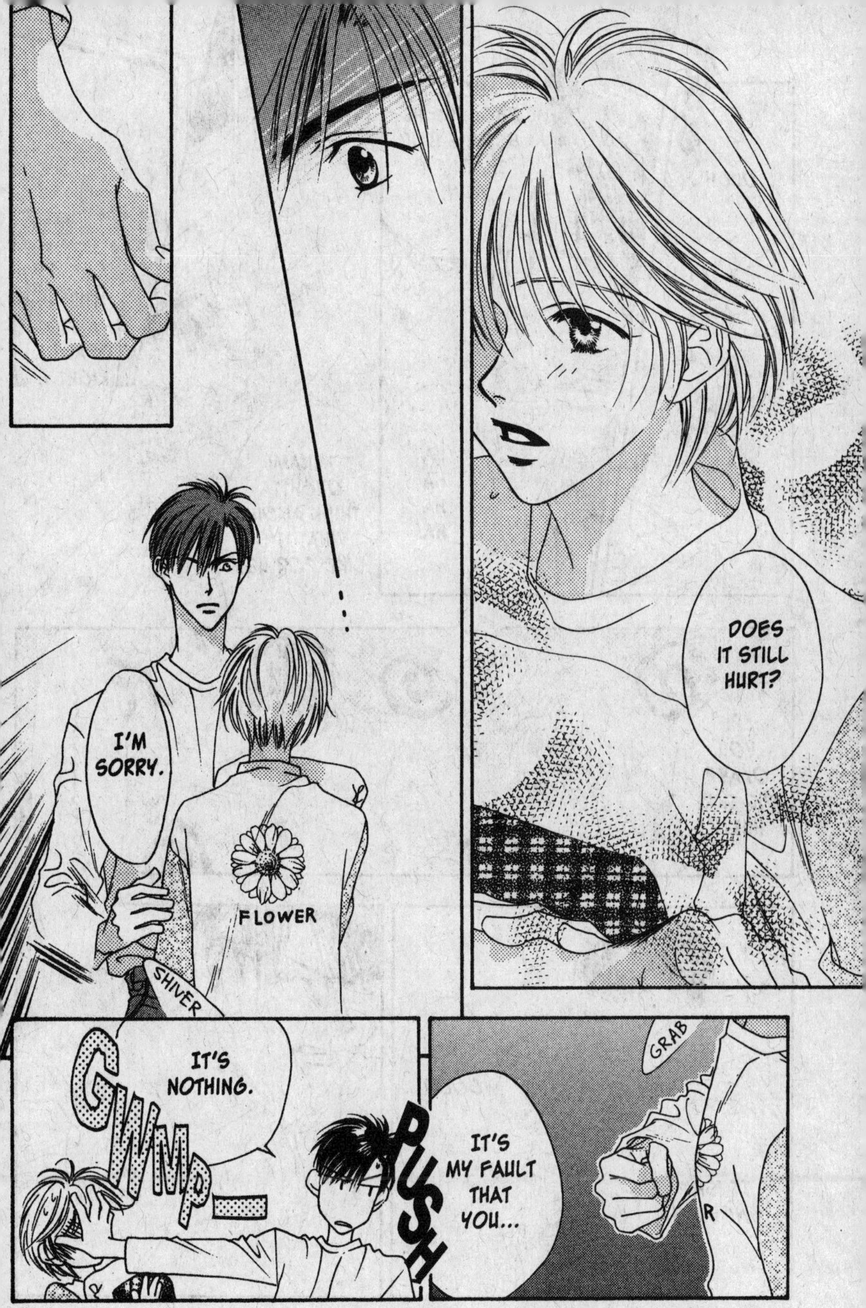
DOES IT STILL HURT?
...
I'M SORRY.
FLOWER
SHIVER
GRAB
IT'S MY FAULT THAT YOU...
R
PUSH!
IT'S NOTHING.
GWMP—

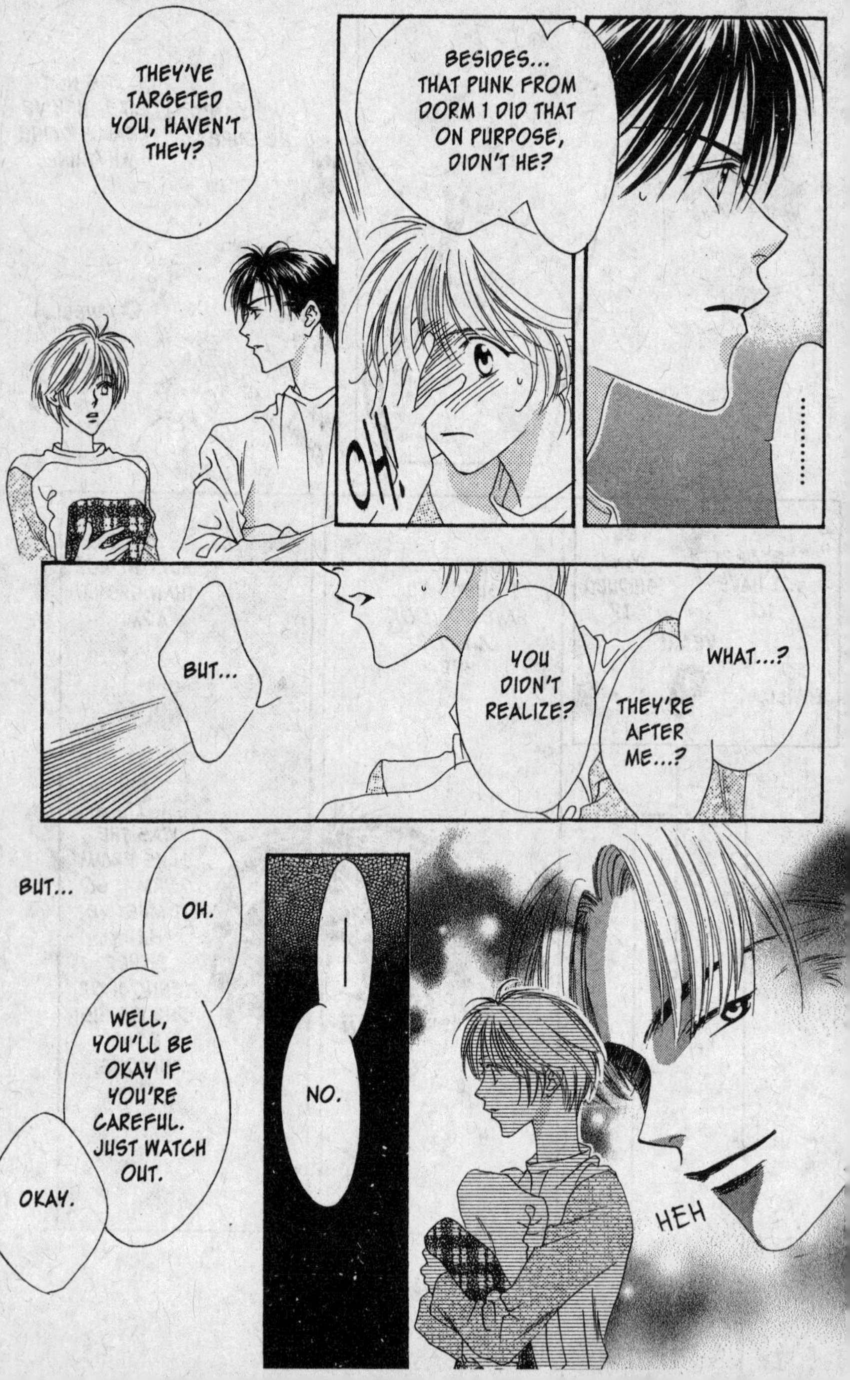
......
BESIDES... THAT PUNK FROM DORM 1 DID THAT ON PURPOSE, DIDN'T HE?
OH!
THEY'VE TARGETED YOU, HAVEN'T THEY?
WHAT...?
THEY'RE AFTER ME...?
YOU DIDN'T REALIZE?
BUT...
HEH
I
NO.
OH.
BUT...
WELL, YOU'LL BE OKAY IF YOU'RE CAREFUL. JUST WATCH OUT.
OKAY.

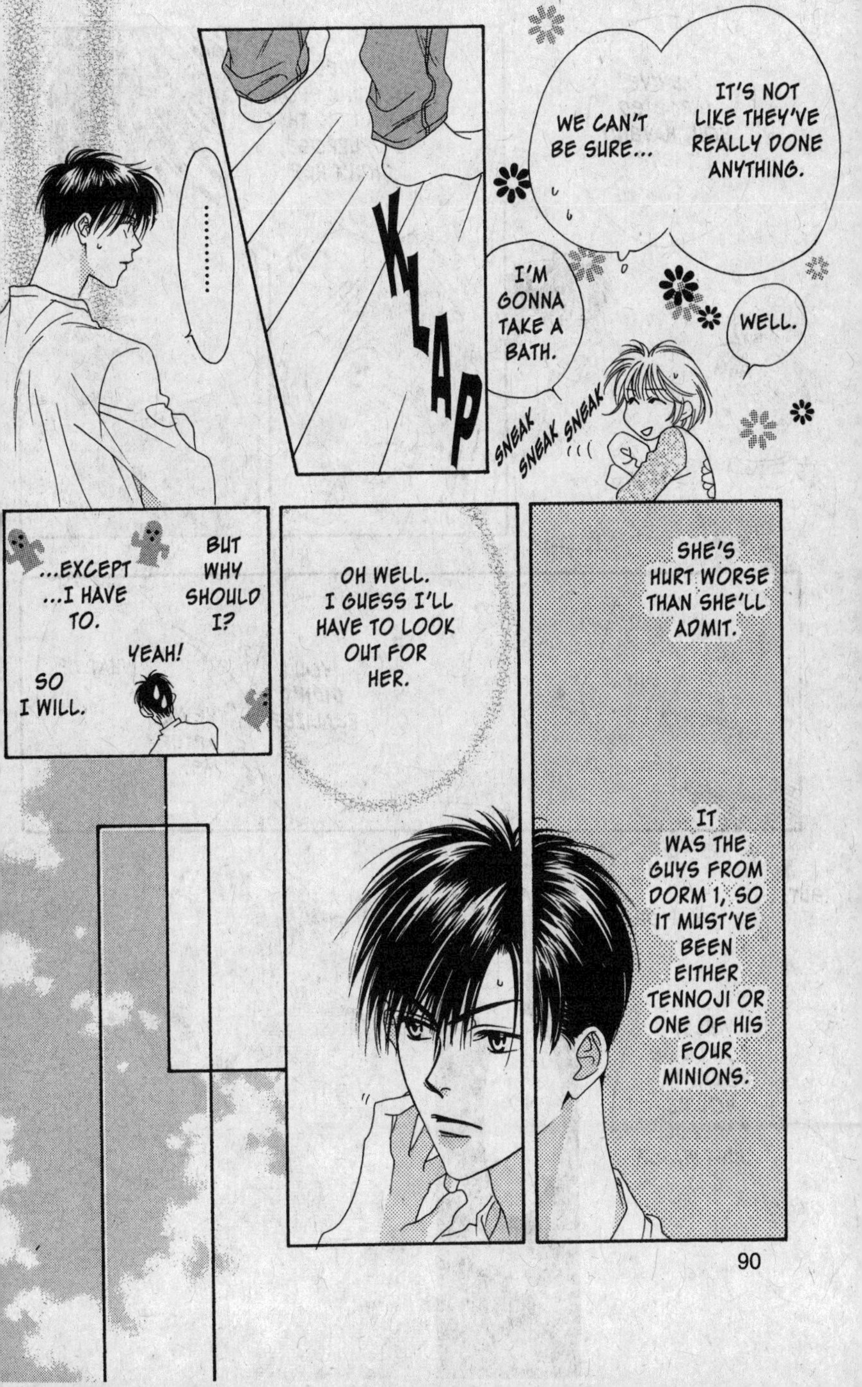

IT'S NOT LIKE THEY'VE REALLY DONE ANYTHING.
WE CAN'T BE SURE...
WELL.
I'M GONNA TAKE A BATH.
SNEAK SNEAK SNEAK
KLAP
......
SHE'S HURT WORSE THAN SHE'LL ADMIT.
IT WAS THE GUYS FROM DORM 1, SO IT MUST'VE BEEN EITHER TENNOJI OR ONE OF HIS FOUR MINIONS.
OH WELL. I GUESS I'LL HAVE TO LOOK OUT FOR HER.
BUT WHY SHOULD I?
...EXCEPT ...I HAVE TO.
YEAH!
SO I WILL.

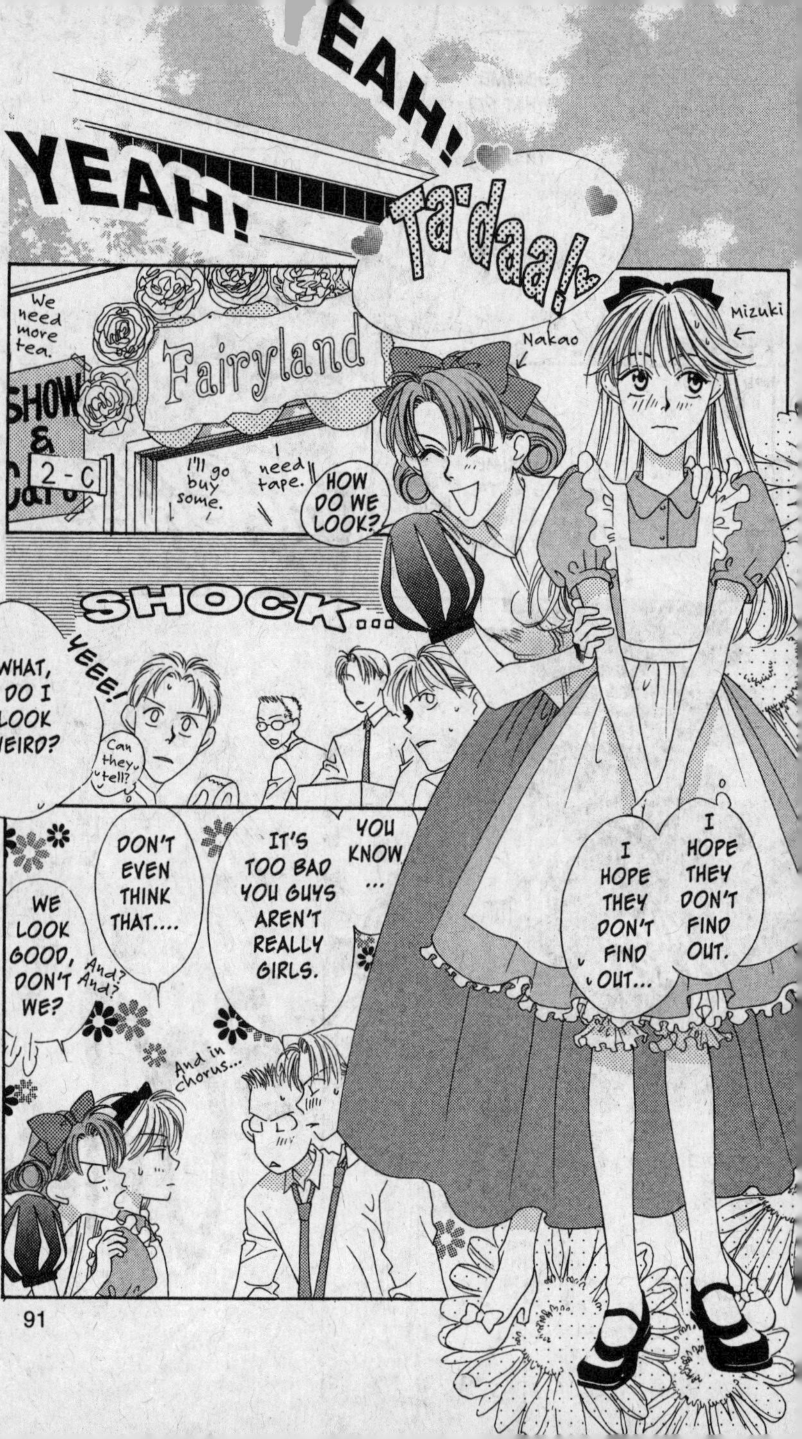
YEAH! YEAH!
Ta'daa!
Mizuki
Nakao
HOW DO WE LOOK?
I need tape.
I'll go buy some.
Fairyland
We need more tea.
SHOW & Caf
2-C
SHOCK...
YEEE!
WHAT, DO I LOOK WEIRD?
Can they tell?
I HOPE THEY DON'T FIND OUT.
I HOPE THEY DON'T FIND OUT...
YOU KNOW...
IT'S TOO BAD YOU GUYS AREN'T REALLY GIRLS.
DON'T EVEN THINK THAT....
WE LOOK GOOD, DON'T WE?
And? And?
And in chorus...

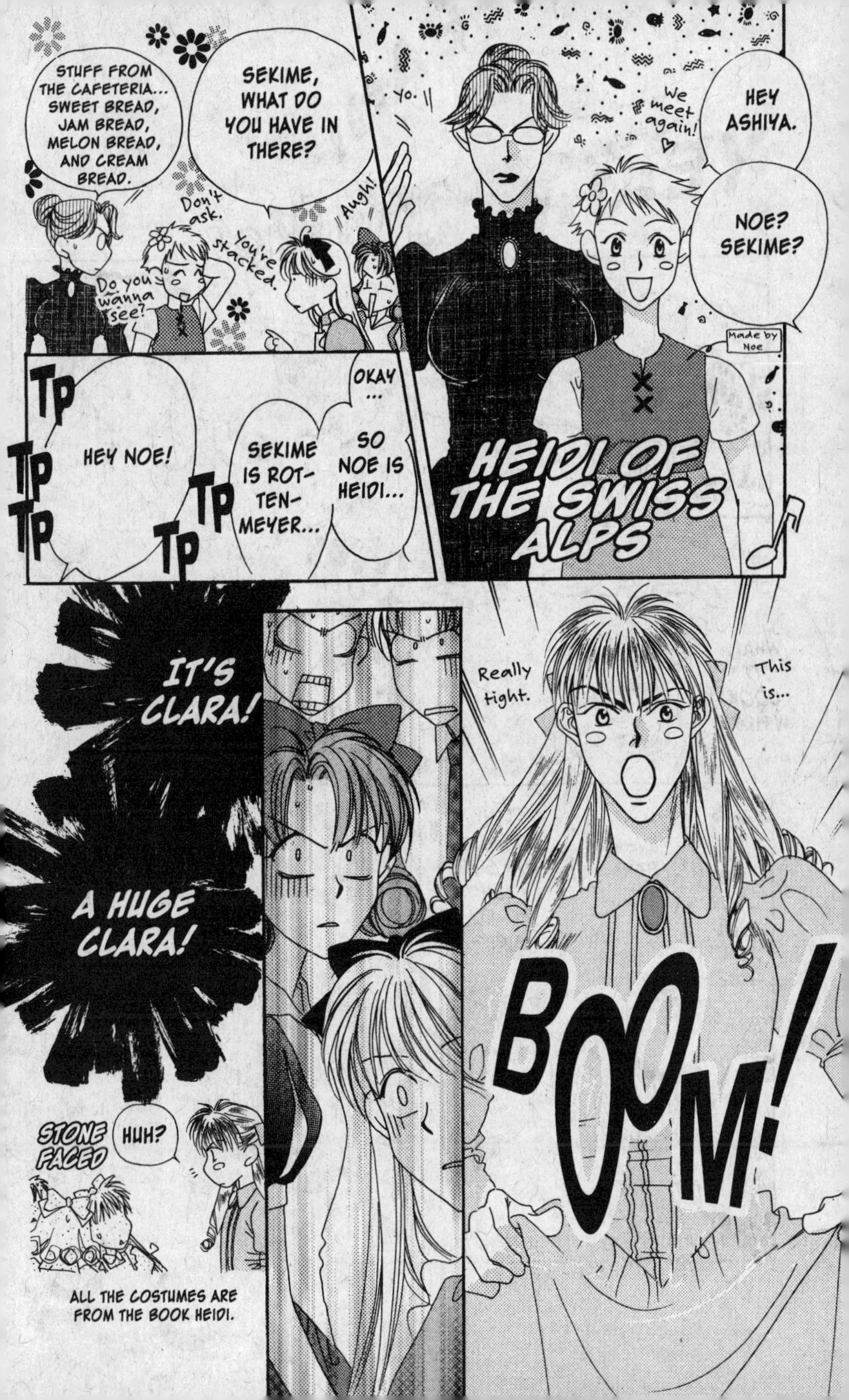
HEY ASHIYA.
NOE? SEKIME?
We meet again!
Yo.
Made by Noe
HEIDI OF THE SWISS ALPS
SEKIME, WHAT DO YOU HAVE IN THERE?
STUFF FROM THE CAFETERIA... SWEET BREAD, JAM BREAD, MELON BREAD, AND CREAM BREAD.
Augh!
Don't ask.
You're stacked.
Do you wanna see?
OKAY ...
SO NOE IS HEIDI...
SEKIME IS ROT-TEN-MEYER...
HEY NOE!
TP TP TP TP TP TP
This is...
Really tight.
BOOM!
IT'S CLARA!
A HUGE CLARA!
HUH?
STONE FACED
ALL THE COSTUMES ARE FROM THE BOOK HEIDI.

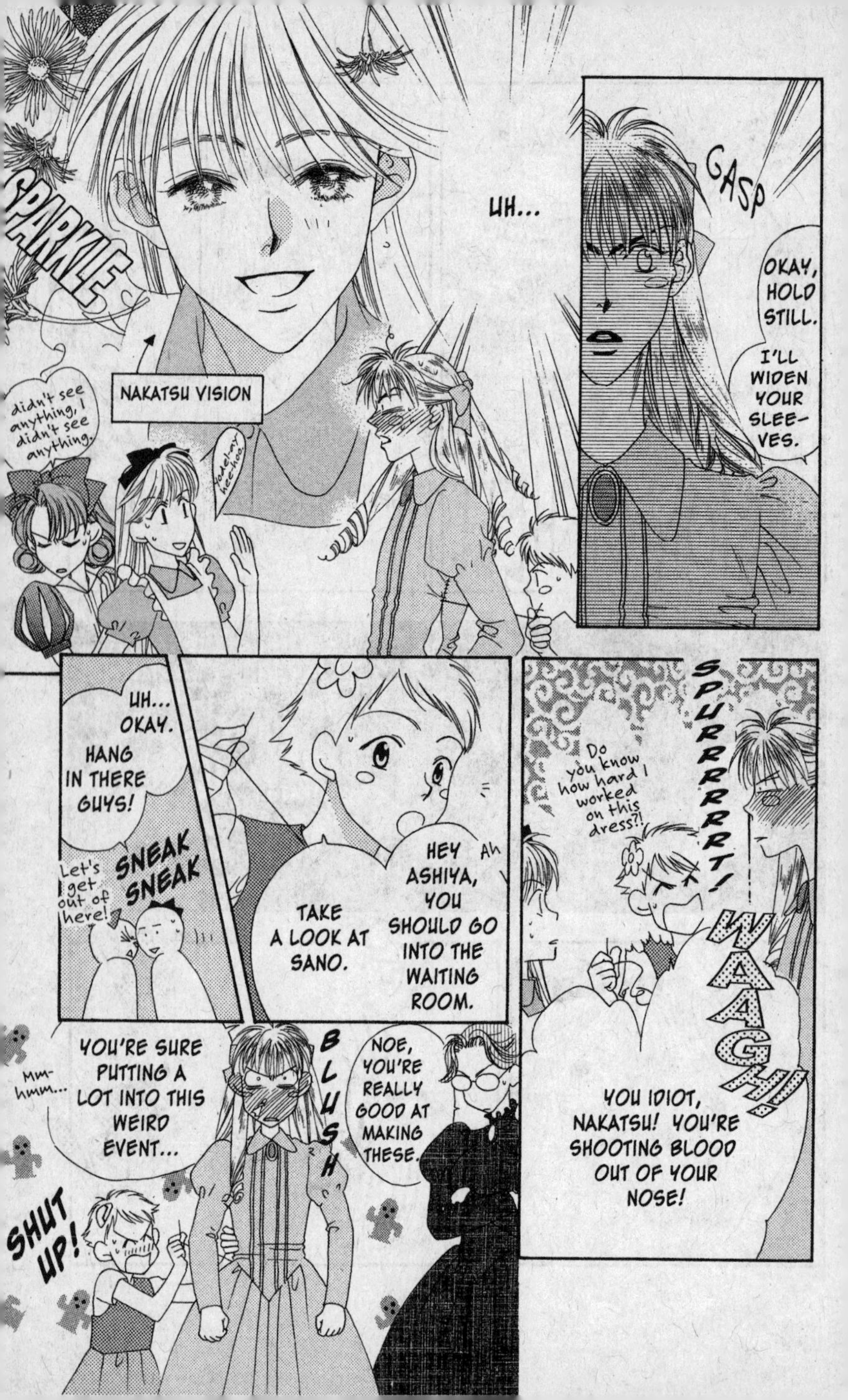
GASP
OKAY, HOLD STILL.
I'LL WIDEN YOUR SLEE-VES.
UH...
Yodel-ay hee-hoo
NAKATSU VISION
SPARKLE
didn't see anything, I didn't see anything.
SPURRRRRT!
WAAGH!!
Do you know how hard I worked on this dress?!
YOU IDIOT, NAKATSU! YOU'RE SHOOTING BLOOD OUT OF YOUR NOSE!
HEY ASHIYA, YOU SHOULD GO INTO THE WAITING ROOM.
Ah
TAKE A LOOK AT SANO.
UH... OKAY. HANG IN THERE GUYS!
SNEAK SNEAK
Let's get out of here!
NOE, YOU'RE REALLY GOOD AT MAKING THESE.
BLUSH
YOU'RE SURE PUTTING A LOT INTO THIS WEIRD EVENT...
Mm-hmm...
SHUT UP!

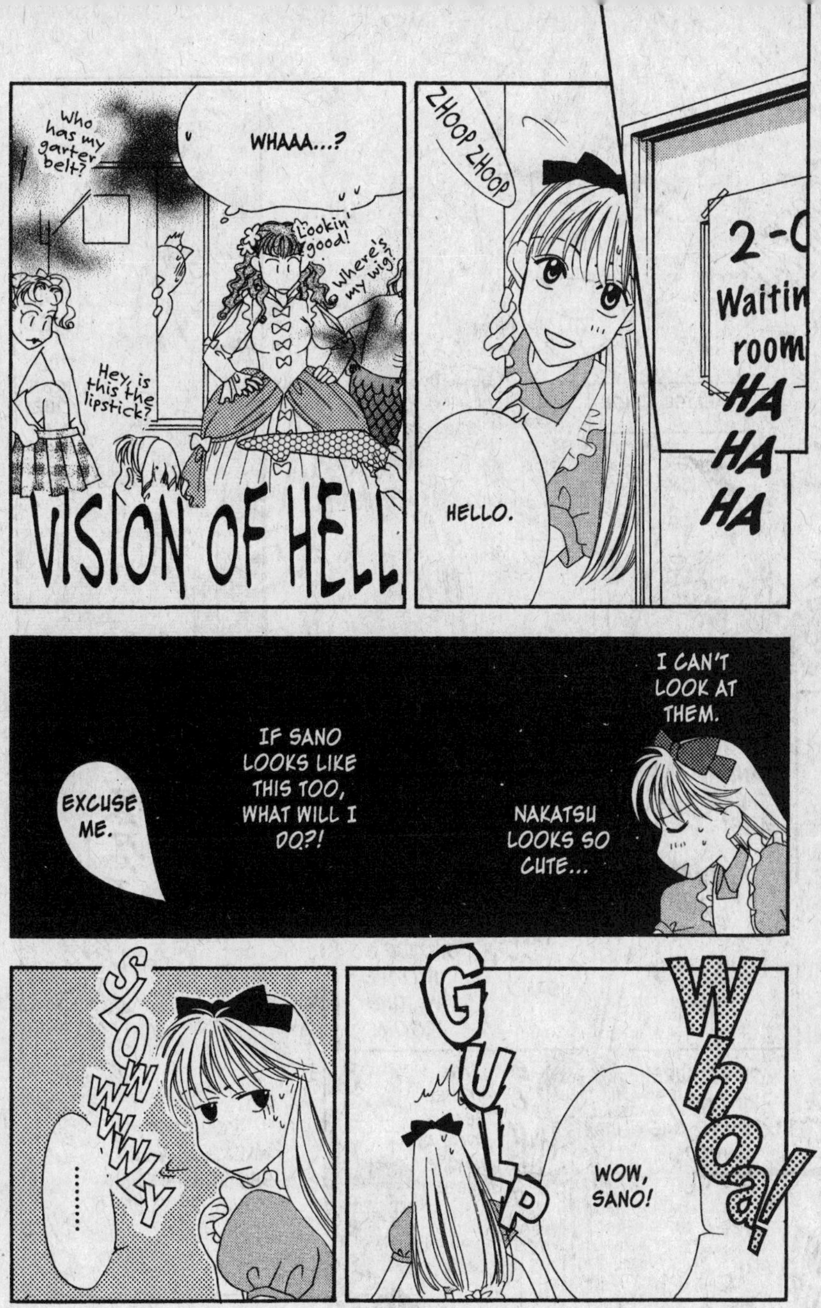

2-
Waitin
room
ZHOOP ZHOOP
HELLO.
HA HA HA HA
WHAAA...?
Who has my garter belt?
Lookin' good!
Where's my wig?
Hey, is this the lipstick?
VISION OF HELL
I CAN'T LOOK AT THEM.
NAKATSU LOOKS SO CUTE...
IF SANO LOOKS LIKE THIS TOO, WHAT WILL I DO?!
EXCUSE ME.
GULP
WHOA!
WOW, SANO!
SLOWWWWLY
......

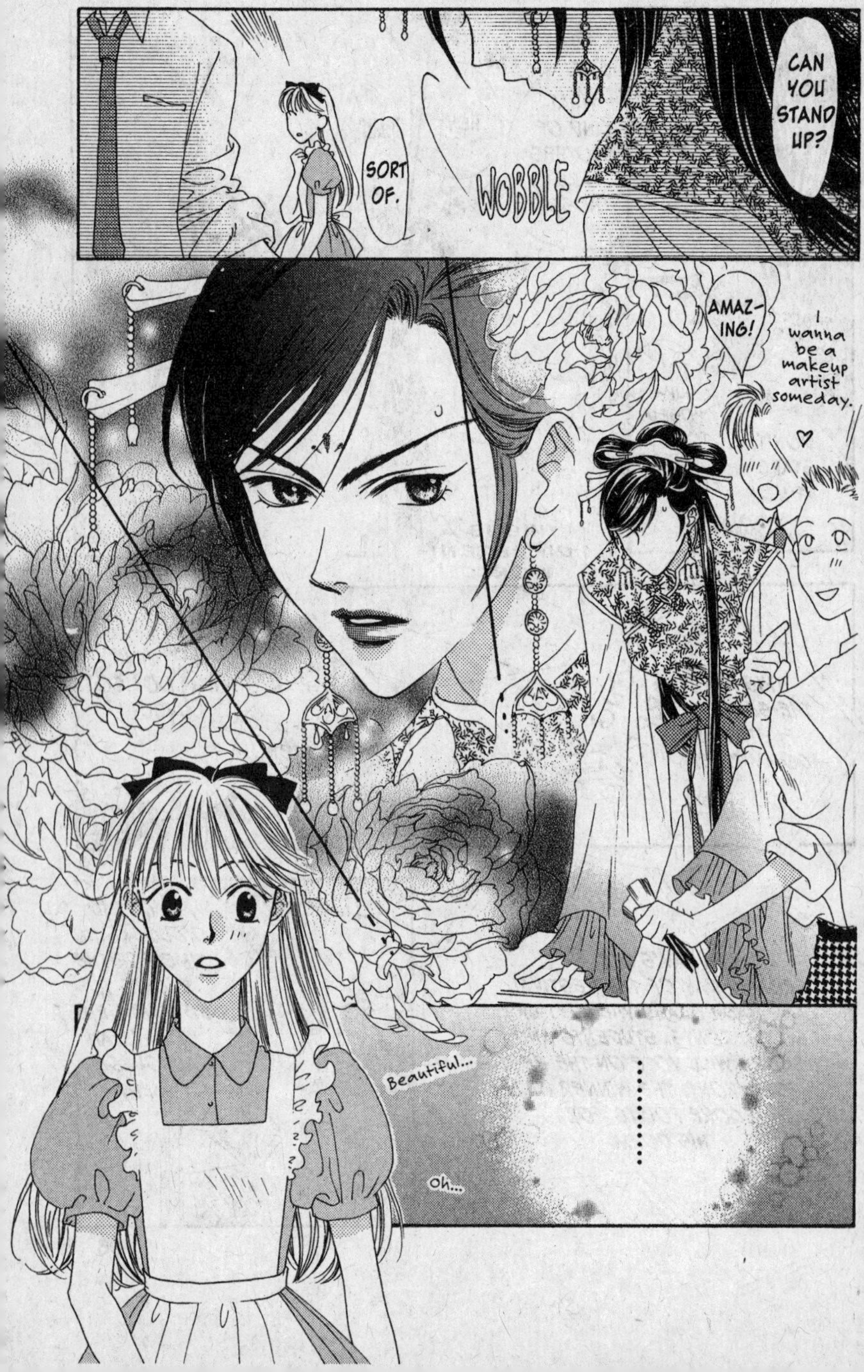
CAN YOU STAND UP?
WOBBLE
SORT OF.
AMAZ-ING!
I wanna be a makeup artist someday.
♥
....
Beautiful...
Oh...

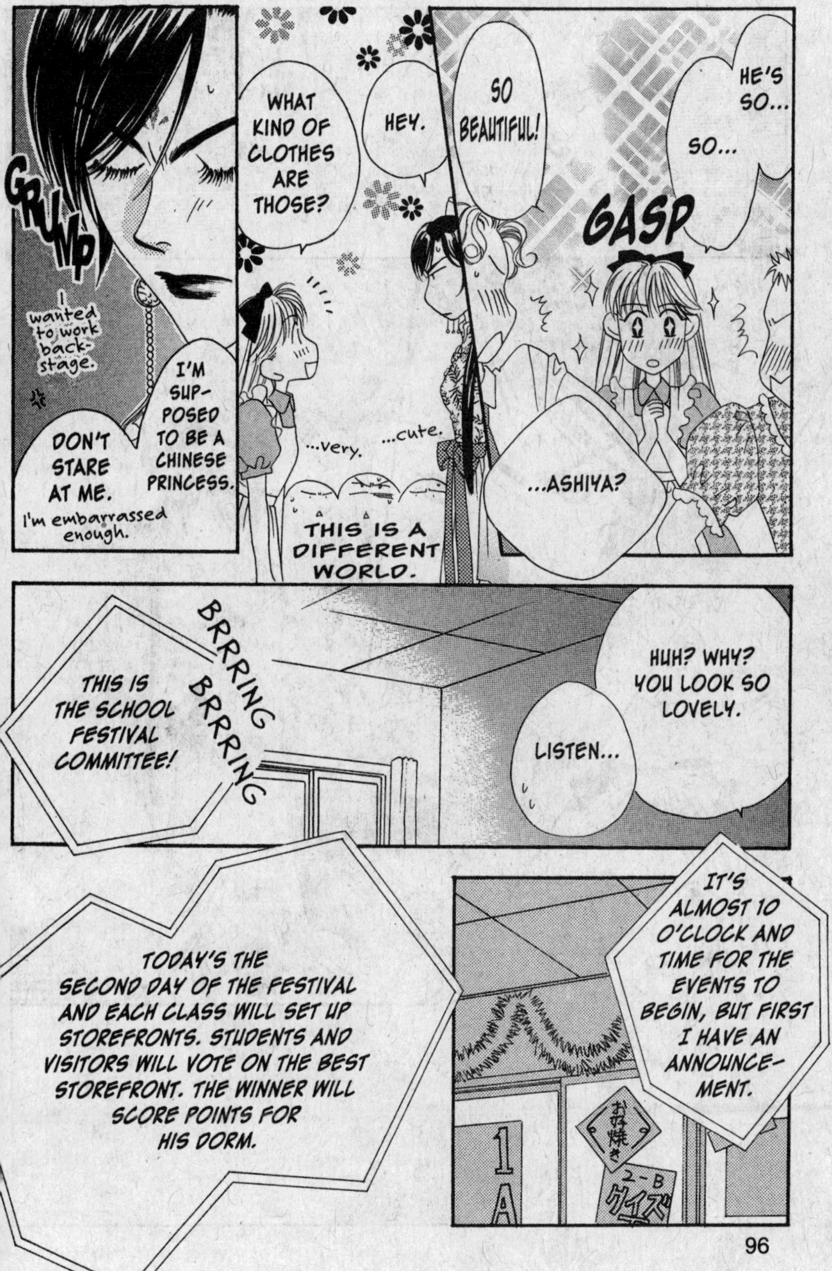
HE'S SO...
SO...
GASP
SO BEAUTIFUL!
...ASHIYA?
HEY.
WHAT KIND OF CLOTHES ARE THOSE?
...very.
...cute.
THIS IS A DIFFERENT WORLD.
GRUMP
I wanted to work back-stage.
I'M SUP-POSED TO BE A CHINESE PRINCESS.
DON'T STARE AT ME.
I'm embarrassed enough.
HUH? WHY? YOU LOOK SO LOVELY.
LISTEN...
BRRRING BRRRING
THIS IS THE SCHOOL FESTIVAL COMMITTEE!
IT'S ALMOST 10 O'CLOCK AND TIME FOR THE EVENTS TO BEGIN, BUT FIRST I HAVE AN ANNOUNCE-MENT.
お好焼き
2-B
1 A
TODAY'S THE SECOND DAY OF THE FESTIVAL AND EACH CLASS WILL SET UP STOREFRONTS. STUDENTS AND VISITORS WILL VOTE ON THE BEST STOREFRONT. THE WINNER WILL SCORE POINTS FOR HIS DORM.

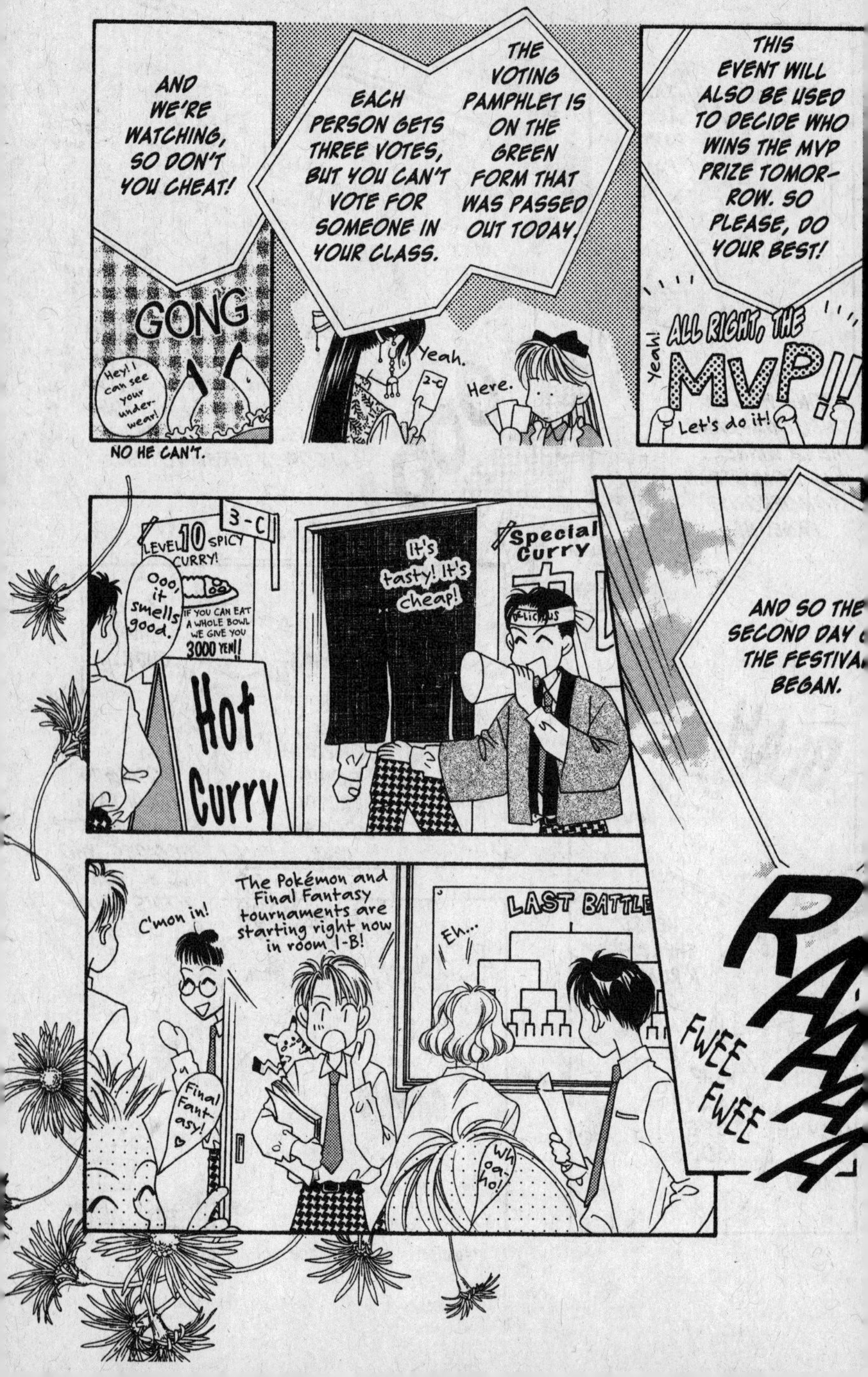
THIS EVENT WILL ALSO BE USED TO DECIDE WHO WINS THE MVP PRIZE TOMORROW. SO PLEASE, DO YOUR BEST!
ALL RIGHT, THE MVP!!
Yeah!
Let's do it!
THE VOTING PAMPHLET IS ON THE GREEN FORM THAT WAS PASSED OUT TODAY.
EACH PERSON GETS THREE VOTES, BUT YOU CAN'T VOTE FOR SOMEONE IN YOUR CLASS.
Yeah.
2-C
Here.
AND WE'RE WATCHING, SO DON'T YOU CHEAT!
GONG
Hey! I can see your underwear!
NO HE CAN'T.
AND SO THE SECOND DAY THE FESTIVA BEGAN.
FWEE FWEE
Special Curry
It's tasty! It's cheap!
3-C
LEVEL 10 SPICY CURRY!
Ooo, it smells good.
IF YOU CAN EAT A WHOLE BOWL WE GIVE YOU 3000 YEN!!
Hot Curry
LAST BATTLE
Eh...
The Pokémon and Final Fantasy tournaments are starting right now in room 1-B!
C'mon in!
Final Fantasy!
Whoa-ho!

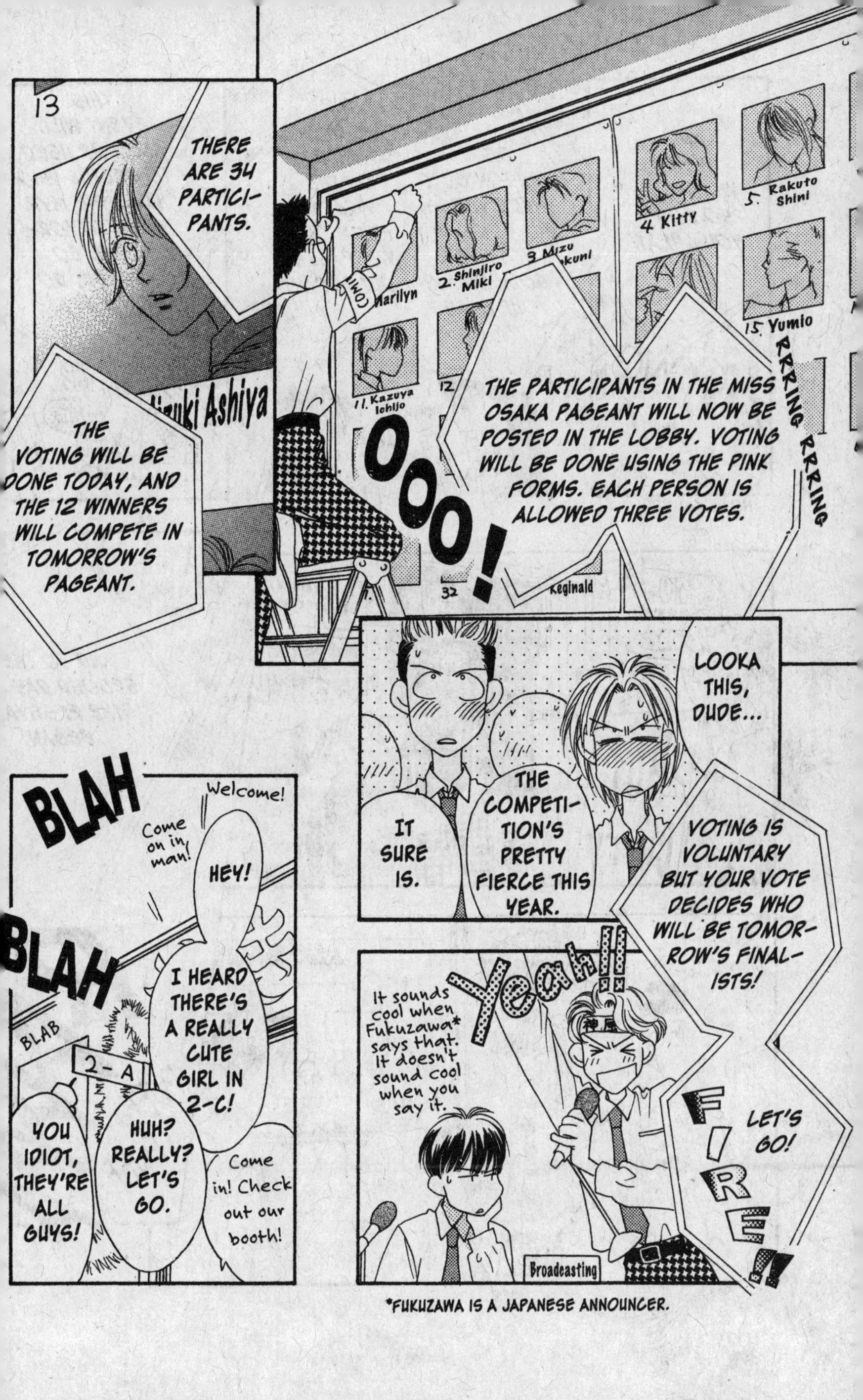
4 Kitty
5. Rakuto Shini
2. Shinjiro Miki
Marilyn
15. Yumio
11. Kazuya Ichijo
32
Reginald
THE PARTICIPANTS IN THE MISS OSAKA PAGEANT WILL NOW BE POSTED IN THE LOBBY. VOTING WILL BE DONE USING THE PINK FORMS. EACH PERSON IS ALLOWED THREE VOTES.
RRRING RRRING
OOO!
13
THERE ARE 34 PARTICIPANTS.
THE VOTING WILL BE DONE TODAY, AND THE 12 WINNERS WILL COMPETE IN TOMORROW'S PAGEANT.
LOOKA THIS, DUDE...
THE COMPETITION'S PRETTY FIERCE THIS YEAR.
IT SURE IS.
VOTING IS VOLUNTARY BUT YOUR VOTE DECIDES WHO WILL BE TOMORROW'S FINALISTS!
Yeah!!
FIRE!!
LET'S GO!
It sounds cool when Fukuzawa* says that. It doesn't sound cool when you say it.
Broadcasting
BLAH
BLAH
Welcome!
Come on in man!
HEY!
I HEARD THERE'S A REALLY CUTE GIRL IN 2-C!
BLAB
2-A
HUH? REALLY? LET'S GO.
YOU IDIOT, THEY'RE ALL GUYS!
Come in! Check out our booth!

*FUKUZAWA IS A JAPANESE ANNOUNCER.

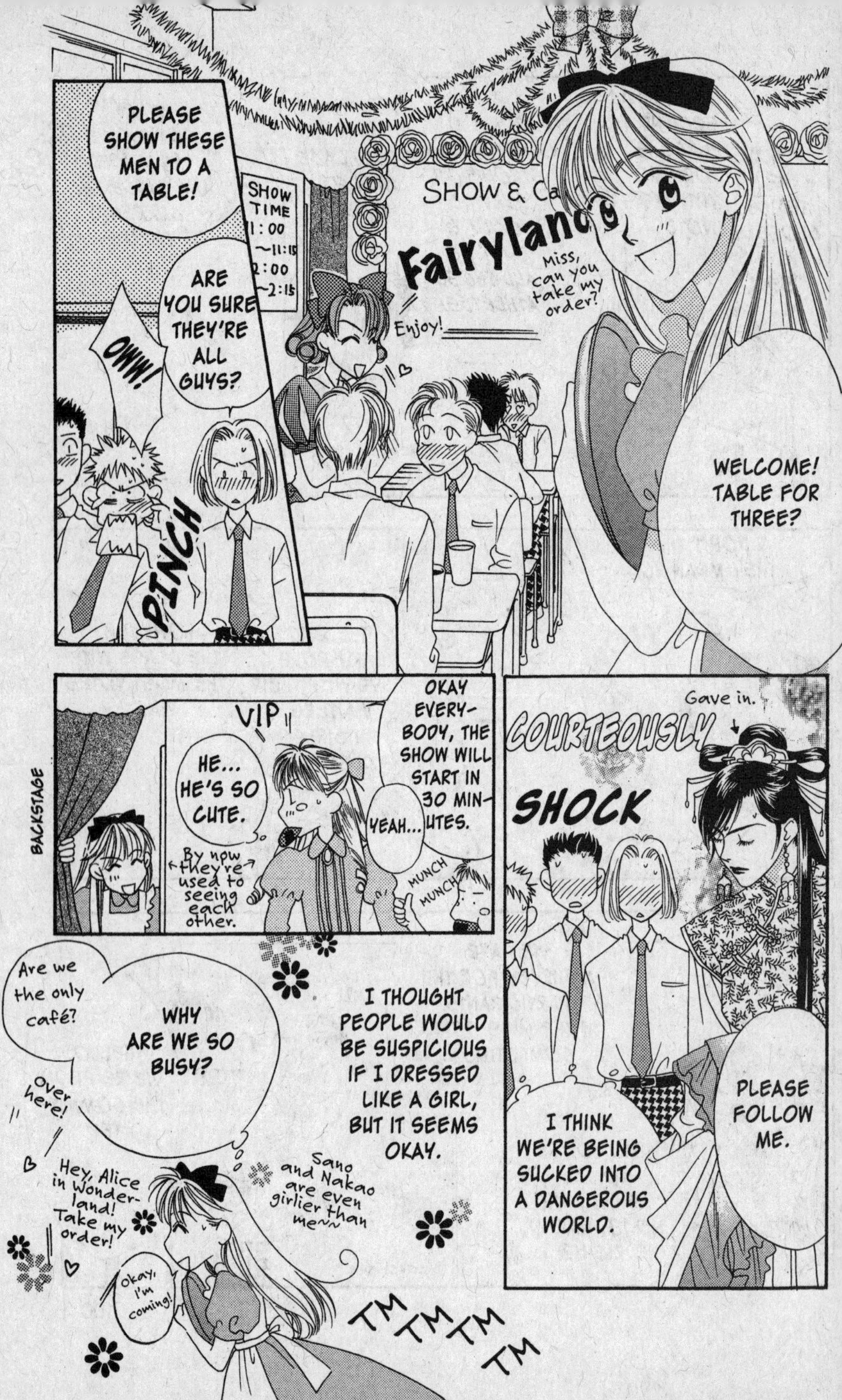
SHOW & Ca
Fairyland
Miss, can you take my order?
WELCOME! TABLE FOR THREE?
Enjoy!
PLEASE SHOW THESE MEN TO A TABLE!
SHOW TIME 11:00 ~11:15 2:00 ~2:15
ARE YOU SURE THEY'RE ALL GUYS?
OWW!
PINCH
Gave in.
COURTEOUSLY
SHOCK
PLEASE FOLLOW ME.
I THINK WE'RE BEING SUCKED INTO A DANGEROUS WORLD.
OKAY EVERYBODY, THE SHOW WILL START IN 30 MINUTES.
YEAH...
VIP
HE... HE'S SO CUTE.
By now they're used to seeing each other.
MUNCH MUNCH
BACKSTAGE
I THOUGHT PEOPLE WOULD BE SUSPICIOUS IF I DRESSED LIKE A GIRL, BUT IT SEEMS OKAY.
Sano and Nakao are even girlier than me~~
WHY ARE WE SO BUSY?
Are we the only café?
Over here!
Hey, Alice in Wonderland! Take my order!
Okay, I'm coming!
TM TM TM TM

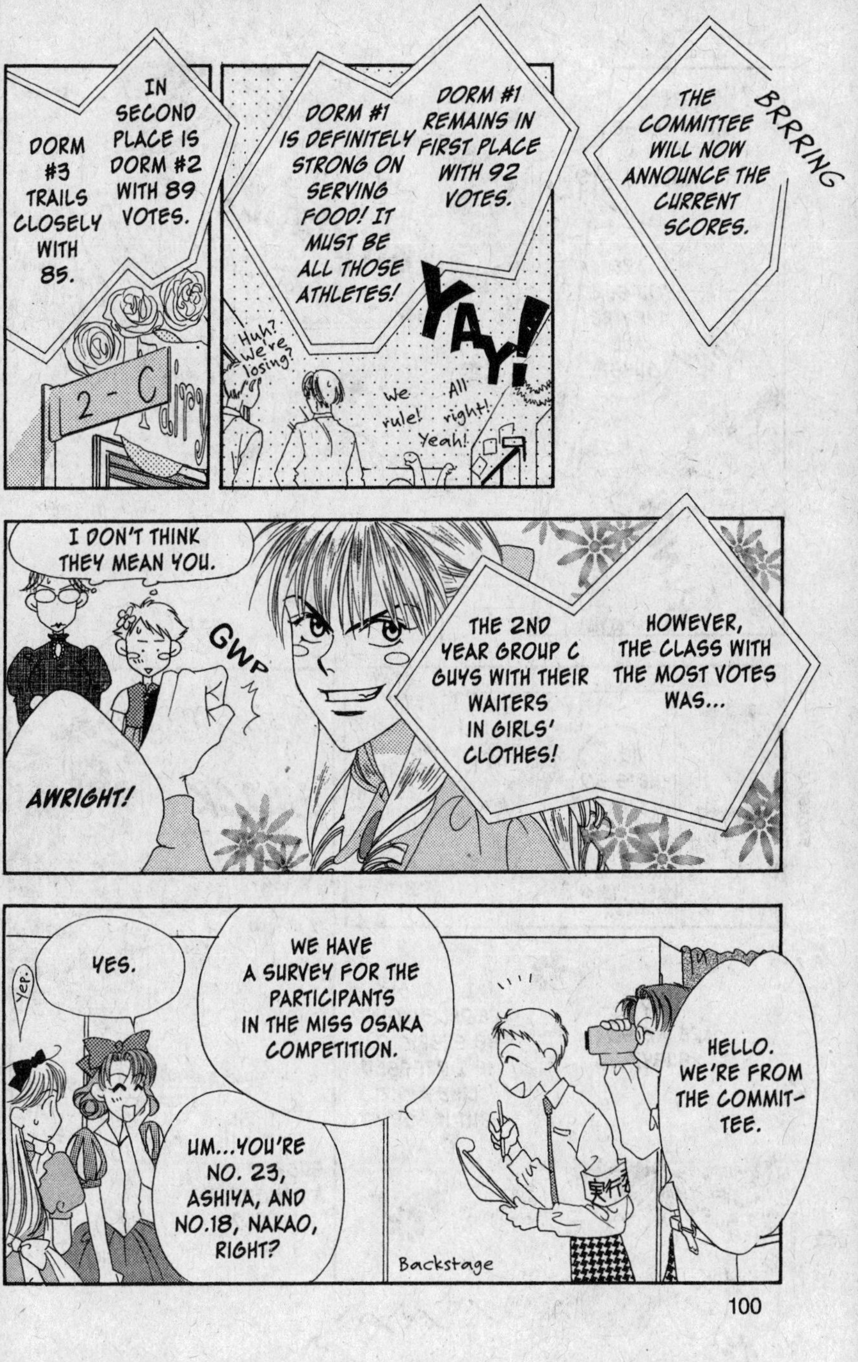

THE COMMITTEE WILL NOW ANNOUNCE THE CURRENT SCORES.
BRRRING
DORM #1 REMAINS IN FIRST PLACE WITH 92 VOTES.
YAY!
DORM #1 IS DEFINITELY STRONG ON SERVING FOOD! IT MUST BE ALL THOSE ATHLETES!
All right!
Yeah!
We rule!
Huh? We're losing?
IN SECOND PLACE IS DORM #2 WITH 89 VOTES.
DORM #3 TRAILS CLOSELY WITH 85.
2 - C
Fairy
HOWEVER, THE CLASS WITH THE MOST VOTES WAS...
THE 2ND YEAR GROUP C GUYS WITH THEIR WAITERS IN GIRLS' CLOTHES!
GWP
AWRIGHT!
I DON'T THINK THEY MEAN YOU.
Backstage
HELLO. WE'RE FROM THE COMMIT-TEE.
WE HAVE A SURVEY FOR THE PARTICIPANTS IN THE MISS OSAKA COMPETITION.
UM...YOU'RE NO. 23, ASHIYA, AND NO.18, NAKAO, RIGHT?
YES.
Yep.

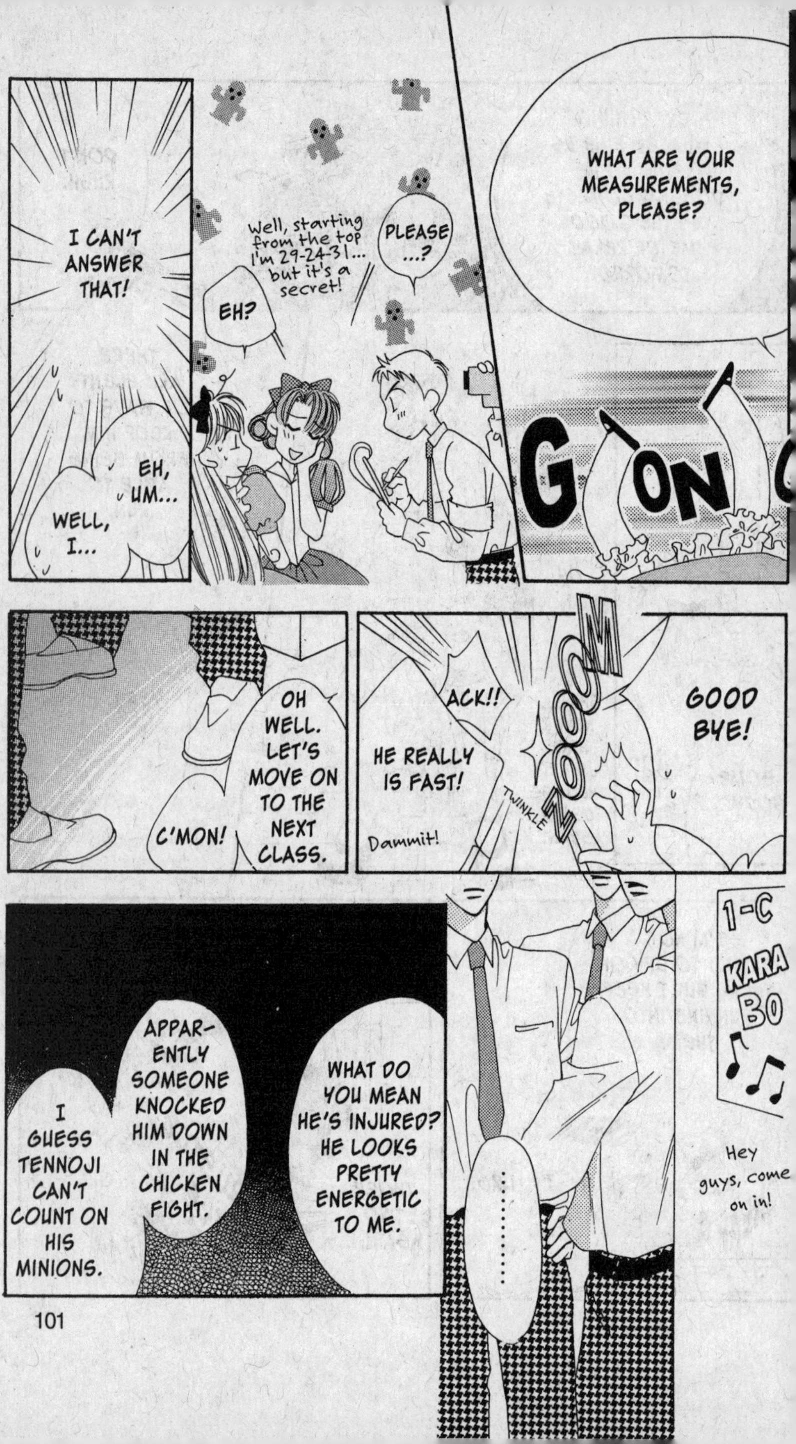
WHAT ARE YOUR MEASUREMENTS, PLEASE?
GON
PLEASE ...?
Well, starting from the top I'm 29-24-31... but it's a secret!
EH?
I CAN'T ANSWER THAT!
EH, UM...
WELL, I...
GOOD BYE!
ZOOOOM
ACK!!
HE REALLY IS FAST!
TWINKLE
Dammit!
OH WELL. LET'S MOVE ON TO THE NEXT CLASS.
C'MON!
1-C KARA BO
Hey guys, come on in!
......
WHAT DO YOU MEAN HE'S INJURED? HE LOOKS PRETTY ENERGETIC TO ME.
APPAR-ENTLY SOMEONE KNOCKED HIM DOWN IN THE CHICKEN FIGHT.
I GUESS TENNOJI CAN'T COUNT ON HIS MINIONS.

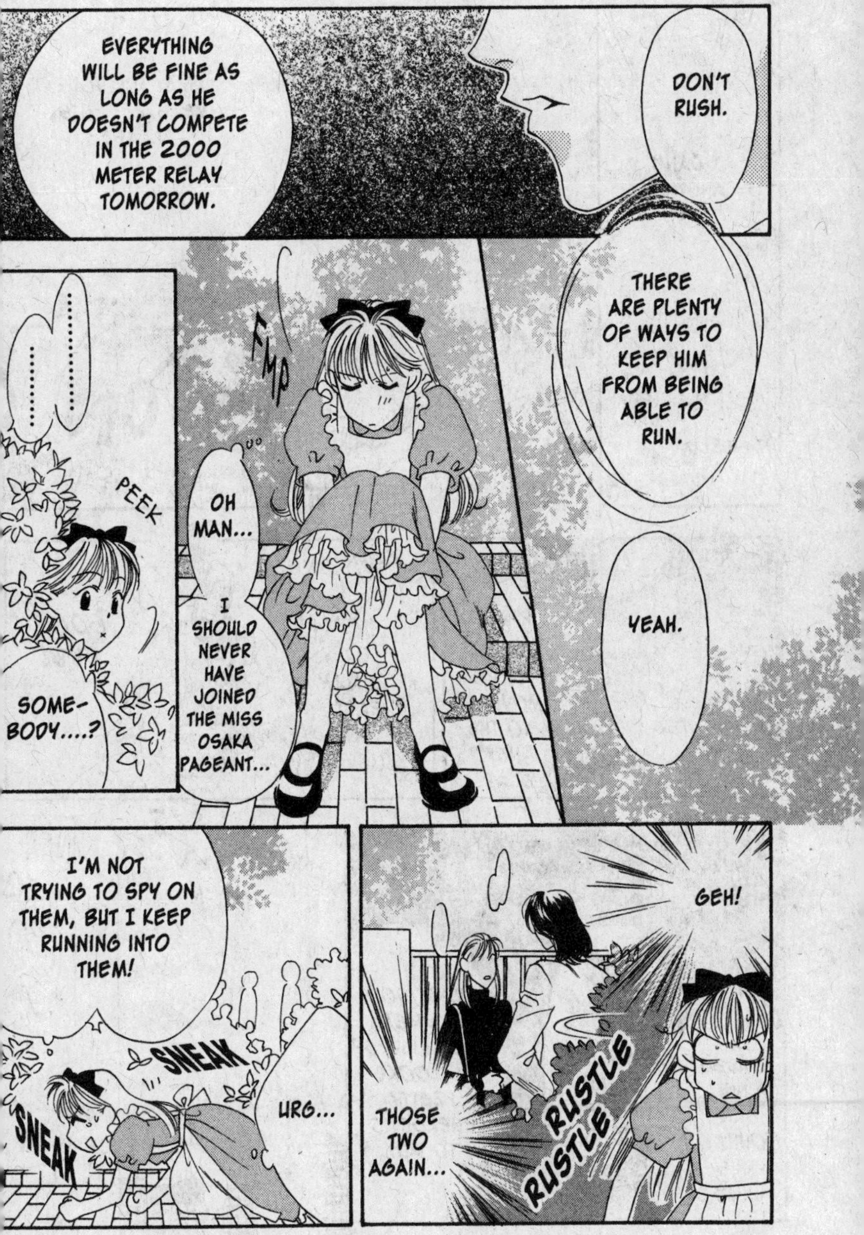
DON'T RUSH.
EVERYTHING WILL BE FINE AS LONG AS HE DOESN'T COMPETE IN THE 2000 METER RELAY TOMORROW.
THERE ARE PLENTY OF WAYS TO KEEP HIM FROM BEING ABLE TO RUN.
YEAH.
FMP
OH MAN...
I SHOULD NEVER HAVE JOINED THE MISS OSAKA PAGEANT...
......
......
PEEK
SOME-BODY.....?
GEH!
RUSTLE RUSTLE
THOSE TWO AGAIN...
I'M NOT TRYING TO SPY ON THEM, BUT I KEEP RUNNING INTO THEM!
URG...
SNEAK SNEAK

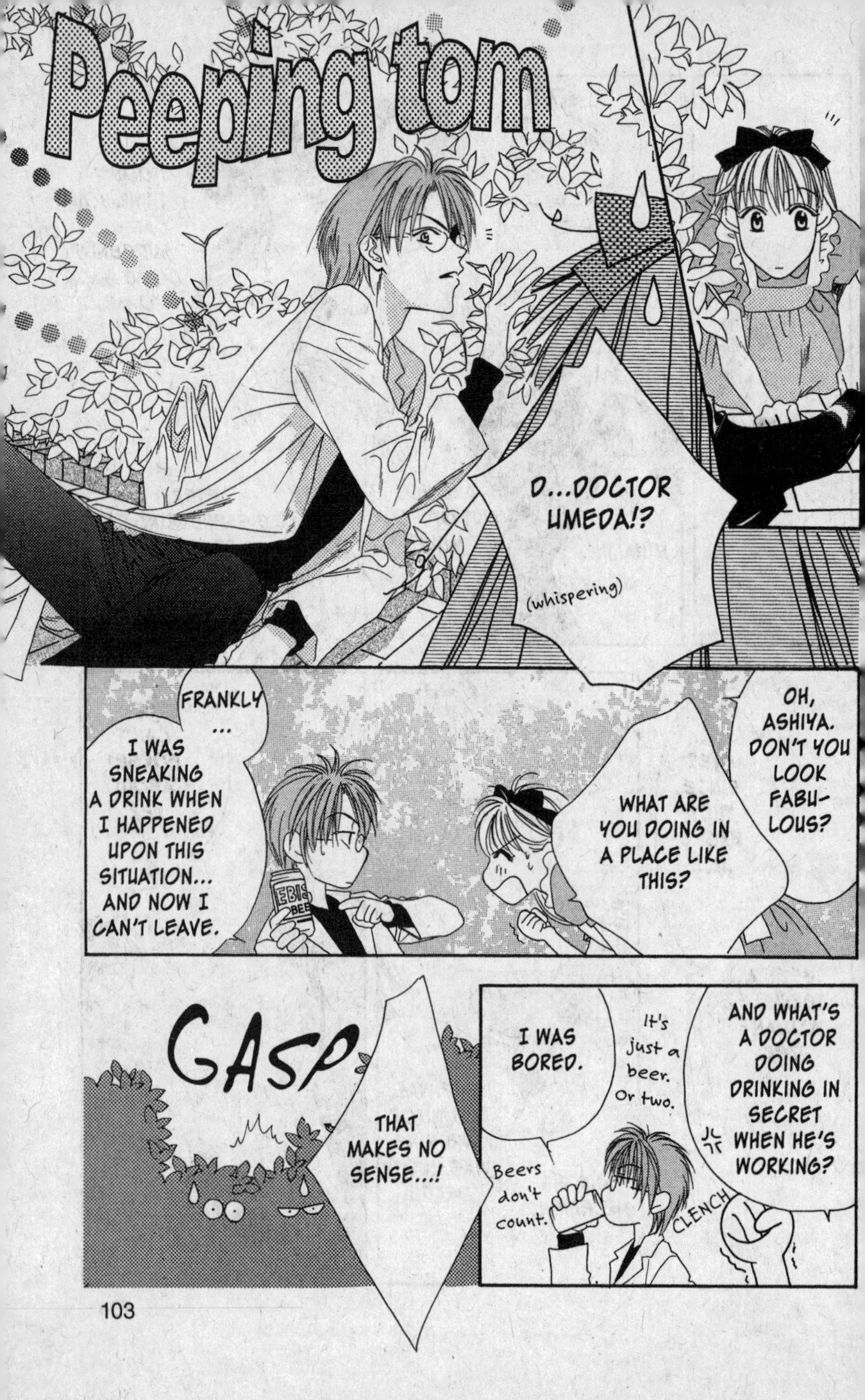
Peeping tom
D...DOCTOR UMEDA!?
(whispering)
OH, ASHIYA. DON'T YOU LOOK FABU-LOUS?
WHAT ARE YOU DOING IN A PLACE LIKE THIS?
FRANKLY ...
I WAS SNEAKING A DRINK WHEN I HAPPENED UPON THIS SITUATION... AND NOW I CAN'T LEAVE.
AND WHAT'S A DOCTOR DOING DRINKING IN SECRET WHEN HE'S WORKING?
CLENCH
It's just a beer. Or two.
I WAS BORED.
Beers don't count.
GASP
THAT MAKES NO SENSE...!

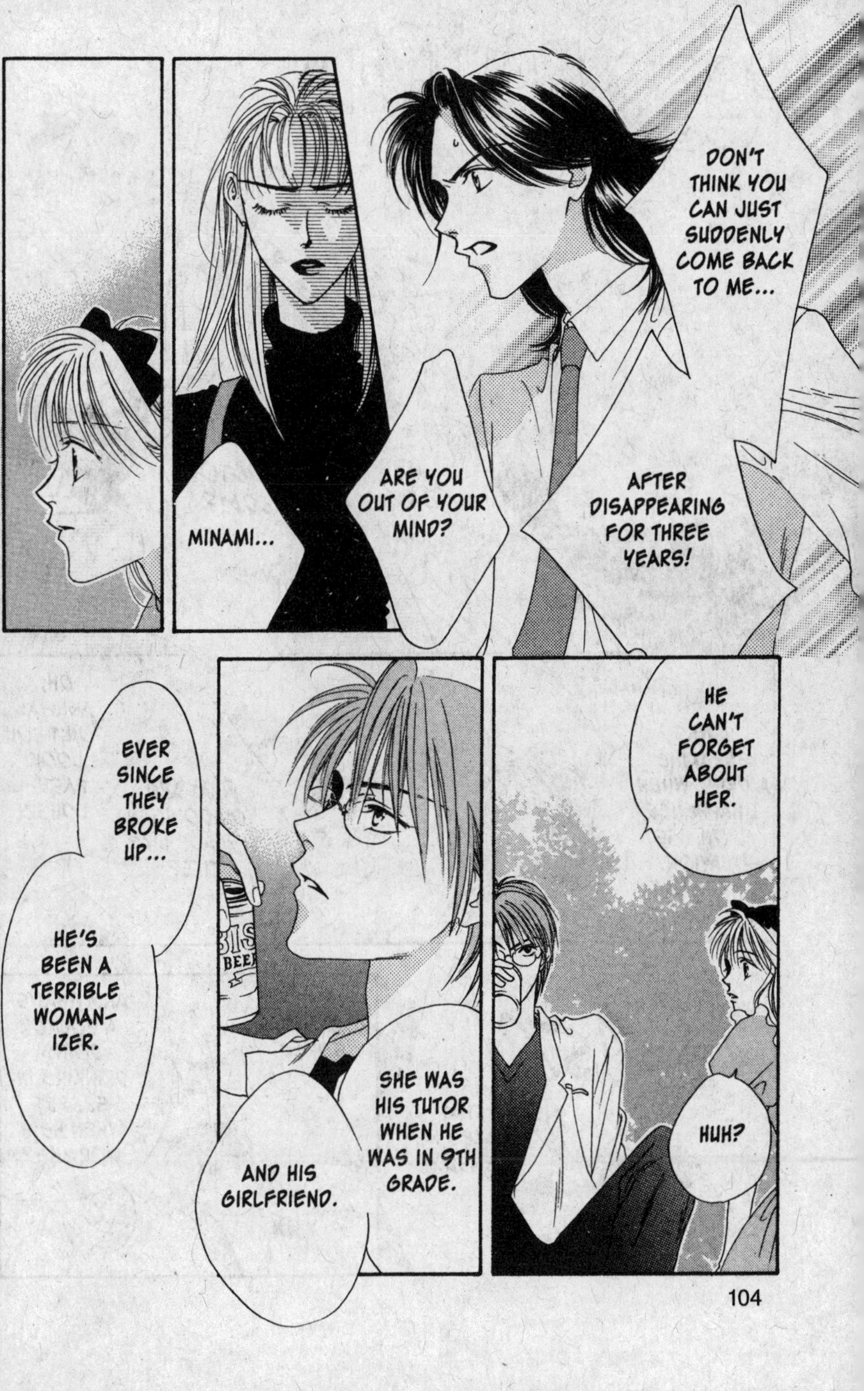
DON'T THINK YOU CAN JUST SUDDENLY COME BACK TO ME...
AFTER DISAPPEARING FOR THREE YEARS!
ARE YOU OUT OF YOUR MIND?
MINAMI...
HE CAN'T FORGET ABOUT HER.
HUH?
SHE WAS HIS TUTOR WHEN HE WAS IN 9TH GRADE.
AND HIS GIRLFRIEND.
EVER SINCE THEY BROKE UP...
HE'S BEEN A TERRIBLE WOMAN-IZER.

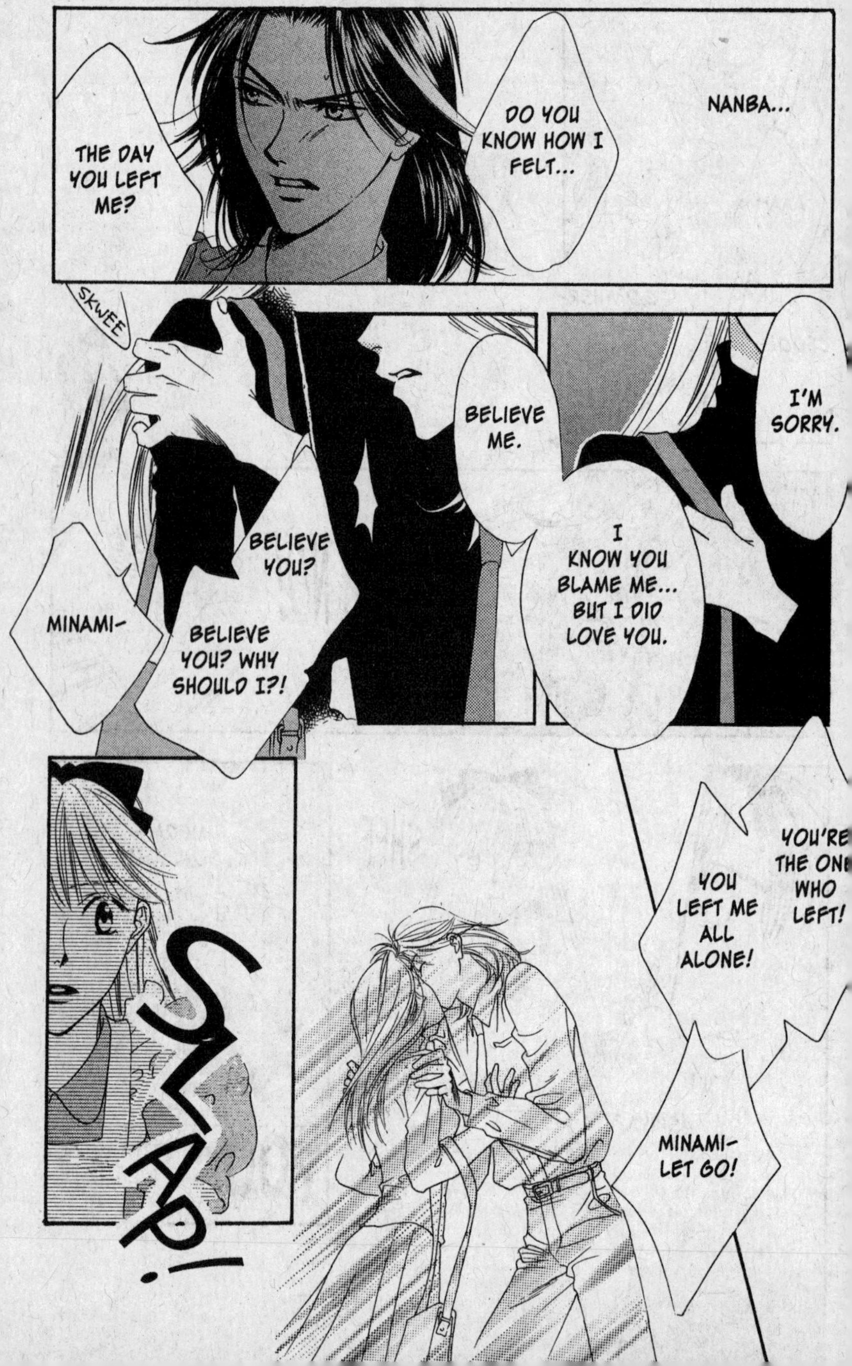
NANBA...
DO YOU KNOW HOW I FELT...
THE DAY YOU LEFT ME?
I'M SORRY.
I KNOW YOU BLAME ME... BUT I DID LOVE YOU.
BELIEVE ME.
SKWEE
BELIEVE YOU?
BELIEVE YOU? WHY SHOULD I?!
MINAMI-
YOU'RE THE ONE WHO LEFT!
YOU LEFT ME ALL ALONE!
MINAMI- LET GO!
SNAP!

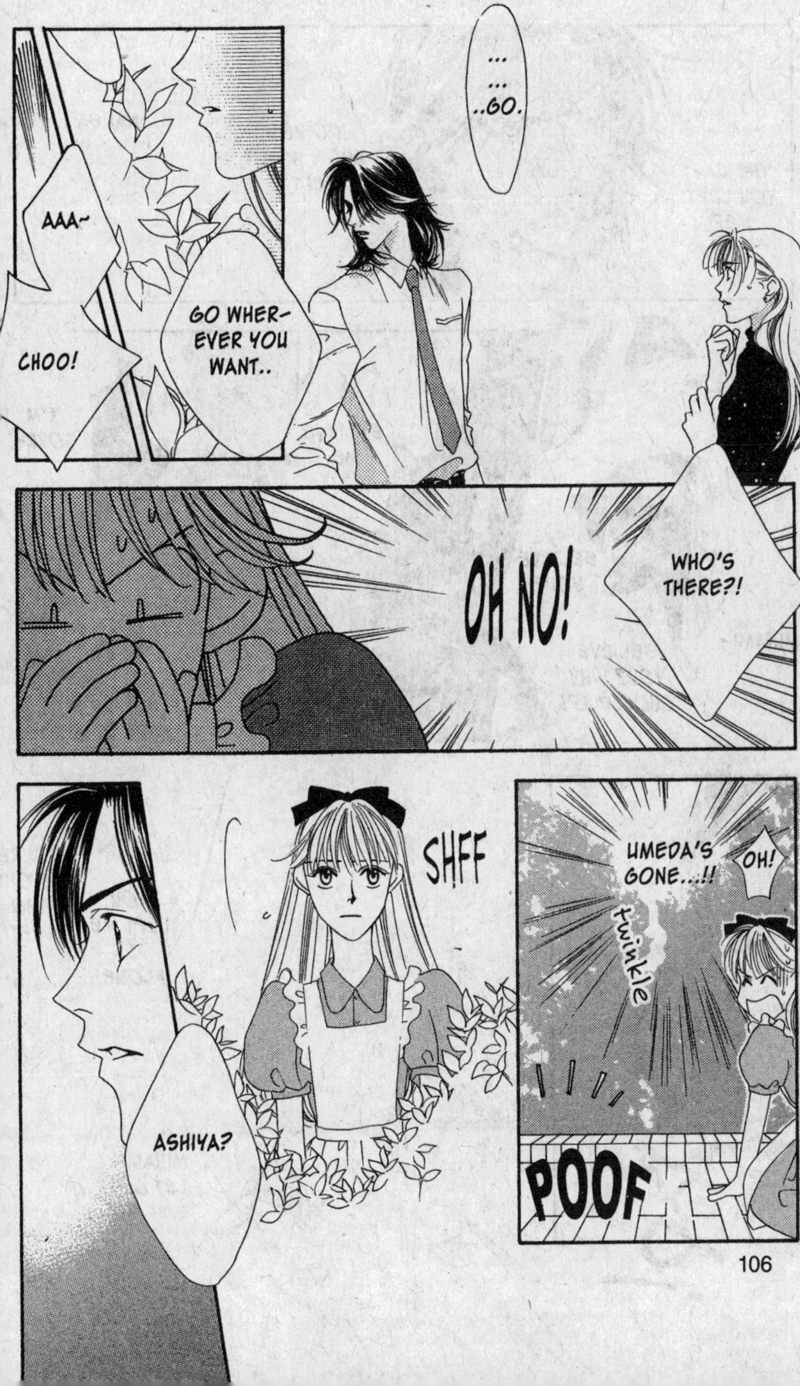
... .GO.
GO WHER-EVER YOU WANT..
AAA~
CHOO!
WHO'S THERE?!
OH NO!
OH!
UMEDA'S GONE...!!
twinkle
POOF
SHFF
ASHIYA?

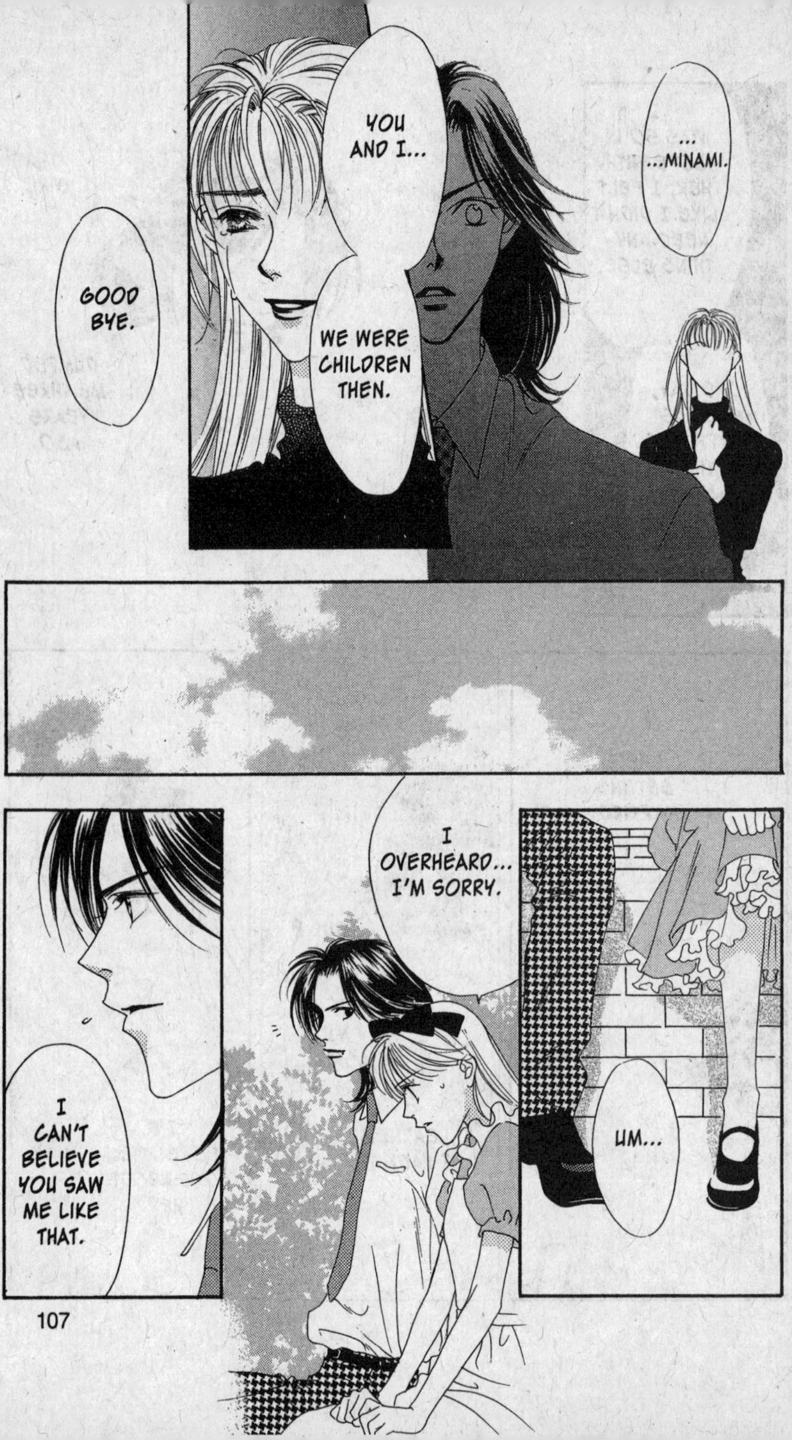
...
...MINAMI.
YOU AND I...
WE WERE CHILDREN THEN.
GOOD BYE.
UM...
I OVERHEARD... I'M SORRY.
I CAN'T BELIEVE YOU SAW ME LIKE THAT.

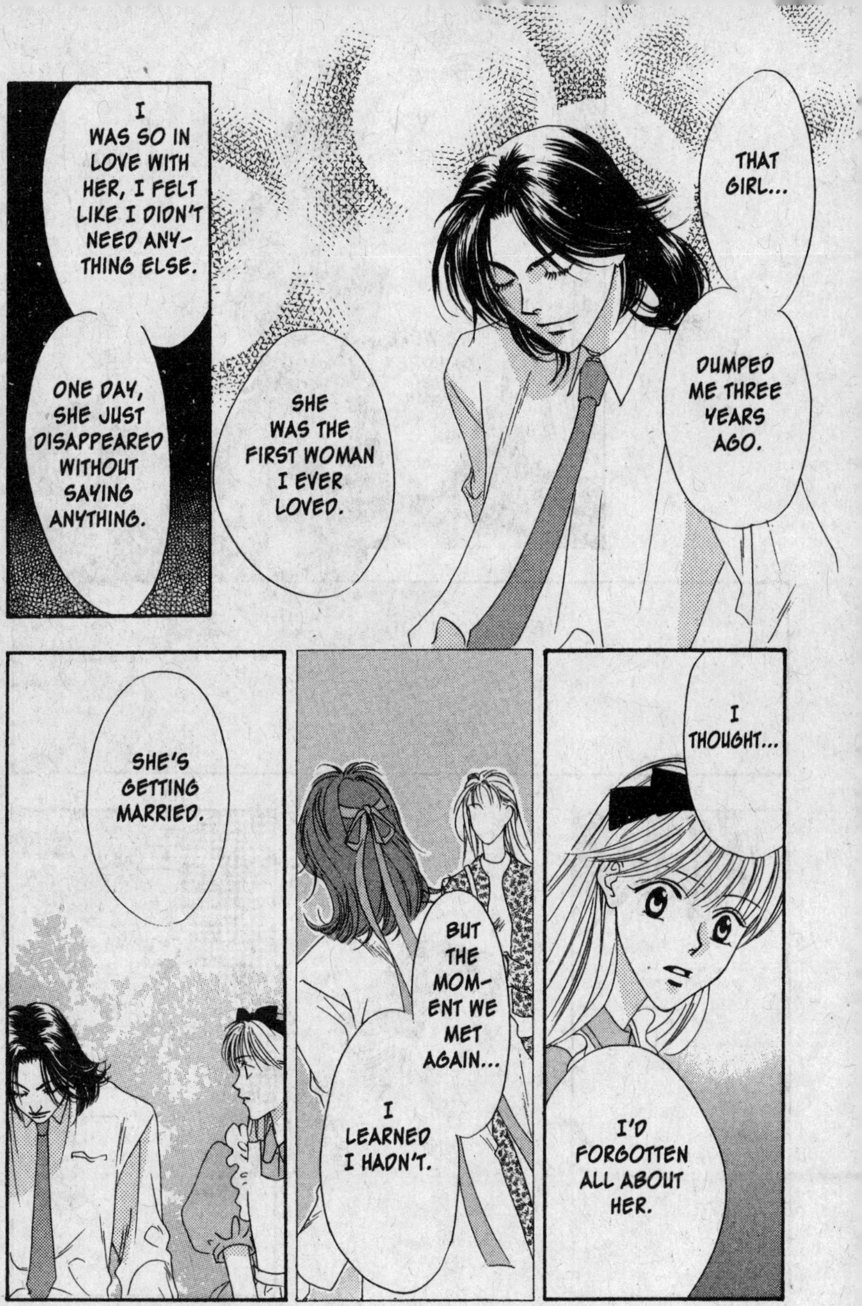
THAT GIRL...
DUMPED ME THREE YEARS AGO.
SHE WAS THE FIRST WOMAN I EVER LOVED.
I WAS SO IN LOVE WITH HER, I FELT LIKE I DIDN'T NEED ANY-THING ELSE.
ONE DAY, SHE JUST DISAPPEARED WITHOUT SAYING ANYTHING.
I THOUGHT...
I'D FORGOTTEN ALL ABOUT HER.
BUT THE MOM-ENT WE MET AGAIN...
I LEARNED I HADN'T.
SHE'S GETTING MARRIED.

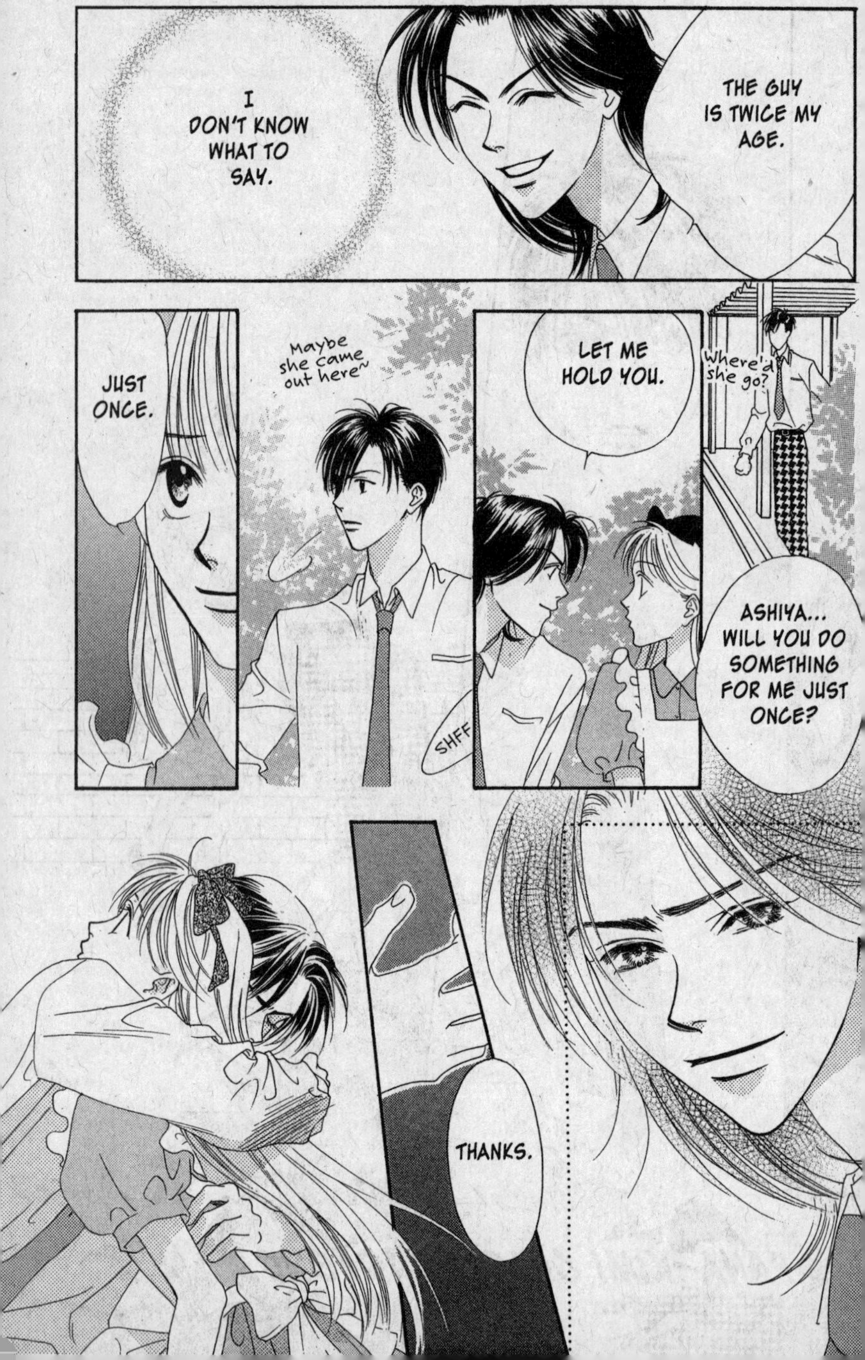
THE GUY IS TWICE MY AGE.
I DON'T KNOW WHAT TO SAY.
Where'd she go?
ASHIYA... WILL YOU DO SOMETHING FOR ME JUST ONCE?
LET ME HOLD YOU.
SHFF
Maybe she came out here~
JUST ONCE.
THANKS.

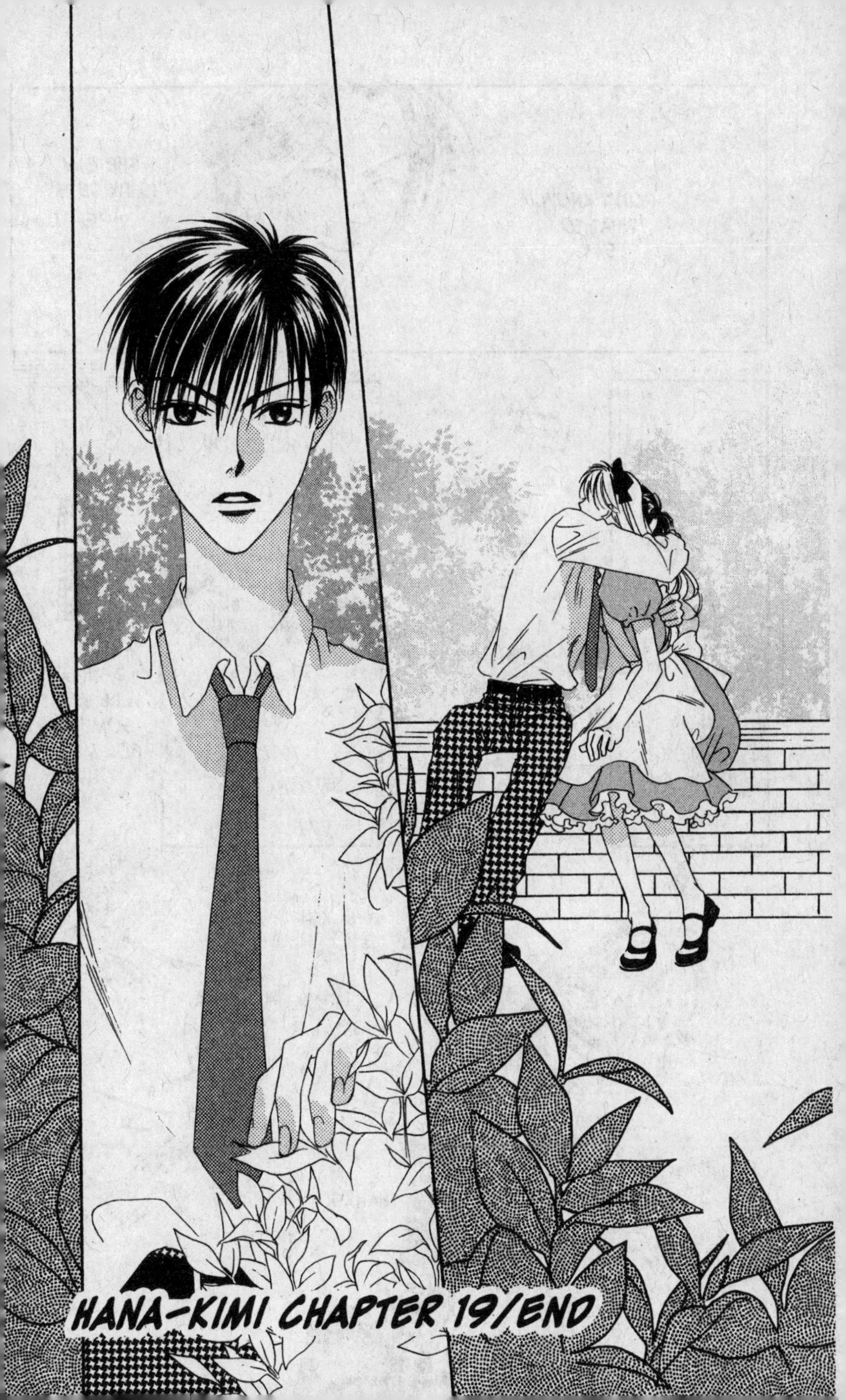
HANA-KIMI CHAPTER 19/END

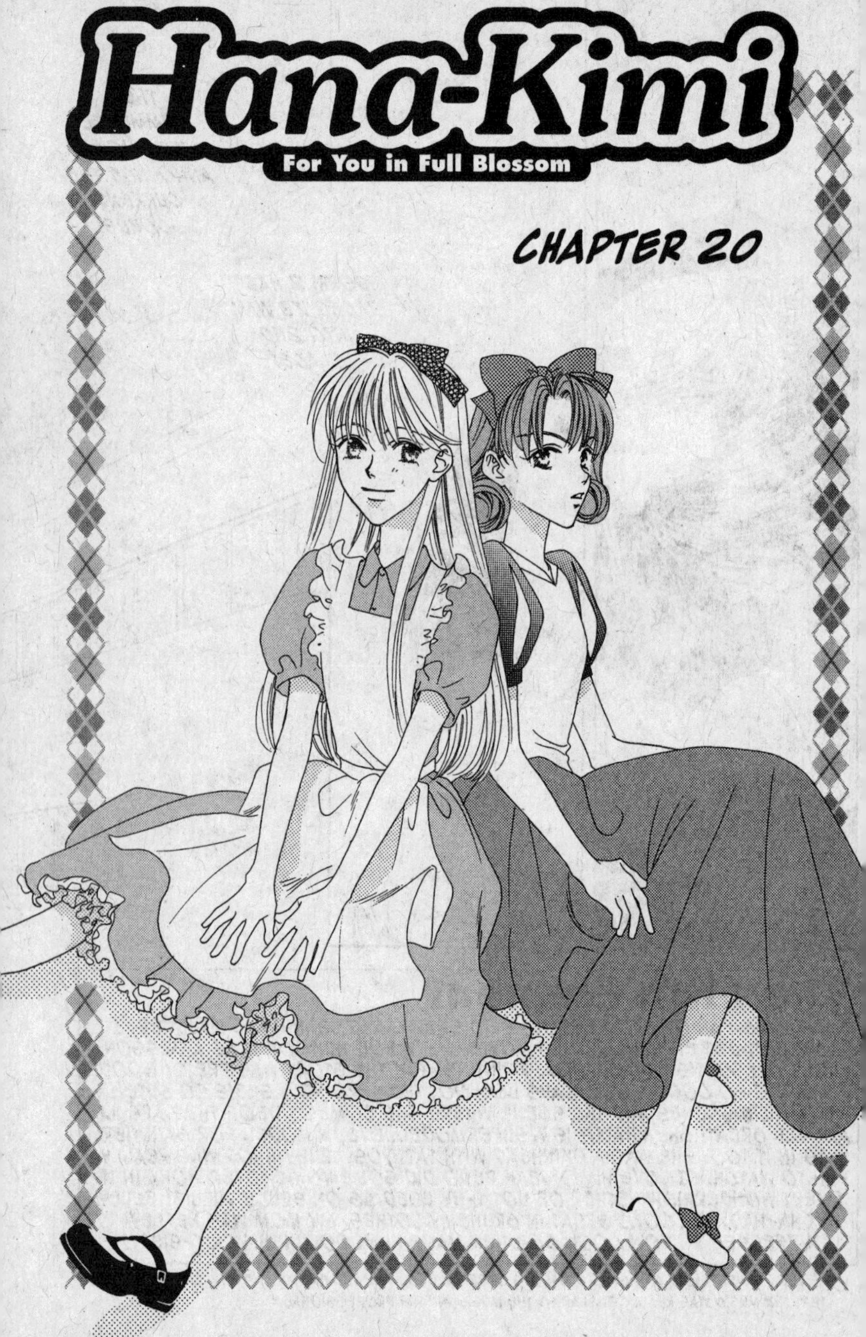
Hana-Kimi
For You in Full Blossom
CHAPTER 20

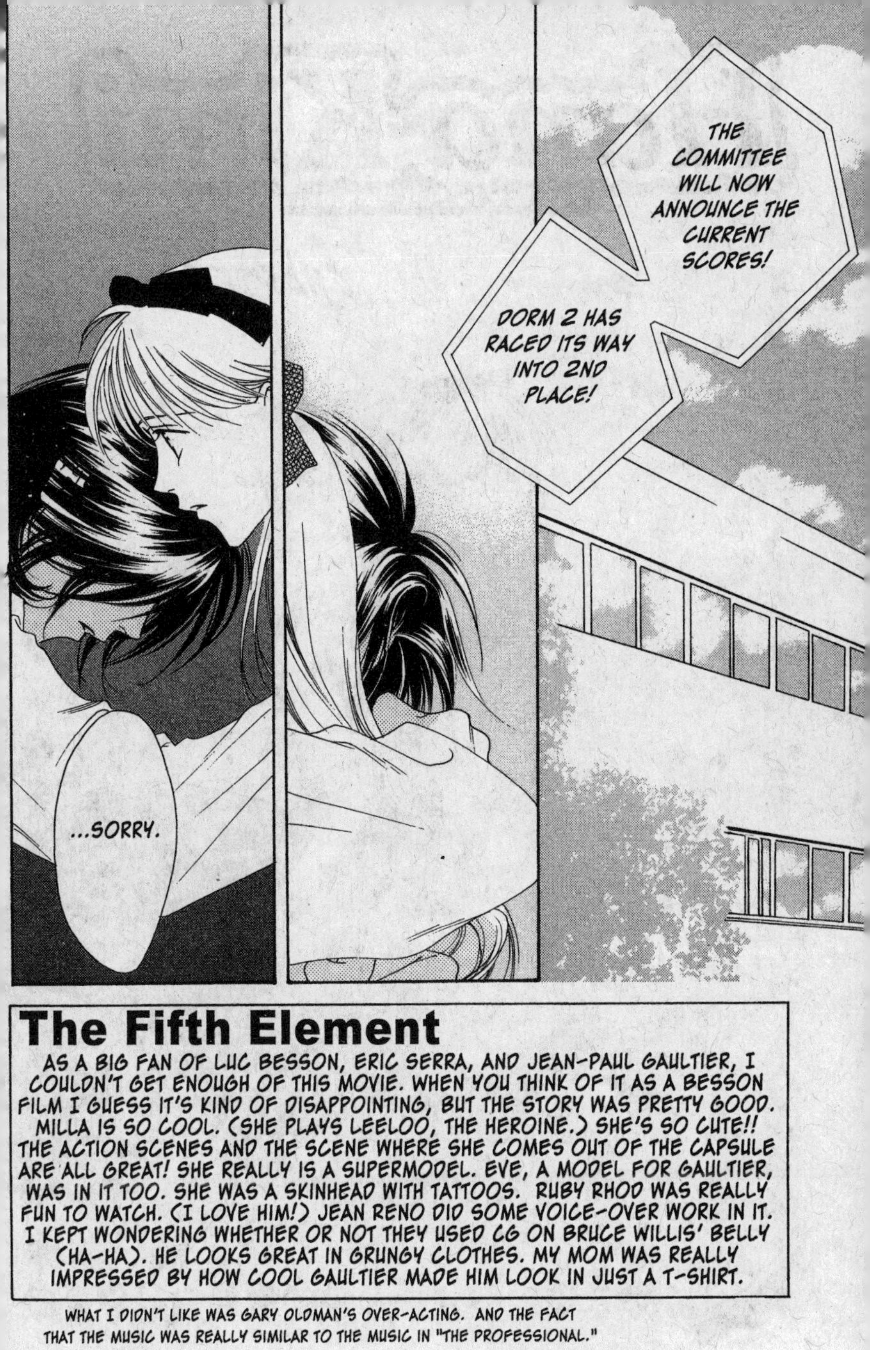
THE COMMITTEE WILL NOW ANNOUNCE THE CURRENT SCORES!
DORM 2 HAS RACED ITS WAY INTO 2ND PLACE!
...SORRY.

The Fifth Element

AS A BIG FAN OF LUC BESSON, ERIC SERRA, AND JEAN-PAUL GAULTIER, I COULDN'T GET ENOUGH OF THIS MOVIE. WHEN YOU THINK OF IT AS A BESSON FILM I GUESS IT'S KIND OF DISAPPOINTING, BUT THE STORY WAS PRETTY GOOD. MILLA IS SO COOL. (SHE PLAYS LEELOO, THE HEROINE.) SHE'S SO CUTE!! THE ACTION SCENES AND THE SCENE WHERE SHE COMES OUT OF THE CAPSULE ARE ALL GREAT! SHE REALLY IS A SUPERMODEL. EVE, A MODEL FOR GAULTIER, WAS IN IT TOO. SHE WAS A SKINHEAD WITH TATTOOS. RUBY RHOD WAS REALLY FUN TO WATCH. (I LOVE HIM!) JEAN RENO DID SOME VOICE-OVER WORK IN IT. I KEPT WONDERING WHETHER OR NOT THEY USED CG ON BRUCE WILLIS' BELLY (HA-HA). HE LOOKS GREAT IN GRUNGY CLOTHES. MY MOM WAS REALLY IMPRESSED BY HOW COOL GAULTIER MADE HIM LOOK IN JUST A T-SHIRT.

WHAT I DIDN'T LIKE WAS GARY OLDMAN'S OVER-ACTING. AND THE FACT THAT THE MUSIC WAS REALLY SIMILAR TO THE MUSIC IN "THE PROFESSIONAL."

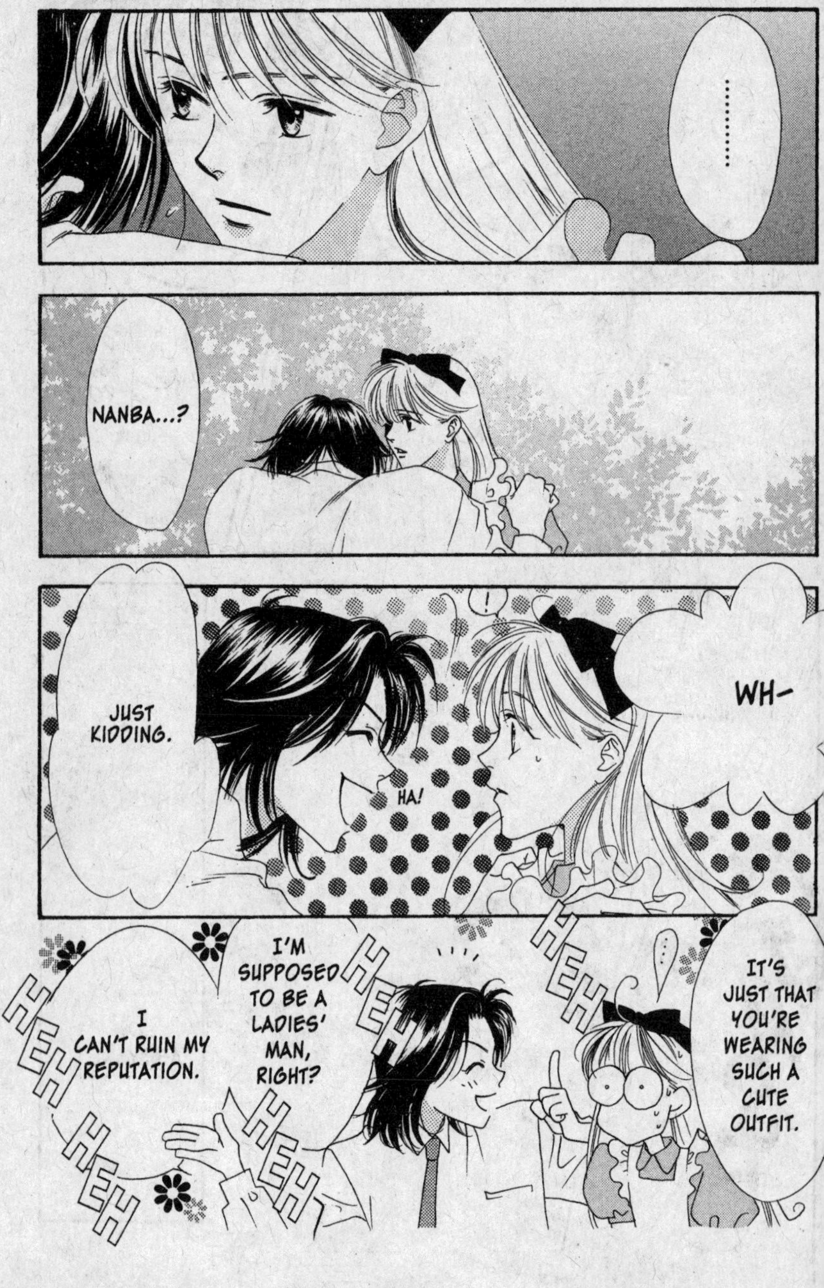
......
NANBA...?
WH-
!
JUST KIDDING.
HA!
IT'S JUST THAT YOU'RE WEARING SUCH A CUTE OUTFIT.
...
HEH HEH
I'M SUPPOSED TO BE A LADIES' MAN, RIGHT?
HEH HEH
I CAN'T RUIN MY REPUTATION.
HEH HEH HEH

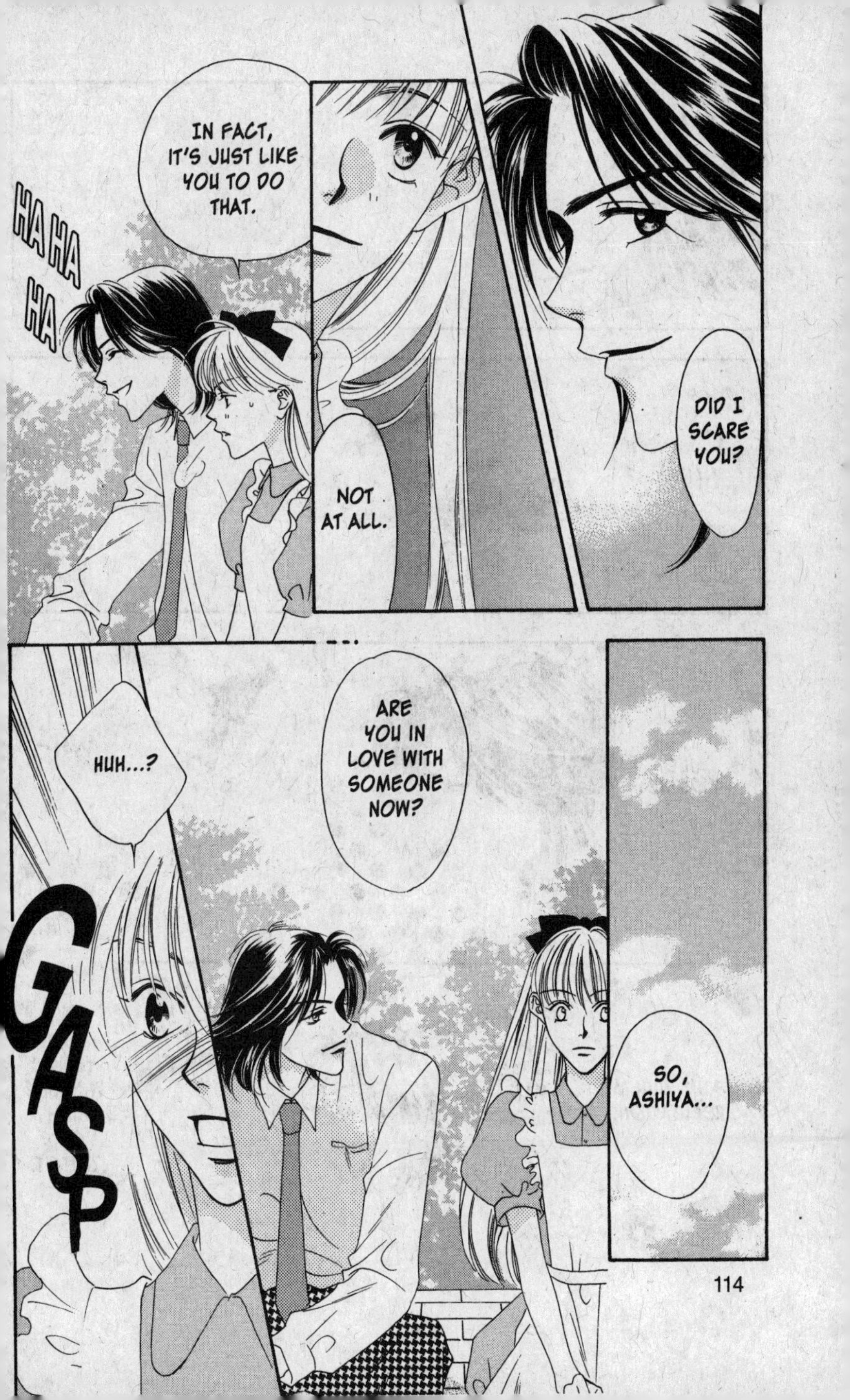
DID I SCARE YOU?
NOT AT ALL.
IN FACT, IT'S JUST LIKE YOU TO DO THAT.
HA HA HA
SO, ASHIYA...
ARE YOU IN LOVE WITH SOMEONE NOW?
HUH...?
GASP

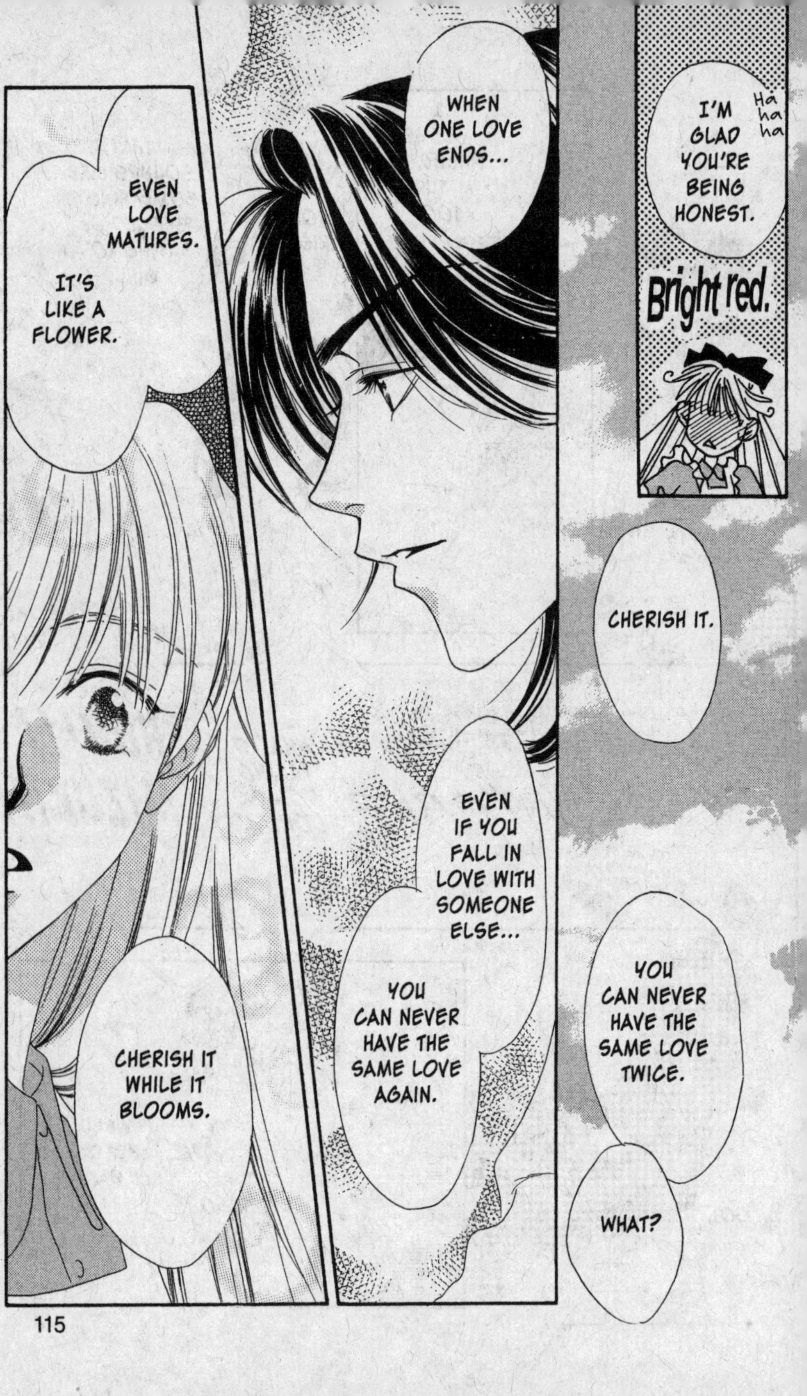
I'M GLAD YOU'RE BEING HONEST.
Ha ha ha
Bright red.
CHERISH IT.
YOU CAN NEVER HAVE THE SAME LOVE TWICE.
WHAT?
WHEN ONE LOVE ENDS...
EVEN IF YOU FALL IN LOVE WITH SOMEONE ELSE...
YOU CAN NEVER HAVE THE SAME LOVE AGAIN.
EVEN LOVE MATURES.
IT'S LIKE A FLOWER.
CHERISH IT WHILE IT BLOOMS.

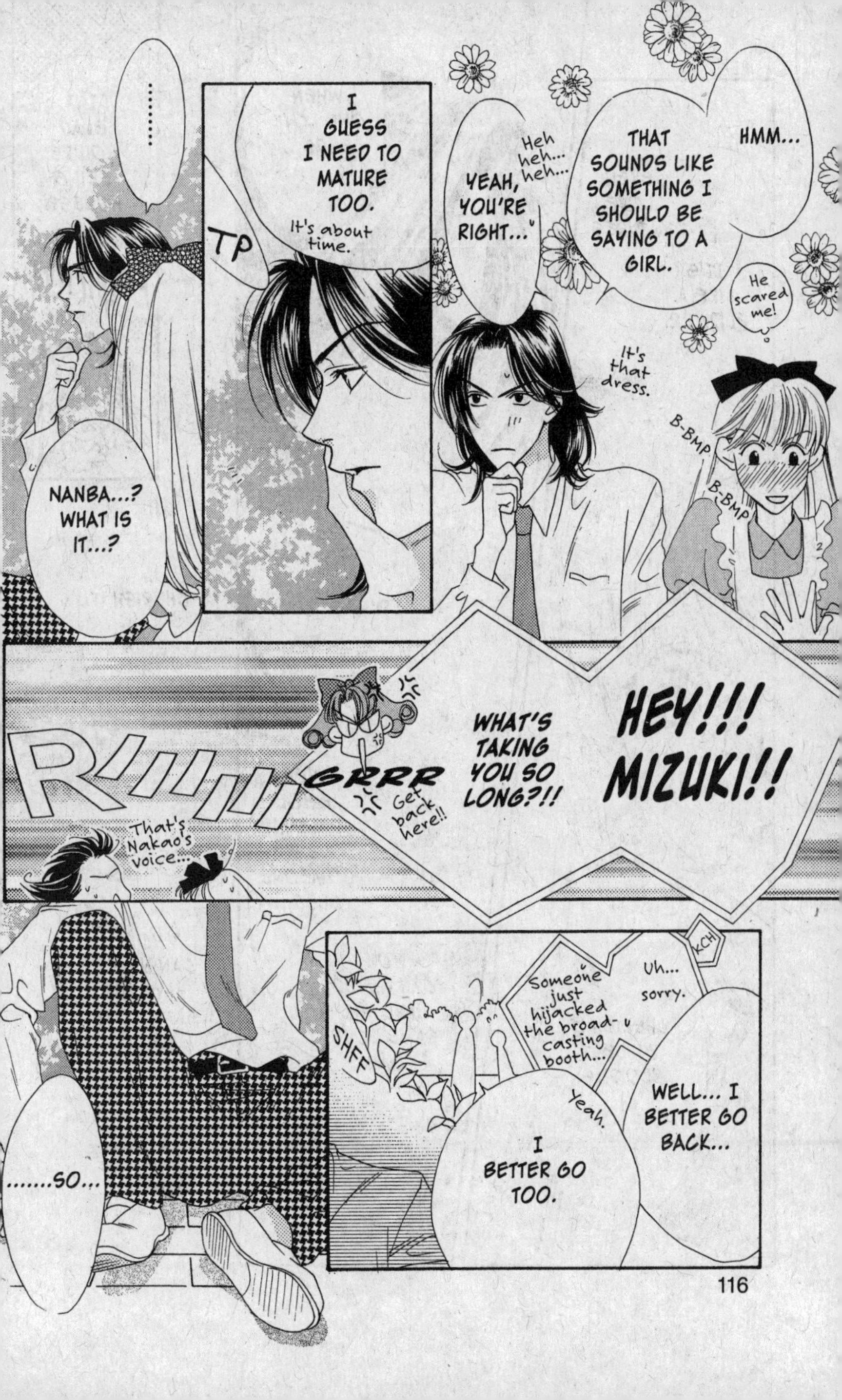
HMM...
THAT SOUNDS LIKE SOMETHING I SHOULD BE SAYING TO A GIRL.
He scared me!
It's that dress.
B-Bmp
B-Bmp
YEAH, YOU'RE RIGHT...
Heh heh... heh...
I GUESS I NEED TO MATURE TOO.
It's about time.
TP
......
NANBA...? WHAT IS IT...?
HEY!!! MIZUKI!!
WHAT'S TAKING YOU SO LONG?!!
GRRR
Get back here!!
RIIIIII
That's Nakao's voice...
KCH
Uh... sorry.
WELL... I BETTER GO BACK...
Someone just hijacked the broad-casting booth...
Yeah.
I BETTER GO TOO.
SHFF
.......SO...

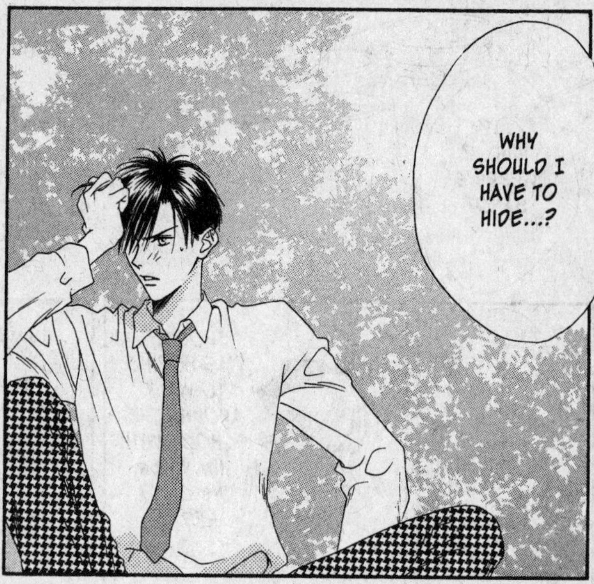
WHY SHOULD I HAVE TO HIDE...?

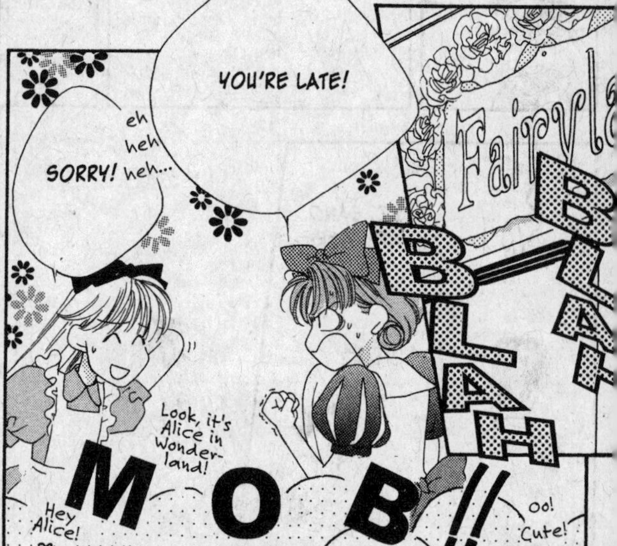
BLAH BLAH
BLAH
YOU'RE LATE!
eh heh heh...
SORRY!
Oo! Cute!
MOB!!
Look, it's Alice in Wonderland!
Hey Alice!

Whispered Secrets

Karate vs. Music

THE CHARACTERS TENNOJI AND KUJO COME FROM MY LOVE FOR KARATE. IN K1, I LIKE ANDY HUG. IN KYOKUSHIN KARATE, I LIKE GLAUBE FEITOSA. HIS ANKLE CHOP AND UPPER FLIP KICKS ARE REALLY COOL. I THINK THIN "REPLICANT" TYPE BODIES ARE BEAUTIFUL, BUT WELL-DEFINED MUSCULAR BODIES ARE NICE TOO. AND OSCAR M. HIMEJIMA IS BASED ON A SINGER FROM MALICE MIZER, NAMED GACKT. WHEN THEY FIRST CAME OUT SOME PEOPLE LIKED THEM AND SOME PEOPLE DIDN'T, BUT NOW THEY'RE GETTING VERY POPULAR!! (HE HAS A NICE VOICE...AND I'VE GOT A VOICE FETISH.)

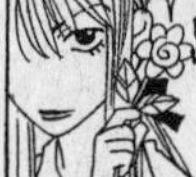

But Himejima's voice is probably more like Koyasu Takehito's.

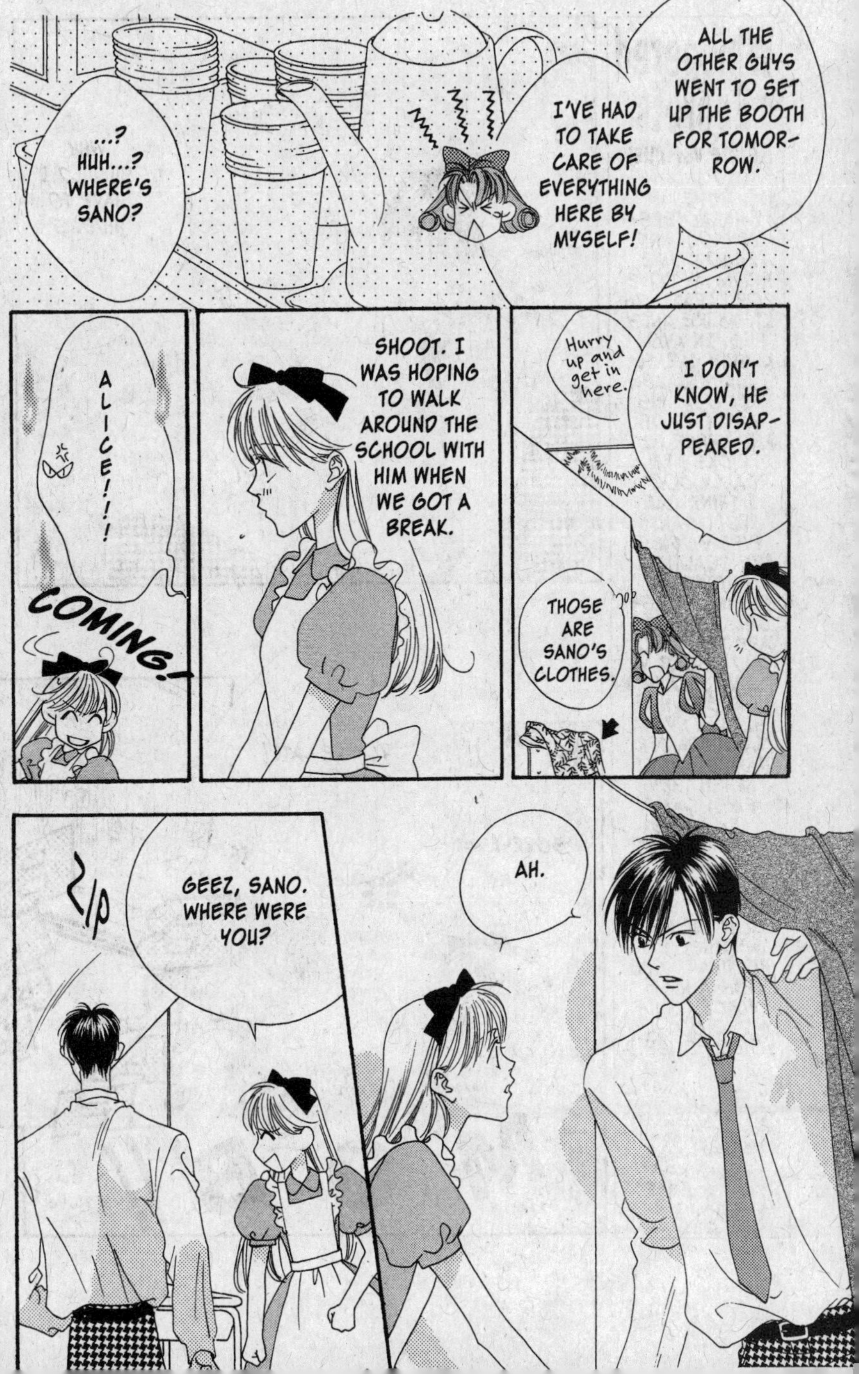
ALL THE OTHER GUYS WENT TO SET UP THE BOOTH FOR TOMORROW.
I'VE HAD TO TAKE CARE OF EVERYTHING HERE BY MYSELF!
...? HUH...? WHERE'S SANO?
I DON'T KNOW, HE JUST DISAPPEARED.
Hurry up and get in here.
THOSE ARE SANO'S CLOTHES.
SHOOT. I WAS HOPING TO WALK AROUND THE SCHOOL WITH HIM WHEN WE GOT A BREAK.
ALICE!!!
COMING!
AH.
GEEZ, SANO. WHERE WERE YOU?
Zip

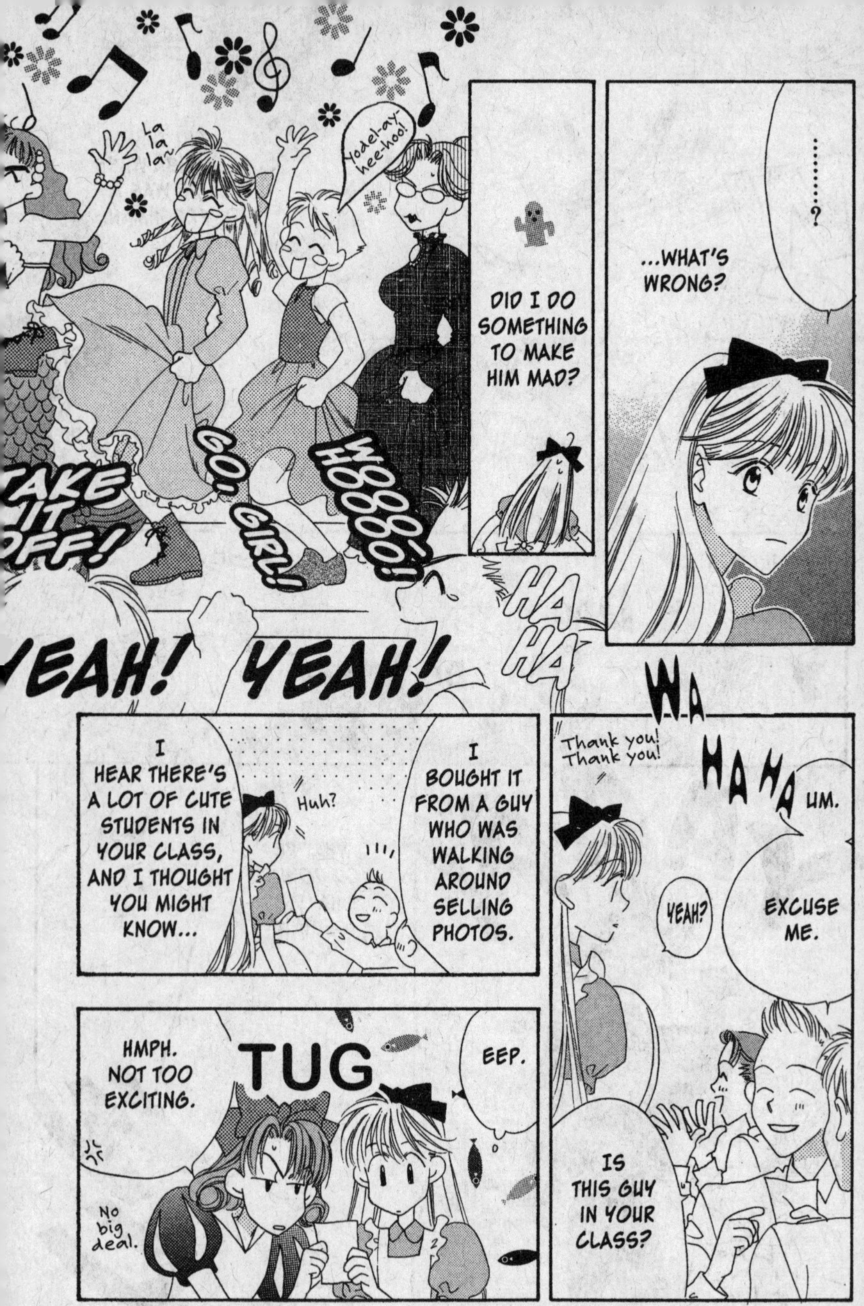

......?
...WHAT'S WRONG?
DID I DO SOMETHING TO MAKE HIM MAD?
Yodel-ay-hee-hoo!
La la la~
WOOOO!
GO, GIRL!
TAKE IT OFF!
HA HA
YEAH! YEAH!
WA HA HA HA
Thank you! Thank you!
UM.
EXCUSE ME.
YEAH?
IS THIS GUY IN YOUR CLASS?
I BOUGHT IT FROM A GUY WHO WAS WALKING AROUND SELLING PHOTOS.
Huh?
I HEAR THERE'S A LOT OF CUTE STUDENTS IN YOUR CLASS, AND I THOUGHT YOU MIGHT KNOW...
EEP.
TUG
HMPH. NOT TOO EXCITING.
No big deal.

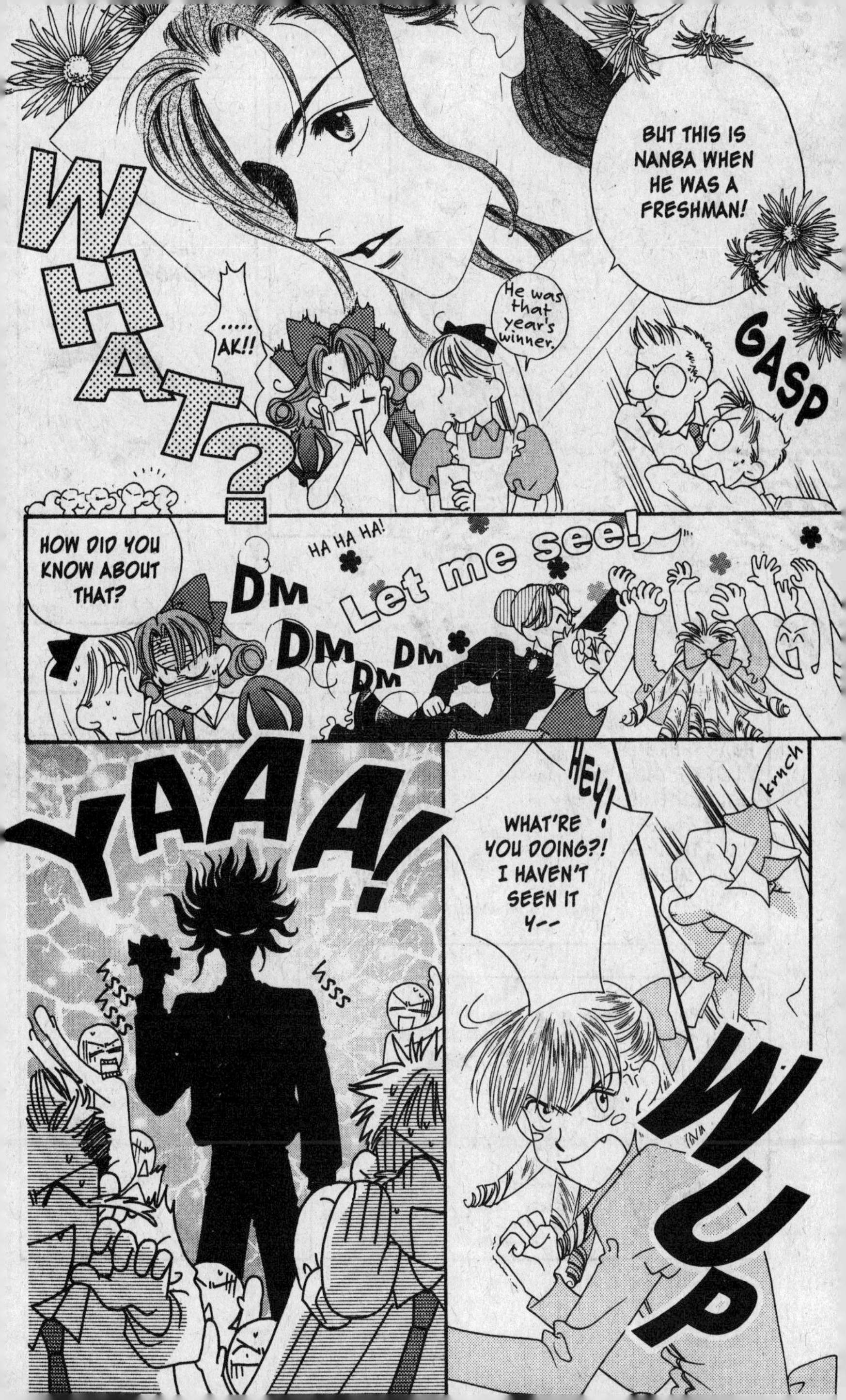
BUT THIS IS NANBA WHEN HE WAS A FRESHMAN!
GASP
He was that year's winner.
.....AK!!
WHAT?
Let me see!
HA HA HA!
DM DM DM DM
HOW DID YOU KNOW ABOUT THAT?
krnch
HEY!
WHAT'RE YOU DOING?! I HAVEN'T SEEN IT Y--
WUP
YAAA!
hssss
hsss
hssss

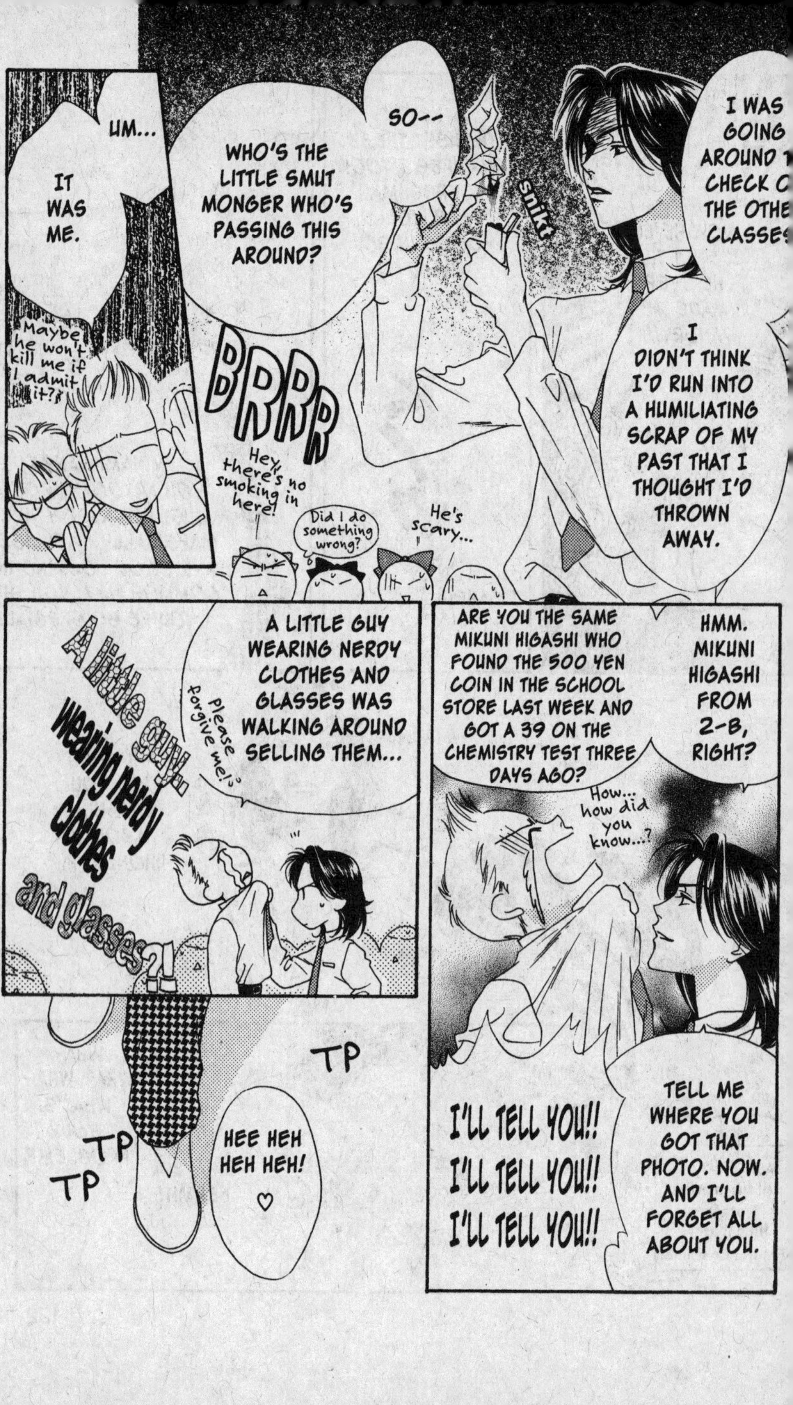
I WAS GOING AROUND T CHECK O THE OTHE CLASSES
I DIDN'T THINK I'D RUN INTO A HUMILIATING SCRAP OF MY PAST THAT I THOUGHT I'D THROWN AWAY.
snikt
SO--
WHO'S THE LITTLE SMUT MONGER WHO'S PASSING THIS AROUND?
BRRRR
Hey, there's no smoking in here!
Did I do something wrong?
He's scary...
UM...
IT WAS ME.
Maybe he won't kill me if I admit it?!
HMM. MIKUNI HIGASHI FROM 2-B, RIGHT?
ARE YOU THE SAME MIKUNI HIGASHI WHO FOUND THE 500 YEN COIN IN THE SCHOOL STORE LAST WEEK AND GOT A 39 ON THE CHEMISTRY TEST THREE DAYS AGO?
How... how did you know...?
TELL ME WHERE YOU GOT THAT PHOTO. NOW. AND I'LL FORGET ALL ABOUT YOU.
I'LL TELL YOU!!
I'LL TELL YOU!!
I'LL TELL YOU!!
A LITTLE GUY WEARING NERDY CLOTHES AND GLASSES WAS WALKING AROUND SELLING THEM...
Please forgive me!
A little guy, wearing nerdy clothes and glasses?!
TP
HEE HEH HEH HEH! ♡
TP
TP

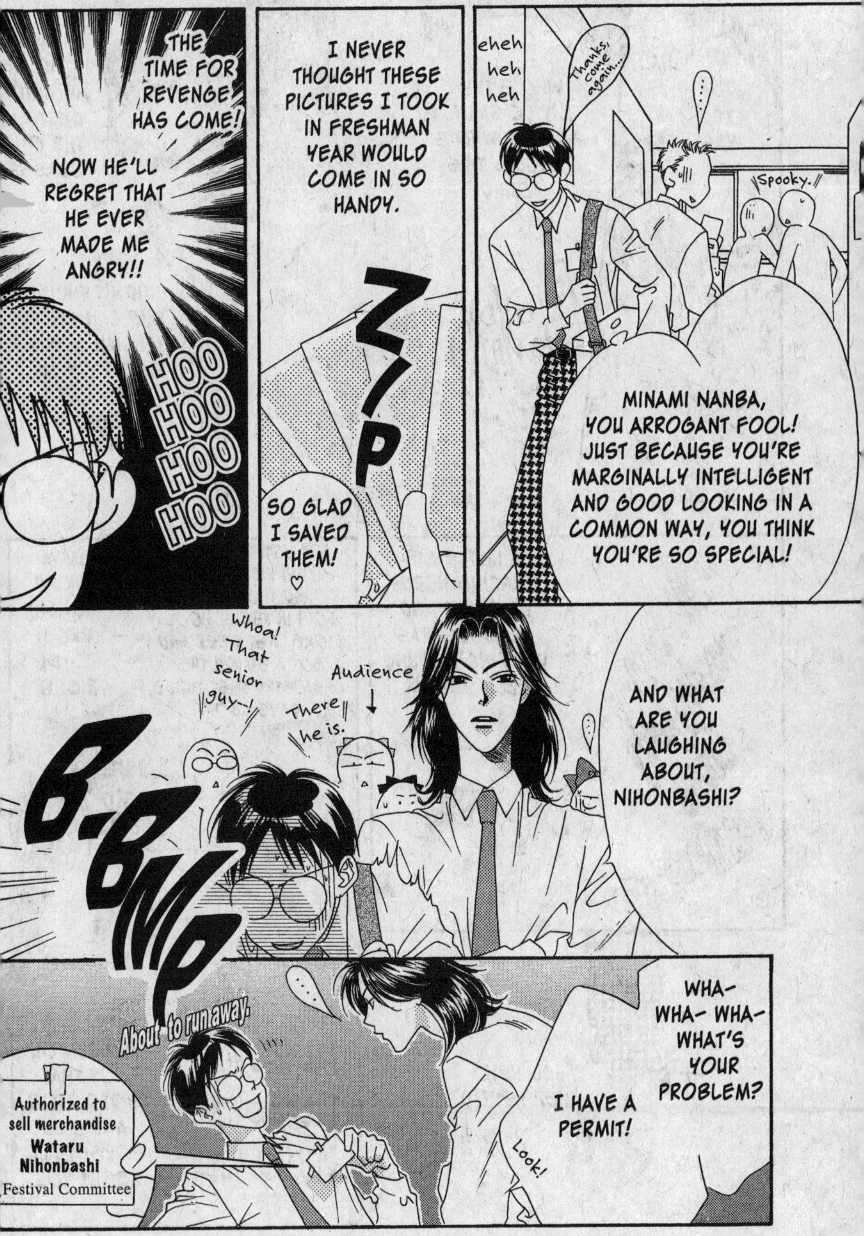

Thanks, come again...
eheh heh heh
...!
Spooky.
MINAMI NANBA, YOU ARROGANT FOOL! JUST BECAUSE YOU'RE MARGINALLY INTELLIGENT AND GOOD LOOKING IN A COMMON WAY, YOU THINK YOU'RE SO SPECIAL!
I NEVER THOUGHT THESE PICTURES I TOOK IN FRESHMAN YEAR WOULD COME IN SO HANDY.
ZIP
SO GLAD I SAVED THEM! ♡
THE TIME FOR REVENGE HAS COME!
NOW HE'LL REGRET THAT HE EVER MADE ME ANGRY!!
HOO HOO HOO HOO HOO
AND WHAT ARE YOU LAUGHING ABOUT, NIHONBASHI?
Audience
There he is.
Whoa! That senior guy--!
B-BMP
WHA- WHA- WHA- WHAT'S YOUR PROBLEM?
I HAVE A PERMIT!
Look!
About to run away.
Authorized to sell merchandise
Wataru Nihonbashi
Festival Committee

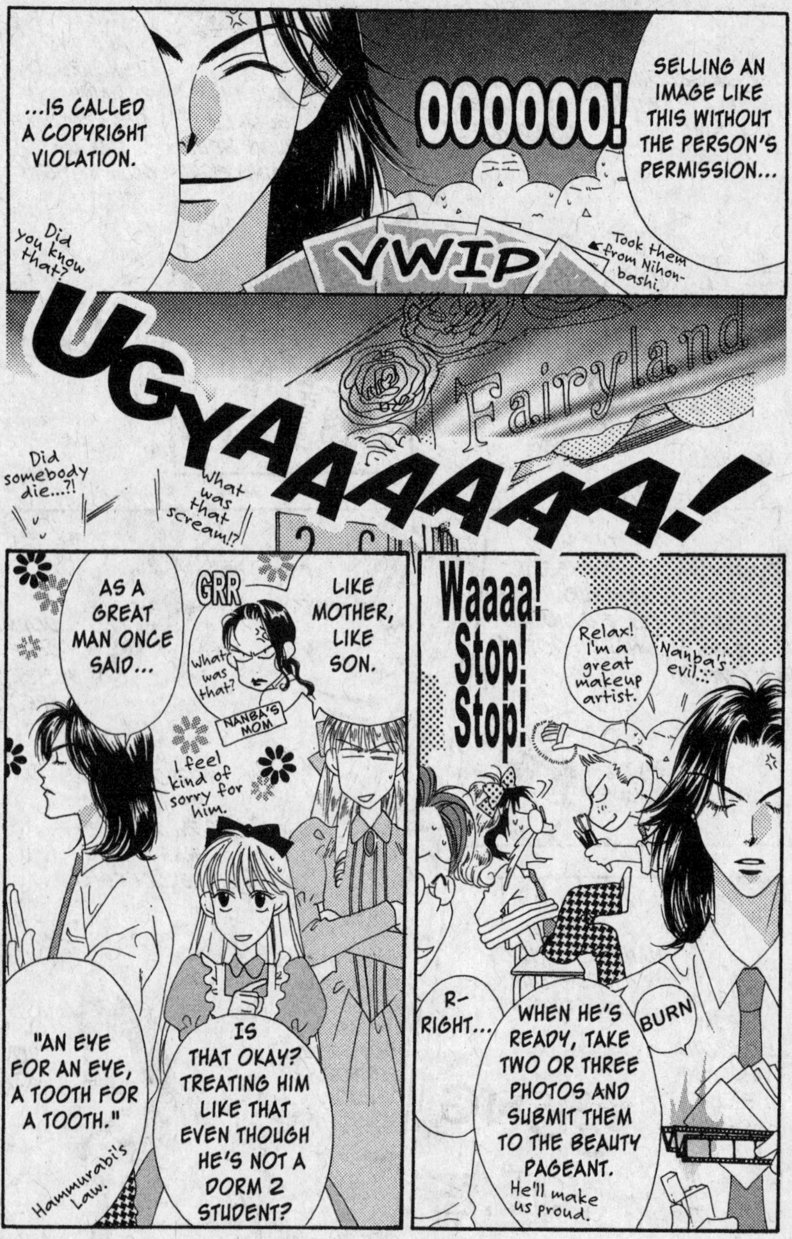
SELLING AN IMAGE LIKE THIS WITHOUT THE PERSON'S PERMISSION...
OOOOOO!
Took them from Nihon-bashi.
YWIP
...IS CALLED A COPYRIGHT VIOLATION.
Did you know that?
UGYAAAAAA!
Fairyland
What was that scream!?
Did somebody die...?!
Waaaa! Stop! Stop!
Relax! I'm a great makeup artist.
Nanba's evil...
BURN
WHEN HE'S READY, TAKE TWO OR THREE PHOTOS AND SUBMIT THEM TO THE BEAUTY PAGEANT.
He'll make us proud.
R-RIGHT...
LIKE MOTHER, LIKE SON.
GRR
What was that?
NANBA'S MOM
AS A GREAT MAN ONCE SAID...
I feel kind of sorry for him.
IS THAT OKAY? TREATING HIM LIKE THAT EVEN THOUGH HE'S NOT A DORM 2 STUDENT?
"AN EYE FOR AN EYE, A TOOTH FOR A TOOTH."
Hammurabi's Law.

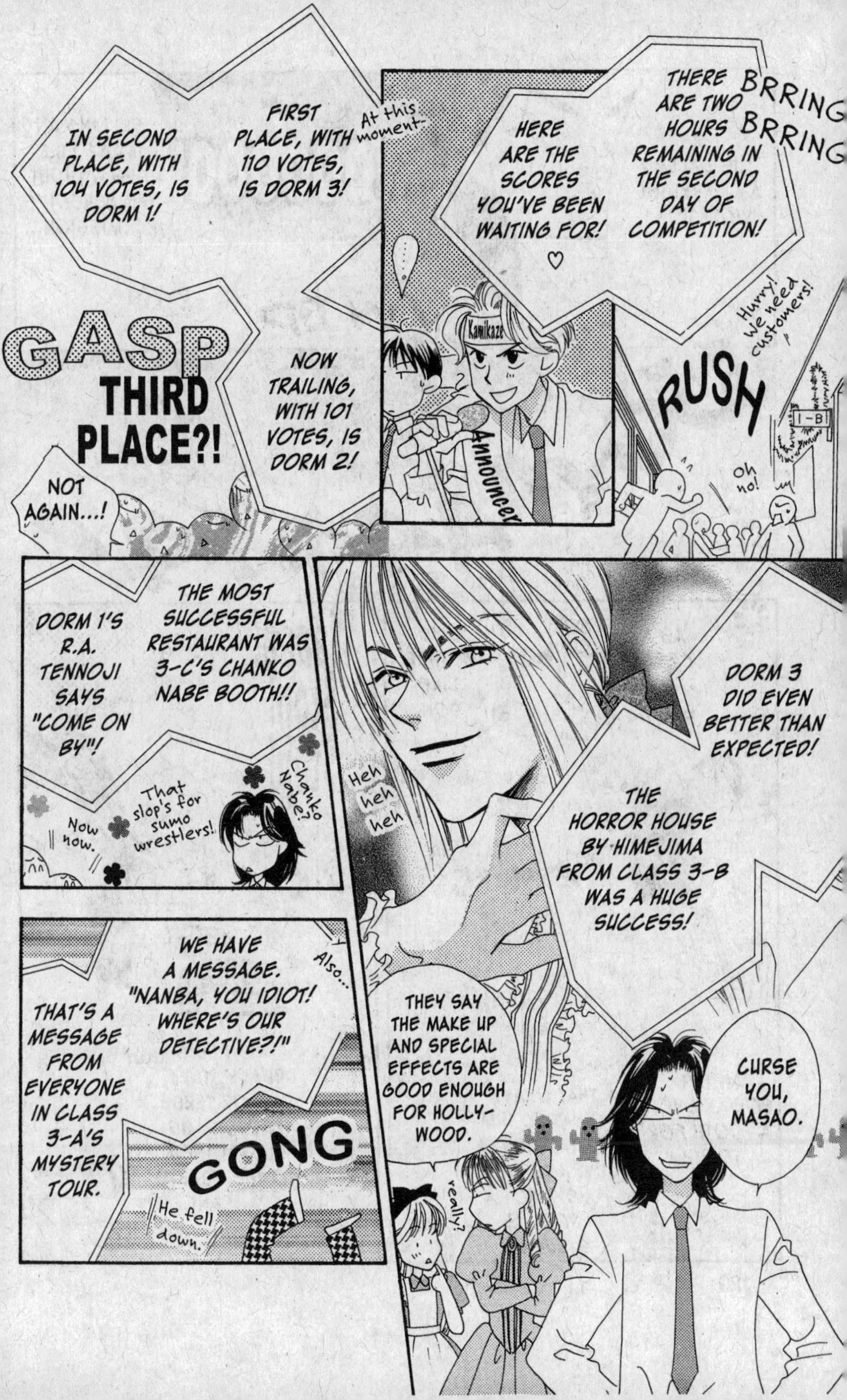
THERE ARE TWO HOURS REMAINING IN THE SECOND DAY OF COMPETITION!
BRRING BRRING
HERE ARE THE SCORES YOU'VE BEEN WAITING FOR! ♡
Hurry! We need customers!
RUSH
Oh no!
I-B
At this moment-
FIRST PLACE, WITH 110 VOTES, IS DORM 3!
IN SECOND PLACE, WITH 104 VOTES, IS DORM 1!
NOW TRAILING, WITH 101 VOTES, IS DORM 2!
GASP
THIRD PLACE?!
NOT AGAIN...!
Kamikaze
Announcer
DORM 3 DID EVEN BETTER THAN EXPECTED!
THE HORROR HOUSE BY HIMEJIMA FROM CLASS 3-B WAS A HUGE SUCCESS!
Heh heh heh
CURSE YOU, MASAO.
THEY SAY THE MAKE UP AND SPECIAL EFFECTS ARE GOOD ENOUGH FOR HOLLY-WOOD.
really?
THE MOST SUCCESSFUL RESTAURANT WAS 3-C'S CHANKO NABE BOOTH!!
DORM 1'S R.A. TENNOJI SAYS "COME ON BY"!
Chanko Nabe?
That slop's for sumo wrestlers!
Now now.
Also...
WE HAVE A MESSAGE. "NANBA, YOU IDIOT! WHERE'S OUR DETECTIVE?!"
THAT'S A MESSAGE FROM EVERYONE IN CLASS 3-A'S MYSTERY TOUR.
GONG
He fell down.

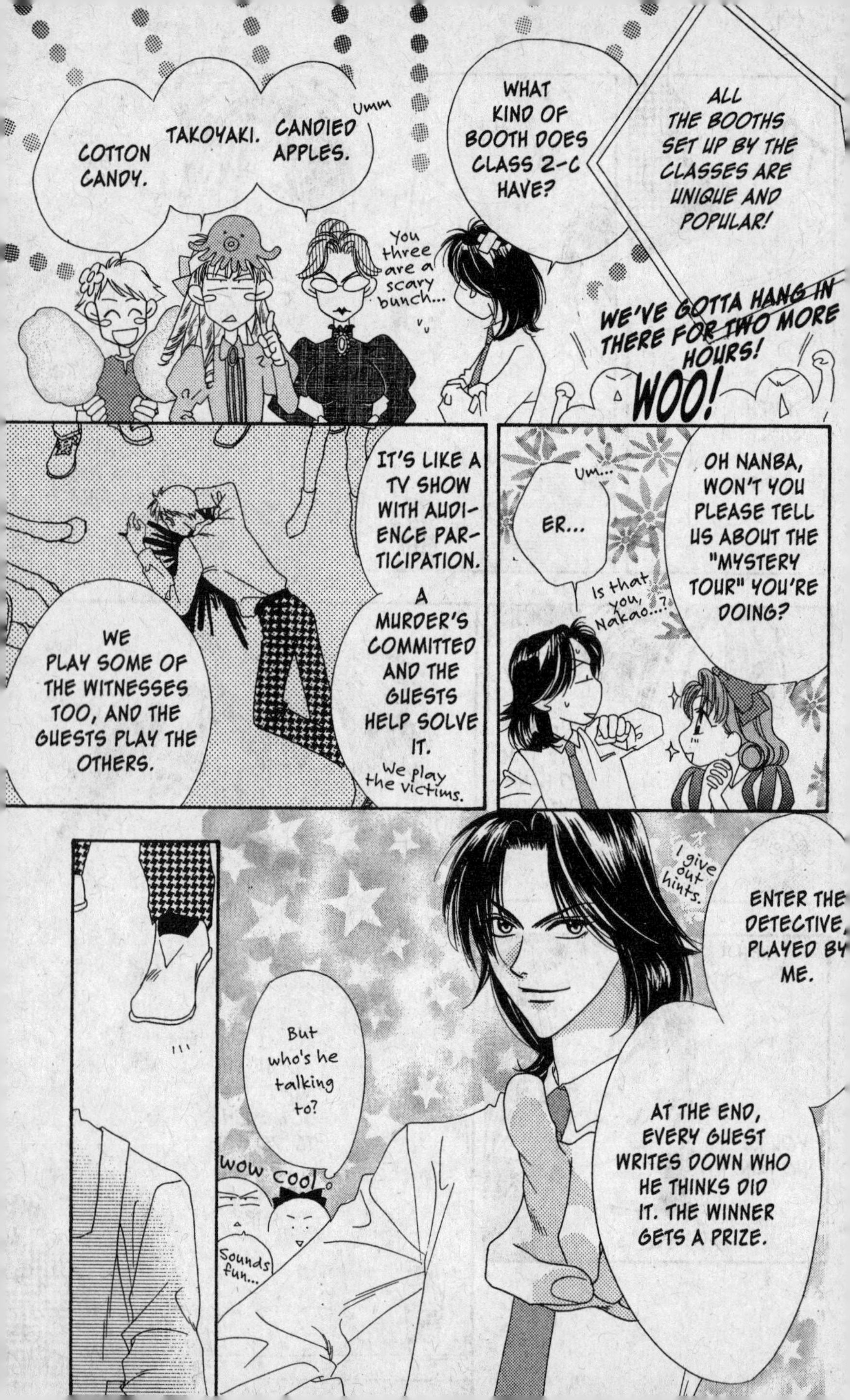
ALL THE BOOTHS SET UP BY THE CLASSES ARE UNIQUE AND POPULAR!
WE'VE GOTTA HANG IN THERE FOR TWO MORE HOURS!
WOO!
WHAT KIND OF BOOTH DOES CLASS 2-C HAVE?
You three are a scary bunch...
Umm
CANDIED APPLES.
TAKOYAKI.
COTTON CANDY.
OH NANBA, WON'T YOU PLEASE TELL US ABOUT THE "MYSTERY TOUR" YOU'RE DOING?
Um...
ER...
Is that you, Nakao...?
IT'S LIKE A TV SHOW WITH AUDIENCE PARTICIPATION.
A MURDER'S COMMITTED AND THE GUESTS HELP SOLVE IT.
We play the victims.
WE PLAY SOME OF THE WITNESSES TOO, AND THE GUESTS PLAY THE OTHERS.
ENTER THE DETECTIVE, PLAYED BY ME.
I give out hints.
AT THE END, EVERY GUEST WRITES DOWN WHO HE THINKS DID IT. THE WINNER GETS A PRIZE.
But who's he talking to?
WOW COOL
Sounds fun...

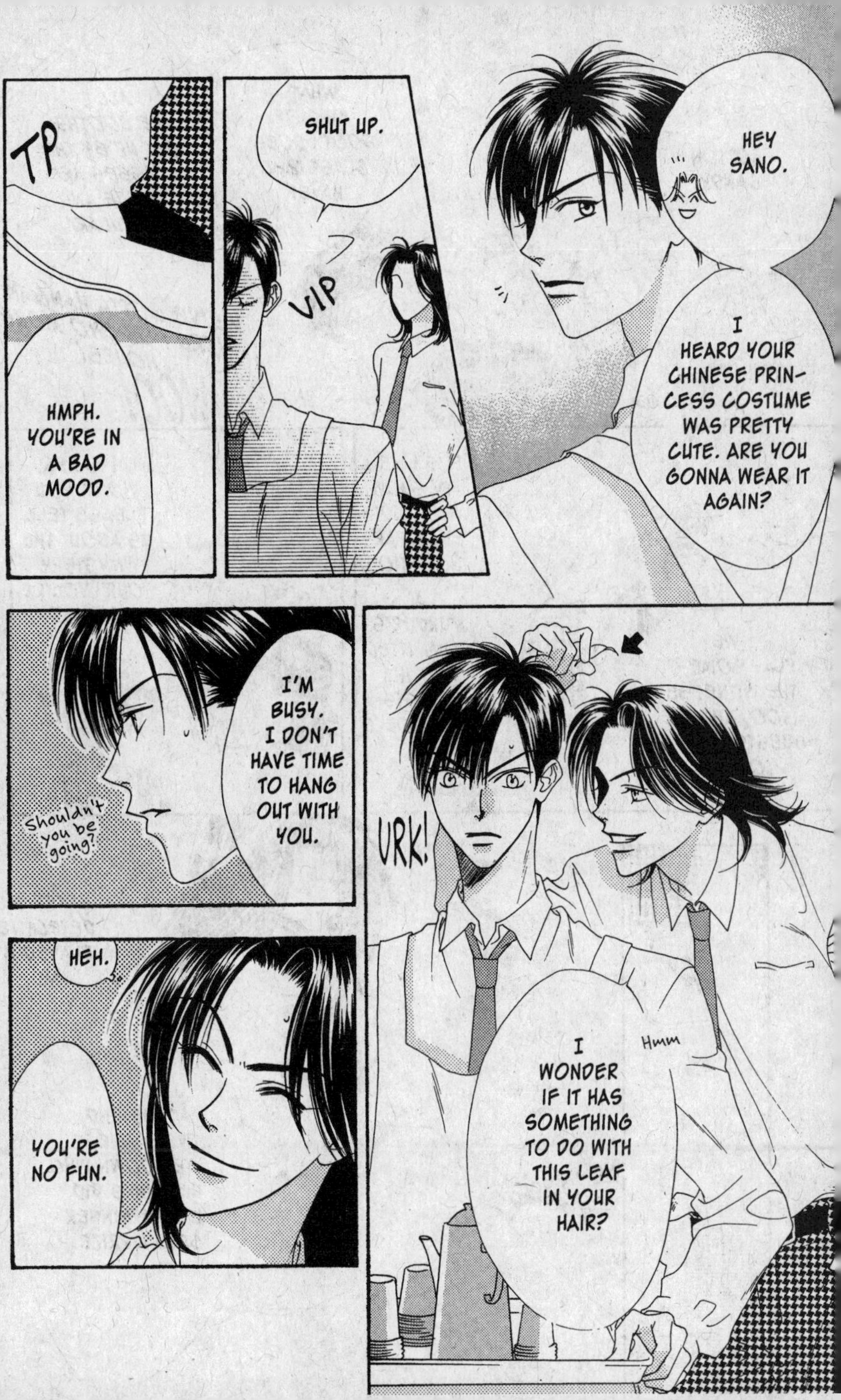
HEY SANO.
I HEARD YOUR CHINESE PRIN-CESS COSTUME WAS PRETTY CUTE. ARE YOU GONNA WEAR IT AGAIN?
SHUT UP.
VIP
TP
HMPH. YOU'RE IN A BAD MOOD.
URK!
Hmm
I WONDER IF IT HAS SOMETHING TO DO WITH THIS LEAF IN YOUR HAIR?
I'M BUSY. I DON'T HAVE TIME TO HANG OUT WITH YOU.
Shouldn't you be going?
HEH.
YOU'RE NO FUN.

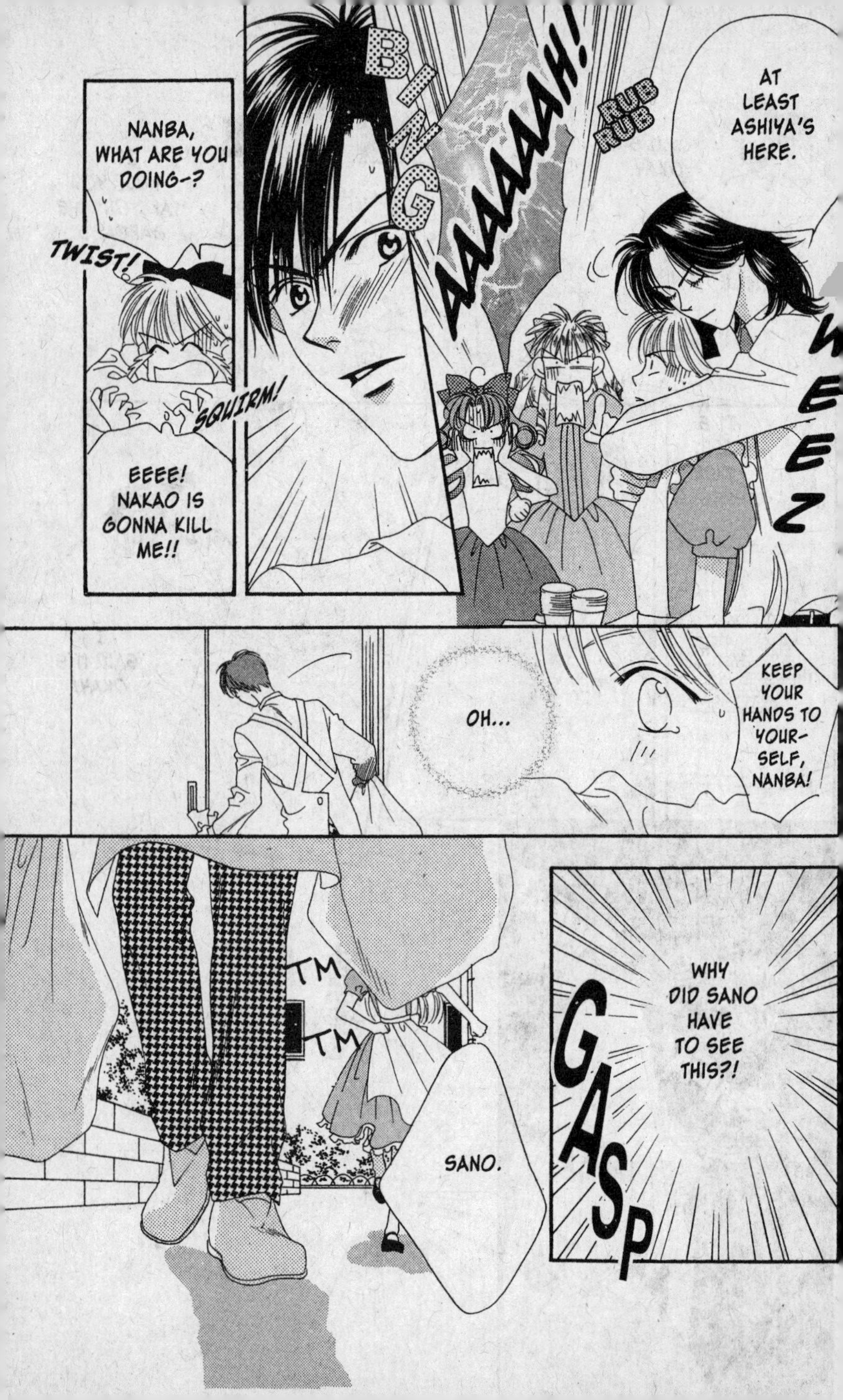

AT LEAST ASHIYA'S HERE.
RUB RUB
WEEZ
BING
AAAAAH!
NANBA, WHAT ARE YOU DOING-?
TWIST!
SQUIRM!
EEEE! NAKAO IS GONNA KILL ME!!
KEEP YOUR HANDS TO YOUR-SELF, NANBA!
OH...
WHY DID SANO HAVE TO SEE THIS?!
GASP
SANO.
TM
TM

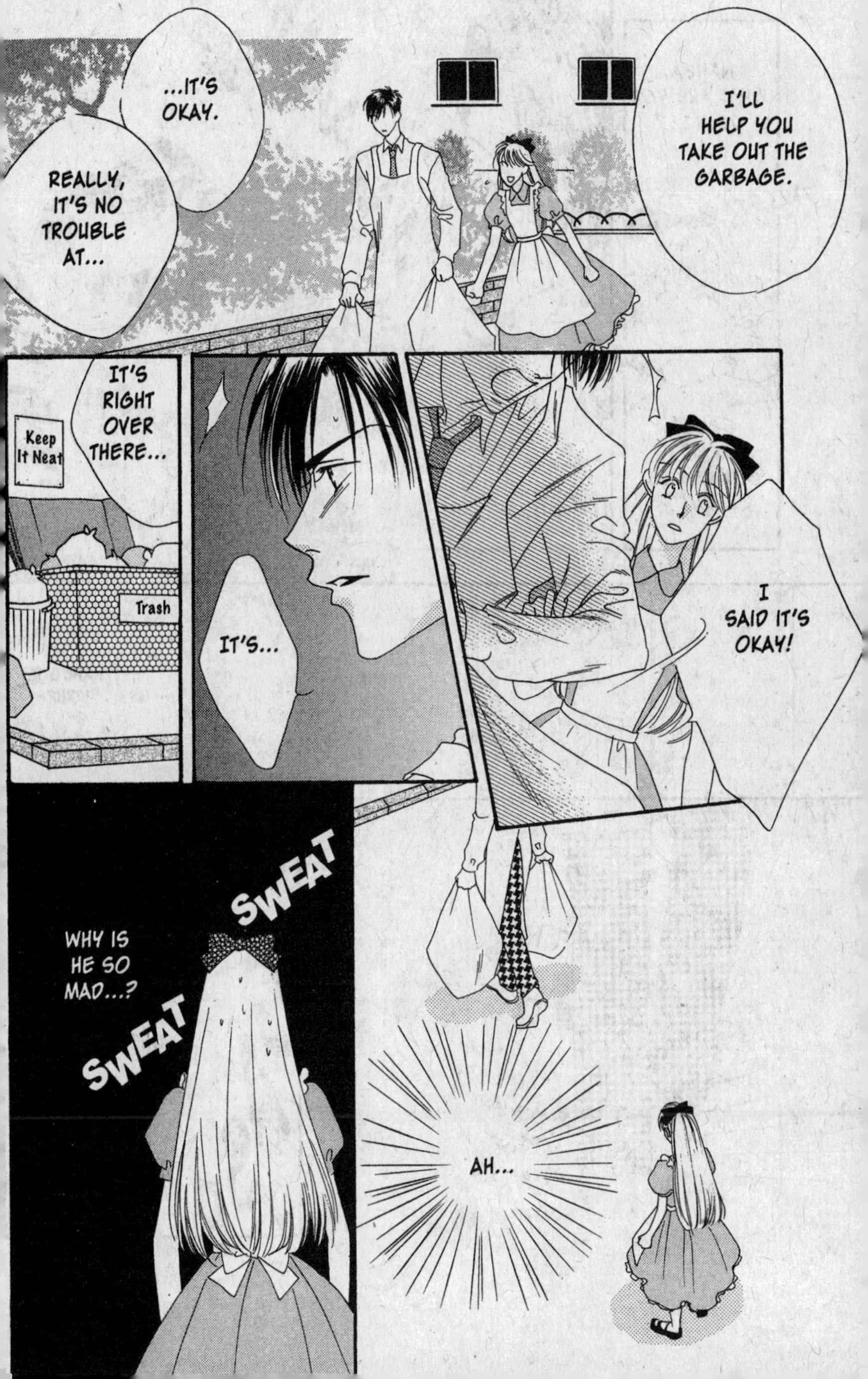
I'LL HELP YOU TAKE OUT THE GARBAGE.
...IT'S OKAY.
REALLY, IT'S NO TROUBLE AT...
I SAID IT'S OKAY!
IT'S...
IT'S RIGHT OVER THERE...
Keep It Neat
Trash
AH...
SWEAT
WHY IS HE SO MAD...?
SWEAT

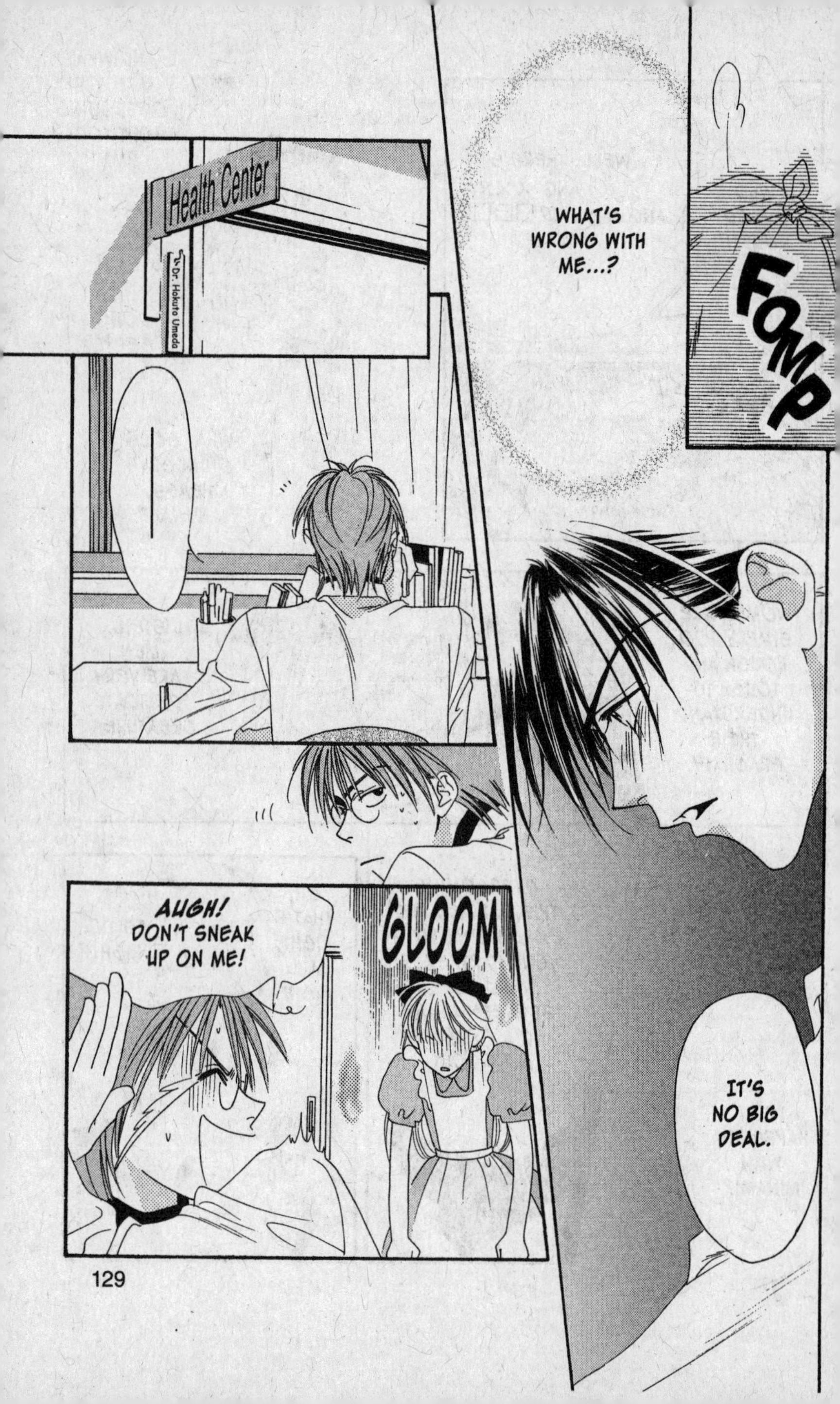
FOMP
WHAT'S WRONG WITH ME...?
IT'S NO BIG DEAL.
Health Center
Dr. Hokuto Umeda
GLOOM
AUGH! DON'T SNEAK UP ON ME!

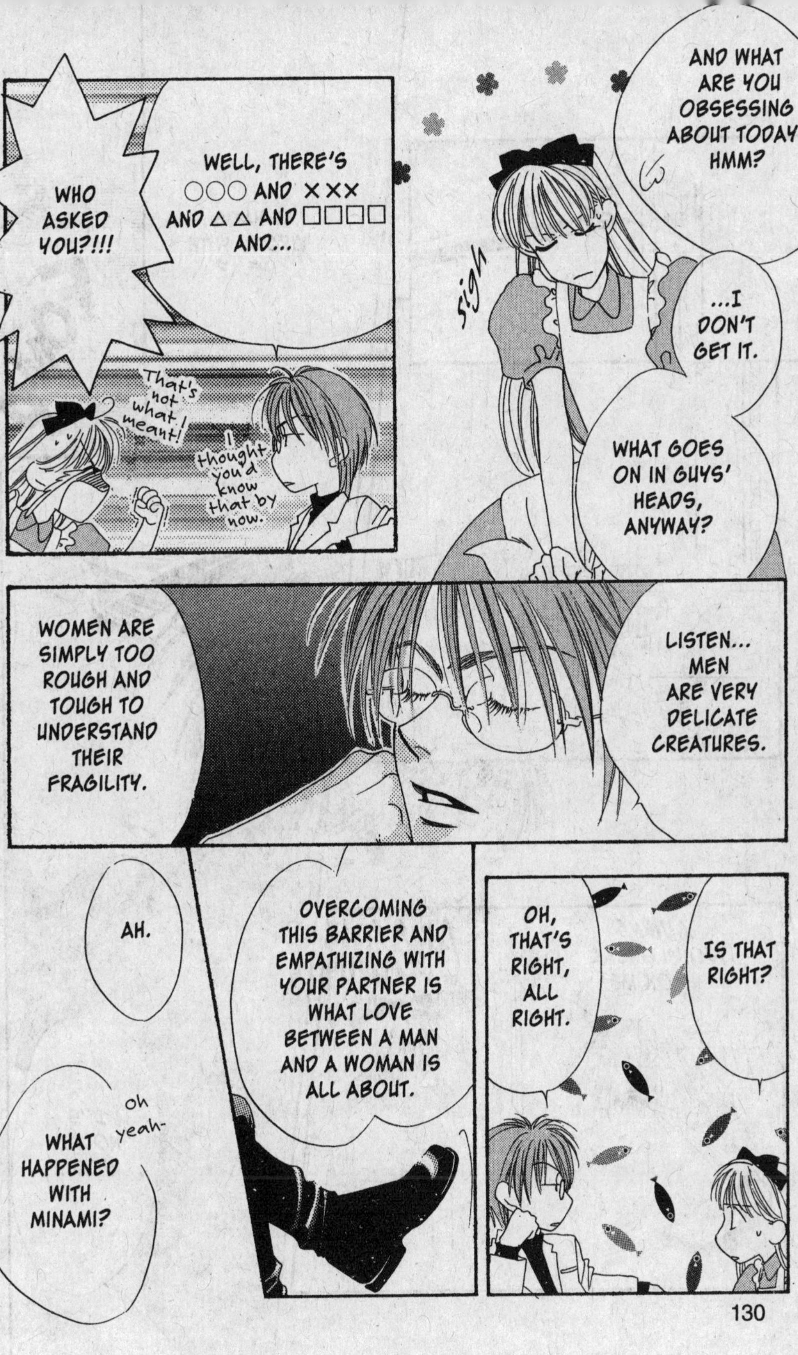
AND WHAT ARE YOU OBSESSING ABOUT TODAY, HMM?
sigh
...I DON'T GET IT.
WHAT GOES ON IN GUYS' HEADS, ANYWAY?
WELL, THERE'S ○○○ AND ××× AND △△ AND □□□□ AND...
WHO ASKED YOU?!!!
That's not what I meant!
I thought you'd know that by now.
LISTEN... MEN ARE VERY DELICATE CREATURES.
WOMEN ARE SIMPLY TOO ROUGH AND TOUGH TO UNDERSTAND THEIR FRAGILITY.
IS THAT RIGHT?
OH, THAT'S RIGHT, ALL RIGHT.
OVERCOMING THIS BARRIER AND EMPATHIZING WITH YOUR PARTNER IS WHAT LOVE BETWEEN A MAN AND A WOMAN IS ALL ABOUT.
AH.
oh yeah-
WHAT HAPPENED WITH MINAMI?

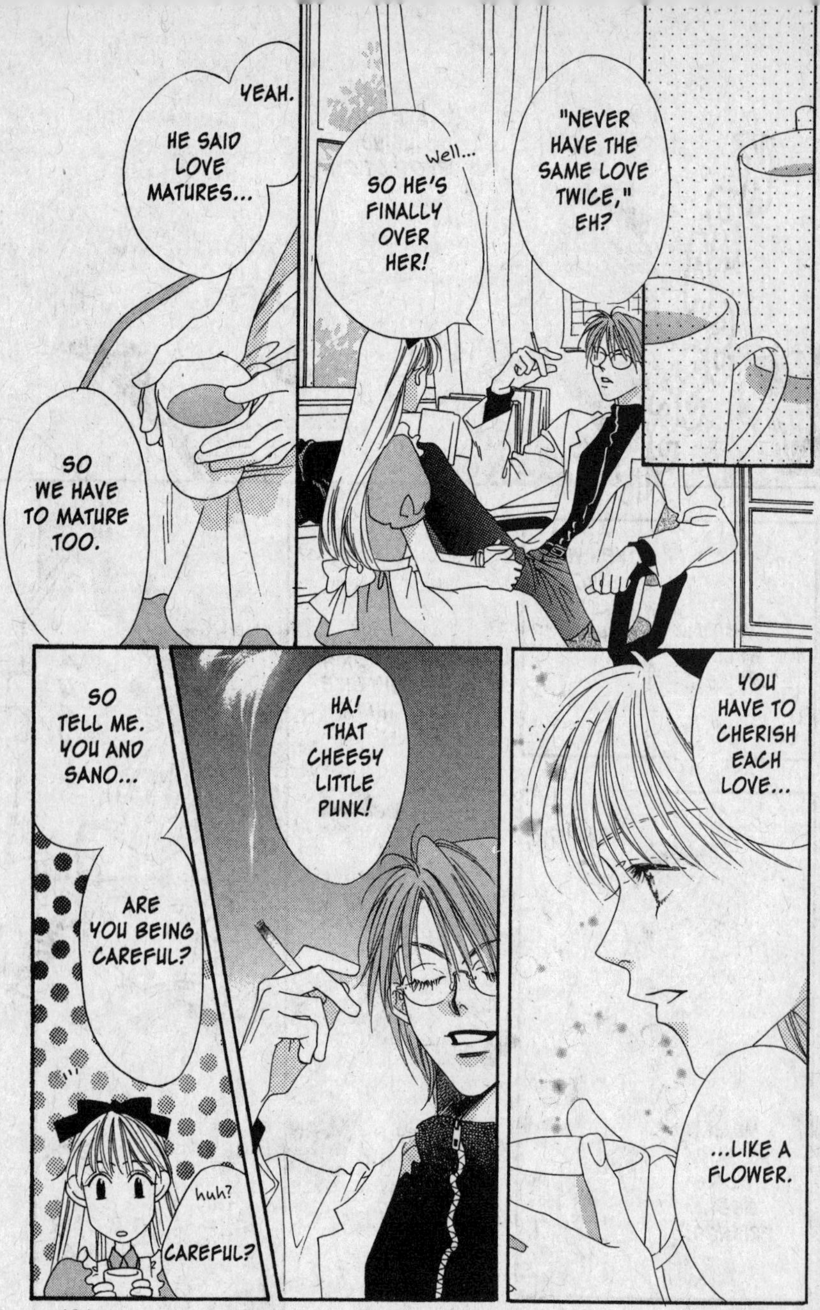
"NEVER HAVE THE SAME LOVE TWICE," EH?
Well...
SO HE'S FINALLY OVER HER!
YEAH.
HE SAID LOVE MATURES...
SO WE HAVE TO MATURE TOO.
YOU HAVE TO CHERISH EACH LOVE...
...LIKE A FLOWER.
HA! THAT CHEESY LITTLE PUNK!
SO TELL ME. YOU AND SANO...
ARE YOU BEING CAREFUL?
huh?
CAREFUL?

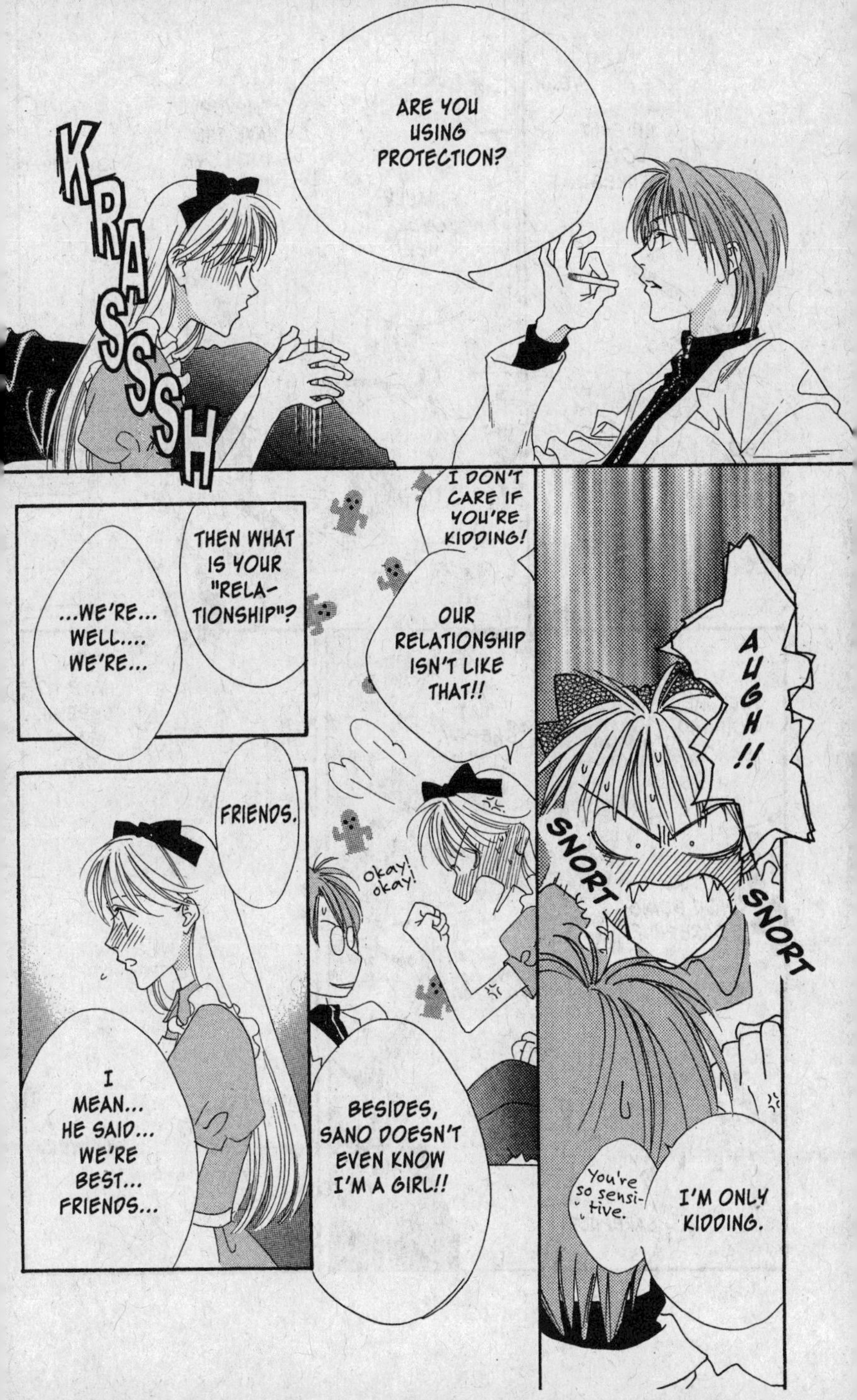
ARE YOU USING PROTECTION?
KRASSSH
AUGH!!
SNORT
SNORT
I'M ONLY KIDDING.
You're so sensitive.
I DON'T CARE IF YOU'RE KIDDING!
OUR RELATIONSHIP ISN'T LIKE THAT!!
okay! okay!
BESIDES, SANO DOESN'T EVEN KNOW I'M A GIRL!!
THEN WHAT IS YOUR "RELATIONSHIP"?
...WE'RE... WELL.... WE'RE...
FRIENDS.
I MEAN... HE SAID... WE'RE BEST... FRIENDS...

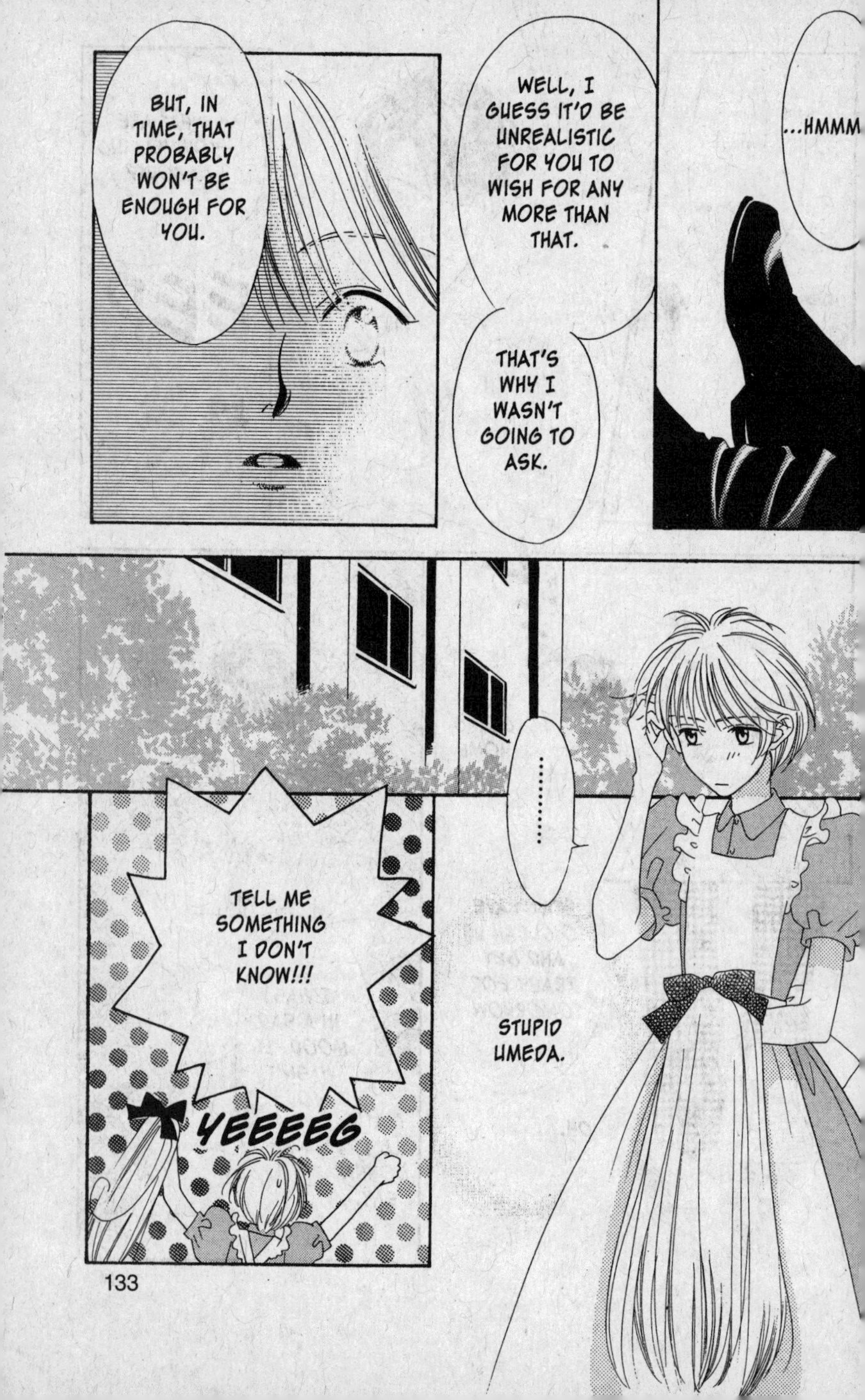
...HMMM
WELL, I GUESS IT'D BE UNREALISTIC FOR YOU TO WISH FOR ANY MORE THAN THAT.
THAT'S WHY I WASN'T GOING TO ASK.
BUT, IN TIME, THAT PROBABLY WON'T BE ENOUGH FOR YOU.
......
STUPID UMEDA.
TELL ME SOMETHING I DON'T KNOW!!!
YEEEEG

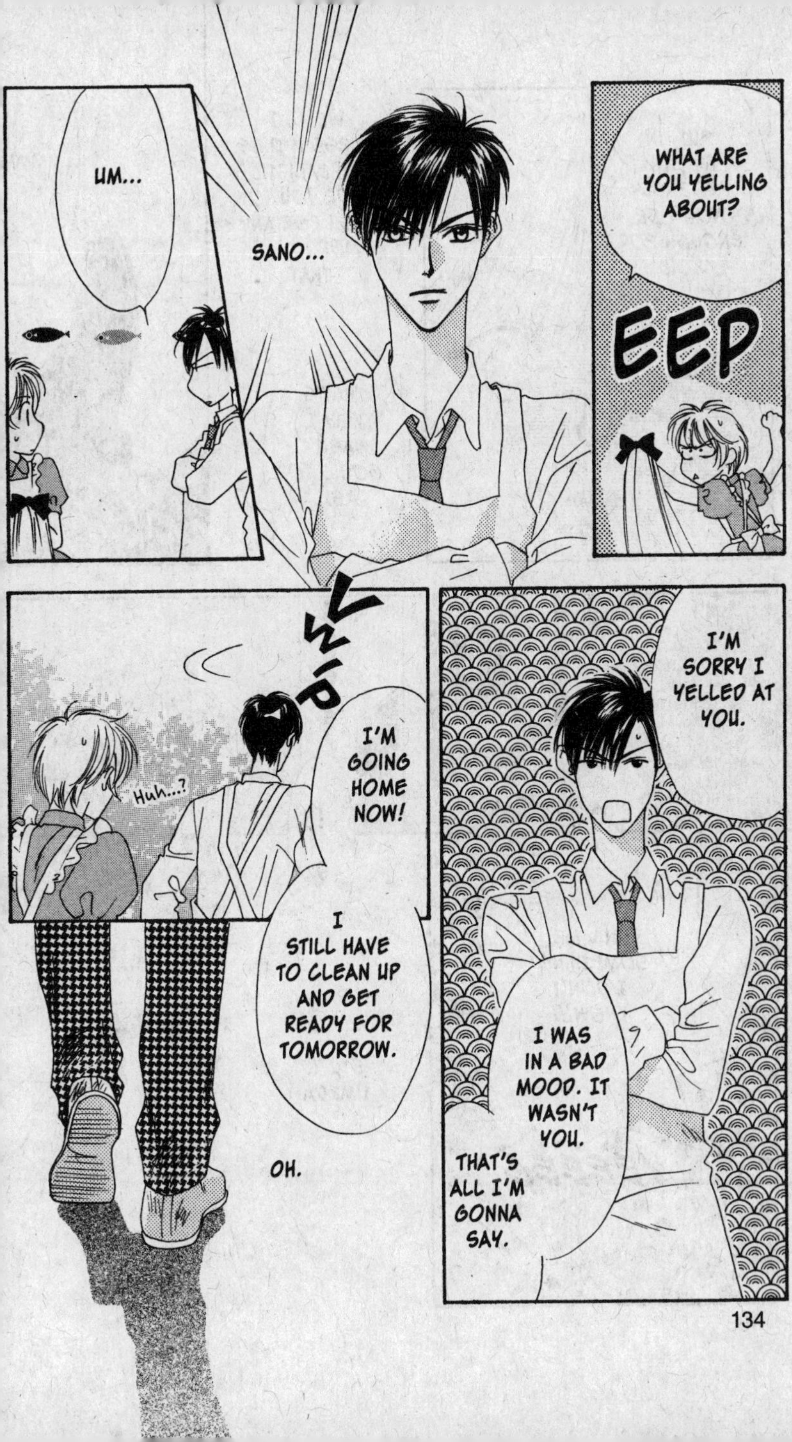
WHAT ARE YOU YELLING ABOUT?
EEP
SANO...
UM...
I'M SORRY I YELLED AT YOU.
I WAS IN A BAD MOOD. IT WASN'T YOU.
THAT'S ALL I'M GONNA SAY.
I'M GOING HOME NOW!
Huh...?
I STILL HAVE TO CLEAN UP AND GET READY FOR TOMORROW.
OH.

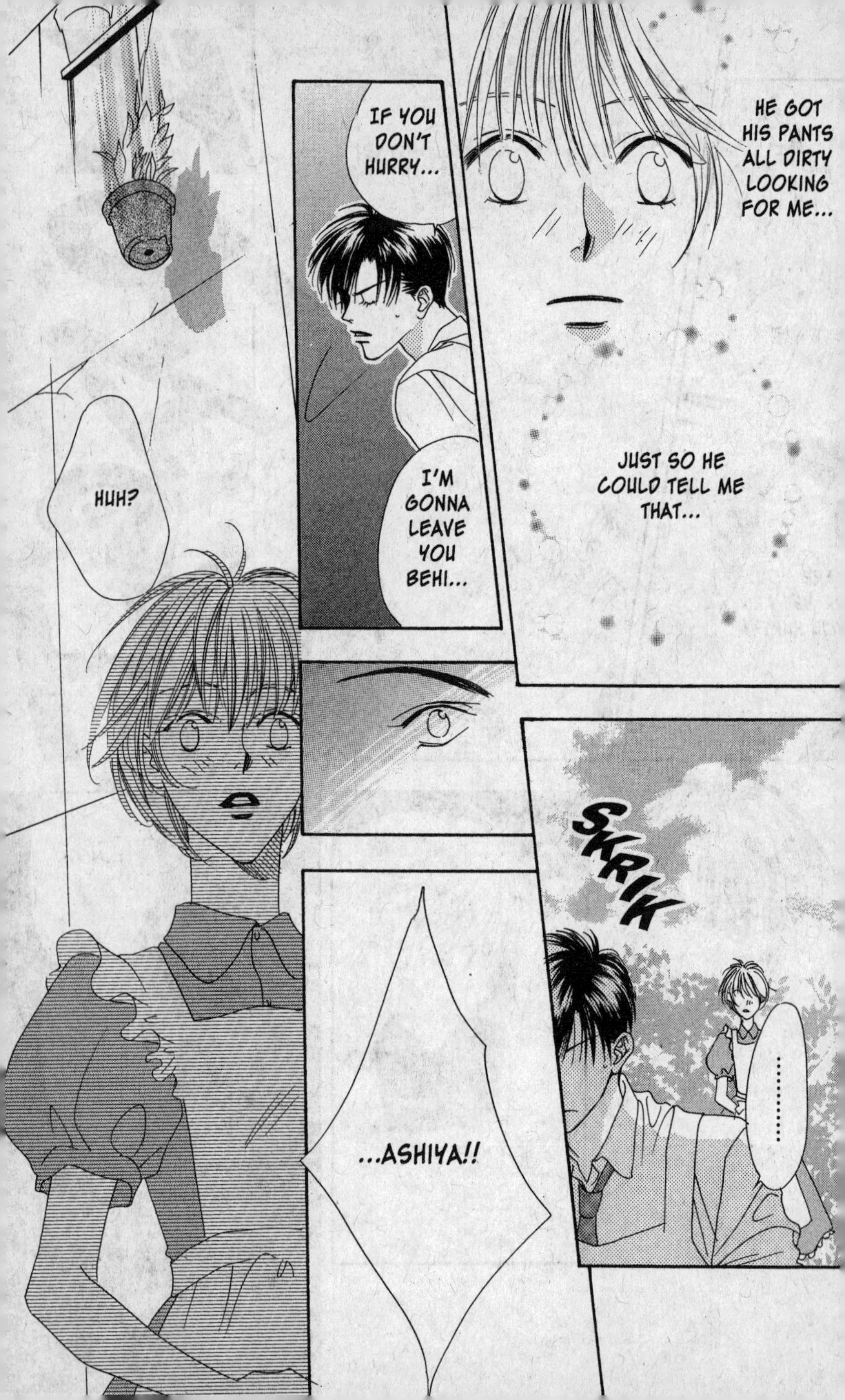
HE GOT HIS PANTS ALL DIRTY LOOKING FOR ME...
JUST SO HE COULD TELL ME THAT...
IF YOU DON'T HURRY...
I'M GONNA LEAVE YOU BEHI...
SKRIK
......
...ASHIYA!!
HUH?

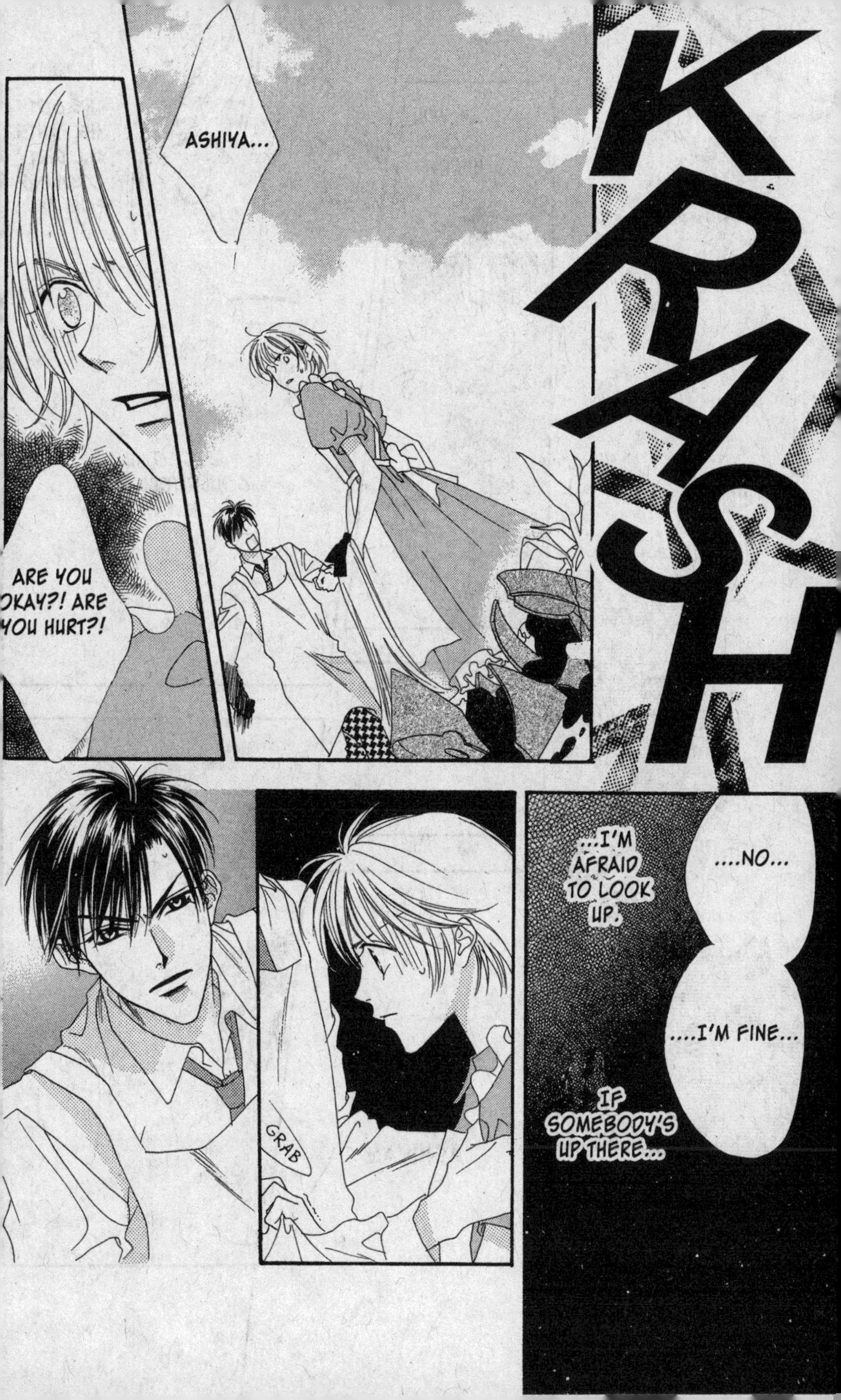
KRASH
ASHIYA...
ARE YOU OKAY?! ARE YOU HURT?!
....NO...
...I'M AFRAID TO LOOK UP.
....I'M FINE...
IF SOMEBODY'S UP THERE...
GRAB

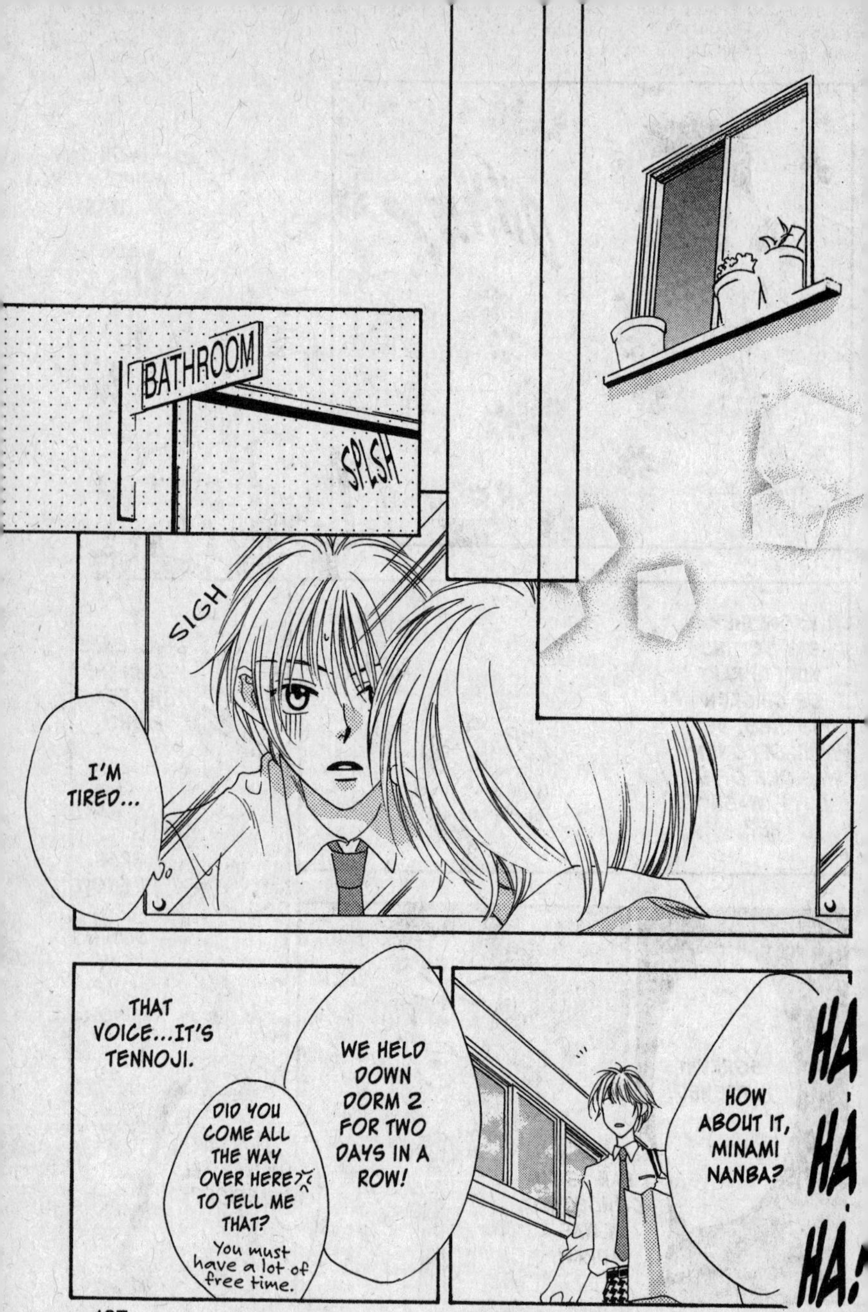
BATHROOM
SPLSH
SIGH
I'M TIRED...
HA HA HA!
HOW ABOUT IT, MINAMI NANBA?
WE HELD DOWN DORM 2 FOR TWO DAYS IN A ROW!
THAT VOICE...IT'S TENNOJI.
DID YOU COME ALL THE WAY OVER HERE TO TELL ME THAT?
You must have a lot of free time.

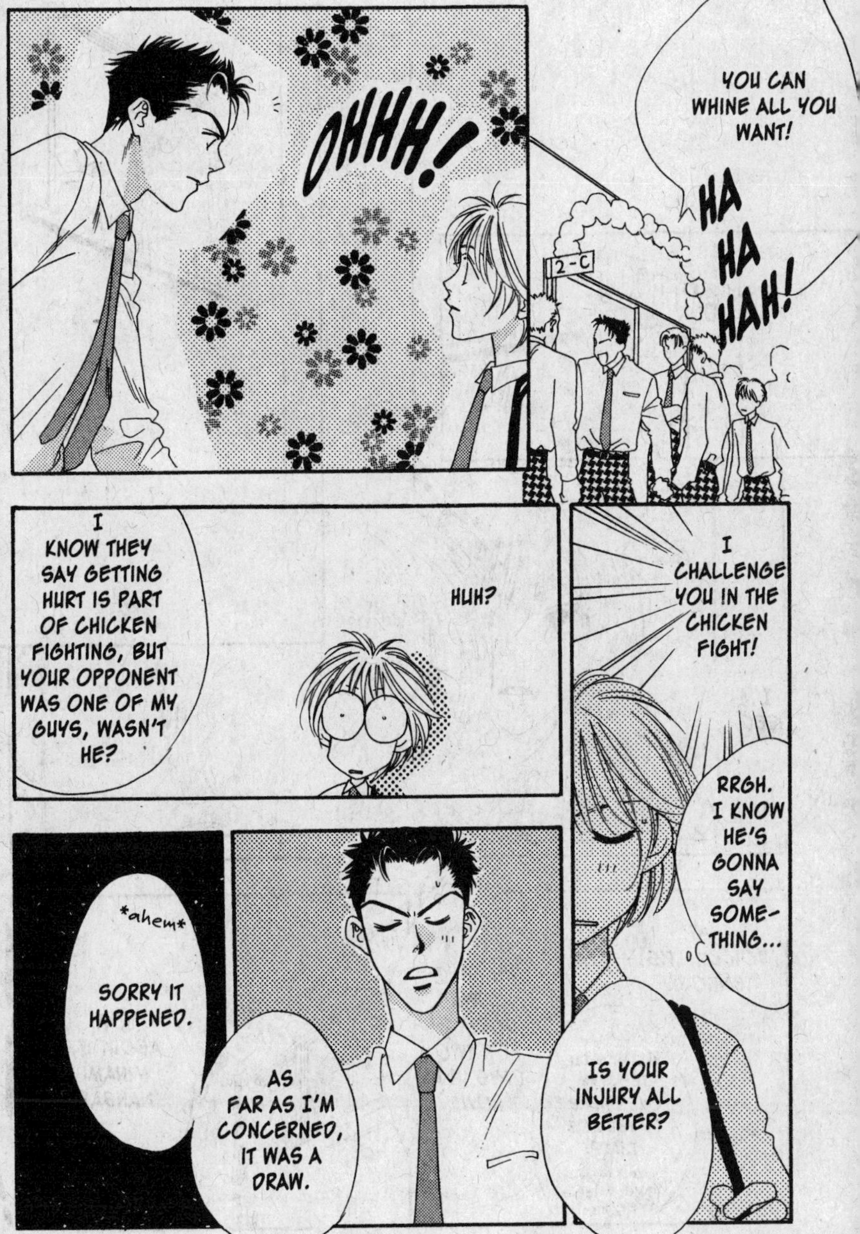
YOU CAN WHINE ALL YOU WANT!
HA HA HAH!
2-C
OHHH!
I CHALLENGE YOU IN THE CHICKEN FIGHT!
RRGH. I KNOW HE'S GONNA SAY SOME-THING...
IS YOUR INJURY ALL BETTER?
HUH?
I KNOW THEY SAY GETTING HURT IS PART OF CHICKEN FIGHTING, BUT YOUR OPPONENT WAS ONE OF MY GUYS, WASN'T HE?
AS FAR AS I'M CONCERNED, IT WAS A DRAW.
ahem
SORRY IT HAPPENED.

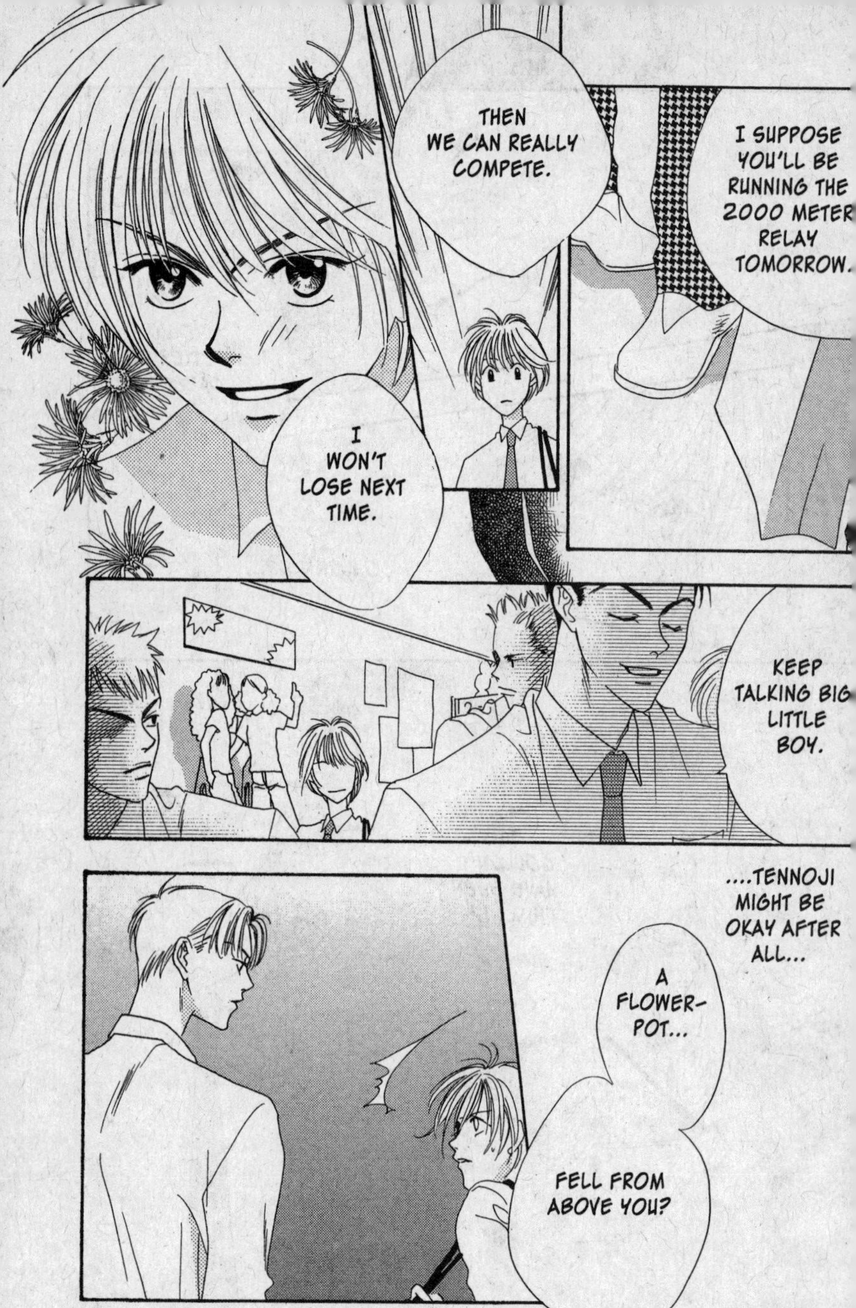

I SUPPOSE YOU'LL BE RUNNING THE 2000 METER RELAY TOMORROW.
THEN WE CAN REALLY COMPETE.
I WON'T LOSE NEXT TIME.
KEEP TALKING BIG LITTLE BOY.
....TENNOJI MIGHT BE OKAY AFTER ALL...
A FLOWER-POT...
FELL FROM ABOVE YOU?

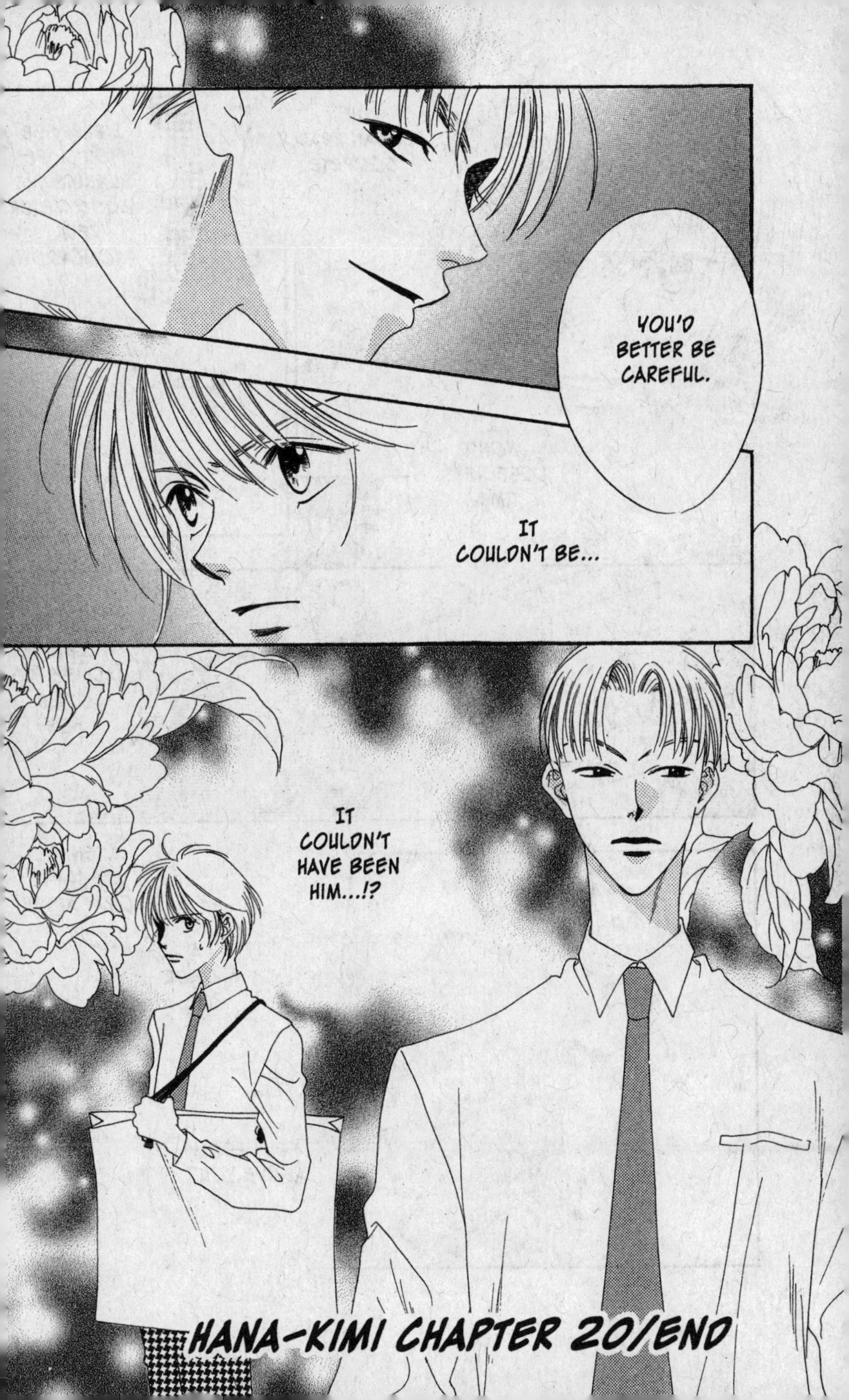
YOU'D BETTER BE CAREFUL.
IT COULDN'T BE...
IT COULDN'T HAVE BEEN HIM...!?
HANA-KIMI CHAPTER 20/END

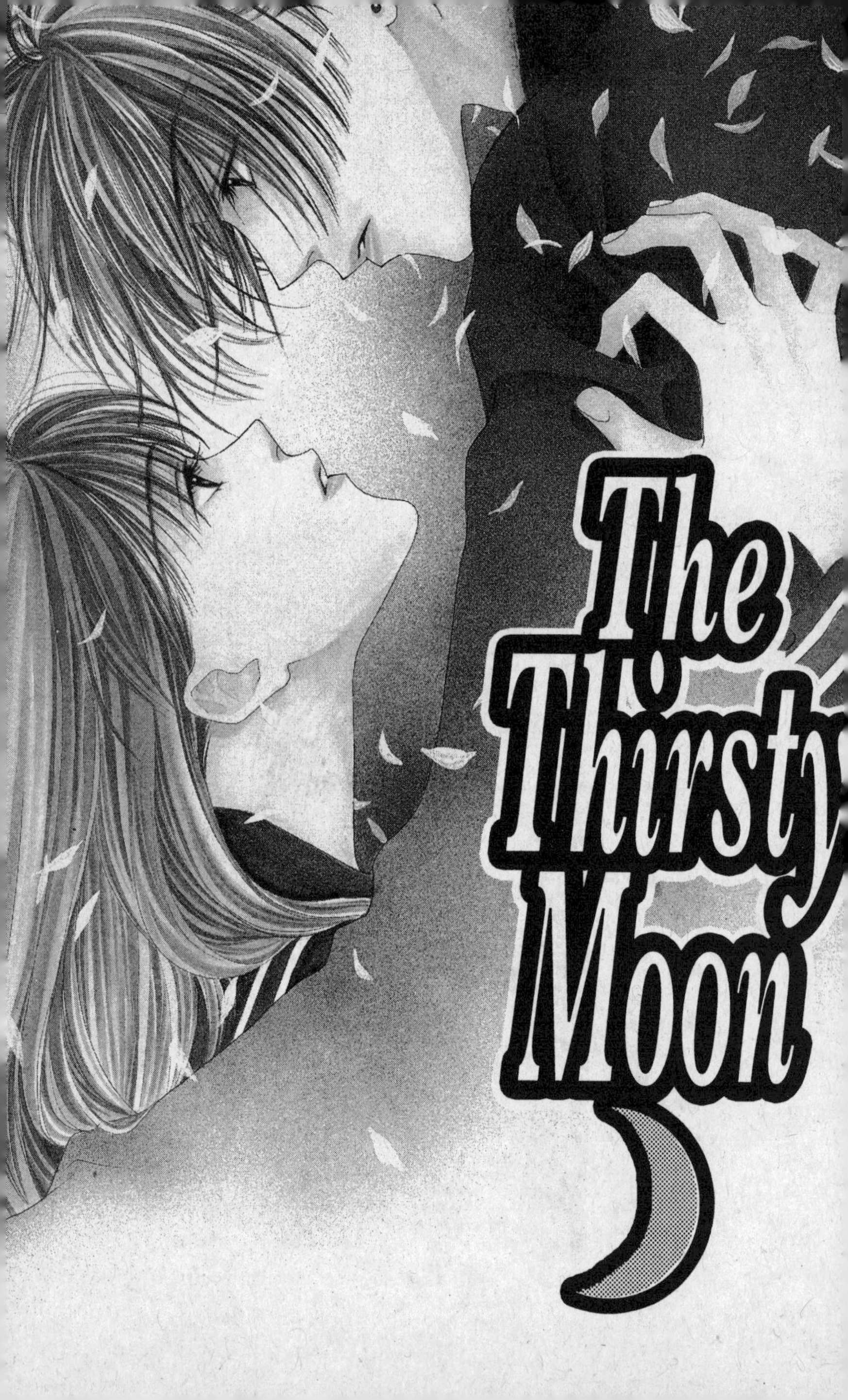
The Thirsty Moon

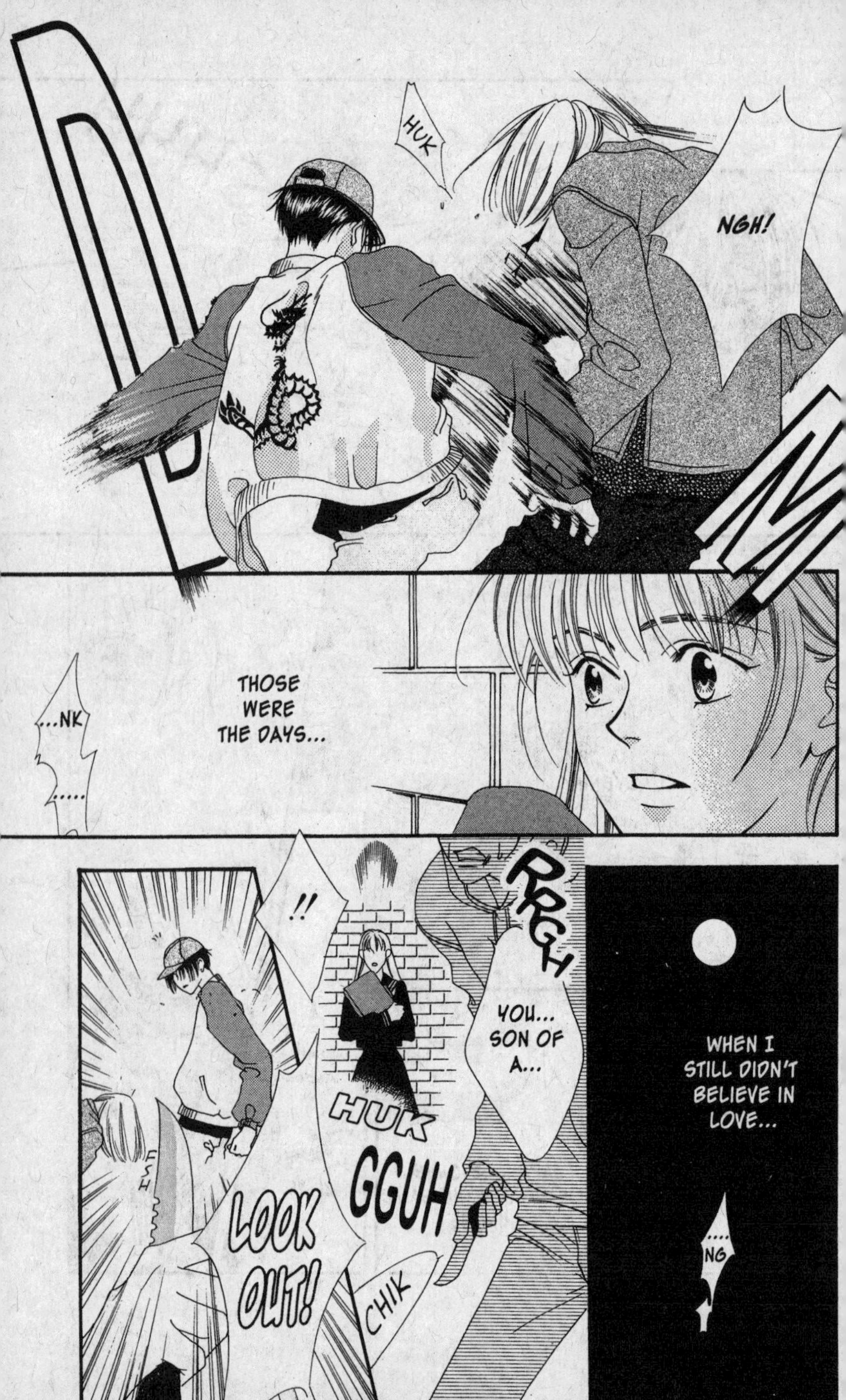
NGH!
HUK
THOSE WERE THE DAYS...
...NK
......
WHEN I STILL DIDN'T BELIEVE IN LOVE...
....NG
RRGH
YOU... SON OF A...
!!
HUK
GGUH
LOOK OUT!
CHIK

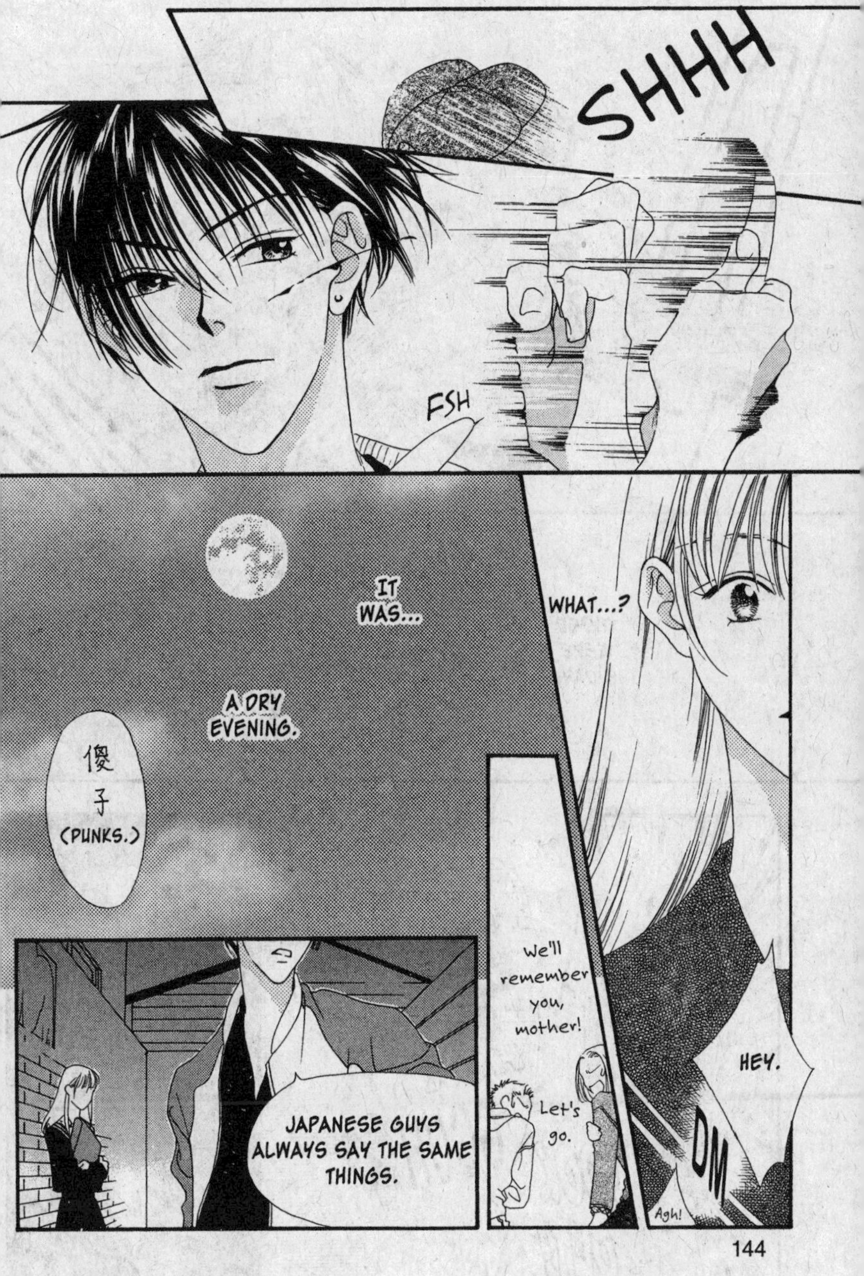
SHHH
FSH
WHAT...?
HEY.
DM
Agh!
IT WAS...
A DRY EVENING.
傻子 (PUNKS.)
We'll remember you, mother!
Let's go.
JAPANESE GUYS ALWAYS SAY THE SAME THINGS.

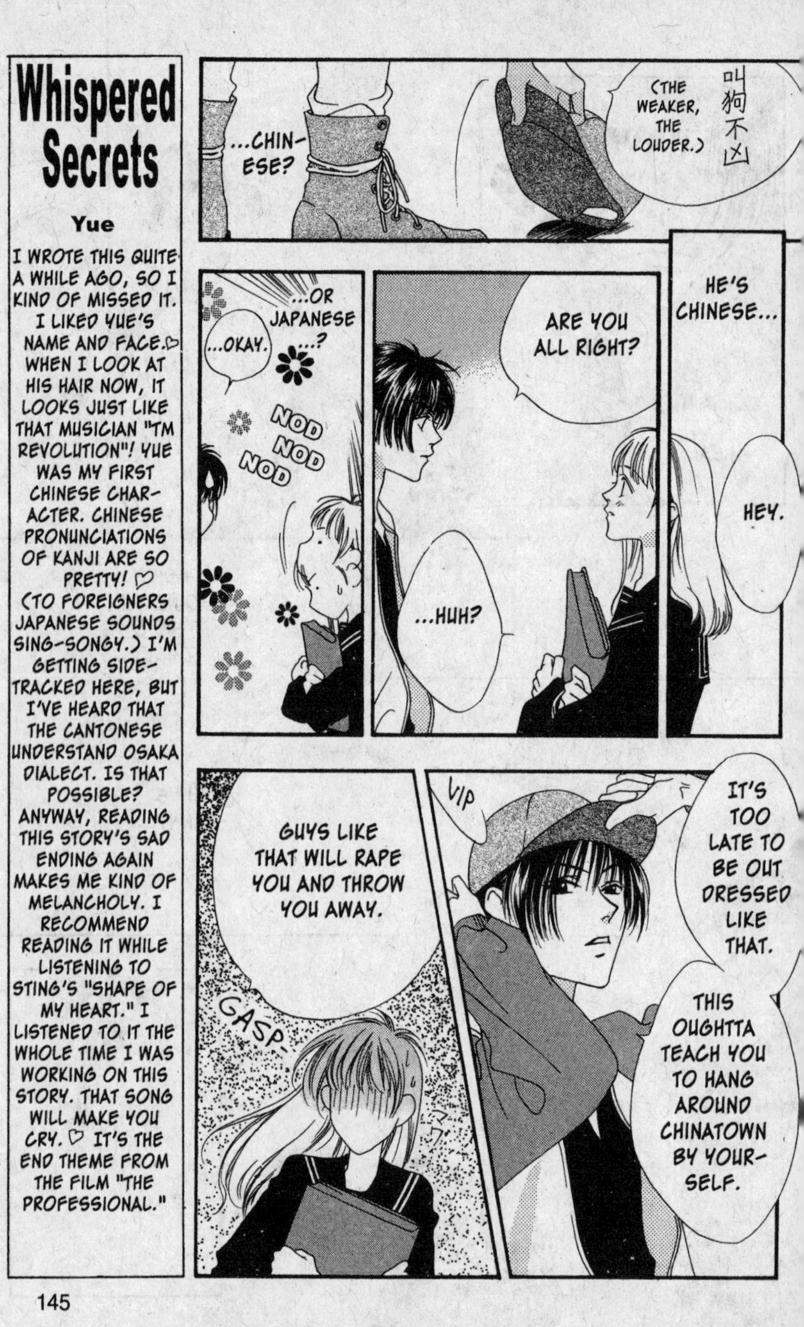
(THE WEAKER, THE LOUDER.)
叫狗不凶
...CHINESE?
HE'S CHINESE...
HEY.
ARE YOU ALL RIGHT?
...HUH?
...OR JAPANESE...?
...OKAY.
NOD NOD NOD
VIP
IT'S TOO LATE TO BE OUT DRESSED LIKE THAT.
THIS OUGHTTA TEACH YOU TO HANG AROUND CHINATOWN BY YOURSELF.
GUYS LIKE THAT WILL RAPE YOU AND THROW YOU AWAY.
GASP

Whispered Secrets

Yue

I WROTE THIS QUITE A WHILE AGO, SO I KIND OF MISSED IT. I LIKED YUE'S NAME AND FACE.♡ WHEN I LOOK AT HIS HAIR NOW, IT LOOKS JUST LIKE THAT MUSICIAN "TM REVOLUTION"! YUE WAS MY FIRST CHINESE CHARACTER. CHINESE PRONUNCIATIONS OF KANJI ARE SO PRETTY! ♡ (TO FOREIGNERS JAPANESE SOUNDS SING-SONGY.) I'M GETTING SIDETRACKED HERE, BUT I'VE HEARD THAT THE CANTONESE UNDERSTAND OSAKA DIALECT. IS THAT POSSIBLE? ANYWAY, READING THIS STORY'S SAD ENDING AGAIN MAKES ME KIND OF MELANCHOLY. I RECOMMEND READING IT WHILE LISTENING TO STING'S "SHAPE OF MY HEART." I LISTENED TO IT THE WHOLE TIME I WAS WORKING ON THIS STORY. THAT SONG WILL MAKE YOU CRY. ♡ IT'S THE END THEME FROM THE FILM "THE PROFESSIONAL."

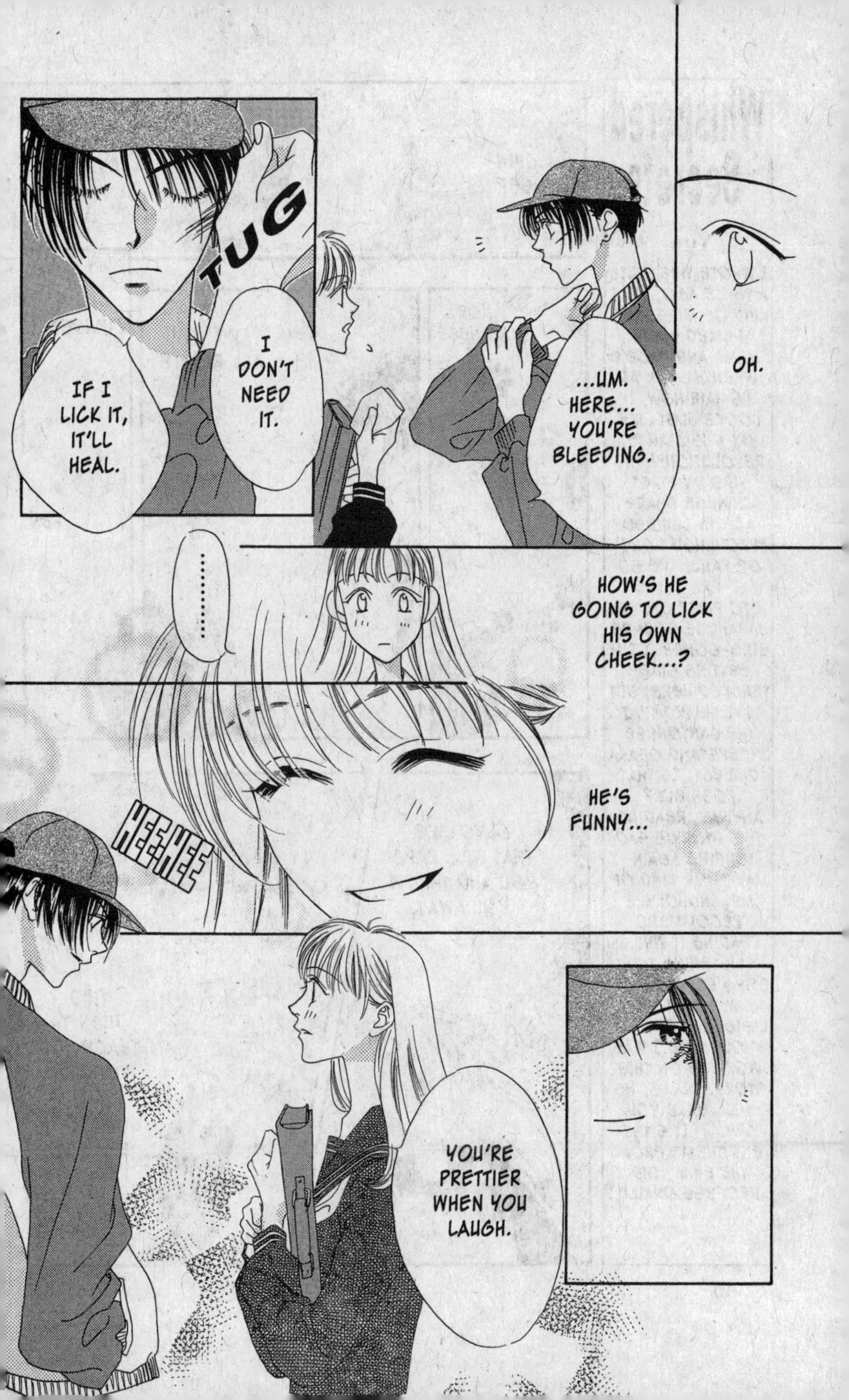
OH.
...UM. HERE... YOU'RE BLEEDING.
TUG
I DON'T NEED IT.
IF I LICK IT, IT'LL HEAL.
HOW'S HE GOING TO LICK HIS OWN CHEEK...?
......
HE'S FUNNY...
HEE HEE
YOU'RE PRETTIER WHEN YOU LAUGH.

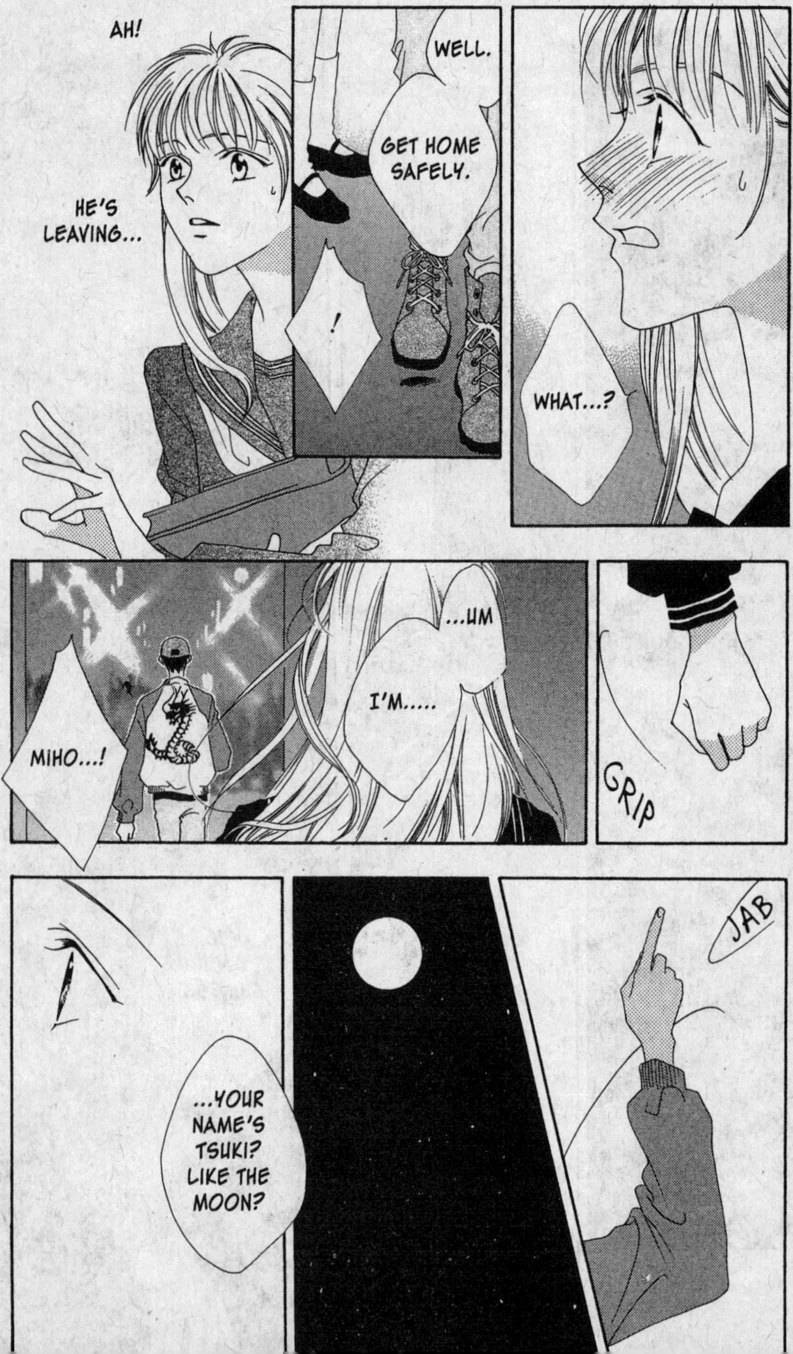
WHAT...?
WELL.
GET HOME SAFELY.
!
AH!
HE'S LEAVING...
GRIP
...UM
I'M.....
MIHO...!
JAB
...YOUR NAME'S TSUKI? LIKE THE MOON?

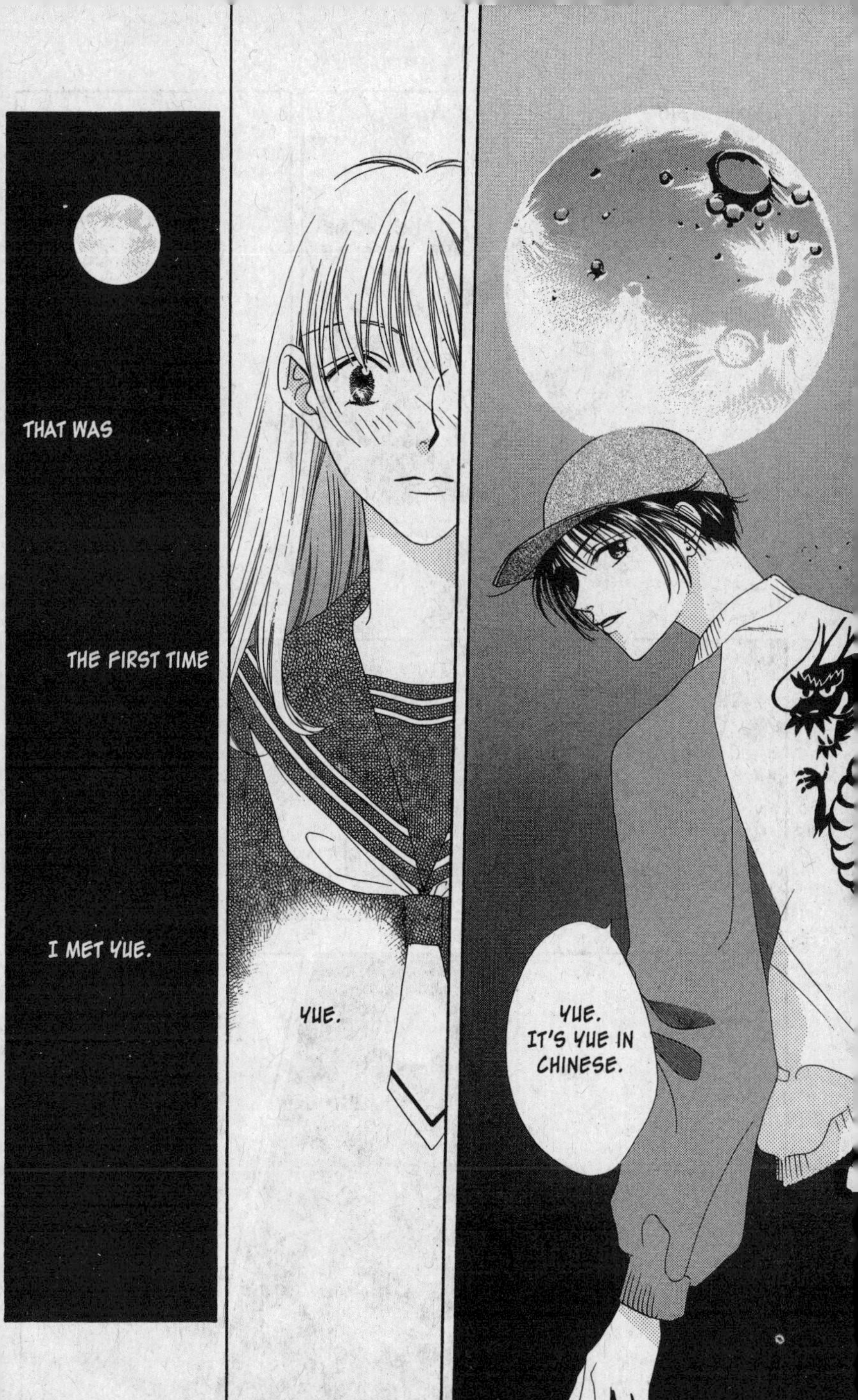
YUE.
IT'S YUE IN
CHINESE.
YUE.
THAT WAS
THE FIRST TIME
I MET YUE.

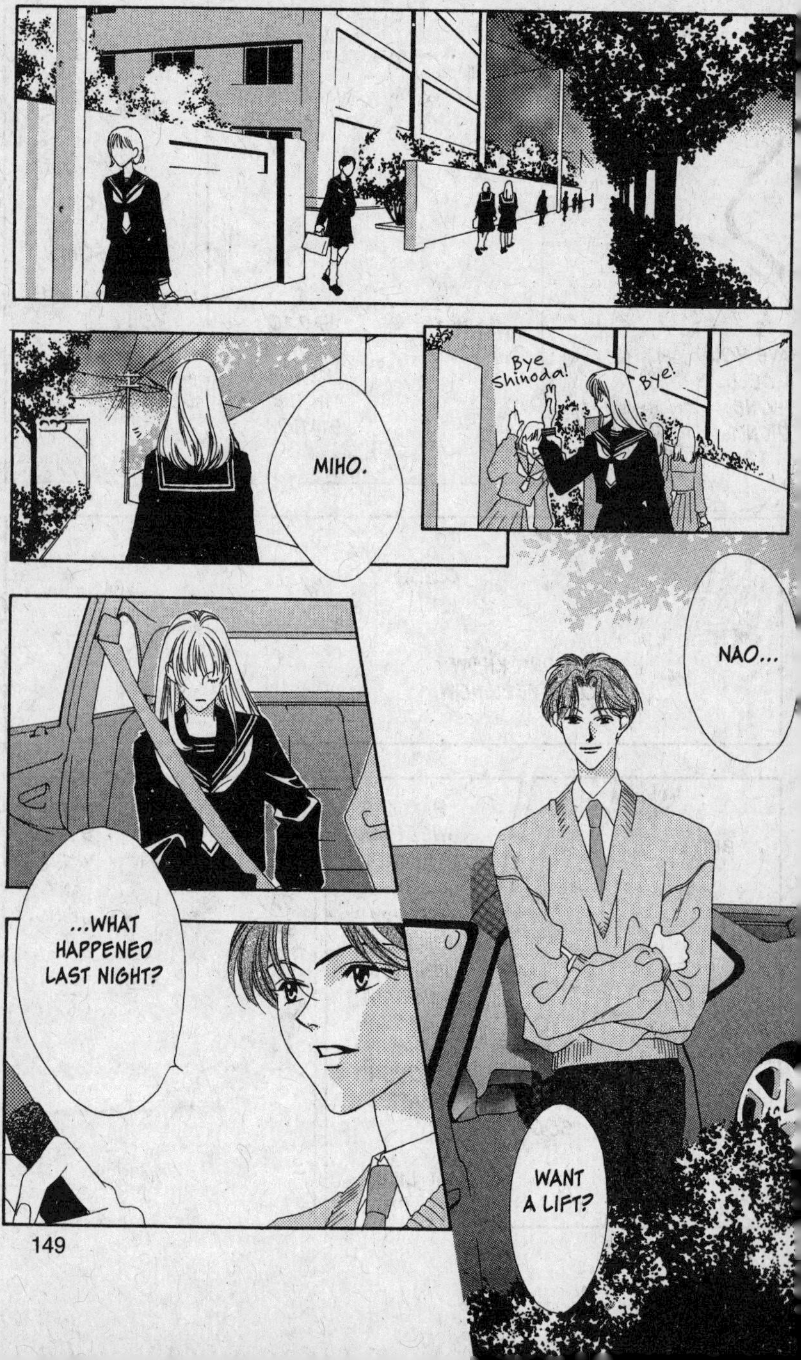
Bye!
Bye Shinoda!
MIHO.
NAO...
WANT A LIFT?
...WHAT HAPPENED LAST NIGHT?

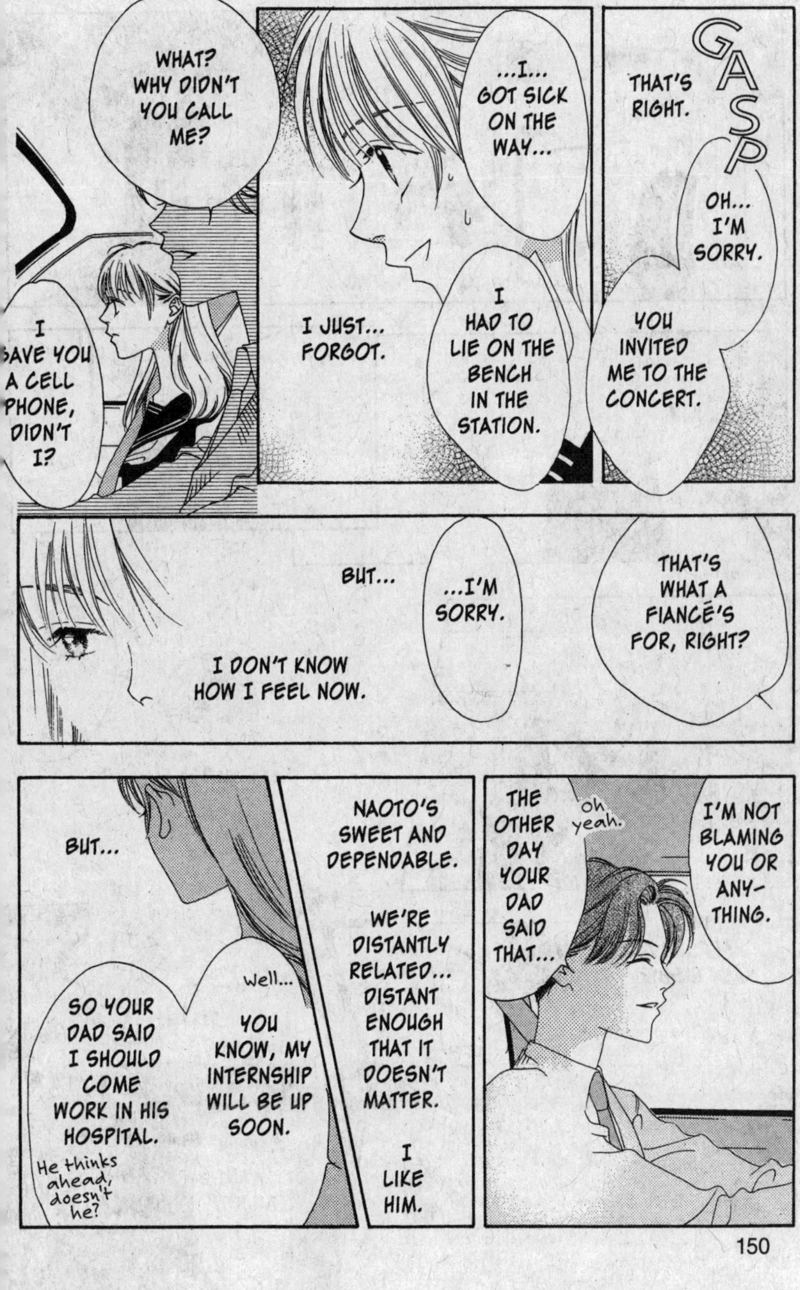

THAT'S RIGHT.
GASP
OH... I'M SORRY.
YOU INVITED ME TO THE CONCERT.
...I... GOT SICK ON THE WAY...
I HAD TO LIE ON THE BENCH IN THE STATION.
I JUST... FORGOT.
WHAT? WHY DIDN'T YOU CALL ME?
I GAVE YOU A CELL PHONE, DIDN'T I?
THAT'S WHAT A FIANCÉ'S FOR, RIGHT?
...I'M SORRY.
BUT...
I DON'T KNOW HOW I FEEL NOW.
I'M NOT BLAMING YOU OR ANY-THING.
Oh yeah.
THE OTHER DAY YOUR DAD SAID THAT...
NAOTO'S SWEET AND DEPENDABLE.
WE'RE DISTANTLY RELATED... DISTANT ENOUGH THAT IT DOESN'T MATTER.
I LIKE HIM.
Well...
YOU KNOW, MY INTERNSHIP WILL BE UP SOON.
SO YOUR DAD SAID I SHOULD COME WORK IN HIS HOSPITAL.
He thinks ahead, doesn't he?
BUT...

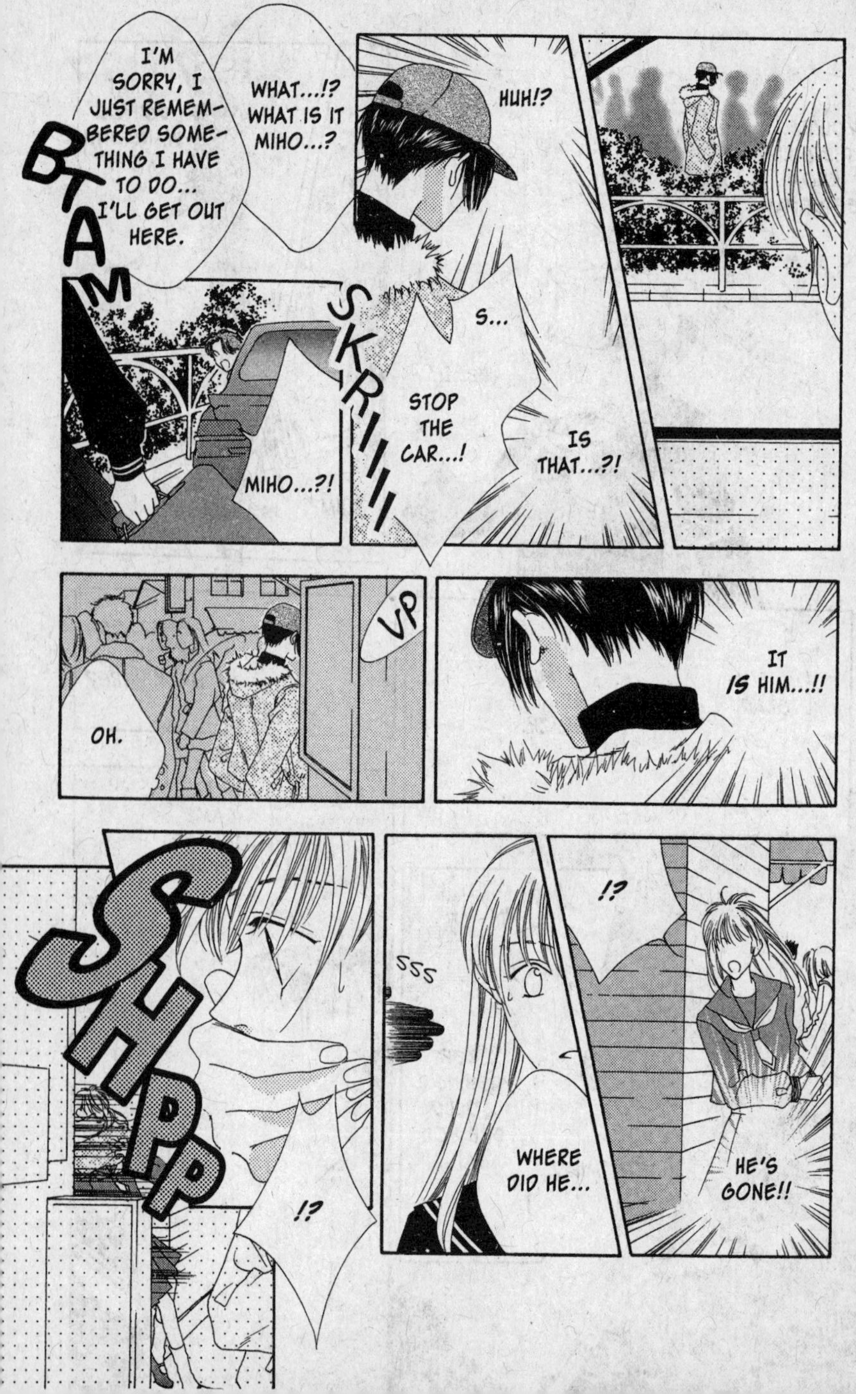
HUH!?
S...
IS THAT...?!
STOP THE CAR...!
SKRIIII
WHAT...!? WHAT IS IT MIHO...?
I'M SORRY, I JUST REMEMBERED SOMETHING I HAVE TO DO... I'LL GET OUT HERE.
BTAM
MIHO...?!
IT IS HIM...!!
VP
OH.
!?
HE'S GONE!!
SSS
WHERE DID HE...
SHPP
!?

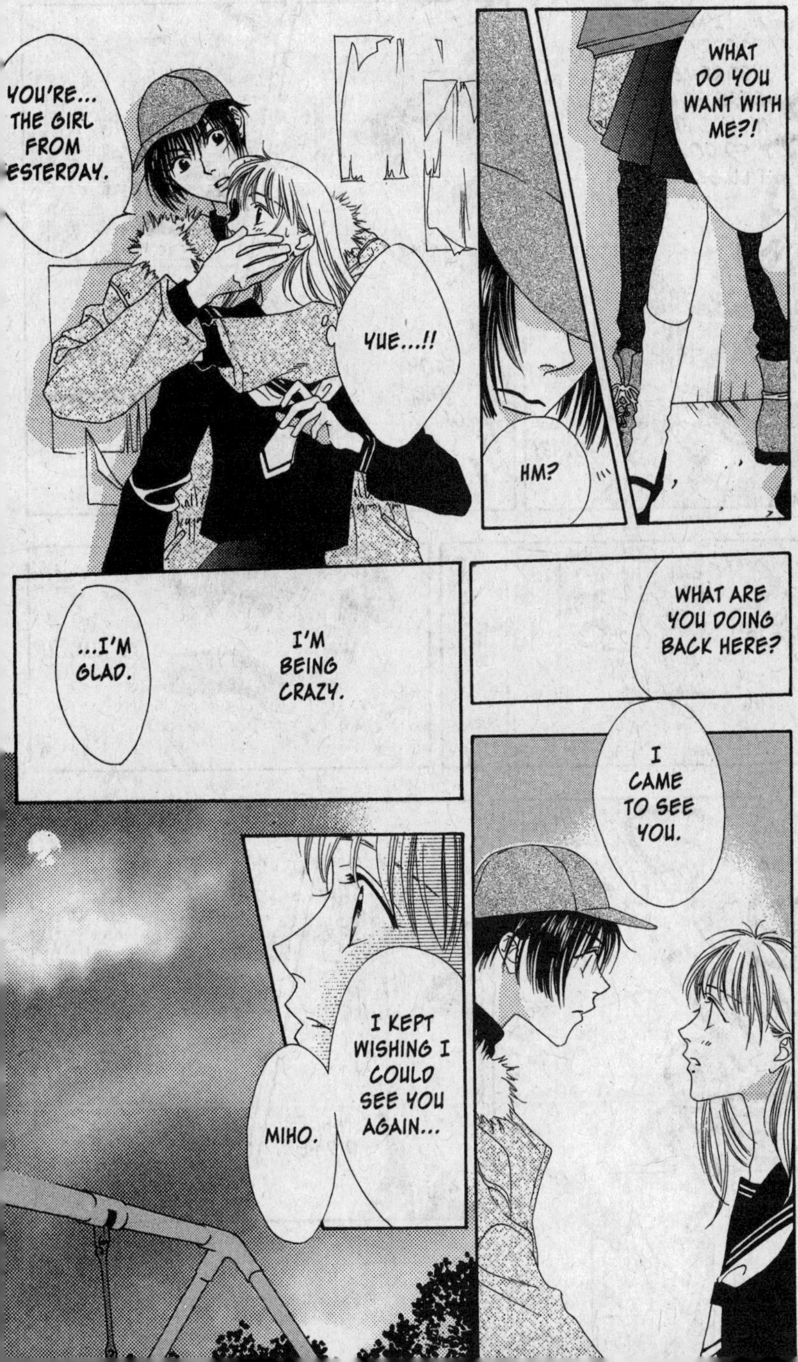
WHAT DO YOU WANT WITH ME?!
HM?
YOU'RE... THE GIRL FROM ESTERDAY.
YUE...!!
WHAT ARE YOU DOING BACK HERE?
I'M BEING CRAZY.
...I'M GLAD.
I CAME TO SEE YOU.
I KEPT WISHING I COULD SEE YOU AGAIN...
MIHO.

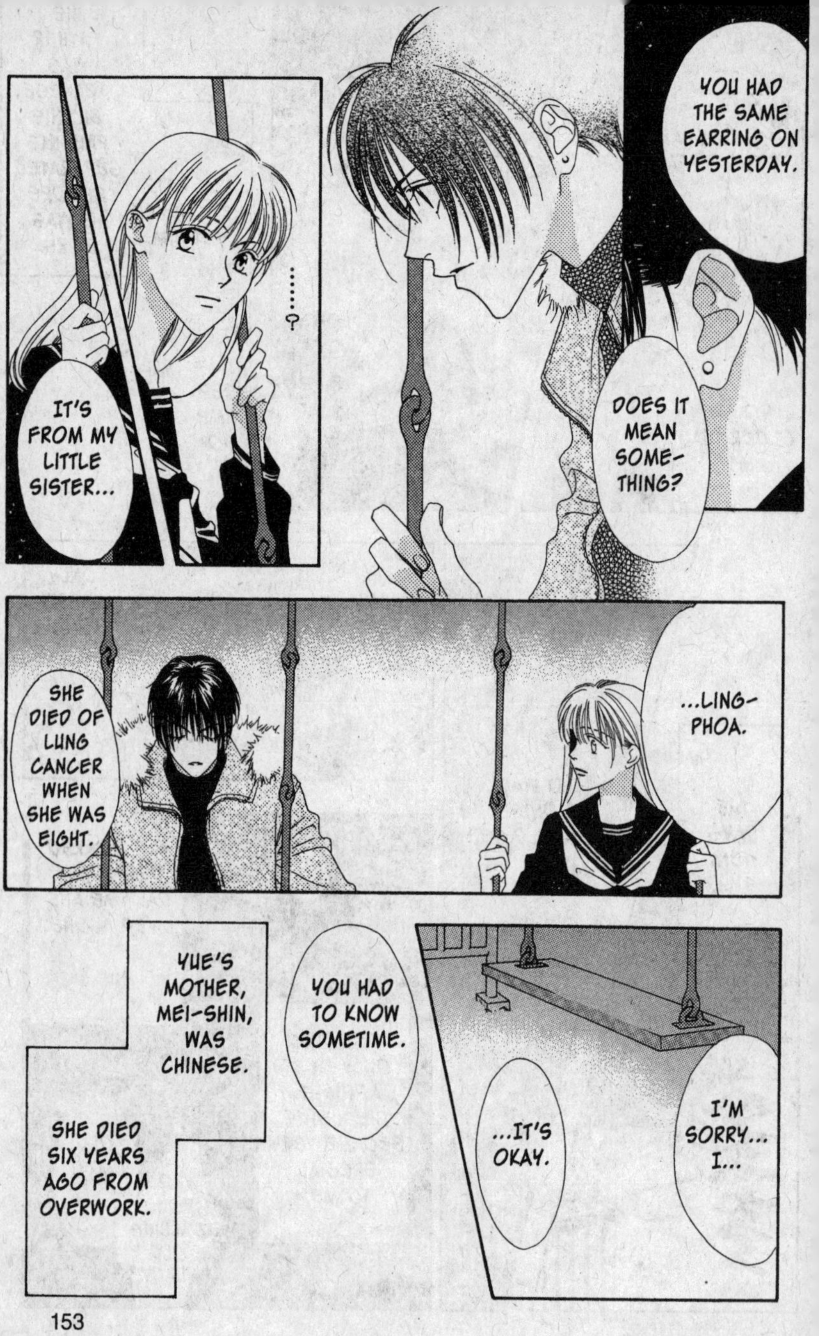
YOU HAD THE SAME EARRING ON YESTERDAY.
DOES IT MEAN SOME-THING?
......?
IT'S FROM MY LITTLE SISTER...
...LING-PHOA.
SHE DIED OF LUNG CANCER WHEN SHE WAS EIGHT.
I'M SORRY... I...
...IT'S OKAY.
YOU HAD TO KNOW SOMETIME.
YUE'S MOTHER, MEI-SHIN, WAS CHINESE.
SHE DIED SIX YEARS AGO FROM OVERWORK.

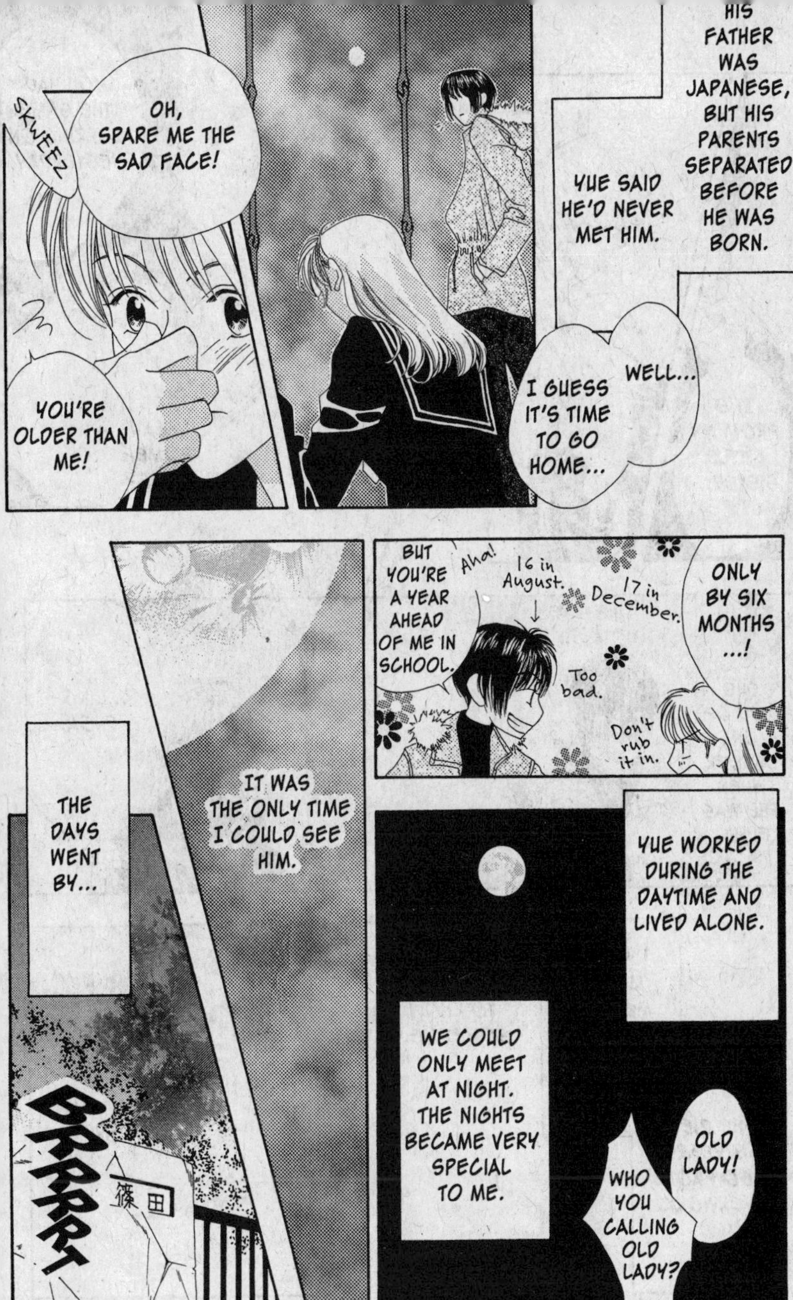
HIS FATHER WAS JAPANESE, BUT HIS PARENTS SEPARATED BEFORE HE WAS BORN.
YUE SAID HE'D NEVER MET HIM.
WELL...
I GUESS IT'S TIME TO GO HOME...
OH, SPARE ME THE SAD FACE!
SKWEEZ
YOU'RE OLDER THAN ME!
ONLY BY SIX MONTHS ...!
17 in December.
16 in August.
Aha!
BUT YOU'RE A YEAR AHEAD OF ME IN SCHOOL.
Too bad.
Don't rub it in.
YUE WORKED DURING THE DAYTIME AND LIVED ALONE.
WE COULD ONLY MEET AT NIGHT. THE NIGHTS BECAME VERY SPECIAL TO ME.
OLD LADY!
WHO YOU CALLING OLD LADY?
IT WAS THE ONLY TIME I COULD SEE HIM.
THE DAYS WENT BY...
BRRRRT
篠田

* Shinoda

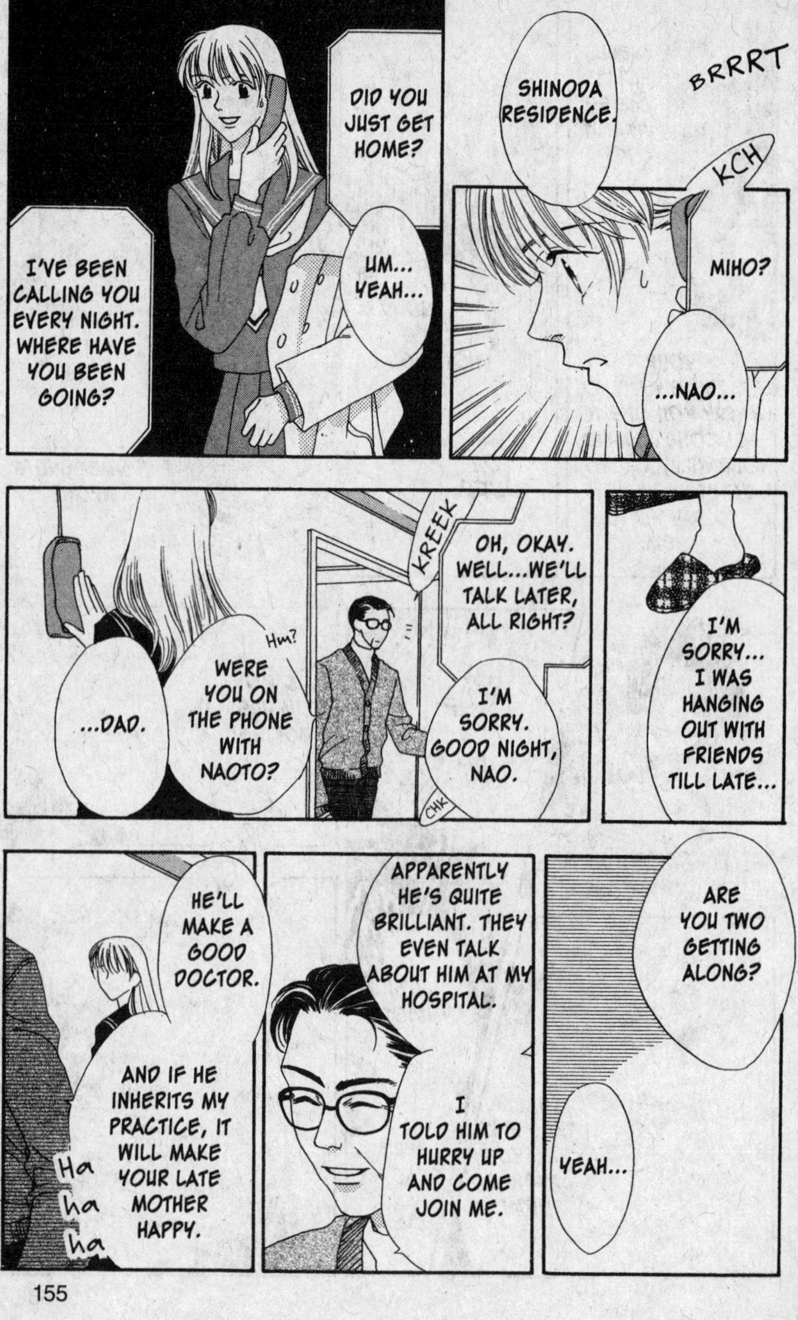
BRRRT
SHINODA RESIDENCE.
KCH
MIHO?
...NAO...
DID YOU JUST GET HOME?
UM... YEAH...
I'VE BEEN CALLING YOU EVERY NIGHT. WHERE HAVE YOU BEEN GOING?
I'M SORRY... I WAS HANGING OUT WITH FRIENDS TILL LATE...
OH, OKAY. WELL...WE'LL TALK LATER, ALL RIGHT?
KREEK
I'M SORRY. GOOD NIGHT, NAO.
CHK
Hm?
WERE YOU ON THE PHONE WITH NAOTO?
...DAD.
ARE YOU TWO GETTING ALONG?
YEAH...
APPARENTLY HE'S QUITE BRILLIANT. THEY EVEN TALK ABOUT HIM AT MY HOSPITAL.
I TOLD HIM TO HURRY UP AND COME JOIN ME.
HE'LL MAKE A GOOD DOCTOR.
AND IF HE INHERITS MY PRACTICE, IT WILL MAKE YOUR LATE MOTHER HAPPY.
Ha ha ha

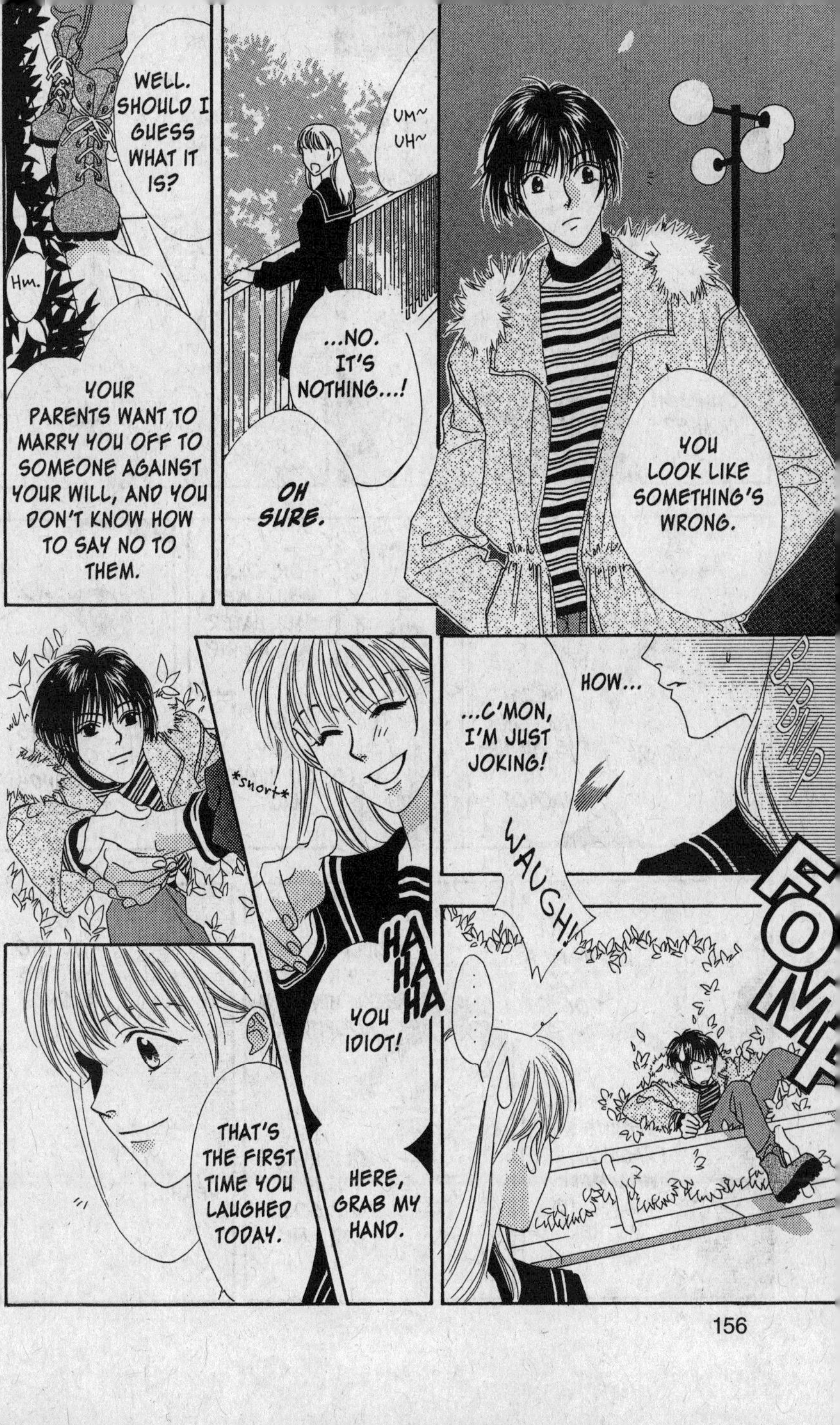
YOU LOOK LIKE SOMETHING'S WRONG.
UM~ UH~
...NO. IT'S NOTHING...!
OH SURE.
WELL. SHOULD I GUESS WHAT IT IS?
Hm.
YOUR PARENTS WANT TO MARRY YOU OFF TO SOMEONE AGAINST YOUR WILL, AND YOU DON'T KNOW HOW TO SAY NO TO THEM.
B-BMP
HOW...
...C'MON, I'M JUST JOKING!
WAUGH!
FOMP
...
snort
HAHAHAHA
YOU IDIOT!
HERE, GRAB MY HAND.
THAT'S THE FIRST TIME YOU LAUGHED TODAY.

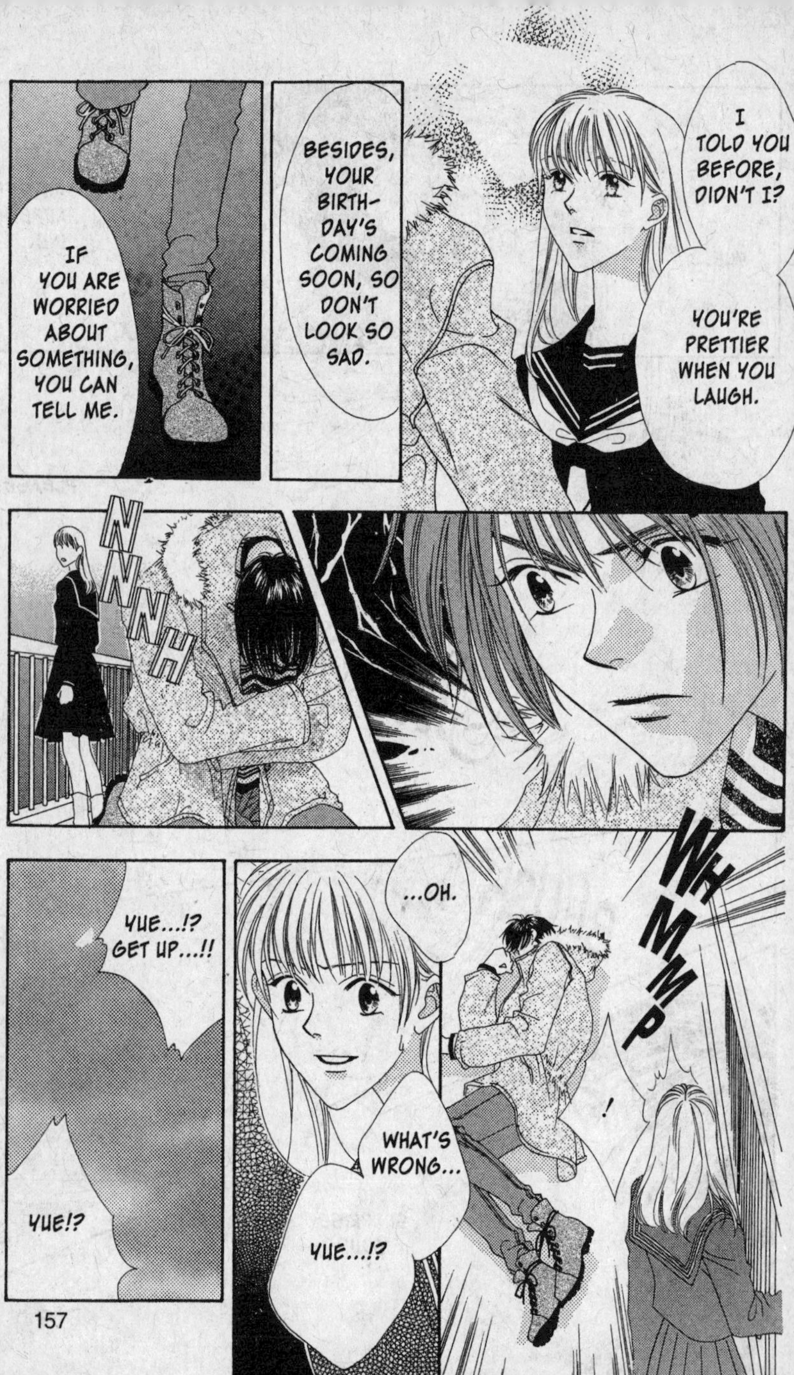
I TOLD YOU BEFORE, DIDN'T I?
YOU'RE PRETTIER WHEN YOU LAUGH.
BESIDES, YOUR BIRTH-DAY'S COMING SOON, SO DON'T LOOK SO SAD.
IF YOU ARE WORRIED ABOUT SOMETHING, YOU CAN TELL ME.
...
NNNNH
WHMMP
!
...OH.
WHAT'S WRONG...
YUE...!?
YUE...!? GET UP...!!
YUE!?

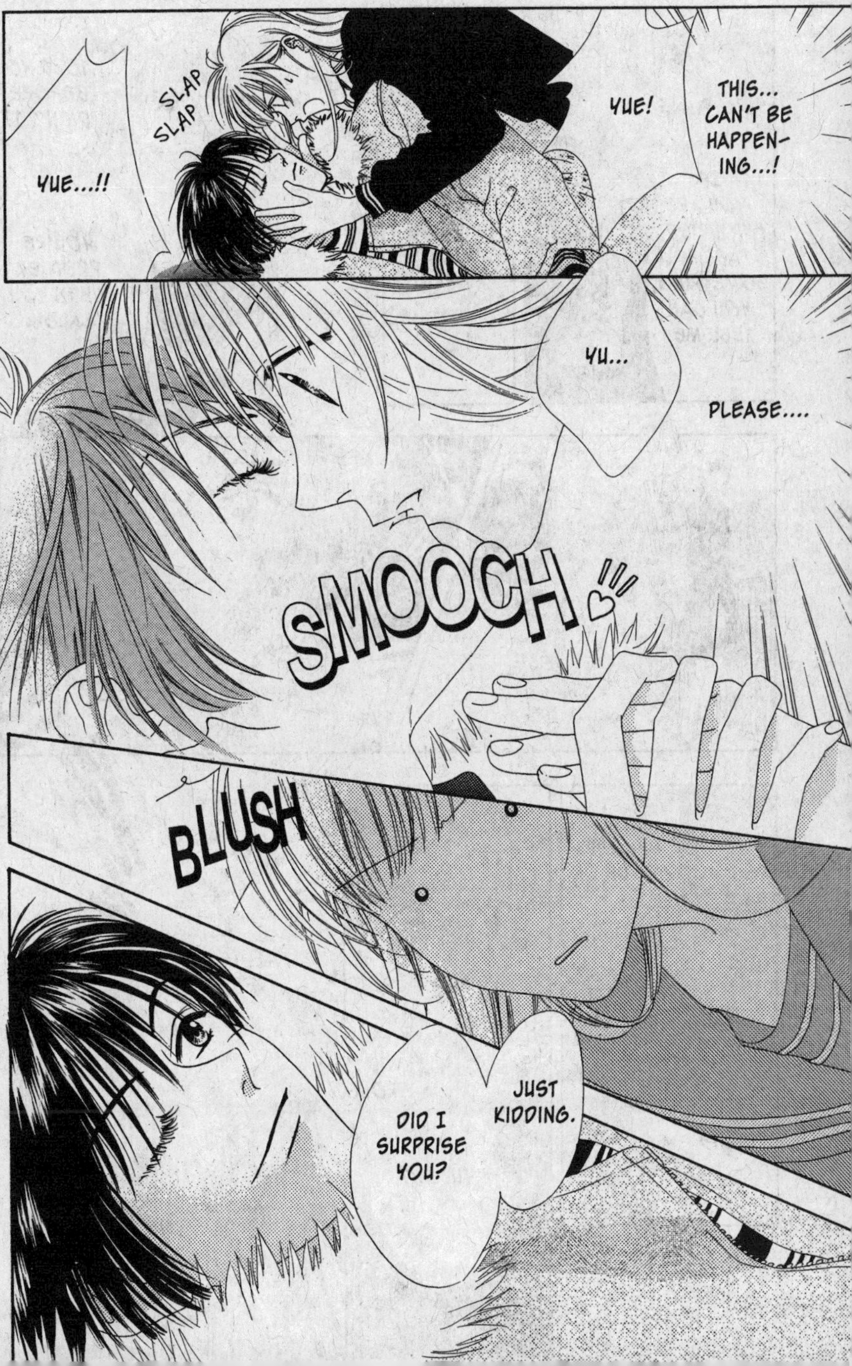
THIS... CAN'T BE HAPPENING...!
YUE!
SLAP SLAP
YUE...!!
YU...
PLEASE....
SMOOCH
BLUSH
JUST KIDDING.
DID I SURPRISE YOU?

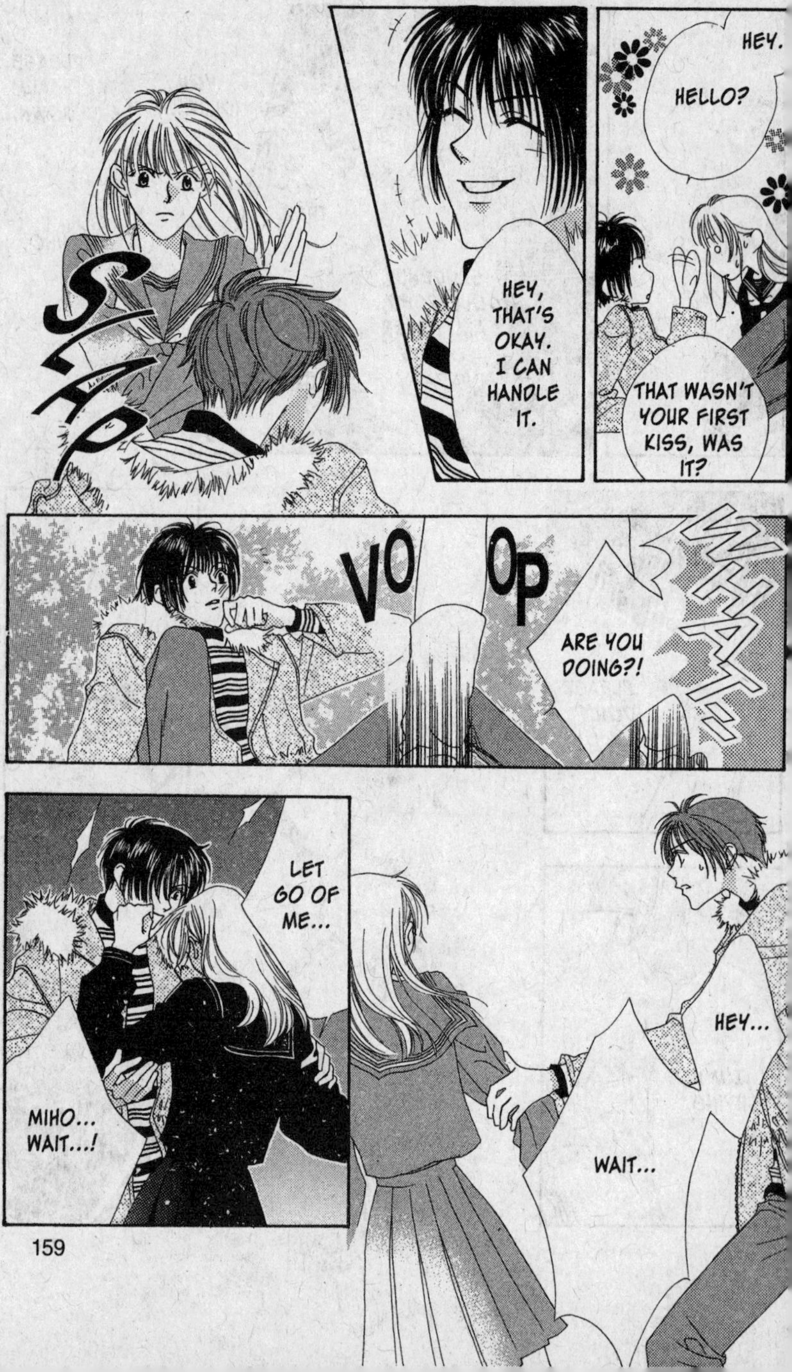
HEY.
HELLO?
THAT WASN'T YOUR FIRST KISS, WAS IT?
HEY, THAT'S OKAY. I CAN HANDLE IT.
SLAP
WHAT!!
ARE YOU DOING?!
VO OP
HEY...
WAIT...
LET GO OF ME...
MIHO... WAIT...!

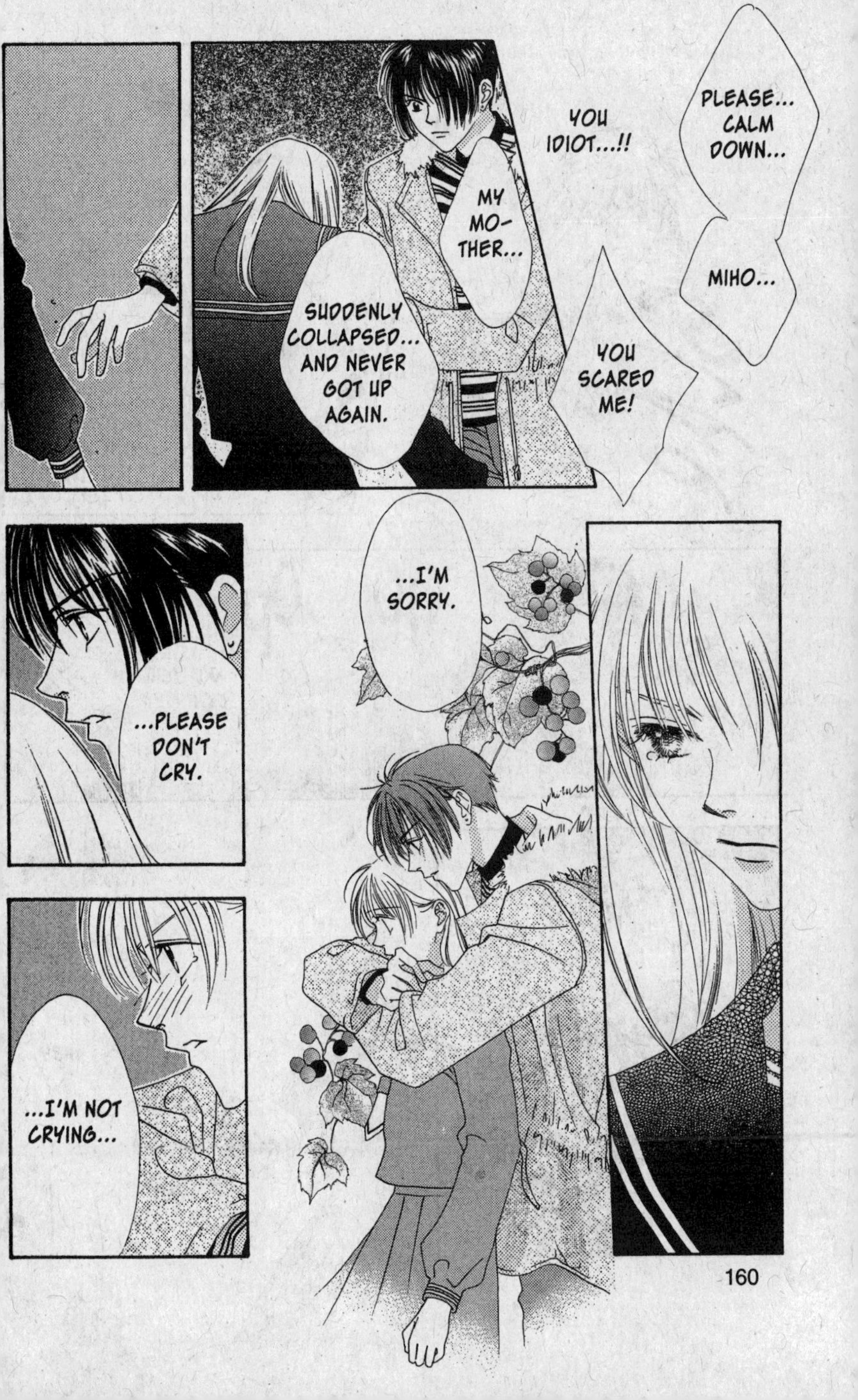
PLEASE... CALM DOWN...
MIHO...
YOU IDIOT...!!
YOU SCARED ME!
MY MO-THER...
SUDDENLY COLLAPSED... AND NEVER GOT UP AGAIN.
...I'M SORRY.
...PLEASE DON'T CRY.
...I'M NOT CRYING...

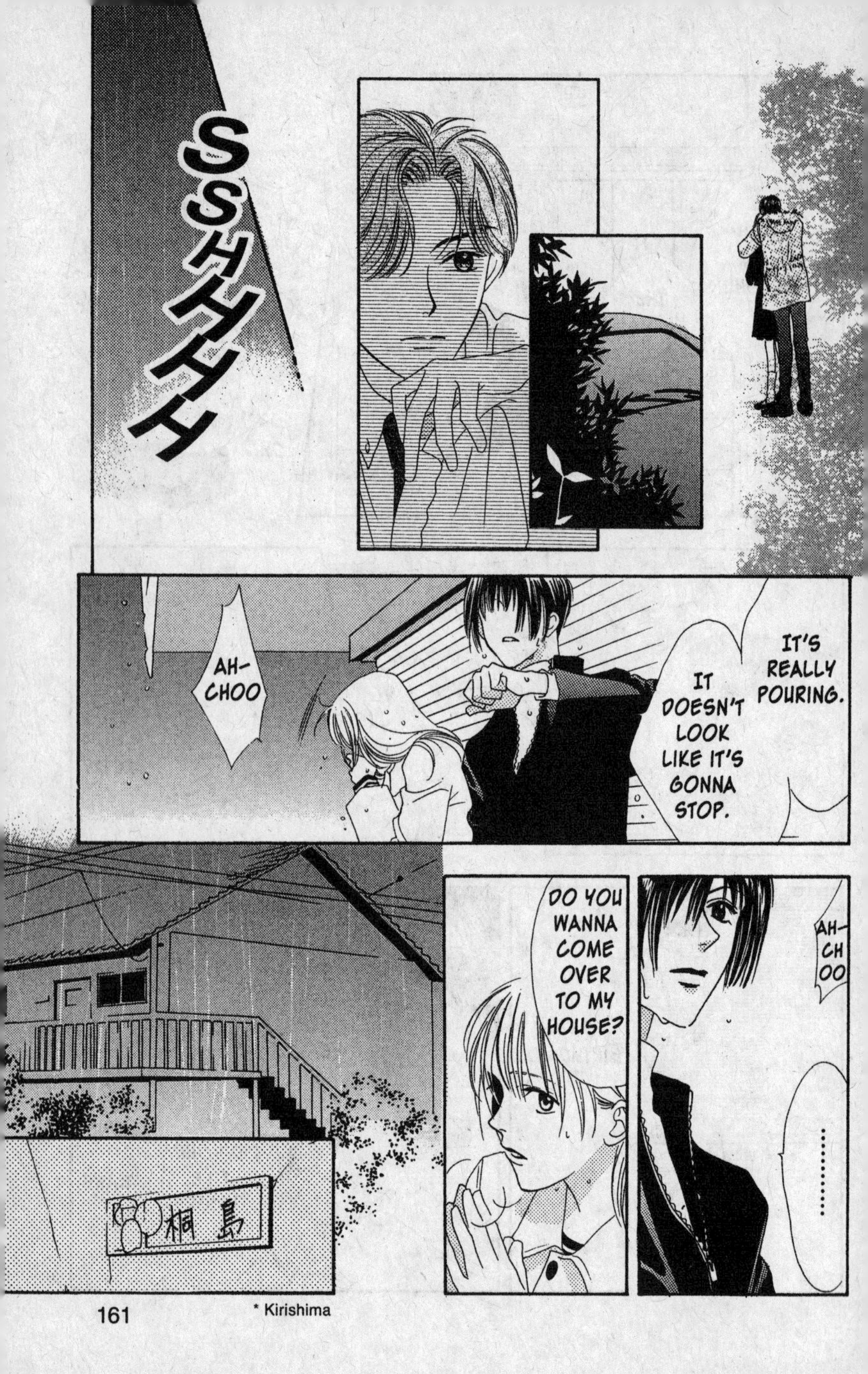
SSHHHH
IT'S REALLY POURING.
IT DOESN'T LOOK LIKE IT'S GONNA STOP.
AH-CHOO
AH-CHOO
......
DO YOU WANNA COME OVER TO MY HOUSE?
桐島

* Kirishima

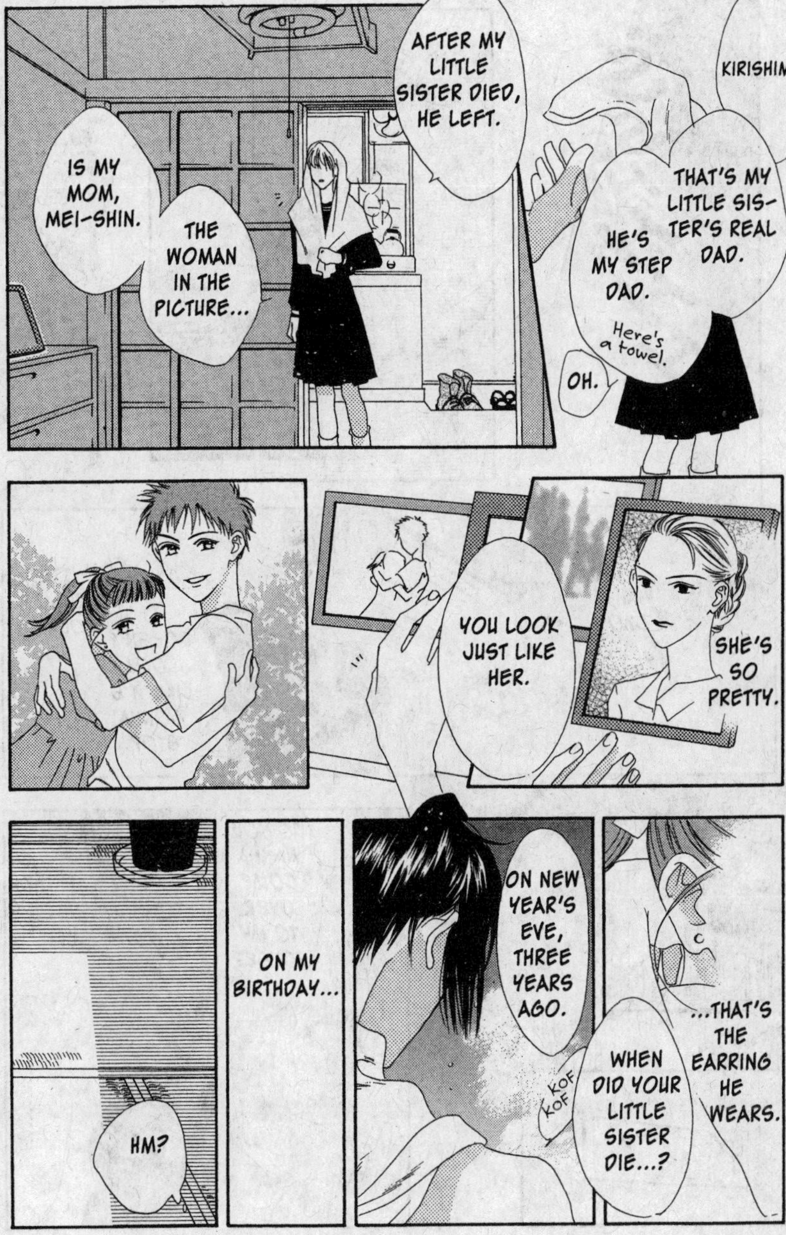
KIRISHIMA?
THAT'S MY LITTLE SISTER'S REAL DAD.
HE'S MY STEP DAD.
Here's a towel.
OH.
AFTER MY LITTLE SISTER DIED, HE LEFT.
THE WOMAN IN THE PICTURE...
IS MY MOM, MEI-SHIN.
SHE'S SO PRETTY.
YOU LOOK JUST LIKE HER.
...THAT'S THE EARRING HE WEARS.
WHEN DID YOUR LITTLE SISTER DIE...?
ON NEW YEAR'S EVE, THREE YEARS AGO.
KOF KOF
ON MY BIRTHDAY...
HM?

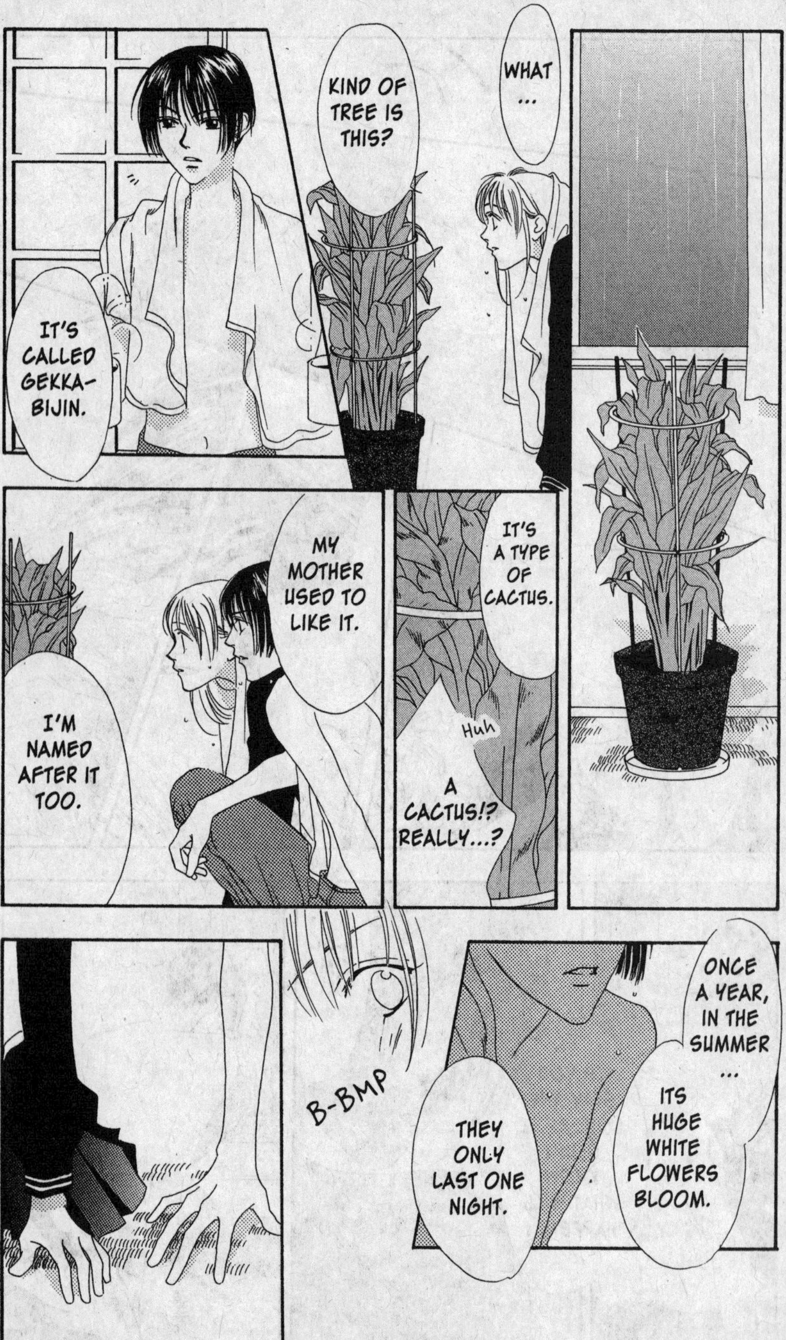
WHAT ...
KIND OF TREE IS THIS?
IT'S CALLED GEKKA-BIJIN.
IT'S A TYPE OF CACTUS.
Huh
A CACTUS!? REALLY...?
MY MOTHER USED TO LIKE IT.
I'M NAMED AFTER IT TOO.
ONCE A YEAR, IN THE SUMMER ...
ITS HUGE WHITE FLOWERS BLOOM.
THEY ONLY LAST ONE NIGHT.
B-BMP

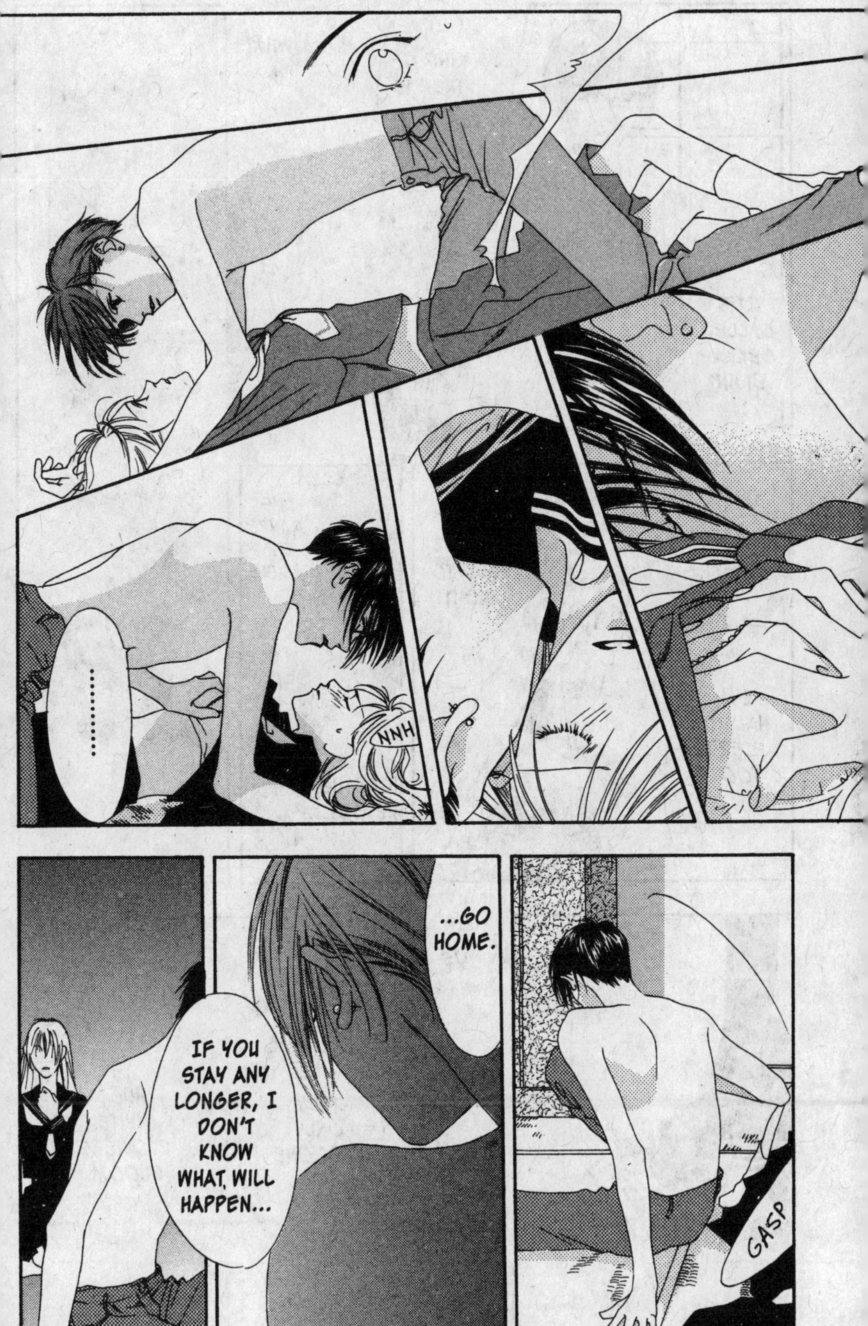
NNH
......
GASP
...GO HOME.
IF YOU STAY ANY LONGER, I DON'T KNOW WHAT WILL HAPPEN...

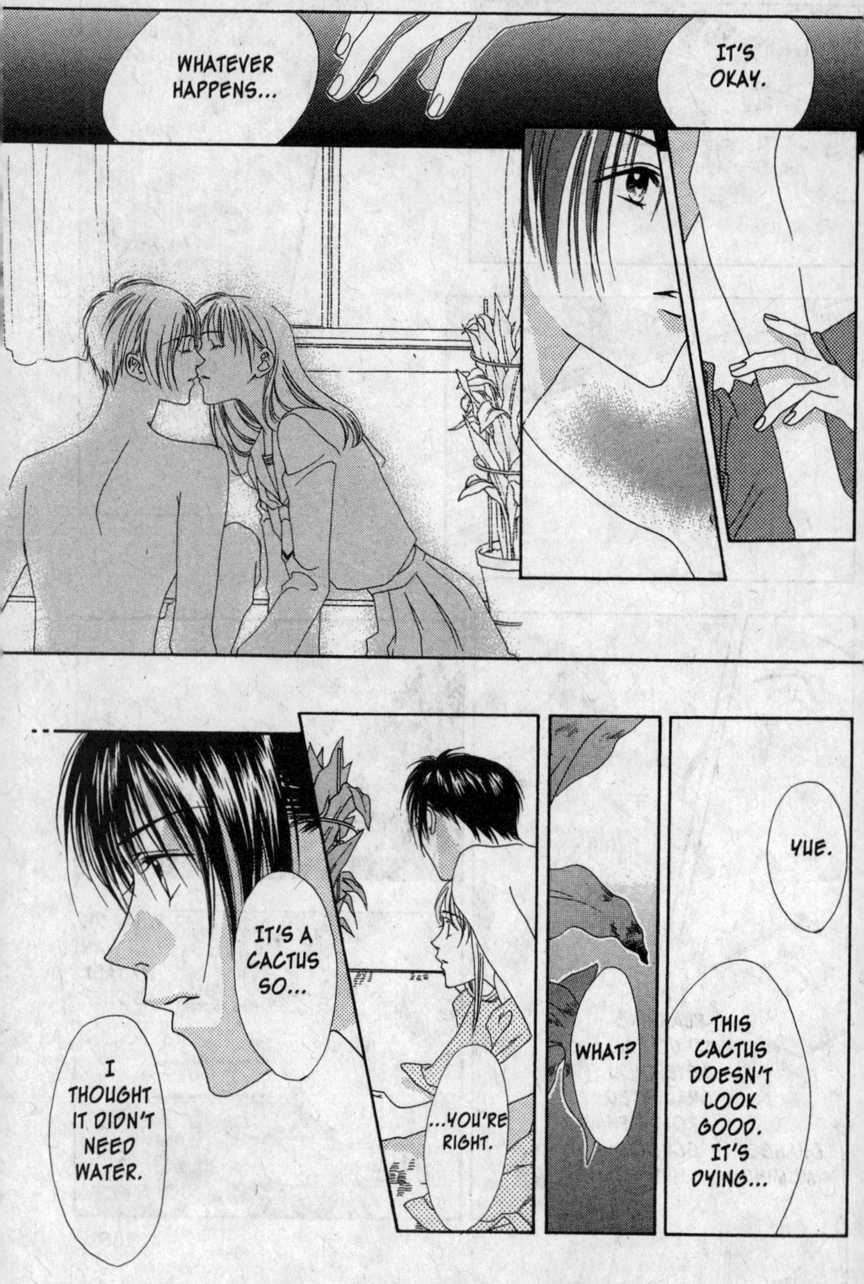
IT'S OKAY.
WHATEVER HAPPENS...
YUE.
THIS CACTUS DOESN'T LOOK GOOD. IT'S DYING...
WHAT?
...YOU'RE RIGHT.
IT'S A CACTUS SO...
I THOUGHT IT DIDN'T NEED WATER.

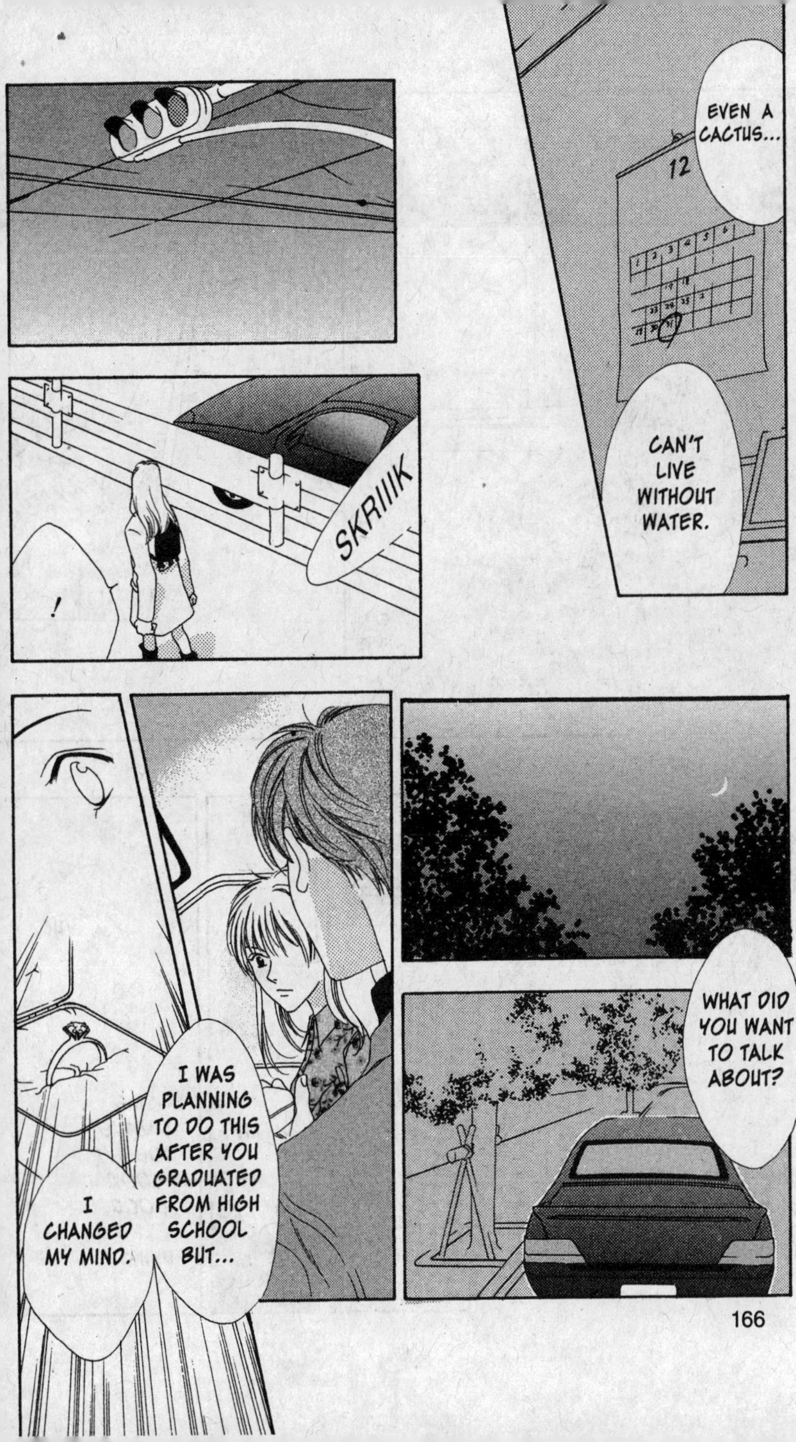

EVEN A CACTUS...
CAN'T LIVE WITHOUT WATER.
SKRIIIK
!
WHAT DID YOU WANT TO TALK ABOUT?
I WAS PLANNING TO DO THIS AFTER YOU GRADUATED FROM HIGH SCHOOL BUT...
I CHANGED MY MIND.

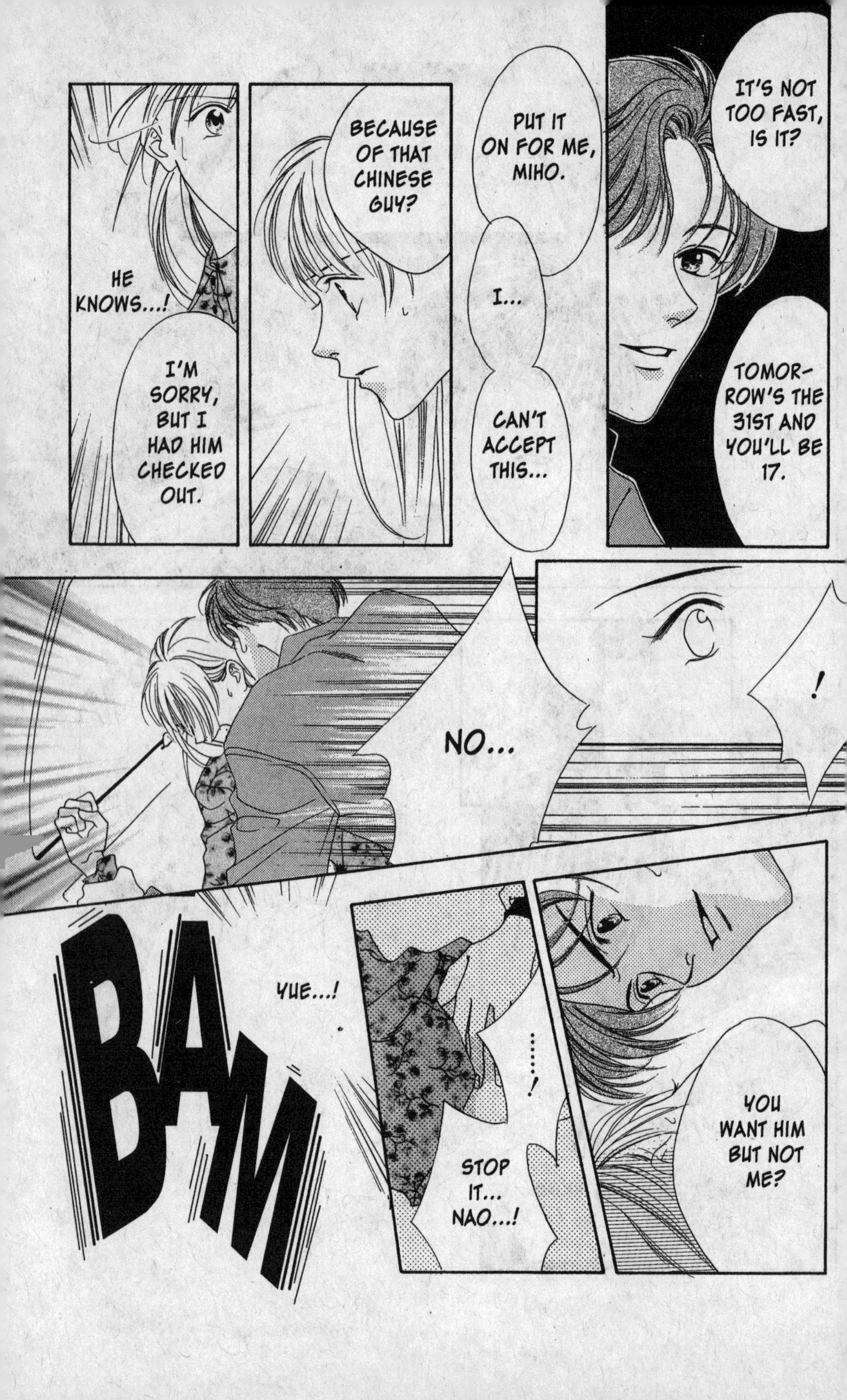
IT'S NOT TOO FAST, IS IT?
TOMORROW'S THE 31ST AND YOU'LL BE 17.
PUT IT ON FOR ME, MIHO.
I...
CAN'T ACCEPT THIS...
BECAUSE OF THAT CHINESE GUY?
HE KNOWS...!
I'M SORRY, BUT I HAD HIM CHECKED OUT.
!
NO...
YOU WANT HIM BUT NOT ME?
.....!
STOP IT... NAO...!
YUE...!
BAM

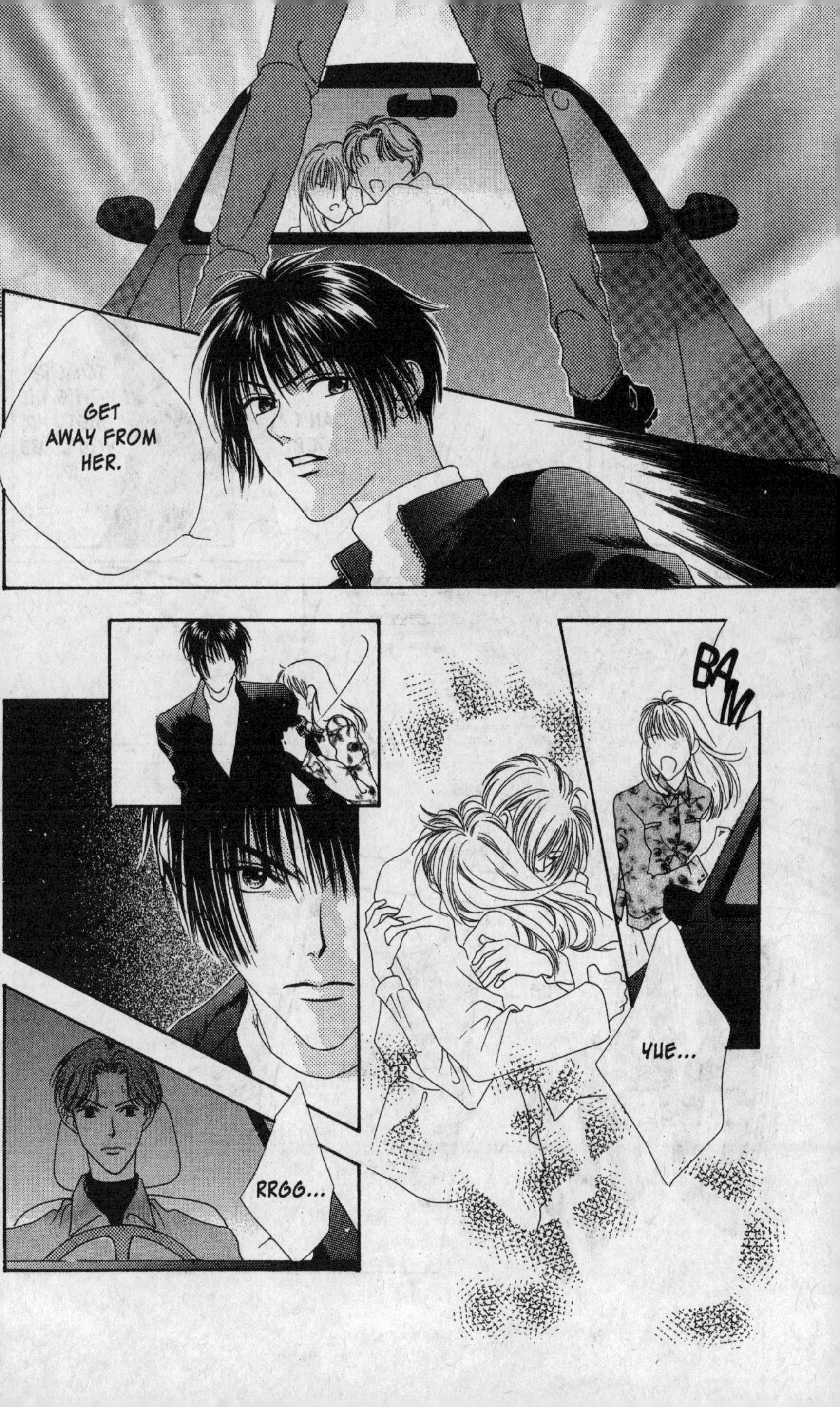
GET AWAY FROM HER.
BAM
YUE...
RRGG...

* Kirishima

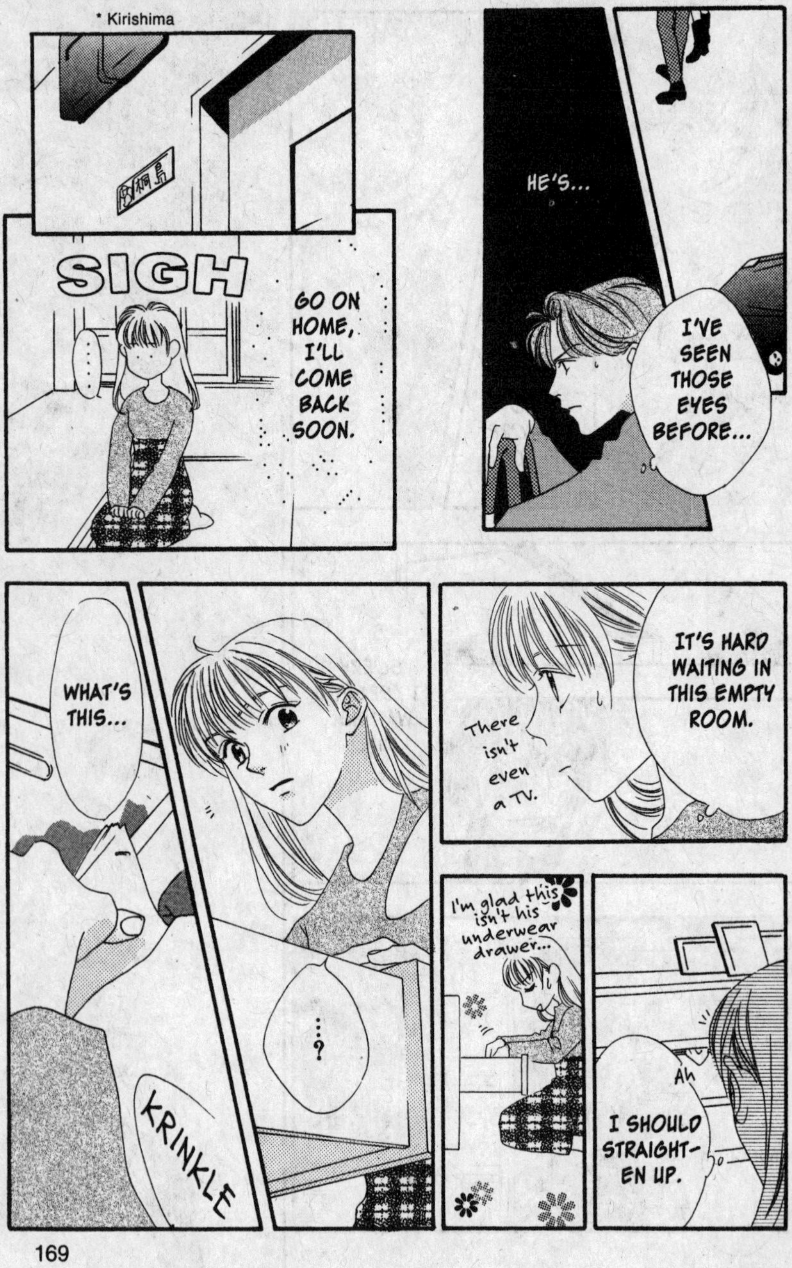
HE'S...
I'VE SEEN THOSE EYES BEFORE...
SIGH
...
GO ON HOME, I'LL COME BACK SOON.
IT'S HARD WAITING IN THIS EMPTY ROOM.
There isn't even a TV.
Ah
I SHOULD STRAIGHT-EN UP.
I'm glad this isn't his underwear drawer...
...?
WHAT'S THIS...
KRINKLE

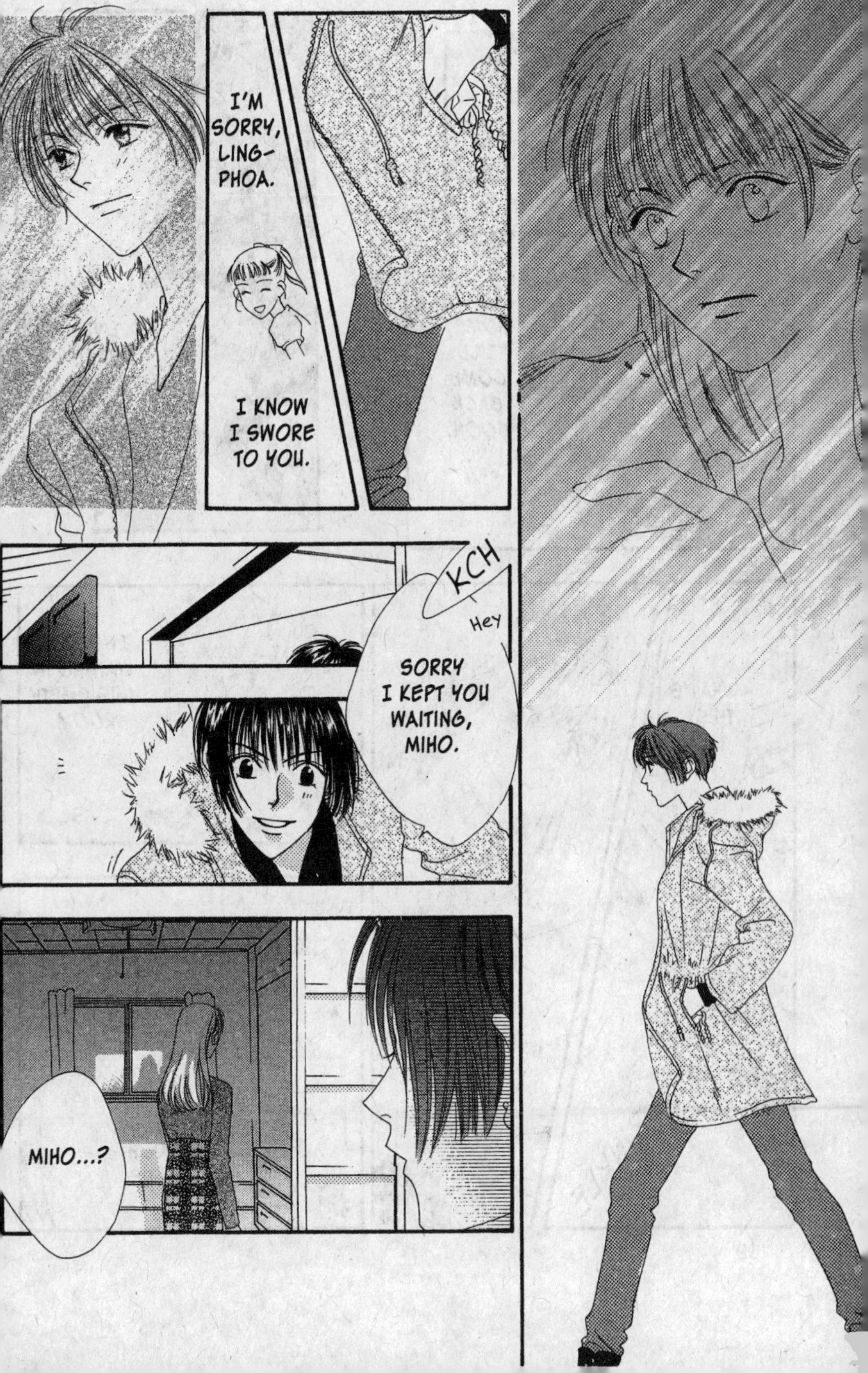
I'M SORRY, LING-PHOA.
I KNOW I SWORE TO YOU.
KCH
Hey
SORRY I KEPT YOU WAITING, MIHO.
MIHO...?

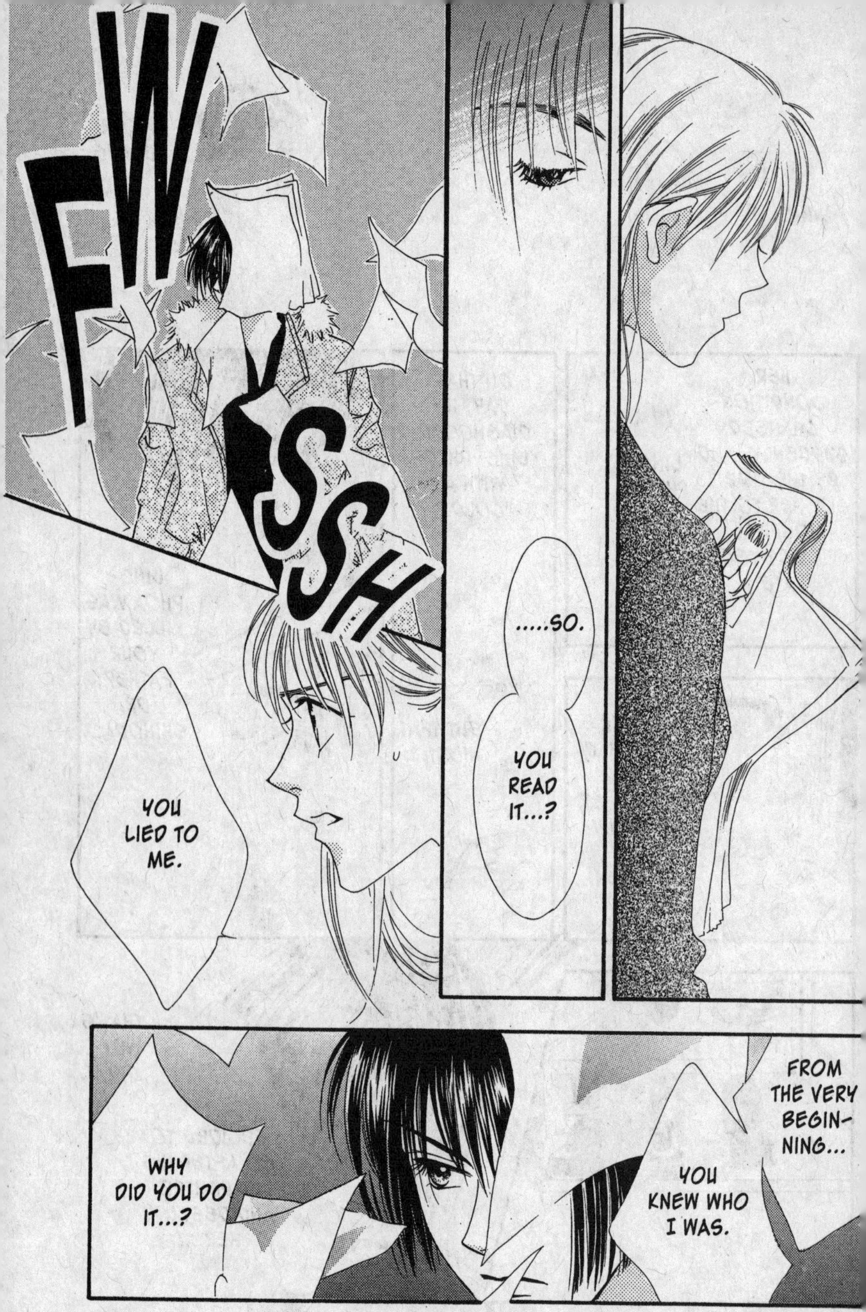
.....SO.
YOU READ IT...?
FWSSH
YOU LIED TO ME.
FROM THE VERY BEGIN-NING...
YOU KNEW WHO I WAS.
WHY DID YOU DO IT...?

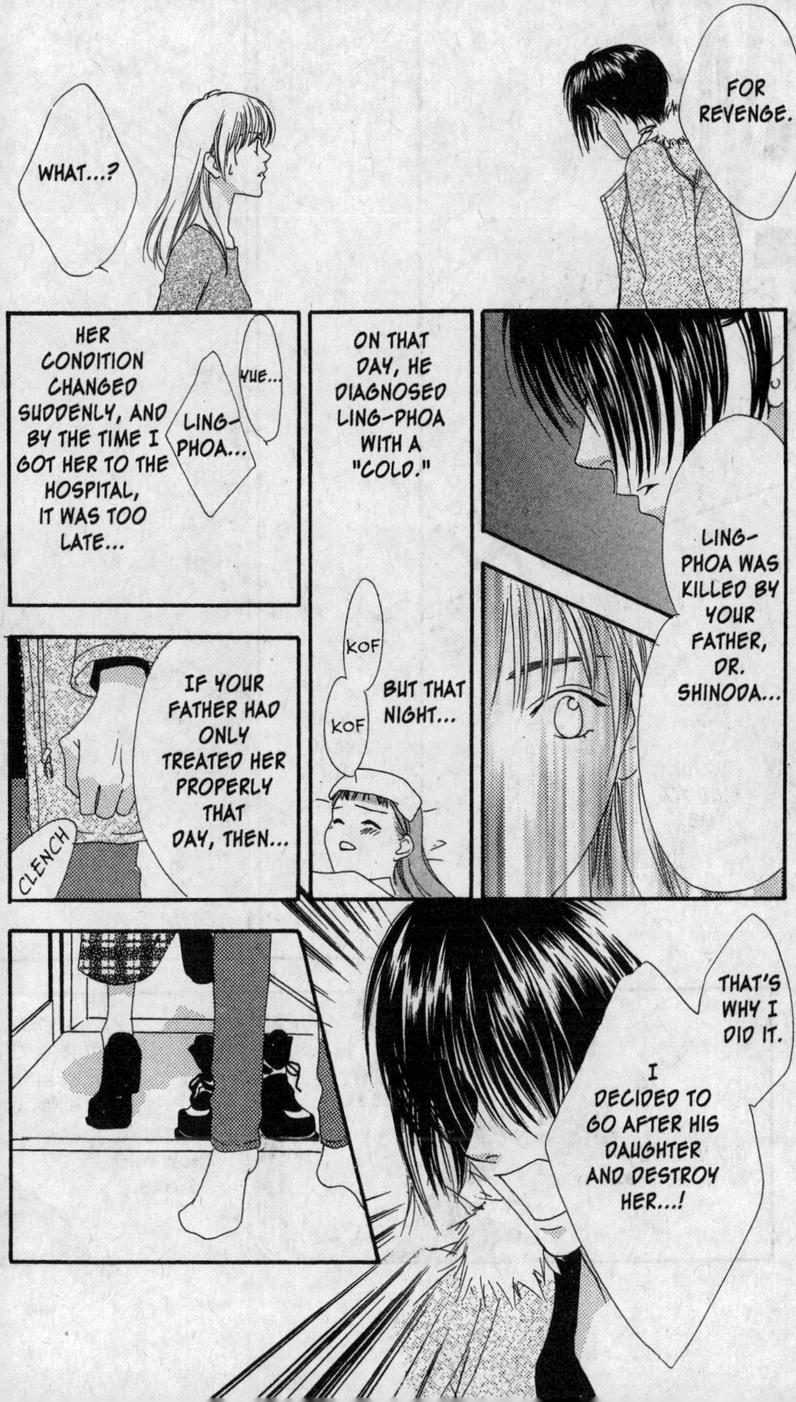
FOR REVENGE.
WHAT...?
LING-PHOA WAS KILLED BY YOUR FATHER, DR. SHINODA...
ON THAT DAY, HE DIAGNOSED LING-PHOA WITH A "COLD."
BUT THAT NIGHT...
KOF
KOF
YUE...
LING-PHOA...
HER CONDITION CHANGED SUDDENLY, AND BY THE TIME I GOT HER TO THE HOSPITAL, IT WAS TOO LATE...
IF YOUR FATHER HAD ONLY TREATED HER PROPERLY THAT DAY, THEN...
CLENCH
THAT'S WHY I DID IT.
I DECIDED TO GO AFTER HIS DAUGHTER AND DESTROY HER...!

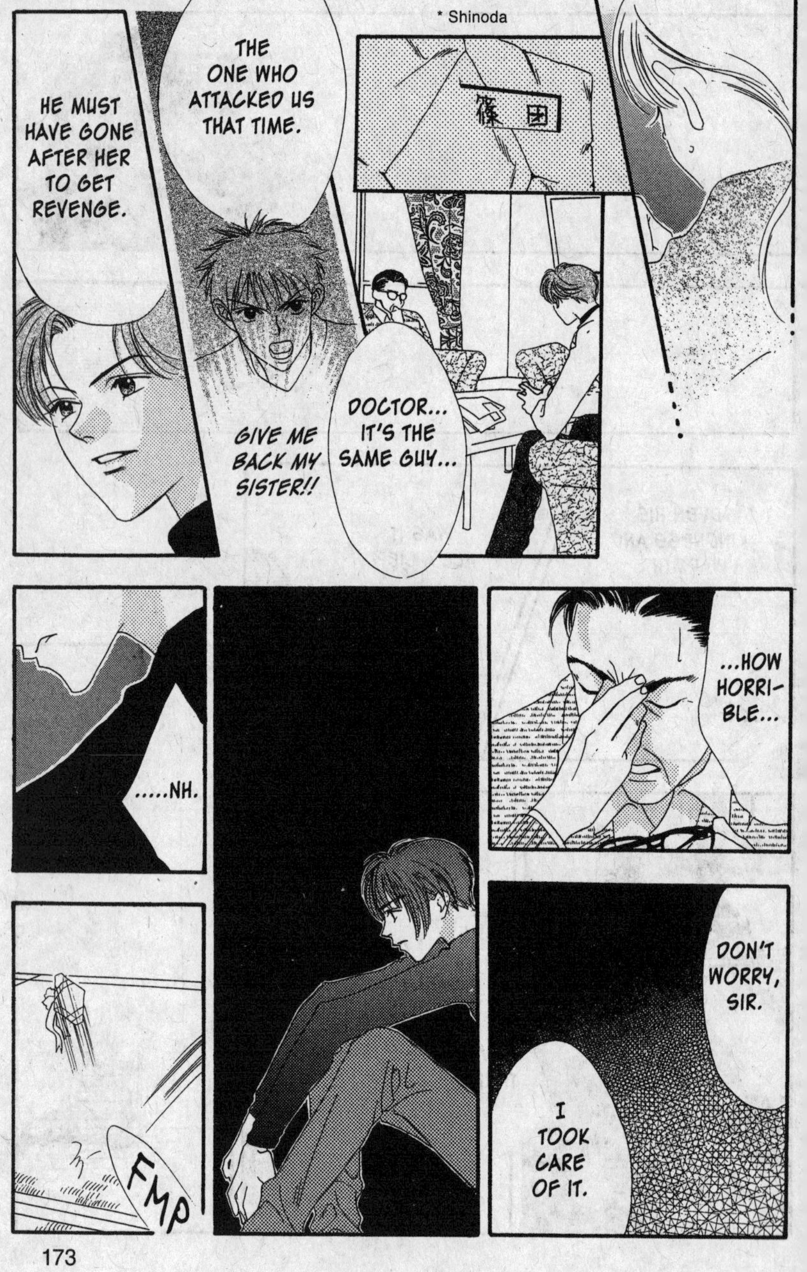
* Shinoda
DOCTOR... IT'S THE SAME GUY...
THE ONE WHO ATTACKED US THAT TIME.
GIVE ME BACK MY SISTER!!
HE MUST HAVE GONE AFTER HER TO GET REVENGE.
...HOW HORRIBLE...
DON'T WORRY, SIR.
I TOOK CARE OF IT.
.....NH.
FMP

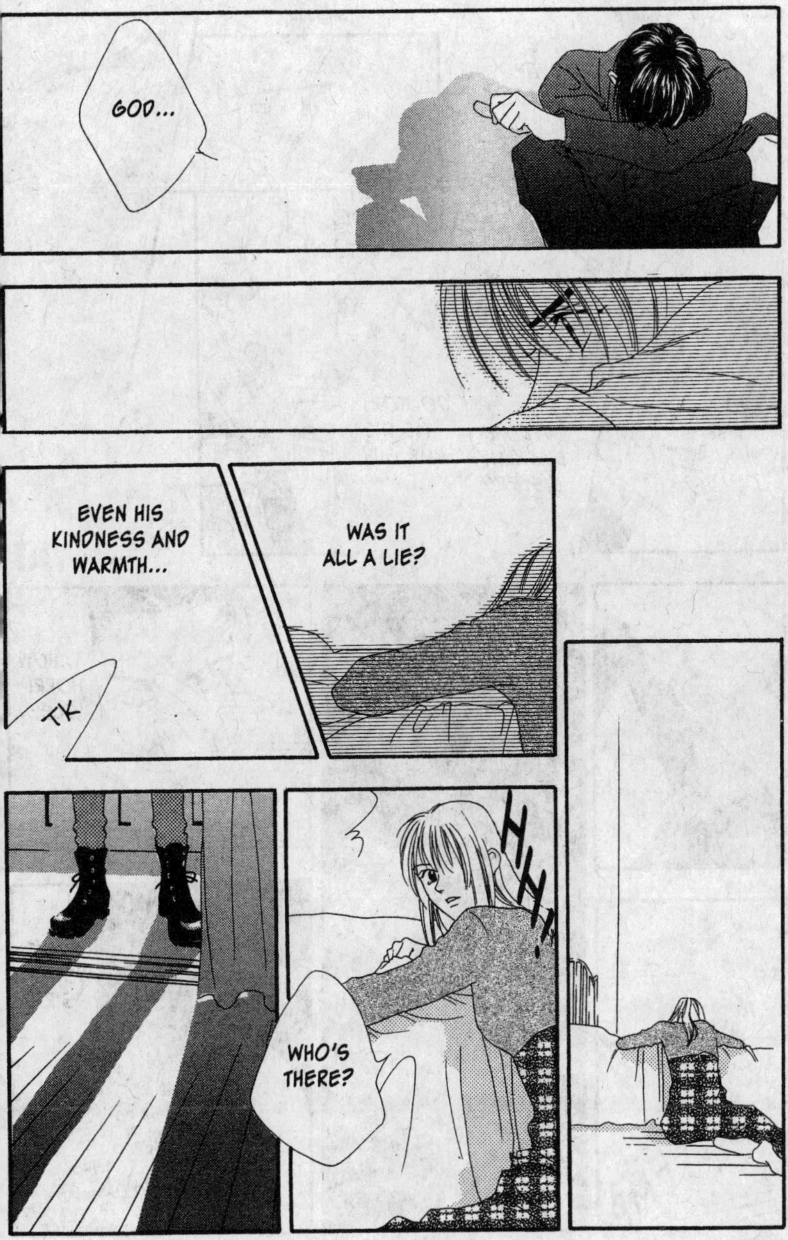
GOD...
WAS IT ALL A LIE?
EVEN HIS KINDNESS AND WARMTH...
TK
WHO'S THERE?

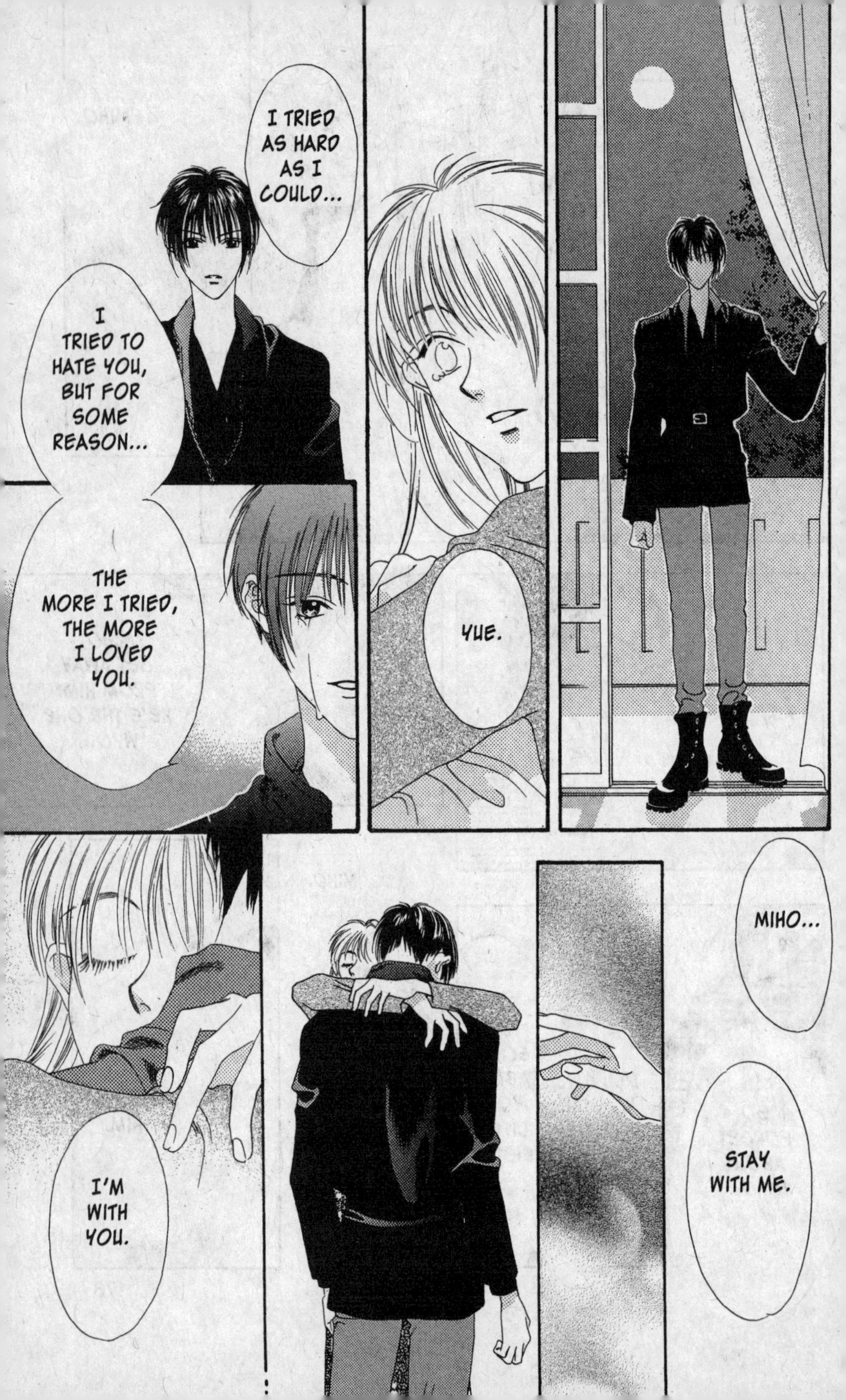
YUE.
I TRIED AS HARD AS I COULD...
I TRIED TO HATE YOU, BUT FOR SOME REASON...
THE MORE I TRIED, THE MORE I LOVED YOU.
MIHO...
STAY WITH ME.
I'M WITH YOU.

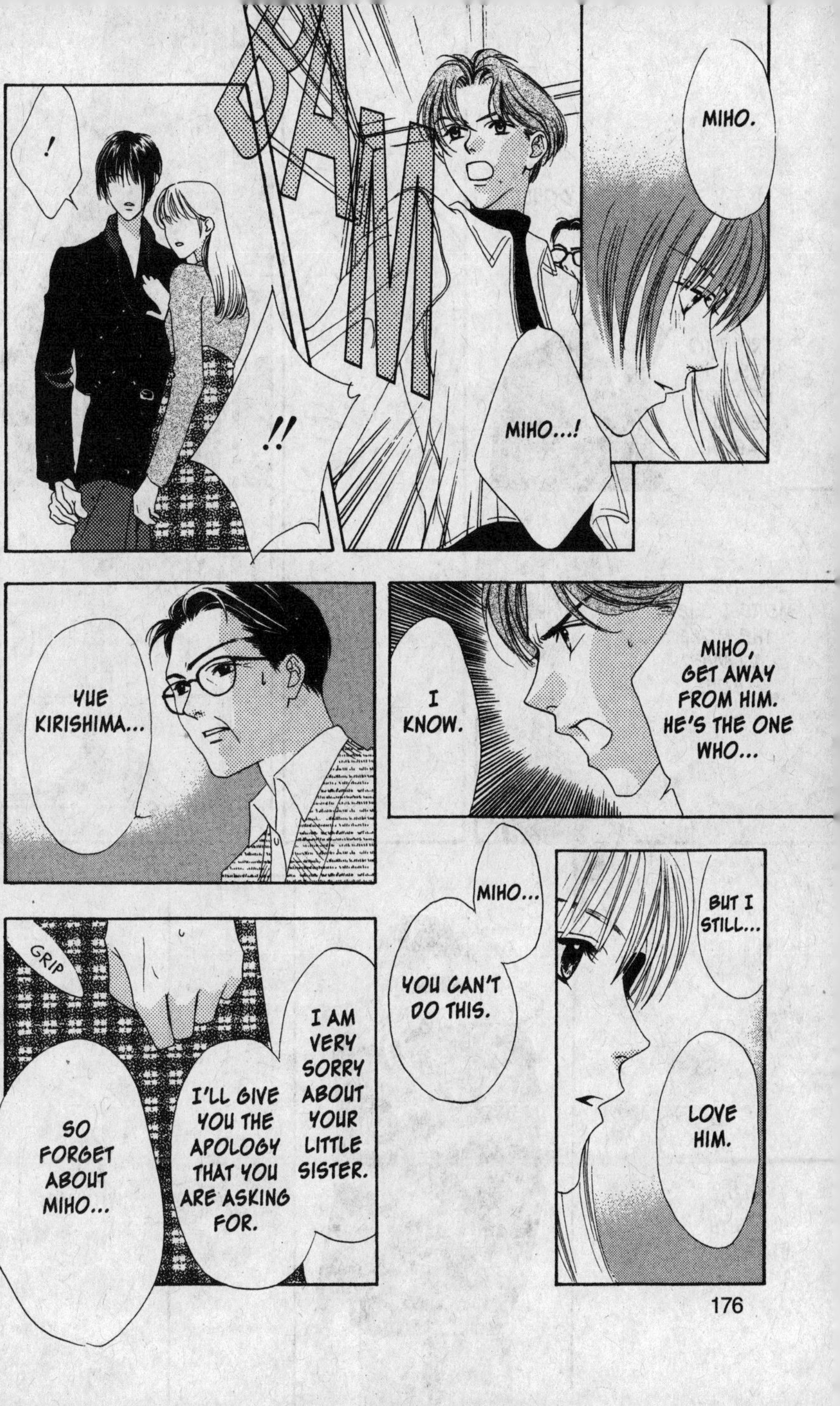
MIHO.
BAM
MIHO...!
!!
!
MIHO, GET AWAY FROM HIM. HE'S THE ONE WHO...
I KNOW.
YUE KIRISHIMA...
BUT I STILL...
LOVE HIM.
MIHO...
YOU CAN'T DO THIS.
I AM VERY SORRY ABOUT YOUR LITTLE SISTER.
I'LL GIVE YOU THE APOLOGY THAT YOU ARE ASKING FOR.
SO FORGET ABOUT MIHO...
GRIP

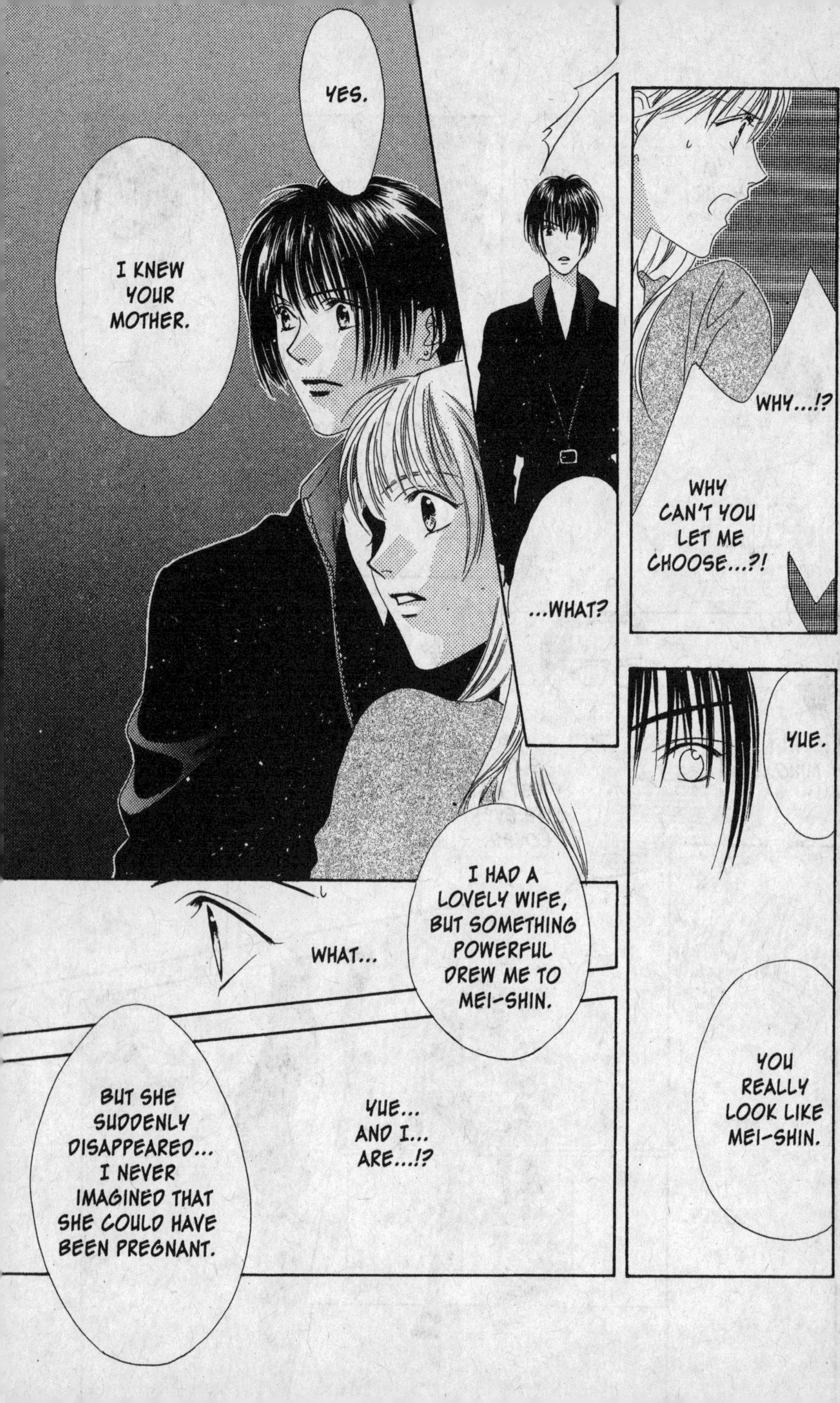
WHY...!?
WHY CAN'T YOU LET ME CHOOSE...?!
YUE.
YOU REALLY LOOK LIKE MEI-SHIN.
...WHAT?
YES.
I KNEW YOUR MOTHER.
I HAD A LOVELY WIFE, BUT SOMETHING POWERFUL DREW ME TO MEI-SHIN.
WHAT...
BUT SHE SUDDENLY DISAPPEARED... I NEVER IMAGINED THAT SHE COULD HAVE BEEN PREGNANT.
YUE... AND I... ARE...!?

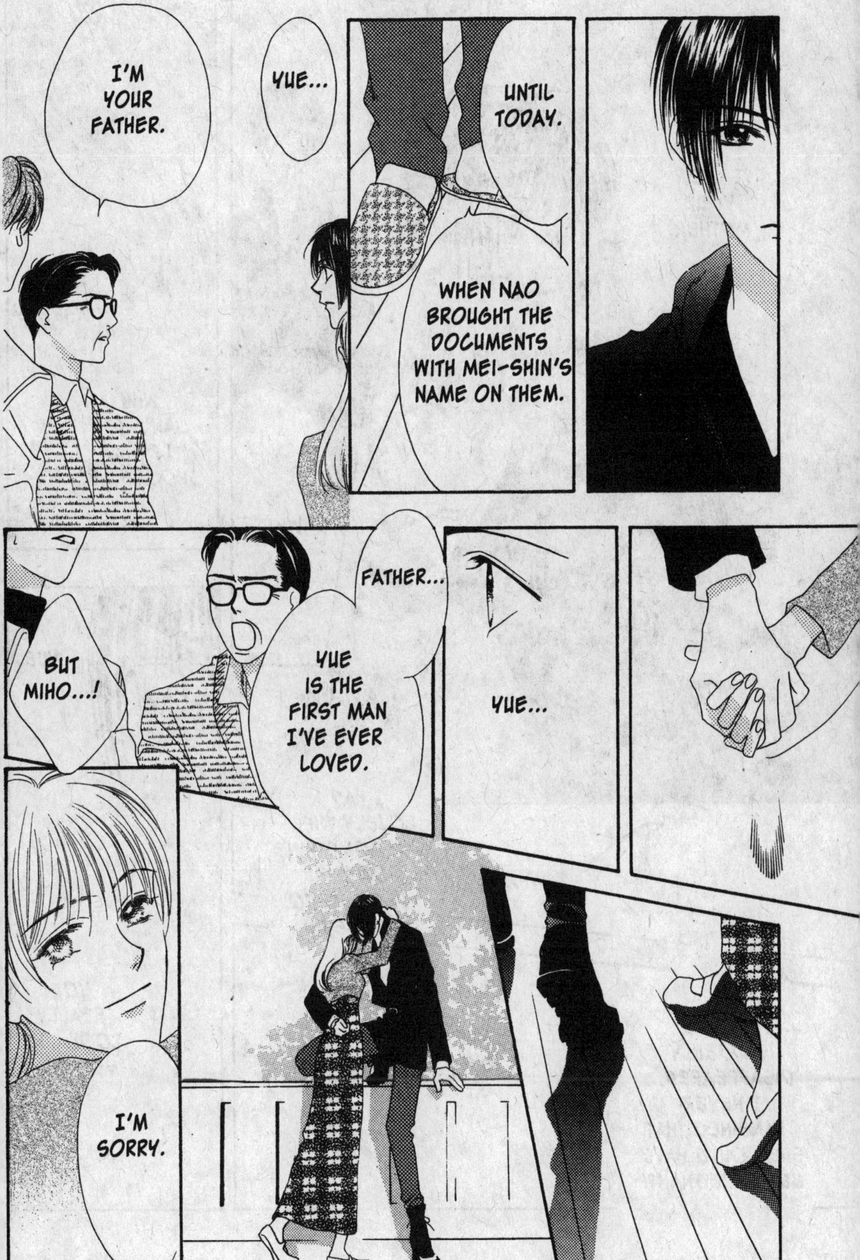
UNTIL TODAY.
WHEN NAO BROUGHT THE DOCUMENTS WITH MEI-SHIN'S NAME ON THEM.
YUE...
I'M YOUR FATHER.
YUE...
FATHER...
YUE IS THE FIRST MAN I'VE EVER LOVED.
BUT MIHO...!
I'M SORRY.

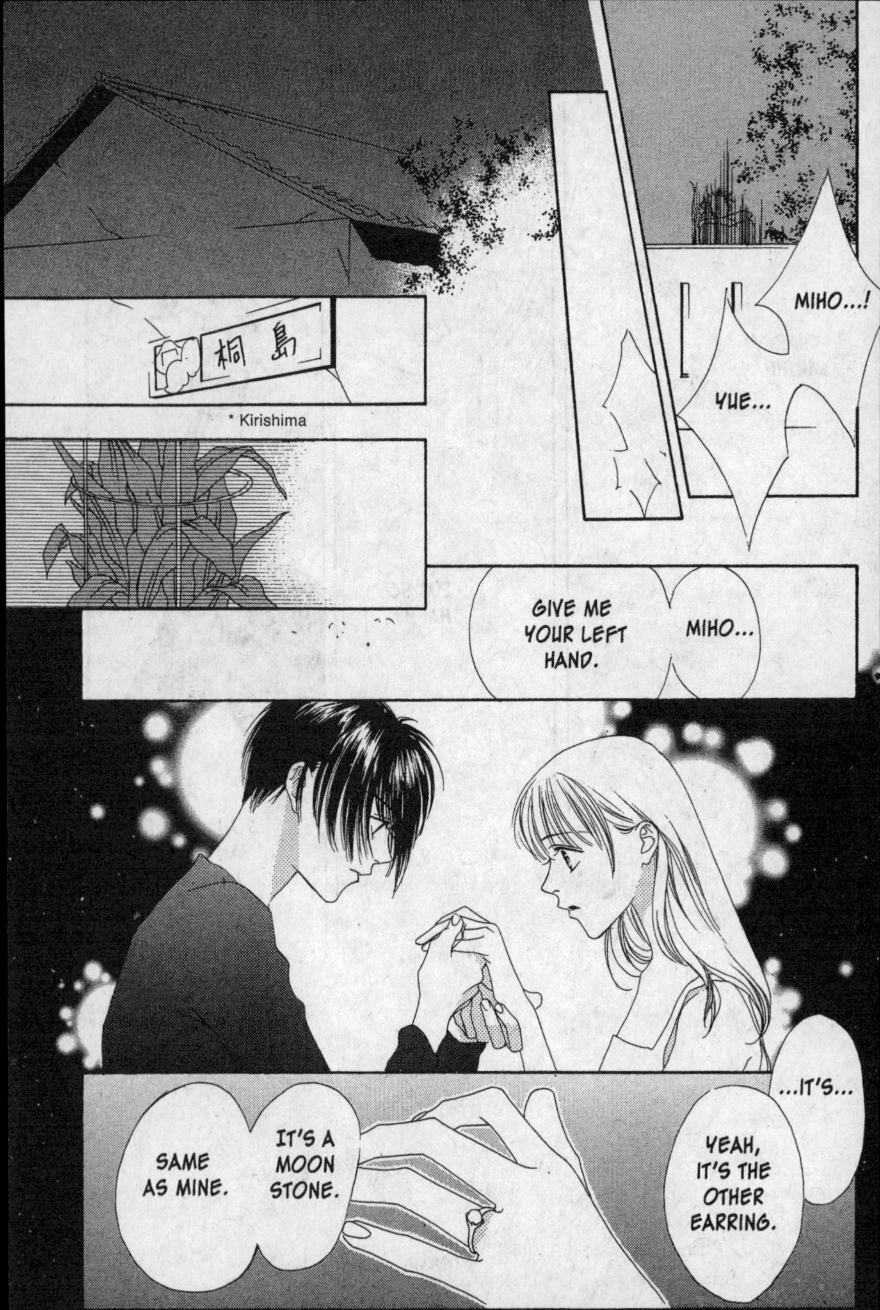
MIHO...!
YUE...
桐島
* Kirishima
MIHO...
GIVE ME YOUR LEFT HAND.
...IT'S...
YEAH, IT'S THE OTHER EARRING.
IT'S A MOON STONE.
SAME AS MINE.

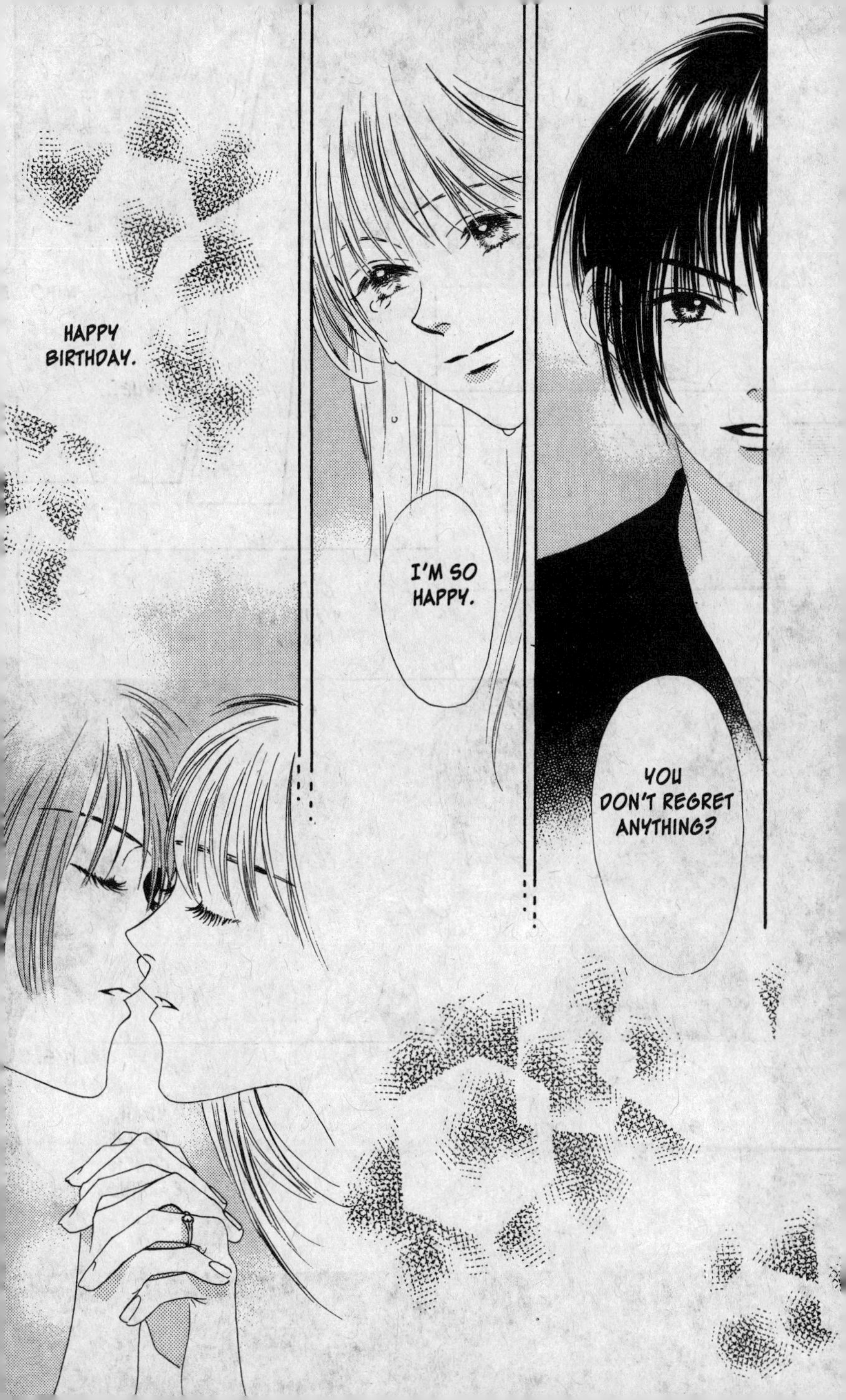
YOU DON'T REGRET ANYTHING?
I'M SO HAPPY.
HAPPY BIRTHDAY.

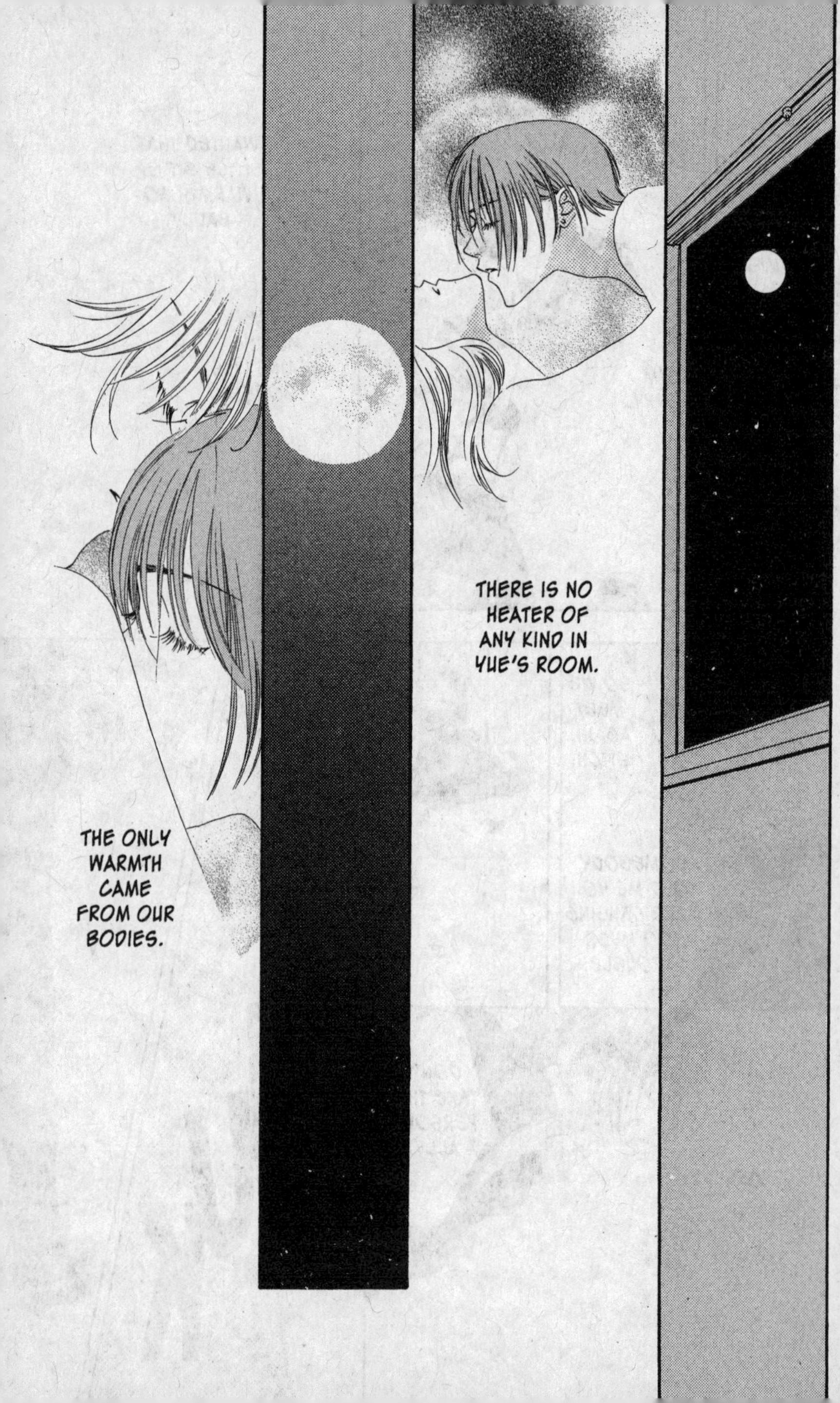
THERE IS NO HEATER OF ANY KIND IN YUE'S ROOM.
THE ONLY WARMTH CAME FROM OUR BODIES.

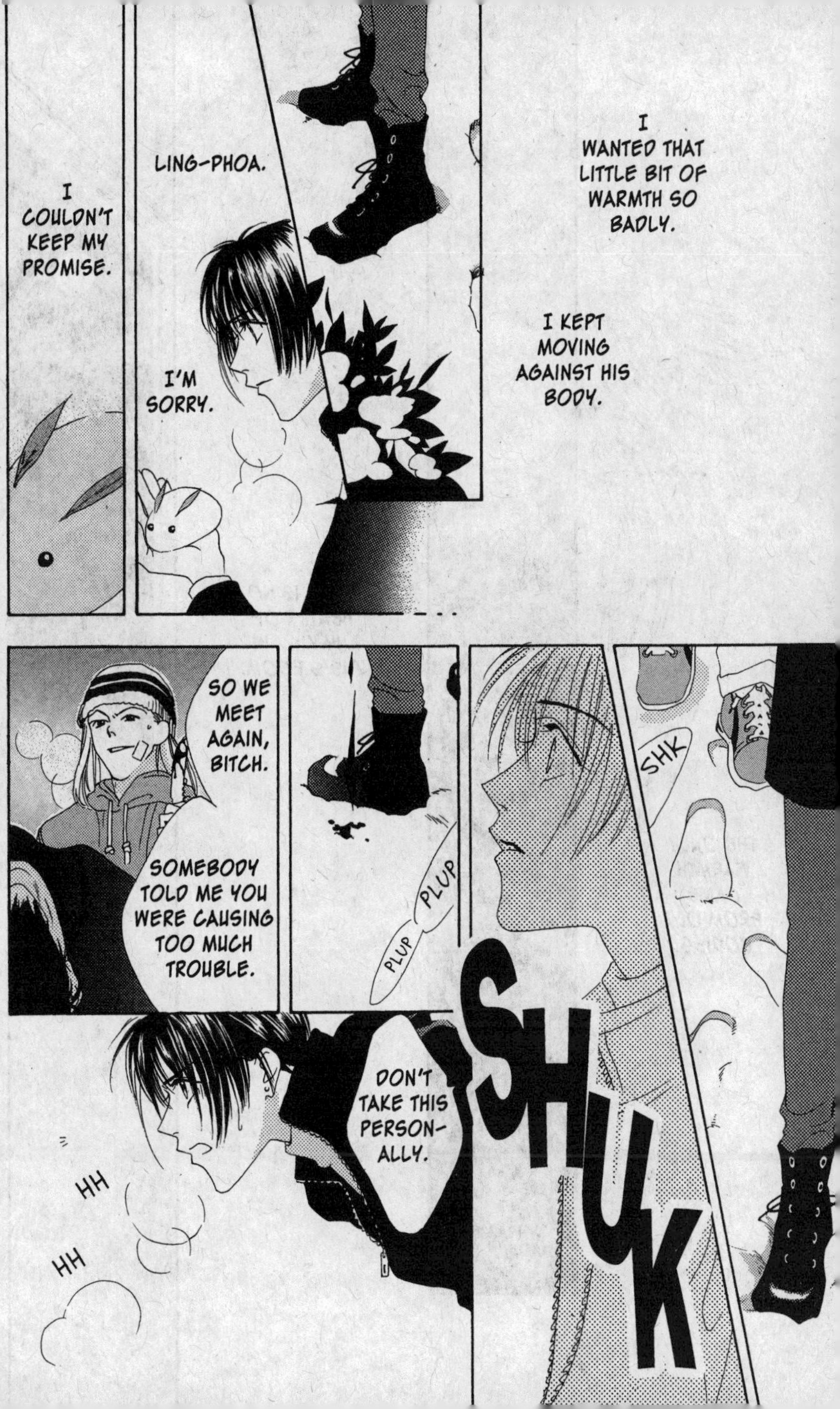
I WANTED THAT LITTLE BIT OF WARMTH SO BADLY.
I KEPT MOVING AGAINST HIS BODY.
LING-PHOA.
I'M SORRY.
I COULDN'T KEEP MY PROMISE.
SHK
SHUK
PLUP PLUP
SO WE MEET AGAIN, BITCH.
SOMEBODY TOLD ME YOU WERE CAUSING TOO MUCH TROUBLE.
DON'T TAKE THIS PERSON-ALLY.
HH
HH

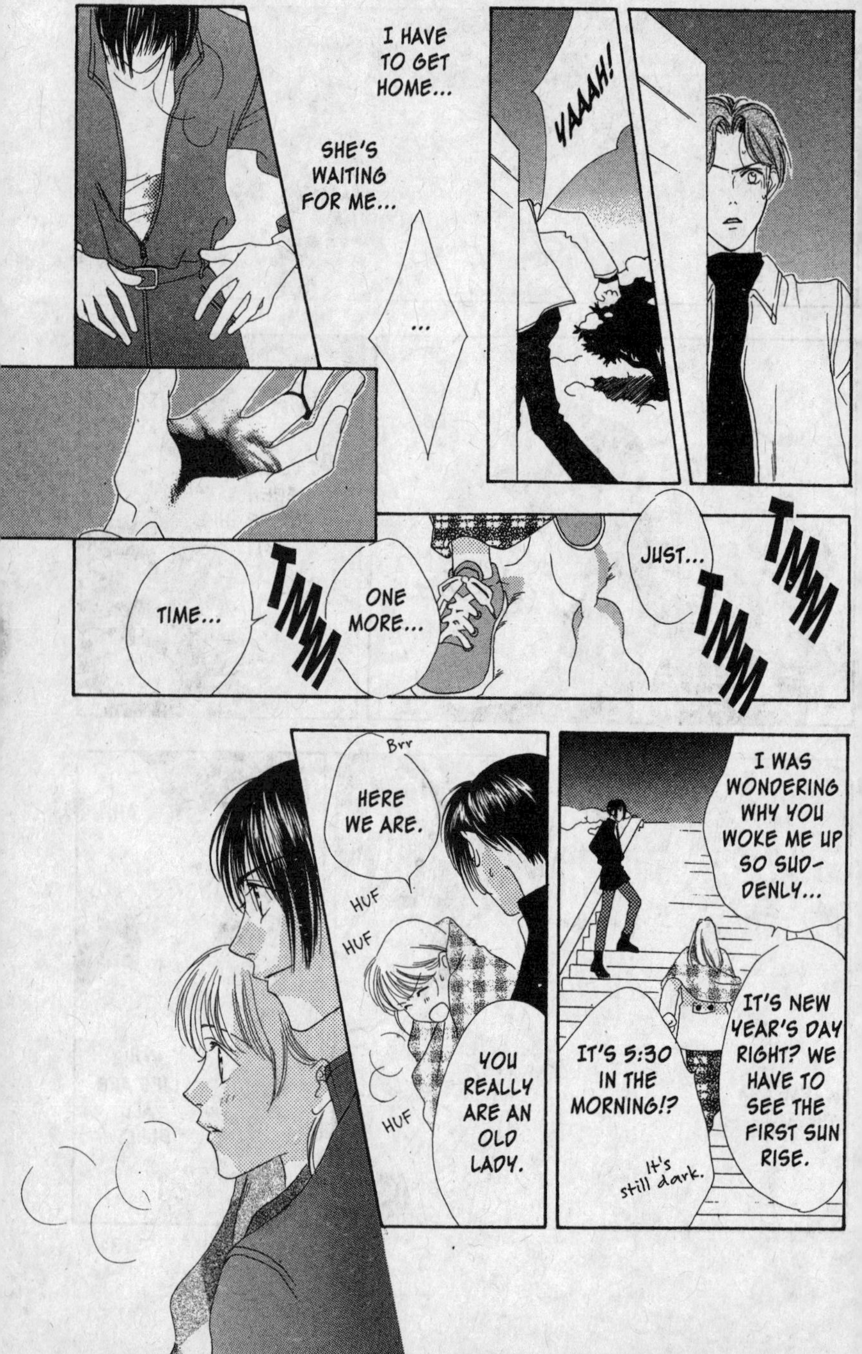
YAAAAH!
I HAVE TO GET HOME...
SHE'S WAITING FOR ME...
...
TMM
TMM
JUST...
ONE MORE...
TMM
TIME...
I WAS WONDERING WHY YOU WOKE ME UP SO SUD-DENLY...
IT'S NEW YEAR'S DAY RIGHT? WE HAVE TO SEE THE FIRST SUN RISE.
IT'S 5:30 IN THE MORNING!?
It's still dark.
Brr
HERE WE ARE.
HUF
HUF
YOU REALLY ARE AN OLD LADY.
HUF

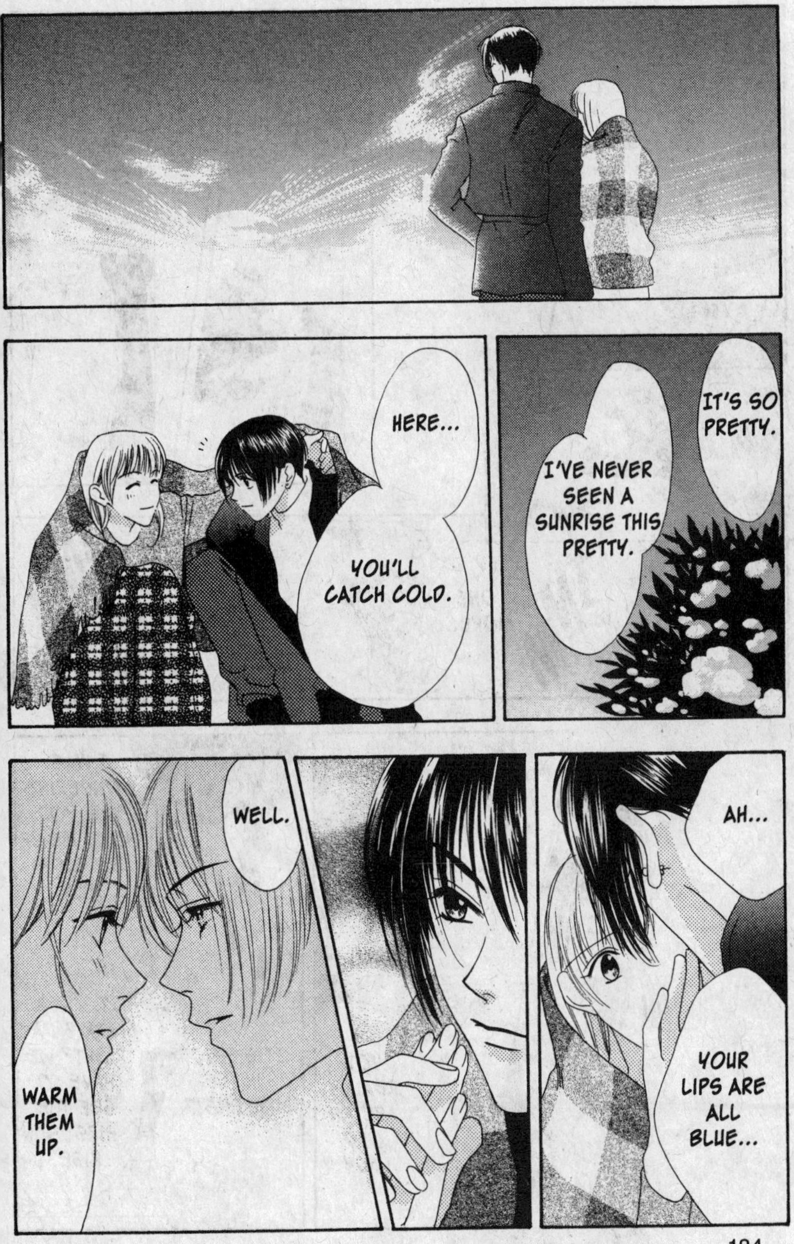
IT'S SO PRETTY.
I'VE NEVER SEEN A SUNRISE THIS PRETTY.
HERE...
YOU'LL CATCH COLD.
AH...
YOUR LIPS ARE ALL BLUE...
WELL.
WARM THEM UP.

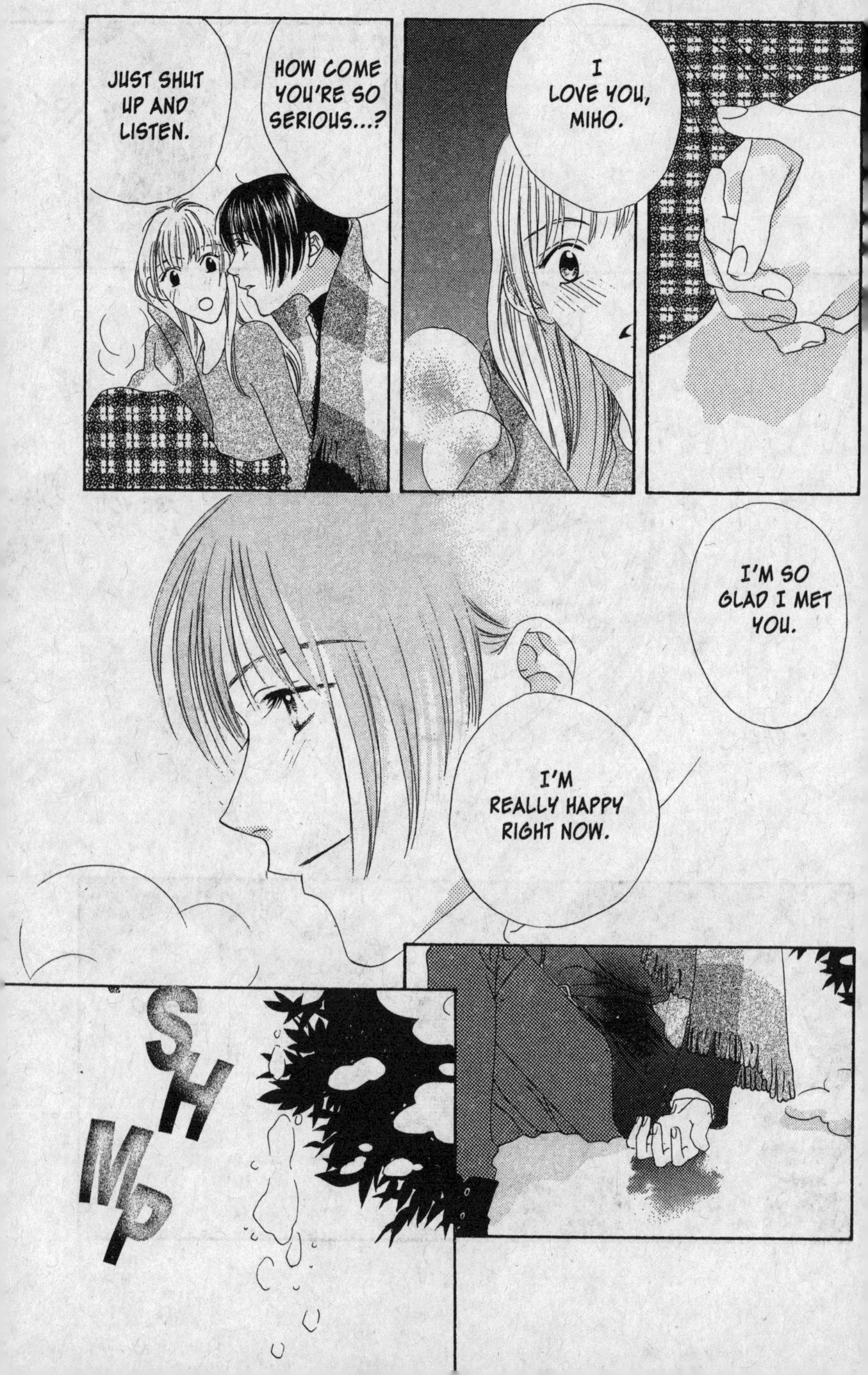
I LOVE YOU, MIHO.
HOW COME YOU'RE SO SERIOUS...?
JUST SHUT UP AND LISTEN.
I'M SO GLAD I MET YOU.
I'M REALLY HAPPY RIGHT NOW.
SHMP

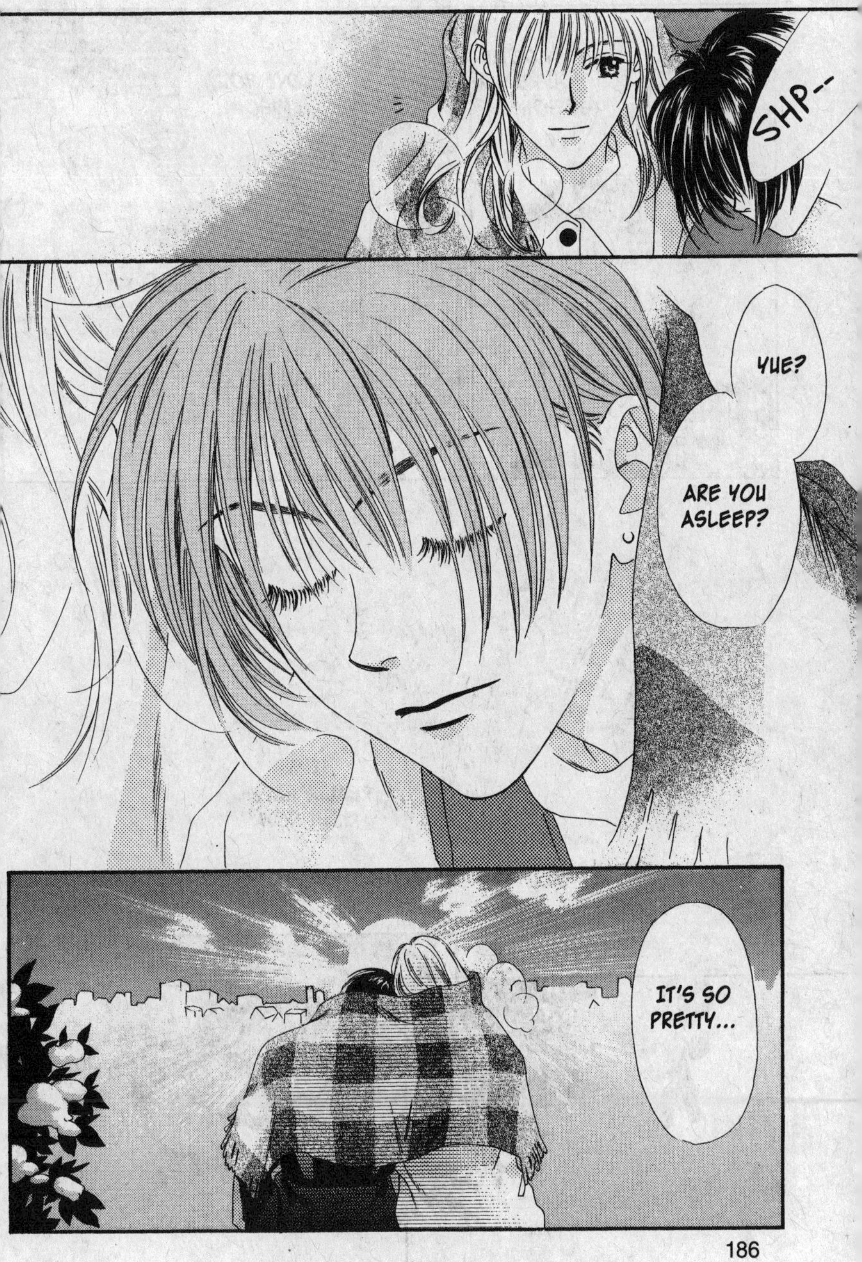
SHP--
YUE?
ARE YOU ASLEEP?
IT'S SO PRETTY...

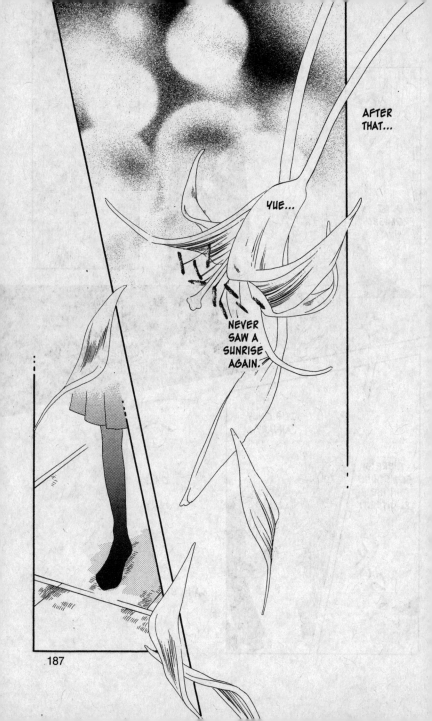

AFTER THAT...

YUE...

NEVER SAW A SUNRISE AGAIN.

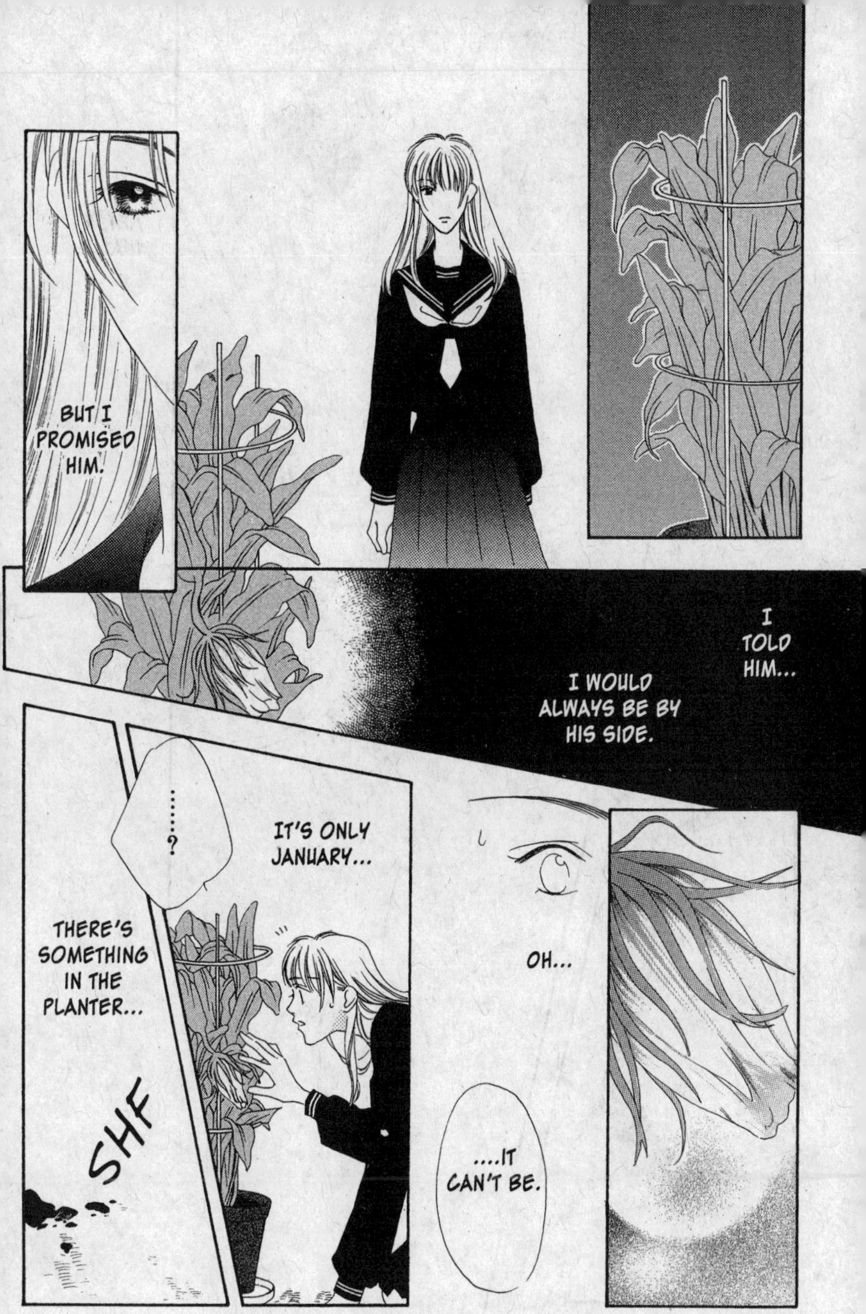
BUT I PROMISED HIM.
I TOLD HIM...
I WOULD ALWAYS BE BY HIS SIDE.
OH...
....IT CAN'T BE.
IT'S ONLY JANUARY...
......?
THERE'S SOMETHING IN THE PLANTER...
SHF

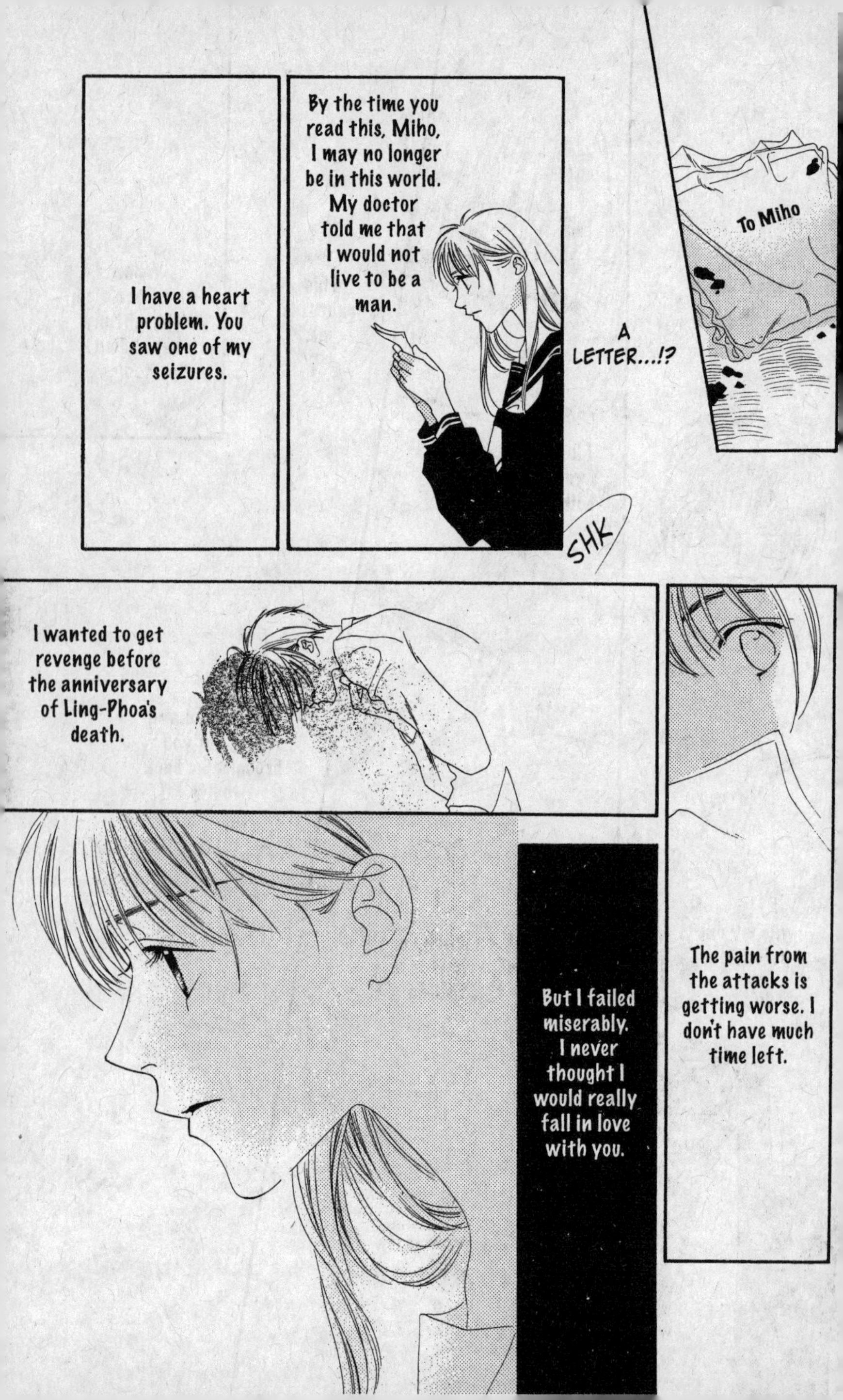
To Miho
A LETTER...!?
SHK
By the time you read this, Miho, I may no longer be in this world. My doctor told me that I would not live to be a man.
I have a heart problem. You saw one of my seizures.
The pain from the attacks is getting worse. I don't have much time left.
I wanted to get revenge before the anniversary of Ling-Phoa's death.
But I failed miserably. I never thought I would really fall in love with you.

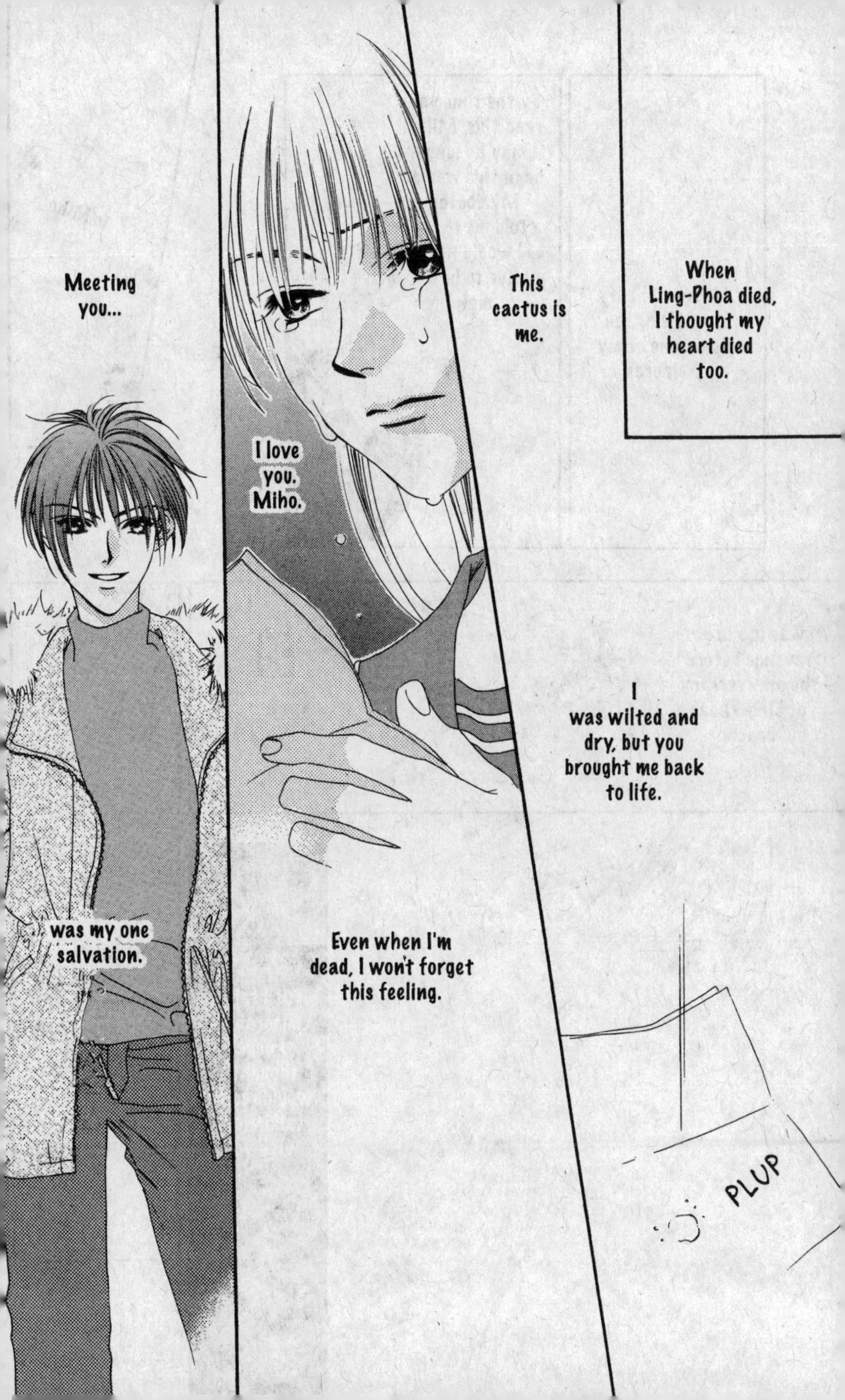
When Ling-Phoa died, I thought my heart died too.
This cactus is me.
I was wilted and dry, but you brought me back to life.
PLUP
I love you. Miho.
Even when I'm dead, I won't forget this feeling.
Meeting you...
...was my one salvation.

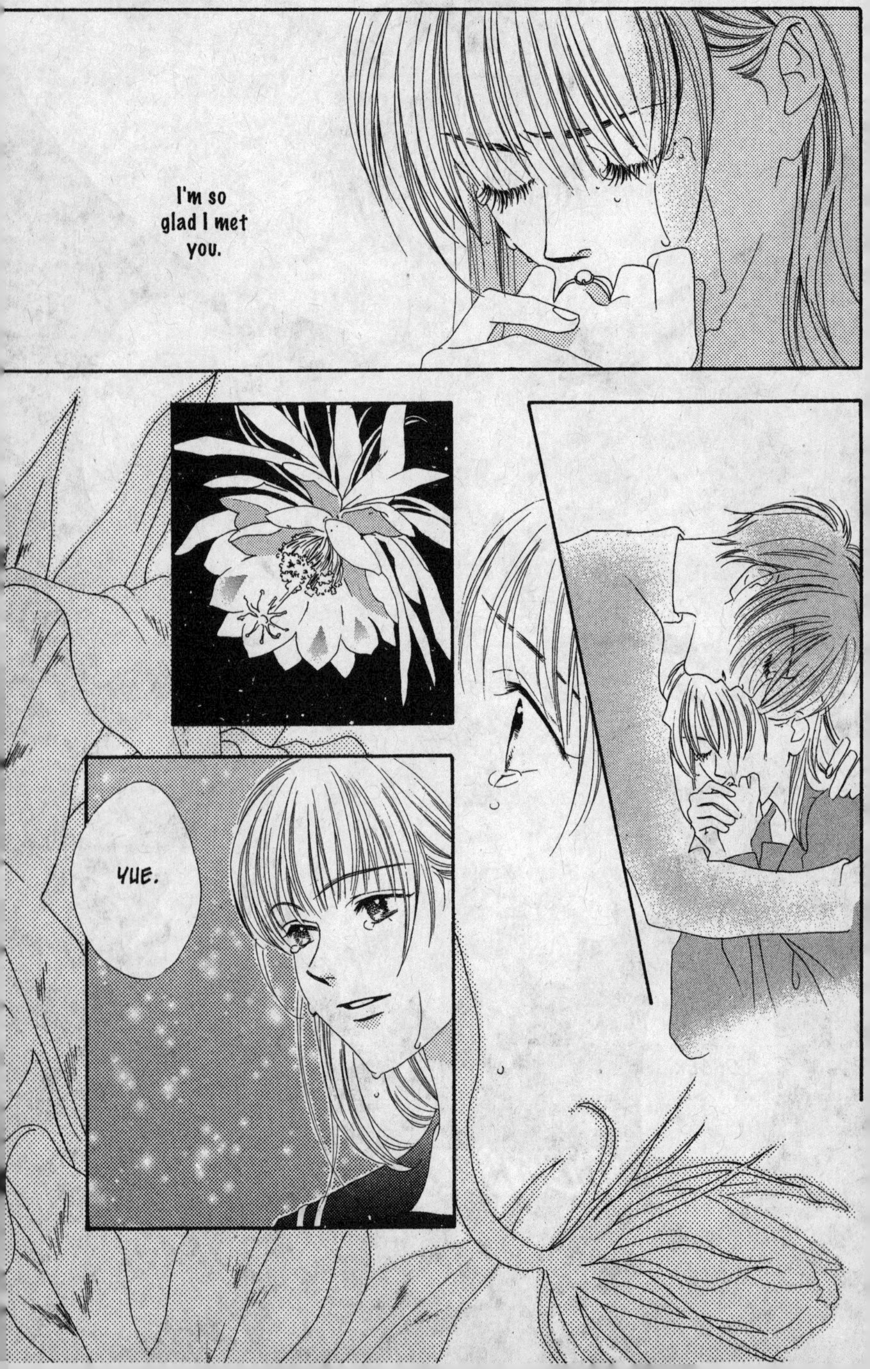
I'm so glad I met you.
YUE.

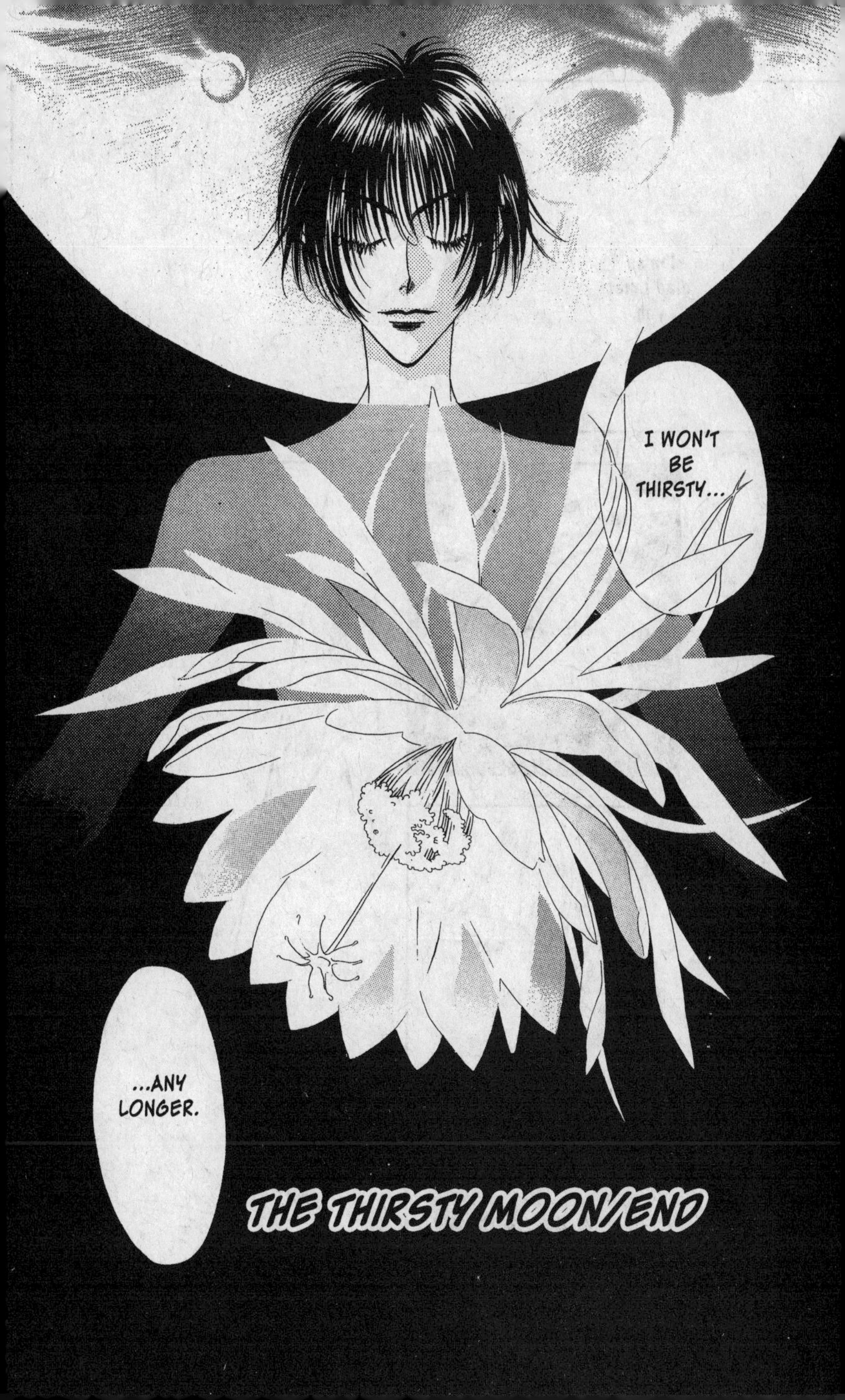
I WON'T BE THIRSTY...
...ANY LONGER.
THE THIRSTY MOON/END

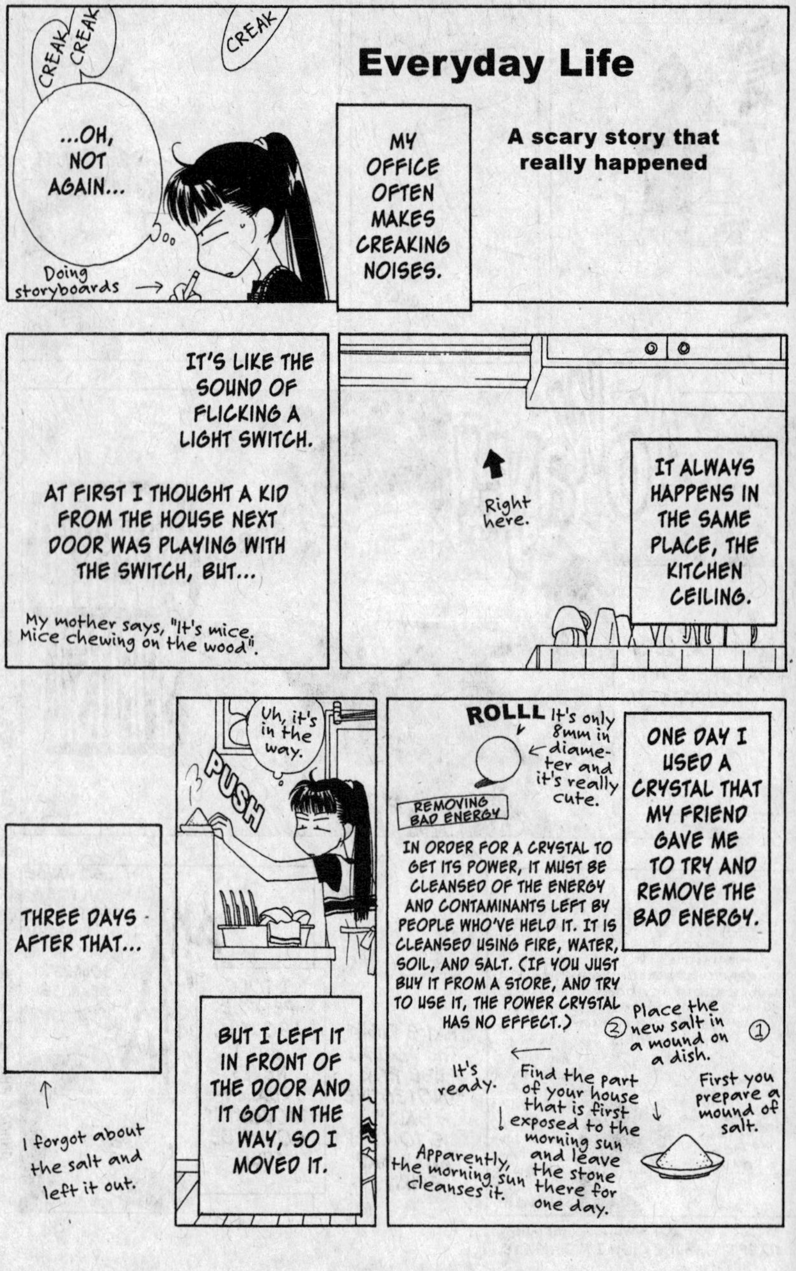

Everyday Life
A scary story that really happened
MY OFFICE OFTEN MAKES CREAKING NOISES.
CREAK
CREAK CREAK
...OH, NOT AGAIN...
Doing storyboards
IT ALWAYS HAPPENS IN THE SAME PLACE, THE KITCHEN CEILING.
Right here.
IT'S LIKE THE SOUND OF FLICKING A LIGHT SWITCH.
AT FIRST I THOUGHT A KID FROM THE HOUSE NEXT DOOR WAS PLAYING WITH THE SWITCH, BUT...
My mother says, "It's mice. Mice chewing on the wood".
ONE DAY I USED A CRYSTAL THAT MY FRIEND GAVE ME TO TRY AND REMOVE THE BAD ENERGY.
ROLLL
It's only 8mm in diameter and it's really cute.
REMOVING BAD ENERGY
IN ORDER FOR A CRYSTAL TO GET ITS POWER, IT MUST BE CLEANSED OF THE ENERGY AND CONTAMINANTS LEFT BY PEOPLE WHO'VE HELD IT. IT IS CLEANSED USING FIRE, WATER, SOIL, AND SALT. (IF YOU JUST BUY IT FROM A STORE, AND TRY TO USE IT, THE POWER CRYSTAL HAS NO EFFECT.)
① First you prepare a mound of salt.
② Place the new salt in a mound on a dish.
Find the part of your house that is first exposed to the morning sun and leave the stone there for one day.
It's ready.
Apparently, the morning sun cleanses it.
Uh, it's in the way.
PUSH
BUT I LEFT IT IN FRONT OF THE DOOR AND IT GOT IN THE WAY, SO I MOVED IT.
THREE DAYS AFTER THAT...
I forgot about the salt and left it out.

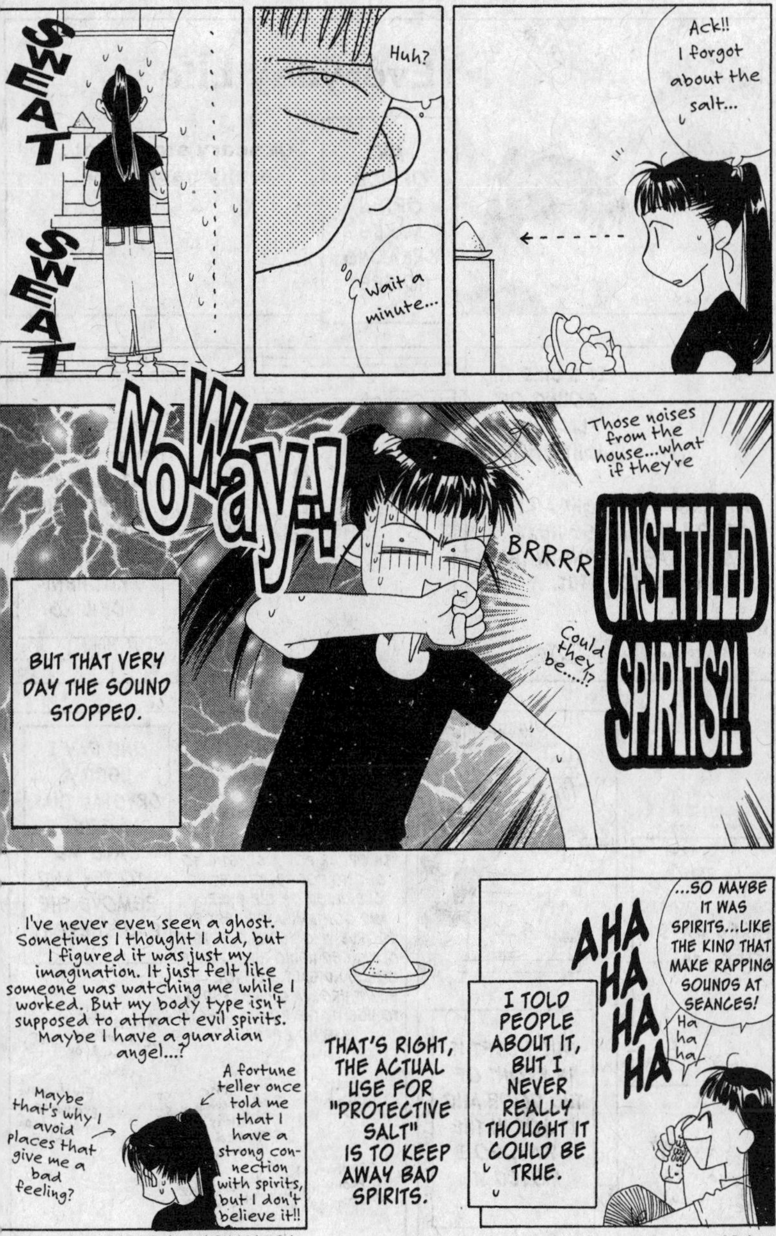
Ack!! I forgot about the salt...
Huh?
Wait a minute...
SWEAT
SWEAT
Those noises from the house...what if they're
UNSETTLED SPIRITS?!
Could they be....!?
BRRRR
No Way-!
BUT THAT VERY DAY THE SOUND STOPPED.
...SO MAYBE IT WAS SPIRITS...LIKE THE KIND THAT MAKE RAPPING SOUNDS AT SEANCES!
AHA HA HA HA
Ha ha ha
I TOLD PEOPLE ABOUT IT, BUT I NEVER REALLY THOUGHT IT COULD BE TRUE.
THAT'S RIGHT, THE ACTUAL USE FOR "PROTECTIVE SALT" IS TO KEEP AWAY BAD SPIRITS.
I've never even seen a ghost. Sometimes I thought I did, but I figured it was just my imagination. It just felt like someone was watching me while I worked. But my body type isn't supposed to attract evil spirits. Maybe I have a guardian angel...?
A fortune teller once told me that I have a strong connection with spirits, but I don't believe it!!
Maybe that's why I avoid places that give me a bad feeling?

WELL, I MAY NOT HAVE A CONNECTION TO SPIRITS, BUT I KNOW I'M SENSITIVE.

*"UNSETTLED SPIRITS" ARE SAID TO MAKE NOISES SO THAT THEIR PRESENCE IS KNOWN. THEY'RE SAID TO SOUND LIKE A LIVE TREE BEING PULLED FROM THE GROUND.

AFTER ALL, LIVING PEOPLE ARE MUCH STRONGER THAN SPIRITS. WE'VE GOT BREATH! WE'VE GOT POWER!

LOTS OF PEOPLE SAY THEY SAW SPIRITS WHO ONLY THINK THEY SAW THEM. ESPECIALLY YOUNG PEOPLE.

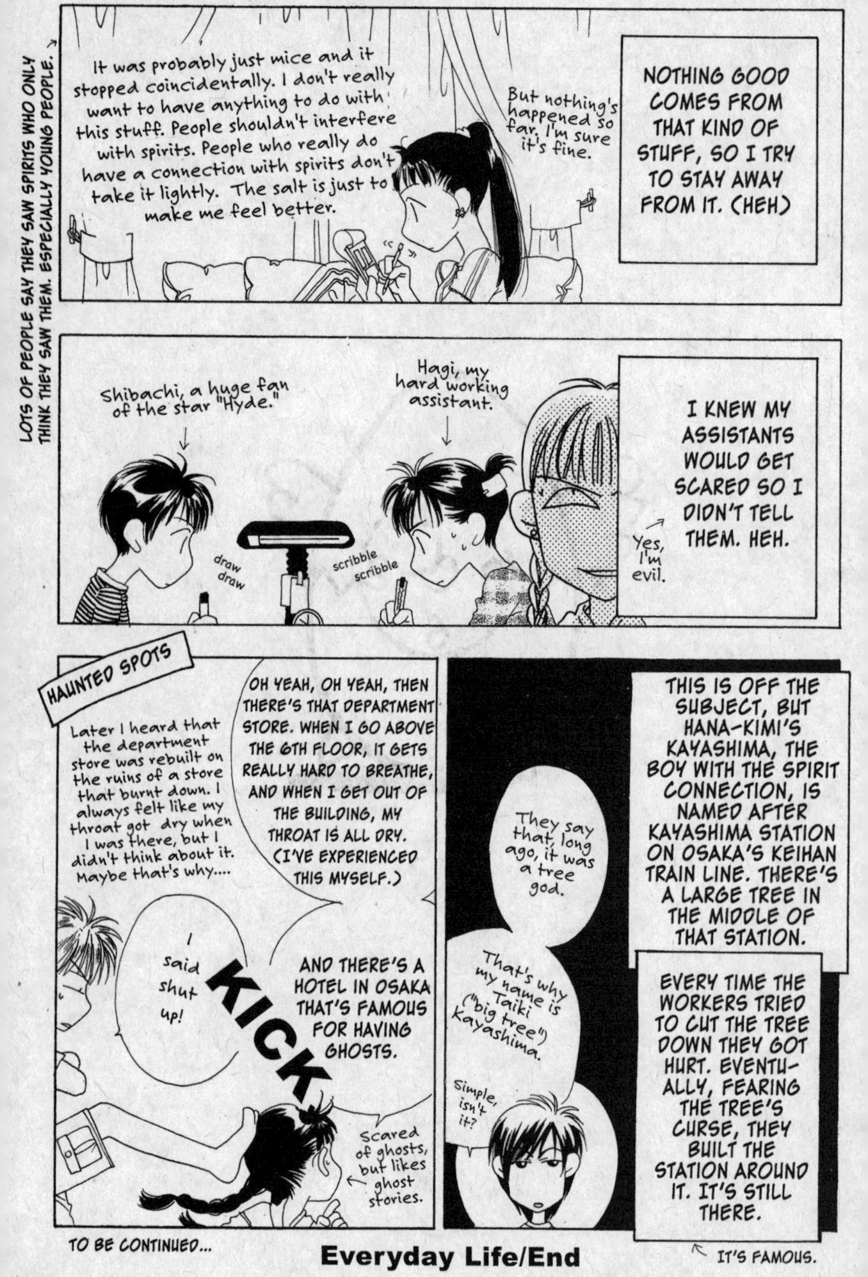
NOTHING GOOD COMES FROM THAT KIND OF STUFF, SO I TRY TO STAY AWAY FROM IT. (HEH)
But nothing's happened so far. I'm sure it's fine.
It was probably just mice and it stopped coincidentally. I don't really want to have anything to do with this stuff. People shouldn't interfere with spirits. People who really do have a connection with spirits don't take it lightly. The salt is just to make me feel better.
I KNEW MY ASSISTANTS WOULD GET SCARED SO I DIDN'T TELL THEM. HEH.
Yes, I'm evil.
Hagi, my hard working assistant.
scribble scribble
Shibachi, a huge fan of the star "Hyde."
draw draw
THIS IS OFF THE SUBJECT, BUT HANA-KIMI'S KAYASHIMA, THE BOY WITH THE SPIRIT CONNECTION, IS NAMED AFTER KAYASHIMA STATION ON OSAKA'S KEIHAN TRAIN LINE. THERE'S A LARGE TREE IN THE MIDDLE OF THAT STATION.
EVERY TIME THE WORKERS TRIED TO CUT THE TREE DOWN THEY GOT HURT. EVENTU-ALLY, FEARING THE TREE'S CURSE, THEY BUILT THE STATION AROUND IT. IT'S STILL THERE.
They say that, long ago, it was a tree god.
That's why my name is Taiki ("big tree") Kayashima.
Simple, isn't it?
HAUNTED SPOTS
OH YEAH, OH YEAH, THEN THERE'S THAT DEPARTMENT STORE. WHEN I GO ABOVE THE 6TH FLOOR, IT GETS REALLY HARD TO BREATHE, AND WHEN I GET OUT OF THE BUILDING, MY THROAT IS ALL DRY. (I'VE EXPERIENCED THIS MYSELF.)
Later I heard that the department store was rebuilt on the ruins of a store that burnt down. I always felt like my throat got dry when I was there, but I didn't think about it. Maybe that's why....
AND THERE'S A HOTEL IN OSAKA THAT'S FAMOUS FOR HAVING GHOSTS.
KICK
I said shut up!
Scared of ghosts, but likes ghost stories.

TO BE CONTINUED...

IT'S FAMOUS.

Everyday Life/End

Hana-Kimi

For You in Full Blossom

5

story and art by
HISAYA NAKAJO

CONTENTS

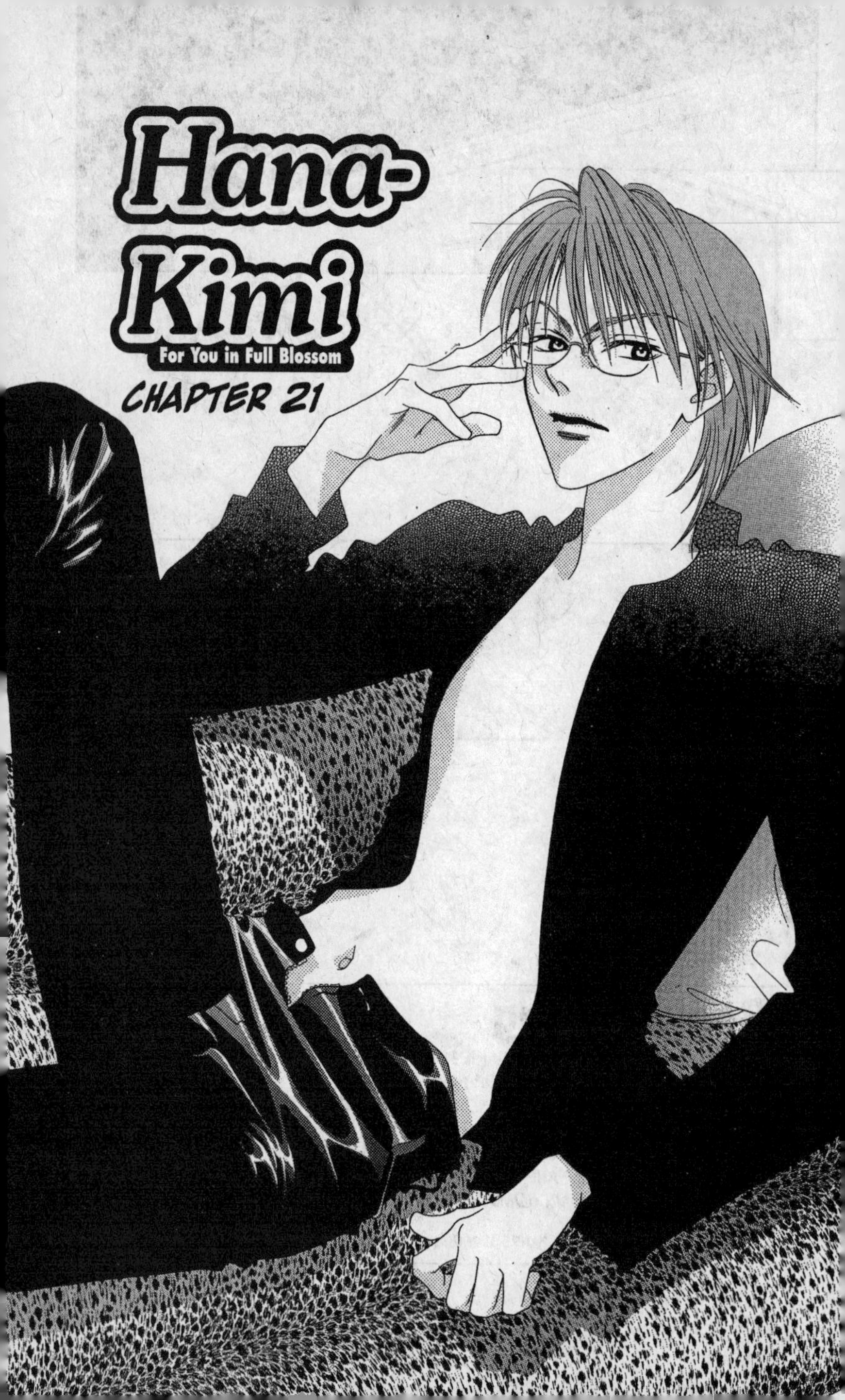
Hana-Kimi
For You in Full Blossom
CHAPTER 21

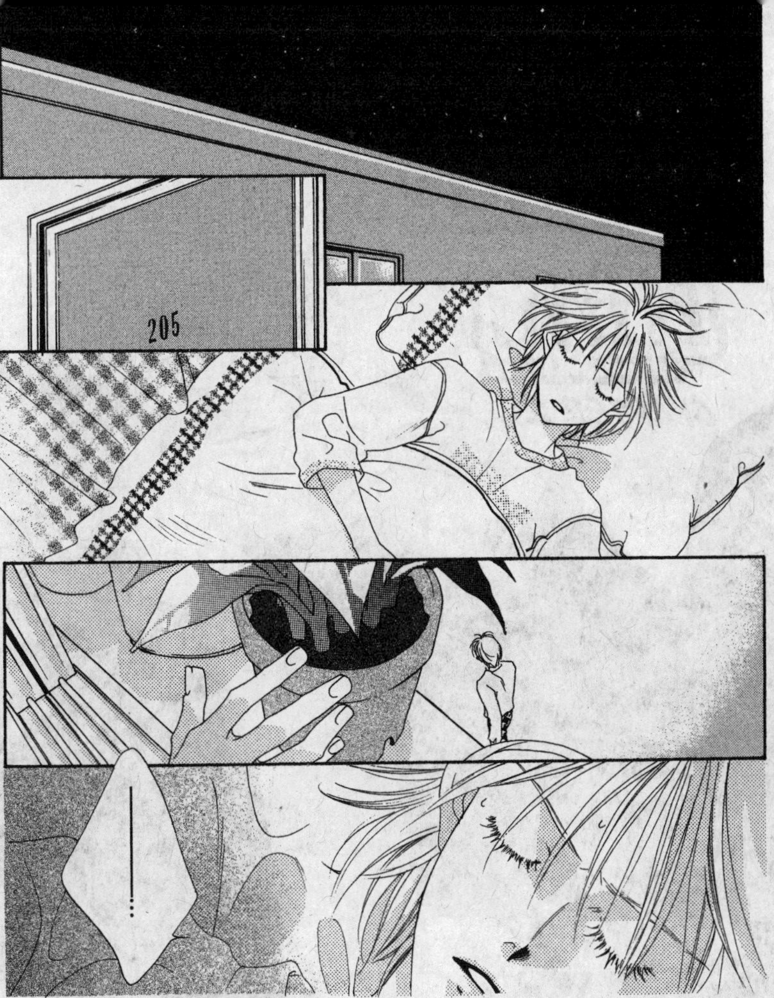
205
......

Book Signing

ON SUNDAY, MAY 24, 1998 I DID MY FIRST BOOK SIGNING!! I WAS SO HAPPY WHEN I SAW A LINE OF FANS WAITING IN THE RAIN JUST TO SEE ME! THANK YOU! NORMALLY I DON'T HAVE THE OPPORTUNITY TO MEET MY FANS, SO IT WAS FUN! ♪ THEY SOLD TICKETS, AND THERE WAS A TIME LIMIT, SO I DIDN'T GET TO SIGN FOR 100% OF THE FANS WHO CAME, BUT I'D LIKE TO DO IT AGAIN SOMETIME.

ALTHOUGH MY HANDS MAY DIE.

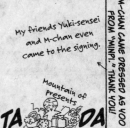

My friends Yuki-sensei and M-chan even came to the signing.

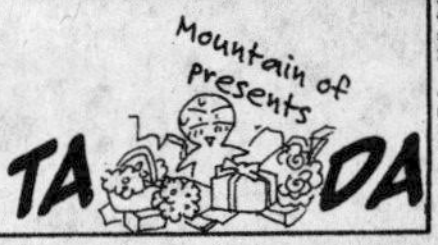
Mountain of Presents
TA
DA

M-CHAN CAME DRESSED AS YOO FROM "MINPI." THANK YOU!!

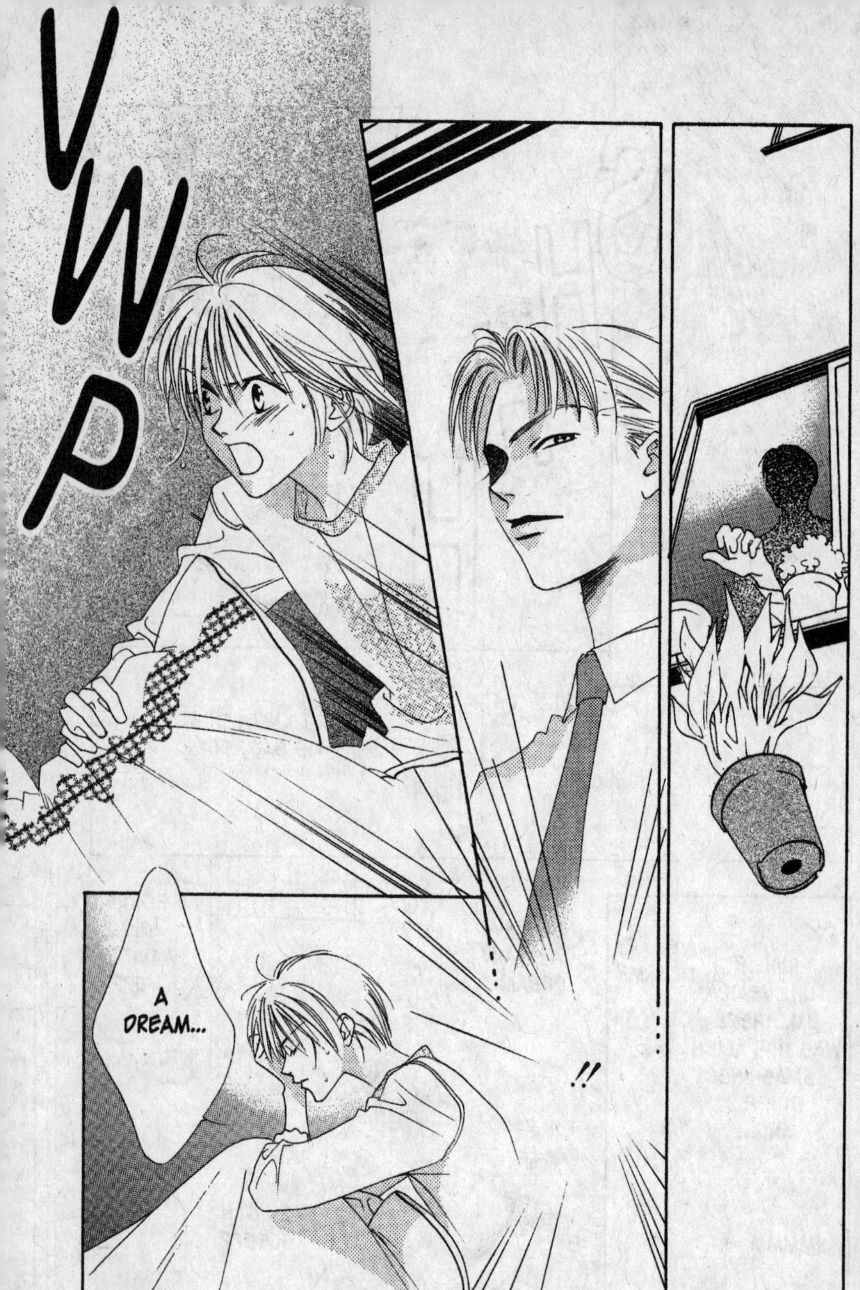
VWP
!!
A DREAM...

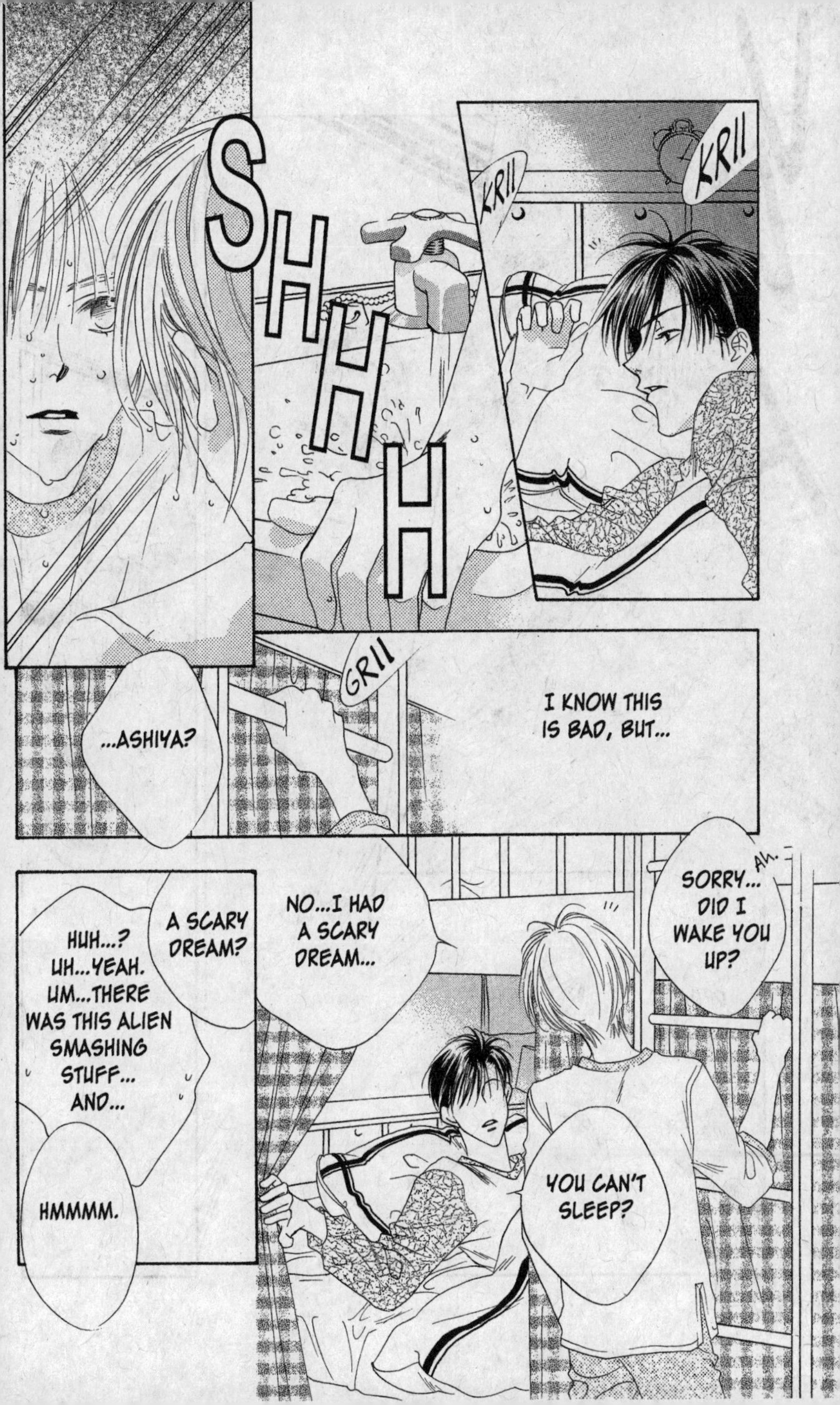
KRII
KRII
SHHHH
I KNOW THIS IS BAD, BUT...
GRII
...ASHIYA?
AH...
SORRY... DID I WAKE YOU UP?
NO...I HAD A SCARY DREAM...
YOU CAN'T SLEEP?
A SCARY DREAM?
HUH...? UH...YEAH. UM...THERE WAS THIS ALIEN SMASHING STUFF... AND...
HMMMM.

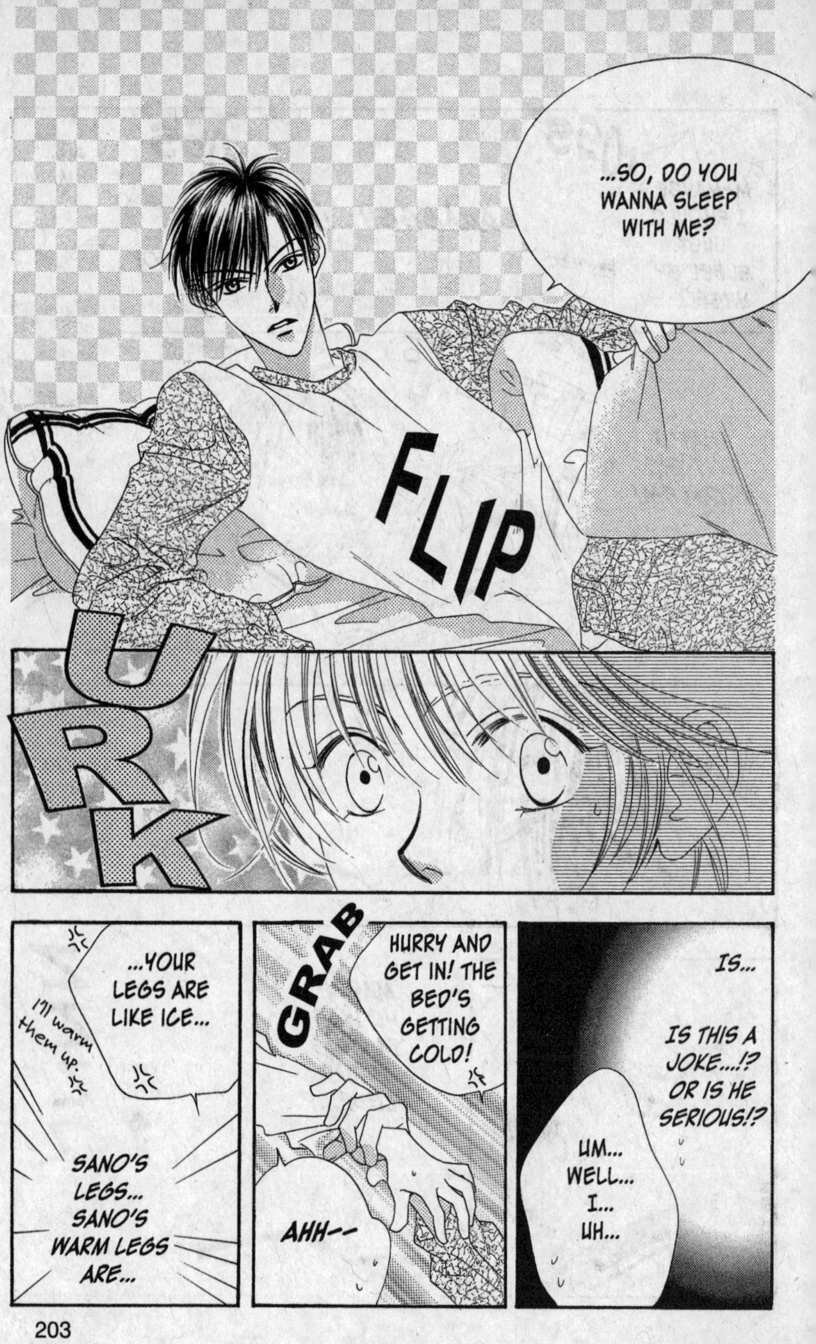
...SO, DO YOU WANNA SLEEP WITH ME?
FLIP
URK
IS...
IS THIS A JOKE...!? OR IS HE SERIOUS!?
UM... WELL... I... UH...
GRAB
HURRY AND GET IN! THE BED'S GETTING COLD!
AHH--
...YOUR LEGS ARE LIKE ICE...
I'll warm them up.
SANO'S LEGS... SANO'S WARM LEGS ARE...

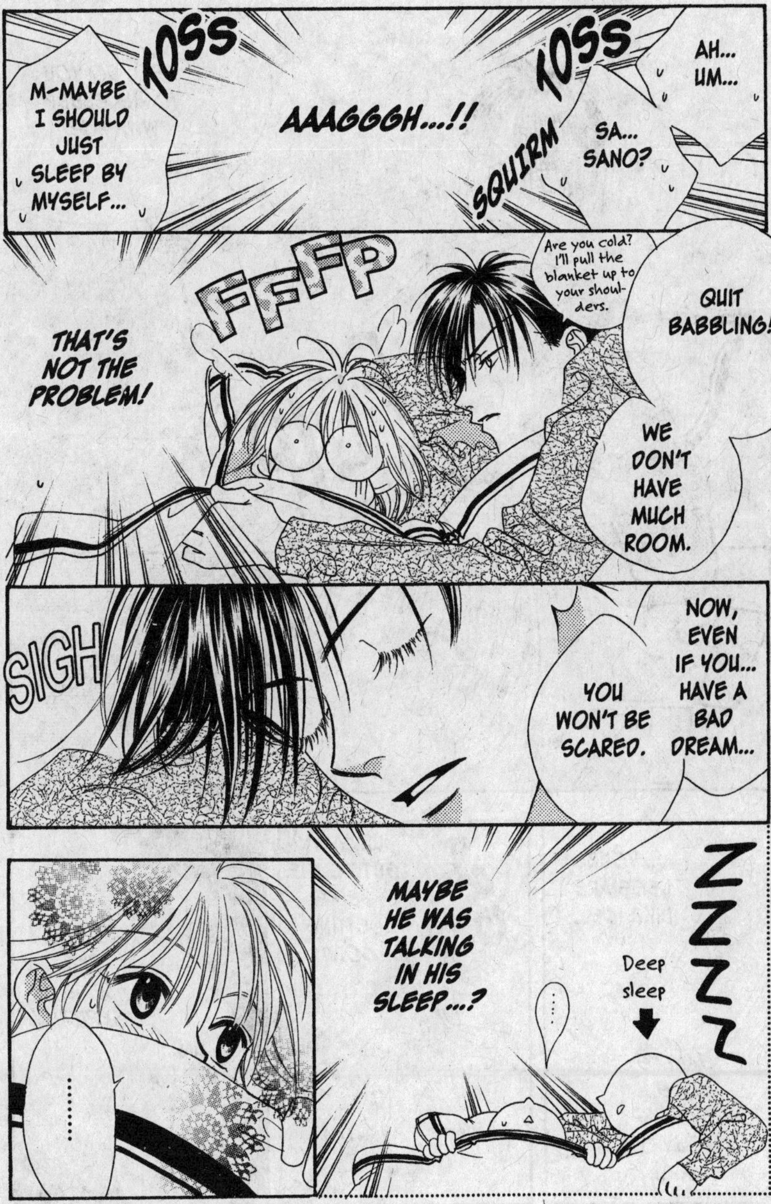
AH... UM...
SA... SANO?
SQUIRM
TOSS
AAAGGGH...!!
TOSS
M-MAYBE I SHOULD JUST SLEEP BY MYSELF...
Are you cold? I'll pull the blanket up to your shoulders.
QUIT BABBLING!
WE DON'T HAVE MUCH ROOM.
FFFP
THAT'S NOT THE PROBLEM!
NOW, EVEN IF YOU... HAVE A BAD DREAM...
YOU WON'T BE SCARED.
SIGH
ZZZZ
Deep sleep
....
MAYBE HE WAS TALKING IN HIS SLEEP...?
......

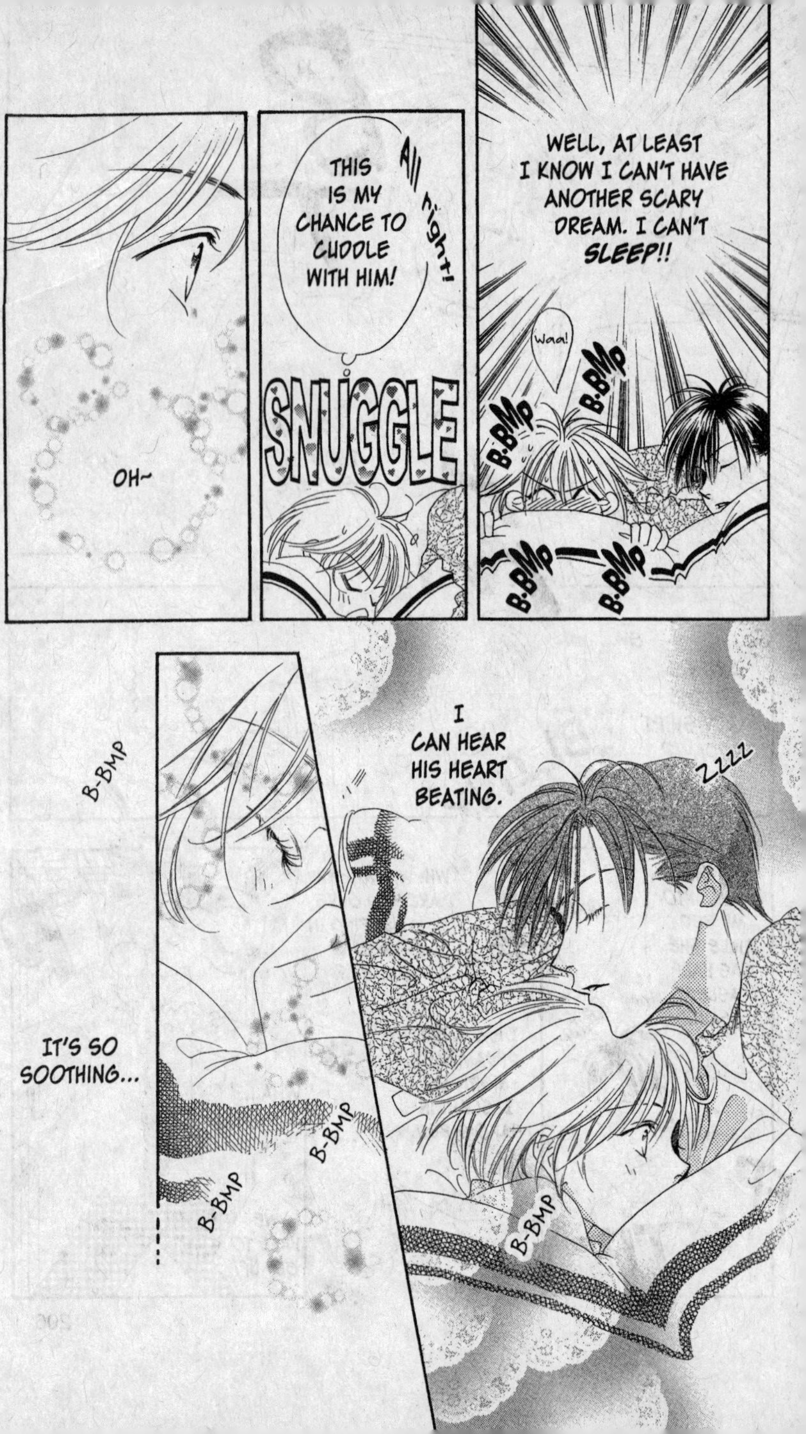
WELL, AT LEAST I KNOW I CAN'T HAVE ANOTHER SCARY DREAM. I CAN'T SLEEP!!
Waa!
B-BMP
B-BMP
B-BMP
B-BMP
All right!
THIS IS MY CHANCE TO CUDDLE WITH HIM!
SNUGGLE
OH~
I CAN HEAR HIS HEART BEATING.
ZZZZ
B-BMP
IT'S SO SOOTHING...
B-BMP
B-BMP
B-BMP

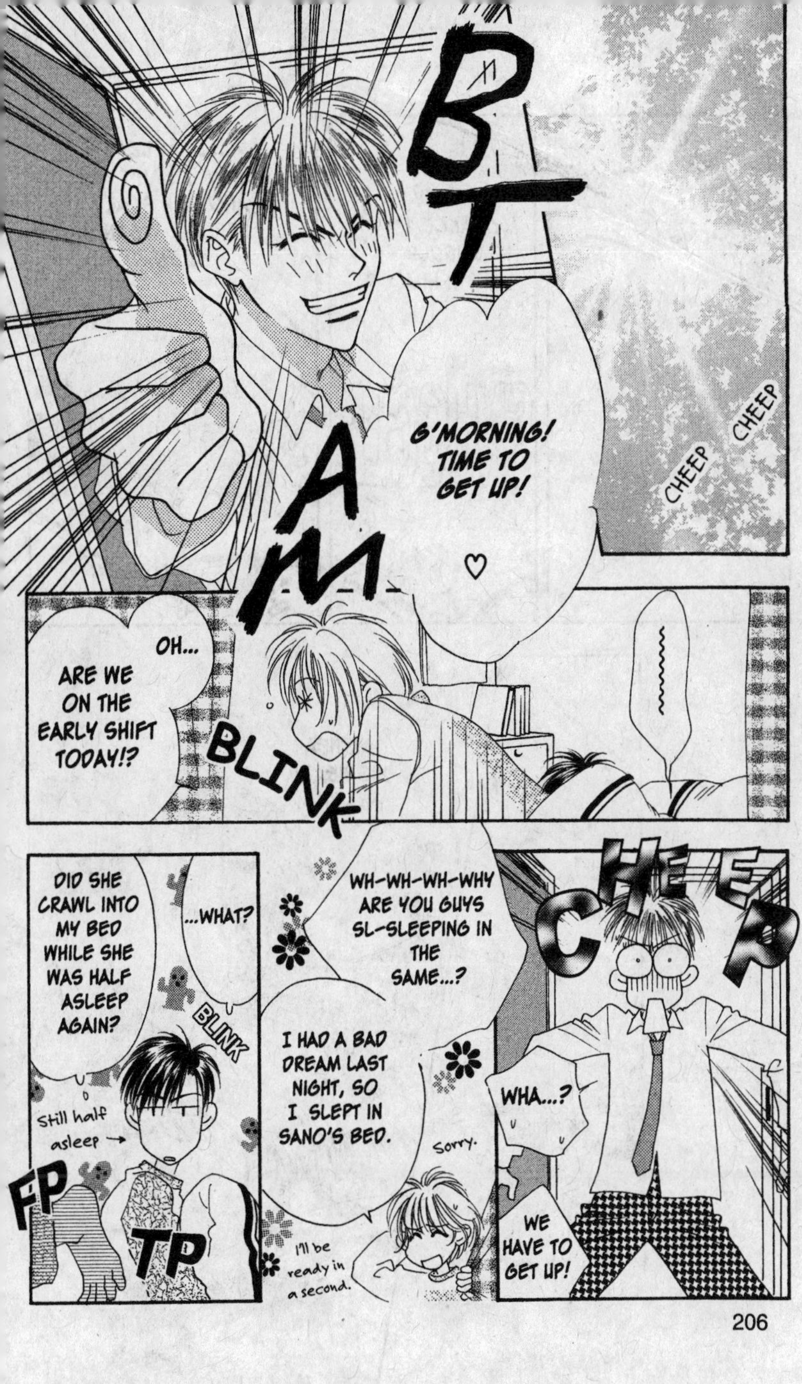
CHEEP CHEEP
G'MORNING! TIME TO GET UP! ♡
~~~
OH... ARE WE ON THE EARLY SHIFT TODAY!?
BLINK
CHEEP
WH-WH-WH-WHY ARE YOU GUYS SL-SLEEPING IN THE SAME...?
WHA...?
WE HAVE TO GET UP!
I HAD A BAD DREAM LAST NIGHT, SO I SLEPT IN SANO'S BED.
Sorry.
I'll be ready in a second.
...WHAT?
DID SHE CRAWL INTO MY BED WHILE SHE WAS HALF ASLEEP AGAIN?
BLINK
Still half asleep →
FP
TP
~~~

O-OKAY THEN. I'LL WAIT OUTSIDE...
'KAY. SORRY.
......
SINCE WHEN DO HIGH SCHOOL GUYS SLEEP TOGETHER JUST BECAUSE THEY HAVE A BAD DREAM!?
HMM... YOUR AURA IS THE COLOR OF JEALOUSY.
What're you doing outside their room?
Purple aura
AGH
GASP
STUDENTS!
THE LAST DAY OF THE FESTIVAL HAS ARRIVED!
FESTIVAL
私立
桜

* SIGN = OSAKA HIGH SCHOOL

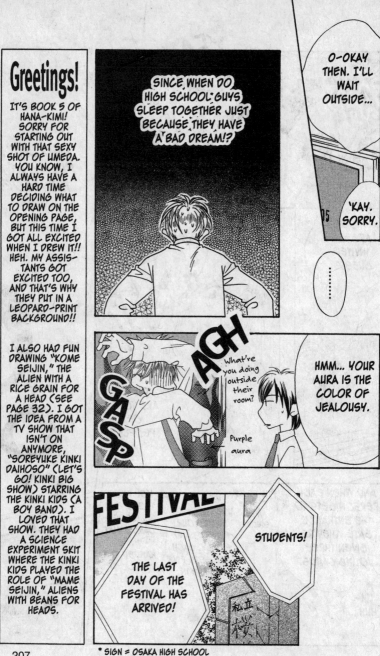

Greetings!

IT'S BOOK 5 OF HANA-KIMI! SORRY FOR STARTING OUT WITH THAT SEXY SHOT OF UMEDA. YOU KNOW, I ALWAYS HAVE A HARD TIME DECIDING WHAT TO DRAW ON THE OPENING PAGE, BUT THIS TIME I GOT ALL EXCITED WHEN I DREW IT!! HEH. MY ASSISTANTS GOT EXCITED TOO, AND THAT'S WHY THEY PUT IN A LEOPARD-PRINT BACKGROUND!!

I ALSO HAD FUN DRAWING "KOME SEIJIN," THE ALIEN WITH A RICE GRAIN FOR A HEAD (SEE PAGE 32). I GOT THE IDEA FROM A TV SHOW THAT ISN'T ON ANYMORE, "SOREYUKE KINKI DAIHOSO" (LET'S GO! KINKI BIG SHOW) STARRING THE KINKI KIDS (A BOY BAND). I LOVED THAT SHOW. THEY HAD A SCIENCE EXPERIMENT SKIT WHERE THE KINKI KIDS PLAYED THE ROLE OF "MAME SEIJIN," ALIENS WITH BEANS FOR HEADS.

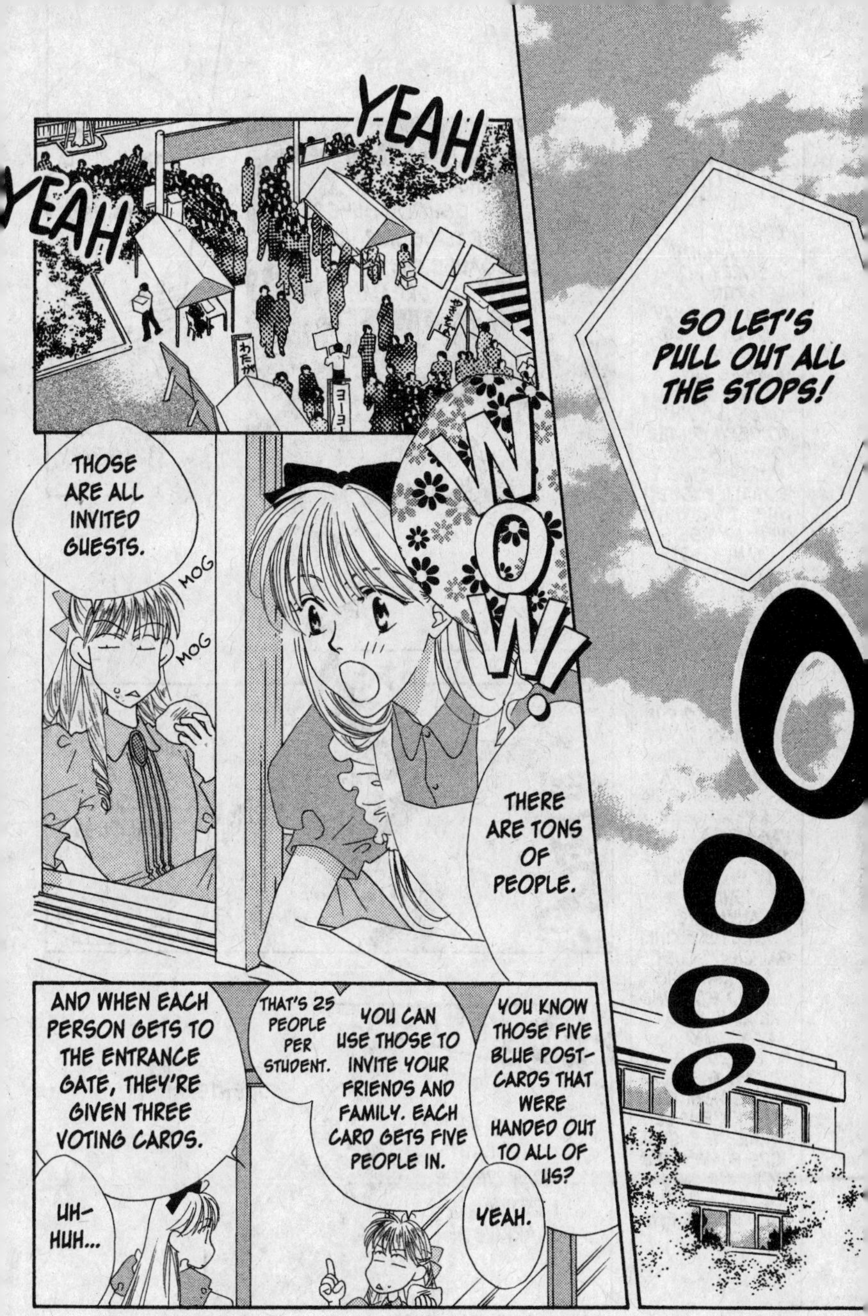
SO LET'S PULL OUT ALL THE STOPS!
OOOO
YEAH
YEAH
WOW!
THERE ARE TONS OF PEOPLE.
THOSE ARE ALL INVITED GUESTS.
MOG
MOG
YOU KNOW THOSE FIVE BLUE POST-CARDS THAT WERE HANDED OUT TO ALL OF US?
YEAH.
YOU CAN USE THOSE TO INVITE YOUR FRIENDS AND FAMILY. EACH CARD GETS FIVE PEOPLE IN.
THAT'S 25 PEOPLE PER STUDENT.
AND WHEN EACH PERSON GETS TO THE ENTRANCE GATE, THEY'RE GIVEN THREE VOTING CARDS.
UH-HUH...

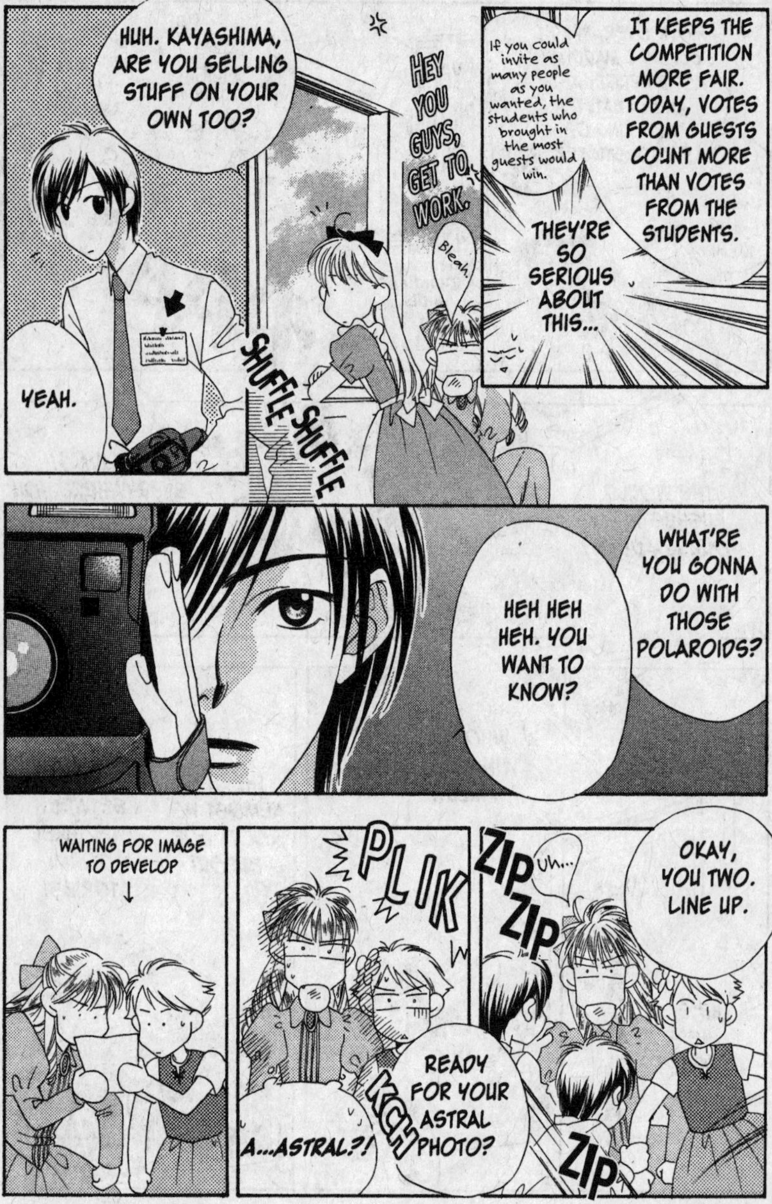

IT KEEPS THE COMPETITION MORE FAIR. TODAY, VOTES FROM GUESTS COUNT MORE THAN VOTES FROM THE STUDENTS.
If you could invite as many people as you wanted, the students who brought in the most guests would win.
THEY'RE SO SERIOUS ABOUT THIS...
HEY YOU GUYS, GET TO WORK.
Bleah.
SHUFFLE SHUFFLE
HUH. KAYASHIMA, ARE YOU SELLING STUFF ON YOUR OWN TOO?
YEAH.
WHAT'RE YOU GONNA DO WITH THOSE POLAROIDS?
HEH HEH HEH. YOU WANT TO KNOW?
OKAY, YOU TWO. LINE UP.
Uh...
ZIP ZIP
ZIP
PLIK
READY FOR YOUR ASTRAL PHOTO?
KCH
A...ASTRAL?!
WAITING FOR IMAGE TO DEVELOP
↓

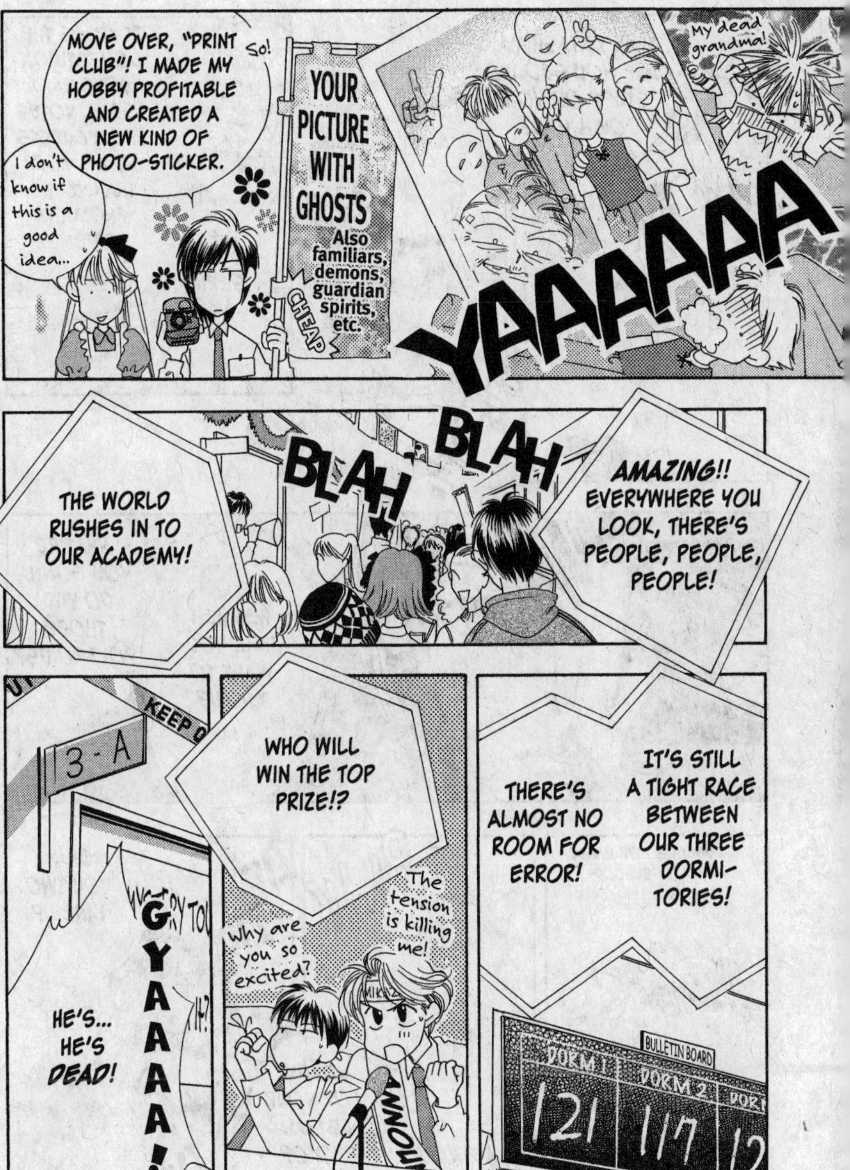
My dead grandma!
YAAAAAA
So!
MOVE OVER, "PRINT CLUB"! I MADE MY HOBBY PROFITABLE AND CREATED A NEW KIND OF PHOTO-STICKER.
YOUR PICTURE WITH GHOSTS
Also familiars, demons, guardian spirits, etc.
CHEAP
I don't know if this is a good idea...
AMAZING!! EVERYWHERE YOU LOOK, THERE'S PEOPLE, PEOPLE, PEOPLE!
BLAH
BLAH
THE WORLD RUSHES IN TO OUR ACADEMY!
IT'S STILL A TIGHT RACE BETWEEN OUR THREE DORMITORIES!
THERE'S ALMOST NO ROOM FOR ERROR!
BULLETIN BOARD
DORM 1
DORM 2
121
117
12
WHO WILL WIN THE TOP PRIZE!?
The tension is killing me!
Why are you so excited?
KEEP O
3-A
GYAAAAA!
HE'S... HE'S DEAD!

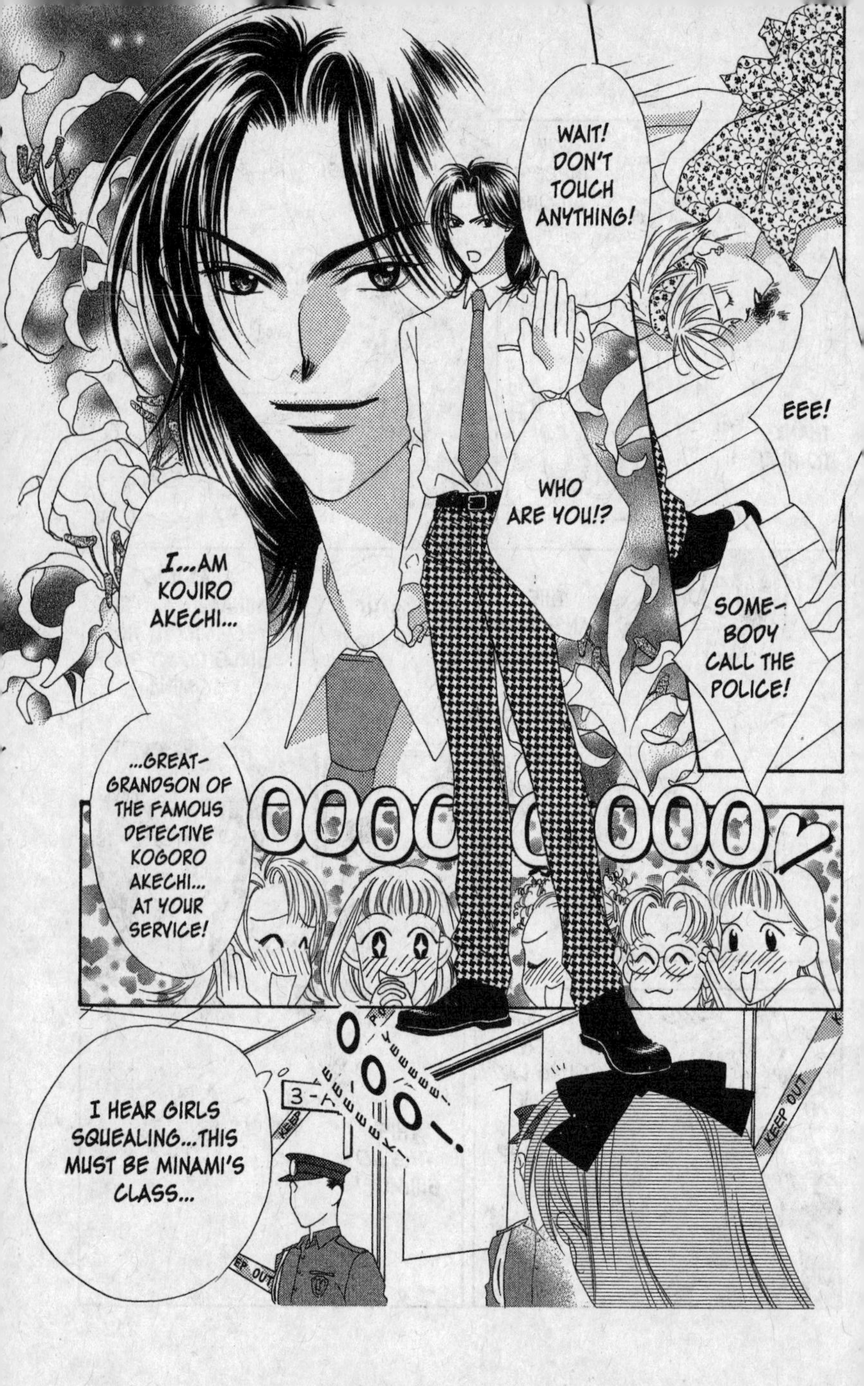
EEE!
SOME-BODY CALL THE POLICE!
WAIT! DON'T TOUCH ANYTHING!
WHO ARE YOU!?
I...AM KOJIRO AKECHI...
...GREAT-GRANDSON OF THE FAMOUS DETECTIVE KOGORO AKECHI... AT YOUR SERVICE!
OOOOOOOO
OOO!
3-A
I HEAR GIRLS SQUEALING...THIS MUST BE MINAMI'S CLASS...
KEEP OUT

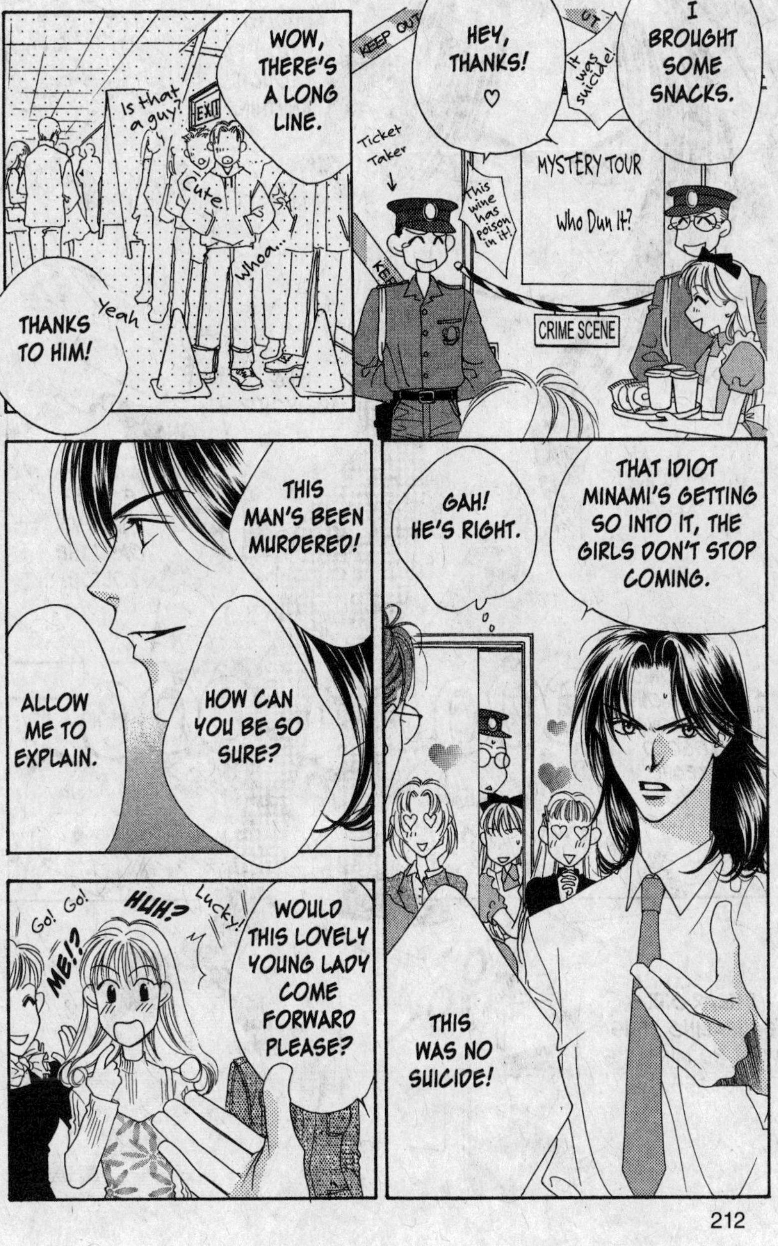
I BROUGHT SOME SNACKS.
It was suicide!
HEY, THANKS! ♡
KEEP OUT
MYSTERY TOUR
Who Dun It?
CRIME SCENE
This wine has poison in it!
Ticket Taker
WOW, THERE'S A LONG LINE.
Is that a guy?
EXIT
Cute
Whoa...
Yeah
THANKS TO HIM!
THAT IDIOT MINAMI'S GETTING SO INTO IT, THE GIRLS DON'T STOP COMING.
GAH! HE'S RIGHT.
THIS WAS NO SUICIDE!
THIS MAN'S BEEN MURDERED!
HOW CAN YOU BE SO SURE?
ALLOW ME TO EXPLAIN.
WOULD THIS LOVELY YOUNG LADY COME FORWARD PLEASE?
Lucky!
HUH?
ME!?
Go! Go!

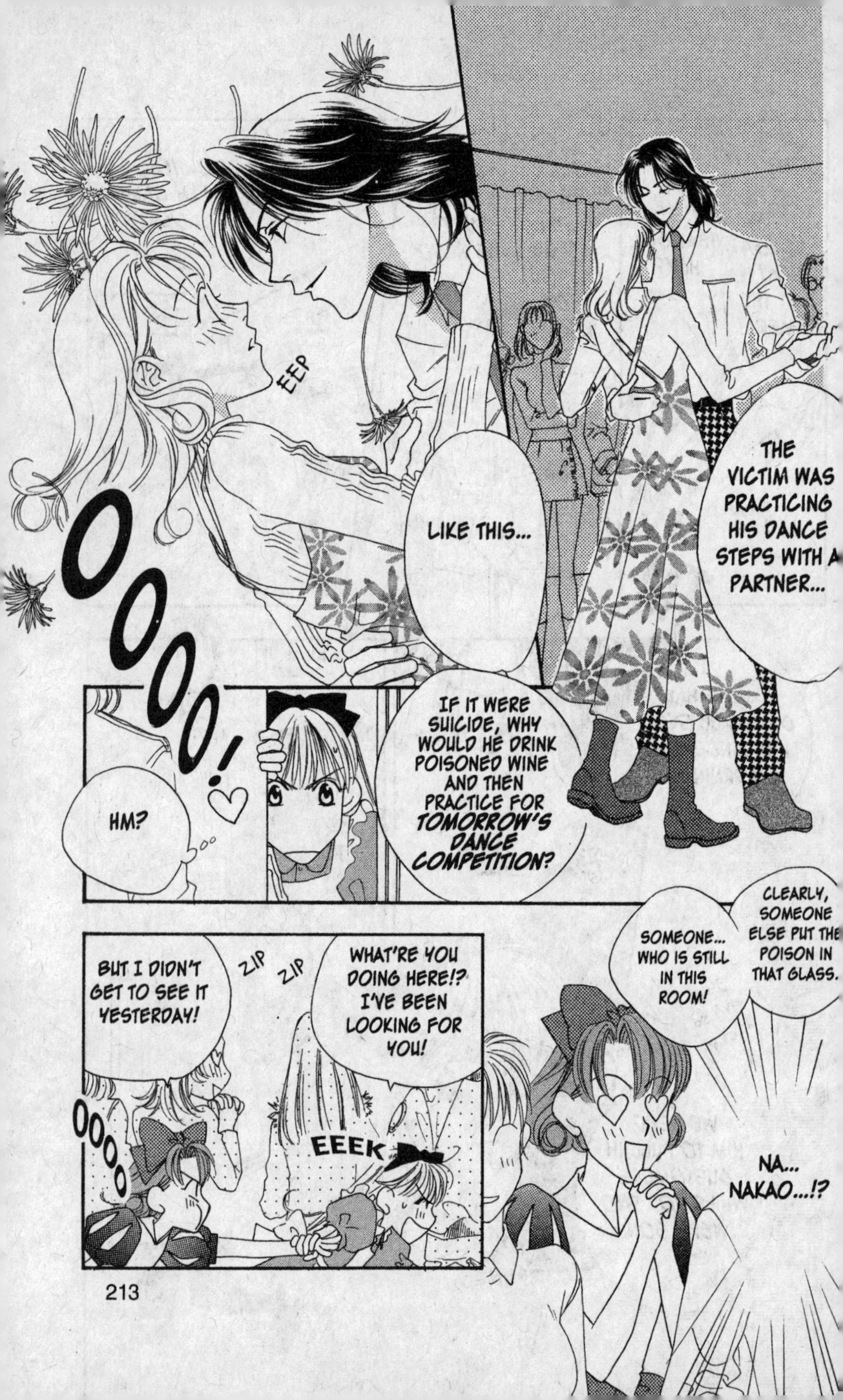

THE VICTIM WAS PRACTICING HIS DANCE STEPS WITH A PARTNER...
LIKE THIS...
EEP
OOOO!
IF IT WERE SUICIDE, WHY WOULD HE DRINK POISONED WINE AND THEN PRACTICE FOR *TOMORROW'S DANCE COMPETITION?*
HM?
CLEARLY, SOMEONE ELSE PUT THE POISON IN THAT GLASS.
SOMEONE... WHO IS STILL IN THIS ROOM!
NA... NAKAO...!?
WHAT'RE YOU DOING HERE!? I'VE BEEN LOOKING FOR YOU!
ZIP
ZIP
BUT I DIDN'T GET TO SEE IT YESTERDAY!
EEEK
OOOO

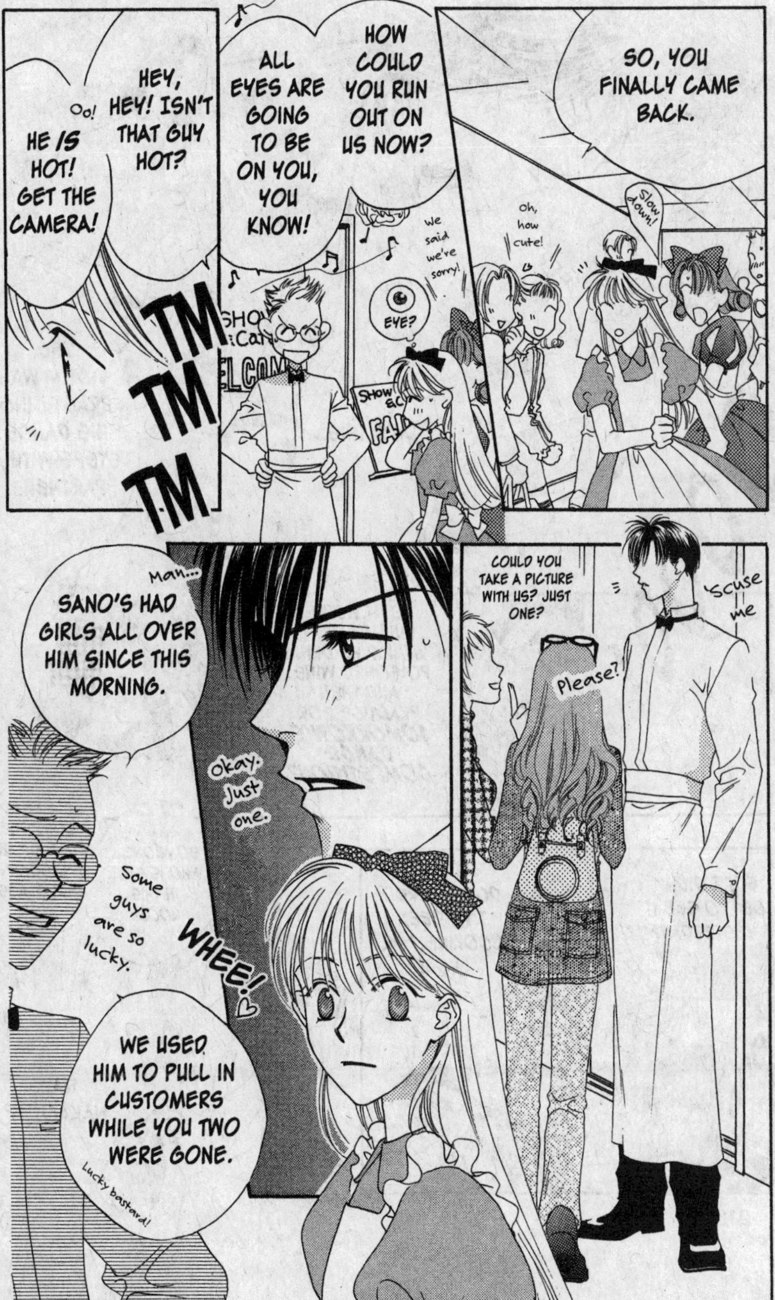

SO, YOU FINALLY CAME BACK.
Slow down!
Oh, how cute!
HOW COULD YOU RUN OUT ON US NOW?
ALL EYES ARE GOING TO BE ON YOU, YOU KNOW!
we said we're sorry!
EYE?
HEY, HEY! ISN'T THAT GUY HOT?
Oo!
HE IS HOT! GET THE CAMERA!
TM TM TM
'Scuse me
COULD YOU TAKE A PICTURE WITH US? JUST ONE?
Please?
Man...
SANO'S HAD GIRLS ALL OVER HIM SINCE THIS MORNING.
Okay. Just one.
Some guys are so lucky.
WHEE!
WE USED HIM TO PULL IN CUSTOMERS WHILE YOU TWO WERE GONE.
Lucky bastard!

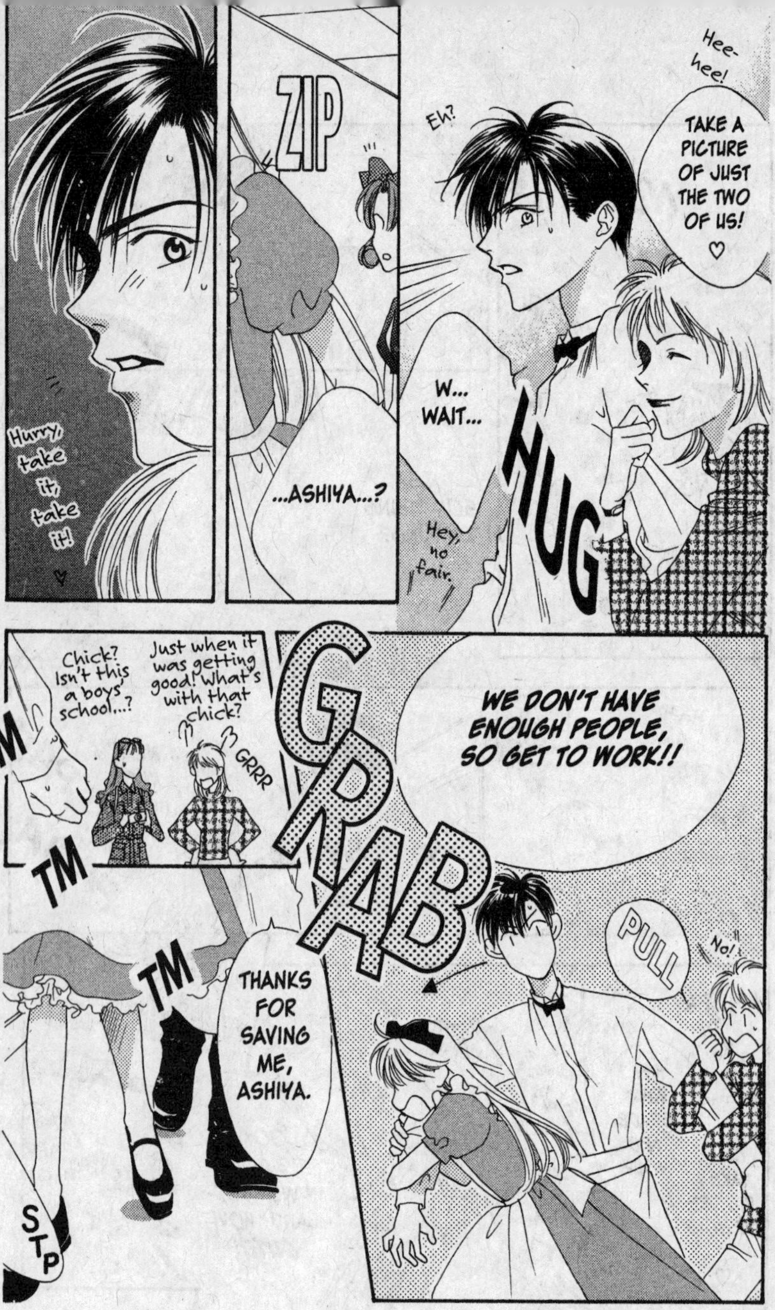
Hee-hee!
TAKE A PICTURE OF JUST THE TWO OF US! ♡
Eh?
W... WAIT...
HUG
Hey, no fair.
ZIP
...ASHIYA...?
Hurry, take it, take it! ♡
GRAB
WE DON'T HAVE ENOUGH PEOPLE, SO GET TO WORK!!
PULL
No!
Just when it was getting good! What's with that chick?
GRRR
Chick? Isn't this a boys' school...?
TM
TM
TM
THANKS FOR SAVING ME, ASHIYA.
STP

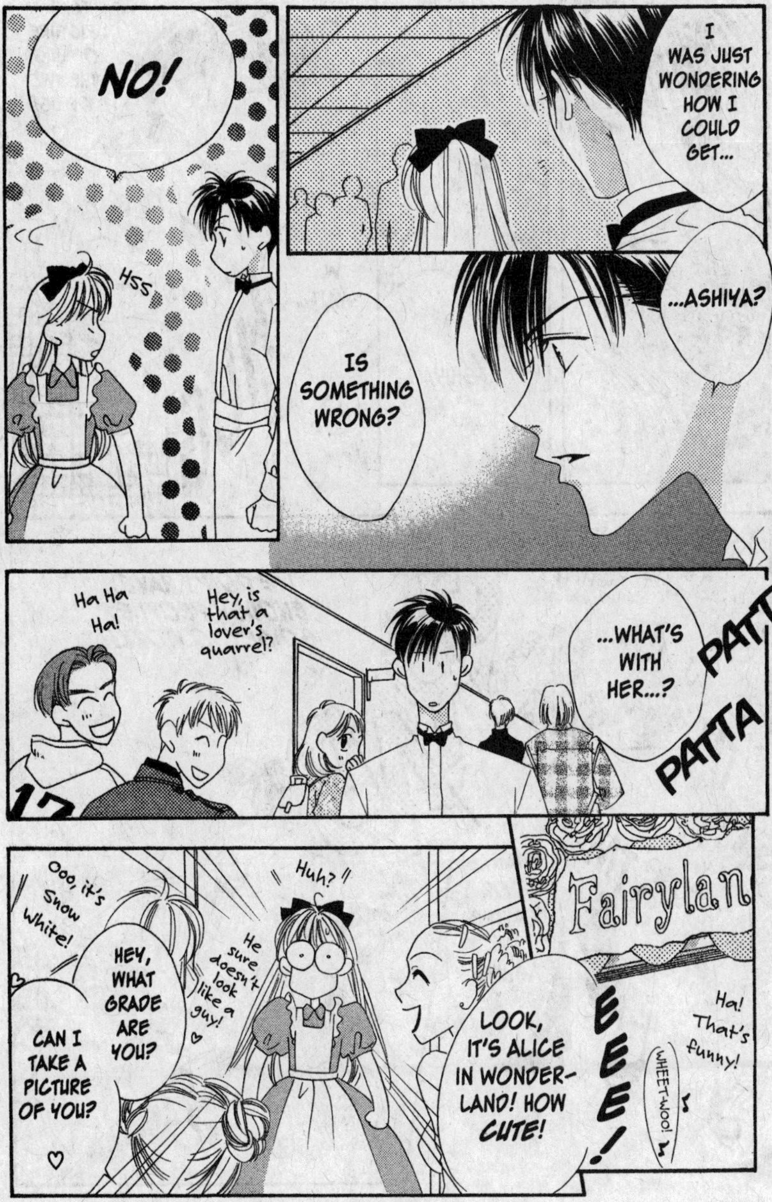
I WAS JUST WONDERING HOW I COULD GET...
...ASHIYA?
IS SOMETHING WRONG?
NO!
HSS
PATTA
PATTA
...WHAT'S WITH HER...?
Hey, is that a lover's quarrel?
Ha Ha Ha!
Ha! That's funny!
EEE!
WHEET-WOO!
LOOK, IT'S ALICE IN WONDER-LAND! HOW CUTE!
Fairylan
Huh?
He sure doesn't look like a guy!
HEY, WHAT GRADE ARE YOU?
Ooo, it's Snow White!
CAN I TAKE A PICTURE OF YOU?

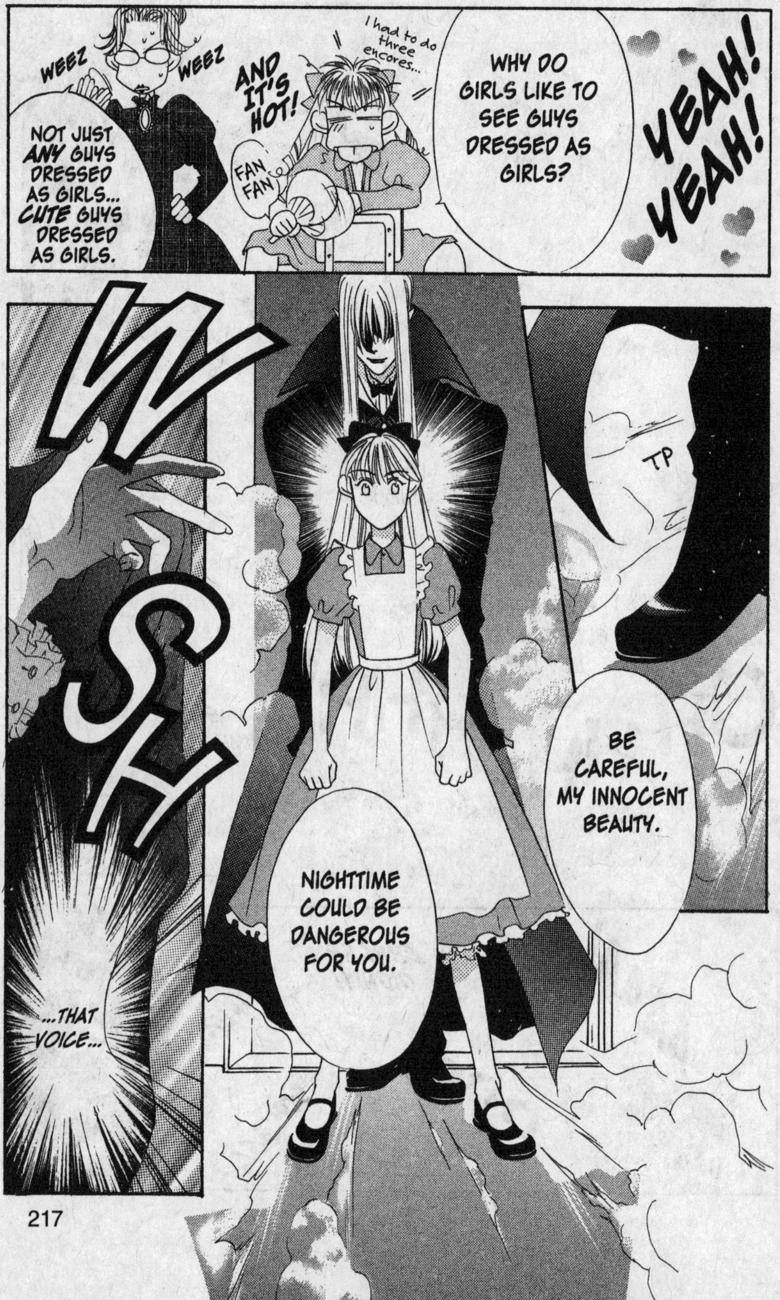
YEAH! YEAH!
WHY DO GIRLS LIKE TO SEE GUYS DRESSED AS GIRLS?
I had to do three encores...
AND IT'S HOT!
FAN FAN
WEEZ WEEZ
NOT JUST ANY GUYS DRESSED AS GIRLS... CUTE GUYS DRESSED AS GIRLS.
TP
BE CAREFUL, MY INNOCENT BEAUTY.
NIGHTTIME COULD BE DANGEROUS FOR YOU.
WSH
...THAT VOICE...

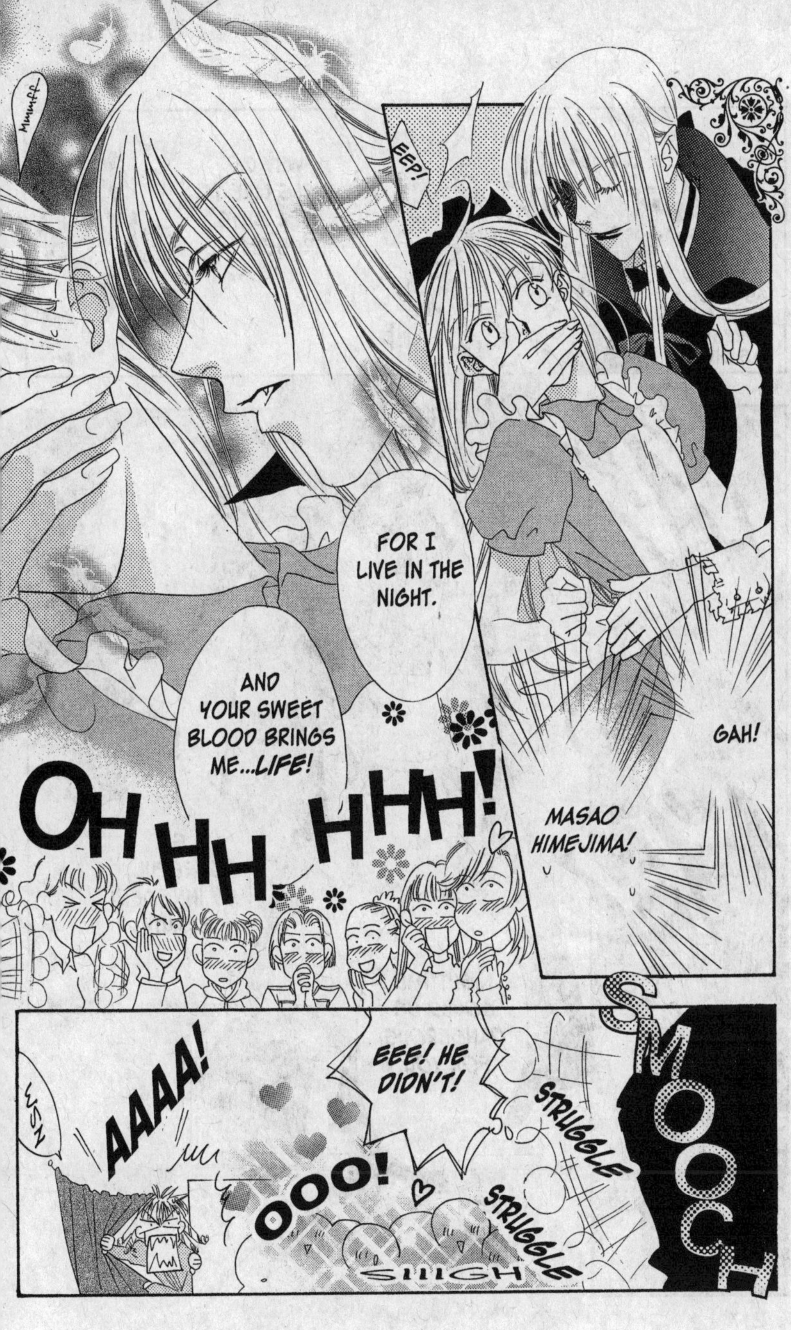
EEP!
GAH!
MASAO HIMEJIMA!
Mmmfff
FOR I LIVE IN THE NIGHT.
AND YOUR SWEET BLOOD BRINGS ME...LIFE!
OHHHHHHH!
SMOOCH
STRUGGLE
STRUGGLE
EEE! HE DIDN'T!
OOOO!
SIIIGH
AAAA!
WSN

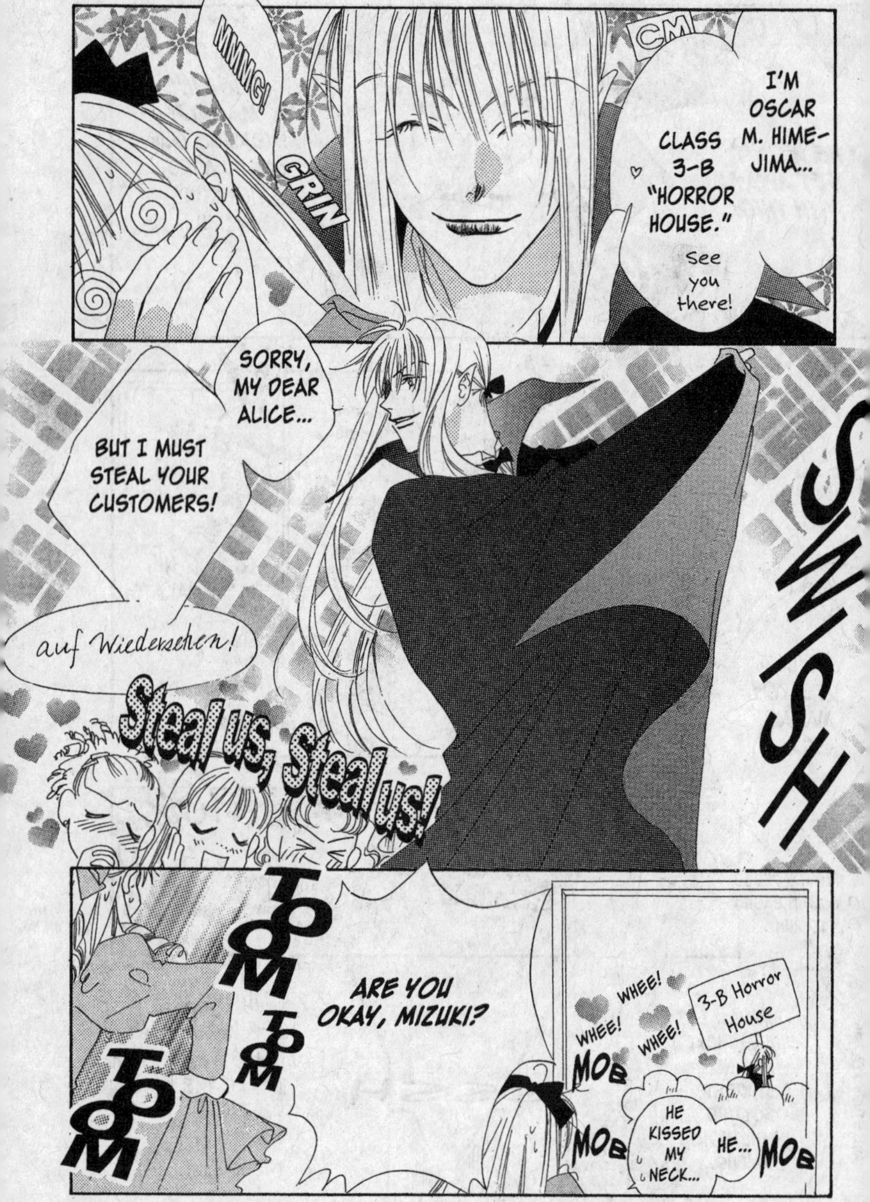
CM
I'M OSCAR M. HIME-JIMA...
CLASS 3-B "HORROR HOUSE."
See you there!
GRIN
MMMG!
SWISH
SORRY, MY DEAR ALICE...
BUT I MUST STEAL YOUR CUSTOMERS!
auf Wiedersehen!
Steal us, Steal us!
3-B Horror House
WHEE! WHEE!
WHEE! WHEE!
MOB
HE...
MOB
HE KISSED MY NECK...
MOB
MOB
ARE YOU OKAY, MIZUKI?
TOOM TOOM
TOOM TOOM

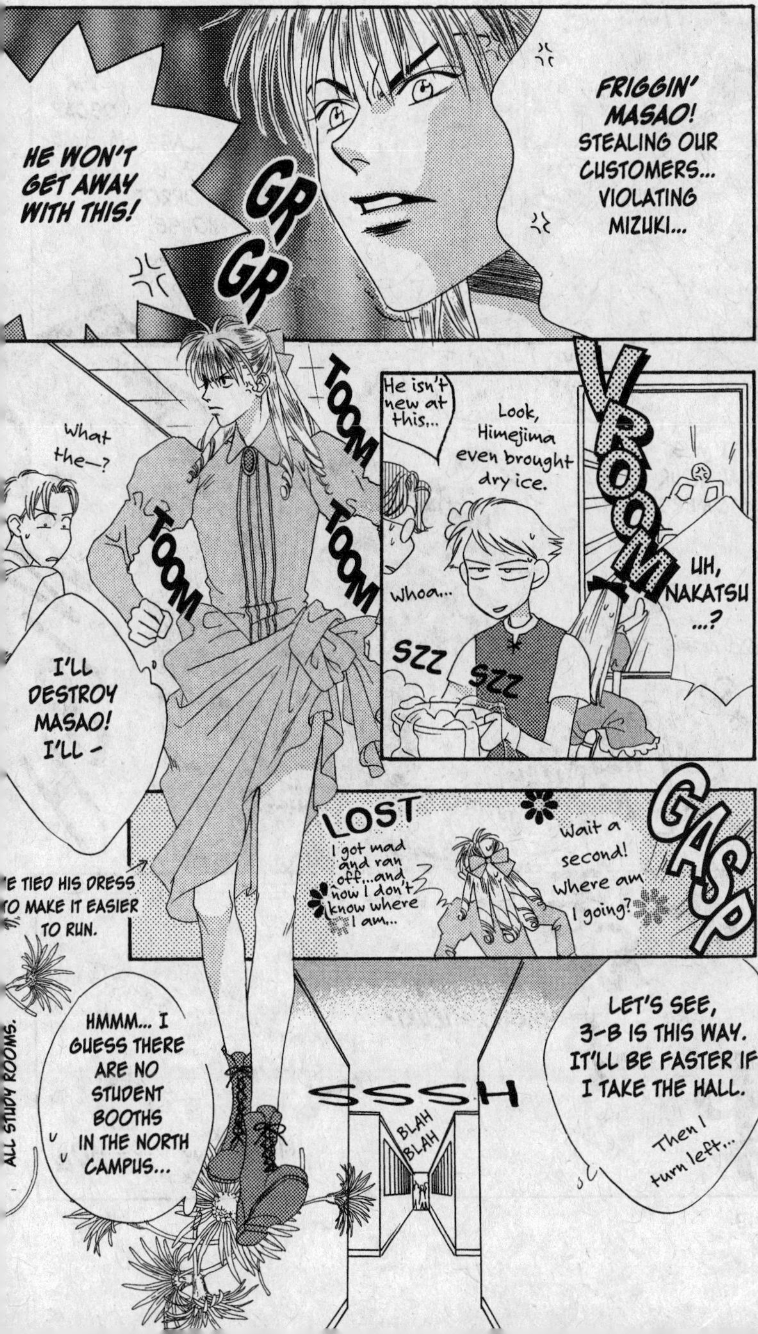
FRIGGIN' MASAO! STEALING OUR CUSTOMERS... VIOLATING MIZUKI...
GR GR
HE WON'T GET AWAY WITH THIS!
VROOM
UH, NAKATSU ...?
Look, Himejima even brought dry ice.
He isn't new at this...
Whoa...
SZZ SZZ
TOOM TOOM
What the—?
TOOM
I'LL DESTROY MASAO! I'LL –
E TIED HIS DRESS TO MAKE IT EASIER TO RUN.
GASP
Wait a second! Where am I going?
LOST
I got mad and ran off...and now I don't know where I am...
LET'S SEE, 3-B IS THIS WAY. IT'LL BE FASTER IF I TAKE THE HALL.
Then I turn left...
SSSH
BLAH BLAH
HMMM... I GUESS THERE ARE NO STUDENT BOOTHS IN THE NORTH CAMPUS...
ALL STUDY ROOMS.

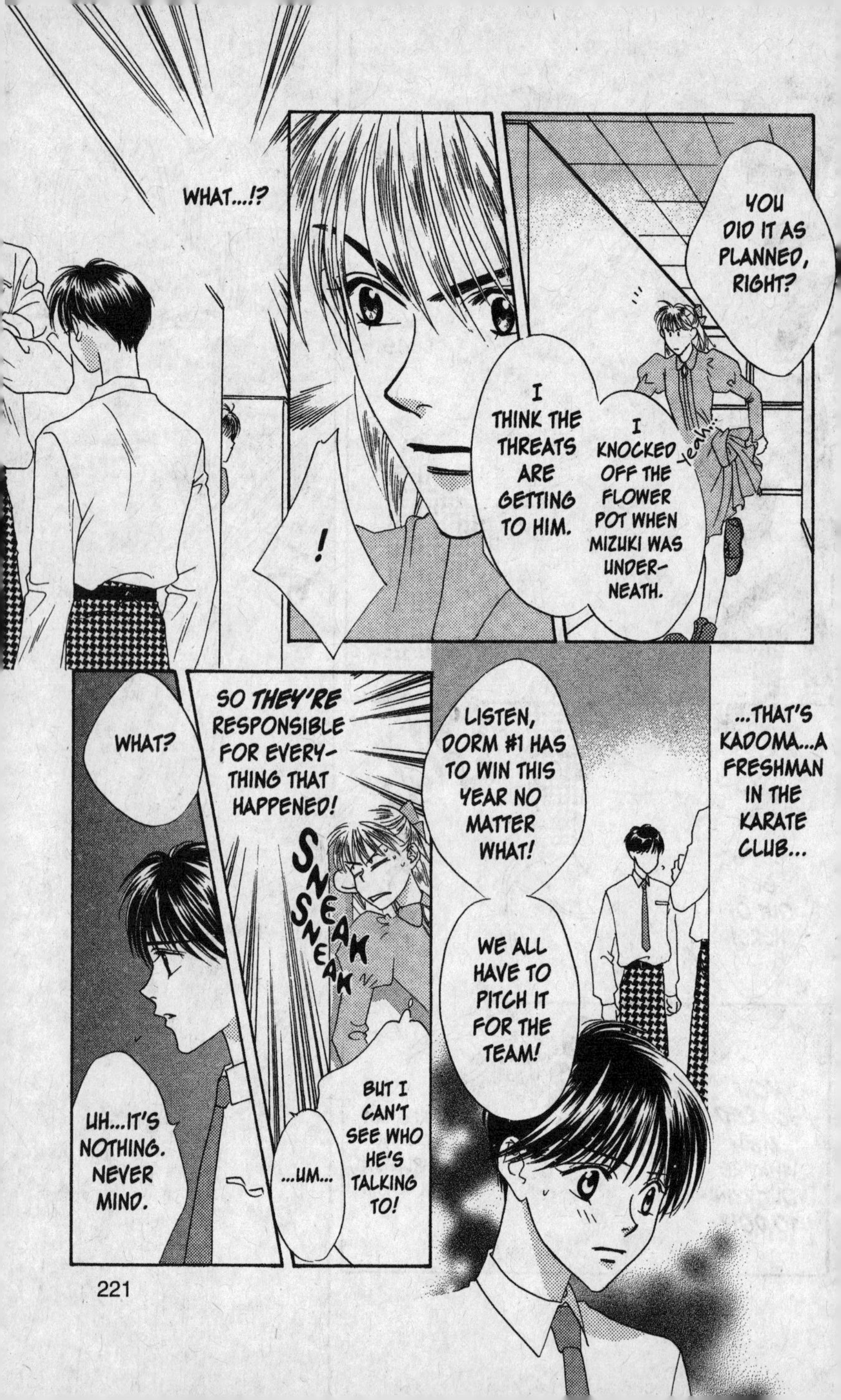

YOU DID IT AS PLANNED, RIGHT?
I KNOCKED OFF THE FLOWER POT WHEN MIZUKI WAS UNDER-NEATH.
Yeah...
I THINK THE THREATS ARE GETTING TO HIM.
!
WHAT...!?
...THAT'S KADOMA...A FRESHMAN IN THE KARATE CLUB...
LISTEN, DORM #1 HAS TO WIN THIS YEAR NO MATTER WHAT!
WE ALL HAVE TO PITCH IT FOR THE TEAM!
SO *THEY'RE* RESPONSIBLE FOR EVERY-THING THAT HAPPENED!
SNEAK SNEAK
BUT I CAN'T SEE WHO HE'S TALKING TO!
...UM...
WHAT?
UH...IT'S NOTHING. NEVER MIND.

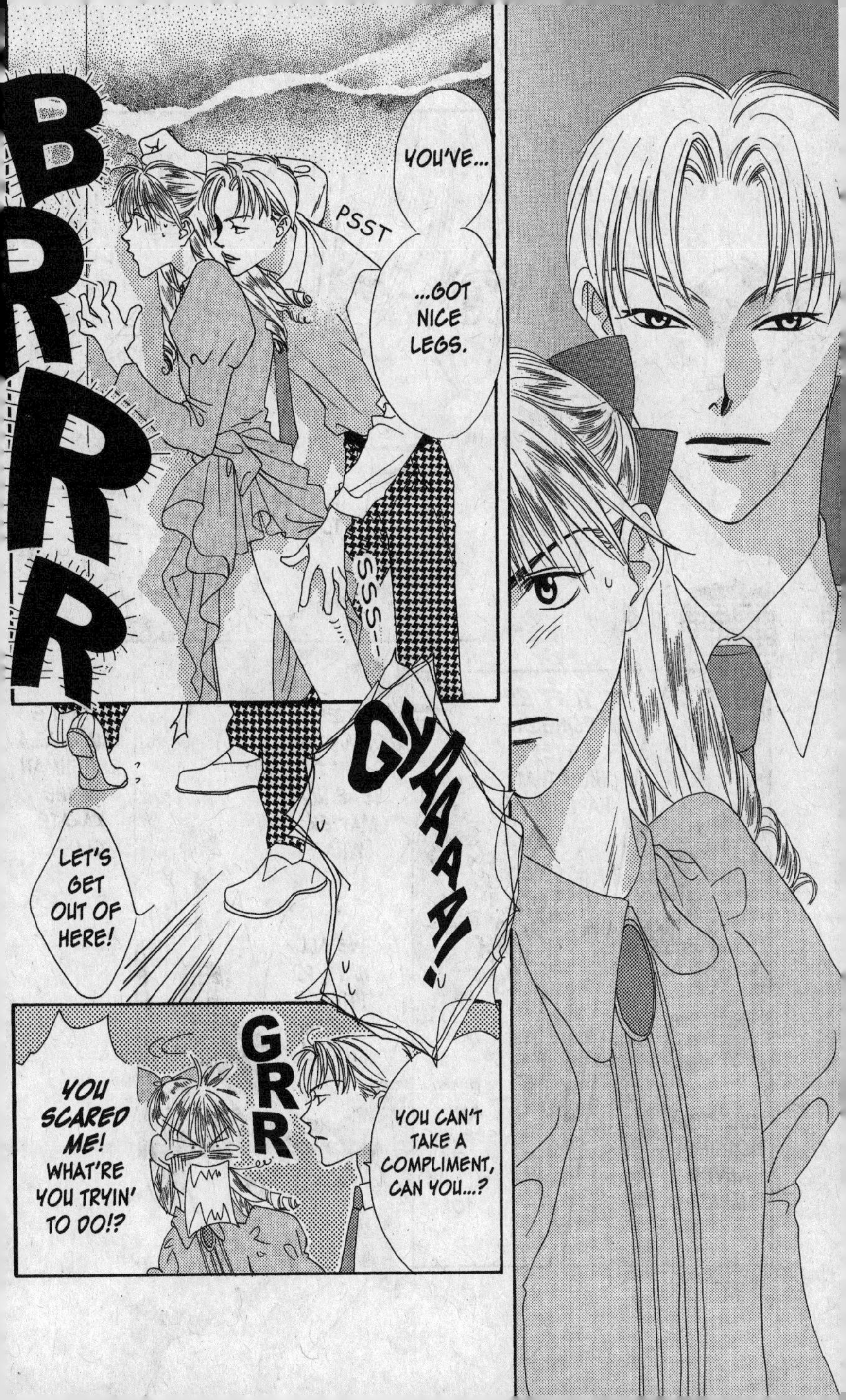
YOU'VE...
PSST
...GOT NICE LEGS.
BRRR
SSS--
GYAAAA!!
LET'S GET OUT OF HERE!
YOU CAN'T TAKE A COMPLIMENT, CAN YOU...?
GRR
YOU SCARED ME! WHAT'RE YOU TRYIN' TO DO!?

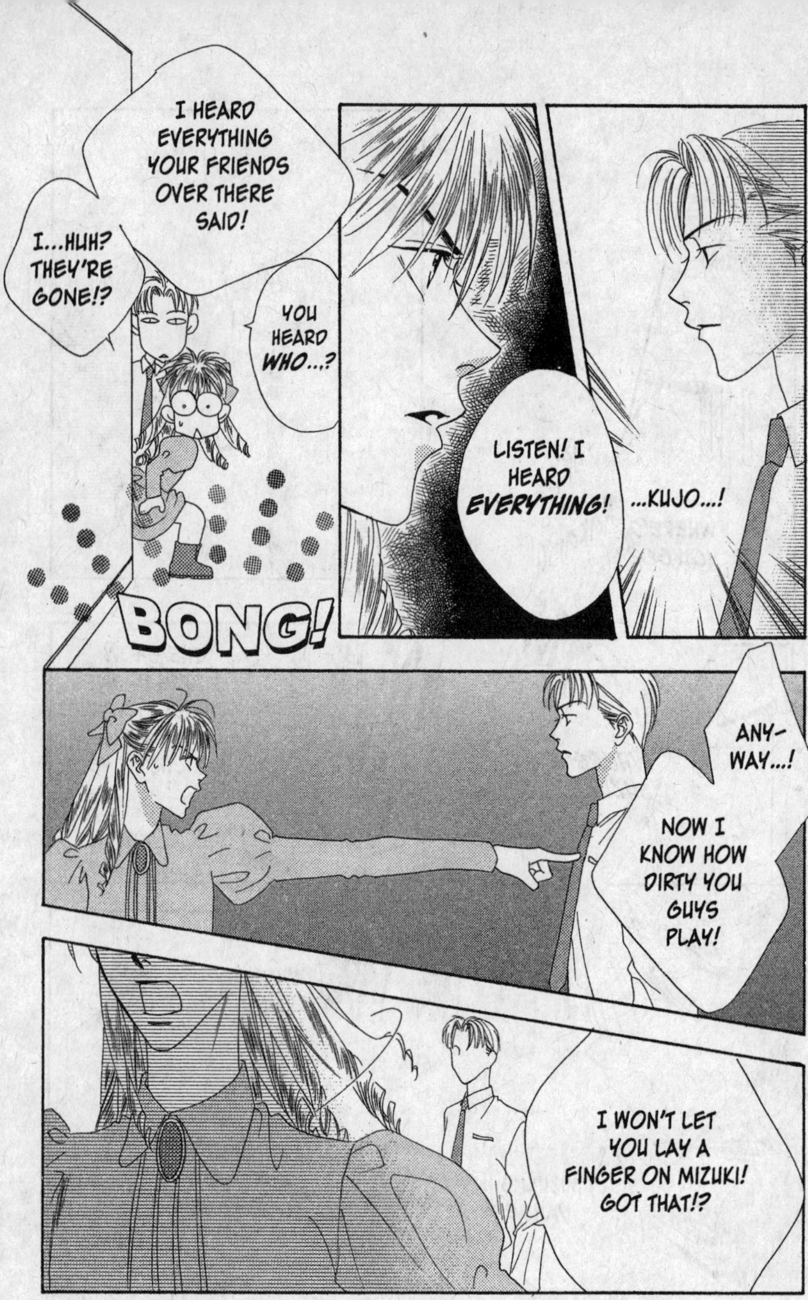
...KUJO...!
LISTEN! I HEARD EVERYTHING!
I HEARD EVERYTHING YOUR FRIENDS OVER THERE SAID!
YOU HEARD WHO...?
I...HUH? THEY'RE GONE!?
BONG!
ANY-WAY...!
NOW I KNOW HOW DIRTY YOU GUYS PLAY!
I WON'T LET YOU LAY A FINGER ON MIZUKI! GOT THAT!?

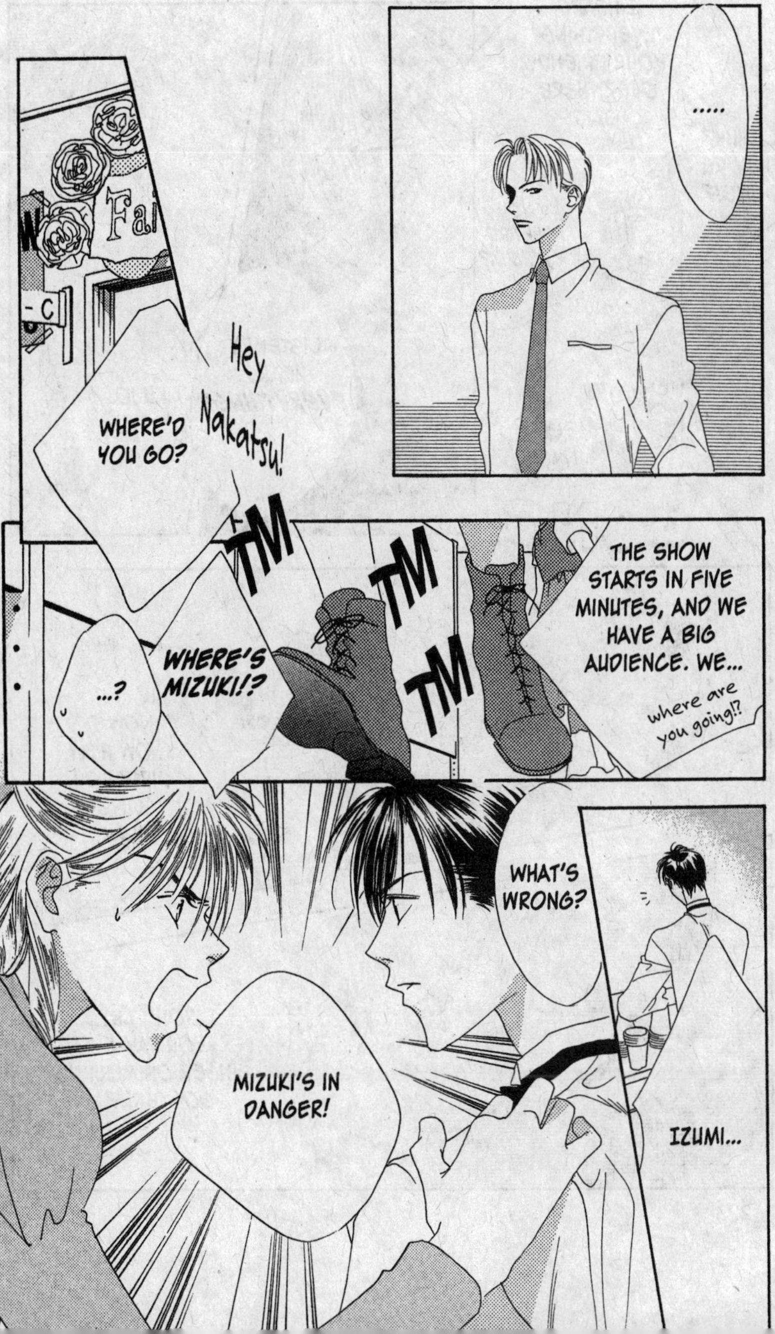
.....
Hey Nakatsu!
WHERE'D YOU GO?
THE SHOW STARTS IN FIVE MINUTES, AND WE HAVE A BIG AUDIENCE. WE...
where are you going!?
TM
TM
TM
WHERE'S MIZUKI!?
...?
IZUMI...
WHAT'S WRONG?
MIZUKI'S IN DANGER!

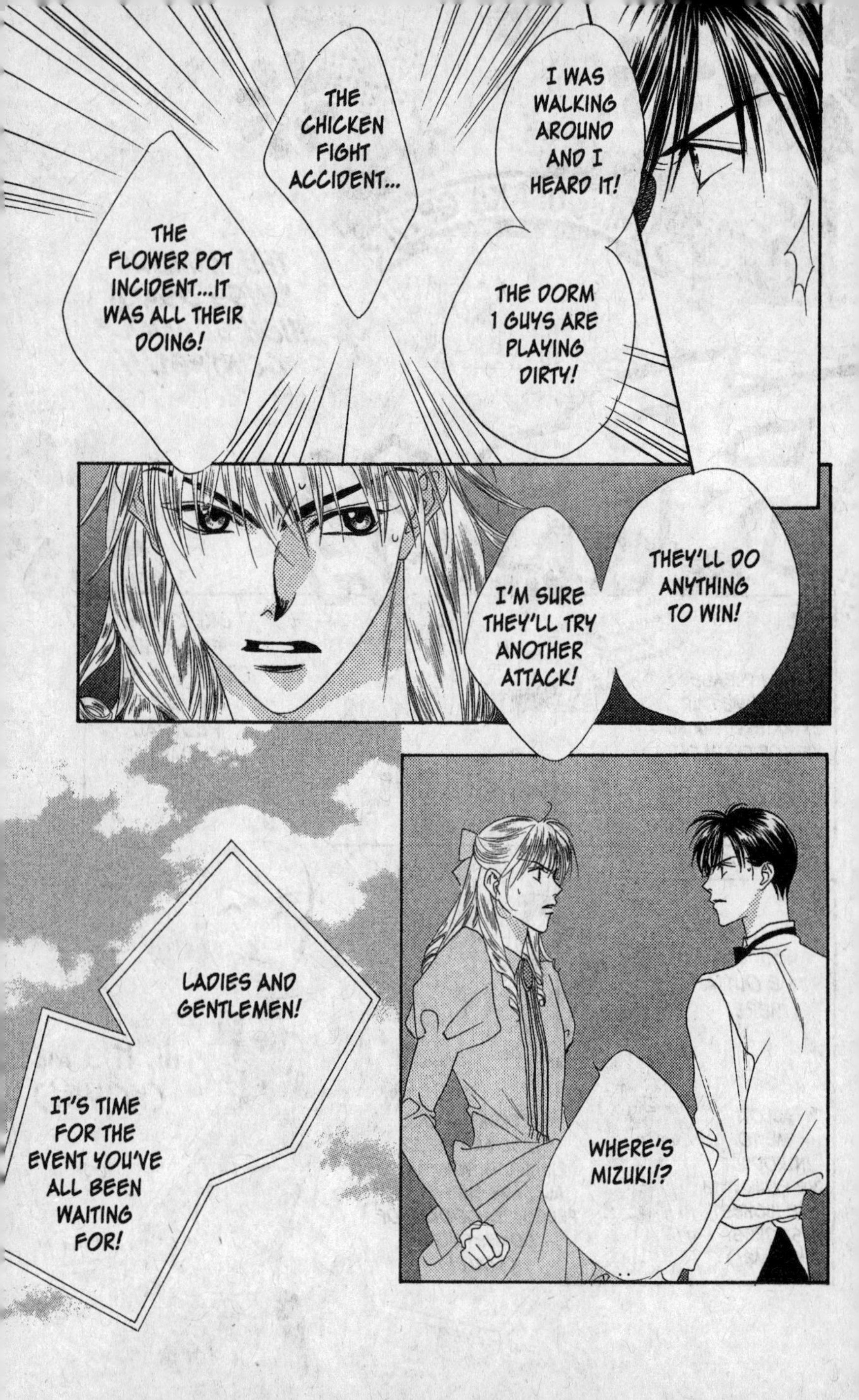
I WAS WALKING AROUND AND I HEARD IT!
THE DORM 1 GUYS ARE PLAYING DIRTY!
THE CHICKEN FIGHT ACCIDENT...
THE FLOWER POT INCIDENT...IT WAS ALL THEIR DOING!
THEY'LL DO ANYTHING TO WIN!
I'M SURE THEY'LL TRY ANOTHER ATTACK!
WHERE'S MIZUKI!?
LADIES AND GENTLEMEN!
IT'S TIME FOR THE EVENT YOU'VE ALL BEEN WAITING FOR!

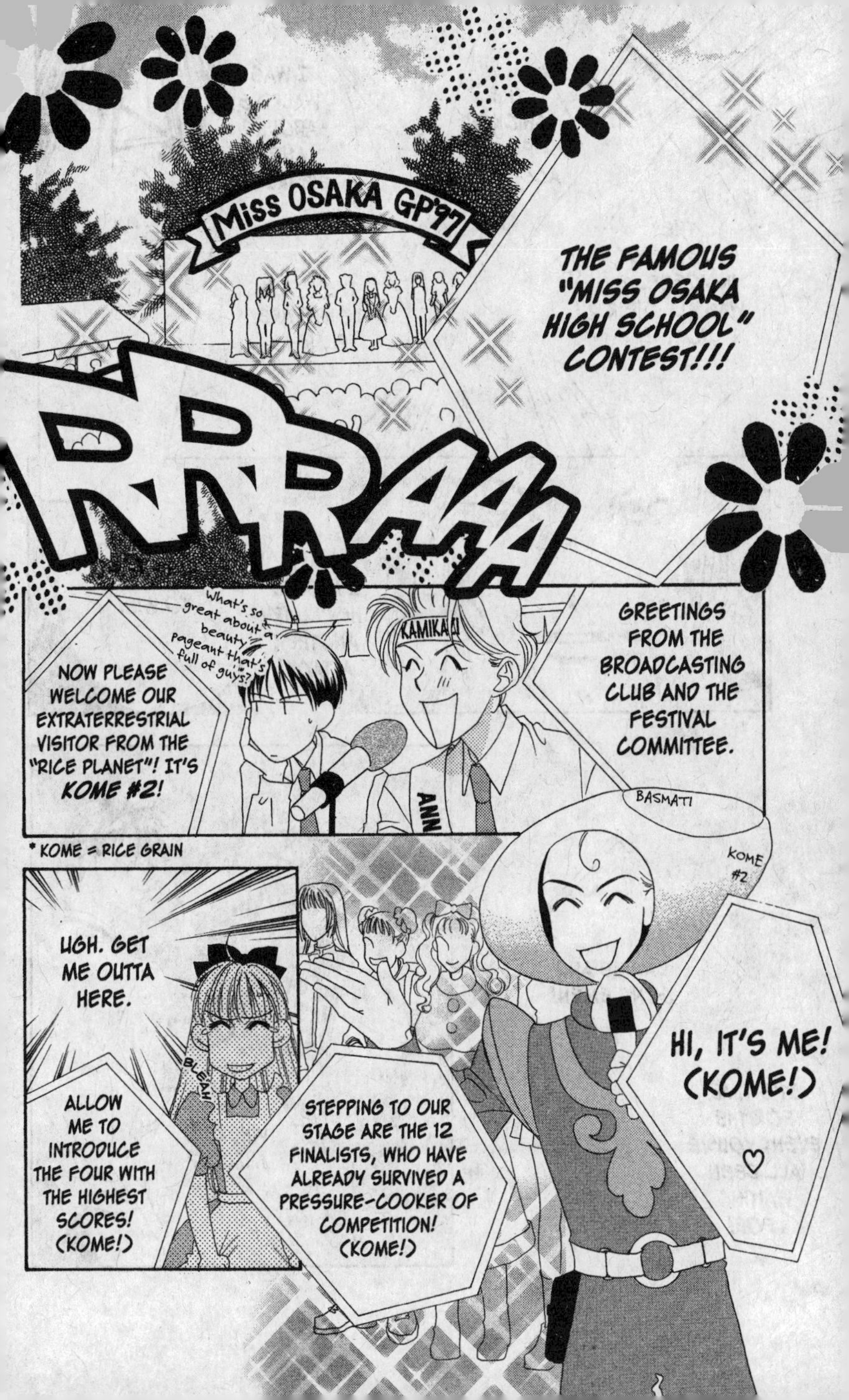
THE FAMOUS "MISS OSAKA HIGH SCHOOL" CONTEST!!!
Miss OSAKA GP'97
RRRAAA
GREETINGS FROM THE BROADCASTING CLUB AND THE FESTIVAL COMMITTEE.
What's so great about a beauty pageant that's full of guys?
NOW PLEASE WELCOME OUR EXTRATERRESTRIAL VISITOR FROM THE "RICE PLANET"! IT'S *KOME #2*!
BASMATI
KOME #2
HI, IT'S ME! (KOME!) ♡
STEPPING TO OUR STAGE ARE THE 12 FINALISTS, WHO HAVE ALREADY SURVIVED A PRESSURE-COOKER OF COMPETITION! (KOME!)
UGH. GET ME OUTTA HERE.
BLEAH
ALLOW ME TO INTRODUCE THE FOUR WITH THE HIGHEST SCORES! (KOME!)

* KOME = RICE GRAIN

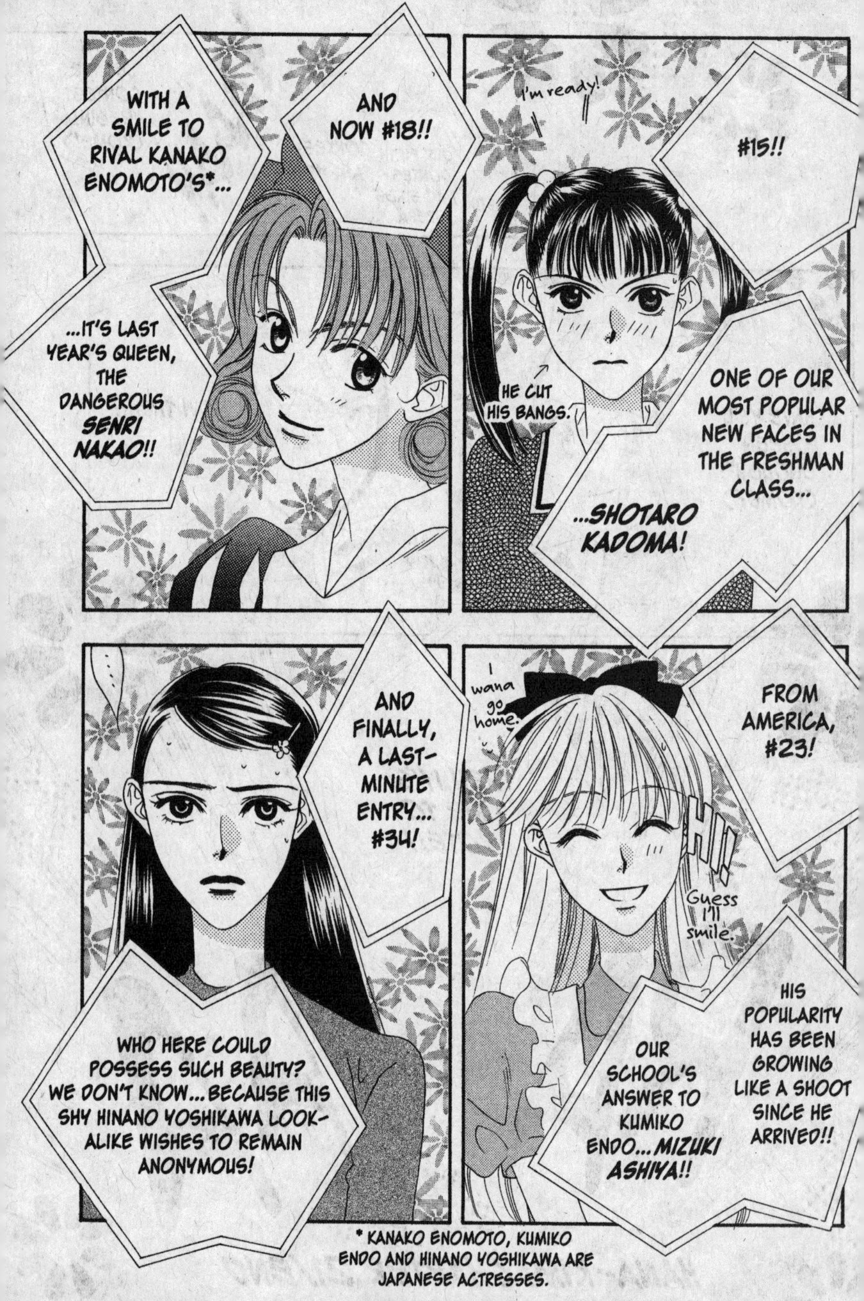

I'm ready!
#15!!
HE CUT HIS BANGS.
ONE OF OUR MOST POPULAR NEW FACES IN THE FRESHMAN CLASS...
...SHOTARO KADOMA!
AND NOW #18!!
WITH A SMILE TO RIVAL KANAKO ENOMOTO'S*...
...IT'S LAST YEAR'S QUEEN, THE DANGEROUS SENRI NAKAO!!
FROM AMERICA, #23!
I wana go home.
HI!
Guess I'll smile.
HIS POPULARITY HAS BEEN GROWING LIKE A SHOOT SINCE HE ARRIVED!!
OUR SCHOOL'S ANSWER TO KUMIKO ENDO... MIZUKI ASHIYA!!
AND FINALLY, A LAST-MINUTE ENTRY... #34!
...
WHO HERE COULD POSSESS SUCH BEAUTY? WE DON'T KNOW... BECAUSE THIS SHY HINANO YOSHIKAWA LOOK-ALIKE WISHES TO REMAIN ANONYMOUS!

* KANAKO ENOMOTO, KUMIKO ENDO AND HINANO YOSHIKAWA ARE JAPANESE ACTRESSES.

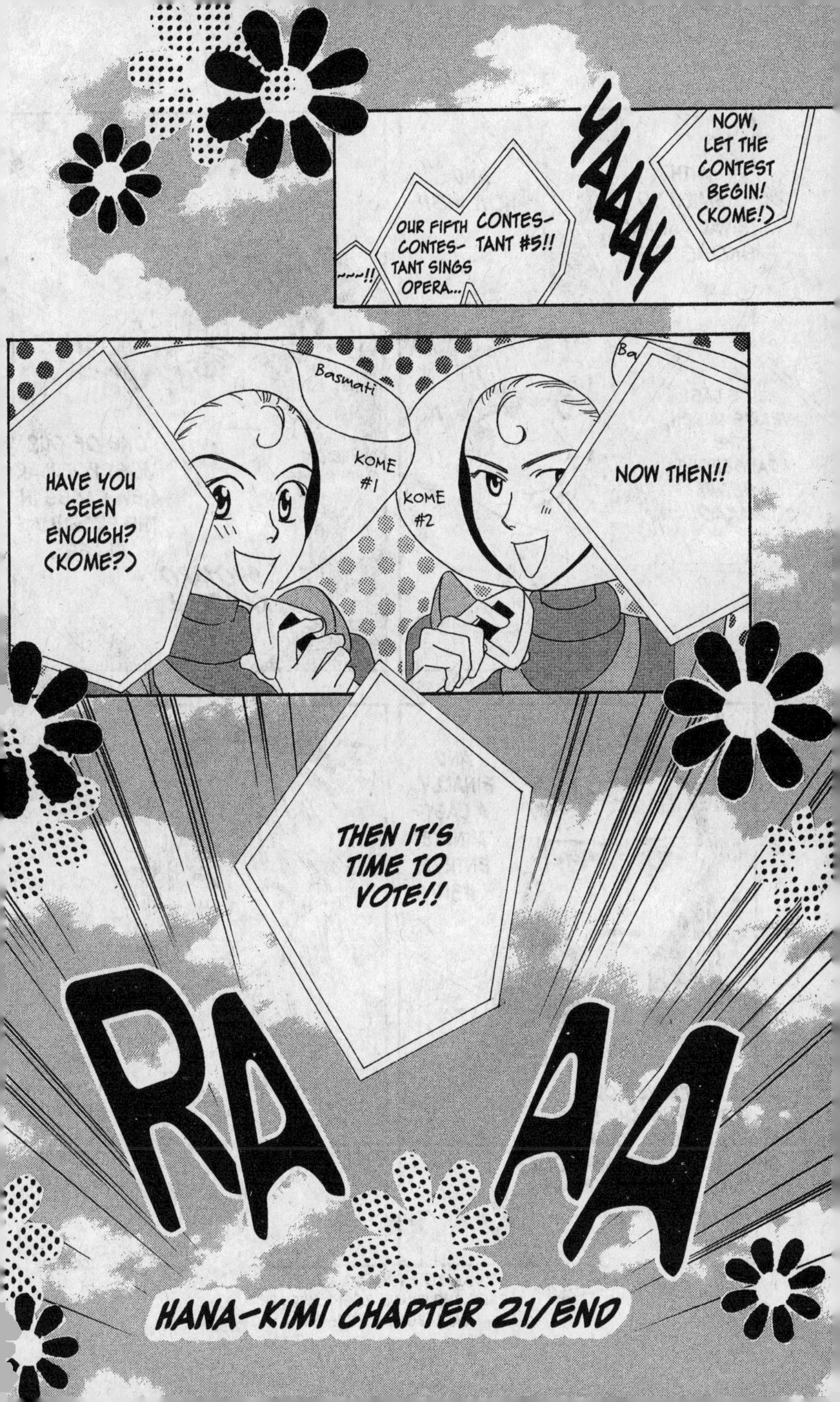
NOW, LET THE CONTEST BEGIN! (KOME!)
YAAAAY
CONTES-TANT #5!!
OUR FIFTH CONTES-TANT SINGS OPERA...
~~~!!
NOW THEN!!
KOME #2
KOME #1
Basmati
HAVE YOU SEEN ENOUGH? (KOME?)
THEN IT'S TIME TO VOTE!!
RAAA
HANA-KIMI CHAPTER 21/END
~~~

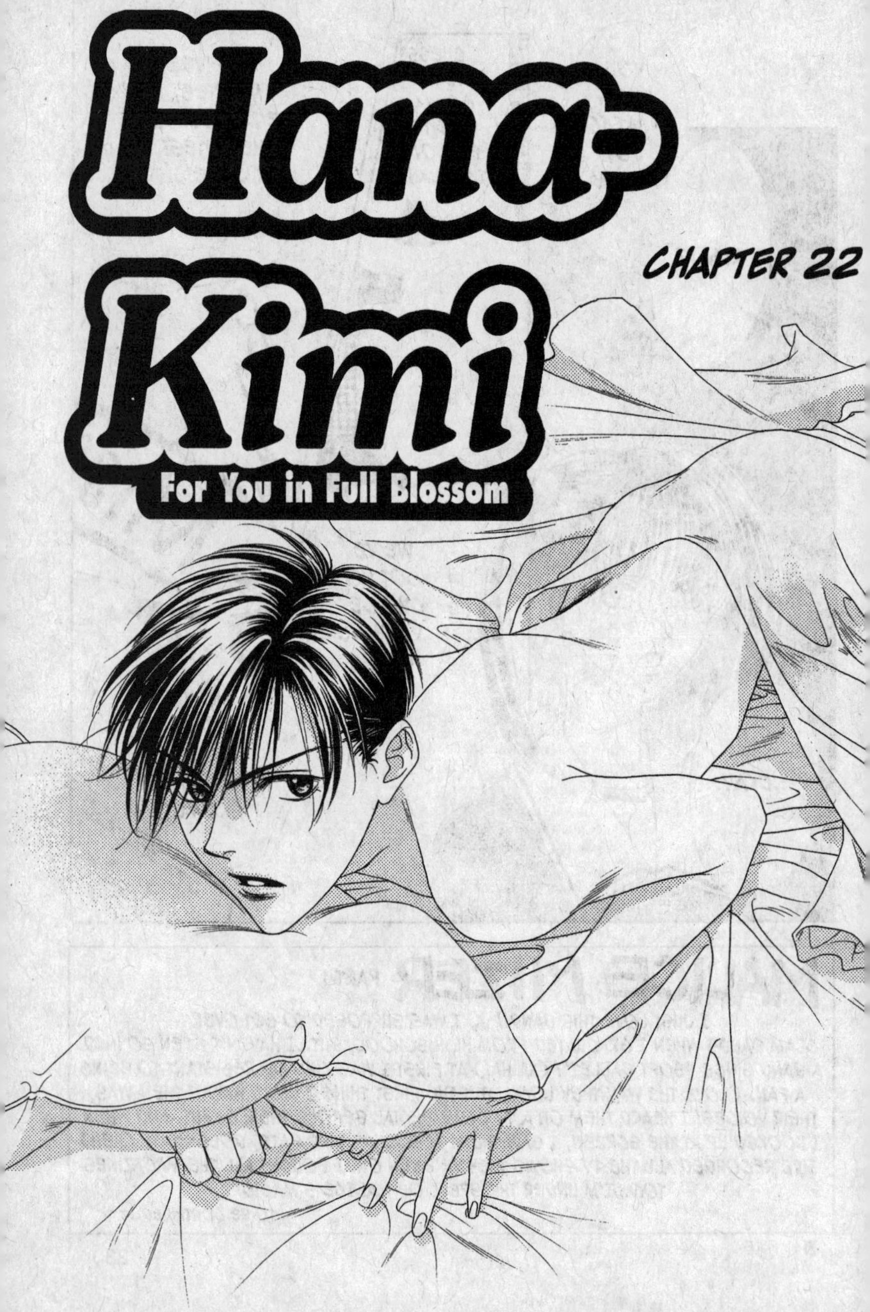
Hana-
Kimi
For You in Full Blossom
CHAPTER 22

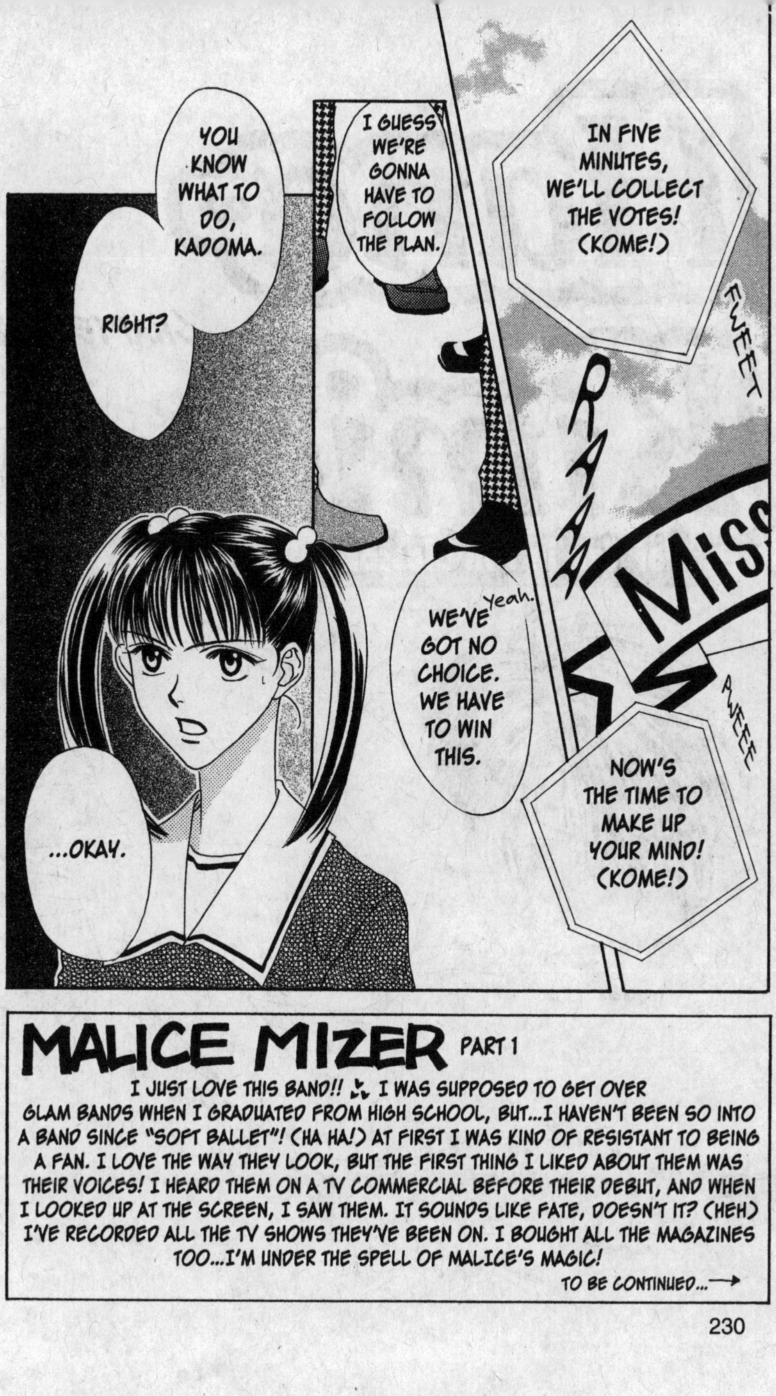
IN FIVE MINUTES, WE'LL COLLECT THE VOTES! (KOME!)
FWEET
RAAAA
MiSS
PWEEE
NOW'S THE TIME TO MAKE UP YOUR MIND! (KOME!)
I GUESS WE'RE GONNA HAVE TO FOLLOW THE PLAN.
Yeah.
WE'VE GOT NO CHOICE. WE HAVE TO WIN THIS.
YOU KNOW WHAT TO DO, KADOMA.
RIGHT?
...OKAY.

MALICE MIZER PART 1

I JUST LOVE THIS BAND!! ♪ I WAS SUPPOSED TO GET OVER GLAM BANDS WHEN I GRADUATED FROM HIGH SCHOOL, BUT...I HAVEN'T BEEN SO INTO A BAND SINCE "SOFT BALLET"! (HA HA!) AT FIRST I WAS KIND OF RESISTANT TO BEING A FAN. I LOVE THE WAY THEY LOOK, BUT THE FIRST THING I LIKED ABOUT THEM WAS THEIR VOICES! I HEARD THEM ON A TV COMMERCIAL BEFORE THEIR DEBUT, AND WHEN I LOOKED UP AT THE SCREEN, I SAW THEM. IT SOUNDS LIKE FATE, DOESN'T IT? (HEH) I'VE RECORDED ALL THE TV SHOWS THEY'VE BEEN ON. I BOUGHT ALL THE MAGAZINES TOO...I'M UNDER THE SPELL OF MALICE'S MAGIC!

TO BE CONTINUED...→

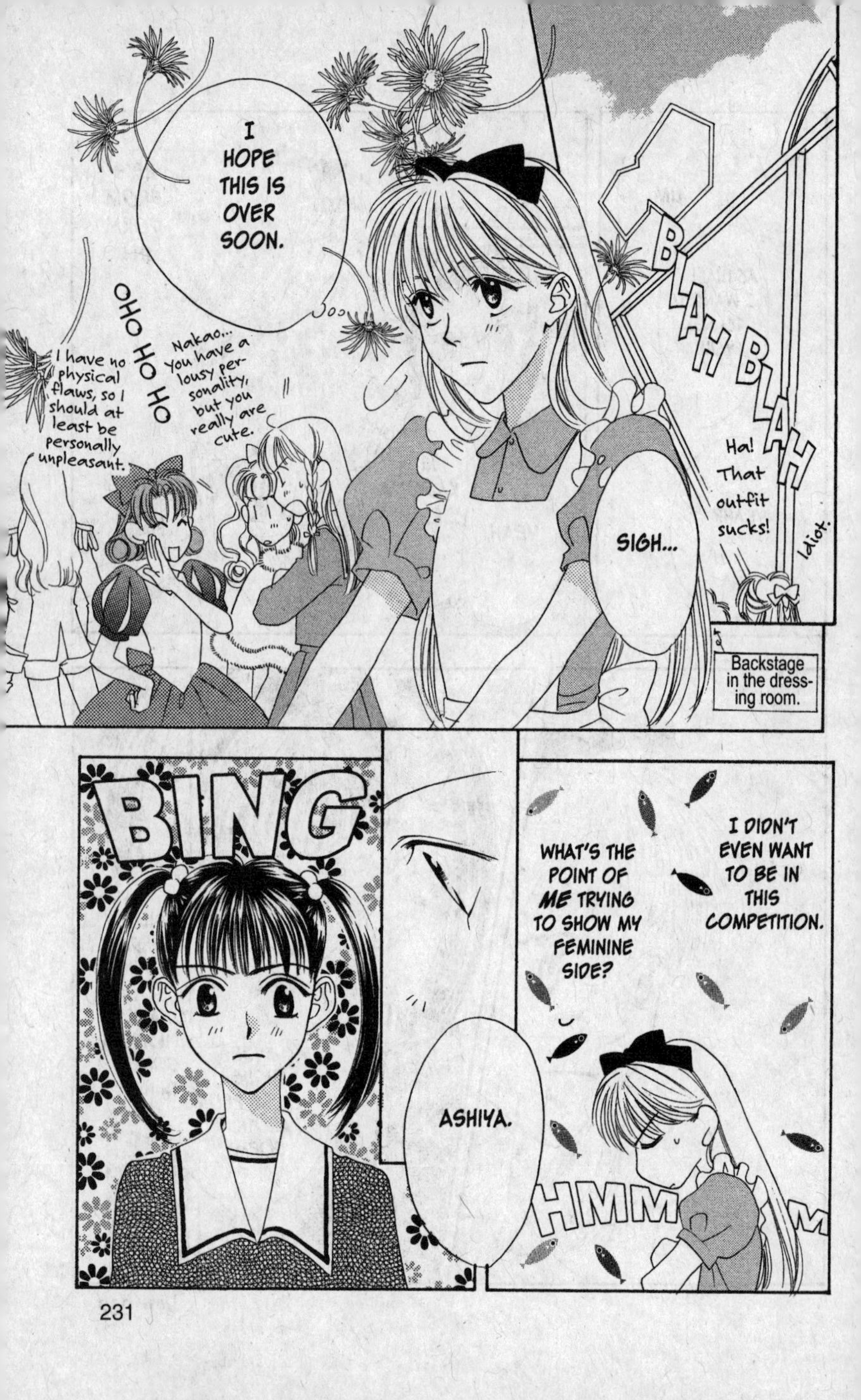
BLAH BLAH
Ha! That outfit sucks!
Idiot.
Backstage in the dressing room.
SIGH...
I HOPE THIS IS OVER SOON.
Nakao... You have a lousy personality, but you really are cute.
OHO HO HO HO
I have no physical flaws, so I should at least be personally unpleasant.
I DIDN'T EVEN WANT TO BE IN THIS COMPETITION.
WHAT'S THE POINT OF *ME* TRYING TO SHOW MY FEMININE SIDE?
HMMMM
ASHIYA.
BING

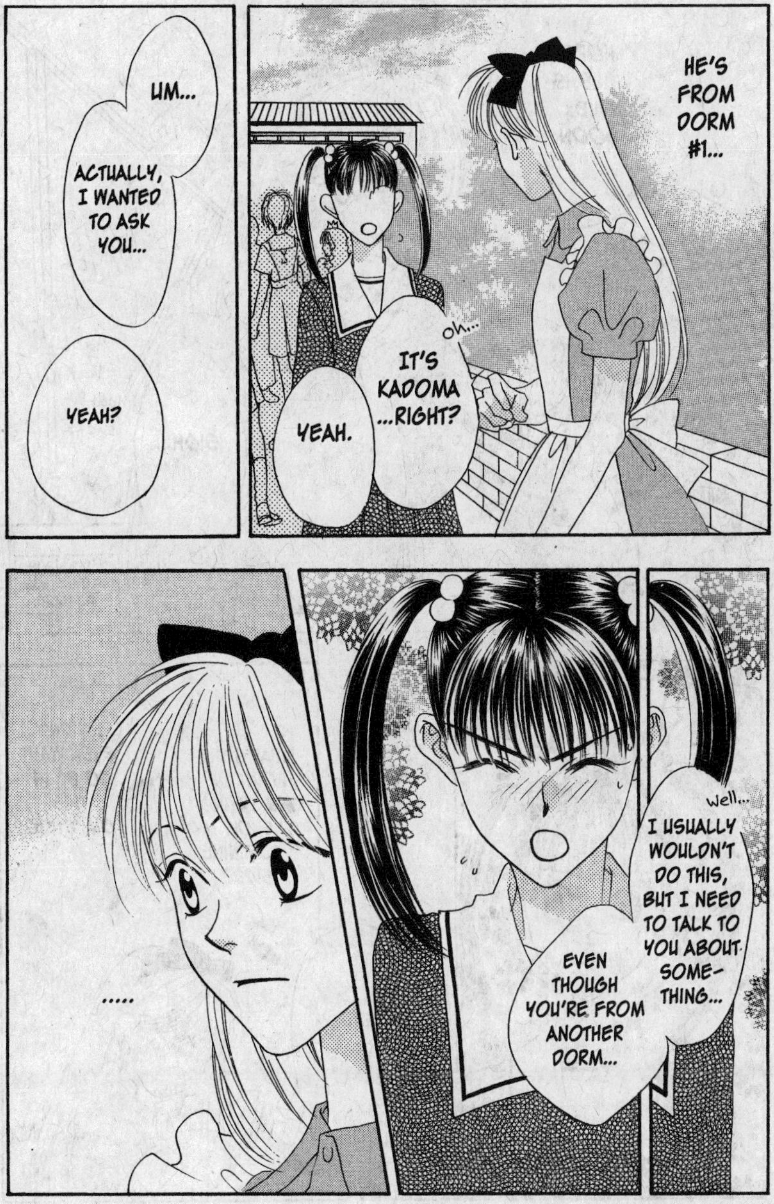
HE'S FROM DORM #1...
oh...
IT'S KADOMA ...RIGHT?
YEAH.
UM...
ACTUALLY, I WANTED TO ASK YOU...
YEAH?
well...
I USUALLY WOULDN'T DO THIS, BUT I NEED TO TALK TO YOU ABOUT SOME-THING...
EVEN THOUGH YOU'RE FROM ANOTHER DORM...
.....

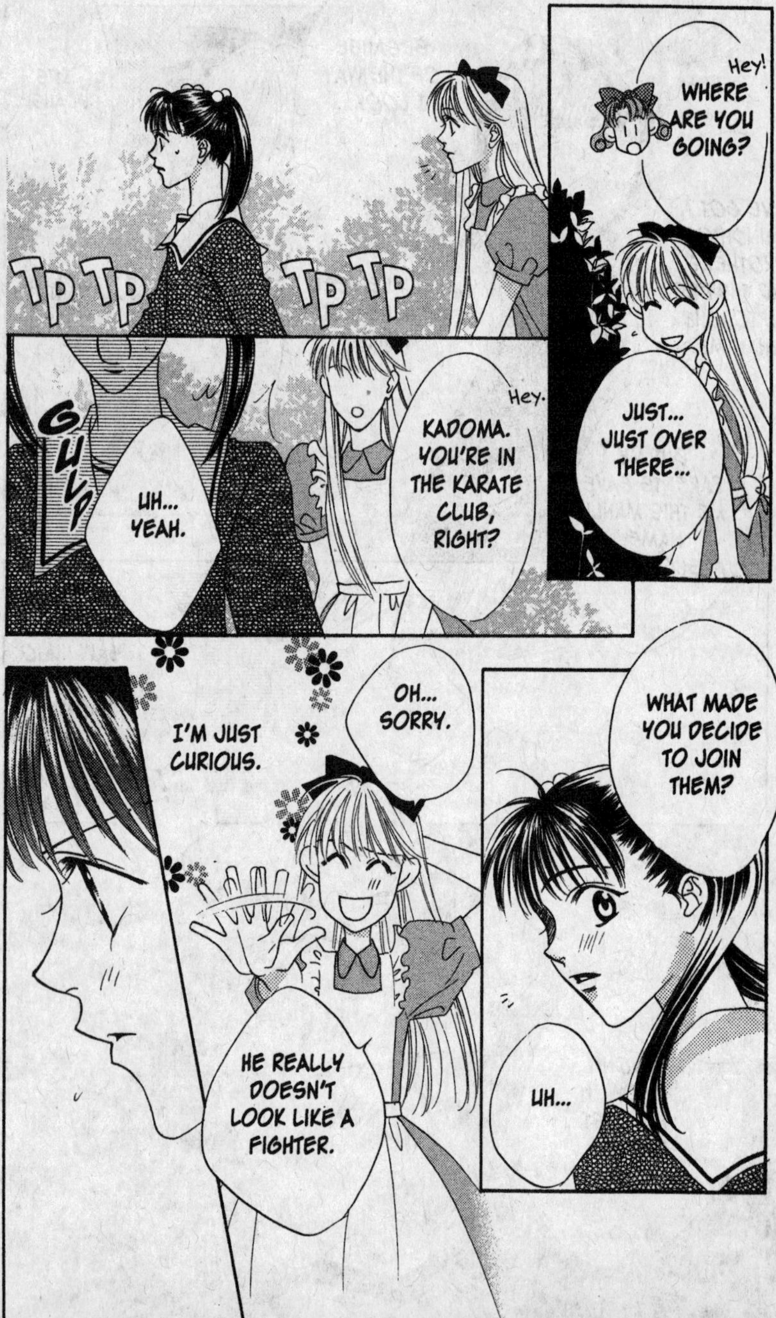
Hey!
WHERE ARE YOU GOING?
JUST... JUST OVER THERE...
TP TP TP TP
Hey.
KADOMA. YOU'RE IN THE KARATE CLUB, RIGHT?
GULP
UH... YEAH.
WHAT MADE YOU DECIDE TO JOIN THEM?
UH...
OH... SORRY.
I'M JUST CURIOUS.
HE REALLY DOESN'T LOOK LIKE A FIGHTER.

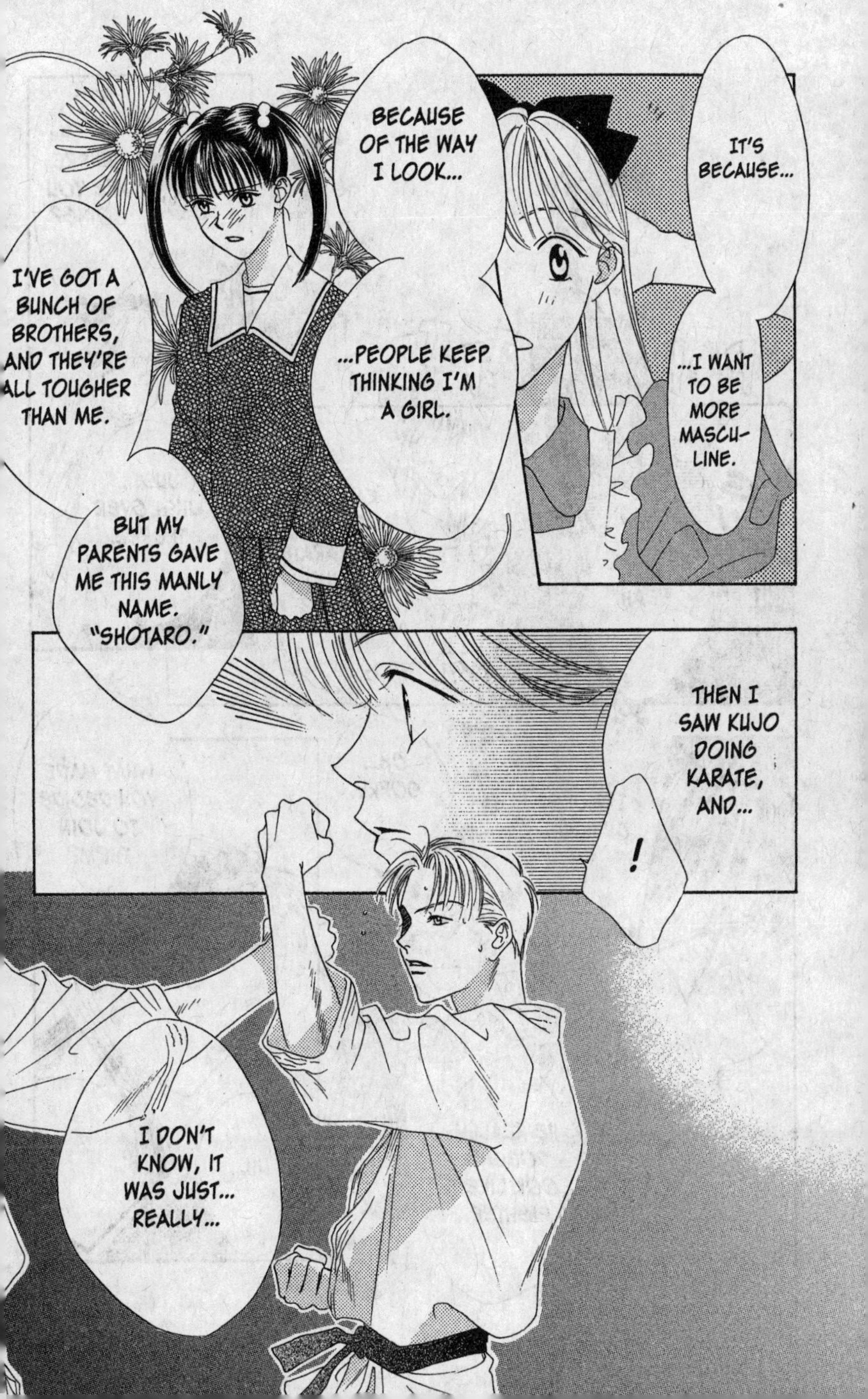
IT'S BECAUSE...
...I WANT TO BE MORE MASCU-LINE.
BECAUSE OF THE WAY I LOOK...
...PEOPLE KEEP THINKING I'M A GIRL.
I'VE GOT A BUNCH OF BROTHERS, AND THEY'RE ALL TOUGHER THAN ME.
BUT MY PARENTS GAVE ME THIS MANLY NAME. "SHOTARO."
THEN I SAW KUJO DOING KARATE, AND...
!
I DON'T KNOW, IT WAS JUST... REALLY...

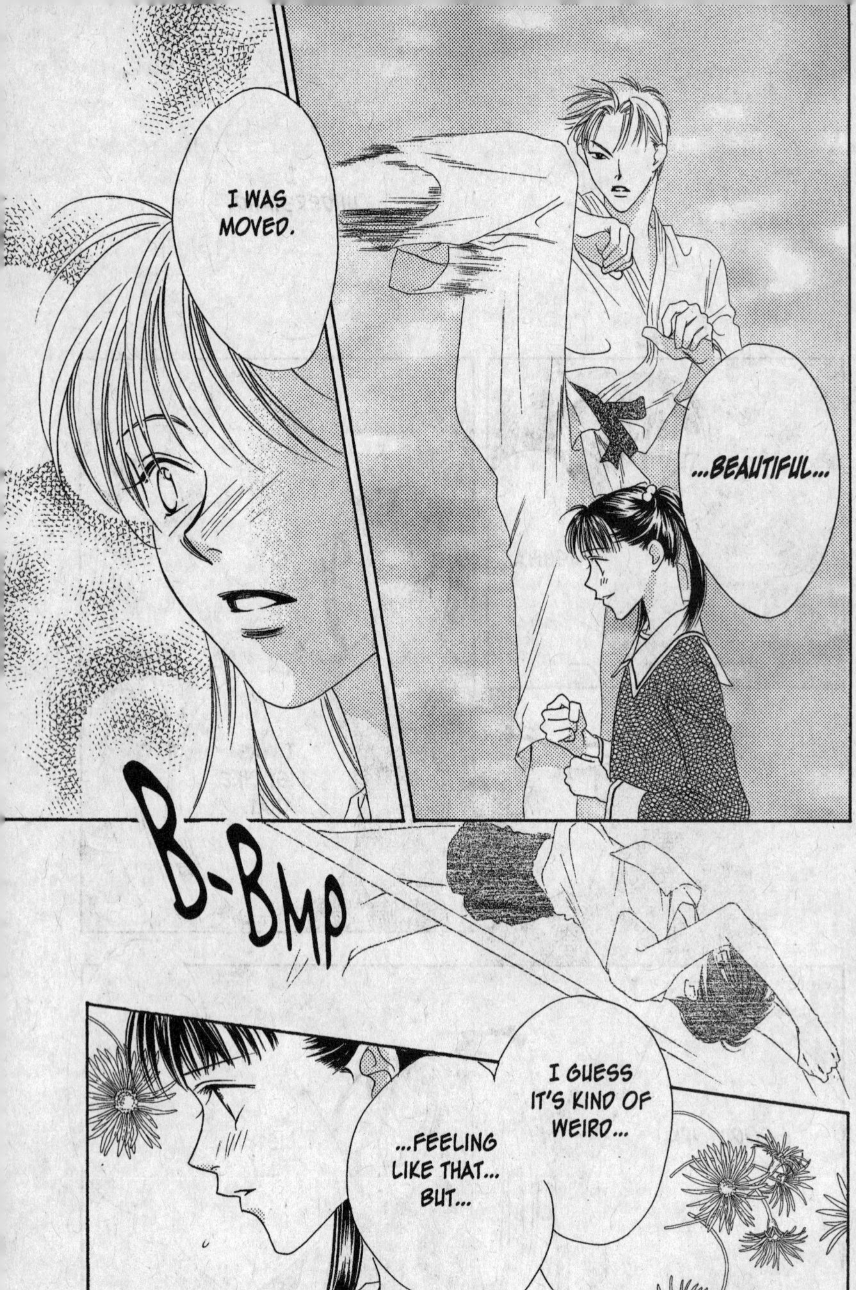
...BEAUTIFUL...
I WAS MOVED.
B-BMP
I GUESS IT'S KIND OF WEIRD...
...FEELING LIKE THAT... BUT...

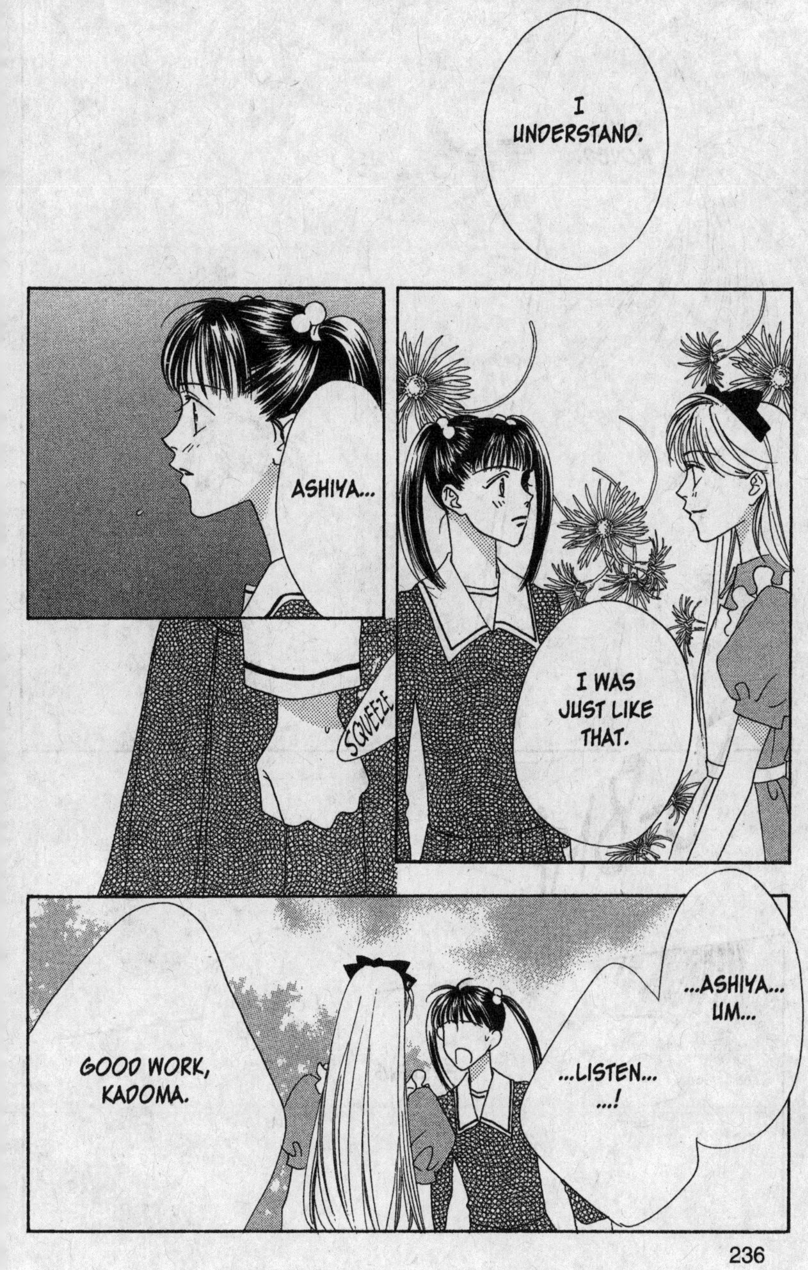
I UNDERSTAND.
I WAS JUST LIKE THAT.
ASHIYA...
SQUEEZE
...ASHIYA... UM...
...LISTEN... ...!
GOOD WORK, KADOMA.

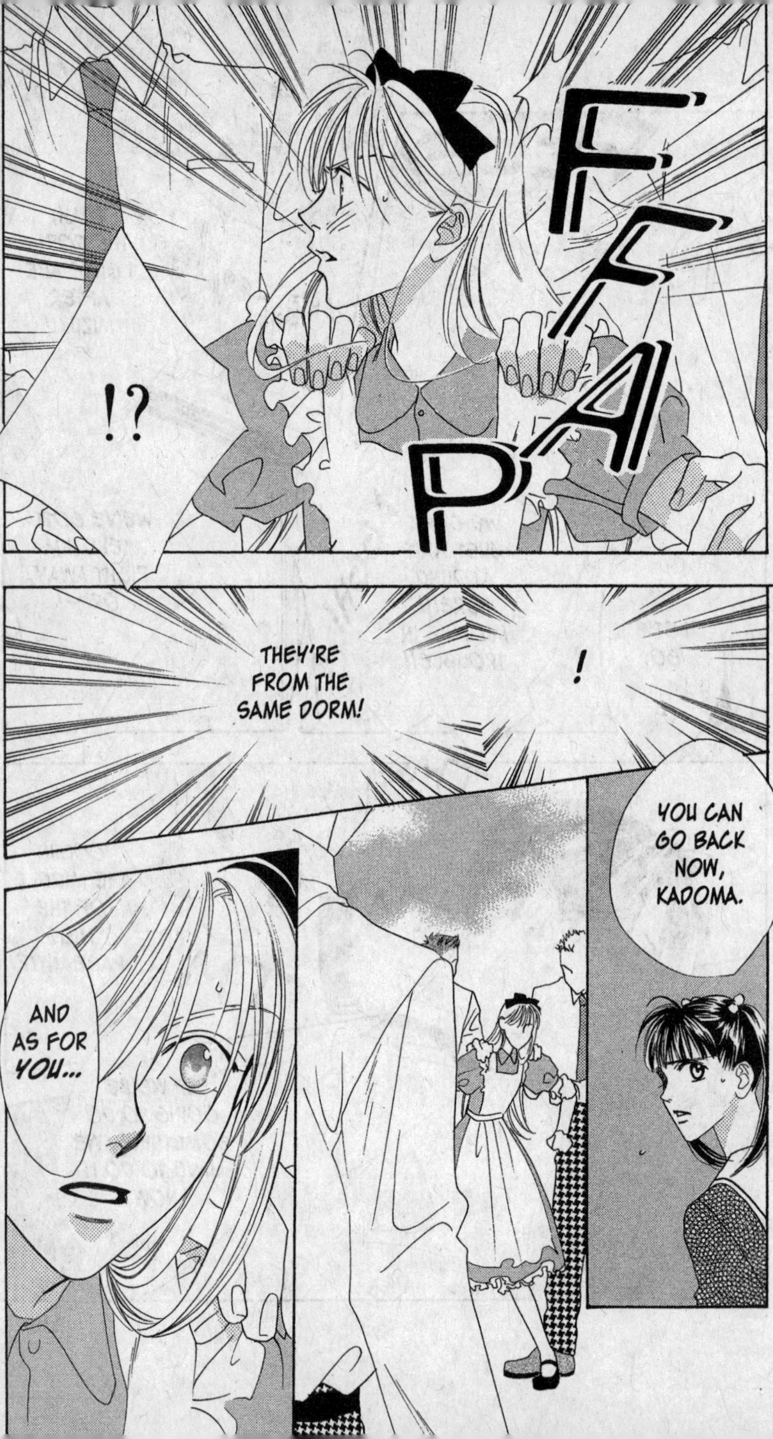
FFAP
!?
!
THEY'RE FROM THE SAME DORM!
YOU CAN GO BACK NOW, KADOMA.
AND AS FOR *YOU*...

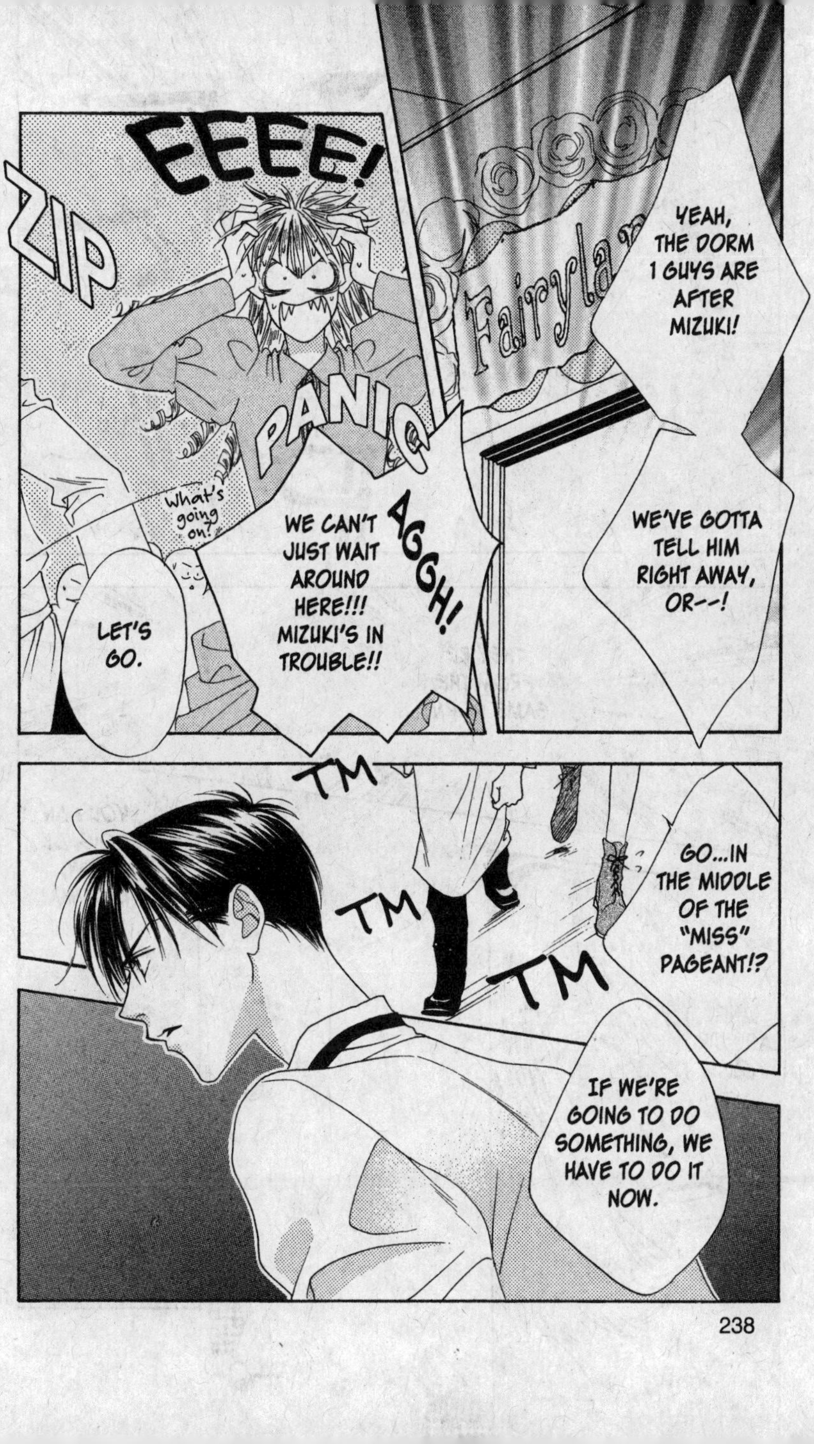
YEAH, THE DORM 1 GUYS ARE AFTER MIZUKI!
WE'VE GOTTA TELL HIM RIGHT AWAY, OR--!
EEEE!
ZIP
PANIC
AGGH!
WE CAN'T JUST WAIT AROUND HERE!!! MIZUKI'S IN TROUBLE!!
What's going on?
LET'S GO.
TM
TM
TM
GO...IN THE MIDDLE OF THE "MISS" PAGEANT!?
IF WE'RE GOING TO DO SOMETHING, WE HAVE TO DO IT NOW.

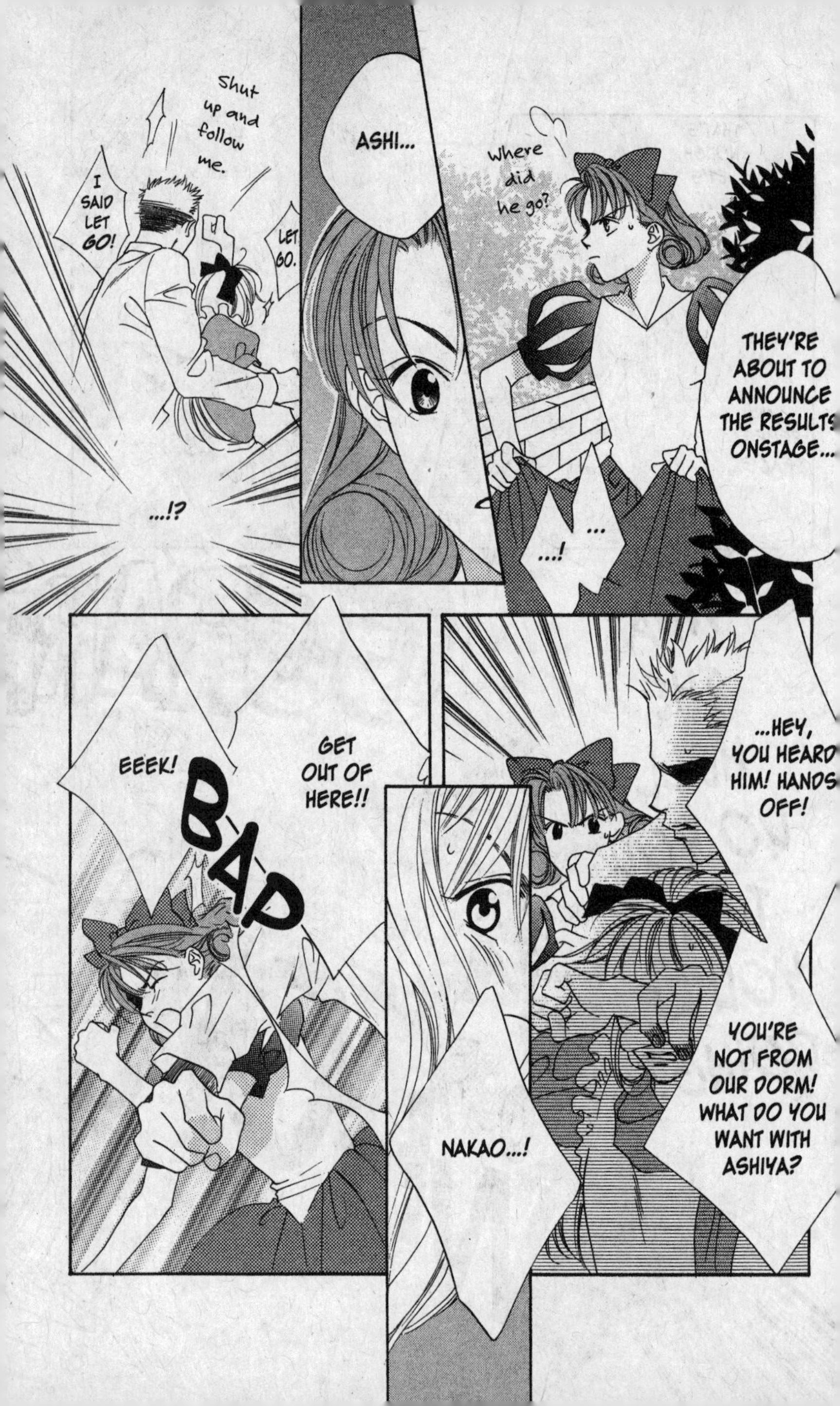

Where did he go?
THEY'RE ABOUT TO ANNOUNCE THE RESULTS ONSTAGE...
...
...!
ASHI...
Shut up and follow me.
LET GO.
I SAID LET GO!
...!?
...HEY, YOU HEARD HIM! HANDS OFF!
YOU'RE NOT FROM OUR DORM! WHAT DO YOU WANT WITH ASHIYA?
NAKAO...!
GET OUT OF HERE!!
EEEK!
BAP

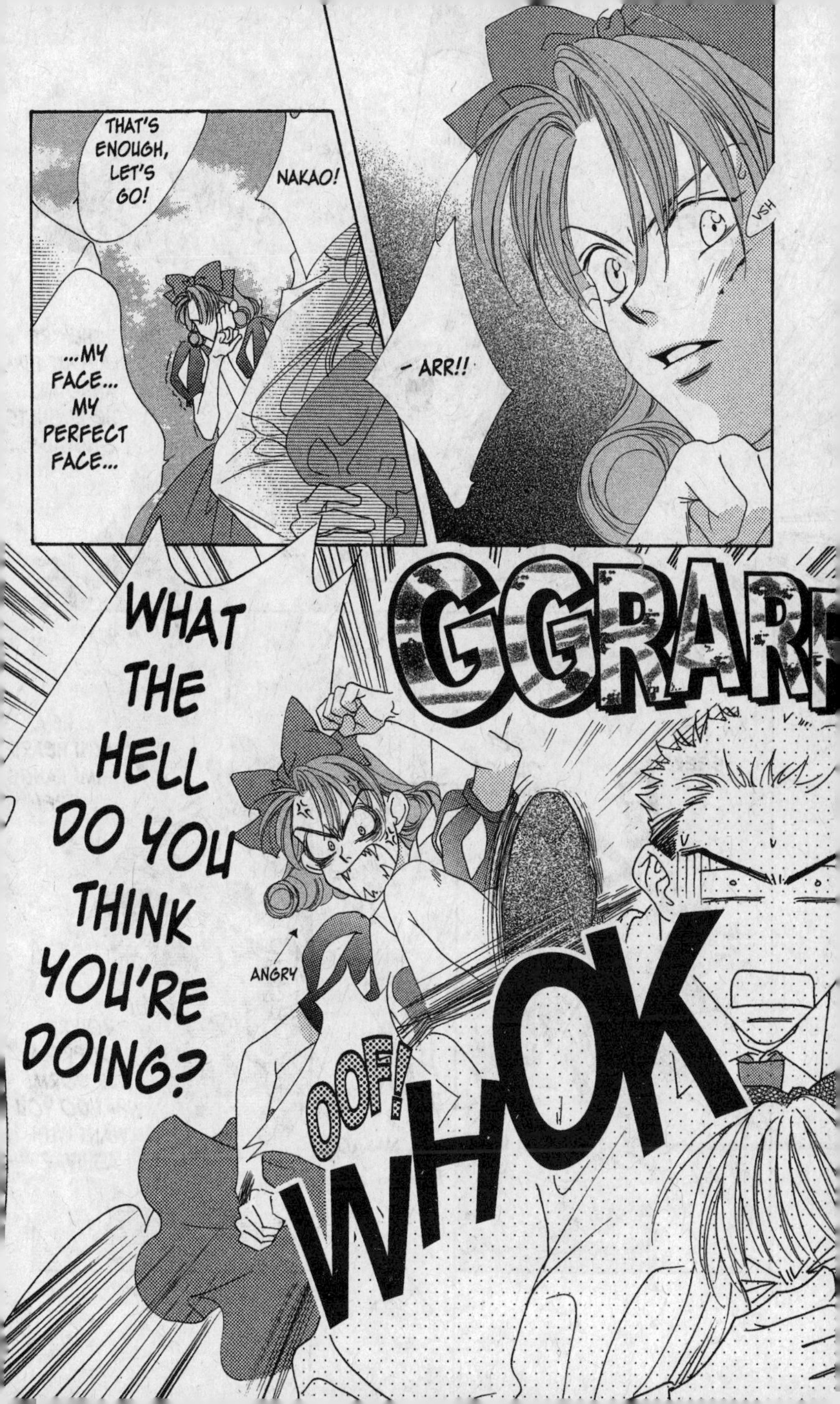
VSH
- ARR!!
NAKAO!
THAT'S ENOUGH, LET'S GO!
...MY FACE... MY PERFECT FACE...
GGRAR
WHAT THE HELL DO YOU THINK YOU'RE DOING?
ANGRY
OOF!
WHOK

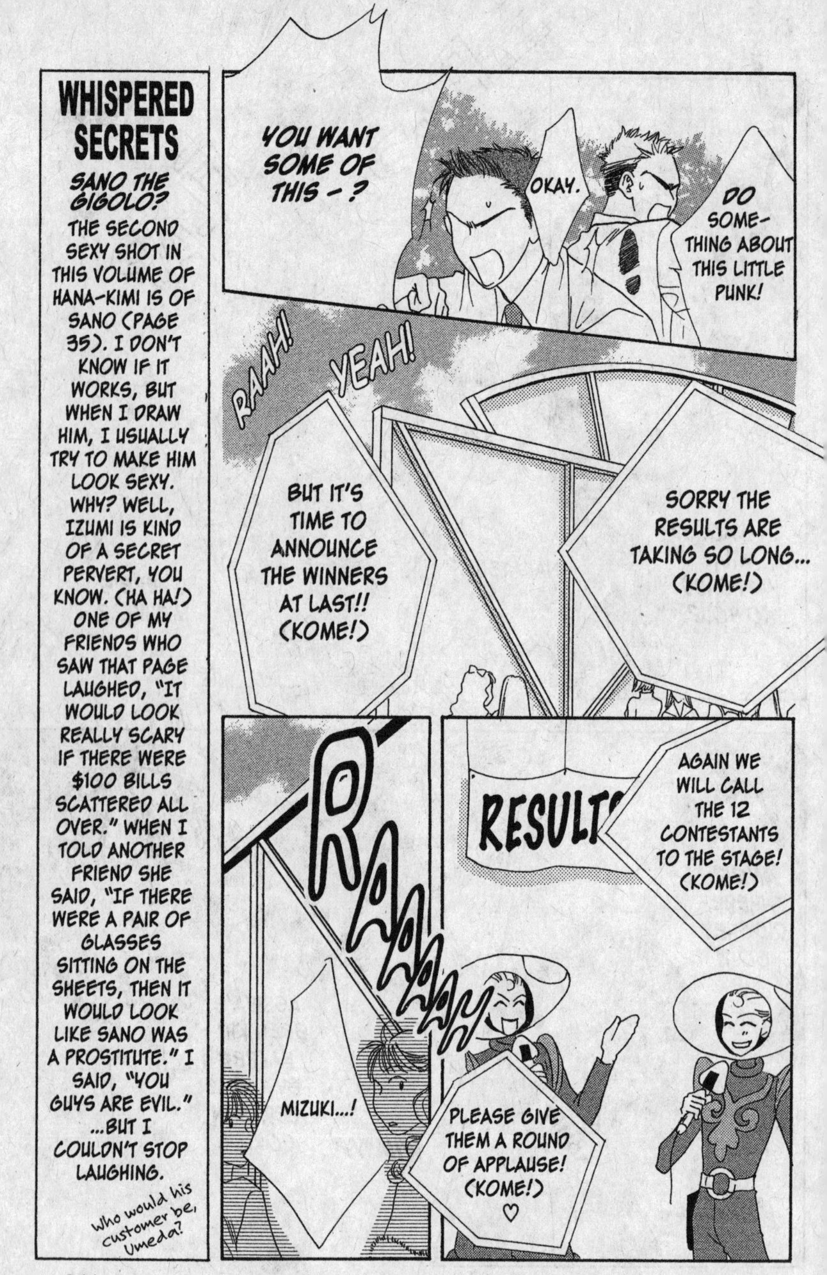
DO SOME-THING ABOUT THIS LITTLE PUNK!
OKAY.
YOU WANT SOME OF THIS -?
YEAH!
RAAH!
SORRY THE RESULTS ARE TAKING SO LONG... (KOME!)
BUT IT'S TIME TO ANNOUNCE THE WINNERS AT LAST!! (KOME!)
RESULTS
AGAIN WE WILL CALL THE 12 CONTESTANTS TO THE STAGE! (KOME!)
PLEASE GIVE THEM A ROUND OF APPLAUSE! (KOME!) ♡
MIZUKI...!

WHISPERED SECRETS

SANO THE GIGOLO?

THE SECOND SEXY SHOT IN THIS VOLUME OF HANA-KIMI IS OF SANO (PAGE 35). I DON'T KNOW IF IT WORKS, BUT WHEN I DRAW HIM, I USUALLY TRY TO MAKE HIM LOOK SEXY. WHY? WELL, IZUMI IS KIND OF A SECRET PERVERT, YOU KNOW. (HA HA!) ONE OF MY FRIENDS WHO SAW THAT PAGE LAUGHED, "IT WOULD LOOK REALLY SCARY IF THERE WERE $100 BILLS SCATTERED ALL OVER." WHEN I TOLD ANOTHER FRIEND SHE SAID, "IF THERE WERE A PAIR OF GLASSES SITTING ON THE SHEETS, THEN IT WOULD LOOK LIKE SANO WAS A PROSTITUTE." I SAID, "YOU GUYS ARE EVIL." ...BUT I COULDN'T STOP LAUGHING.

Who would his customer be, Umeda?

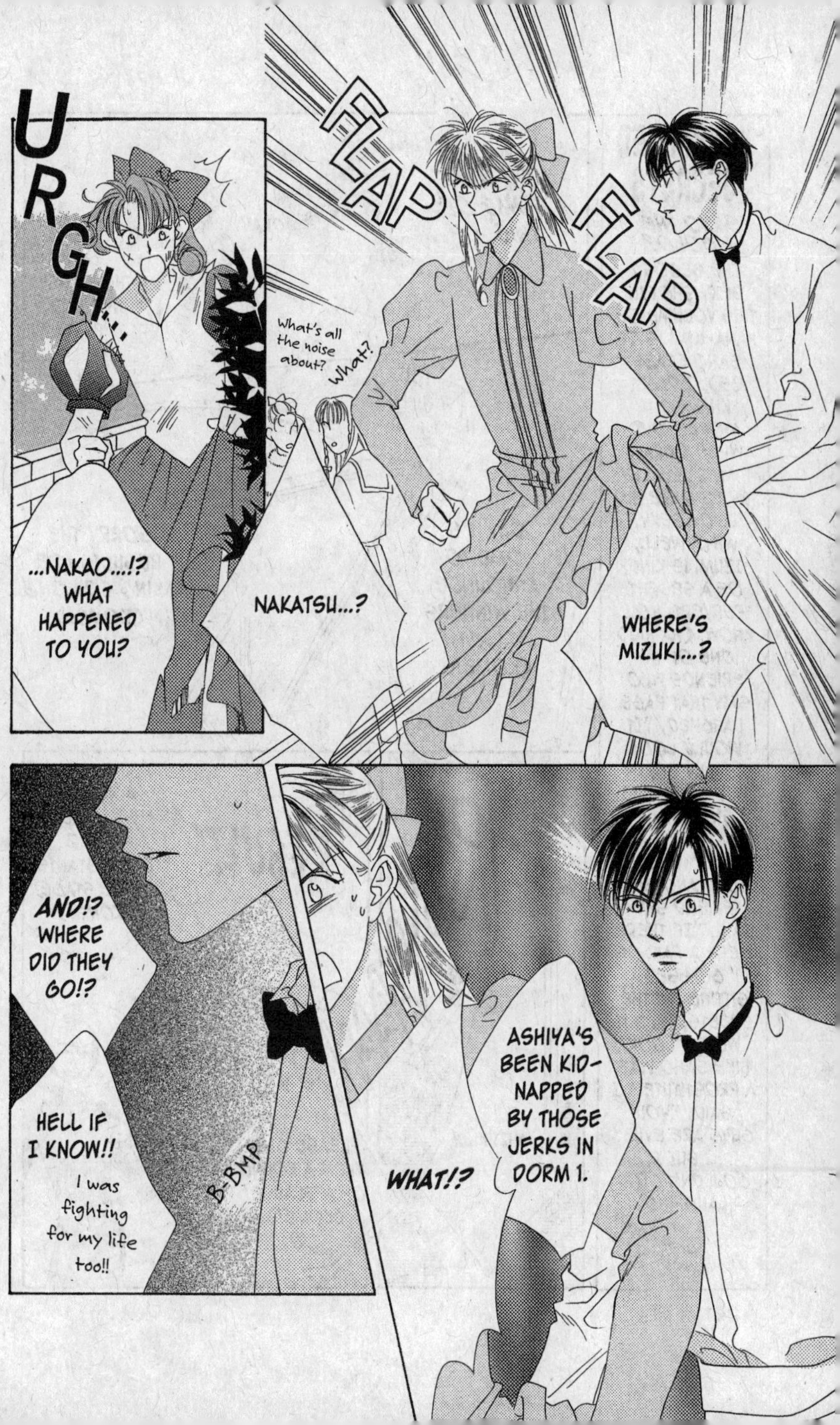
FLAP
FLAP
What?
What's all the noise about?
WHERE'S MIZUKI...?
NAKATSU...?
URGH...
...NAKAO...!? WHAT HAPPENED TO YOU?
ASHIYA'S BEEN KID-NAPPED BY THOSE JERKS IN DORM 1.
WHAT!?
B-BMP
AND!? WHERE DID THEY GO!?
HELL IF I KNOW!!
I was fighting for my life too!!

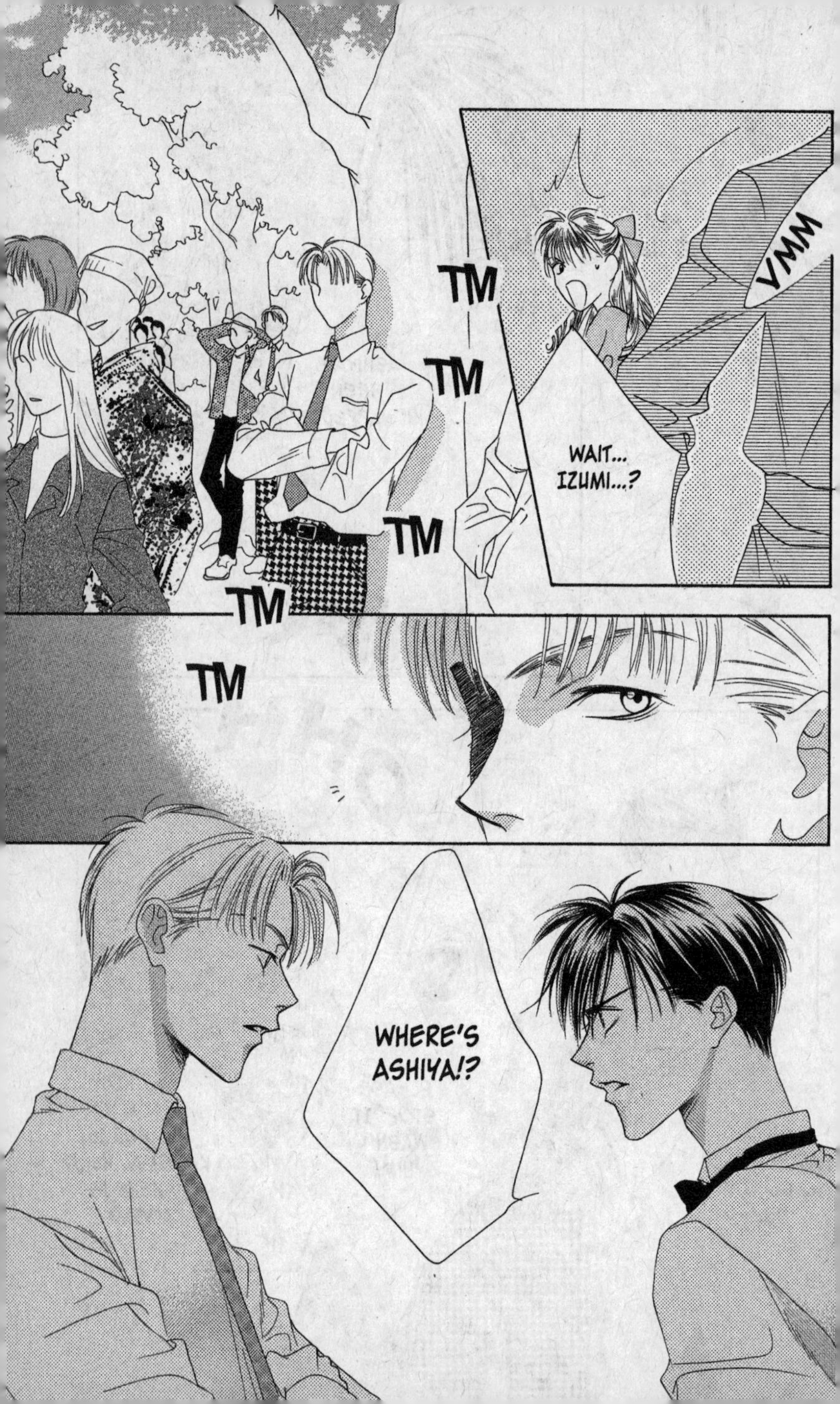
VMM
WAIT... IZUMI...?
TM
TM
TM
TM
TM
WHERE'S ASHIYA!?

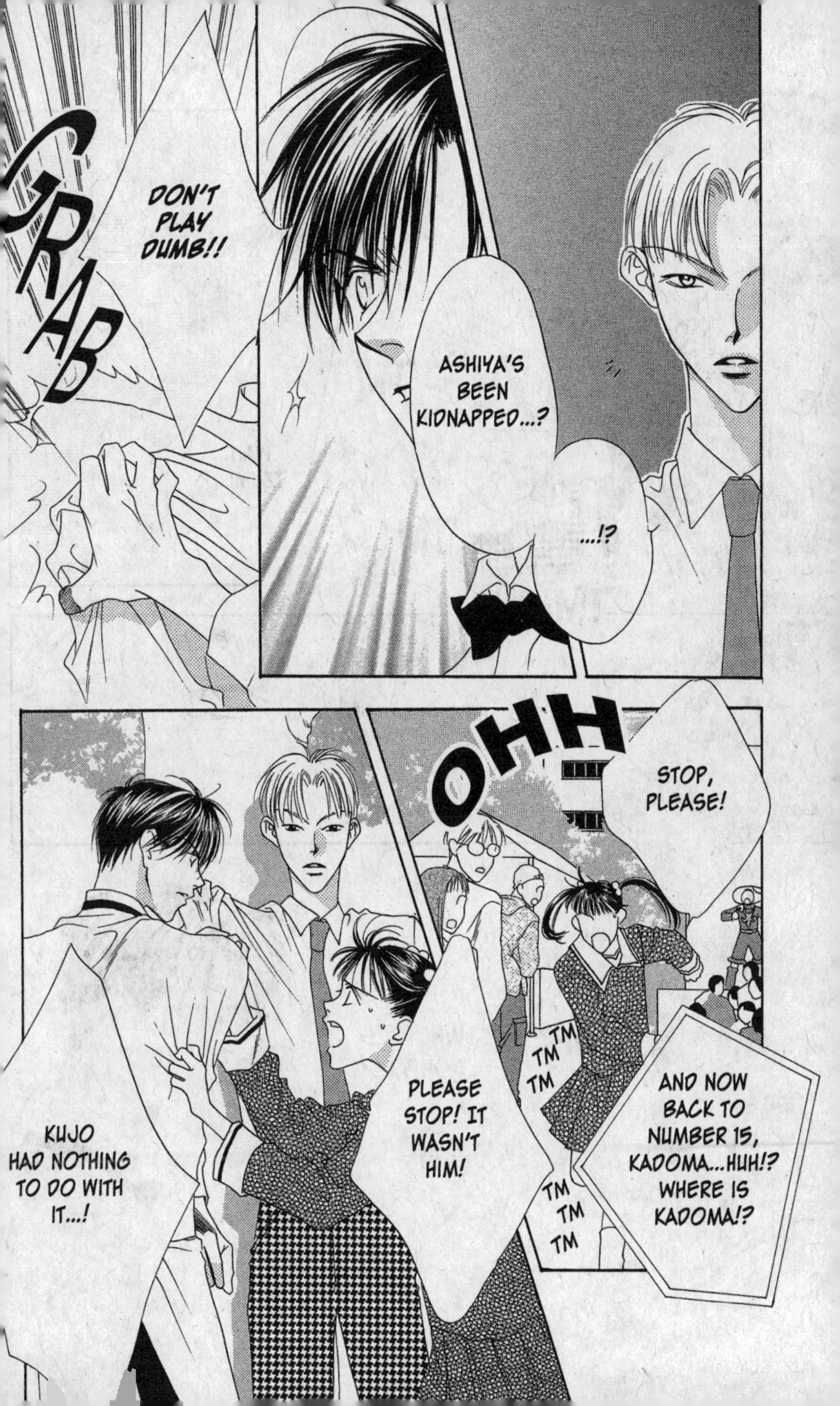
...!?
ASHIYA'S BEEN KIDNAPPED...?
GRAB
DON'T PLAY DUMB!!
OHH
STOP, PLEASE!
AND NOW BACK TO NUMBER 15, KADOMA...HUH!? WHERE IS KADOMA!?
TM TM TM
TM TM TM
PLEASE STOP! IT WASN'T HIM!
KUJO HAD NOTHING TO DO WITH IT...!

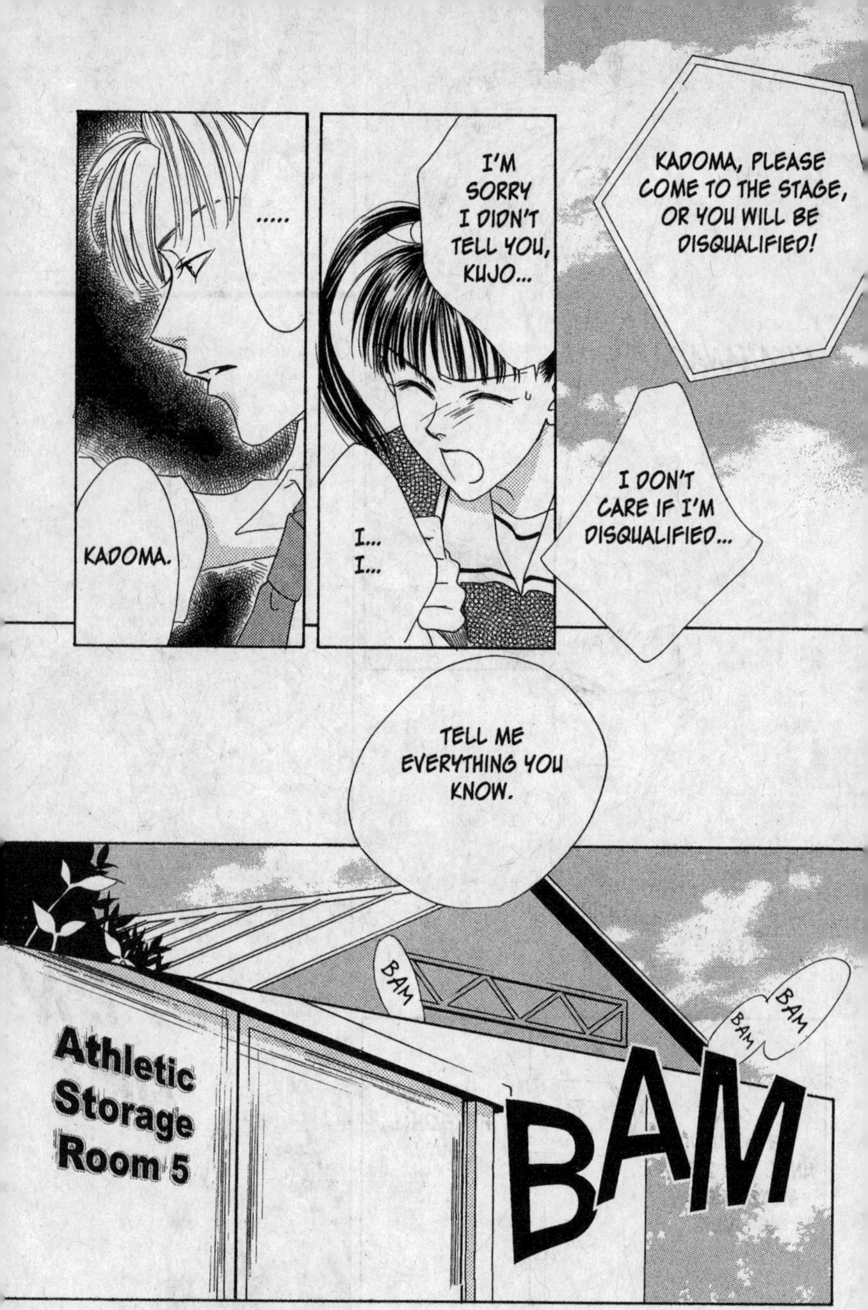
KADOMA, PLEASE COME TO THE STAGE, OR YOU WILL BE DISQUALIFIED!
I DON'T CARE IF I'M DISQUALIFIED...
I'M SORRY I DIDN'T TELL YOU, KUJO...
I... I...
.....
KADOMA.
TELL ME EVERYTHING YOU KNOW.
BAM
BAM
BAM
BAM
Athletic Storage Room 5

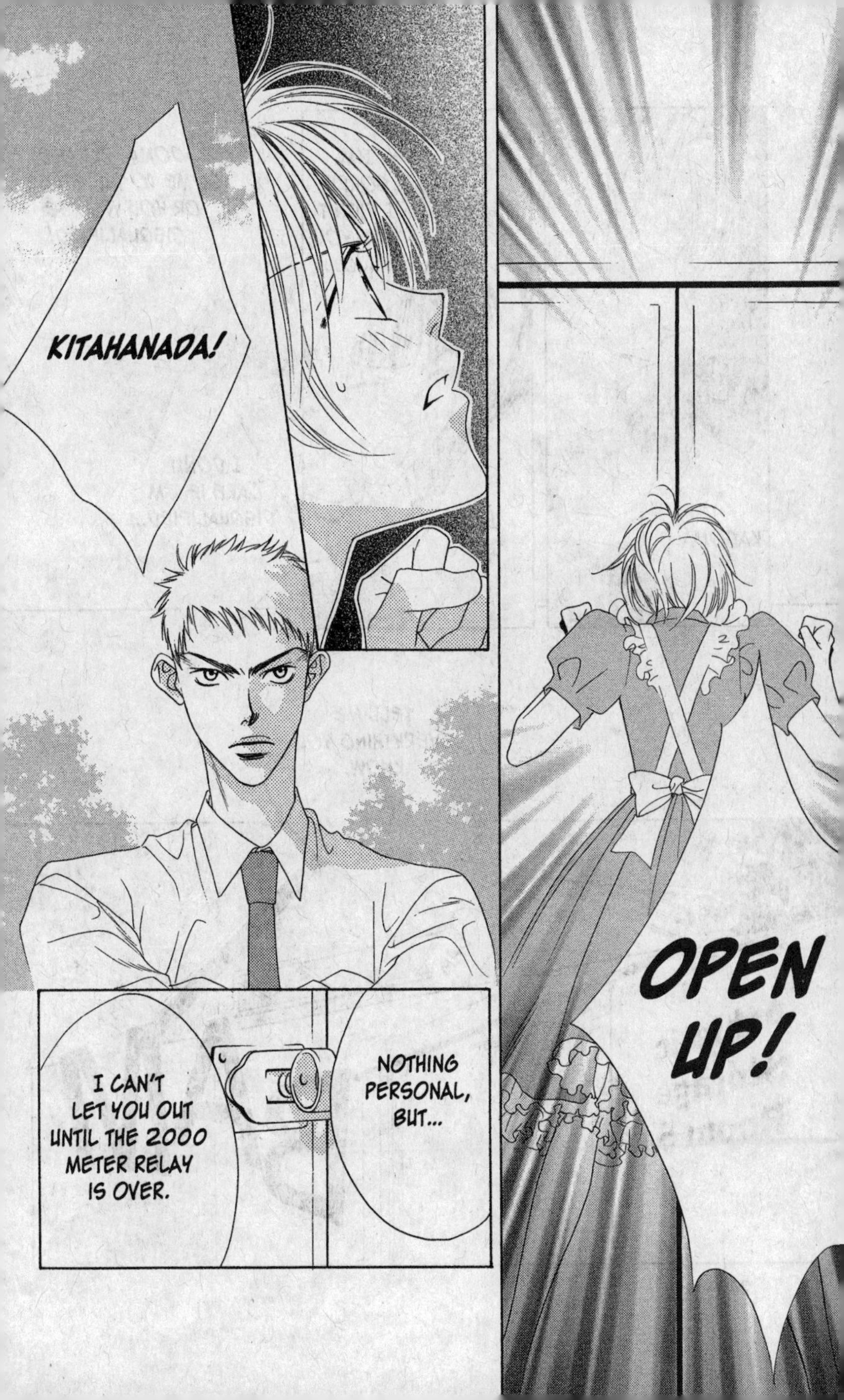
OPEN UP!
KITAHANADA!
NOTHING PERSONAL, BUT...
I CAN'T LET YOU OUT UNTIL THE 2000 METER RELAY IS OVER.

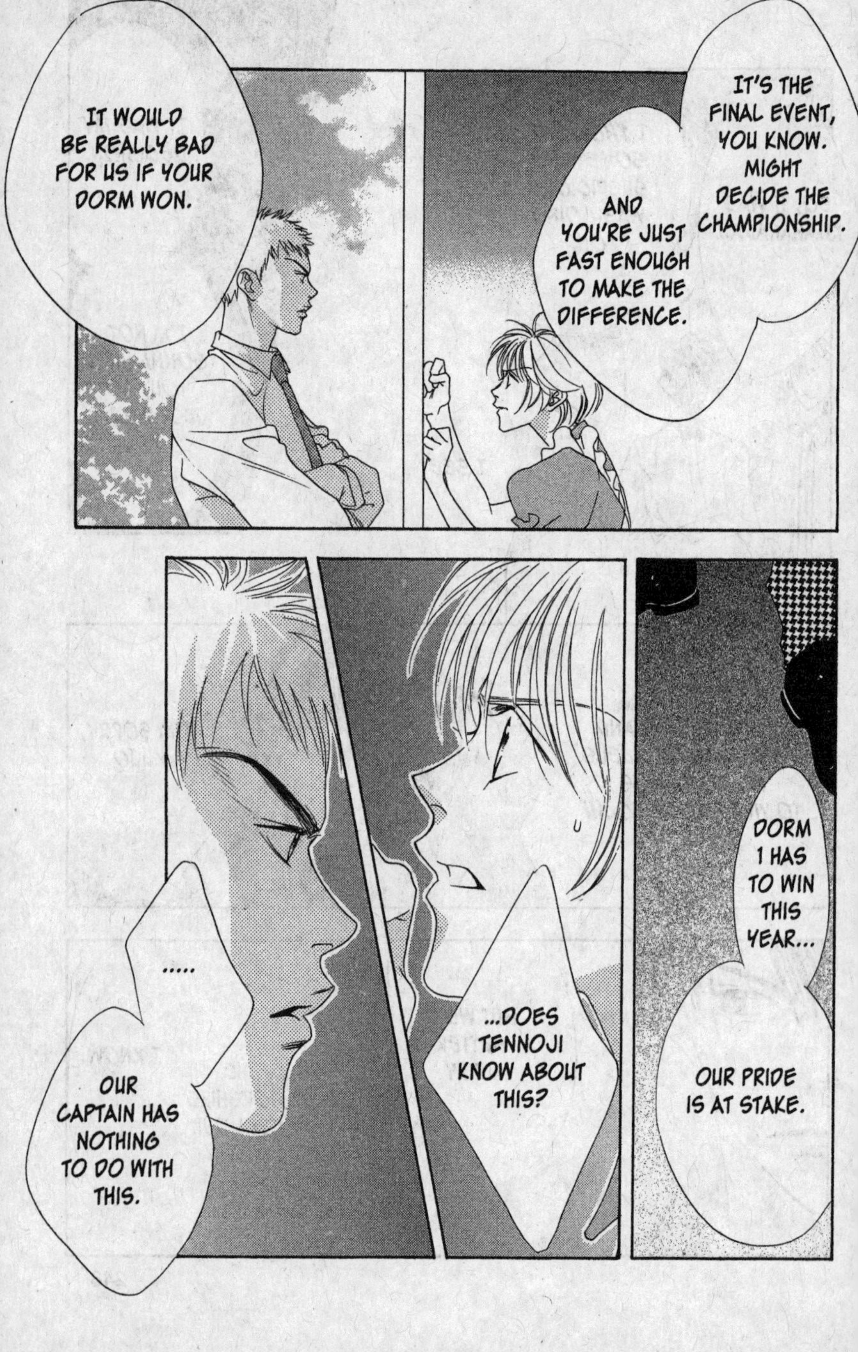
IT'S THE FINAL EVENT, YOU KNOW. MIGHT DECIDE THE CHAMPIONSHIP.
AND YOU'RE JUST FAST ENOUGH TO MAKE THE DIFFERENCE.
IT WOULD BE REALLY BAD FOR US IF YOUR DORM WON.
DORM 1 HAS TO WIN THIS YEAR...
OUR PRIDE IS AT STAKE.
...DOES TENNOJI KNOW ABOUT THIS?
.....
OUR CAPTAIN HAS NOTHING TO DO WITH THIS.

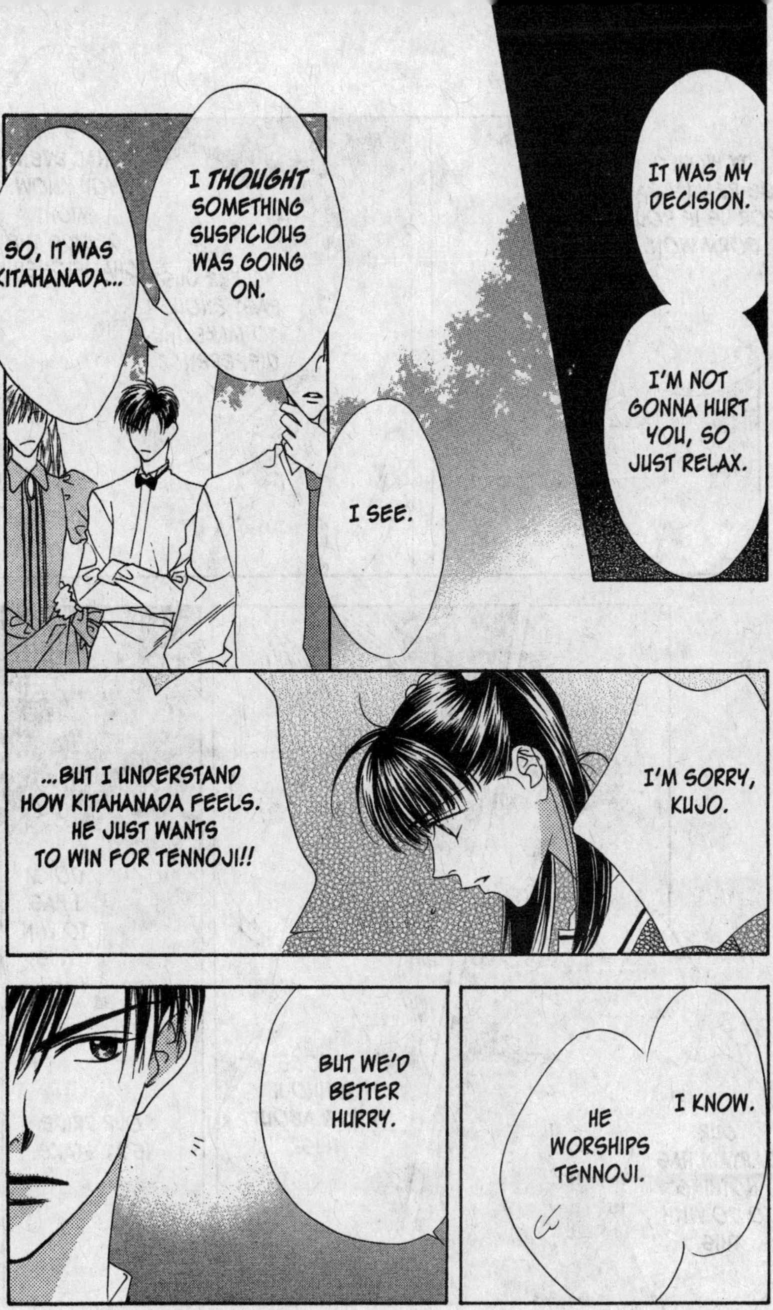
IT WAS MY DECISION.
I'M NOT GONNA HURT YOU, SO JUST RELAX.
I SEE.
I *THOUGHT* SOMETHING SUSPICIOUS WAS GOING ON.
SO, IT WAS KITAHANADA...
I'M SORRY, KUJO.
...BUT I UNDERSTAND HOW KITAHANADA FEELS. HE JUST WANTS TO WIN FOR TENNOJI!!
I KNOW.
HE WORSHIPS TENNOJI.
BUT WE'D BETTER HURRY.

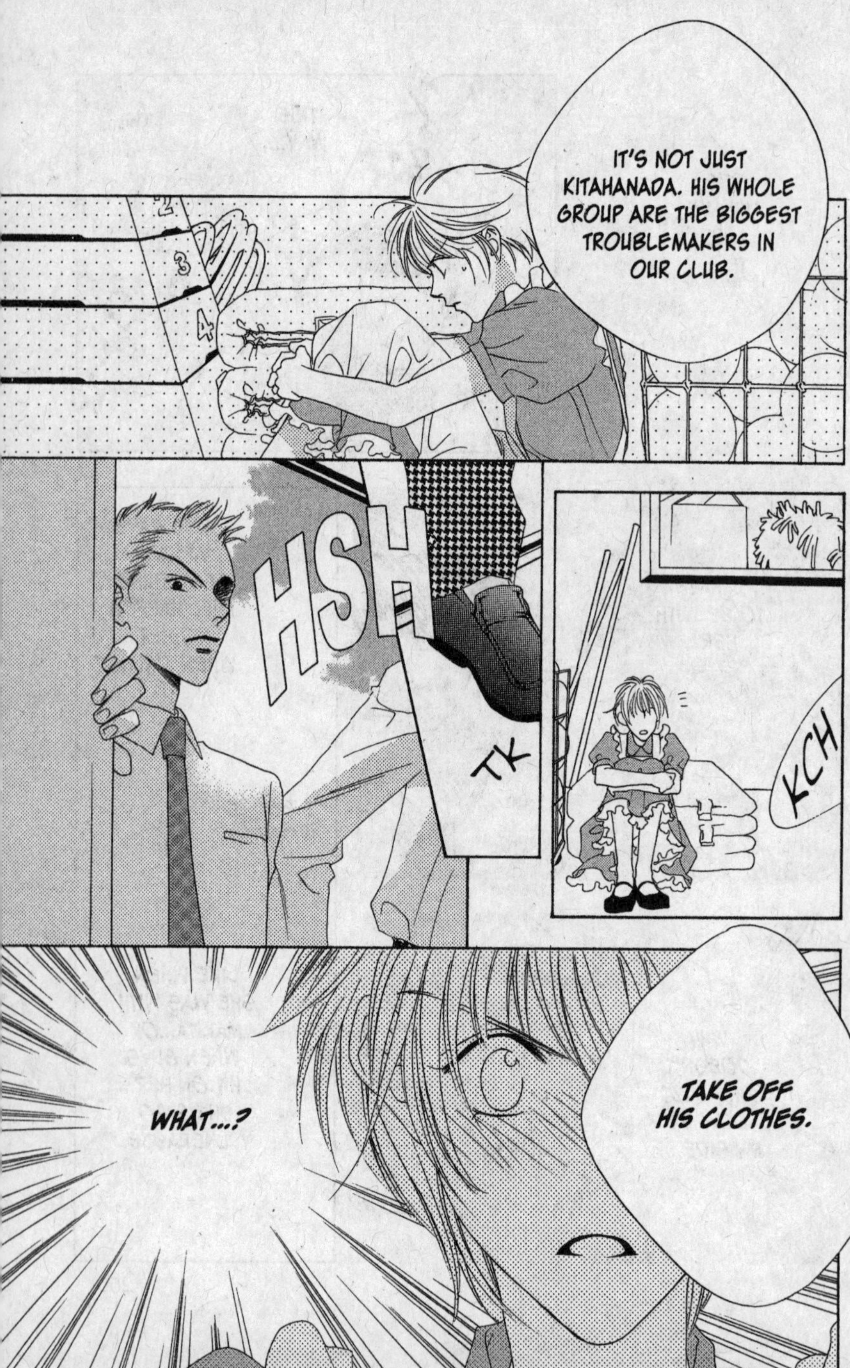
IT'S NOT JUST KITAHANADA. HIS WHOLE GROUP ARE THE BIGGEST TROUBLEMAKERS IN OUR CLUB.
KCH
HSH
TK
TAKE OFF HIS CLOTHES.
WHAT...?

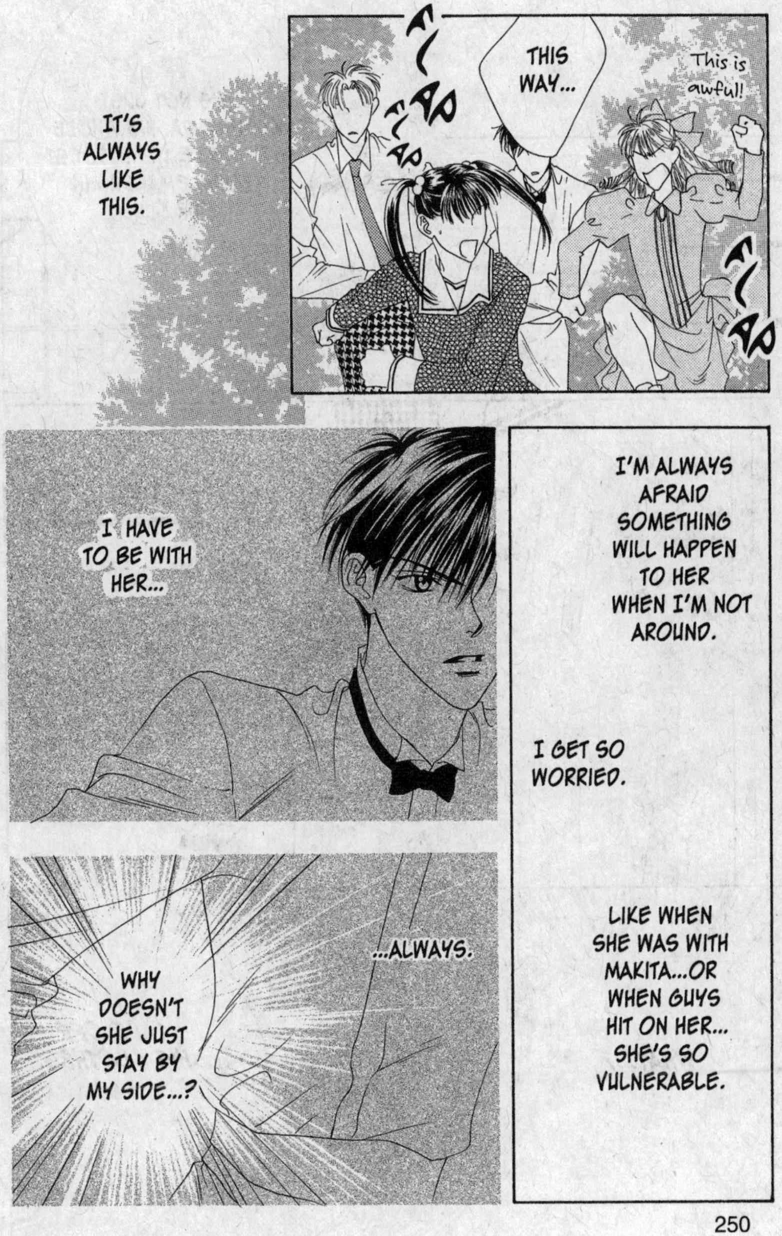
This is awful!
FLAP
THIS WAY...
FLAP FLAP FLAP
IT'S ALWAYS LIKE THIS.
I'M ALWAYS AFRAID SOMETHING WILL HAPPEN TO HER WHEN I'M NOT AROUND.
I GET SO WORRIED.
LIKE WHEN SHE WAS WITH MAKITA...OR WHEN GUYS HIT ON HER... SHE'S SO VULNERABLE.
I HAVE TO BE WITH HER...
...ALWAYS.
WHY DOESN'T SHE JUST STAY BY MY SIDE...?

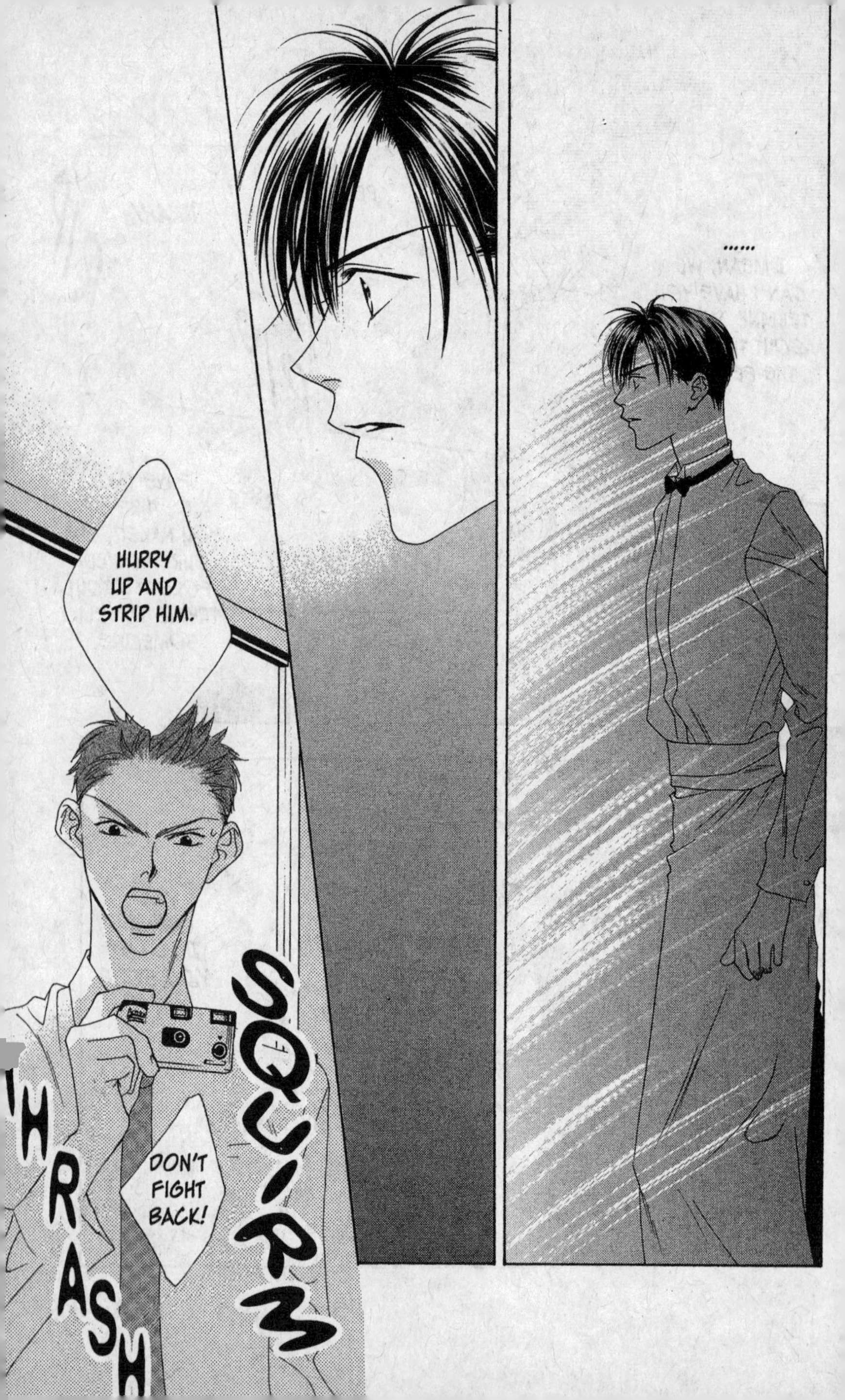
......
HURRY UP AND STRIP HIM.
SQUIRM
DON'T FIGHT BACK!
HRASH

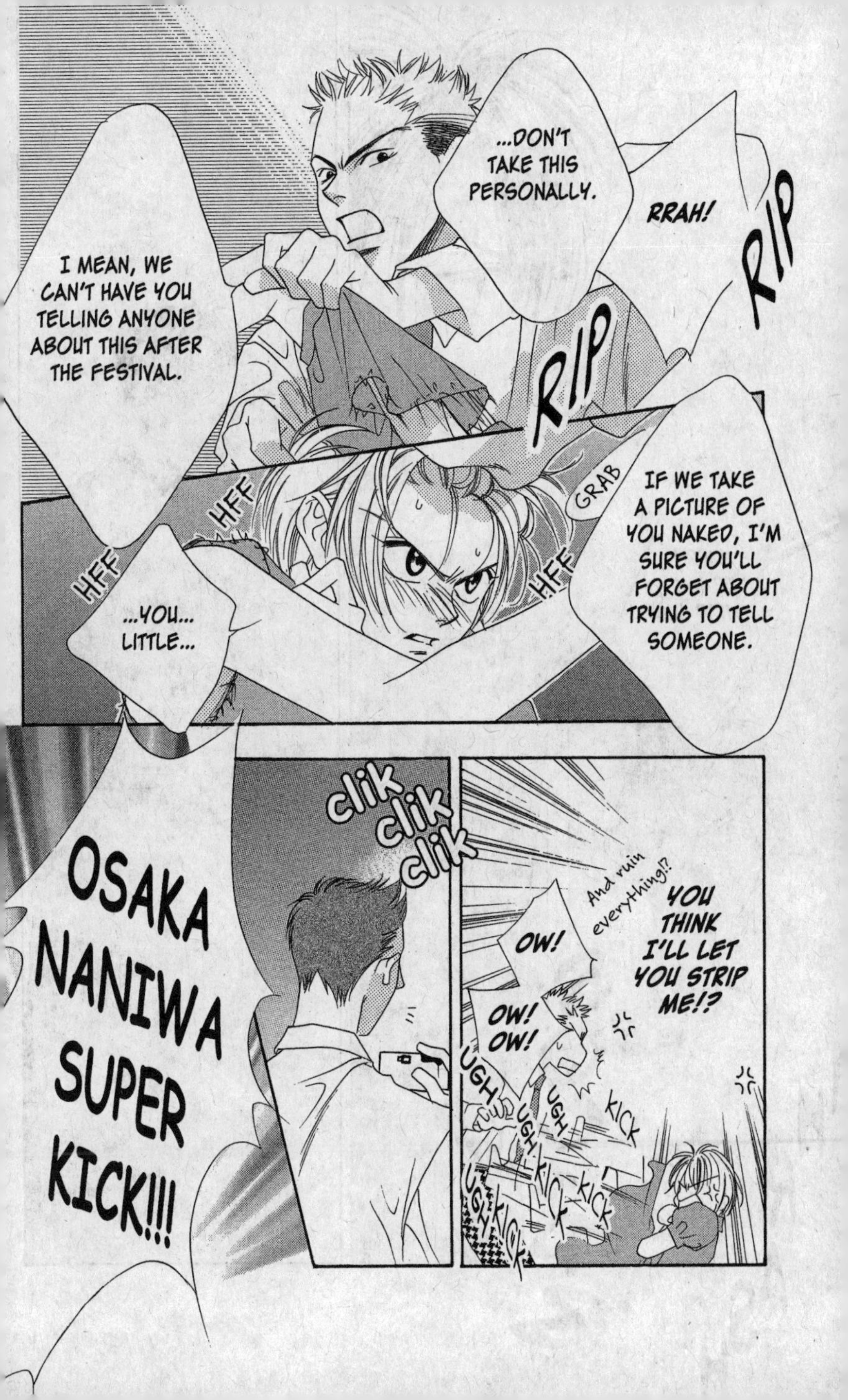

RIP
...DON'T TAKE THIS PERSONALLY.
RRAH!
RIP
I MEAN, WE CAN'T HAVE YOU TELLING ANYONE ABOUT THIS AFTER THE FESTIVAL.
IF WE TAKE A PICTURE OF YOU NAKED, I'M SURE YOU'LL FORGET ABOUT TRYING TO TELL SOMEONE.
GRAB
HFF
HFF
HFF
...YOU... LITTLE...
YOU THINK I'LL LET YOU STRIP ME!?
And ruin everything!?
OW!
OW! OW!
KICK
KICK
KICK
KICK
UGH
UGH
UGH
UGH
clik clik clik
OSAKA NANIWA SUPER KICK!!!

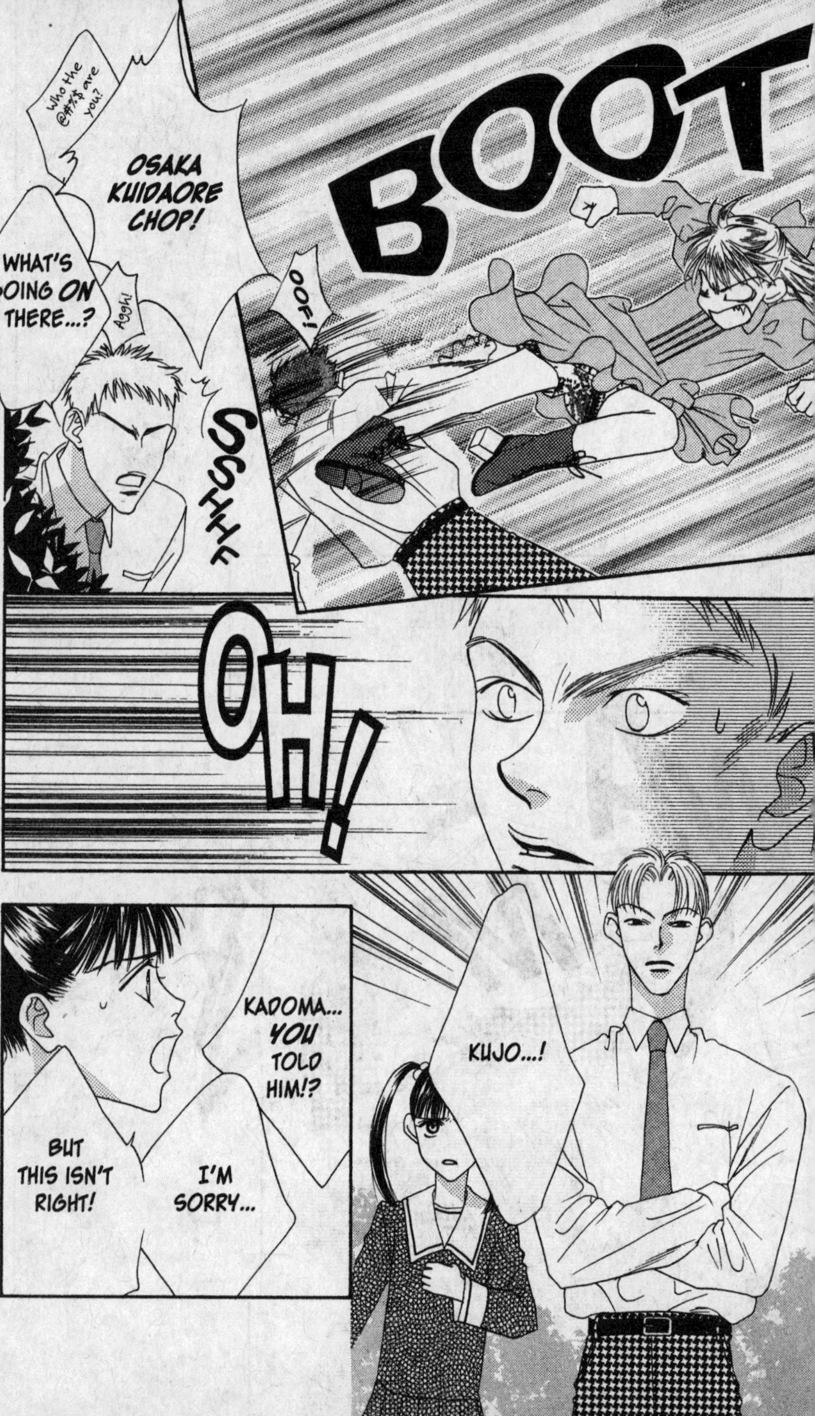
BOOT
OOF!
OSAKA KUIDAORE CHOP!
Who the @#%$ are you?
Aggh!
WHAT'S GOING ON IN THERE...?
SSHHF
OH!
KUJO...!
KADOMA... YOU TOLD HIM!?
I'M SORRY...
BUT THIS ISN'T RIGHT!

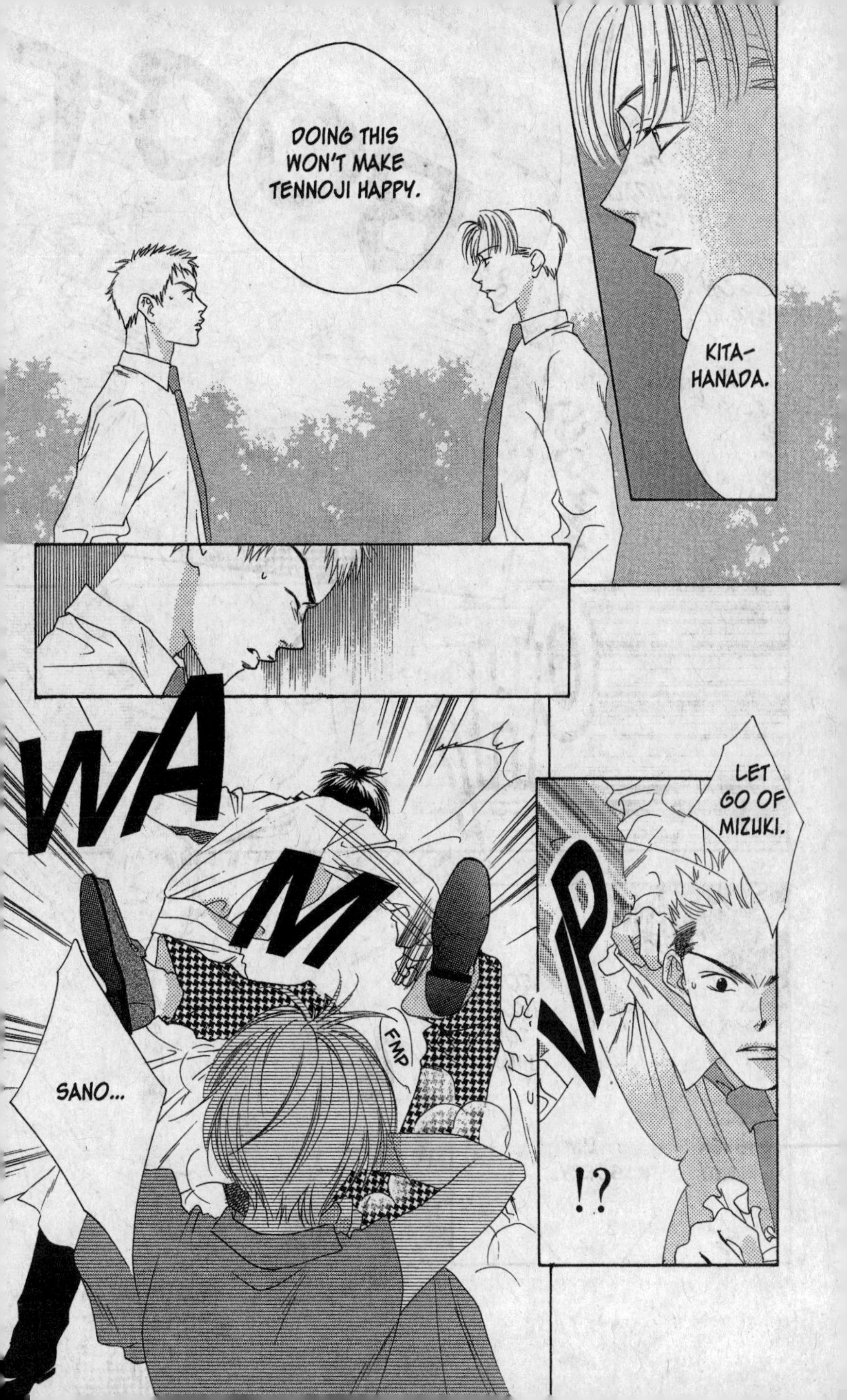
KITA-HANADA.
DOING THIS WON'T MAKE TENNOJI HAPPY.
LET GO OF MIZUKI.
!?
WHAMP
FMP
SANO...

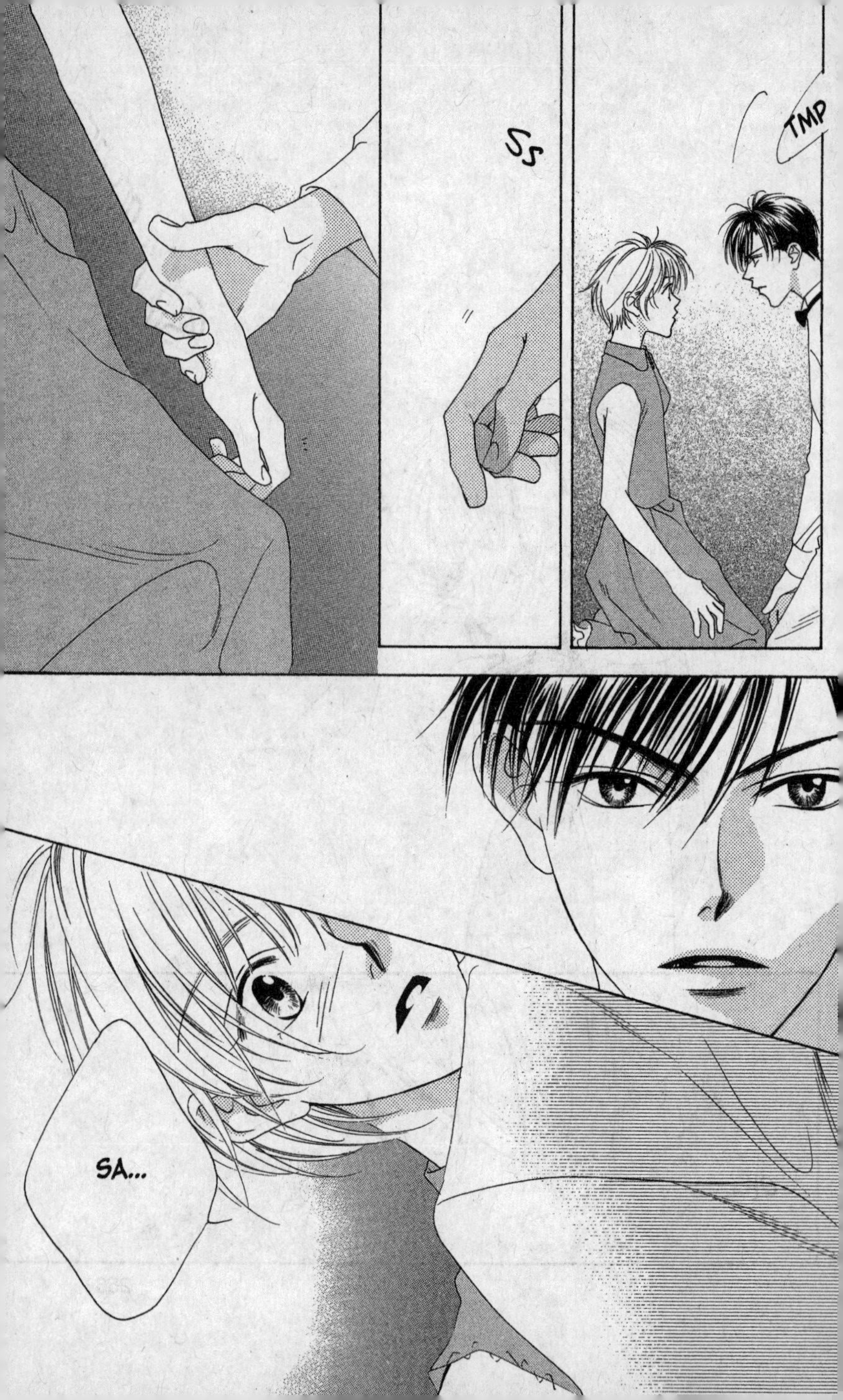
TMP
Ss
SA...

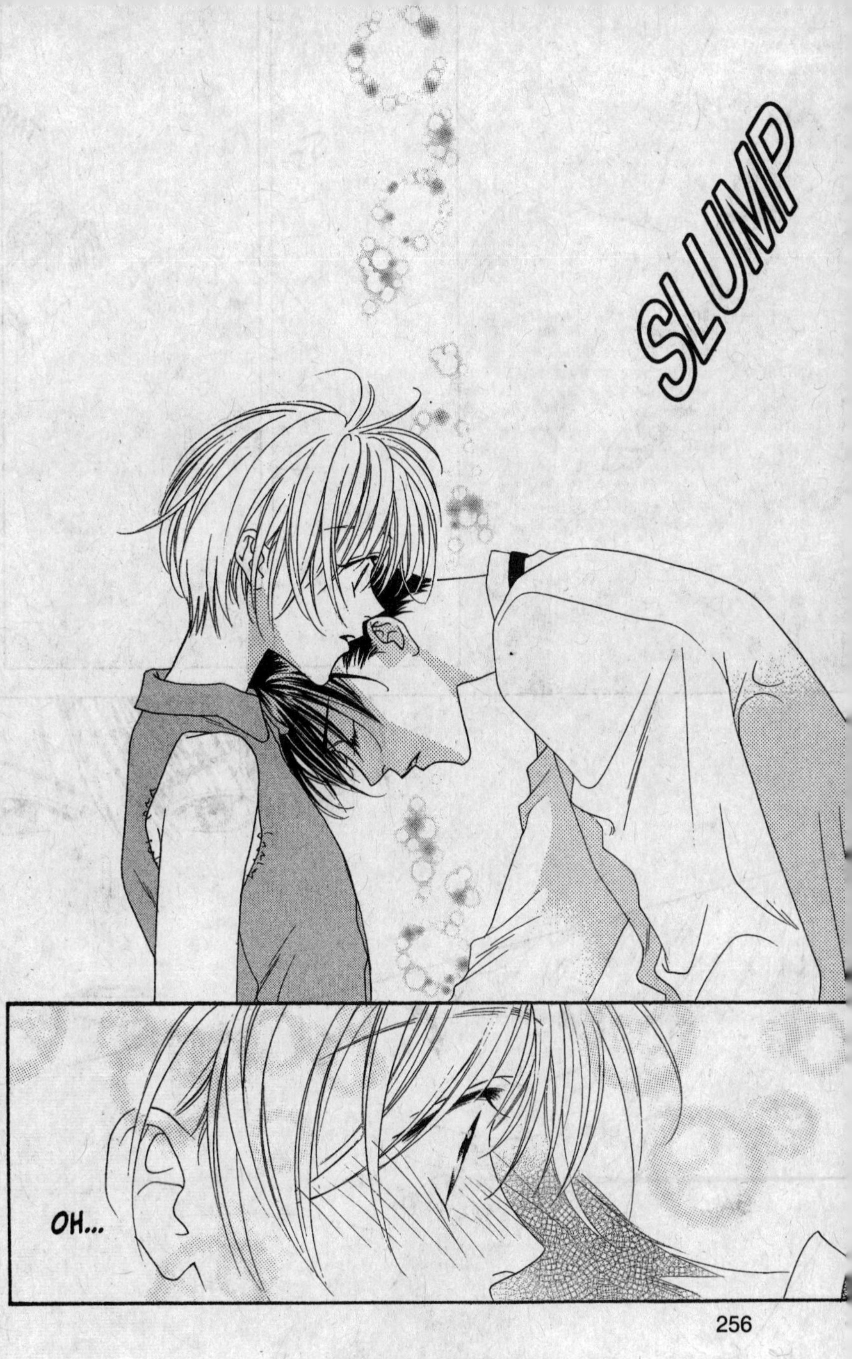
SLUMP
OH...

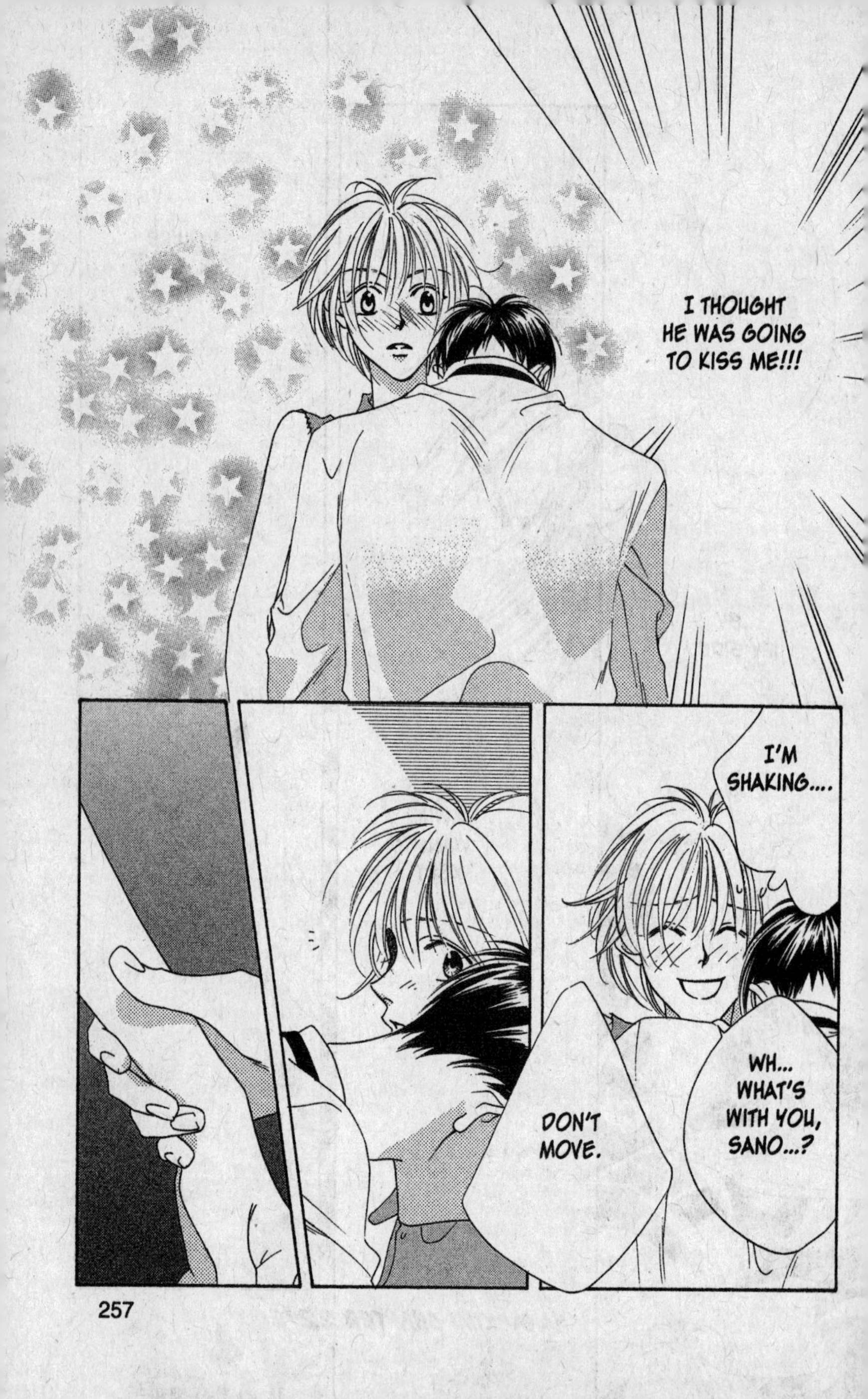
I THOUGHT HE WAS GOING TO KISS ME!!!
I'M SHAKING....
WH... WHAT'S WITH YOU, SANO...?
DON'T MOVE.

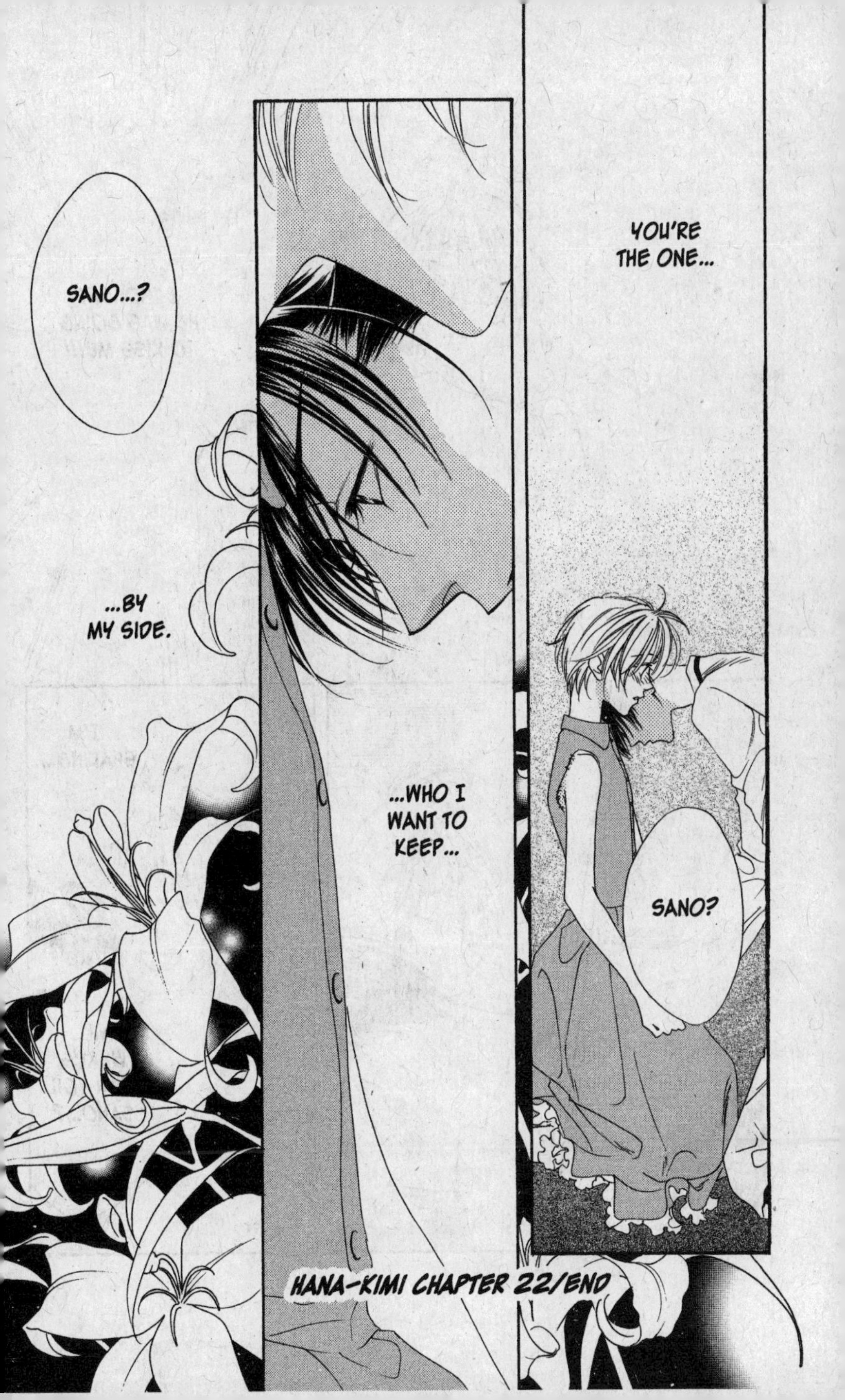
YOU'RE THE ONE...
SANO?
...WHO I WANT TO KEEP...
SANO...?
...BY MY SIDE.
HANA-KIMI CHAPTER 22/END

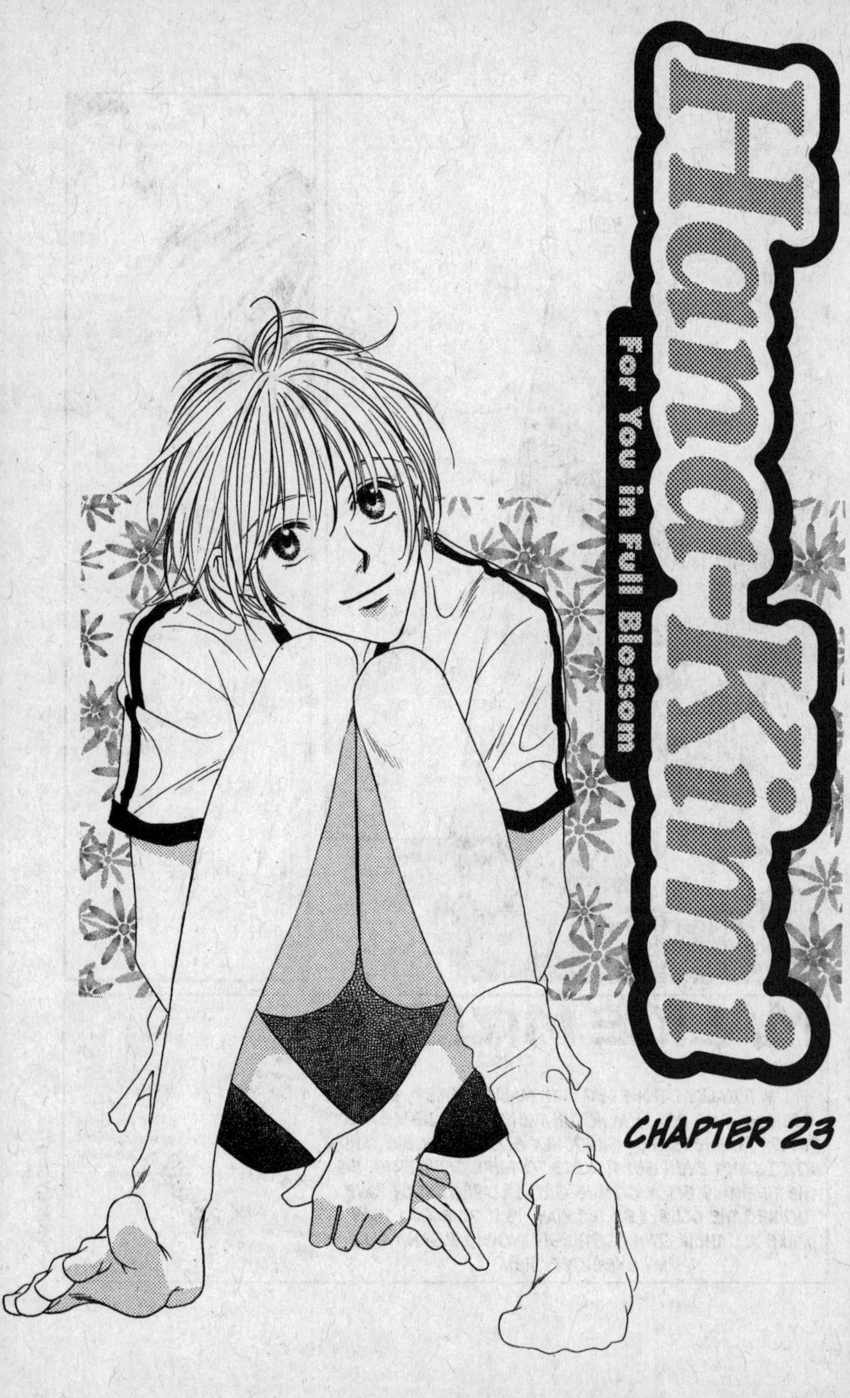
Hana-Kimi
For You in Full Blossom
CHAPTER 23

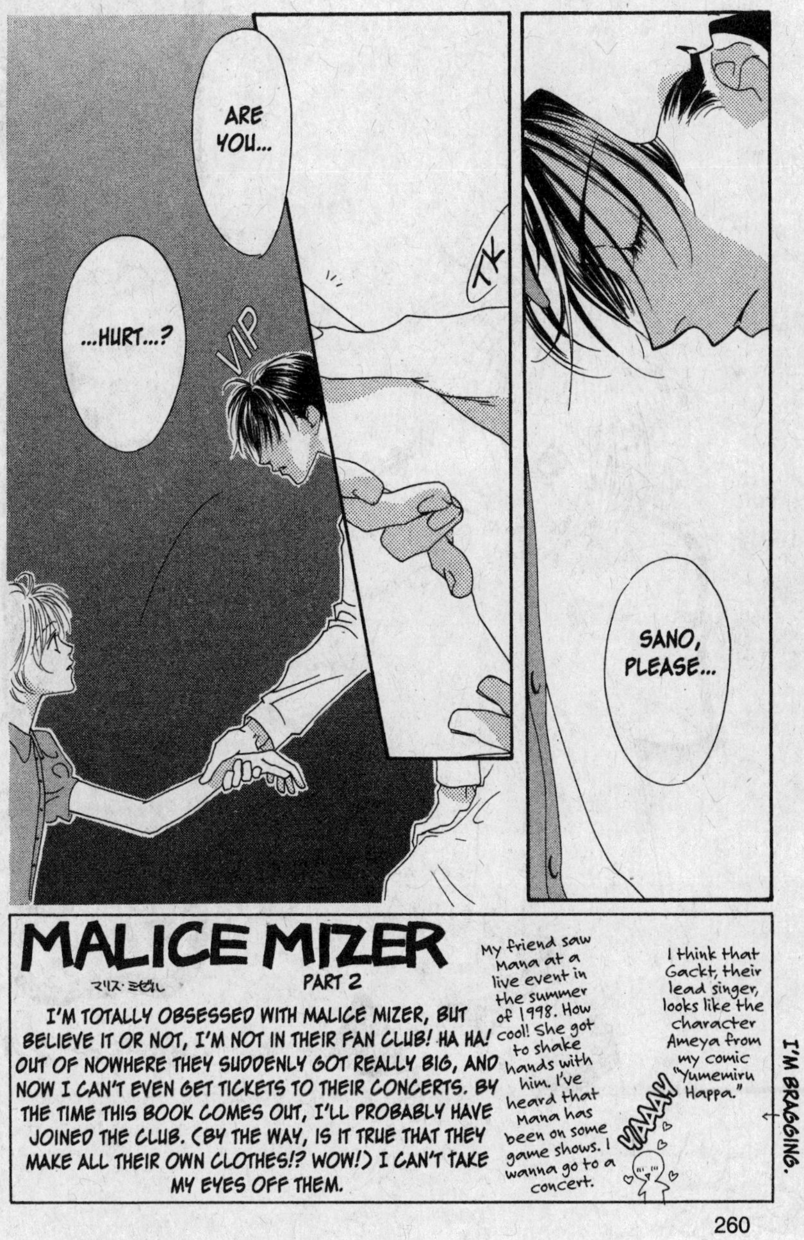
SANO, PLEASE...
TK
ARE YOU...
...HURT...?
VIP

MALICE MIZER

マリス・ミゼル

PART 2

I'M TOTALLY OBSESSED WITH MALICE MIZER, BUT BELIEVE IT OR NOT, I'M NOT IN THEIR FAN CLUB! HA HA! OUT OF NOWHERE THEY SUDDENLY GOT REALLY BIG, AND NOW I CAN'T EVEN GET TICKETS TO THEIR CONCERTS. BY THE TIME THIS BOOK COMES OUT, I'LL PROBABLY HAVE JOINED THE CLUB. (BY THE WAY, IS IT TRUE THAT THEY MAKE ALL THEIR OWN CLOTHES!? WOW!) I CAN'T TAKE MY EYES OFF THEM.

My friend saw Mana at a live event in the summer of 1998. How cool! She got to shake hands with him. I've heard that Mana has been on some game shows. I wanna go to a concert.

I think that Gackt, their lead singer, looks like the character Ameya from my comic "Yumemiru Happa."

YAAAAY

I'M BRAGGING.

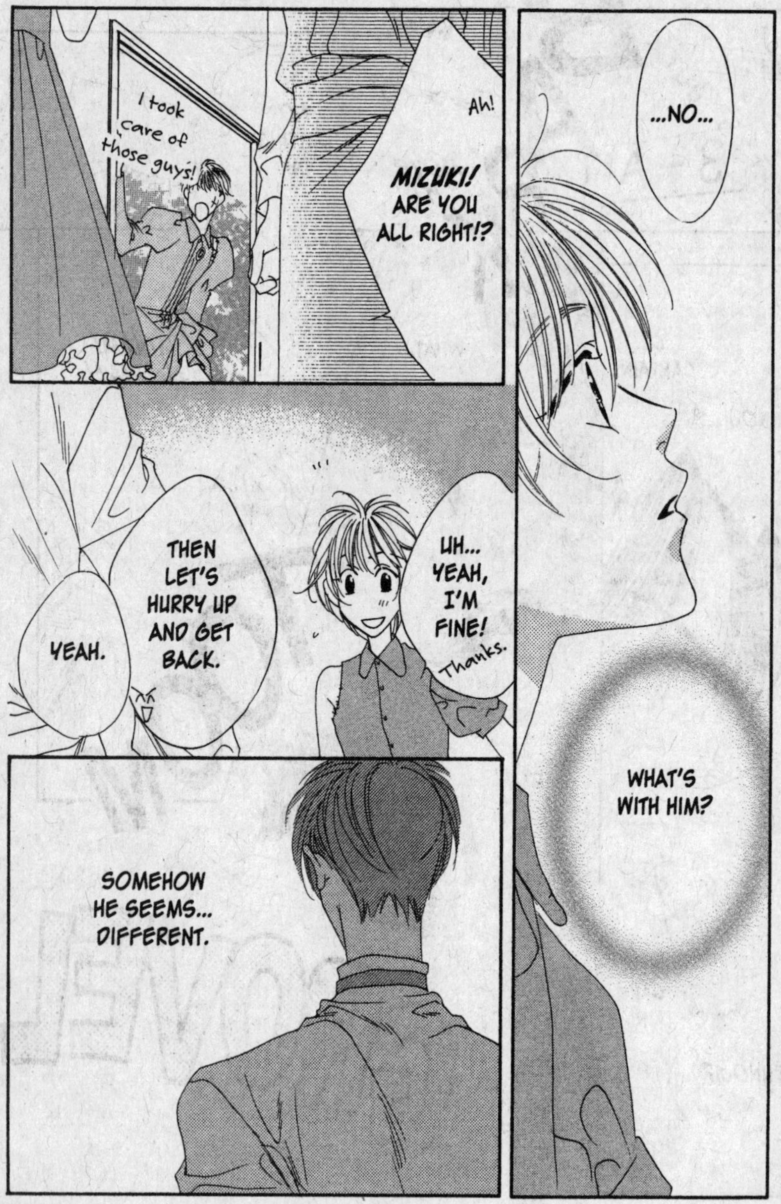
...NO...
WHAT'S WITH HIM?
Ah!
MIZUKI! ARE YOU ALL RIGHT!?
I took care of those guys!
UH... YEAH, I'M FINE!
Thanks.
THEN LET'S HURRY UP AND GET BACK.
YEAH.
SOMEHOW HE SEEMS... DIFFERENT.

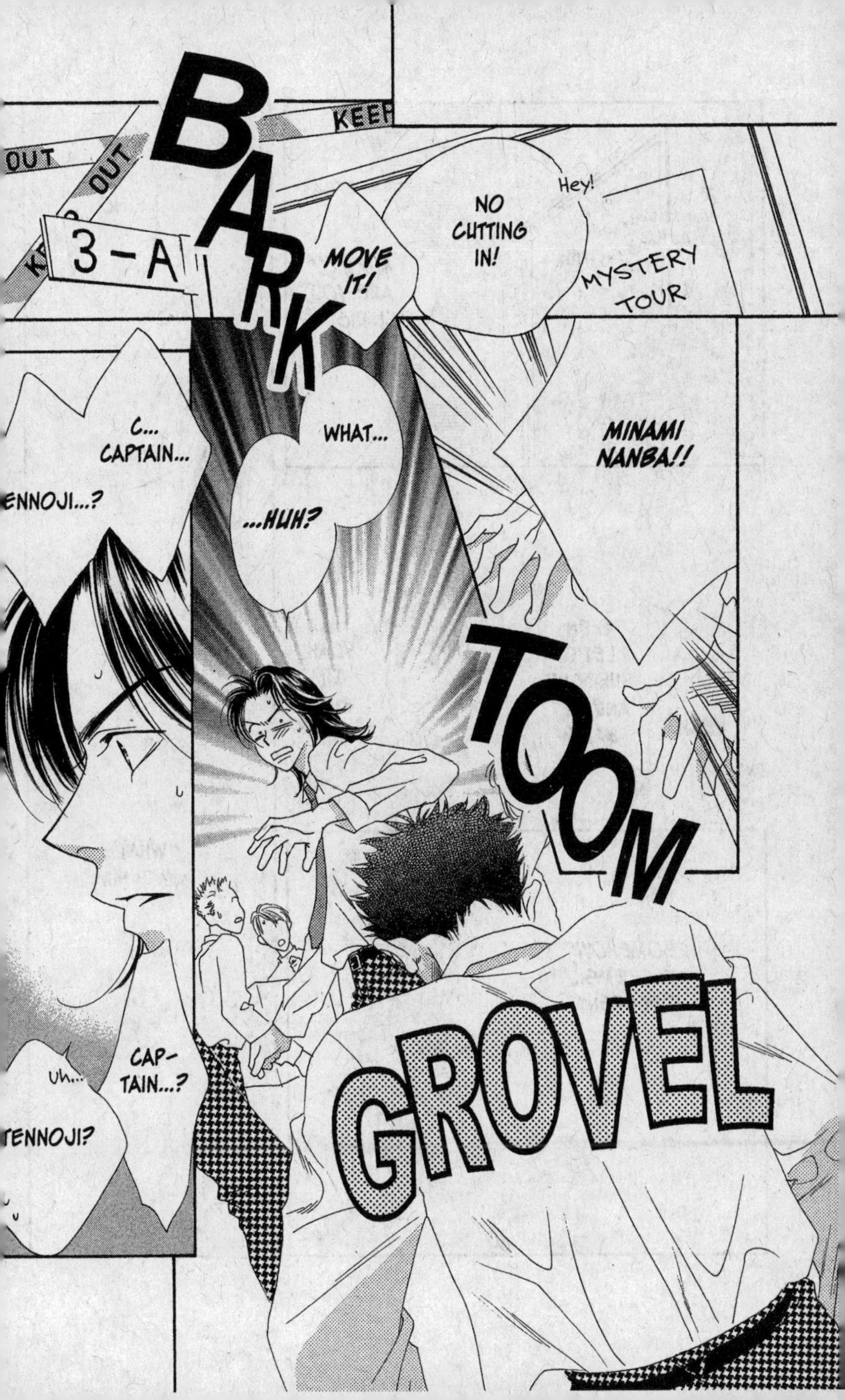

Hey!
NO CUTTING IN!
MYSTERY TOUR
MOVE IT!
BARK
3-A
OUT
OUT
MINAMI NANBA!!
WHAT...
...HUH?
TOOM
GROVEL
C... CAPTAIN...
TENNOJI...?
CAP-TAIN...?
Uh...
TENNOJI?

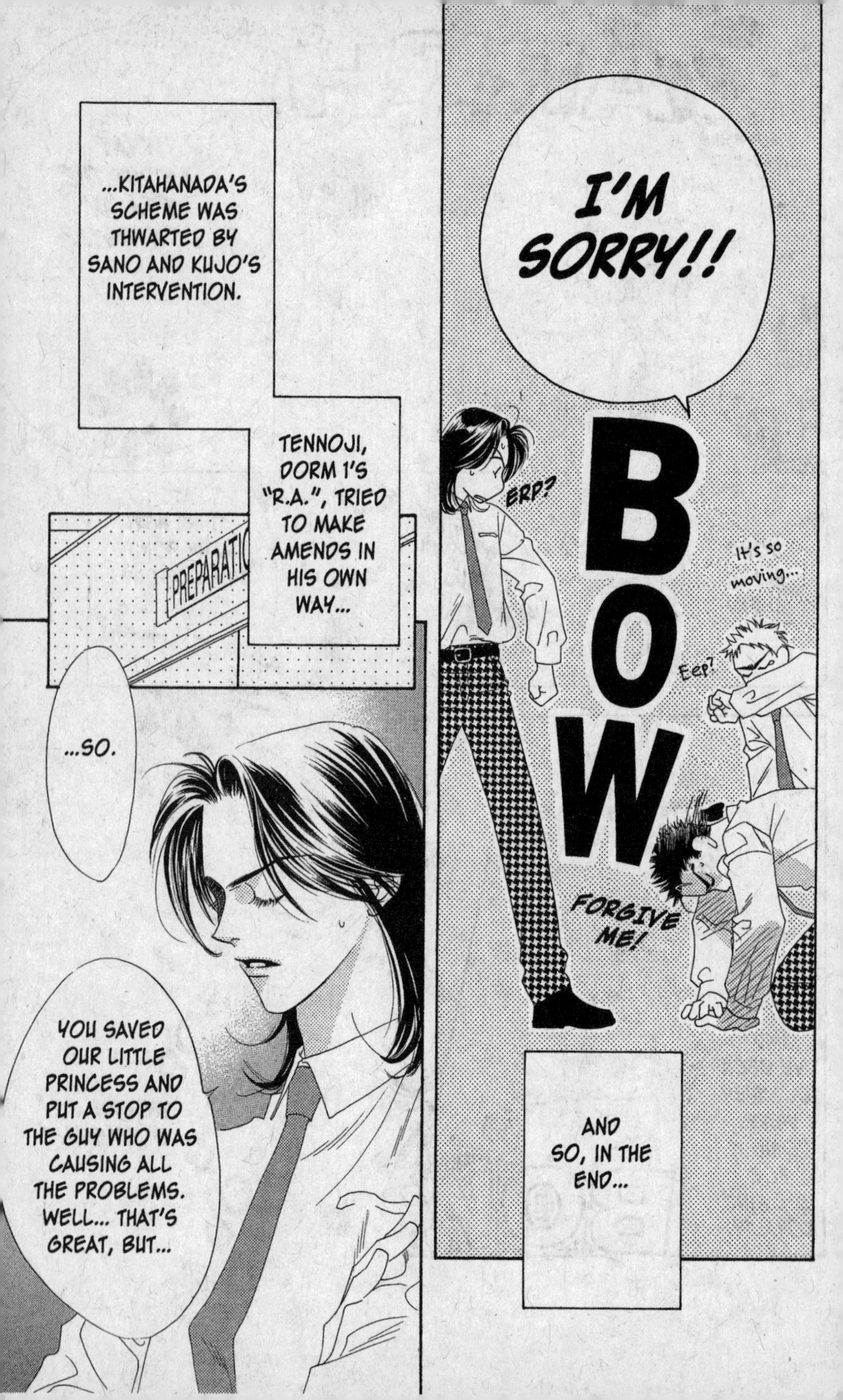
I'M SORRY!!
BOW
ERP?
It's so moving...
Eep?
FORGIVE ME!
AND SO, IN THE END...
...KITAHANADA'S SCHEME WAS THWARTED BY SANO AND KUJO'S INTERVENTION.
TENNOJI, DORM 1'S "R.A.", TRIED TO MAKE AMENDS IN HIS OWN WAY...
PREPARATIO
...SO.
YOU SAVED OUR LITTLE PRINCESS AND PUT A STOP TO THE GUY WHO WAS CAUSING ALL THE PROBLEMS. WELL... THAT'S GREAT, BUT...

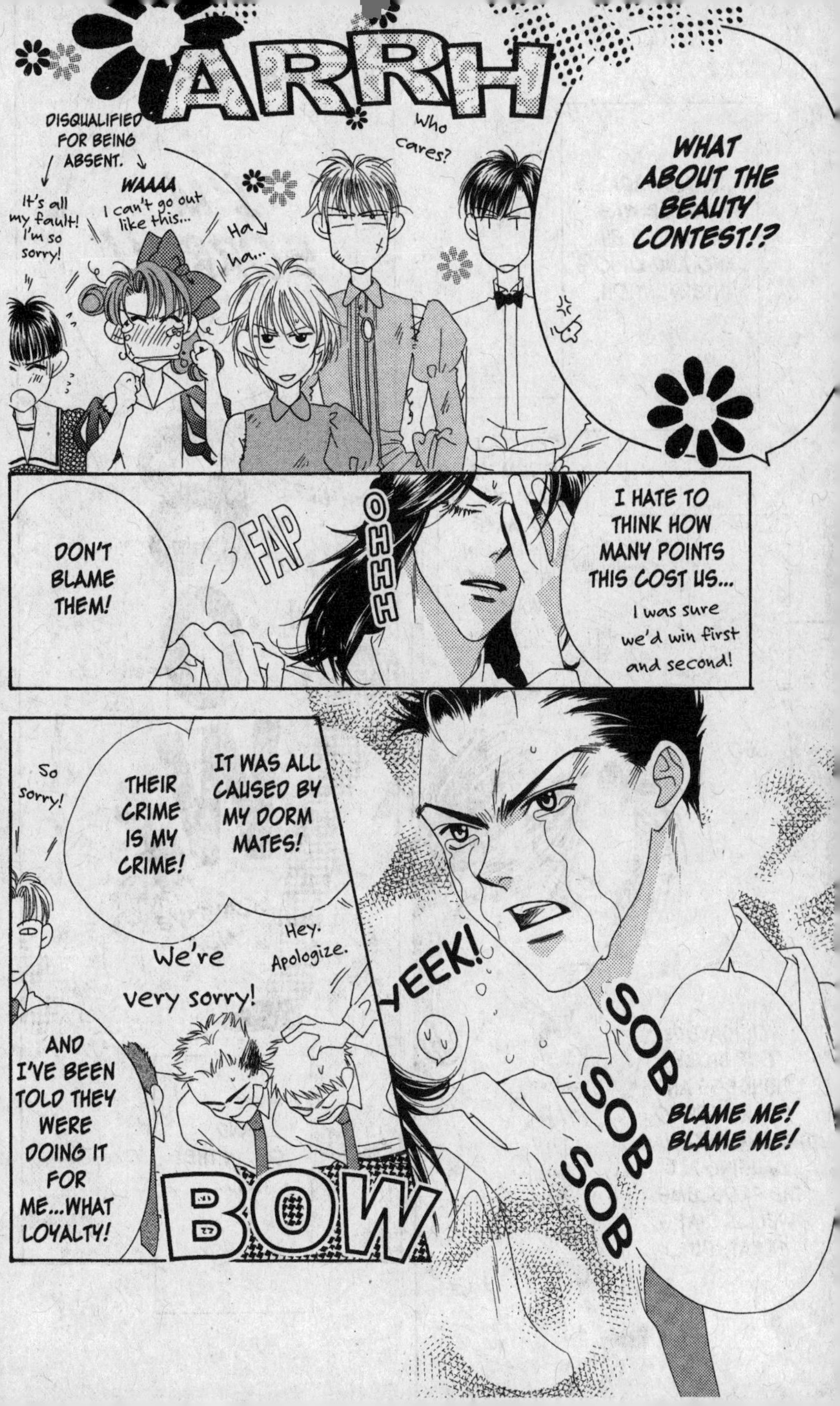
WHAT ABOUT THE BEAUTY CONTEST!?
ARRH
Who cares?
DISQUALIFIED FOR BEING ABSENT.
WAAAA
I can't go out like this...
Ha ha...
It's all my fault! I'm so sorry!
I HATE TO THINK HOW MANY POINTS THIS COST US...
I was sure we'd win first and second!
OHHHH
FAP
DON'T BLAME THEM!
SOB SOB SOB
BLAME ME! BLAME ME!
YEEK!
IT WAS ALL CAUSED BY MY DORM MATES!
THEIR CRIME IS MY CRIME!
So sorry!
Hey. Apologize.
We're very sorry!
BOW
AND I'VE BEEN TOLD THEY WERE DOING IT FOR ME...WHAT LOYALTY!

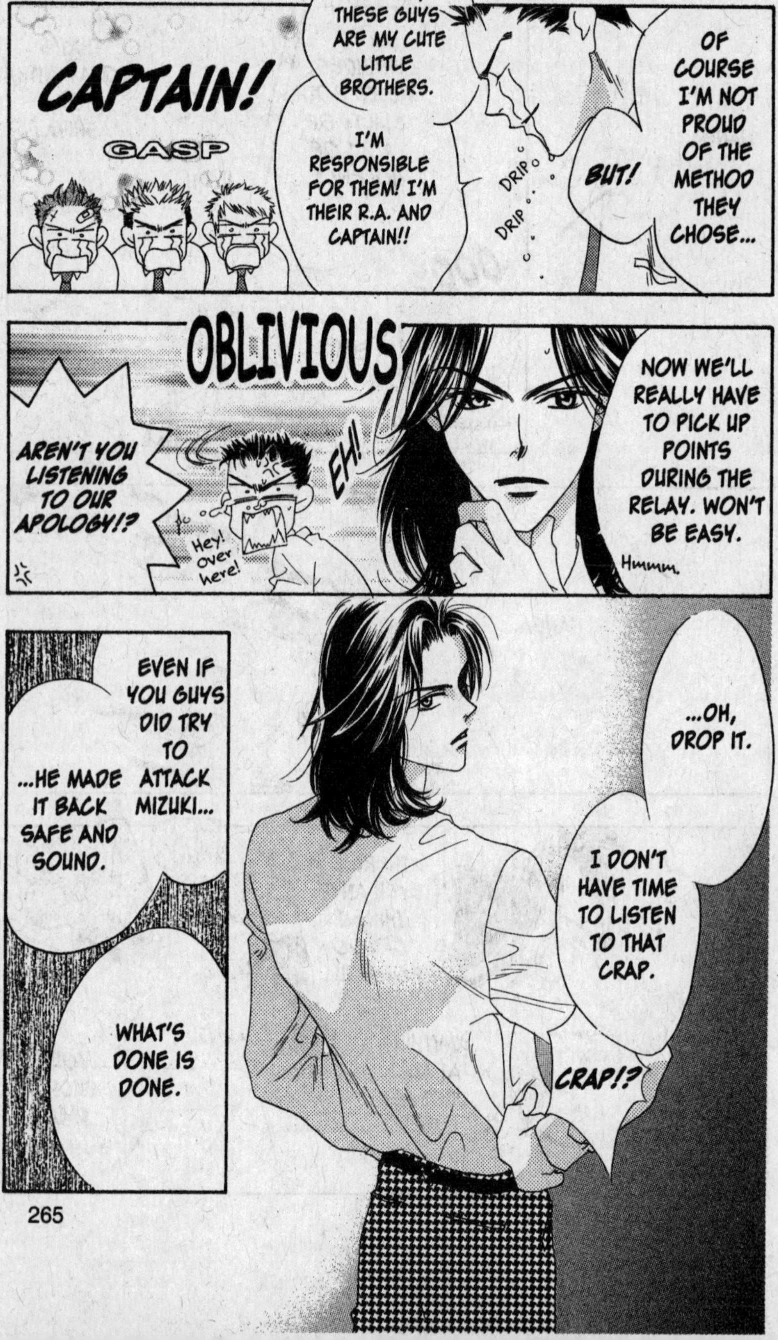
OF COURSE I'M NOT PROUD OF THE METHOD THEY CHOSE...
BUT!
...TO ME, THESE GUYS ARE MY CUTE LITTLE BROTHERS.
I'M RESPONSIBLE FOR THEM! I'M THEIR R.A. AND CAPTAIN!!
DRIP
DRIP
CAPTAIN!
GASP
NOW WE'LL REALLY HAVE TO PICK UP POINTS DURING THE RELAY. WON'T BE EASY.
Hmmm.
EH!
OBLIVIOUS
Hey! over here!
AREN'T YOU LISTENING TO OUR APOLOGY!?
...OH, DROP IT.
I DON'T HAVE TIME TO LISTEN TO THAT CRAP.
CRAP!?
EVEN IF YOU GUYS DID TRY TO ATTACK MIZUKI...
...HE MADE IT BACK SAFE AND SOUND.
WHAT'S DONE IS DONE.

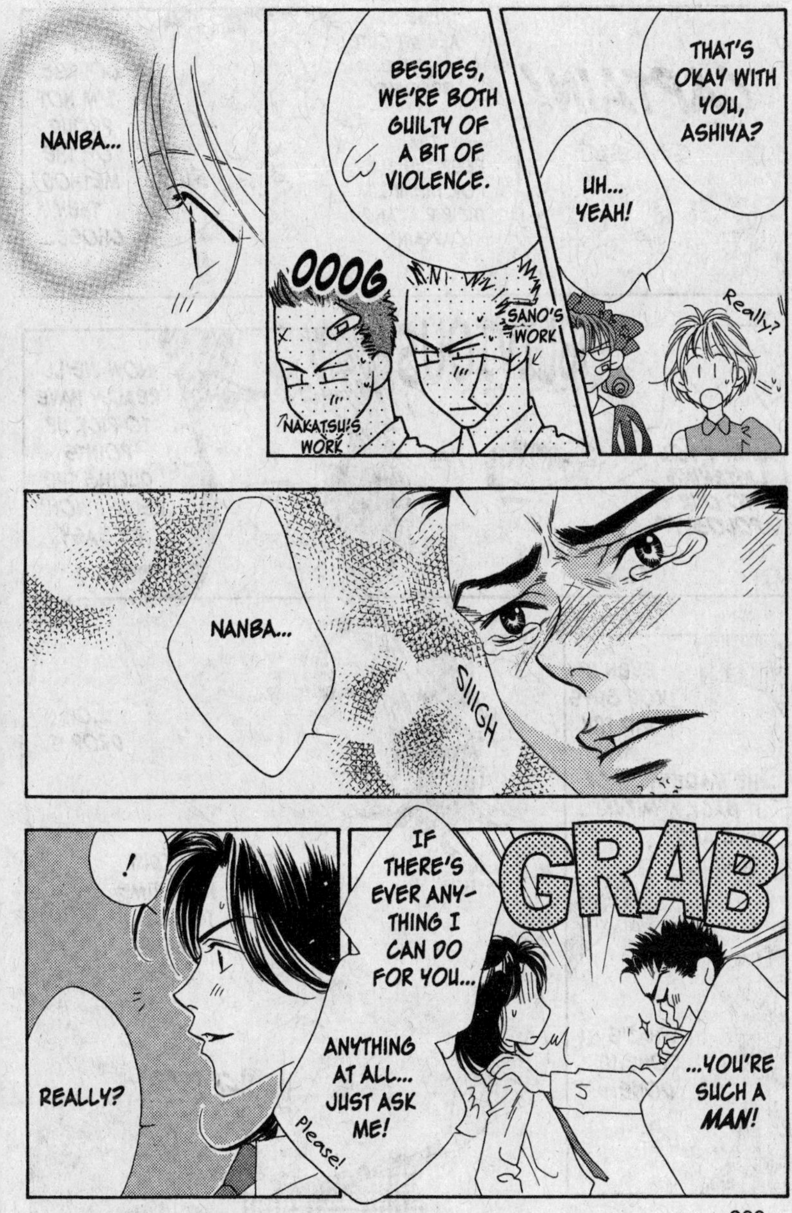
THAT'S OKAY WITH YOU, ASHIYA?
UH... YEAH!
Really?
BESIDES, WE'RE BOTH GUILTY OF A BIT OF VIOLENCE.
OOOG
SANO'S WORK
NAKATSU'S WORK
NANBA...
NANBA...
SIIIGH
GRAB
...YOU'RE SUCH A *MAN*!
IF THERE'S EVER ANY-THING I CAN DO FOR YOU...
ANYTHING AT ALL... JUST ASK ME!
Please!
!
REALLY?

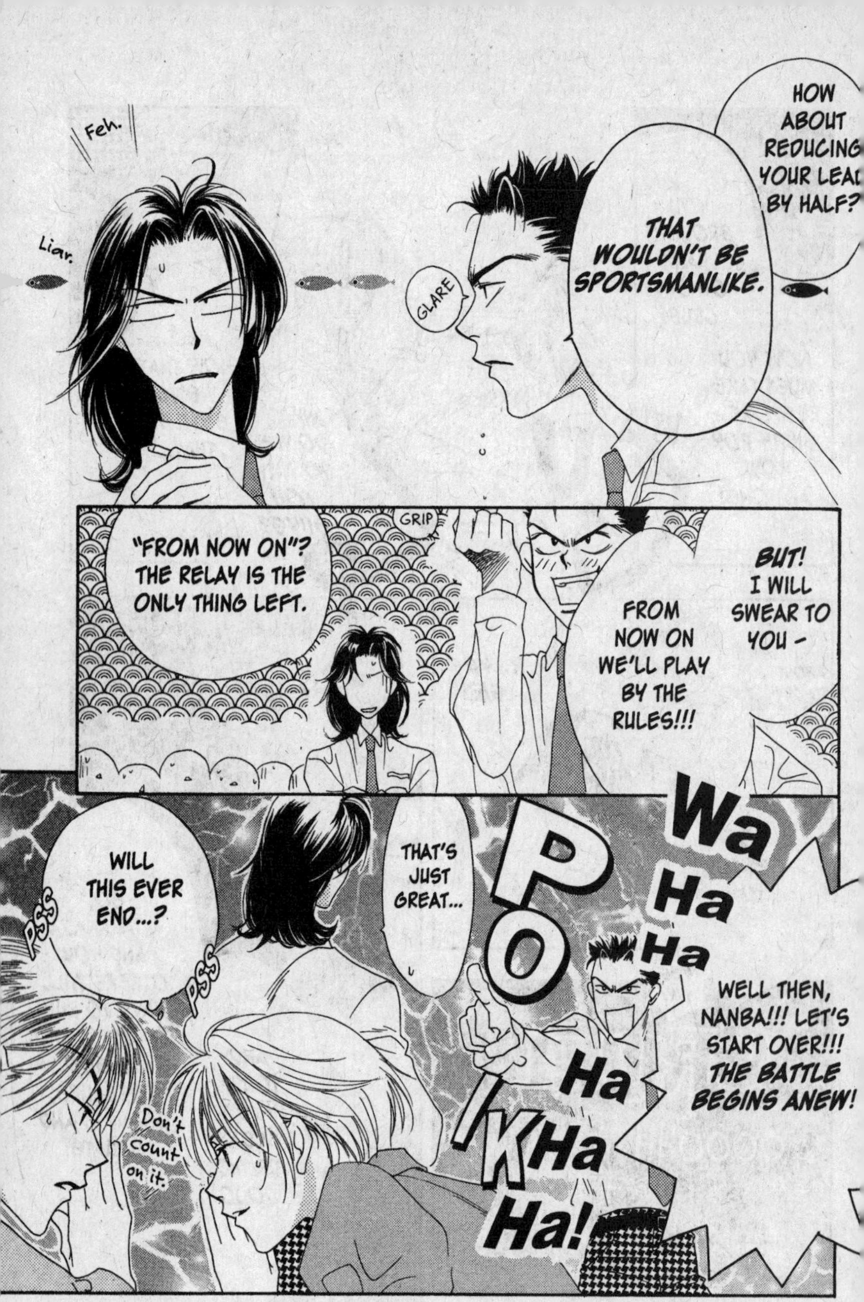
HOW ABOUT REDUCING YOUR LEA BY HALF?
THAT WOULDN'T BE SPORTSMANLIKE.
GLARE
Feh.
Liar.
BUT! I WILL SWEAR TO YOU -
FROM NOW ON WE'LL PLAY BY THE RULES!!!
GRIP
"FROM NOW ON"? THE RELAY IS THE ONLY THING LEFT.
WELL THEN, NANBA!!! LET'S START OVER!!! THE BATTLE BEGINS ANEW!
Wa Ha Ha Ha Ha Ha Ha!
POIK
THAT'S JUST GREAT...
WILL THIS EVER END...?
PSS
PSS
Don't count on it.

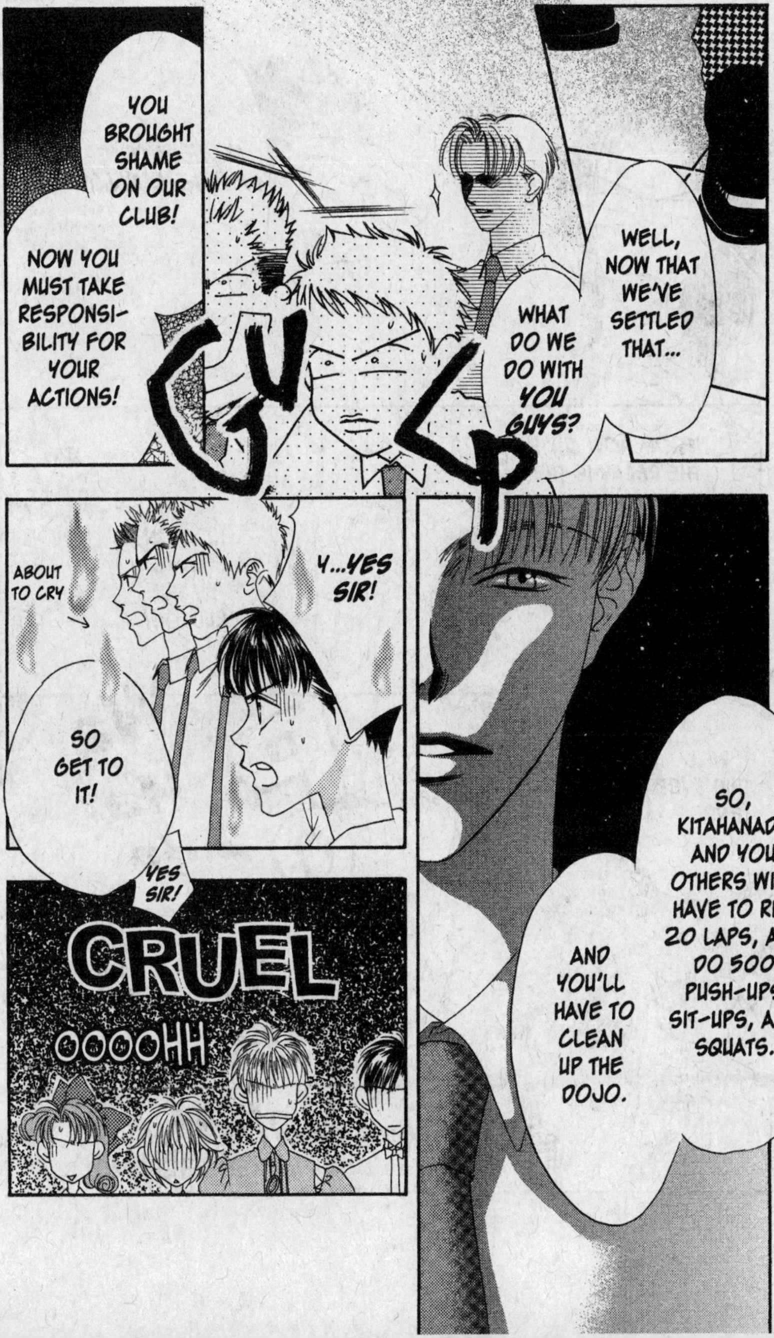
WELL, NOW THAT WE'VE SETTLED THAT...
WHAT DO WE DO WITH YOU GUYS?
GULP
YOU BROUGHT SHAME ON OUR CLUB!
NOW YOU MUST TAKE RESPONSI-BILITY FOR YOUR ACTIONS!
SO, KITAHANADA AND YOU OTHERS WILL HAVE TO RUN 20 LAPS, AND DO 500 PUSH-UPS, SIT-UPS, AND SQUATS.
AND YOU'LL HAVE TO CLEAN UP THE DOJO.
Y...YES SIR!
ABOUT TO CRY
SO GET TO IT!
YES SIR!
CRUEL
OOOOHH

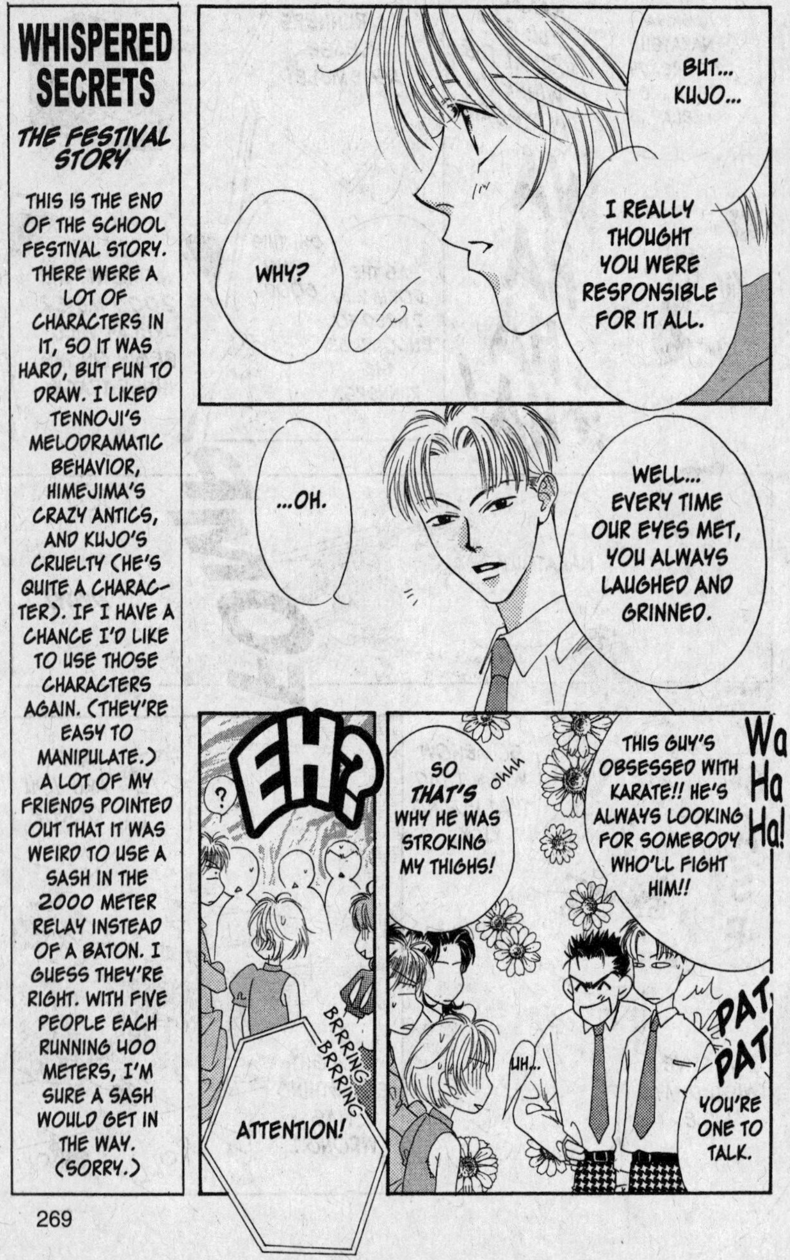
BUT... KUJO...
I REALLY THOUGHT YOU WERE RESPONSIBLE FOR IT ALL.
WHY?
WELL... EVERY TIME OUR EYES MET, YOU ALWAYS LAUGHED AND GRINNED.
...OH.
Wa Ha Ha!
THIS GUY'S OBSESSED WITH KARATE!! HE'S ALWAYS LOOKING FOR SOMEBODY WHO'LL FIGHT HIM!!
SO *THAT'S* WHY HE WAS STROKING MY THIGHS!
OHHH
PAT PAT
YOU'RE ONE TO TALK.
UH...
EH?
?
BRRRING BRRRING
ATTENTION!

WHISPERED SECRETS

THE FESTIVAL STORY

THIS IS THE END OF THE SCHOOL FESTIVAL STORY. THERE WERE A LOT OF CHARACTERS IN IT, SO IT WAS HARD, BUT FUN TO DRAW. I LIKED TENNOJI'S MELODRAMATIC BEHAVIOR, HIMEJIMA'S CRAZY ANTICS, AND KUJO'S CRUELTY (HE'S QUITE A CHARACTER). IF I HAVE A CHANCE I'D LIKE TO USE THOSE CHARACTERS AGAIN. (THEY'RE EASY TO MANIPULATE.) A LOT OF MY FRIENDS POINTED OUT THAT IT WAS WEIRD TO USE A SASH IN THE 2000 METER RELAY INSTEAD OF A BATON. I GUESS THEY'RE RIGHT. WITH FIVE PEOPLE EACH RUNNING 400 METERS, I'M SURE A SASH WOULD GET IN THE WAY. (SORRY.)

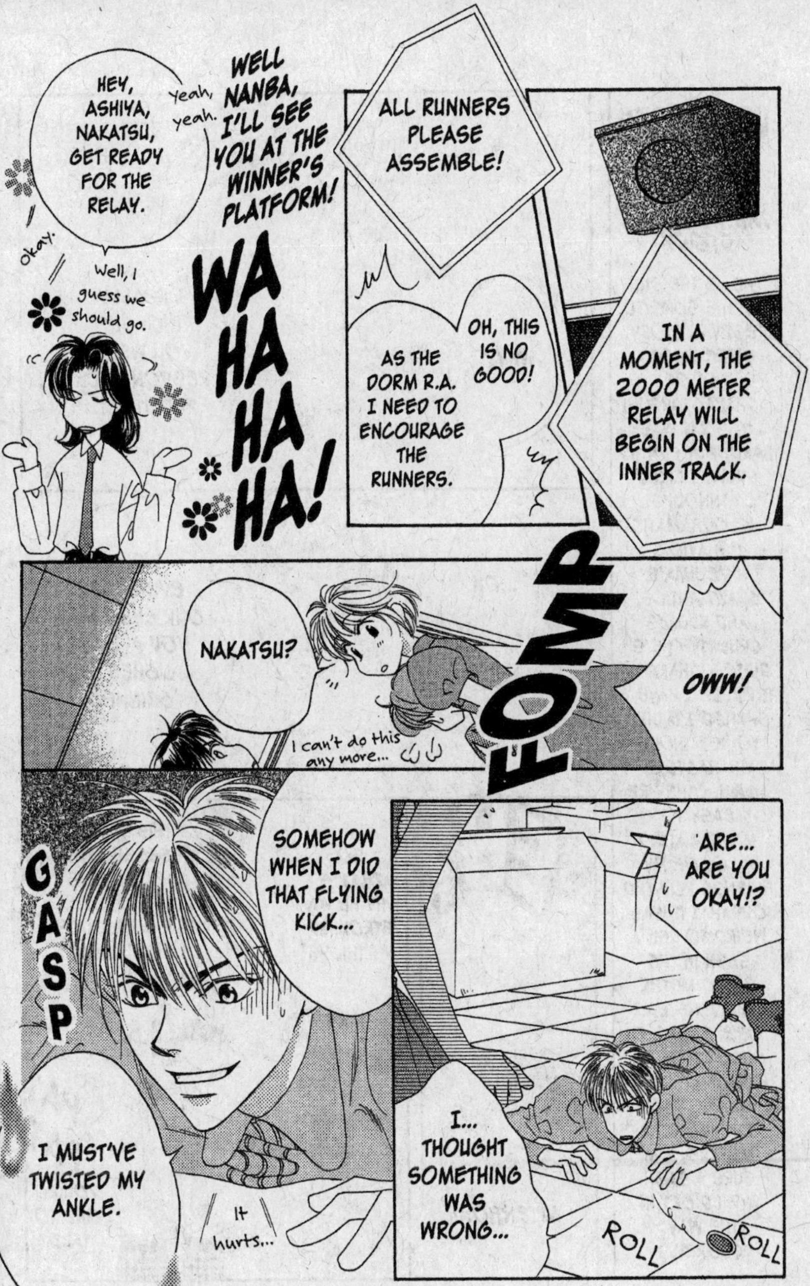
ALL RUNNERS PLEASE ASSEMBLE!
IN A MOMENT, THE 2000 METER RELAY WILL BEGIN ON THE INNER TRACK.
OH, THIS IS NO GOOD!
AS THE DORM R.A. I NEED TO ENCOURAGE THE RUNNERS.
WELL NANBA, I'LL SEE YOU AT THE WINNER'S PLATFORM!
WA HA HA HA!
HEY, ASHIYA, NAKATSU, GET READY FOR THE RELAY.
Yeah, yeah.
Okay.
Well, I guess we should go.
FOMP
OWW!
NAKATSU?
I can't do this any more...
ARE... ARE YOU OKAY!?
I... THOUGHT SOMETHING WAS WRONG...
ROLL
ROLL
GASP
SOMEHOW WHEN I DID THAT FLYING KICK...
I MUST'VE TWISTED MY ANKLE.
It hurts...

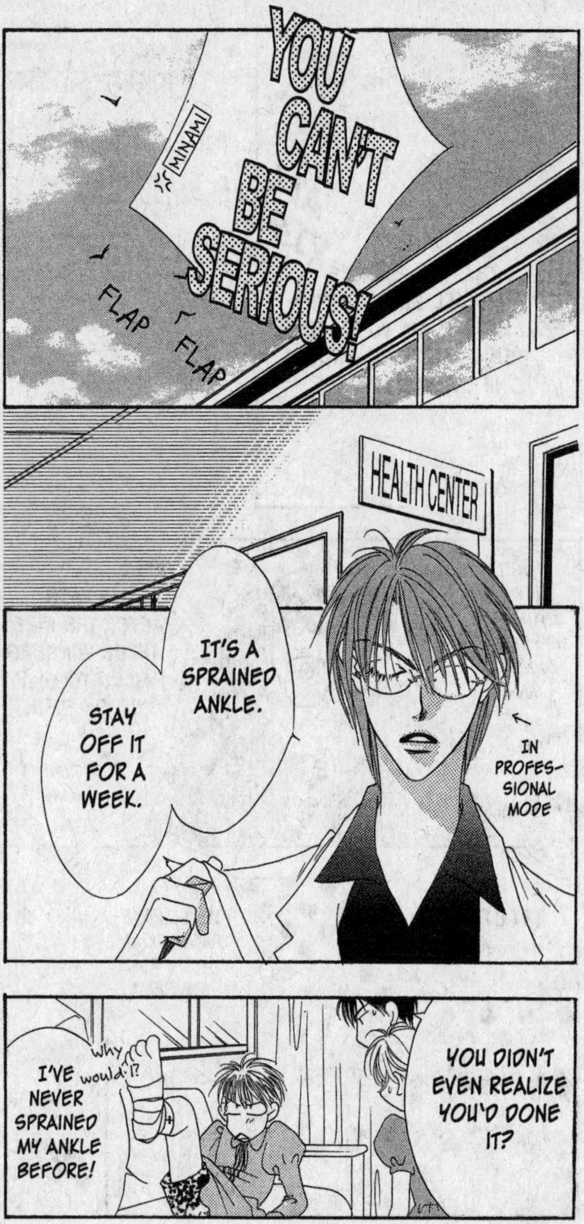
YOU CAN'T BE SERIOUS!
MINAMI
FLAP
FLAP
HEALTH CENTER
IT'S A SPRAINED ANKLE.
STAY OFF IT FOR A WEEK.
IN PROFES-SIONAL MODE
YOU DIDN'T EVEN REALIZE YOU'D DONE IT?
I'VE NEVER SPRAINED MY ANKLE BEFORE!
Why would I?

WHISPERED SECRETS

STUDIO GHIBLI

I JUST SAW "PRINCESS MONONOKE."♥ I LIKED THE FAMILY OF WOLF SPIRITS♥ ...THEY WERE SO GREAT!♥ YAKKURU WAS CUTE TOO!♥ RIGHT NOW STUDIO GHIBLI VIDEOS ARE VERY CHEAP! THEY USED TO BE TOO EXPENSIVE FOR ME, SO I'M HAPPY THEY LOWERED THE PRICE. MY FAVORITE IS "LAPUTA." DORA HAD A LOT OF CHARACTER (I LOVE HATSUI, NOW DECEASED). IT GETS A 100% FOR ITS DRAMATIC QUALITY TOO. I ALSO LIKE "MIMI WO SUMASEBA" (WHISPER OF THE HEART). IF YOU HAVE A DREAM, YOU CAN REALLY RELATE TO IT! IT'S HEARTWARMING!♥ MY MOTHER LOVES "TOTORO," AND SHE'S ALWAYS SINGING THE SONG "ARUKO ARUKO" FROM THE OPENING CREDITS.

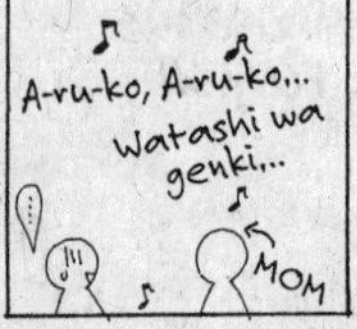
A-ru-ko, A-ru-ko...
Watashi wa genki...
MOM

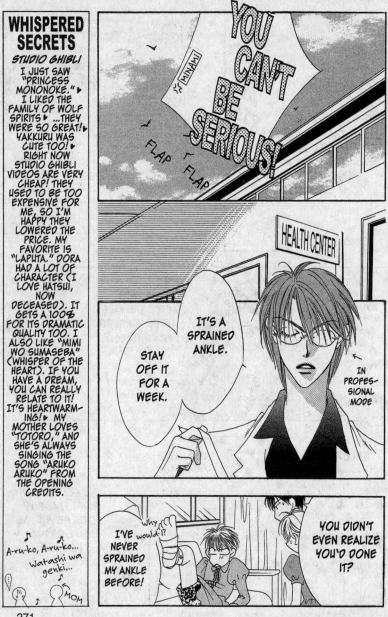

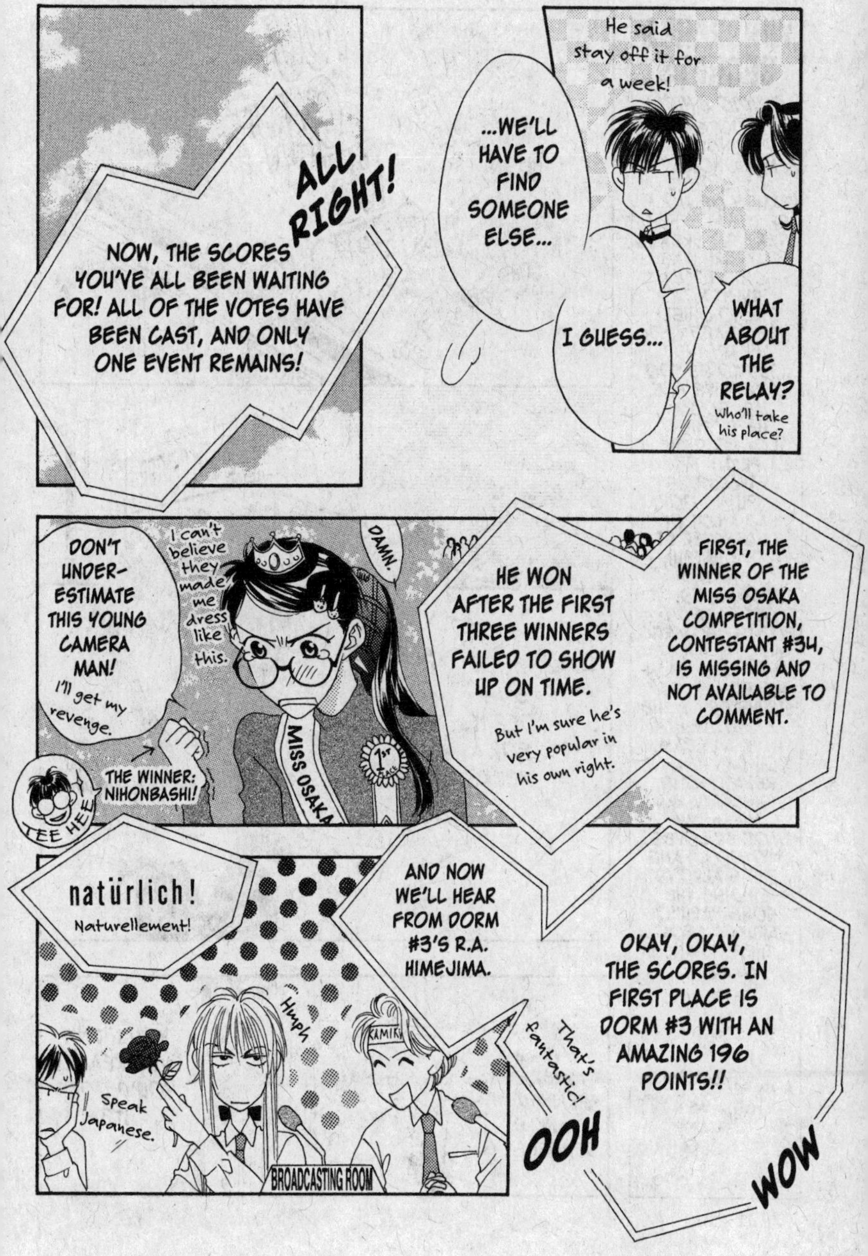
He said stay off it for a week!
...WE'LL HAVE TO FIND SOMEONE ELSE...
WHAT ABOUT THE RELAY? Who'll take his place?
I GUESS...
ALL RIGHT!
NOW, THE SCORES YOU'VE ALL BEEN WAITING FOR! ALL OF THE VOTES HAVE BEEN CAST, AND ONLY ONE EVENT REMAINS!
FIRST, THE WINNER OF THE MISS OSAKA COMPETITION, CONTESTANT #34, IS MISSING AND NOT AVAILABLE TO COMMENT.
HE WON AFTER THE FIRST THREE WINNERS FAILED TO SHOW UP ON TIME.
But I'm sure he's very popular in his own right.
DAMN.
I can't believe they made me dress like this.
MISS OSAKA
1ST PLACE
DON'T UNDER-ESTIMATE THIS YOUNG CAMERA MAN!
I'll get my revenge.
THE WINNER: NIHONBASHI!
TEE HEE
OKAY, OKAY, THE SCORES. IN FIRST PLACE IS DORM #3 WITH AN AMAZING 196 POINTS!!
WOW
AND NOW WE'LL HEAR FROM DORM #3'S R.A. HIMEJIMA.
OOH
That's fantastic!
natürlich!
Naturellement!
Hmph
Speak Japanese.
BROADCASTING ROOM

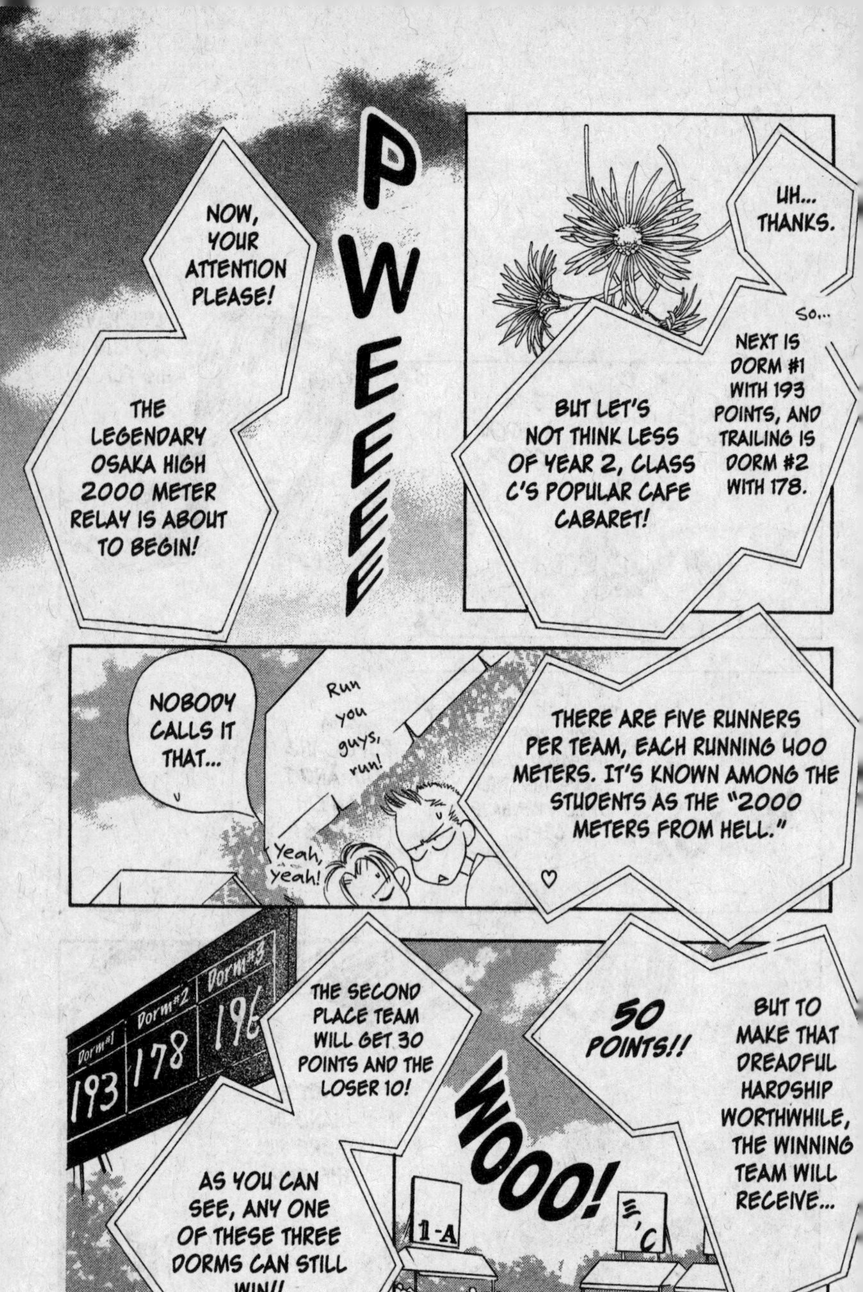

UH... THANKS.
So...
NEXT IS DORM #1 WITH 193 POINTS, AND TRAILING IS DORM #2 WITH 178.
BUT LET'S NOT THINK LESS OF YEAR 2, CLASS C'S POPULAR CAFE CABARET!
PWEEEE
NOW, YOUR ATTENTION PLEASE!
THE LEGENDARY OSAKA HIGH 2000 METER RELAY IS ABOUT TO BEGIN!
THERE ARE FIVE RUNNERS PER TEAM, EACH RUNNING 400 METERS. IT'S KNOWN AMONG THE STUDENTS AS THE "2000 METERS FROM HELL."
Run you guys, run!
Yeah, yeah!
NOBODY CALLS IT THAT...
BUT TO MAKE THAT DREADFUL HARDSHIP WORTHWHILE, THE WINNING TEAM WILL RECEIVE...
50 POINTS!!
WOOOO!
1-A
C
Dorm#1
193
Dorm#2
178
Dorm#3
196
THE SECOND PLACE TEAM WILL GET 30 POINTS AND THE LOSER 10!
AS YOU CAN SEE, ANY ONE OF THESE THREE DORMS CAN STILL WIN!!

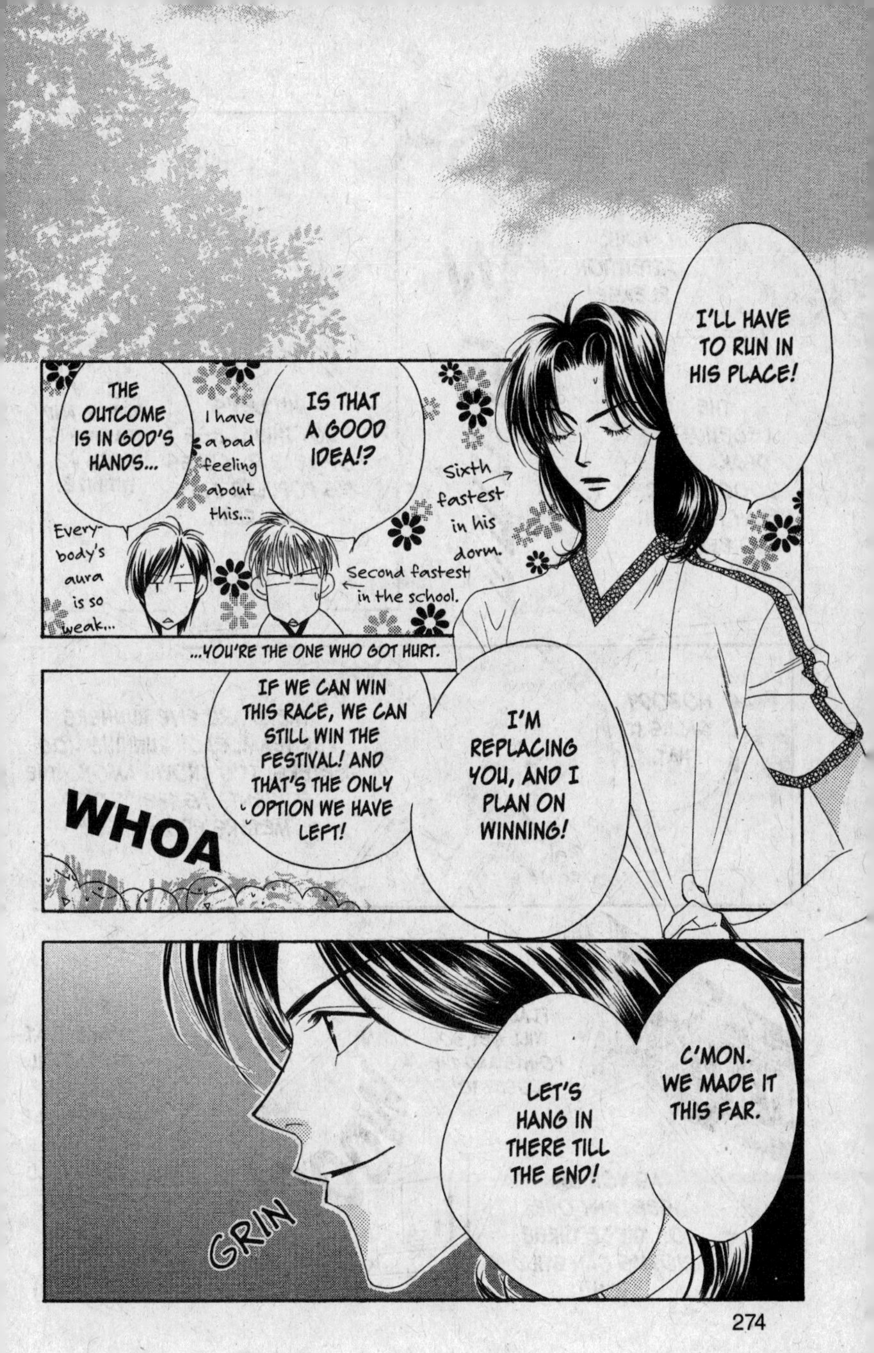
I'LL HAVE TO RUN IN HIS PLACE!
Sixth fastest in his dorm.
IS THAT A GOOD IDEA!?
Second fastest in the school.
I have a bad feeling about this...
THE OUTCOME IS IN GOD'S HANDS...
Everybody's aura is so weak...
...YOU'RE THE ONE WHO GOT HURT.
I'M REPLACING YOU, AND I PLAN ON WINNING!
IF WE CAN WIN THIS RACE, WE CAN STILL WIN THE FESTIVAL! AND THAT'S THE ONLY OPTION WE HAVE LEFT!
WHOA
C'MON. WE MADE IT THIS FAR.
LET'S HANG IN THERE TILL THE END!
GRIN

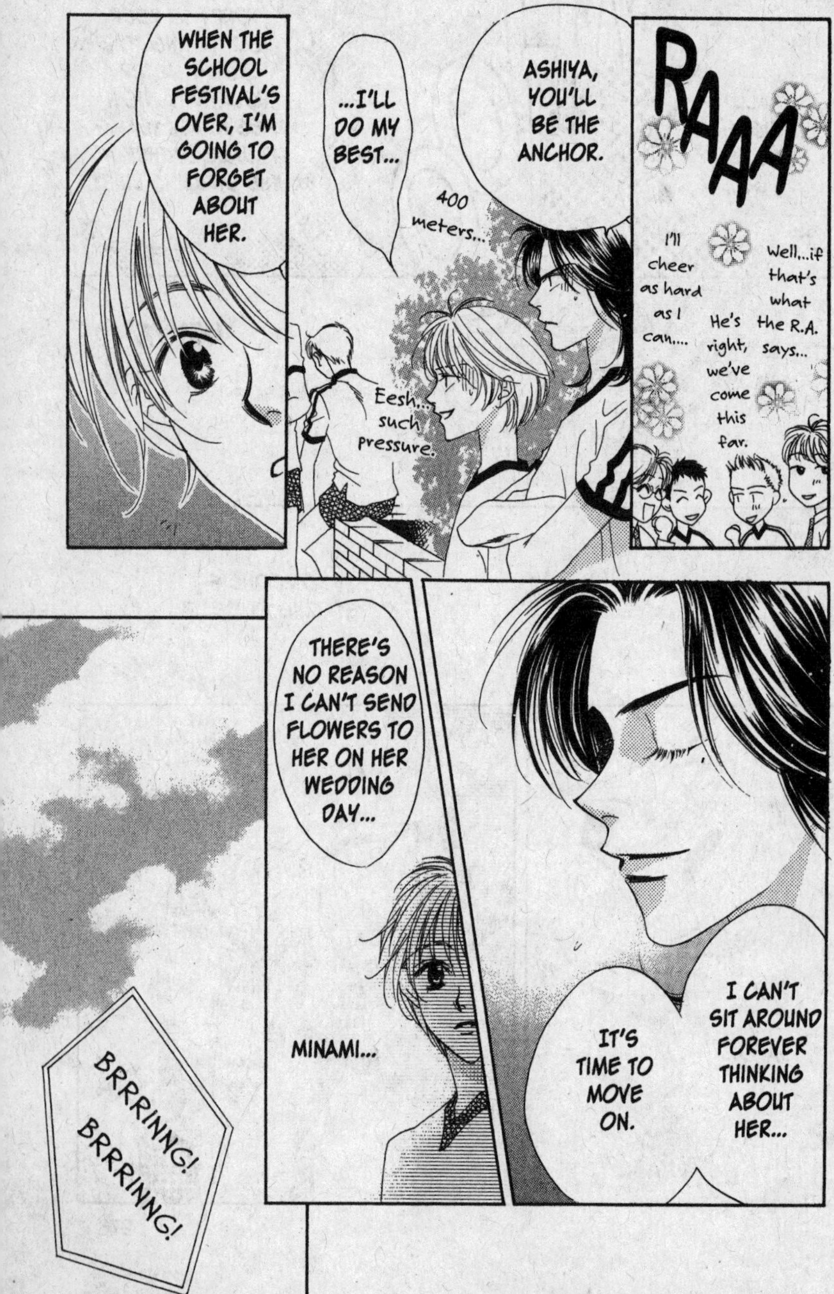
RAAA
Well...if that's what the R.A. says...
He's right, we've come this far.
I'll cheer as hard as I can....
ASHIYA, YOU'LL BE THE ANCHOR.
...I'LL DO MY BEST...
400 meters...
Eesh... such pressure.
WHEN THE SCHOOL FESTIVAL'S OVER, I'M GOING TO FORGET ABOUT HER.
I CAN'T SIT AROUND FOREVER THINKING ABOUT HER...
IT'S TIME TO MOVE ON.
THERE'S NO REASON I CAN'T SEND FLOWERS TO HER ON HER WEDDING DAY...
MINAMI...
BRRRINNG! BRRRINNG!

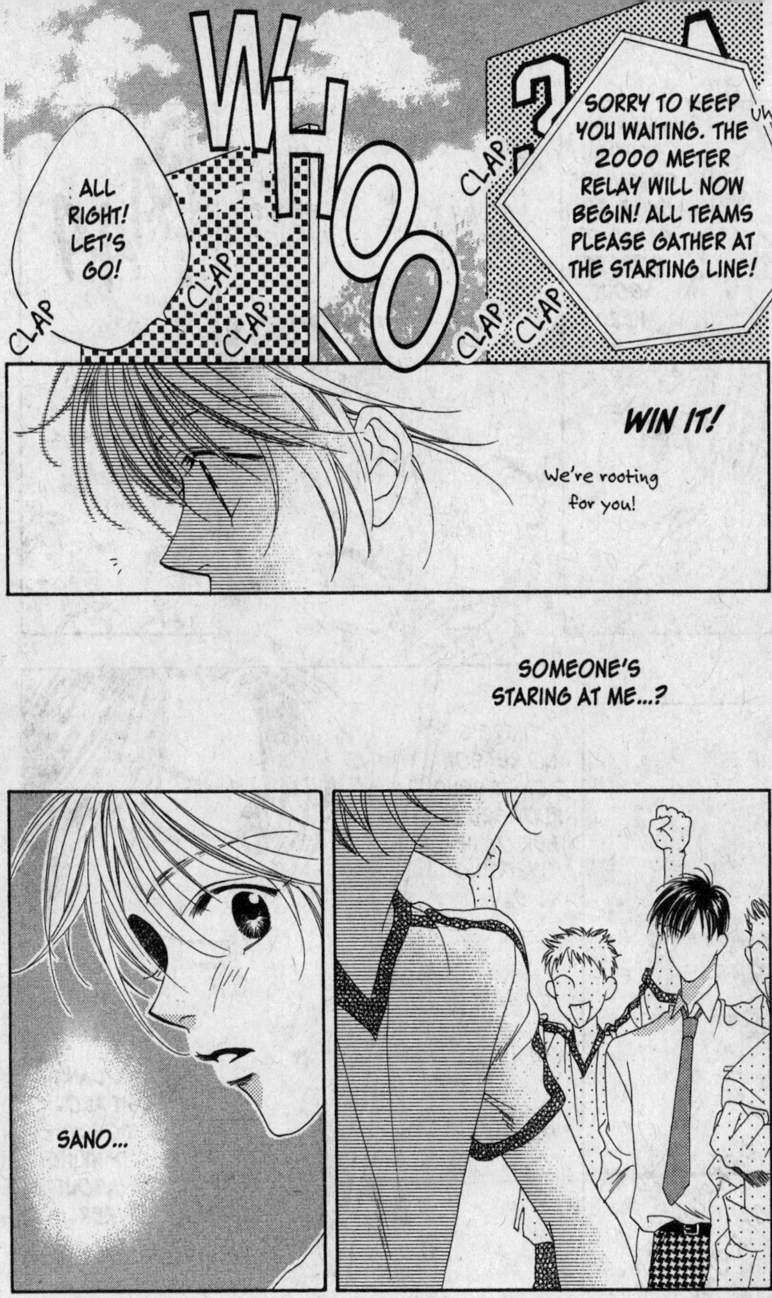
Uh...
SORRY TO KEEP YOU WAITING. THE 2000 METER RELAY WILL NOW BEGIN! ALL TEAMS PLEASE GATHER AT THE STARTING LINE!
?
CLAP
WHOO
CLAP CLAP
ALL RIGHT! LET'S GO!
CLAP CLAP CLAP
CLAP
WIN IT!
We're rooting for you!
SOMEONE'S STARING AT ME...?
SANO...

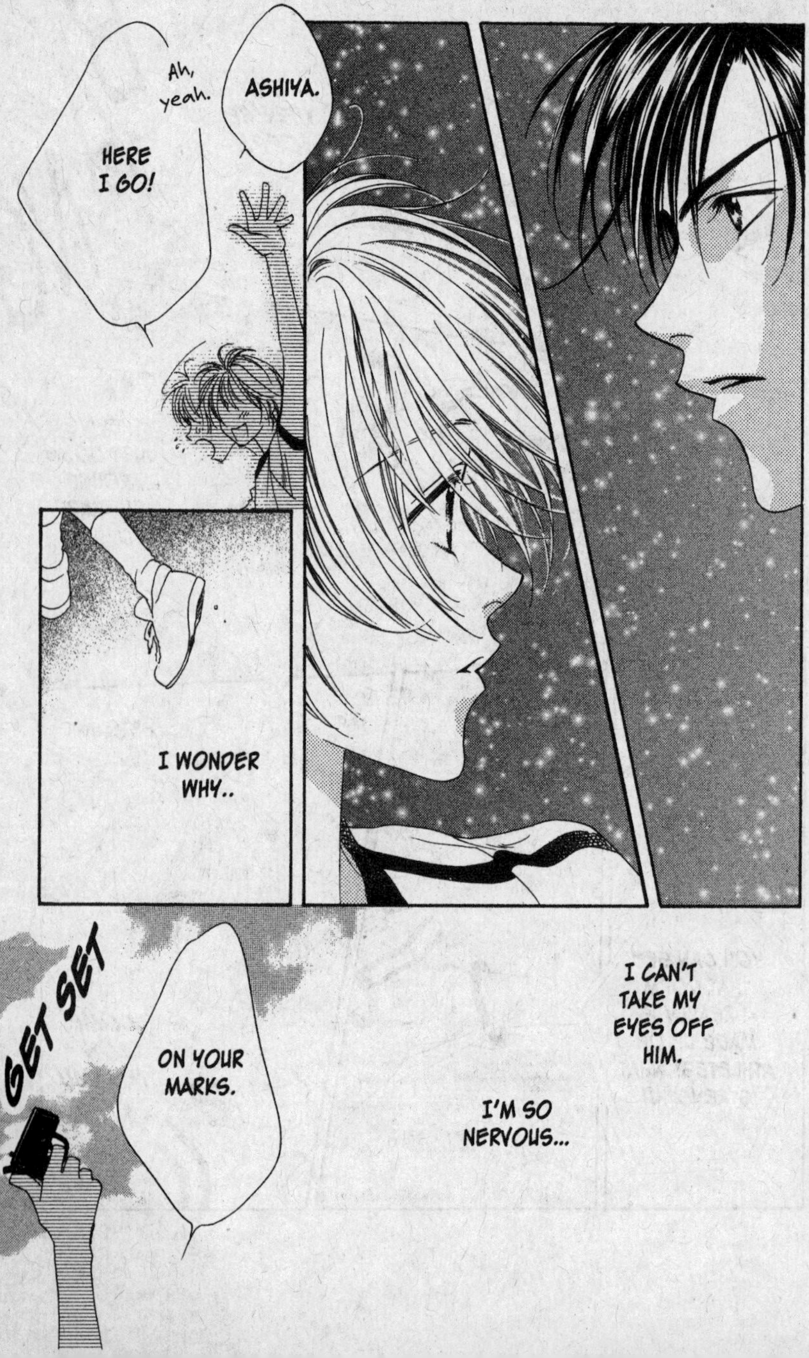

ASHIYA.
Ah, yeah.
HERE I GO!
I WONDER WHY..
I CAN'T TAKE MY EYES OFF HIM.
I'M SO NERVOUS...
ON YOUR MARKS.
GET SET

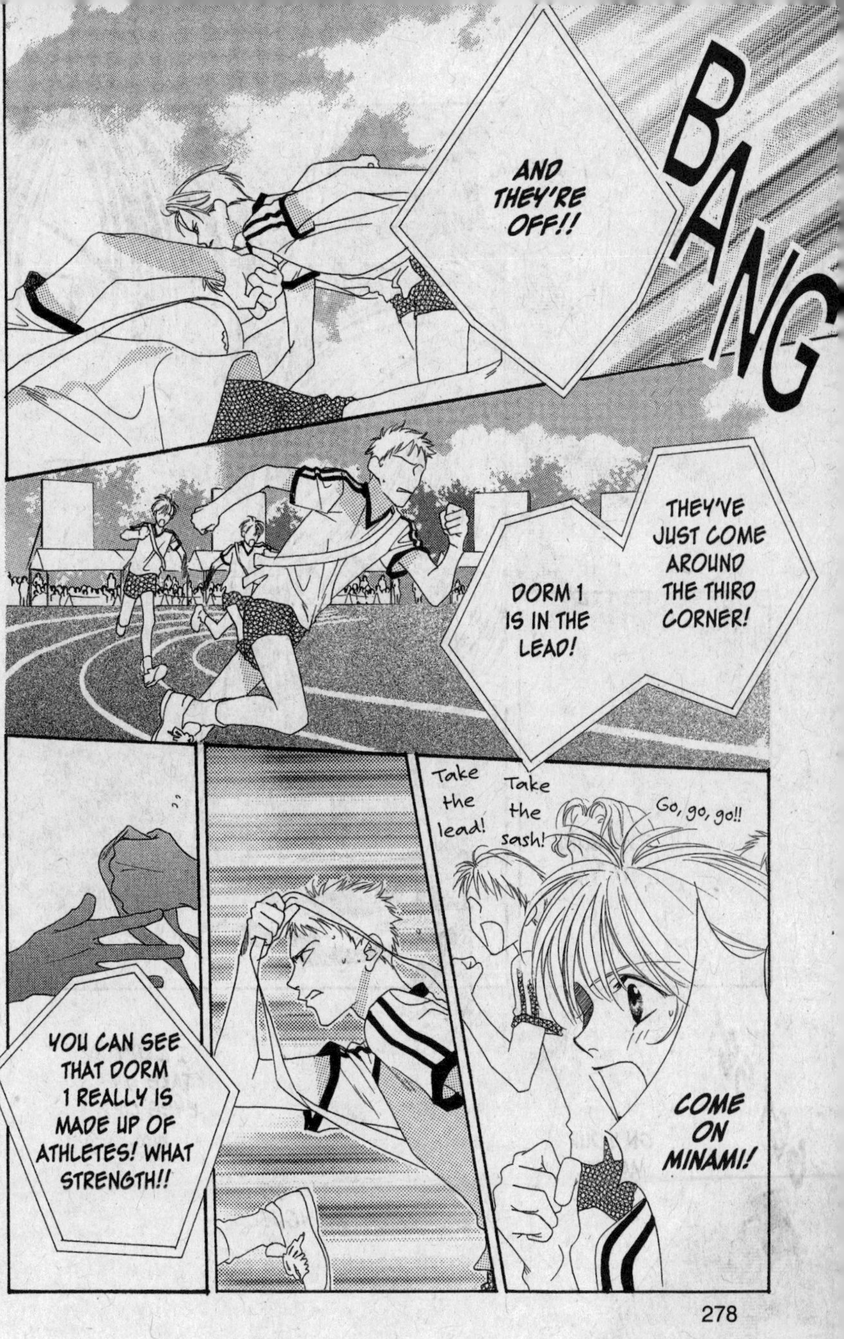
BANG
AND THEY'RE OFF!!
THEY'VE JUST COME AROUND THE THIRD CORNER!
DORM 1 IS IN THE LEAD!
Go, go, go!!
Take the sash!
Take the lead!
COME ON MINAMI!
YOU CAN SEE THAT DORM 1 REALLY IS MADE UP OF ATHLETES! WHAT STRENGTH!!

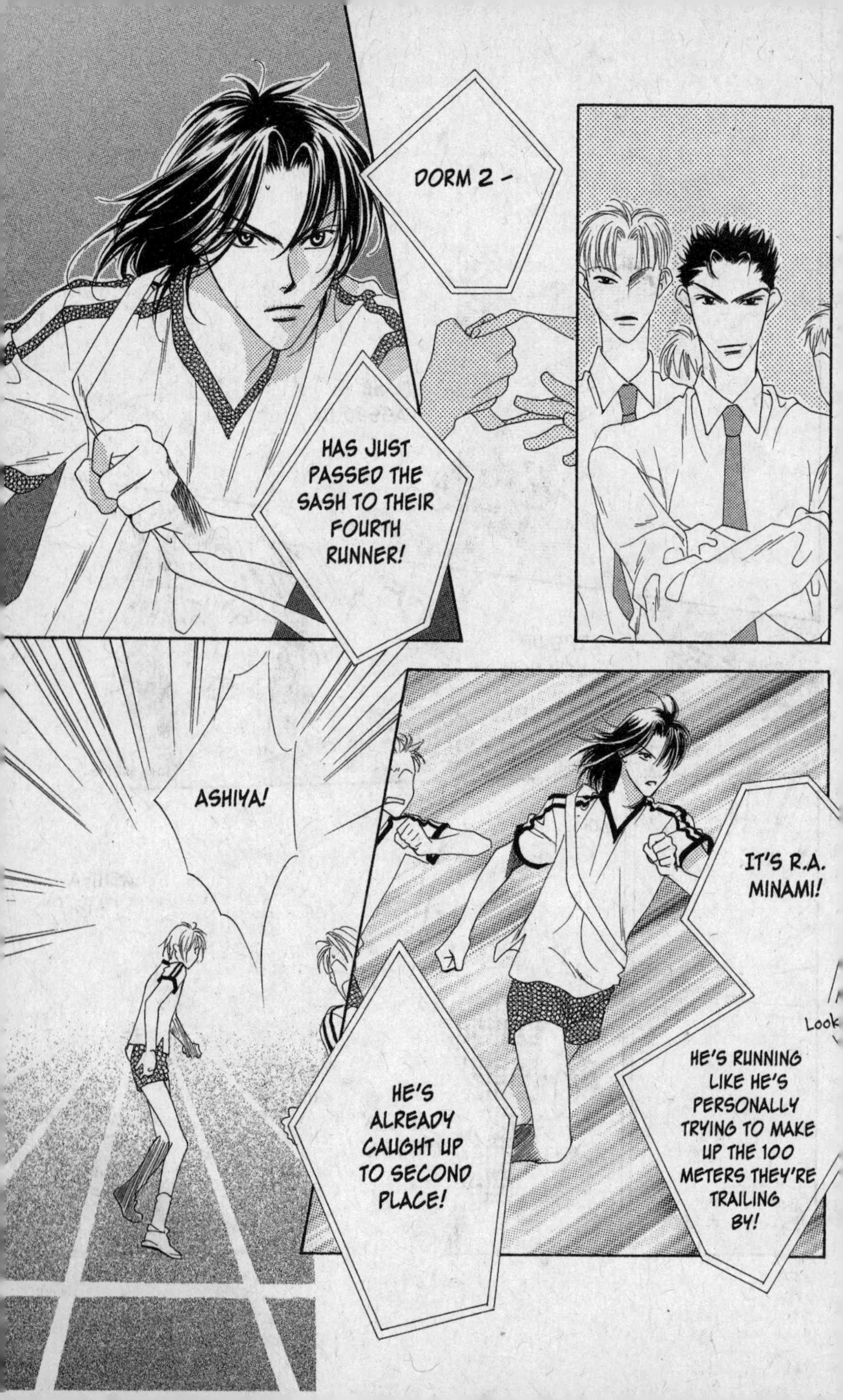
DORM 2 -
HAS JUST PASSED THE SASH TO THEIR FOURTH RUNNER!
IT'S R.A. MINAMI!
Look
HE'S RUNNING LIKE HE'S PERSONALLY TRYING TO MAKE UP THE 100 METERS THEY'RE TRAILING BY!
HE'S ALREADY CAUGHT UP TO SECOND PLACE!
ASHIYA!

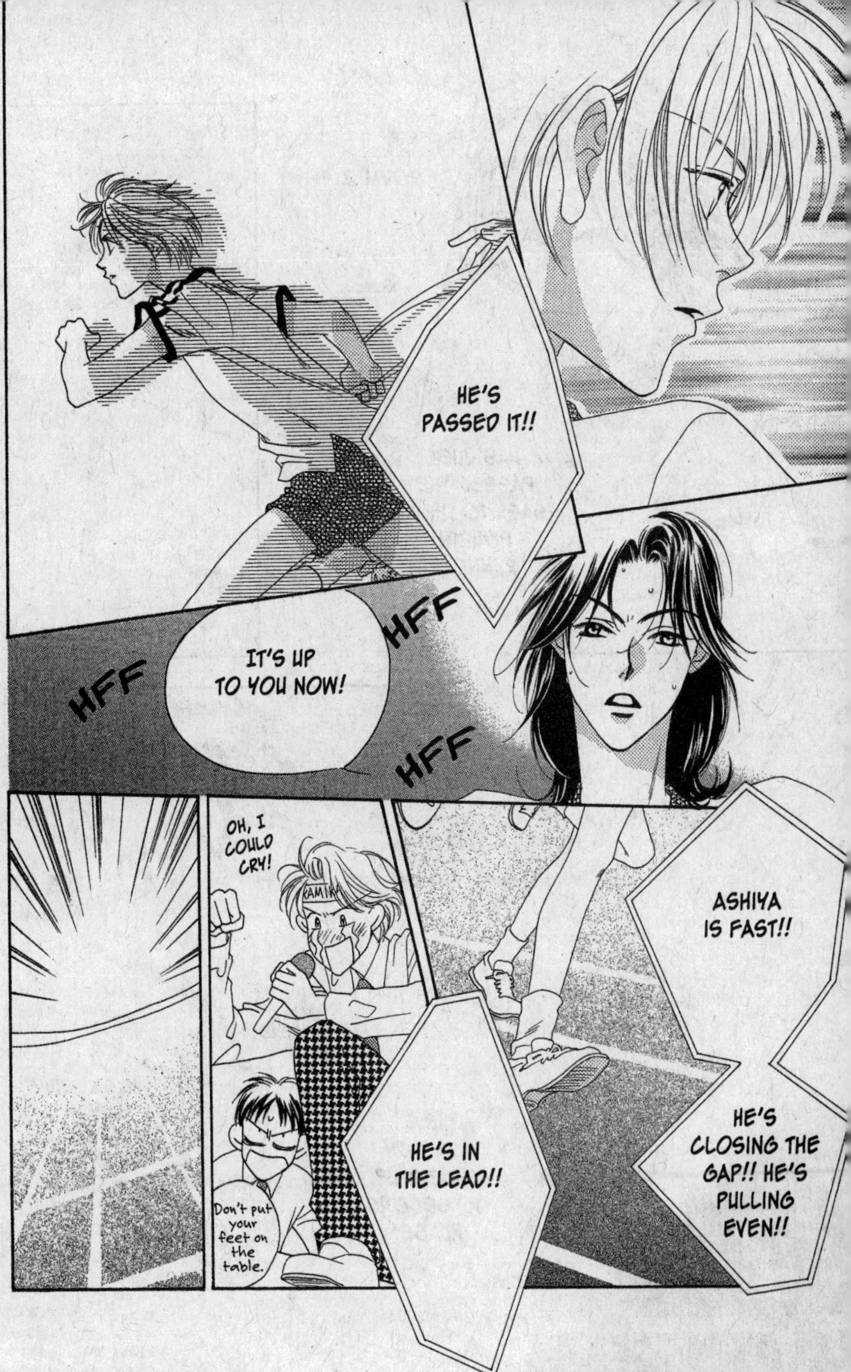
HE'S PASSED IT!!
HFF
IT'S UP TO YOU NOW!
HFF
HFF
ASHIYA IS FAST!!
HE'S CLOSING THE GAP!! HE'S PULLING EVEN!!
HE'S IN THE LEAD!!
OH, I COULD CRY!
KAMIKA
Don't put your feet on the table.

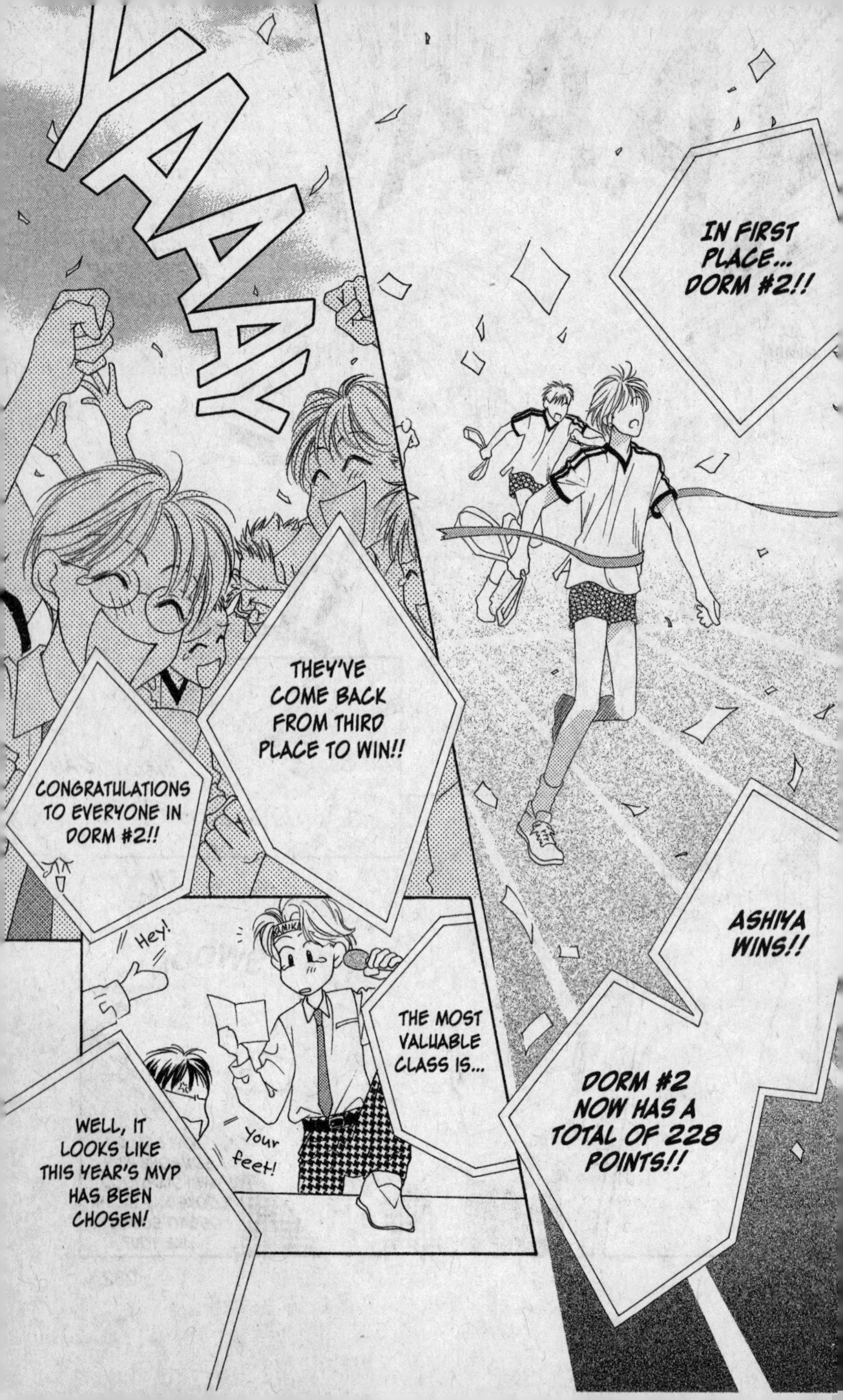
IN FIRST PLACE... DORM #2!!
ASHIYA WINS!!
DORM #2 NOW HAS A TOTAL OF 228 POINTS!!
YAAAAY
THEY'VE COME BACK FROM THIRD PLACE TO WIN!!
CONGRATULATIONS TO EVERYONE IN DORM #2!!
THE MOST VALUABLE CLASS IS...
Hey!
Your feet!
WELL, IT LOOKS LIKE THIS YEAR'S MVP HAS BEEN CHOSEN!

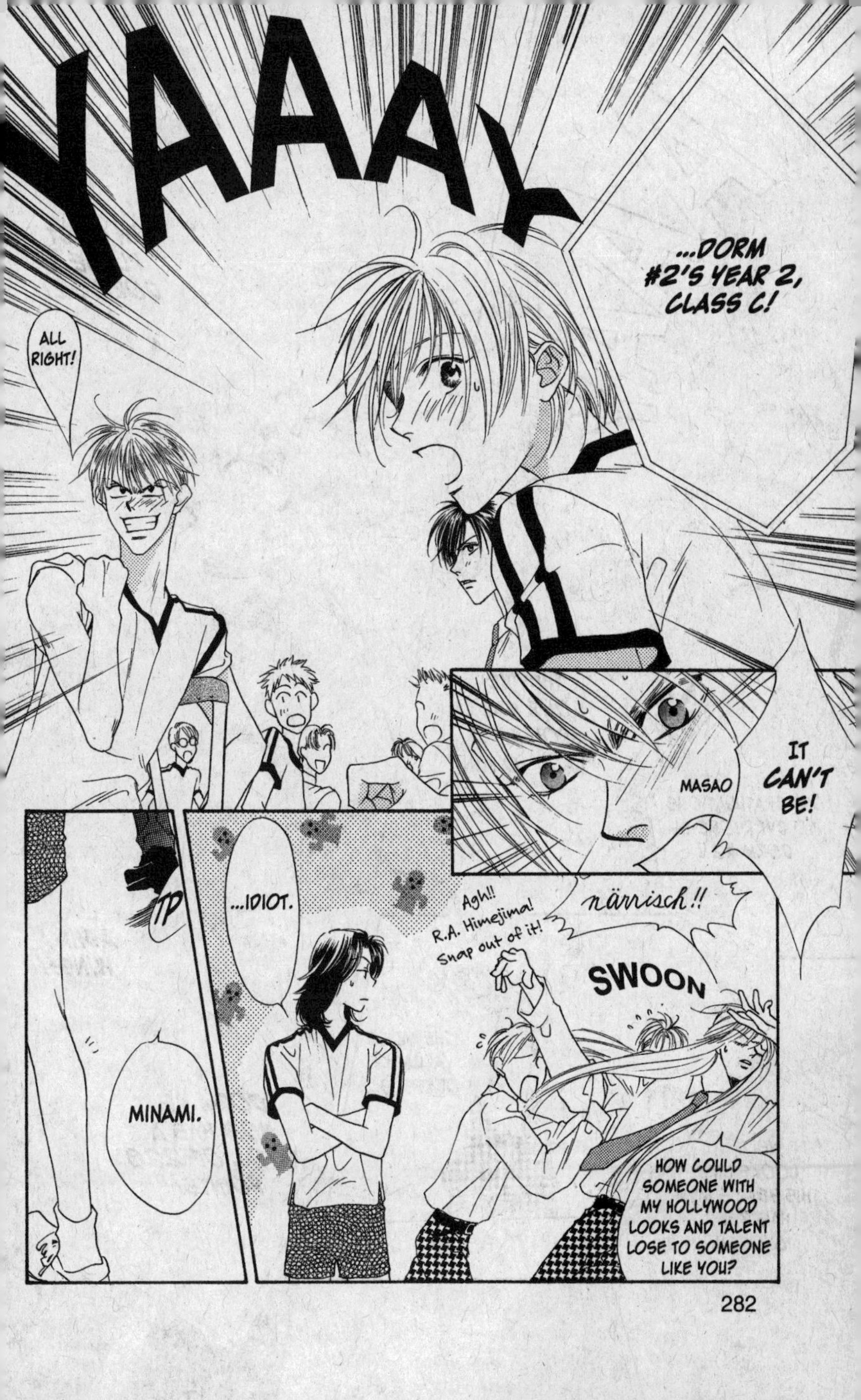
...DORM #2'S YEAR 2, CLASS C!
YAAAY
ALL RIGHT!
IT CAN'T BE!
MASAO
närrisch!!
Agh!! R.A. Himejima! Snap out of it!
SWOON
HOW COULD SOMEONE WITH MY HOLLYWOOD LOOKS AND TALENT LOSE TO SOMEONE LIKE YOU?
...IDIOT.
TP
MINAMI.

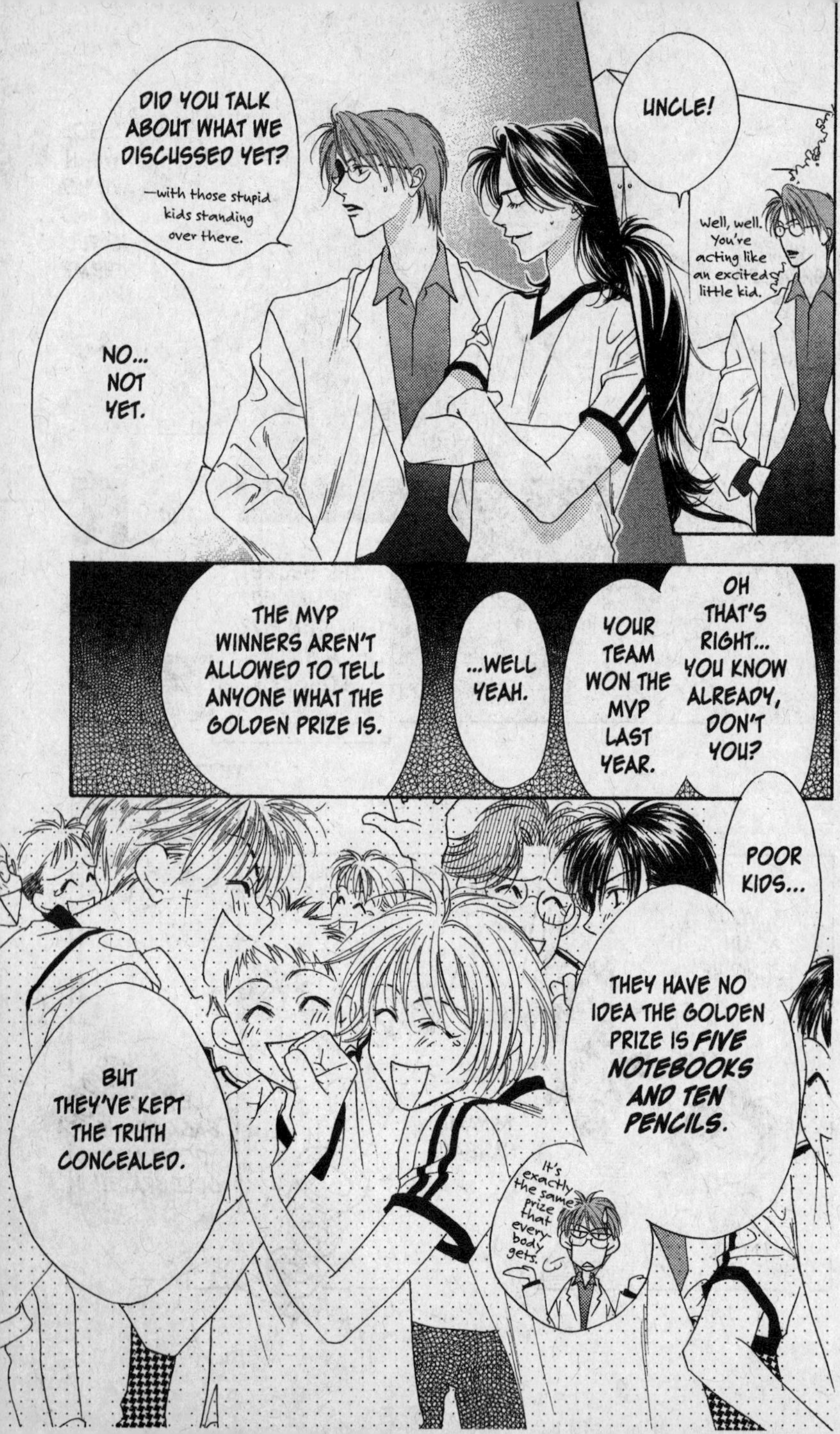
UNCLE!
Well, well. You're acting like an excited little kid.
DID YOU TALK ABOUT WHAT WE DISCUSSED YET?
—with those stupid kids standing over there.
NO... NOT YET.
OH THAT'S RIGHT... YOU KNOW ALREADY, DON'T YOU?
YOUR TEAM WON THE MVP LAST YEAR.
...WELL YEAH.
THE MVP WINNERS AREN'T ALLOWED TO TELL ANYONE WHAT THE GOLDEN PRIZE IS.
POOR KIDS...
THEY HAVE NO IDEA THE GOLDEN PRIZE IS *FIVE NOTEBOOKS AND TEN PENCILS*.
It's exactly the same prize that every-body gets.
BUT THEY'VE KEPT THE TRUTH CONCEALED.

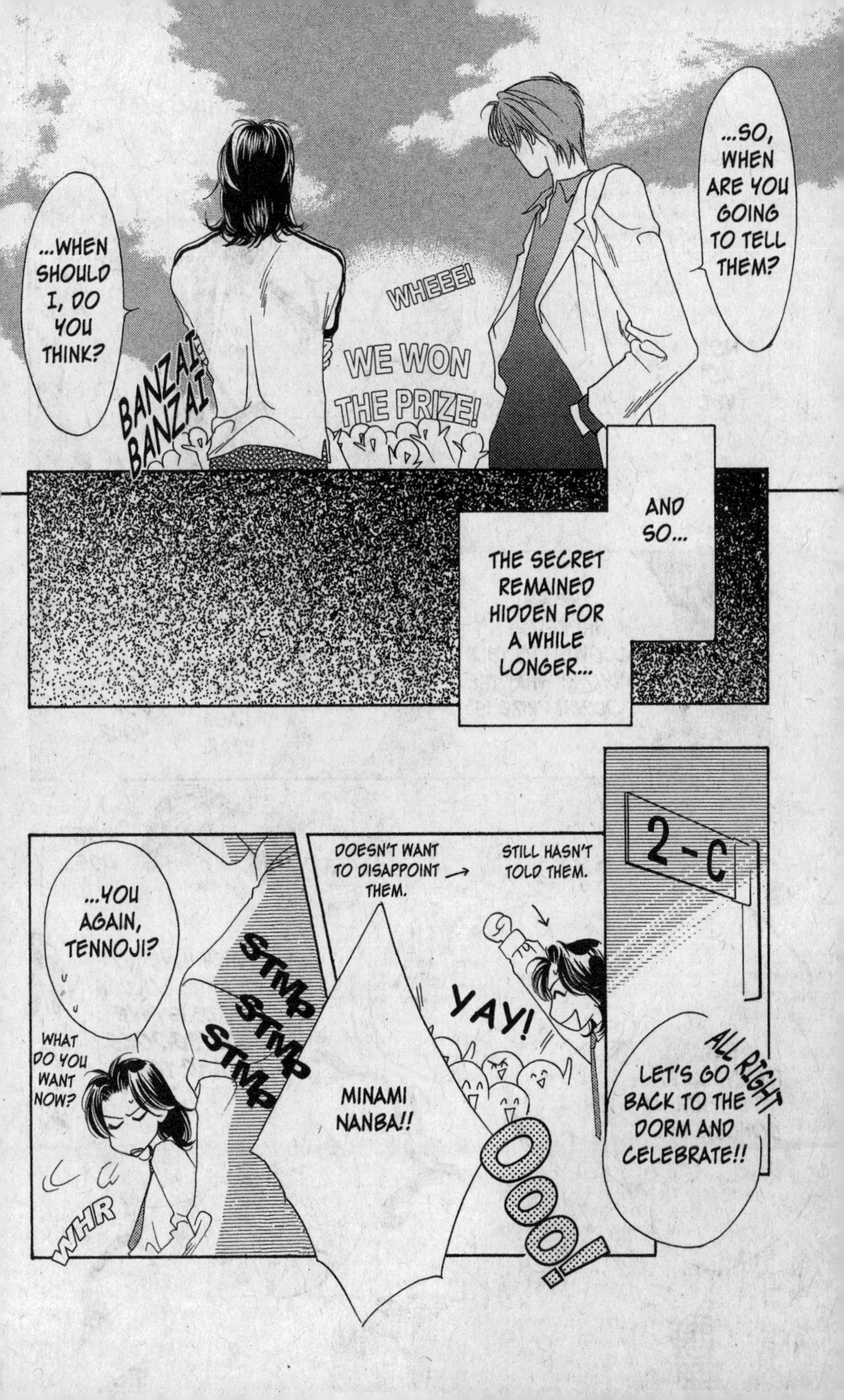
...SO, WHEN ARE YOU GOING TO TELL THEM?
WHEEE!
WE WON THE PRIZE!
BANZAI BANZAI
...WHEN SHOULD I, DO YOU THINK?
AND SO...
THE SECRET REMAINED HIDDEN FOR A WHILE LONGER...
2-C
ALL RIGHT
LET'S GO BACK TO THE DORM AND CELEBRATE!!
STILL HASN'T TOLD THEM.
YAY!
DOESN'T WANT TO DISAPPOINT THEM.
MINAMI NANBA!!
OOOO!
...YOU AGAIN, TENNOJI?
STMP STMP STMP
WHAT DO YOU WANT NOW?
WHR

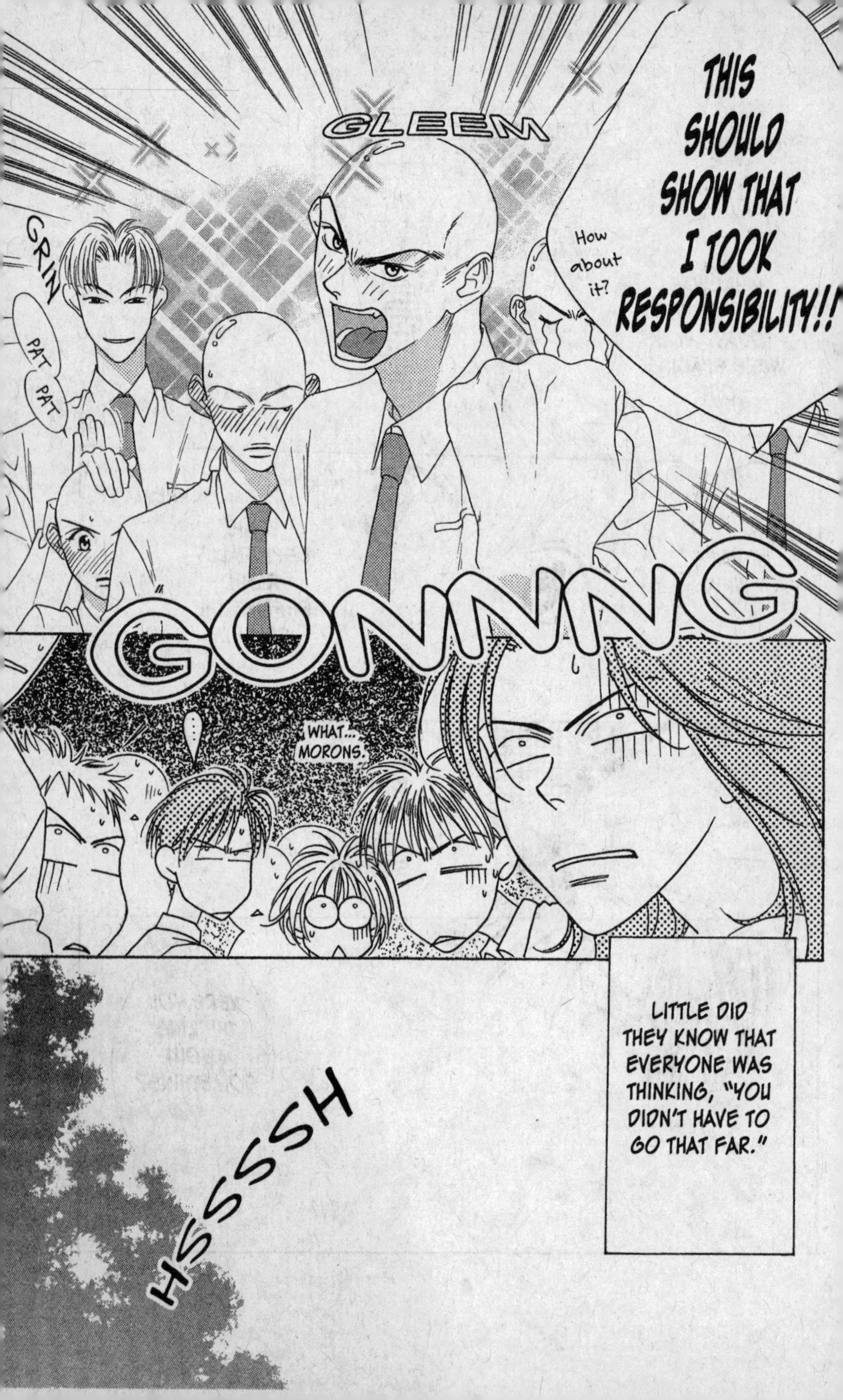
THIS SHOULD SHOW THAT I TOOK RESPONSIBILITY!!
How about it?
GLEEM
GRIN
PAT PAT
GONNNG
WHAT... MORONS.
LITTLE DID THEY KNOW THAT EVERYONE WAS THINKING, "YOU DIDN'T HAVE TO GO THAT FAR."
HSSSSH

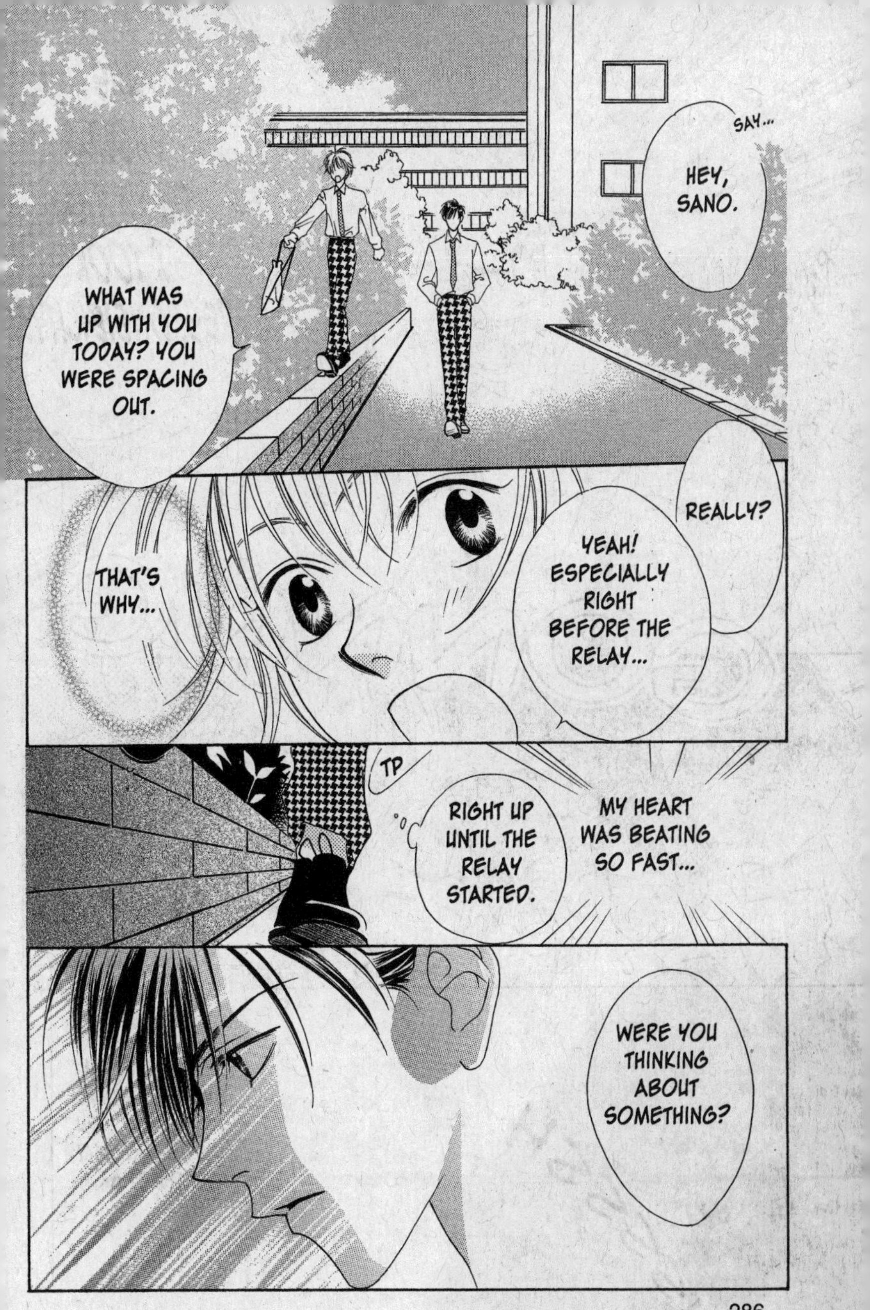
SAY...
HEY, SANO.
WHAT WAS UP WITH YOU TODAY? YOU WERE SPACING OUT.
REALLY?
YEAH! ESPECIALLY RIGHT BEFORE THE RELAY...
THAT'S WHY...
MY HEART WAS BEATING SO FAST...
TP
RIGHT UP UNTIL THE RELAY STARTED.
WERE YOU THINKING ABOUT SOMETHING?

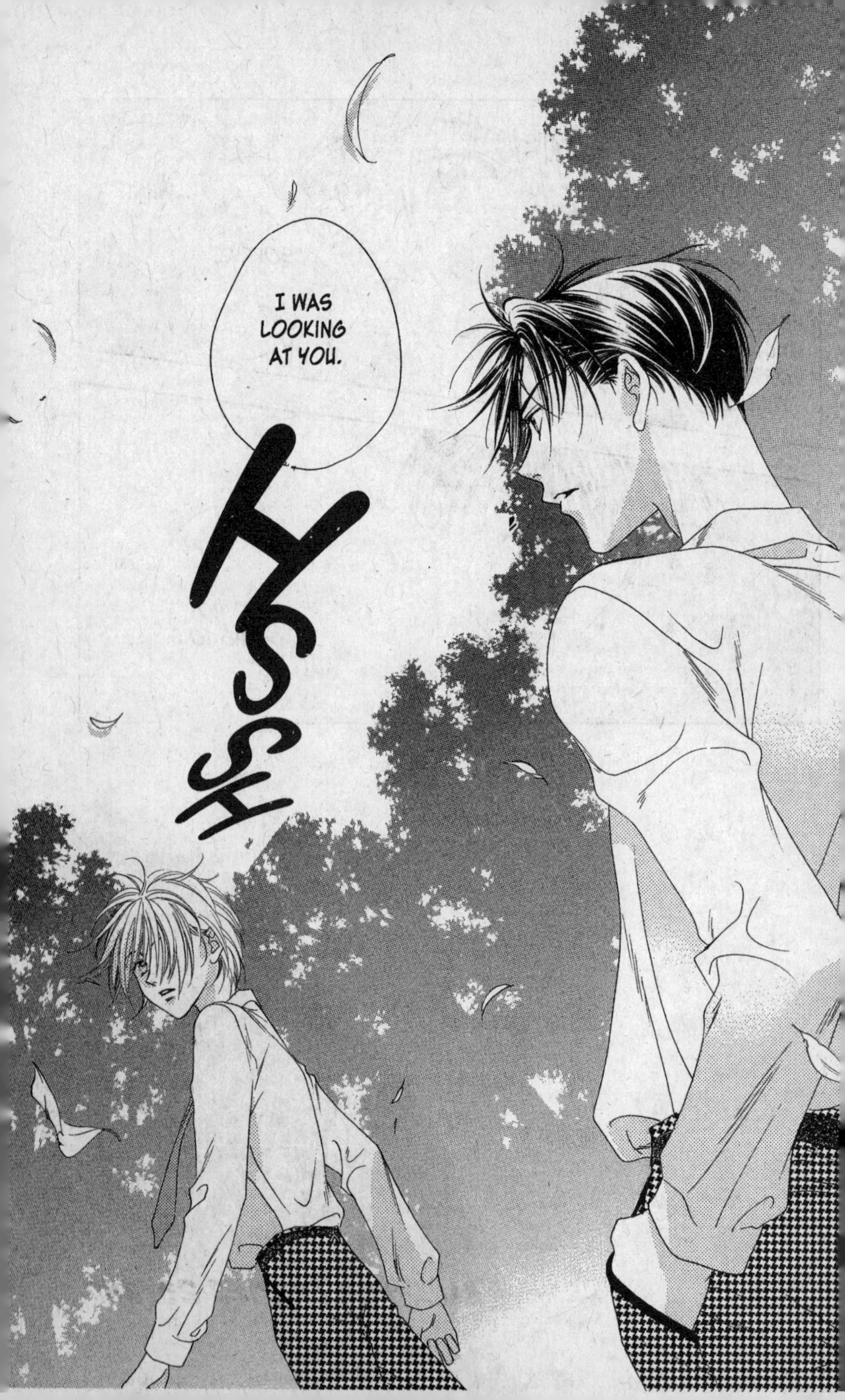
I WAS LOOKING AT YOU.
HSSH

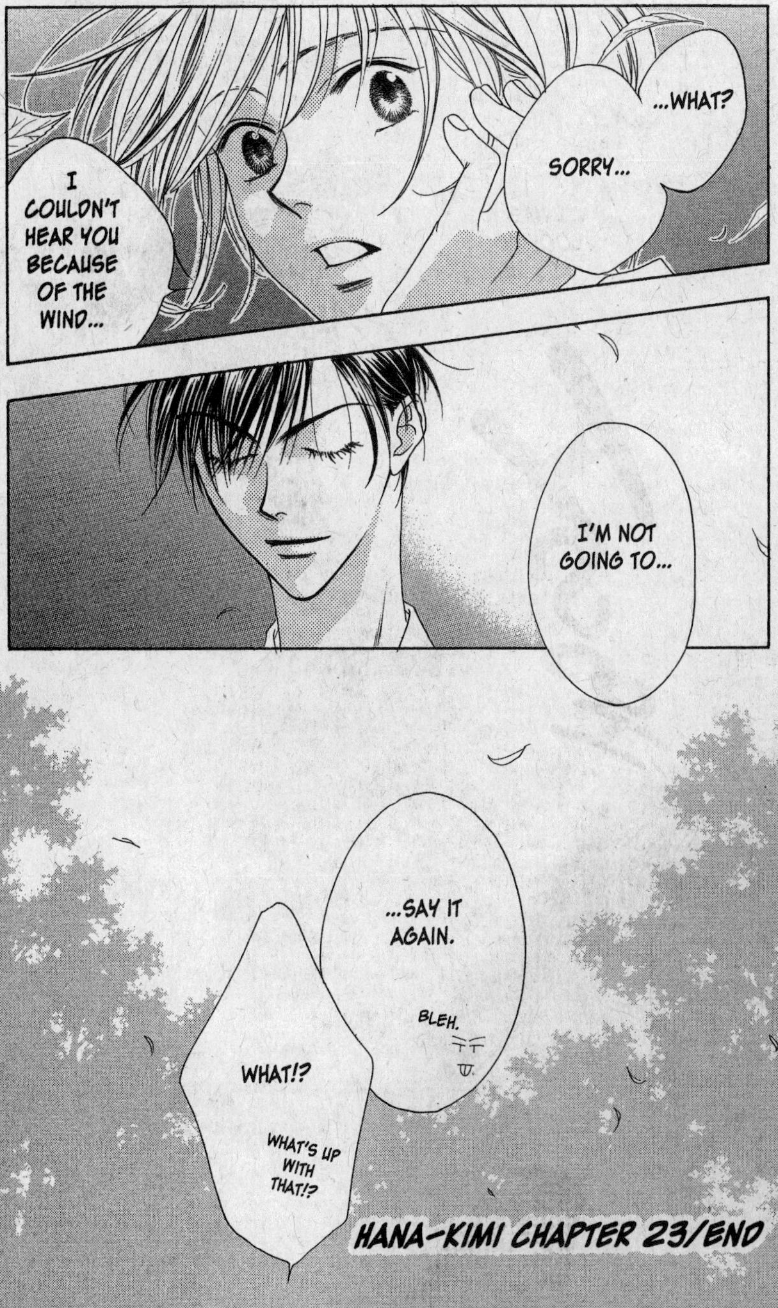
...WHAT?
SORRY...
I COULDN'T HEAR YOU BECAUSE OF THE WIND...
I'M NOT GOING TO...
...SAY IT AGAIN.
BLEH.
WHAT!?
WHAT'S UP WITH THAT!?
HANA-KIMI CHAPTER 23/END

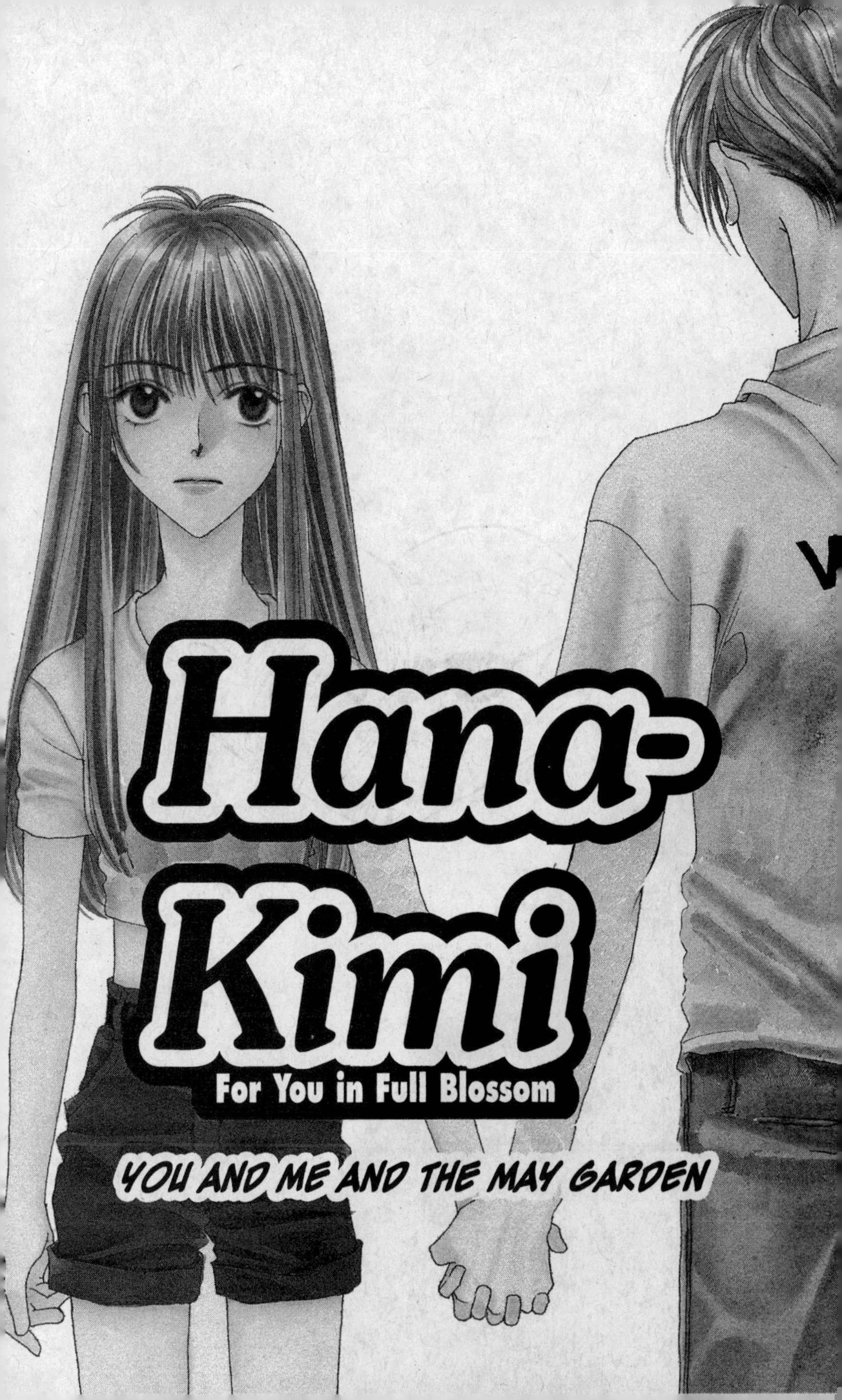
Hana-Kimi
For You in Full Blossom
YOU AND ME AND THE MAY GARDEN

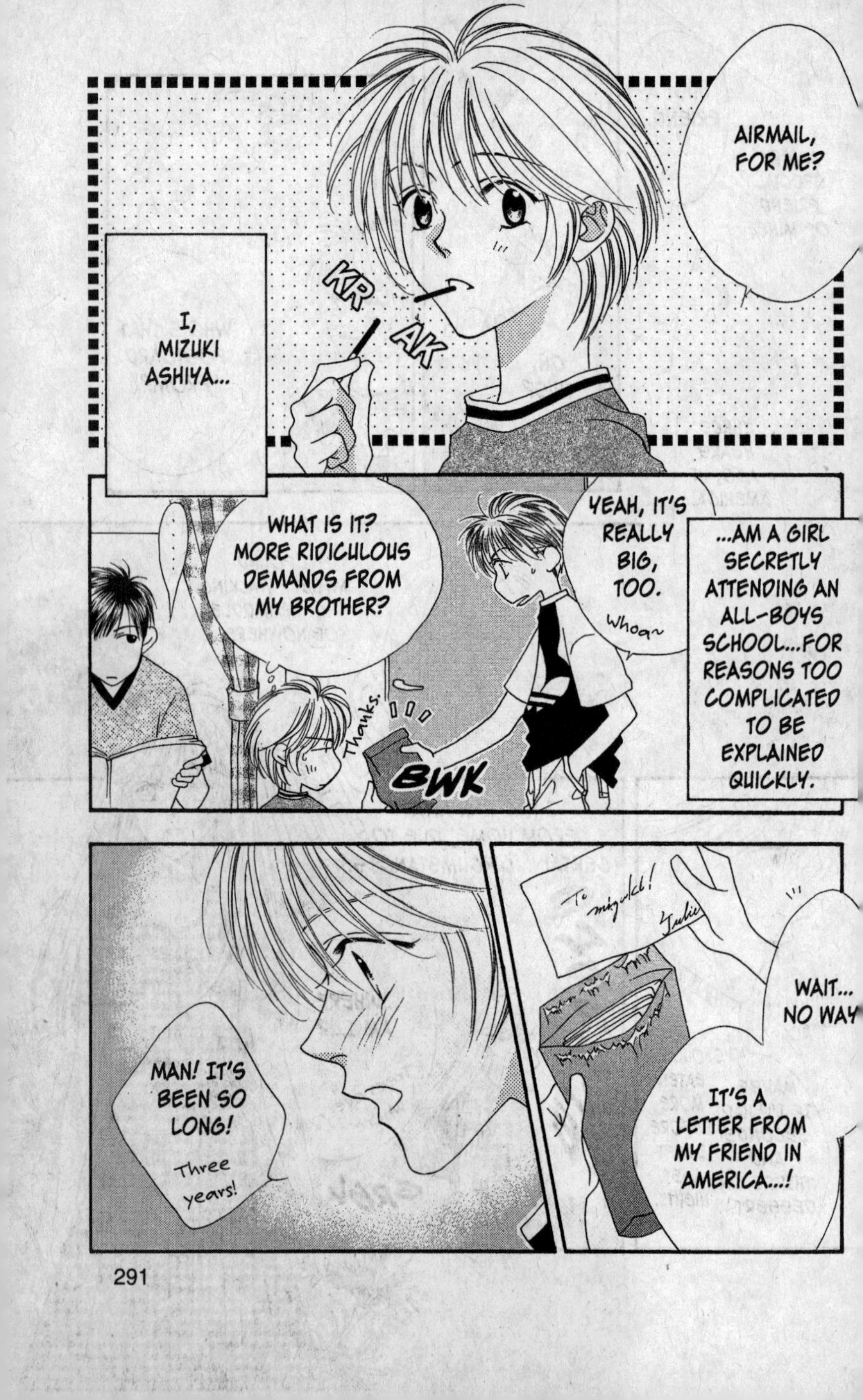
AIRMAIL, FOR ME?
KR AK
I, MIZUKI ASHIYA...
...AM A GIRL SECRETLY ATTENDING AN ALL-BOYS SCHOOL...FOR REASONS TOO COMPLICATED TO BE EXPLAINED QUICKLY.
YEAH, IT'S REALLY BIG, TOO.
Whoa~
Thanks.
BWK
WHAT IS IT? MORE RIDICULOUS DEMANDS FROM MY BROTHER?
WAIT... NO WAY
To mizuki!
Julie
IT'S A LETTER FROM MY FRIEND IN AMERICA...!
MAN! IT'S BEEN SO LONG!
Three years!

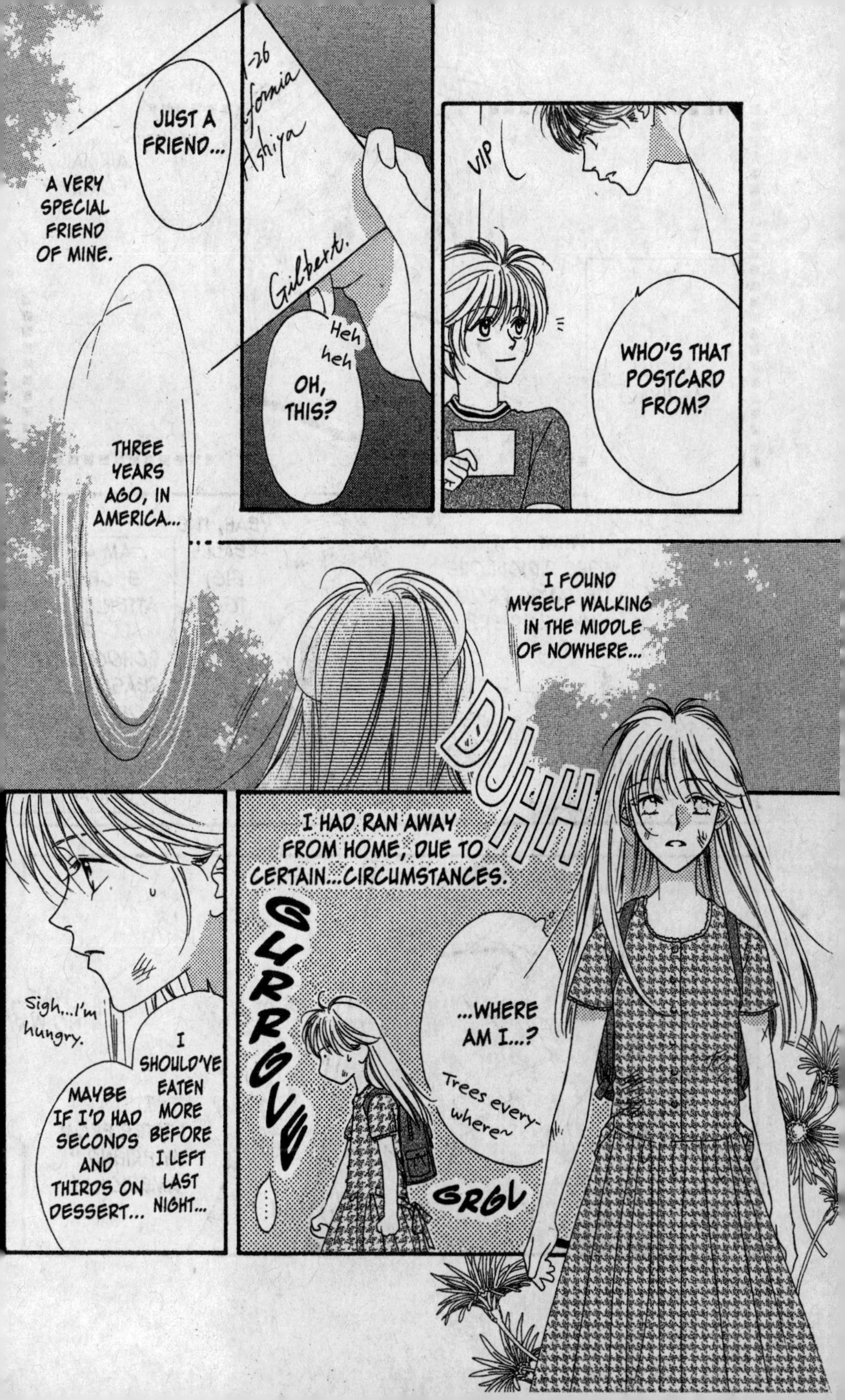
VIP
WHO'S THAT POSTCARD FROM?
Heh heh
OH, THIS?
1-26
fornia
Ashiya
Gilbert.
JUST A FRIEND...
A VERY SPECIAL FRIEND OF MINE.
THREE YEARS AGO, IN AMERICA...
I FOUND MYSELF WALKING IN THE MIDDLE OF NOWHERE...
DUHH
I HAD RAN AWAY FROM HOME, DUE TO CERTAIN...CIRCUMSTANCES.
GURRGVE
...WHERE AM I...?
Trees everywhere~
GRGV
...
Sigh...I'm hungry.
I SHOULD'VE EATEN MORE BEFORE I LEFT LAST NIGHT...
MAYBE IF I'D HAD SECONDS AND THIRDS ON DESSERT...

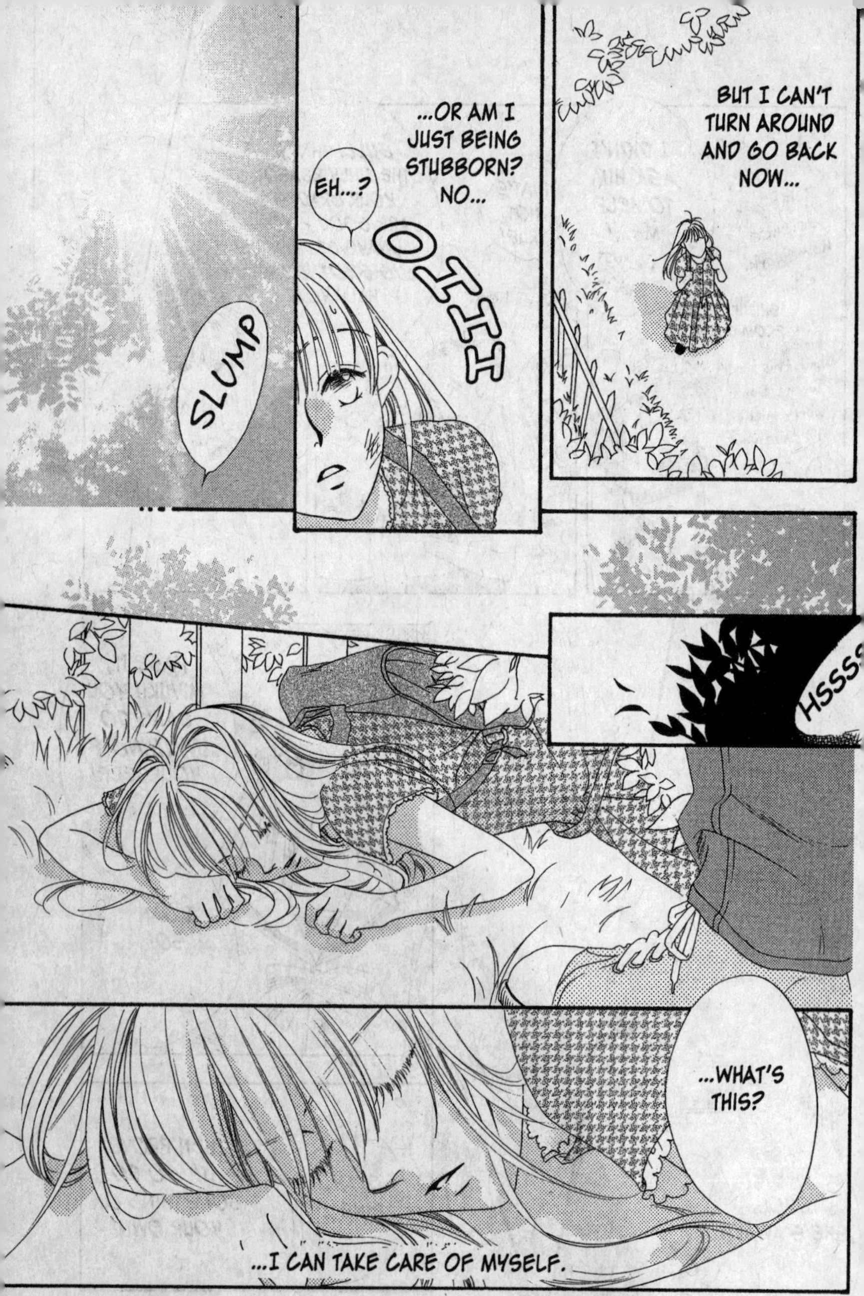
BUT I CAN'T TURN AROUND AND GO BACK NOW...
...OR AM I JUST BEING STUBBORN? NO...
EH...?
SLUMP
...
HSSS
...WHAT'S THIS?
...I CAN TAKE CARE OF MYSELF.

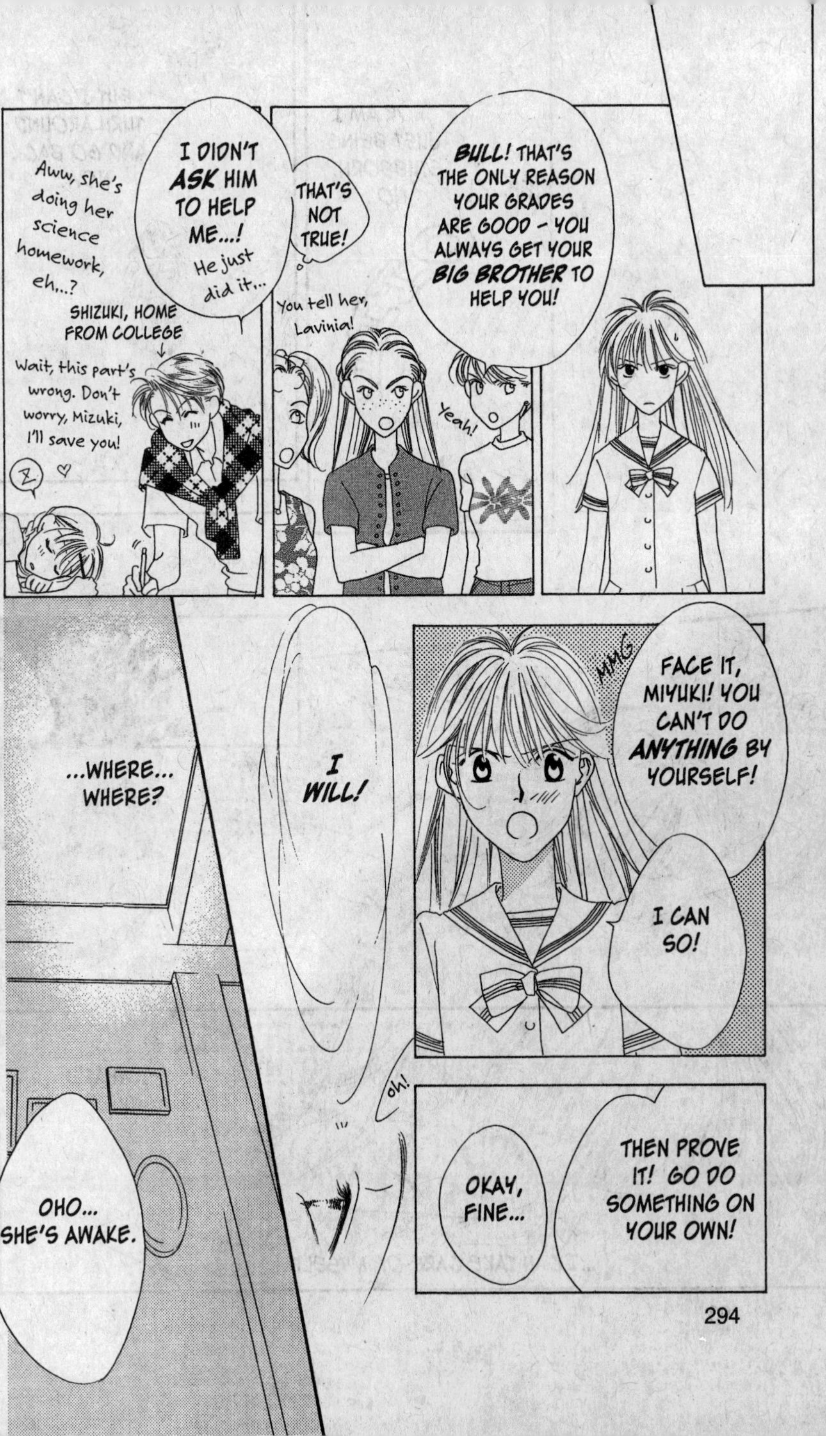
BULL! THAT'S THE ONLY REASON YOUR GRADES ARE GOOD - YOU ALWAYS GET YOUR BIG BROTHER TO HELP YOU!
THAT'S NOT TRUE!
You tell her, Lavinia!
Yeah!
I DIDN'T ASK HIM TO HELP ME...!
He just did it...
Aww, she's doing her science homework, eh...?
SHIZUKI, HOME FROM COLLEGE
Wait, this part's wrong. Don't worry, Mizuki, I'll save you!
Z
FACE IT, MIYUKI! YOU CAN'T DO ANYTHING BY YOURSELF!
MMG
I CAN SO!
THEN PROVE IT! GO DO SOMETHING ON YOUR OWN!
OKAY, FINE...
I WILL!
oh!
...WHERE... WHERE?
OHO... SHE'S AWAKE.

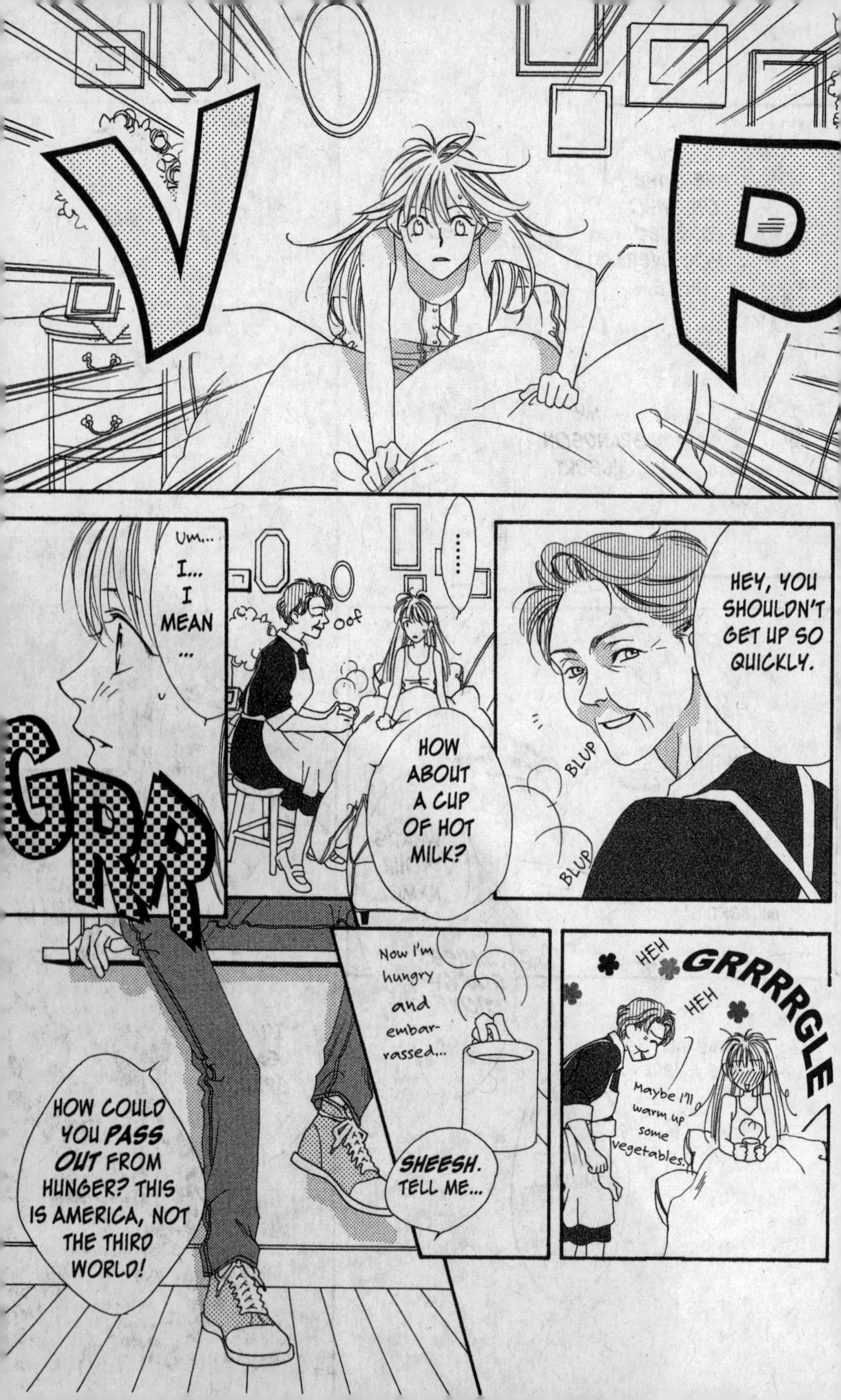
VP
HEY, YOU SHOULDN'T GET UP SO QUICKLY.
BLUP
BLUP
......
Oof
HOW ABOUT A CUP OF HOT MILK?
Um... I... I MEAN ...
GRR
HEH
HEH
GRRRRGLE
Maybe I'll warm up some vegetables.
Now I'm hungry and embar-rassed...
SHEESH. TELL ME...
HOW COULD YOU *PASS OUT* FROM HUNGER? THIS IS AMERICA, NOT THE THIRD WORLD!

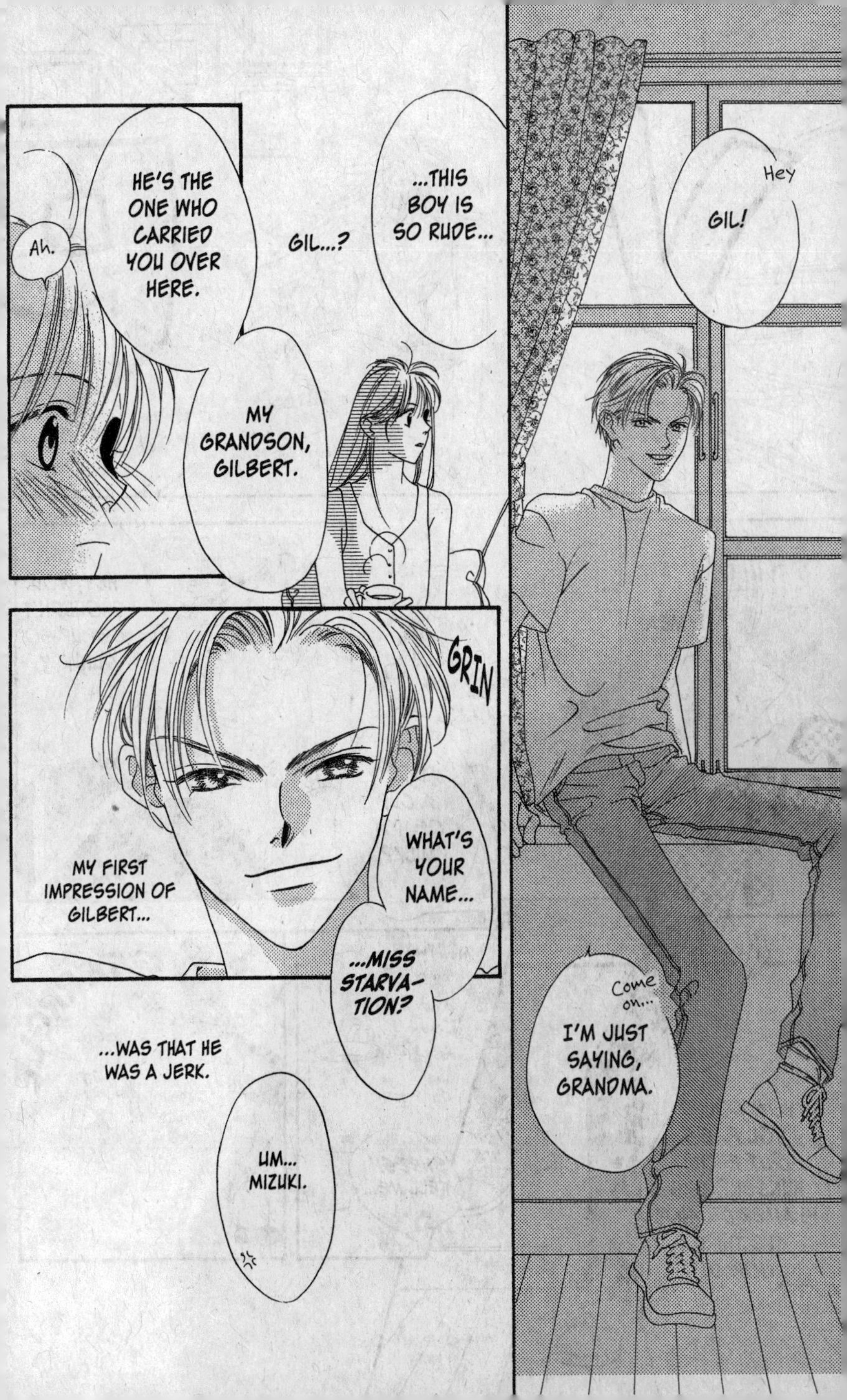
Hey
GIL!
Come on...
I'M JUST SAYING, GRANDMA.
...THIS BOY IS SO RUDE...
GIL...?
HE'S THE ONE WHO CARRIED YOU OVER HERE.
Ah.
MY GRANDSON, GILBERT.
GRIN
WHAT'S YOUR NAME...
...MISS STARVATION?
MY FIRST IMPRESSION OF GILBERT...
...WAS THAT HE WAS A JERK.
UM... MIZUKI.

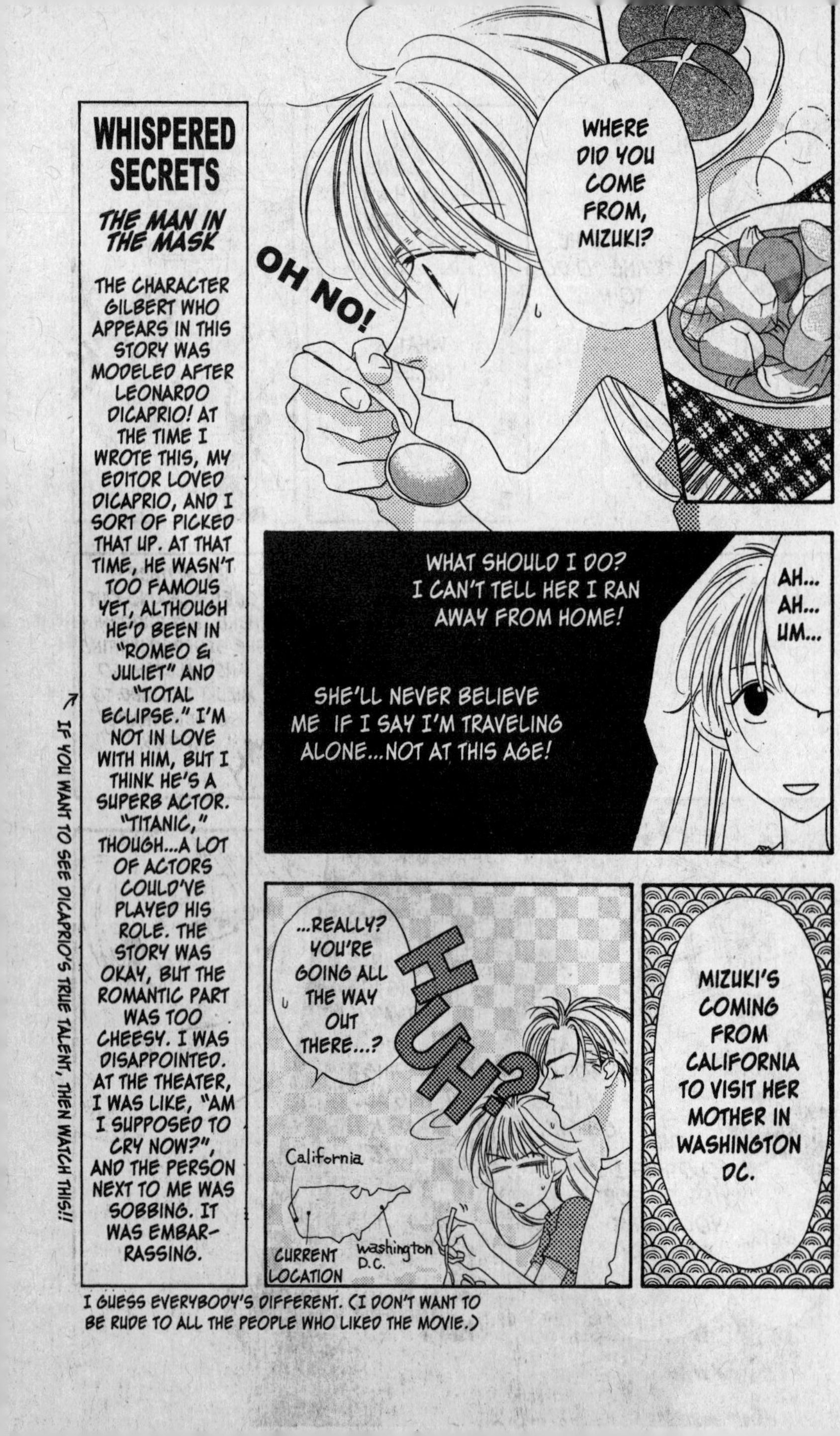
WHERE DID YOU COME FROM, MIZUKI?
OH NO!
AH... AH... UM...
WHAT SHOULD I DO? I CAN'T TELL HER I RAN AWAY FROM HOME!
SHE'LL NEVER BELIEVE ME IF I SAY I'M TRAVELING ALONE...NOT AT THIS AGE!
MIZUKI'S COMING FROM CALIFORNIA TO VISIT HER MOTHER IN WASHINGTON DC.
HUH?
...REALLY? YOU'RE GOING ALL THE WAY OUT THERE...?
California
CURRENT LOCATION
washington D.C.

WHISPERED SECRETS

THE MAN IN THE MASK

THE CHARACTER GILBERT WHO APPEARS IN THIS STORY WAS MODELED AFTER LEONARDO DICAPRIO! AT THE TIME I WROTE THIS, MY EDITOR LOVED DICAPRIO, AND I SORT OF PICKED THAT UP. AT THAT TIME, HE WASN'T TOO FAMOUS YET, ALTHOUGH HE'D BEEN IN "ROMEO & JULIET" AND "TOTAL ECLIPSE." I'M NOT IN LOVE WITH HIM, BUT I THINK HE'S A SUPERB ACTOR. "TITANIC," THOUGH...A LOT OF ACTORS COULD'VE PLAYED HIS ROLE. THE STORY WAS OKAY, BUT THE ROMANTIC PART WAS TOO CHEESY. I WAS DISAPPOINTED. AT THE THEATER, I WAS LIKE, "AM I SUPPOSED TO CRY NOW?", AND THE PERSON NEXT TO ME WAS SOBBING. IT WAS EMBARRASSING.

← IF YOU WANT TO SEE DICAPRIO'S TRUE TALENT, THEN WATCH THIS!!

I GUESS EVERYBODY'S DIFFERENT. (I DON'T WANT TO BE RUDE TO ALL THE PEOPLE WHO LIKED THE MOVIE.)

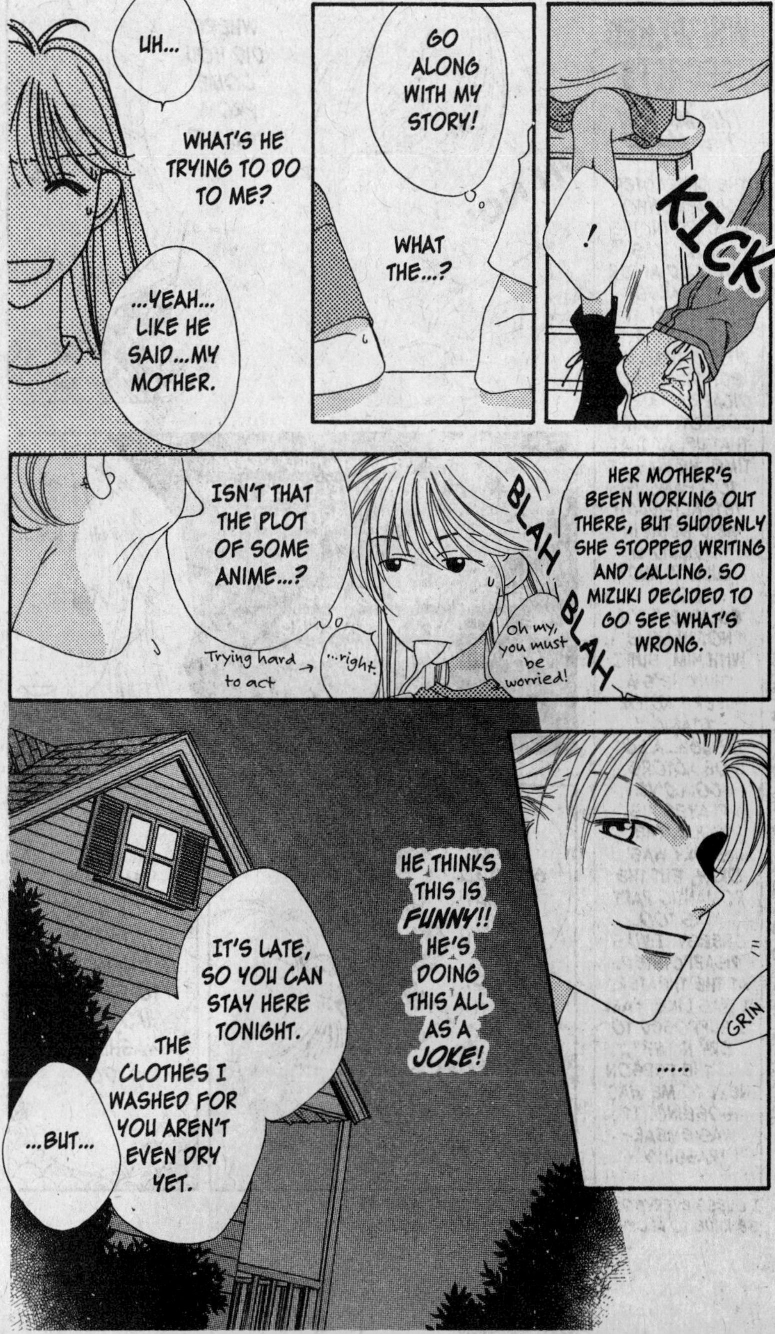
KICK
!
GO ALONG WITH MY STORY!
WHAT THE...?
UH...
WHAT'S HE TRYING TO DO TO ME?
...YEAH... LIKE HE SAID...MY MOTHER.
HER MOTHER'S BEEN WORKING OUT THERE, BUT SUDDENLY SHE STOPPED WRITING AND CALLING. SO MIZUKI DECIDED TO GO SEE WHAT'S WRONG.
BLAH BLAH BLAH
Oh my, you must be worried!
...right.
Trying hard to act
ISN'T THAT THE PLOT OF SOME ANIME...?
GRIN
.....
HE THINKS THIS IS FUNNY!! HE'S DOING THIS ALL AS A JOKE!
IT'S LATE, SO YOU CAN STAY HERE TONIGHT.
THE CLOTHES I WASHED FOR YOU AREN'T EVEN DRY YET.
...BUT...

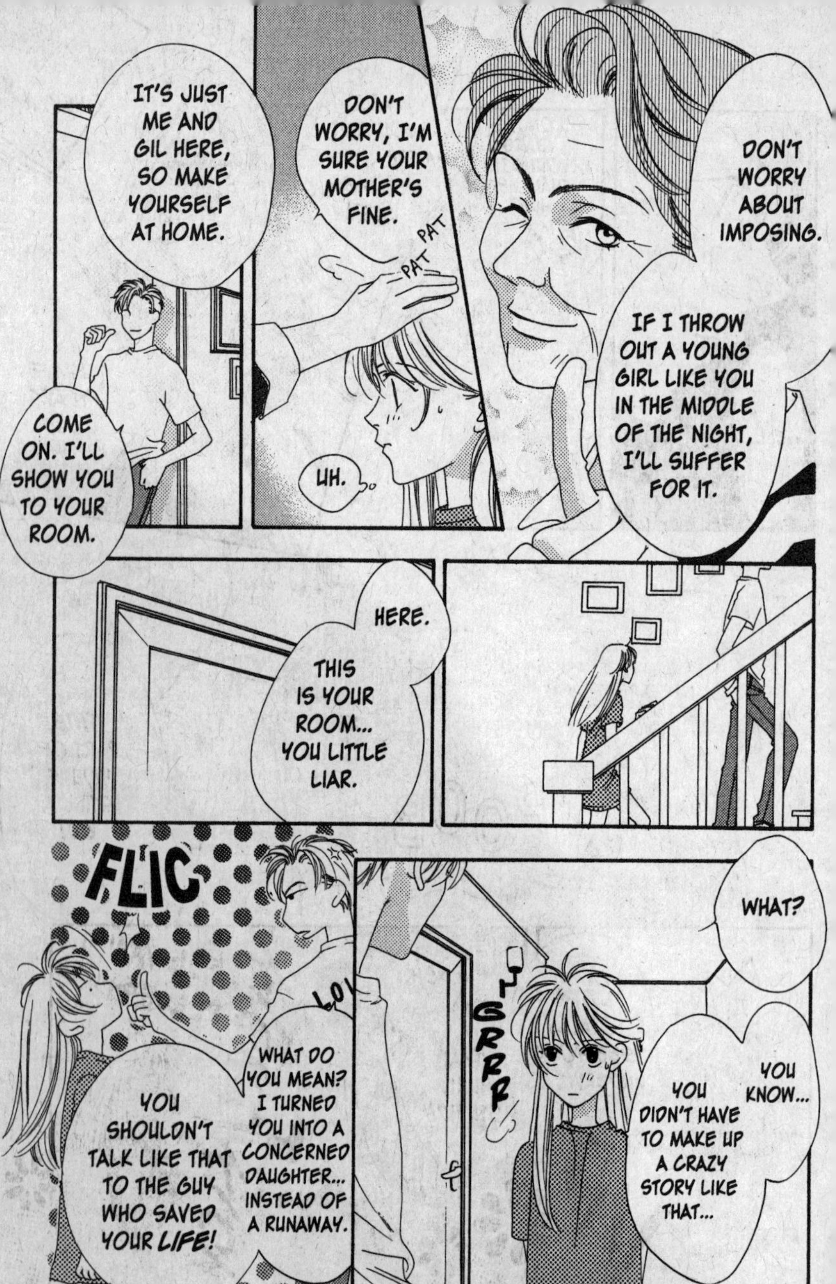
DON'T WORRY ABOUT IMPOSING.
IF I THROW OUT A YOUNG GIRL LIKE YOU IN THE MIDDLE OF THE NIGHT, I'LL SUFFER FOR IT.
DON'T WORRY, I'M SURE YOUR MOTHER'S FINE.
PAT PAT
UH.
IT'S JUST ME AND GIL HERE, SO MAKE YOURSELF AT HOME.
COME ON. I'LL SHOW YOU TO YOUR ROOM.
HERE.
THIS IS YOUR ROOM... YOU LITTLE LIAR.
WHAT?
YOU KNOW...
YOU DIDN'T HAVE TO MAKE UP A CRAZY STORY LIKE THAT...
GRRR
FLIC
WHAT DO YOU MEAN? I TURNED YOU INTO A CONCERNED DAUGHTER... INSTEAD OF A RUNAWAY.
YOU SHOULDN'T TALK LIKE THAT TO THE GUY WHO SAVED YOUR *LIFE*!

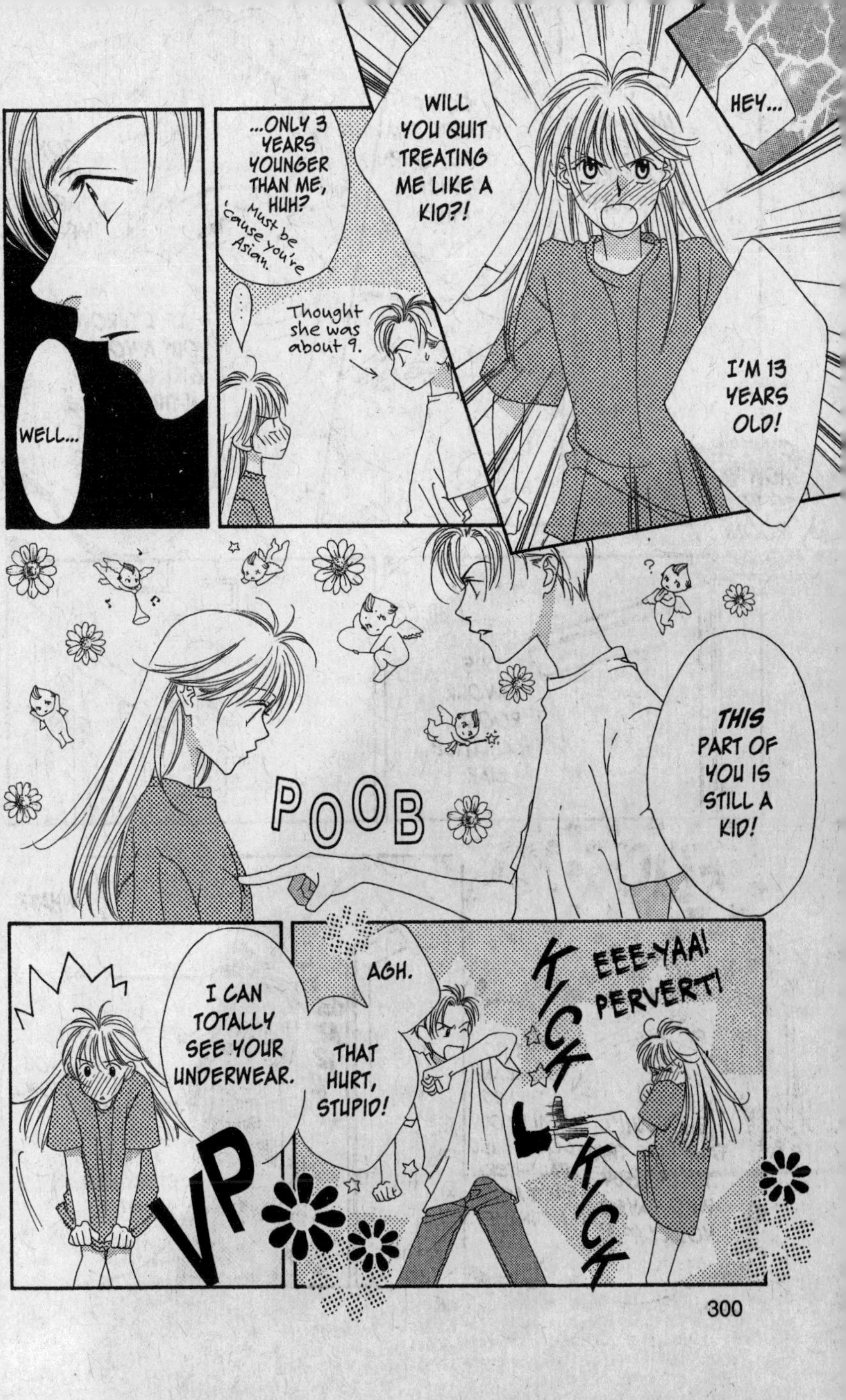
HEY...
WILL YOU QUIT TREATING ME LIKE A KID?!
I'M 13 YEARS OLD!
...ONLY 3 YEARS YOUNGER THAN ME, HUH?
Must be 'cause you're Asian.
...
Thought she was about 9.
WELL...
THIS PART OF YOU IS STILL A KID!
POOB
EEE-YAA! PERVERT!
KICK
KICK
KICK
AGH.
THAT HURT, STUPID!
I CAN TOTALLY SEE YOUR UNDERWEAR.
VP

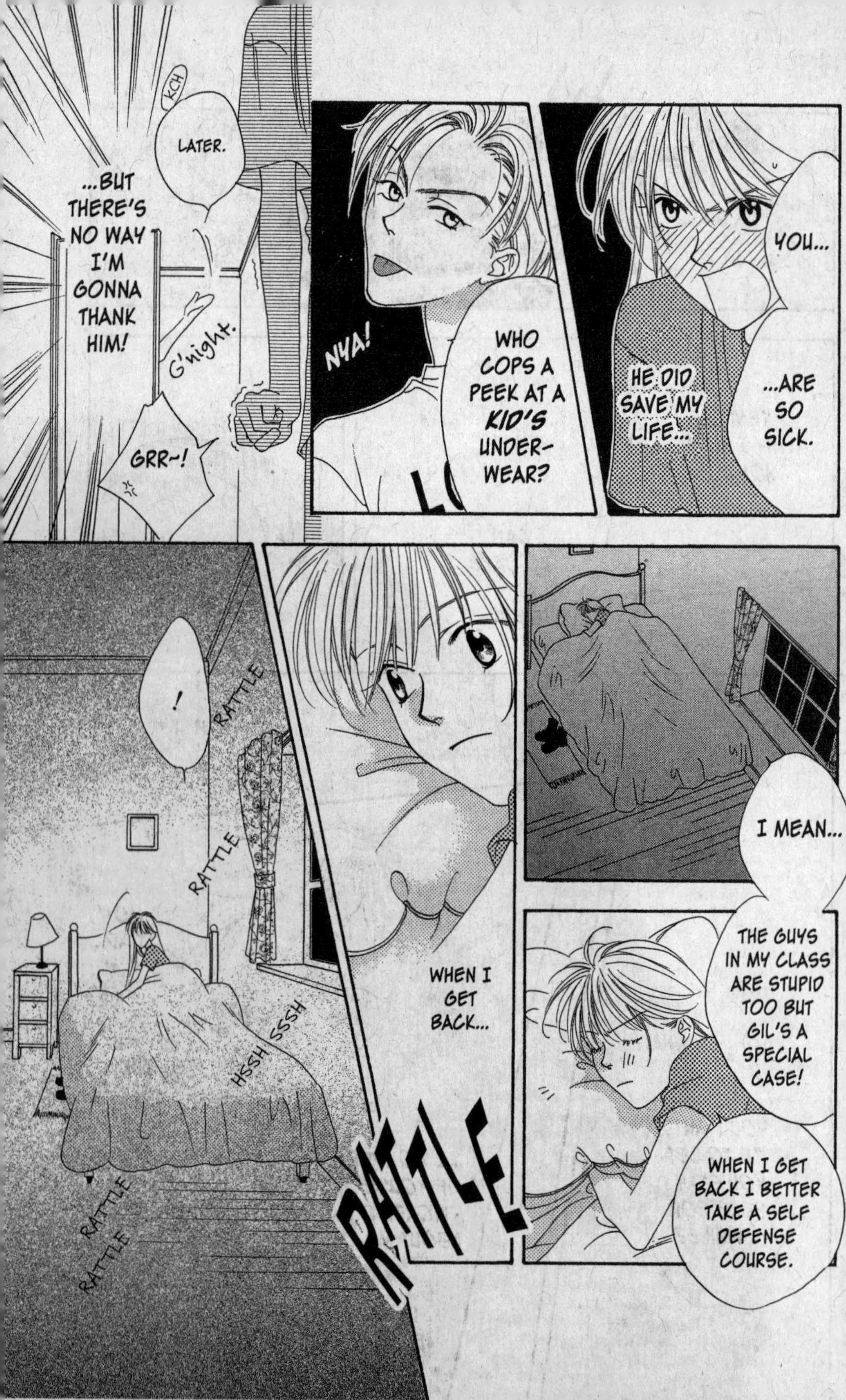

YOU...
...ARE SO SICK.
HE DID SAVE MY LIFE...
NYA!
WHO COPS A PEEK AT A KID'S UNDER-WEAR?
KCH
LATER.
G'night.
GRR~!
...BUT THERE'S NO WAY I'M GONNA THANK HIM!
I MEAN...
THE GUYS IN MY CLASS ARE STUPID TOO BUT GIL'S A SPECIAL CASE!
WHEN I GET BACK I BETTER TAKE A SELF DEFENSE COURSE.
WHEN I GET BACK...
RATTLE
!
RATTLE
RATTLE
HSSH SSSH
RATTLE
RATTLE

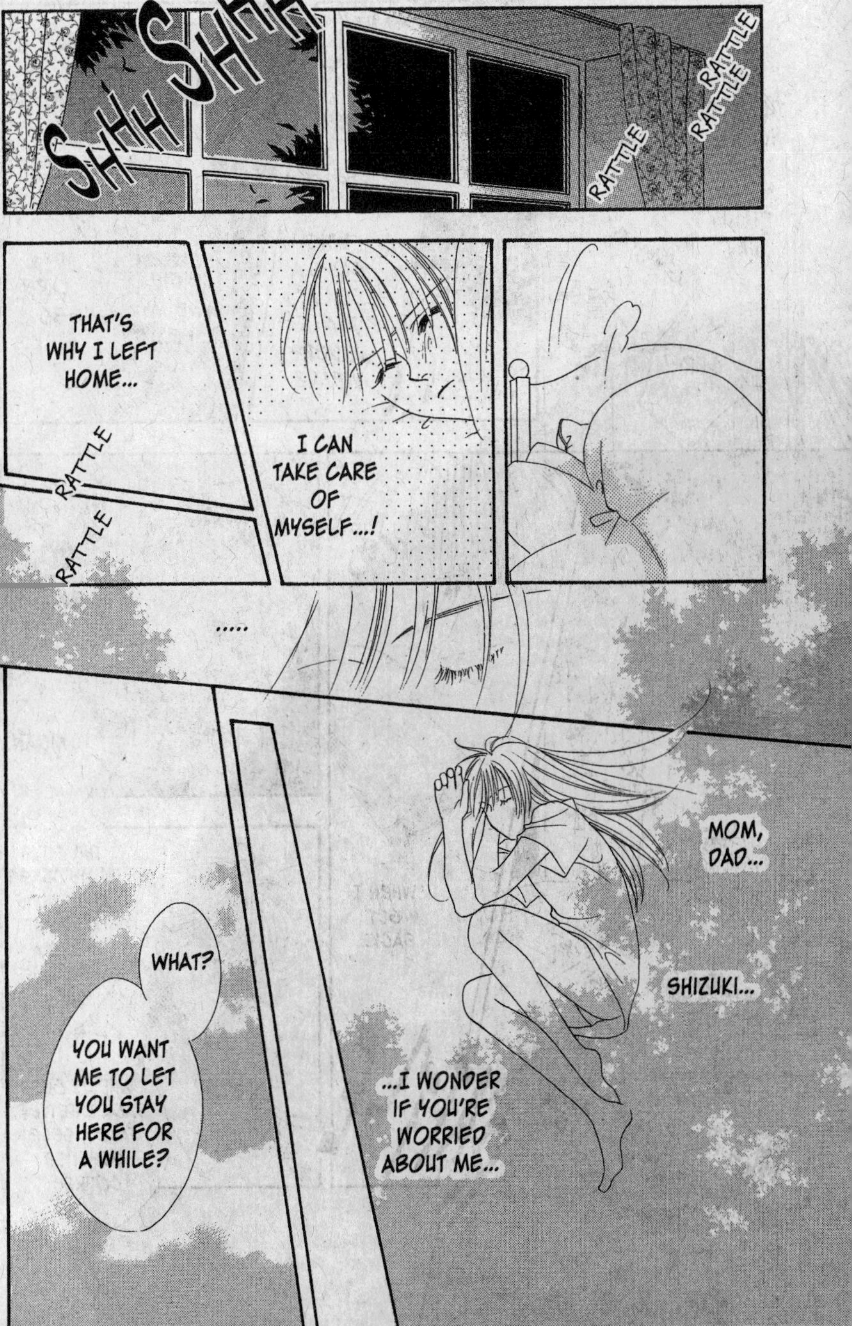
RATTLE
RATTLE
RATTLE
SHH SHH SHH
I CAN TAKE CARE OF MYSELF...!
THAT'S WHY I LEFT HOME...
RATTLE
RATTLE
.....
MOM, DAD...
SHIZUKI...
...I WONDER IF YOU'RE WORRIED ABOUT ME...
WHAT?
YOU WANT ME TO LET YOU STAY HERE FOR A WHILE?

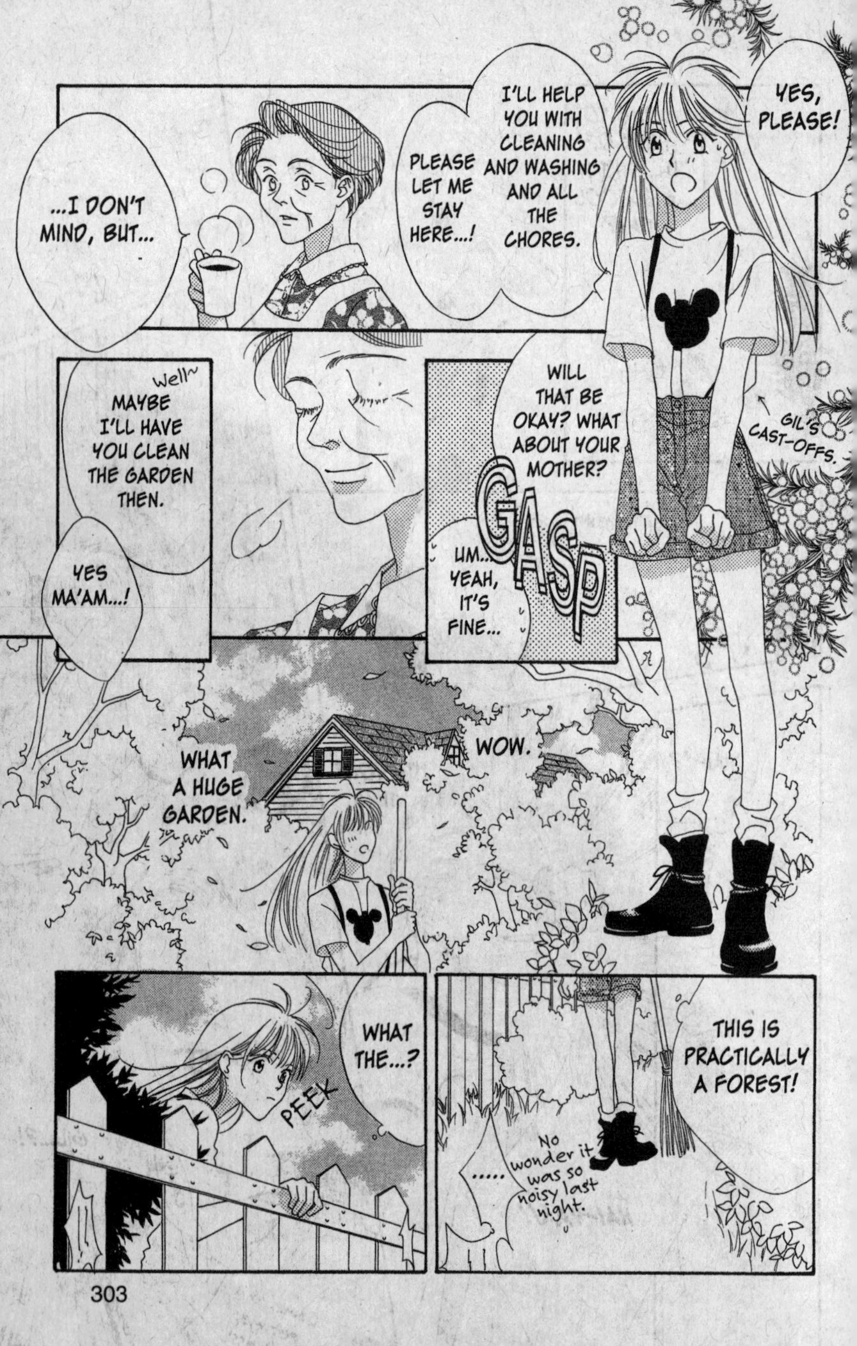
YES, PLEASE!
GIL'S CAST-OFFS.
I'LL HELP YOU WITH CLEANING AND WASHING AND ALL THE CHORES.
PLEASE LET ME STAY HERE...!
...I DON'T MIND, BUT...
WILL THAT BE OKAY? WHAT ABOUT YOUR MOTHER?
GASP
UM... YEAH, IT'S FINE...
Well~
MAYBE I'LL HAVE YOU CLEAN THE GARDEN THEN.
YES MA'AM...!
WOW.
WHAT A HUGE GARDEN.
THIS IS PRACTICALLY A FOREST!
.....
No wonder it was so noisy last night.
WHAT THE...?
PEEK

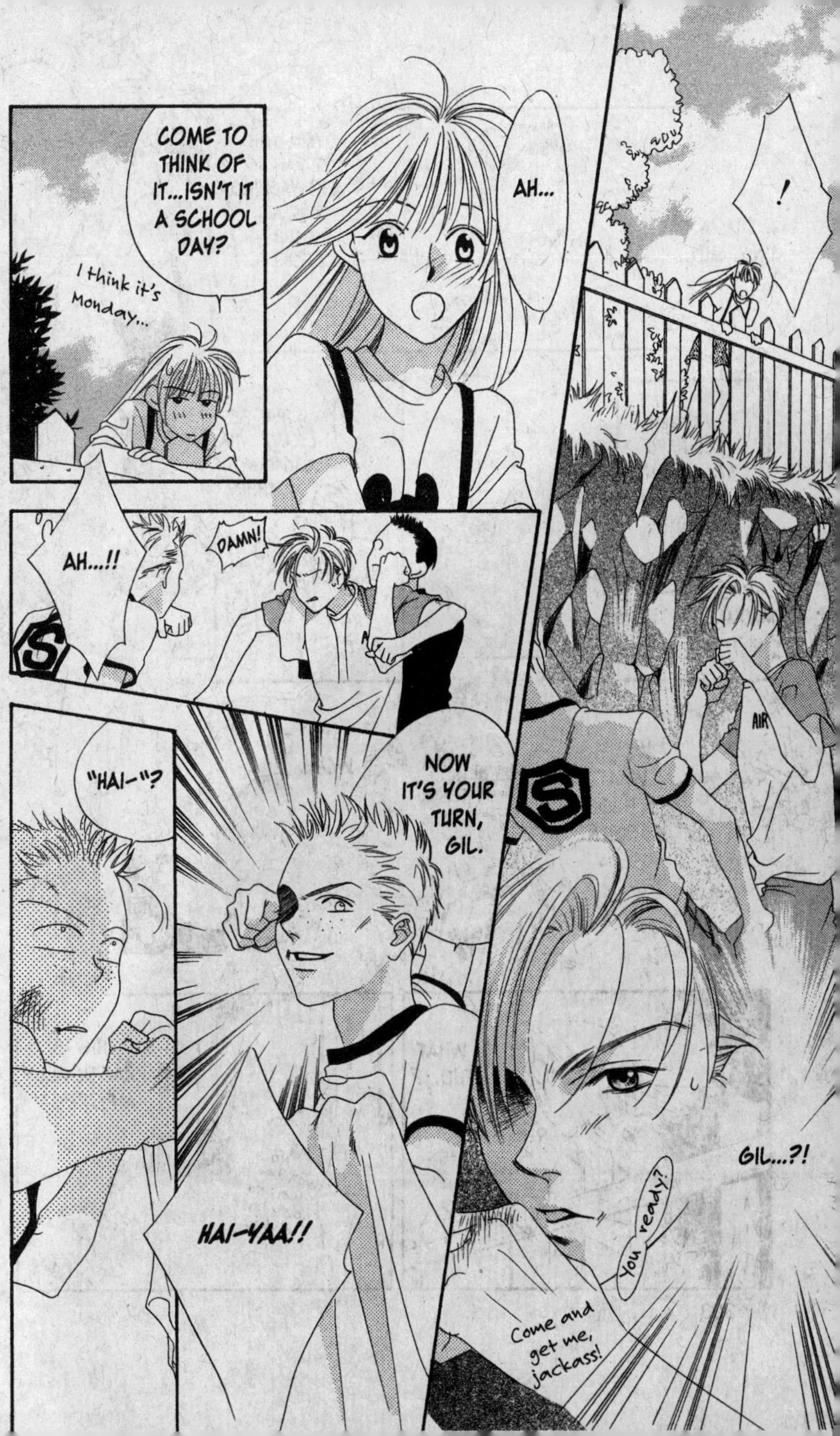
!
GIL...?!
You ready?
Come and get me, jackass!
AH...
COME TO THINK OF IT...ISN'T IT A SCHOOL DAY?
I think it's Monday...
DAMN!
AH...!!
NOW IT'S YOUR TURN, GIL.
HAI-YAA!!
"HAI-"?

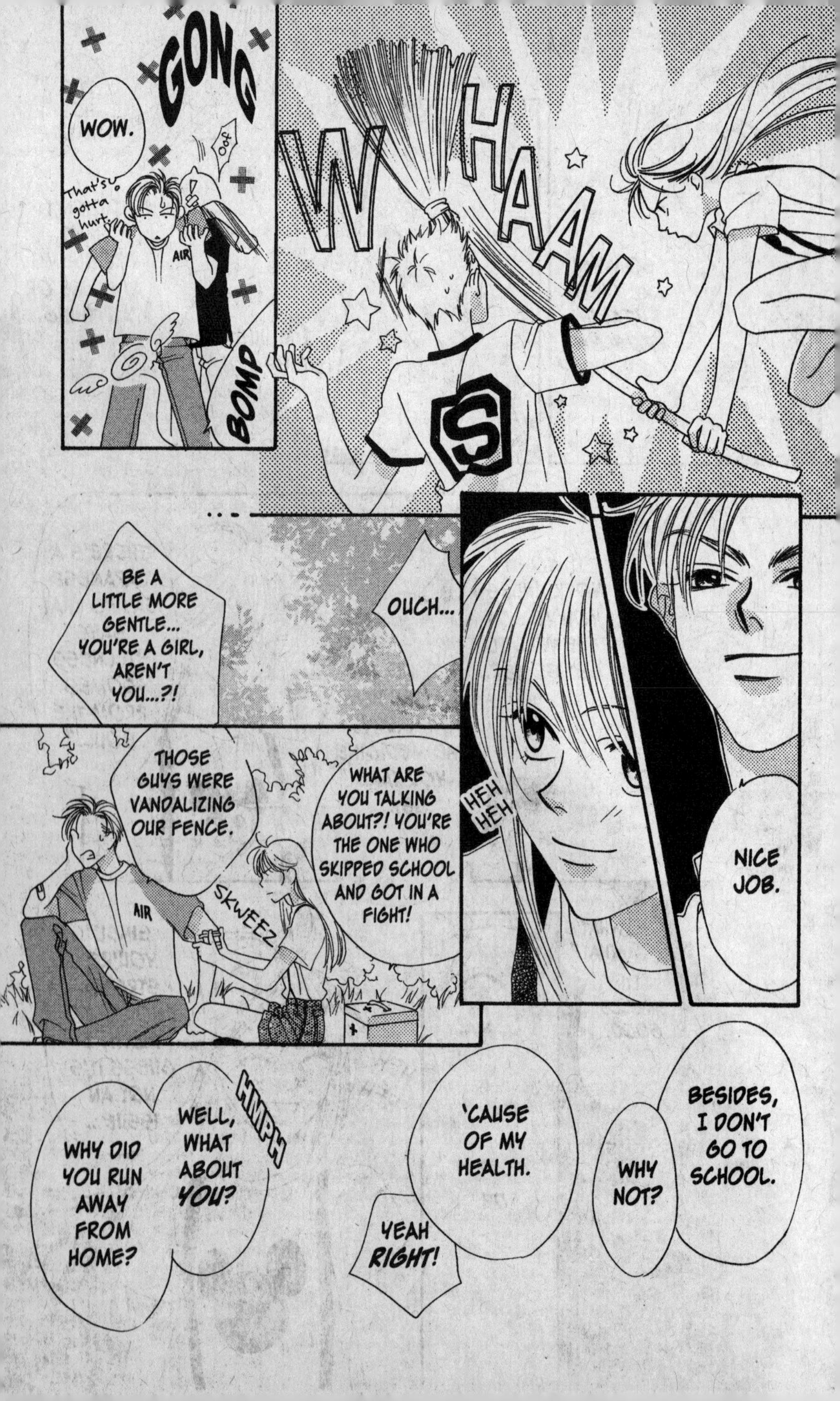

WHAAM
GONG
WOW.
oof
That's gotta hurt.
BOMP
HEH HEH
NICE JOB.
...
OUCH...
BE A LITTLE MORE GENTLE... YOU'RE A GIRL, AREN'T YOU...?!
WHAT ARE YOU TALKING ABOUT?! YOU'RE THE ONE WHO SKIPPED SCHOOL AND GOT IN A FIGHT!
SKWEEZ
THOSE GUYS WERE VANDALIZING OUR FENCE.
BESIDES, I DON'T GO TO SCHOOL.
WHY NOT?
'CAUSE OF MY HEALTH.
YEAH RIGHT!
HMPH
WELL, WHAT ABOUT YOU?
WHY DID YOU RUN AWAY FROM HOME?

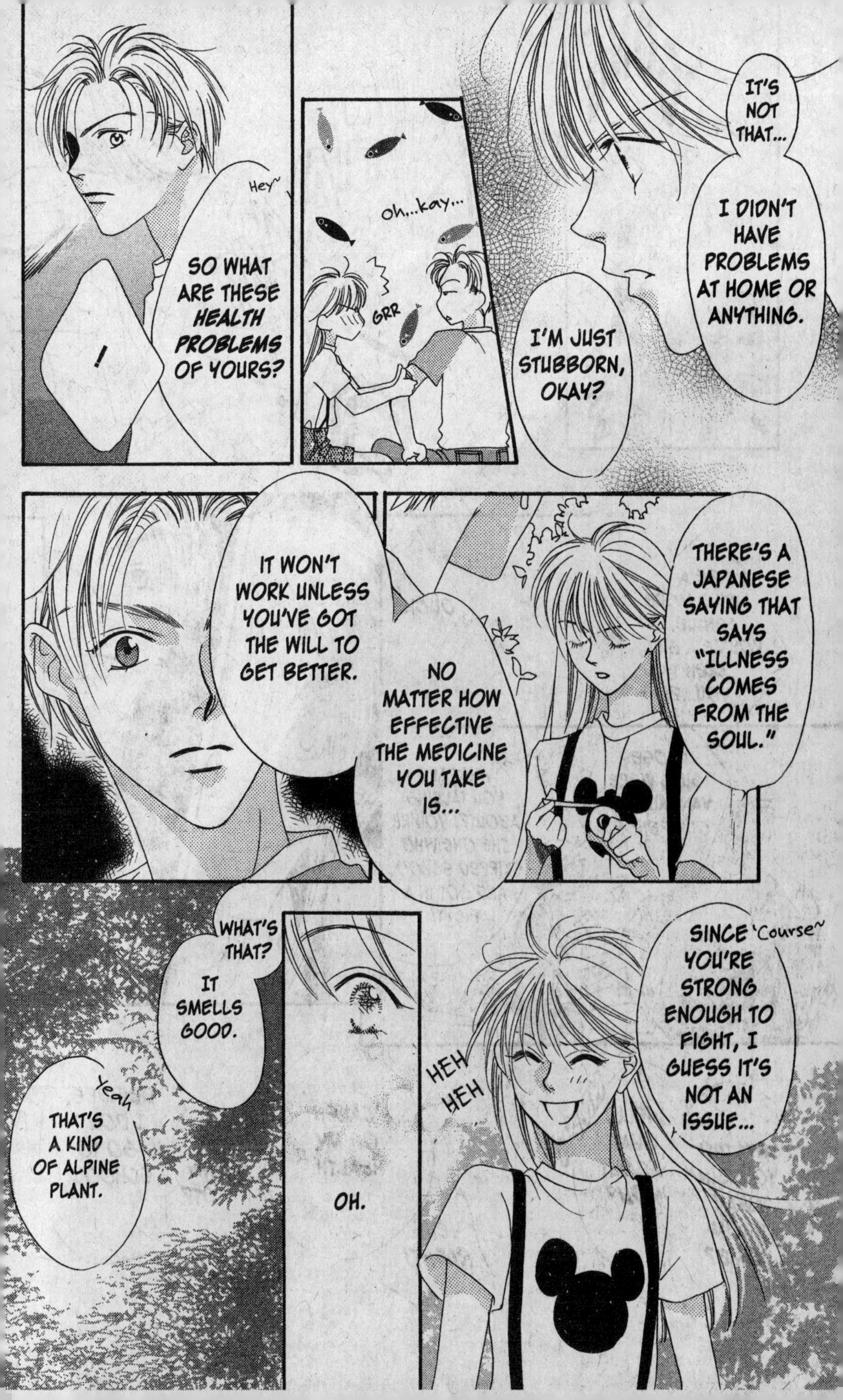
IT'S NOT THAT...
I DIDN'T HAVE PROBLEMS AT HOME OR ANYTHING.
I'M JUST STUBBORN, OKAY?
Oh...kay...
GRR
Hey~
SO WHAT ARE THESE *HEALTH PROBLEMS* OF YOURS?
!
THERE'S A JAPANESE SAYING THAT SAYS "ILLNESS COMES FROM THE SOUL."
NO MATTER HOW EFFECTIVE THE MEDICINE YOU TAKE IS...
IT WON'T WORK UNLESS YOU'VE GOT THE WILL TO GET BETTER.
SINCE YOU'RE STRONG ENOUGH TO FIGHT, I GUESS IT'S NOT AN ISSUE...
'Course~
HEH HEH
OH.
WHAT'S THAT?
IT SMELLS GOOD.
Yeah
THAT'S A KIND OF ALPINE PLANT.

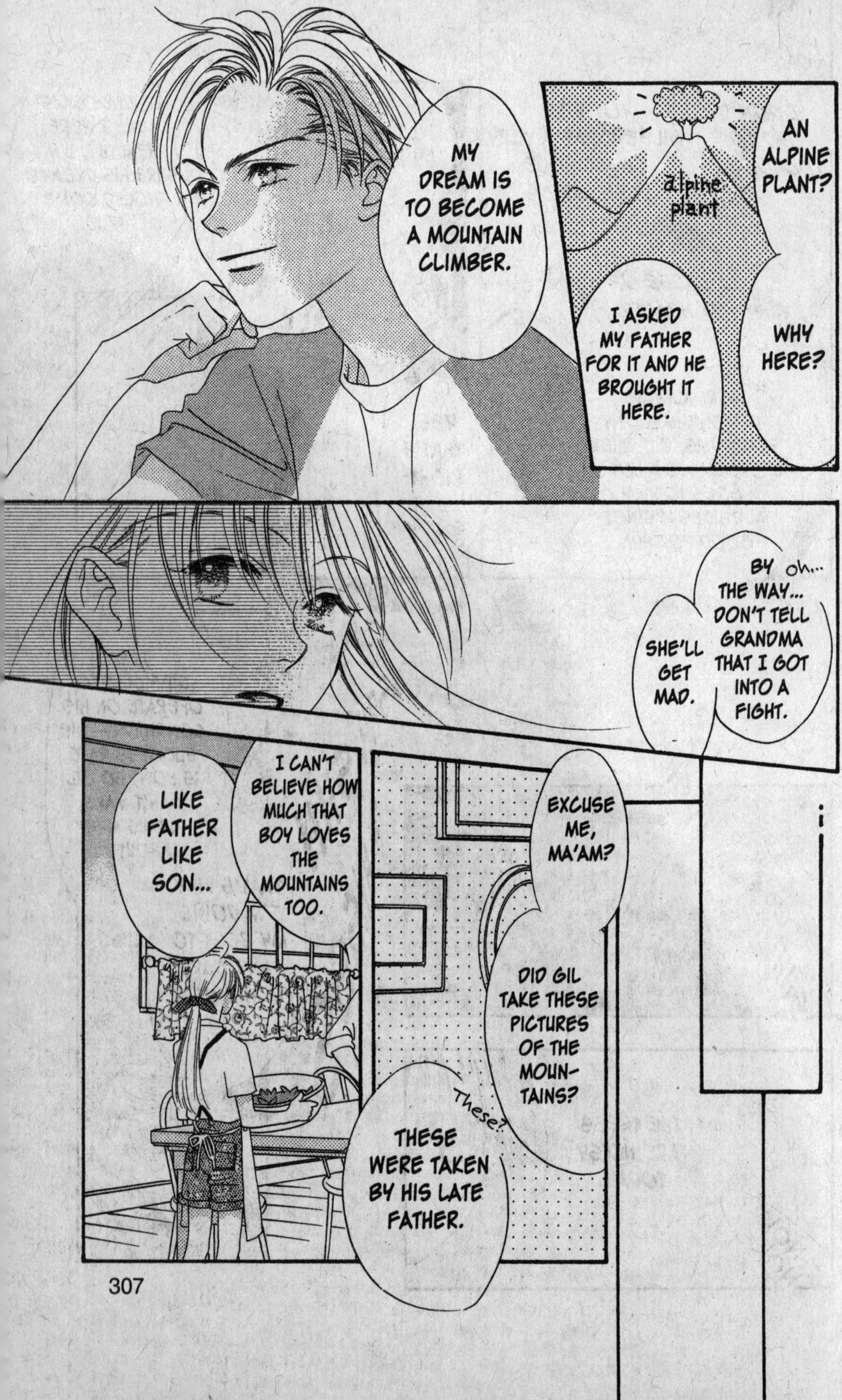
AN ALPINE PLANT?
alpine plant
WHY HERE?
I ASKED MY FATHER FOR IT AND HE BROUGHT IT HERE.
MY DREAM IS TO BECOME A MOUNTAIN CLIMBER.
oh...
BY THE WAY... DON'T TELL GRANDMA THAT I GOT INTO A FIGHT.
SHE'LL GET MAD.
EXCUSE ME, MA'AM?
DID GIL TAKE THESE PICTURES OF THE MOUN-TAINS?
These?
THESE WERE TAKEN BY HIS LATE FATHER.
I CAN'T BELIEVE HOW MUCH THAT BOY LOVES THE MOUNTAINS TOO.
LIKE FATHER LIKE SON...

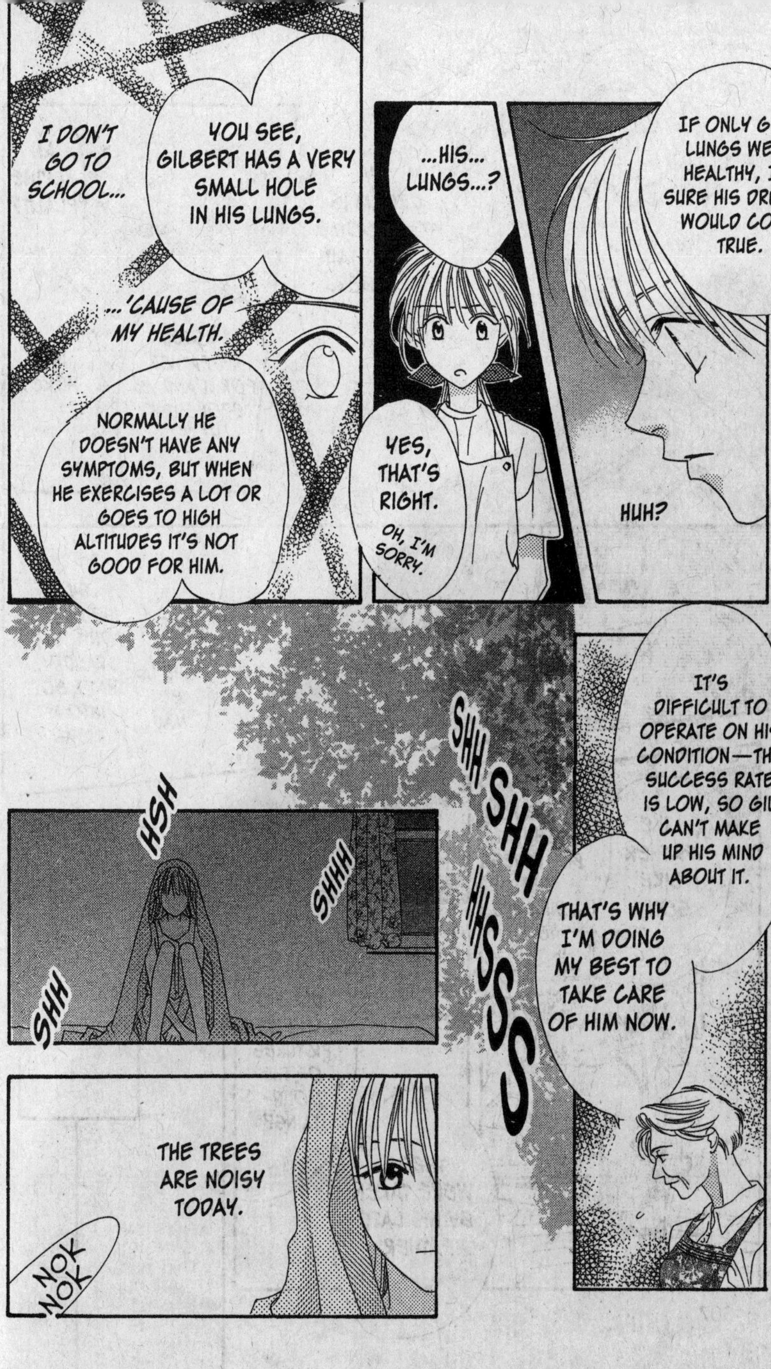
IF ONLY GIL'S LUNGS WERE HEALTHY, I'M SURE HIS DREAMS WOULD COME TRUE.
HUH?
...HIS... LUNGS...?
YES, THAT'S RIGHT.
OH, I'M SORRY.
I DON'T GO TO SCHOOL...
YOU SEE, GILBERT HAS A VERY SMALL HOLE IN HIS LUNGS.
...'CAUSE OF MY HEALTH.
NORMALLY HE DOESN'T HAVE ANY SYMPTOMS, BUT WHEN HE EXERCISES A LOT OR GOES TO HIGH ALTITUDES IT'S NOT GOOD FOR HIM.
IT'S DIFFICULT TO OPERATE ON HIS CONDITION—THE SUCCESS RATE IS LOW, SO GIL CAN'T MAKE UP HIS MIND ABOUT IT.
THAT'S WHY I'M DOING MY BEST TO TAKE CARE OF HIM NOW.
SHH SHH HSSSS
HSH
SHHH
SHH
THE TREES ARE NOISY TODAY.
NOK NOK

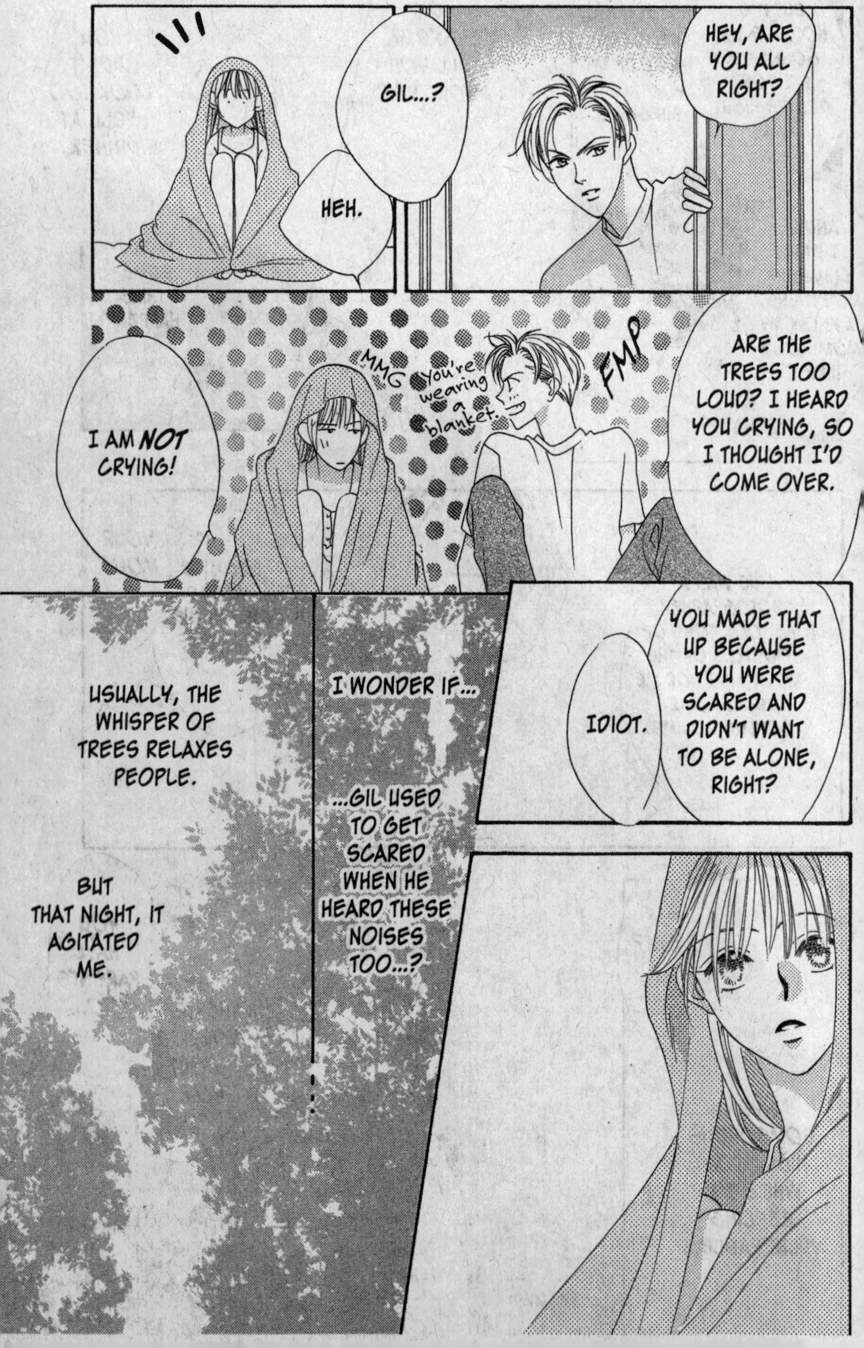

HEY, ARE YOU ALL RIGHT?
GIL...?
HEH.
ARE THE TREES TOO LOUD? I HEARD YOU CRYING, SO I THOUGHT I'D COME OVER.
FMP
You're wearing a blanket.
MMG
I AM *NOT* CRYING!
YOU MADE THAT UP BECAUSE YOU WERE SCARED AND DIDN'T WANT TO BE ALONE, RIGHT?
IDIOT.
I WONDER IF...
...GIL USED TO GET SCARED WHEN HE HEARD THESE NOISES TOO...?
USUALLY, THE WHISPER OF TREES RELAXES PEOPLE.
BUT THAT NIGHT, IT AGITATED ME.

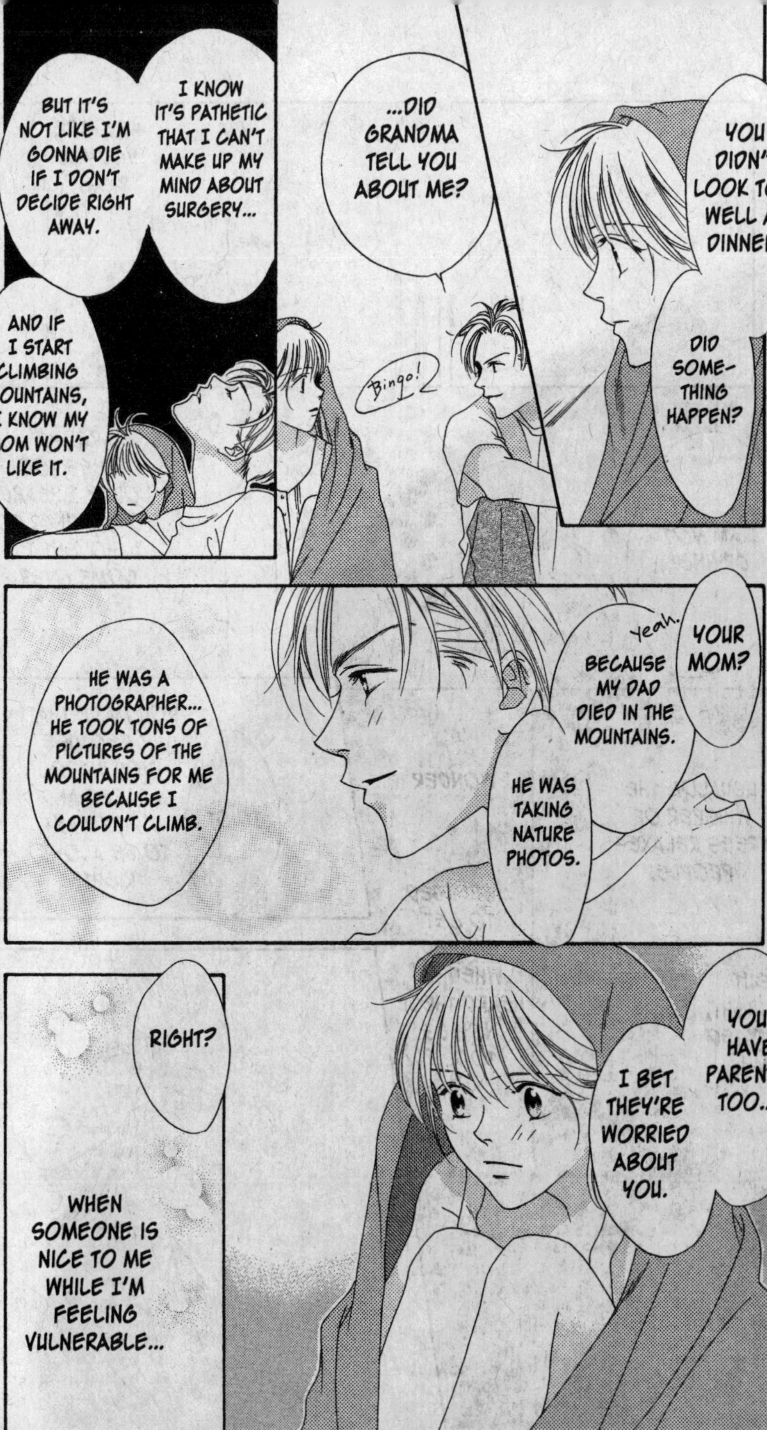
YOU DIDN'T LOOK TOO WELL AT DINNER.
DID SOMETHING HAPPEN?
...DID GRANDMA TELL YOU ABOUT ME?
Bingo!
I KNOW IT'S PATHETIC THAT I CAN'T MAKE UP MY MIND ABOUT SURGERY...
BUT IT'S NOT LIKE I'M GONNA DIE IF I DON'T DECIDE RIGHT AWAY.
AND IF I START CLIMBING MOUNTAINS, I KNOW MY MOM WON'T LIKE IT.
YOUR MOM?
Yeah.
BECAUSE MY DAD DIED IN THE MOUNTAINS.
HE WAS TAKING NATURE PHOTOS.
HE WAS A PHOTOGRAPHER... HE TOOK TONS OF PICTURES OF THE MOUNTAINS FOR ME BECAUSE I COULDN'T CLIMB.
YOU HAVE PARENTS TOO...
I BET THEY'RE WORRIED ABOUT YOU.
RIGHT?
WHEN SOMEONE IS NICE TO ME WHILE I'M FEELING VULNERABLE...

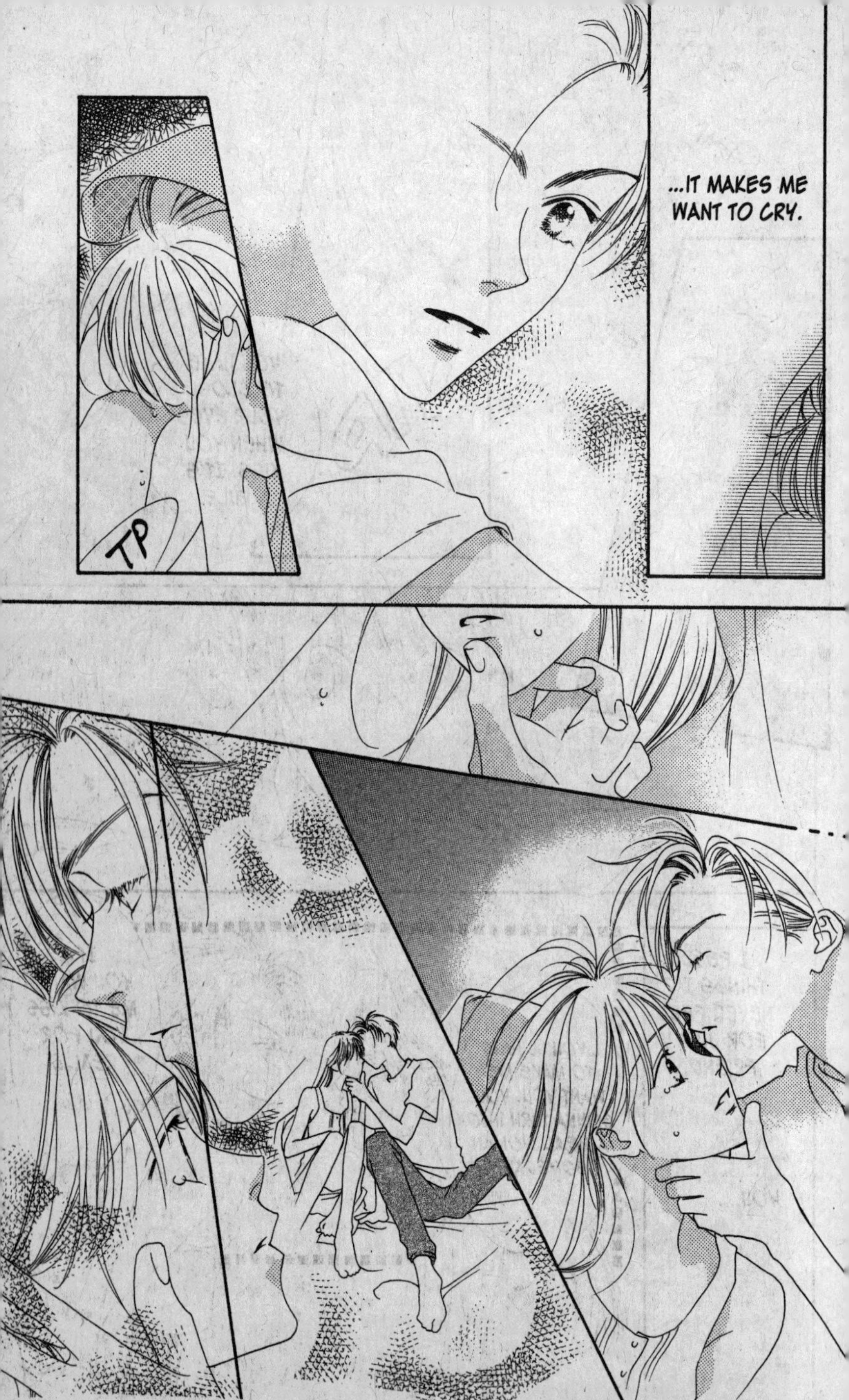
...IT MAKES ME WANT TO CRY.
TP

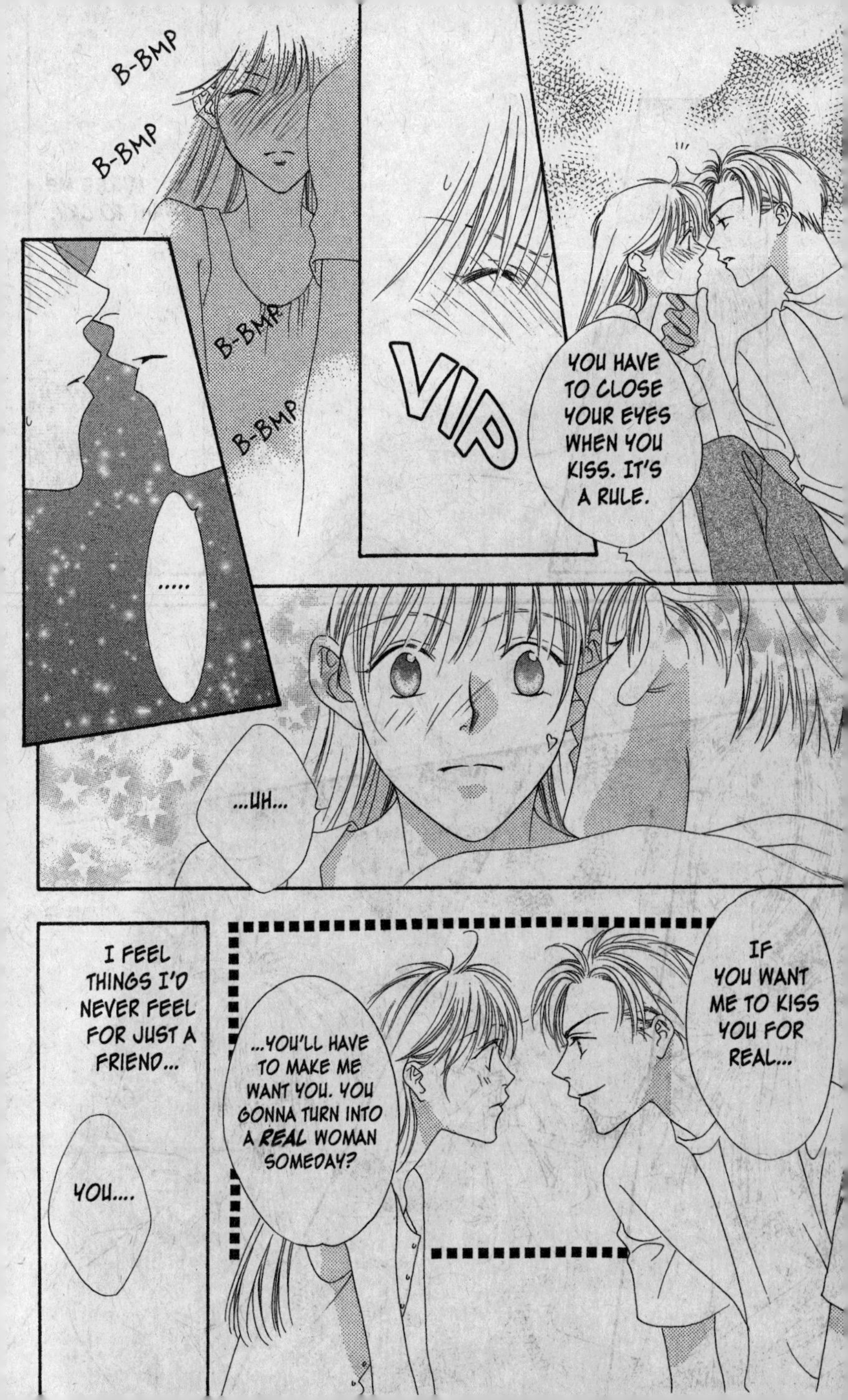
YOU HAVE TO CLOSE YOUR EYES WHEN YOU KISS. IT'S A RULE.
VIP
B-BMP
B-BMP
B-BMP
B-BMP
.....
...UH...
IF YOU WANT ME TO KISS YOU FOR REAL...
...YOU'LL HAVE TO MAKE ME WANT YOU. YOU GONNA TURN INTO A *REAL* WOMAN SOMEDAY?
I FEEL THINGS I'D NEVER FEEL FOR JUST A FRIEND...
YOU....

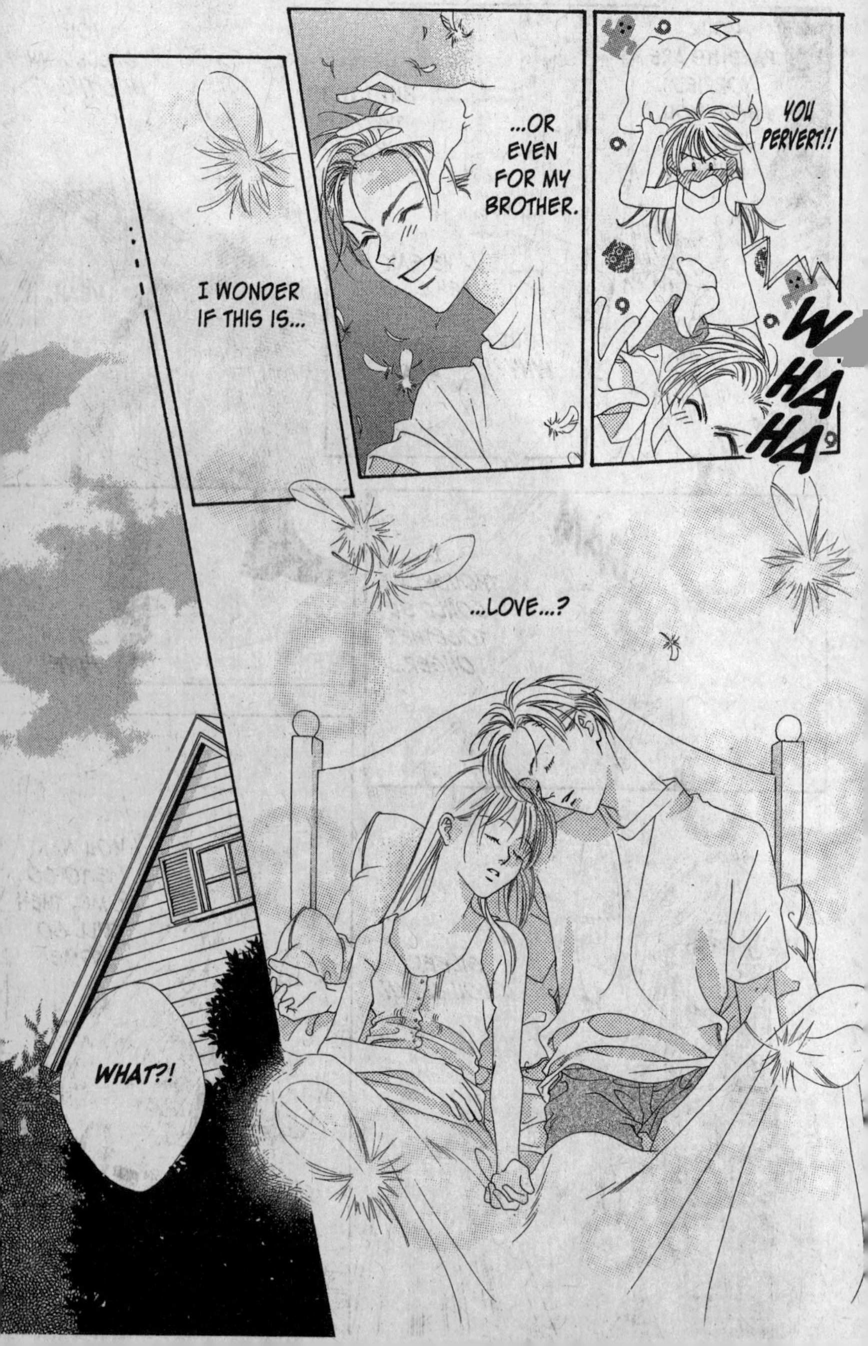
YOU PERVERT!!
WHA HA HA
...OR EVEN FOR MY BROTHER.
...
I WONDER IF THIS IS...
...LOVE...?
WHAT?!

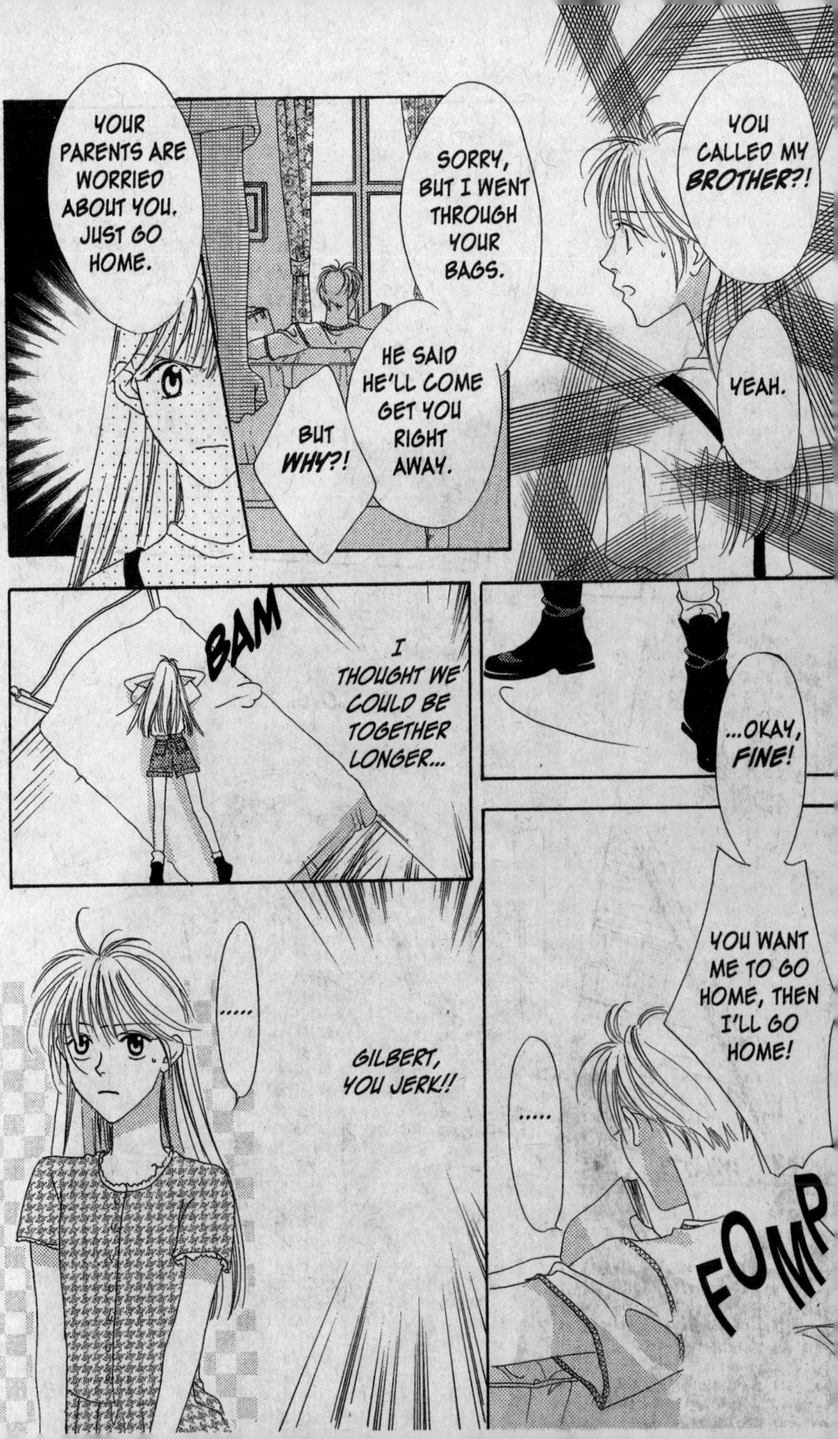
YOU CALLED MY BROTHER?!
YEAH.
SORRY, BUT I WENT THROUGH YOUR BAGS.
HE SAID HE'LL COME GET YOU RIGHT AWAY.
BUT WHY?!
YOUR PARENTS ARE WORRIED ABOUT YOU. JUST GO HOME.
...OKAY, FINE!
BAM
I THOUGHT WE COULD BE TOGETHER LONGER...
YOU WANT ME TO GO HOME, THEN I'LL GO HOME!
.....
FOMP
GILBERT, YOU JERK!!
.....

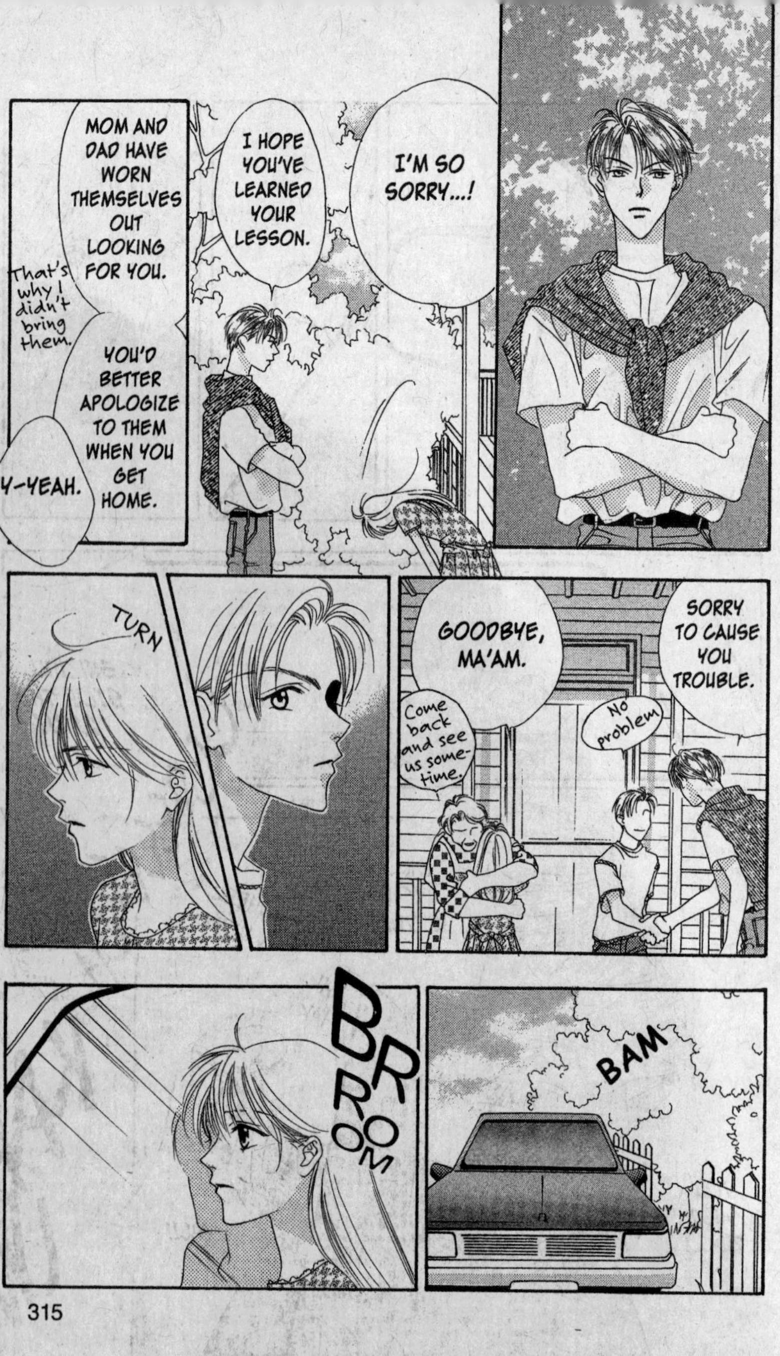
I'M SO SORRY...!
I HOPE YOU'VE LEARNED YOUR LESSON.
MOM AND DAD HAVE WORN THEMSELVES OUT LOOKING FOR YOU.
That's why I didn't bring them.
YOU'D BETTER APOLOGIZE TO THEM WHEN YOU GET HOME.
Y-YEAH.
SORRY TO CAUSE YOU TROUBLE.
No problem
GOODBYE, MA'AM.
Come back and see us sometime.
TURN
BAM
BRROOM

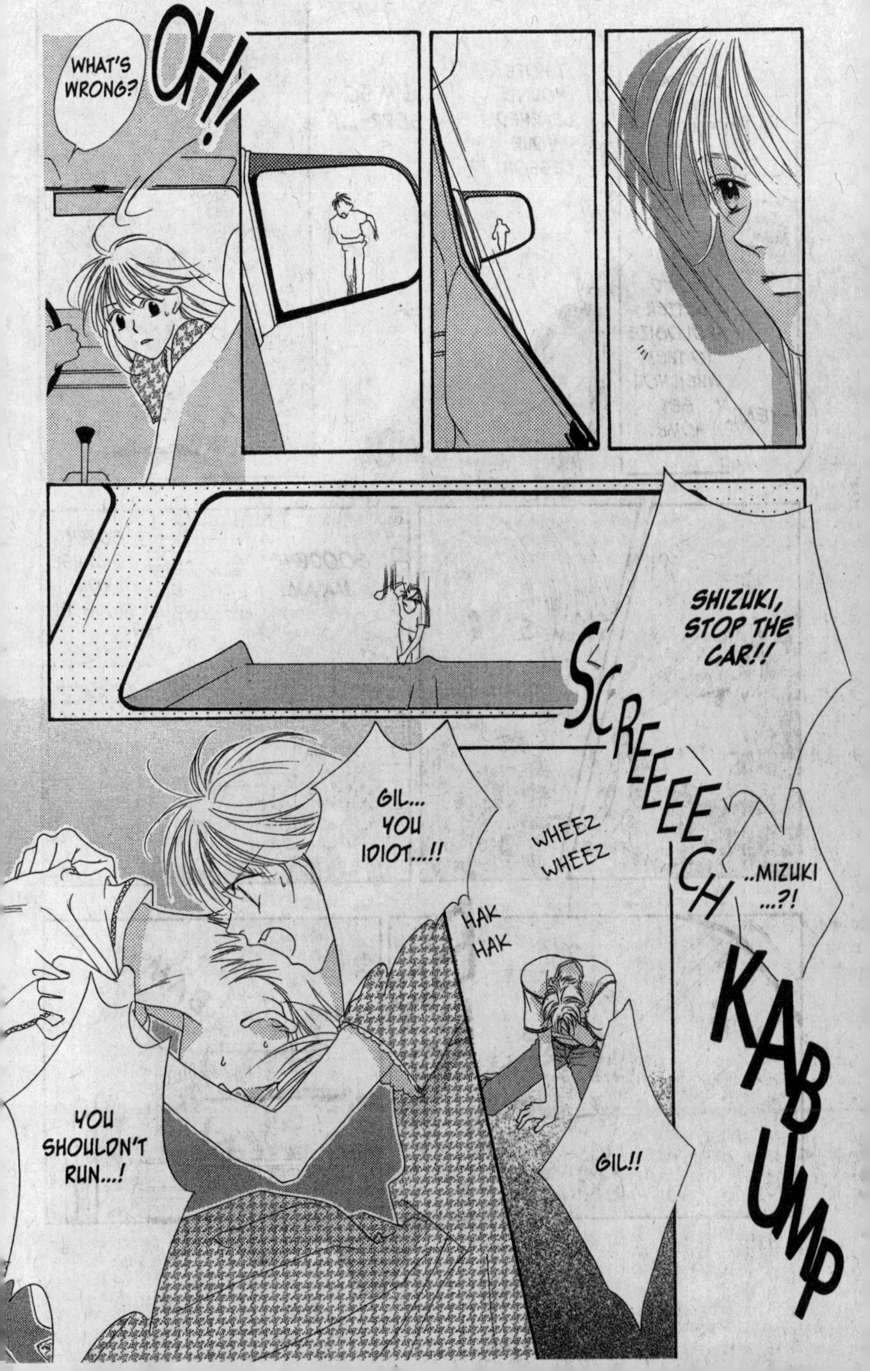
OH!!
WHAT'S WRONG?
SHIZUKI, STOP THE CAR!!
SCREEEEECH
..MIZUKI ...?!
KABUMP
GIL!!
HAK HAK
WHEEZ WHEEZ
GIL... YOU IDIOT...!!
YOU SHOULDN'T RUN...!

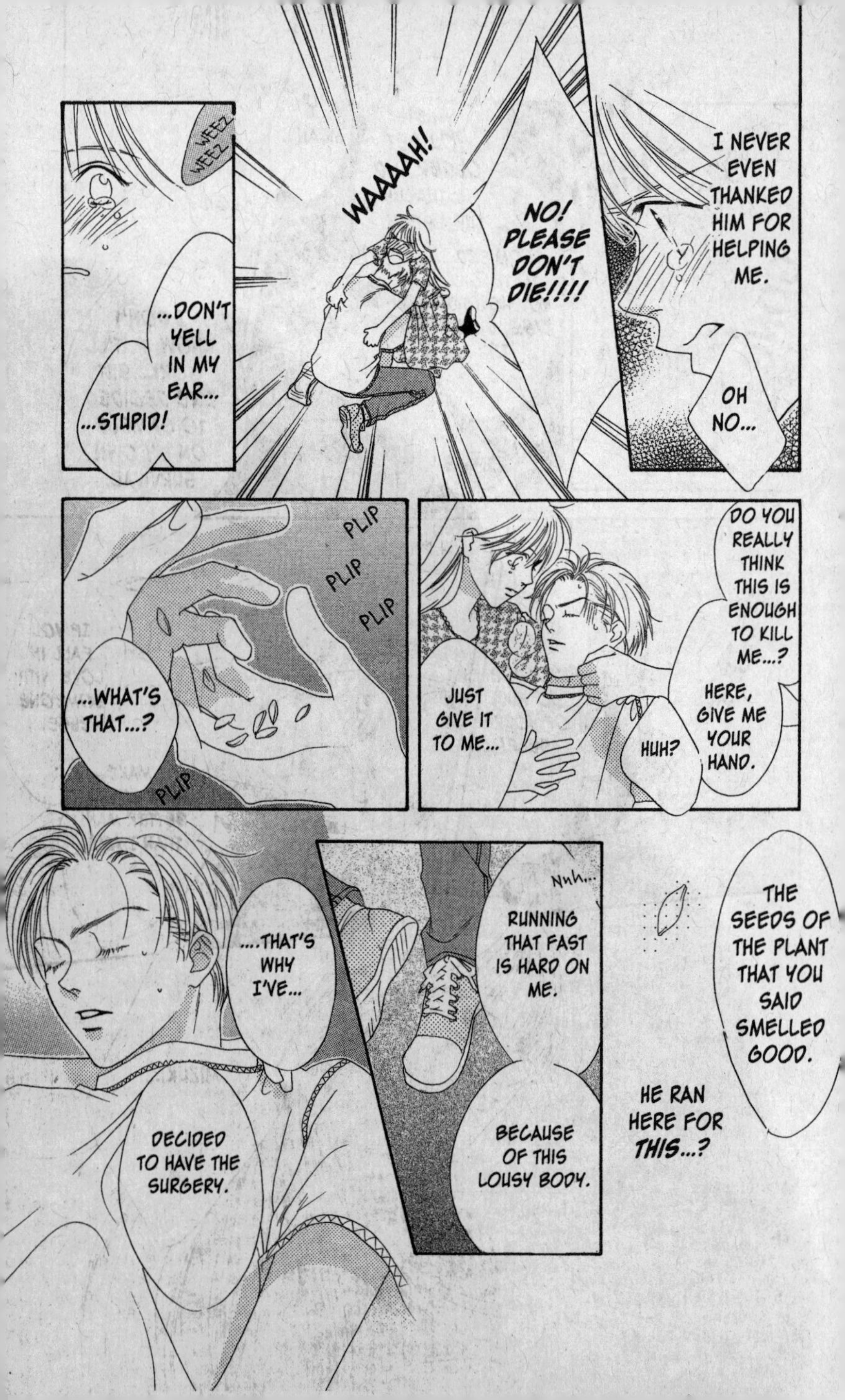
I NEVER EVEN THANKED HIM FOR HELPING ME.
OH NO...
NO! PLEASE DON'T DIE!!!!
WAAAAH!
WEEZ WEEZ
...DON'T YELL IN MY EAR...
...STUPID!
DO YOU REALLY THINK THIS IS ENOUGH TO KILL ME...?
HERE, GIVE ME YOUR HAND.
HUH?
JUST GIVE IT TO ME...
PLIP PLIP PLIP
...WHAT'S THAT...?
PLIP
THE SEEDS OF THE PLANT THAT YOU SAID SMELLED GOOD.
HE RAN HERE FOR *THIS*...?
Nnh...
RUNNING THAT FAST IS HARD ON ME.
BECAUSE OF THIS LOUSY BODY.
....THAT'S WHY I'VE...
DECIDED TO HAVE THE SURGERY.

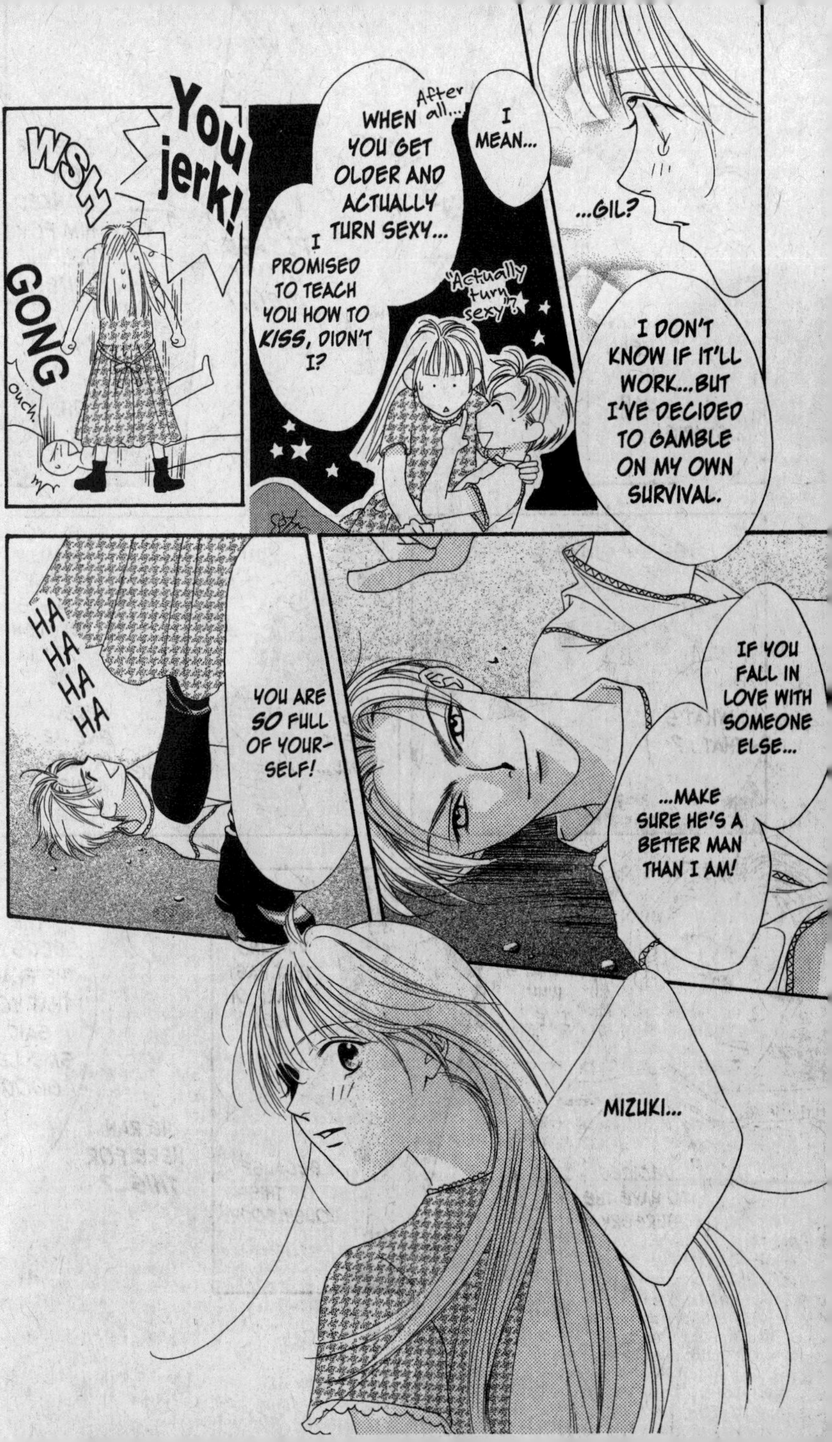

...GIL?
I DON'T KNOW IF IT'LL WORK...BUT I'VE DECIDED TO GAMBLE ON MY OWN SURVIVAL.
I MEAN...
After all...
WHEN YOU GET OLDER AND ACTUALLY TURN SEXY...
I PROMISED TO TEACH YOU HOW TO KISS, DIDN'T I?
"Actually turn sexy"?
You jerk!
WSH
GONG
ouch.
IF YOU FALL IN LOVE WITH SOMEONE ELSE...
...MAKE SURE HE'S A BETTER MAN THAN I AM!
YOU ARE SO FULL OF YOUR-SELF!
HA HA HA HA
MIZUKI...

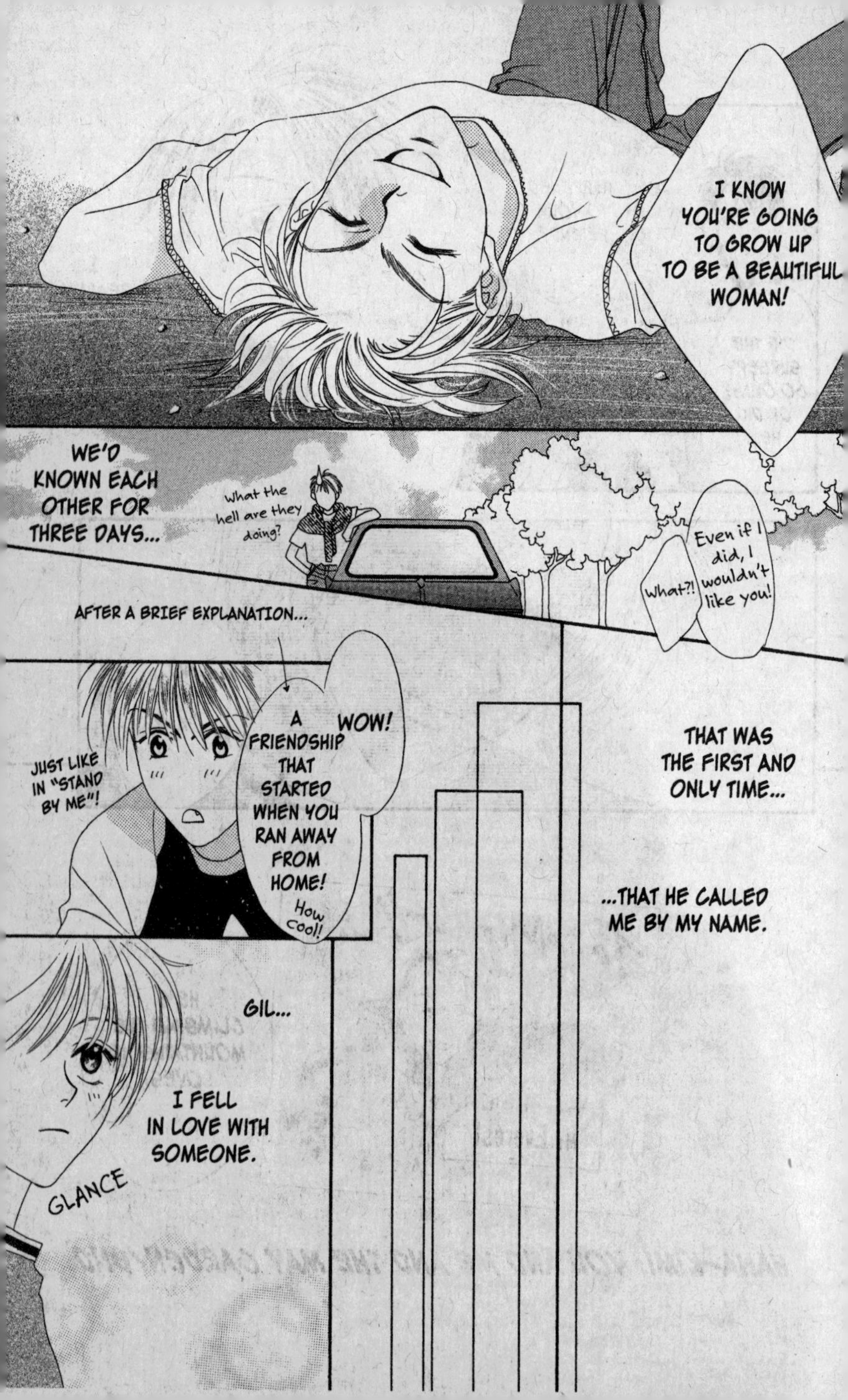
I KNOW YOU'RE GOING TO GROW UP TO BE A BEAUTIFUL WOMAN!
Even if I did, I wouldn't like you!
What?!
What the hell are they doing?
WE'D KNOWN EACH OTHER FOR THREE DAYS...
THAT WAS THE FIRST AND ONLY TIME...
AFTER A BRIEF EXPLANATION...
WOW!
A FRIENDSHIP THAT STARTED WHEN YOU RAN AWAY FROM HOME!
How cool!
JUST LIKE IN "STAND BY ME"!
...THAT HE CALLED ME BY MY NAME.
GIL...
I FELL IN LOVE WITH SOMEONE.
GLANCE

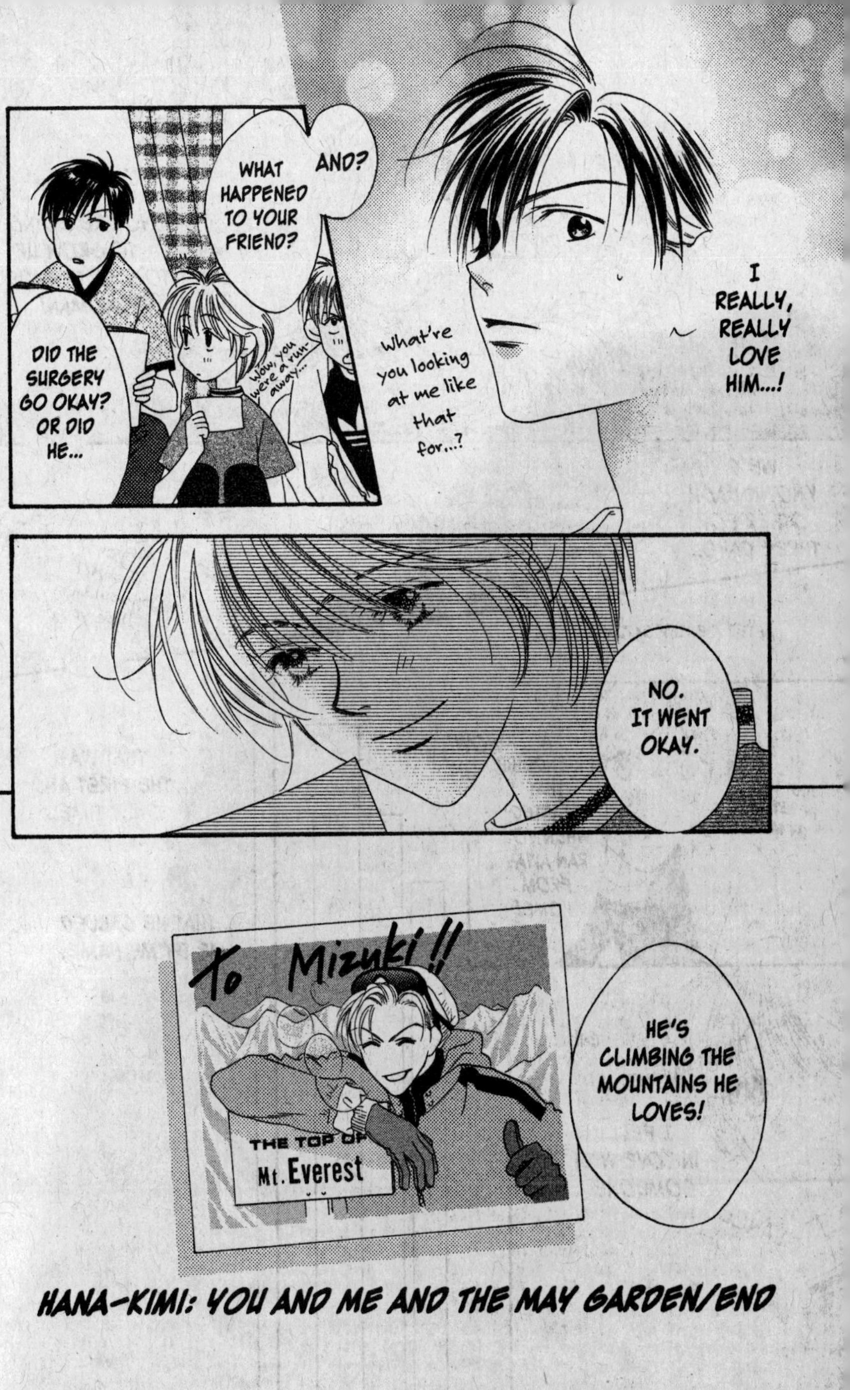
I REALLY, REALLY LOVE HIM...!
What're you looking at me like that for...?
AND?
WHAT HAPPENED TO YOUR FRIEND?
Wow, you were a run-away...
DID THE SURGERY GO OKAY? OR DID HE...
NO. IT WENT OKAY.
To Mizuki!!
THE TOP OF Mt. Everest
HE'S CLIMBING THE MOUNTAINS HE LOVES!

HANA-KIMI: YOU AND ME AND THE MAY GARDEN/END

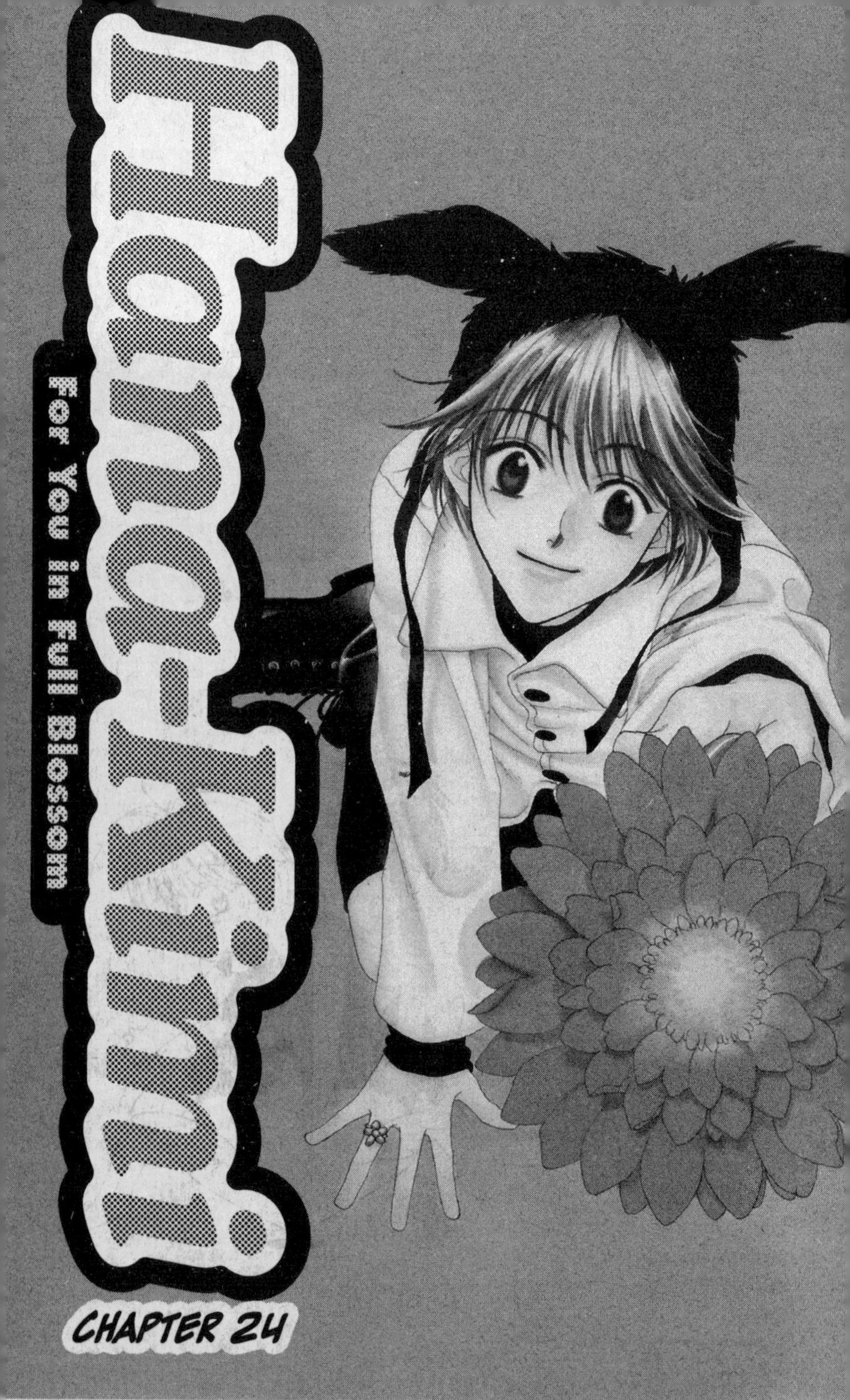
Hana-Kimi!
For You in Full Blossom
CHAPTER 24

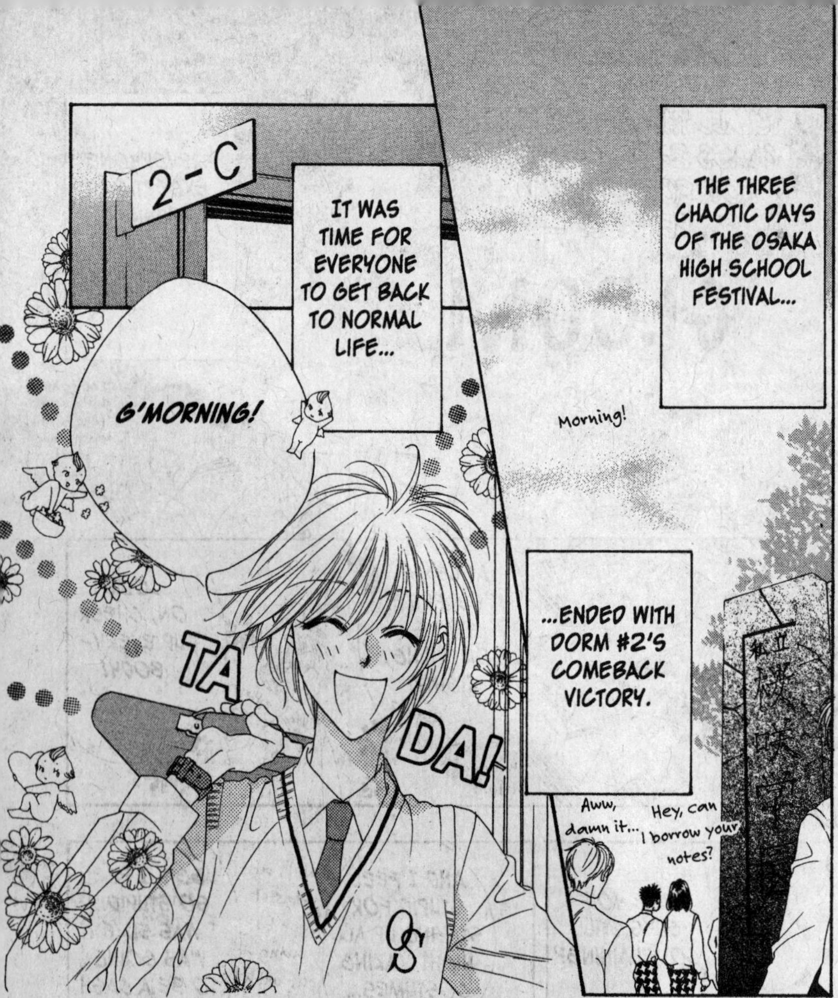

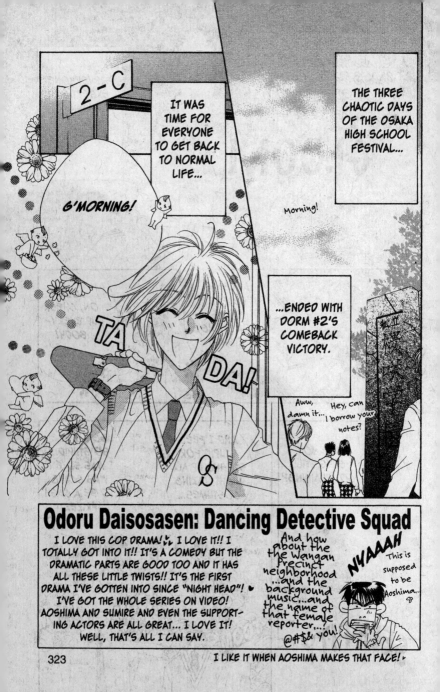

THE THREE CHAOTIC DAYS OF THE OSAKA HIGH SCHOOL FESTIVAL...
Morning!
...ENDED WITH DORM #2'S COMEBACK VICTORY.
Hey, can I borrow your notes?
Aww, damn it...
2-C
IT WAS TIME FOR EVERYONE TO GET BACK TO NORMAL LIFE...
G'MORNING!
TA
DA!

Odoru Daisosasen: Dancing Detective Squad

I LOVE THIS COP DRAMA! I LOVE IT!! I TOTALLY GOT INTO IT!! IT'S A COMEDY BUT THE DRAMATIC PARTS ARE GOOD TOO AND IT HAS ALL THESE LITTLE TWISTS!! IT'S THE FIRST DRAMA I'VE GOTTEN INTO SINCE "NIGHT HEAD"! I'VE GOT THE WHOLE SERIES ON VIDEO! AOSHIMA AND SUMIRE AND EVEN THE SUPPORTING ACTORS ARE ALL GREAT... I LOVE IT! WELL, THAT'S ALL I CAN SAY.

And how about the the Wangan Precinct neighborhood ...and the background music...and the name of that female reporter...? @#$& you!

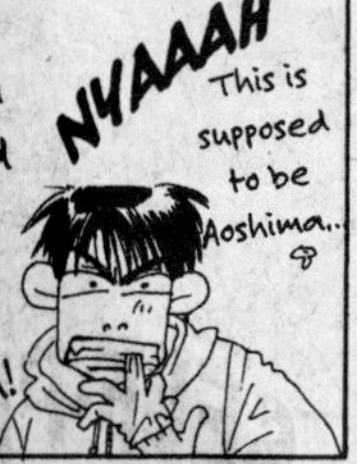

NYAAAH
This is supposed to be Aoshima..

I LIKE IT WHEN AOSHIMA MAKES THAT FACE!

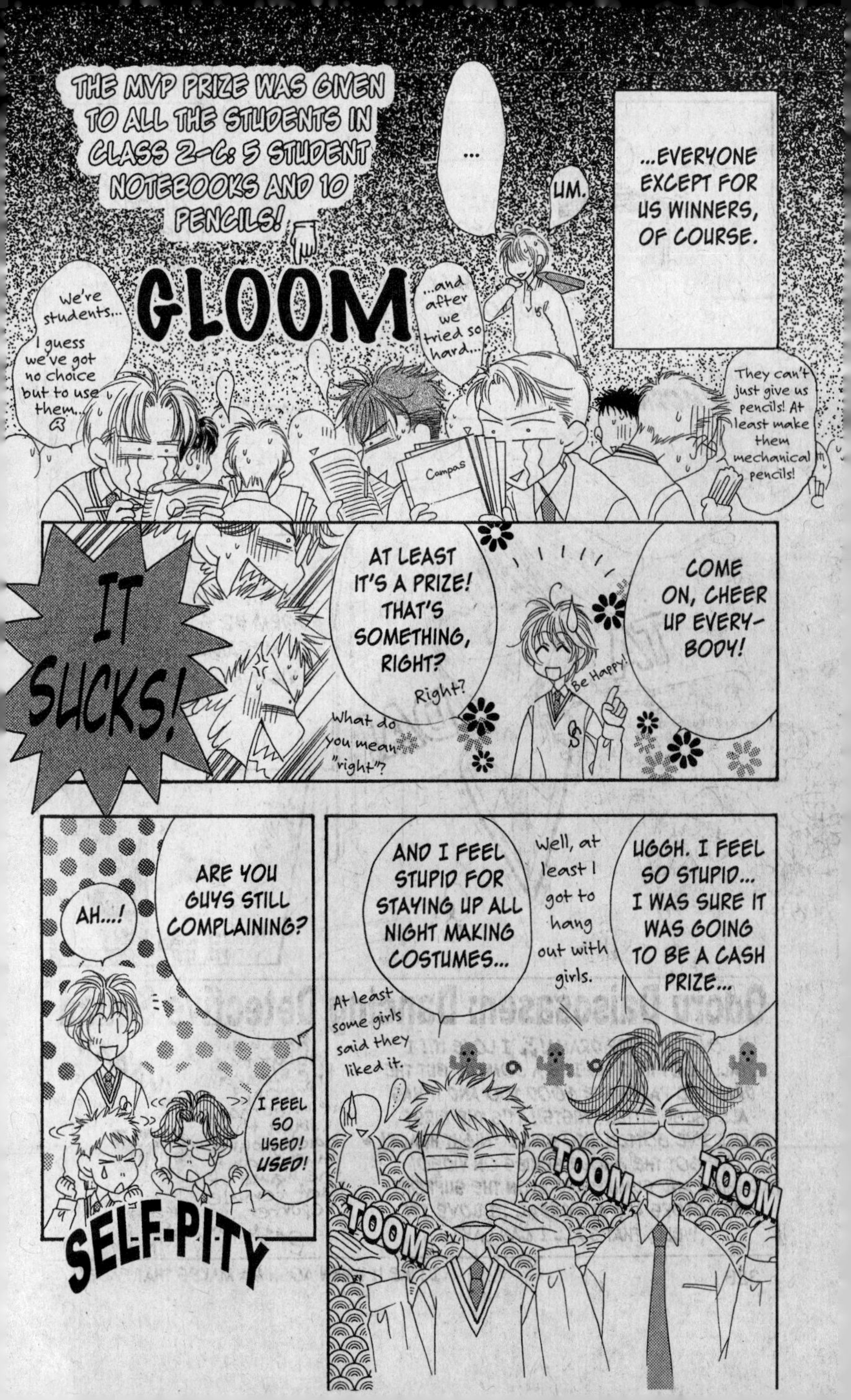
...EVERYONE EXCEPT FOR US WINNERS, OF COURSE.
UM.
...
THE MVP PRIZE WAS GIVEN TO ALL THE STUDENTS IN CLASS 2-C: 5 STUDENT NOTEBOOKS AND 10 PENCILS!
GLOOM
They can't just give us pencils! At least make them mechanical pencils!
...and after we tried so hard...
We're students... I guess we've got no choice but to use them...
Campas
COME ON, CHEER UP EVERYBODY!
Be Happy!
AT LEAST IT'S A PRIZE! THAT'S SOMETHING, RIGHT?
Right?
What do you mean "right"?
IT SUCKS!
UGGH. I FEEL SO STUPID... I WAS SURE IT WAS GOING TO BE A CASH PRIZE...
Well, at least I got to hang out with girls.
AND I FEEL STUPID FOR STAYING UP ALL NIGHT MAKING COSTUMES...
At least some girls said they liked it.
TOOM
TOOM
TOOM
ARE YOU GUYS STILL COMPLAINING?
AH...!
I FEEL SO USED! USED!
SELF-PITY

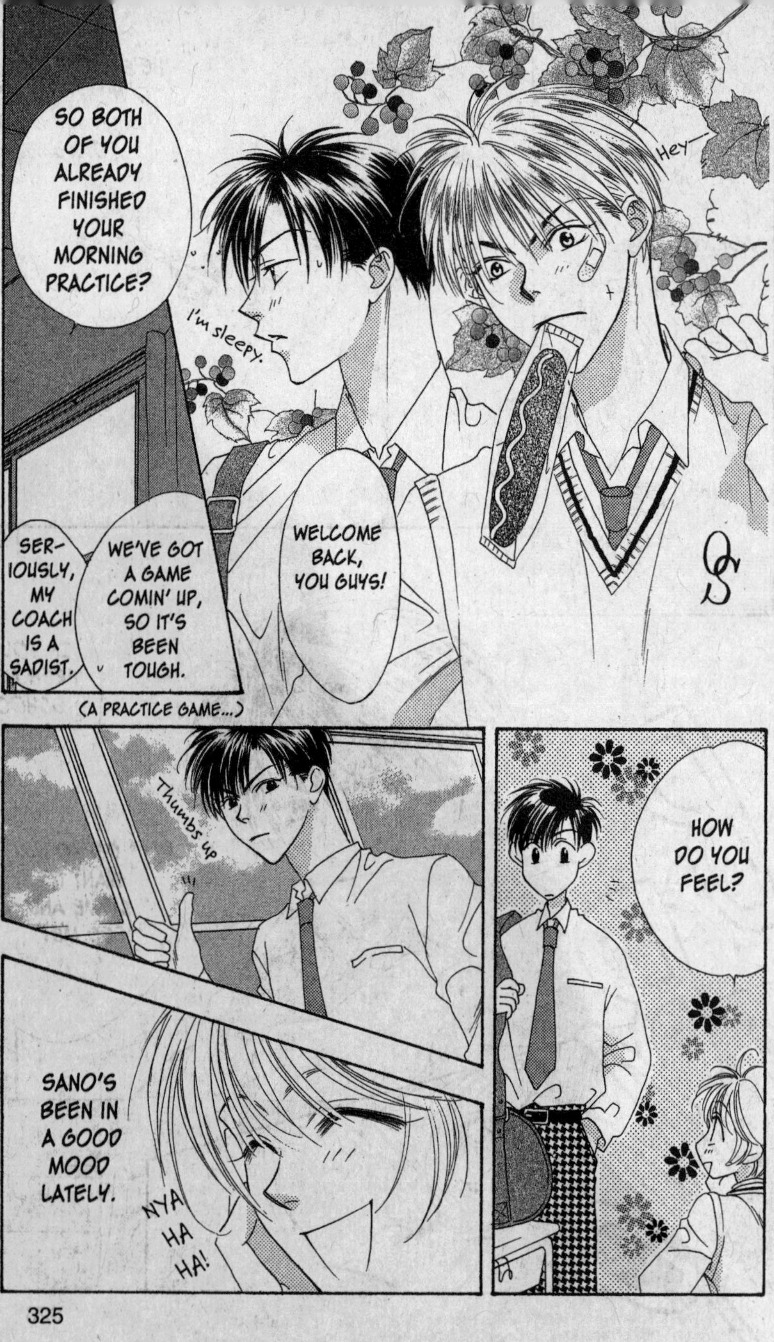
Hey—
SO BOTH OF YOU ALREADY FINISHED YOUR MORNING PRACTICE?
I'm sleepy.
WELCOME BACK, YOU GUYS!
WE'VE GOT A GAME COMIN' UP, SO IT'S BEEN TOUGH.
SER-IOUSLY, MY COACH IS A SADIST.
(A PRACTICE GAME...)
HOW DO YOU FEEL?
Thumbs up
SANO'S BEEN IN A GOOD MOOD LATELY.
NYA HA HA!

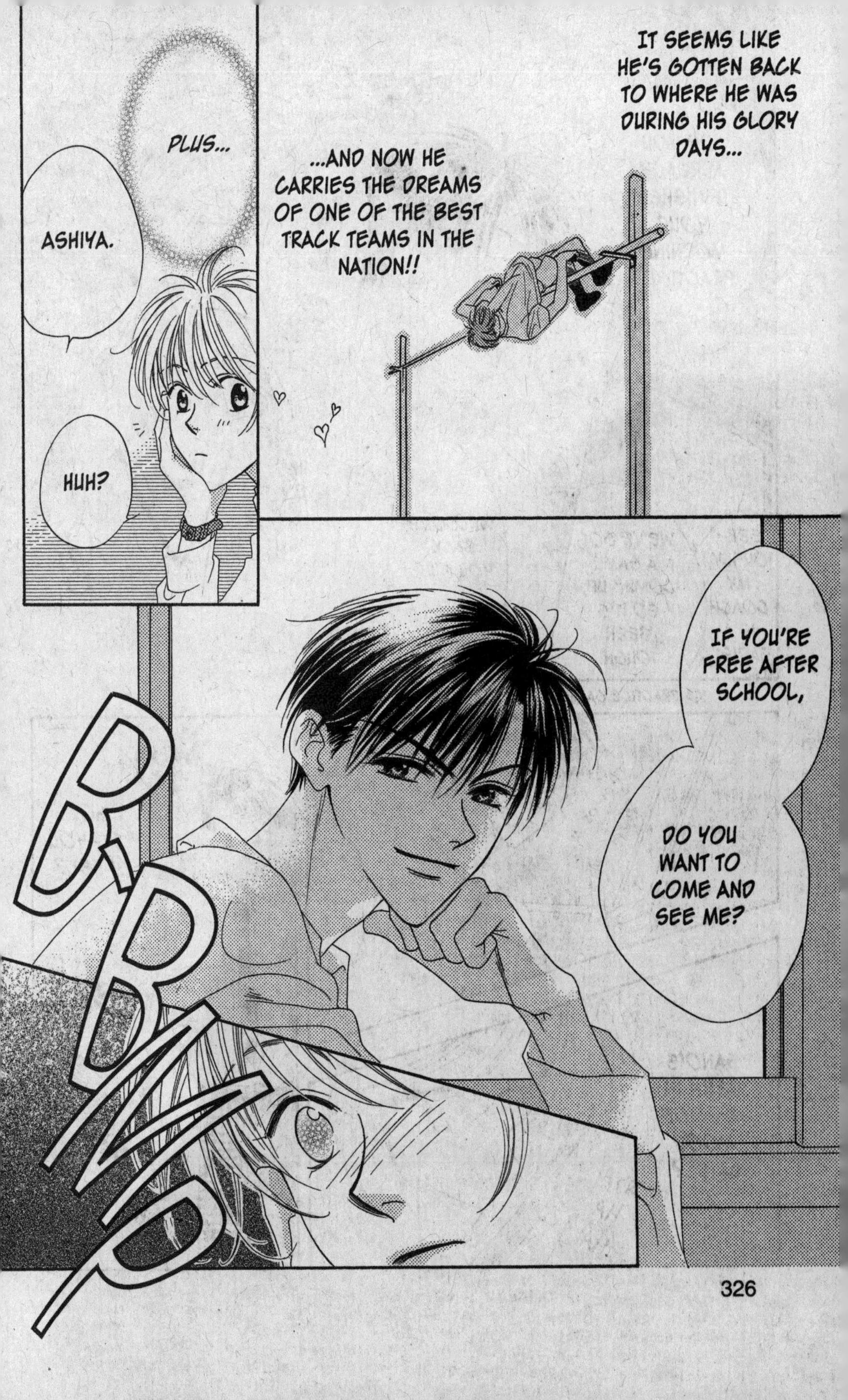
IT SEEMS LIKE HE'S GOTTEN BACK TO WHERE HE WAS DURING HIS GLORY DAYS...
...AND NOW HE CARRIES THE DREAMS OF ONE OF THE BEST TRACK TEAMS IN THE NATION!!
PLUS...
ASHIYA.
HUH?
IF YOU'RE FREE AFTER SCHOOL,
DO YOU WANT TO COME AND SEE ME?
B-BUMP

UH... YEAH, OF COURSE...!
...NOW HE SMILES ALL THE TIME.
EVER SINCE THAT DAY DURING THE FESTIVAL...
HSSH
...HIS SMILE HAS BEEN BLAZING IN ME.
OH, THIS IS BAD FOR MY HEART...
B-BMP B-BMP
Sound of her heart
B-BMP
?

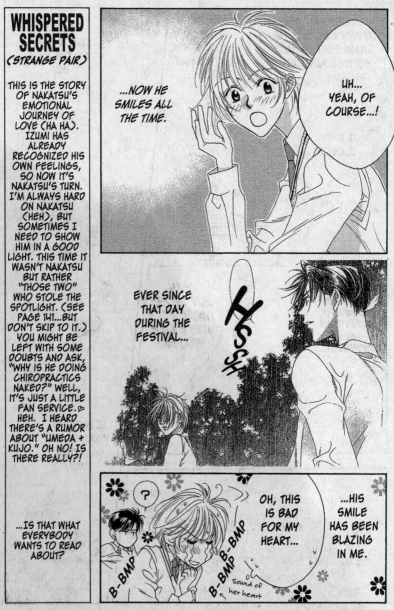

WHISPERED SECRETS
(STRANGE PAIR)

THIS IS THE STORY OF NAKATSU'S EMOTIONAL JOURNEY OF LOVE (HA HA). IZUMI HAS ALREADY RECOGNIZED HIS OWN FEELINGS, SO NOW IT'S NAKATSU'S TURN. I'M ALWAYS HARD ON NAKATSU (HEH), BUT SOMETIMES I NEED TO SHOW HIM IN A GOOD LIGHT. THIS TIME IT WASN'T NAKATSU BUT RATHER "THOSE TWO" WHO STOLE THE SPOTLIGHT. (SEE PAGE 141...BUT DON'T SKIP TO IT.) YOU MIGHT BE LEFT WITH SOME DOUBTS AND ASK, "WHY IS HE DOING CHIROPRACTICS NAKED?" WELL, IT'S JUST A LITTLE FAN SERVICE.♡ HEH. I HEARD THERE'S A RUMOR ABOUT "UMEDA + KUJO." OH NO! IS THERE REALLY?!

...IS THAT WHAT EVERYBODY WANTS TO READ ABOUT?

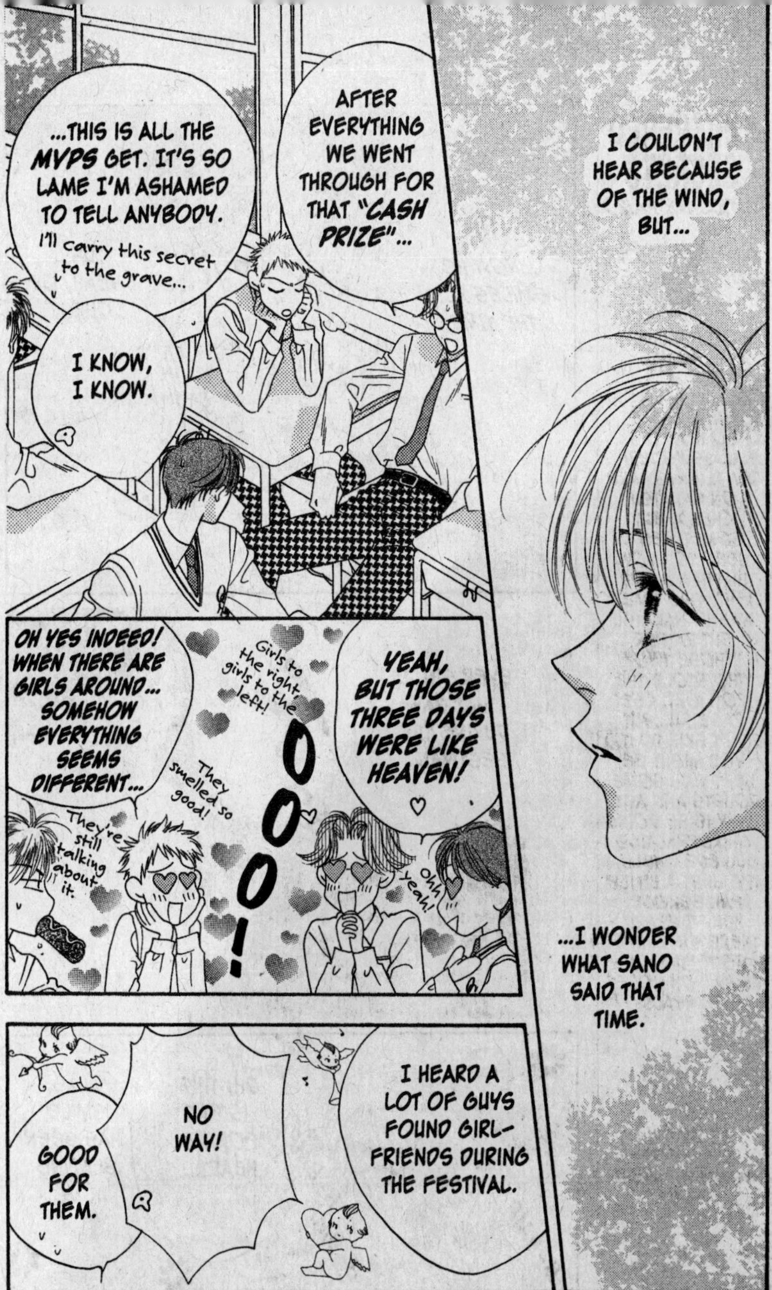
I COULDN'T HEAR BECAUSE OF THE WIND, BUT...
...I WONDER WHAT SANO SAID THAT TIME.
AFTER EVERYTHING WE WENT THROUGH FOR THAT "CASH PRIZE"...
...THIS IS ALL THE MVPS GET. IT'S SO LAME I'M ASHAMED TO TELL ANYBODY.
I'll carry this secret to the grave...
I KNOW, I KNOW.
YEAH, BUT THOSE THREE DAYS WERE LIKE HEAVEN!
Ohh yeah!
OOOO!
Girls to the right girls to the left!
OH YES INDEED! WHEN THERE ARE GIRLS AROUND... SOMEHOW EVERYTHING SEEMS DIFFERENT...
They smelled so good!
They're still talking about it.
I HEARD A LOT OF GUYS FOUND GIRL-FRIENDS DURING THE FESTIVAL.
NO WAY!
GOOD FOR THEM.

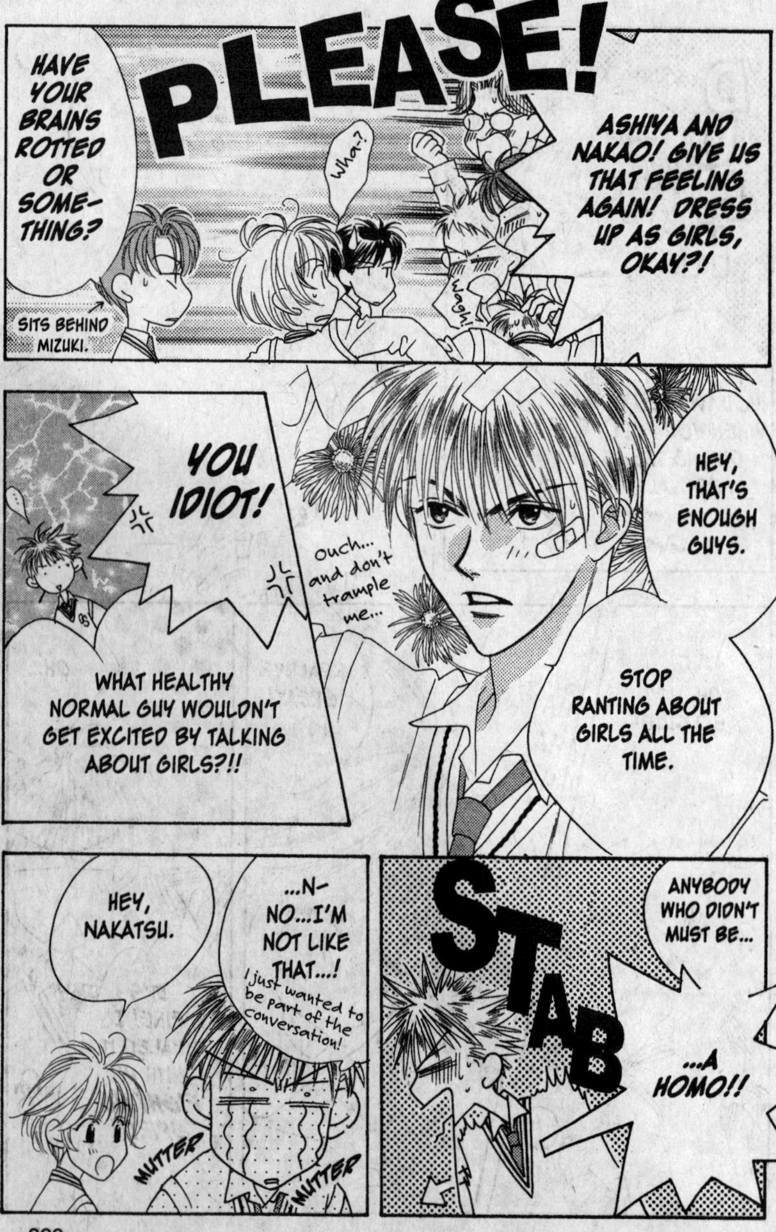
PLEASE!
ASHIYA AND NAKAO! GIVE US THAT FEELING AGAIN! DRESS UP AS GIRLS, OKAY?!
Wagh!
Wha-?
HAVE YOUR BRAINS ROTTED OR SOME-THING?
SITS BEHIND MIZUKI.
HEY, THAT'S ENOUGH GUYS.
STOP RANTING ABOUT GIRLS ALL THE TIME.
YOU IDIOT!
ouch... and don't trample me...
WHAT HEALTHY NORMAL GUY WOULDN'T GET EXCITED BY TALKING ABOUT GIRLS?!!
ANYBODY WHO DIDN'T MUST BE...
STAB
...A HOMO!!
...N-NO...I'M NOT LIKE THAT...!
I just wanted to be part of the conversation!
HEY, NAKATSU.
MUTTER
MUTTER

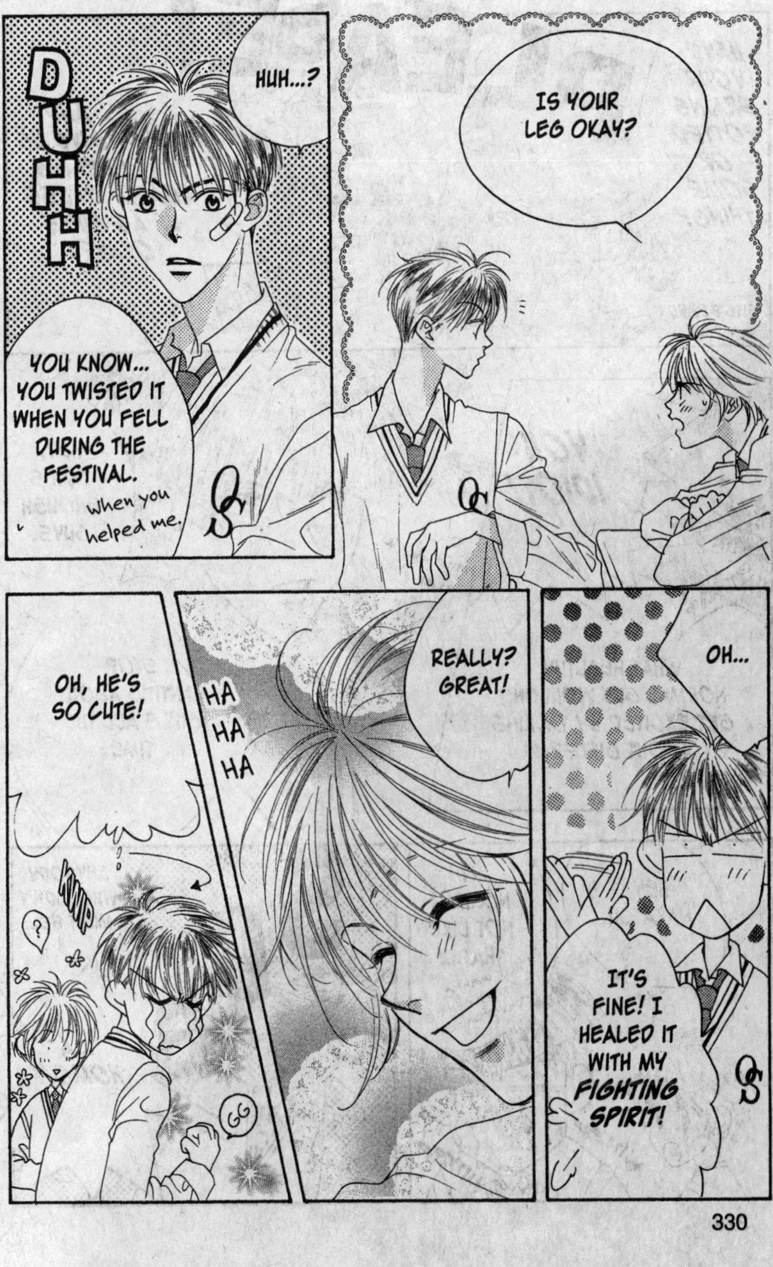
IS YOUR LEG OKAY?
HUH...?
DUHH
YOU KNOW... YOU TWISTED IT WHEN YOU FELL DURING THE FESTIVAL.
When you helped me.
OH...
IT'S FINE! I HEALED IT WITH MY FIGHTING SPIRIT!
REALLY? GREAT!
HA HA HA
OH, HE'S SO CUTE!
KNIP
?
GG

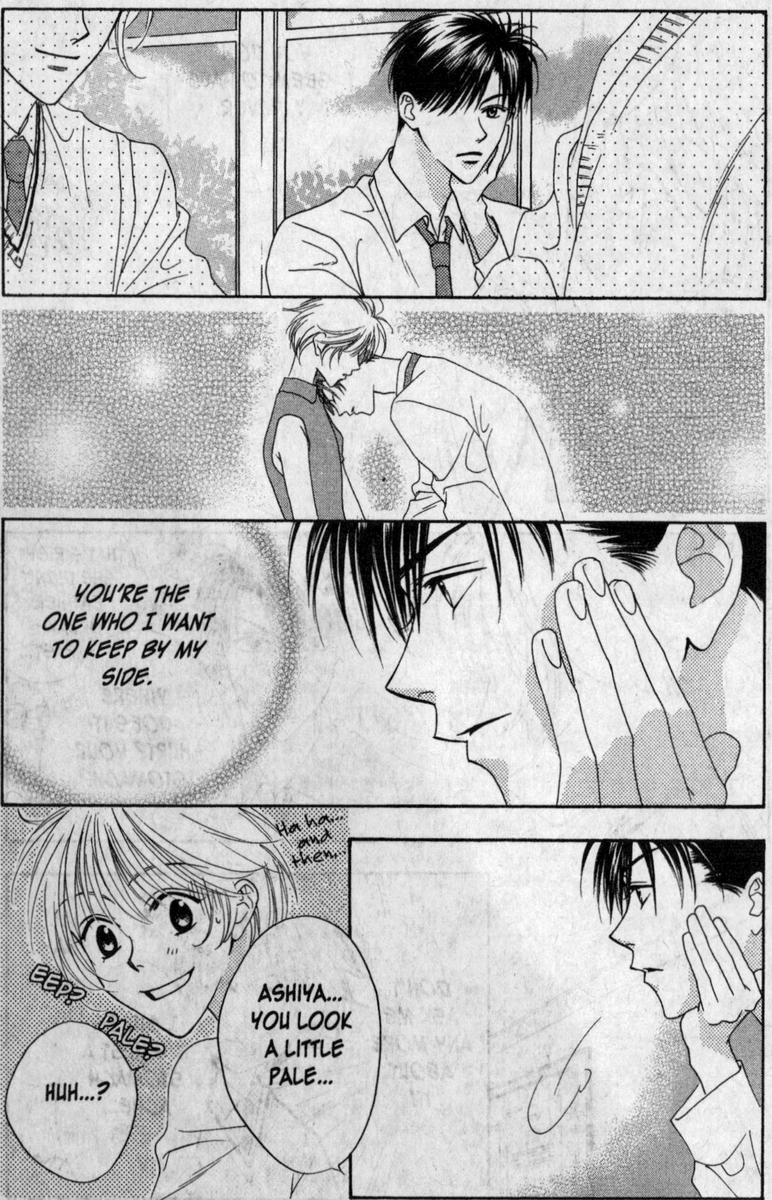
YOU'RE THE ONE WHO I WANT TO KEEP BY MY SIDE.
Ha ha... and then...
ASHIYA... YOU LOOK A LITTLE PALE...
EEP? PALE?
HUH...?

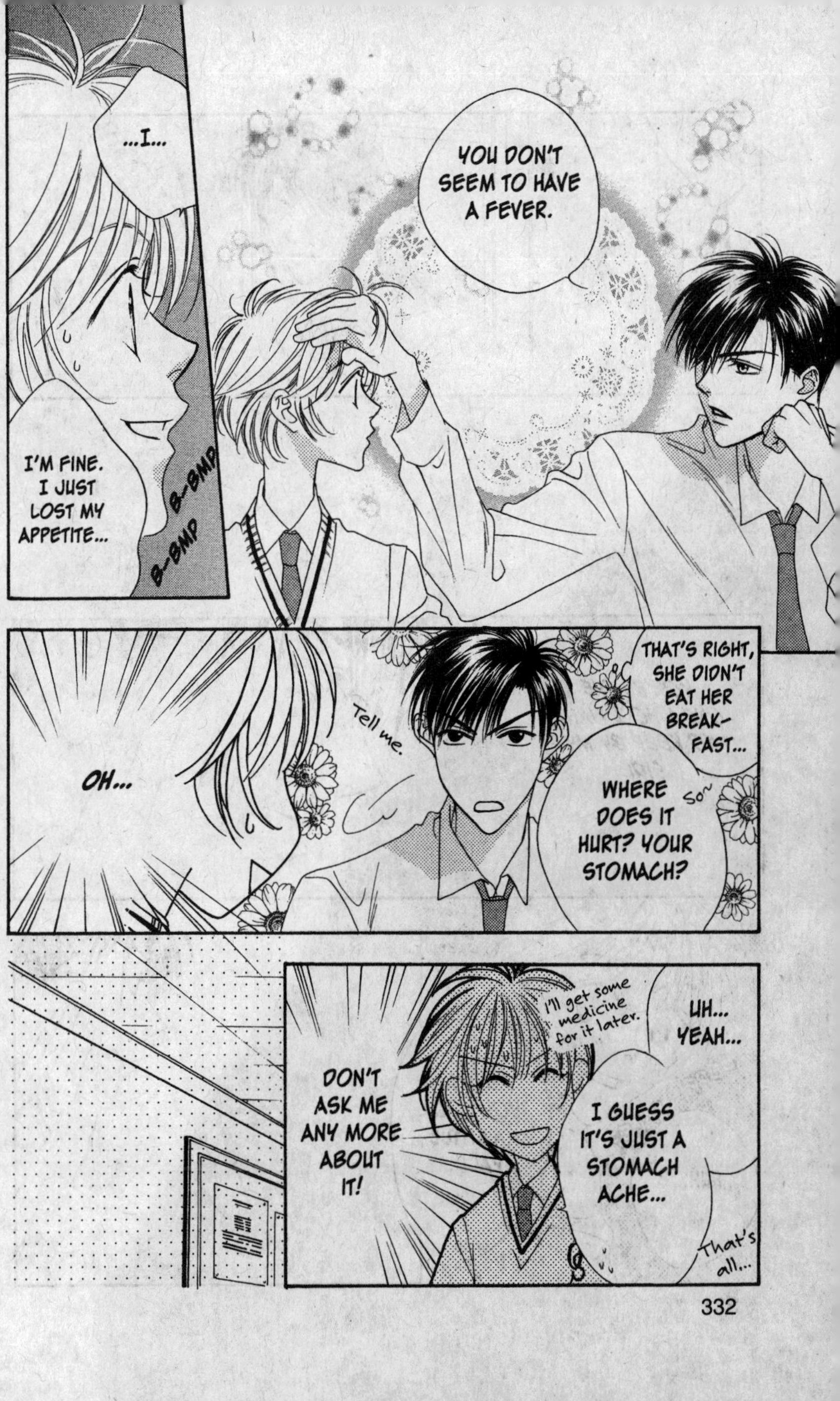
YOU DON'T SEEM TO HAVE A FEVER.
...I...
I'M FINE. I JUST LOST MY APPETITE...
B-BMP
B-BMP
THAT'S RIGHT, SHE DIDN'T EAT HER BREAK-FAST...
WHERE DOES IT HURT? YOUR STOMACH?
Tell me.
OH...
UH... YEAH...
I'll get some medicine for it later.
I GUESS IT'S JUST A STOMACH ACHE...
That's all...
DON'T ASK ME ANY MORE ABOUT IT!

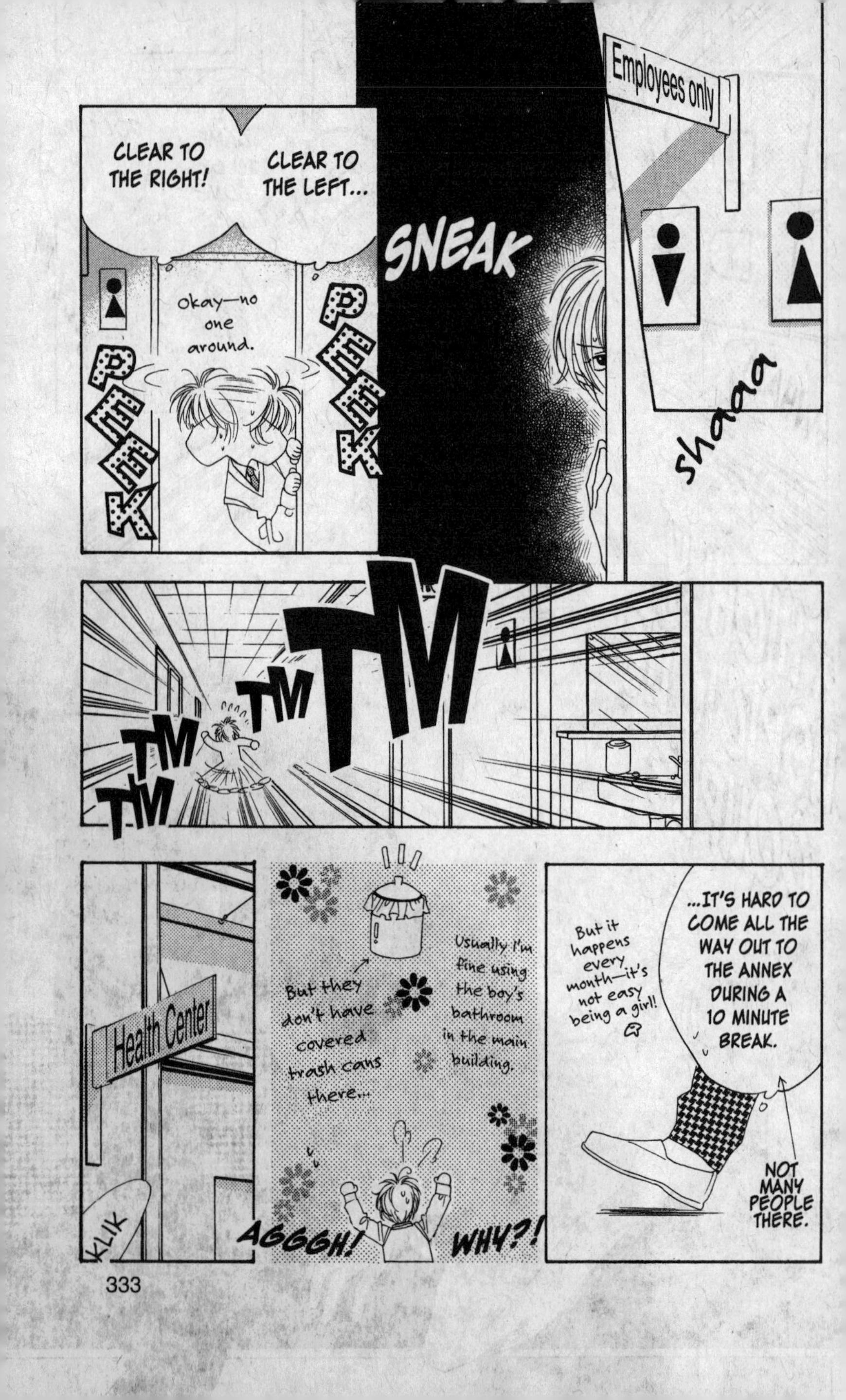
Employees only
shaaa
SNEAK
CLEAR TO THE RIGHT!
CLEAR TO THE LEFT...
PEEK
PEEK
Okay—no one around.
T-TM
TM
TM
TM
...IT'S HARD TO COME ALL THE WAY OUT TO THE ANNEX DURING A 10 MINUTE BREAK.
But it happens every month—it's not easy being a girl!
NOT MANY PEOPLE THERE.
Usually I'm fine using the boy's bathroom in the main building.
But they don't have covered trash cans there...
AGGGH!
WHY?!
Health Center
KLIK

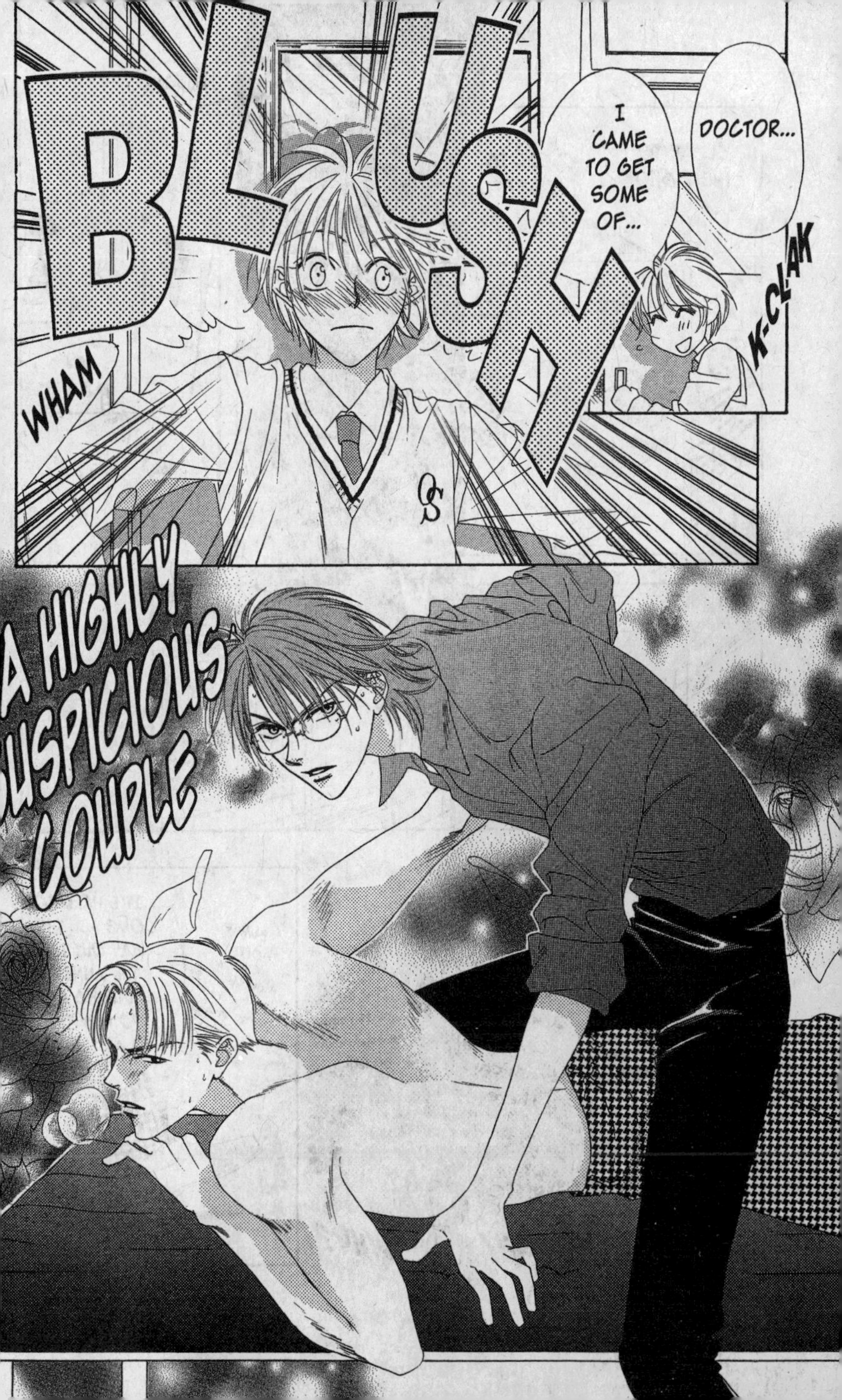
DOCTOR...
I CAME TO GET SOME OF...
K-CLAK
BLUSH
WHAM
A HIGHLY SUSPICIOUS COUPLE

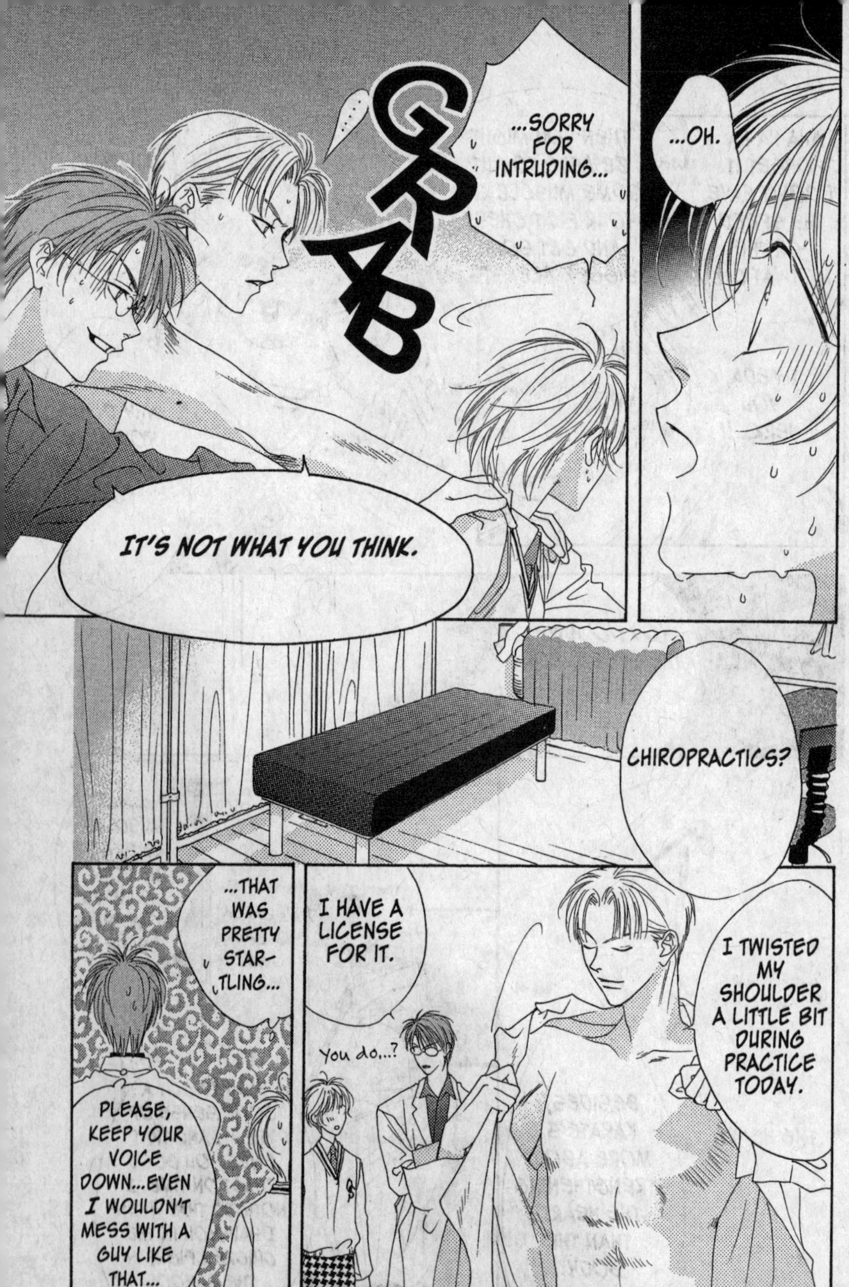
...OH.
...SORRY FOR INTRUDING...
GRAB
IT'S NOT WHAT YOU THINK.
CHIROPRACTICS?
I TWISTED MY SHOULDER A LITTLE BIT DURING PRACTICE TODAY.
I HAVE A LICENSE FOR IT.
You do...?
...THAT WAS PRETTY STAR-TLING...
PLEASE, KEEP YOUR VOICE DOWN...EVEN I WOULDN'T MESS WITH A GUY LIKE THAT...

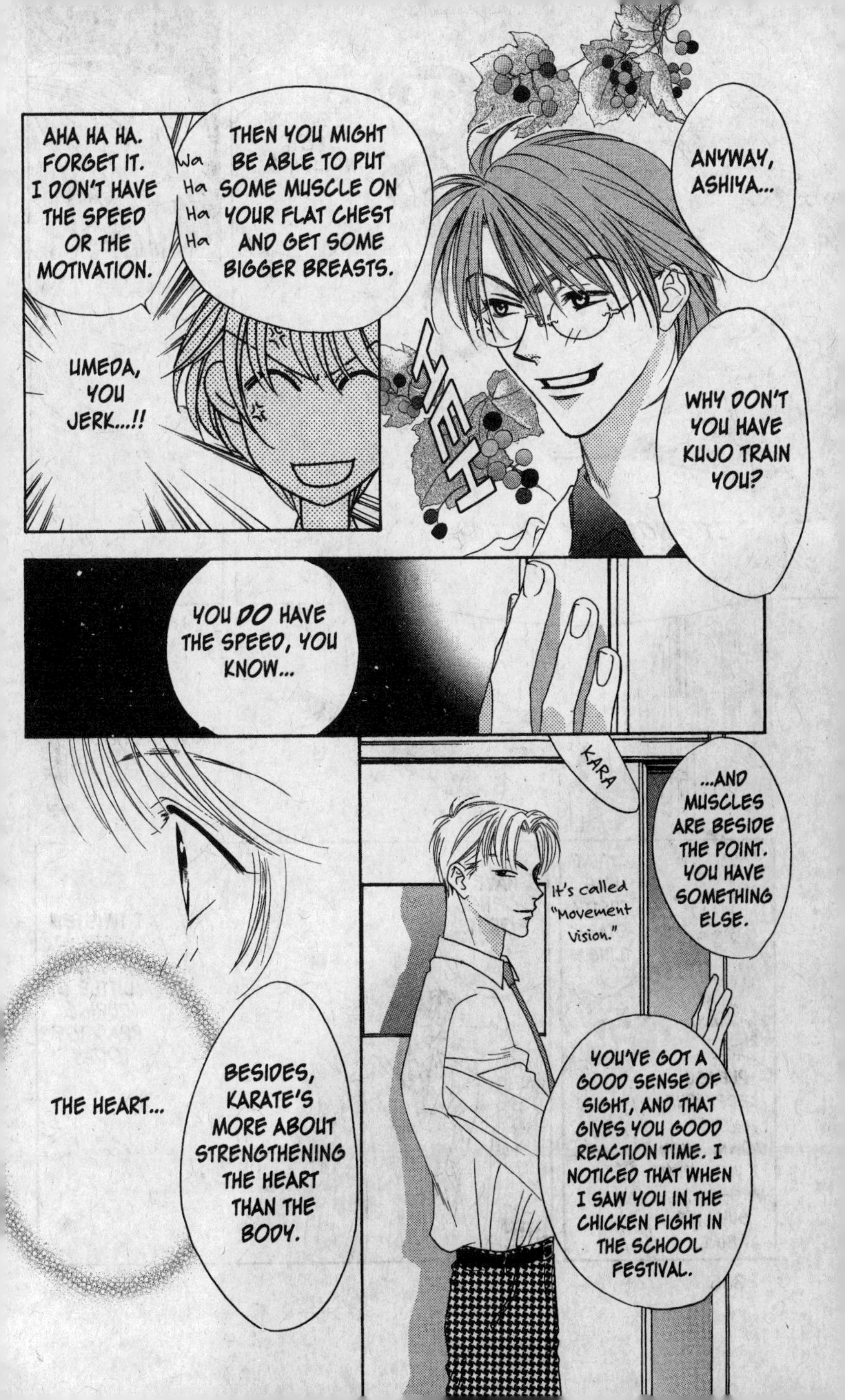
ANYWAY, ASHIYA...
HEH
WHY DON'T YOU HAVE KUJO TRAIN YOU?
THEN YOU MIGHT BE ABLE TO PUT SOME MUSCLE ON YOUR FLAT CHEST AND GET SOME BIGGER BREASTS.
Wa Ha Ha Ha
AHA HA HA. FORGET IT. I DON'T HAVE THE SPEED OR THE MOTIVATION.
UMEDA, YOU JERK...!!
YOU *DO* HAVE THE SPEED, YOU KNOW...
KARA
...AND MUSCLES ARE BESIDE THE POINT. YOU HAVE SOMETHING ELSE.
It's called "Movement Vision."
YOU'VE GOT A GOOD SENSE OF SIGHT, AND THAT GIVES YOU GOOD REACTION TIME. I NOTICED THAT WHEN I SAW YOU IN THE CHICKEN FIGHT IN THE SCHOOL FESTIVAL.
BESIDES, KARATE'S MORE ABOUT STRENGTHENING THE HEART THAN THE BODY.
THE HEART...

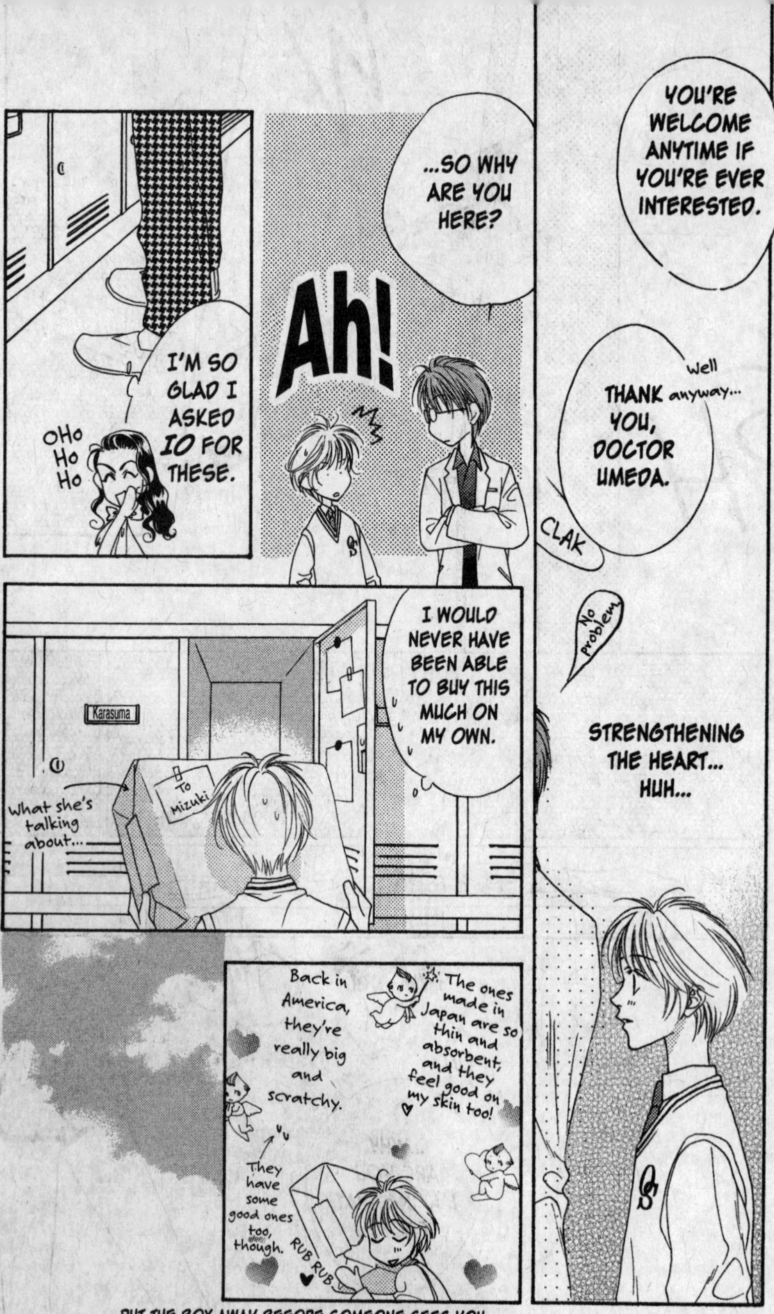
YOU'RE WELCOME ANYTIME IF YOU'RE EVER INTERESTED.
Well anyway...
THANK YOU, DOCTOR UMEDA.
CLAK
No problem
STRENGTHENING THE HEART... HUH...
...SO WHY ARE YOU HERE?
Ah!
I'M SO GLAD I ASKED IO FOR THESE.
OHo Ho Ho
I WOULD NEVER HAVE BEEN ABLE TO BUY THIS MUCH ON MY OWN.
Karasuma
To Mizuki
What she's talking about...
The ones made in Japan are so thin and absorbent, and they feel good on my skin too!
Back in America, they're really big and scratchy.
They have some good ones too, though.
RUB RUB

PUT THE BOX AWAY BEFORE SOMEONE SEES YOU...

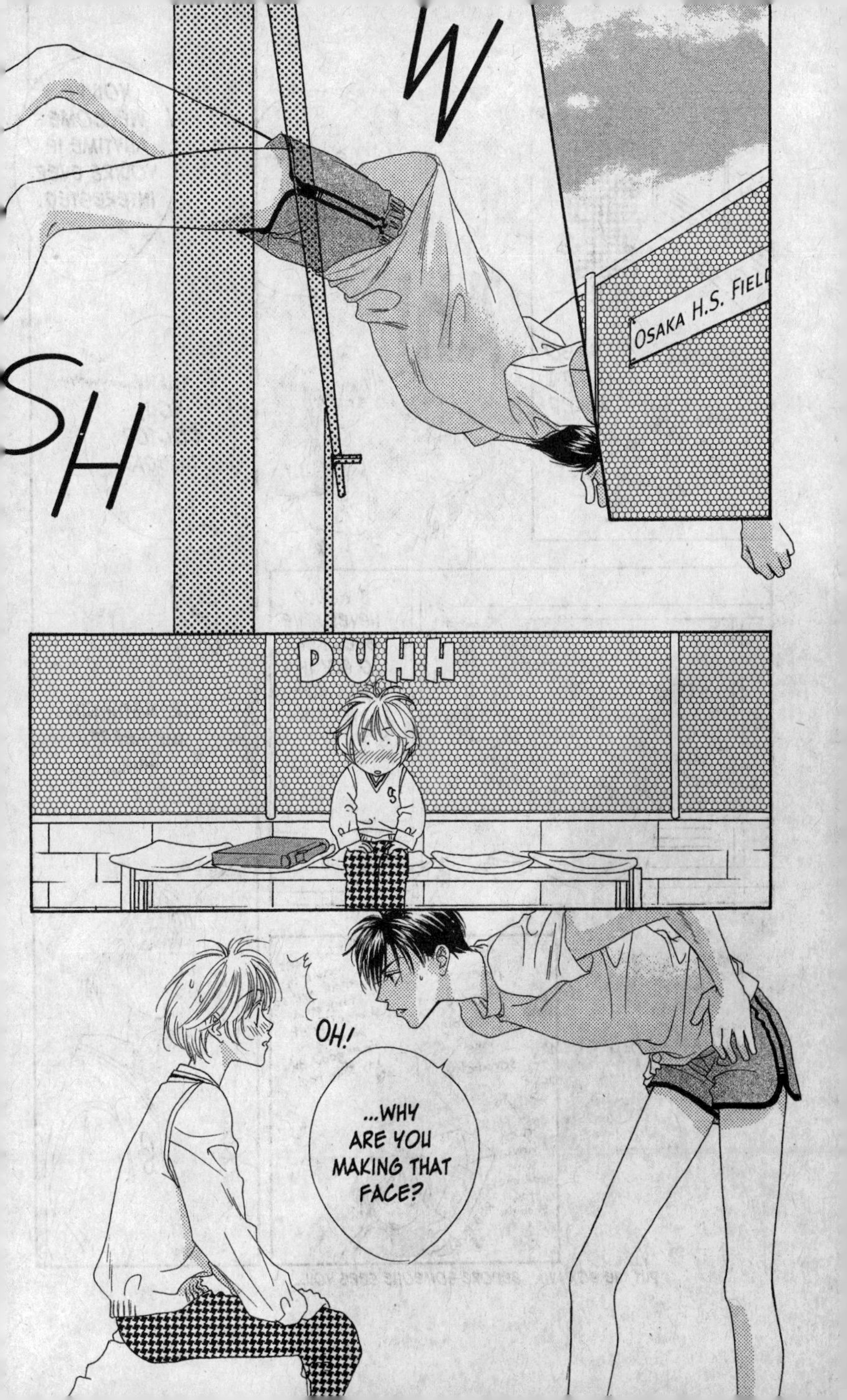
W
OSAKA H.S. FIELD
SH
DUHH
OH!
...WHY ARE YOU MAKING THAT FACE?

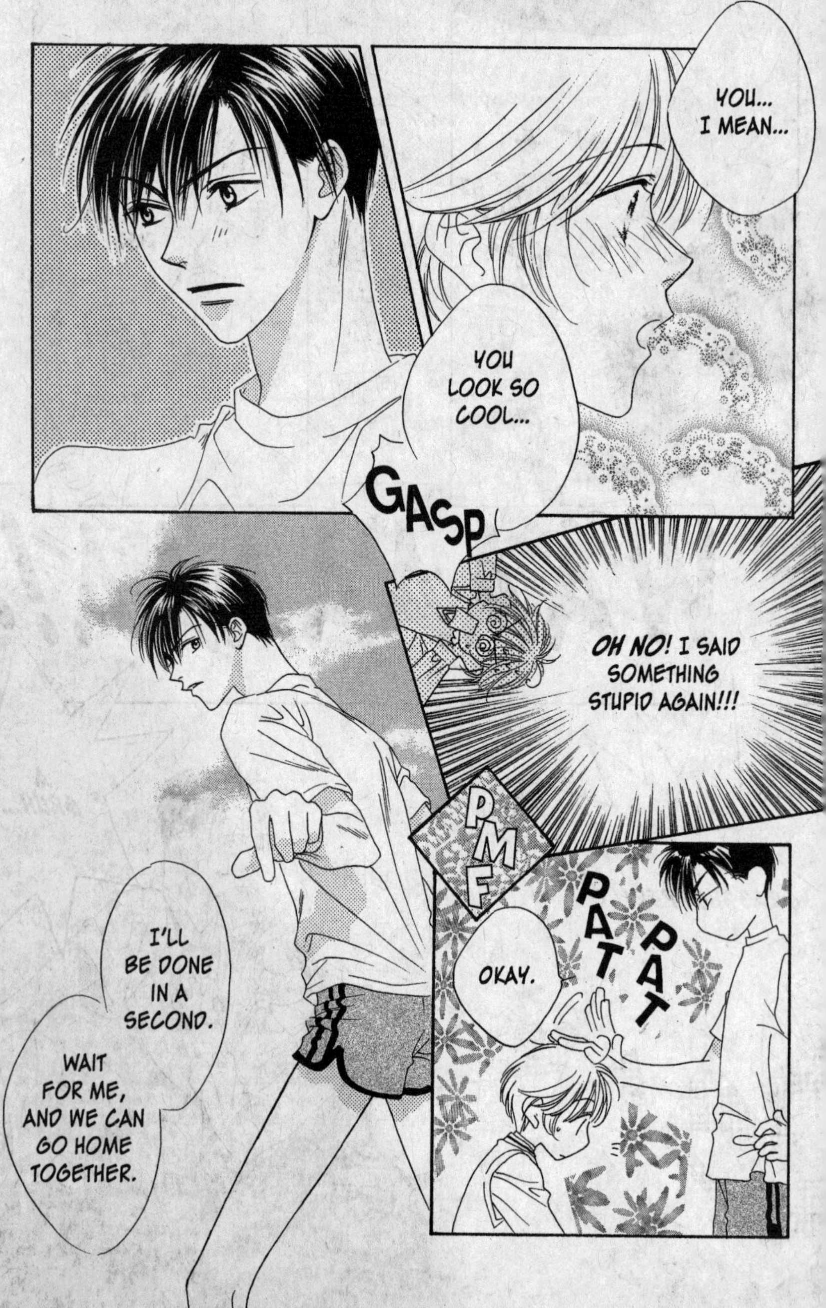
YOU... I MEAN...
YOU LOOK SO COOL...
GASP
OH NO! I SAID SOMETHING STUPID AGAIN!!!
PMF
PAT PAT
OKAY.
I'LL BE DONE IN A SECOND.
WAIT FOR ME, AND WE CAN GO HOME TOGETHER.

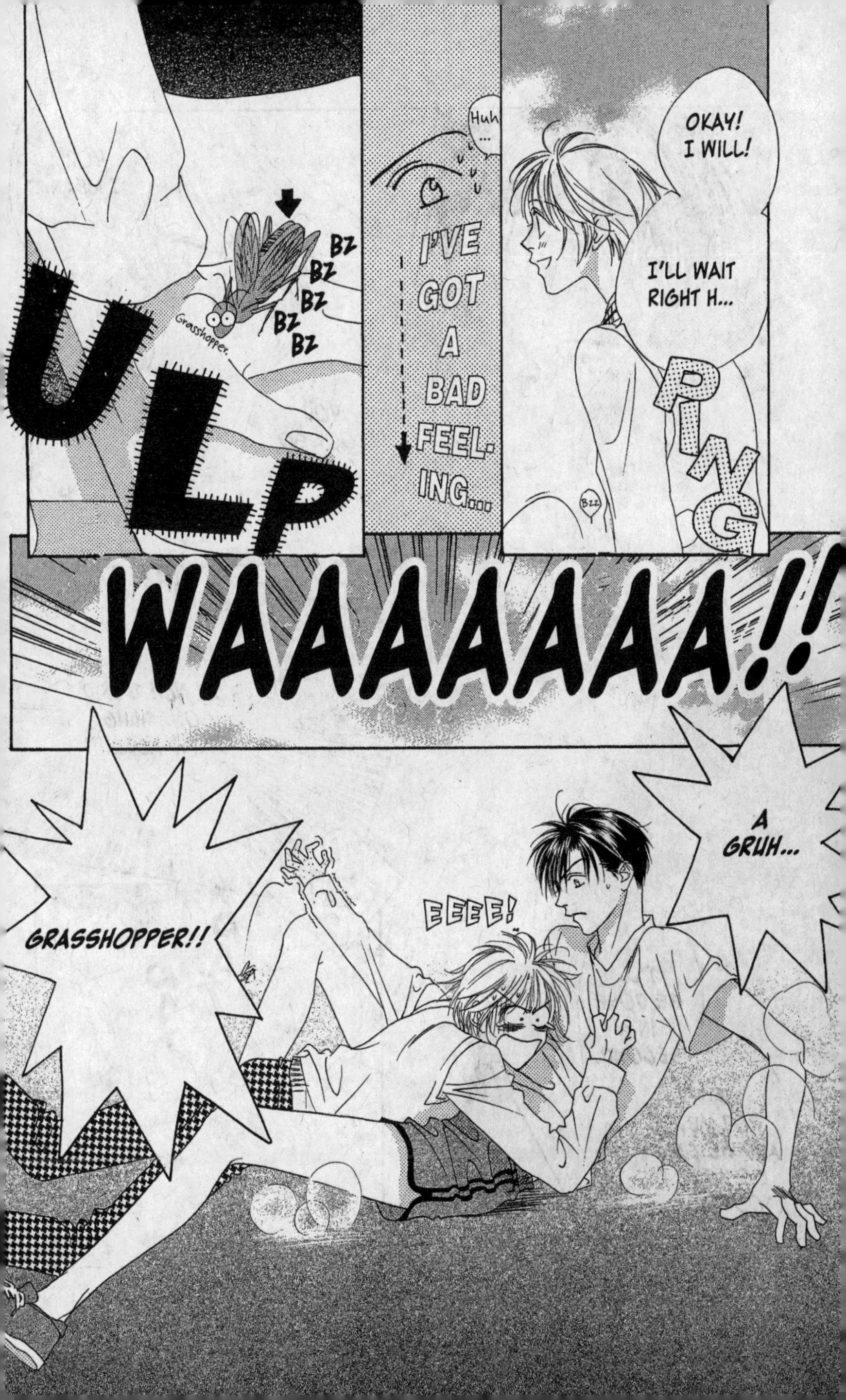
OKAY! I WILL!
I'LL WAIT RIGHT H...
PING
Bzz
Huh...
I'VE GOT A BAD FEEL-ING...
BZ BZ BZ BZ BZ
Grasshopper.
ULP
WAAAAAAA!!
A GRUH...
EEEE!
GRASSHOPPER!!

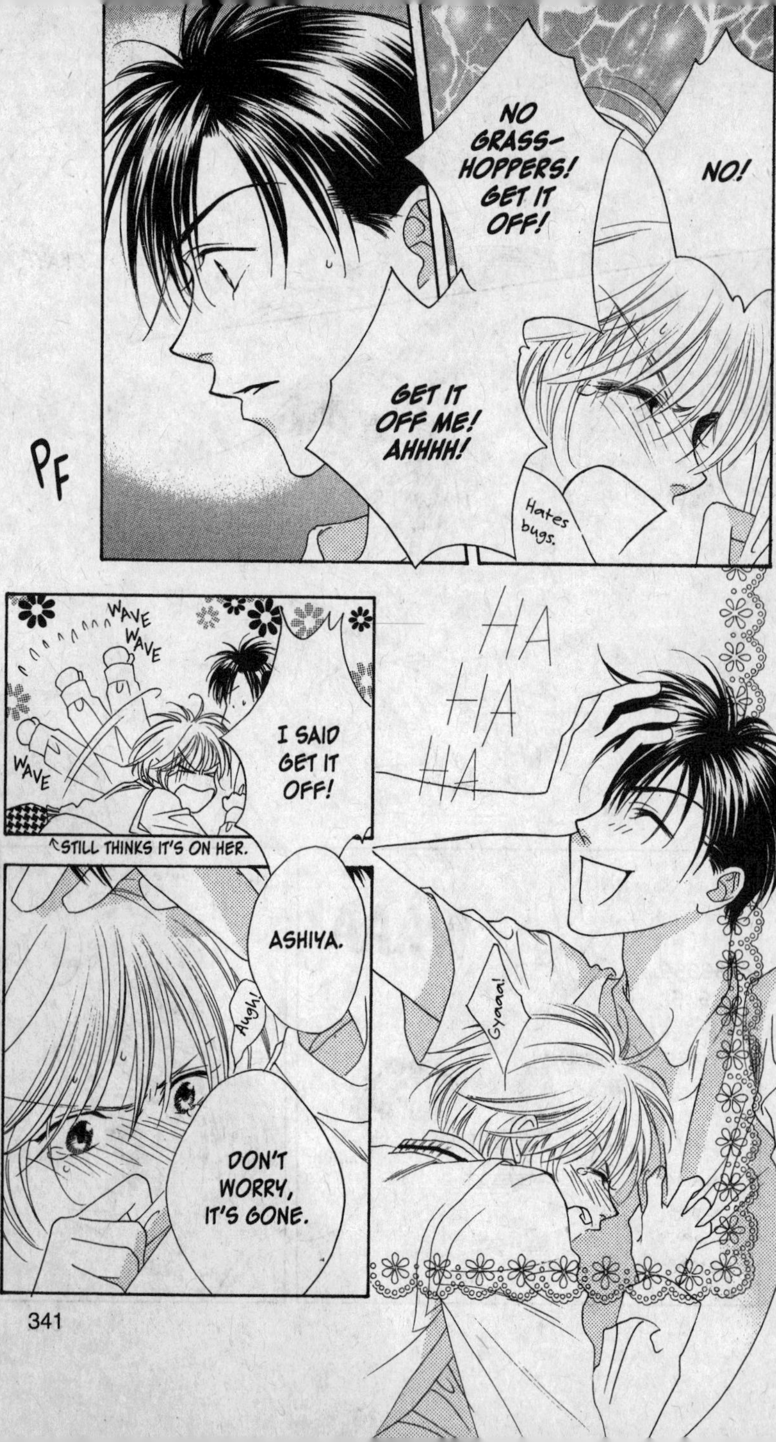
NO!
NO GRASS-HOPPERS! GET IT OFF!
GET IT OFF ME! AHHHH!
Hates bugs.
PF
HA HA HA
Gyaaa!
WAVE WAVE WAVE
I SAID GET IT OFF!
↖STILL THINKS IT'S ON HER.
ASHIYA.
Augh!
DON'T WORRY, IT'S GONE.

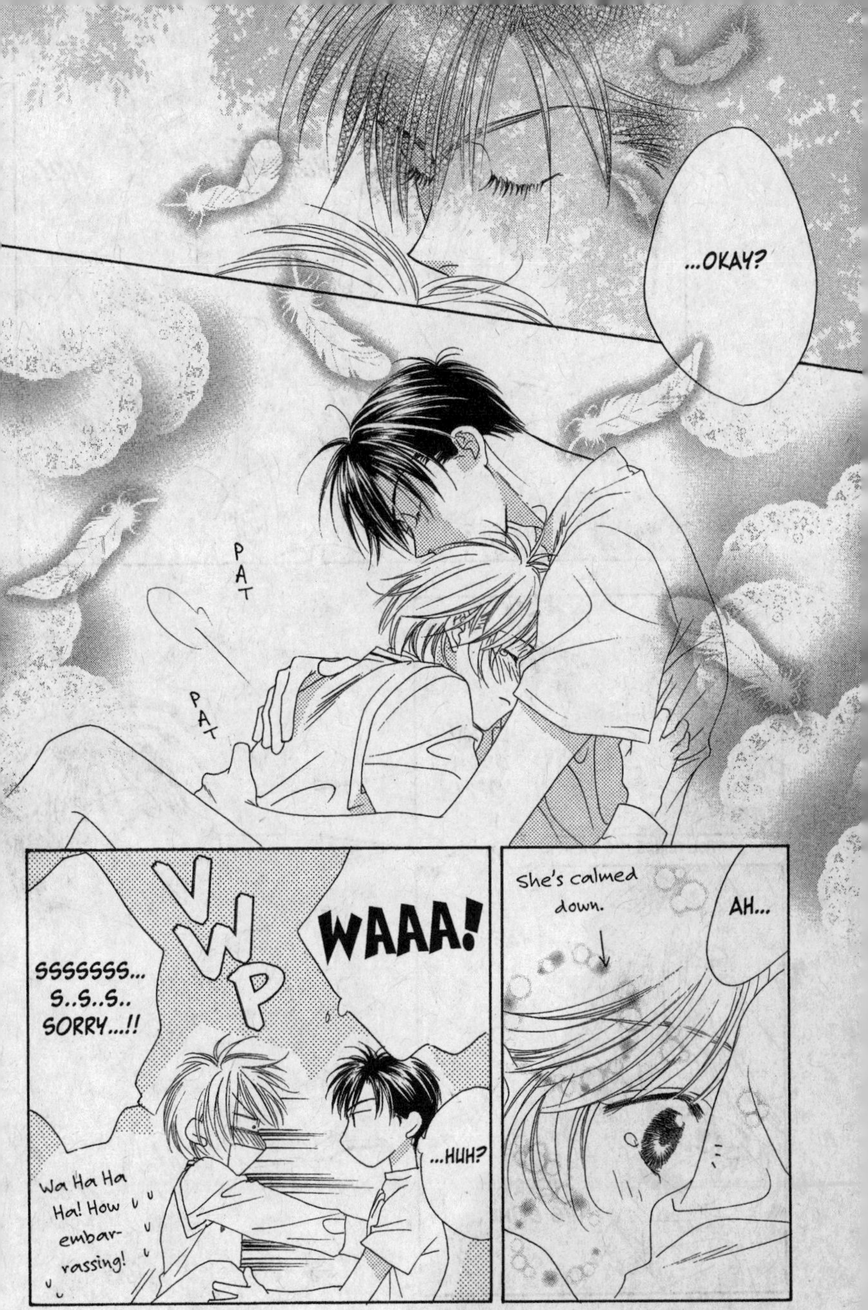
...OKAY?
PAT
PAT
AH...
She's calmed down.
WAAA!
VWP
SSSSSSS... S..S..S.. SORRY...!!
...HUH?
Wa Ha Ha Ha! How embar-rassing!

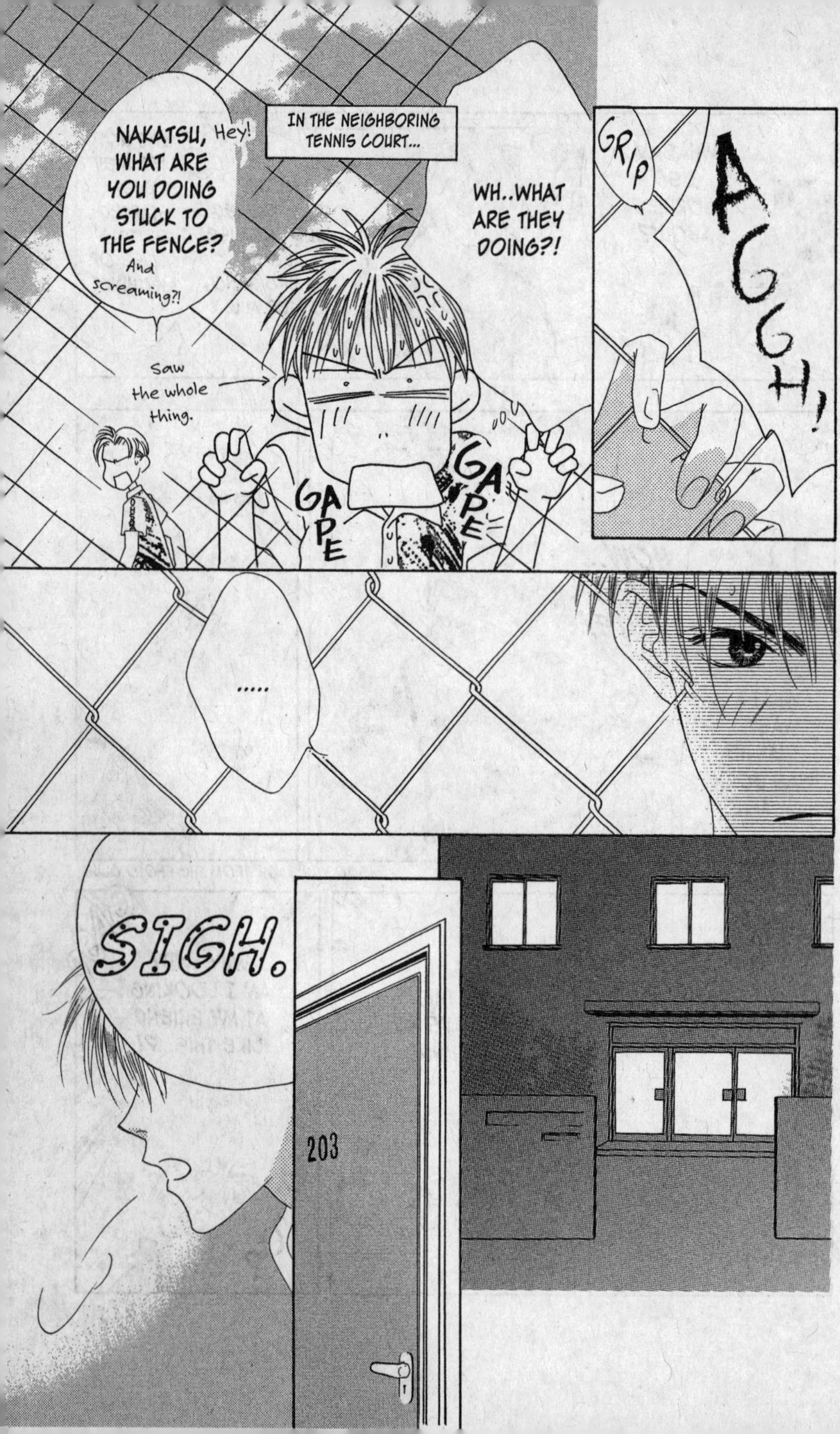
GRIP
AGGH!
IN THE NEIGHBORING TENNIS COURT...
WH..WHAT ARE THEY DOING?!
NAKATSU, WHAT ARE YOU DOING STUCK TO THE FENCE?
Hey!
And screaming?!
Saw the whole thing.
GAPE
GAPE
.....
SIGH.
203

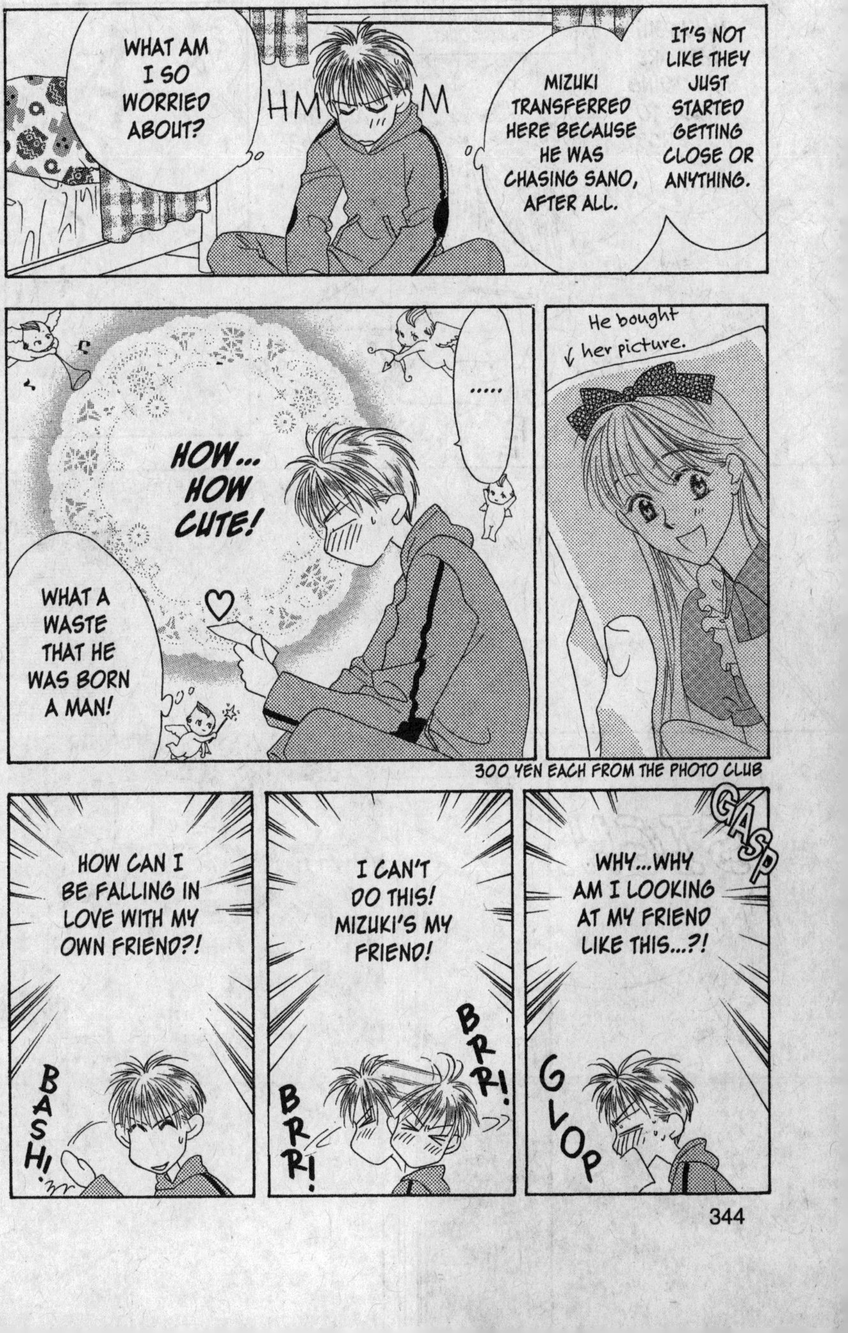
IT'S NOT LIKE THEY JUST STARTED GETTING CLOSE OR ANYTHING.
MIZUKI TRANSFERRED HERE BECAUSE HE WAS CHASING SANO, AFTER ALL.
HMM
WHAT AM I SO WORRIED ABOUT?
He bought her picture.
300 YEN EACH FROM THE PHOTO CLUB
.....
HOW... HOW CUTE!
WHAT A WASTE THAT HE WAS BORN A MAN!
GASP
WHY...WHY AM I LOOKING AT MY FRIEND LIKE THIS...?!
GLOP
I CAN'T DO THIS! MIZUKI'S MY FRIEND!
BRRR!
BRRR!
HOW CAN I BE FALLING IN LOVE WITH MY OWN FRIEND?!
BASH!

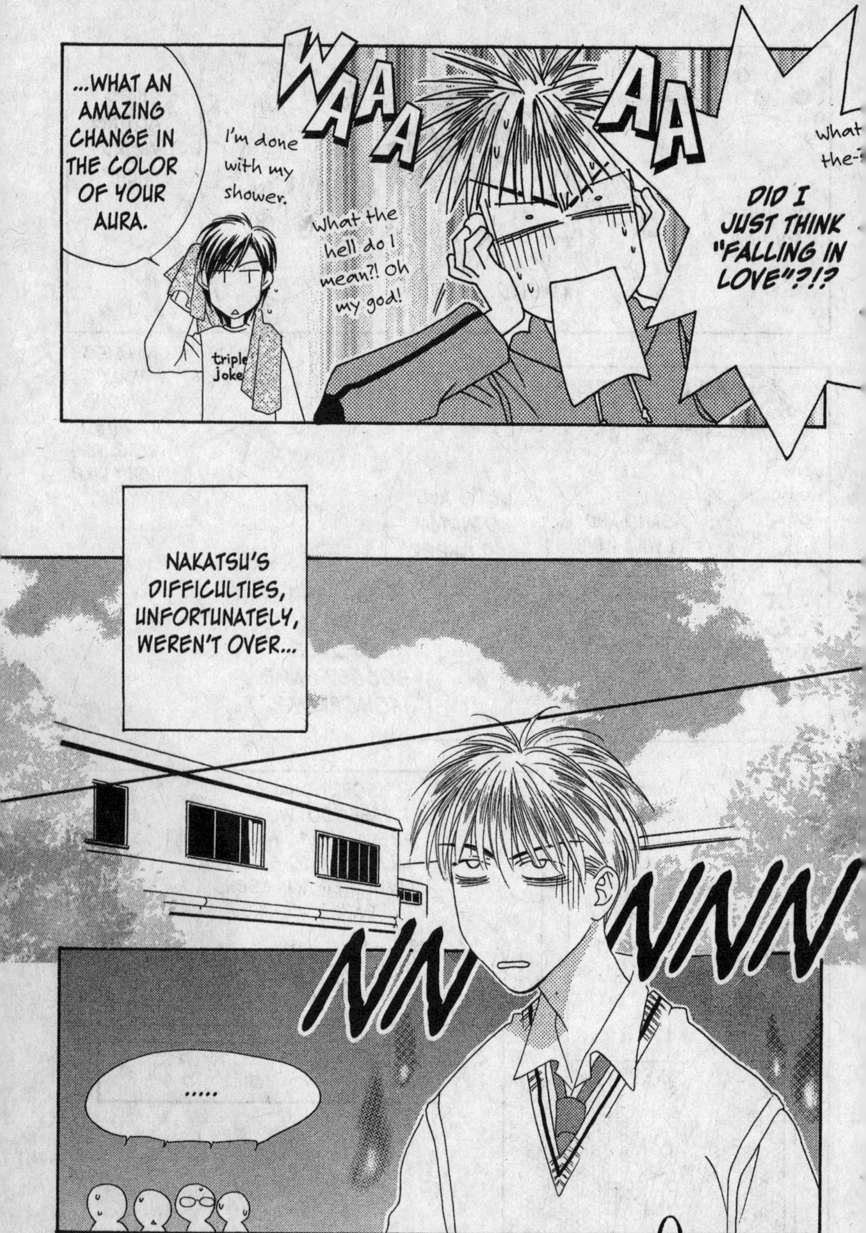

what the-
DID I JUST THINK "FALLING IN LOVE"?!?
WAAAAAA
what the hell do I mean?! Oh my god!
I'm done with my shower.
...WHAT AN AMAZING CHANGE IN THE COLOR OF YOUR AURA.
triple joke
NAKATSU'S DIFFICULTIES, UNFORTUNATELY, WEREN'T OVER...
NNNNNN
.....

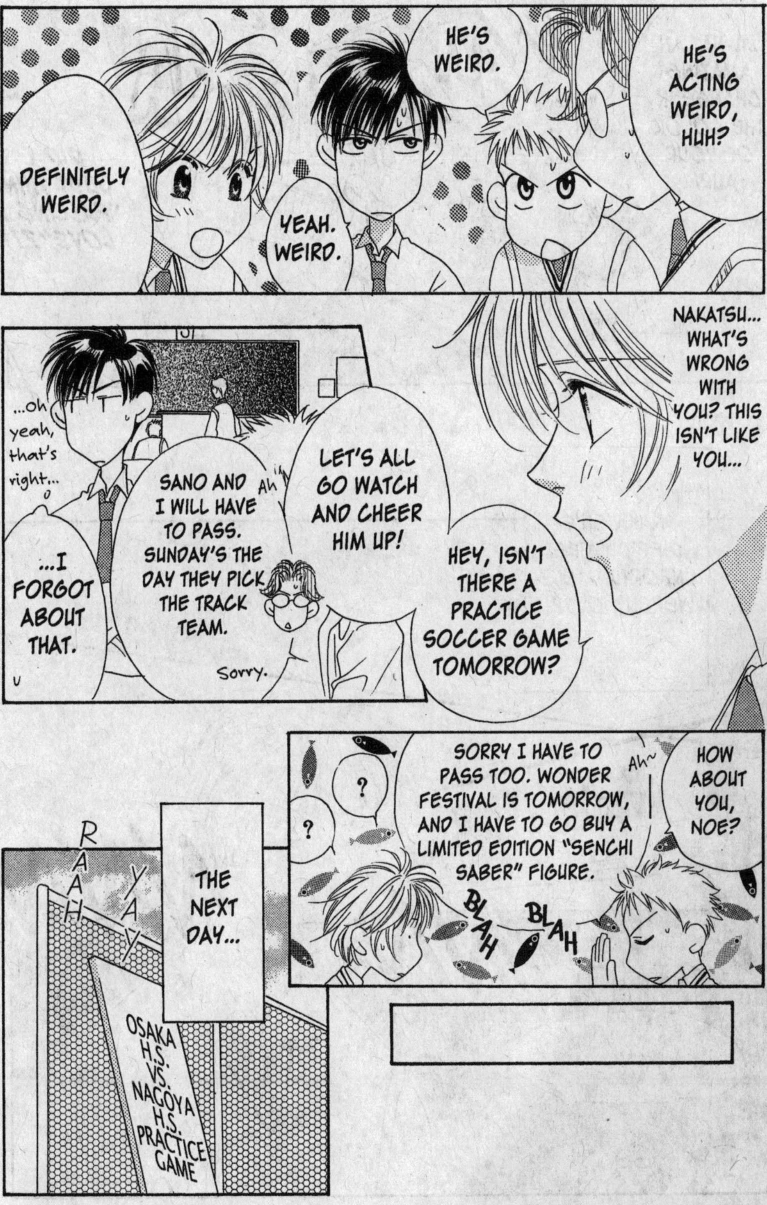
HE'S ACTING WEIRD, HUH?
HE'S WEIRD.
YEAH. WEIRD.
DEFINITELY WEIRD.
NAKATSU... WHAT'S WRONG WITH YOU? THIS ISN'T LIKE YOU...
HEY, ISN'T THERE A PRACTICE SOCCER GAME TOMORROW?
LET'S ALL GO WATCH AND CHEER HIM UP!
Ah
SANO AND I WILL HAVE TO PASS. SUNDAY'S THE DAY THEY PICK THE TRACK TEAM.
...oh yeah, that's right...
...I FORGOT ABOUT THAT.
Sorry.
HOW ABOUT YOU, NOE?
Ah~
SORRY I HAVE TO PASS TOO. WONDER FESTIVAL IS TOMORROW, AND I HAVE TO GO BUY A LIMITED EDITION "SENCHI SABER" FIGURE.
?
?
BLAH
BLAH
THE NEXT DAY...
YAY
RAAH
OSAKA H.S. VS. NAGOYA H.S. PRACTICE GAME

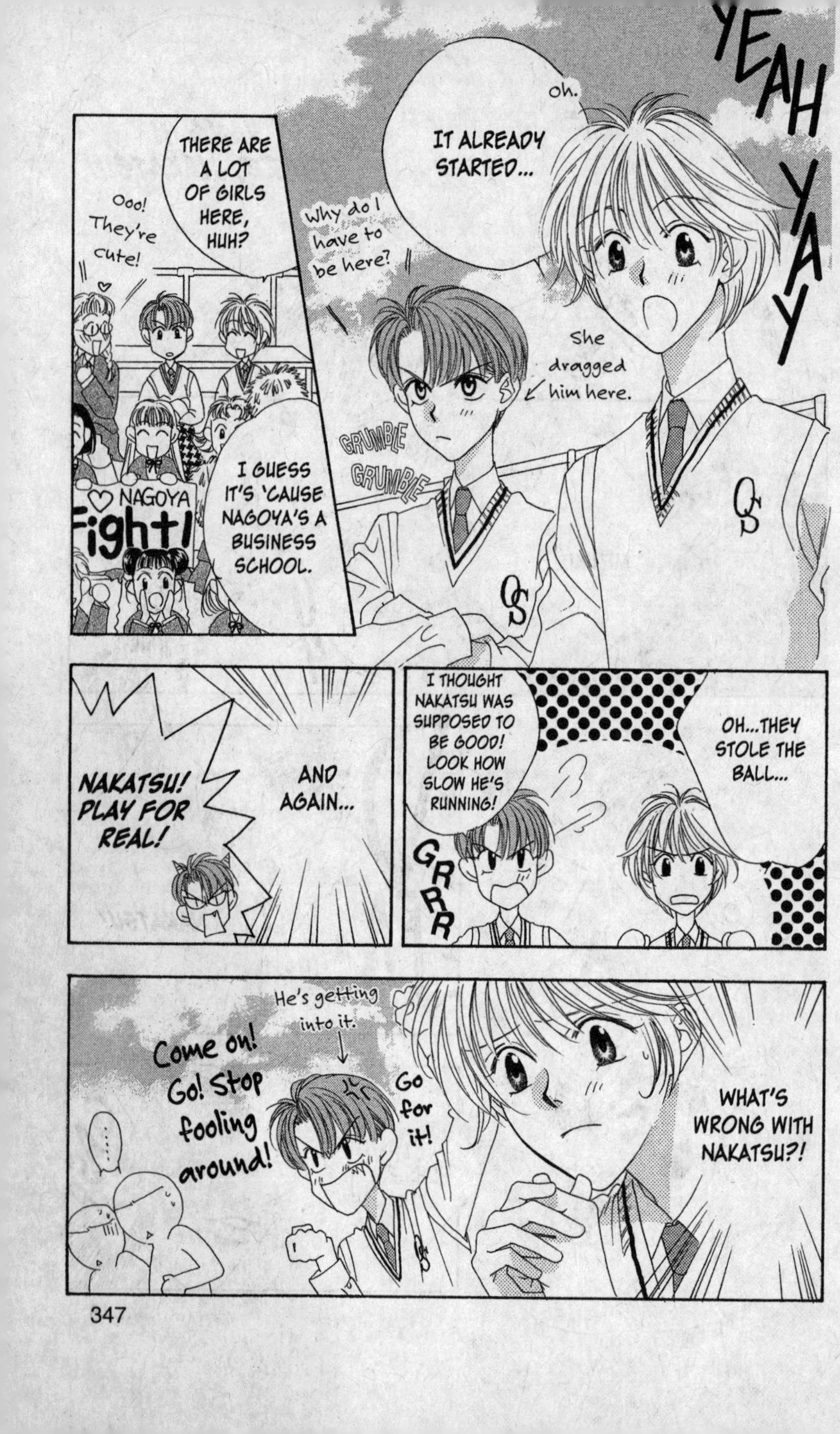
YEAH YAY
oh.
IT ALREADY STARTED...
why do I have to be here?
She dragged him here.
GRUMBLE GRUMBLE
THERE ARE A LOT OF GIRLS HERE, HUH?
Ooo! They're cute!
I GUESS IT'S 'CAUSE NAGOYA'S A BUSINESS SCHOOL.
♥ NAGOYA Fight!
OH...THEY STOLE THE BALL...
I THOUGHT NAKATSU WAS SUPPOSED TO BE GOOD! LOOK HOW SLOW HE'S RUNNING!
GRRR
AND AGAIN...
NAKATSU! PLAY FOR REAL!
WHAT'S WRONG WITH NAKATSU?!
Go for it!
He's getting into it.
Come on! Go! Stop fooling around!
......

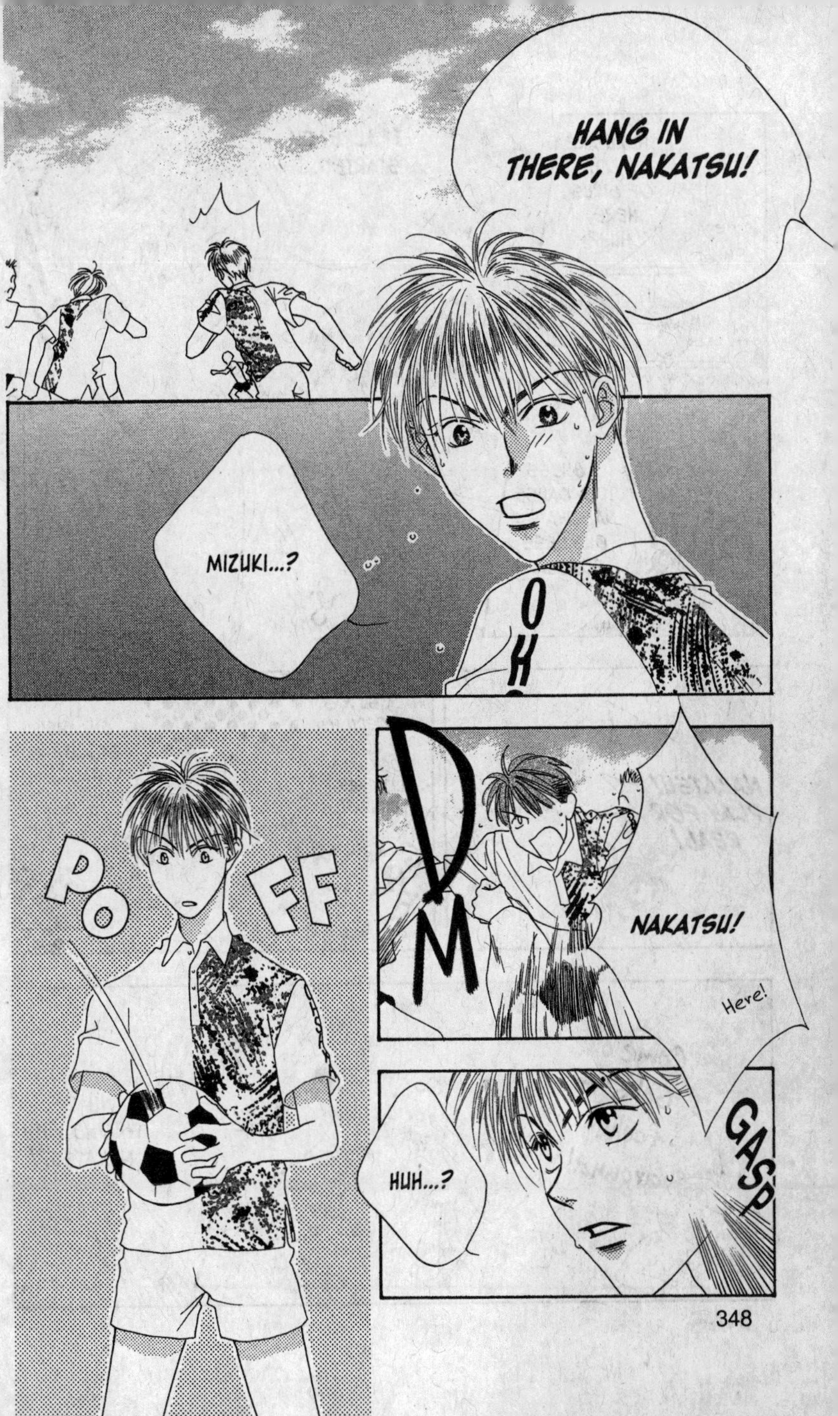
HANG IN THERE, NAKATSU!
MIZUKI...?
NAKATSU!
Here!
GASP
HUH...?
POFF

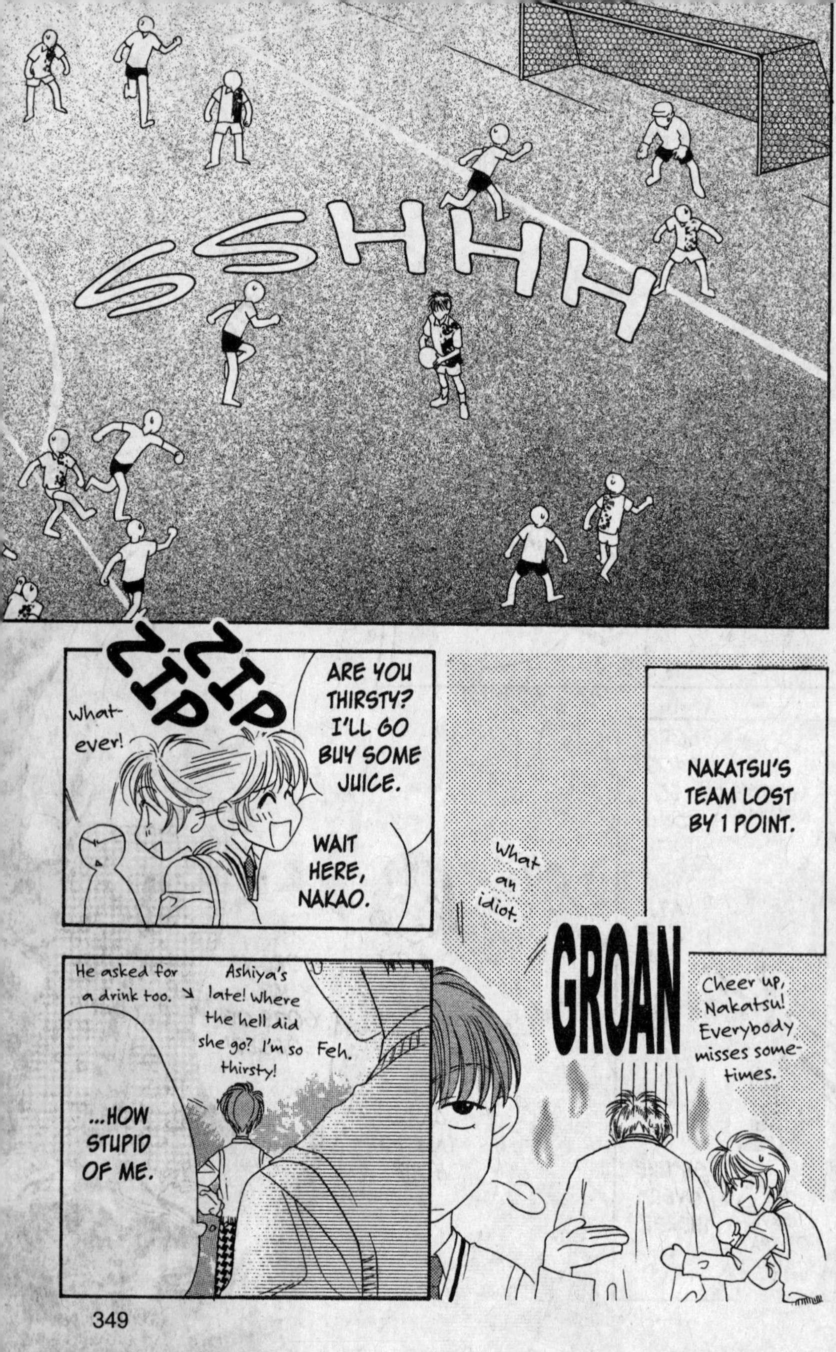
SSHHH
NAKATSU'S TEAM LOST BY 1 POINT.
What an idiot.
GROAN
Cheer up, Nakatsu! Everybody misses some-times.
ARE YOU THIRSTY? I'LL GO BUY SOME JUICE.
WAIT HERE, NAKAO.
ZIP ZIP
What-ever!
Ashiya's late! Where the hell did she go? I'm so thirsty!
Feh.
He asked for a drink too.
...HOW STUPID OF ME.

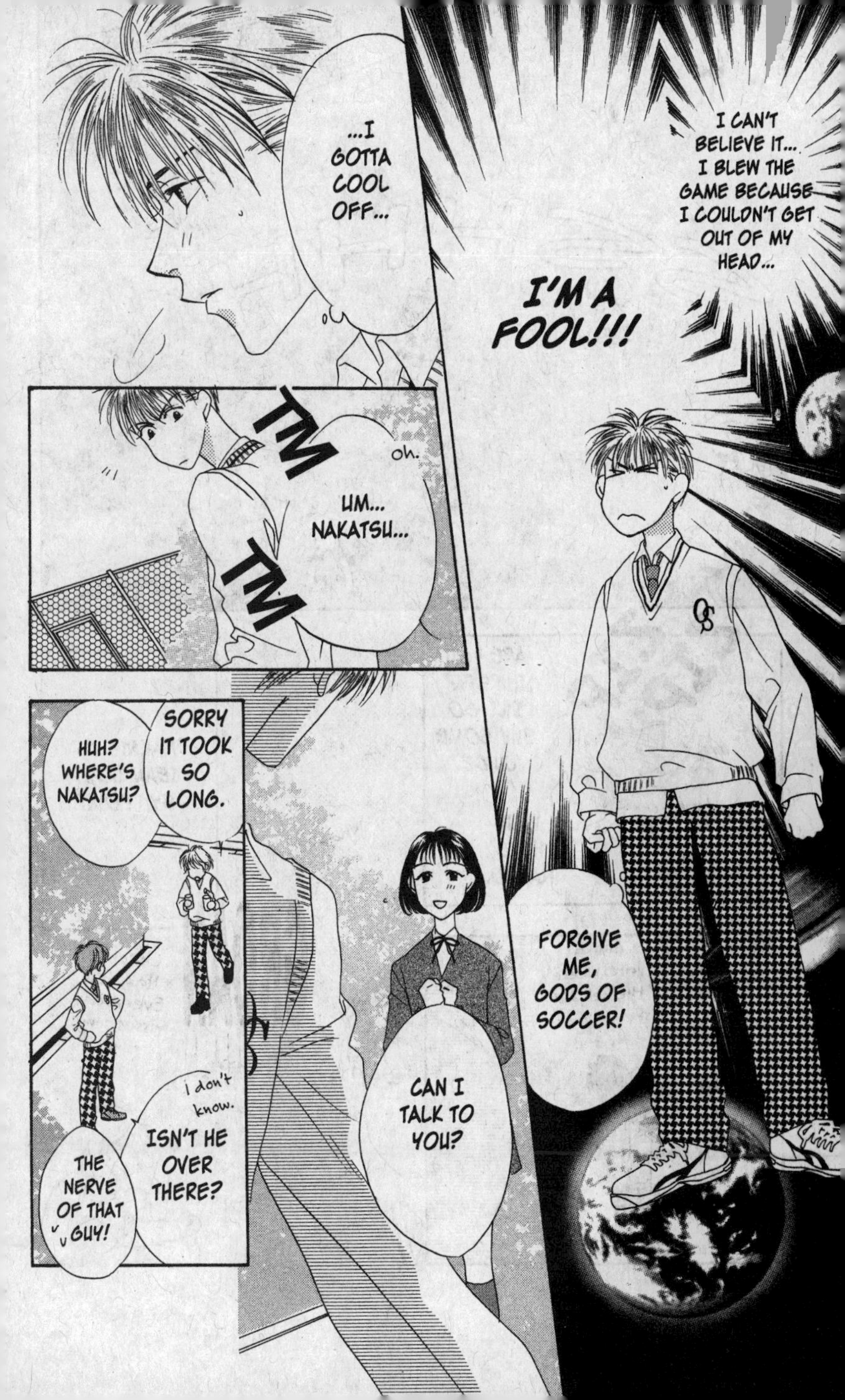
I CAN'T BELIEVE IT... I BLEW THE GAME BECAUSE I COULDN'T GET OUT OF MY HEAD...
I'M A FOOL!!!
FORGIVE ME, GODS OF SOCCER!
...I GOTTA COOL OFF...
TM
TM
oh.
UM... NAKATSU...
CAN I TALK TO YOU?
SORRY IT TOOK SO LONG.
HUH? WHERE'S NAKATSU?
I don't know.
ISN'T HE OVER THERE?
THE NERVE OF THAT GUY!

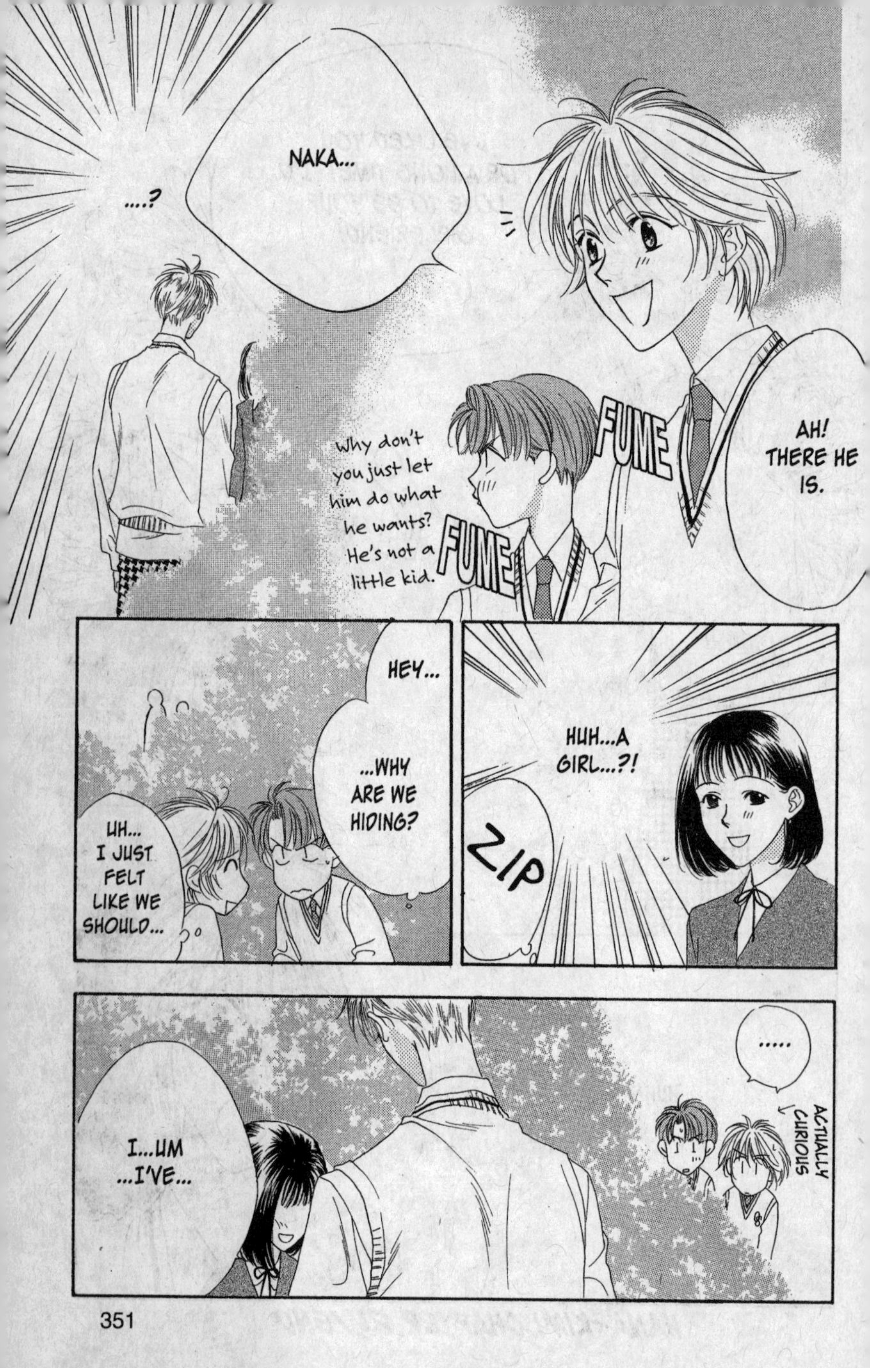
AH! THERE HE IS.
FUME
FUME
Why don't you just let him do what he wants? He's not a little kid.
NAKA...
....?
HUH...A GIRL...?!
ZIP
HEY...
...WHY ARE WE HIDING?
UH... I JUST FELT LIKE WE SHOULD...
.....
ACTUALLY CURIOUS
I...UM ...I'VE...

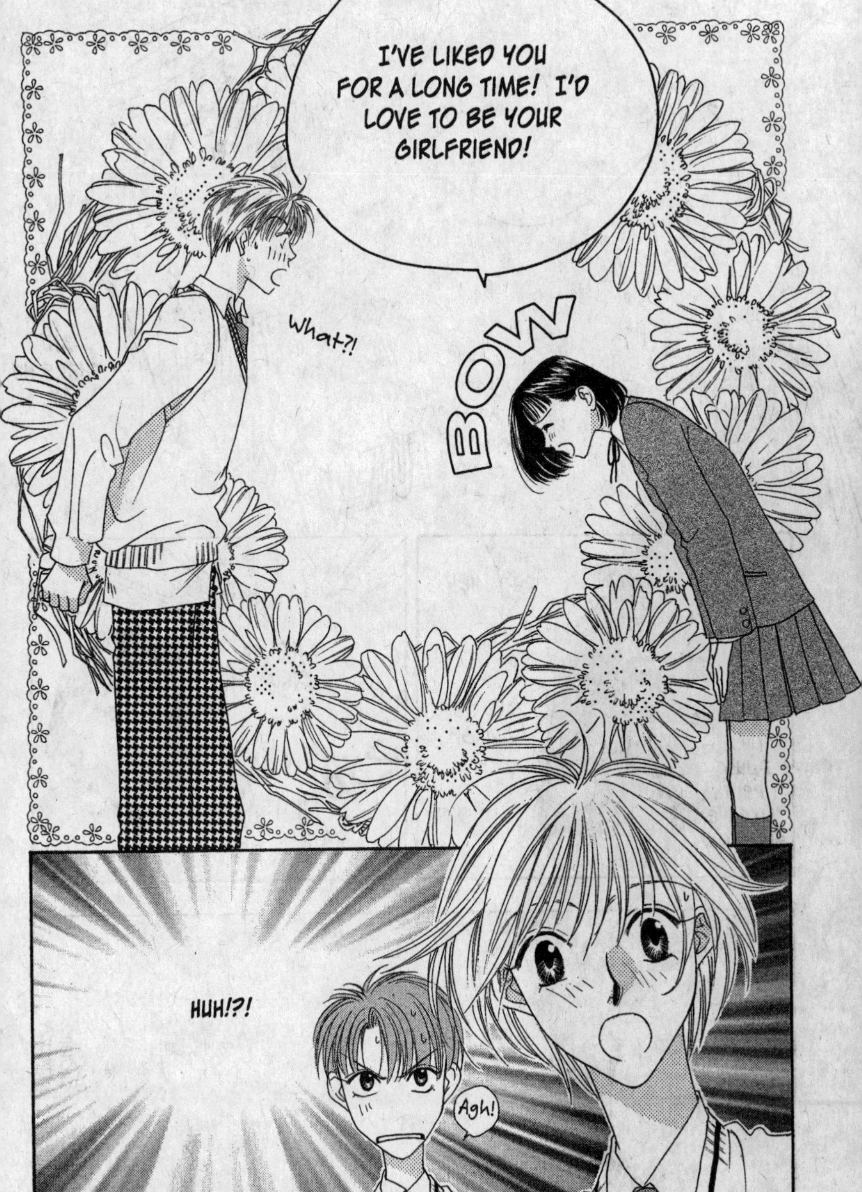
I'VE LIKED YOU FOR A LONG TIME! I'D LOVE TO BE YOUR GIRLFRIEND!
BOW
What?!
HUH!?!
Agh!

HANA-KIMI CHAPTER 24/END

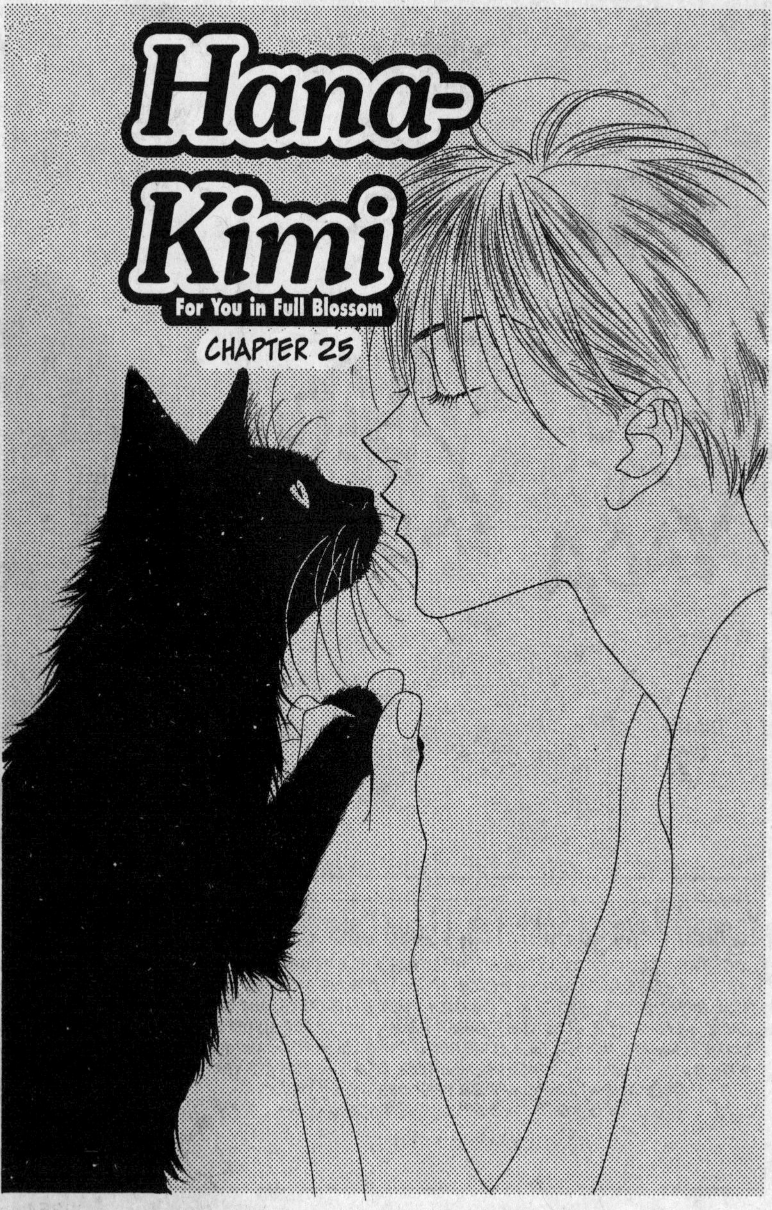
Hana-
Kimi
For You in Full Blossom
CHAPTER 25

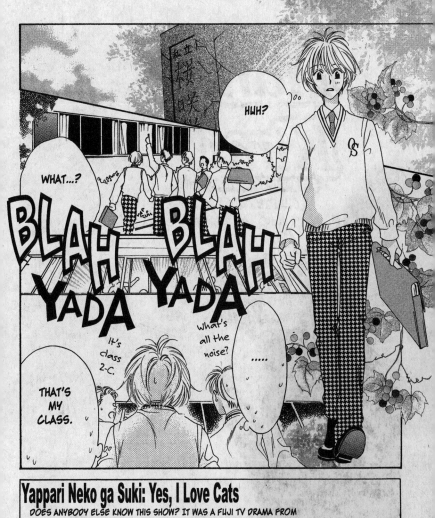

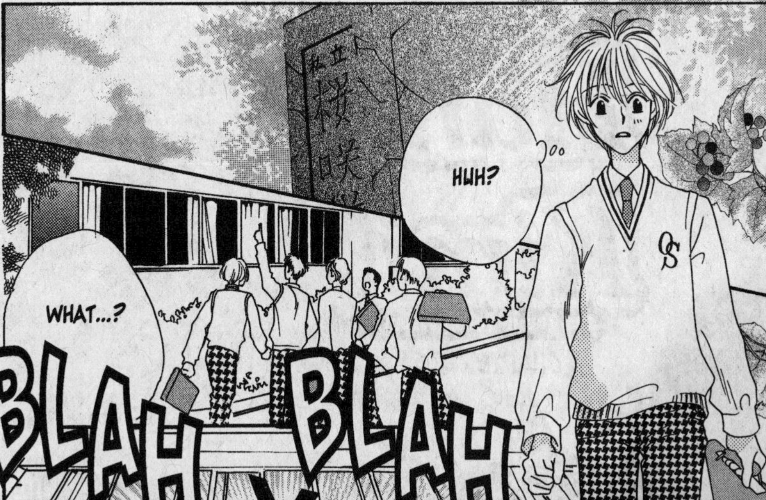
HUH?
WHAT...?
BLAH BLAH
YADA YADA
What's all the noise?
.....
It's class 2-C.
THAT'S MY CLASS.

Yappari Neko ga Suki: Yes, I Love Cats

DOES ANYBODY ELSE KNOW THIS SHOW? IT WAS A FUJI TV DRAMA FROM ABOUT 10 YEARS AGO (WRITTEN BY KOKI MITANI). IT'S THE STORY OF THE THREE ONDA SISTERS. (THOSE ARE THE ONLY THREE CHARACTERS, AND THEN THERE'S SACHIKO THE CAT.) IT'S A FAMILY DRAMA. THE OLDER SISTER IS KAYANO (MASAKO MOTAI), THE NEXT IS REIKO (SHIGERU MUROI), AND THE YOUNGEST IS KIMIE (SATOMI KOBAYASHI). THEIR RELATIONSHIPS ARE VERY INTERESTING♥. THERE ARE 26 EPISODES OUT ON VIDEO. (A NEW ONE CAME OUT THIS YEAR TOO.)

See it if you get a chance!

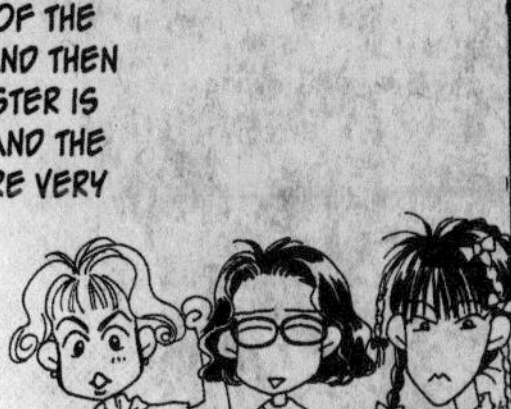

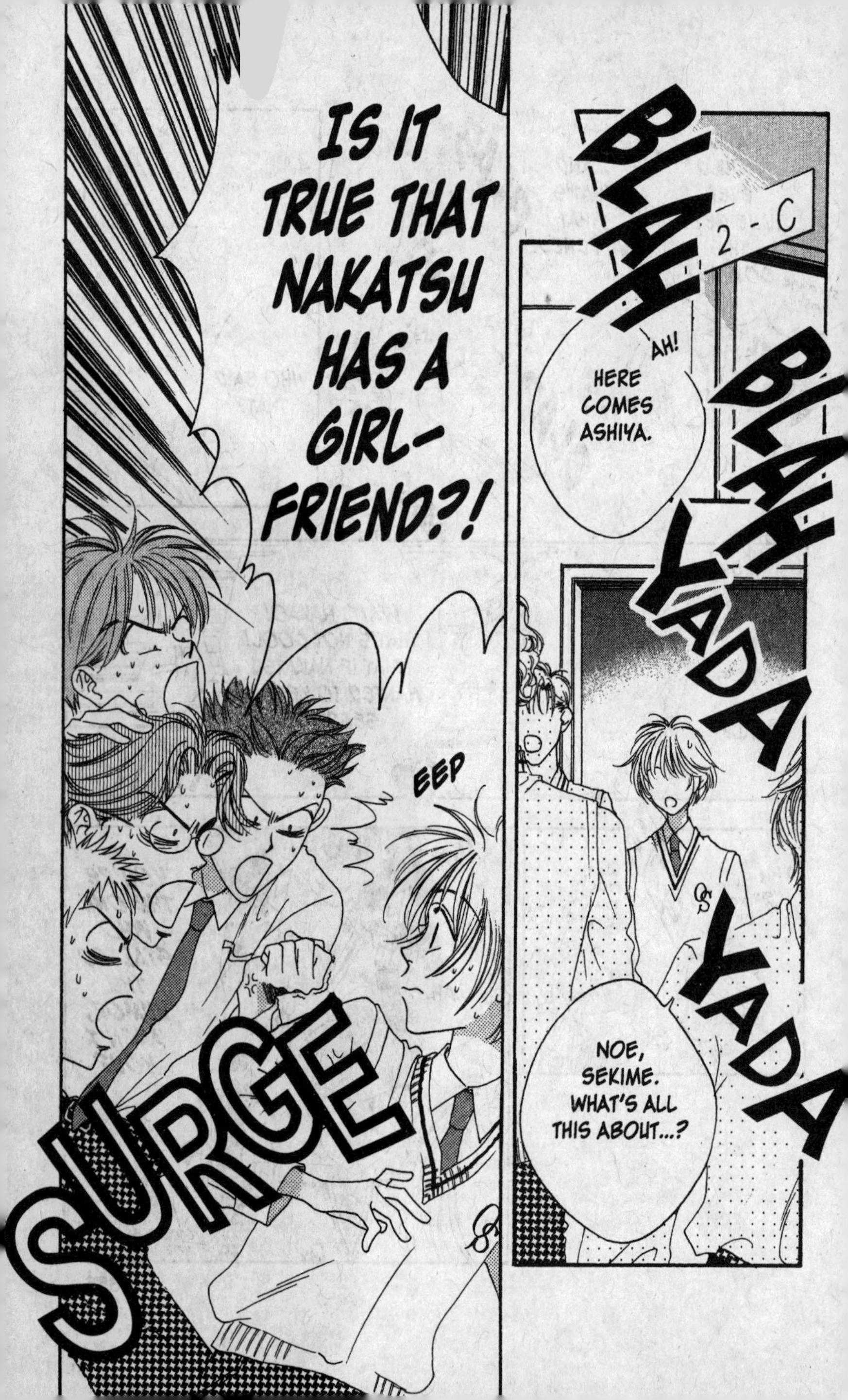
BLAH BLAH
2-C
AH!
HERE COMES ASHIYA.
YADA YADA
YADA YADA
NOE, SEKIME. WHAT'S ALL THIS ABOUT...?
IS IT TRUE THAT NAKATSU HAS A GIRL-FRIEND?!
EEP
SURGE

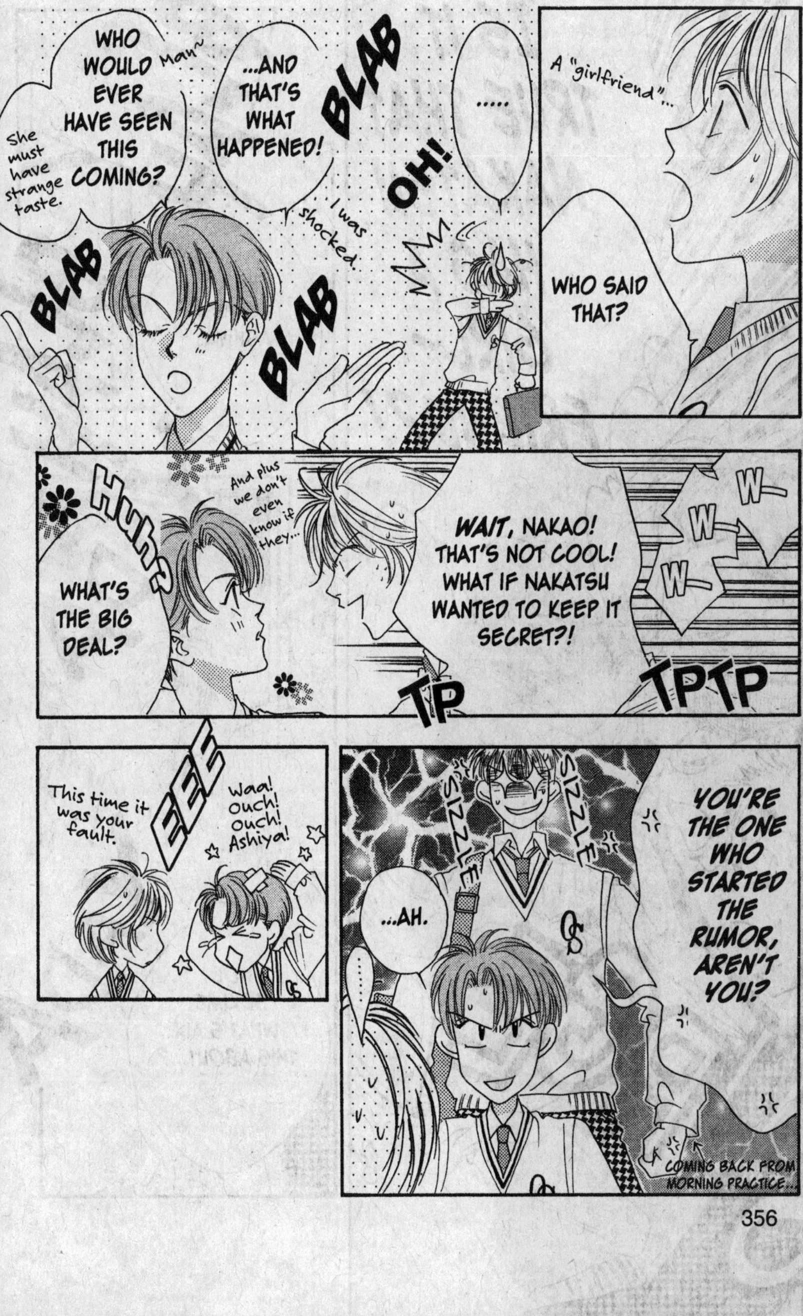
A "girlfriend"...
WHO SAID THAT?
.....
OH!
I was shocked.
BLAB
...AND THAT'S WHAT HAPPENED!
WHO WOULD EVER HAVE SEEN THIS COMING?
Man~
She must have strange taste.
BLAB
BLAB
W
W
W
WAIT, NAKAO! THAT'S NOT COOL! WHAT IF NAKATSU WANTED TO KEEP IT SECRET?!
TPTP
TP
And plus we don't even know if they...
Huh?
WHAT'S THE BIG DEAL?
YOU'RE THE ONE WHO STARTED THE RUMOR, AREN'T YOU?
SIZZLE
SIZZLE
...AH.
COMING BACK FROM MORNING PRACTICE...
EEE
Waa! Ouch! Ouch! Ashiya!
This time it was your fault.

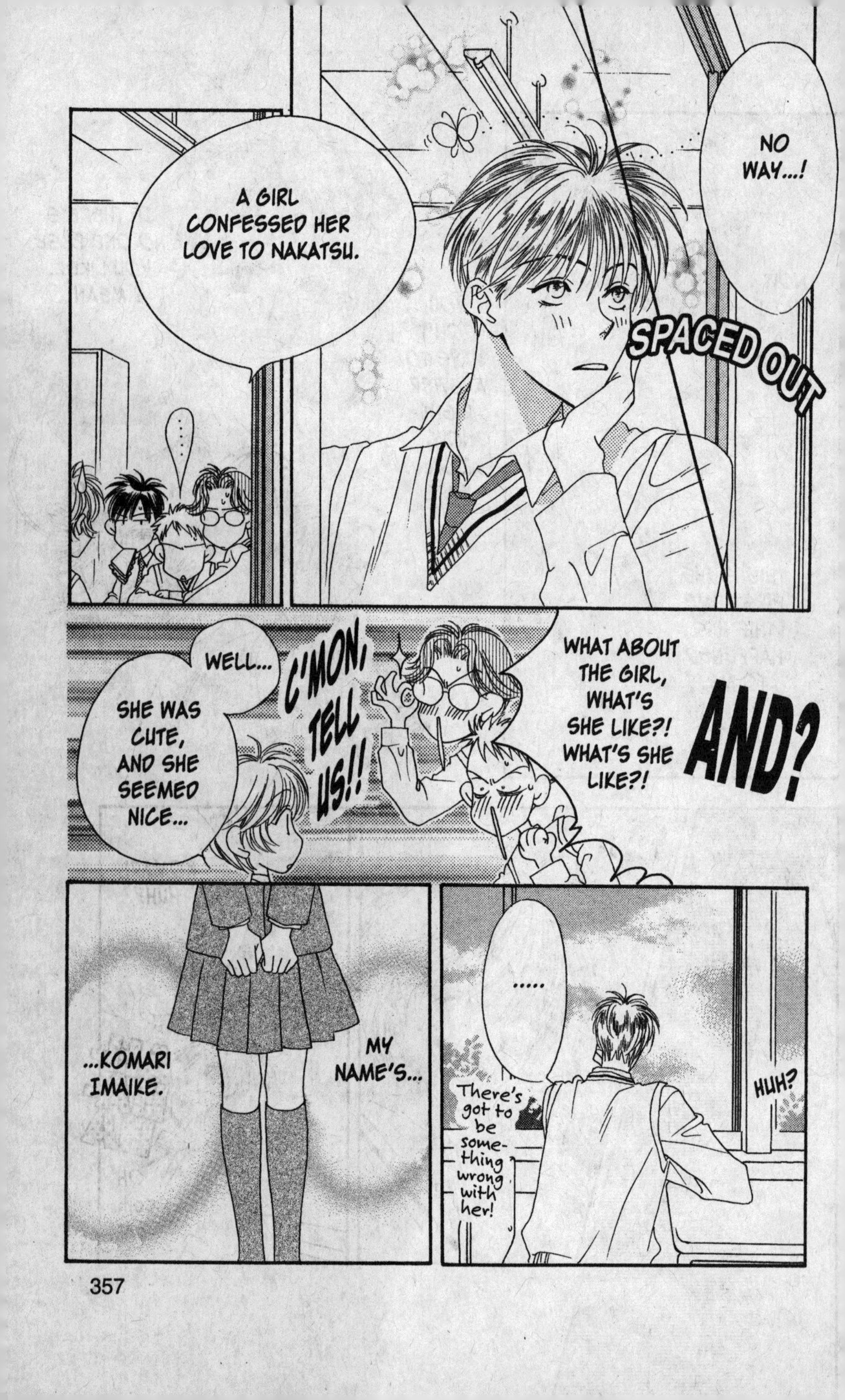
NO WAY...!
SPACED OUT
A GIRL CONFESSED HER LOVE TO NAKATSU.
...
AND?
WHAT ABOUT THE GIRL, WHAT'S SHE LIKE?! WHAT'S SHE LIKE?!
C'MON, TELL US!!
WELL...
SHE WAS CUTE, AND SHE SEEMED NICE...
HUH?
.....
There's got to be some-thing wrong with her!
MY NAME'S...
...KOMARI IMAIKE.

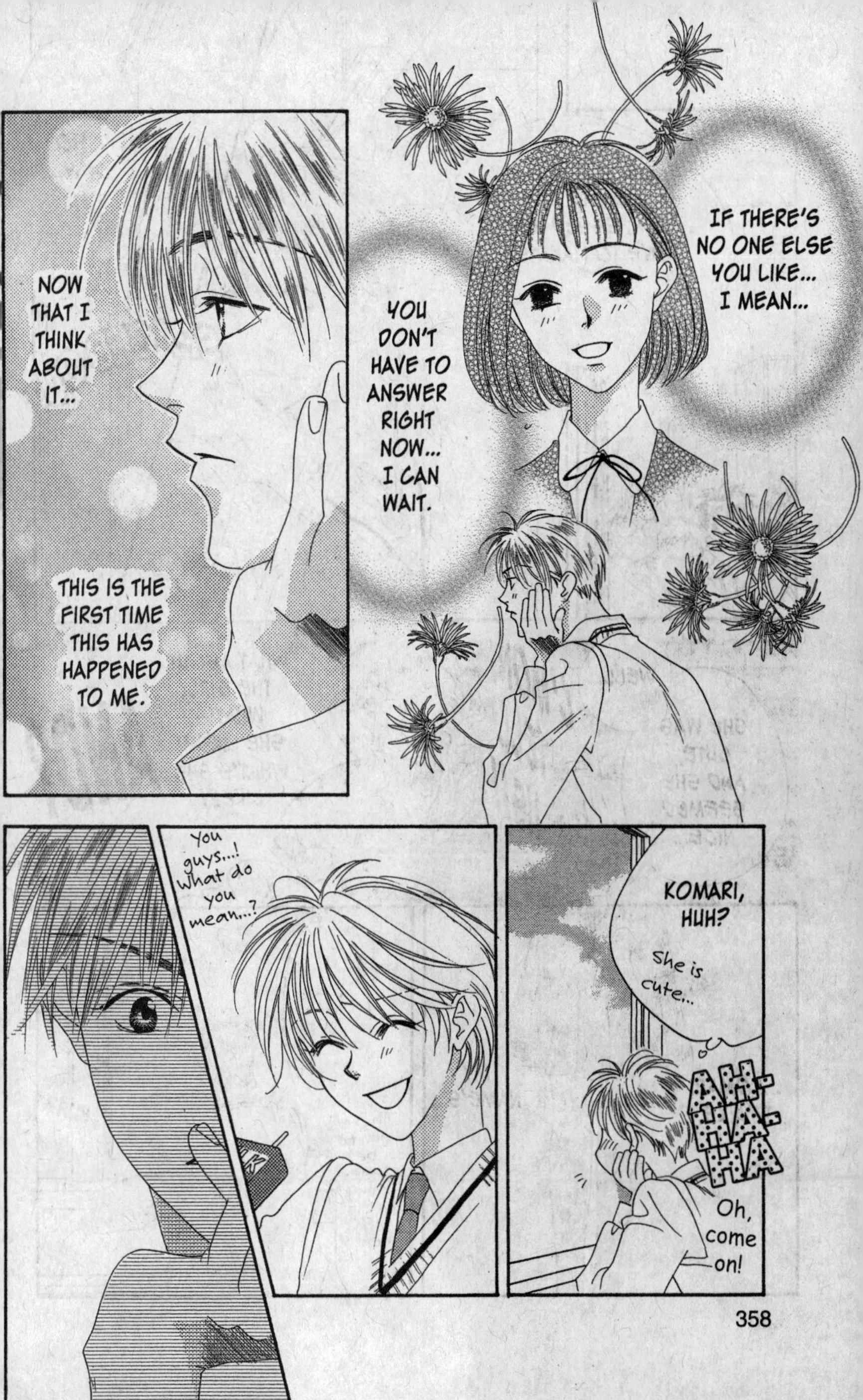
IF THERE'S NO ONE ELSE YOU LIKE... I MEAN...
YOU DON'T HAVE TO ANSWER RIGHT NOW... I CAN WAIT.
NOW THAT I THINK ABOUT IT...
THIS IS THE FIRST TIME THIS HAS HAPPENED TO ME.
KOMARI, HUH?
She is cute...
AH-HA-HA
Oh, come on!
You guys...! what do you mean...?

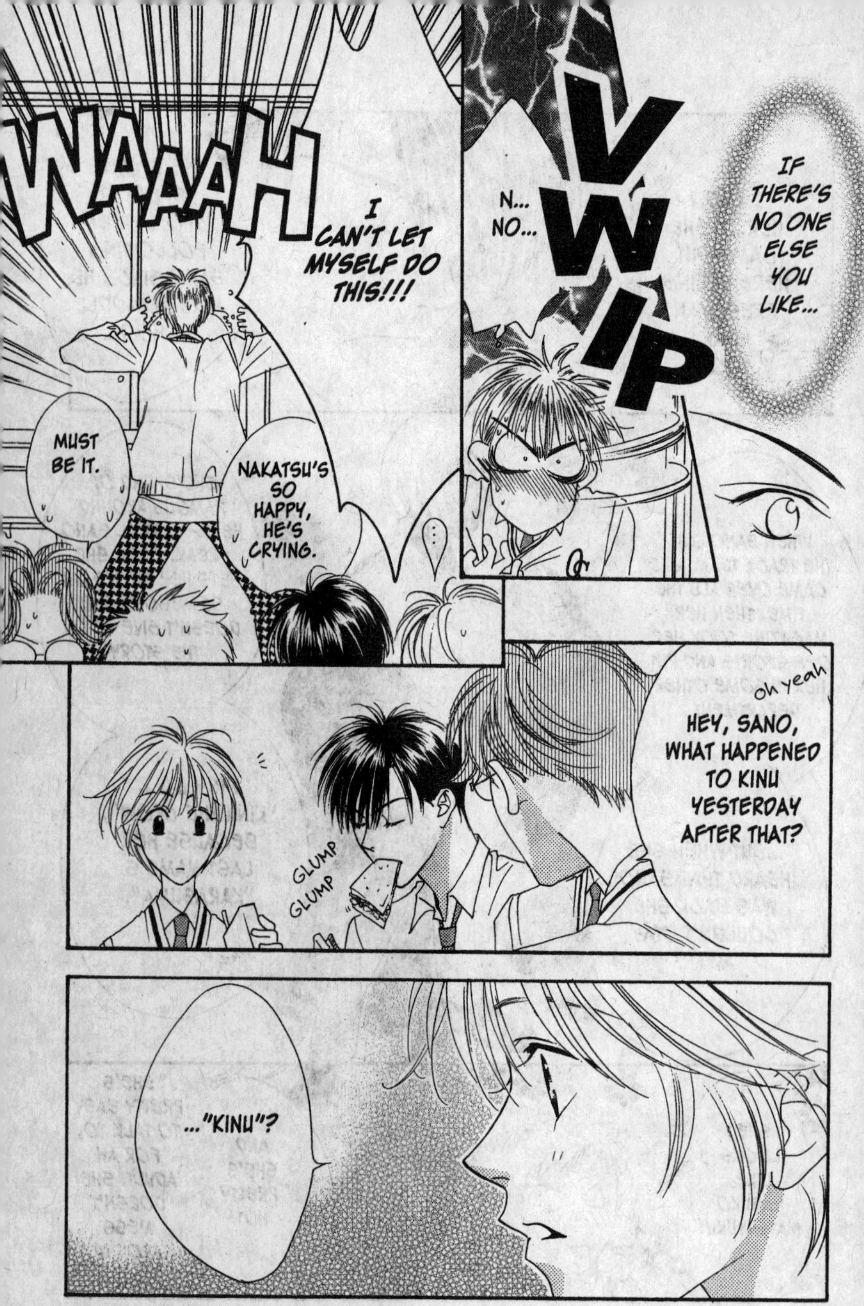
IF THERE'S NO ONE ELSE YOU LIKE...
WIP
N... NO...
WAAAH
I CAN'T LET MYSELF DO THIS!!!
NAKATSU'S SO HAPPY, HE'S CRYING.
MUST BE IT.
Oh yeah
HEY, SANO, WHAT HAPPENED TO KINU YESTERDAY AFTER THAT?
GLUMP GLUMP
..."KINU"?

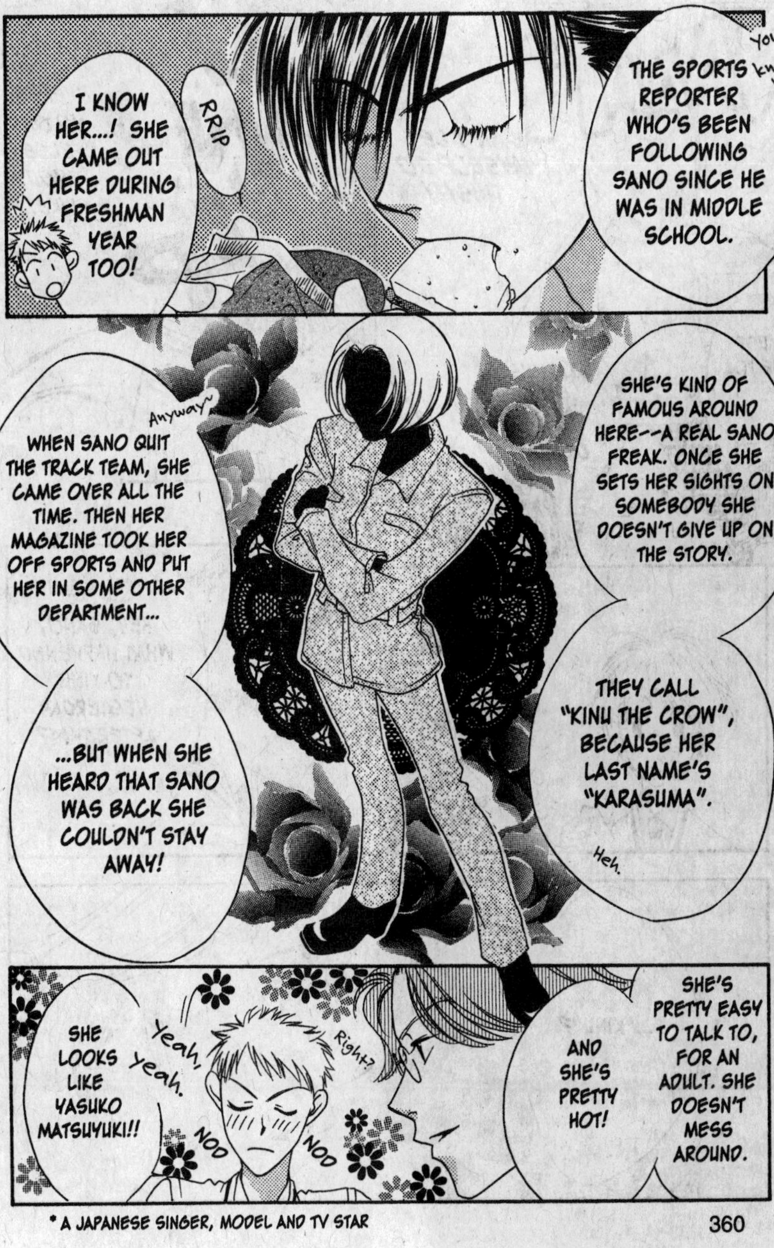
THE SPORTS REPORTER WHO'S BEEN FOLLOWING SANO SINCE HE WAS IN MIDDLE SCHOOL.
You know
RRIP
I KNOW HER...! SHE CAME OUT HERE DURING FRESHMAN YEAR TOO!
SHE'S KIND OF FAMOUS AROUND HERE--A REAL SANO FREAK. ONCE SHE SETS HER SIGHTS ON SOMEBODY SHE DOESN'T GIVE UP ON THE STORY.
THEY CALL "KINU THE CROW", BECAUSE HER LAST NAME'S "KARASUMA".
Heh.
Anyway~
WHEN SANO QUIT THE TRACK TEAM, SHE CAME OVER ALL THE TIME. THEN HER MAGAZINE TOOK HER OFF SPORTS AND PUT HER IN SOME OTHER DEPARTMENT...
...BUT WHEN SHE HEARD THAT SANO WAS BACK SHE COULDN'T STAY AWAY!
SHE'S PRETTY EASY TO TALK TO, FOR AN ADULT. SHE DOESN'T MESS AROUND.
AND SHE'S PRETTY HOT!
Right?
Yeah, yeah.
NOO
NOO
SHE LOOKS LIKE YASUKO MATSUYUKI!!

* A JAPANESE SINGER, MODEL AND TV STAR

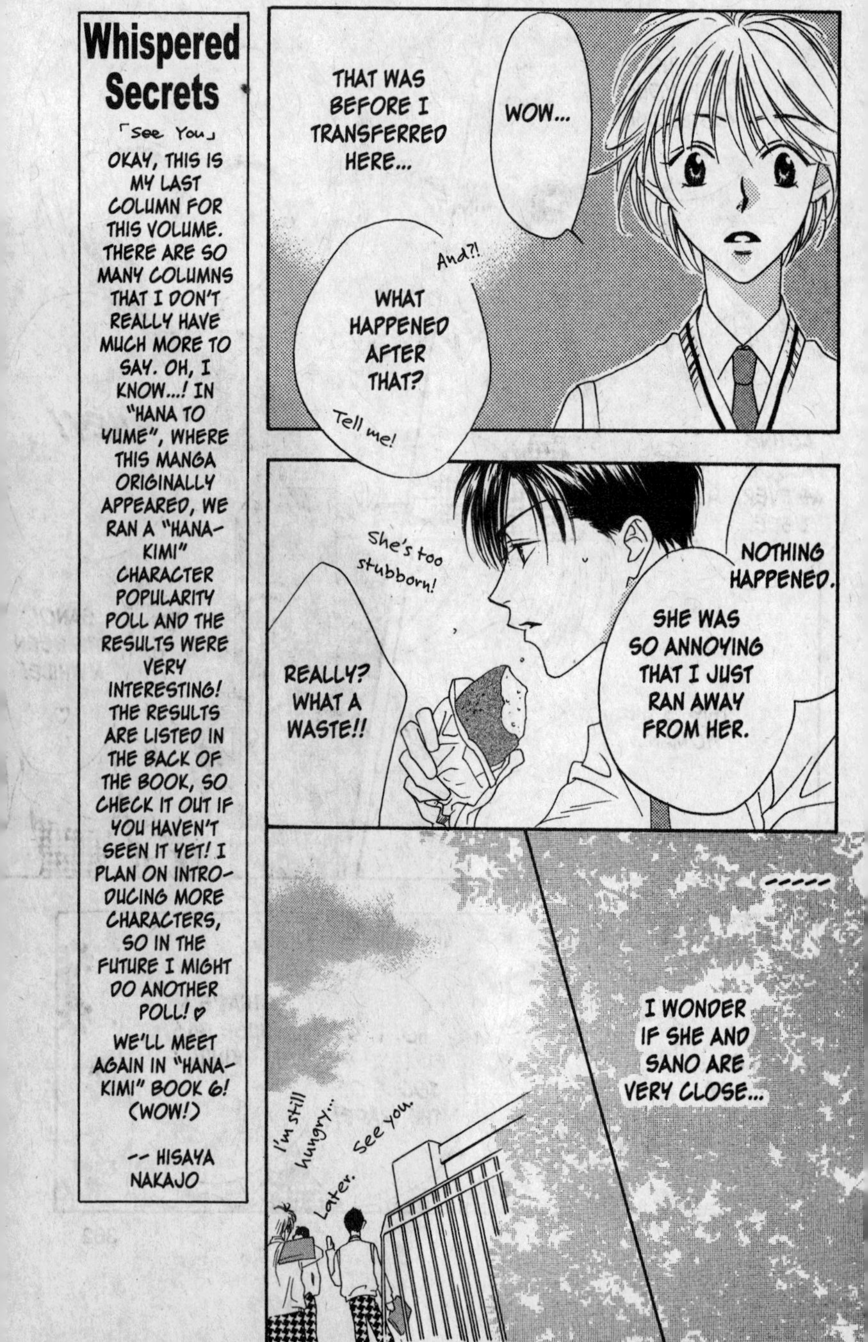
WOW...
THAT WAS BEFORE I TRANSFERRED HERE...
And?!
WHAT HAPPENED AFTER THAT?
Tell me!
NOTHING HAPPENED.
SHE WAS SO ANNOYING THAT I JUST RAN AWAY FROM HER.
She's too stubborn!
REALLY? WHAT A WASTE!!

I WONDER IF SHE AND SANO ARE VERY CLOSE...
See you.
Later.
I'm still hungry...

Whispered Secrets

「See You」

OKAY, THIS IS MY LAST COLUMN FOR THIS VOLUME. THERE ARE SO MANY COLUMNS THAT I DON'T REALLY HAVE MUCH MORE TO SAY. OH, I KNOW...! IN "HANA TO YUME", WHERE THIS MANGA ORIGINALLY APPEARED, WE RAN A "HANA-KIMI" CHARACTER POPULARITY POLL AND THE RESULTS WERE VERY INTERESTING! THE RESULTS ARE LISTED IN THE BACK OF THE BOOK, SO CHECK IT OUT IF YOU HAVEN'T SEEN IT YET! I PLAN ON INTRODUCING MORE CHARACTERS, SO IN THE FUTURE I MIGHT DO ANOTHER POLL! ♡

WE'LL MEET AGAIN IN "HANA-KIMI" BOOK 6! (WOW!)

-- HISAYA NAKAJO

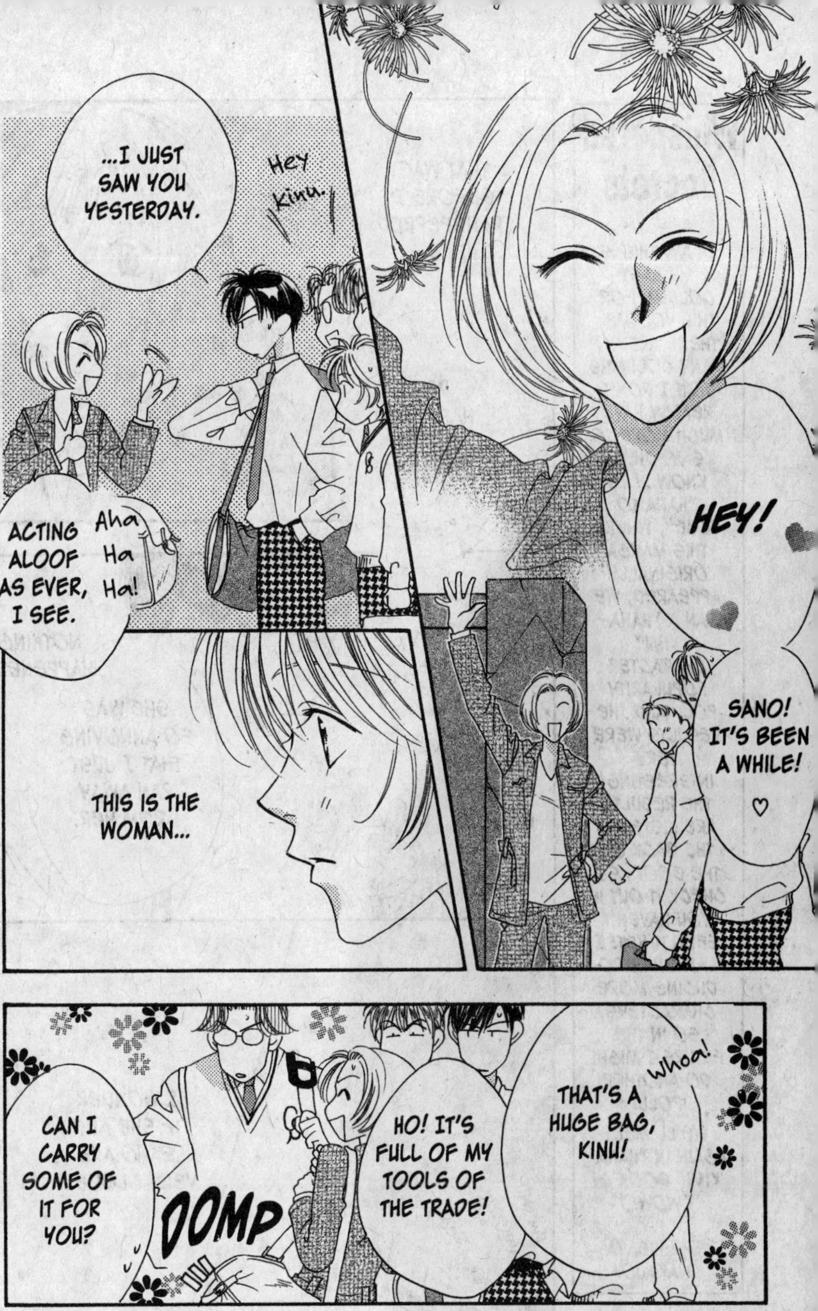
HEY!
SANO! IT'S BEEN A WHILE!
Hey Kinu.
...I JUST SAW YOU YESTERDAY.
Aha Ha Ha!
ACTING ALOOF AS EVER, I SEE.
THIS IS THE WOMAN...
Whoa!
THAT'S A HUGE BAG, KINU!
HO! IT'S FULL OF MY TOOLS OF THE TRADE!
DOMP
CAN I CARRY SOME OF IT FOR YOU?

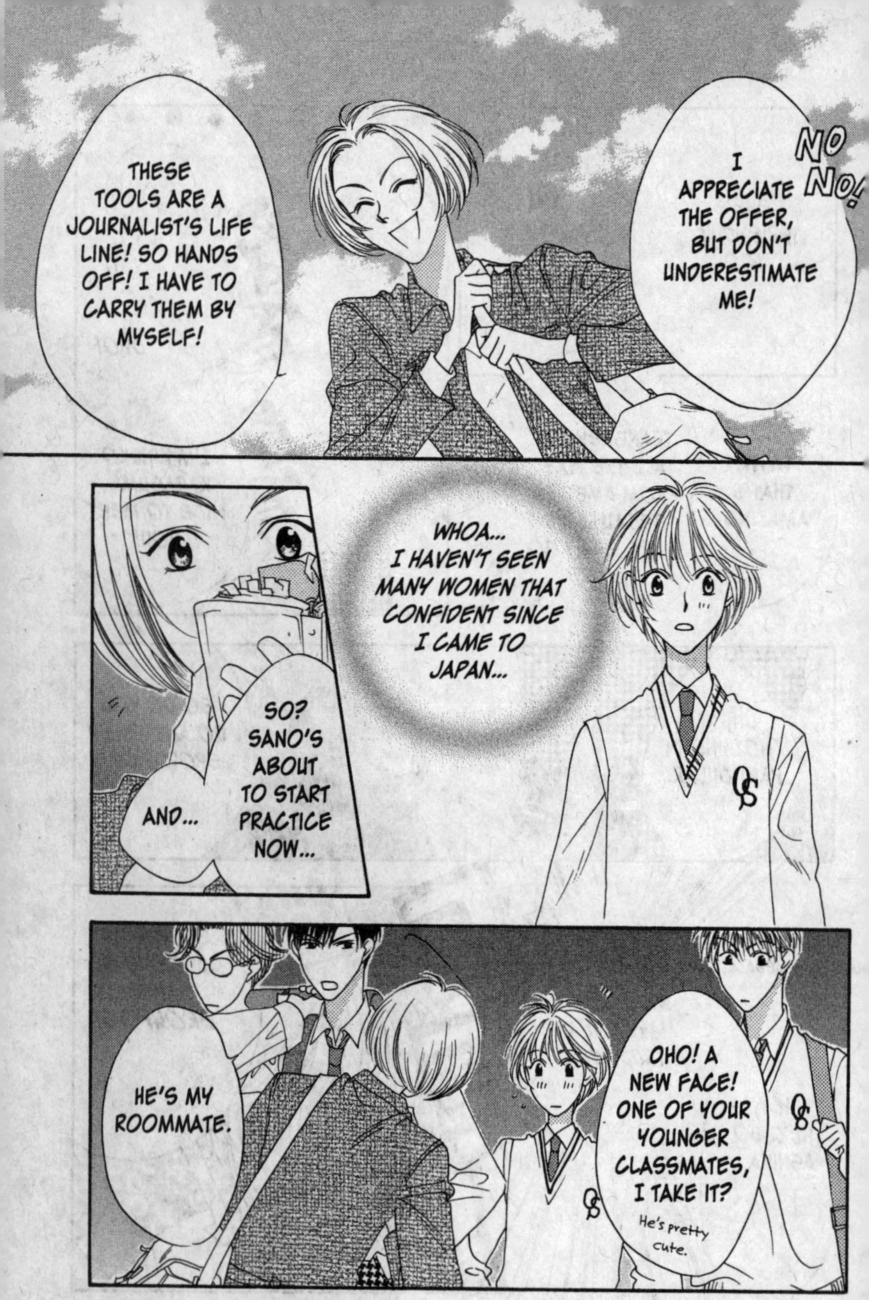
NO NO!
I APPRECIATE THE OFFER, BUT DON'T UNDERESTIMATE ME!
THESE TOOLS ARE A JOURNALIST'S LIFE LINE! SO HANDS OFF! I HAVE TO CARRY THEM BY MYSELF!
WHOA... I HAVEN'T SEEN MANY WOMEN THAT CONFIDENT SINCE I CAME TO JAPAN...
SO? SANO'S ABOUT TO START PRACTICE NOW...
AND...
OHO! A NEW FACE! ONE OF YOUR YOUNGER CLASSMATES, I TAKE IT?
He's pretty cute.
HE'S MY ROOMMATE.

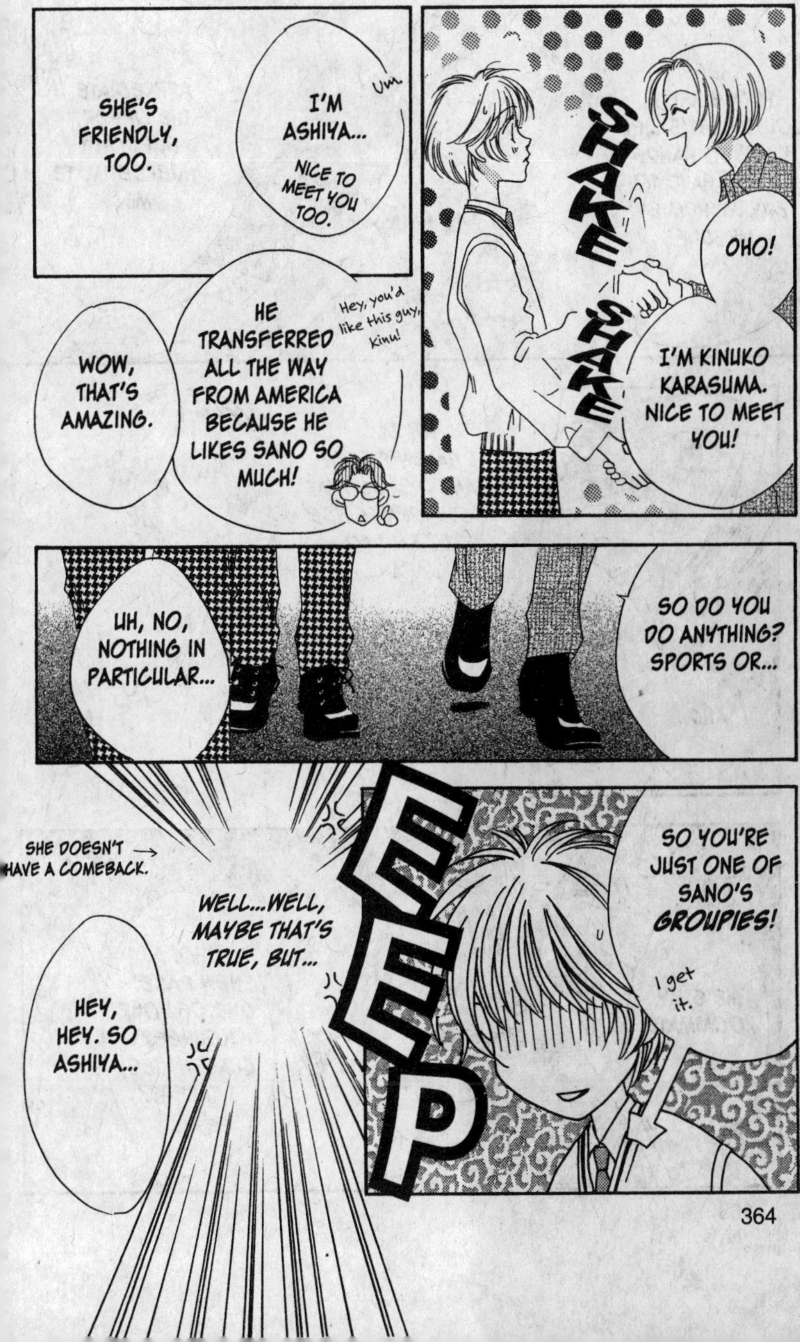
SHAKE SHAKE
OHO!
I'M KINUKO KARASUMA. NICE TO MEET YOU!
Um.
I'M ASHIYA...
NICE TO MEET YOU TOO.
SHE'S FRIENDLY, TOO.
Hey, you'd like this guy, Kinu!
HE TRANSFERRED ALL THE WAY FROM AMERICA BECAUSE HE LIKES SANO SO MUCH!
WOW, THAT'S AMAZING.
SO DO YOU DO ANYTHING? SPORTS OR...
UH, NO, NOTHING IN PARTICULAR...
SO YOU'RE JUST ONE OF SANO'S GROUPIES!
I get it.
EEEP
WELL...WELL, MAYBE THAT'S TRUE, BUT...
SHE DOESN'T HAVE A COMEBACK.
HEY, HEY. SO ASHIYA...

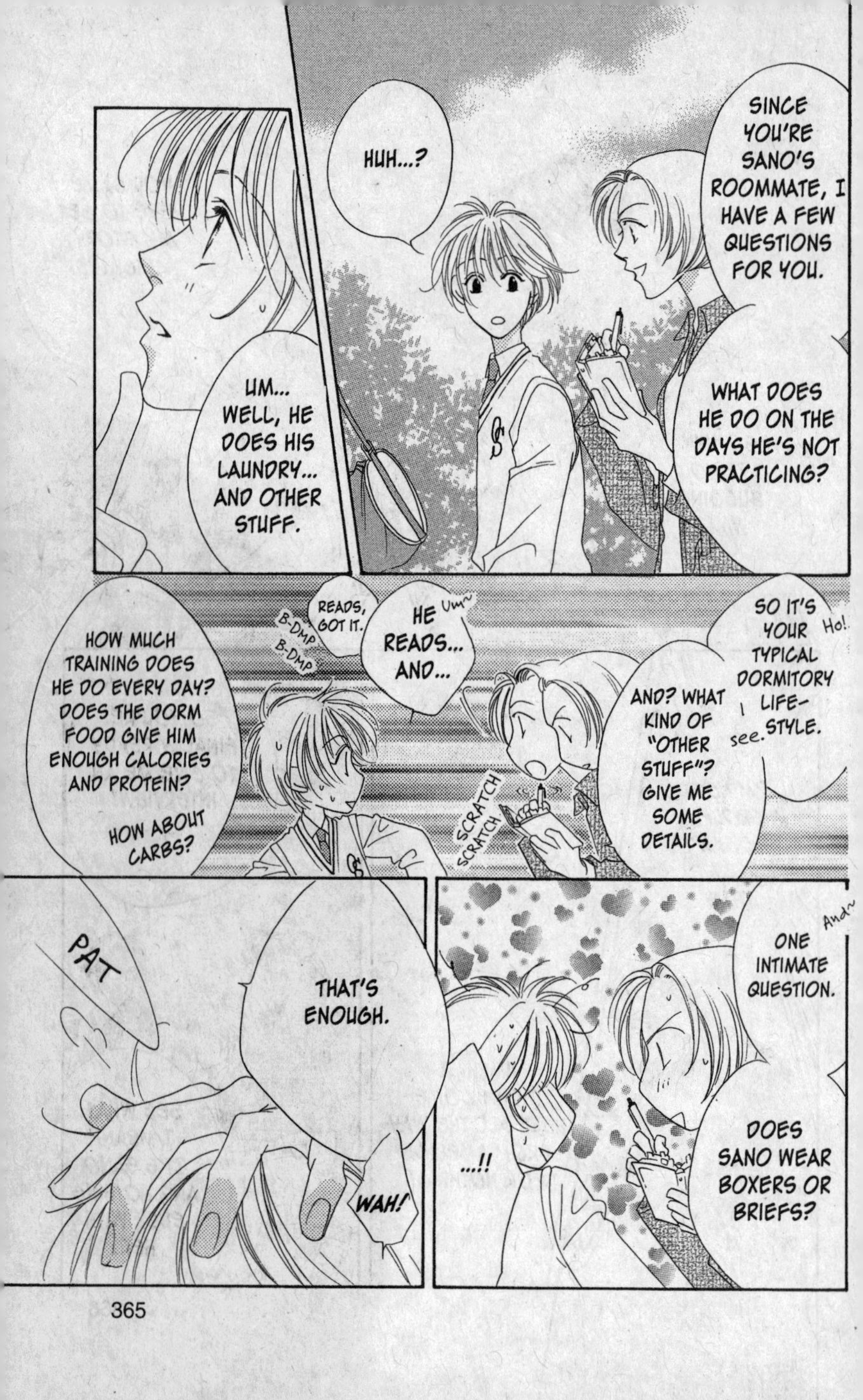
SINCE YOU'RE SANO'S ROOMMATE, I HAVE A FEW QUESTIONS FOR YOU.
HUH...?
WHAT DOES HE DO ON THE DAYS HE'S NOT PRACTICING?
UM... WELL, HE DOES HIS LAUNDRY... AND OTHER STUFF.
SO IT'S YOUR TYPICAL DORMITORY LIFE-STYLE.
Ho!
I see.
AND? WHAT KIND OF "OTHER STUFF"? GIVE ME SOME DETAILS.
HE READS... AND...
Um~
READS, GOT IT.
B-DMP B-DMP
SCRATCH SCRATCH
HOW MUCH TRAINING DOES HE DO EVERY DAY? DOES THE DORM FOOD GIVE HIM ENOUGH CALORIES AND PROTEIN?
HOW ABOUT CARBS?
And~
ONE INTIMATE QUESTION.
DOES SANO WEAR BOXERS OR BRIEFS?
...!!
THAT'S ENOUGH.
WAH!
PAT

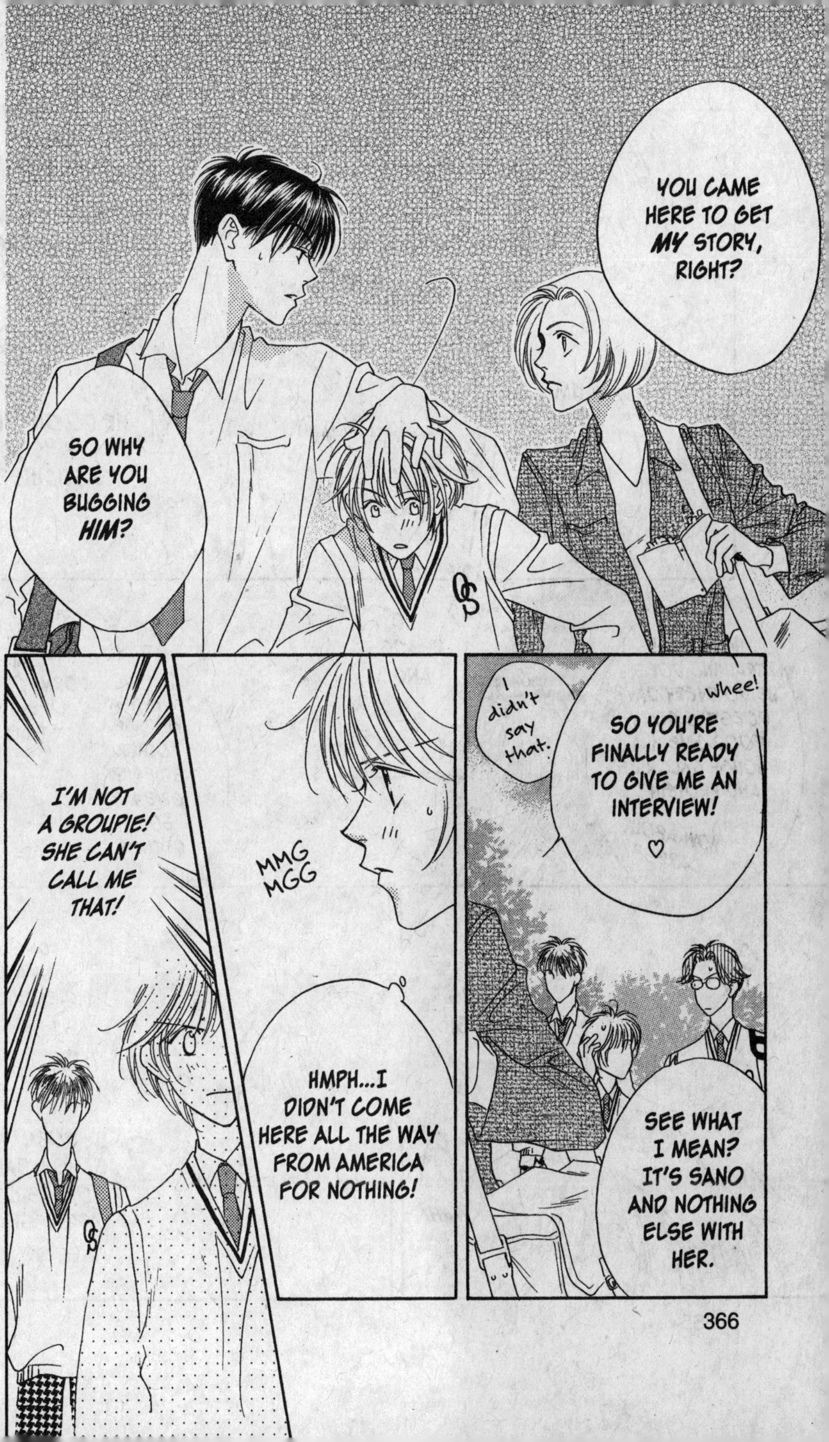
YOU CAME HERE TO GET MY STORY, RIGHT?
SO WHY ARE YOU BUGGING HIM?
Whee!
SO YOU'RE FINALLY READY TO GIVE ME AN INTERVIEW! ♡
I didn't say that.
SEE WHAT I MEAN? IT'S SANO AND NOTHING ELSE WITH HER.
MMG MGG
HMPH...I DIDN'T COME HERE ALL THE WAY FROM AMERICA FOR NOTHING!
I'M NOT A GROUPIE! SHE CAN'T CALL ME THAT!

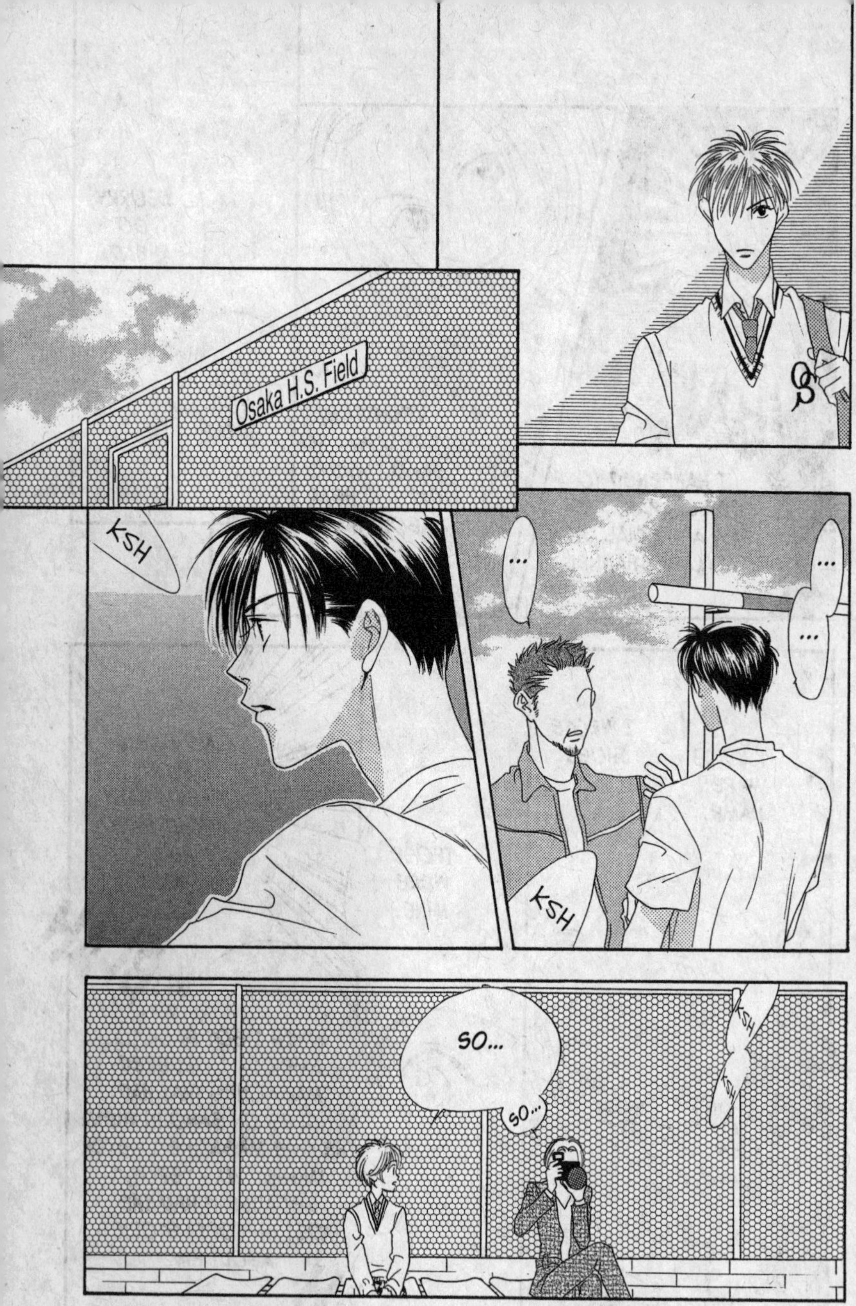
Osaka H.S. Field
...
...
...
KSH
KSH
KSH
KSH
SO...
SO...

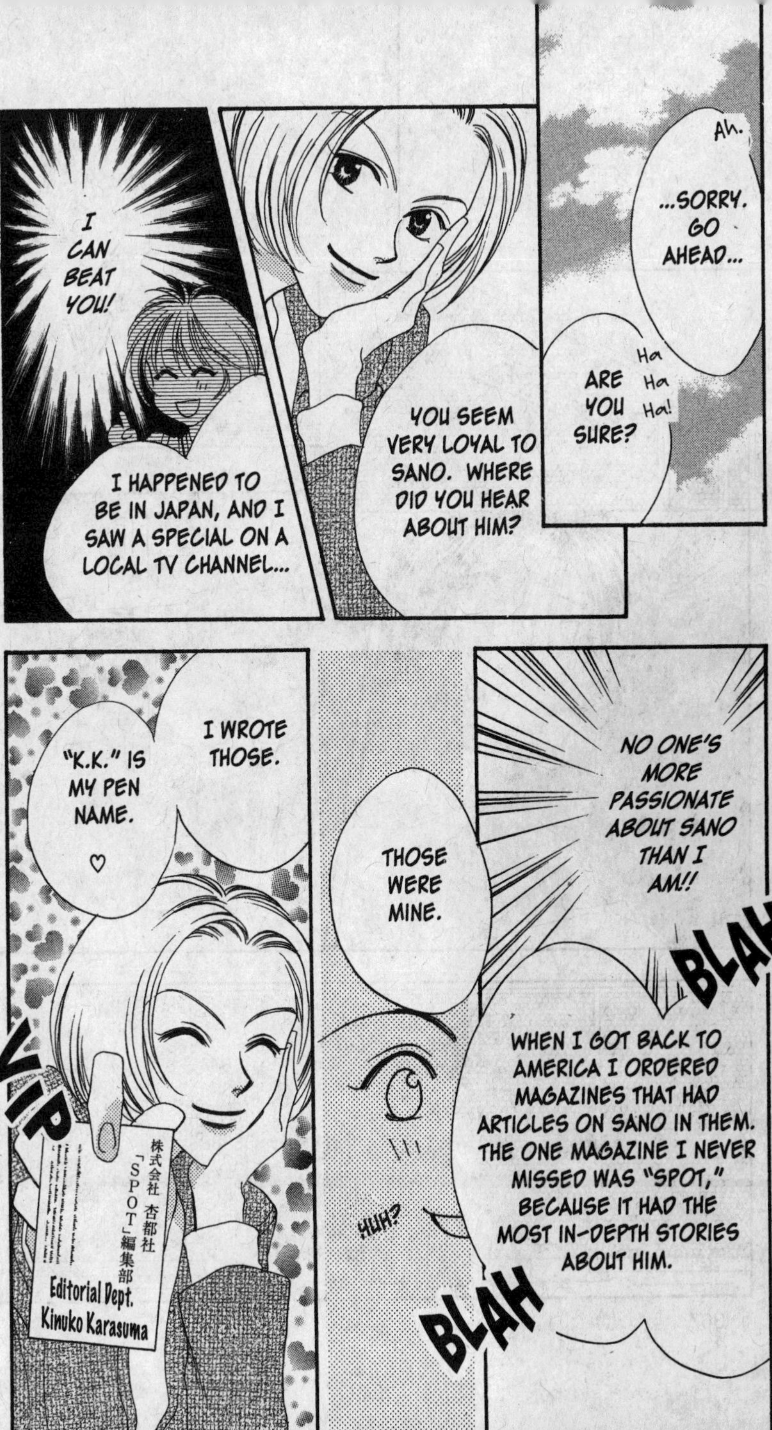
Ah.
...SORRY. GO AHEAD...
ARE YOU SURE?
Ha Ha Ha!
YOU SEEM VERY LOYAL TO SANO. WHERE DID YOU HEAR ABOUT HIM?
I CAN BEAT YOU!
I HAPPENED TO BE IN JAPAN, AND I SAW A SPECIAL ON A LOCAL TV CHANNEL...
NO ONE'S MORE PASSIONATE ABOUT SANO THAN I AM!!
BLAH
WHEN I GOT BACK TO AMERICA I ORDERED MAGAZINES THAT HAD ARTICLES ON SANO IN THEM. THE ONE MAGAZINE I NEVER MISSED WAS "SPOT," BECAUSE IT HAD THE MOST IN-DEPTH STORIES ABOUT HIM.
BLAH
HUH?
THOSE WERE MINE.
I WROTE THOSE.
"K.K." IS MY PEN NAME. ♡
VIP
株式会社 杏都社
「SPOT」編集部
Editorial Dept.
Kinuko Karasuma

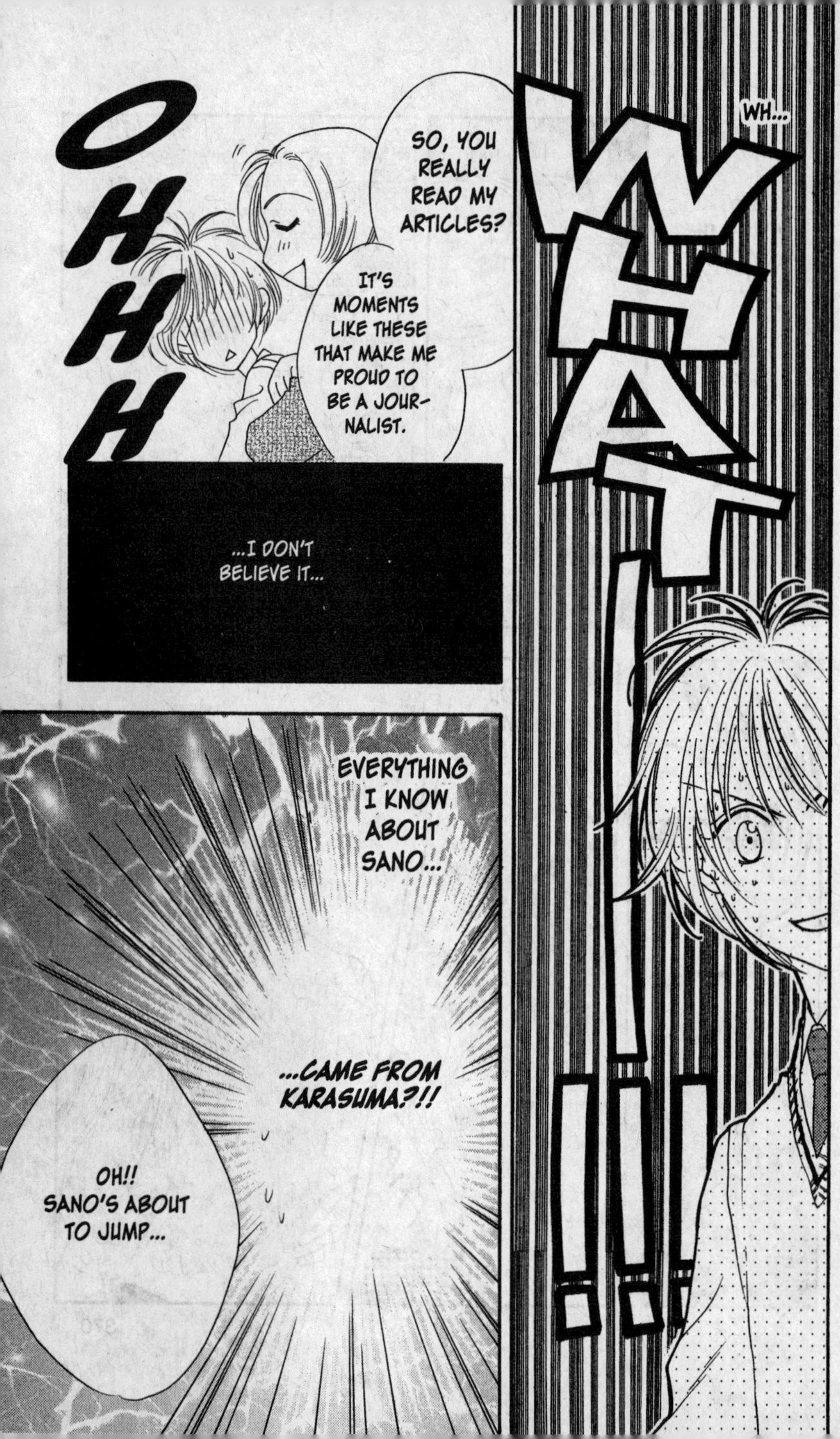
WH...
WHAT!!!
SO, YOU REALLY READ MY ARTICLES?
IT'S MOMENTS LIKE THESE THAT MAKE ME PROUD TO BE A JOURNALIST.
OHHHH
...I DON'T BELIEVE IT...
EVERYTHING I KNOW ABOUT SANO...
...CAME FROM KARASUMA?!!
OH!! SANO'S ABOUT TO JUMP...

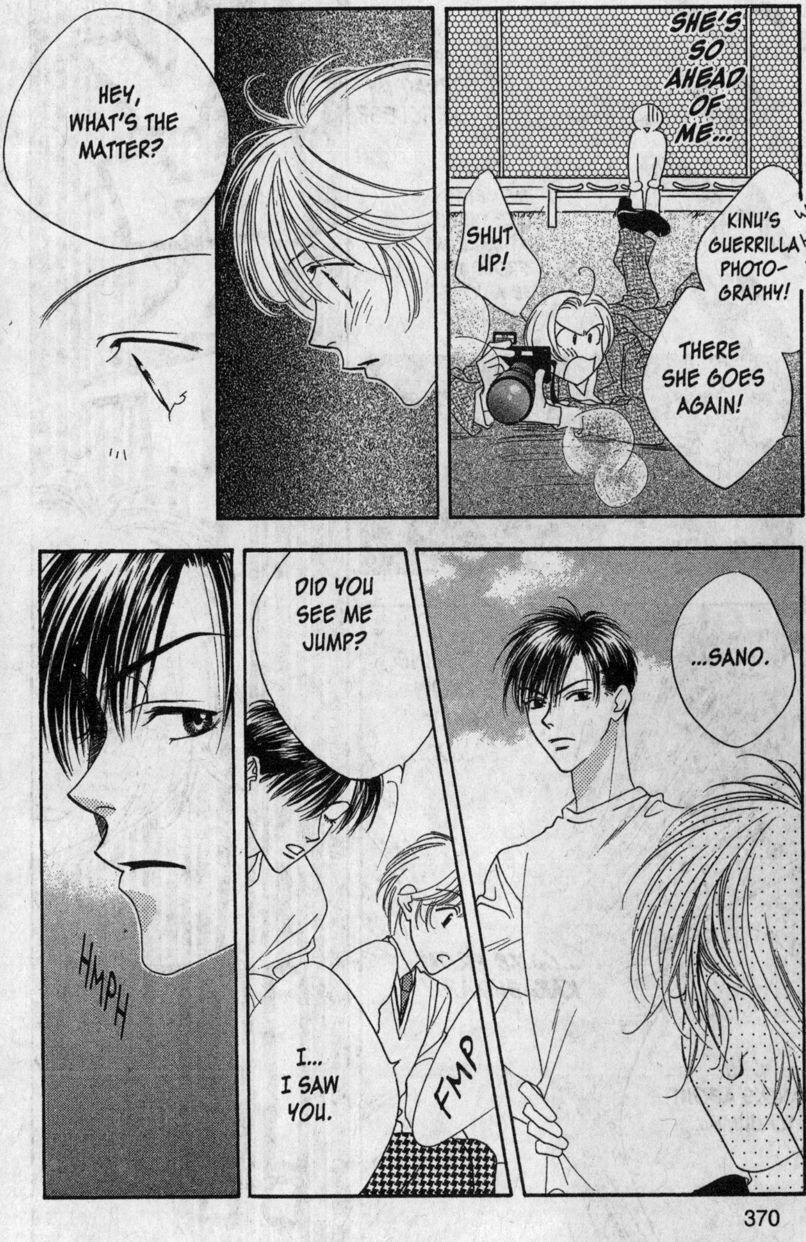
SHE'S SO AHEAD OF ME...
Wa Ha Ha!
KINU'S GUERRILLA PHOTOGRAPHY!
SHUT UP!
THERE SHE GOES AGAIN!
HEY, WHAT'S THE MATTER?
...SANO.
DID YOU SEE ME JUMP?
FMP
I... I SAW YOU.
HMPH

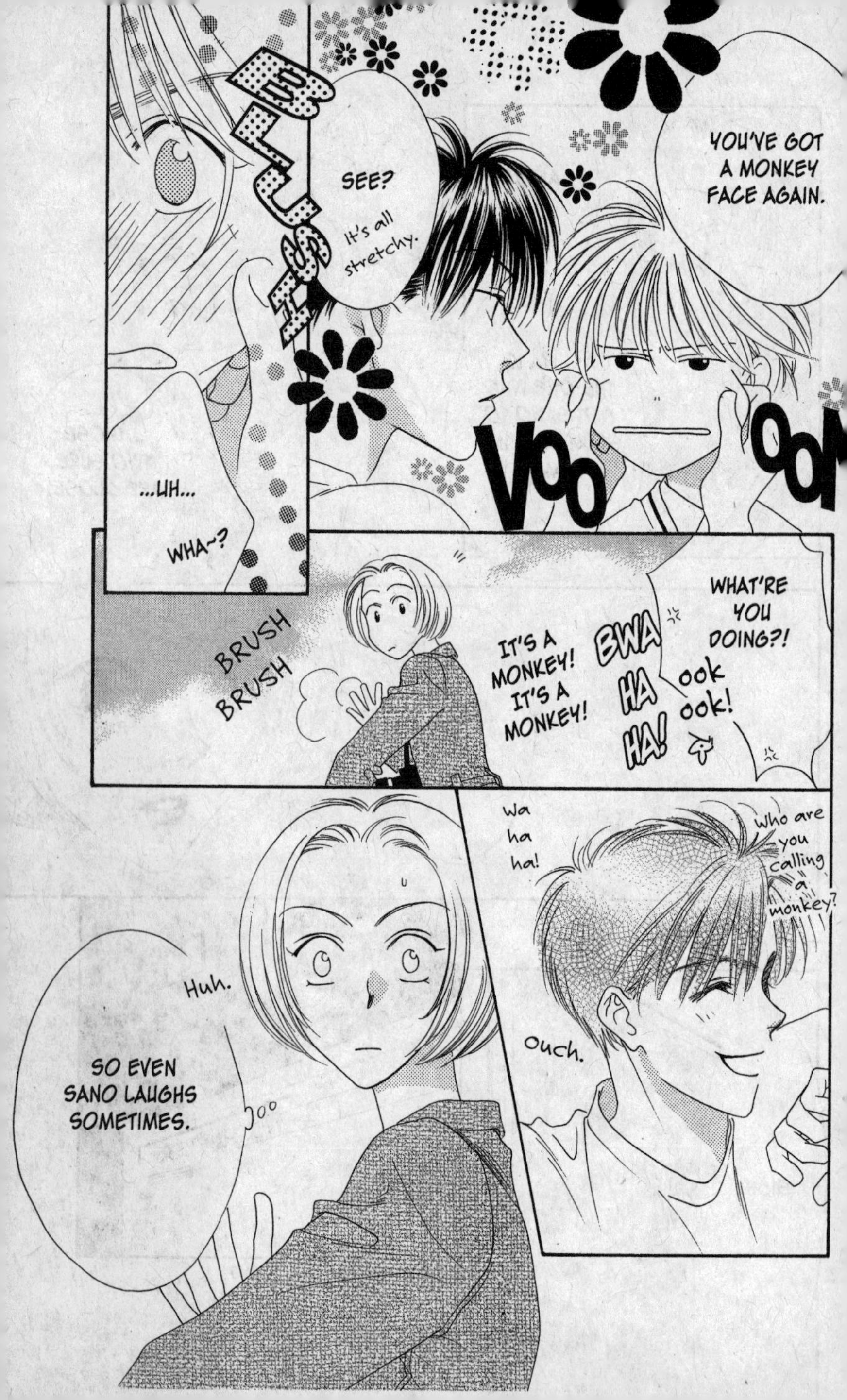
YOU'VE GOT A MONKEY FACE AGAIN.
SEE?
It's all stretchy.
VOOOM
BLUSH
...UH...
WHA~?
WHAT'RE YOU DOING?!
ook ook!
BWA HA HA!
IT'S A MONKEY! IT'S A MONKEY!
BRUSH BRUSH
Who are you calling a monkey?
Wa ha ha!
Ouch.
Huh.
SO EVEN SANO LAUGHS SOMETIMES.

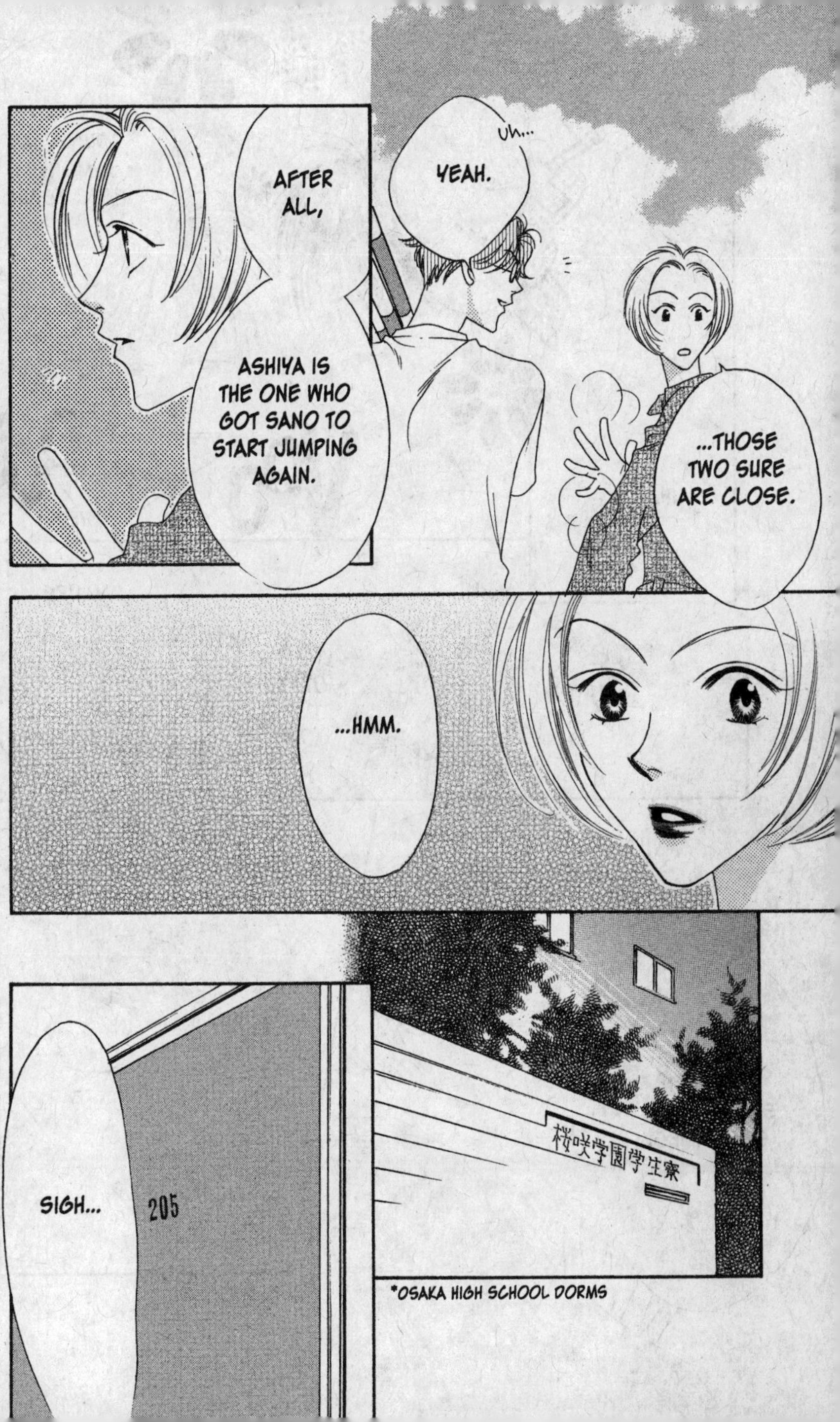
...THOSE TWO SURE ARE CLOSE.
Uh...
YEAH.
AFTER ALL,
ASHIYA IS THE ONE WHO GOT SANO TO START JUMPING AGAIN.
...HMM.
桜咲学園学生寮
*OSAKA HIGH SCHOOL DORMS
205
SIGH...

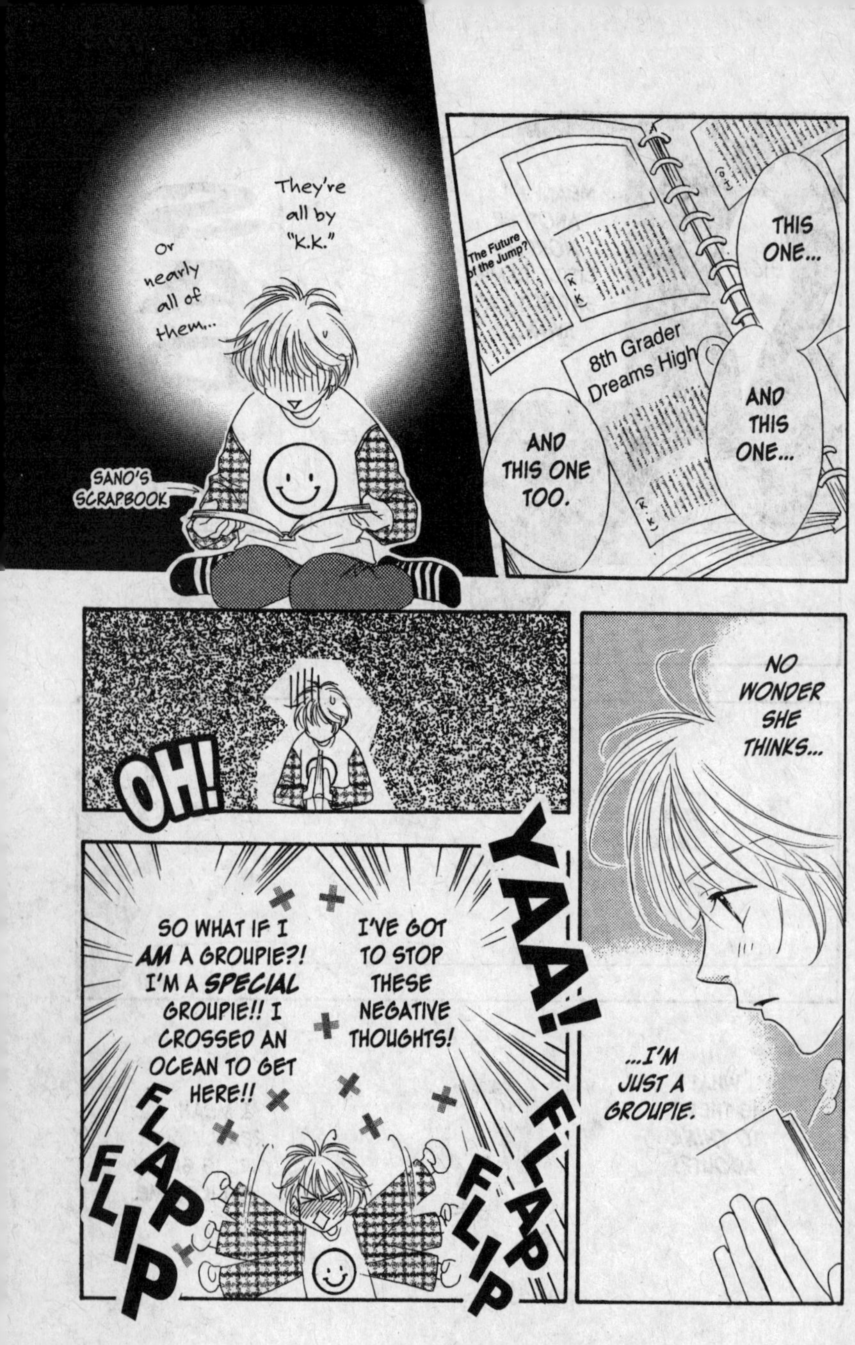

The Future of the Jump?
8th Grader Dreams High
THIS ONE...
AND THIS ONE...
AND THIS ONE TOO.
They're all by "K.K."
Or nearly all of them...
SANO'S SCRAPBOOK
NO WONDER SHE THINKS...
...I'M JUST A GROUPIE.
OH!
YAAA!
I'VE GOT TO STOP THESE NEGATIVE THOUGHTS!
SO WHAT IF I *AM* A GROUPIE?! I'M A *SPECIAL* GROUPIE!! I CROSSED AN OCEAN TO GET HERE!!
FLAP FLIP
FLAP FLIP

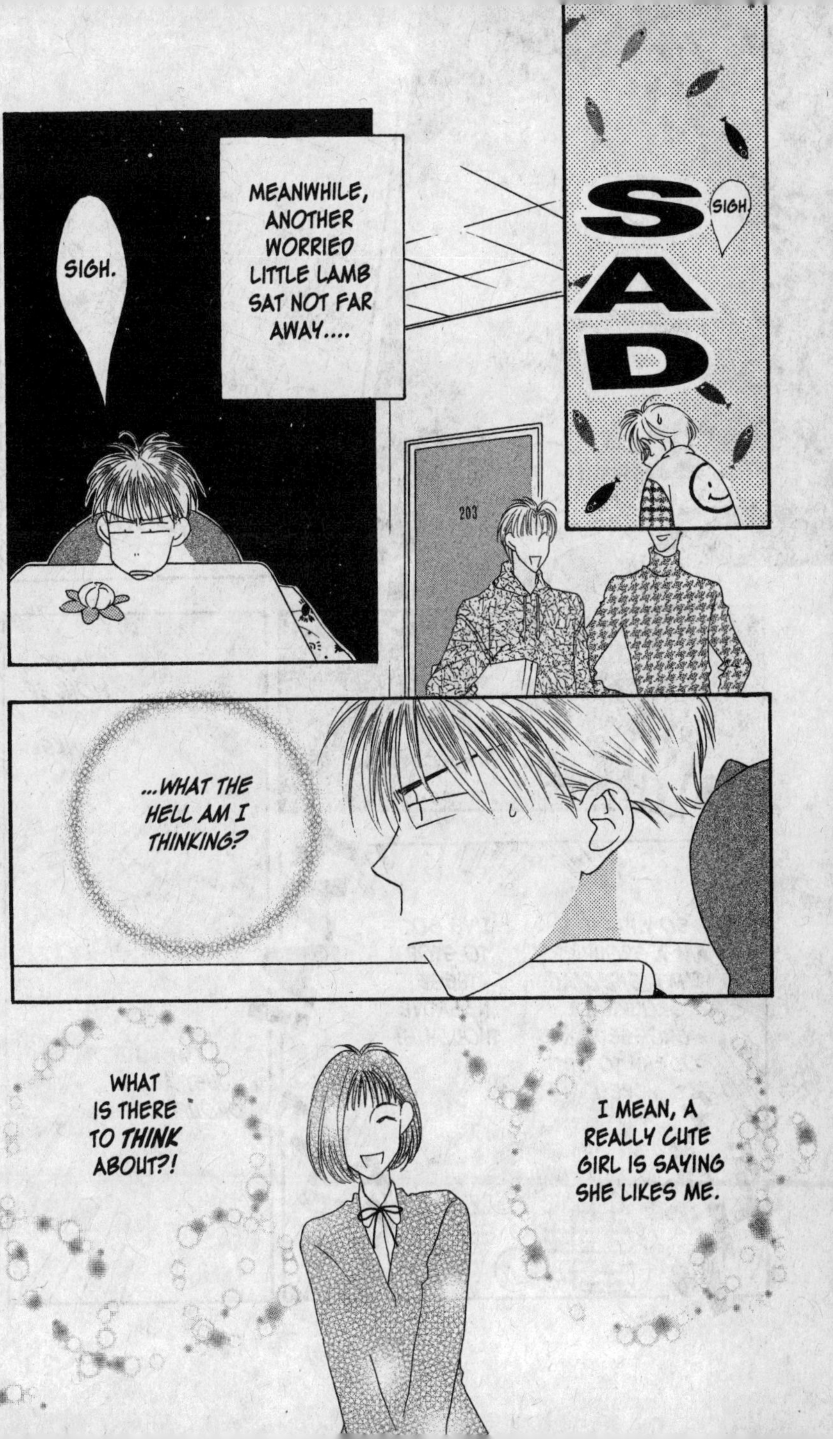
SAD
SIGH.
MEANWHILE, ANOTHER WORRIED LITTLE LAMB SAT NOT FAR AWAY....
SIGH.
...WHAT THE HELL AM I THINKING?
I MEAN, A REALLY CUTE GIRL IS SAYING SHE LIKES ME.
WHAT IS THERE TO THINK ABOUT?!

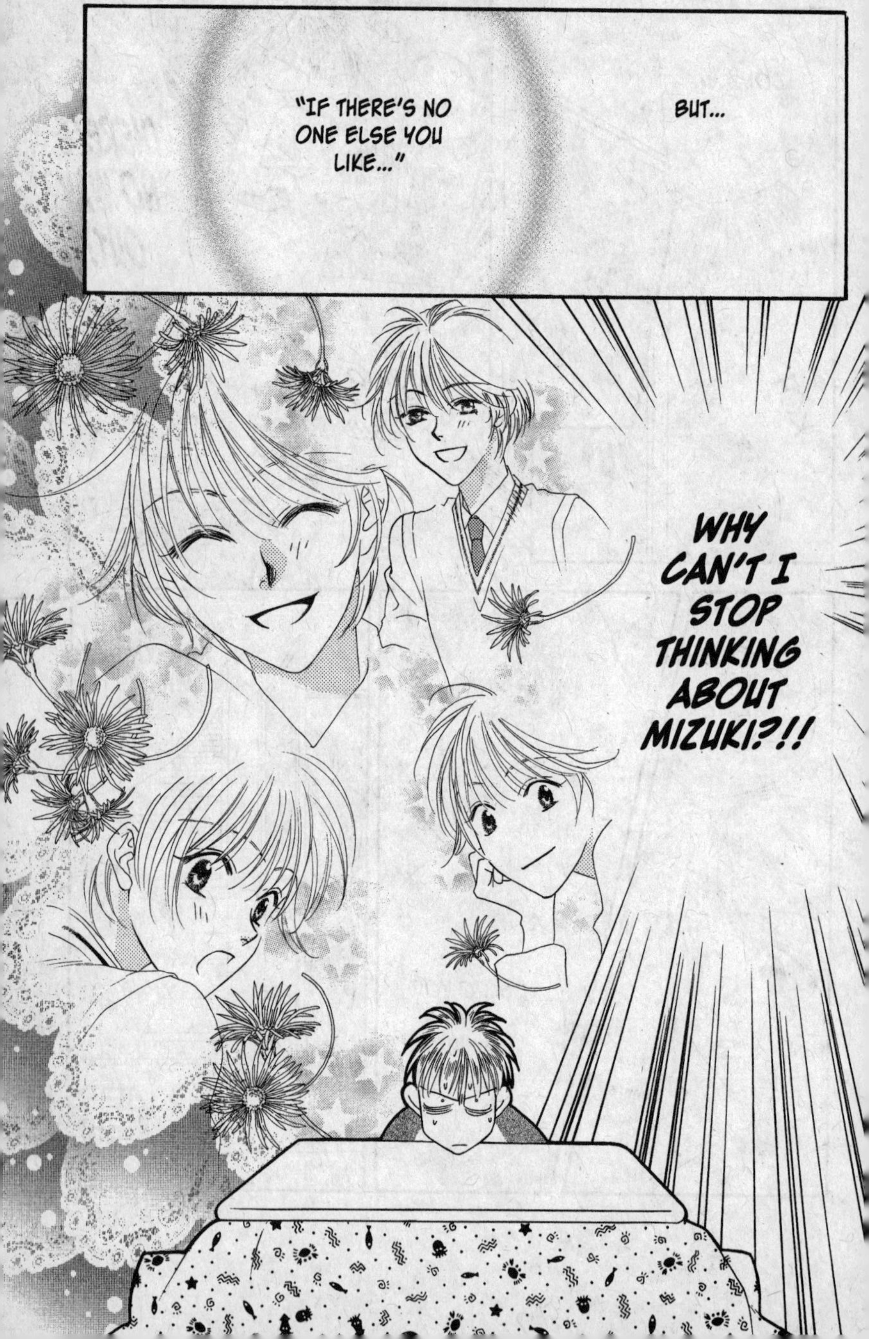
BUT...
"IF THERE'S NO ONE ELSE YOU LIKE..."
WHY CAN'T I STOP THINKING ABOUT MIZUKI?!!

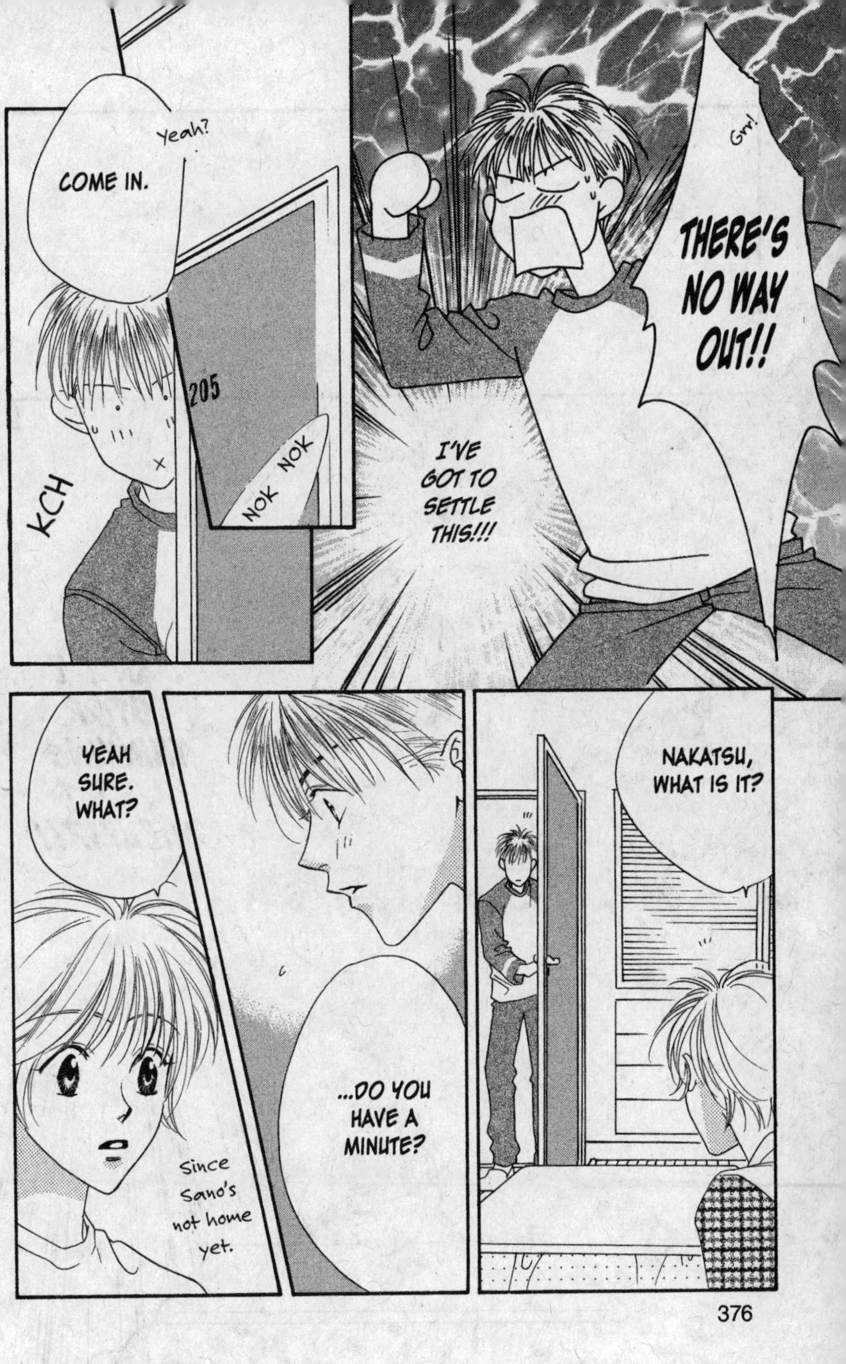
Grr!
THERE'S NO WAY OUT!!
I'VE GOT TO SETTLE THIS!!!
Yeah?
COME IN.
205
NOK NOK
KCH
NAKATSU, WHAT IS IT?
...DO YOU HAVE A MINUTE?
YEAH SURE. WHAT?
Since Sano's not home yet.

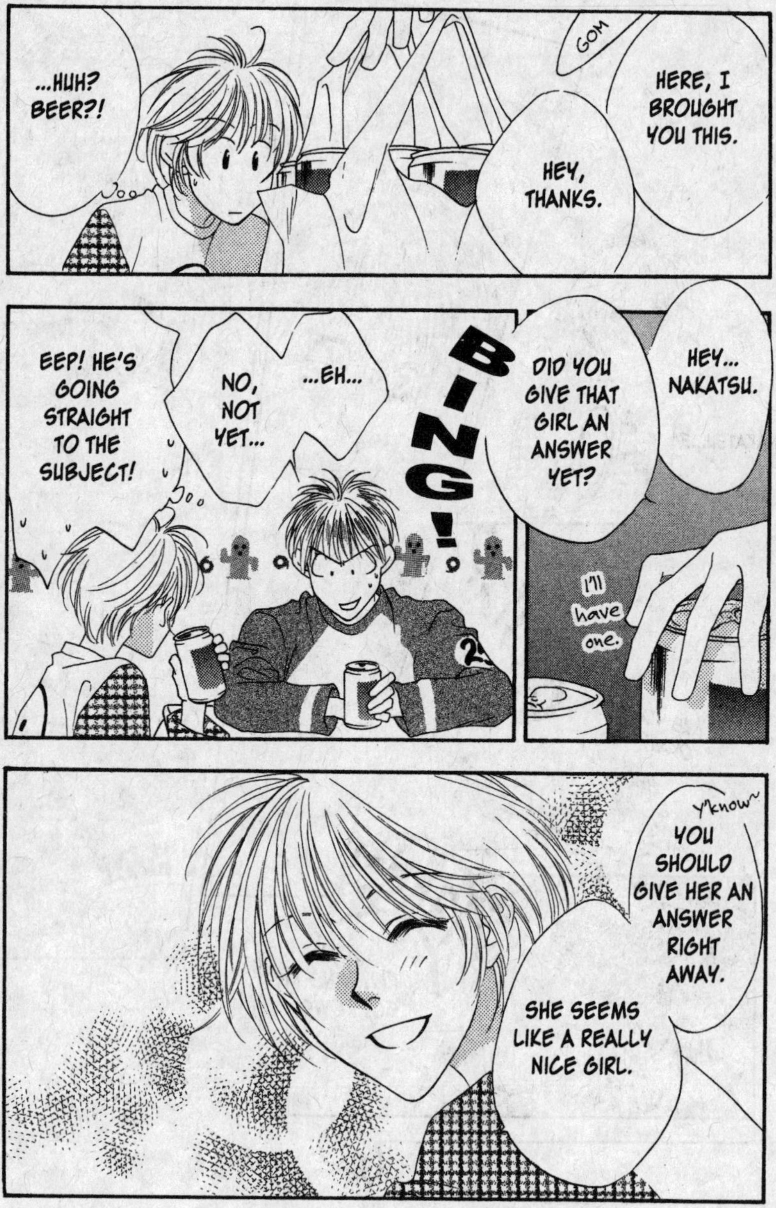
GOM
HERE, I BROUGHT YOU THIS.
HEY, THANKS.
...HUH? BEER?!
HEY... NAKATSU.
DID YOU GIVE THAT GIRL AN ANSWER YET?
I'll have one.
BING!
...EH...
NO, NOT YET...
EEP! HE'S GOING STRAIGHT TO THE SUBJECT!
Y'know~
YOU SHOULD GIVE HER AN ANSWER RIGHT AWAY.
SHE SEEMS LIKE A REALLY NICE GIRL.

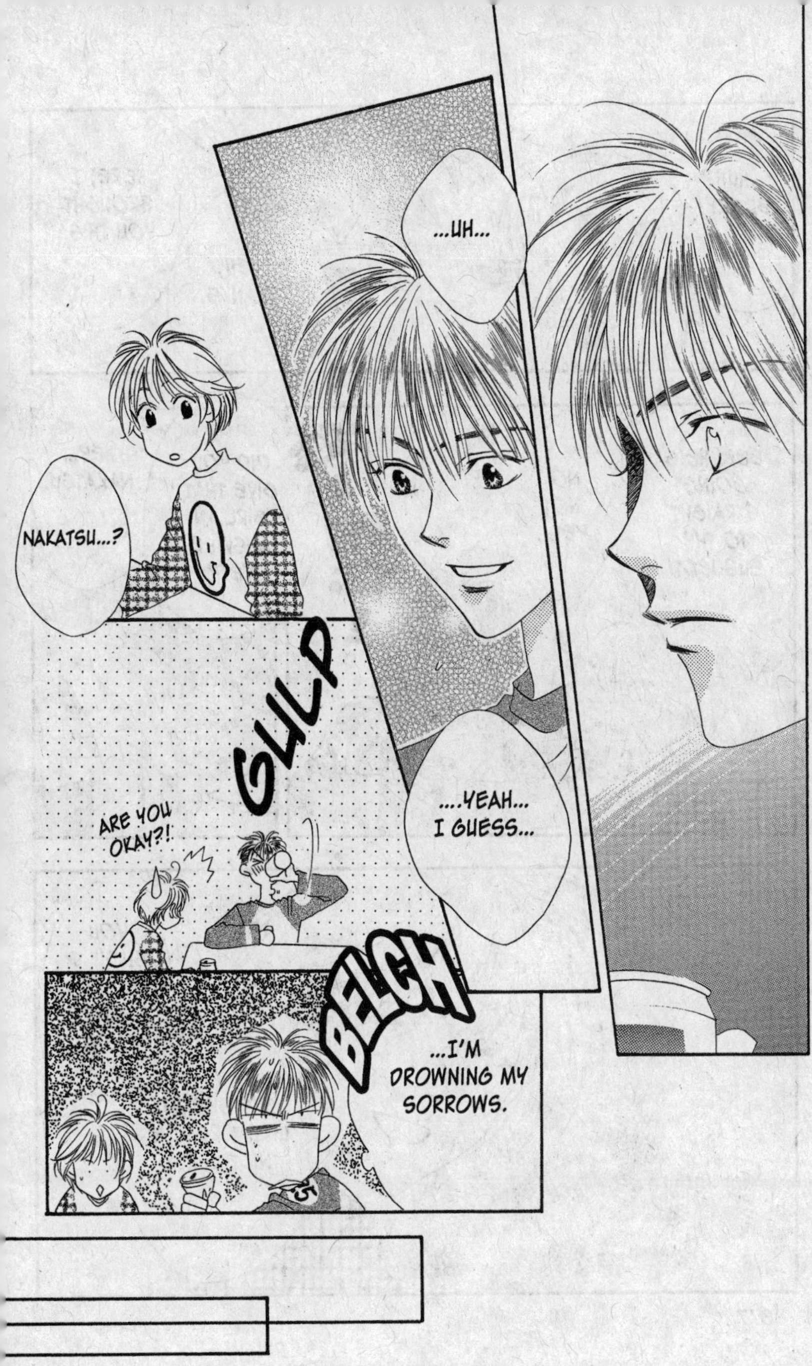
...UH...
....YEAH... I GUESS...
NAKATSU...?
GULP
ARE YOU OKAY?!
BELCH
...I'M DROWNING MY SORROWS.

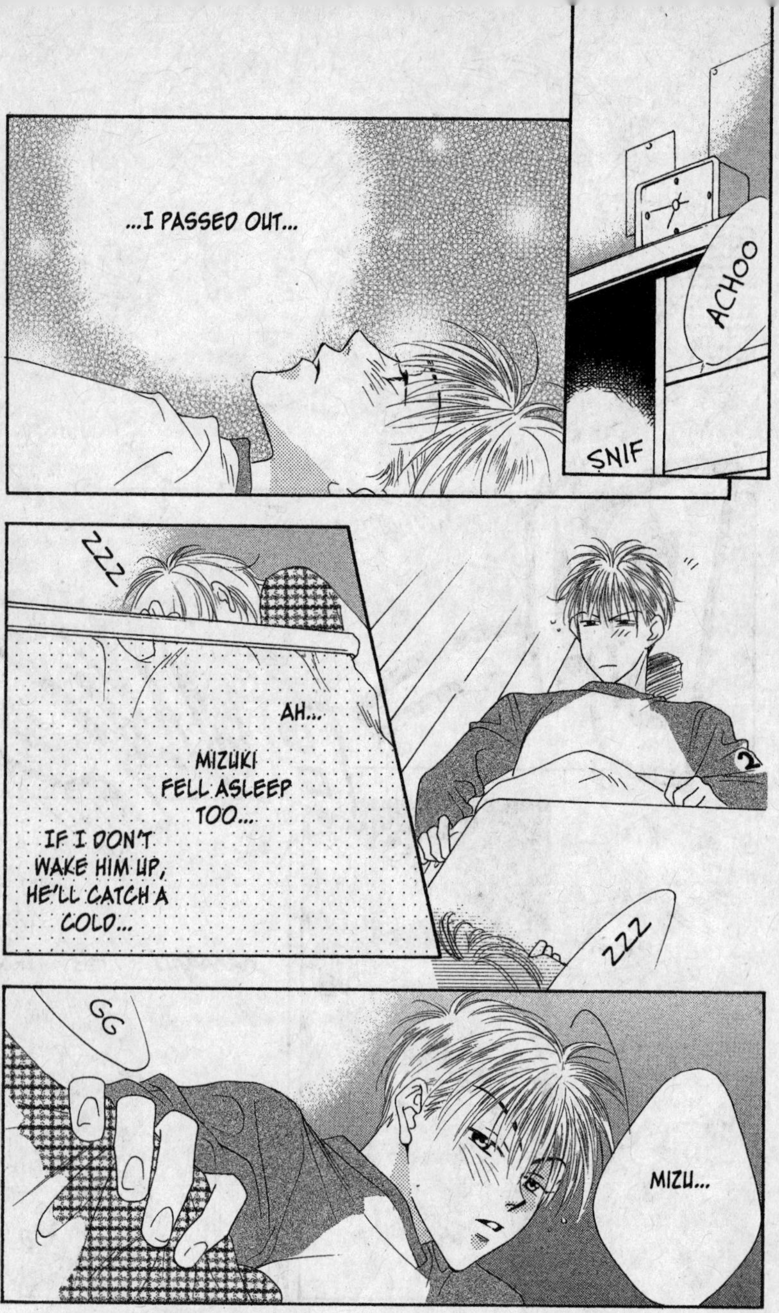
ACHOO
SNIF
...I PASSED OUT...
ZZZ
ZZZ
AH...
MIZUKI FELL ASLEEP TOO...
IF I DON'T WAKE HIM UP, HE'LL CATCH A COLD...
MIZU...
GG

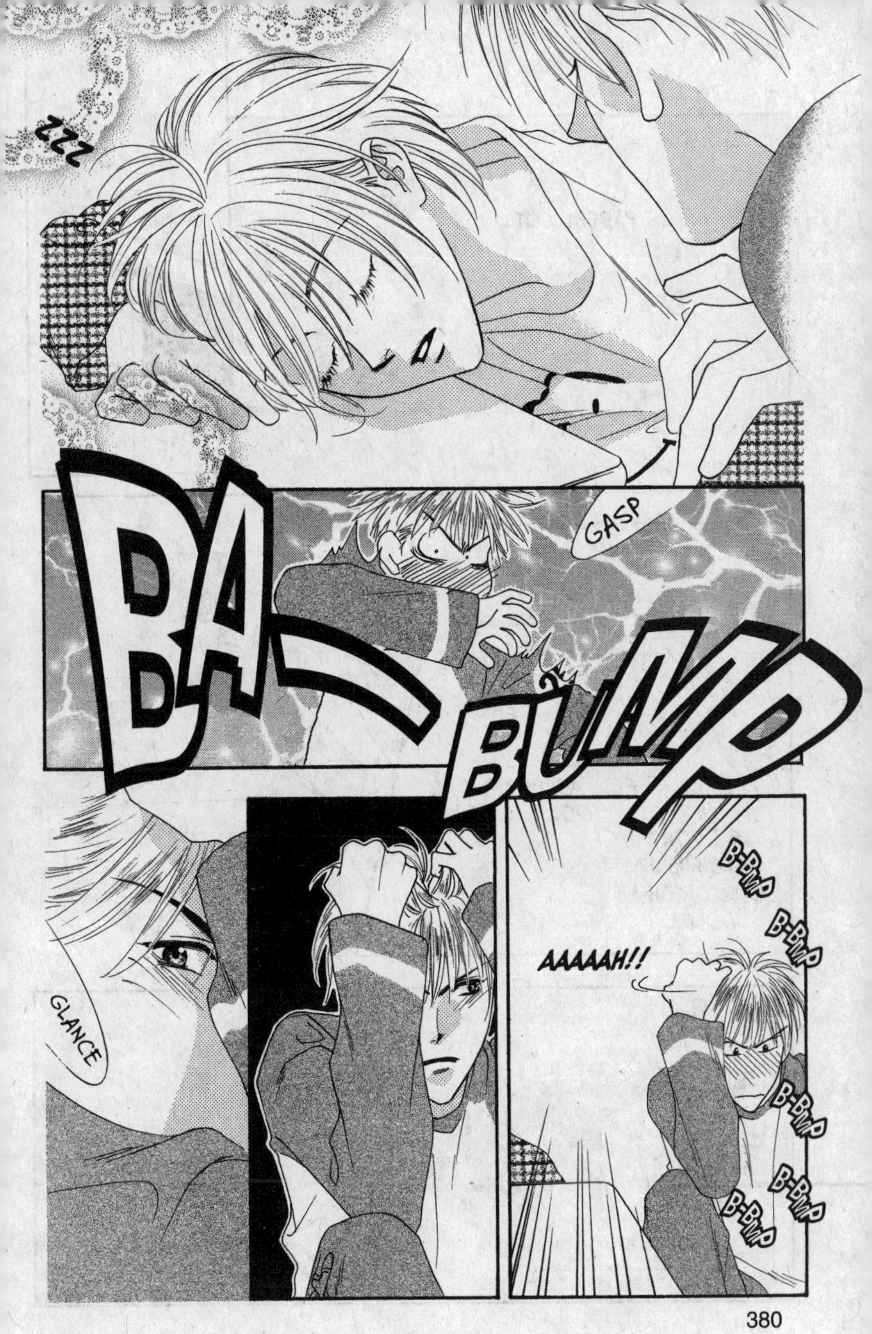
zzz
GASP
BA—
BUMP
B-BMP
B-BMP
AAAAAH!!
B-BMP
B-BMP
B-BMP
GLANCE

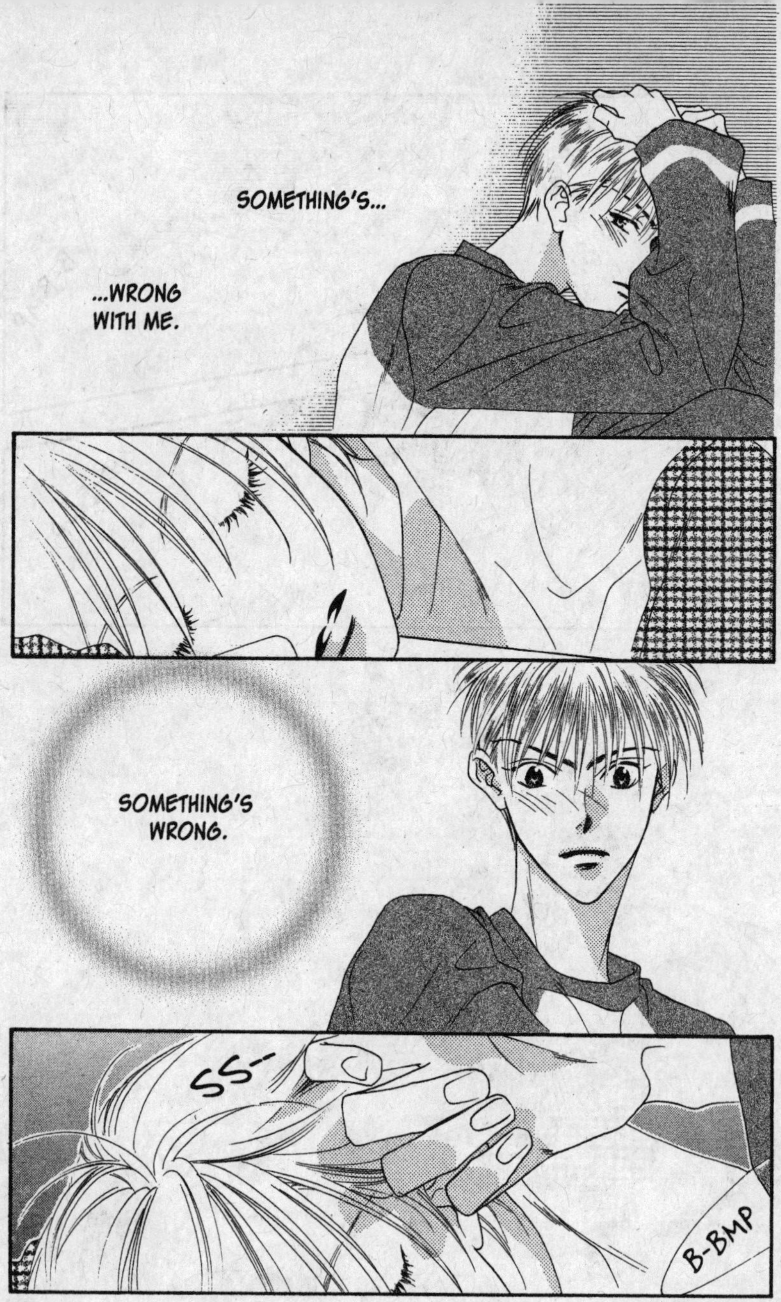
SOMETHING'S...
...WRONG WITH ME.
SOMETHING'S WRONG.
B-BMP
SS-

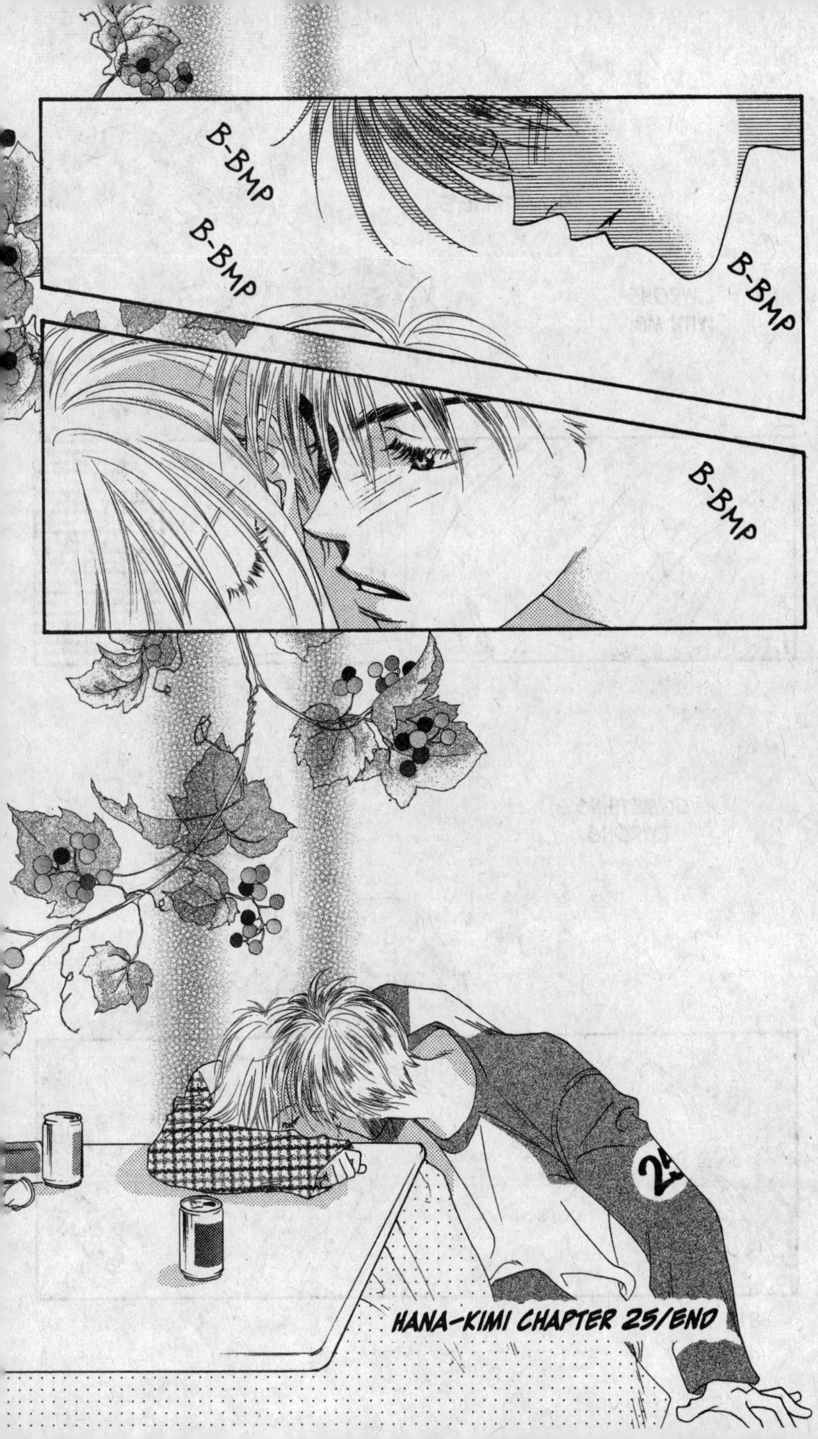
B-BMP
B-BMP
B-BMP
B-BMP
HANA-KIMI CHAPTER 25/END

HANA-KIMI POPULARITY POLL

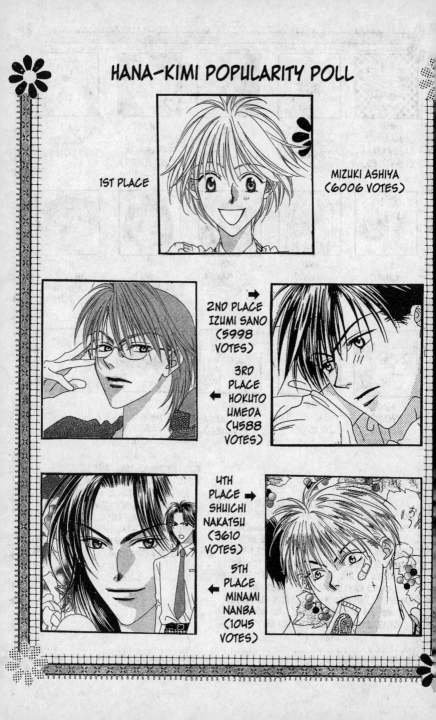

1ST PLACE

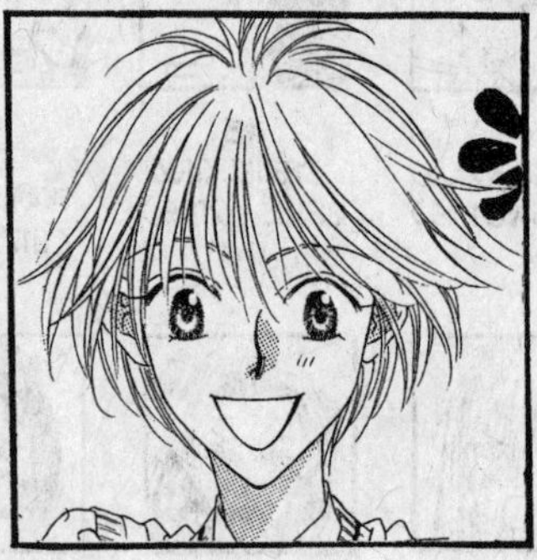

MIZUKI ASHIYA (6006 VOTES)

2ND PLACE IZUMI SANO (5998 VOTES)

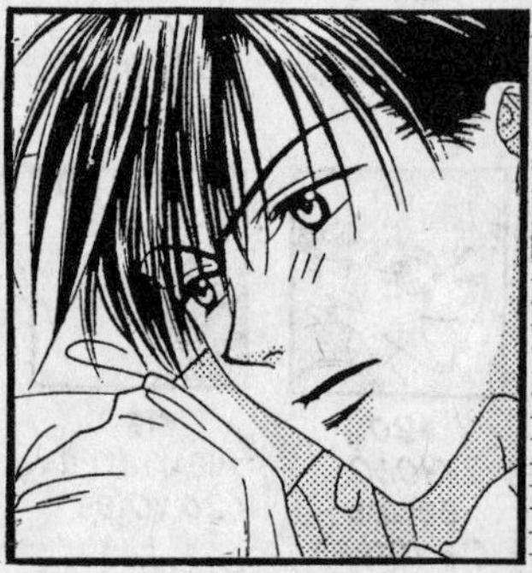

3RD PLACE HOKUTO UMEDA (4588 VOTES)

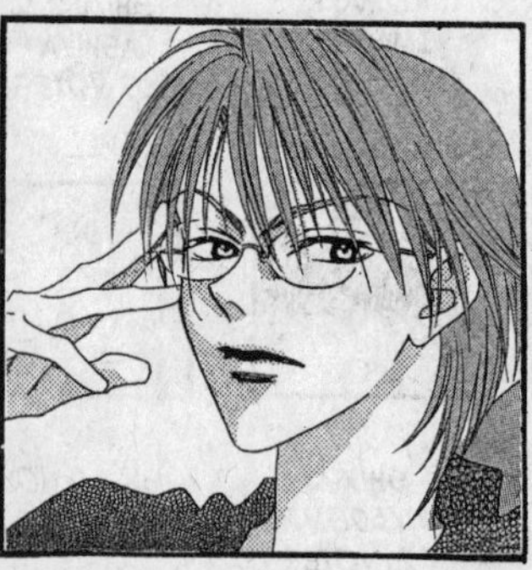

4TH PLACE SHUICHI NAKATSU (3610 VOTES)

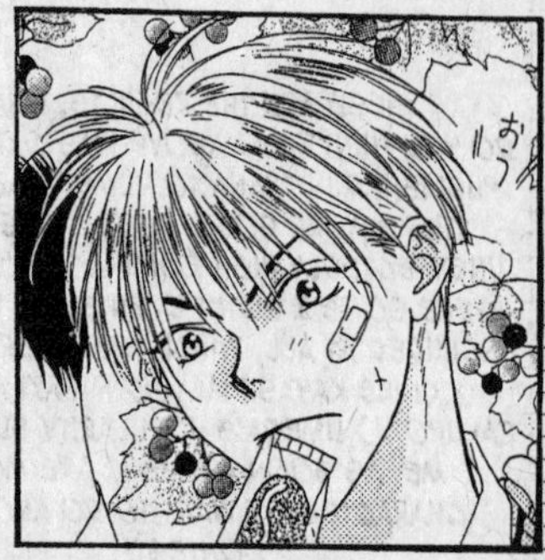
おう

5TH PLACE MINAMI NANBA (1045 VOTES)

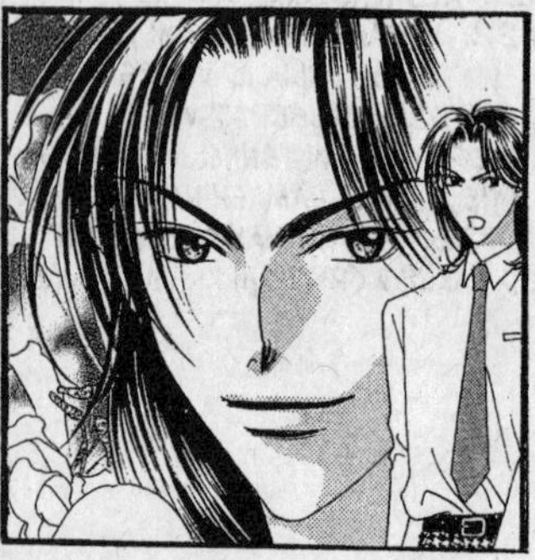

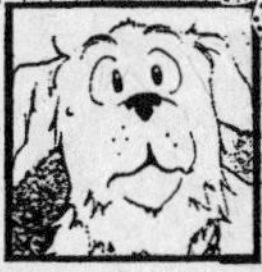

#6
YUJIRO
(440 VOTES)

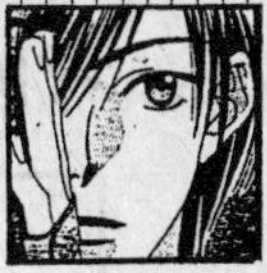

#7
DAIKI
KAYASHIMA
(317 VOTES)

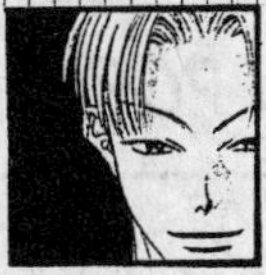

#8
ITSUKI KUJO
(248 VOTES)

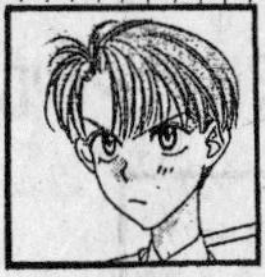

#9
SENRI NAKAO
(223 VOTES)

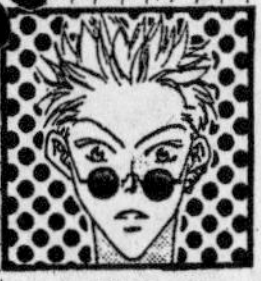

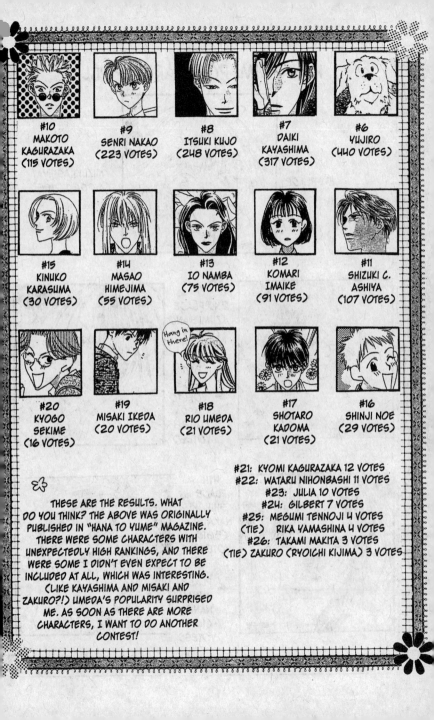

#10
MAKOTO
KAGURAZAKA
(115 VOTES)

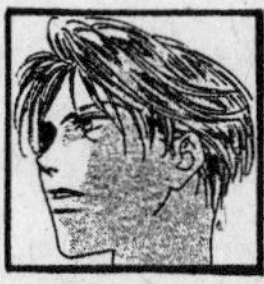

#11
SHIZUKI C.
ASHIYA
(107 VOTES)

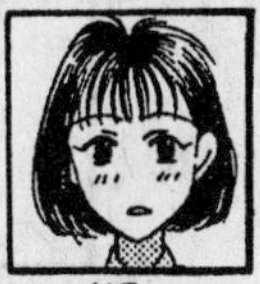

#12
KOMARI
IMAIKE
(91 VOTES)

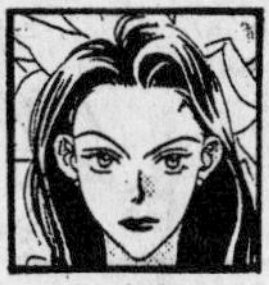

#13
IO NAMBA
(75 VOTES)

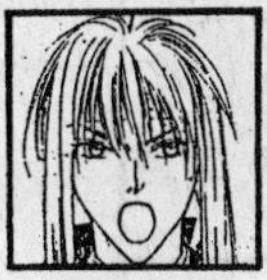

#14
MASAO
HIMEJIMA
(55 VOTES)

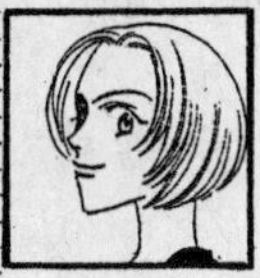

#15
KINUKO
KARASUMA
(30 VOTES)

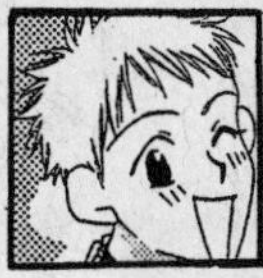

#16
SHINJI NOE
(29 VOTES)

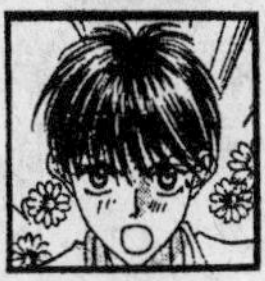

#17
SHOTARO
KADOMA
(21 VOTES)

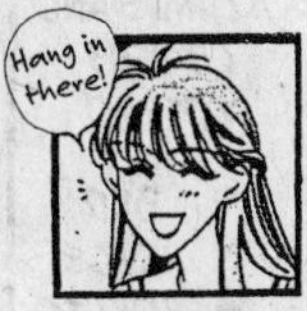
Hang in there!

#18
RIO UMEDA
(21 VOTES)

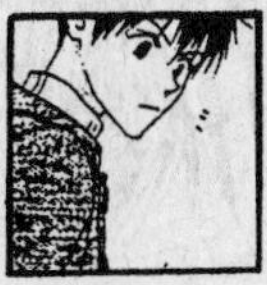

#19
MISAKI IKEDA
(20 VOTES)

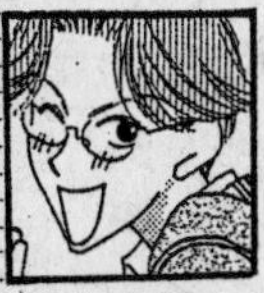

#20
KYOGO
SEKIME
(16 VOTES)

#21: KYOMI KAGURAZAKA 12 VOTES
#22: WATARU NIHONBASHI 11 VOTES
#23: JULIA 10 VOTES
#24: GILBERT 7 VOTES
#25: MEGUMI TENNOJI 4 VOTES
(TIE) RIKA YAMASHINA 4 VOTES
#26: TAKAMI MAKITA 3 VOTES
(TIE) ZAKURO (RYOICHI KIJIMA) 3 VOTES

THESE ARE THE RESULTS. WHAT DO YOU THINK? THE ABOVE WAS ORIGINALLY PUBLISHED IN "HANA TO YUME" MAGAZINE. THERE WERE SOME CHARACTERS WITH UNEXPECTEDLY HIGH RANKINGS, AND THERE WERE SOME I DIDN'T EVEN EXPECT TO BE INCLUDED AT ALL, WHICH WAS INTERESTING. (LIKE KAYASHIMA AND MISAKI AND ZAKURO?!) UMEDA'S POPULARITY SURPRISED ME. AS SOON AS THERE ARE MORE CHARACTERS, I WANT TO DO ANOTHER CONTEST!

For You in Full Blossom

6

story and art by
HISAYA NAKAJO

CONTENTS

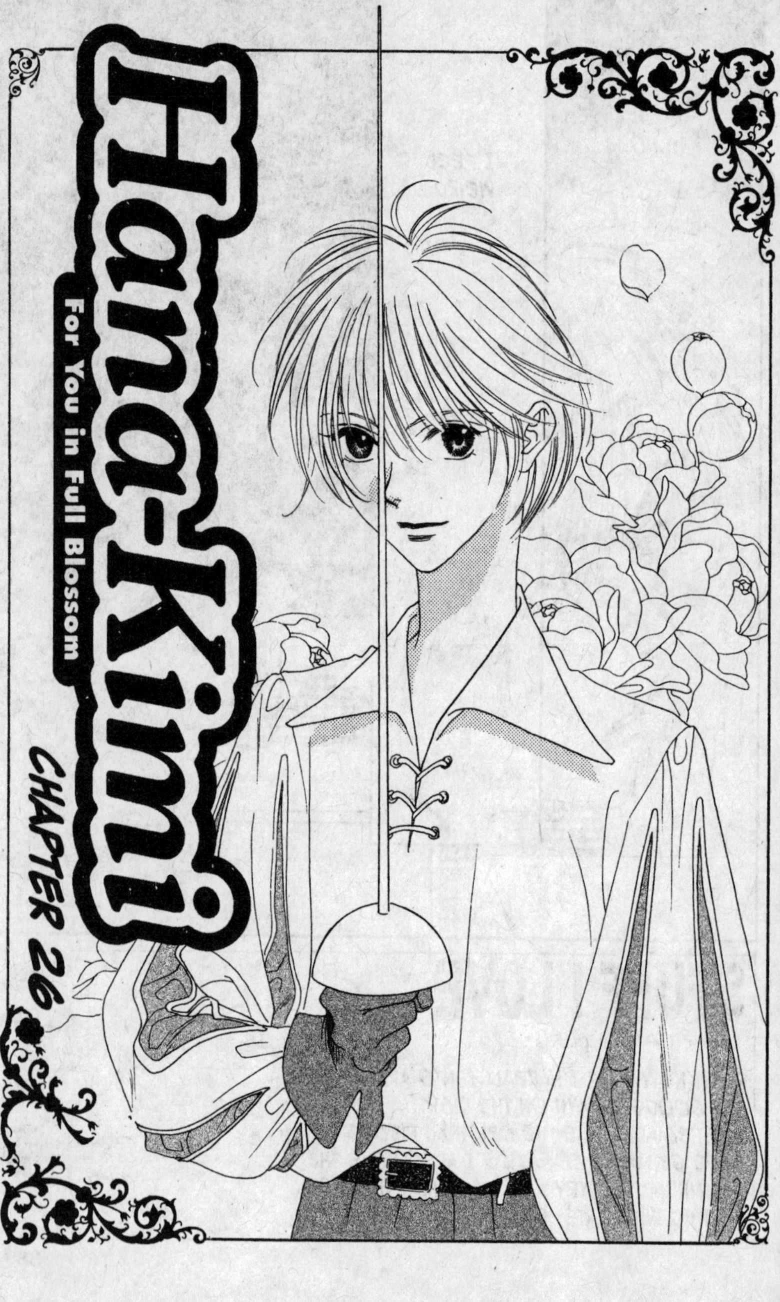
Hana-Kimi
For You in Full Blossom
CHAPTER 26

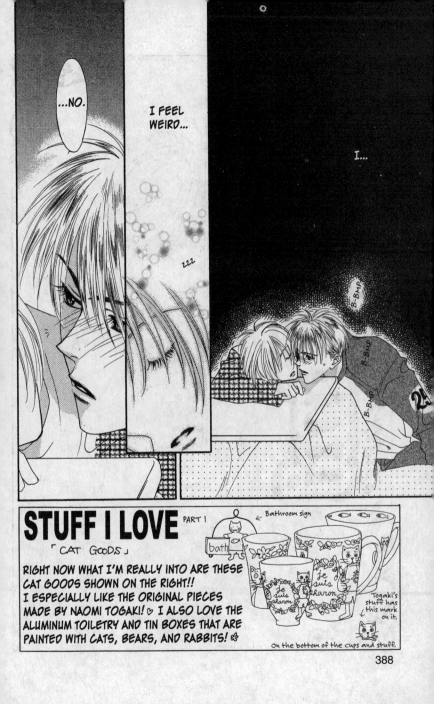

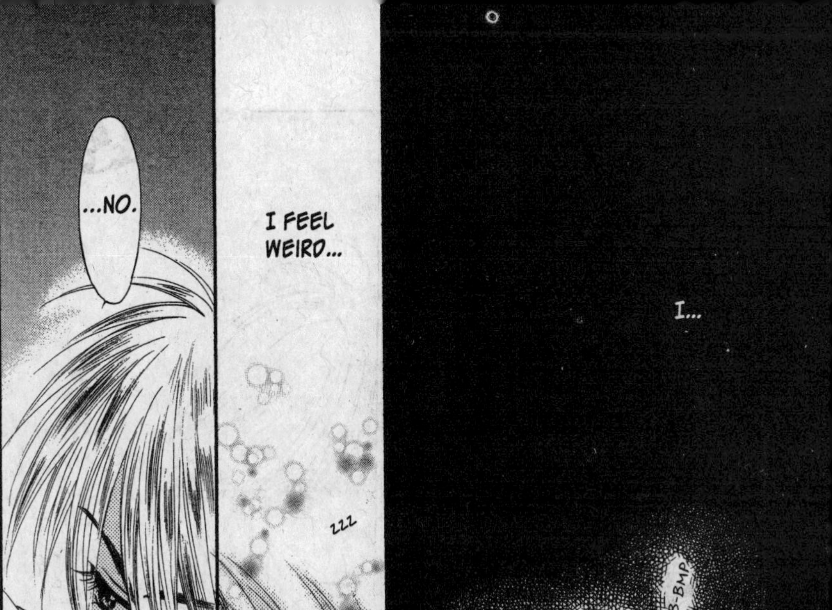
I...
B-BMP
B-BMP
B-BMP
I FEEL WEIRD...
ZZZ
...NO.

STUFF I LOVE PART 1

「CAT GOODS」

RIGHT NOW WHAT I'M REALLY INTO ARE THESE CAT GOODS SHOWN ON THE RIGHT!! I ESPECIALLY LIKE THE ORIGINAL PIECES MADE BY NAOMI TOGAKI! ♡ I ALSO LOVE THE ALUMINUM TOILETRY AND TIN BOXES THAT ARE PAINTED WITH CATS, BEARS, AND RABBITS! ✿

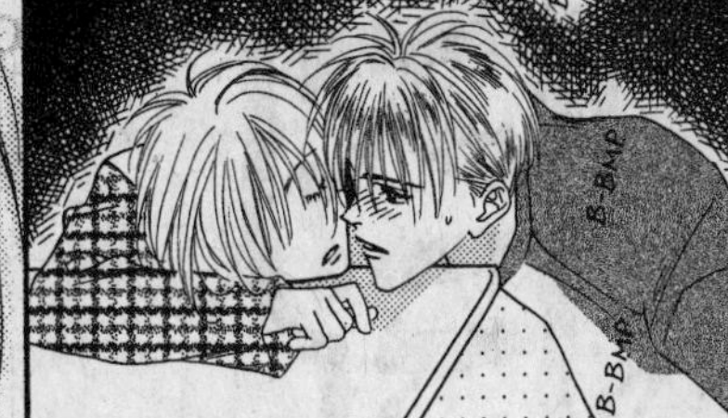
Bathroom sign
bath
je suis sharon
je suis sharon
Togaki's stuff has this mark on it.
On the bottom of the cups and stuff.

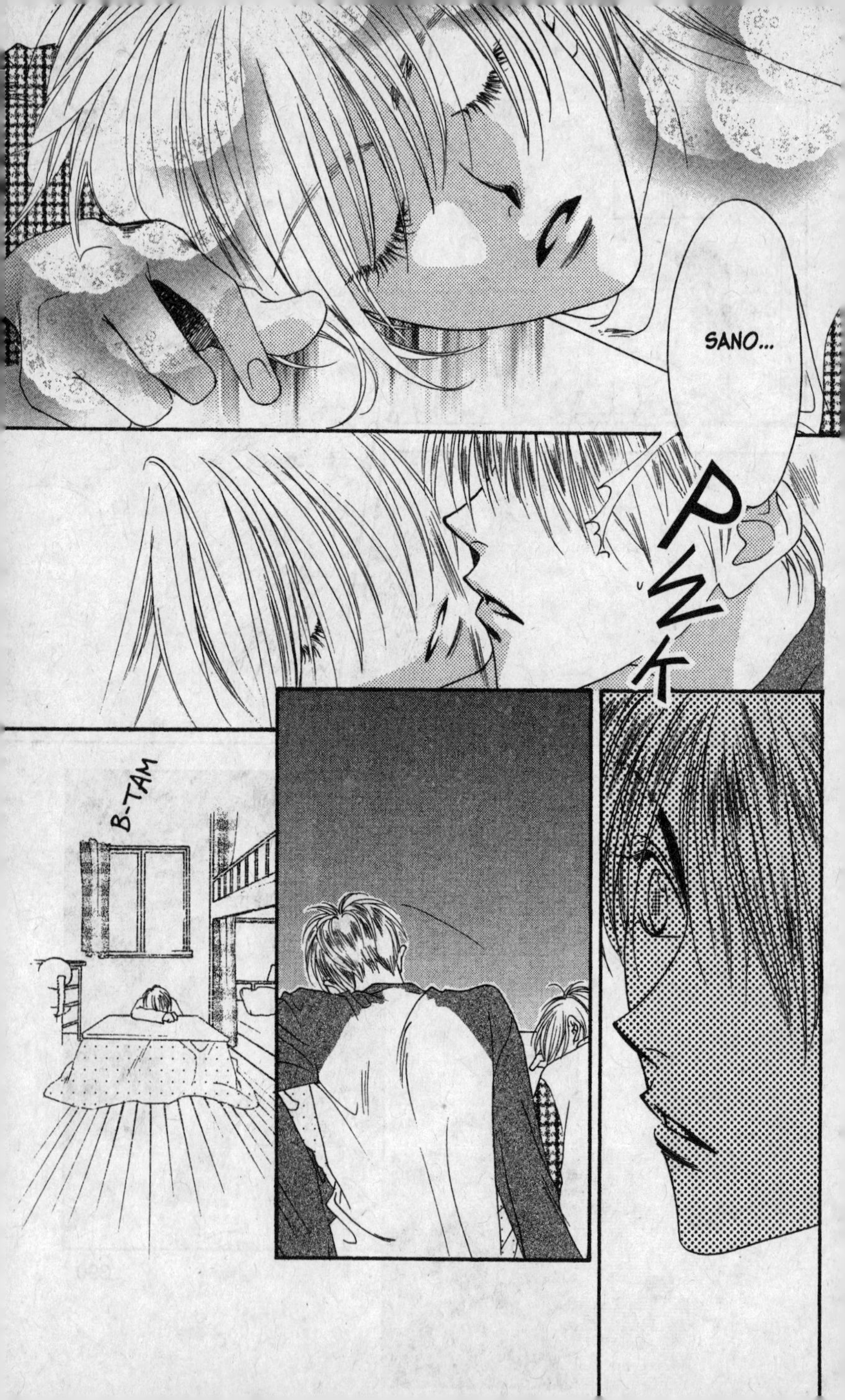
SANO...
PWK
B-TAM

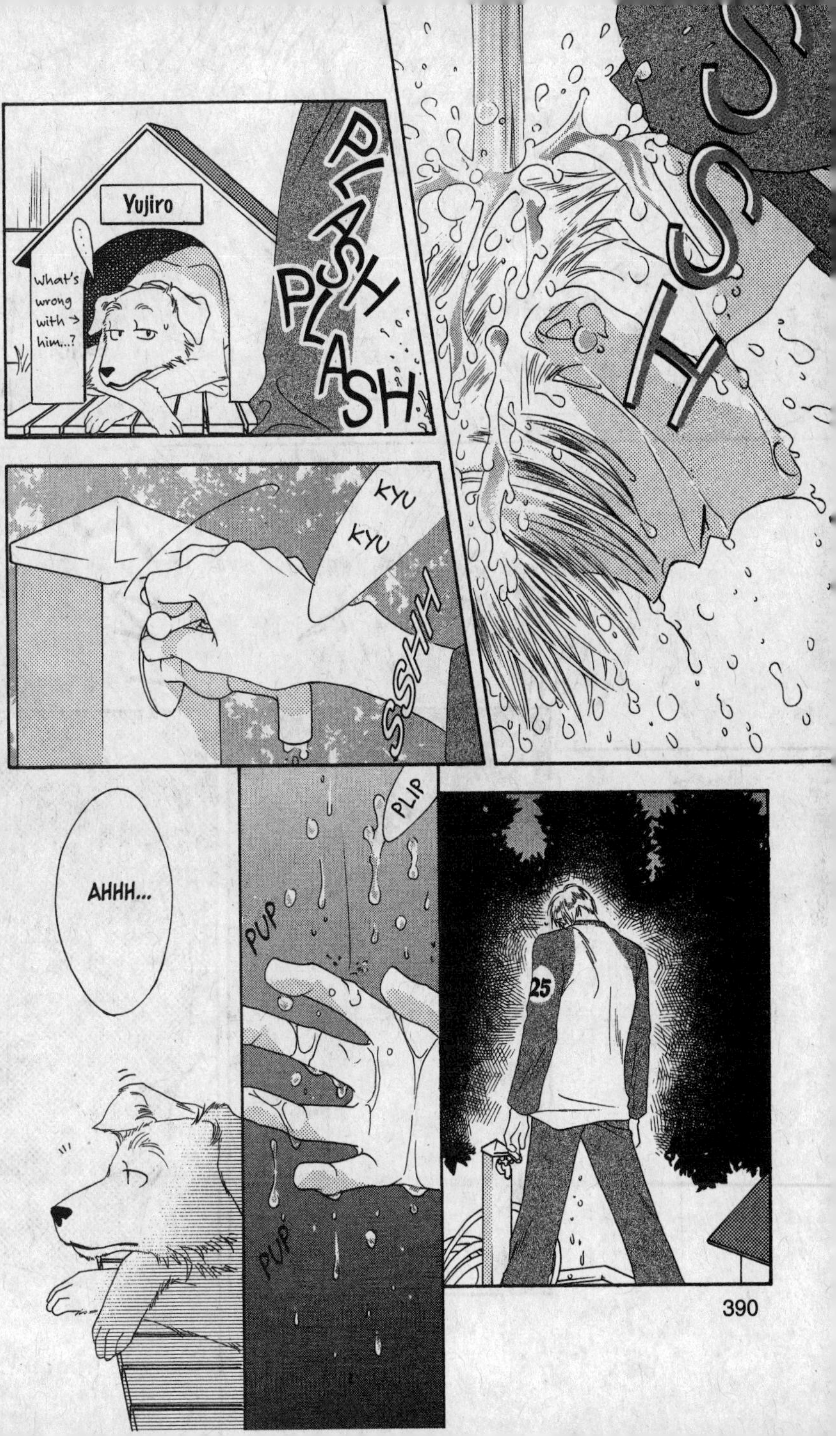
SSSH
Yujiro
What's wrong with → him...?
PLASH PLASH PLASH
KYU KYU
SSHH
PLIP
PUP
PUP
AHHH...

WHISPERED SECRETS

THAT'S RIGHT!

HELLO HELLO! IT'S HANA-KIMI VOL. 6! THIS VOLUME'S COVER FEATURES UMEDA, THE MOST REQUESTED CHARACTER. I DREW IT ESPECIALLY FOR THIS BOOK!! MY EDITOR TOLD ME THAT IT WAS SCARY. (WHY?) THIS IS UNRELATED, BUT SOMEBODY POINTED OUT THAT UMEDA'S FAMILY LOOKS A LOT LIKE THE FAMILY FROM SAZAE-SAN. AND I GUESS THEY'RE RIGHT! THIS MEANS UMEDA IS KATSUO, RIO IS WAKAME, AND NANBA IS TARA-CHAN! HA HA!

IN THIS BOOK, NOE AND SEKIME IMITATE THE (FEMALE) IDOL GROUP PAIRETSU (SEE PAGE 10). THEY WEREN'T THAT POPULAR WHEN I WROTE THIS, SO I WASN'T SURE IF ANYONE WOULD GET IT OR NOT.

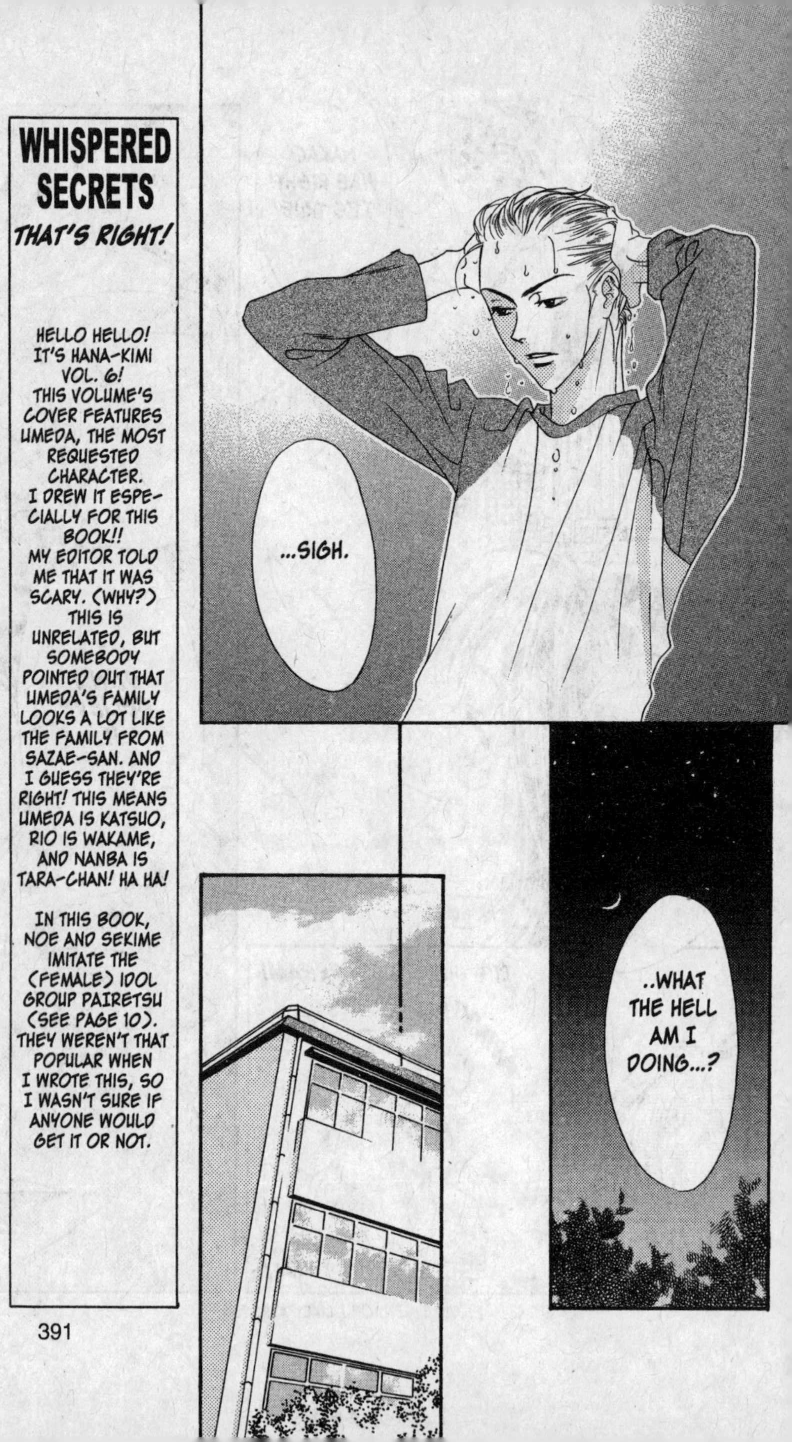
...SIGH.
..WHAT THE HELL AM I DOING...?

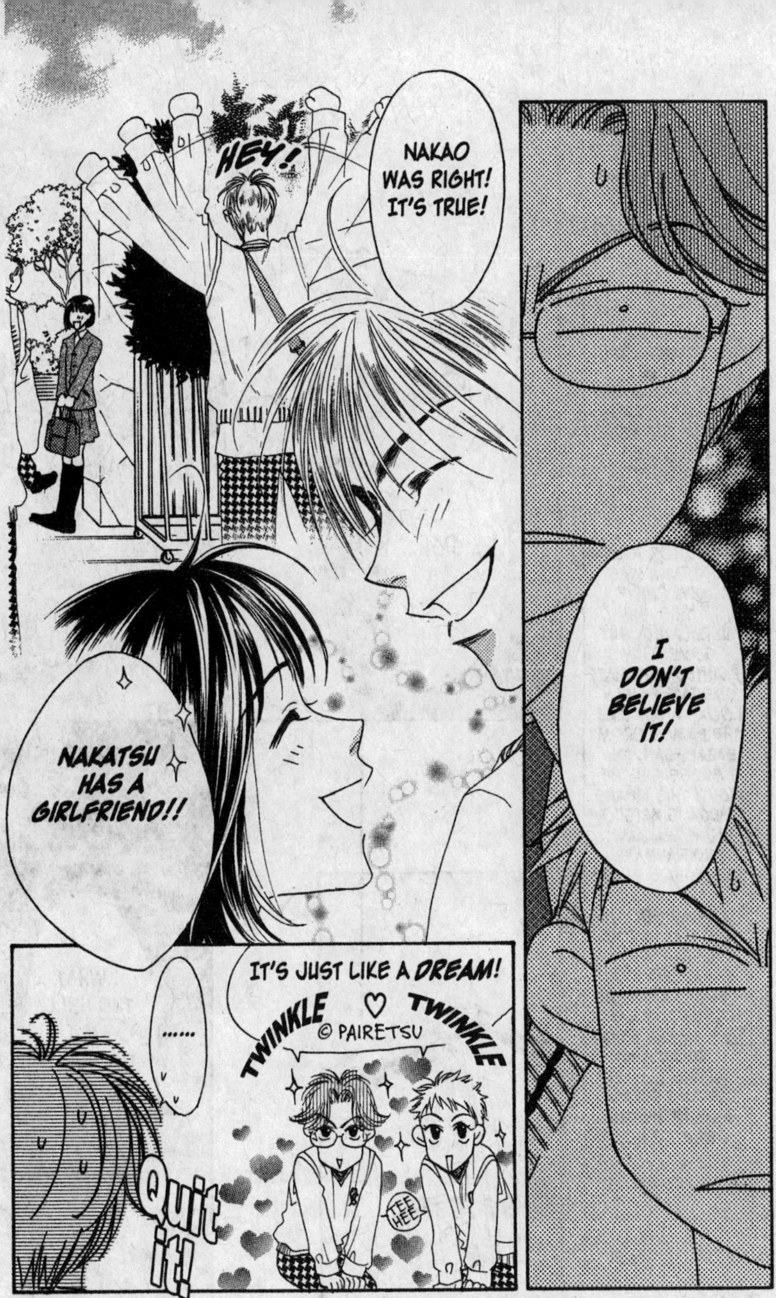
I DON'T BELIEVE IT!
HEY!
NAKAO WAS RIGHT! IT'S TRUE!
NAKATSU HAS A GIRLFRIEND!!
IT'S JUST LIKE A DREAM!
TWINKLE ♡ TWINKLE
© PAIRETSU
TEE HEE
......
Quit it!

...DID I MENTION I LIKE PAIRETSU?

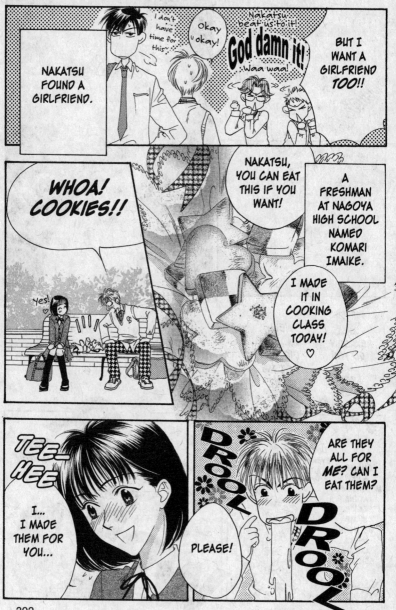

BUT I WANT A GIRLFRIEND *TOO*!!
Nakatsu beat us to it!
God damn it!
Waa waa!
Okay okay!
I don't have time for this~
NAKATSU FOUND A GIRLFRIEND.
A FRESHMAN AT NAGOYA HIGH SCHOOL NAMED KOMARI IMAIKE.
NAKATSU, YOU CAN EAT THIS IF YOU WANT!
I MADE IT IN COOKING CLASS TODAY! ♡
WHOA! COOKIES!!
Yes! ♡
ARE THEY ALL FOR *ME*? CAN I EAT THEM?
DROOL
DROOL
PLEASE!
TEE-HEE
I... I MADE THEM FOR YOU...

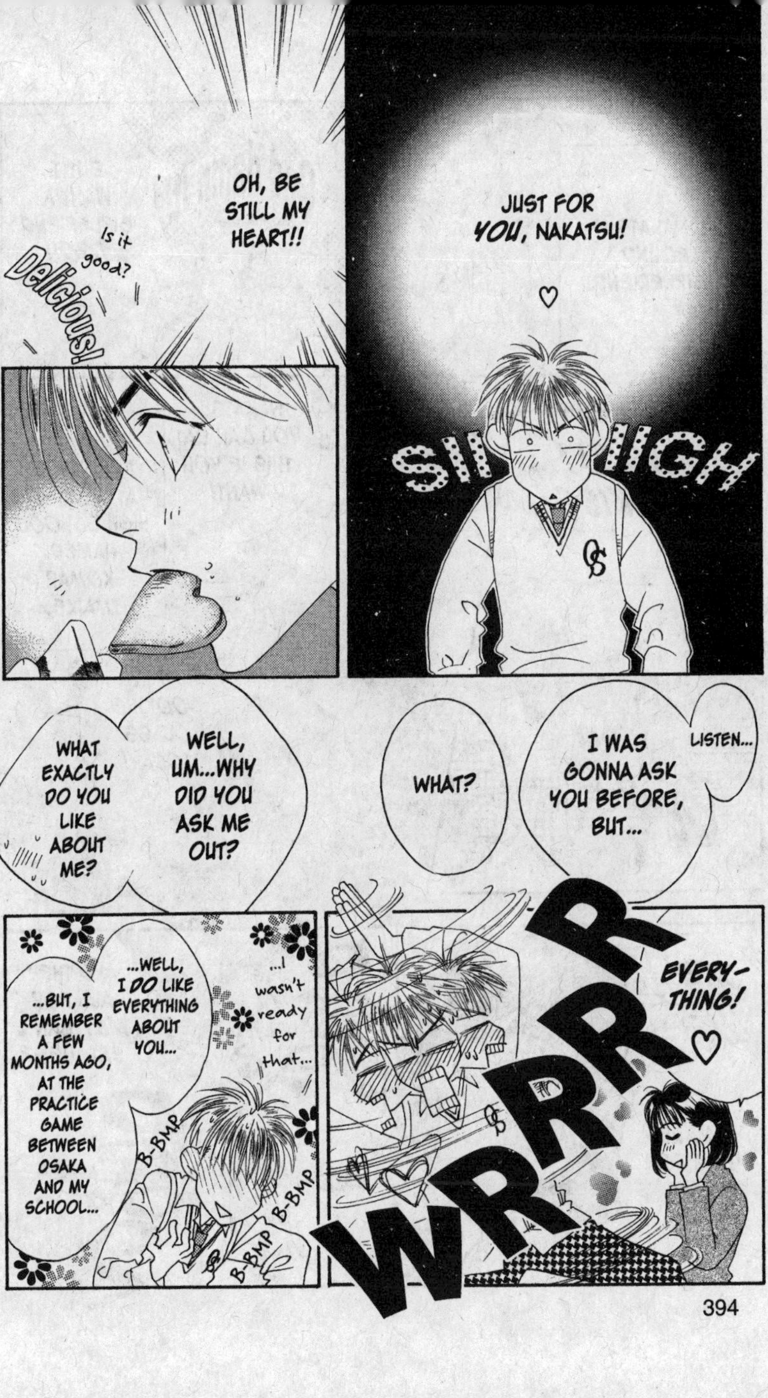
JUST FOR YOU, NAKATSU!
SIIIIGH
OH, BE STILL MY HEART!!
Is it good?
Delicious!
LISTEN...
I WAS GONNA ASK YOU BEFORE, BUT...
WHAT?
WELL, UM...WHY DID YOU ASK ME OUT?
WHAT EXACTLY DO YOU LIKE ABOUT ME?
EVERY-THING!
WRRRR
...I wasn't ready for that...
...WELL, I DO LIKE EVERYTHING ABOUT YOU...
...BUT, I REMEMBER A FEW MONTHS AGO, AT THE PRACTICE GAME BETWEEN OSAKA AND MY SCHOOL...
B-BMP
B-BMP
B-BMP

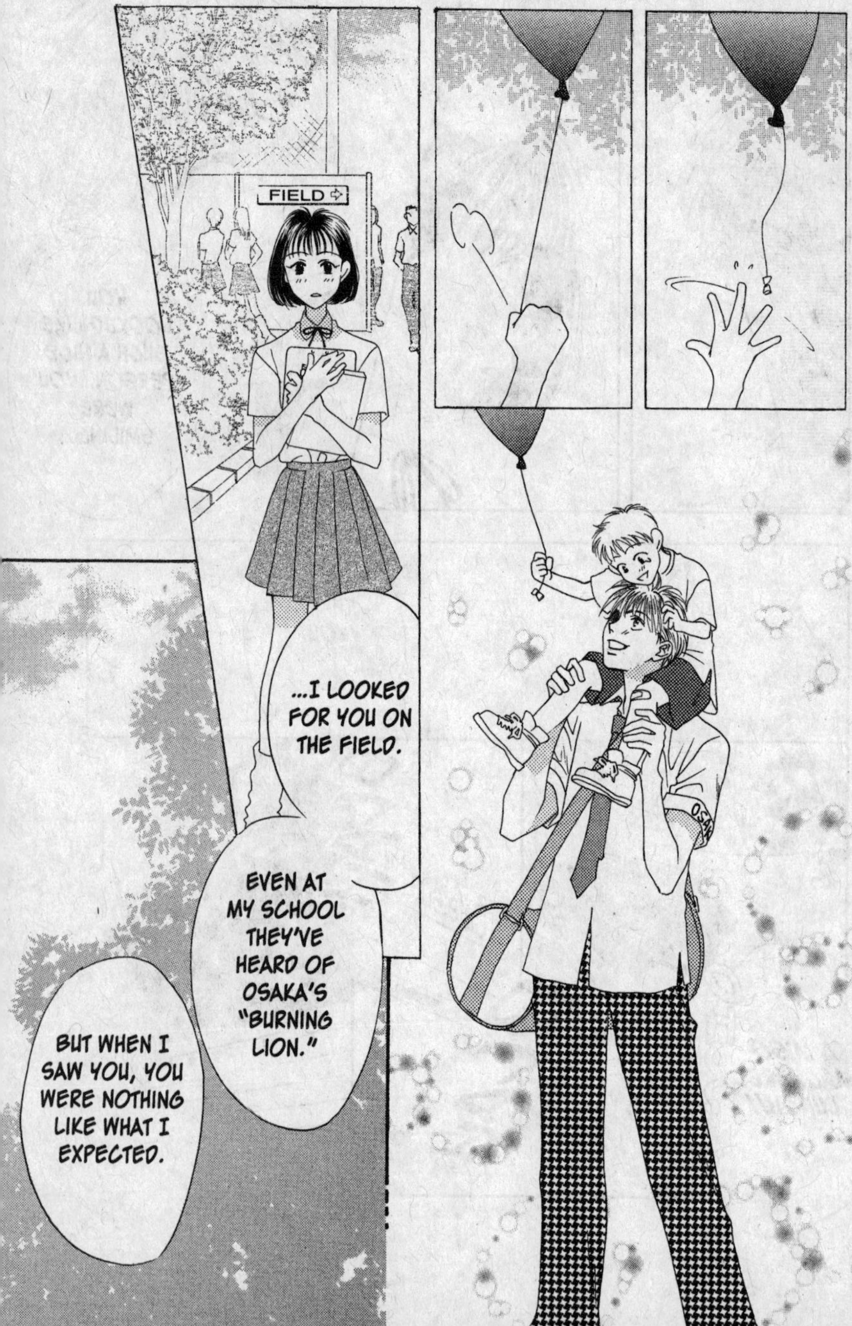
FIELD
...I LOOKED FOR YOU ON THE FIELD.
EVEN AT MY SCHOOL THEY'VE HEARD OF OSAKA'S "BURNING LION."
BUT WHEN I SAW YOU, YOU WERE NOTHING LIKE WHAT I EXPECTED.

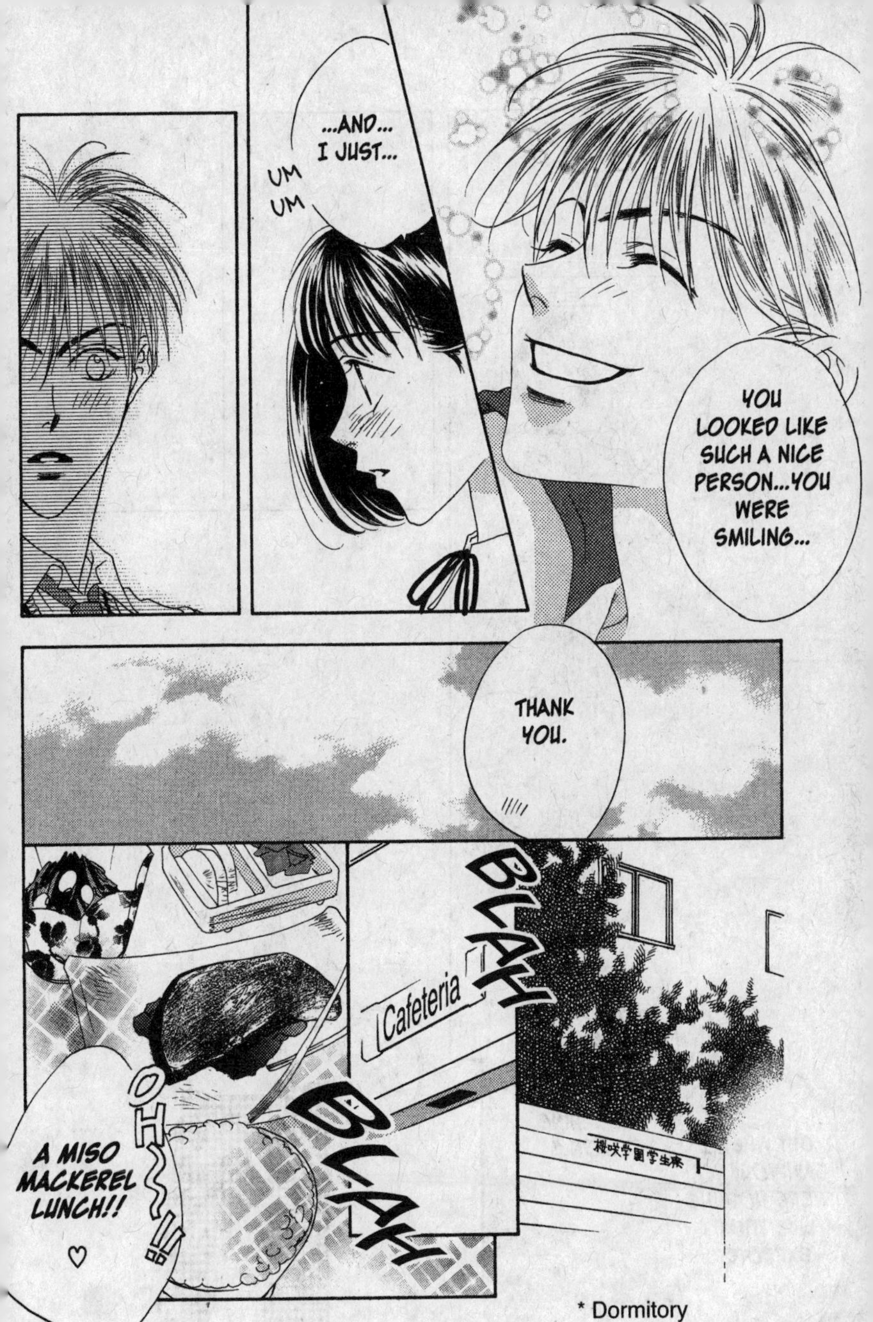
...AND... I JUST...
UM UM
YOU LOOKED LIKE SUCH A NICE PERSON...YOU WERE SMILING...
THANK YOU.
BLAH
BLAH
Cafeteria
桜咲学園学生寮
OH~!!
A MISO MACKEREL LUNCH!! ♡

* Dormitory

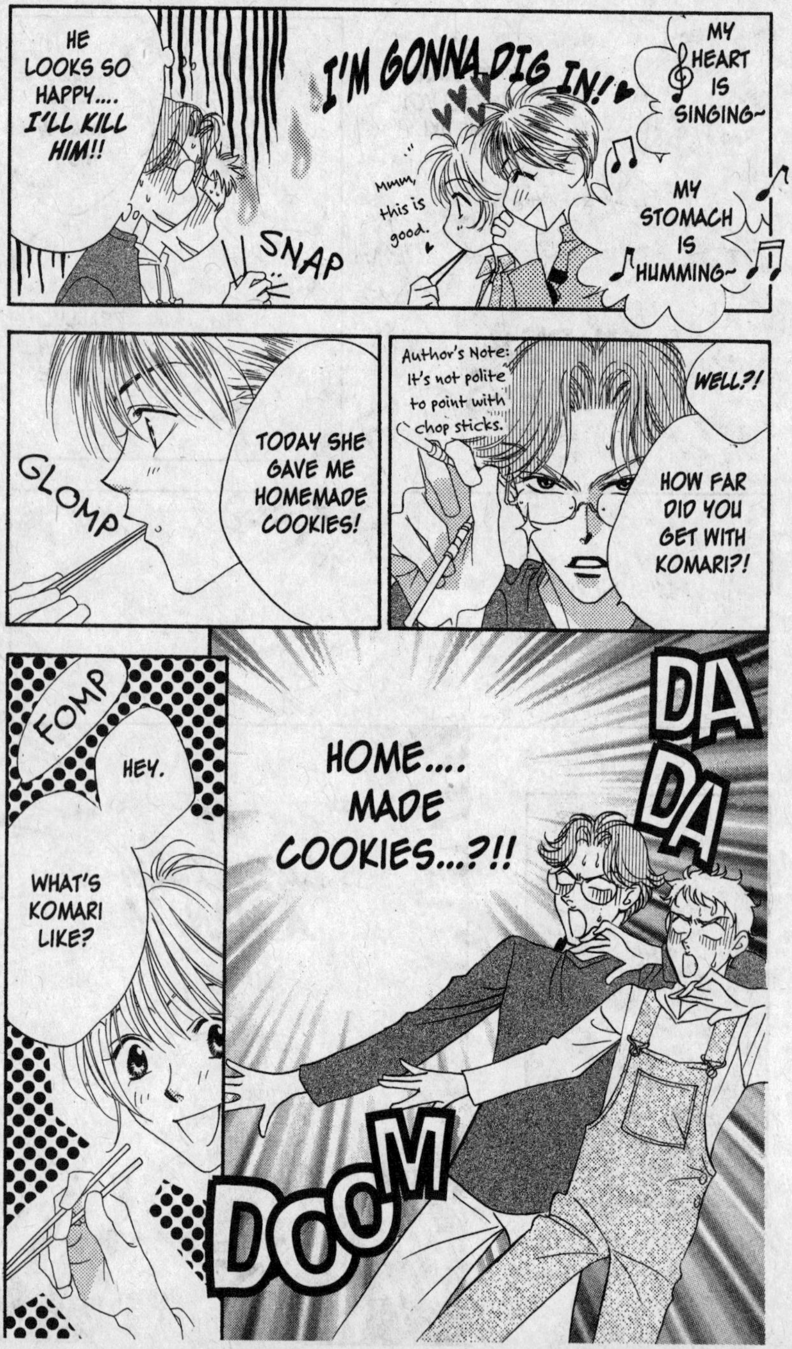
MY HEART IS SINGING~
MY STOMACH IS HUMMING~
I'M GONNA DIG IN!
Mmm, this is good.
SNAP
HE LOOKS SO HAPPY.... I'LL KILL HIM!!
WELL?!
Author's Note: It's not polite to point with chop sticks.
HOW FAR DID YOU GET WITH KOMARI?!
TODAY SHE GAVE ME HOMEMADE COOKIES!
GLOMP
DA DA
HOME.... MADE COOKIES...?!!
DOOM
FOMP
HEY.
WHAT'S KOMARI LIKE?

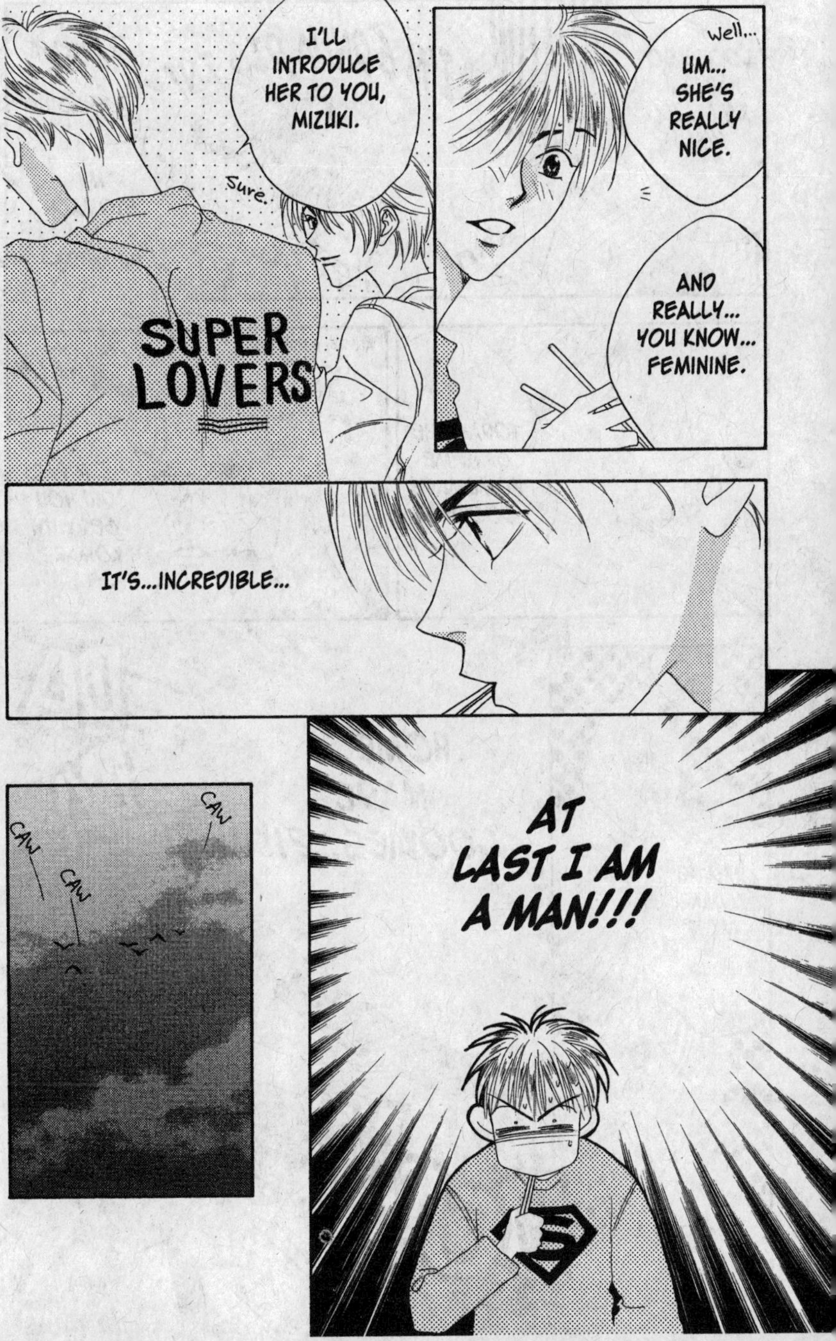
Well...
UM... SHE'S REALLY NICE.
AND REALLY... YOU KNOW... FEMININE.
I'LL INTRODUCE HER TO YOU, MIZUKI.
Sure.
SUPER LOVERS
IT'S...INCREDIBLE...
AT LAST I AM A MAN!!!
CAW
CAW
CAW

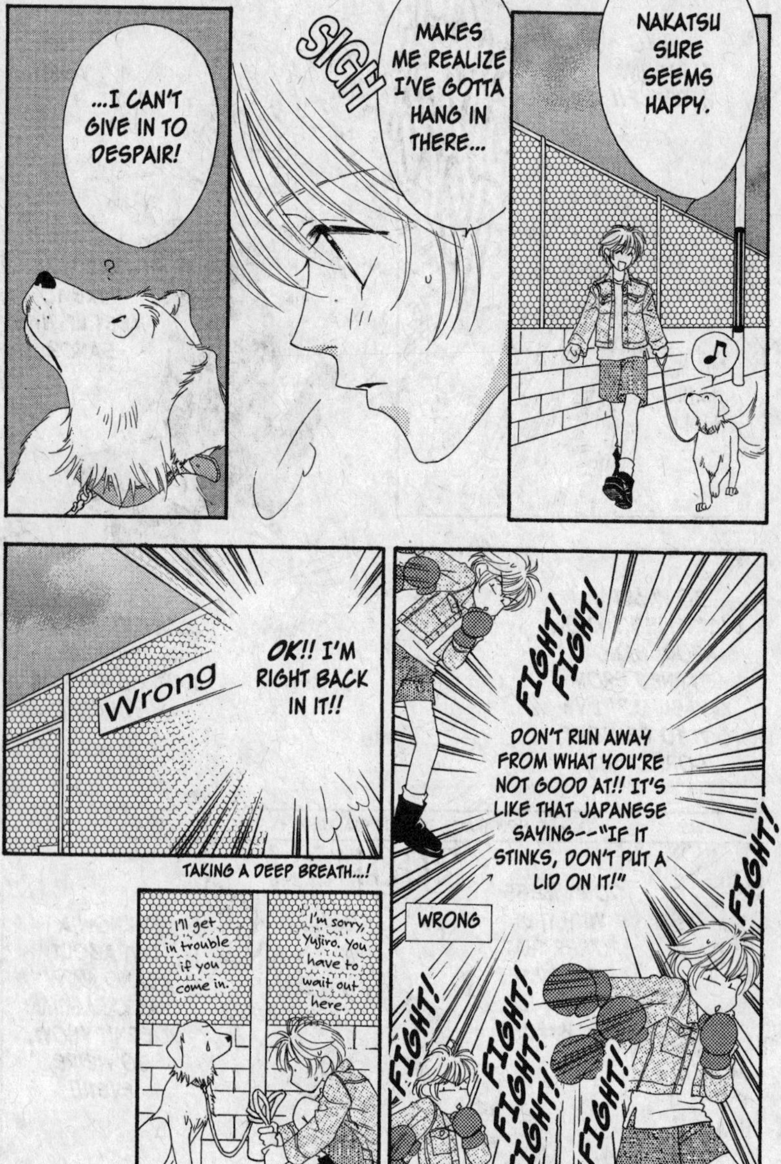
NAKATSU SURE SEEMS HAPPY.
♪
SIGH
MAKES ME REALIZE I'VE GOTTA HANG IN THERE...
...I CAN'T GIVE IN TO DESPAIR!
?
FIGHT! FIGHT!
DON'T RUN AWAY FROM WHAT YOU'RE NOT GOOD AT!! IT'S LIKE THAT JAPANESE SAYING--"IF IT STINKS, DON'T PUT A LID ON IT!"
FIGHT!
WRONG
FIGHT!
FIGHT! FIGHT! FIGHT!
FIGHT!
Wrong
OK!! I'M RIGHT BACK IN IT!!
TAKING A DEEP BREATH...!
I'm sorry, Yujiro. You have to wait out here.
I'll get in trouble if you come in.

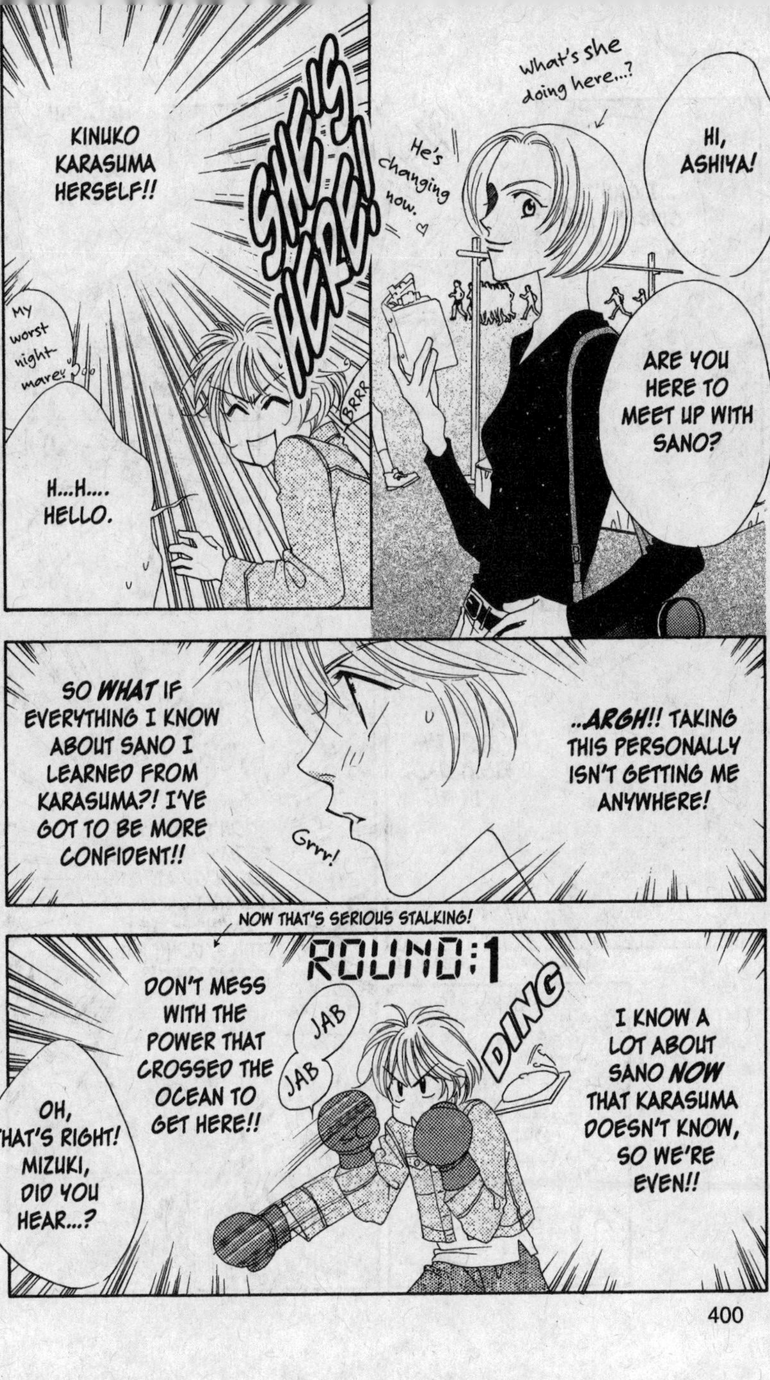
What's she doing here...?
HI, ASHIYA!
He's changing now. ♡
ARE YOU HERE TO MEET UP WITH SANO?
SHE'S HERE!!
KINUKO KARASUMA HERSELF!!
My worst nightmare...
BRRR
H...H.... HELLO.
...ARGH!! TAKING THIS PERSONALLY ISN'T GETTING ME ANYWHERE!
SO WHAT IF EVERYTHING I KNOW ABOUT SANO I LEARNED FROM KARASUMA?! I'VE GOT TO BE MORE CONFIDENT!!
Grrr!
NOW THAT'S SERIOUS STALKING!
ROUND:1
DING
I KNOW A LOT ABOUT SANO NOW THAT KARASUMA DOESN'T KNOW, SO WE'RE EVEN!!
DON'T MESS WITH THE POWER THAT CROSSED THE OCEAN TO GET HERE!!
JAB
JAB
OH, THAT'S RIGHT! MIZUKI, DID YOU HEAR...?

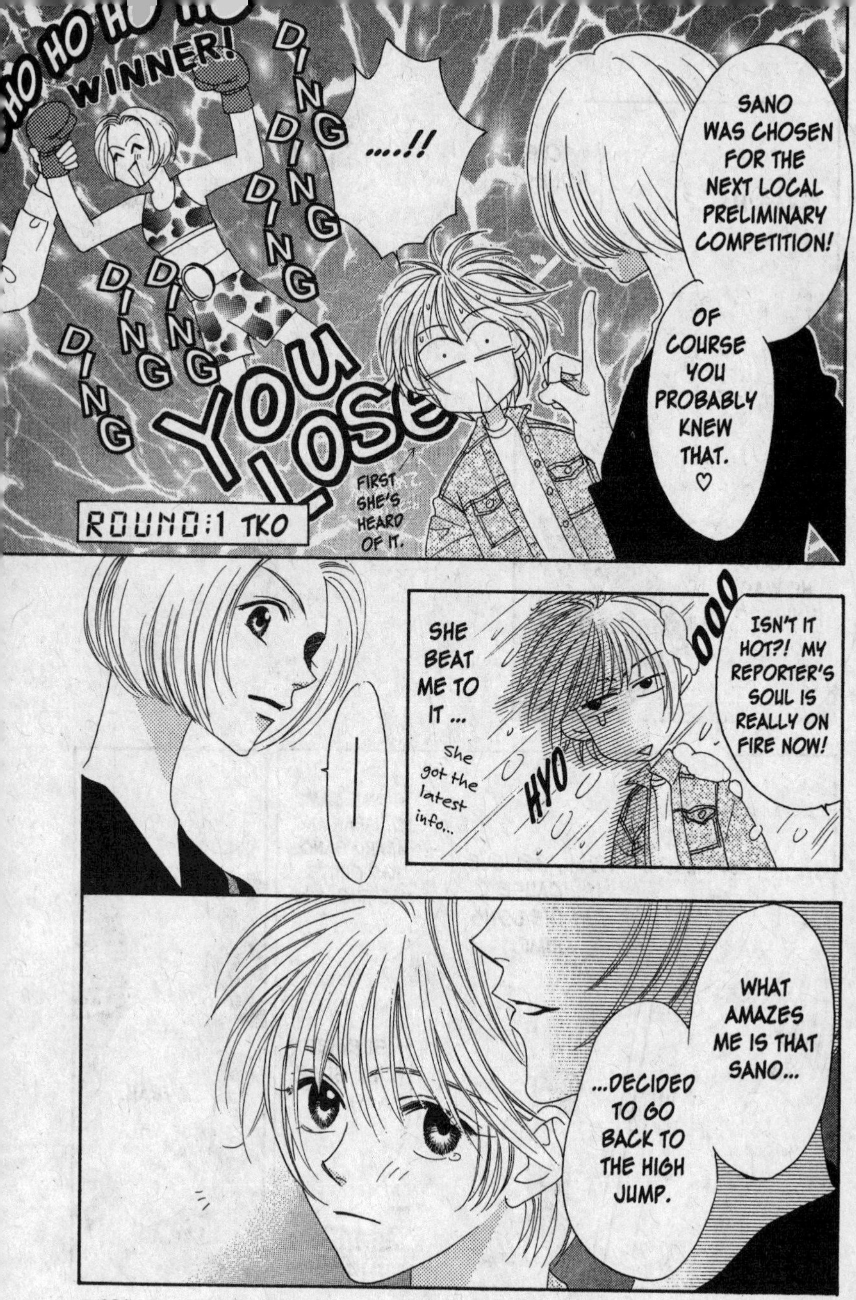
SANO WAS CHOSEN FOR THE NEXT LOCAL PRELIMINARY COMPETITION!
OF COURSE YOU PROBABLY KNEW THAT. ♡
....!!
HO HO HO
WINNER!
DING DING DING DING DING
YOU LOSE
FIRST SHE'S HEARD OF IT.
ROUND:1 TKO
ISN'T IT HOT?! MY REPORTER'S SOUL IS REALLY ON FIRE NOW!
OOO
HYO
SHE BEAT ME TO IT ...
She got the latest info...
—
WHAT AMAZES ME IS THAT SANO...
...DECIDED TO GO BACK TO THE HIGH JUMP.

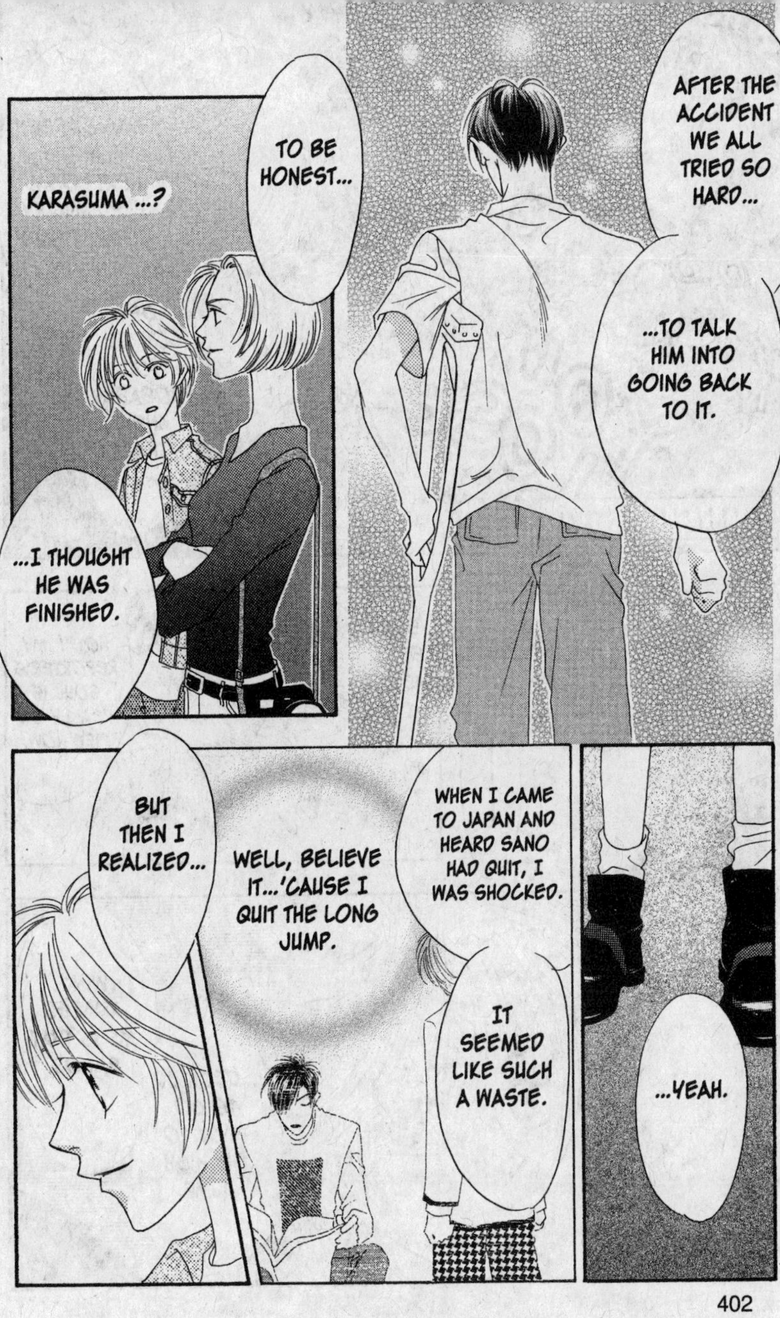
AFTER THE ACCIDENT WE ALL TRIED SO HARD...
...TO TALK HIM INTO GOING BACK TO IT.
TO BE HONEST...
KARASUMA ...?
...I THOUGHT HE WAS FINISHED.
...YEAH.
WHEN I CAME TO JAPAN AND HEARD SANO HAD QUIT, I WAS SHOCKED.
IT SEEMED LIKE SUCH A WASTE.
WELL, BELIEVE IT...'CAUSE I QUIT THE LONG JUMP.
BUT THEN I REALIZED...

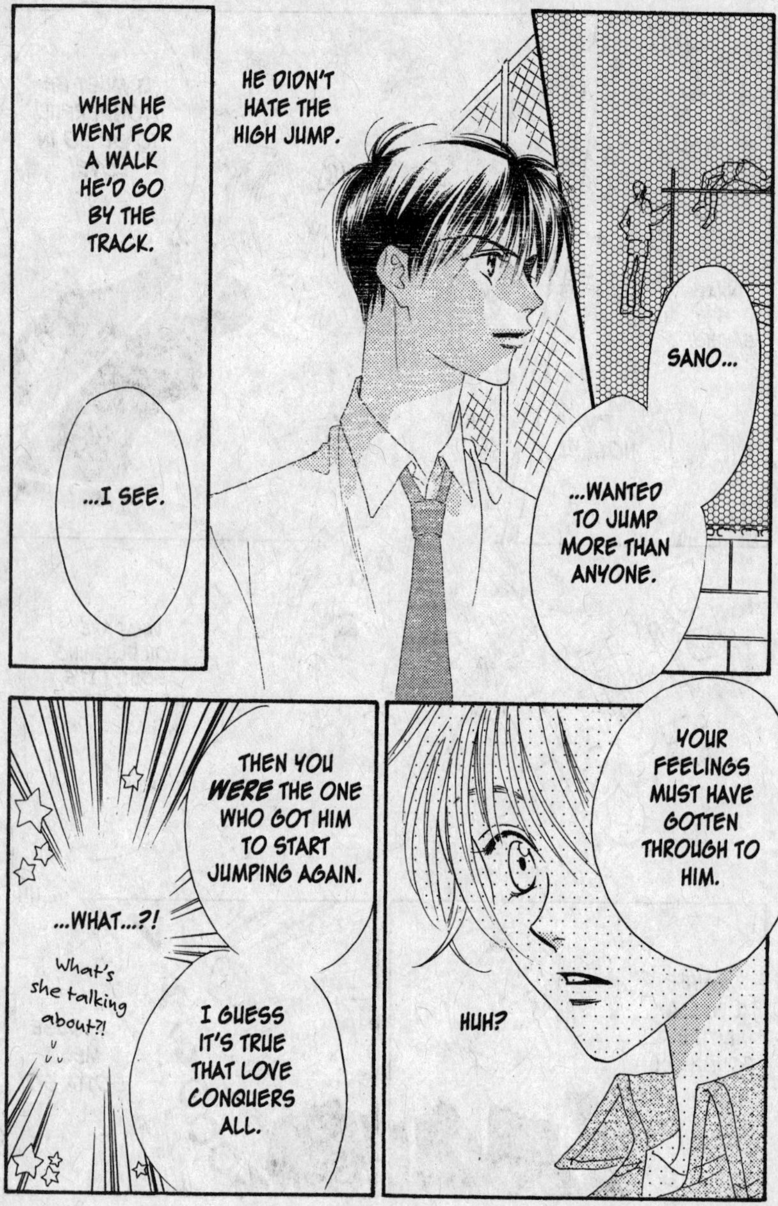
SANO...
...WANTED TO JUMP MORE THAN ANYONE.
HE DIDN'T HATE THE HIGH JUMP.
WHEN HE WENT FOR A WALK HE'D GO BY THE TRACK.
...I SEE.
YOUR FEELINGS MUST HAVE GOTTEN THROUGH TO HIM.
HUH?
THEN YOU *WERE* THE ONE WHO GOT HIM TO START JUMPING AGAIN.
...WHAT...?!
What's she talking about?!
I GUESS IT'S TRUE THAT LOVE CONQUERS ALL.

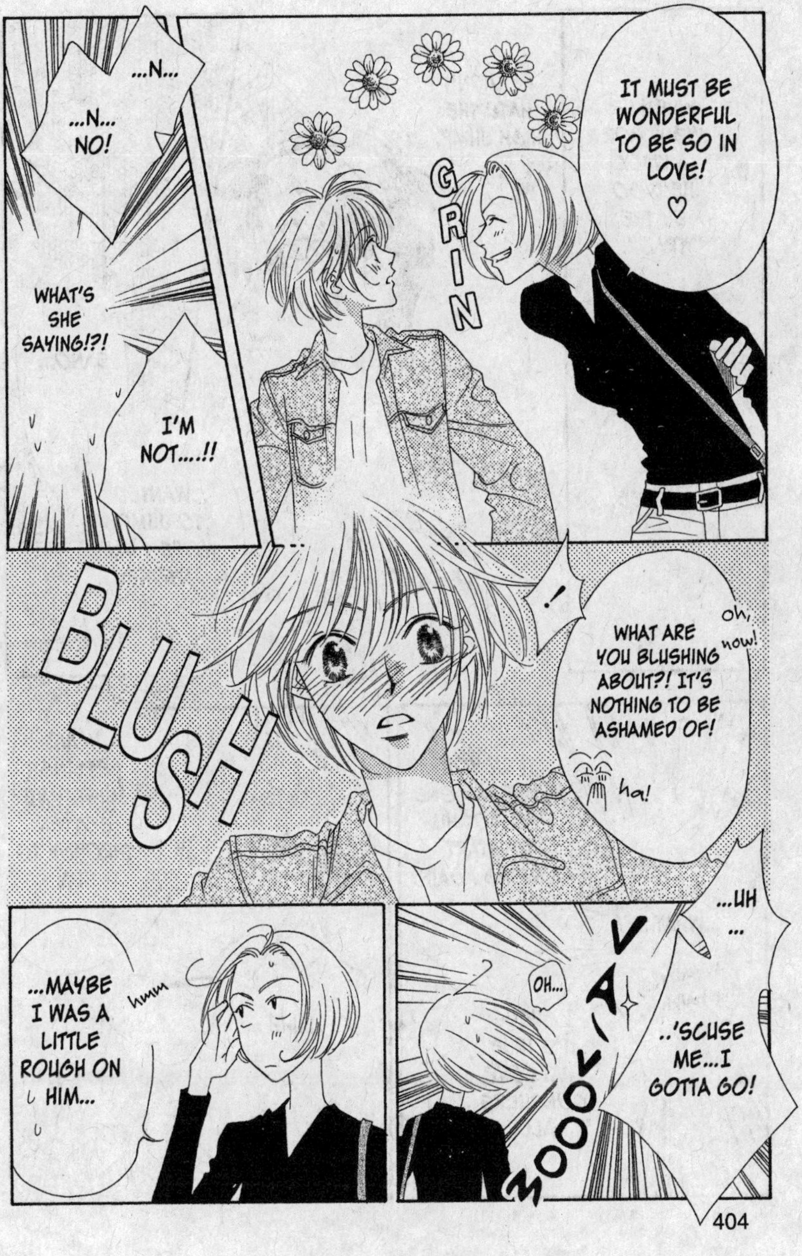
IT MUST BE WONDERFUL TO BE SO IN LOVE! ♡
GRIN
...N...
...N... NO!
WHAT'S SHE SAYING!?!
I'M NOT....!!
BLUSH
!
WHAT ARE YOU BLUSHING ABOUT?! IT'S NOTHING TO BE ASHAMED OF!
oh, now!
ha ha!
...UH ...
..'SCUSE ME...I GOTTA GO!
OH...
...MAYBE I WAS A LITTLE ROUGH ON HIM...
hmm

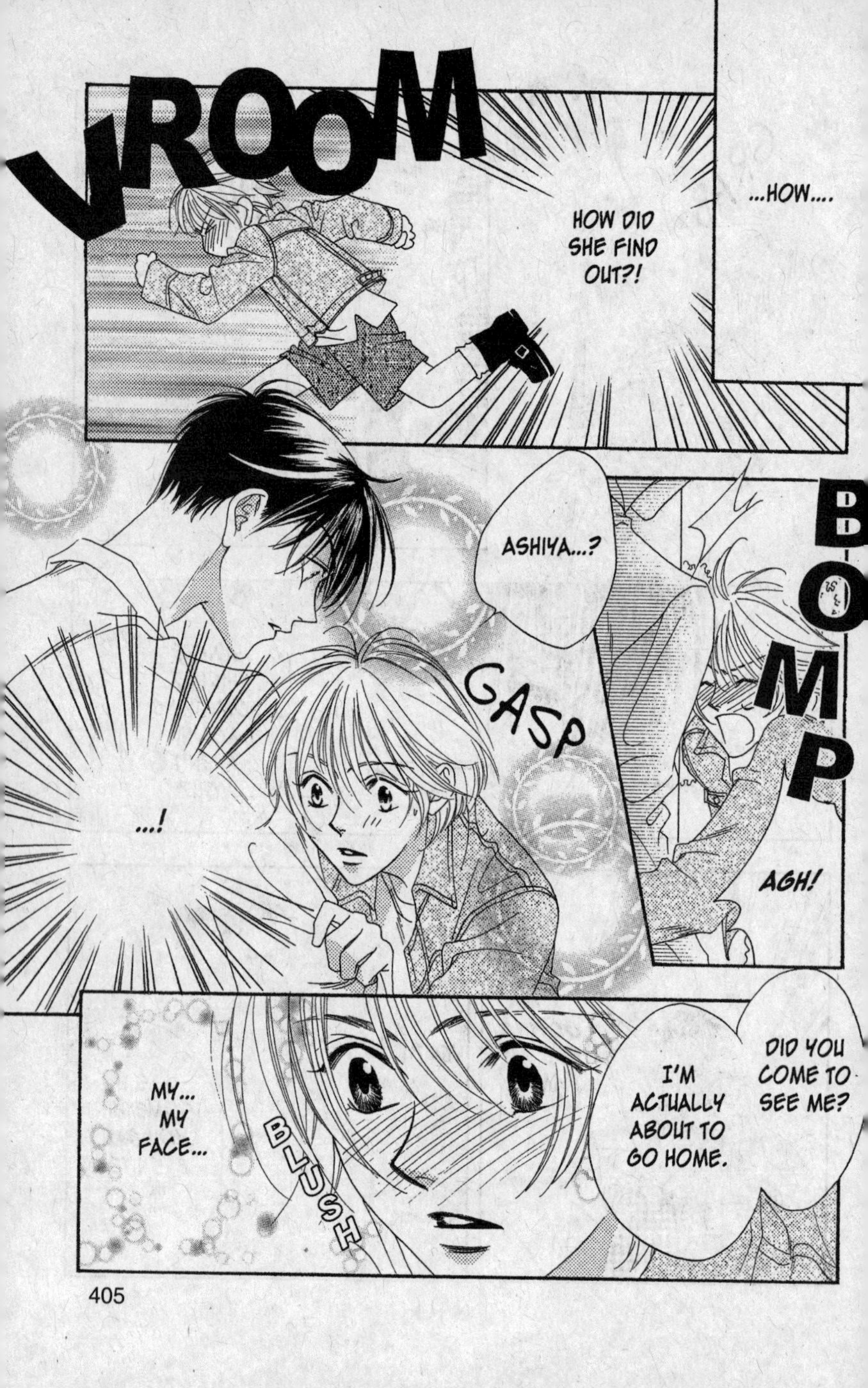
...HOW....
VROOM
HOW DID SHE FIND OUT?!
BOMP
AGH!
ASHIYA...?
GASP
...!
DID YOU COME TO SEE ME?
I'M ACTUALLY ABOUT TO GO HOME.
BLUSH
MY... MY FACE...

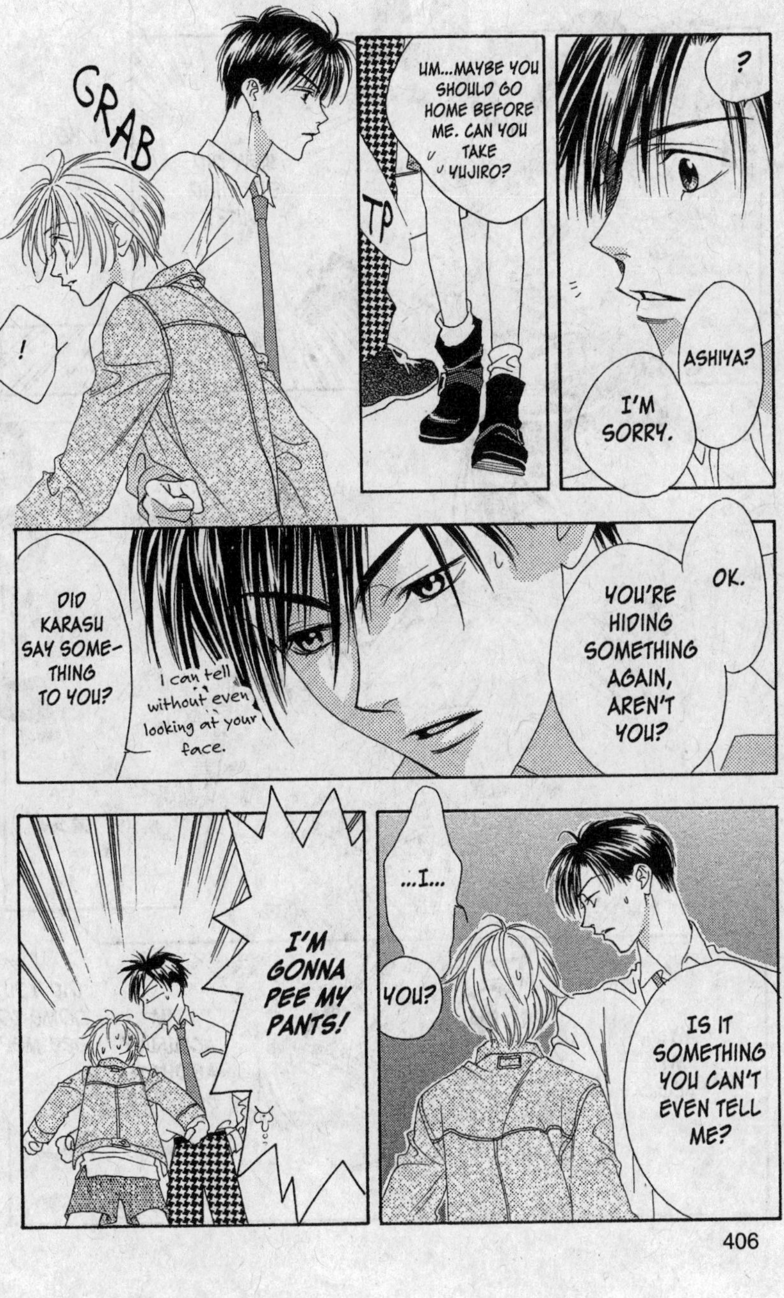
?
ASHIYA?
I'M SORRY.
UM...MAYBE YOU SHOULD GO HOME BEFORE ME. CAN YOU TAKE YUJIRO?
TP
GRAB
!
OK.
YOU'RE HIDING SOMETHING AGAIN, AREN'T YOU?
DID KARASU SAY SOME-THING TO YOU?
I can tell without even looking at your face.
...I...
YOU?
IS IT SOMETHING YOU CAN'T EVEN TELL ME?
I'M GONNA PEE MY PANTS!

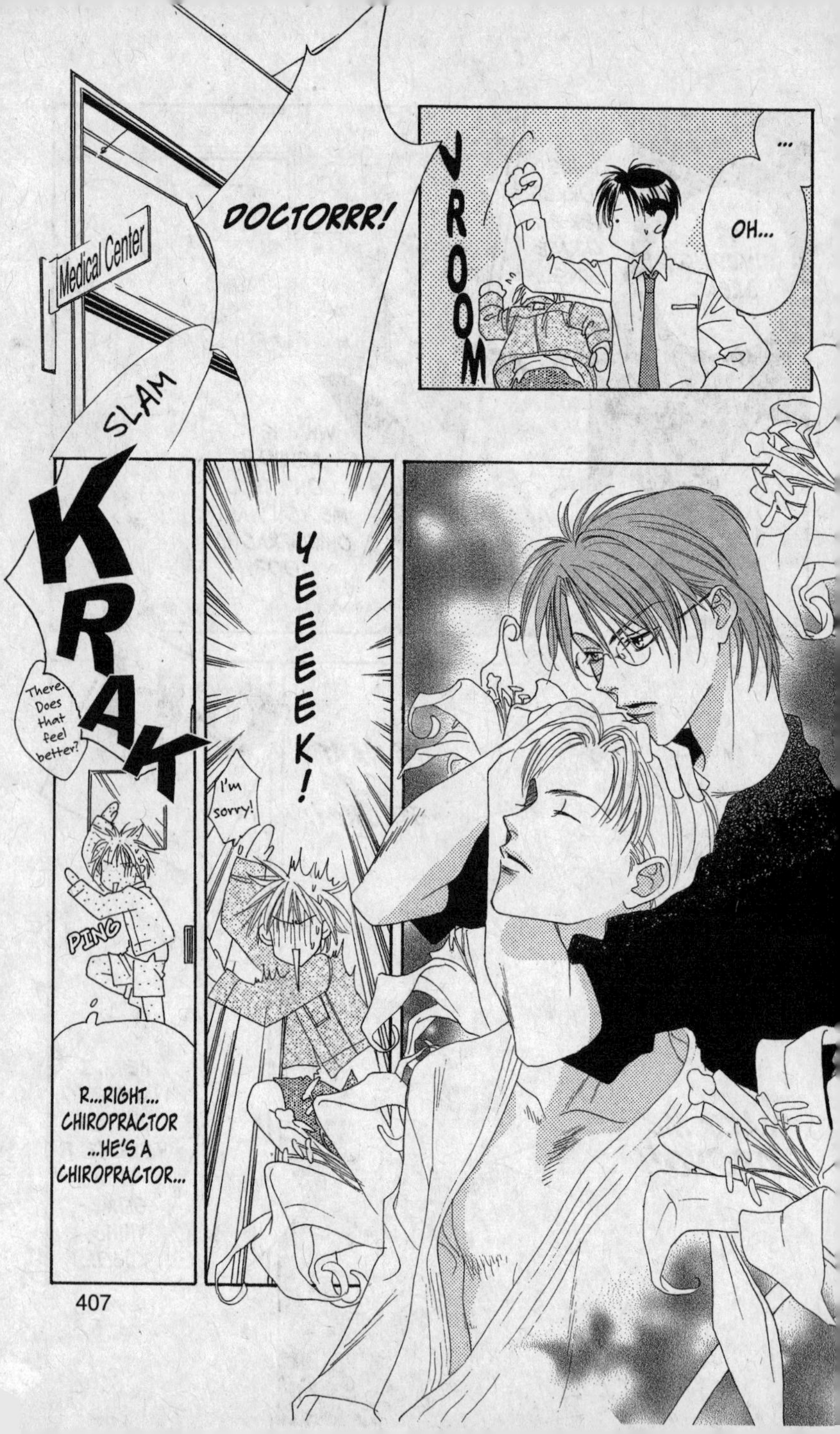
...
OH...
VROOM
DOCTORRR!
Medical Center
SLAM
YEEEEK!
I'm sorry!
KRAK
There. Does that feel better?
PING
R...RIGHT... CHIROPRACTOR ...HE'S A CHIROPRACTOR...

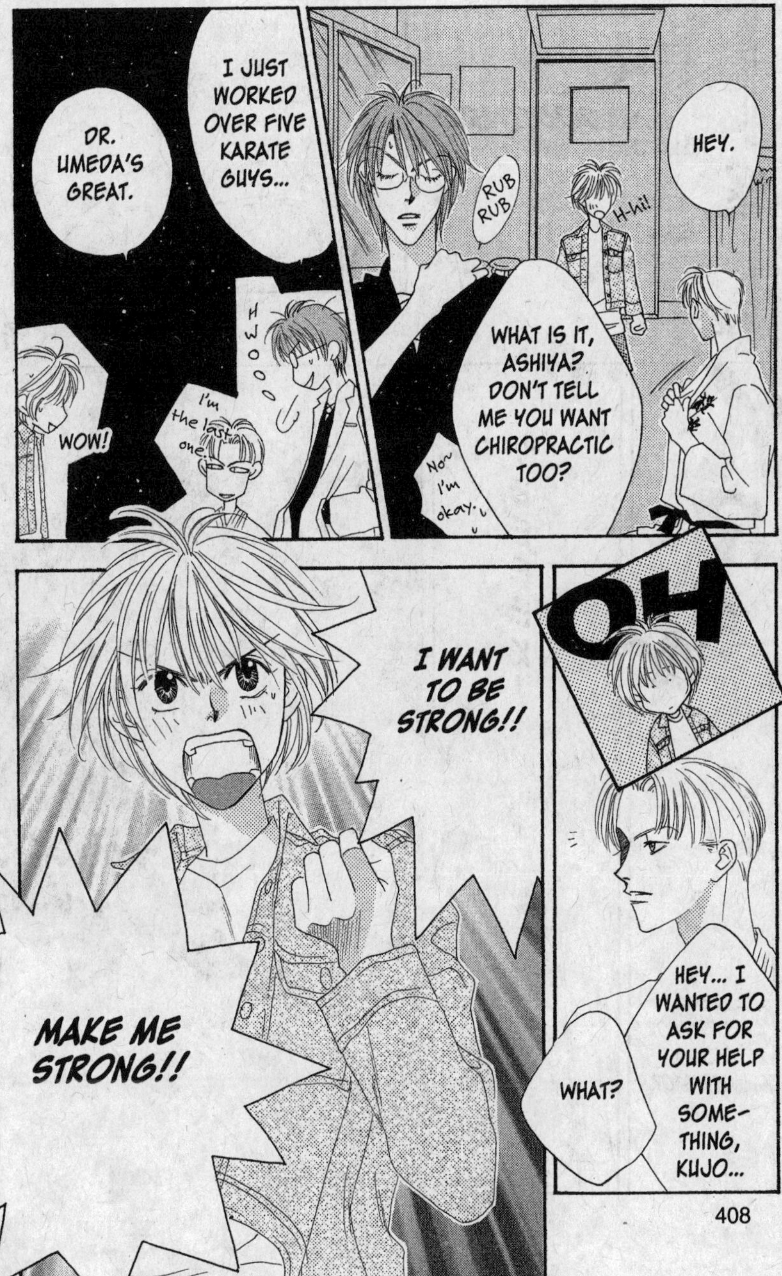
HEY.
H-hi!
RUB RUB
WHAT IS IT, ASHIYA? DON'T TELL ME YOU WANT CHIROPRACTIC TOO?
No~ I'm okay.
I JUST WORKED OVER FIVE KARATE GUYS...
DR. UMEDA'S GREAT.
HWOOO
I'm the last one.
WOW!
OH
HEY... I WANTED TO ASK FOR YOUR HELP WITH SOME-THING, KUJO...
WHAT?
I WANT TO BE STRONG!!
MAKE ME STRONG!!

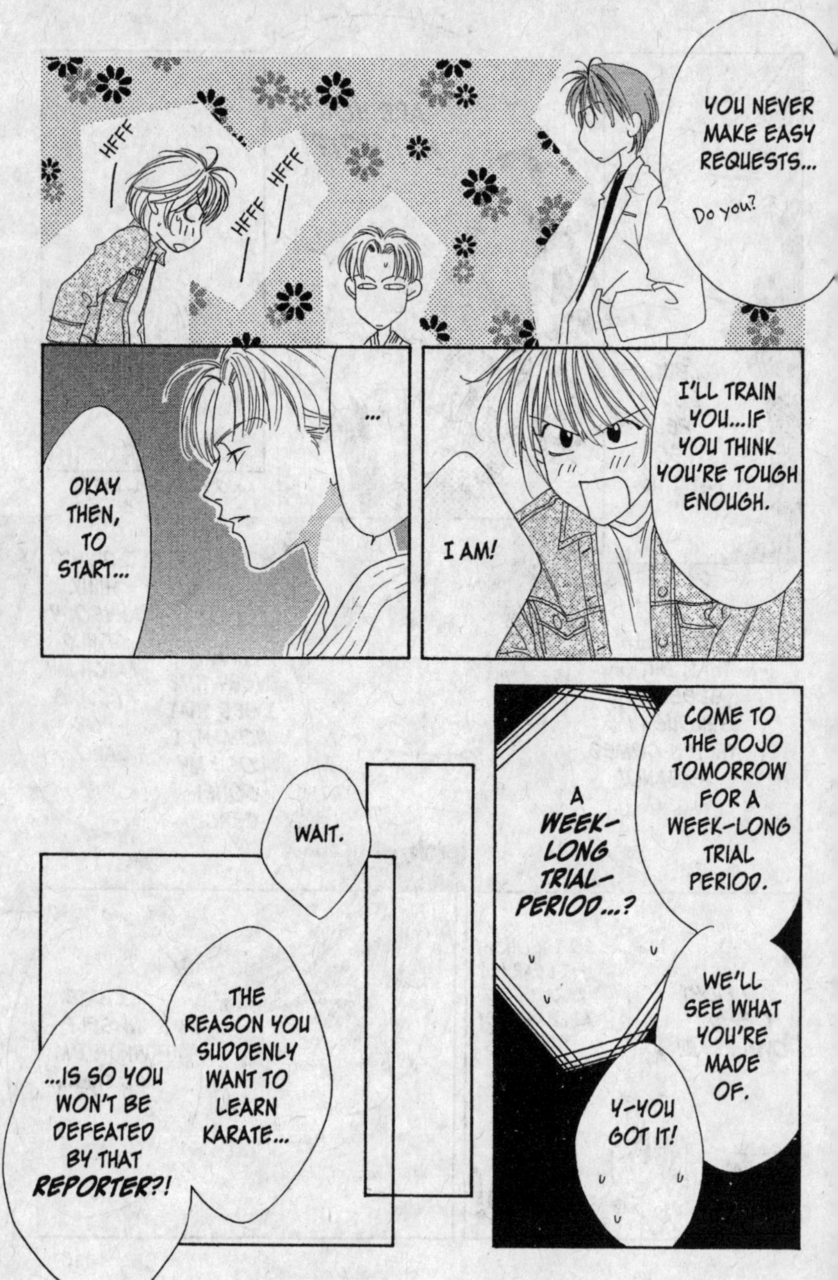
YOU NEVER MAKE EASY REQUESTS...
Do you?
HFFF HFFF
HFFF
I'LL TRAIN YOU...IF YOU THINK YOU'RE TOUGH ENOUGH.
I AM!
...
OKAY THEN, TO START...
COME TO THE DOJO TOMORROW FOR A WEEK-LONG TRIAL PERIOD.
A WEEK-LONG TRIAL-PERIOD...?
WE'LL SEE WHAT YOU'RE MADE OF.
Y-YOU GOT IT!
WAIT.
THE REASON YOU SUDDENLY WANT TO LEARN KARATE...
...IS SO YOU WON'T BE DEFEATED BY THAT REPORTER?!

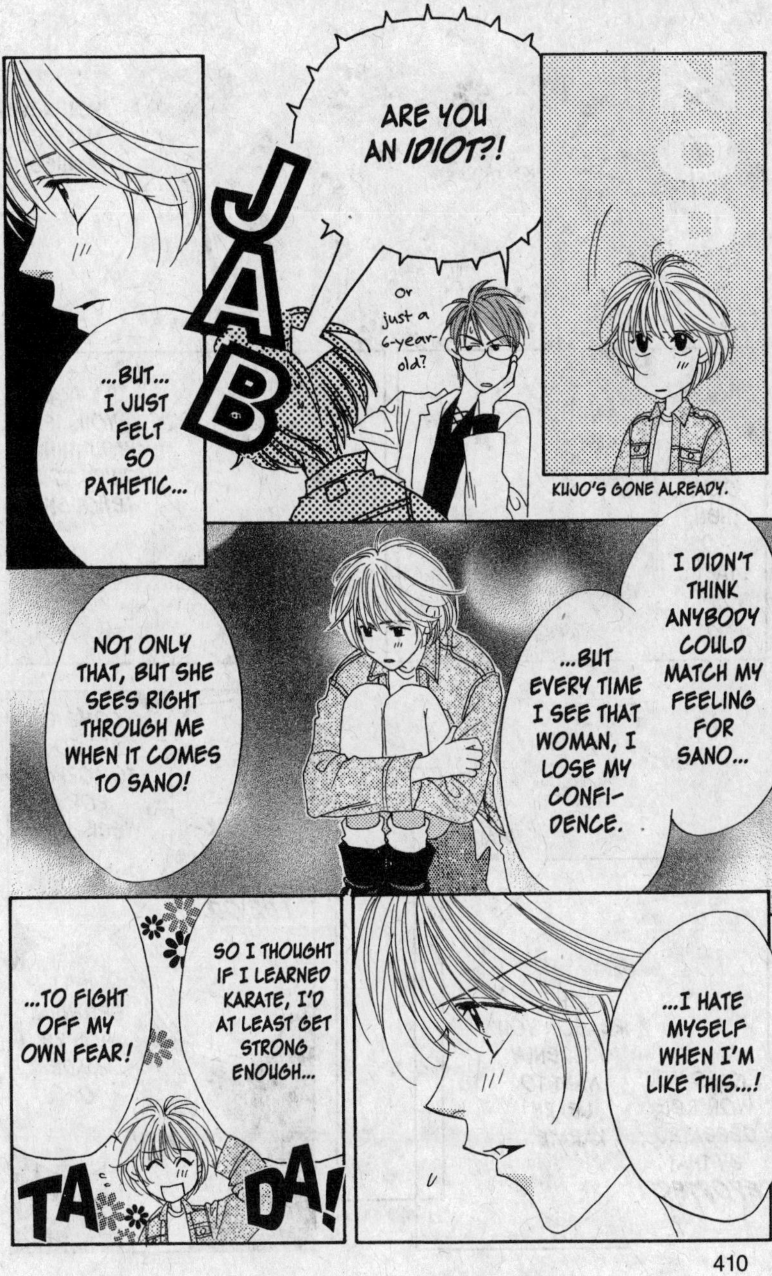
NOD
KUJO'S GONE ALREADY.
ARE YOU AN *IDIOT*?!
Or just a 6-year-old?
JAB
...BUT... I JUST FELT SO PATHETIC...
I DIDN'T THINK ANYBODY COULD MATCH MY FEELING FOR SANO...
...BUT EVERY TIME I SEE THAT WOMAN, I LOSE MY CONFI-DENCE.
NOT ONLY THAT, BUT SHE SEES RIGHT THROUGH ME WHEN IT COMES TO SANO!
...I HATE MYSELF WHEN I'M LIKE THIS...!
SO I THOUGHT IF I LEARNED KARATE, I'D AT LEAST GET STRONG ENOUGH...
...TO FIGHT OFF MY OWN FEAR!
TA DA!

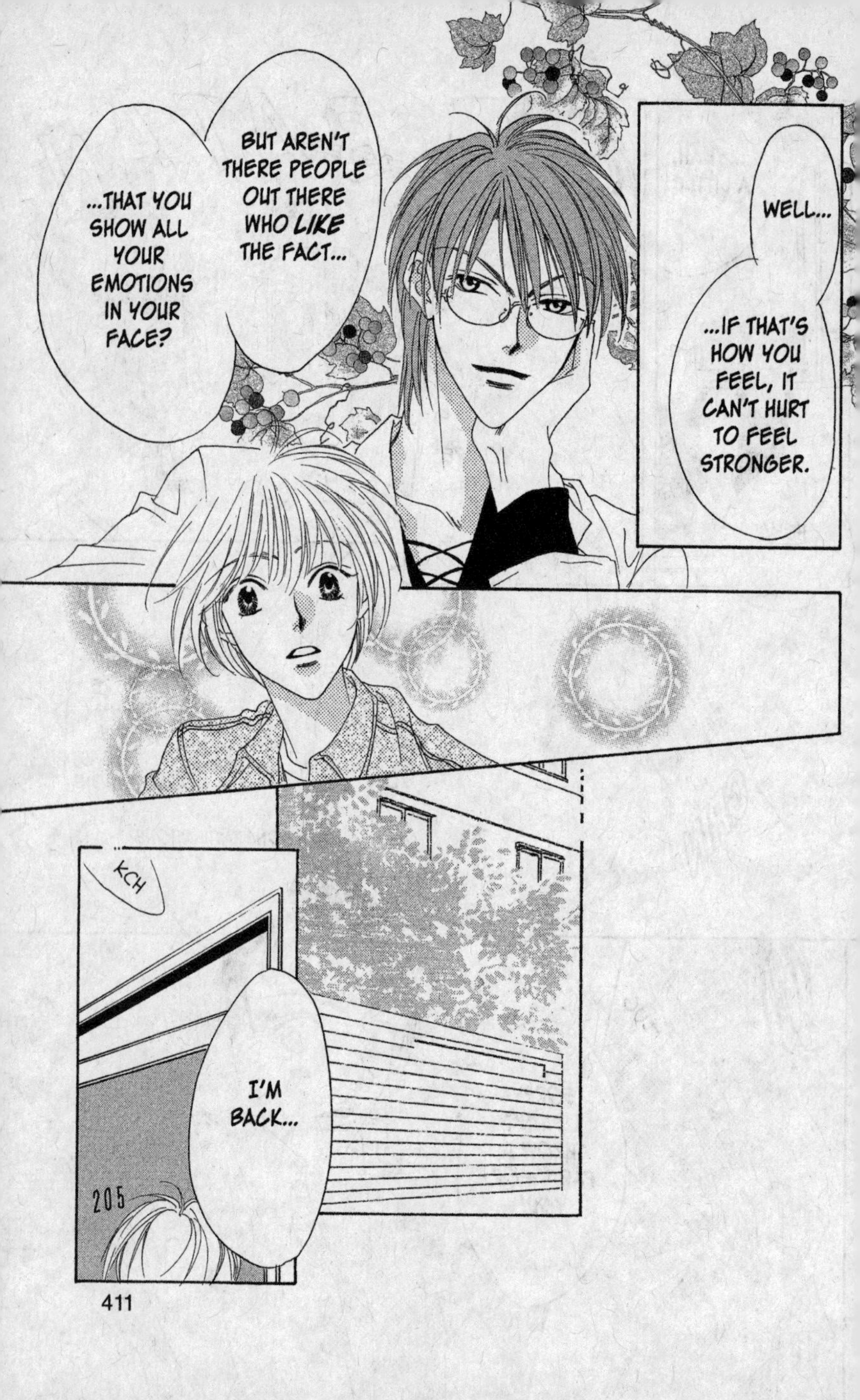
WELL...
...IF THAT'S HOW YOU FEEL, IT CAN'T HURT TO FEEL STRONGER.
BUT AREN'T THERE PEOPLE OUT THERE WHO *LIKE* THE FACT...
...THAT YOU SHOW ALL YOUR EMOTIONS IN YOUR FACE?
KCH
I'M BACK...

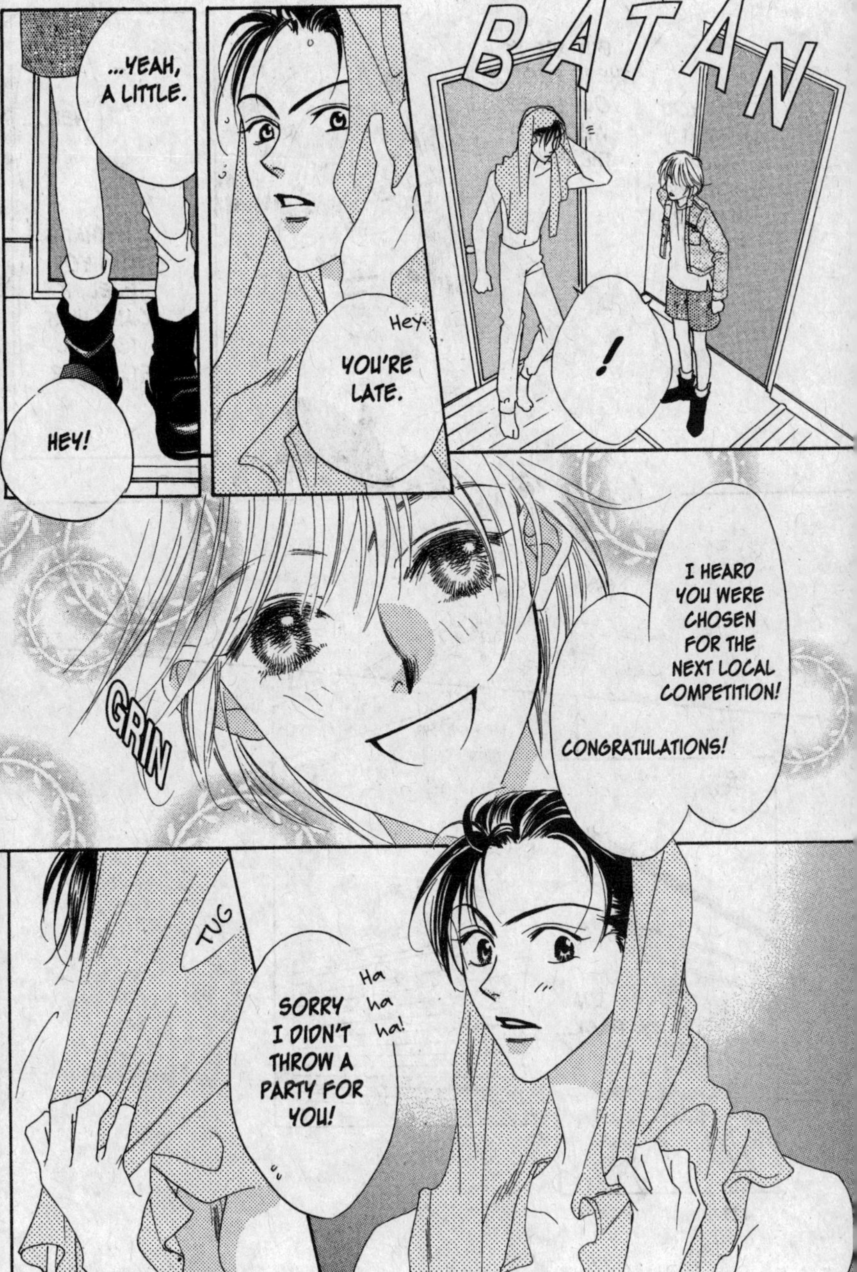
BATAN
!
Hey.
YOU'RE LATE.
...YEAH, A LITTLE.
HEY!
I HEARD YOU WERE CHOSEN FOR THE NEXT LOCAL COMPETITION!
CONGRATULATIONS!
GRIN
Ha ha ha!
SORRY I DIDN'T THROW A PARTY FOR YOU!
TUG

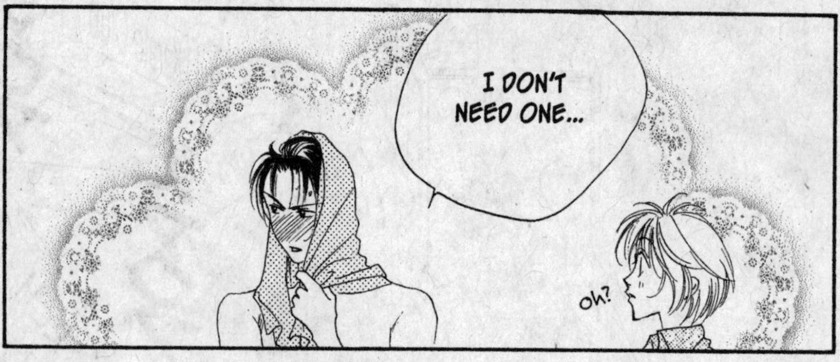
I DON'T NEED ONE...
Oh?

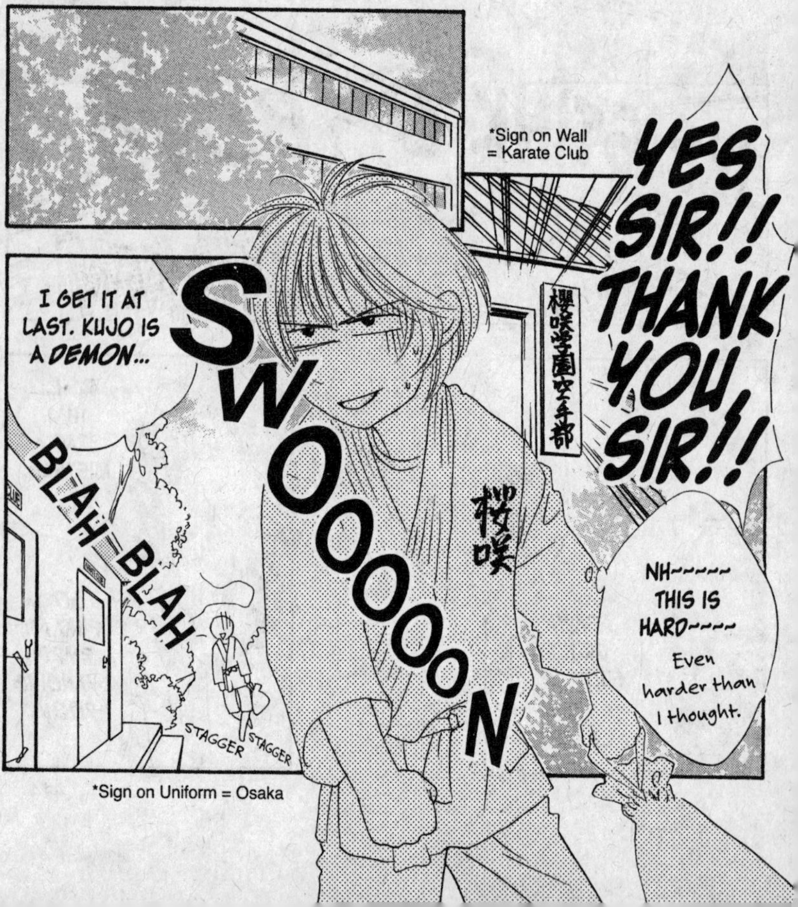
*Sign on Wall = Karate Club
YES SIR!! THANK YOU SIR!!
櫻咲学園空手部
NH~~~~~ THIS IS HARD~~~~
Even harder than I thought.
桜咲
SWOOOOOON
I GET IT AT LAST. KUJO IS A DEMON...
BLAH BLAH BLAH
STAGGER STAGGER
*Sign on Uniform = Osaka

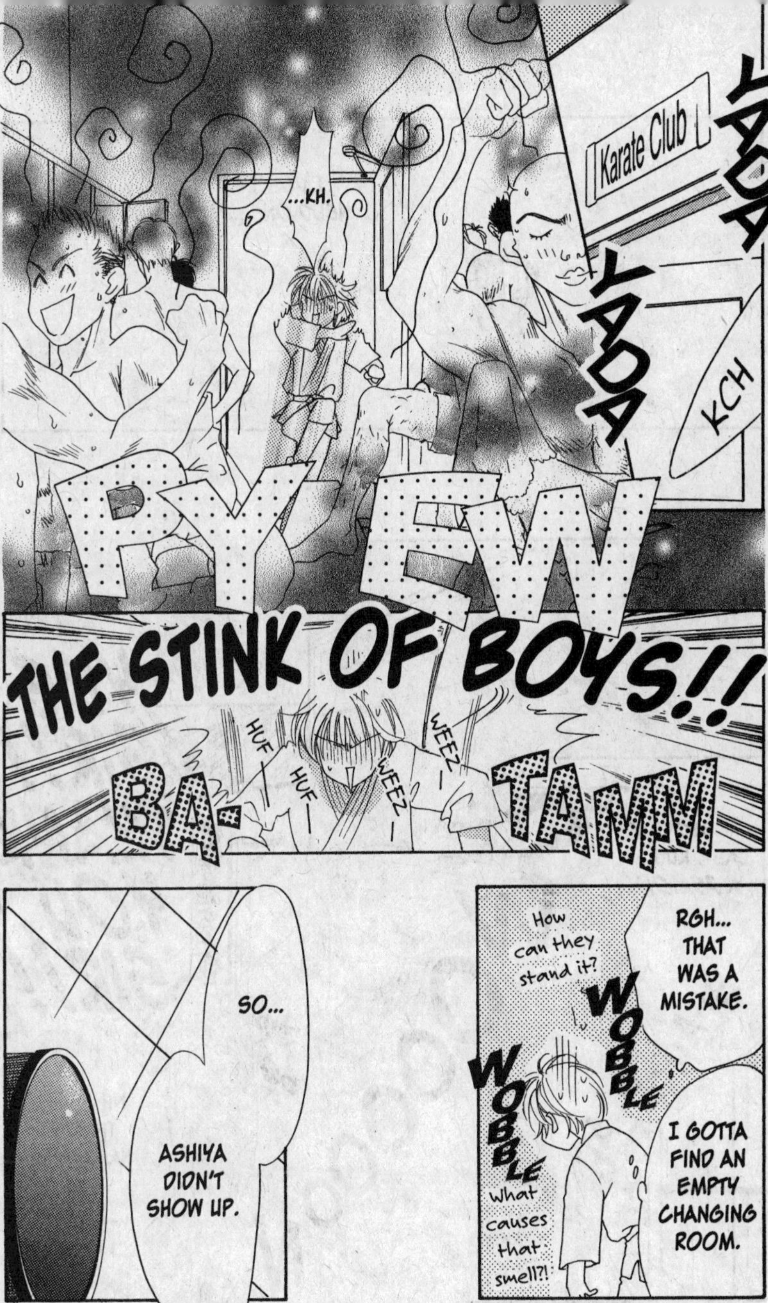
Karate Club
YADA
YADA
KCH
...KH.
PYEW
THE STINK OF BOYS!!
WEEZ
WEEZ
HUF
HUF
BA-TAMM
RGH... THAT WAS A MISTAKE.
How can they stand it?
WOBBLE
WOBBLE
I GOTTA FIND AN EMPTY CHANGING ROOM.
what causes that smell?!
SO...
ASHIYA DIDN'T SHOW UP.

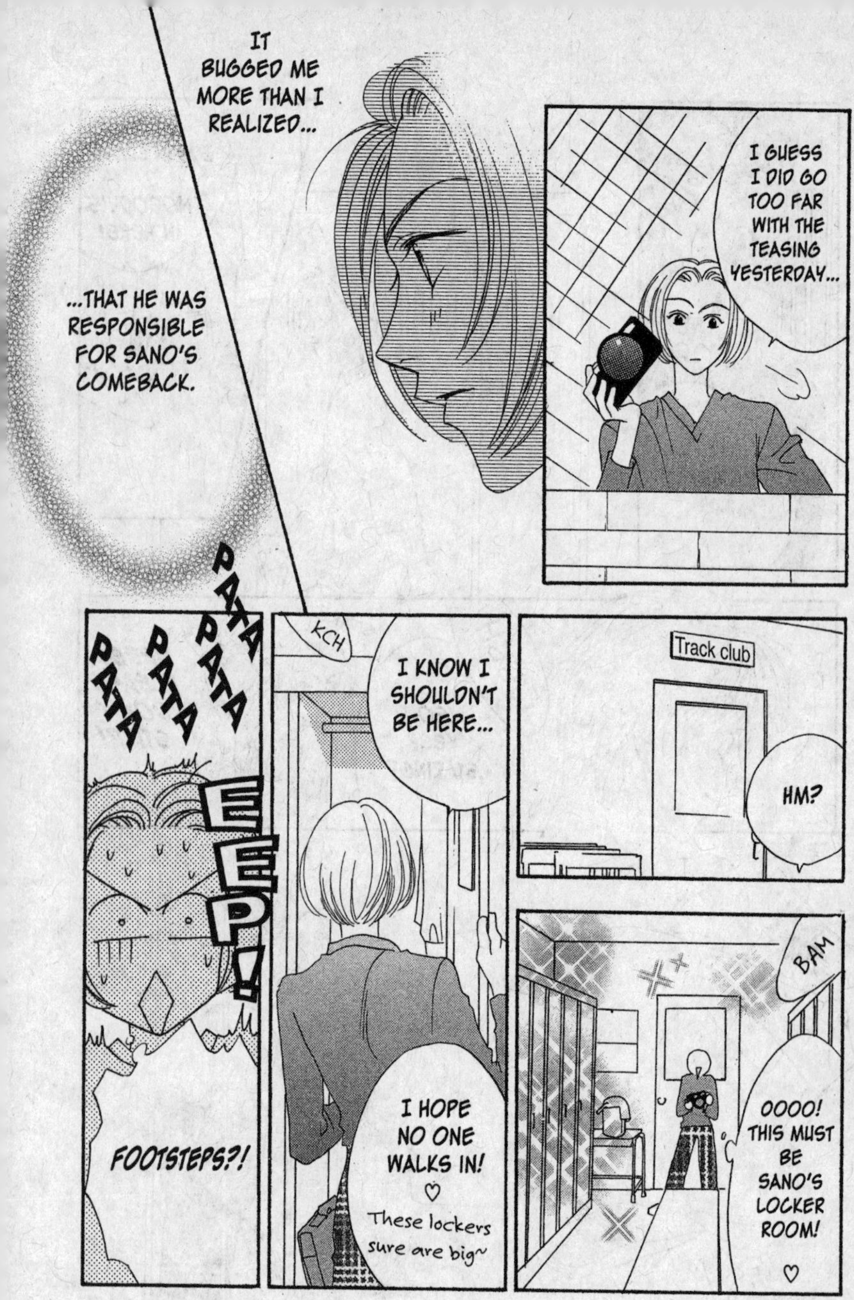
I GUESS I DID GO TOO FAR WITH THE TEASING YESTERDAY...
IT BUGGED ME MORE THAN I REALIZED...
...THAT HE WAS RESPONSIBLE FOR SANO'S COMEBACK.
Track club
HM?
BAM
OOOO! THIS MUST BE SANO'S LOCKER ROOM! ♡
KCH
I KNOW I SHOULDN'T BE HERE...
I HOPE NO ONE WALKS IN! ♡
These lockers sure are big~
PATA PATA PATA PATA
EEEP!
FOOTSTEPS?!

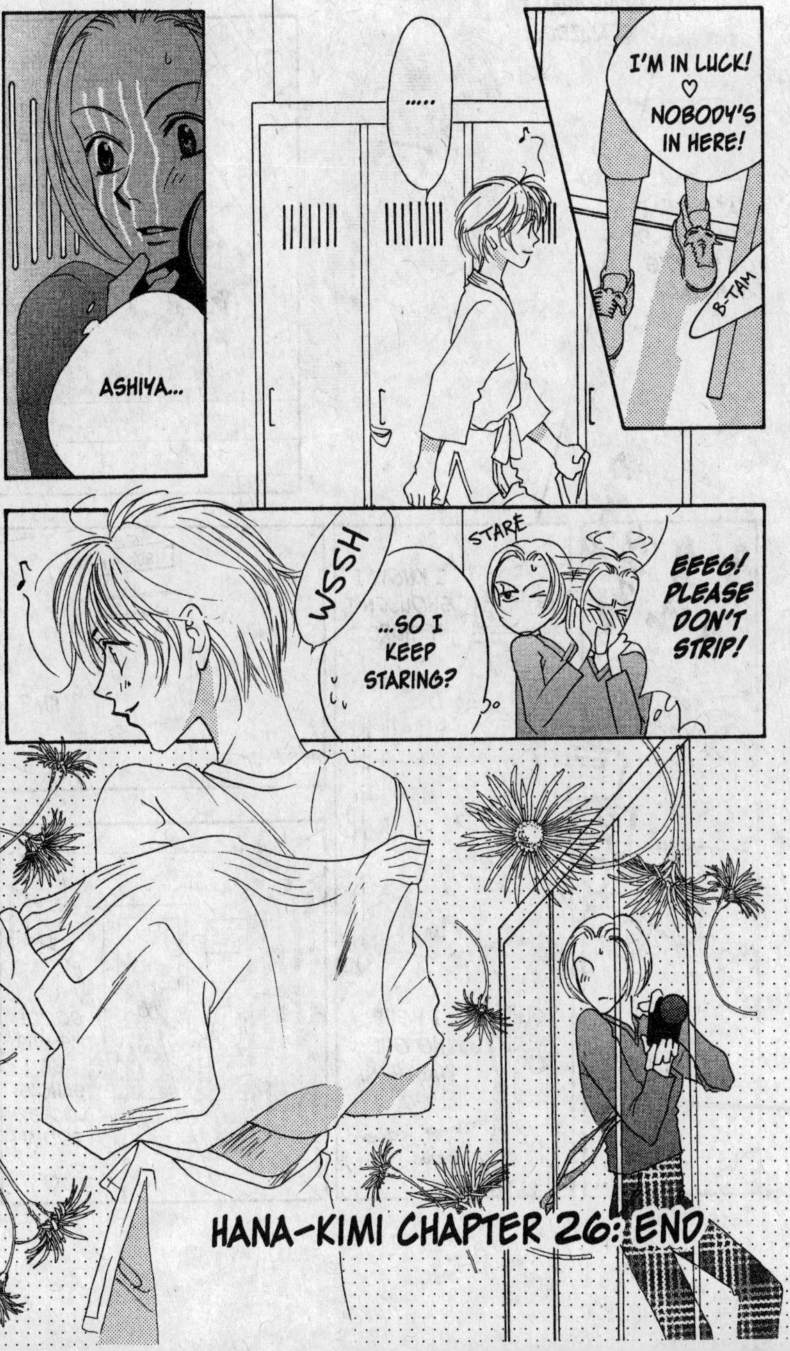
I'M IN LUCK! ♡ NOBODY'S IN HERE!
B-TAM
......
ASHIYA...
STARE
EEEG! PLEASE DON'T STRIP!
WSSH
...SO I KEEP STARING?
HANA-KIMI CHAPTER 26: END

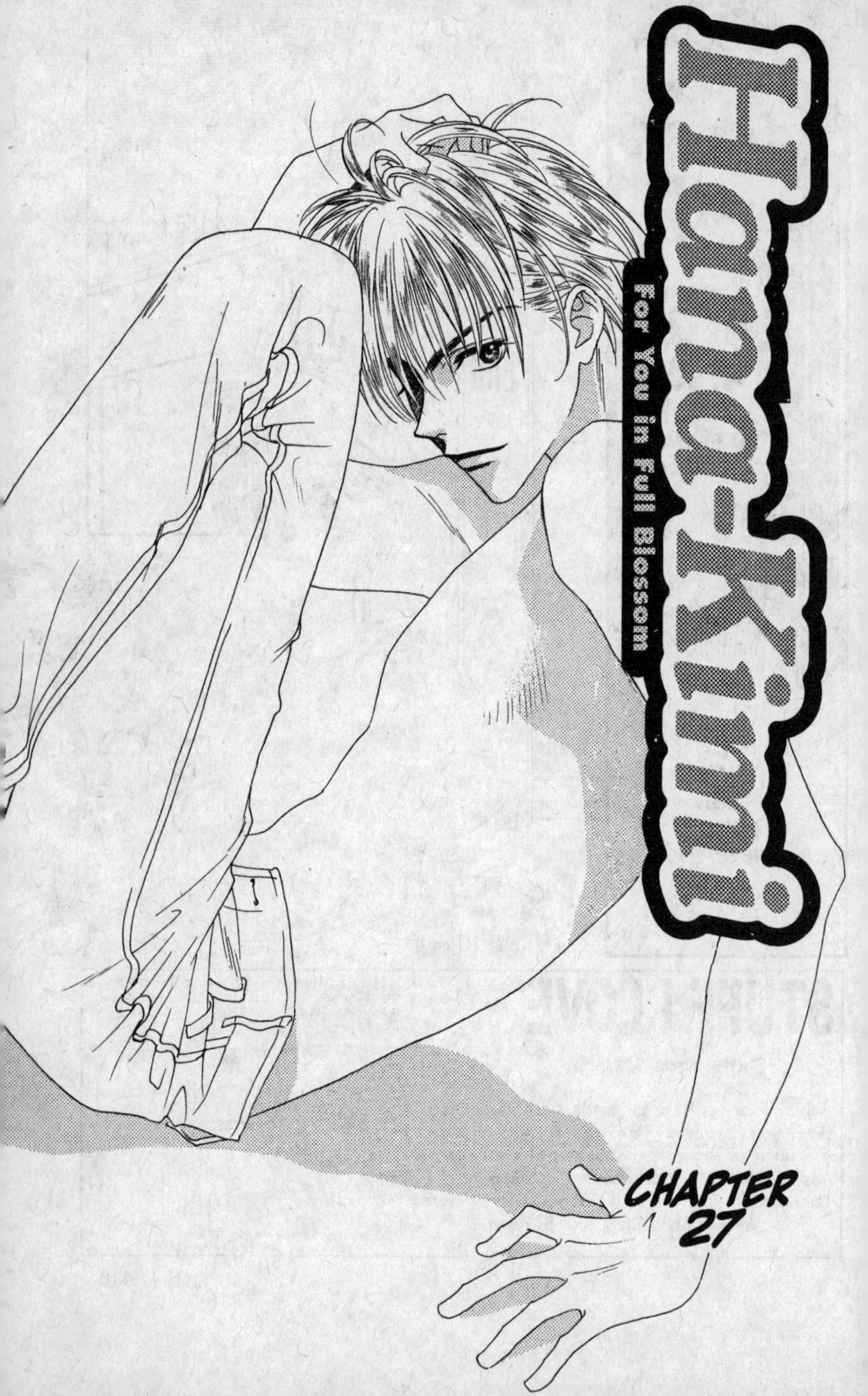
Hana-Kimi
For You in Full Blossom
CHAPTER 27

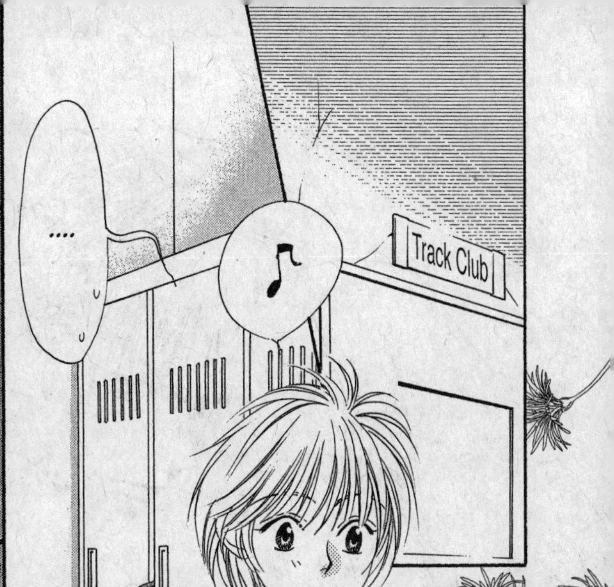
....
♪
Track Club

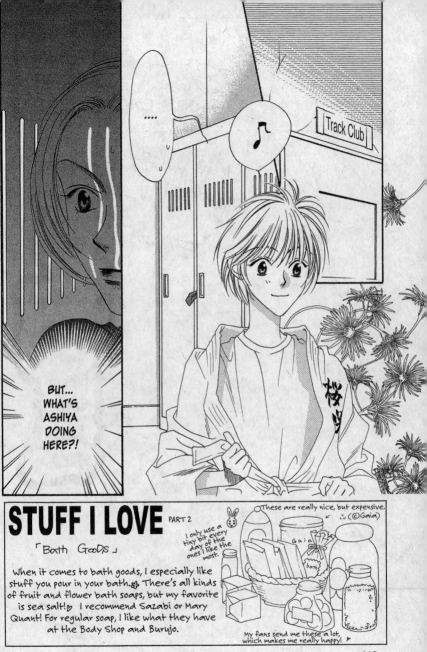

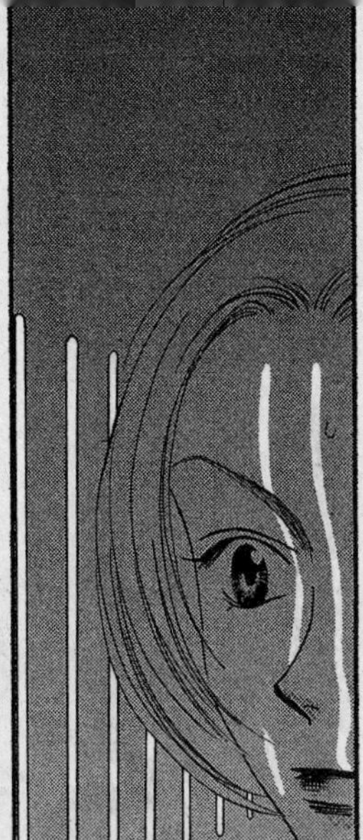
BUT... WHAT'S ASHIYA DOING HERE?!

STUFF I LOVE PART 2

「Bath GooDs」

When it comes to bath goods, I especially like stuff you pour in your bath. There's all kinds of fruit and flower bath soaps, but my favorite is sea salt! I recommend Sazabi or Mary Quant! For regular soap, I like what they have at the Body Shop and Buryjo.

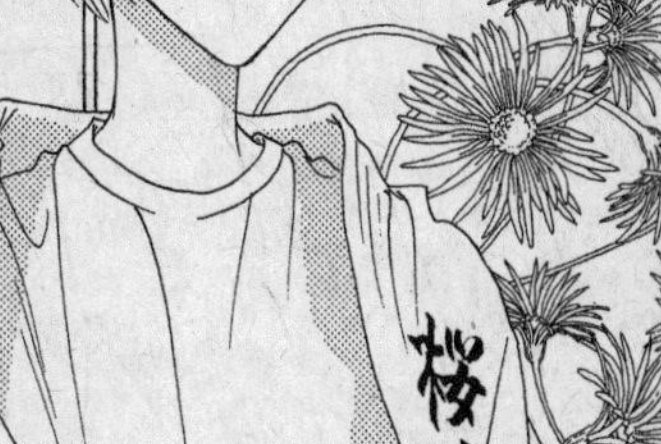
These are really nice, but expensive.
(©Gaia)
I only use a tiny bit every day of the ones I like the most.
Gaia
bath
My fans send me these a lot, which makes me really happy!

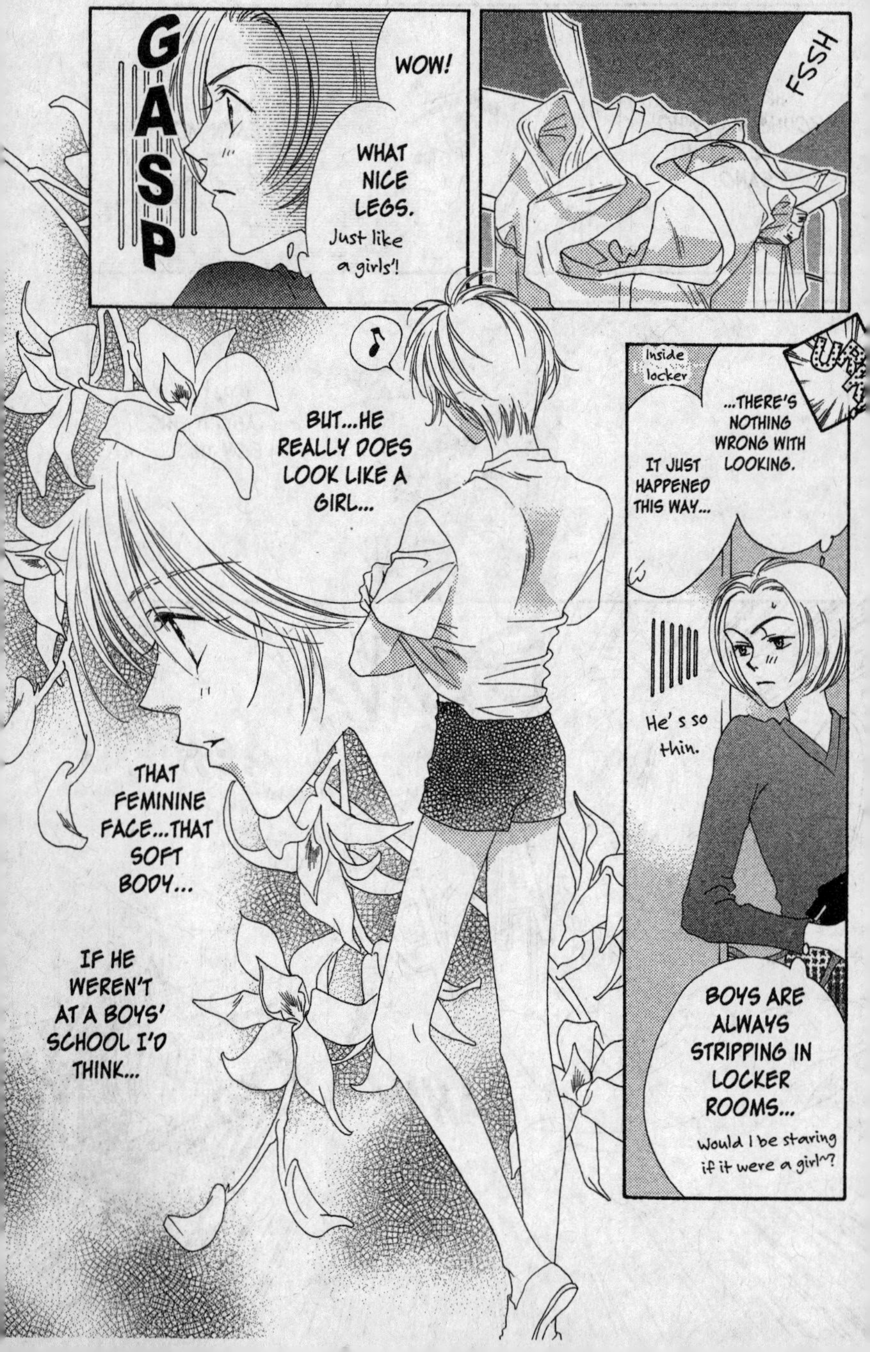
FSSH
GASP
WOW!
WHAT NICE LEGS.
Just like a girls'!
Inside locker
...THERE'S NOTHING WRONG WITH LOOKING.
IT JUST HAPPENED THIS WAY...
He's so thin.
BOYS ARE ALWAYS STRIPPING IN LOCKER ROOMS...
Would I be staring if it were a girl~?
♪
BUT...HE REALLY DOES LOOK LIKE A GIRL...
THAT FEMININE FACE...THAT SOFT BODY...
IF HE WEREN'T AT A BOYS' SCHOOL I'D THINK...

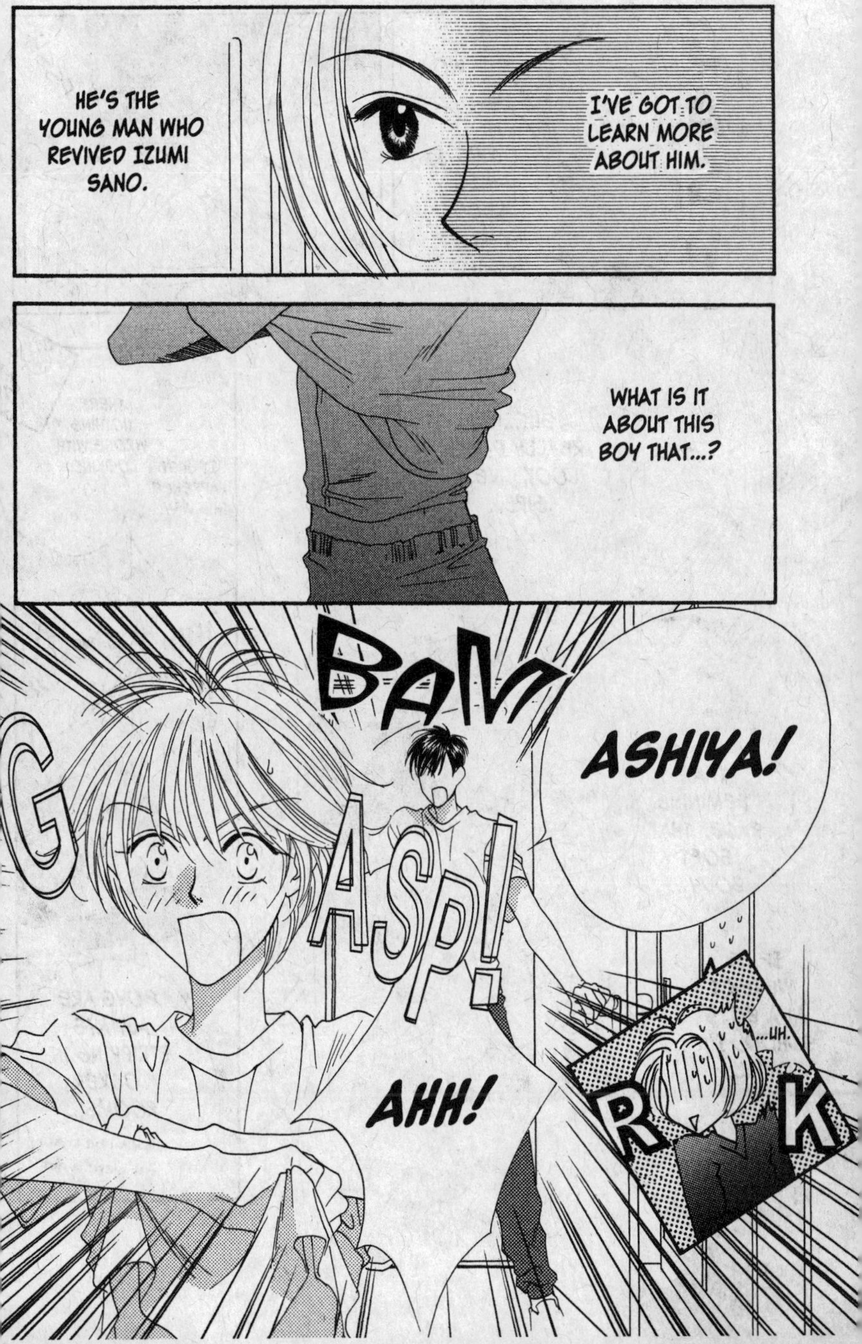
I'VE GOT TO LEARN MORE ABOUT HIM.
HE'S THE YOUNG MAN WHO REVIVED IZUMI SANO.
WHAT IS IT ABOUT THIS BOY THAT...?
ASHIYA!
BAM
...UH.
R K
GASP!
AHH!

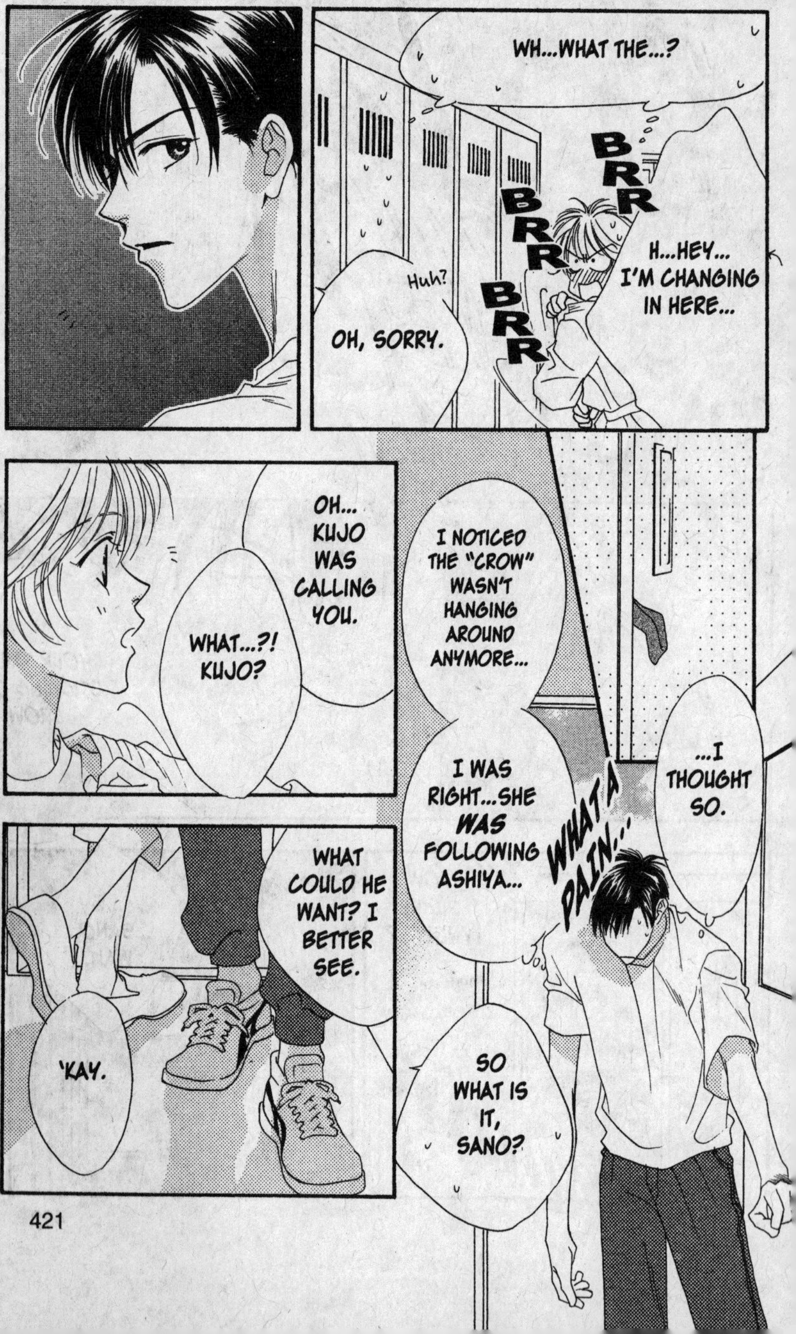
WH...WHAT THE...?
BRR
BRR
BRR
H...HEY... I'M CHANGING IN HERE...
Huh?
OH, SORRY.
...I THOUGHT SO.
WHAT A PAIN...
I NOTICED THE "CROW" WASN'T HANGING AROUND ANYMORE...
I WAS RIGHT...SHE *WAS* FOLLOWING ASHIYA...
SO WHAT IS IT, SANO?
OH... KUJO WAS CALLING YOU.
WHAT...?! KUJO?
WHAT COULD HE WANT? I BETTER SEE.
'KAY.

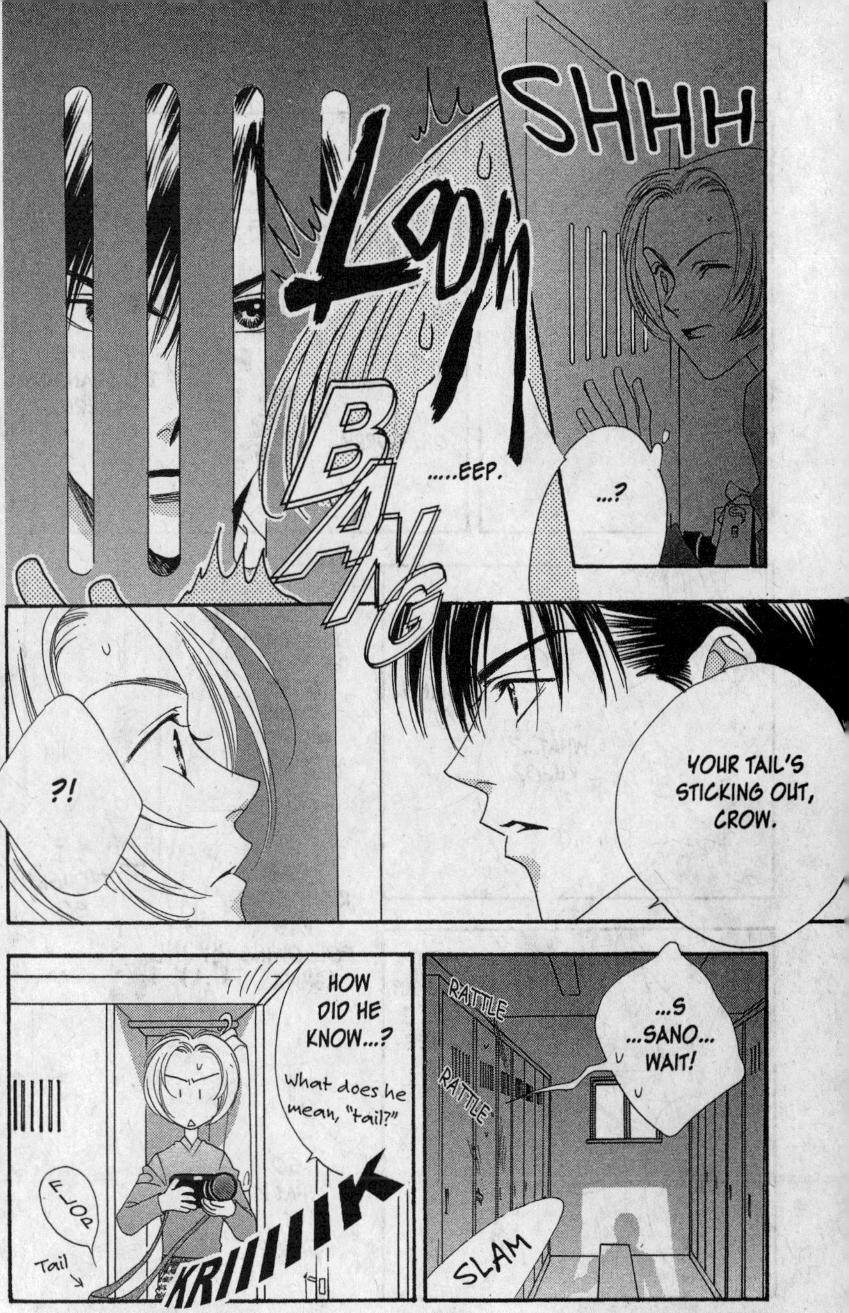
SHHH
...?
Loom
BANG
.....EEP.
YOUR TAIL'S STICKING OUT, CROW.
?!
RATTLE
RATTLE
...S ...SANO... WAIT!
SLAM
HOW DID HE KNOW...?
What does he mean, "tail?"
KRIIIIIK
FLOP
Tail

* Osaka High School

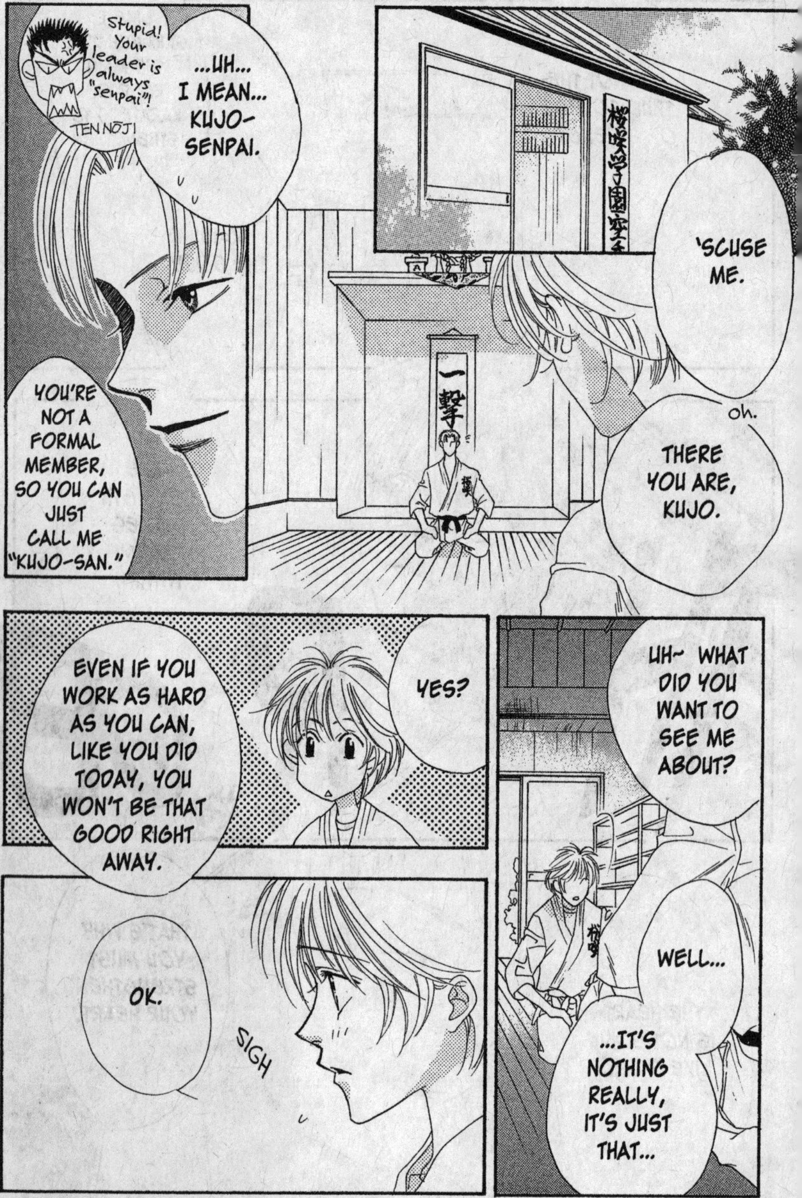

'SCUSE ME.
oh.
THERE YOU ARE, KUJO.
...UH... I MEAN... KUJO-SENPAI.
Stupid! Your leader is always "senpai"!
TENNŌJI
YOU'RE NOT A FORMAL MEMBER, SO YOU CAN JUST CALL ME "KUJO-SAN."
UH~ WHAT DID YOU WANT TO SEE ME ABOUT?
WELL...
...IT'S NOTHING REALLY, IT'S JUST THAT...
YES?
EVEN IF YOU WORK AS HARD AS YOU CAN, LIKE YOU DID TODAY, YOU WON'T BE THAT GOOD RIGHT AWAY.
OK.
SIGH

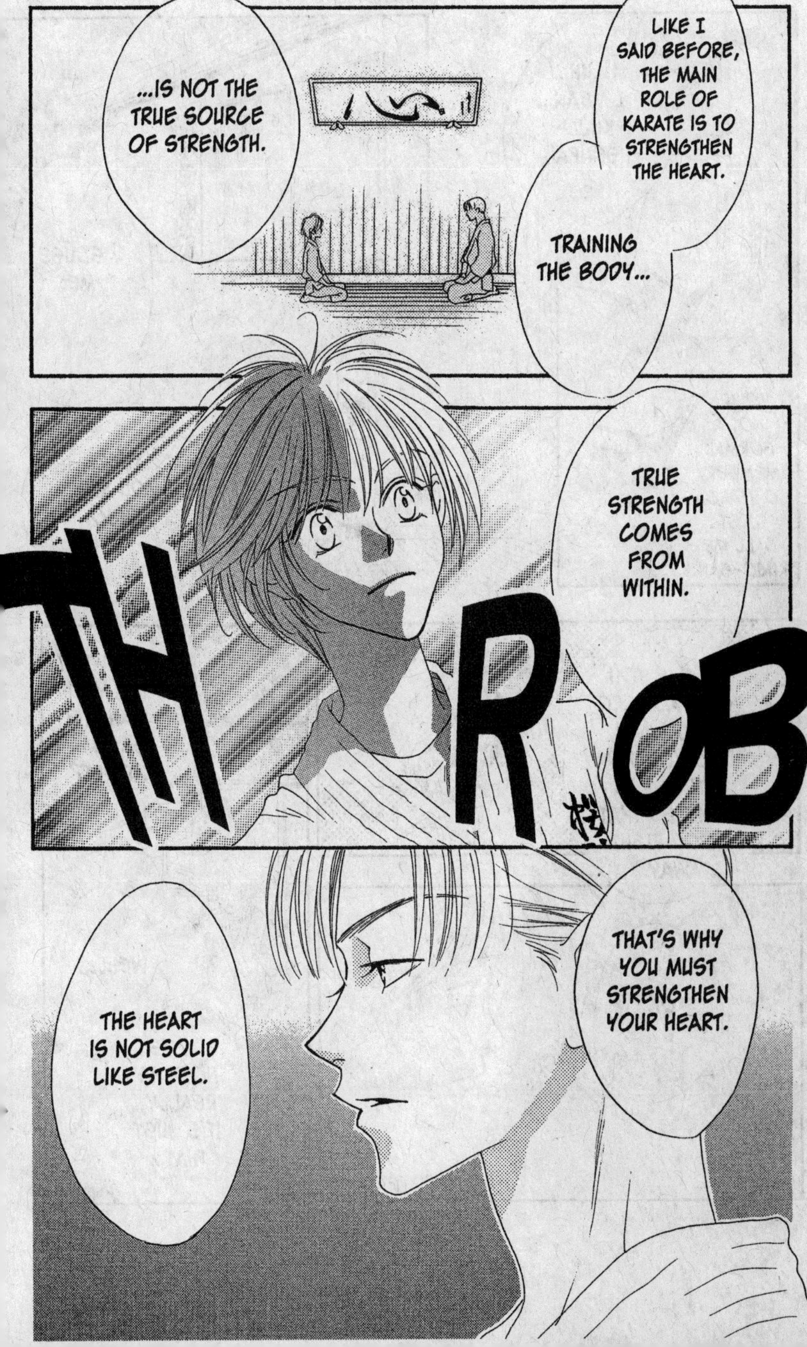
LIKE I SAID BEFORE, THE MAIN ROLE OF KARATE IS TO STRENGTHEN THE HEART.
TRAINING THE BODY...
...IS NOT THE TRUE SOURCE OF STRENGTH.
TRUE STRENGTH COMES FROM WITHIN.
THROB
THAT'S WHY YOU MUST STRENGTHEN YOUR HEART.
THE HEART IS NOT SOLID LIKE STEEL.

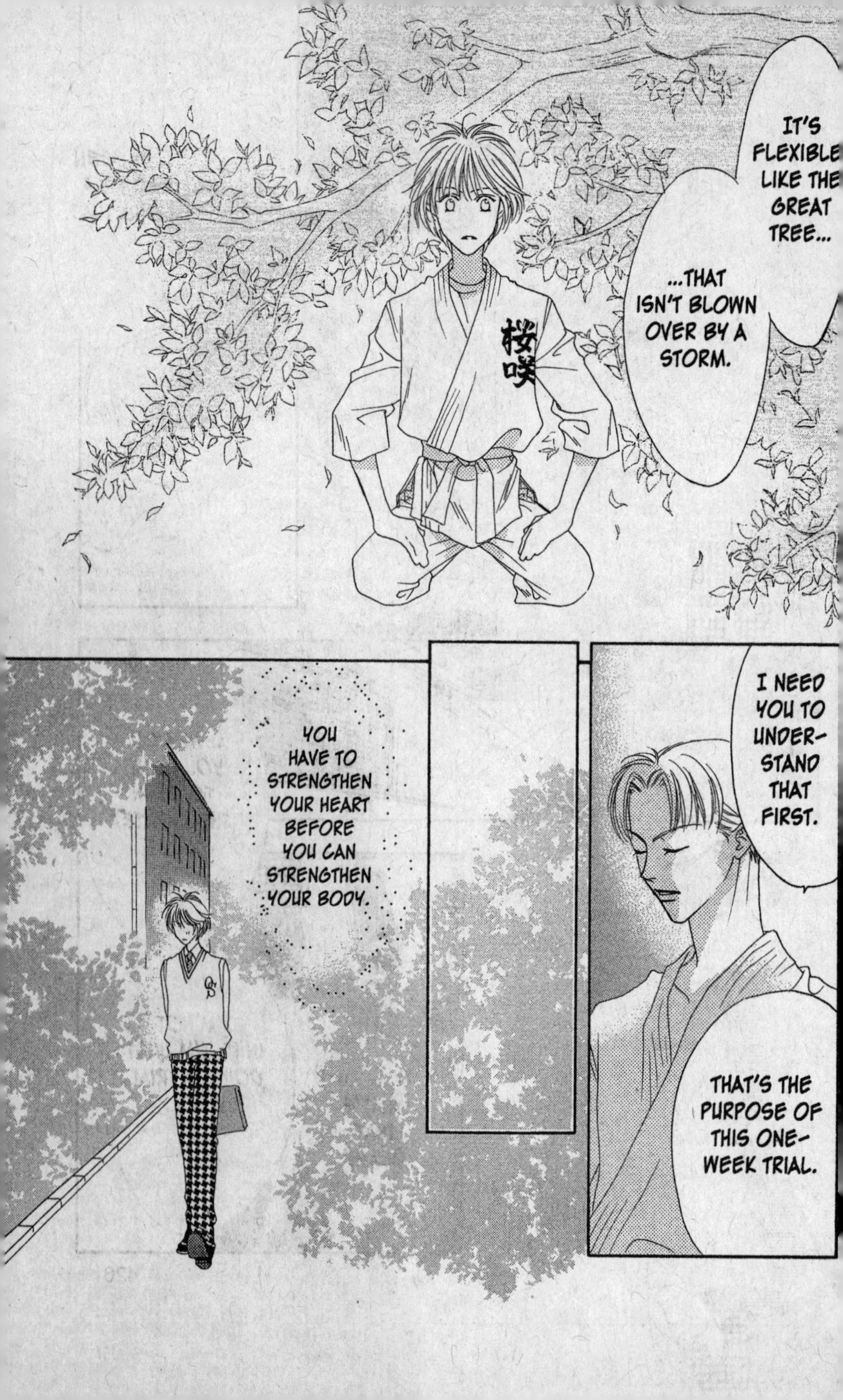
IT'S FLEXIBLE LIKE THE GREAT TREE...
...THAT ISN'T BLOWN OVER BY A STORM.
桜咲
I NEED YOU TO UNDER-STAND THAT FIRST.
THAT'S THE PURPOSE OF THIS ONE-WEEK TRIAL.
YOU HAVE TO STRENGTHEN YOUR HEART BEFORE YOU CAN STRENGTHEN YOUR BODY.

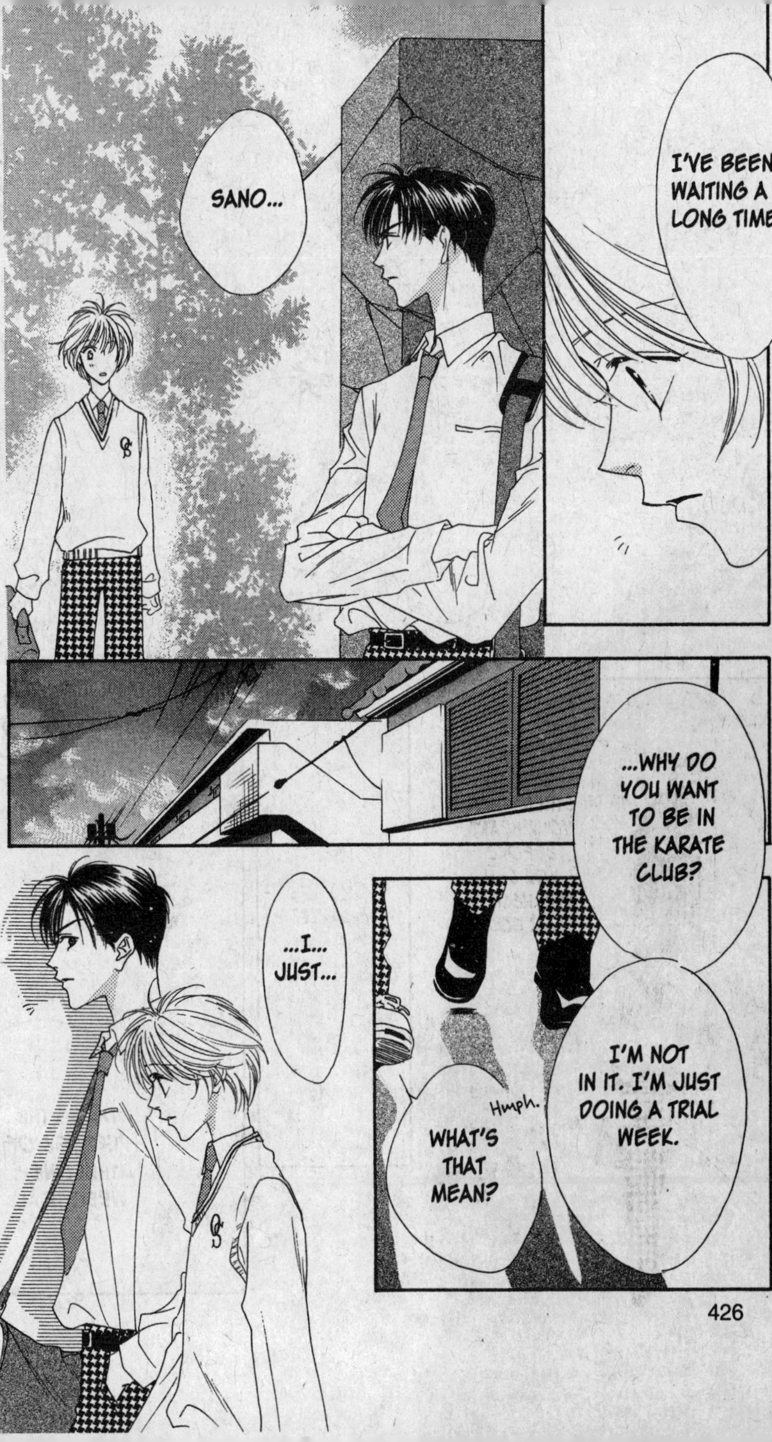
I'VE BEEN WAITING A LONG TIME.
SANO...
...WHY DO YOU WANT TO BE IN THE KARATE CLUB?
I'M NOT IN IT. I'M JUST DOING A TRIAL WEEK.
Hmph.
WHAT'S THAT MEAN?
...I... JUST...

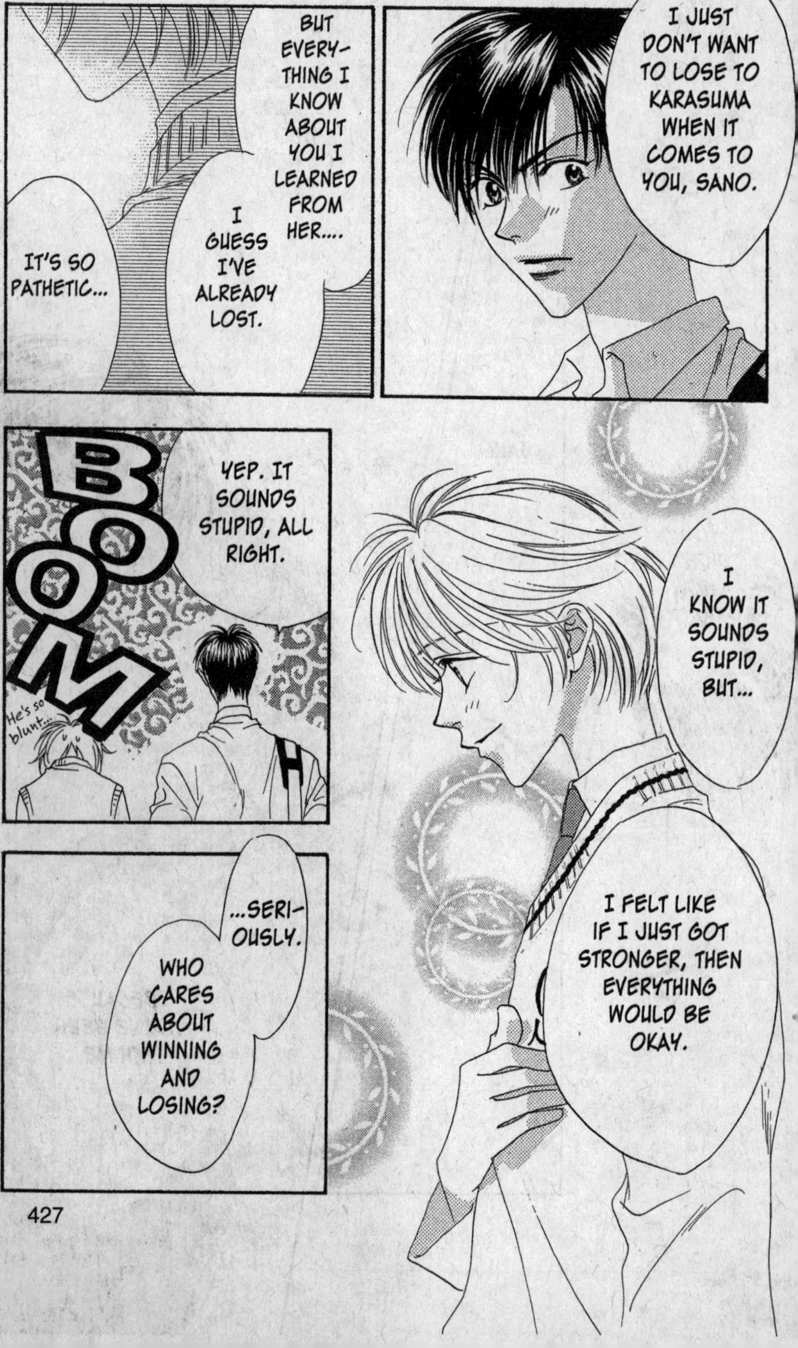

I JUST DON'T WANT TO LOSE TO KARASUMA WHEN IT COMES TO YOU, SANO.
BUT EVERYTHING I KNOW ABOUT YOU I LEARNED FROM HER....
I GUESS I'VE ALREADY LOST.
IT'S SO PATHETIC...
I KNOW IT SOUNDS STUPID, BUT...
I FELT LIKE IF I JUST GOT STRONGER, THEN EVERYTHING WOULD BE OKAY.
YEP. IT SOUNDS STUPID, ALL RIGHT.
BOOM
He's so blunt...
...SERIOUSLY.
WHO CARES ABOUT WINNING AND LOSING?

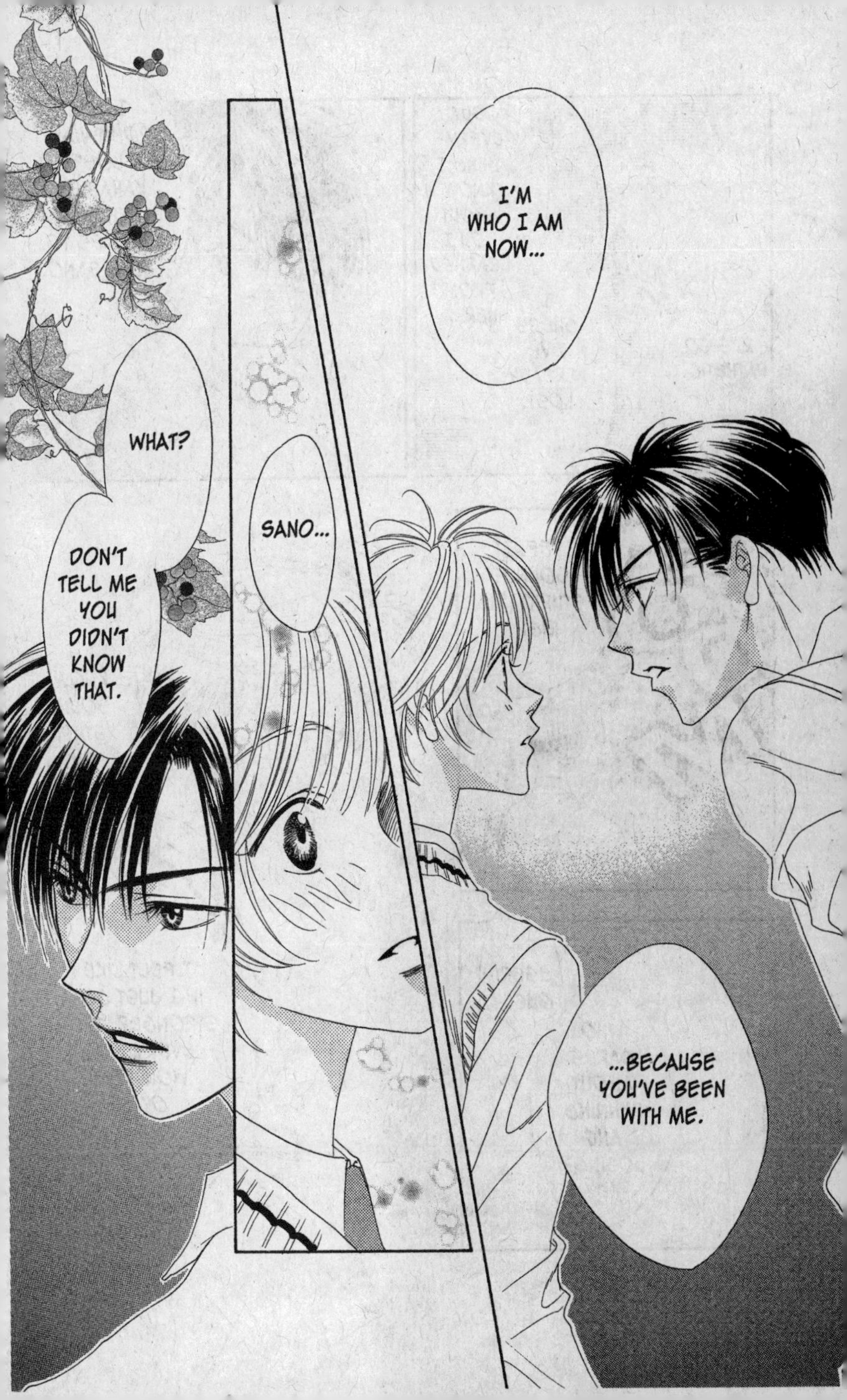
I'M WHO I AM NOW...
...BECAUSE YOU'VE BEEN WITH ME.
SANO...
WHAT?
DON'T TELL ME YOU DIDN'T KNOW THAT.

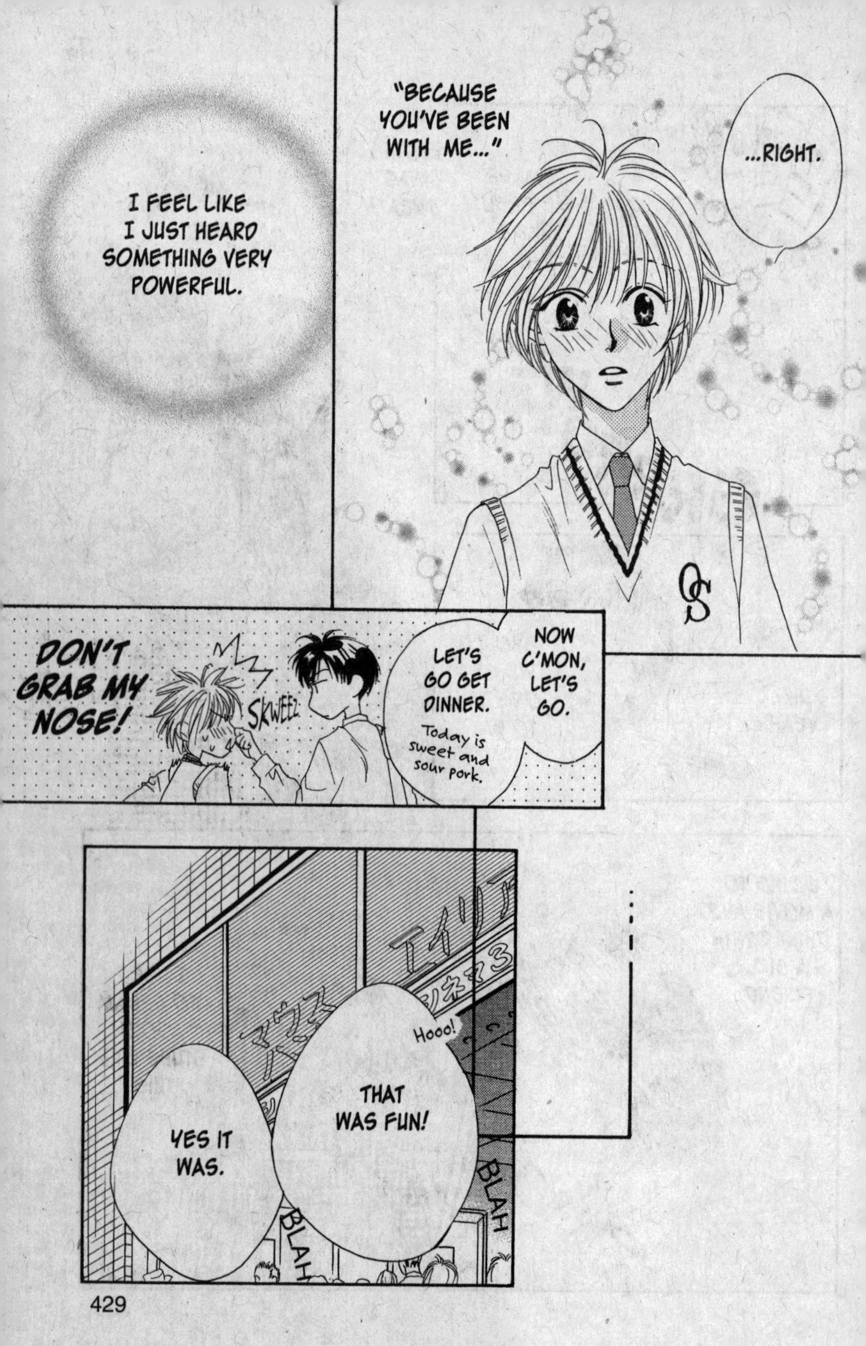
"BECAUSE YOU'VE BEEN WITH ME..."
...RIGHT.
I FEEL LIKE I JUST HEARD SOMETHING VERY POWERFUL.
NOW C'MON, LET'S GO.
LET'S GO GET DINNER.
Today is sweet and sour pork.
SKWEEZ
DON'T GRAB MY NOSE!
Hooo!
THAT WAS FUN!
BLAH
YES IT WAS.
BLAH

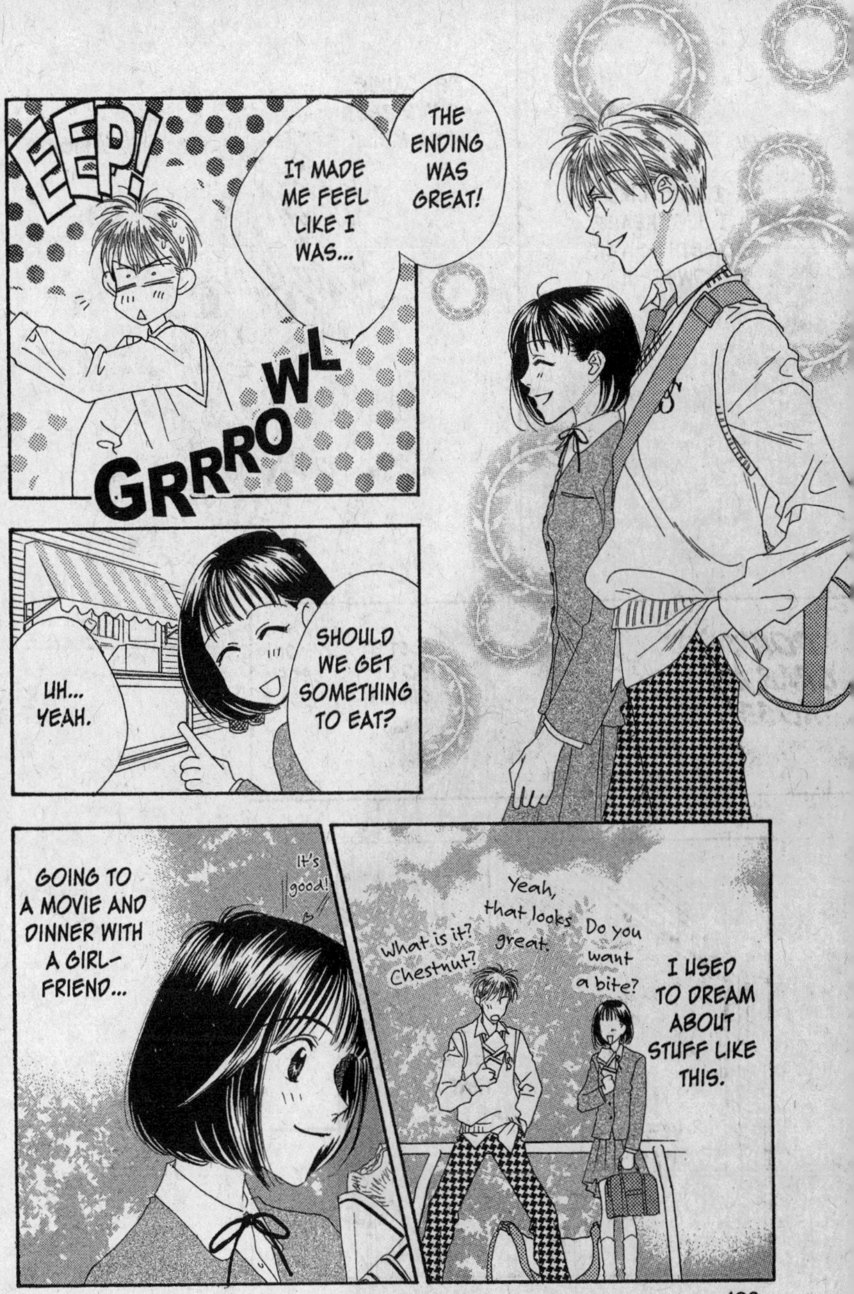
THE ENDING WAS GREAT!
IT MADE ME FEEL LIKE I WAS...
EEP!
GRRROWL
SHOULD WE GET SOMETHING TO EAT?
UH... YEAH.
I USED TO DREAM ABOUT STUFF LIKE THIS.
Do you want a bite?
Yeah, that looks great.
What is it? Chestnut?
It's good!
GOING TO A MOVIE AND DINNER WITH A GIRL-FRIEND...

WHISPERED SECRETS

FIGURE SKATING

MIZUKI'S OUTFIT IN CHAPTER 26 IS FROM THE FIGURE SKATER PHILIPPE CANDELORO, WHO WAS AT THE NAGANO WINTER OLYMPICS!♥ FOR HIS PROGRAM HE WORE A COSTUME BASED ON "THE THREE MUSKETEERS." THE MUSIC THEY PLAYED HAD THE SOUNDS OF SWORDS CLASHING AND HE MIMICKED FENCING MOVES AS HE SKATED. IT WAS SO COOL!! HE ALSO LOOKED REALLY COOL ON THE NHK SPECIAL YEARS AGO WHEN HE WORE ALL BLACK (AND THE MUSIC WAS THE "GODFATHER" THEME)!! I LIKE THE FACT THAT HE DOESN'T WEAR THE FRILLY STUFF THAT'S POPULAR WITH OTHER SKATERS RIGHT NOW!!

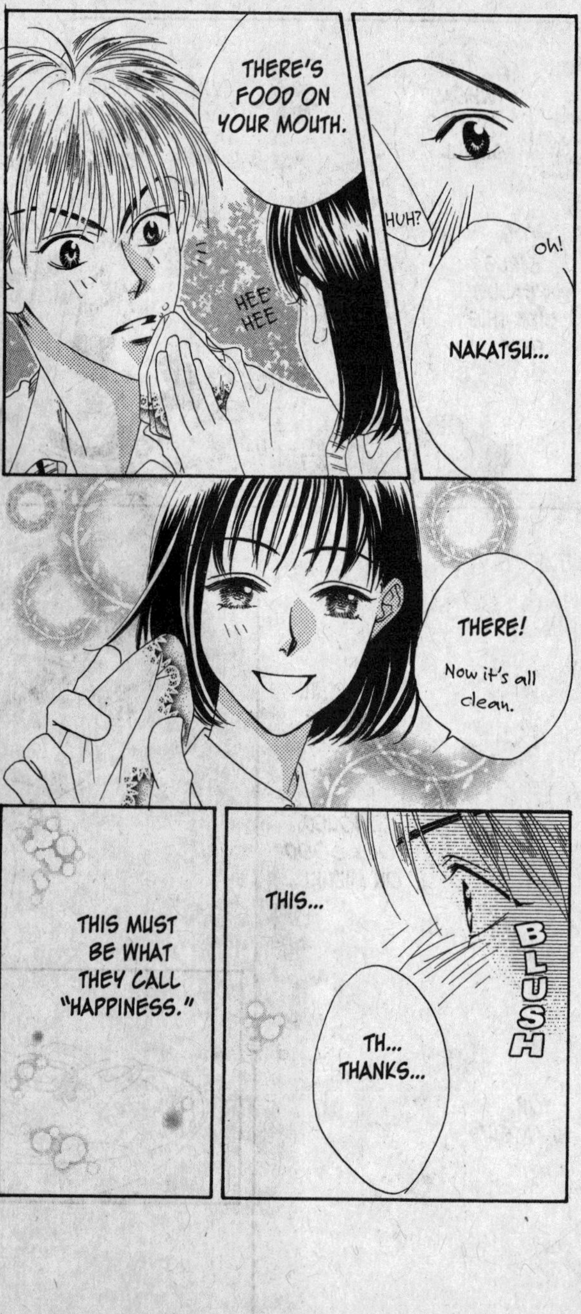
HUH?
Oh!
NAKATSU...
THERE'S FOOD ON YOUR MOUTH.
HEE HEE
THERE!
Now it's all clean.
THIS...
TH... THANKS...
BLUSH
THIS MUST BE WHAT THEY CALL "HAPPINESS."

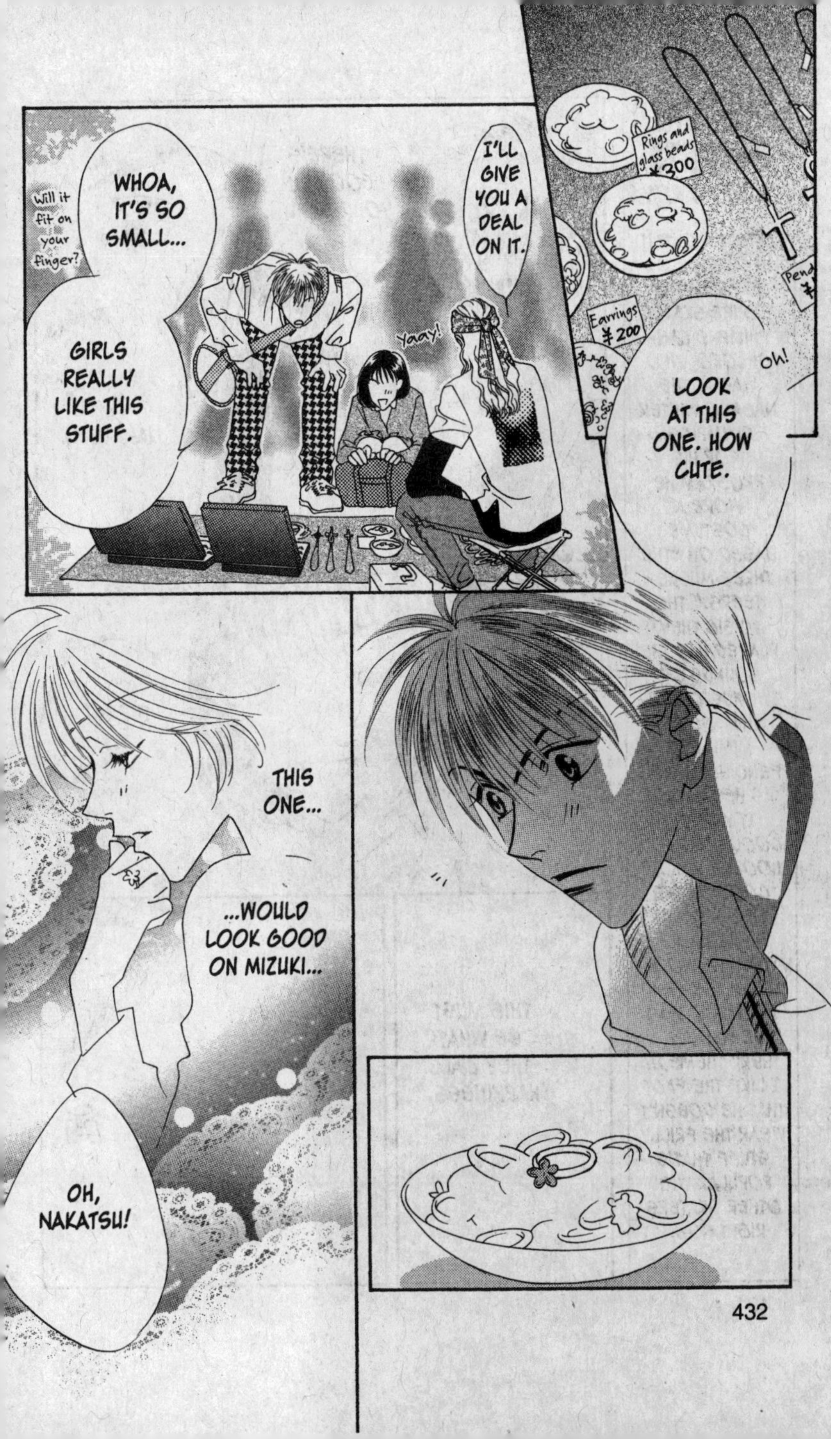
Rings and glass beads ¥300
Earrings ¥200
Oh!
LOOK AT THIS ONE. HOW CUTE.
I'LL GIVE YOU A DEAL ON IT.
Yaaay!
WHOA, IT'S SO SMALL...
Will it fit on your finger?
GIRLS REALLY LIKE THIS STUFF.
THIS ONE...
...WOULD LOOK GOOD ON MIZUKI...
OH, NAKATSU!

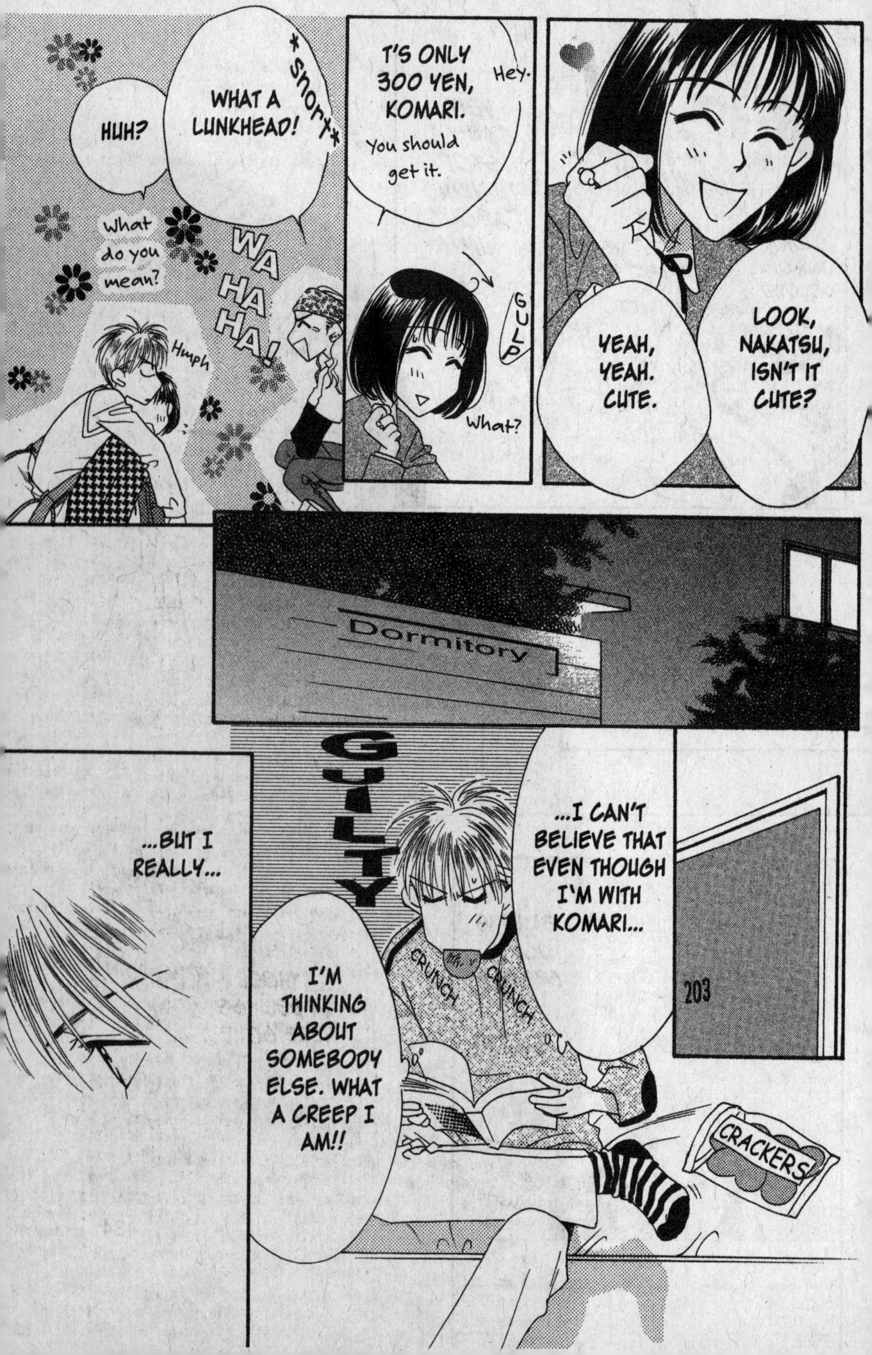
LOOK, NAKATSU, ISN'T IT CUTE?
YEAH, YEAH. CUTE.
T'S ONLY 300 YEN, KOMARI.
You should get it.
Hey.
GULP
What?
Snort
WHAT A LUNKHEAD!
HUH?
WA HA HA!
What do you mean?
Hmph
Dormitory
...I CAN'T BELIEVE THAT EVEN THOUGH I'M WITH KOMARI...
203
GUILTY
CRUNCH
CRUNCH
I'M THINKING ABOUT SOMEBODY ELSE. WHAT A CREEP I AM!!
CRACKERS
...BUT I REALLY...

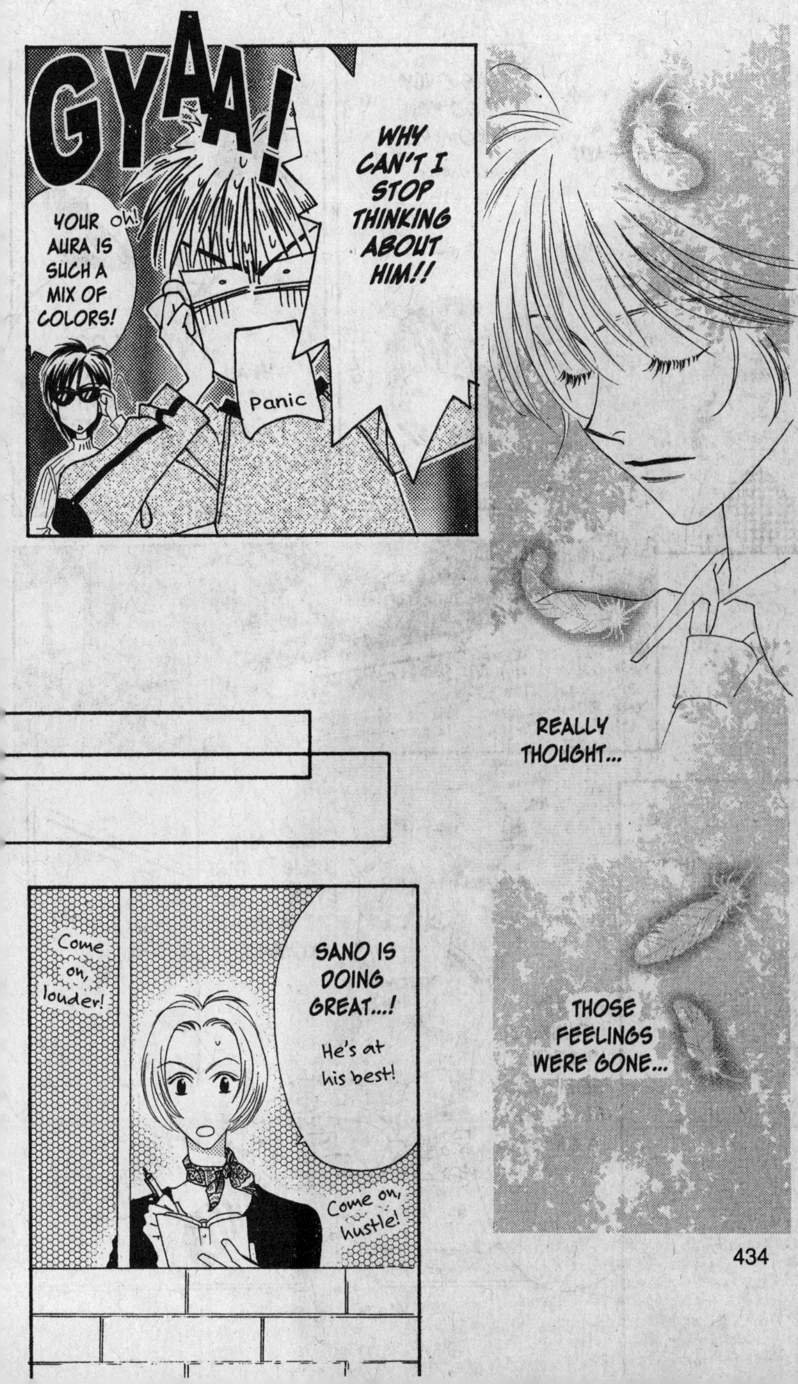
REALLY THOUGHT...
THOSE FEELINGS WERE GONE...
GYAA!
WHY CAN'T I STOP THINKING ABOUT HIM!!
Oh!
YOUR AURA IS SUCH A MIX OF COLORS!
Panic
SANO IS DOING GREAT...!
He's at his best!
Come on, louder!
Come on, hustle!

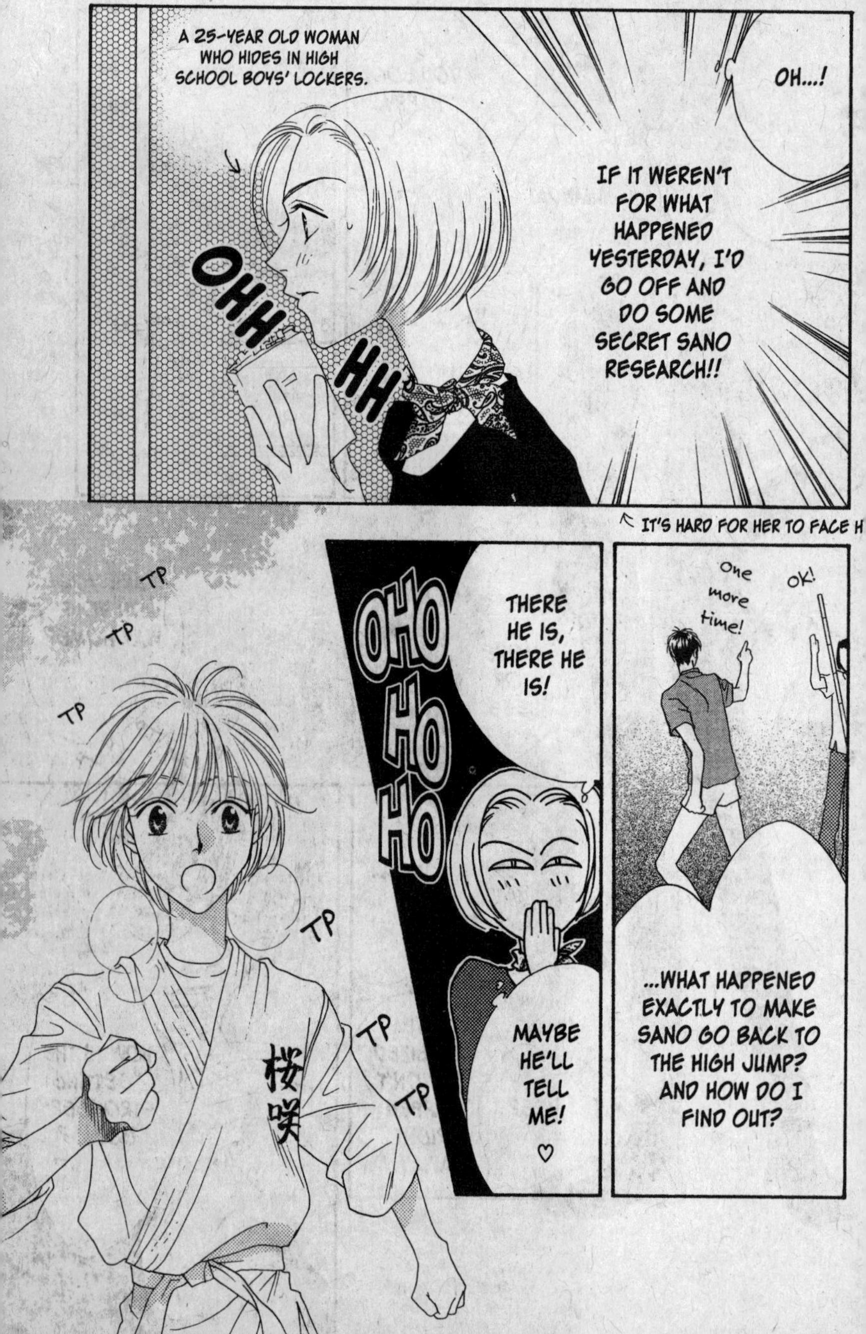
OH...!
IF IT WEREN'T FOR WHAT HAPPENED YESTERDAY, I'D GO OFF AND DO SOME SECRET SANO RESEARCH!!
A 25-YEAR OLD WOMAN WHO HIDES IN HIGH SCHOOL BOYS' LOCKERS.
OHHHH
IT'S HARD FOR HER TO FACE H
OK!
One more time!
...WHAT HAPPENED EXACTLY TO MAKE SANO GO BACK TO THE HIGH JUMP? AND HOW DO I FIND OUT?
THERE HE IS, THERE HE IS!
OHOHOHO
MAYBE HE'LL TELL ME! ♡
TP
TP
TP
TP
TP
TP
桜咲

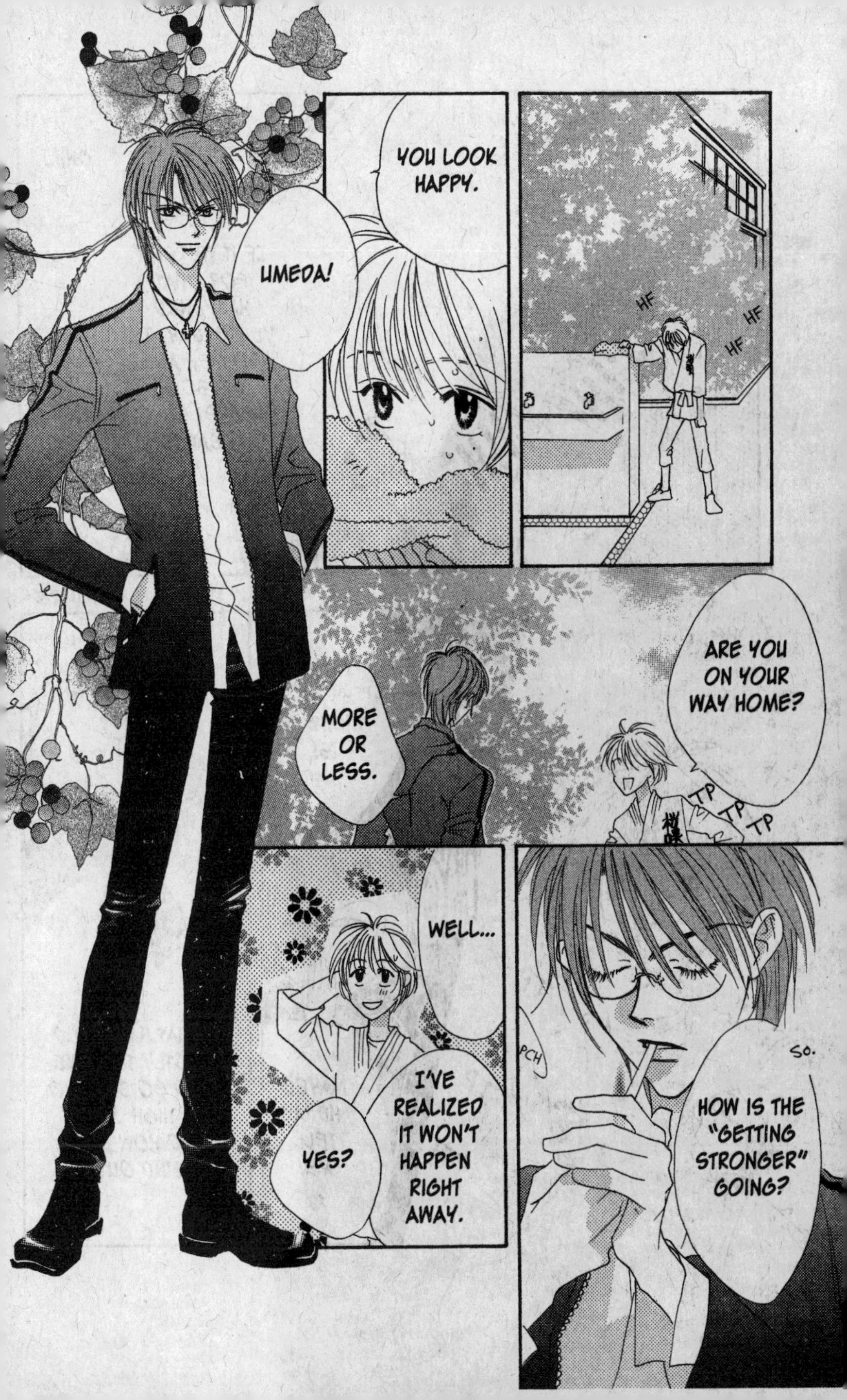
HF
HF
HF
UMEDA!
YOU LOOK HAPPY.
ARE YOU ON YOUR WAY HOME?
TP TP TP
MORE OR LESS.
SO.
HOW IS THE "GETTING STRONGER" GOING?
PCH
WELL...
I'VE REALIZED IT WON'T HAPPEN RIGHT AWAY.
YES?

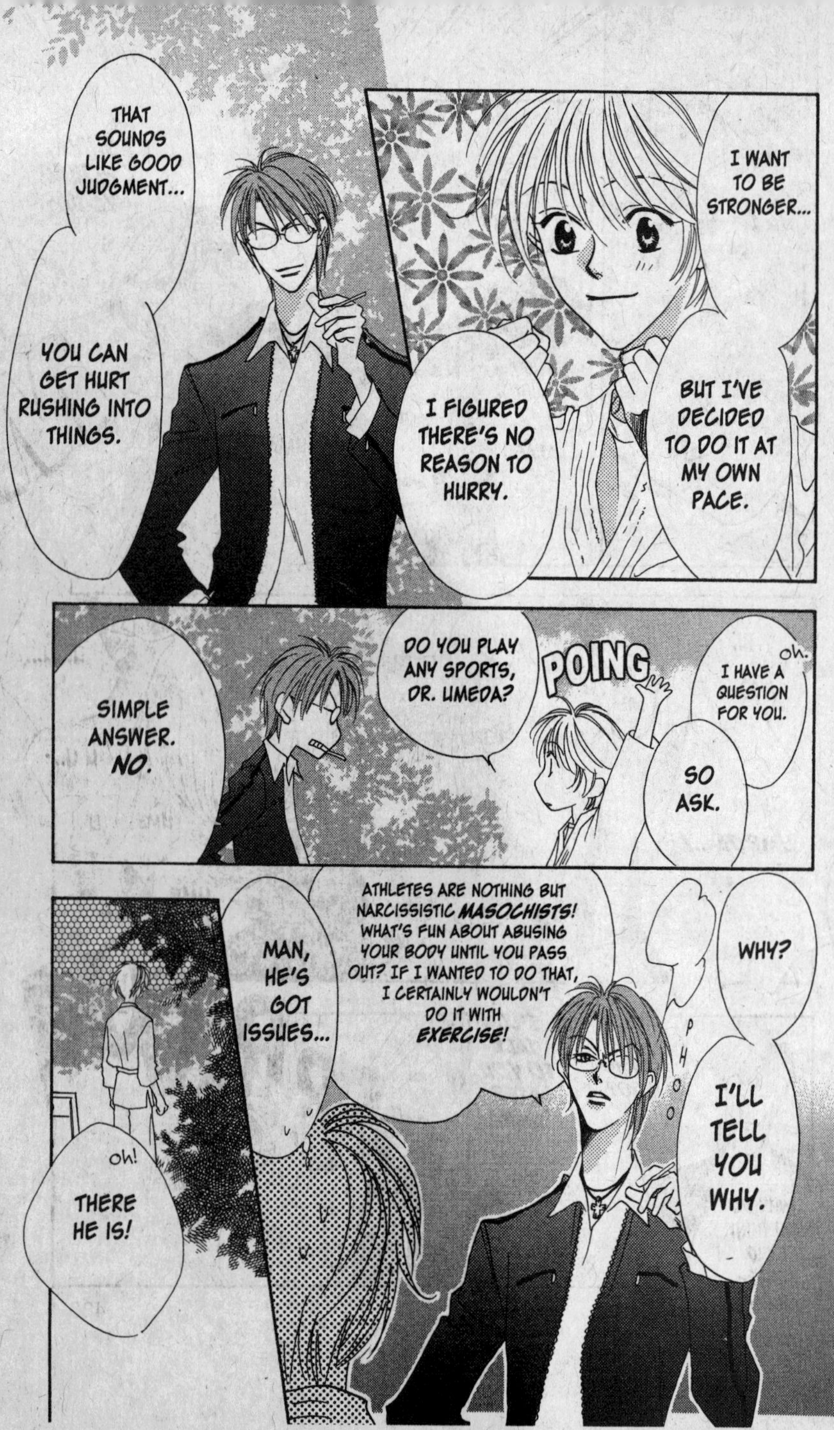
I WANT TO BE STRONGER...
BUT I'VE DECIDED TO DO IT AT MY OWN PACE.
I FIGURED THERE'S NO REASON TO HURRY.
THAT SOUNDS LIKE GOOD JUDGMENT...
YOU CAN GET HURT RUSHING INTO THINGS.
oh.
I HAVE A QUESTION FOR YOU.
SO ASK.
POING
DO YOU PLAY ANY SPORTS, DR. UMEDA?
SIMPLE ANSWER. NO.
WHY?
I'LL TELL YOU WHY.
PHOO
ATHLETES ARE NOTHING BUT NARCISSISTIC MASOCHISTS! WHAT'S FUN ABOUT ABUSING YOUR BODY UNTIL YOU PASS OUT? IF I WANTED TO DO THAT, I CERTAINLY WOULDN'T DO IT WITH EXERCISE!
MAN, HE'S GOT ISSUES...
oh!
THERE HE IS!

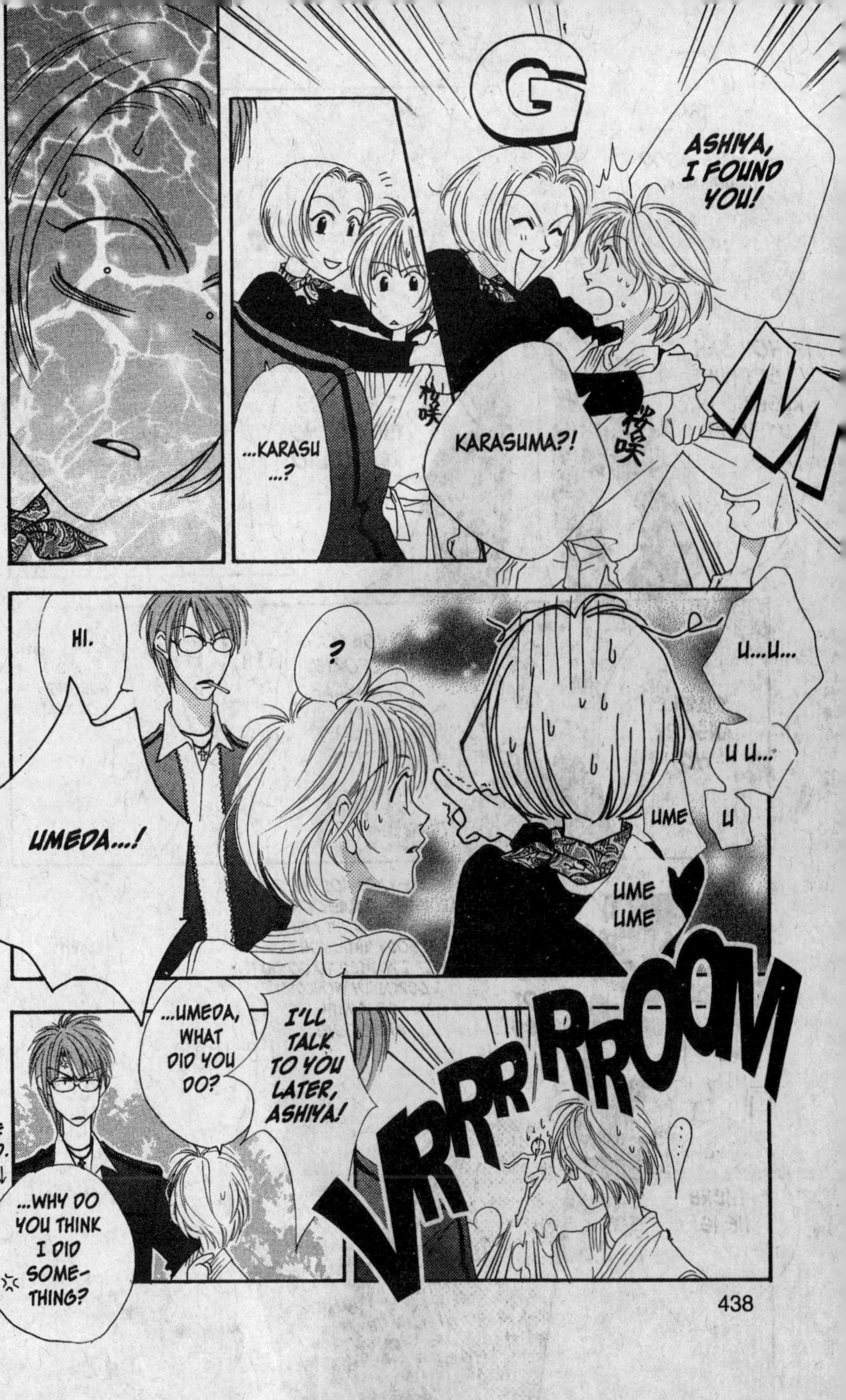
G
M
ASHIYA, I FOUND YOU!
KARASUMA?!
桜咲
桜咲
...KARASU ...?
U...U...
U U...
U
UME
UME UME
?
HI.
UMEDA...!
I'LL TALK TO YOU LATER, ASHIYA!
VRRRRROOM
...UMEDA, WHAT DID YOU DO?
HE DID.
...WHY DO YOU THINK I DID SOME-THING?

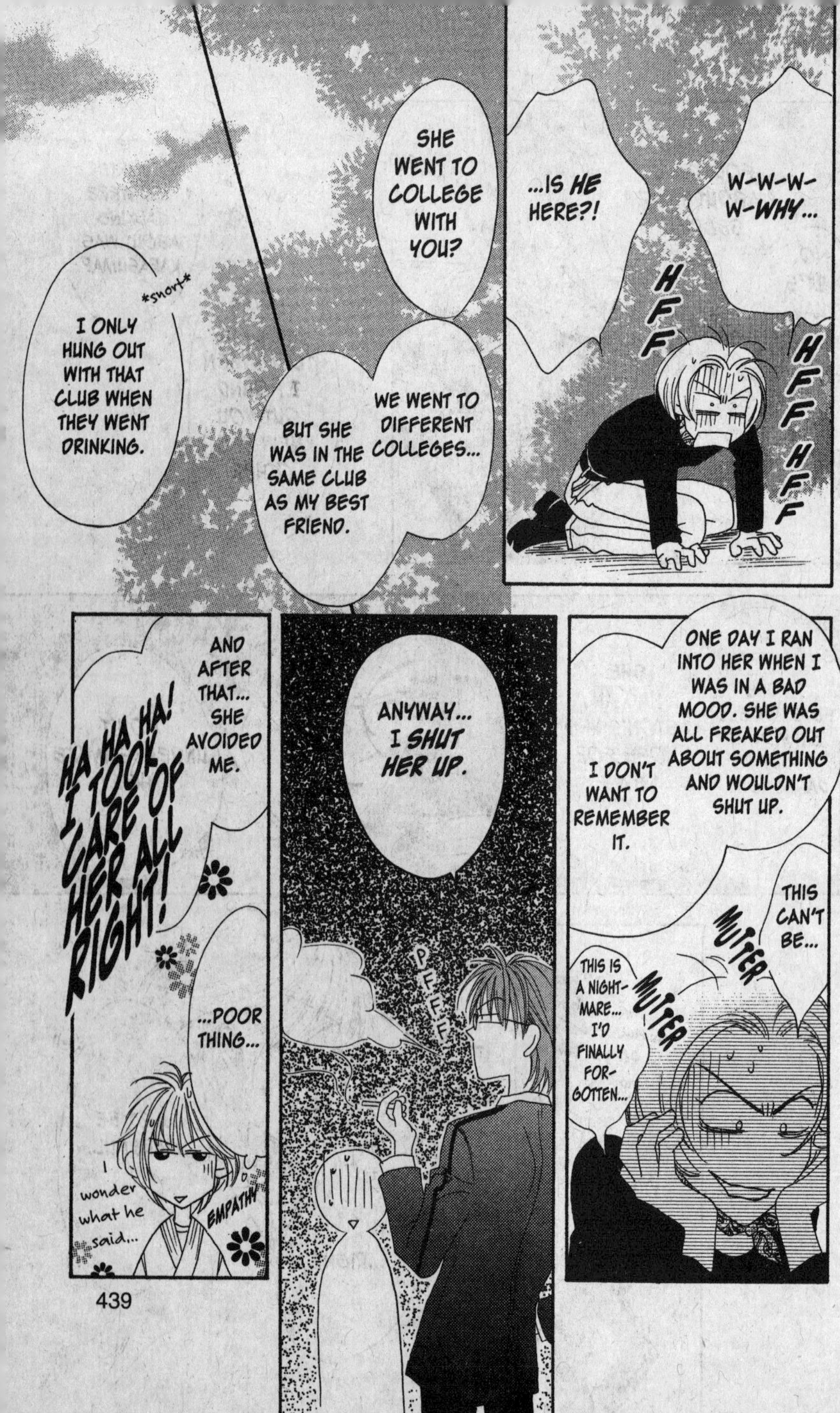
W-W-W-W-WHY...
...IS HE HERE?!
HFF HFF HFF HFF
SHE WENT TO COLLEGE WITH YOU?
WE WENT TO DIFFERENT COLLEGES...
BUT SHE WAS IN THE SAME CLUB AS MY BEST FRIEND.
snort
I ONLY HUNG OUT WITH THAT CLUB WHEN THEY WENT DRINKING.
ONE DAY I RAN INTO HER WHEN I WAS IN A BAD MOOD. SHE WAS ALL FREAKED OUT ABOUT SOMETHING AND WOULDN'T SHUT UP.
I DON'T WANT TO REMEMBER IT.
THIS CAN'T BE...
MUTTER
THIS IS A NIGHTMARE... I'D FINALLY FORGOTTEN...
MUTTER
ANYWAY... I SHUT HER UP.
PFFF
AND AFTER THAT... SHE AVOIDED ME.
HA HA HA! I TOOK CARE OF HER ALL RIGHT!
...POOR THING...
EMPATHY
I wonder what he said...

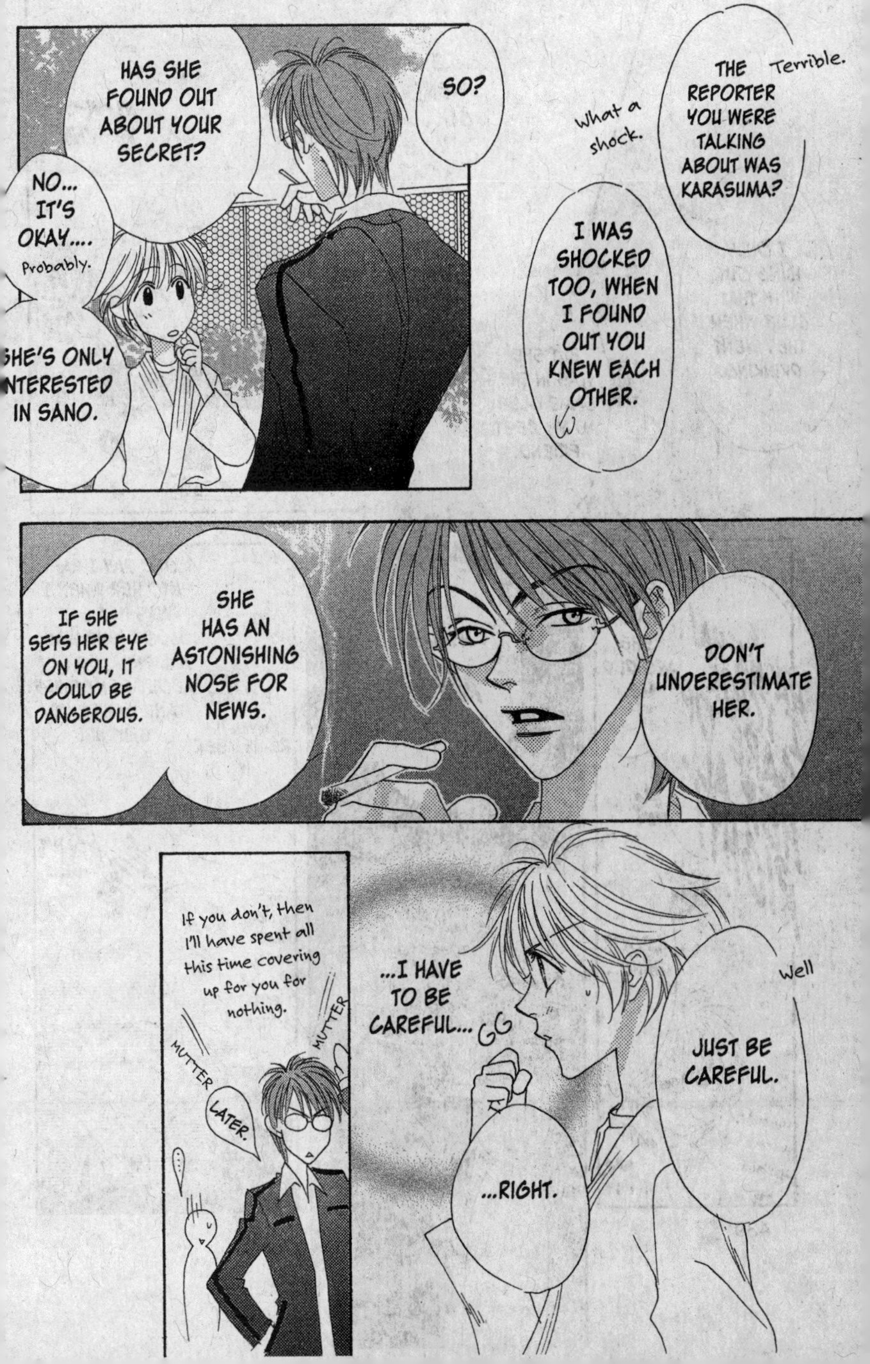
THE REPORTER YOU WERE TALKING ABOUT WAS KARASUMA?
Terrible.
What a shock.
I WAS SHOCKED TOO, WHEN I FOUND OUT YOU KNEW EACH OTHER.
SO?
HAS SHE FOUND OUT ABOUT YOUR SECRET?
NO... IT'S OKAY....
Probably.
HE'S ONLY NTERESTED IN SANO.
DON'T UNDERESTIMATE HER.
SHE HAS AN ASTONISHING NOSE FOR NEWS.
IF SHE SETS HER EYE ON YOU, IT COULD BE DANGEROUS.
Well
JUST BE CAREFUL.
...RIGHT.
...I HAVE TO BE CAREFUL...
GG
If you don't, then I'll have spent all this time covering up for you for nothing.
MUTTER
MUTTER
LATER.
...

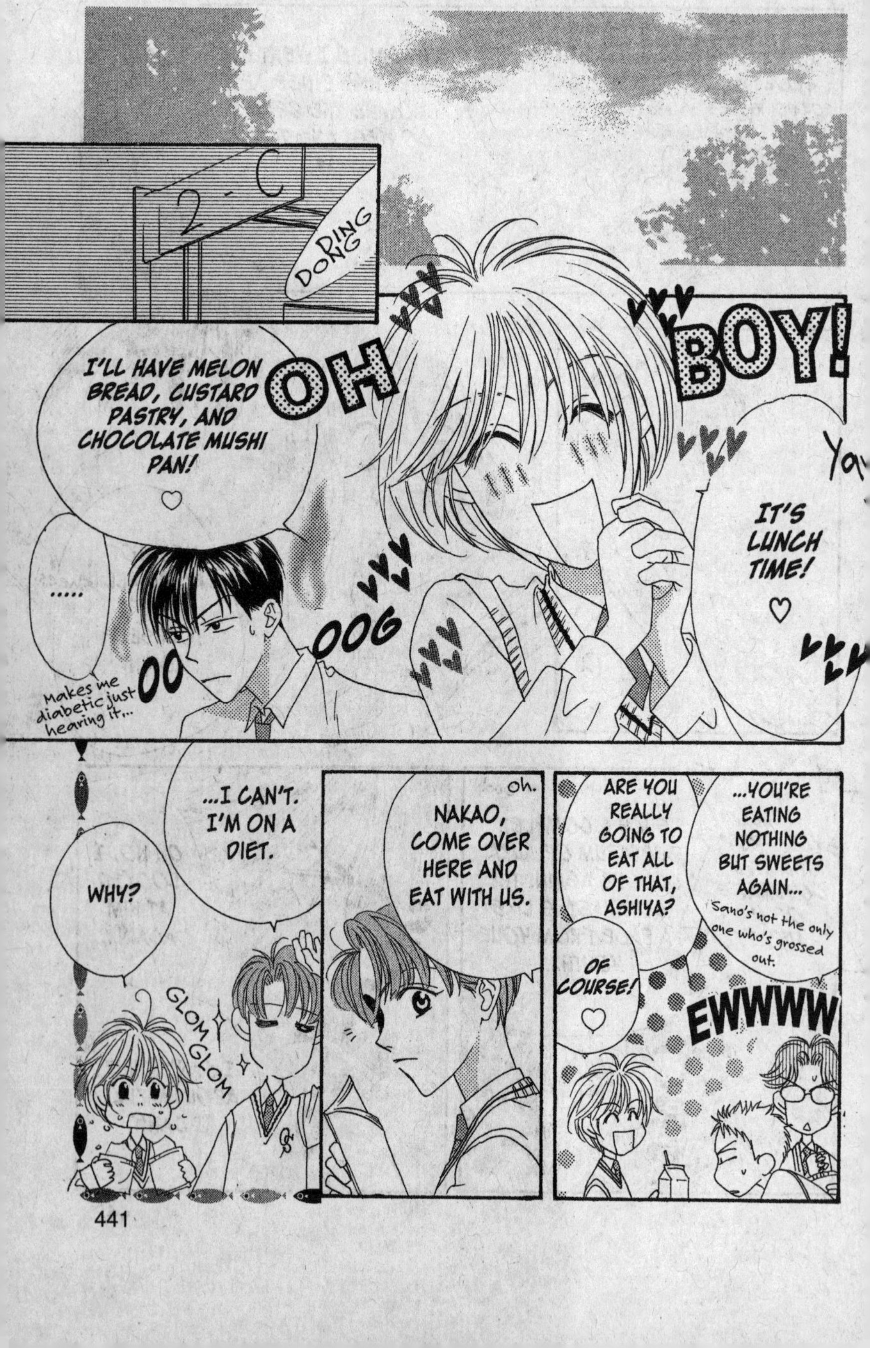
DING DONG
Yay
IT'S LUNCH TIME!
OH BOY!
I'LL HAVE MELON BREAD, CUSTARD PASTRY, AND CHOCOLATE MUSHI PAN!
OOOOG
.....
Makes me diabetic just hearing it...
...YOU'RE EATING NOTHING BUT SWEETS AGAIN...
ARE YOU REALLY GOING TO EAT ALL OF THAT, ASHIYA?
Sano's not the only one who's grossed out.
OF COURSE!
EWWWW
oh.
NAKAO, COME OVER HERE AND EAT WITH US.
...I CAN'T. I'M ON A DIET.
WHY?
GLOM GLOM

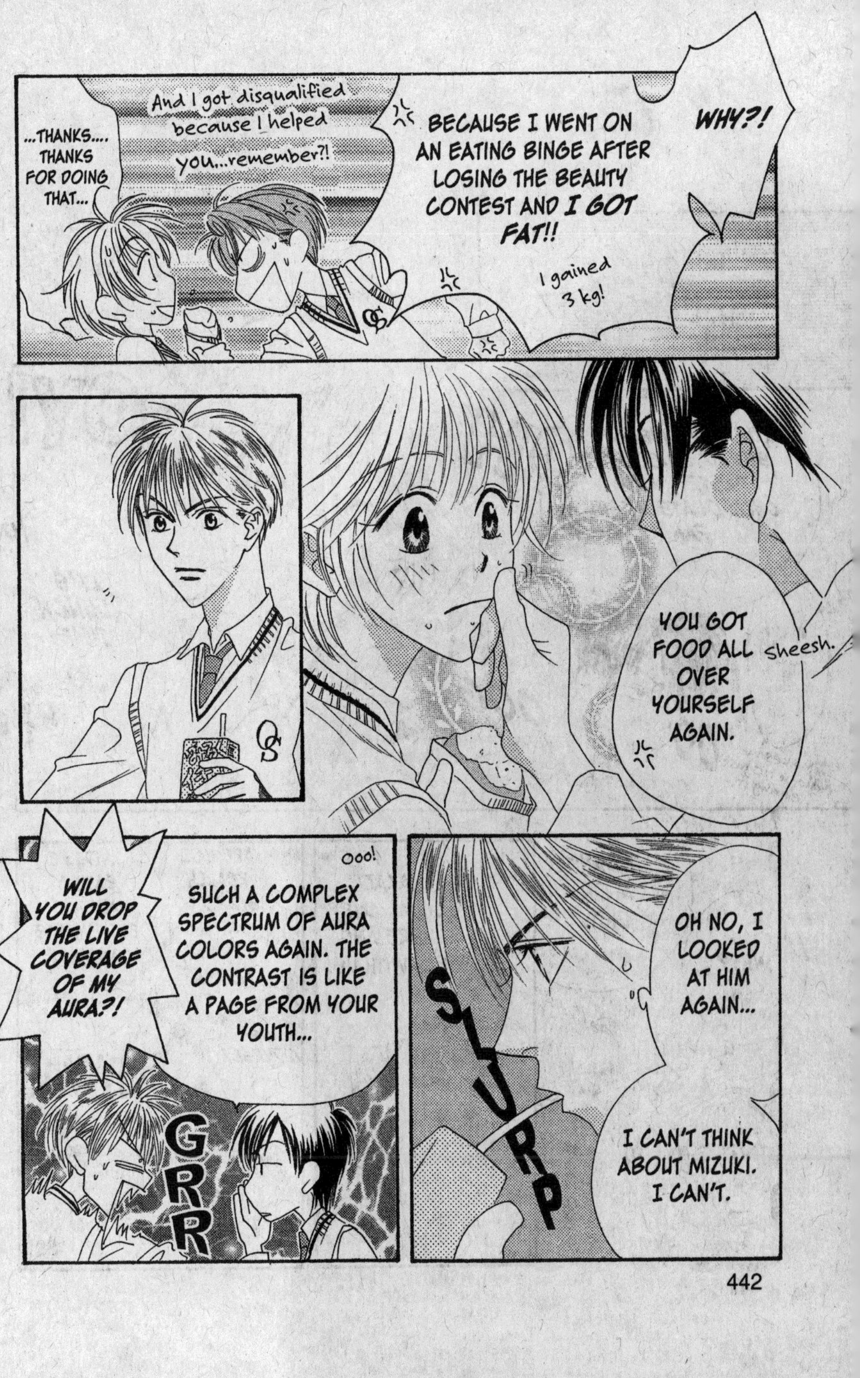
WHY?!
BECAUSE I WENT ON AN EATING BINGE AFTER LOSING THE BEAUTY CONTEST AND I GOT FAT!!
I gained 3 kg!
And I got disqualified because I helped you...remember?!
...THANKS.... THANKS FOR DOING THAT...
YOU GOT FOOD ALL OVER YOURSELF AGAIN.
Sheesh.
OH NO, I LOOKED AT HIM AGAIN...
SLURP
I CAN'T THINK ABOUT MIZUKI. I CAN'T.
Ooo!
SUCH A COMPLEX SPECTRUM OF AURA COLORS AGAIN. THE CONTRAST IS LIKE A PAGE FROM YOUR YOUTH...
WILL YOU DROP THE LIVE COVERAGE OF MY AURA?!
GRR

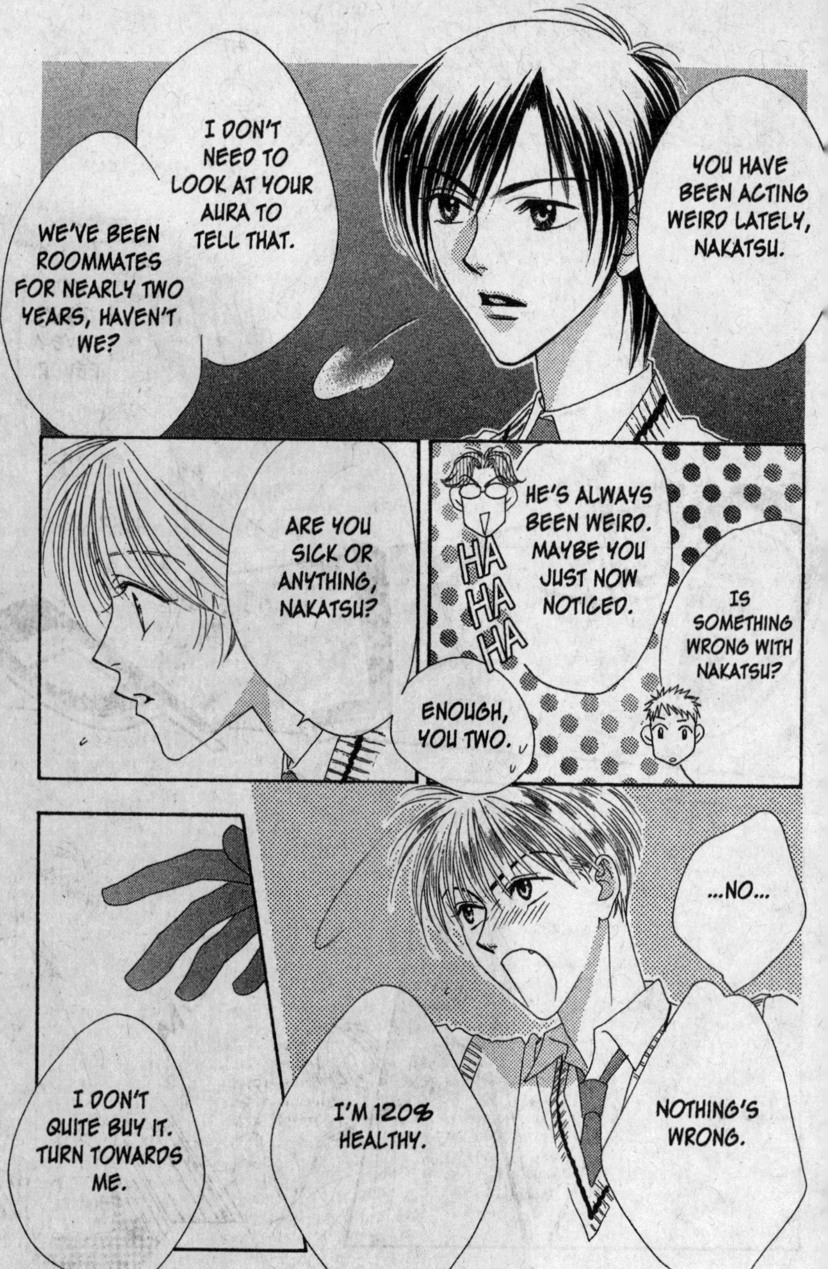

YOU HAVE BEEN ACTING WEIRD LATELY, NAKATSU.
I DON'T NEED TO LOOK AT YOUR AURA TO TELL THAT.
WE'VE BEEN ROOMMATES FOR NEARLY TWO YEARS, HAVEN'T WE?
IS SOMETHING WRONG WITH NAKATSU?
HE'S ALWAYS BEEN WEIRD. MAYBE YOU JUST NOW NOTICED.
HA HA HA
ENOUGH, YOU TWO.
ARE YOU SICK OR ANYTHING, NAKATSU?
...NO...
NOTHING'S WRONG.
I'M 120% HEALTHY.
I DON'T QUITE BUY IT. TURN TOWARDS ME.

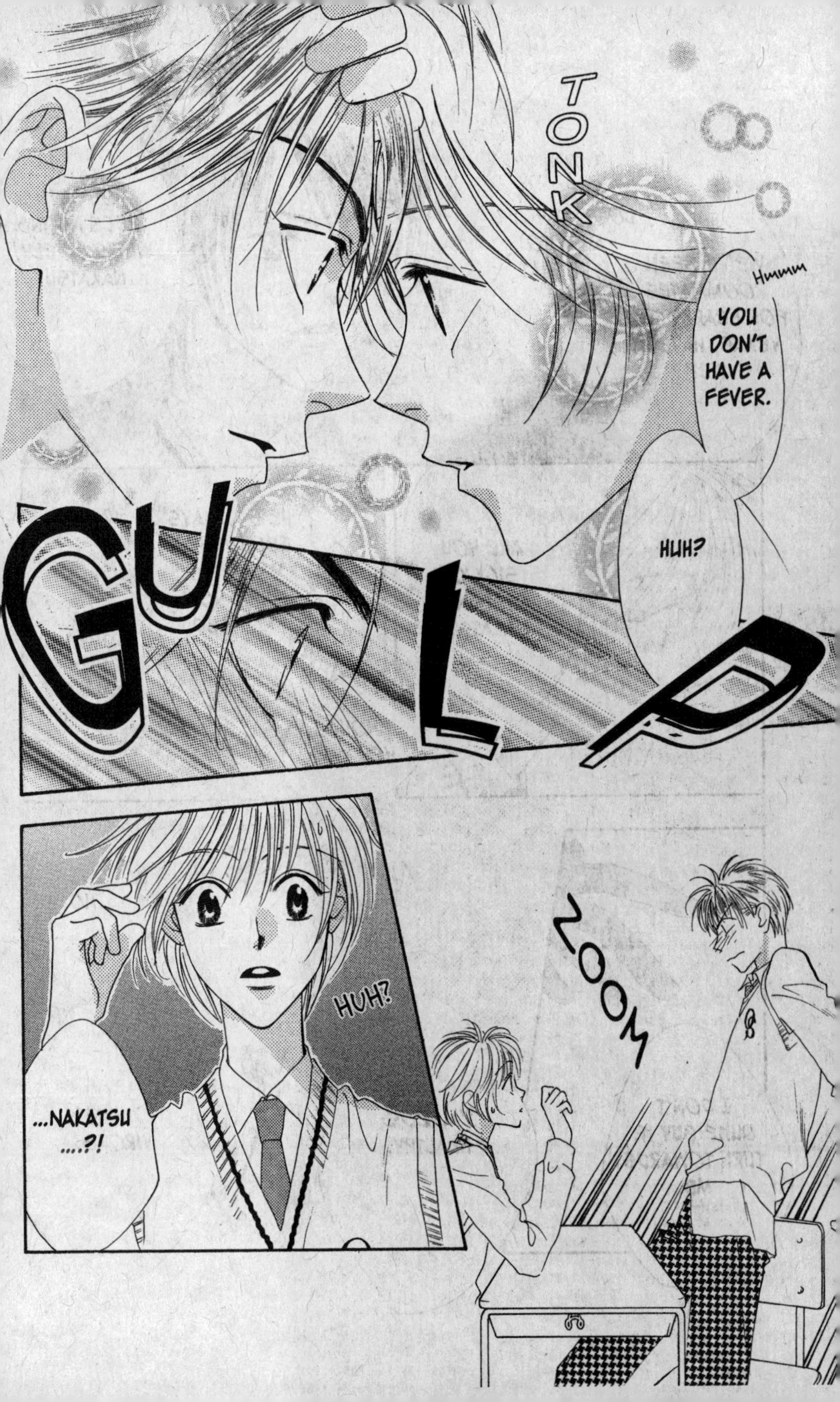
TONK
Hmmm
YOU DON'T HAVE A FEVER.
HUH?
GULP
ZOOM
HUH?
...NAKATSU ....?!

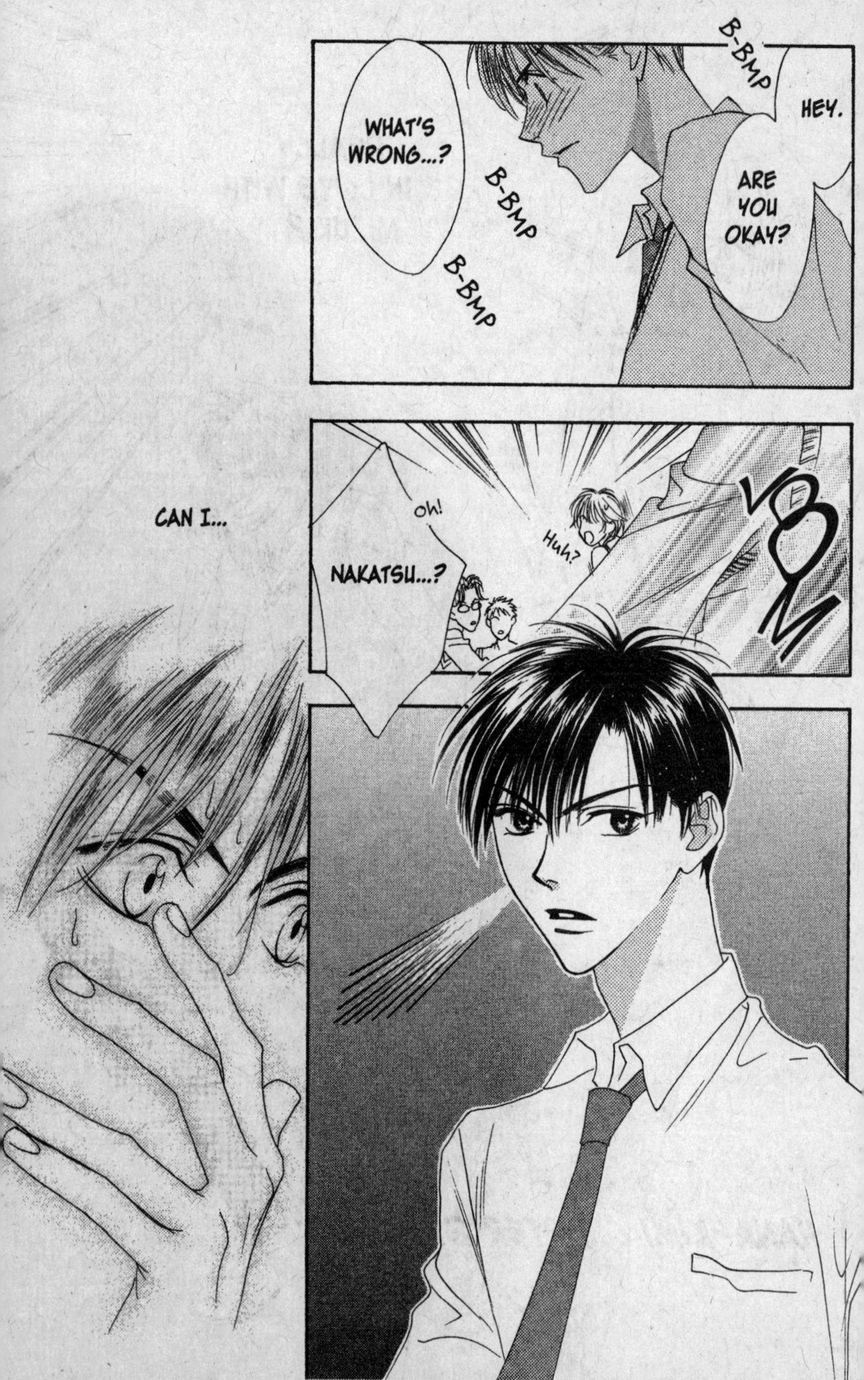
B-BMP
HEY.
ARE YOU OKAY?
WHAT'S WRONG...?
B-BMP
B-BMP
VROOM
Huh?
Oh!
NAKATSU...?
CAN I...

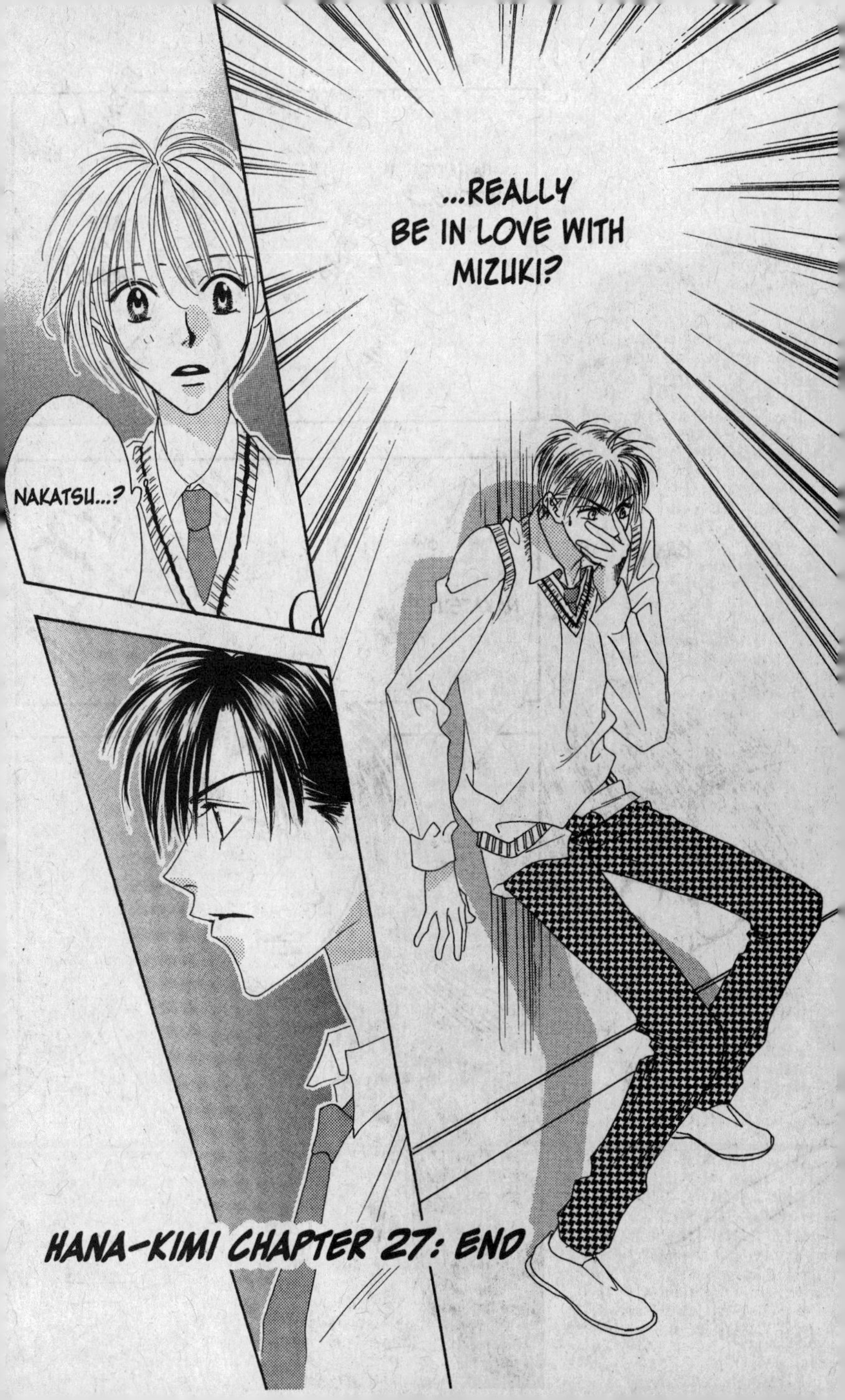
...REALLY BE IN LOVE WITH MIZUKI?
NAKATSU...?
HANA-KIMI CHAPTER 27: END

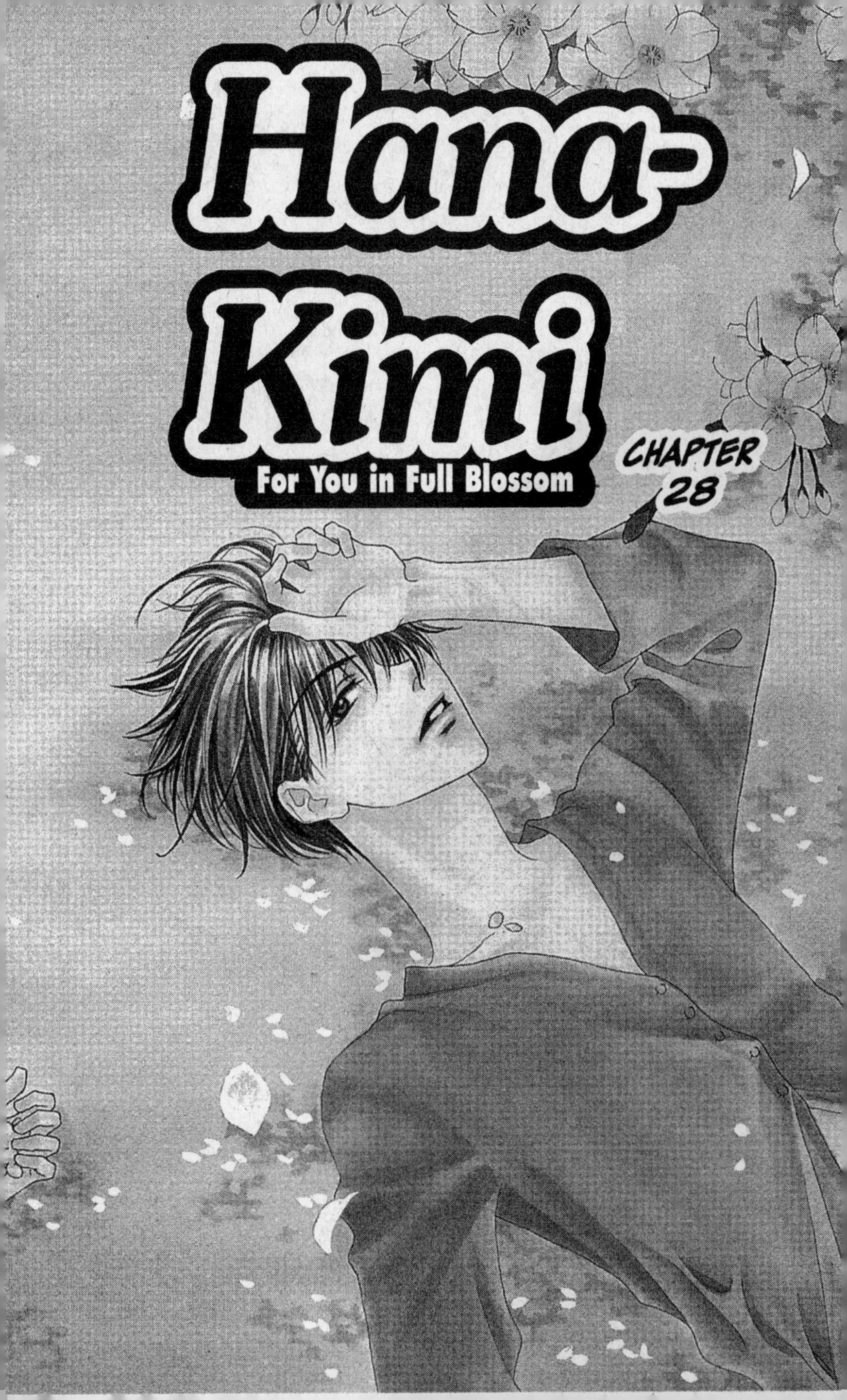
Hana-Kimi
For You in Full Blossom
CHAPTER 28

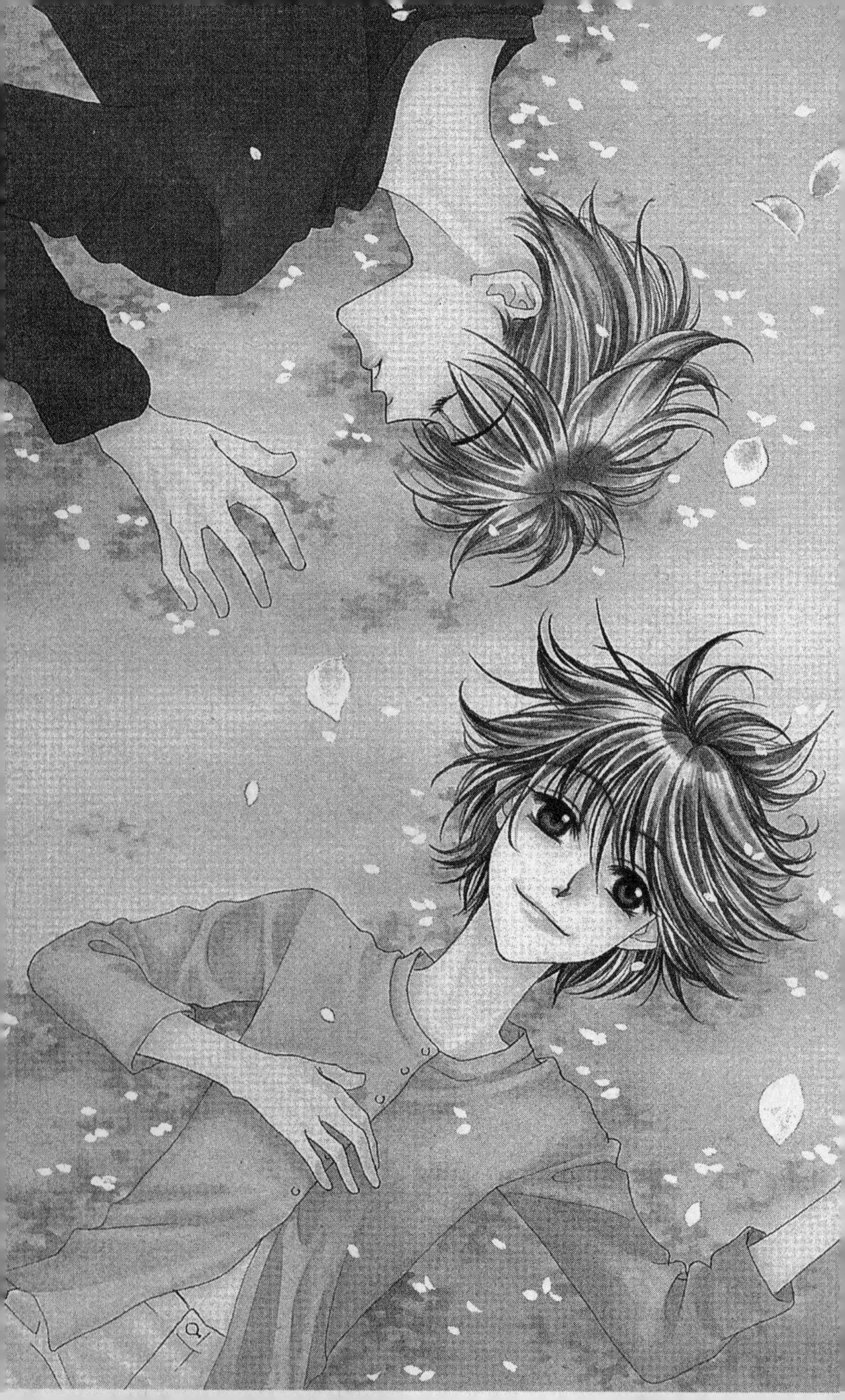

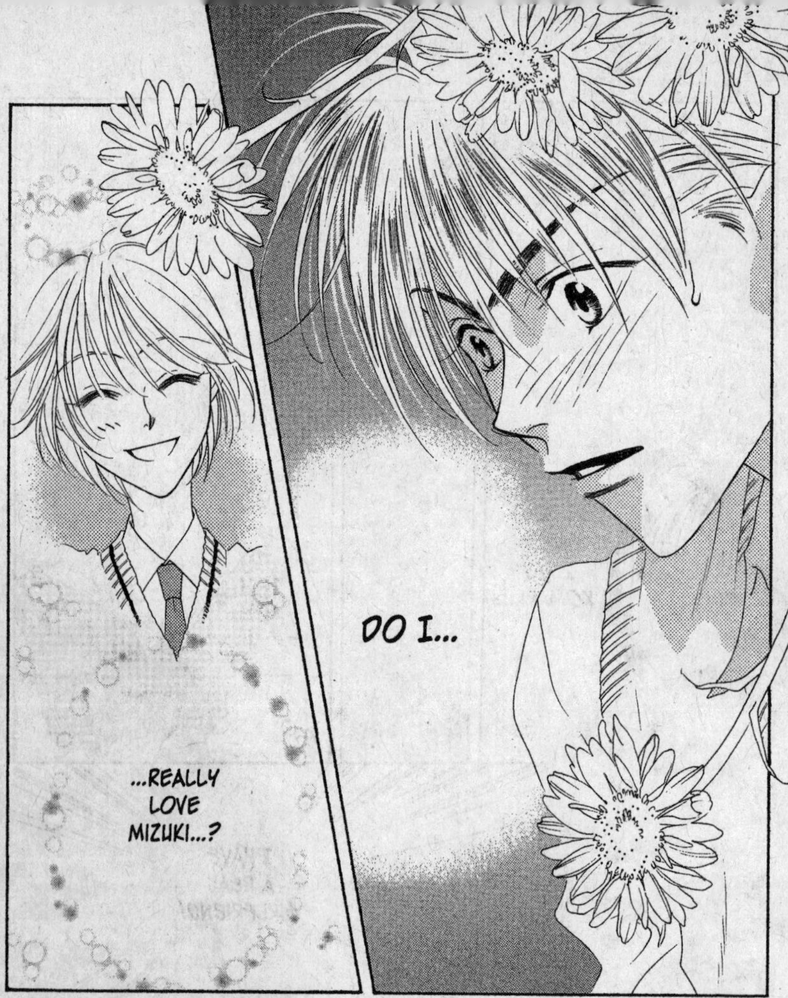
DO I...
...REALLY LOVE MIZUKI...?

STUFF I LOVE Part 3

「 DOLLS 」

I LOVE TEDDY BEARS!!! WHEN IT COMES TO STUFFED ANIMALS, IT'S ALL ABOUT BEARS!! NOTHING BUT BEARS!! (HA HA!) EVEN AT MY AGE, I STILL LIKE STUFFED ANIMALS (AND THERE'S NOTHING WRONG WITH THAT! REALLY!) I'D LIKE TO GET A STEIFF TEDDY BEAR. I LIKE SOME CATS, TOO, BUT ONLY REALLY WELL-DESIGNED ONES. I ALSO HAVE A FROG.

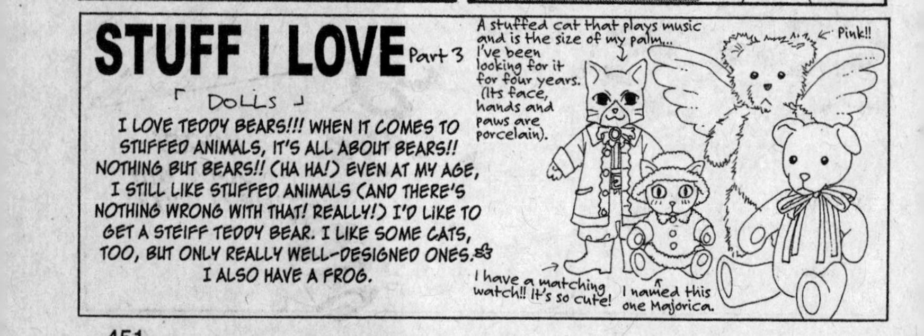
A stuffed cat that plays music and is the size of my palm... I've been looking for it for four years. (Its face, hands and paws are porcelain).
Pink!!
I have a matching watch!! It's so cute!
I named this one Majorica.

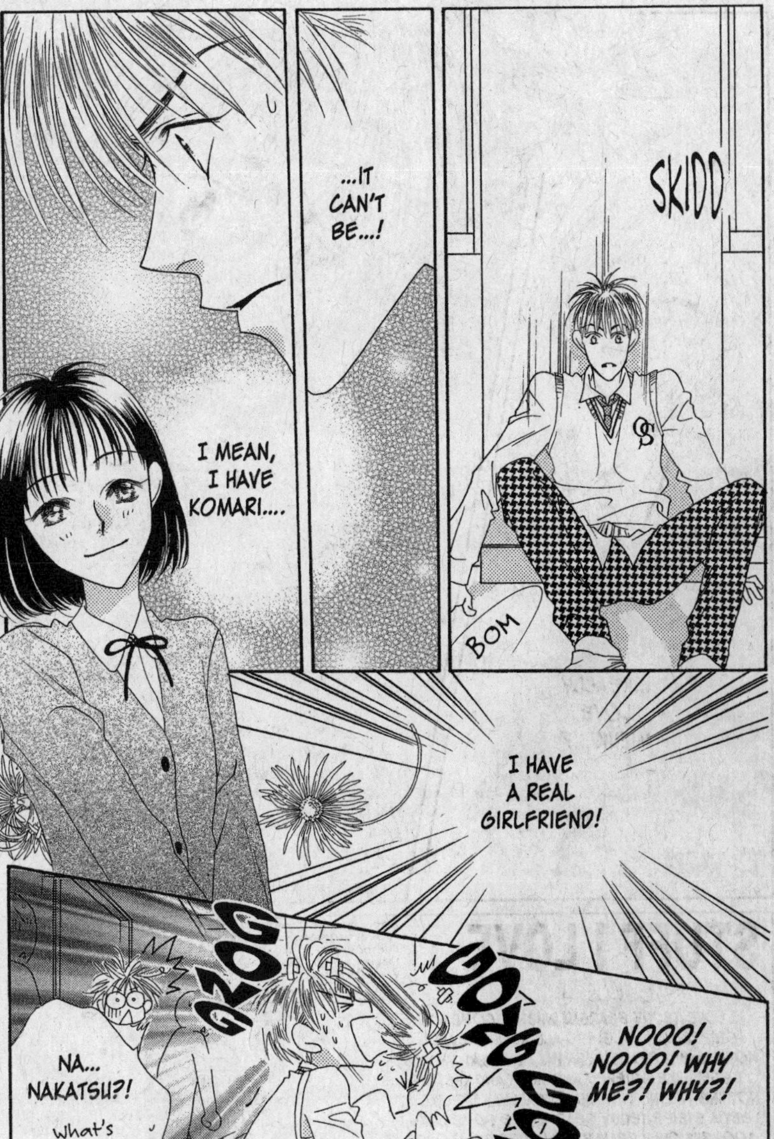
SKIDD
BOM
...IT CAN'T BE...!
I MEAN, I HAVE KOMARI....
I HAVE A REAL GIRLFRIEND!
NOOO! NOOO! WHY ME?! WHY?!
GONG GONG GONG
GONG
NA... NAKATSU?!
what's wrong?

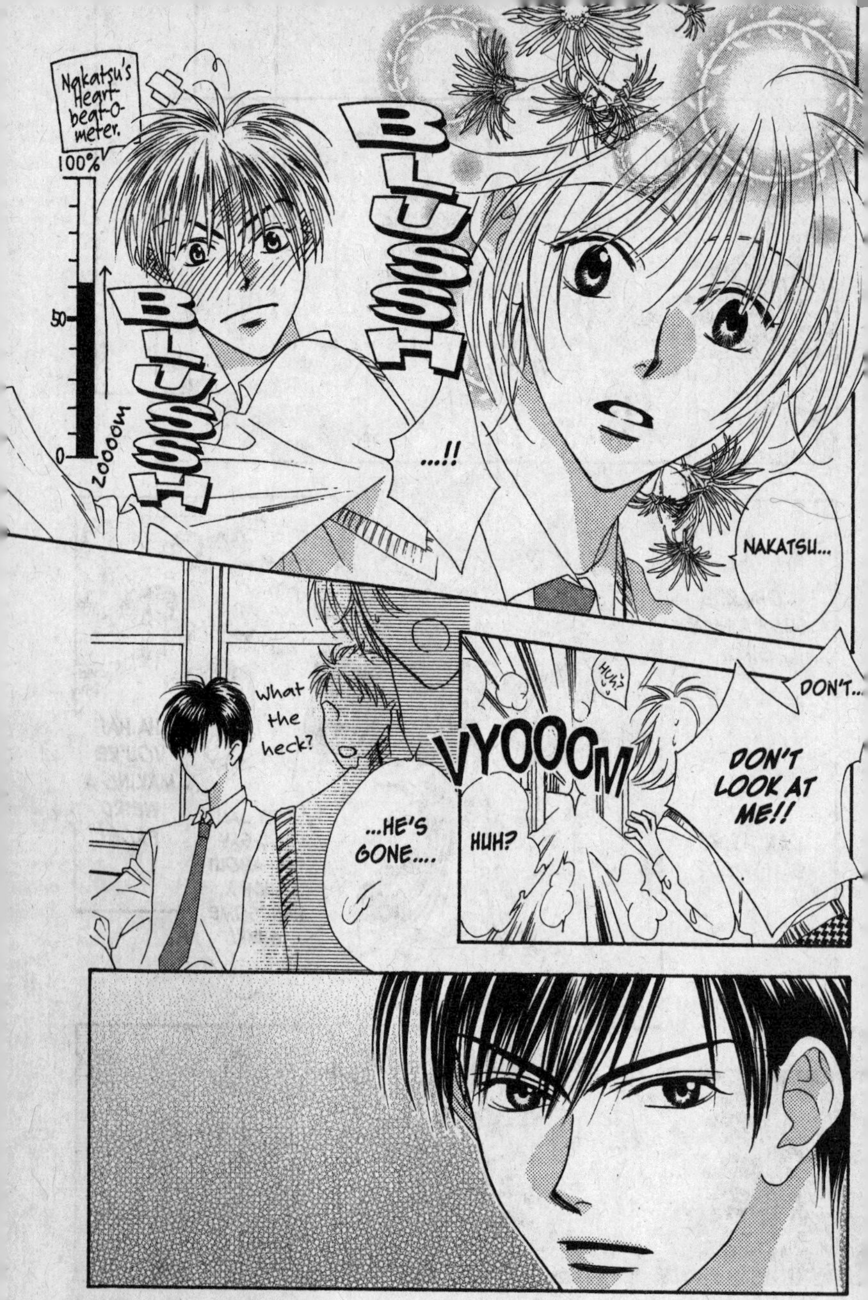
NAKATSU...
BLUSSH
...!!
BLUSSH
Nakatsu's Heart beat-o-meter.
100%
50
0
zoooom
DON'T...
DON'T LOOK AT ME!!
HUH?
VYOOOM
HUH?
...HE'S GONE....
What the heck?

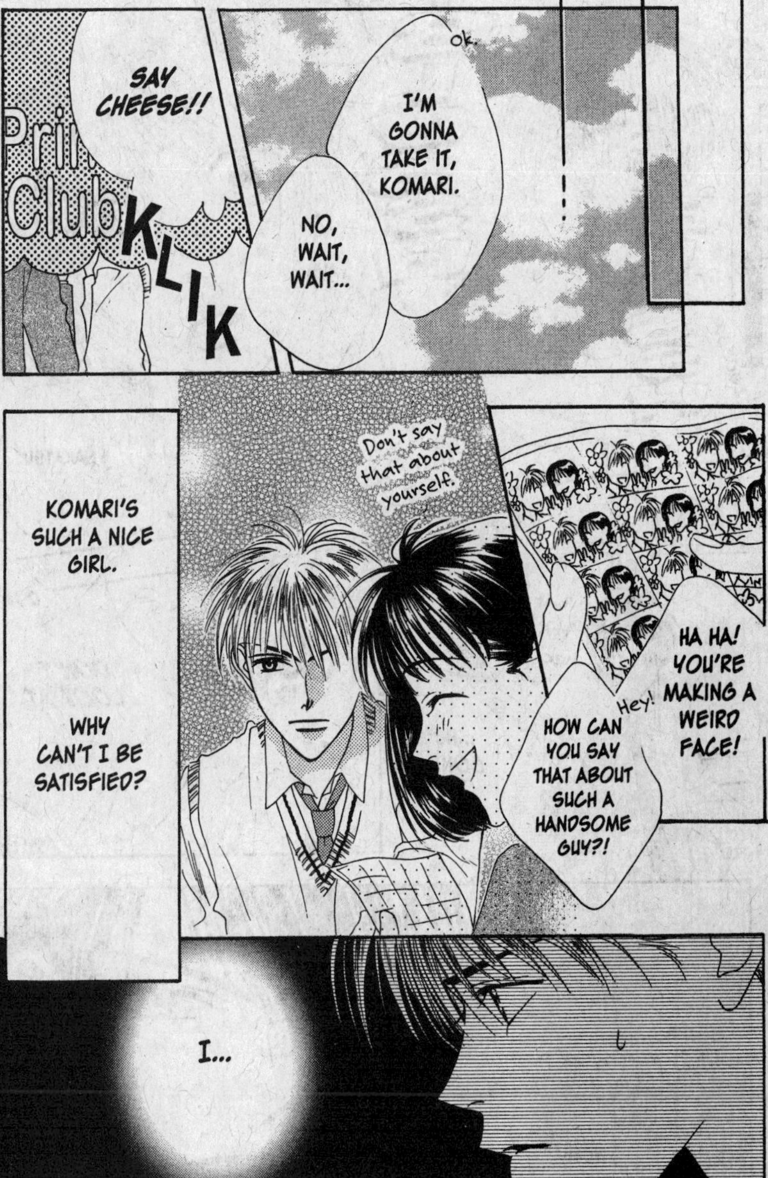
Ok.
I'M GONNA TAKE IT, KOMARI.
NO, WAIT, WAIT...
SAY CHEESE!!
Club
KLIK
HA HA! YOU'RE MAKING A WEIRD FACE!
Hey!
HOW CAN YOU SAY THAT ABOUT SUCH A HANDSOME GUY?!
Don't say that about yourself.
KOMARI'S SUCH A NICE GIRL.
WHY CAN'T I BE SATISFIED?
I...

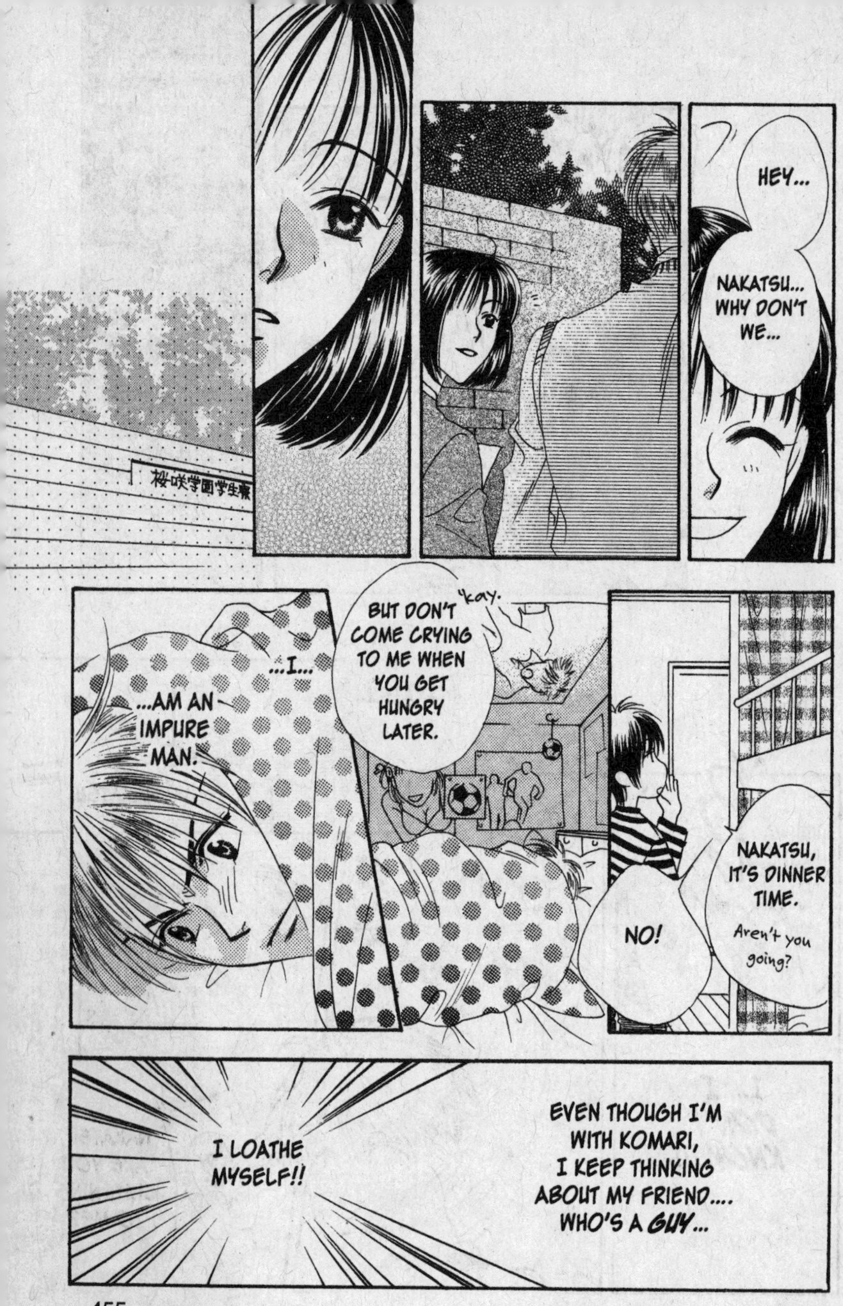
HEY...
NAKATSU... WHY DON'T WE...
桜咲学園学生寮
NAKATSU, IT'S DINNER TIME.
Aren't you going?
NO!
'kay.
BUT DON'T COME CRYING TO ME WHEN YOU GET HUNGRY LATER.
...I...
...AM AN IMPURE MAN.
EVEN THOUGH I'M WITH KOMARI, I KEEP THINKING ABOUT MY FRIEND.... WHO'S A *GUY*...
I LOATHE MYSELF!!

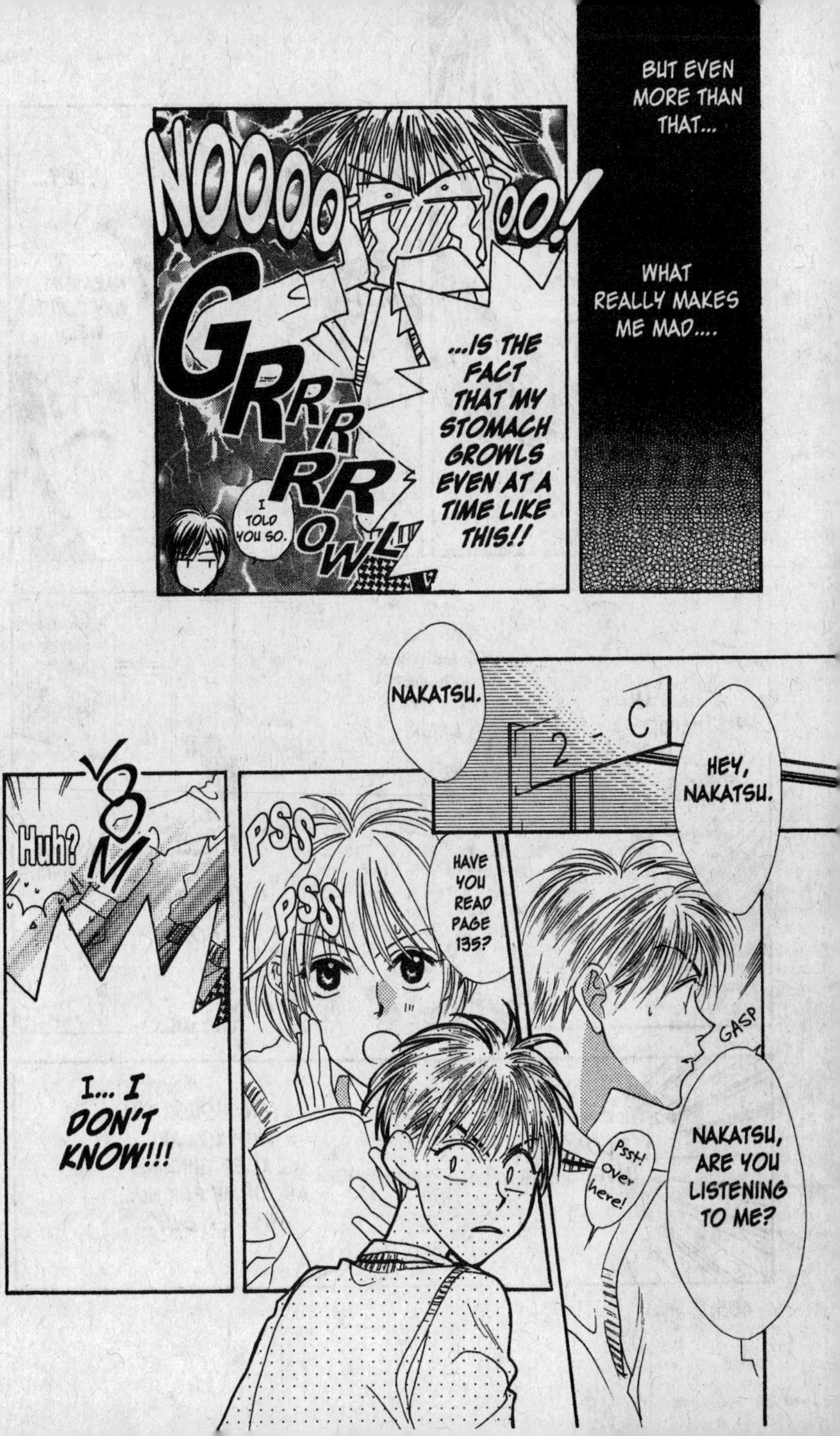

BUT EVEN MORE THAN THAT...
WHAT REALLY MAKES ME MAD....
NOOOOOOO!
GRRRRRROWL
...IS THE FACT THAT MY STOMACH GROWLS EVEN AT A TIME LIKE THIS!!
I TOLD YOU SO.
NAKATSU.
HEY, NAKATSU.
HAVE YOU READ PAGE 135?
PSS
PSS
GASP
NAKATSU, ARE YOU LISTENING TO ME?
Psst! Over here!
VOOM
Huh?
I... I DON'T KNOW!!!

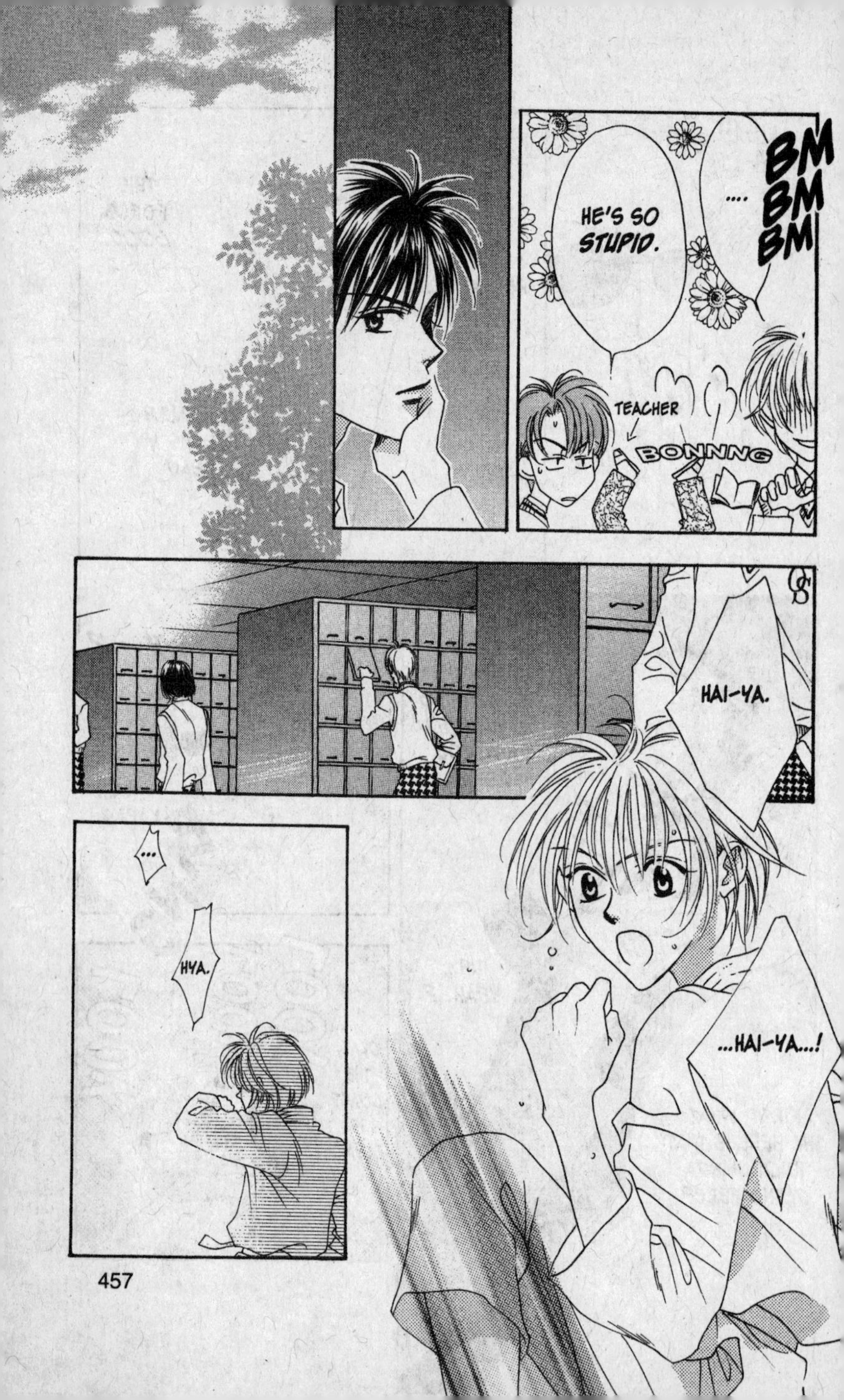
BM
BM
BM
....
HE'S SO STUPID.
TEACHER
BONNNG
HAI-YA.
...HAI-YA...!
...
HYA.

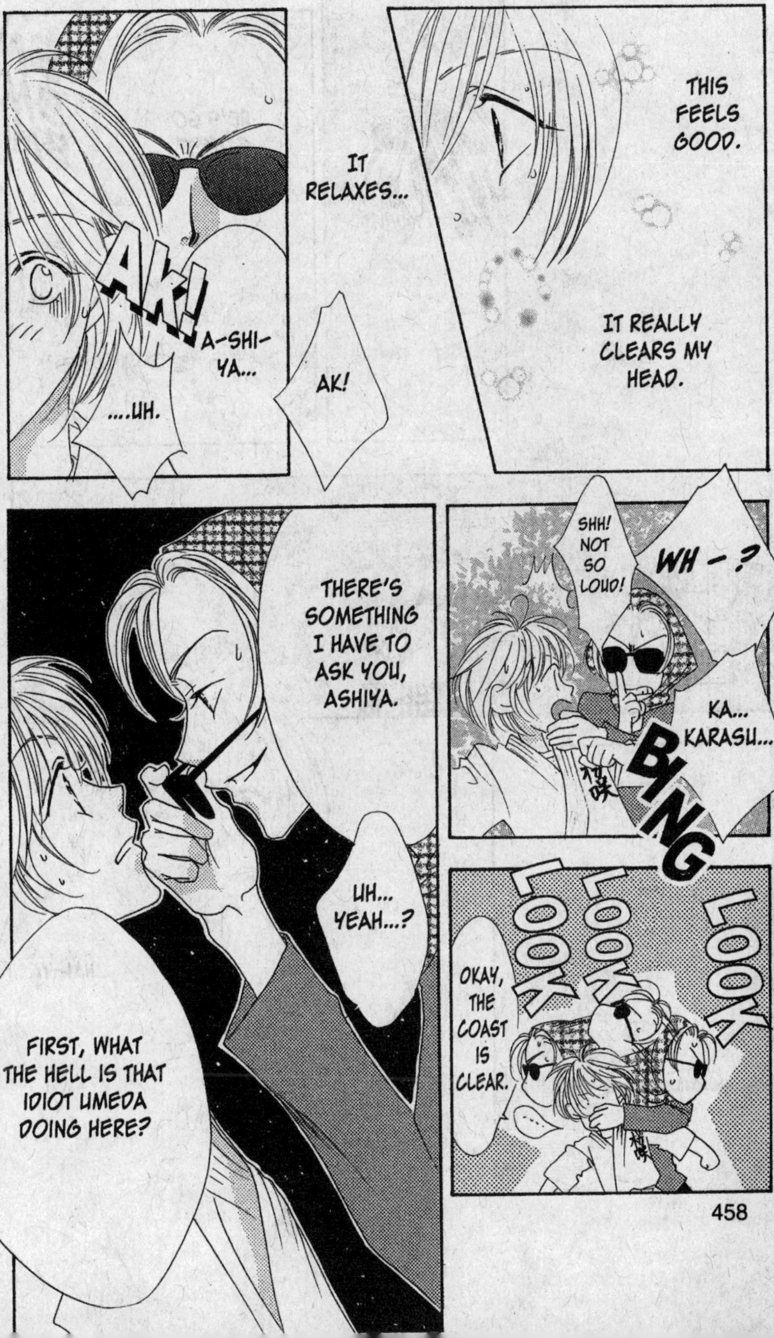
THIS FEELS GOOD.
IT REALLY CLEARS MY HEAD.
IT RELAXES...
AK!
AK!
A-SHI-YA...
....UH.
WH-?
SHH! NOT SO LOUD!
KA... KARASU...
BING
LOOK LOOK LOOK
OKAY, THE COAST IS CLEAR.
THERE'S SOMETHING I HAVE TO ASK YOU, ASHIYA.
UH... YEAH...?
FIRST, WHAT THE HELL IS THAT IDIOT UMEDA DOING HERE?

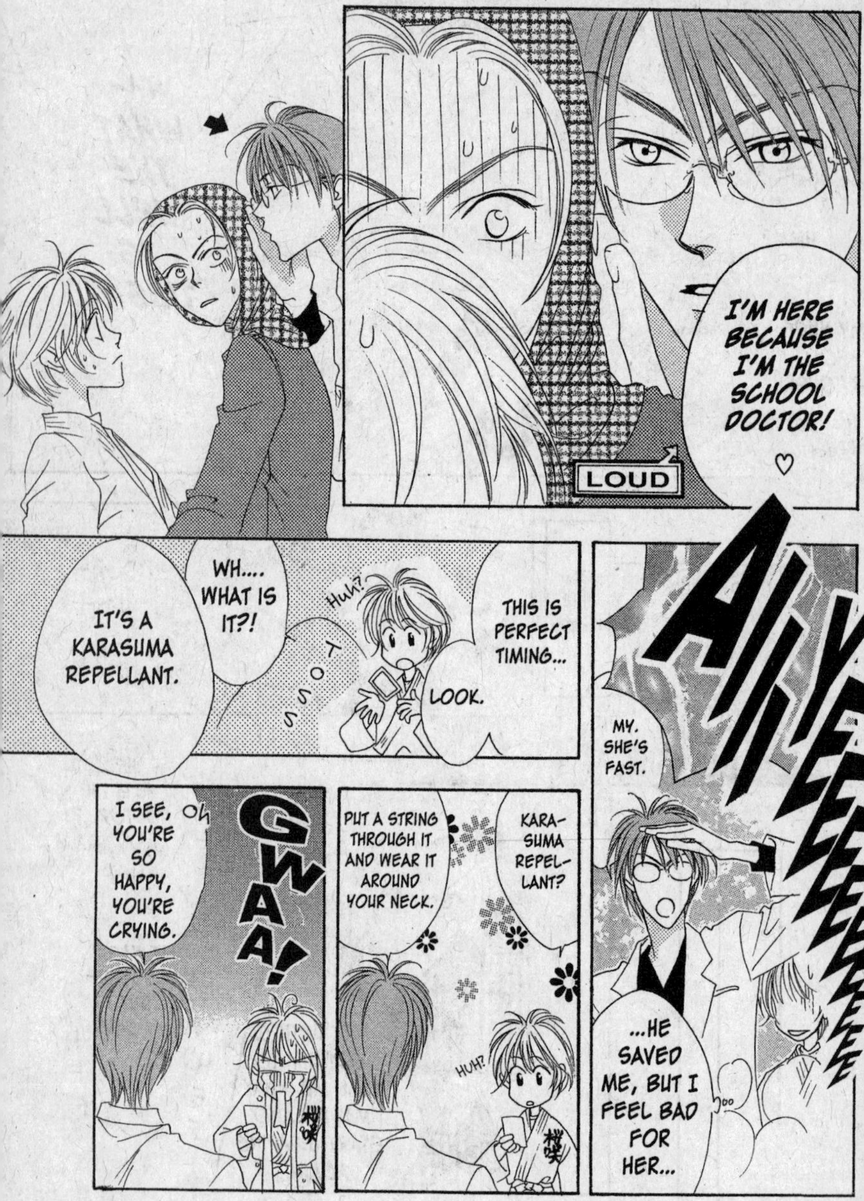

I'M HERE BECAUSE I'M THE SCHOOL DOCTOR! ♡
LOUD
AIYEEEEEEEEEEEE
MY. SHE'S FAST.
...HE SAVED ME, BUT I FEEL BAD FOR HER...
THIS IS PERFECT TIMING...
LOOK.
Huh?
TOSS
WH.... WHAT IS IT?!
IT'S A KARASUMA REPELLANT.
KARA-SUMA REPEL-LANT?
PUT A STRING THROUGH IT AND WEAR IT AROUND YOUR NECK.
HUH?
GWAA!
I SEE, YOU'RE SO HAPPY, YOU'RE CRYING.
Oh

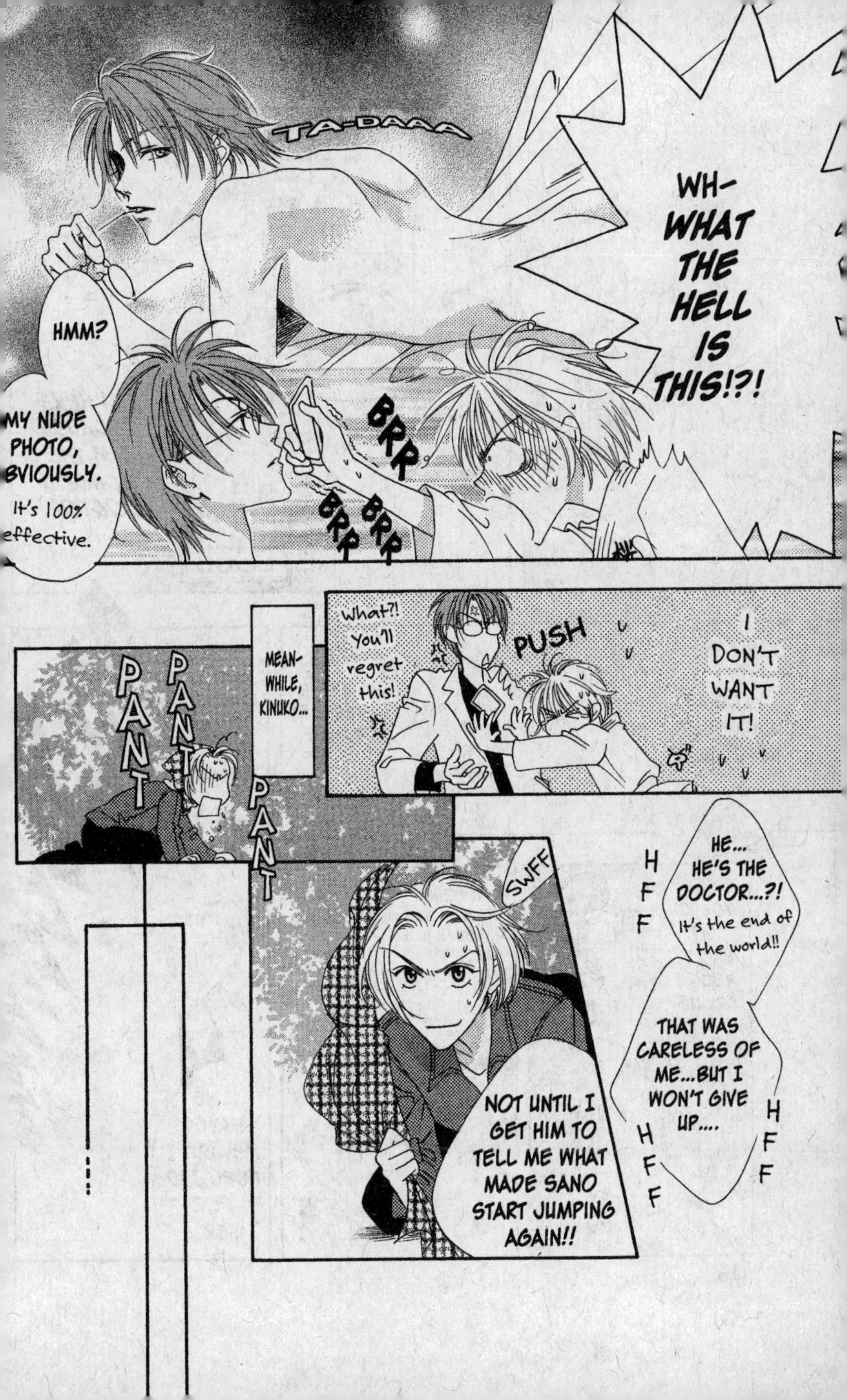
WH- WHAT THE HELL IS THIS!?!
TA-DAAA
HMM?
BRR
BRR
BRR
MY NUDE PHOTO, BVIOUSLY.
It's 100% effective.
I DON'T WANT IT!
PUSH
What?! You'll regret this!
MEAN-WHILE, KINUKO...
PANT
PANT
PANT
HE... HE'S THE DOCTOR...?!
It's the end of the world!!
HFF
SWFF
THAT WAS CARELESS OF ME...BUT I WON'T GIVE UP....
HFF
HFF
NOT UNTIL I GET HIM TO TELL ME WHAT MADE SANO START JUMPING AGAIN!!
...

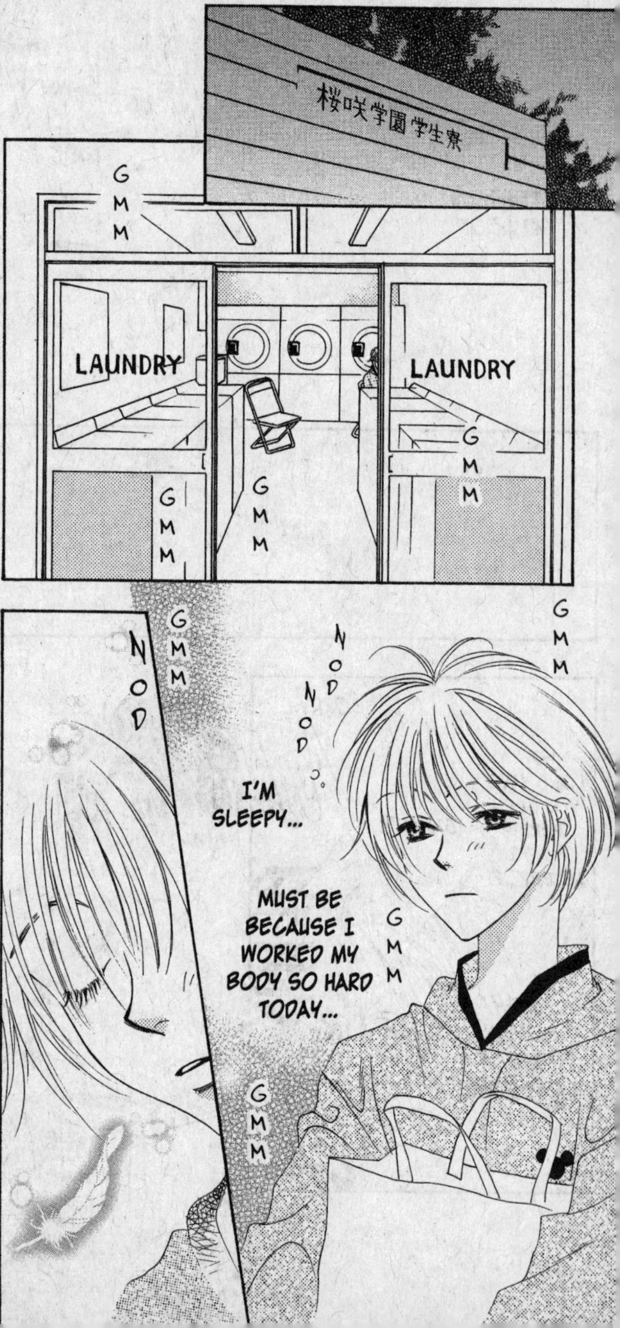
桜咲学園学生寮
GMM
LAUNDRY
LAUNDRY
GMM
GMM
GMM
GMM
GMM
NOD
NOD
NOD
I'M SLEEPY...
MUST BE BECAUSE I WORKED MY BODY SO HARD TODAY...
GMM
GMM

WHISPERED SECRETS

LOVE AND COURAGE

I WROTE THIS STORY FOR NAKATSU. YOU FINALLY BECAME A MAN, NAKATSU! (!?) LOVE TAKES COURAGE! ...BUT POOR KOMARI! MY REPUTATION FOR PURITY WAS FINALLY DESTROYED BY THE APPEARANCE OF UMEDA'S NUDE PHOTO (SEE FACING PAGE)! HA! RIGHT NOW, I'M REALLY INTO SMAP X SMAP'S "TAKE NO ZUKA KAGEKI DAN"! I MELT WHEN I HEAR THEIR THEME SONG "OTOKO" (MAN), AND KIMUTAKU'S "AI YUKI" (LOVE AND COURAGE).

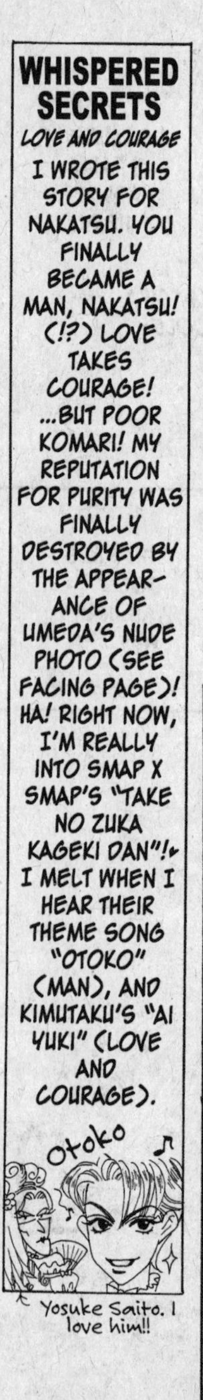
Otoko ♪

Yosuke Saito. I love him!!

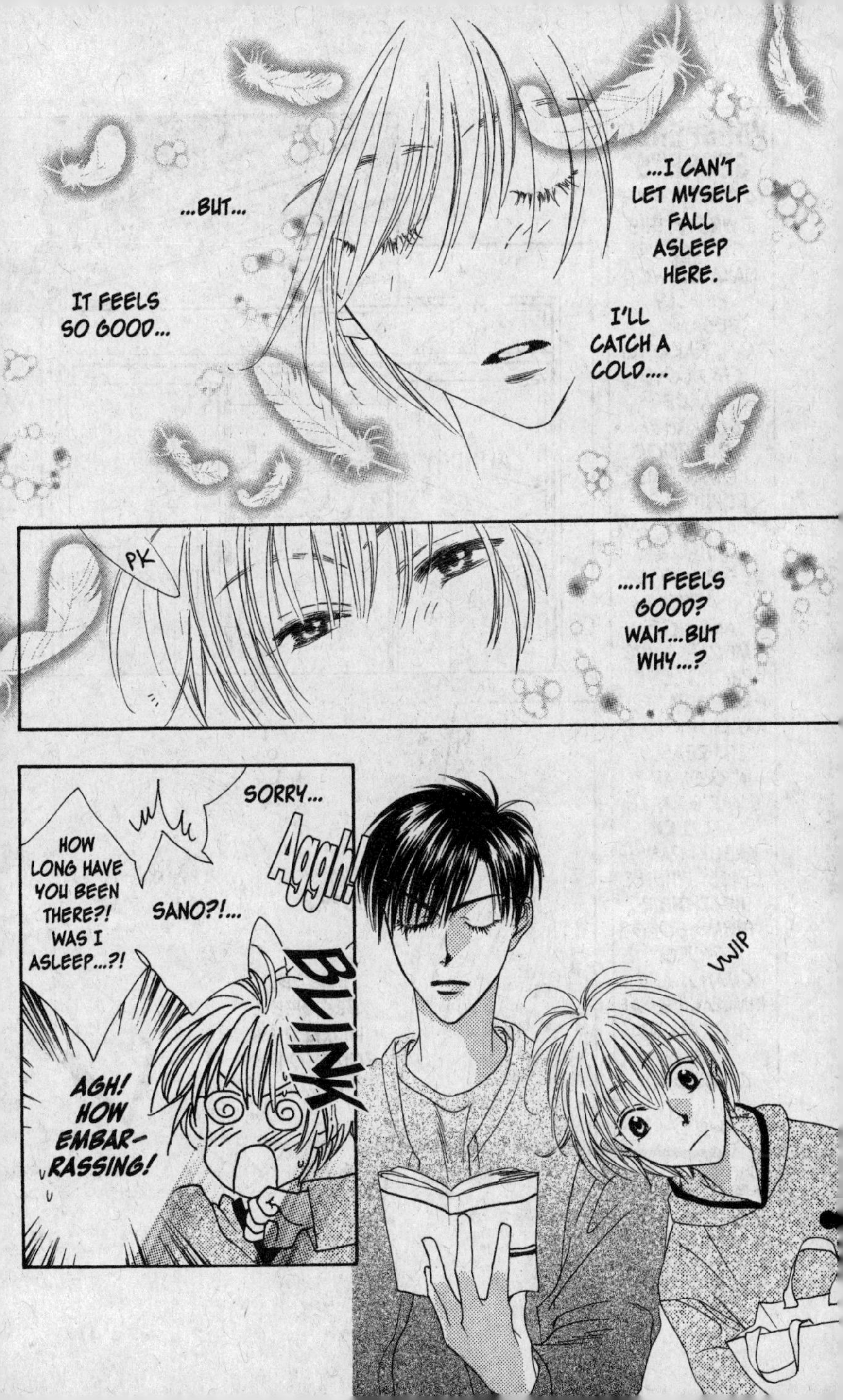
...I CAN'T LET MYSELF FALL ASLEEP HERE.
I'LL CATCH A COLD....
...BUT...
IT FEELS SO GOOD...
....IT FEELS GOOD? WAIT...BUT WHY...?
PK
VWIP
BLINK
Agggh!
SORRY...
SANO?!...
HOW LONG HAVE YOU BEEN THERE?! WAS I ASLEEP...?!
AGH! HOW EMBAR-RASSING!

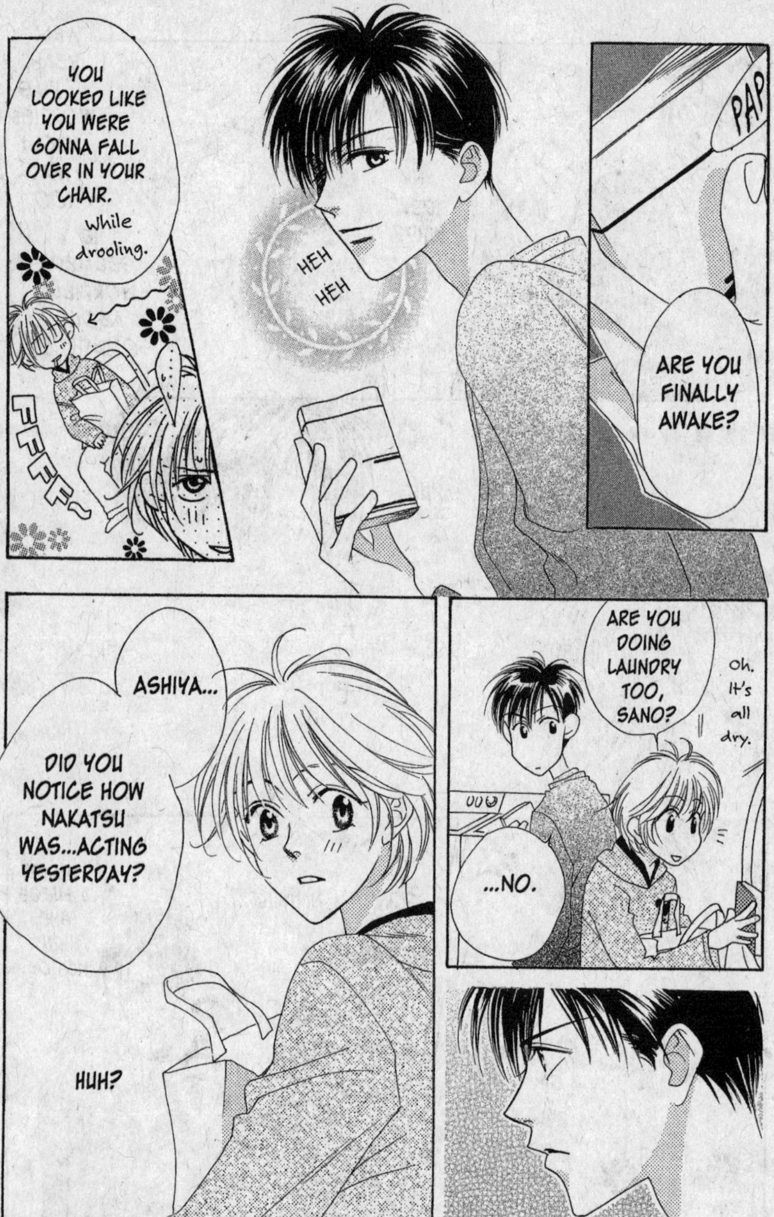
PAP
ARE YOU FINALLY AWAKE?
HEH HEH
YOU LOOKED LIKE YOU WERE GONNA FALL OVER IN YOUR CHAIR.
While drooling.
FFFF~
ARE YOU DOING LAUNDRY TOO, SANO?
Oh. It's all dry.
...NO.
ASHIYA...
DID YOU NOTICE HOW NAKATSU WAS...ACTING YESTERDAY?
HUH?

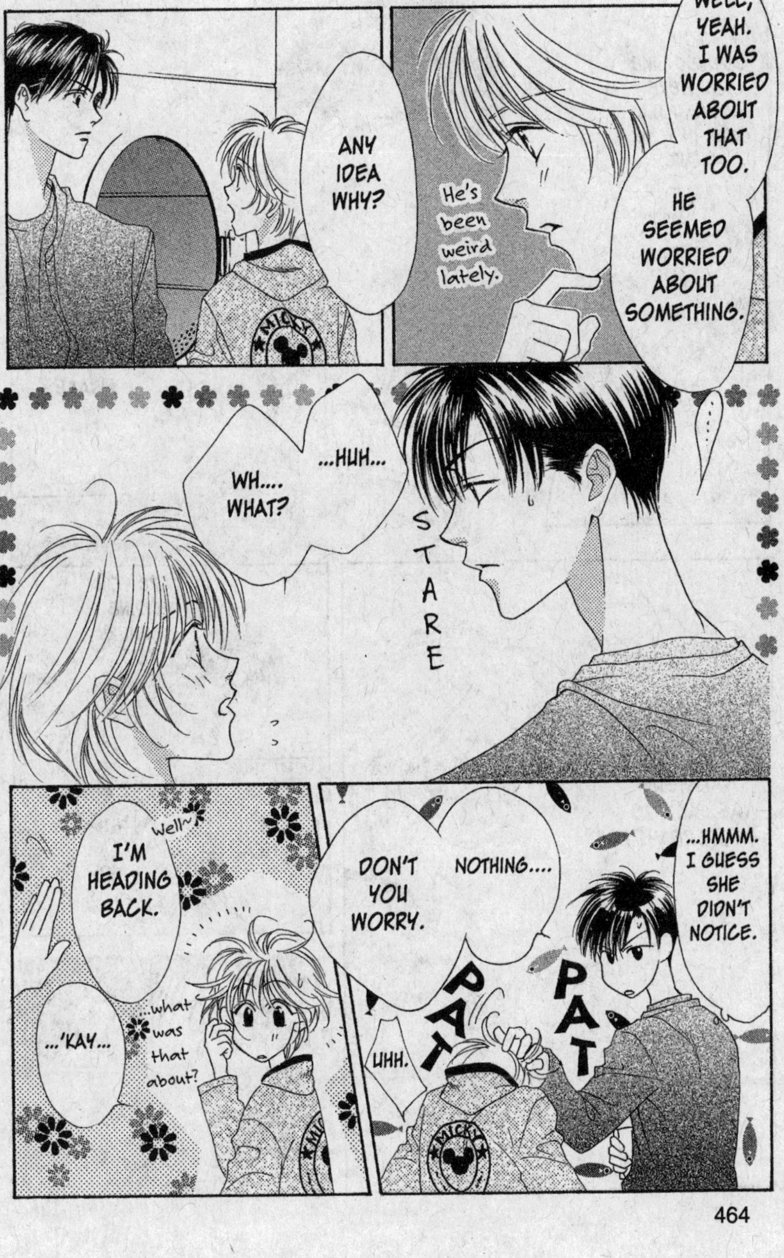
WELL, YEAH. I WAS WORRIED ABOUT THAT TOO.
HE SEEMED WORRIED ABOUT SOMETHING.
He's been weird lately.
ANY IDEA WHY?
...
...HUH...
WH.... WHAT?
STARE
...HMMM. I GUESS SHE DIDN'T NOTICE.
NOTHING....
DON'T YOU WORRY.
PAT
PAT
UHH.
well~
I'M HEADING BACK.
...'KAY...
...what was that about?

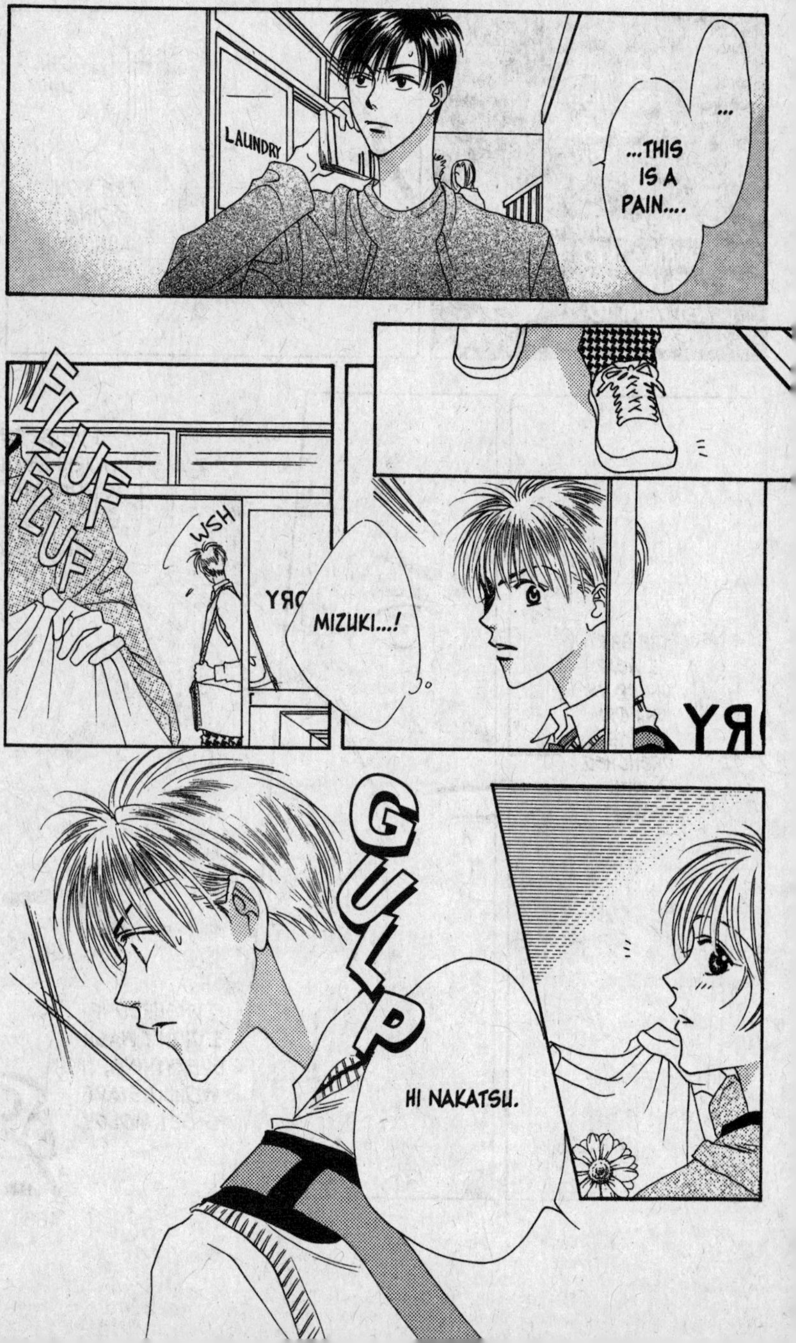

...
...THIS IS A PAIN....
LAUNDRY
MIZUKI...!
FLUF FLUF
WSH
GULP
HI NAKATSU.

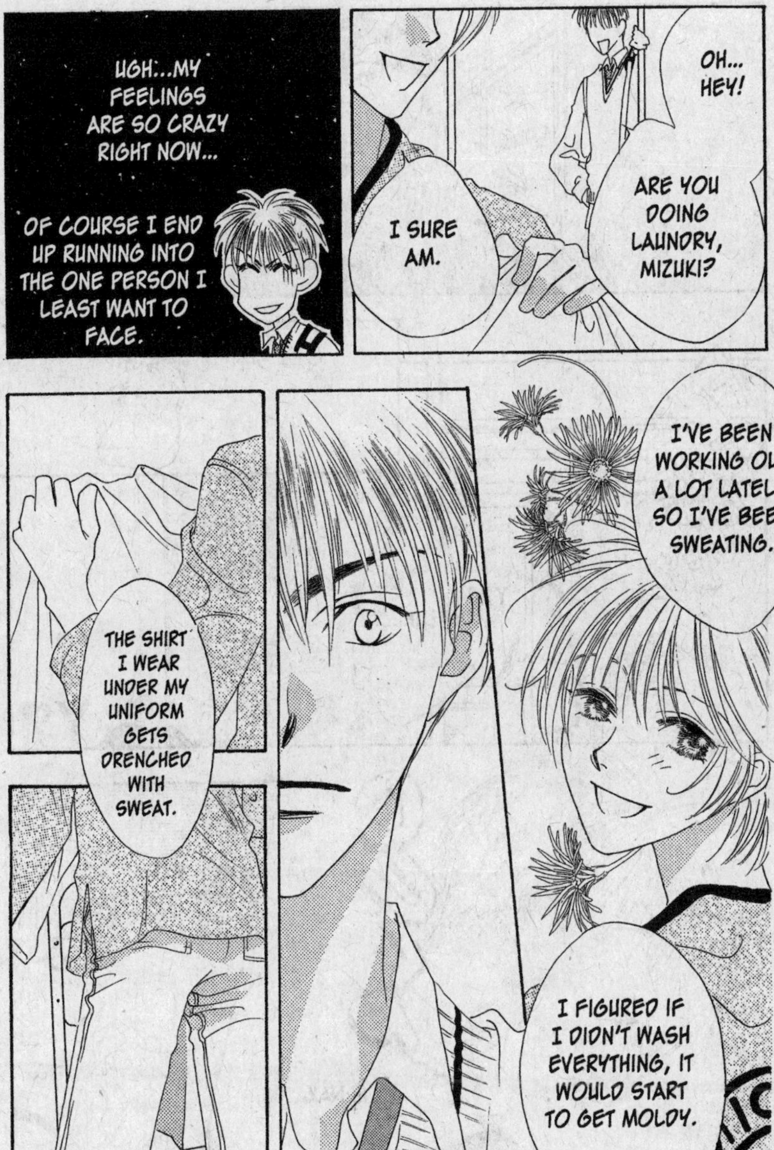
OH... HEY!
ARE YOU DOING LAUNDRY, MIZUKI?
I SURE AM.
UGH...MY FEELINGS ARE SO CRAZY RIGHT NOW...
OF COURSE I END UP RUNNING INTO THE ONE PERSON I LEAST WANT TO FACE.
I'VE BEEN WORKING OUT A LOT LATELY, SO I'VE BEEN SWEATING.
I FIGURED IF I DIDN'T WASH EVERYTHING, IT WOULD START TO GET MOLDY.
THE SHIRT I WEAR UNDER MY UNIFORM GETS DRENCHED WITH SWEAT.

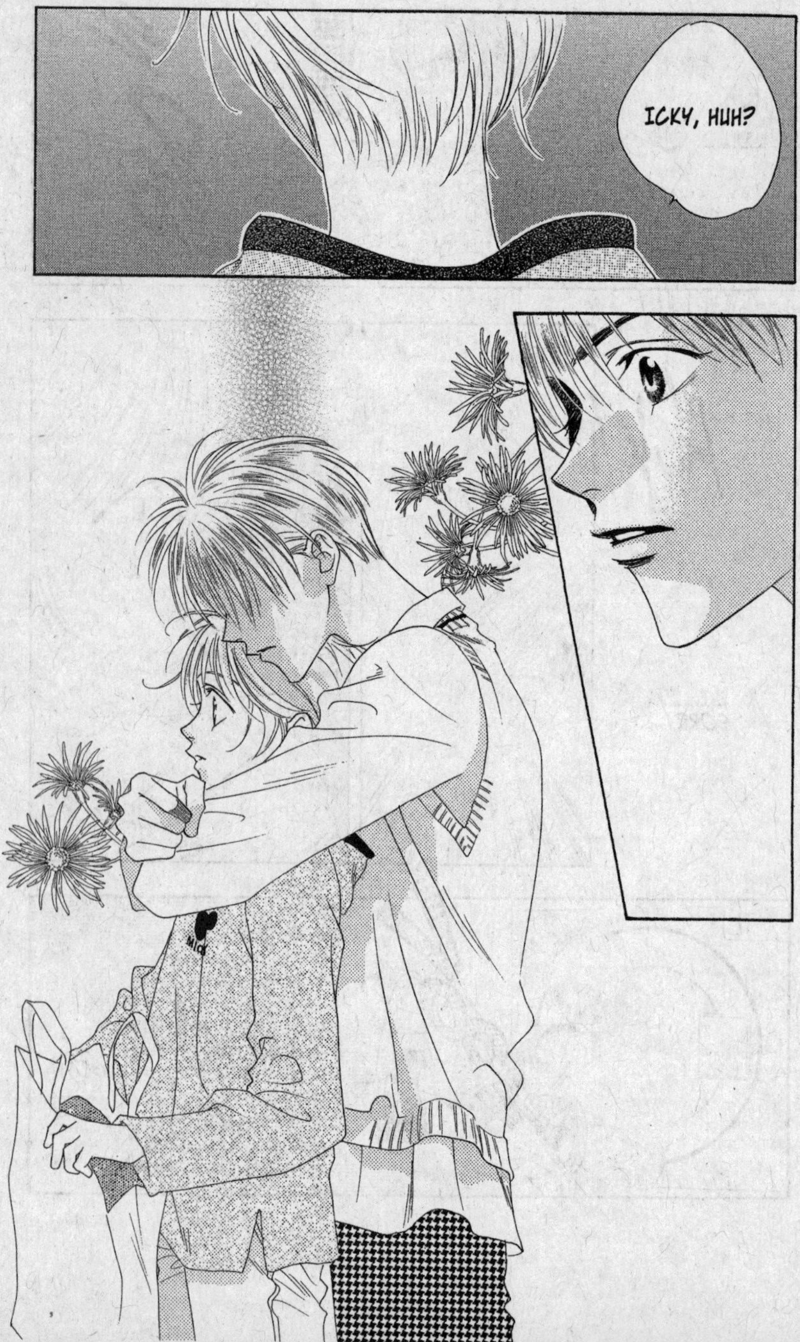
ICKY, HUH?

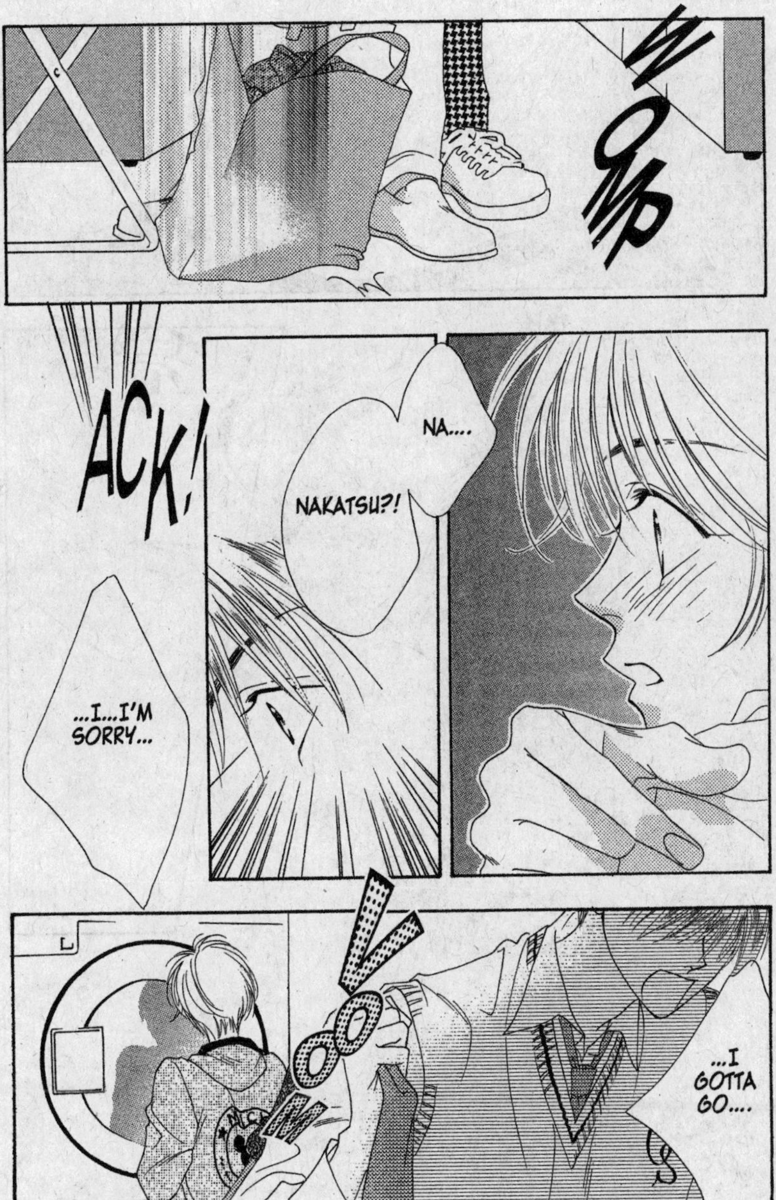
WOMP
NA....
NAKATSU?!
ACK!
...I...I'M SORRY...
...I GOTTA GO....
VOOOM

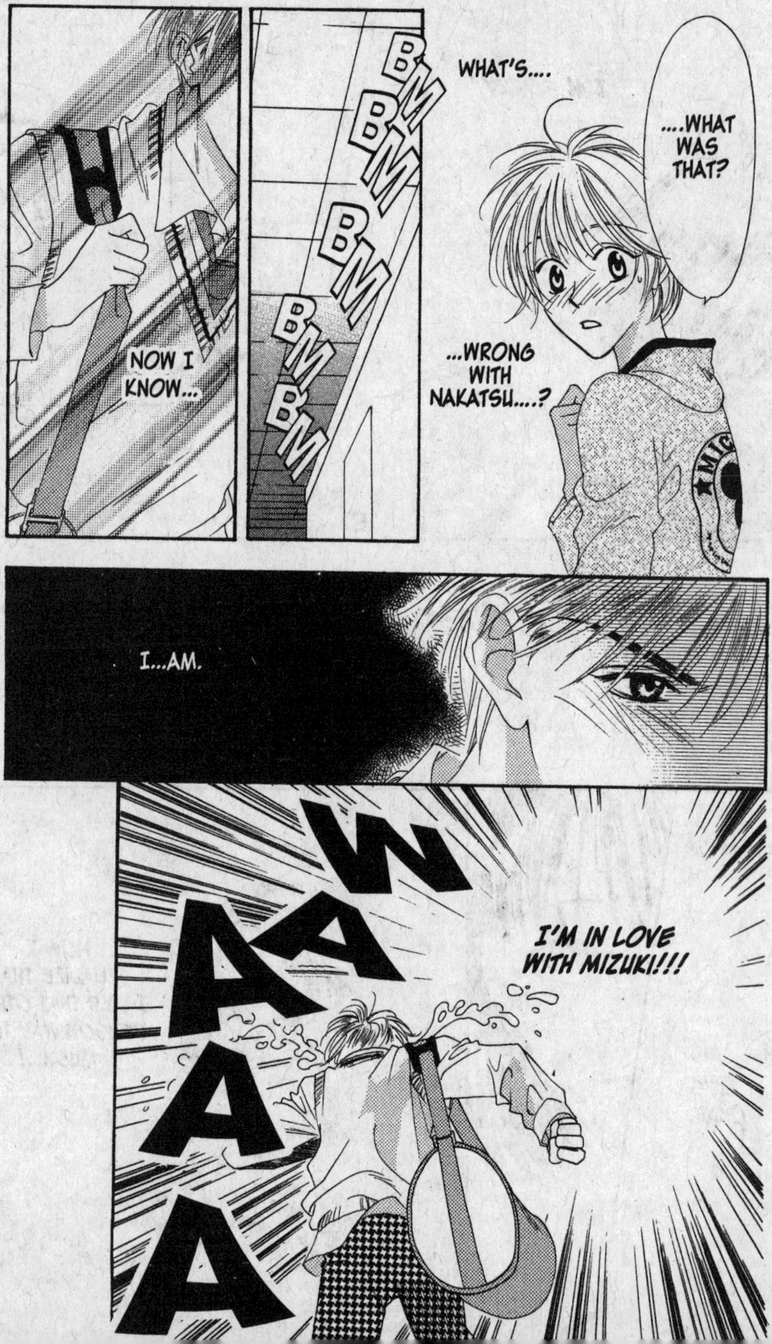
....WHAT WAS THAT?
WHAT'S....
...WRONG WITH NAKATSU....?
BMBMBMBMBM
NOW I KNOW...
I...AM.
WAAAA
I'M IN LOVE WITH MIZUKI!!!

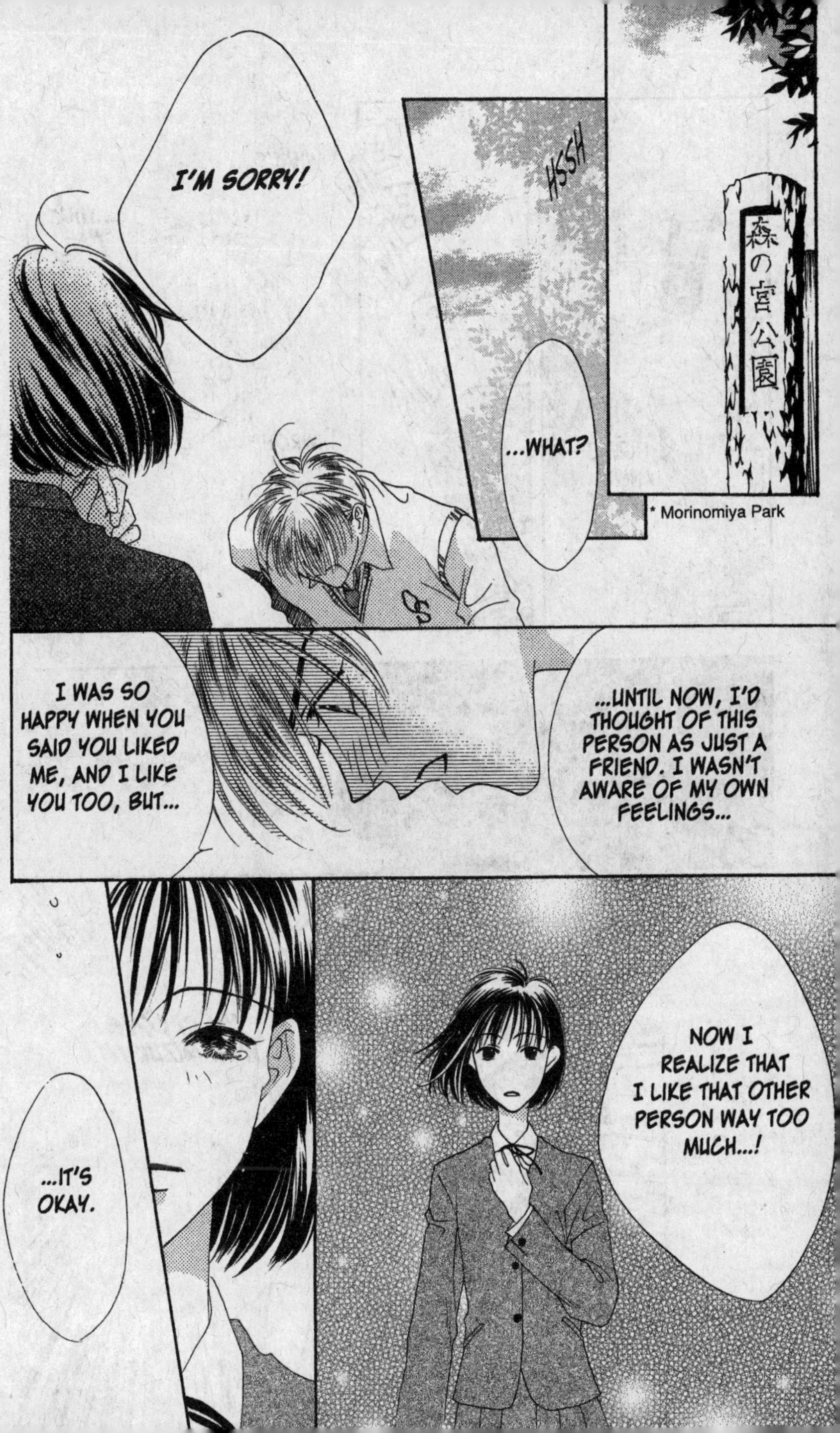

森の宮公園
* Morinomiya Park
HSSH
...WHAT?
I'M SORRY!
...UNTIL NOW, I'D THOUGHT OF THIS PERSON AS JUST A FRIEND. I WASN'T AWARE OF MY OWN FEELINGS...
I WAS SO HAPPY WHEN YOU SAID YOU LIKED ME, AND I LIKE YOU TOO, BUT...
NOW I REALIZE THAT I LIKE THAT OTHER PERSON WAY TOO MUCH...!
...IT'S OKAY.

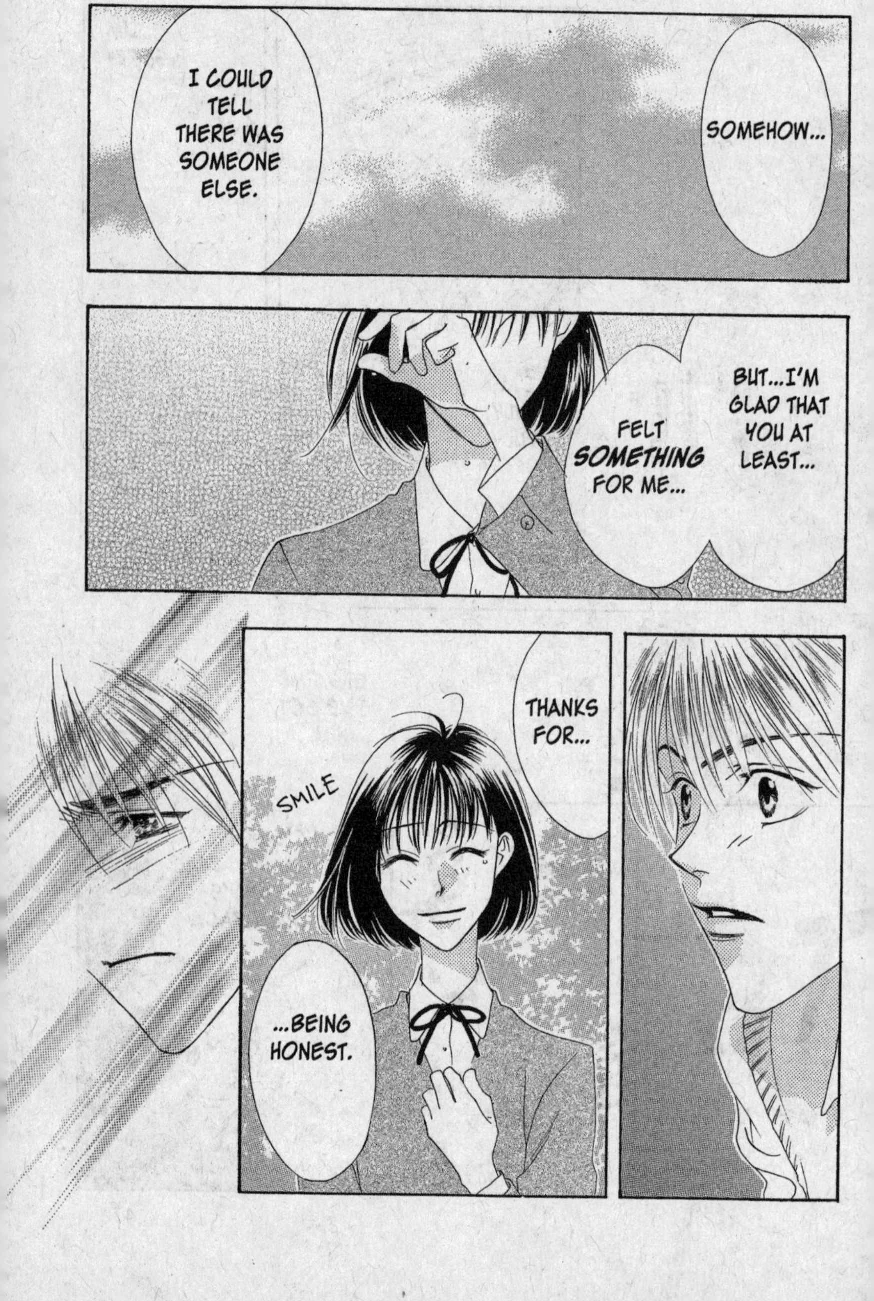
SOMEHOW...
I COULD TELL THERE WAS SOMEONE ELSE.
BUT...I'M GLAD THAT YOU AT LEAST...
FELT **SOMETHING** FOR ME...
THANKS FOR...
SMILE
...BEING HONEST.

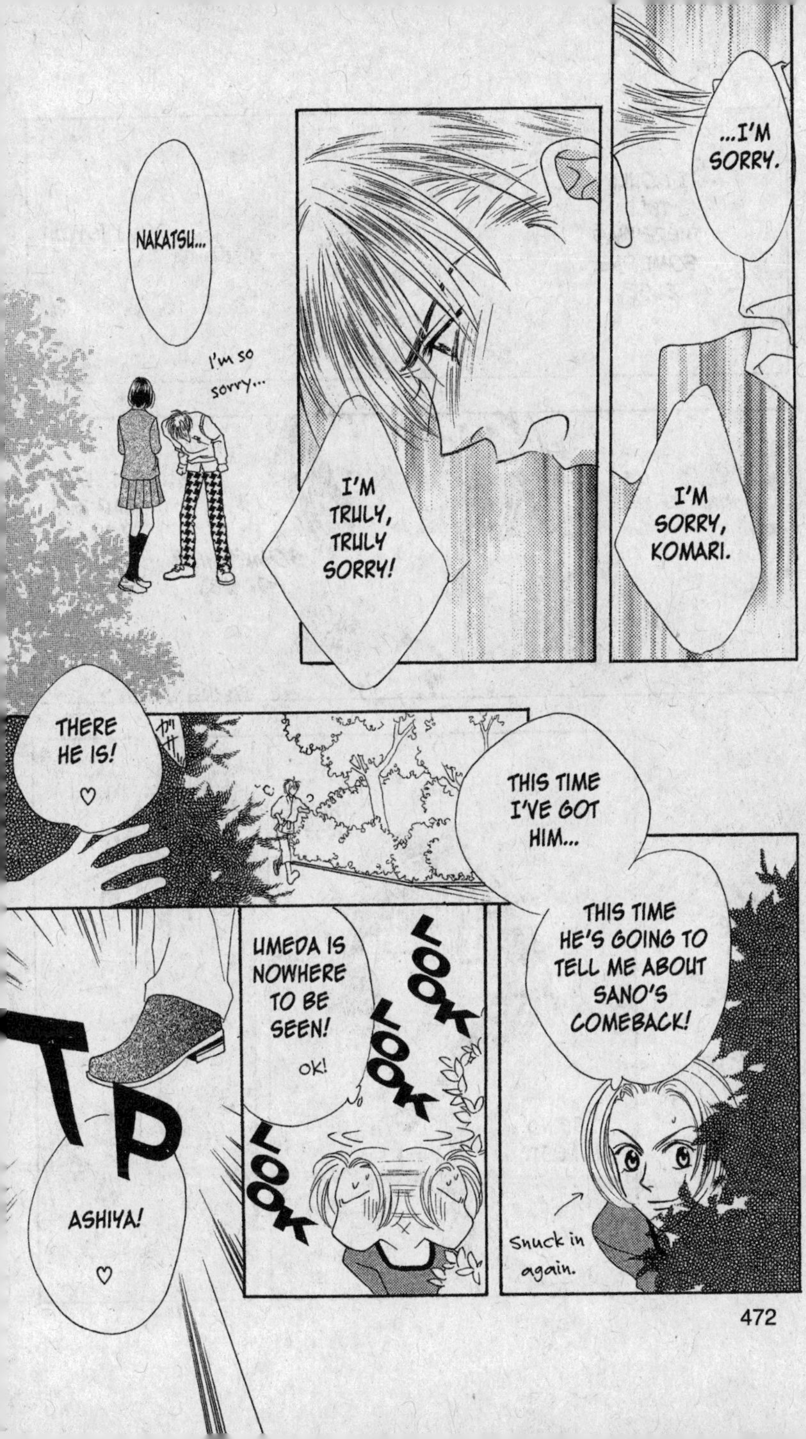
...I'M SORRY.
I'M SORRY, KOMARI.
I'M TRULY, TRULY SORRY!
NAKATSU...
I'm so sorry...
THERE HE IS! ♡
THIS TIME I'VE GOT HIM...
THIS TIME HE'S GOING TO TELL ME ABOUT SANO'S COMEBACK!
Snuck in again.
UMEDA IS NOWHERE TO BE SEEN!
OK!
LOOK
LOOK
LOOK
LOOK
TP
ASHIYA! ♡

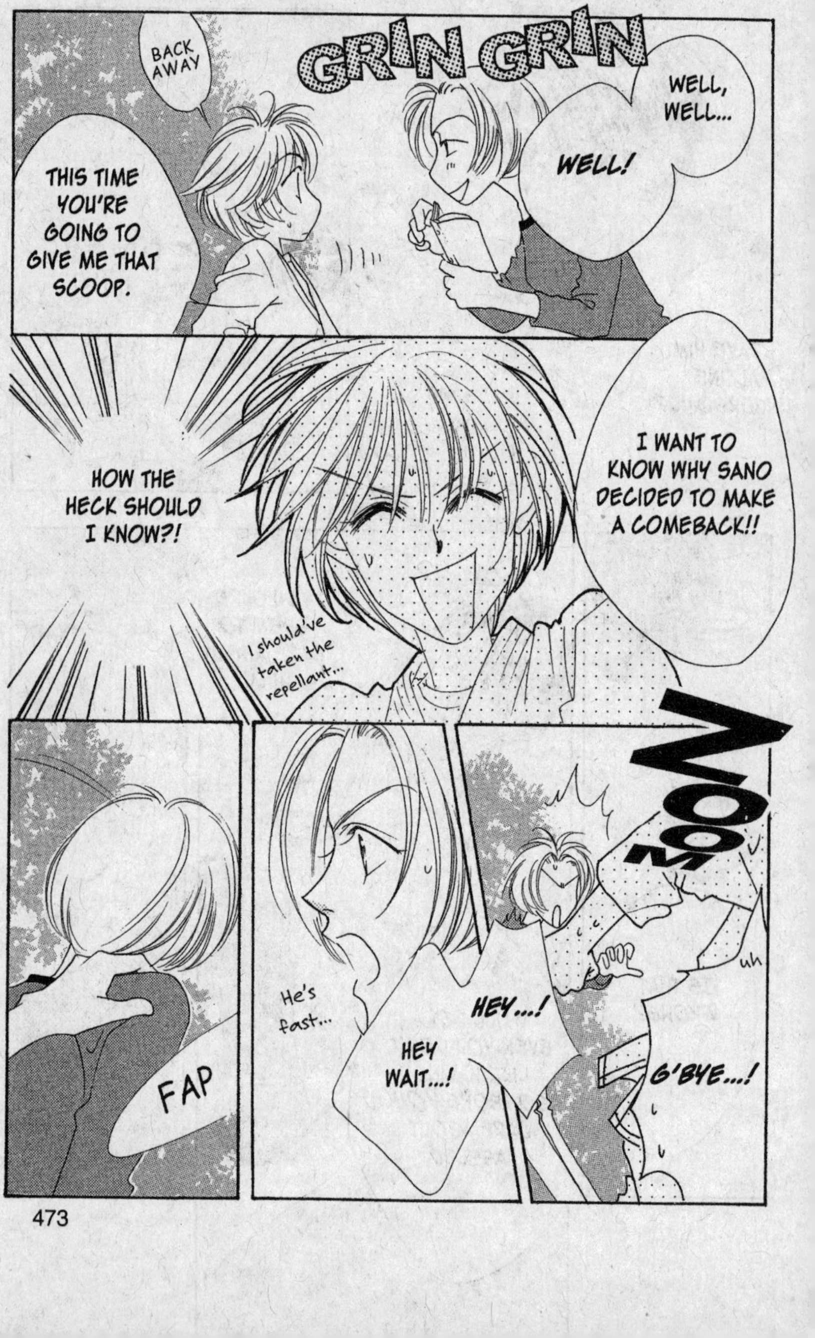
GRIN GRIN
WELL, WELL...
WELL!
BACK AWAY
THIS TIME YOU'RE GOING TO GIVE ME THAT SCOOP.
I WANT TO KNOW WHY SANO DECIDED TO MAKE A COMEBACK!!
HOW THE HECK SHOULD I KNOW?!
I should've taken the repellant...
VOOM
uh
G'BYE...!
HEY...!
HEY WAIT...!
He's fast...
FAP

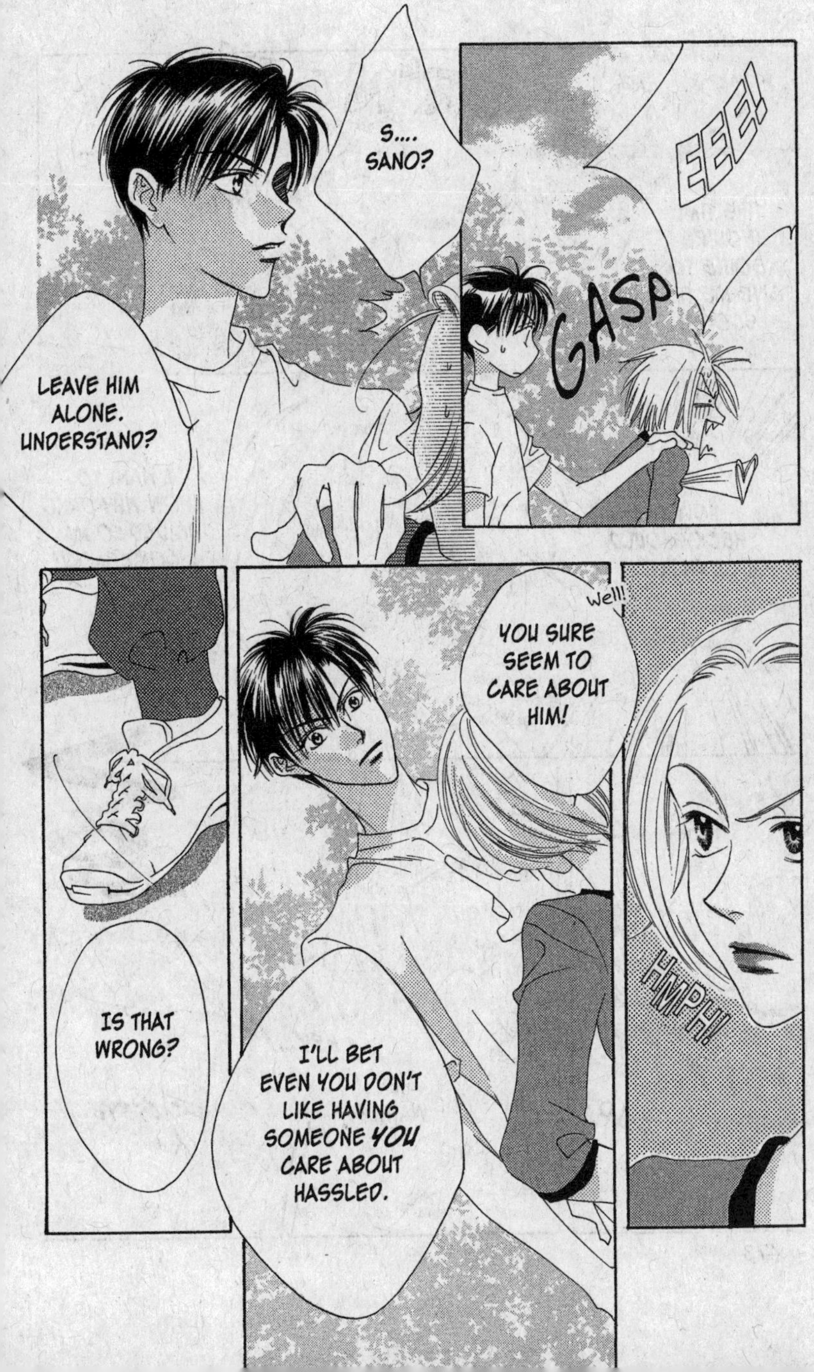
EEE!
GASP
S.... SANO?
LEAVE HIM ALONE. UNDERSTAND?
HMPH!
Well!
YOU SURE SEEM TO CARE ABOUT HIM!
IS THAT WRONG?
I'LL BET EVEN YOU DON'T LIKE HAVING SOMEONE *YOU* CARE ABOUT HASSLED.

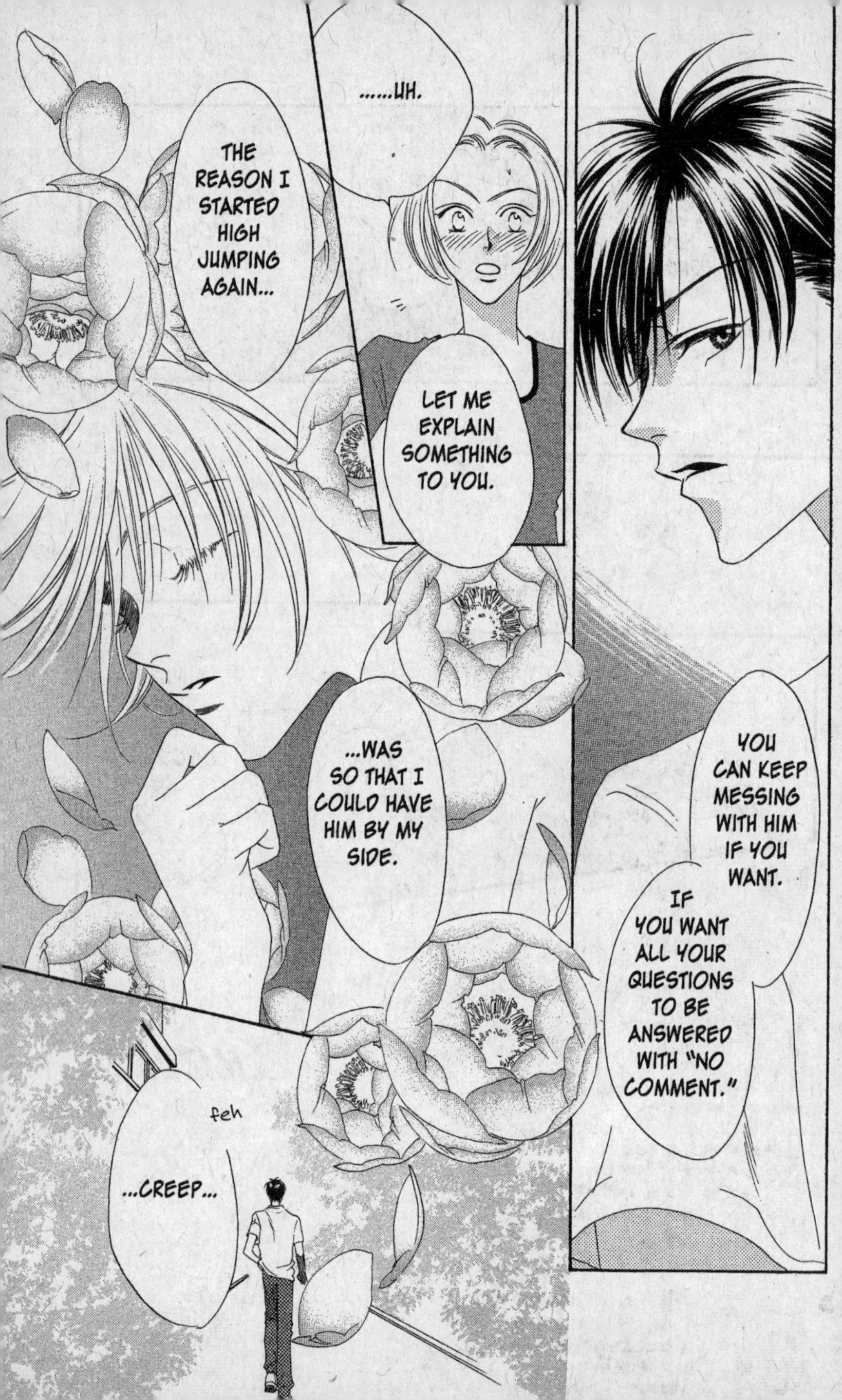
YOU CAN KEEP MESSING WITH HIM IF YOU WANT.
IF YOU WANT ALL YOUR QUESTIONS TO BE ANSWERED WITH "NO COMMENT."
......UH.
LET ME EXPLAIN SOMETHING TO YOU.
THE REASON I STARTED HIGH JUMPING AGAIN...
...WAS SO THAT I COULD HAVE HIM BY MY SIDE.
feh
...CREEP...

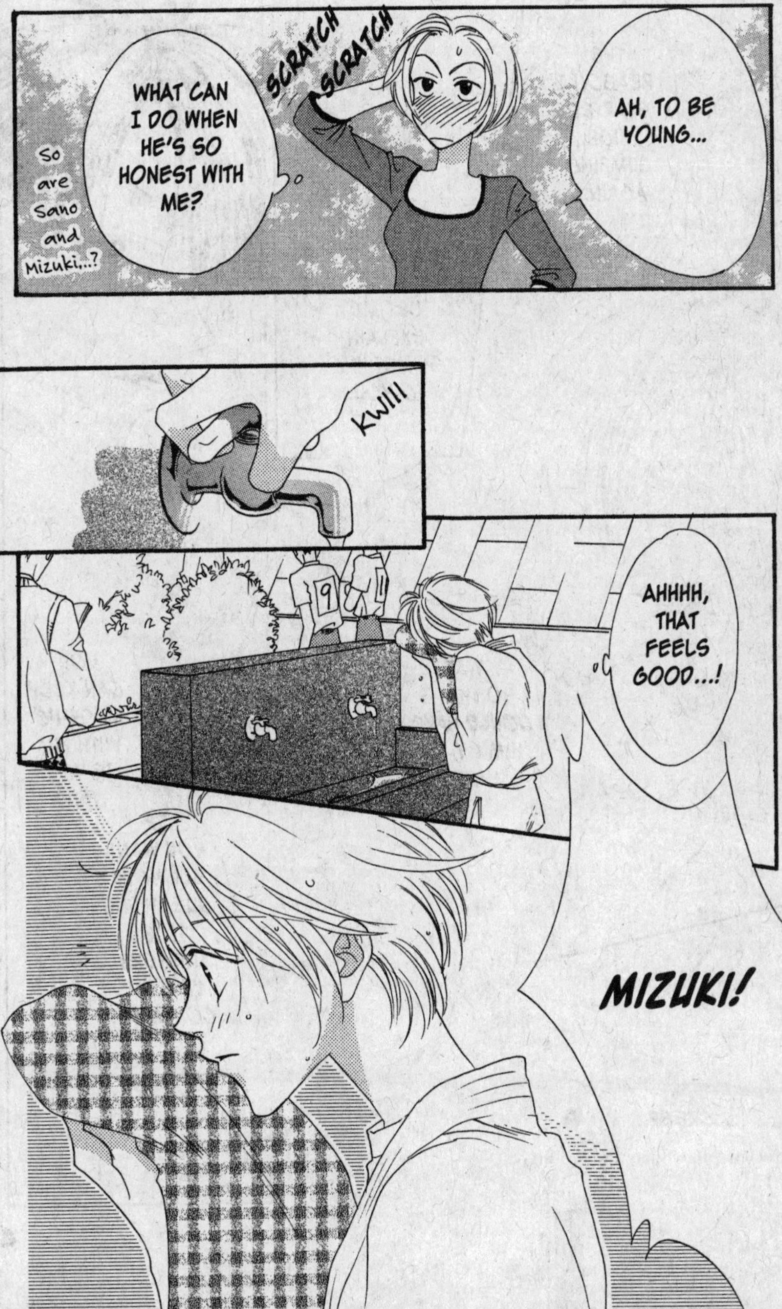
AH, TO BE YOUNG...
SCRATCH SCRATCH
WHAT CAN I DO WHEN HE'S SO HONEST WITH ME?
So are Sano and Mizuki...?
KWIII
AHHHH, THAT FEELS GOOD...!
MIZUKI!

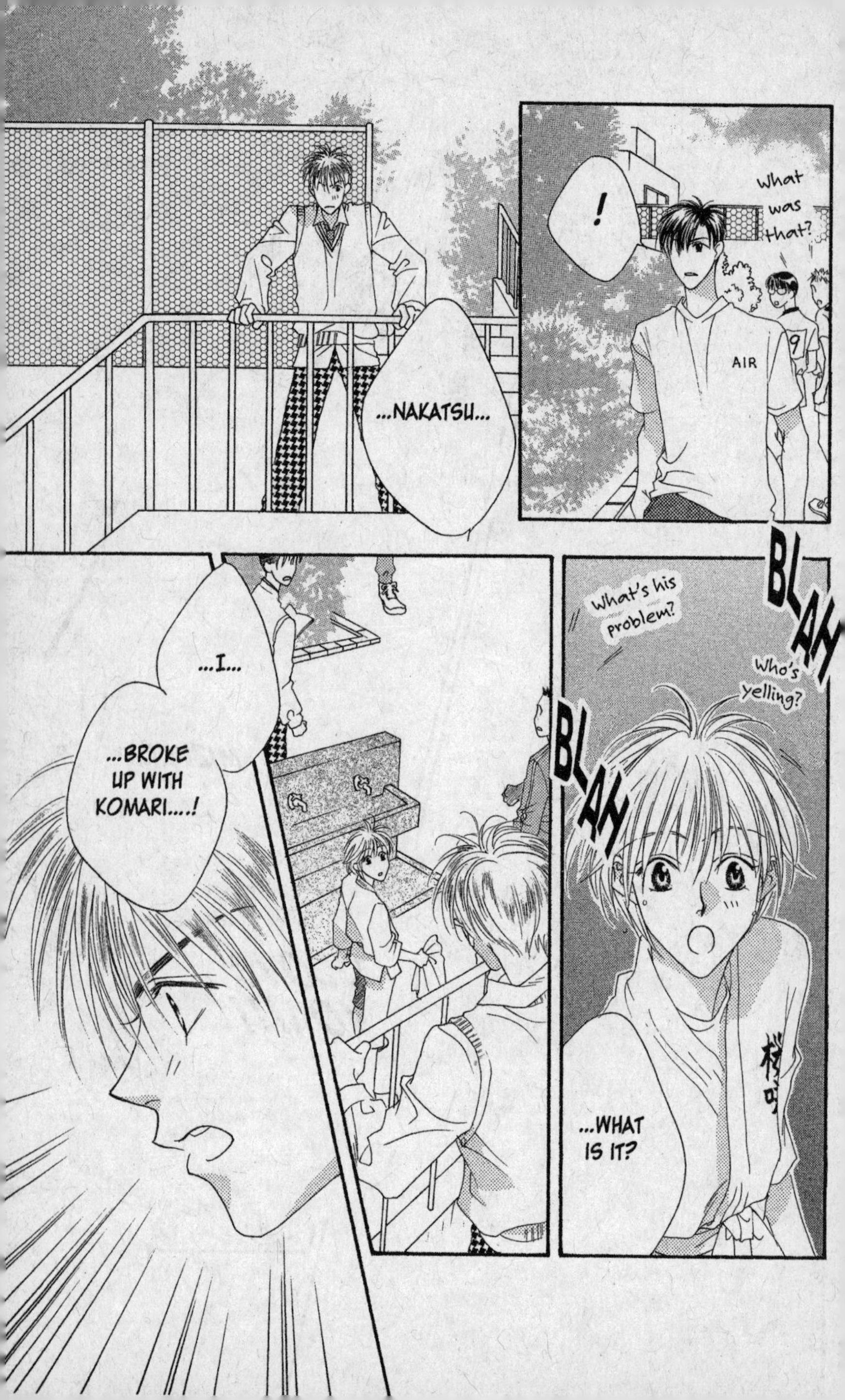
What was that?
!
...NAKATSU...
BLAH
Who's yelling?
What's his problem?
BLAH
...WHAT IS IT?
...I...
...BROKE UP WITH KOMARI....!

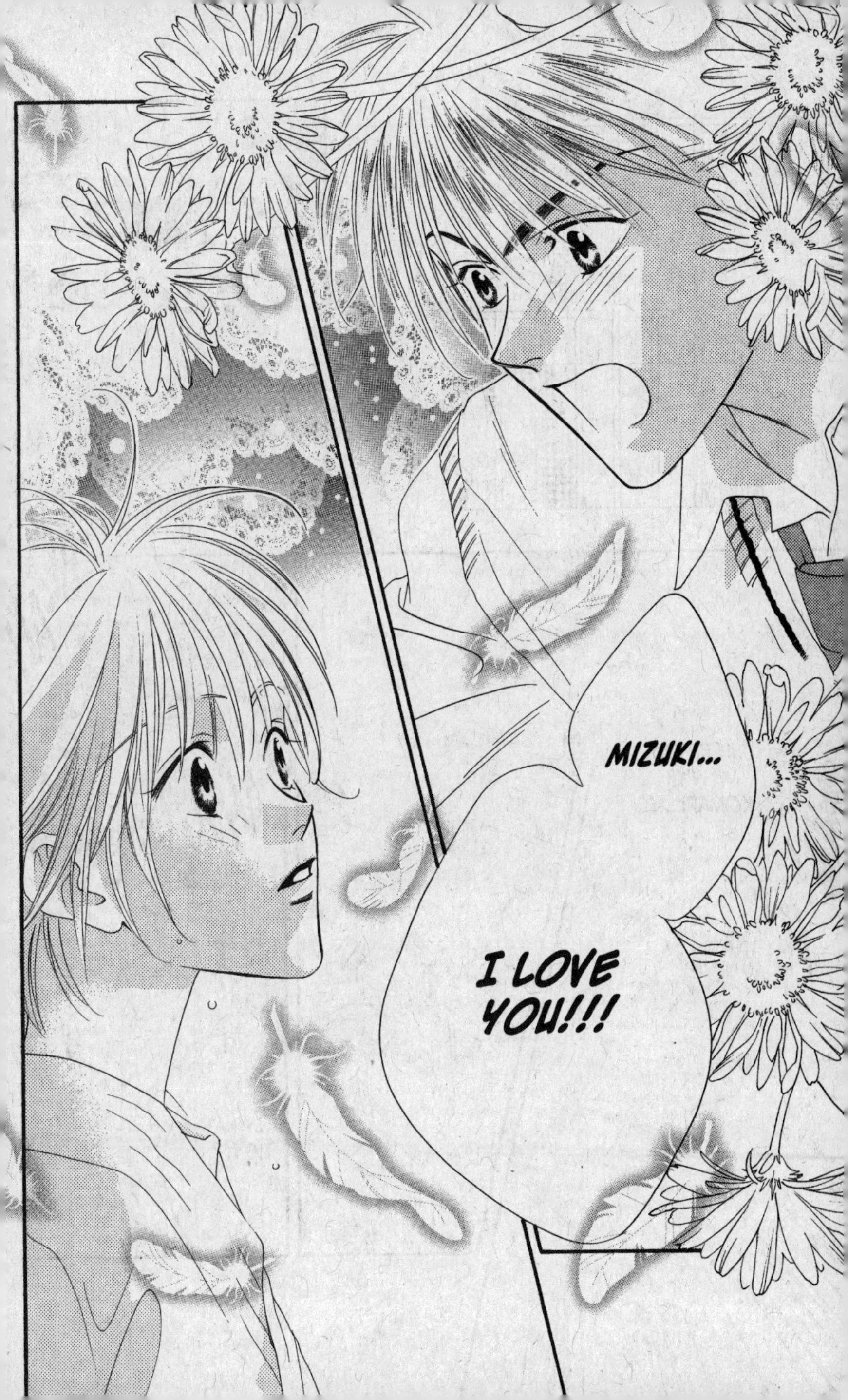
MIZUKI...
I LOVE YOU!!!

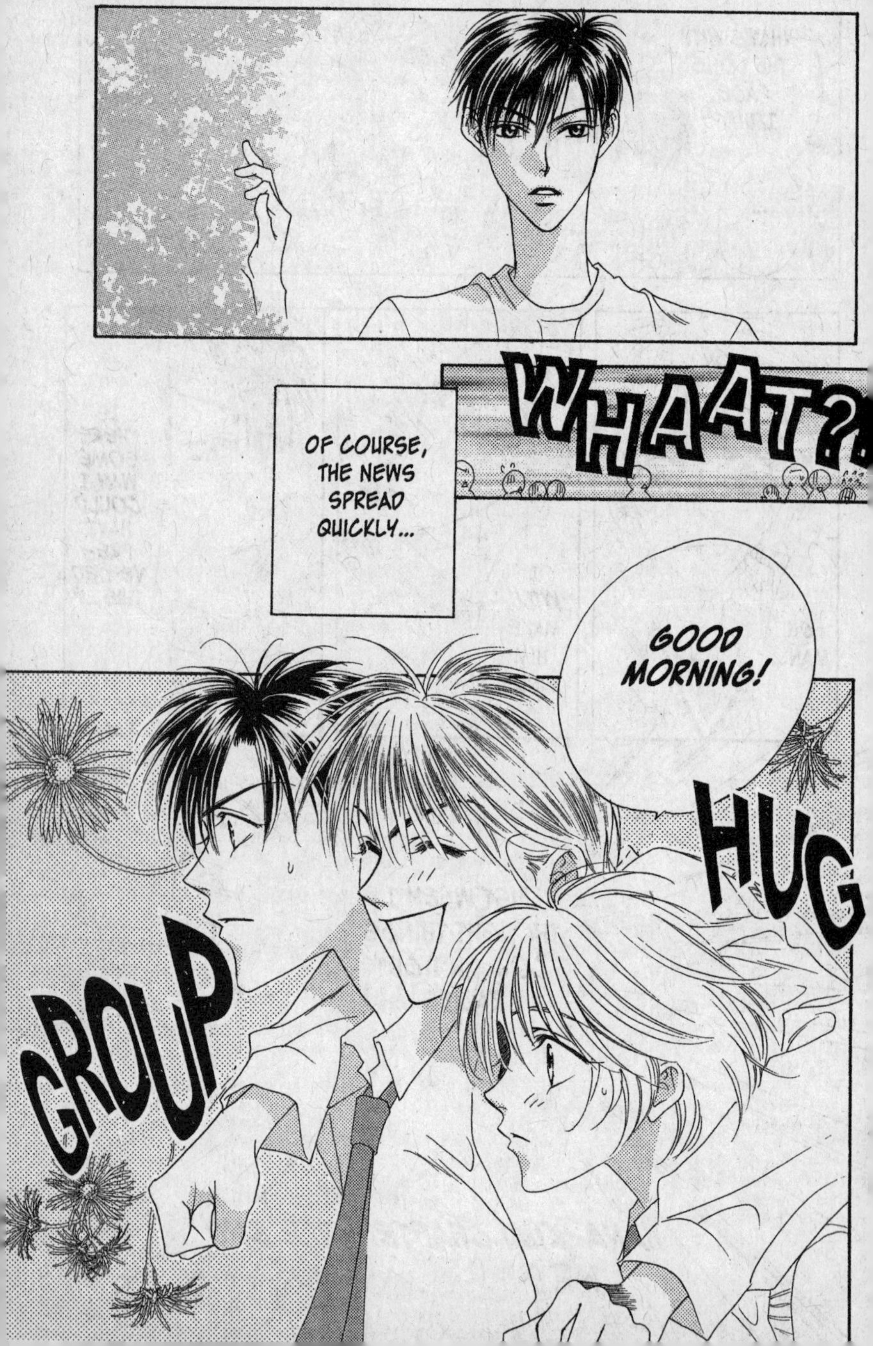
WHAAAT?!
OF COURSE, THE NEWS SPREAD QUICKLY...
GOOD MORNING!
HUG
GROUP

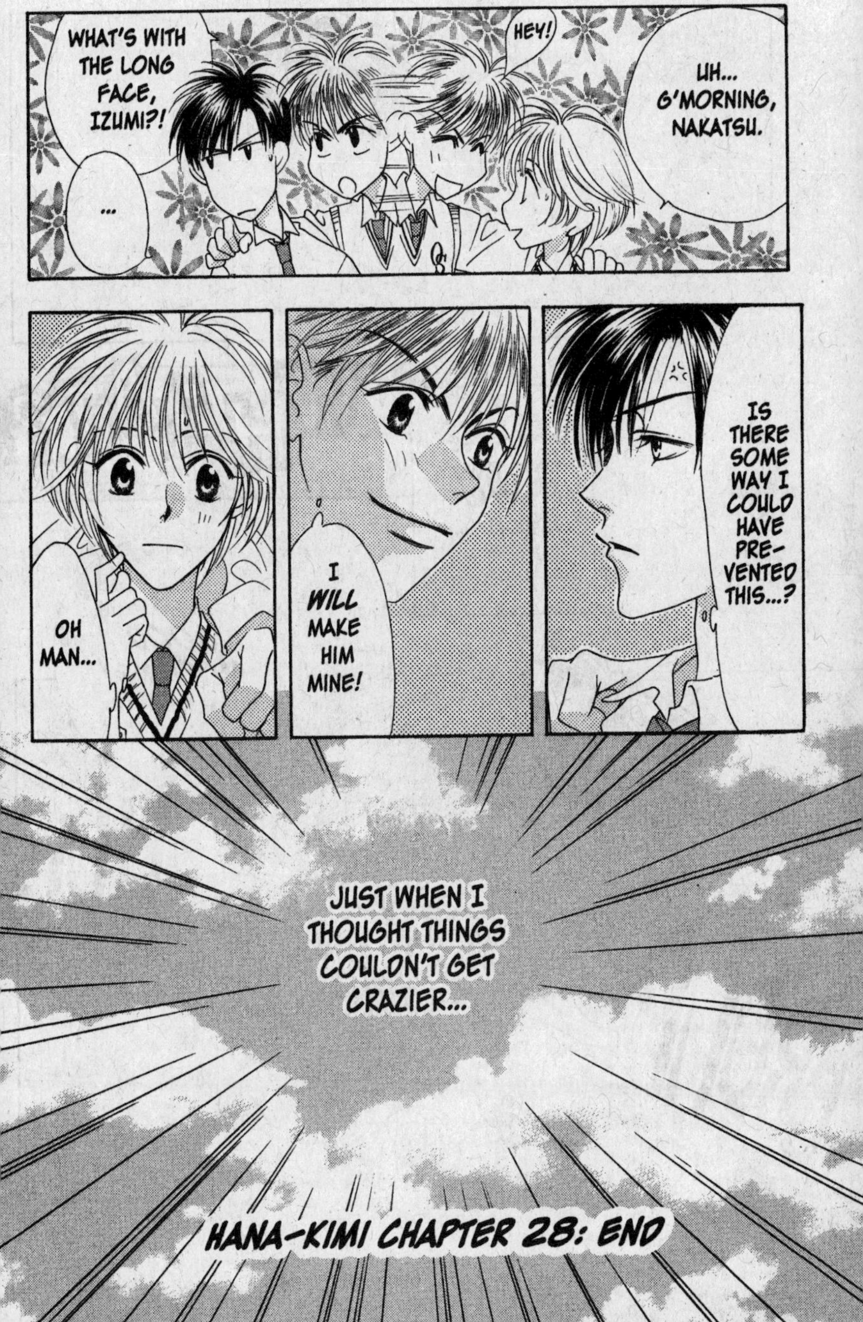
HEY!
UH... G'MORNING, NAKATSU.
WHAT'S WITH THE LONG FACE, IZUMI?!
...
IS THERE SOME WAY I COULD HAVE PRE-VENTED THIS...?
I WILL MAKE HIM MINE!
OH MAN...
JUST WHEN I THOUGHT THINGS COULDN'T GET CRAZIER...
HANA-KIMI CHAPTER 28: END

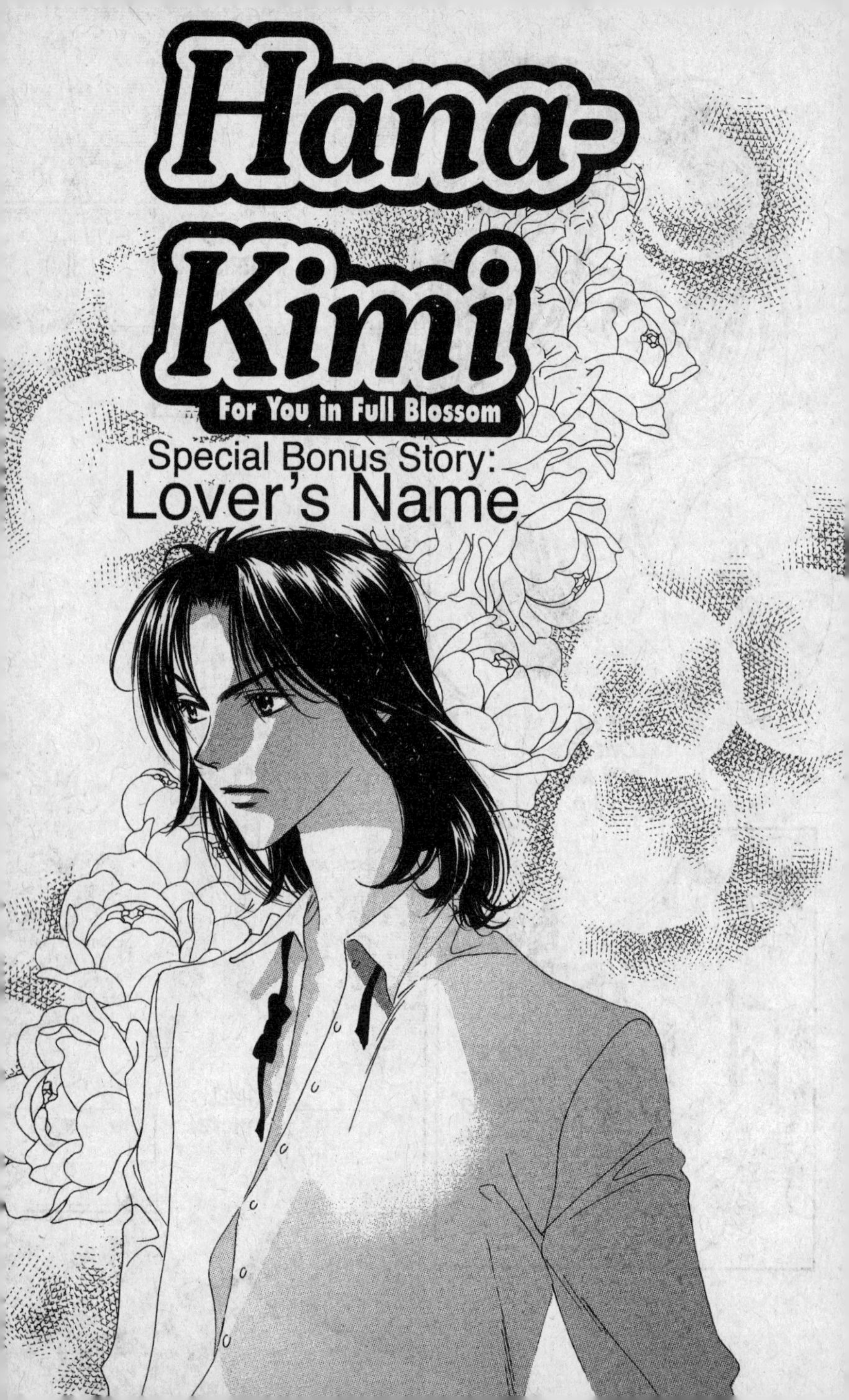
Hana-Kimi
For You in Full Blossom
Special Bonus Story:
Lover's Name

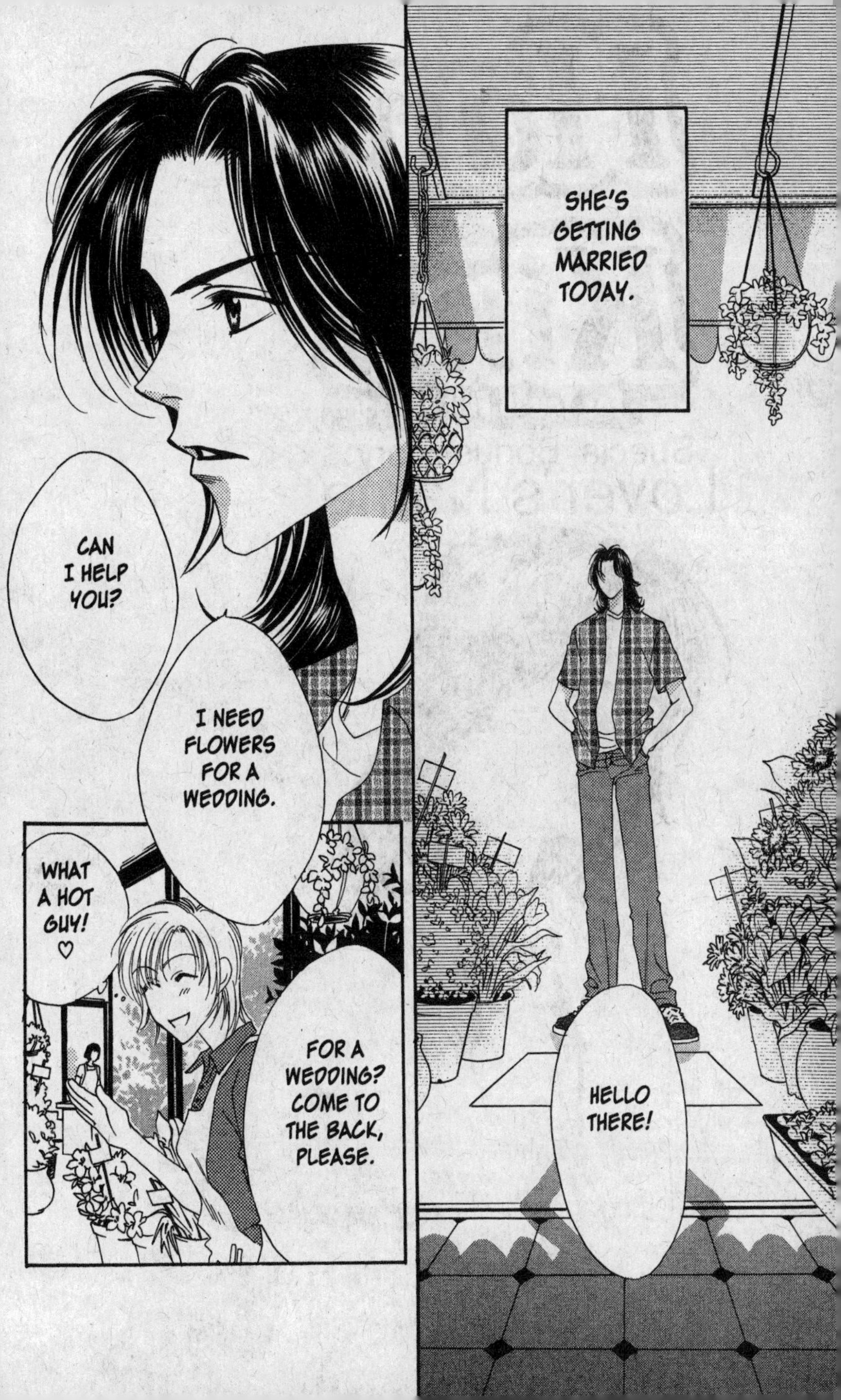

SHE'S GETTING MARRIED TODAY.
HELLO THERE!
CAN I HELP YOU?
I NEED FLOWERS FOR A WEDDING.
FOR A WEDDING? COME TO THE BACK, PLEASE.
WHAT A HOT GUY! ♡

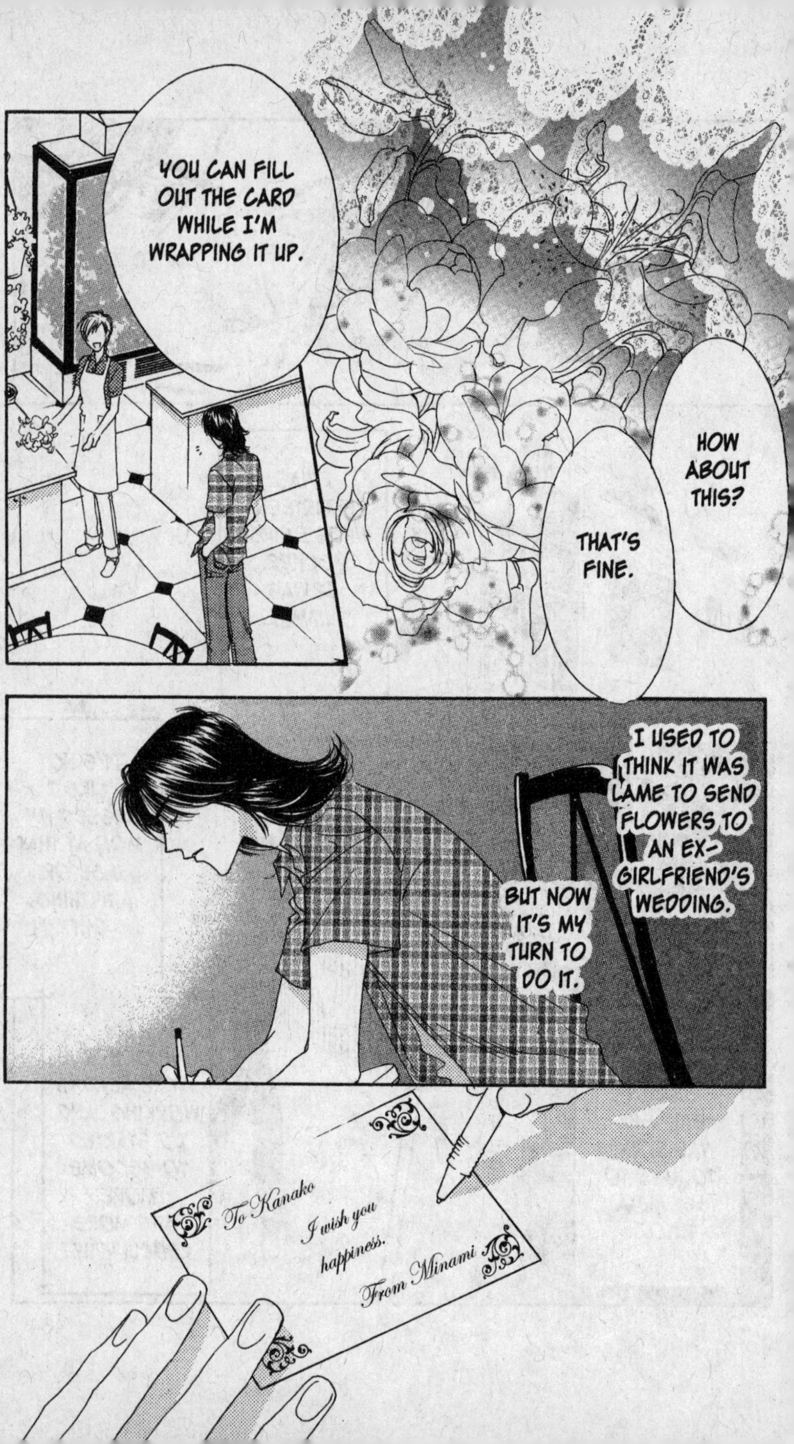
HOW ABOUT THIS?
THAT'S FINE.
YOU CAN FILL OUT THE CARD WHILE I'M WRAPPING IT UP.
I USED TO THINK IT WAS LAME TO SEND FLOWERS TO AN EX-GIRLFRIEND'S WEDDING.
BUT NOW IT'S MY TURN TO DO IT.
To Kanako
I wish you happiness.
From Minami

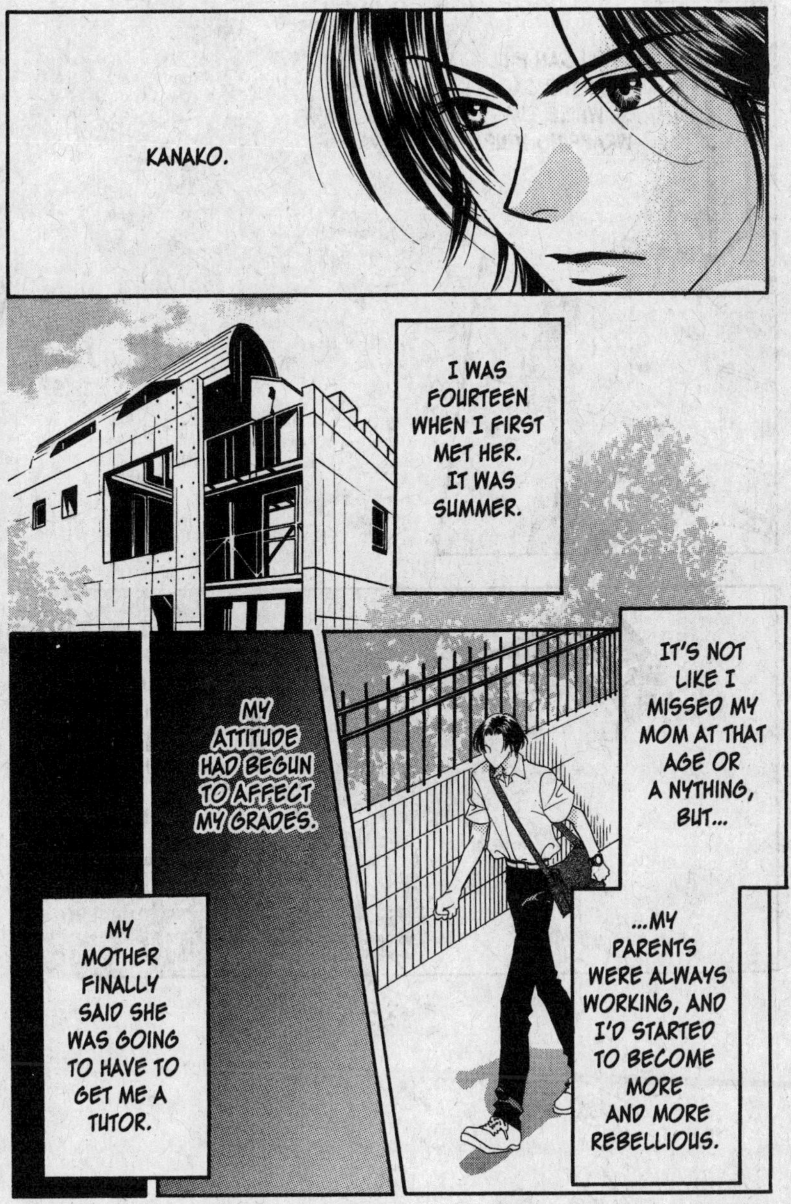
KANAKO.
I WAS FOURTEEN WHEN I FIRST MET HER. IT WAS SUMMER.
IT'S NOT LIKE I MISSED MY MOM AT THAT AGE OR A NYTHING, BUT...
...MY PARENTS WERE ALWAYS WORKING, AND I'D STARTED TO BECOME MORE AND MORE REBELLIOUS.
MY ATTITUDE HAD BEGUN TO AFFECT MY GRADES.
MY MOTHER FINALLY SAID SHE WAS GOING TO HAVE TO GET ME A TUTOR.

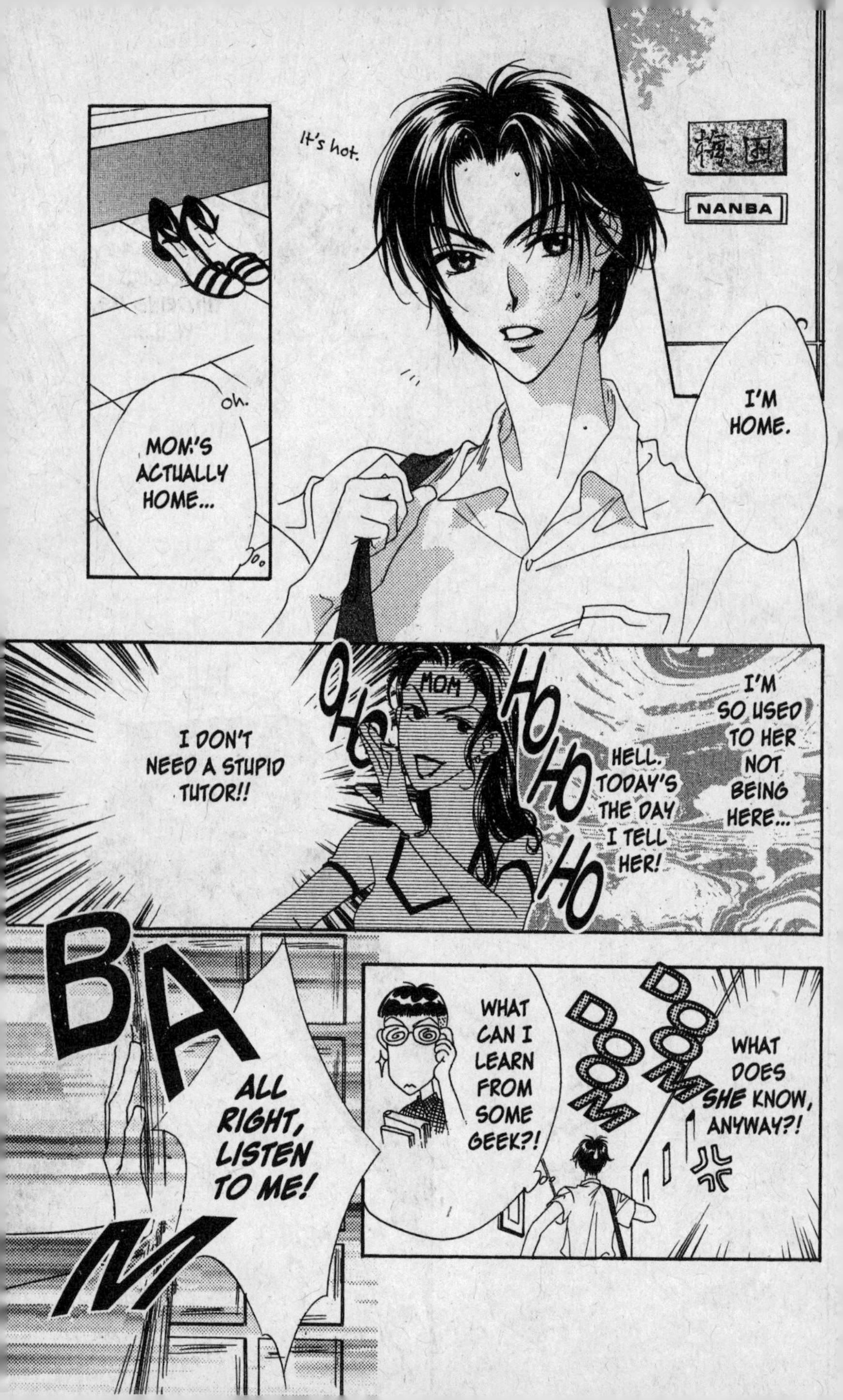
NANBA
I'M HOME.
It's hot.
Oh.
MOM'S ACTUALLY HOME...
I'M SO USED TO HER NOT BEING HERE...
HELL. TODAY'S THE DAY I TELL HER!
HOHOHO
MOM
OHO
I DON'T NEED A STUPID TUTOR!!
WHAT DOES SHE KNOW, ANYWAY?!
DOOM DOOM
WHAT CAN I LEARN FROM SOME GEEK?!
BAM
ALL RIGHT, LISTEN TO ME!

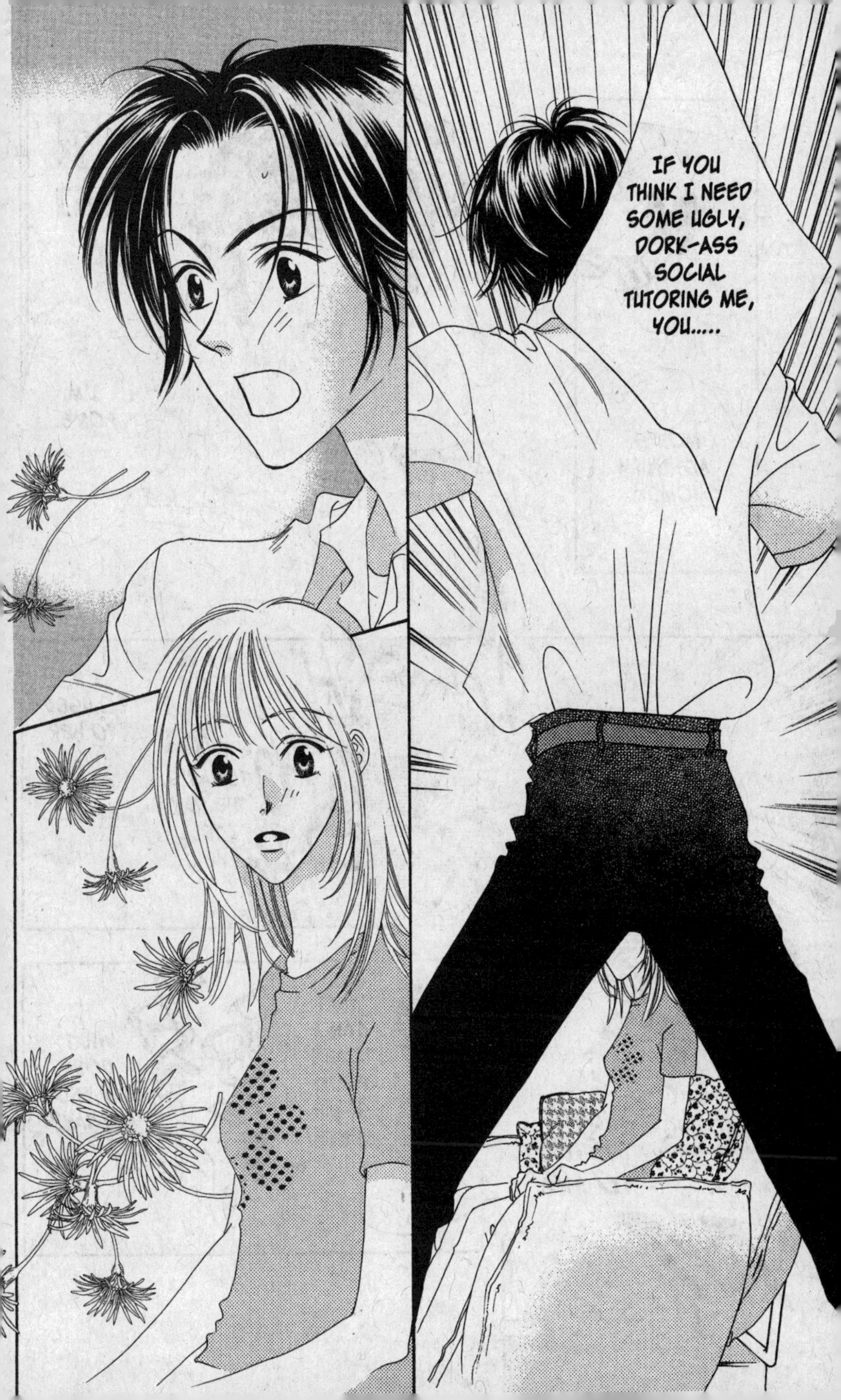
IF YOU THINK I NEED SOME UGLY, DORK-ASS SOCIAL TUTORING ME, YOU.....

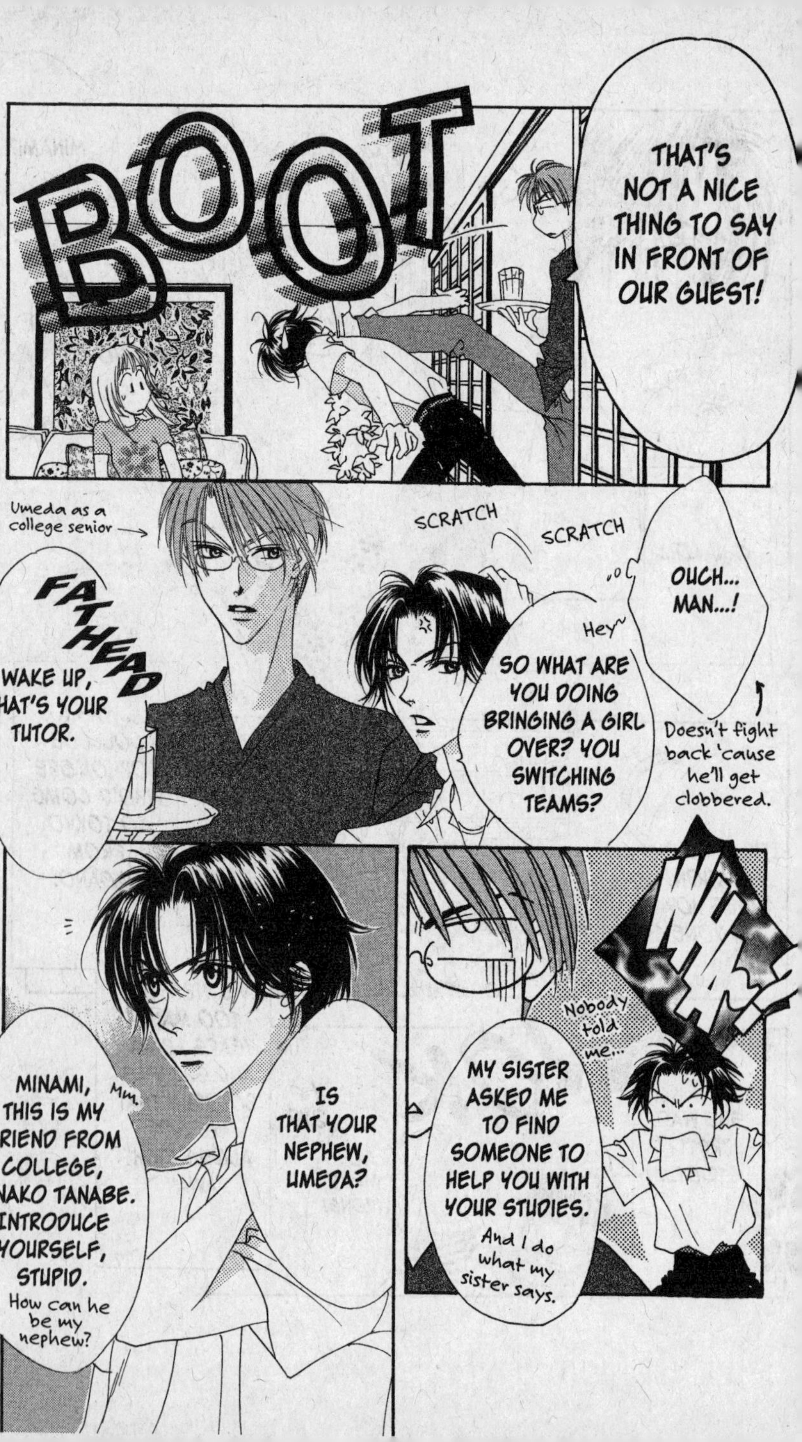
THAT'S NOT A NICE THING TO SAY IN FRONT OF OUR GUEST!
BOOT
OUCH... MAN...!
Doesn't fight back 'cause he'll get clobbered.
SCRATCH
SCRATCH
Hey~
SO WHAT ARE YOU DOING BRINGING A GIRL OVER? YOU SWITCHING TEAMS?
Umeda as a college senior
FATHEAD
WAKE UP, THAT'S YOUR TUTOR.
WHAM!
Nobody told me...
MY SISTER ASKED ME TO FIND SOMEONE TO HELP YOU WITH YOUR STUDIES.
And I do what my sister says.
IS THAT YOUR NEPHEW, UMEDA?
Mm.
MINAMI, THIS IS MY FRIEND FROM COLLEGE, KANAKO TANABE. INTRODUCE YOURSELF, STUPID.
How can he be my nephew?

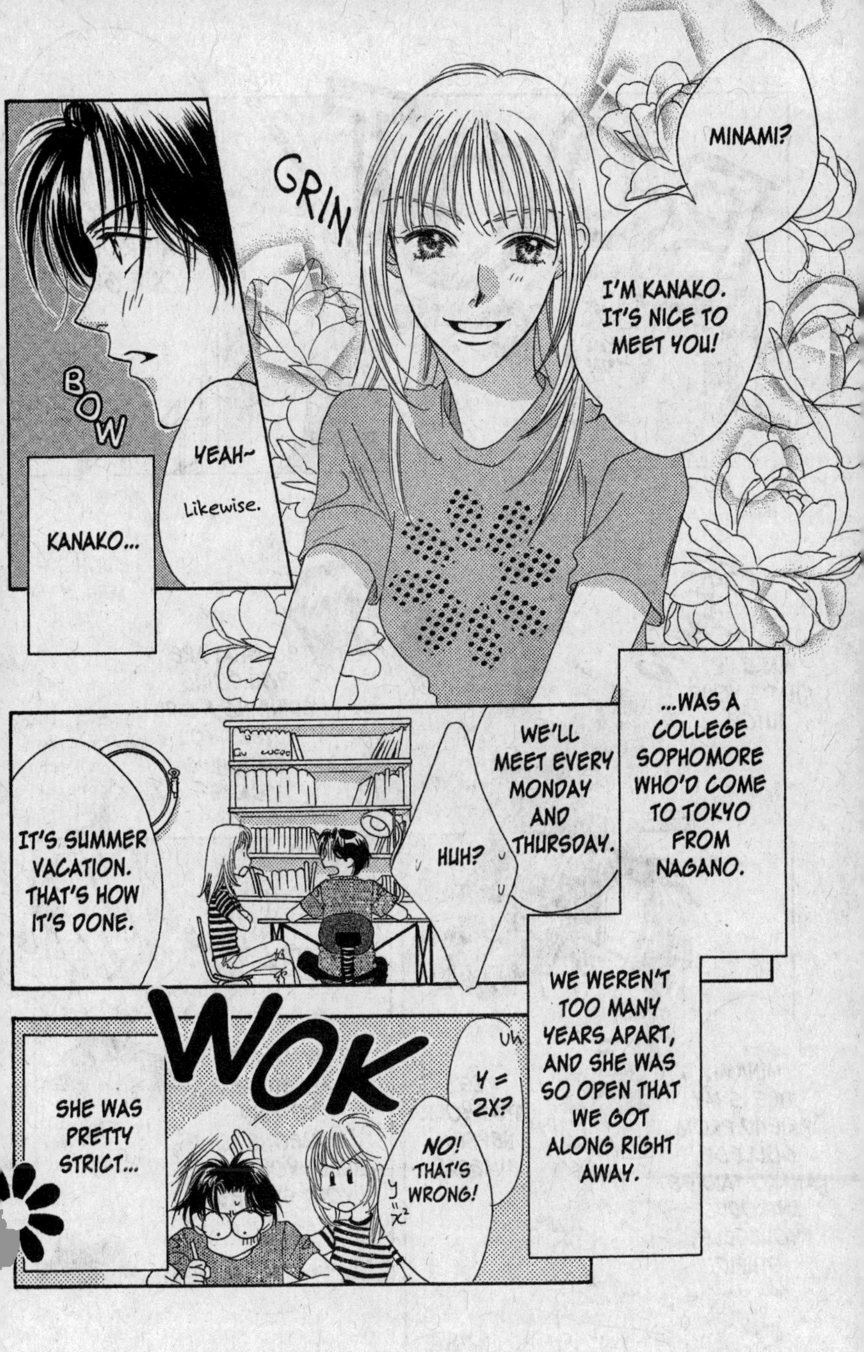
MINAMI?
I'M KANAKO. IT'S NICE TO MEET YOU!
GRIN
BOW
YEAH~
Likewise.
KANAKO...
...WAS A COLLEGE SOPHOMORE WHO'D COME TO TOKYO FROM NAGANO.
WE'LL MEET EVERY MONDAY AND THURSDAY.
HUH?
IT'S SUMMER VACATION. THAT'S HOW IT'S DONE.
WE WEREN'T TOO MANY YEARS APART, AND SHE WAS SO OPEN THAT WE GOT ALONG RIGHT AWAY.
WOK
Uh
Y = 2X?
NO! THAT'S WRONG!
SHE WAS PRETTY STRICT...

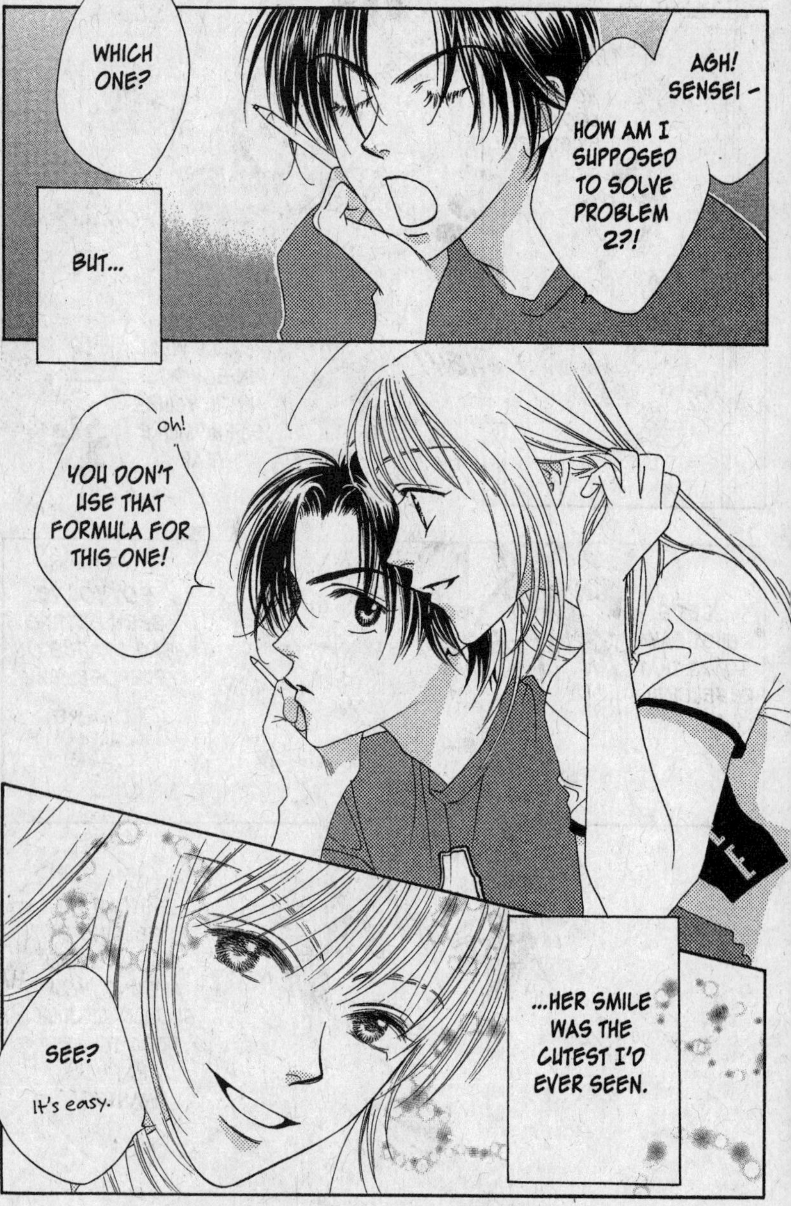
AGH! SENSEI - HOW AM I SUPPOSED TO SOLVE PROBLEM 2?!
WHICH ONE?
BUT...
oh!
YOU DON'T USE THAT FORMULA FOR THIS ONE!
...HER SMILE WAS THE CUTEST I'D EVER SEEN.
SEE?
It's easy.

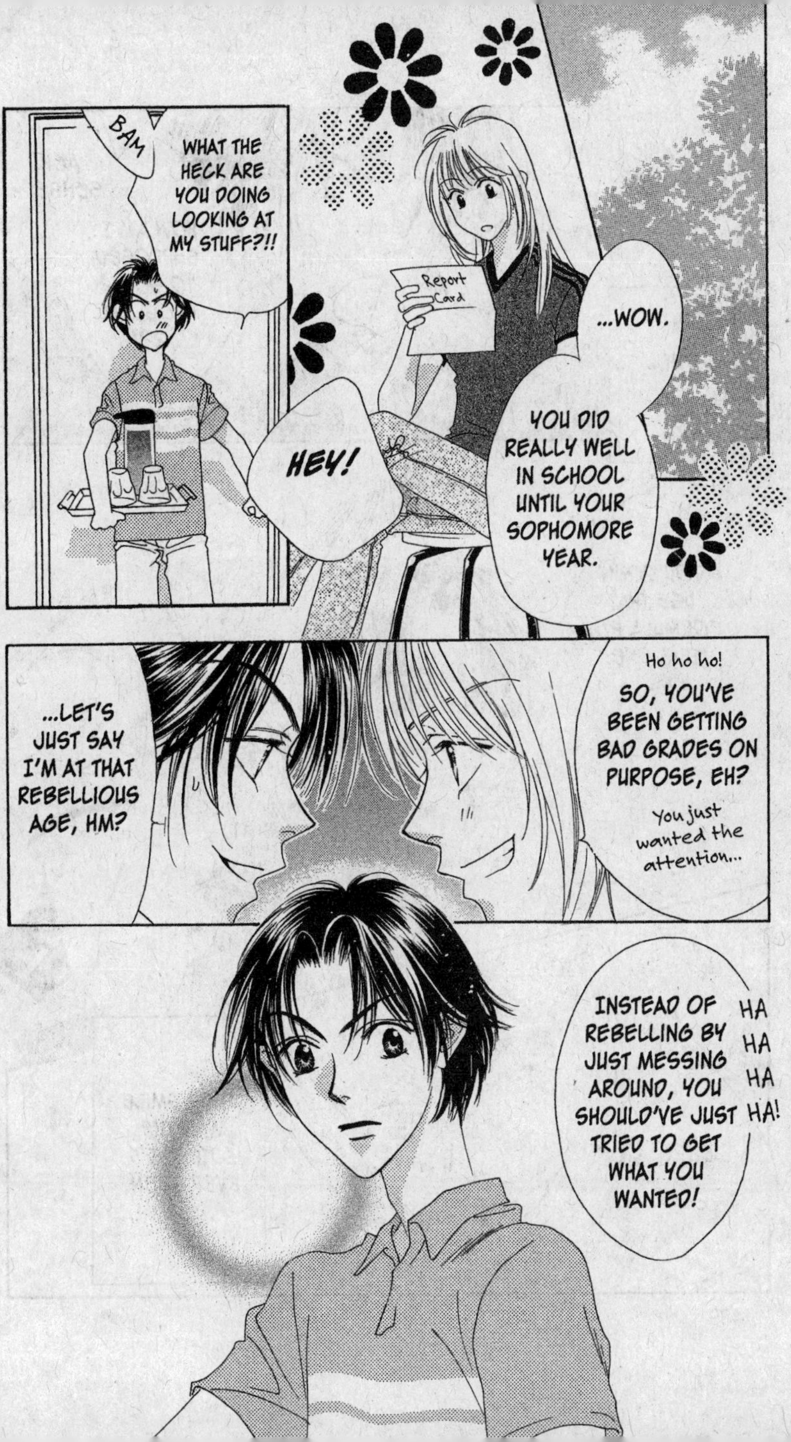
...WOW.
YOU DID REALLY WELL IN SCHOOL UNTIL YOUR SOPHOMORE YEAR.
Report Card
BAM
WHAT THE HECK ARE YOU DOING LOOKING AT MY STUFF?!!
HEY!
Ho ho ho!
SO, YOU'VE BEEN GETTING BAD GRADES ON PURPOSE, EH?
You just wanted the attention...
...LET'S JUST SAY I'M AT THAT REBELLIOUS AGE, HM?
INSTEAD OF REBELLING BY JUST MESSING AROUND, YOU SHOULD'VE JUST TRIED TO GET WHAT YOU WANTED!
HA HA HA HA!

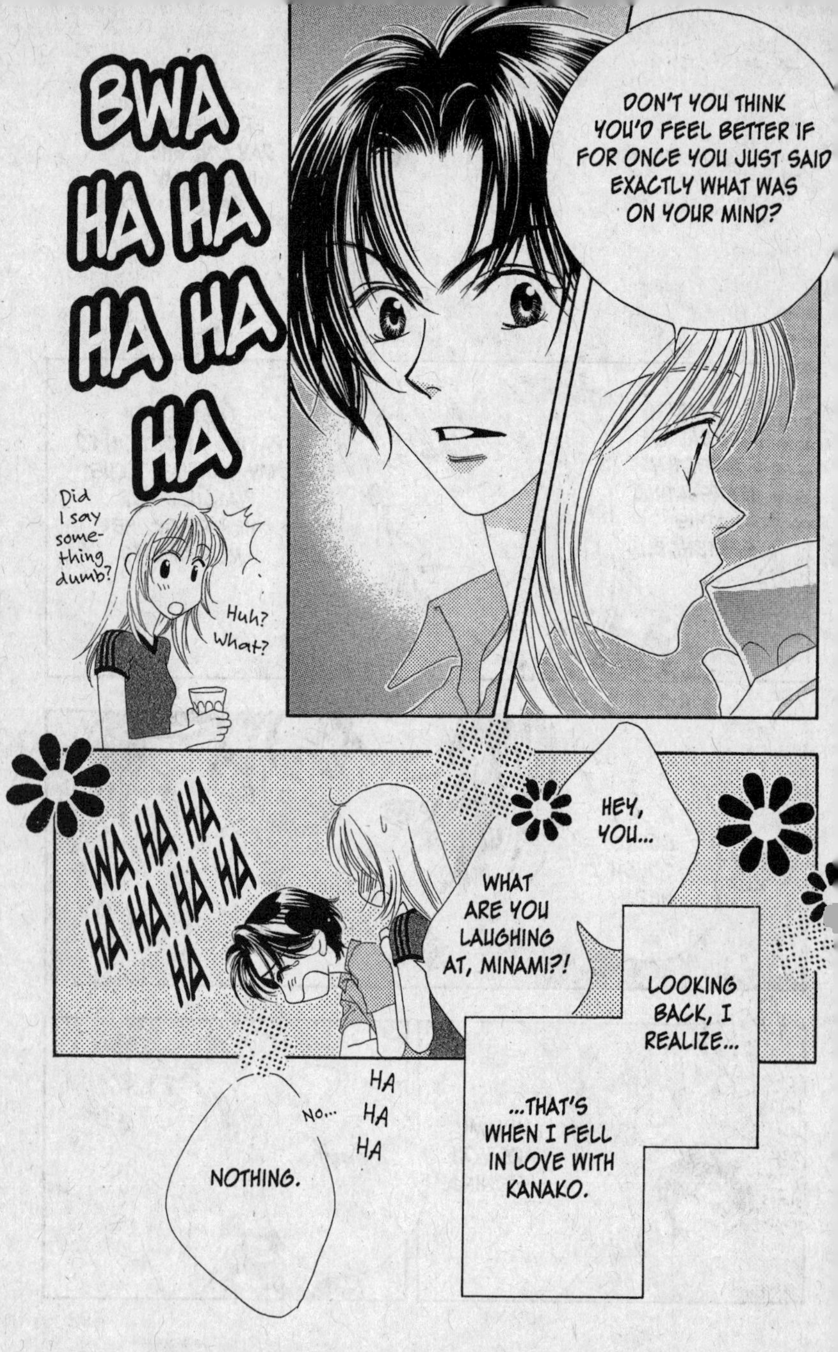
DON'T YOU THINK YOU'D FEEL BETTER IF FOR ONCE YOU JUST SAID EXACTLY WHAT WAS ON YOUR MIND?
BWA HA HA HA HA HA
Huh? What?
Did I say some-thing dumb?
HEY, YOU...
WHAT ARE YOU LAUGHING AT, MINAMI?!
WA HA HA HA HA HA HA HA
LOOKING BACK, I REALIZE...
...THAT'S WHEN I FELL IN LOVE WITH KANAKO.
HA HA HA
No...
NOTHING.

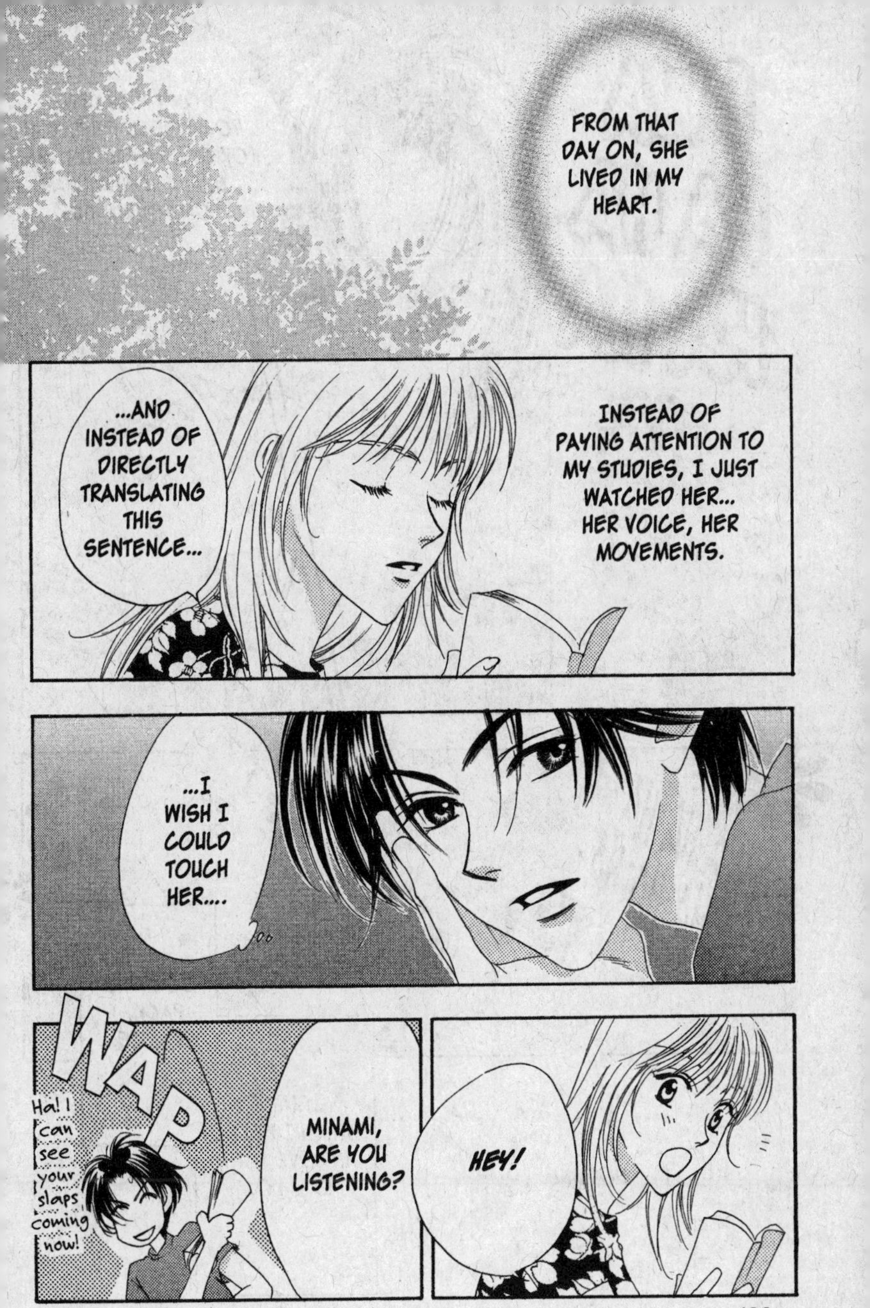
FROM THAT DAY ON, SHE LIVED IN MY HEART.
INSTEAD OF PAYING ATTENTION TO MY STUDIES, I JUST WATCHED HER... HER VOICE, HER MOVEMENTS.
...AND INSTEAD OF DIRECTLY TRANSLATING THIS SENTENCE...
...I WISH I COULD TOUCH HER....
HEY!
MINAMI, ARE YOU LISTENING?
WAP
Ha! I can see your slaps coming now!

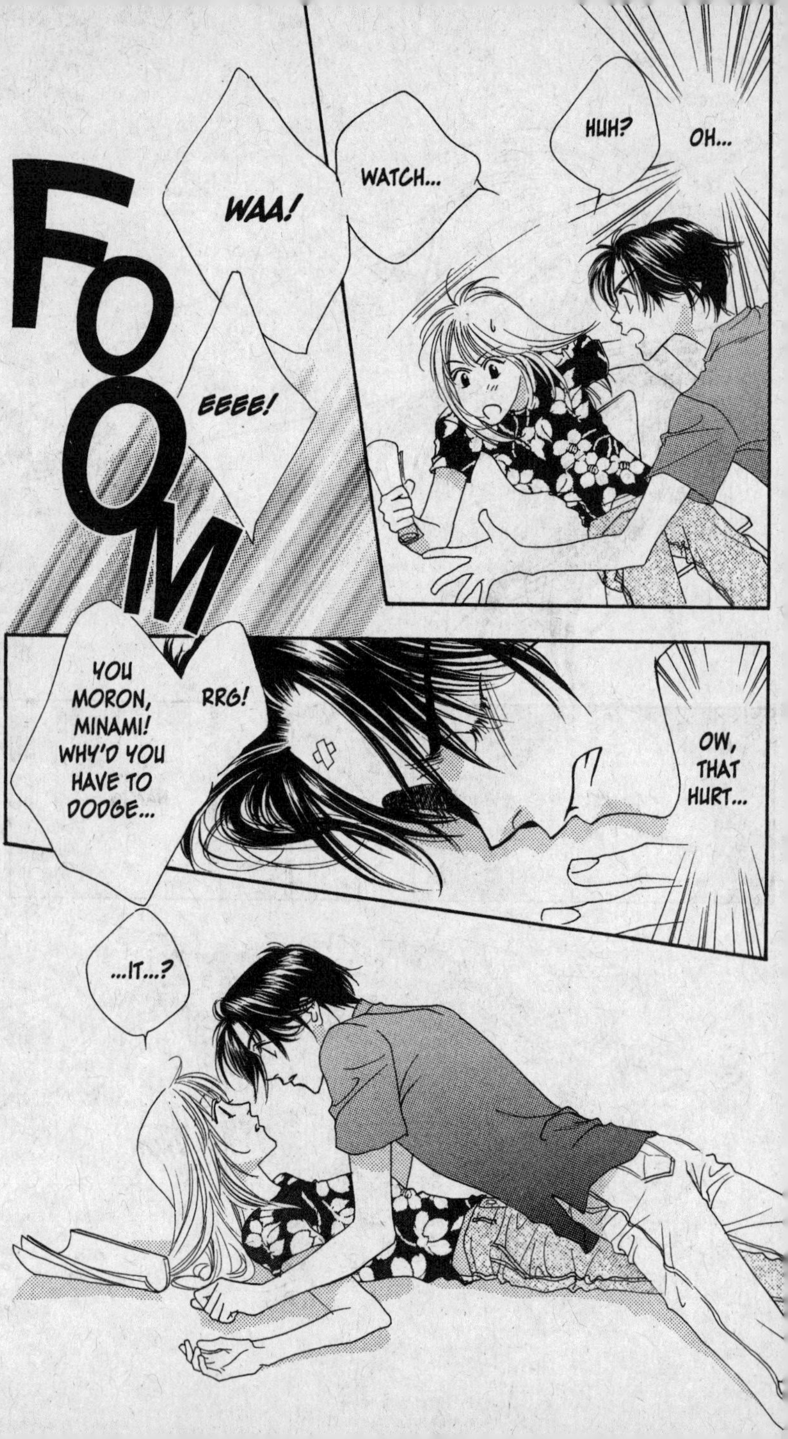
OH...
HUH?
WATCH...
WAA!
EEEE!
FOOM
OW, THAT HURT...
RRG!
YOU MORON, MINAMI! WHY'D YOU HAVE TO DODGE...
...IT...?

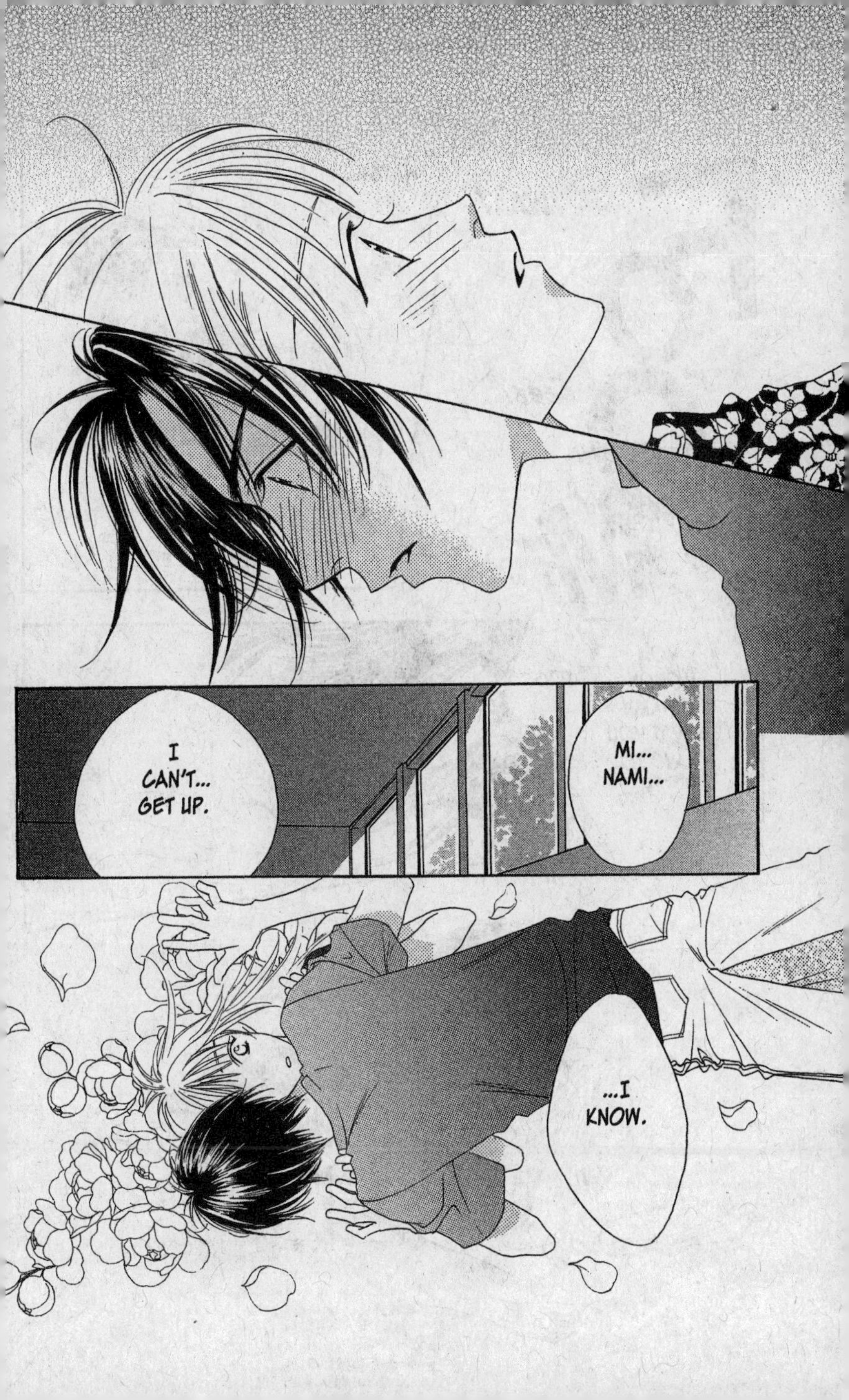
MI... NAMI...
I CAN'T... GET UP.
...I KNOW.

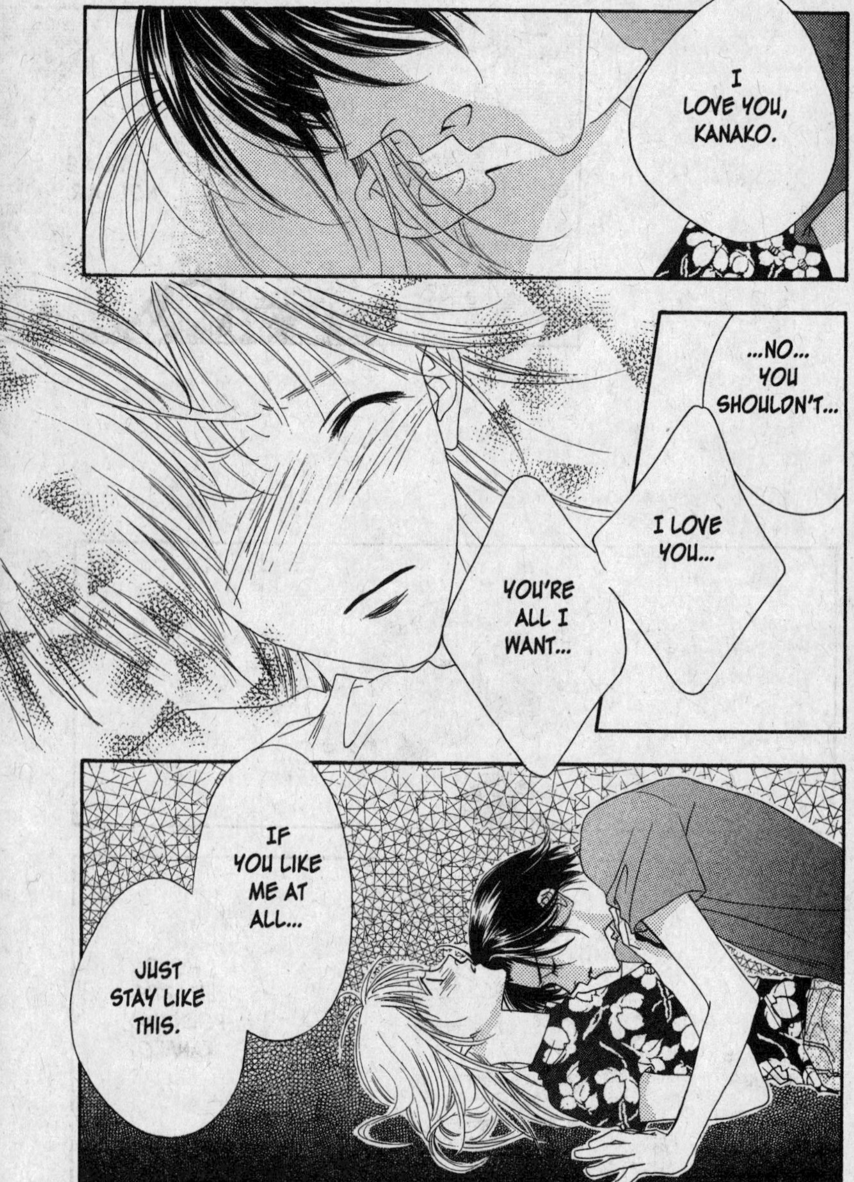
I LOVE YOU, KANAKO.
...NO... YOU SHOULDN'T...
I LOVE YOU...
YOU'RE ALL I WANT...
IF YOU LIKE ME AT ALL...
JUST STAY LIKE THIS.

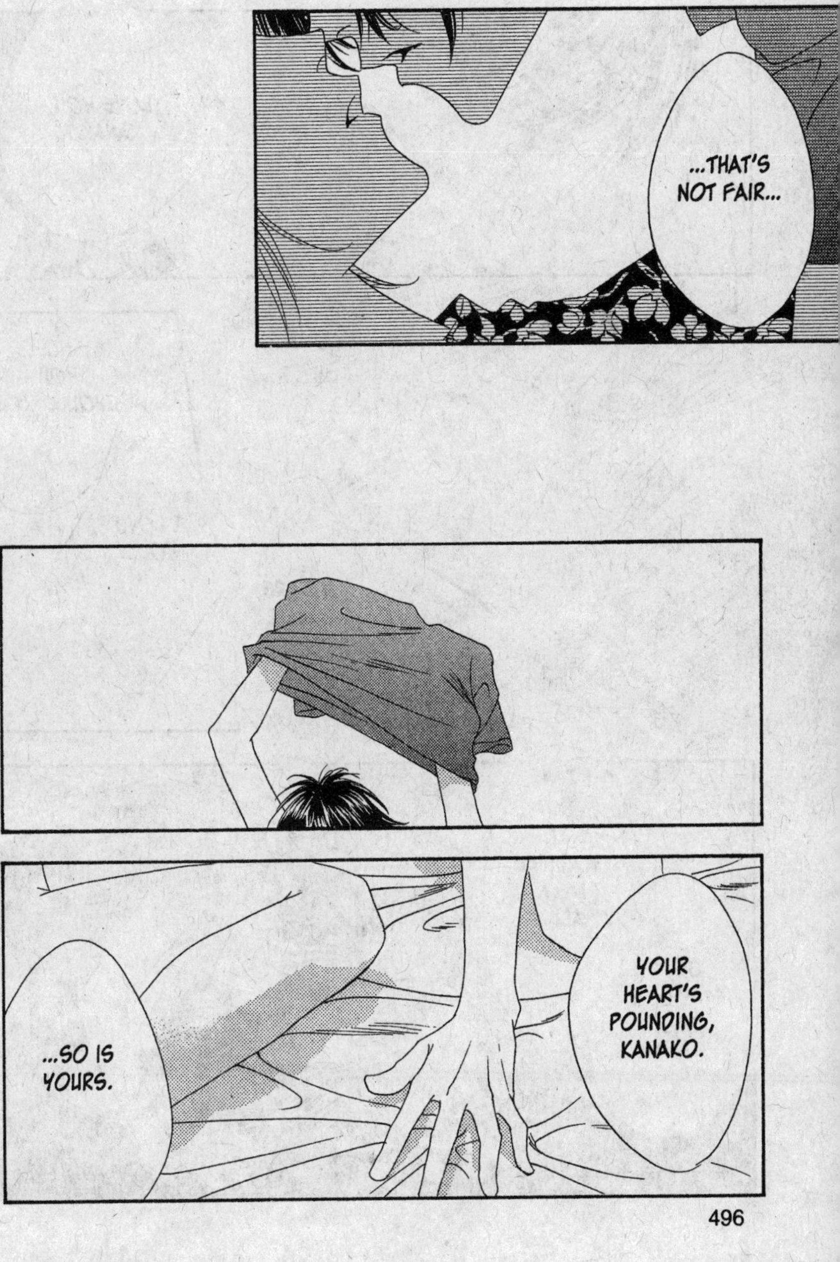
...THAT'S NOT FAIR...
YOUR HEART'S POUNDING, KANAKO.
...SO IS YOURS.

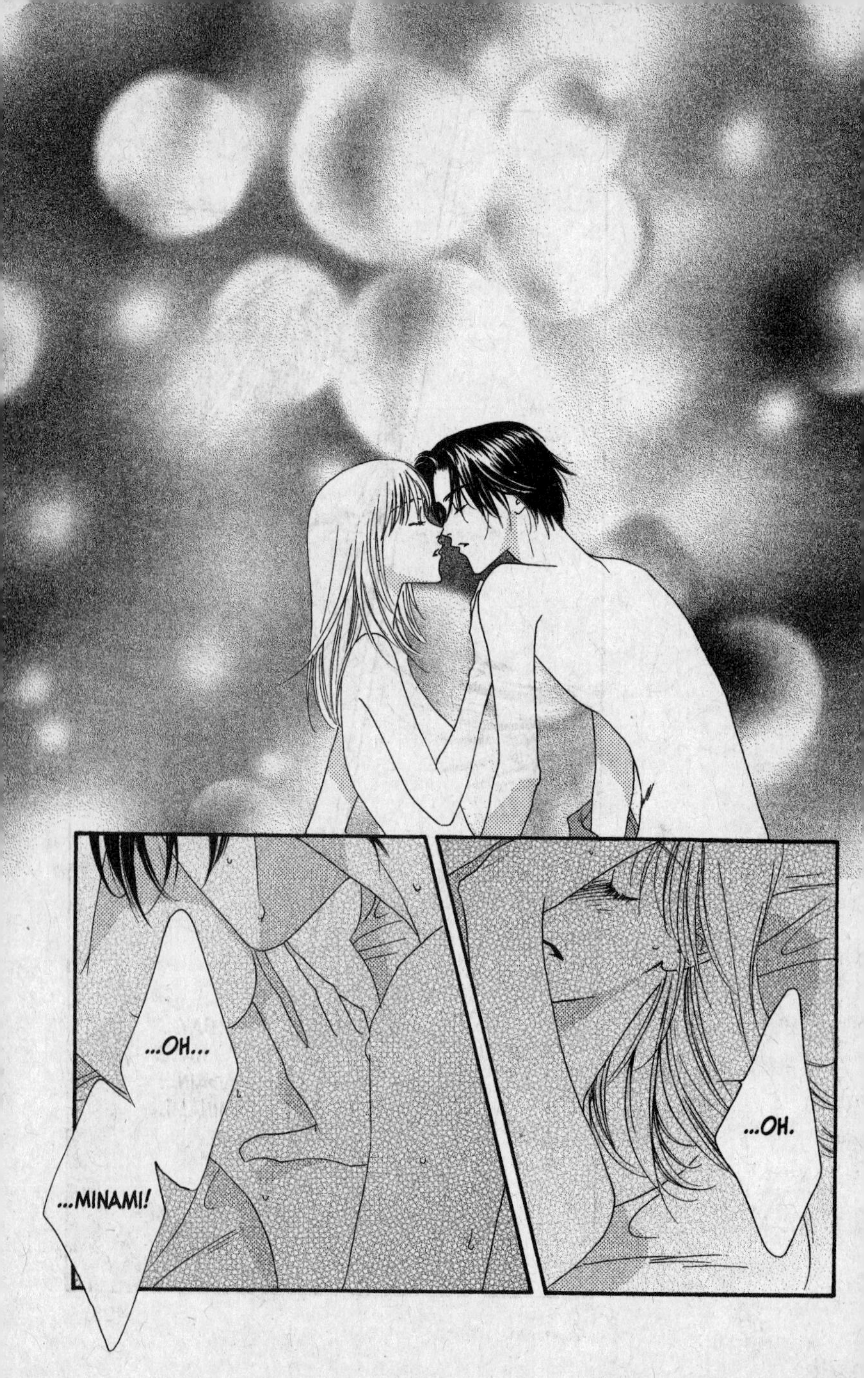
...OH.
...OH...
...MINAMI!

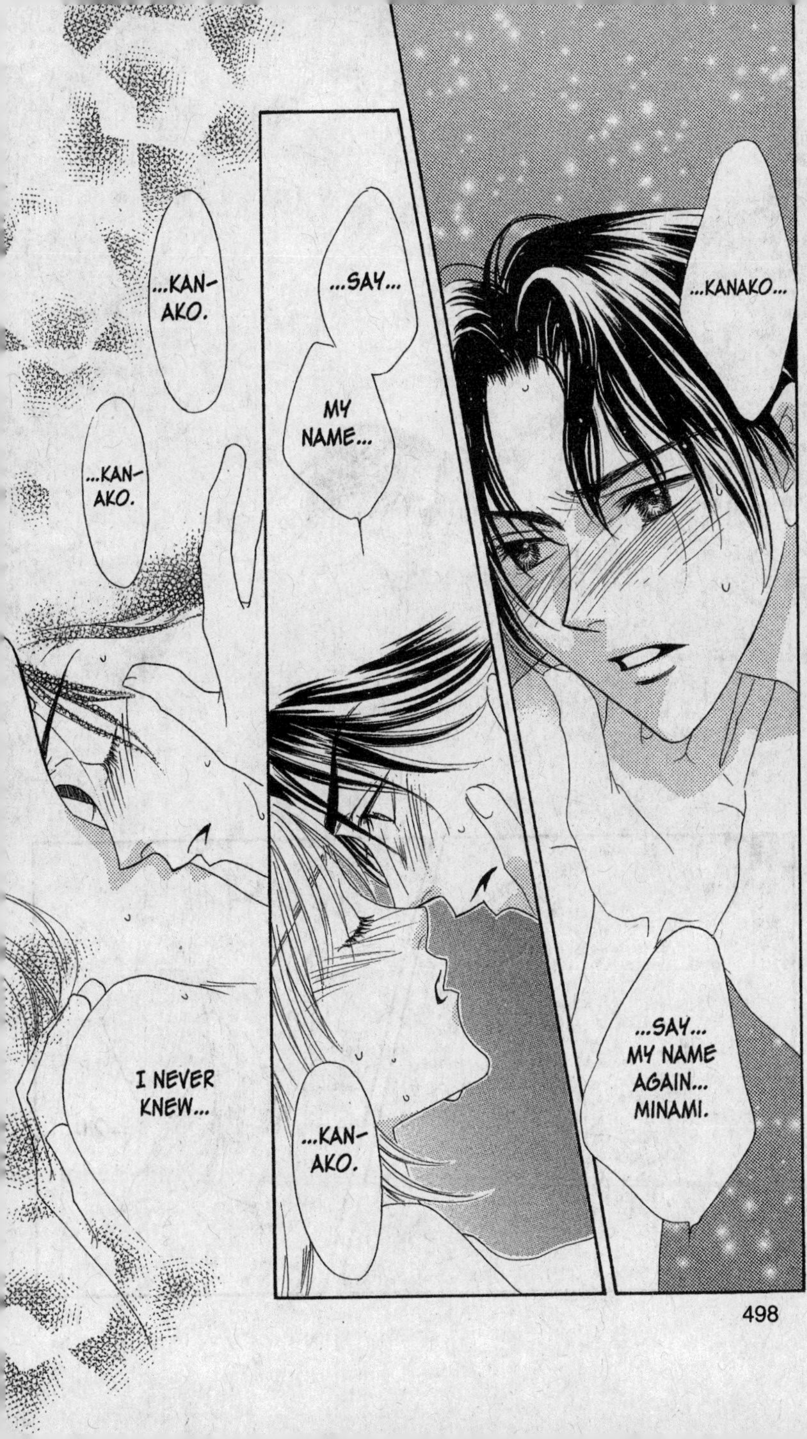
...KANAKO...
...SAY... MY NAME AGAIN... MINAMI.
...SAY...
MY NAME...
...KAN-AKO.
...KAN-AKO.
...KAN-AKO.
I NEVER KNEW...

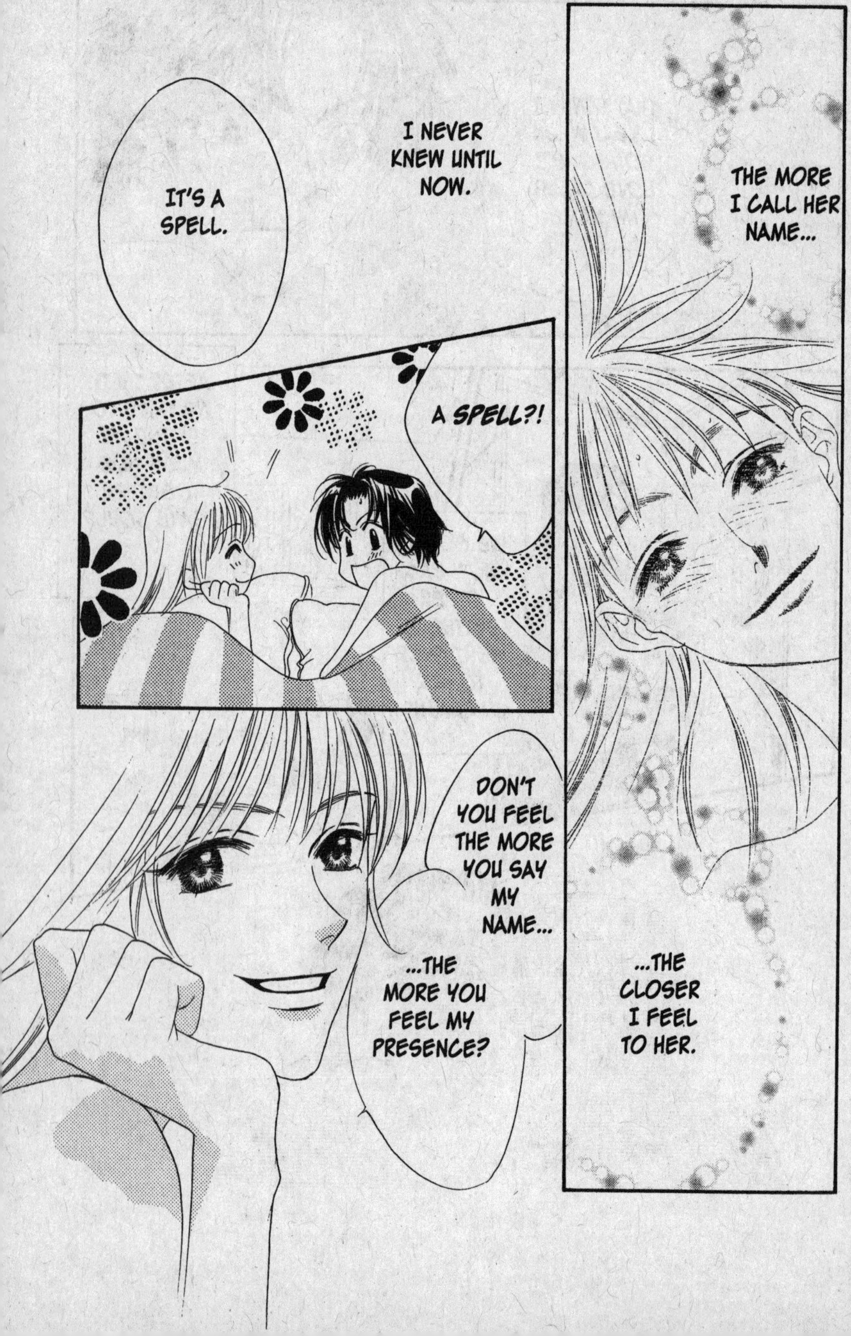

THE MORE I CALL HER NAME...
...THE CLOSER I FEEL TO HER.
I NEVER KNEW UNTIL NOW.
IT'S A SPELL.
A SPELL?!
DON'T YOU FEEL THE MORE YOU SAY MY NAME...
...THE MORE YOU FEEL MY PRESENCE?

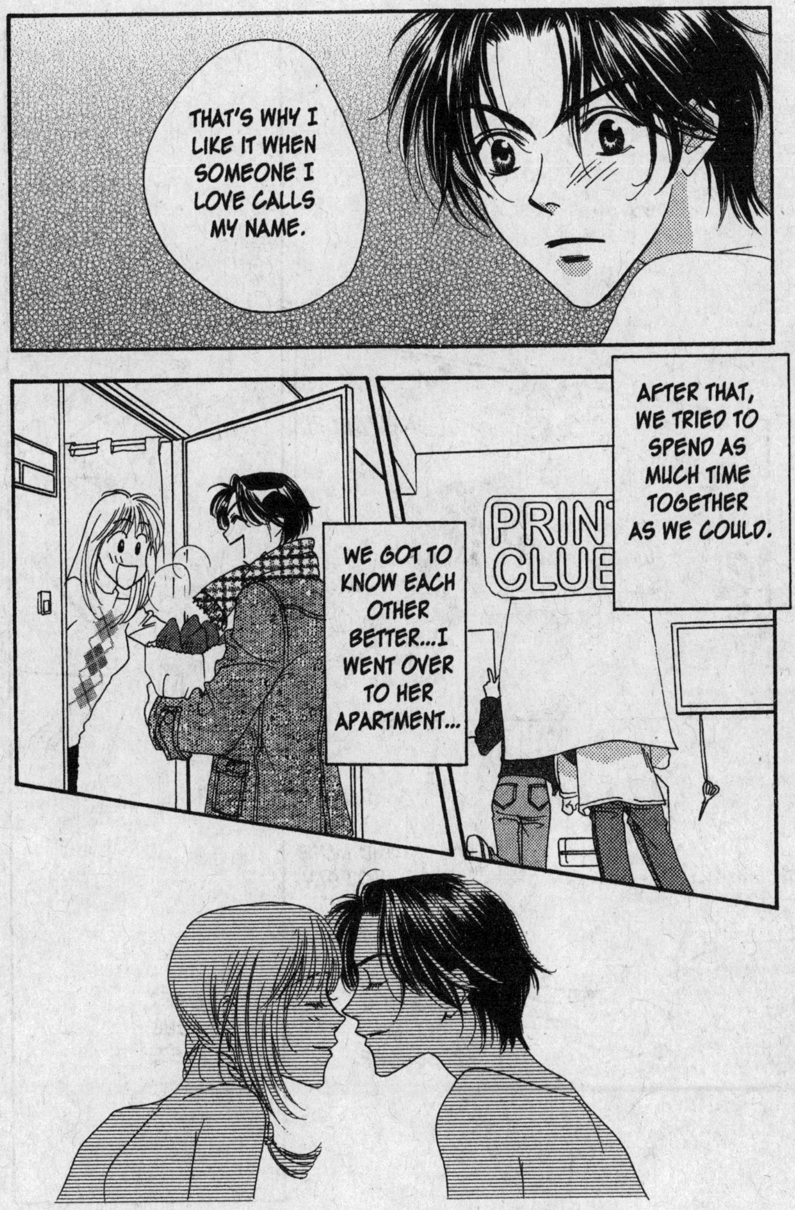
THAT'S WHY I LIKE IT WHEN SOMEONE I LOVE CALLS MY NAME.
AFTER THAT, WE TRIED TO SPEND AS MUCH TIME TOGETHER AS WE COULD.
WE GOT TO KNOW EACH OTHER BETTER...I WENT OVER TO HER APARTMENT...

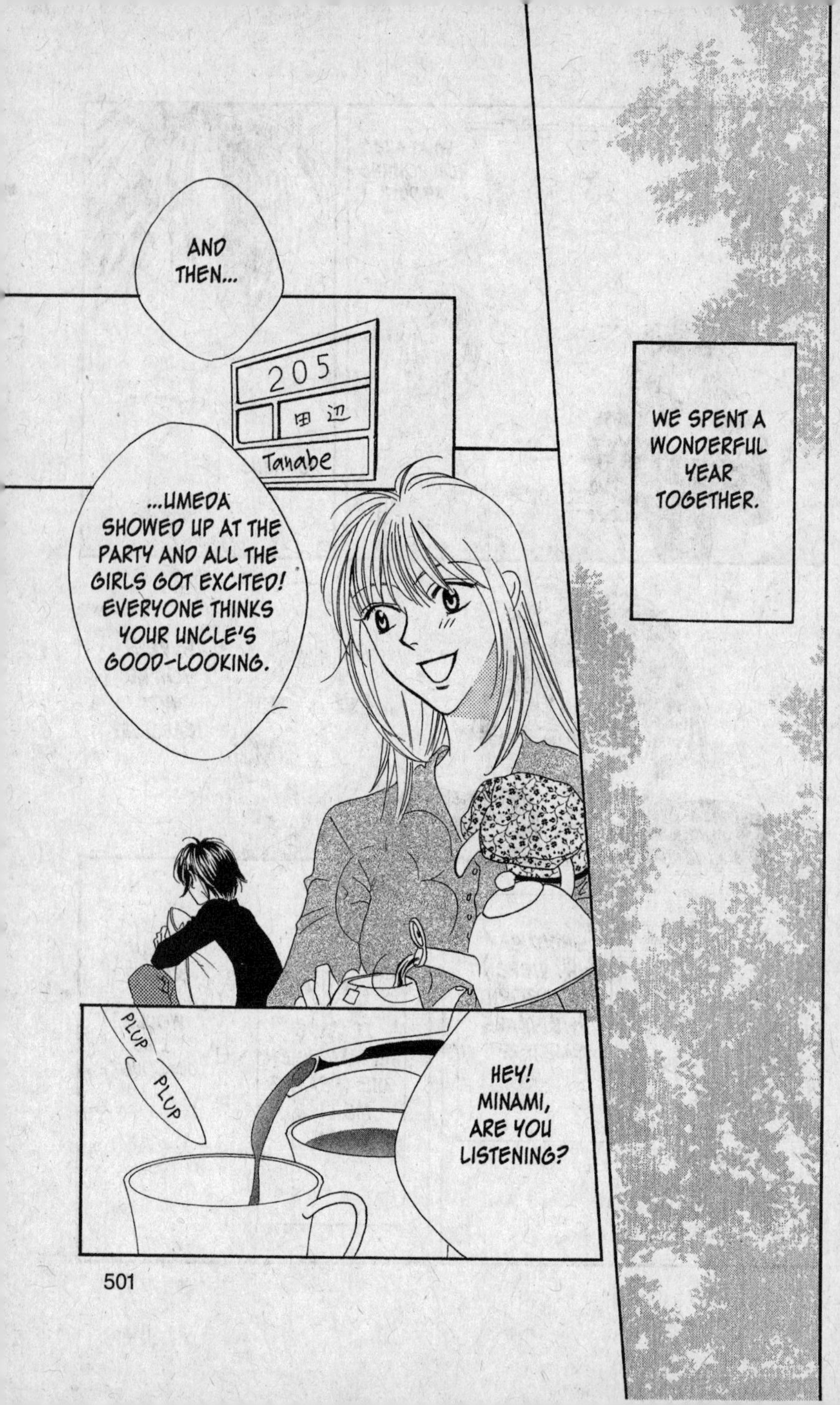
WE SPENT A WONDERFUL YEAR TOGETHER.
AND THEN...
205
田辺
Tanabe
...UMEDA SHOWED UP AT THE PARTY AND ALL THE GIRLS GOT EXCITED! EVERYONE THINKS YOUR UNCLE'S GOOD-LOOKING.
HEY! MINAMI, ARE YOU LISTENING?
PLUP PLUP

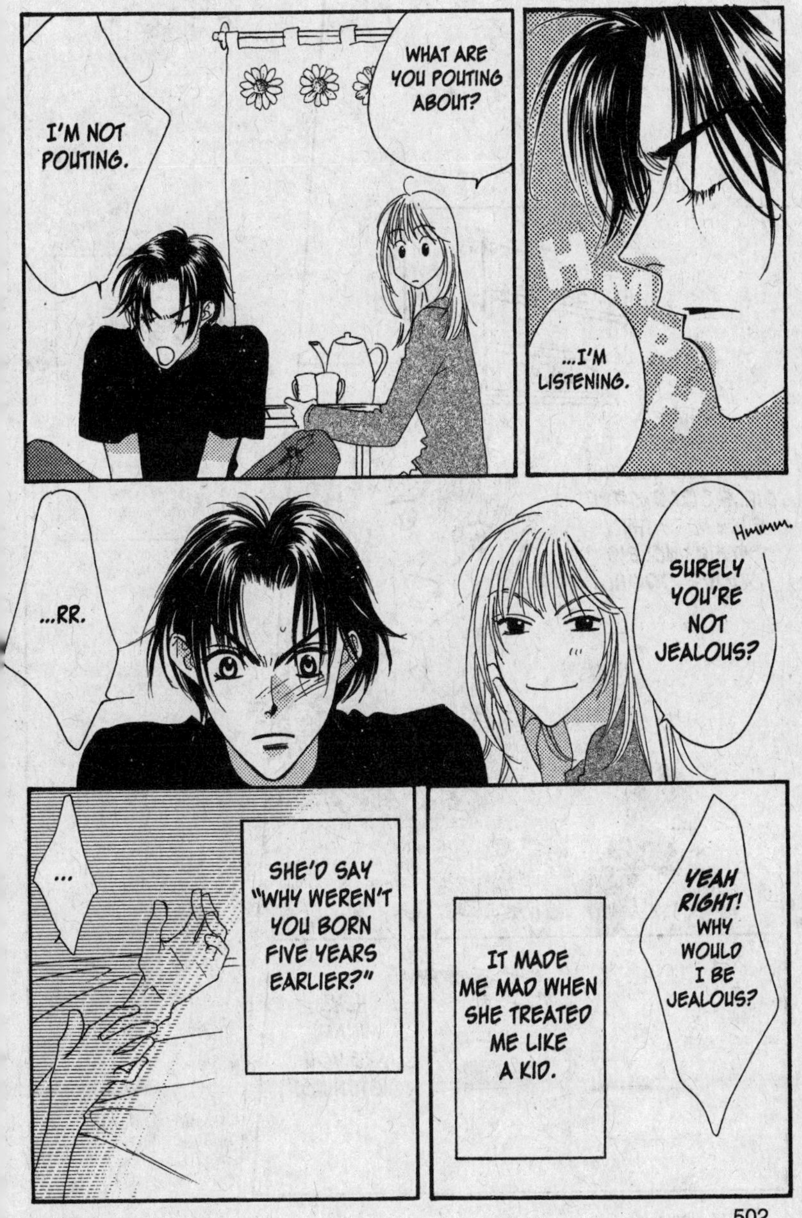
HMPH
...I'M LISTENING.
WHAT ARE YOU POUTING ABOUT?
I'M NOT POUTING.
Hmmm.
SURELY YOU'RE NOT JEALOUS?
...RR.
YEAH RIGHT! WHY WOULD I BE JEALOUS?
IT MADE ME MAD WHEN SHE TREATED ME LIKE A KID.
SHE'D SAY "WHY WEREN'T YOU BORN FIVE YEARS EARLIER?"
...

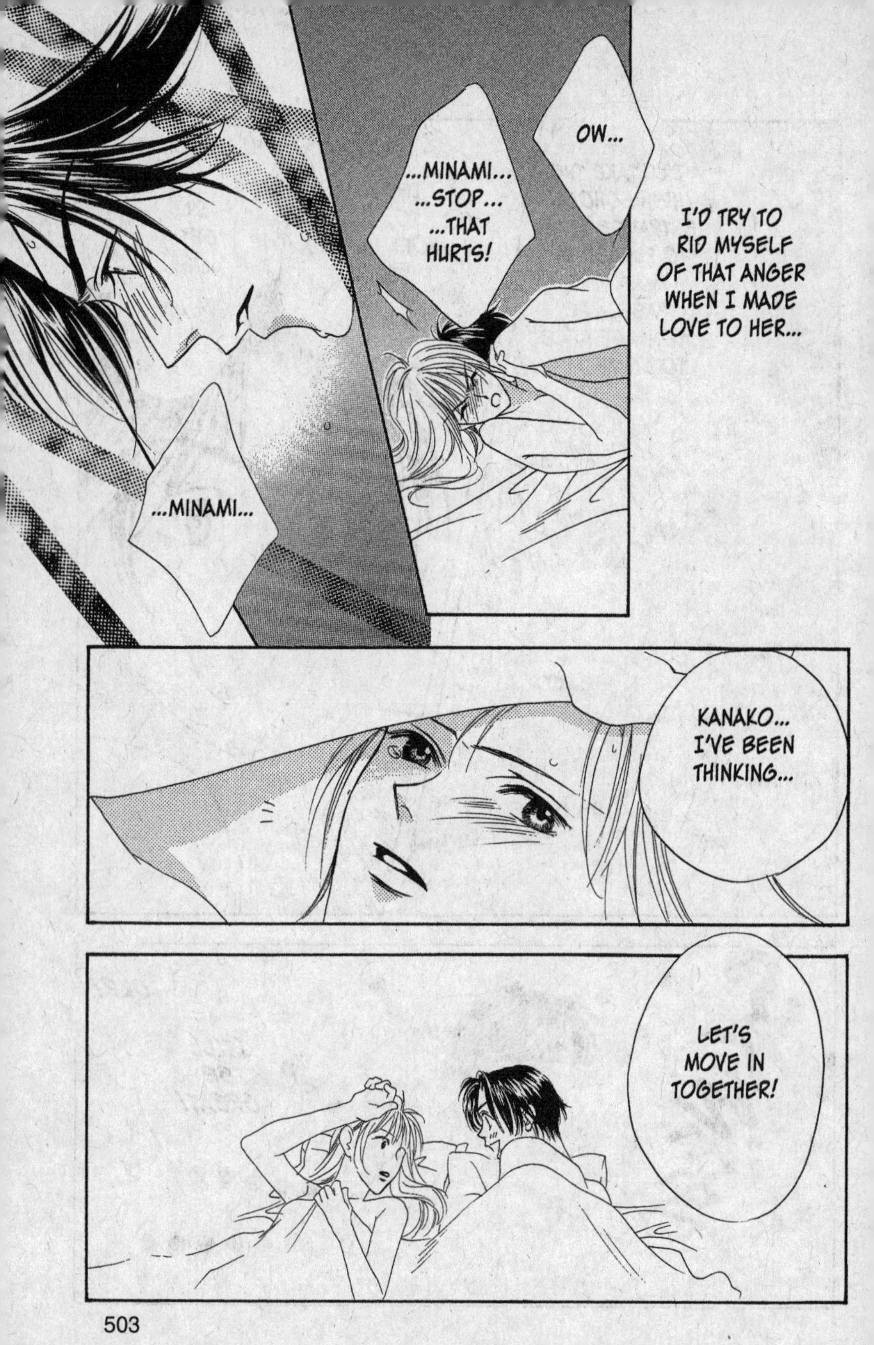
I'D TRY TO RID MYSELF OF THAT ANGER WHEN I MADE LOVE TO HER...
OW...
...MINAMI... ...STOP... ...THAT HURTS!
...MINAMI...
KANAKO... I'VE BEEN THINKING...
LET'S MOVE IN TOGETHER!

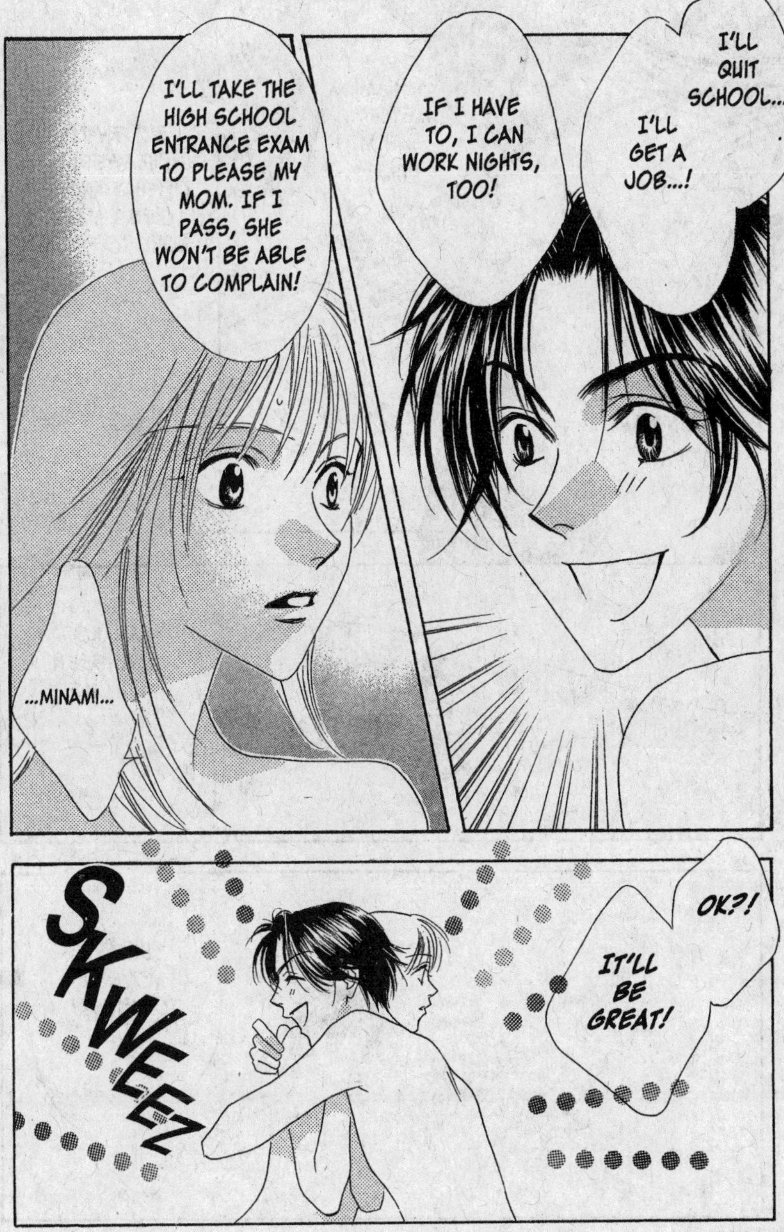
I'LL QUIT SCHOOL...
I'LL GET A JOB...!
IF I HAVE TO, I CAN WORK NIGHTS, TOO!
I'LL TAKE THE HIGH SCHOOL ENTRANCE EXAM TO PLEASE MY MOM. IF I PASS, SHE WON'T BE ABLE TO COMPLAIN!
...MINAMI...
OK?!
IT'LL BE GREAT!
SKWEEZ

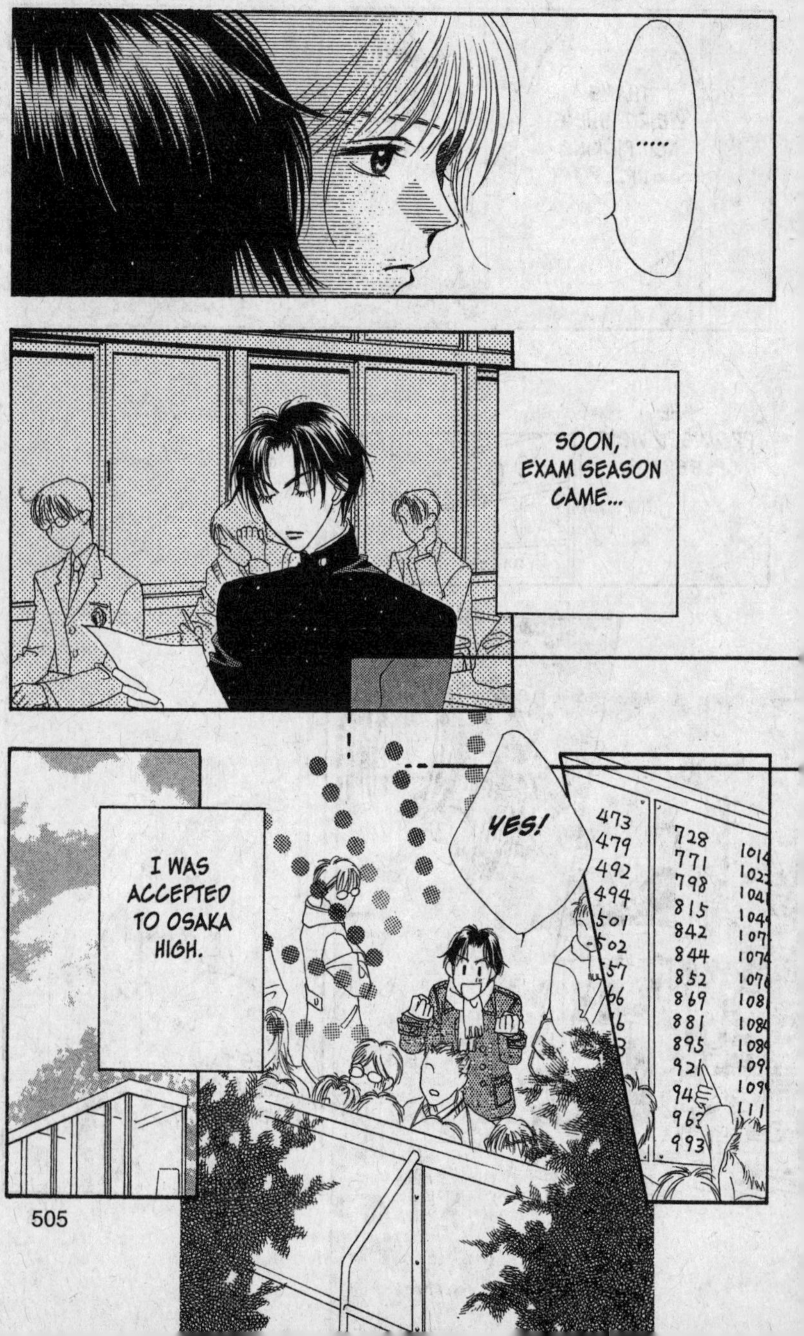
.....
SOON, EXAM SEASON CAME...
YES!
I WAS ACCEPTED TO OSAKA HIGH.

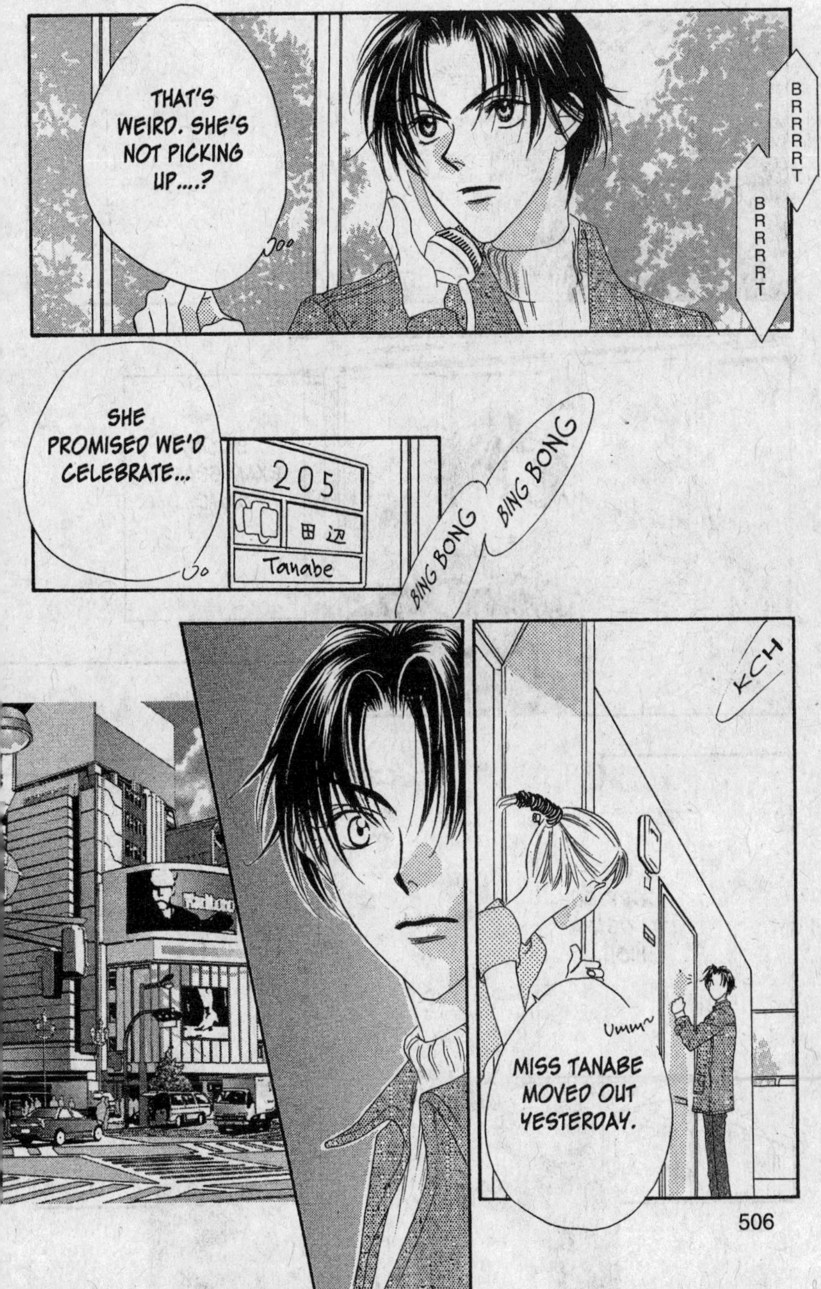
BRRRRT
BRRRRT
THAT'S WEIRD. SHE'S NOT PICKING UP....?
BING BONG
BING BONG
205
田辺
Tanabe
SHE PROMISED WE'D CELEBRATE...
KCH
Umm~
MISS TANABE MOVED OUT YESTERDAY.

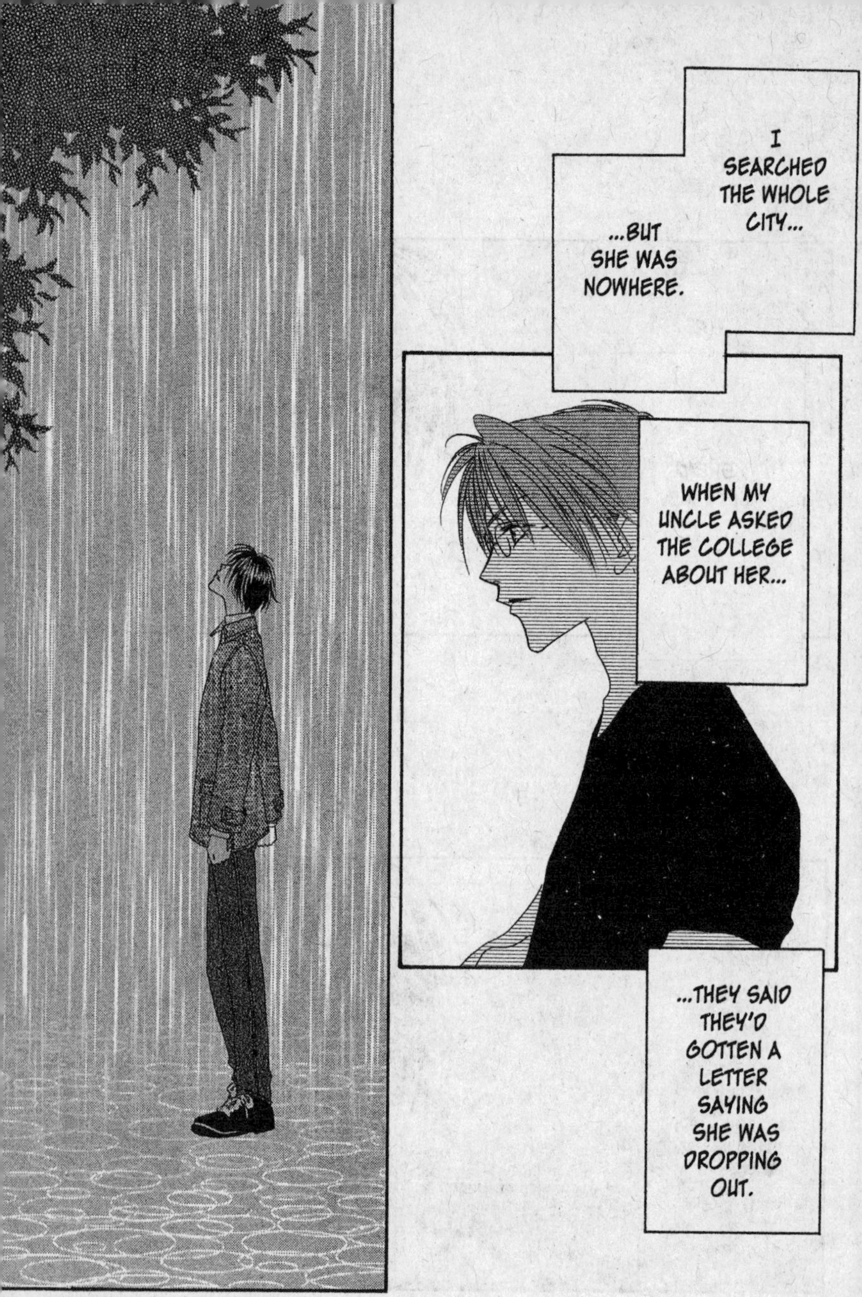
I SEARCHED THE WHOLE CITY...
...BUT SHE WAS NOWHERE.
WHEN MY UNCLE ASKED THE COLLEGE ABOUT HER...
...THEY SAID THEY'D GOTTEN A LETTER SAYING SHE WAS DROPPING OUT.

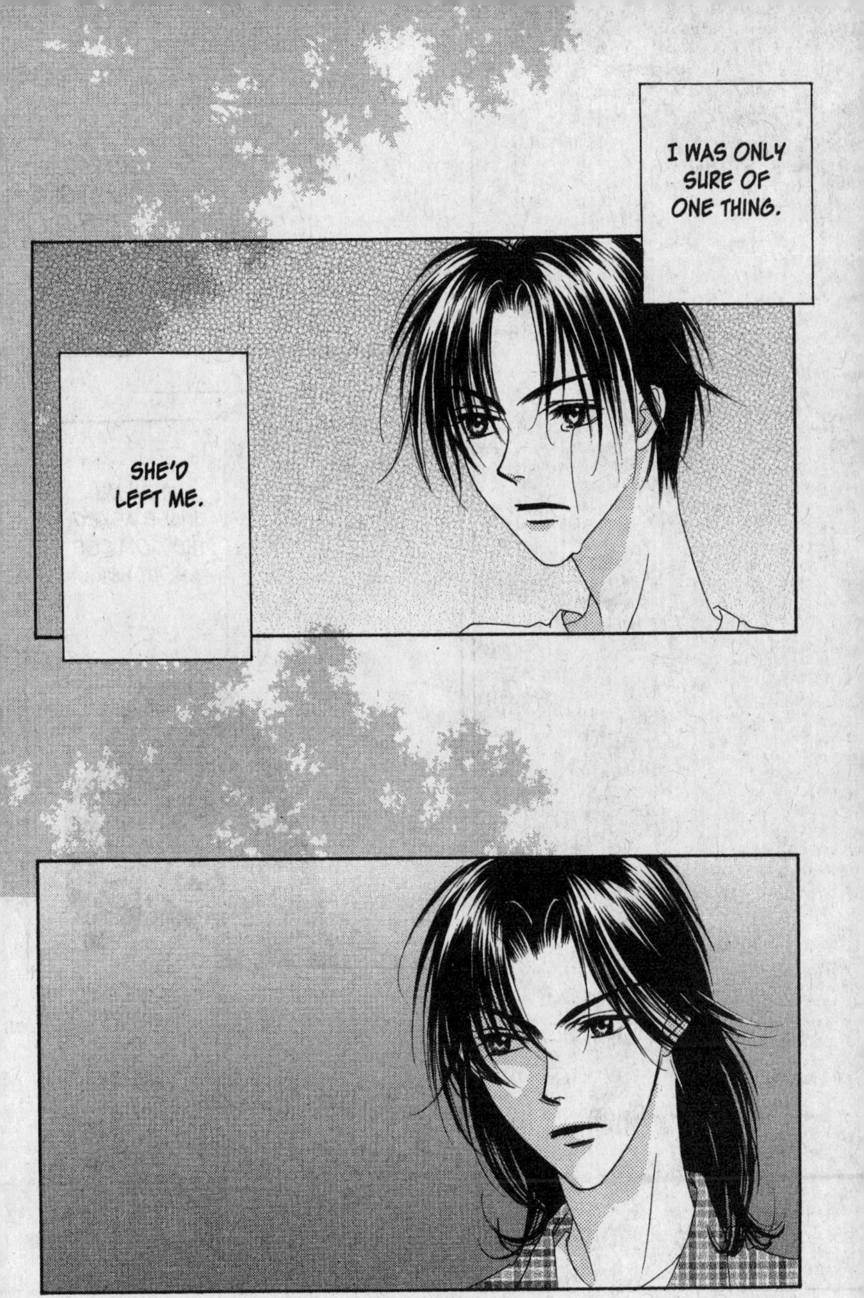
I WAS ONLY SURE OF ONE THING.
SHE'D LEFT ME.

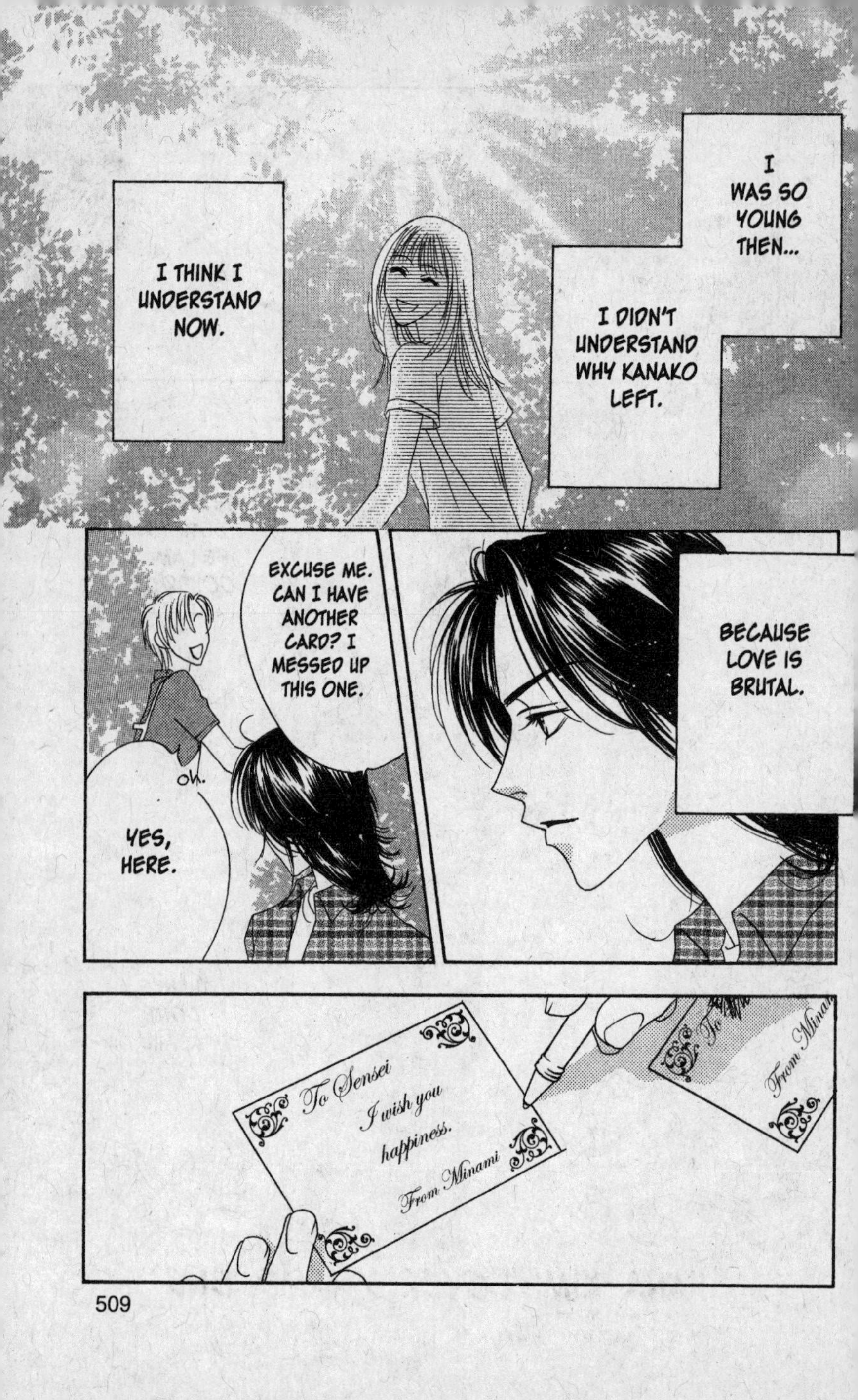
I WAS SO YOUNG THEN...
I DIDN'T UNDERSTAND WHY KANAKO LEFT.
I THINK I UNDERSTAND NOW.
BECAUSE LOVE IS BRUTAL.
EXCUSE ME. CAN I HAVE ANOTHER CARD? I MESSED UP THIS ONE.
OH.
YES, HERE.
To Sensei
I wish you happiness.
From Minami

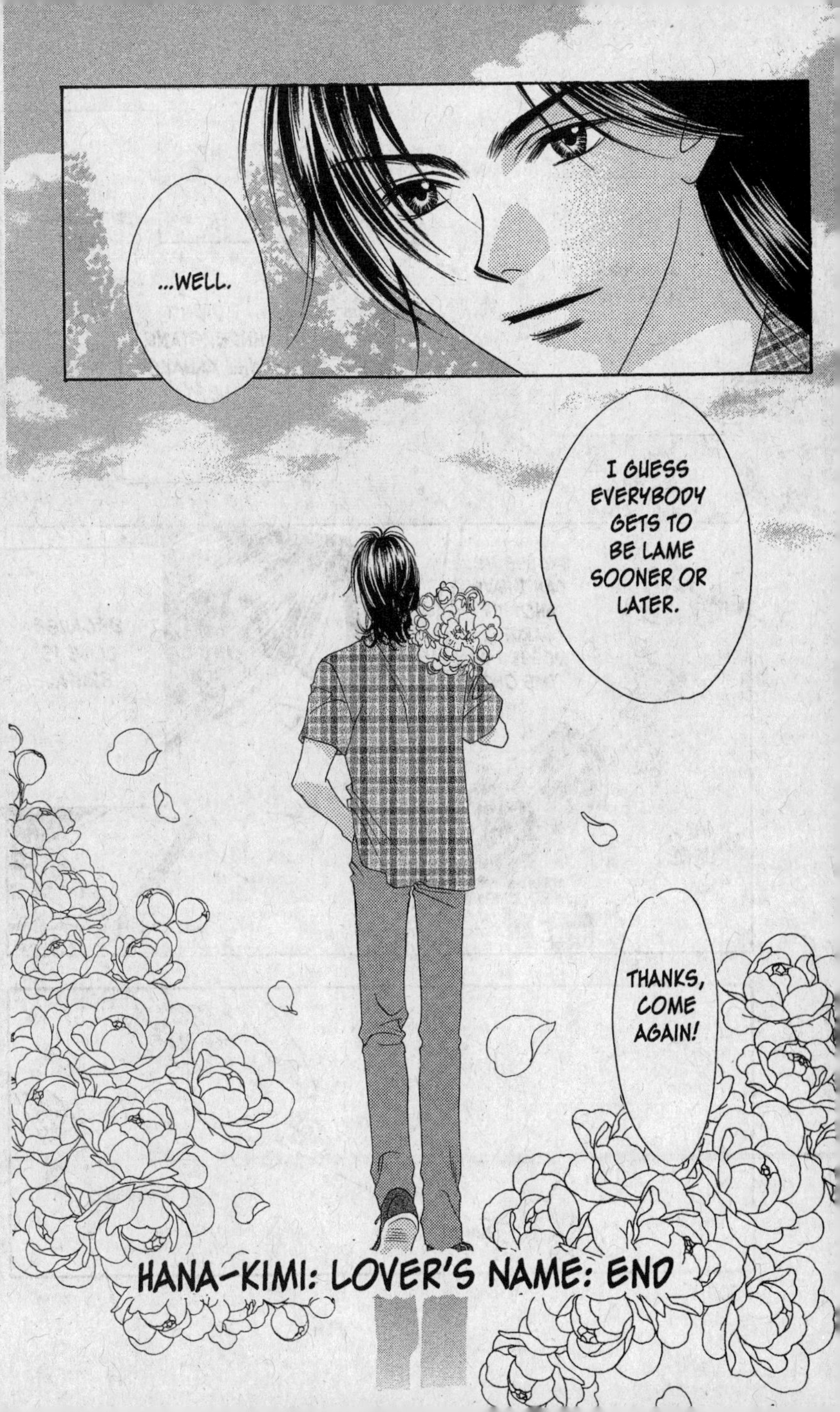
...WELL.
I GUESS EVERYBODY GETS TO BE LAME SOONER OR LATER.
THANKS, COME AGAIN!
HANA-KIMI: LOVER'S NAME: END

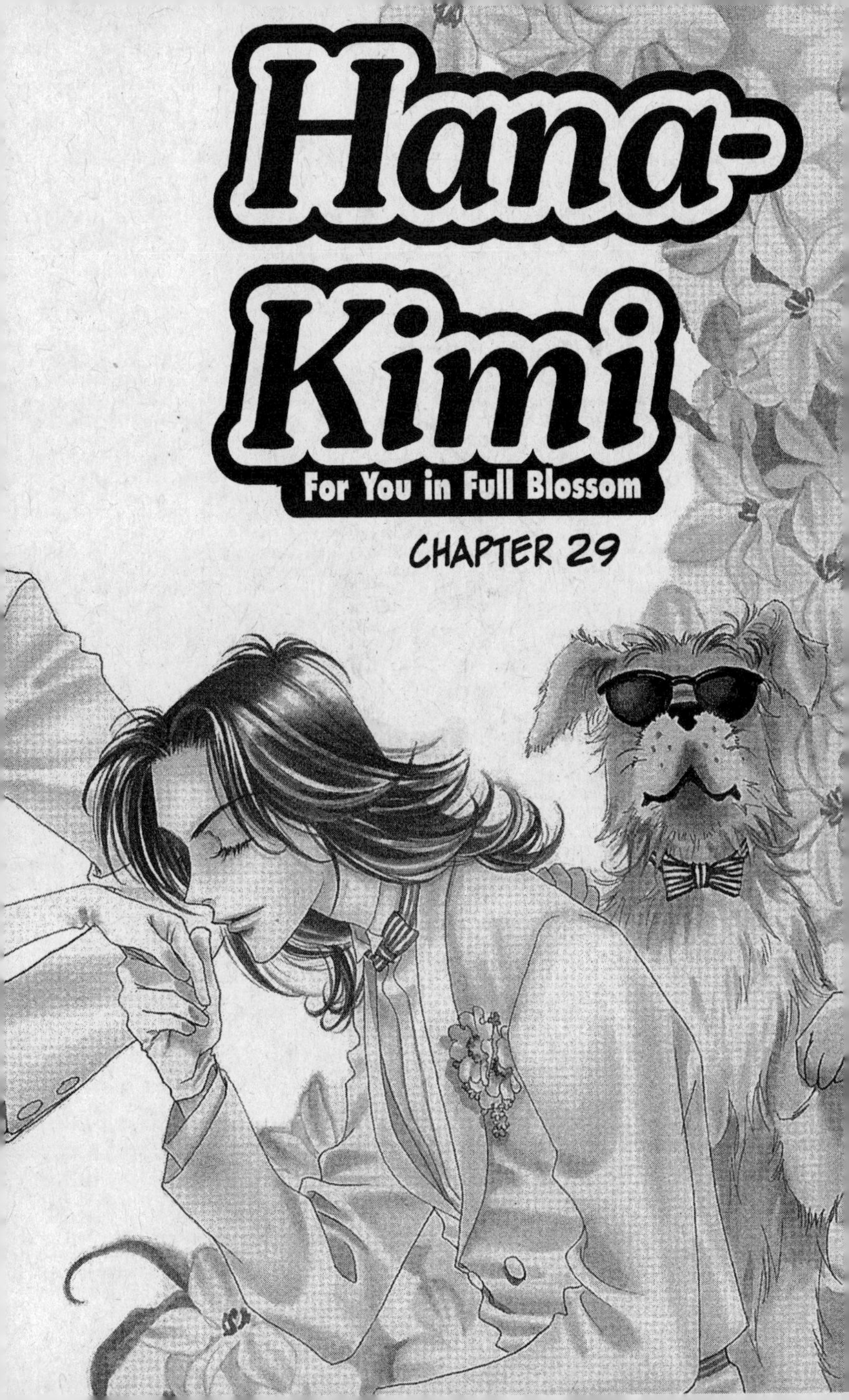
Hana-
Kimi
For You in Full Blossom
CHAPTER 29

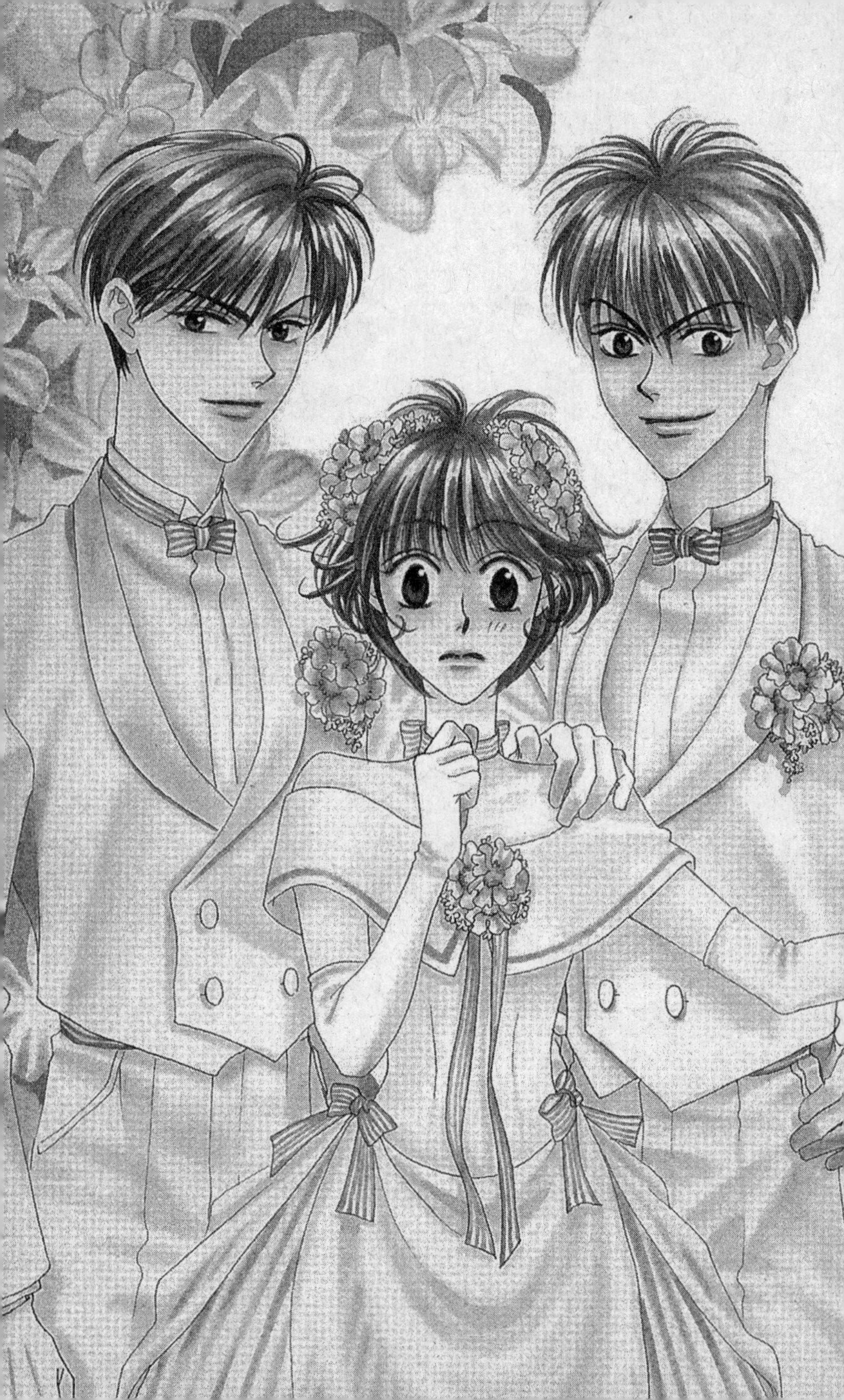

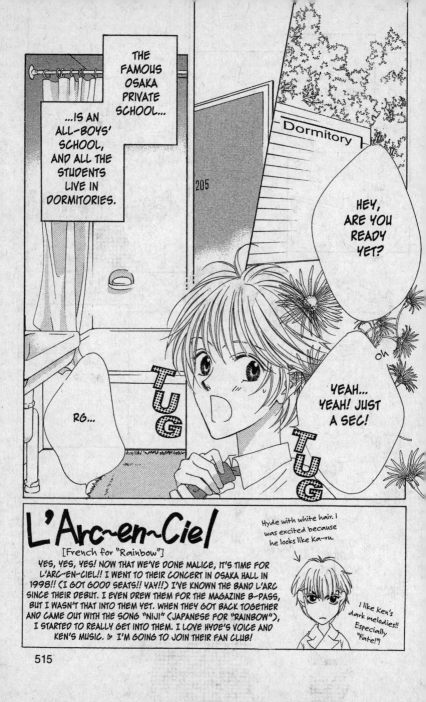

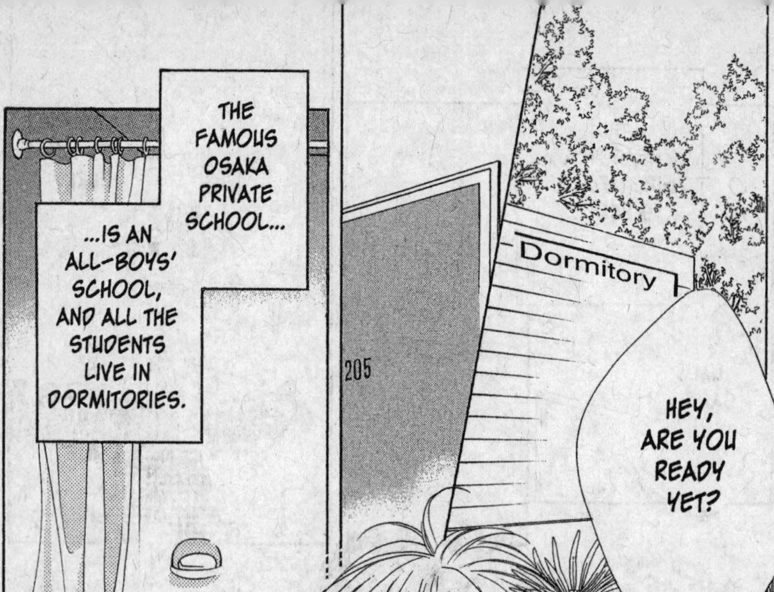
THE FAMOUS OSAKA PRIVATE SCHOOL...
...IS AN ALL-BOYS' SCHOOL, AND ALL THE STUDENTS LIVE IN DORMITORIES.
Dormitory
205
HEY, ARE YOU READY YET?
oh
YEAH... YEAH! JUST A SEC!
TUG
TUG
RG...

L'Arc~en~Ciel

[French for "Rainbow"]

YES, YES, YES! NOW THAT WE'VE DONE MALICE, IT'S TIME FOR L'ARC~EN~CIEL!! I WENT TO THEIR CONCERT IN OSAKA HALL IN 1998!! (I GOT GOOD SEATS!! YAY!!) I'VE KNOWN THE BAND L'ARC SINCE THEIR DEBUT. I EVEN DREW THEM FOR THE MAGAZINE B-PASS, BUT I WASN'T THAT INTO THEM YET. WHEN THEY GOT BACK TOGETHER AND CAME OUT WITH THE SONG "NIJI" (JAPANESE FOR "RAINBOW"), I STARTED TO REALLY GET INTO THEM. I LOVE HYDE'S VOICE AND KEN'S MUSIC. ♥ I'M GOING TO JOIN THEIR FAN CLUB!

Hyde with white hair. I was excited because he looks like Ka-ru.

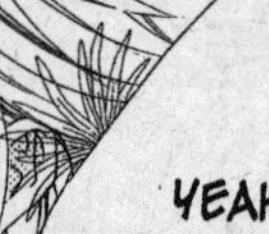

I like Ken's dark melodies!! Especially "Fate!"!

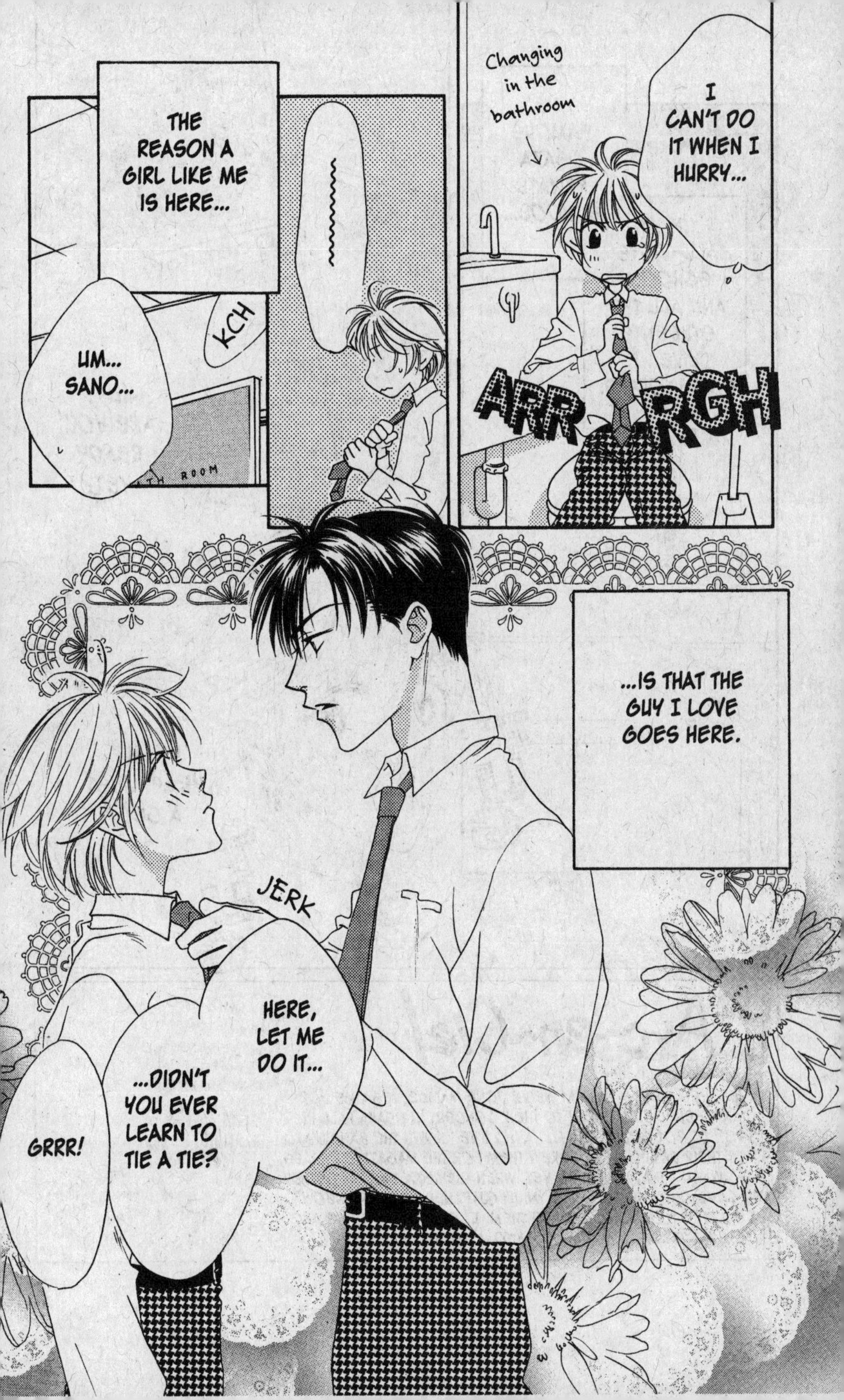

Changing in the bathroom
I CAN'T DO IT WHEN I HURRY...
ARRRGH
THE REASON A GIRL LIKE ME IS HERE...
KCH
UM... SANO...
...IS THAT THE GUY I LOVE GOES HERE.
JERK
HERE, LET ME DO IT...
...DIDN'T YOU EVER LEARN TO TIE A TIE?
GRRR!

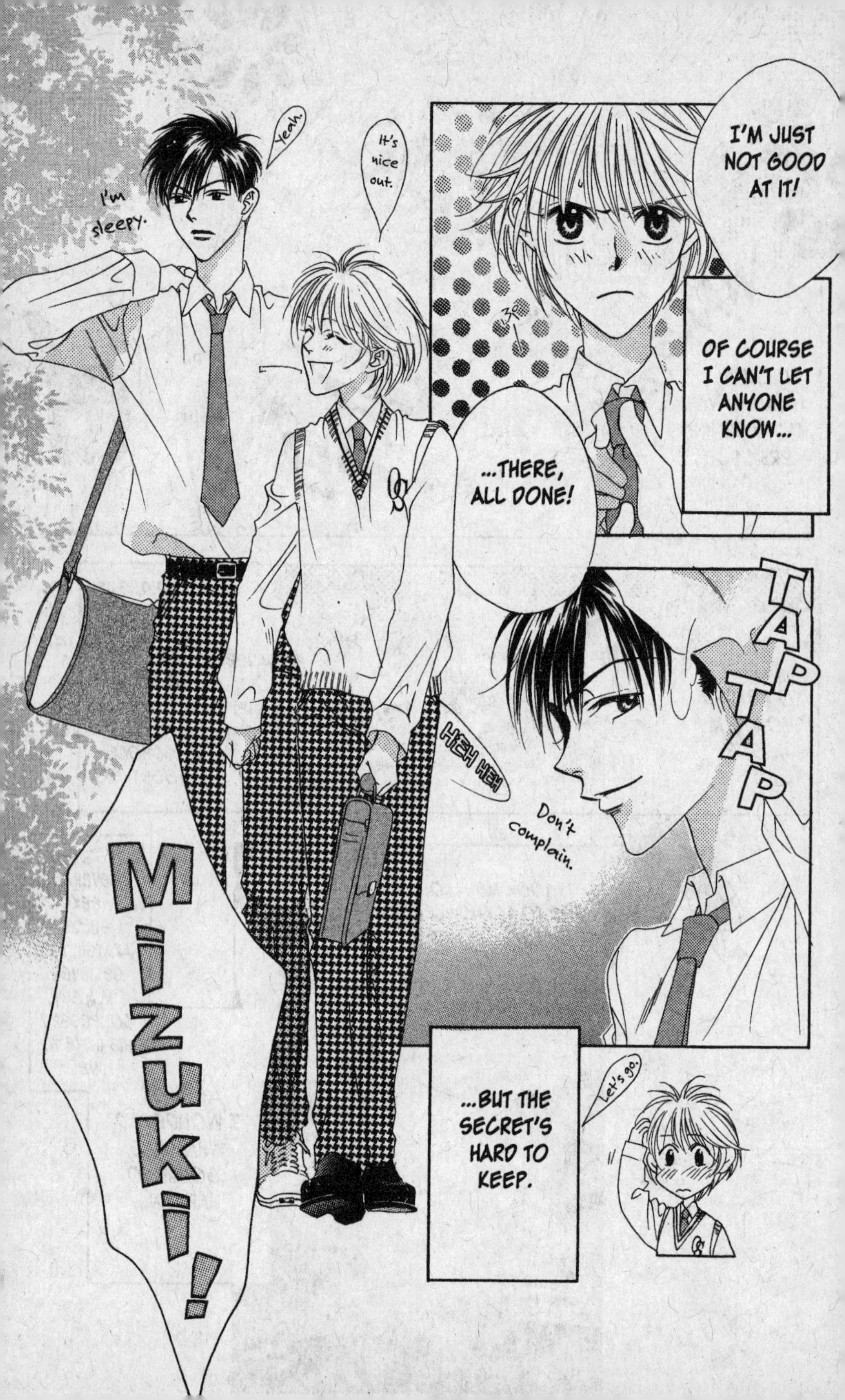
I'M JUST NOT GOOD AT IT!
OF COURSE I CAN'T LET ANYONE KNOW...
...THERE, ALL DONE!
TAP TAP
Don't complain.
HEH HEH
Let's go.
...BUT THE SECRET'S HARD TO KEEP.
Mizuki!
It's nice out.
Yeah.
I'm sleepy.

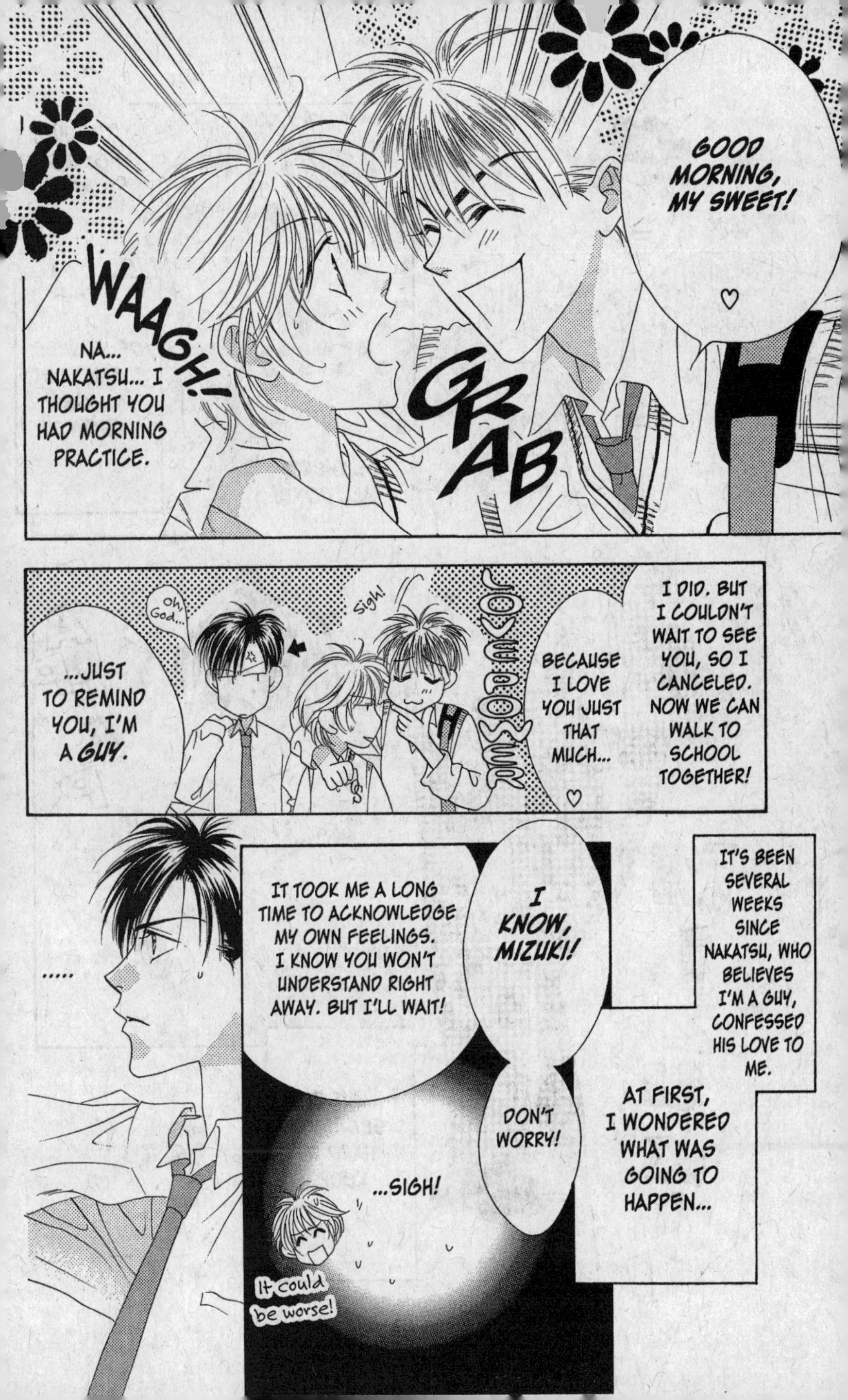
GOOD MORNING, MY SWEET! ♡
WAAGH!
GRAB
NA... NAKATSU... I THOUGHT YOU HAD MORNING PRACTICE.
I DID. BUT I COULDN'T WAIT TO SEE YOU, SO I CANCELED. NOW WE CAN WALK TO SCHOOL TOGETHER!
BECAUSE I LOVE YOU JUST THAT MUCH... ♡
LOVE POWER
Sigh!
Oh, God...
...JUST TO REMIND YOU, I'M A GUY.
IT'S BEEN SEVERAL WEEKS SINCE NAKATSU, WHO BELIEVES I'M A GUY, CONFESSED HIS LOVE TO ME.
I KNOW, MIZUKI!
IT TOOK ME A LONG TIME TO ACKNOWLEDGE MY OWN FEELINGS. I KNOW YOU WON'T UNDERSTAND RIGHT AWAY. BUT I'LL WAIT!
.....
AT FIRST, I WONDERED WHAT WAS GOING TO HAPPEN...
DON'T WORRY!
...SIGH!
It could be worse!

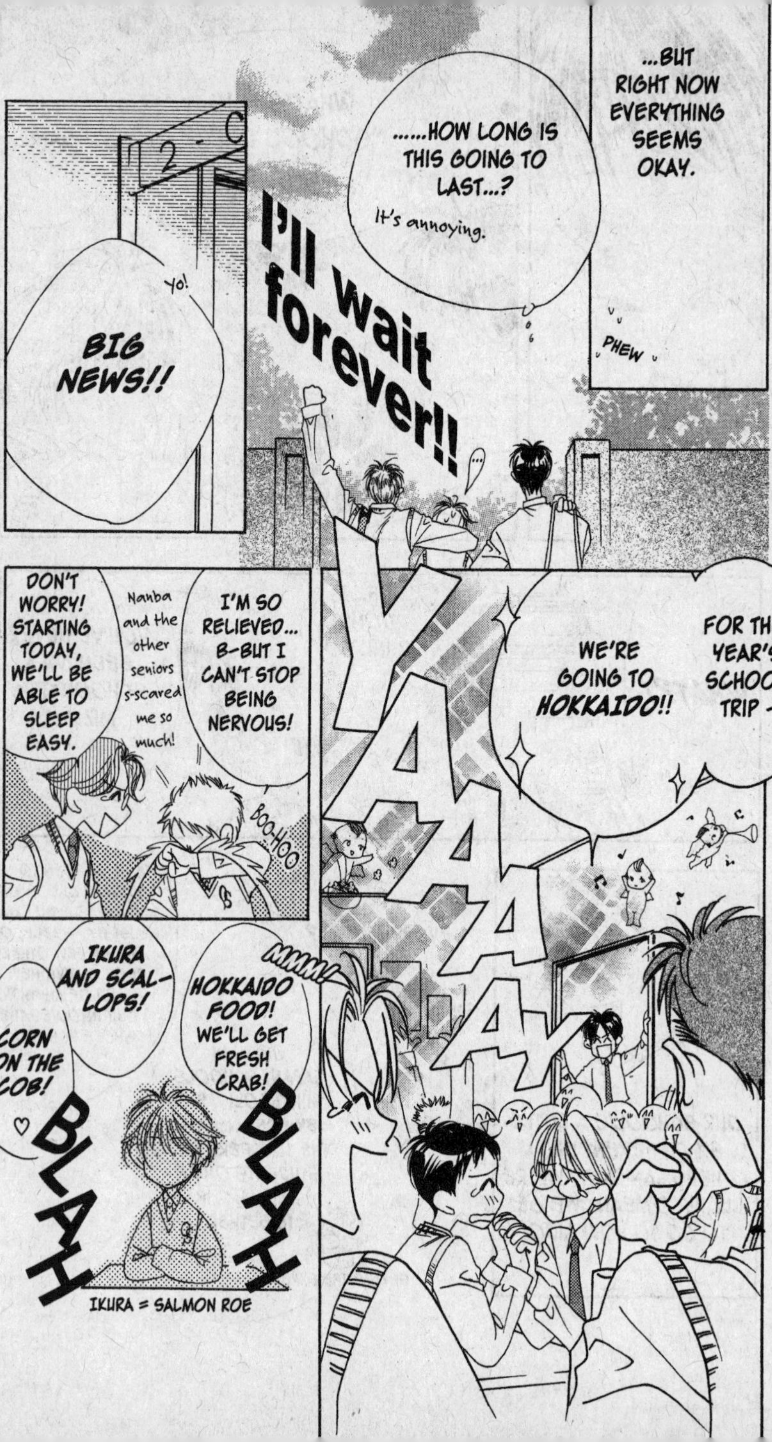

...BUT RIGHT NOW EVERYTHING SEEMS OKAY.
......HOW LONG IS THIS GOING TO LAST...?
It's annoying.
PHEW
I'll wait forever!!
Yo!
BIG NEWS!!
FOR THIS YEAR'S SCHOOL TRIP -
WE'RE GOING TO HOKKAIDO!!
YAAAAY
I'M SO RELIEVED... B-BUT I CAN'T STOP BEING NERVOUS!
Nanba and the other seniors s-scared me so much!
DON'T WORRY! STARTING TODAY, WE'LL BE ABLE TO SLEEP EASY.
BOO-HOO
MMM!
HOKKAIDO FOOD! WE'LL GET FRESH CRAB!
IKURA AND SCAL-LOPS!
CORN ON THE COB!
BLAH
BLAH
IKURA = SALMON ROE

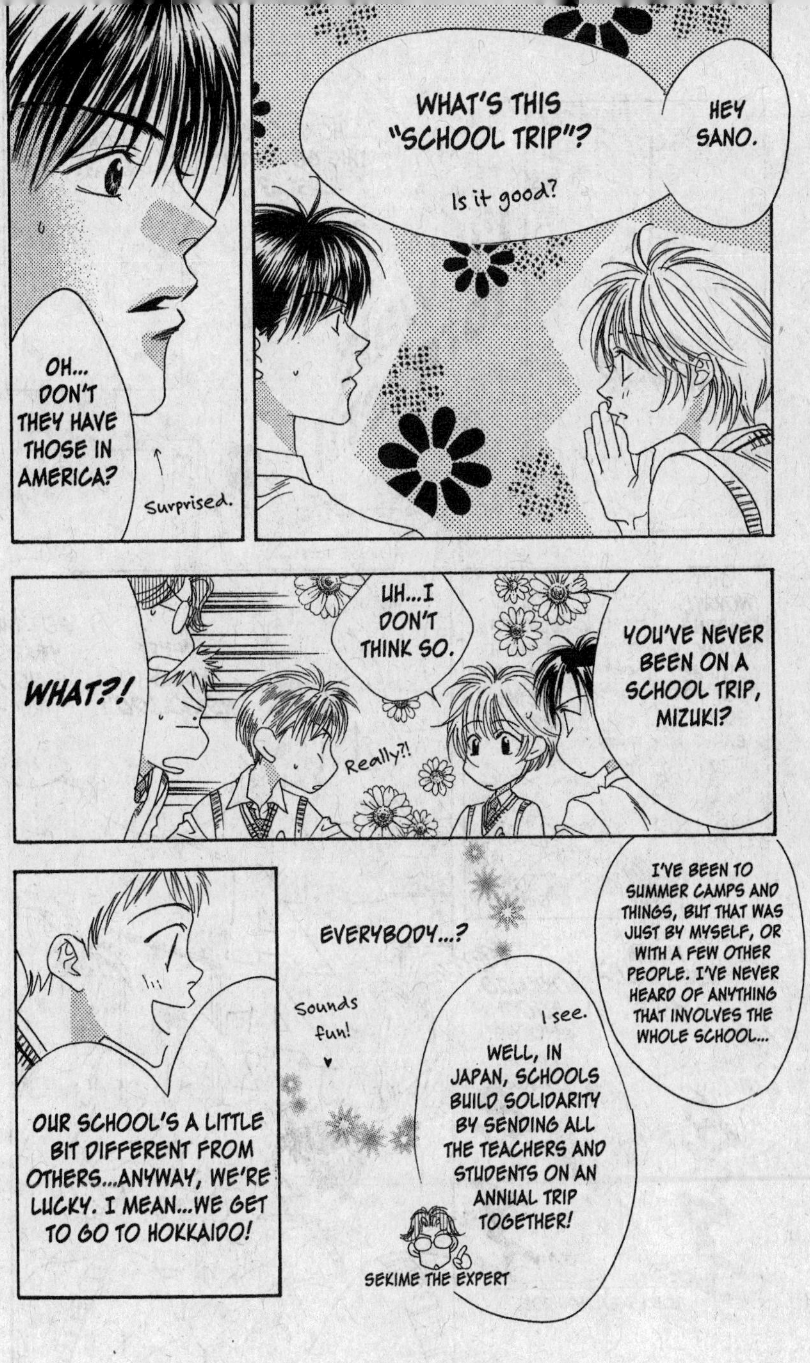
HEY SANO.
WHAT'S THIS "SCHOOL TRIP"?
Is it good?
OH... DON'T THEY HAVE THOSE IN AMERICA?
Surprised.
YOU'VE NEVER BEEN ON A SCHOOL TRIP, MIZUKI?
UH...I DON'T THINK SO.
Really?!
WHAT?!
I'VE BEEN TO SUMMER CAMPS AND THINGS, BUT THAT WAS JUST BY MYSELF, OR WITH A FEW OTHER PEOPLE. I'VE NEVER HEARD OF ANYTHING THAT INVOLVES THE WHOLE SCHOOL...
EVERYBODY...?
Sounds fun!
I see.
WELL, IN JAPAN, SCHOOLS BUILD SOLIDARITY BY SENDING ALL THE TEACHERS AND STUDENTS ON AN ANNUAL TRIP TOGETHER!
SEKIME THE EXPERT
OUR SCHOOL'S A LITTLE BIT DIFFERENT FROM OTHERS...ANYWAY, WE'RE LUCKY. I MEAN...WE GET TO GO TO HOKKAIDO!

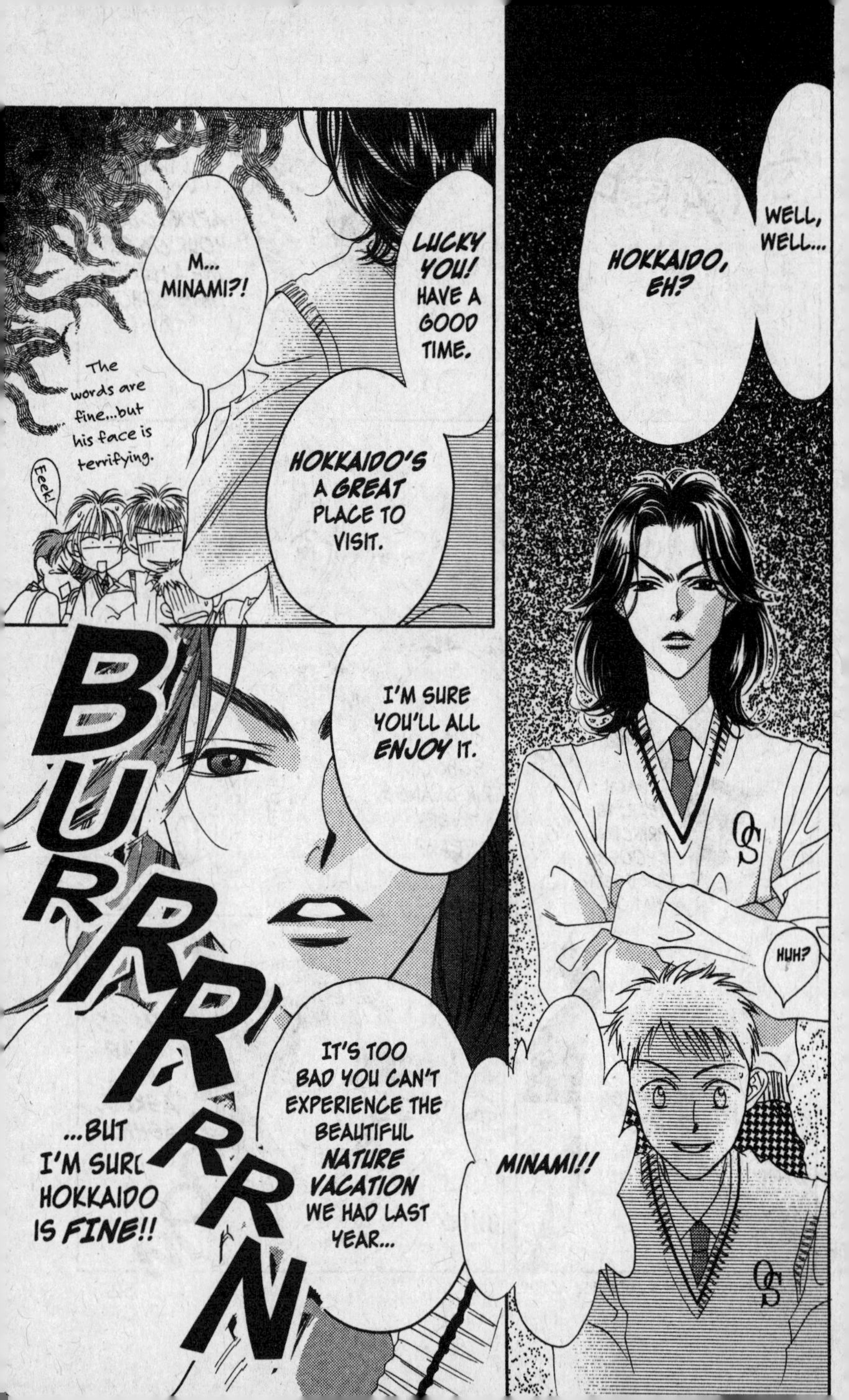
WELL, WELL...
HOKKAIDO, EH?
HUH?
MINAMI!!
LUCKY YOU! HAVE A GOOD TIME.
HOKKAIDO'S A GREAT PLACE TO VISIT.
M... MINAMI?!
The words are fine...but his face is terrifying.
Eeek!
I'M SURE YOU'LL ALL ENJOY IT.
IT'S TOO BAD YOU CAN'T EXPERIENCE THE BEAUTIFUL NATURE VACATION WE HAD LAST YEAR...
...BUT I'M SURE HOKKAIDO IS FINE!!
BURRRRRN

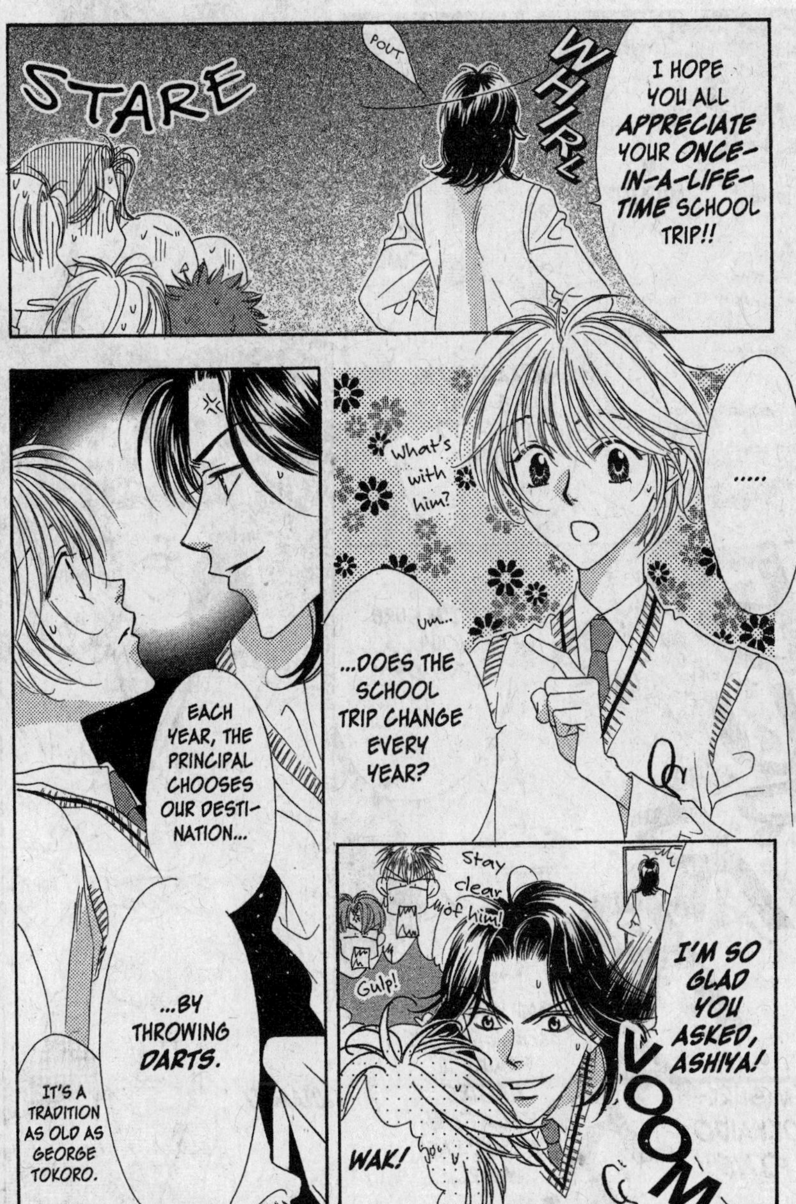

I HOPE YOU ALL APPRECIATE YOUR ONCE-IN-A-LIFE-TIME SCHOOL TRIP!!
WHIRL
POUT
STARE
.....
What's with him?
um...
...DOES THE SCHOOL TRIP CHANGE EVERY YEAR?
I'M SO GLAD YOU ASKED, ASHIYA!
VOOM
Stay clear of him!
Gulp!
WAK!
EACH YEAR, THE PRINCIPAL CHOOSES OUR DESTI-NATION...
...BY THROWING DARTS.
IT'S A TRADITION AS OLD AS GEORGE TOKORO.

GEORGE TOKORO = A JAPANESE ACTOR

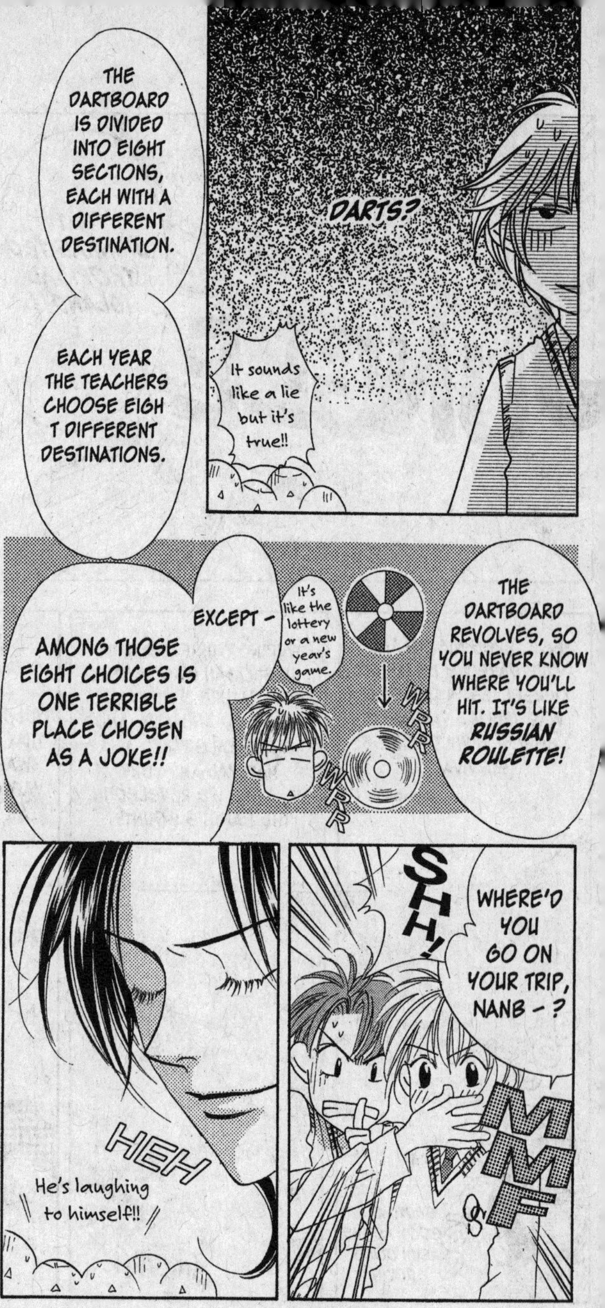
DARTS?
It sounds like a lie but it's true!!
THE DARTBOARD IS DIVIDED INTO EIGHT SECTIONS, EACH WITH A DIFFERENT DESTINATION.
EACH YEAR THE TEACHERS CHOOSE EIGH T DIFFERENT DESTINATIONS.
THE DARTBOARD REVOLVES, SO YOU NEVER KNOW WHERE YOU'LL HIT. IT'S LIKE RUSSIAN ROULETTE!
WRR
WRR
It's like the lottery or a new year's game.
EXCEPT -
AMONG THOSE EIGHT CHOICES IS ONE TERRIBLE PLACE CHOSEN AS A JOKE!!
WHERE'D YOU GO ON YOUR TRIP, NANB - ?
SHH!
MMF
HEH
He's laughing to himself!!

Whispered Secrets

FIGURE SKATING AGAIN

ALONG WITH CANDELORO, I'M ALSO WATCHING RUSSIA'S ILIA KULIK!! ILIA'S REALLY CUTE. IF CANDELORO IS A "GIGOLO ON ICE," THEN HE'S A "PRINCE ON ICE." (THAT'S WHAT NHK TV CALLS THEM.) THE WAY HE SKATES IS REALLY ARISTOCRATIC!! YEAH!! WHEN HE STAYS IN THE RINK TOO LONG, HIS CHEEKS GET RED AND IT'S SO CUTE! ♥ HE LOOKS REALLY GOOD IN FLOWING, FRILLY COSTUMES. AND HIS SKATING TECHNIQUE IS PERFECT!! HE LOOKS SO COOL WHEN HE DOES THOSE GRACEFUL MOVES WITH SO LITTLE EFFORT!! I LOVE HIM!!

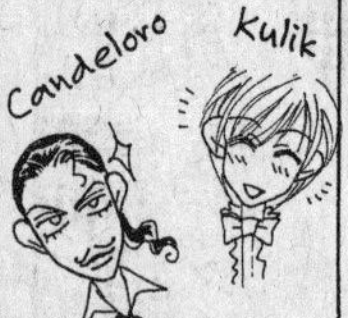
Candeloro
Kulik

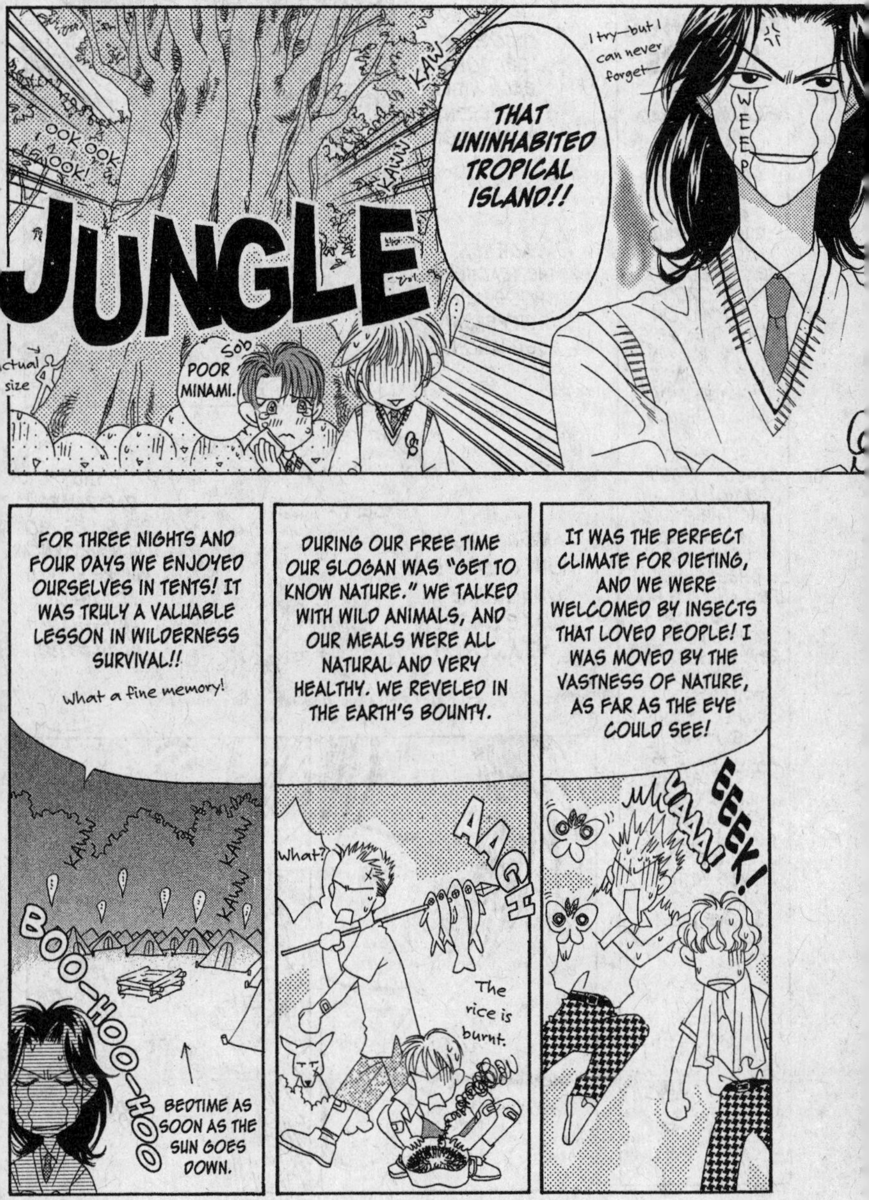
I try—but I can never forget—
WEEP
THAT UNINHABITED TROPICAL ISLAND!!
KAW
KAWW
OOK OOK OOK!
JUNGLE
Sob
POOR MINAMI.
ctual size
IT WAS THE PERFECT CLIMATE FOR DIETING, AND WE WERE WELCOMED BY INSECTS THAT LOVED PEOPLE! I WAS MOVED BY THE VASTNESS OF NATURE, AS FAR AS THE EYE COULD SEE!
EEEEK!
YAAAA!
DURING OUR FREE TIME OUR SLOGAN WAS "GET TO KNOW NATURE." WE TALKED WITH WILD ANIMALS, AND OUR MEALS WERE ALL NATURAL AND VERY HEALTHY. WE REVELED IN THE EARTH'S BOUNTY.
AAGH
What?
The rice is burnt.
FOR THREE NIGHTS AND FOUR DAYS WE ENJOYED OURSELVES IN TENTS! IT WAS TRULY A VALUABLE LESSON IN WILDERNESS SURVIVAL!!
What a fine memory!
KAWW
KAWW
BOO-HOO-HOO-HOO
BEDTIME AS SOON AS THE SUN GOES DOWN.

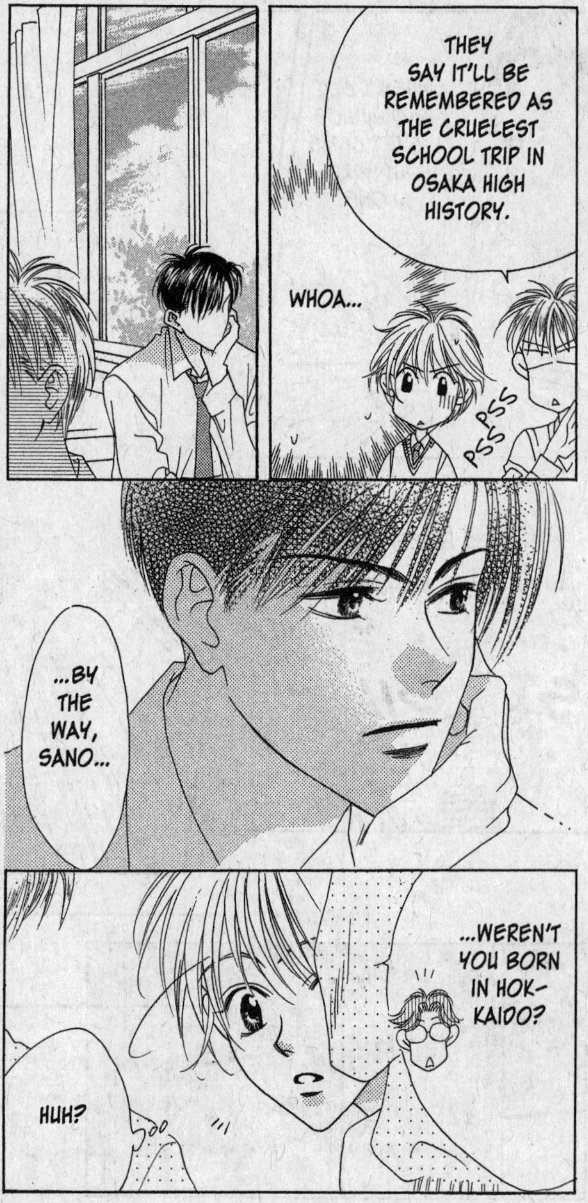
THEY SAY IT'LL BE REMEMBERED AS THE CRUELEST SCHOOL TRIP IN OSAKA HIGH HISTORY.
WHOA...
PSS PSS
...BY THE WAY, SANO...
...WEREN'T YOU BORN IN HOK-KAIDO?
HUH?

Whispered Secrets

ARRIVING IN TAIWAN

HANA-KIMI JUST CAME OUT IN TAIWAN! ✿ IN TAIWAN, THE TITLE OF "HANA-KIMI" IS "TO TO AI JA NI." APPARENTLY IT MEANS SOMETHING LIKE "I LOVE YOU FROM THE BOTTOM OF MY HEART" (I'M NOT REALLY SURE). IT FEELS DIFFERENT AND NEW TO SEE "HANA-KIMI" IN ANOTHER LANGUAGE!! IT'S WRITTEN IN KANJI, SO I CAN SORT OF GUESS THE MEANING, WHICH IS FUN. ✿ WHAT I REALLY NOTICED WAS THE SOUND EFFECTS. SOUND EFFECTS ARE DIFFERENT IN EVERY LANGUAGE. IN TAIWAN, "GOSO" (THE SOUND OF RUSTLING) IS "MO SA KU" AND "SHIIN" (THE SOUND OF SILENCE) IS "SEI." "PORO PORO," THE SOUND OF TEARS, IS "RIU RUI RIU RUI." APPARENTLY, THE KANJI THEY USE FOR THE SOUND EFFECTS HAVE SOME INHERENT MEANING.

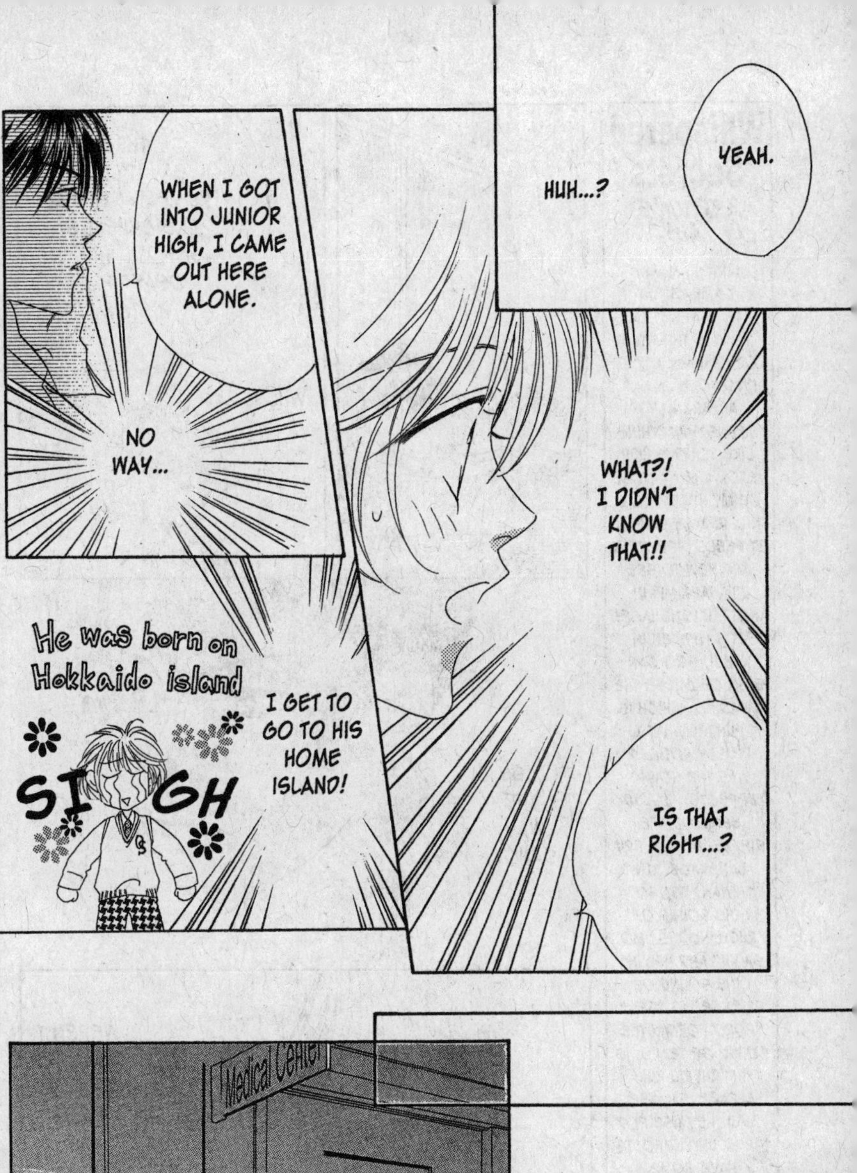
YEAH.
HUH...?
WHAT?! I DIDN'T KNOW THAT!!
IS THAT RIGHT...?
WHEN I GOT INTO JUNIOR HIGH, I CAME OUT HERE ALONE.
NO WAY...
He was born on Hokkaido island
I GET TO GO TO HIS HOME ISLAND!
SIGH
Medical Center

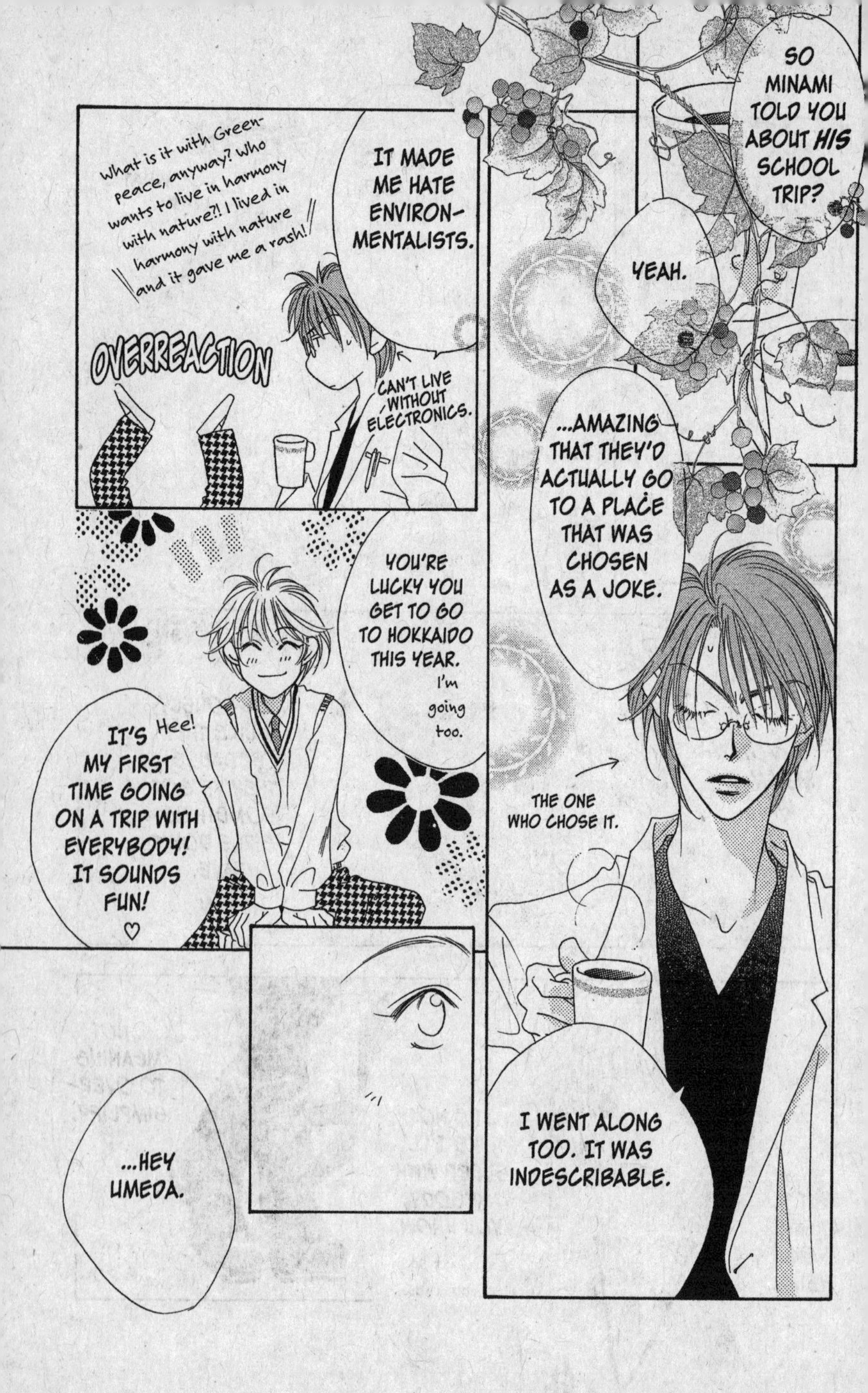
SO MINAMI TOLD YOU ABOUT *HIS* SCHOOL TRIP?
YEAH.
...AMAZING THAT THEY'D ACTUALLY GO TO A PLACE THAT WAS CHOSEN AS A JOKE.
THE ONE WHO CHOSE IT.
I WENT ALONG TOO. IT WAS INDESCRIBABLE.
IT MADE ME HATE ENVIRONMENTALISTS.
What is it with Greenpeace, anyway? Who wants to live in harmony with nature?! I lived in harmony with nature and it gave me a rash!
OVERREACTION
CAN'T LIVE WITHOUT ELECTRONICS.
YOU'RE LUCKY YOU GET TO GO TO HOKKAIDO THIS YEAR.
I'm going too.
Hee!
IT'S MY FIRST TIME GOING ON A TRIP WITH EVERYBODY! IT SOUNDS FUN! ♡
...HEY UMEDA.

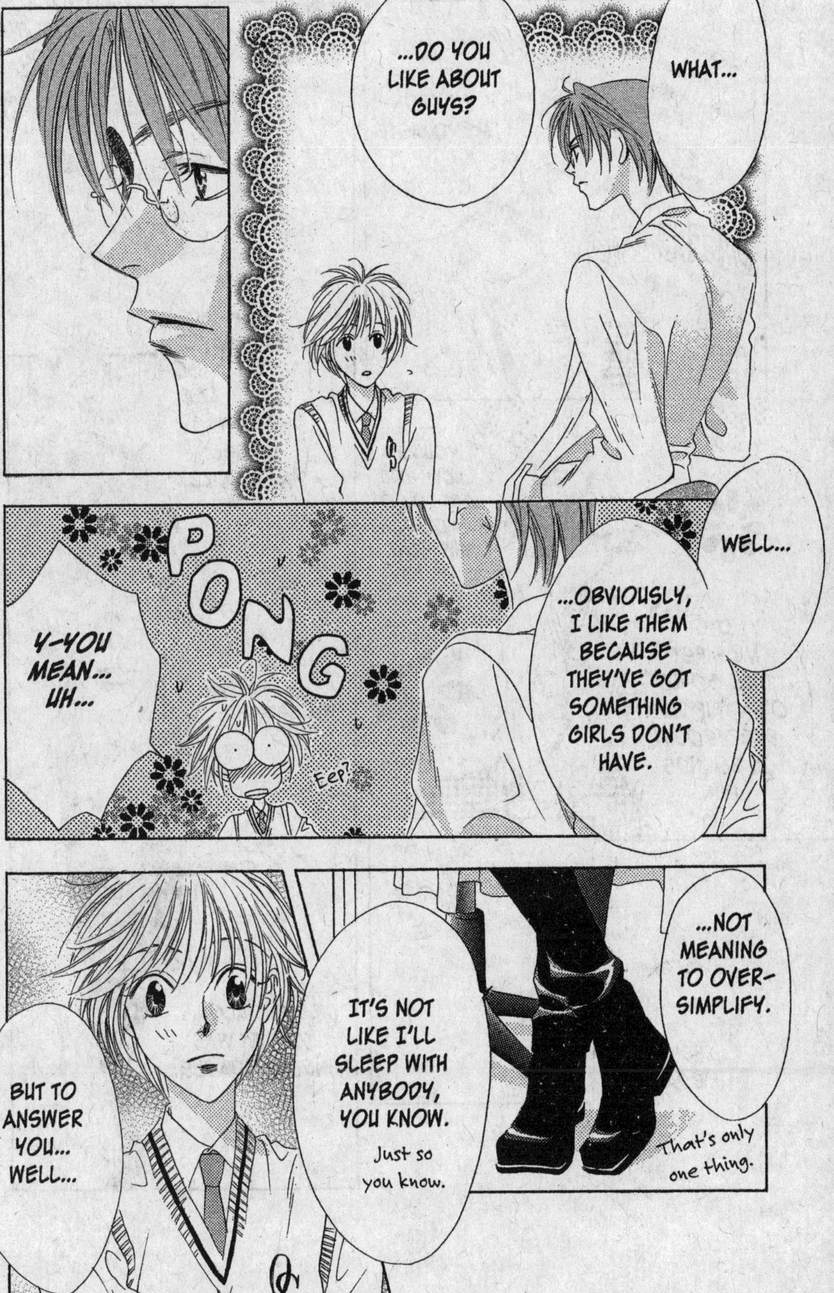

WHAT...
...DO YOU LIKE ABOUT GUYS?
WELL...
...OBVIOUSLY, I LIKE THEM BECAUSE THEY'VE GOT SOMETHING GIRLS DON'T HAVE.
PONG
Eep?
Y-YOU MEAN... UH...
...NOT MEANING TO OVER-SIMPLIFY.
That's only one thing.
IT'S NOT LIKE I'LL SLEEP WITH ANYBODY, YOU KNOW.
Just so you know.
BUT TO ANSWER YOU... WELL...

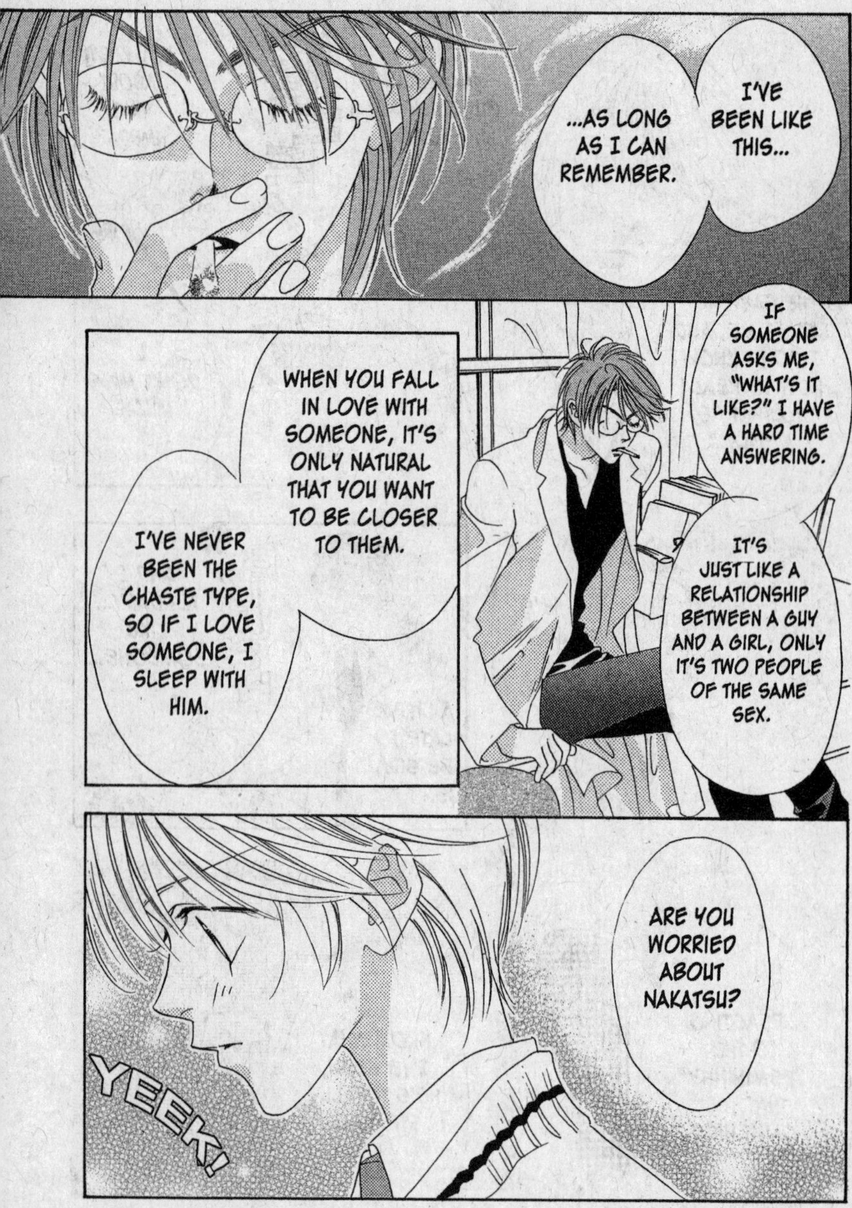
I'VE BEEN LIKE THIS...
...AS LONG AS I CAN REMEMBER.
IF SOMEONE ASKS ME, "WHAT'S IT LIKE?" I HAVE A HARD TIME ANSWERING.
IT'S JUST LIKE A RELATIONSHIP BETWEEN A GUY AND A GIRL, ONLY IT'S TWO PEOPLE OF THE SAME SEX.
WHEN YOU FALL IN LOVE WITH SOMEONE, IT'S ONLY NATURAL THAT YOU WANT TO BE CLOSER TO THEM.
I'VE NEVER BEEN THE CHASTE TYPE, SO IF I LOVE SOMEONE, I SLEEP WITH HIM.
ARE YOU WORRIED ABOUT NAKATSU?
YEEK!

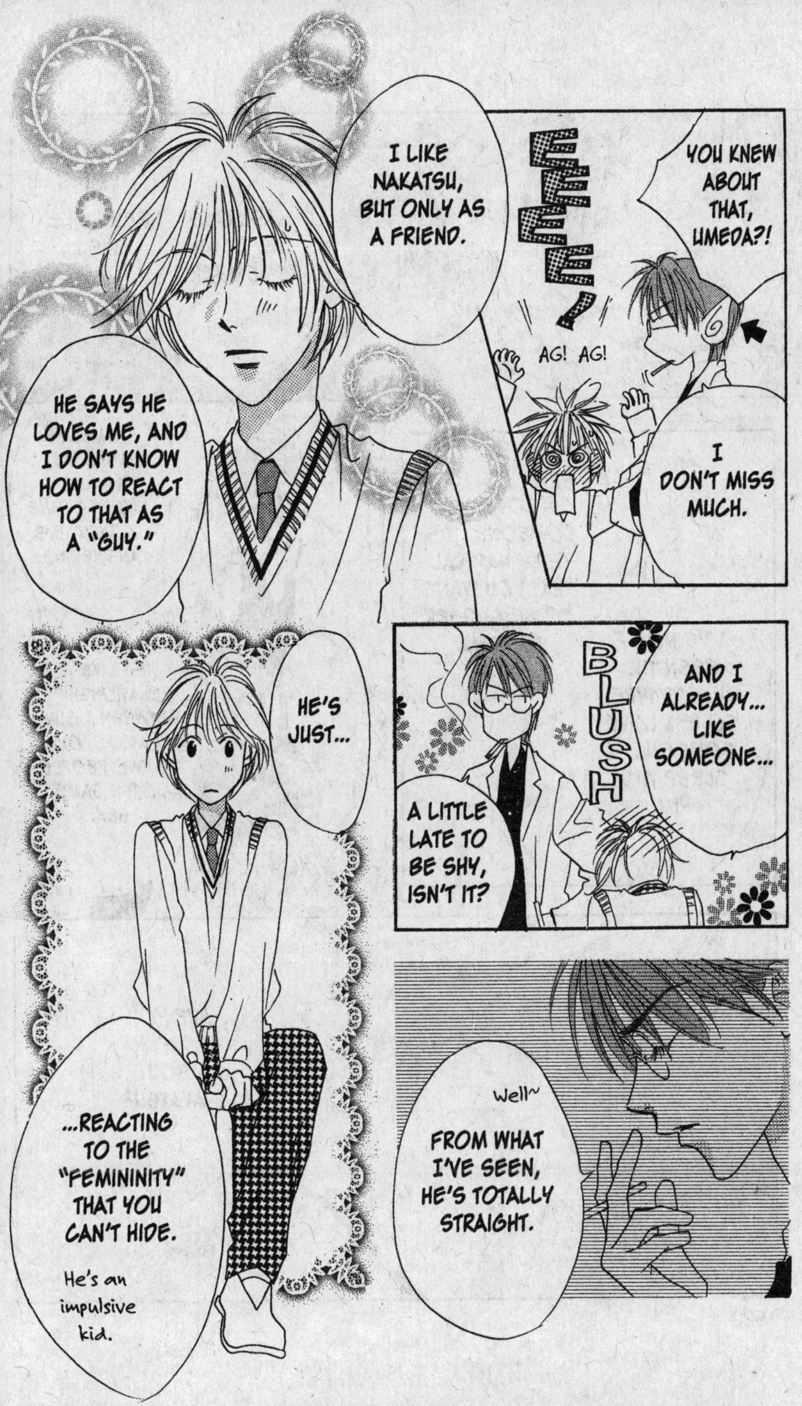
YOU KNEW ABOUT THAT, UMEDA?!
EEEE?
AG! AG!
I DON'T MISS MUCH.
I LIKE NAKATSU, BUT ONLY AS A FRIEND.
HE SAYS HE LOVES ME, AND I DON'T KNOW HOW TO REACT TO THAT AS A "GUY."
AND I ALREADY... LIKE SOMEONE...
BLUSH
A LITTLE LATE TO BE SHY, ISN'T IT?
Well~
FROM WHAT I'VE SEEN, HE'S TOTALLY STRAIGHT.
HE'S JUST...
...REACTING TO THE "FEMININITY" THAT YOU CAN'T HIDE.
He's an impulsive kid.

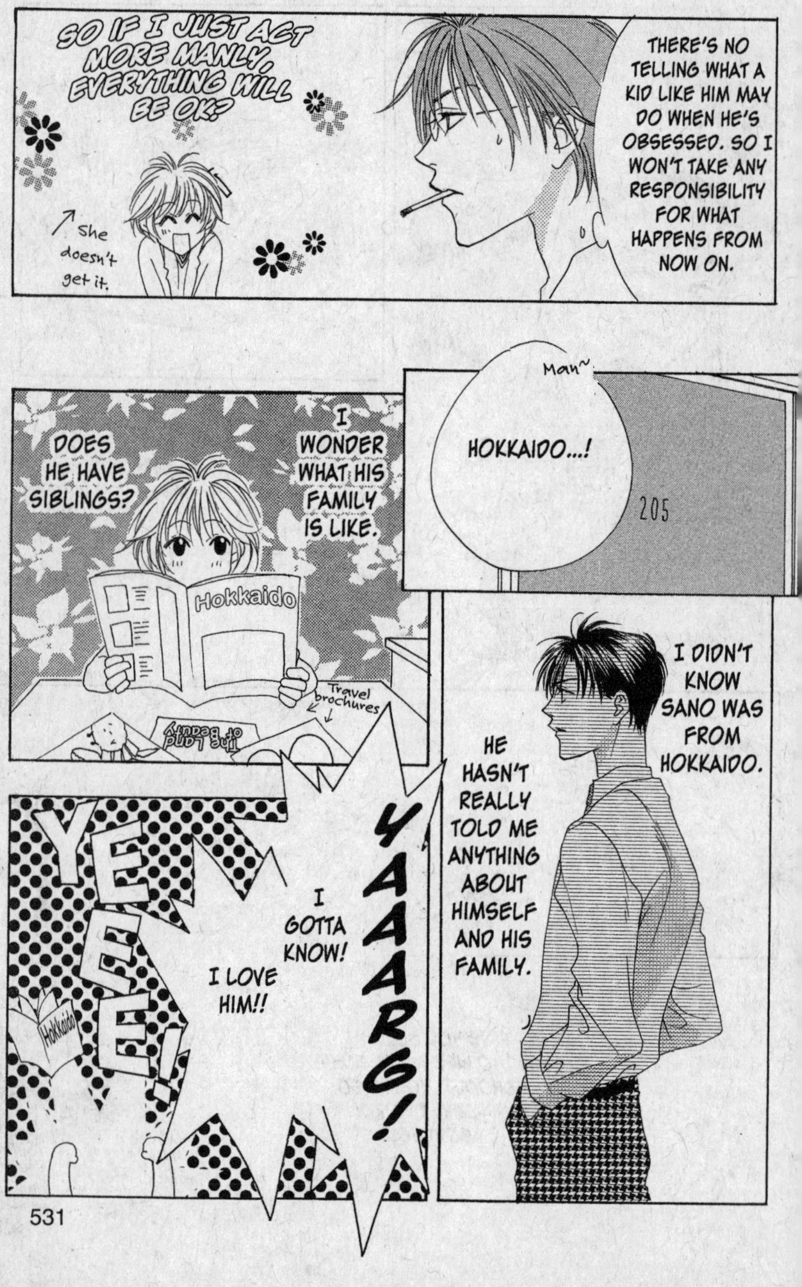
THERE'S NO TELLING WHAT A KID LIKE HIM MAY DO WHEN HE'S OBSESSED. SO I WON'T TAKE ANY RESPONSIBILITY FOR WHAT HAPPENS FROM NOW ON.
SO IF I JUST ACT MORE MANLY, EVERYTHING WILL BE OK?
She doesn't get it.
Man~
HOKKAIDO...!
205
I DIDN'T KNOW SANO WAS FROM HOKKAIDO.
HE HASN'T REALLY TOLD ME ANYTHING ABOUT HIMSELF AND HIS FAMILY.
I WONDER WHAT HIS FAMILY IS LIKE.
DOES HE HAVE SIBLINGS?
Hokkaido
Travel brochures
The Land of Beauty
YAAARG!
I GOTTA KNOW!
I LOVE HIM!!
YEEEE!
Hokkaido

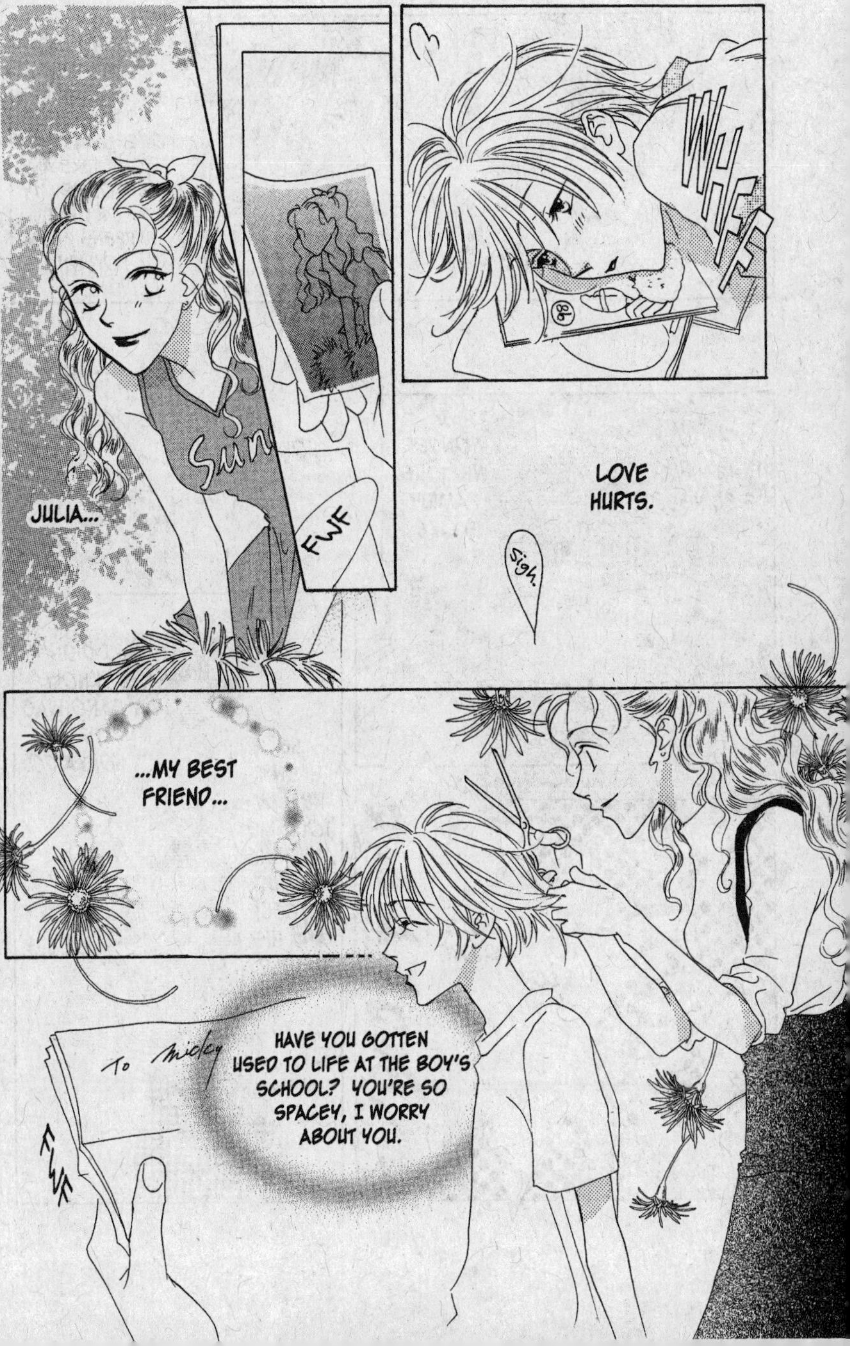
WHFF
LOVE HURTS.
Sigh.
FWF
JULIA...
...MY BEST FRIEND...
HAVE YOU GOTTEN USED TO LIFE AT THE BOY'S SCHOOL? YOU'RE SO SPACEY, I WORRY ABOUT YOU.
To Micky
FWF

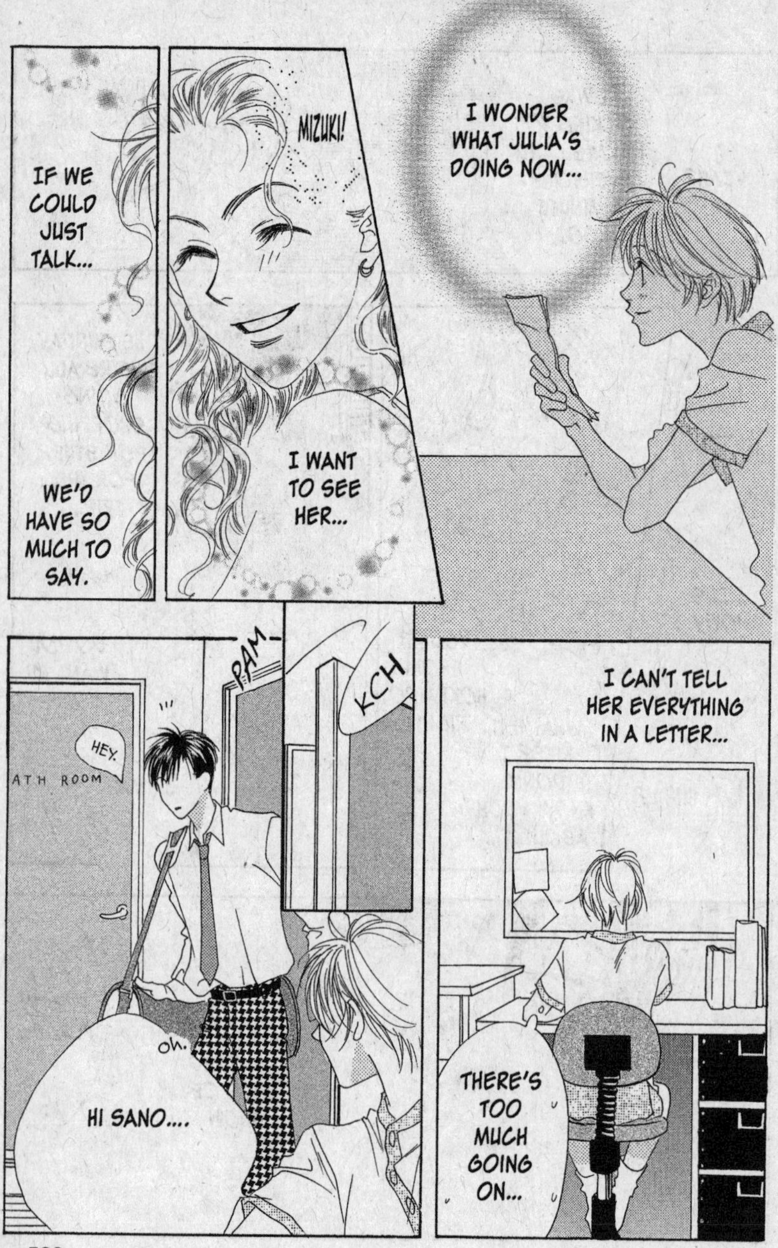
I WONDER WHAT JULIA'S DOING NOW...
MIZUKI!
I WANT TO SEE HER...
IF WE COULD JUST TALK...
WE'D HAVE SO MUCH TO SAY.
I CAN'T TELL HER EVERYTHING IN A LETTER...
THERE'S TOO MUCH GOING ON...
KCH
PAM
HEY.
ATH ROOM
oh.
HI SANO....

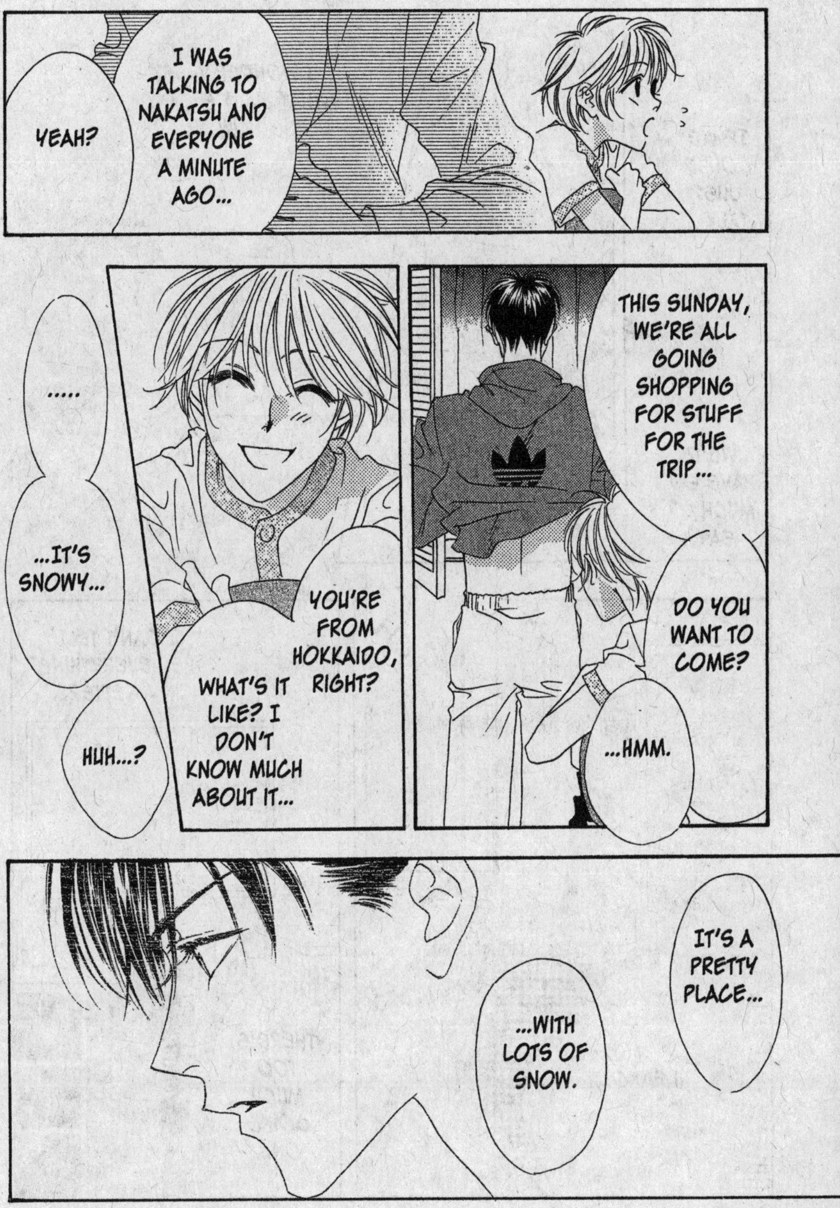
I WAS TALKING TO NAKATSU AND EVERYONE A MINUTE AGO...
YEAH?
THIS SUNDAY, WE'RE ALL GOING SHOPPING FOR STUFF FOR THE TRIP...
DO YOU WANT TO COME?
...HMM.
.....
YOU'RE FROM HOKKAIDO, RIGHT?
WHAT'S IT LIKE? I DON'T KNOW MUCH ABOUT IT...
...IT'S SNOWY...
HUH...?
IT'S A PRETTY PLACE...
...WITH LOTS OF SNOW.

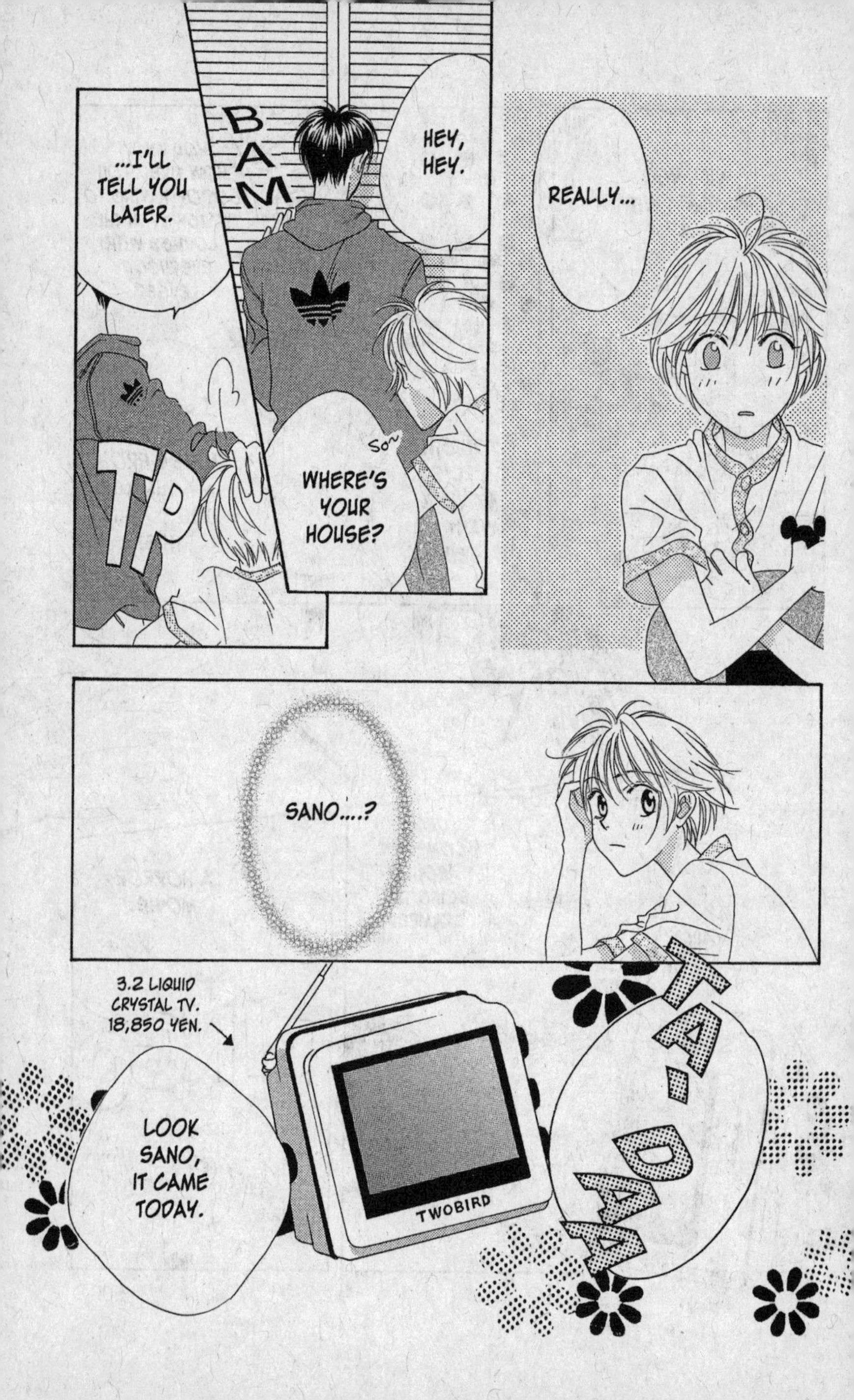
REALLY...
HEY, HEY.
BAM
SO~
WHERE'S YOUR HOUSE?
...I'LL TELL YOU LATER.
TP
SANO....?
TA-DAA
3.2 LIQUID CRYSTAL TV. 18,850 YEN.
TWOBIRD
LOOK SANO, IT CAME TODAY.

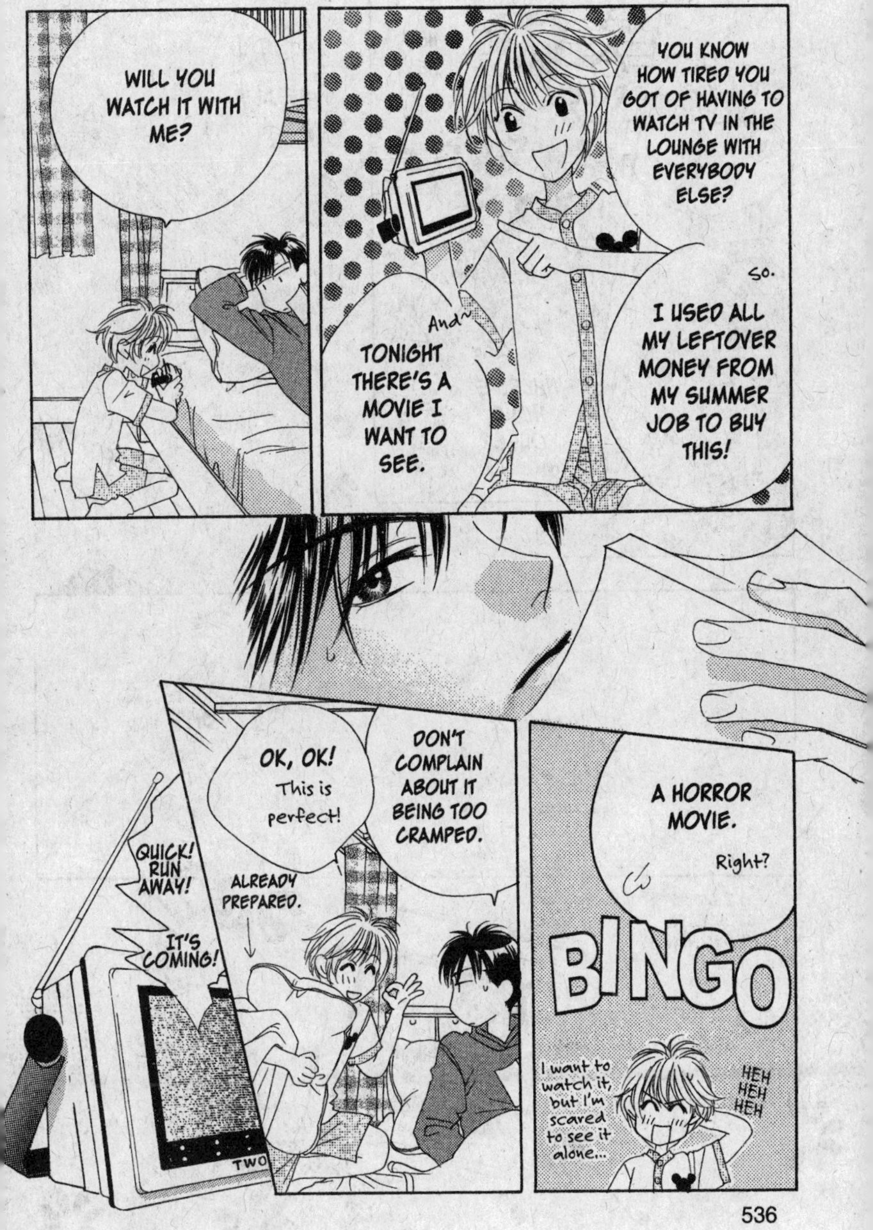
YOU KNOW HOW TIRED YOU GOT OF HAVING TO WATCH TV IN THE LOUNGE WITH EVERYBODY ELSE?
So.
I USED ALL MY LEFTOVER MONEY FROM MY SUMMER JOB TO BUY THIS!
And~
TONIGHT THERE'S A MOVIE I WANT TO SEE.
WILL YOU WATCH IT WITH ME?
A HORROR MOVIE.
Right?
BINGO
HEH HEH HEH
I want to watch it, but I'm scared to see it alone...
DON'T COMPLAIN ABOUT IT BEING TOO CRAMPED.
OK, OK! This is perfect!
ALREADY PREPARED.
QUICK! RUN AWAY!
IT'S COMING!
TWO

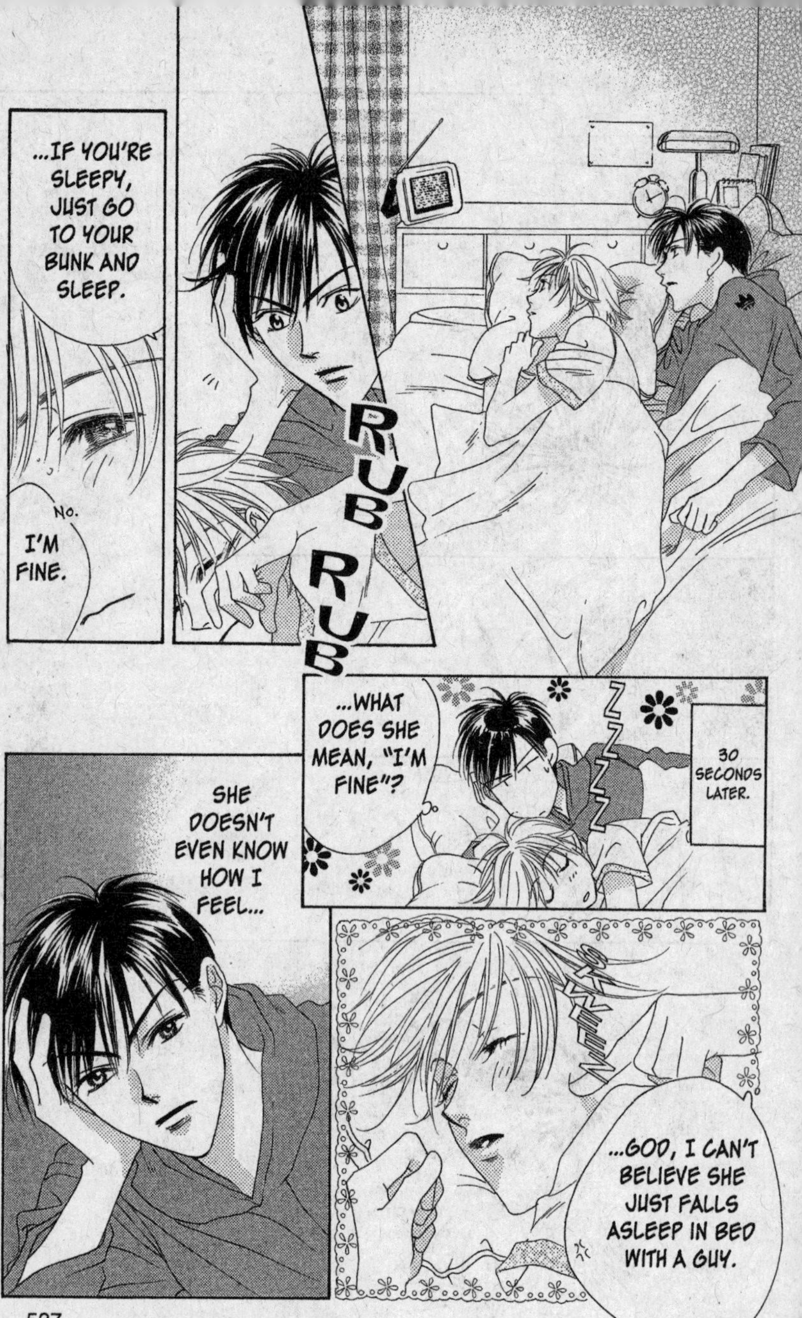
RUB RUB
...IF YOU'RE SLEEPY, JUST GO TO YOUR BUNK AND SLEEP.
NO.
I'M FINE.
30 SECONDS LATER.
ZZZZ
...WHAT DOES SHE MEAN, "I'M FINE"?
...GOD, I CAN'T BELIEVE SHE JUST FALLS ASLEEP IN BED WITH A GUY.
SHE DOESN'T EVEN KNOW HOW I FEEL...

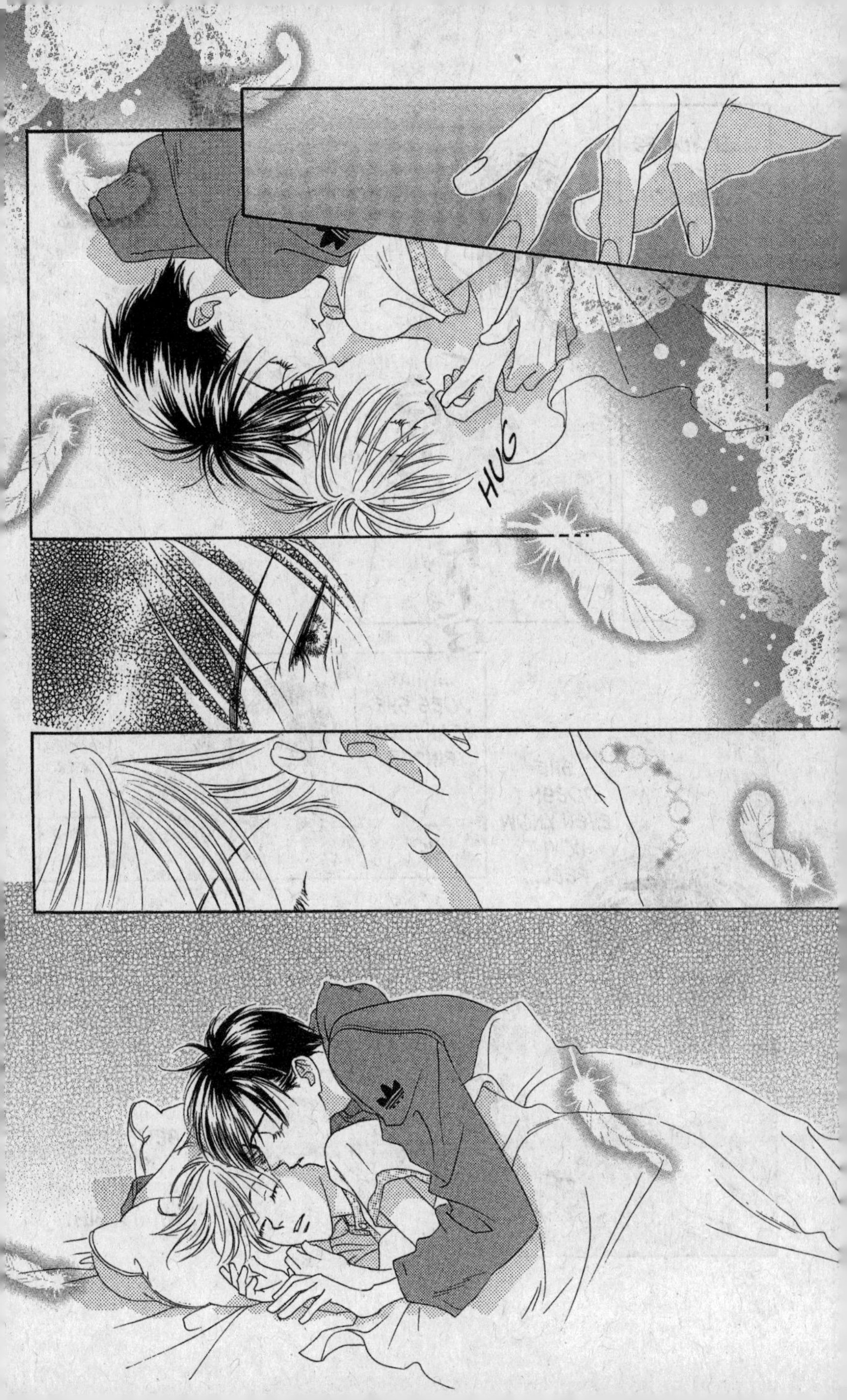
HUG

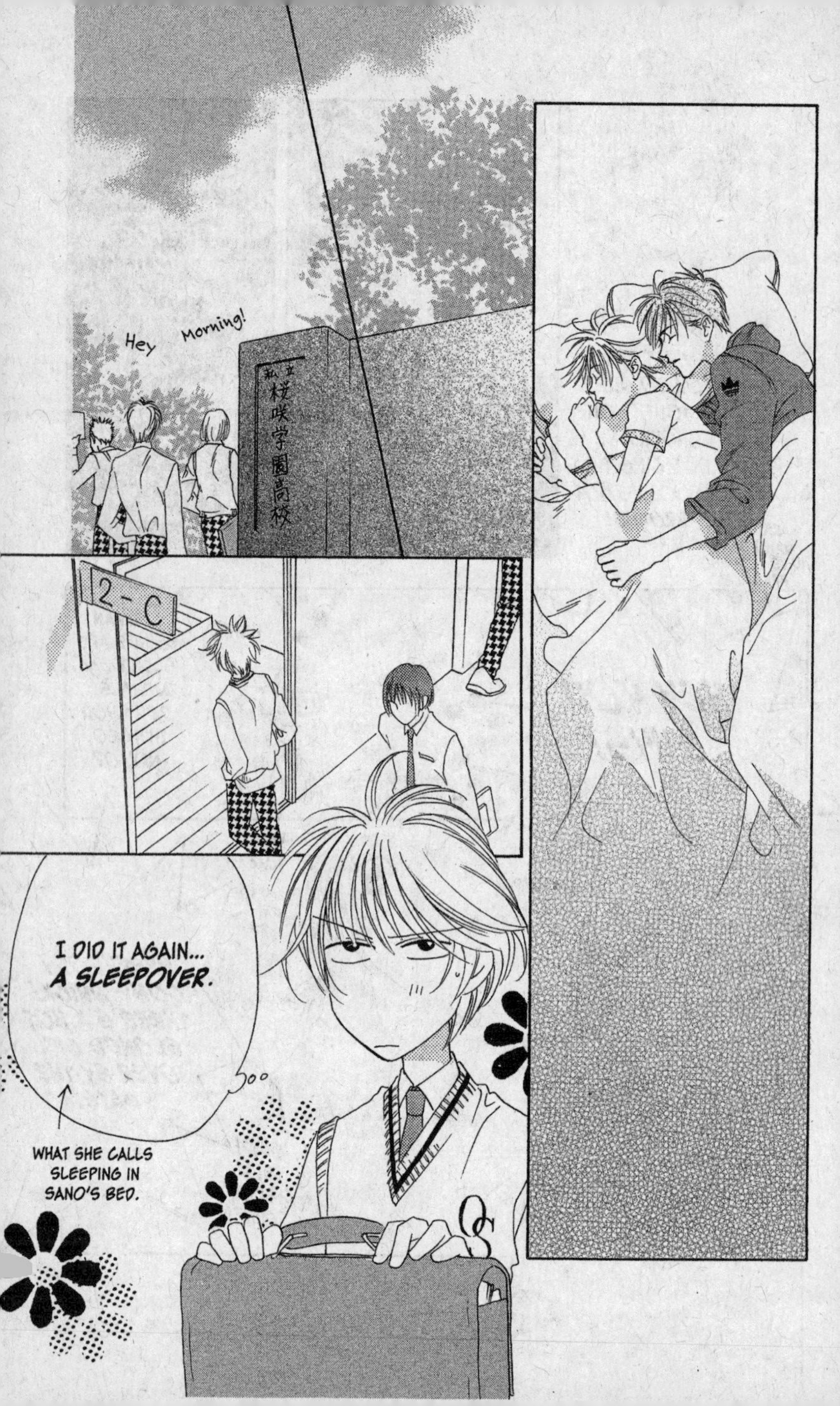
Morning!
Hey
私立 桜咲学園高校
2-C
I DID IT AGAIN... A SLEEPOVER.
WHAT SHE CALLS SLEEPING IN SANO'S BED.

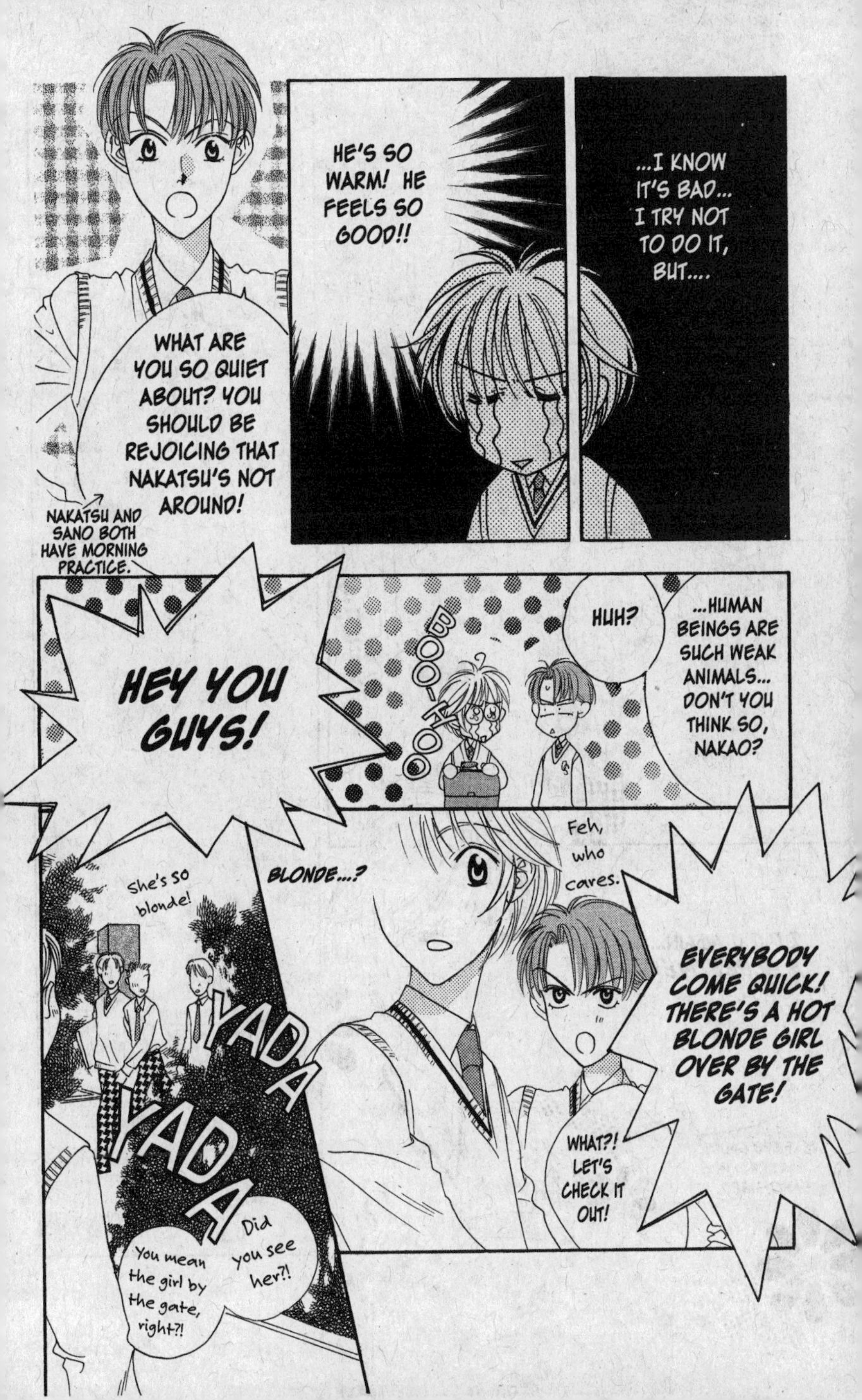
...I KNOW IT'S BAD... I TRY NOT TO DO IT, BUT....
HE'S SO WARM! HE FEELS SO GOOD!!
WHAT ARE YOU SO QUIET ABOUT? YOU SHOULD BE REJOICING THAT NAKATSU'S NOT AROUND!
NAKATSU AND SANO BOTH HAVE MORNING PRACTICE.
...HUMAN BEINGS ARE SUCH WEAK ANIMALS... DON'T YOU THINK SO, NAKAO?
HUH?
BOO-HOO
HEY YOU GUYS!
EVERYBODY COME QUICK! THERE'S A HOT BLONDE GIRL OVER BY THE GATE!
Feh, who cares.
WHAT?! LET'S CHECK IT OUT!
BLONDE...?
She's so blonde!
YADA YADA
Did you see her?!
You mean the girl by the gate, right?!

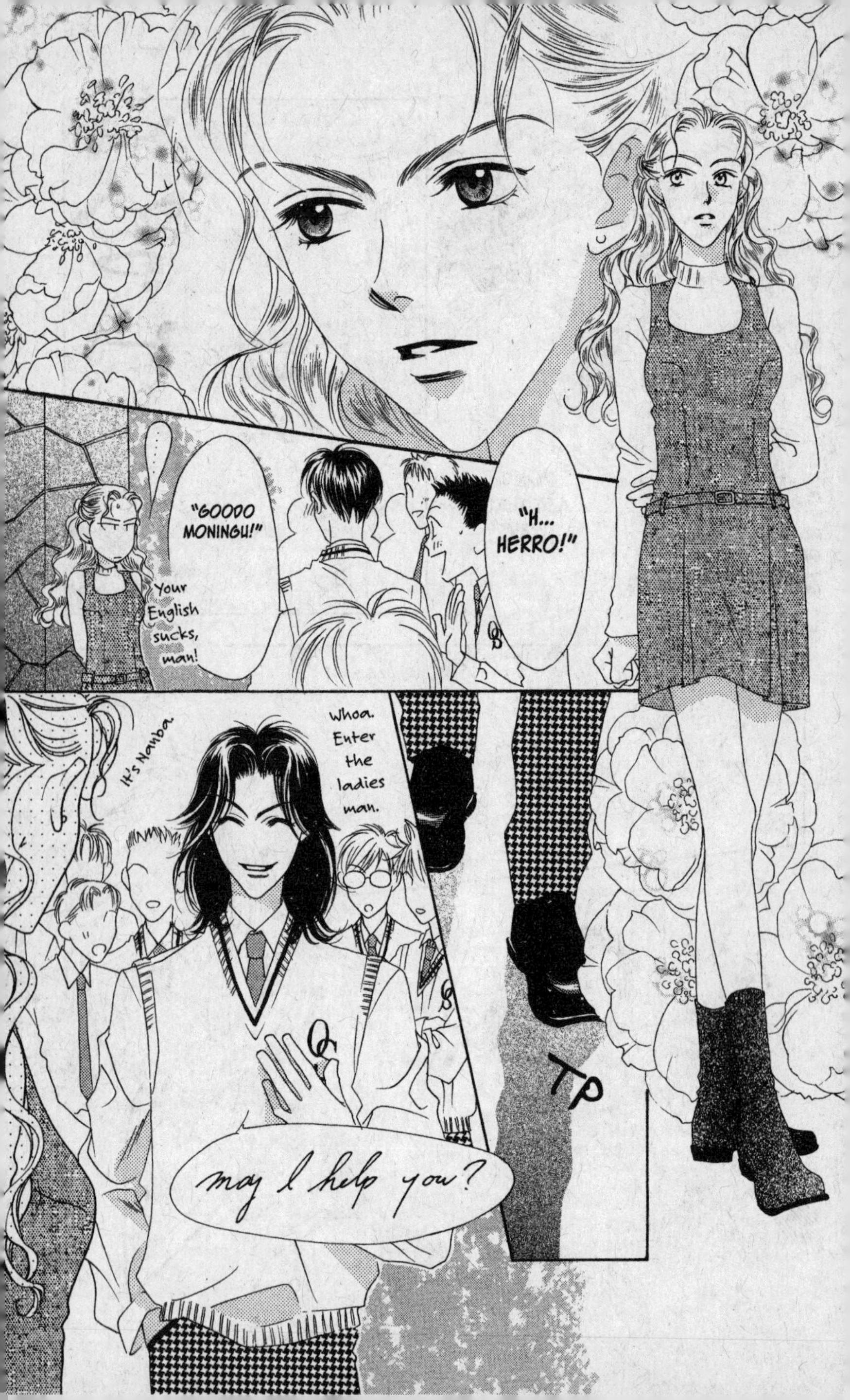
"H... HERRO!"
"GOODO MONINGU!"
Your English sucks, man!
TP
Whoa. Enter the ladies man.
It's Nanba.
may I help you?

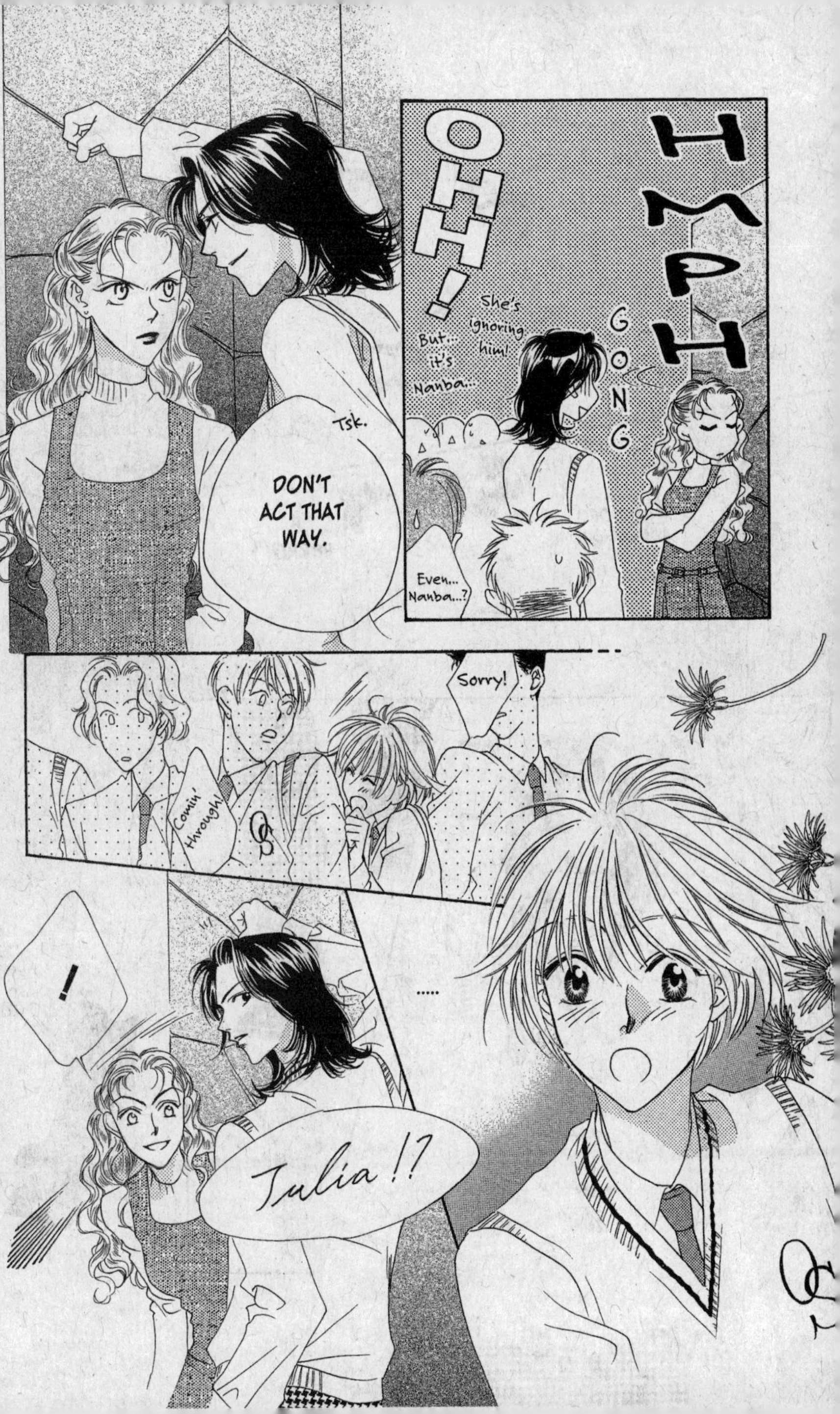
HMPH
OHH!
She's ignoring him!
But... it's Nanba...
GONG
Even... Nanba...?
Tsk.
DON'T ACT THAT WAY.
Sorry!
Comin' through!
.....
!
Julia!?

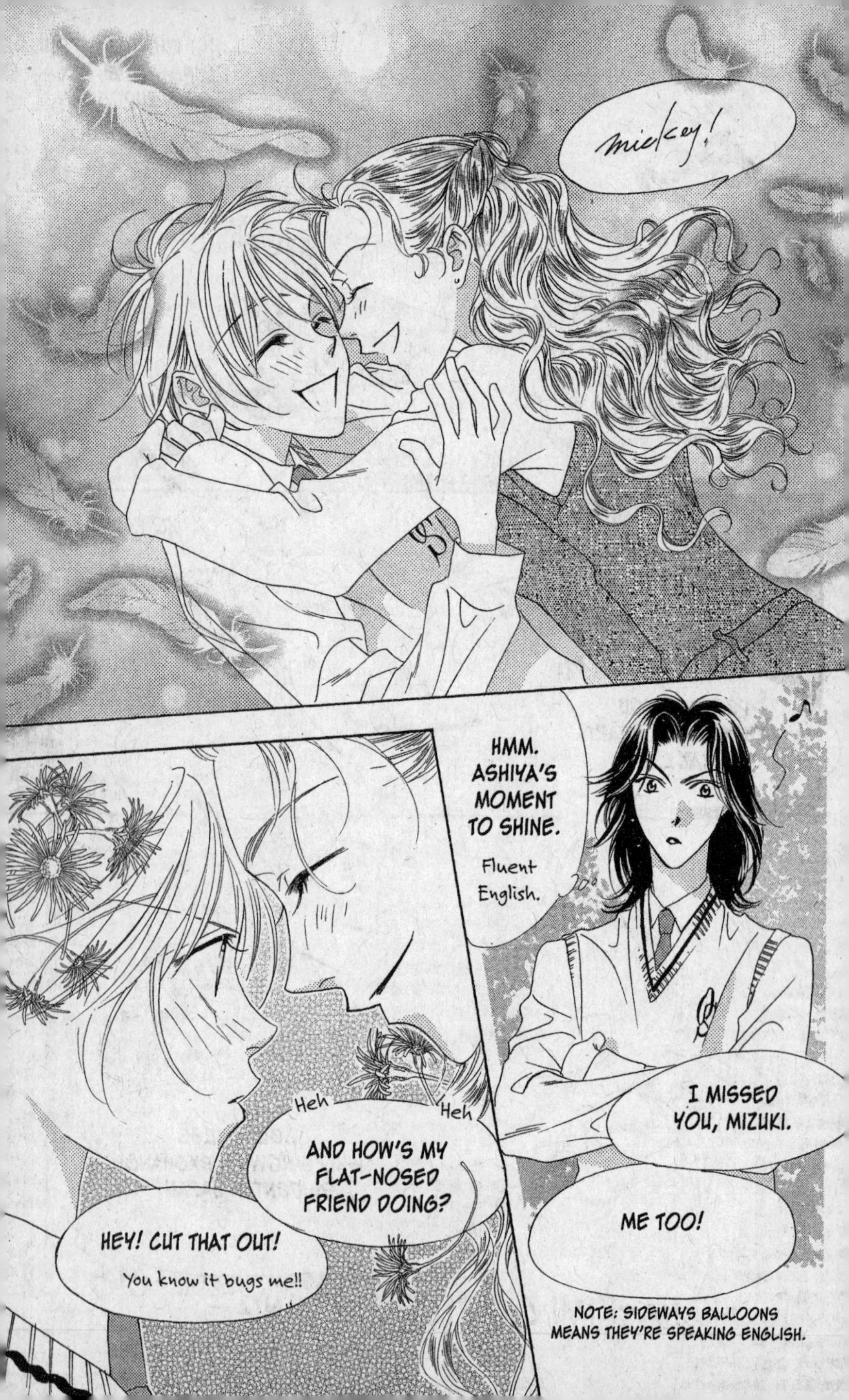
mickey!
HMM. ASHIYA'S MOMENT TO SHINE.
Fluent English.
I MISSED YOU, MIZUKI.
ME TOO!
Heh Heh
AND HOW'S MY FLAT-NOSED FRIEND DOING?
HEY! CUT THAT OUT!
You know it bugs me!!
NOTE: SIDEWAYS BALLOONS MEANS THEY'RE SPEAKING ENGLISH.

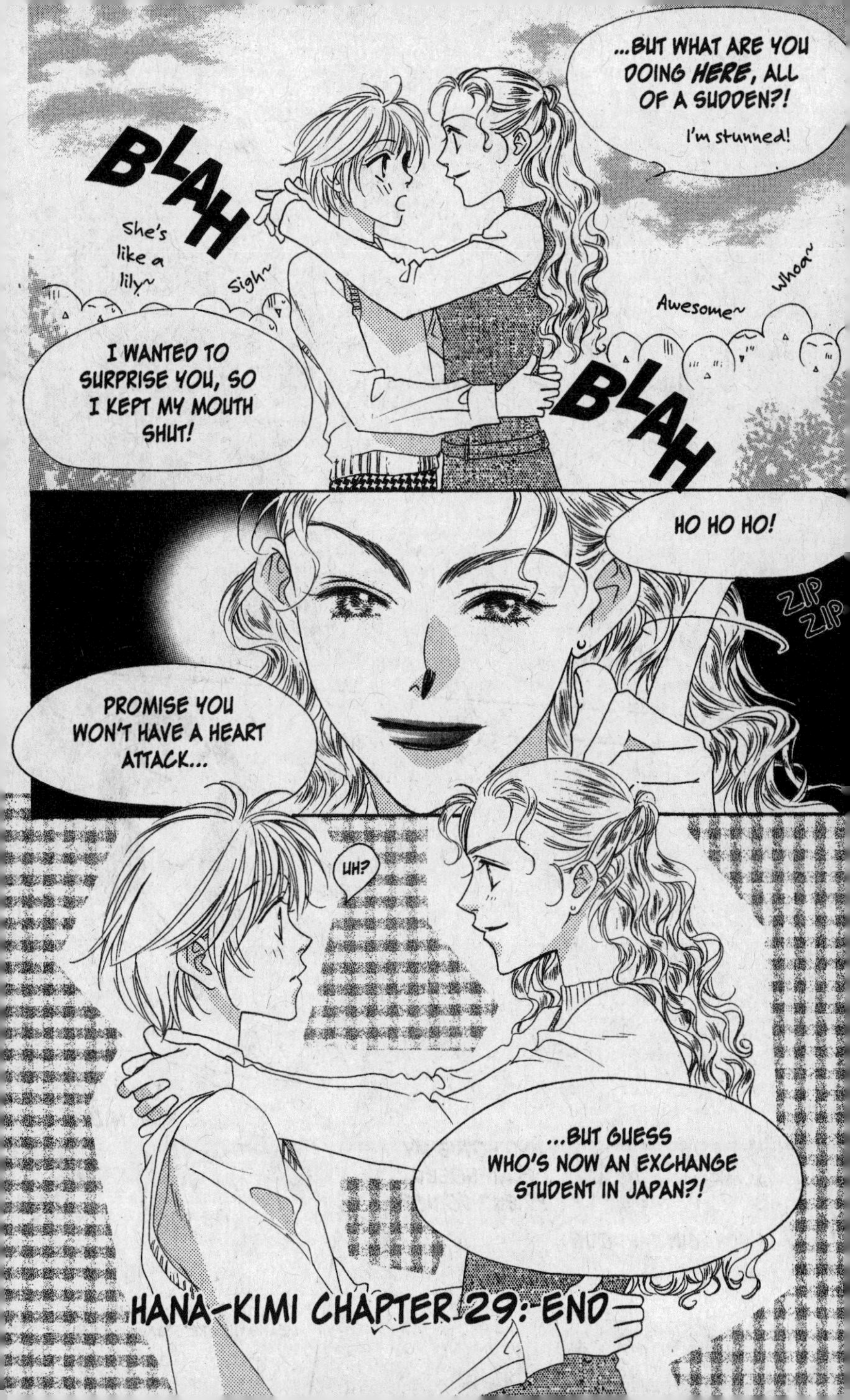
...BUT WHAT ARE YOU DOING *HERE*, ALL OF A SUDDEN?!
I'm stunned!
Whoa~
Awesome~
BLAH
BLAH
Sigh~
She's like a lily~
I WANTED TO SURPRISE YOU, SO I KEPT MY MOUTH SHUT!
HO HO HO!
ZIP ZIP
PROMISE YOU WON'T HAVE A HEART ATTACK...
UH?
...BUT GUESS WHO'S NOW AN EXCHANGE STUDENT IN JAPAN?!
HANA-KIMI CHAPTER 29: END

Hana-Kimi

For You in Full Blossom

CHAPTER 30

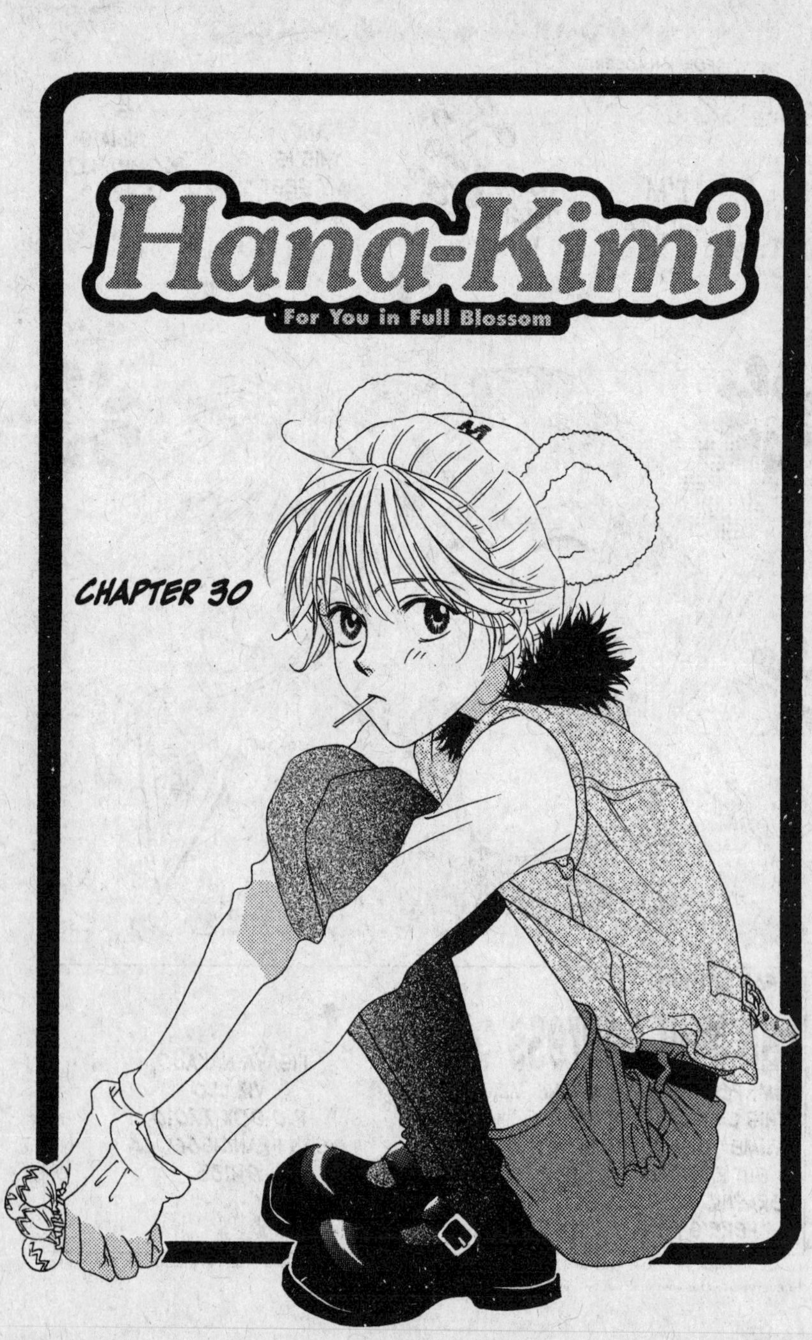

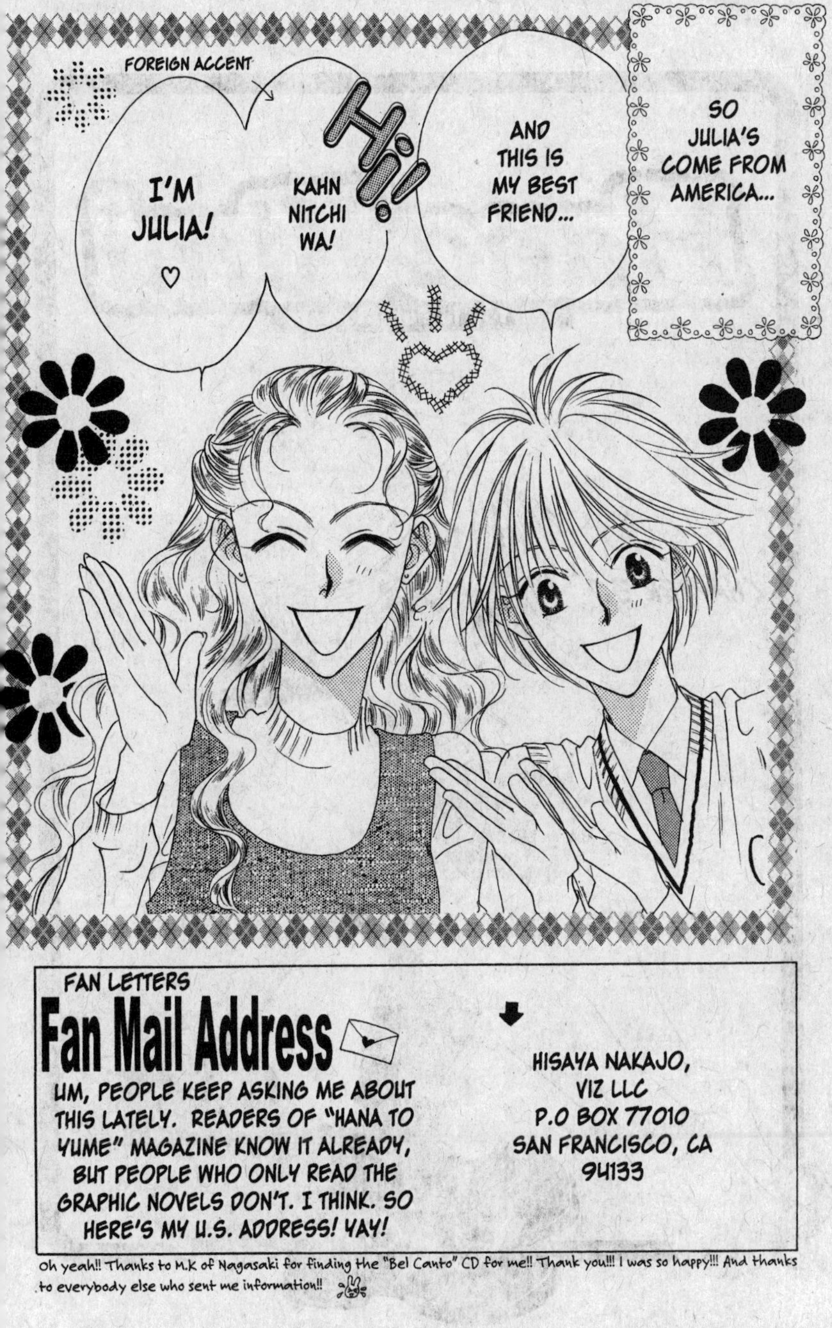
SO JULIA'S COME FROM AMERICA...
AND THIS IS MY BEST FRIEND...
HI!
KAHN NITCHI WA!
I'M JULIA! ♡
FOREIGN ACCENT

FAN LETTERS

Fan Mail Address

UM, PEOPLE KEEP ASKING ME ABOUT THIS LATELY. READERS OF "HANA TO YUME" MAGAZINE KNOW IT ALREADY, BUT PEOPLE WHO ONLY READ THE GRAPHIC NOVELS DON'T. I THINK. SO HERE'S MY U.S. ADDRESS! YAY!

HISAYA NAKAJO,
VIZ LLC
P.O BOX 77010
SAN FRANCISCO, CA
94133

Oh yeah!! Thanks to M.K of Nagasaki for finding the "Bel Canto" CD for me!! Thank you!!! I was so happy!!! And thanks to everybody else who sent me information!!

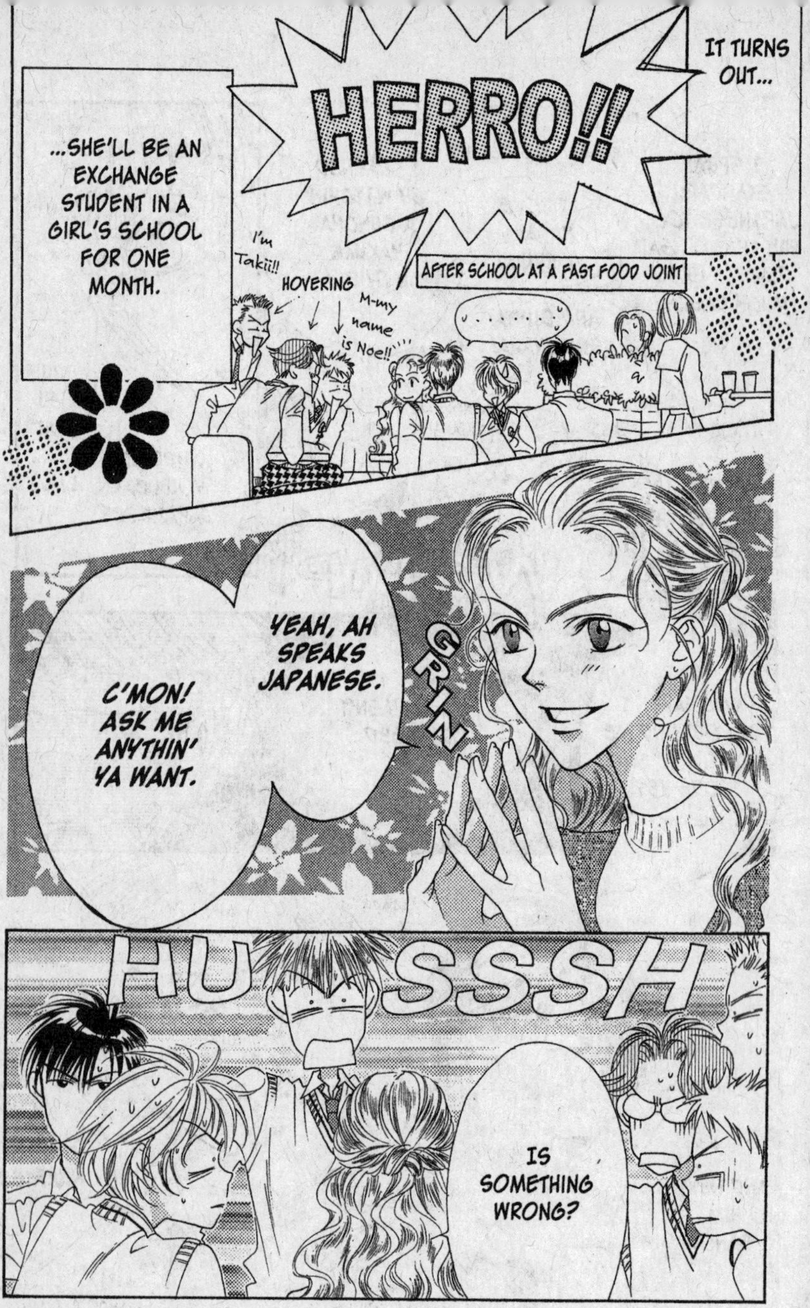
IT TURNS OUT...
HERRO!!
AFTER SCHOOL AT A FAST FOOD JOINT
...SHE'LL BE AN EXCHANGE STUDENT IN A GIRL'S SCHOOL FOR ONE MONTH.
I'm Takii!!
HOVERING
M-my name is Noe!!
GRIN
YEAH, AH SPEAKS JAPANESE.
C'MON! ASK ME ANYTHIN' YA WANT.
HUSSSH
IS SOMETHING WRONG?

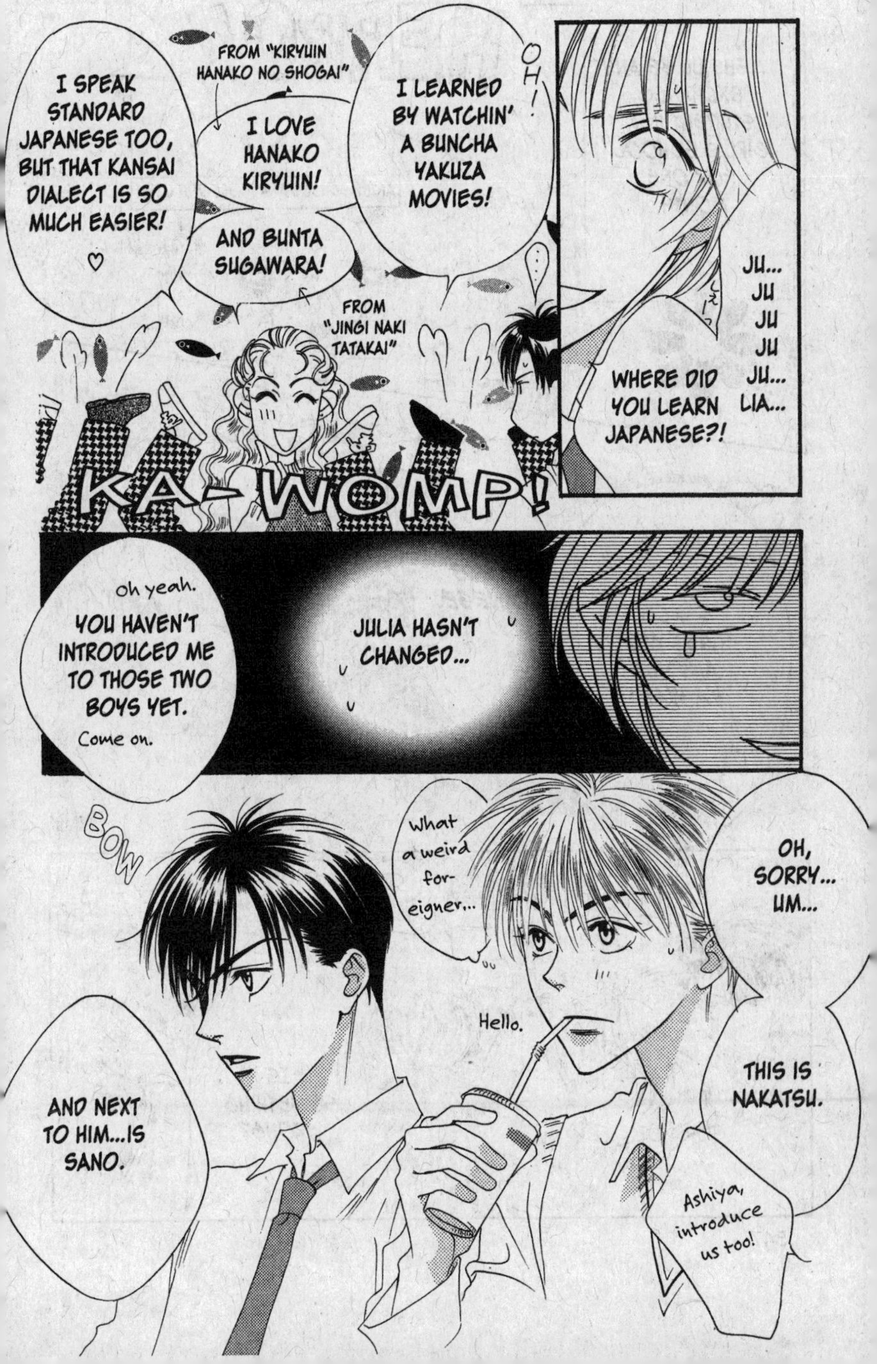
JU... JU JU JU JU... LIA...
WHERE DID YOU LEARN JAPANESE?!
OH!
I LEARNED BY WATCHIN' A BUNCHA YAKUZA MOVIES!
FROM "KIRYUIN HANAKO NO SHOGAI"
I LOVE HANAKO KIRYUIN!
AND BUNTA SUGAWARA!
FROM "JINGI NAKI TATAKAI"
I SPEAK STANDARD JAPANESE TOO, BUT THAT KANSAI DIALECT IS SO MUCH EASIER! ♡
KA-WOMP!
JULIA HASN'T CHANGED...
Oh yeah. YOU HAVEN'T INTRODUCED ME TO THOSE TWO BOYS YET. Come on.
OH, SORRY... UM...
What a weird for-eigner...
THIS IS NAKATSU.
Hello.
BOW
AND NEXT TO HIM...IS SANO.
Ashiya, introduce us too!

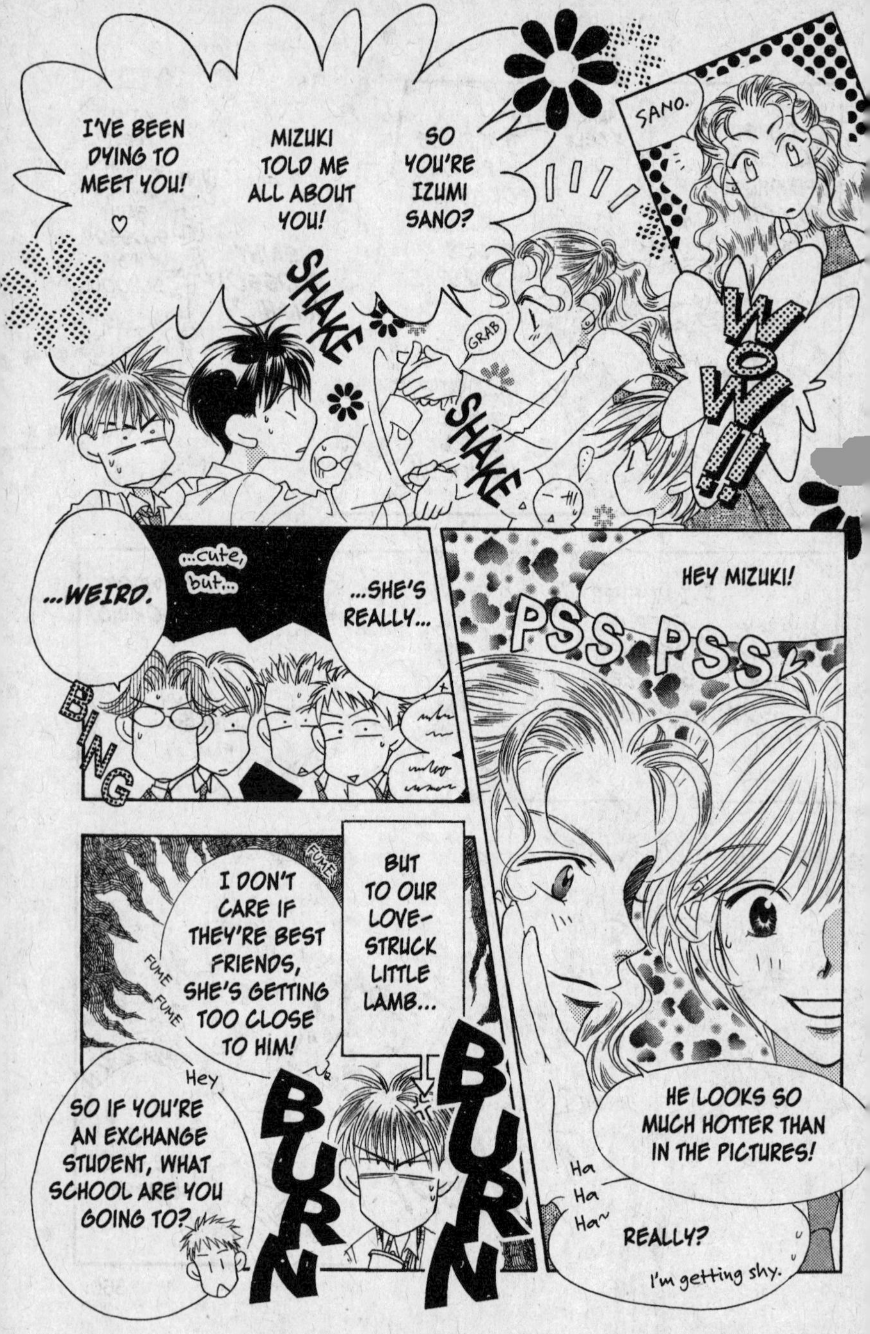
SANO.
WOW!!
SO YOU'RE IZUMI SANO?
MIZUKI TOLD ME ALL ABOUT YOU!
I'VE BEEN DYING TO MEET YOU! ♡
GRAB
SHAKE
SHAKE
HEY MIZUKI!
PSS PSS
HE LOOKS SO MUCH HOTTER THAN IN THE PICTURES!
Ha Ha Ha~
REALLY?
I'm getting shy.
...SHE'S REALLY...
...cute, but...
...WEIRD.
BING
BUT TO OUR LOVE-STRUCK LITTLE LAMB...
FUME
I DON'T CARE IF THEY'RE BEST FRIENDS, SHE'S GETTING TOO CLOSE TO HIM!
FUME
FUME
BURN
BURN
Hey
SO IF YOU'RE AN EXCHANGE STUDENT, WHAT SCHOOL ARE YOU GOING TO?

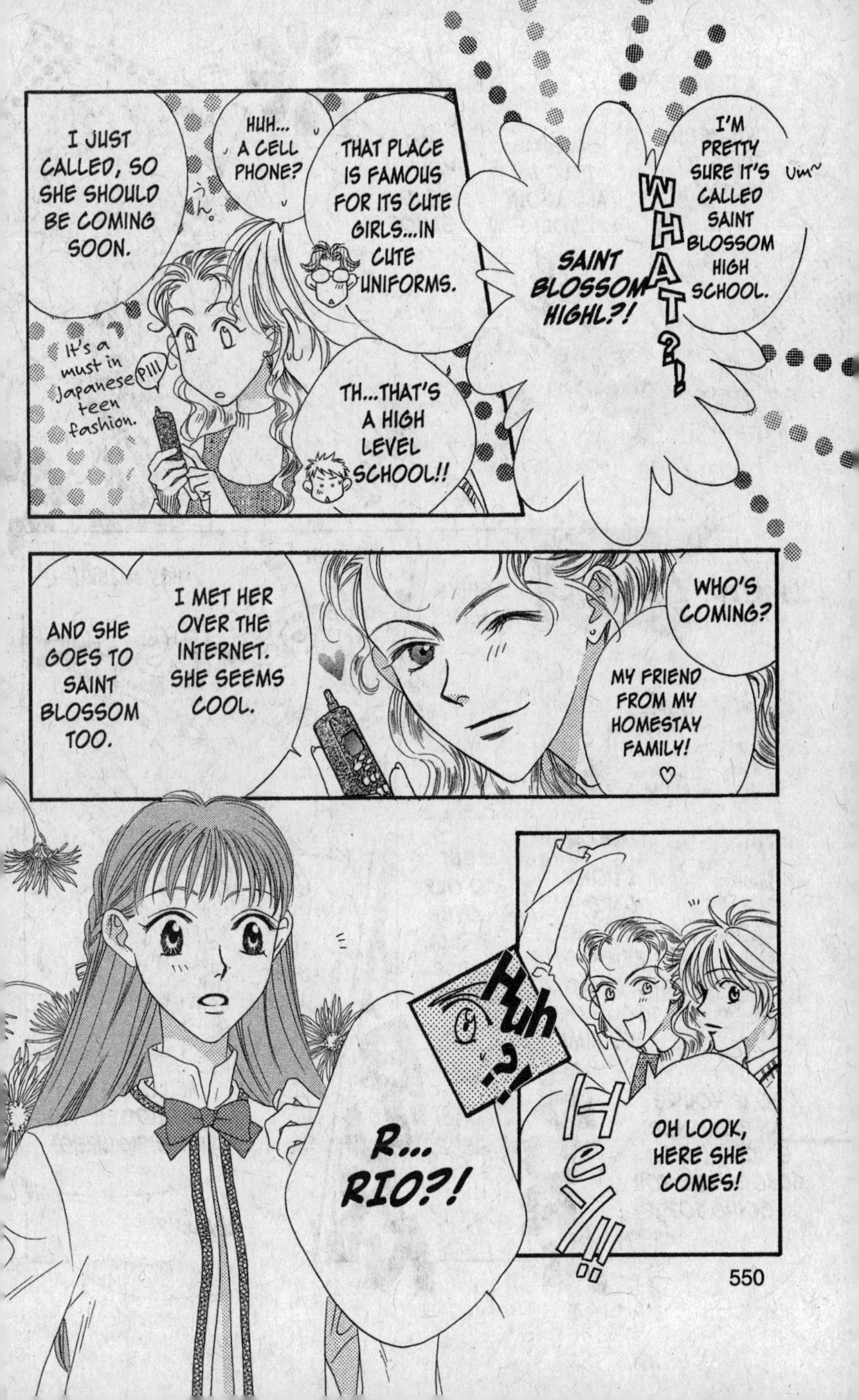
I'M PRETTY SURE IT'S CALLED SAINT BLOSSOM HIGH SCHOOL.
Um~
WHAT?!
SAINT BLOSSOM HIGH!?!
THAT PLACE IS FAMOUS FOR ITS CUTE GIRLS...IN CUTE UNIFORMS.
TH...THAT'S A HIGH LEVEL SCHOOL!!
HUH... A CELL PHONE?
うん。
I JUST CALLED, SO SHE SHOULD BE COMING SOON.
PIII
It's a must in Japanese teen fashion.
WHO'S COMING?
MY FRIEND FROM MY HOMESTAY FAMILY! ♡
I MET HER OVER THE INTERNET. SHE SEEMS COOL.
AND SHE GOES TO SAINT BLOSSOM TOO.
OH LOOK, HERE SHE COMES!
Hey!!
Huh?!
R... RIO?!

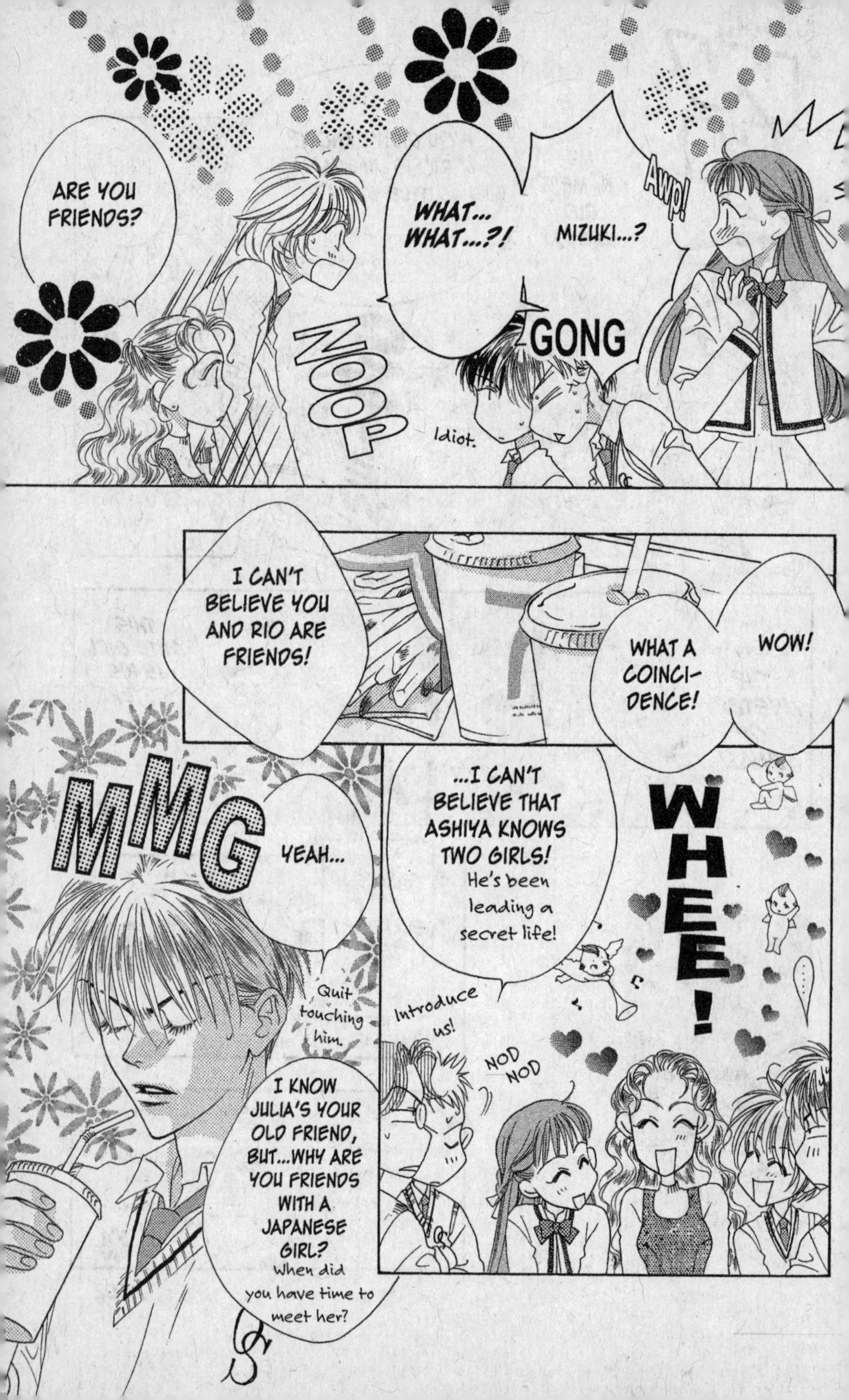
Awp!
MIZUKI...?
WHAT... WHAT...?!
ARE YOU FRIENDS?
GONG
Idiot.
NOOP
WOW!
WHAT A COINCI-DENCE!
I CAN'T BELIEVE YOU AND RIO ARE FRIENDS!
WHEE!
...I CAN'T BELIEVE THAT ASHIYA KNOWS TWO GIRLS!
He's been leading a secret life!
Introduce us!
NOD NOD
MMG
YEAH...
Quit touching him.
I KNOW JULIA'S YOUR OLD FRIEND, BUT...WHY ARE YOU FRIENDS WITH A JAPANESE GIRL?
When did you have time to meet her?

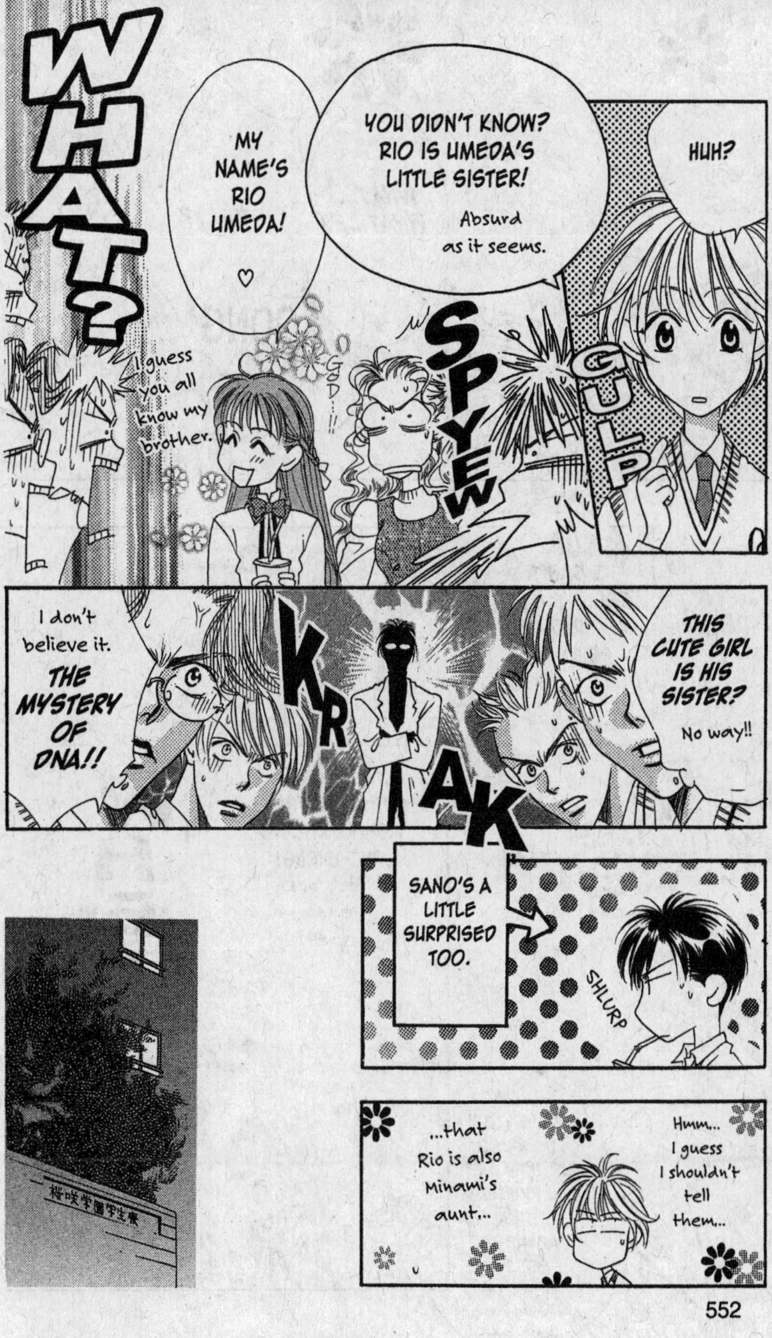
HUH?
GULP
YOU DIDN'T KNOW? RIO IS UMEDA'S LITTLE SISTER!
Absurd as it seems.
MY NAME'S RIO UMEDA! ♡
SPYEW
GOD...!!
I guess you all know my brother.
WHAT?
THIS CUTE GIRL IS HIS SISTER?
No way!!
KRAK
I don't believe it.
THE MYSTERY OF DNA!!
SANO'S A LITTLE SURPRISED TOO.
SHLURP
Hmm... I guess I shouldn't tell them...
...that Rio is also Minami's aunt...

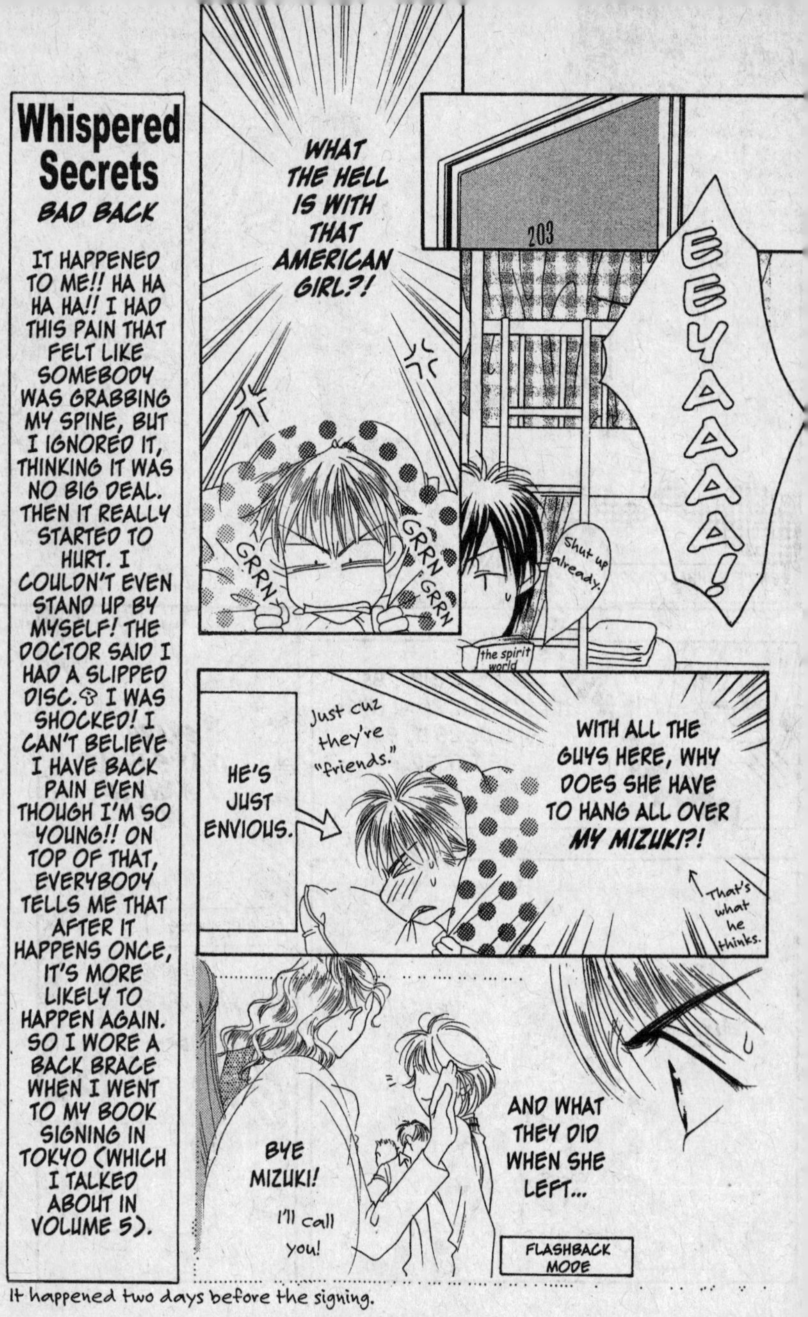
203
EEYAAAA!
Shut up already.
the spirit world
WHAT THE HELL IS WITH THAT AMERICAN GIRL?!
GRRN GRRN GRRN
WITH ALL THE GUYS HERE, WHY DOES SHE HAVE TO HANG ALL OVER MY MIZUKI?!
That's what he thinks.
Just cuz they're "friends."
HE'S JUST ENVIOUS.
AND WHAT THEY DID WHEN SHE LEFT...
BYE MIZUKI!
I'll call you!
FLASHBACK MODE

Whispered Secrets

BAD BACK

IT HAPPENED TO ME!! HA HA HA HA!! I HAD THIS PAIN THAT FELT LIKE SOMEBODY WAS GRABBING MY SPINE, BUT I IGNORED IT, THINKING IT WAS NO BIG DEAL. THEN IT REALLY STARTED TO HURT. I COULDN'T EVEN STAND UP BY MYSELF! THE DOCTOR SAID I HAD A SLIPPED DISC. I WAS SHOCKED! I CAN'T BELIEVE I HAVE BACK PAIN EVEN THOUGH I'M SO YOUNG!! ON TOP OF THAT, EVERYBODY TELLS ME THAT AFTER IT HAPPENS ONCE, IT'S MORE LIKELY TO HAPPEN AGAIN. SO I WORE A BACK BRACE WHEN I WENT TO MY BOOK SIGNING IN TOKYO (WHICH I TALKED ABOUT IN VOLUME 5).

It happened two days before the signing.

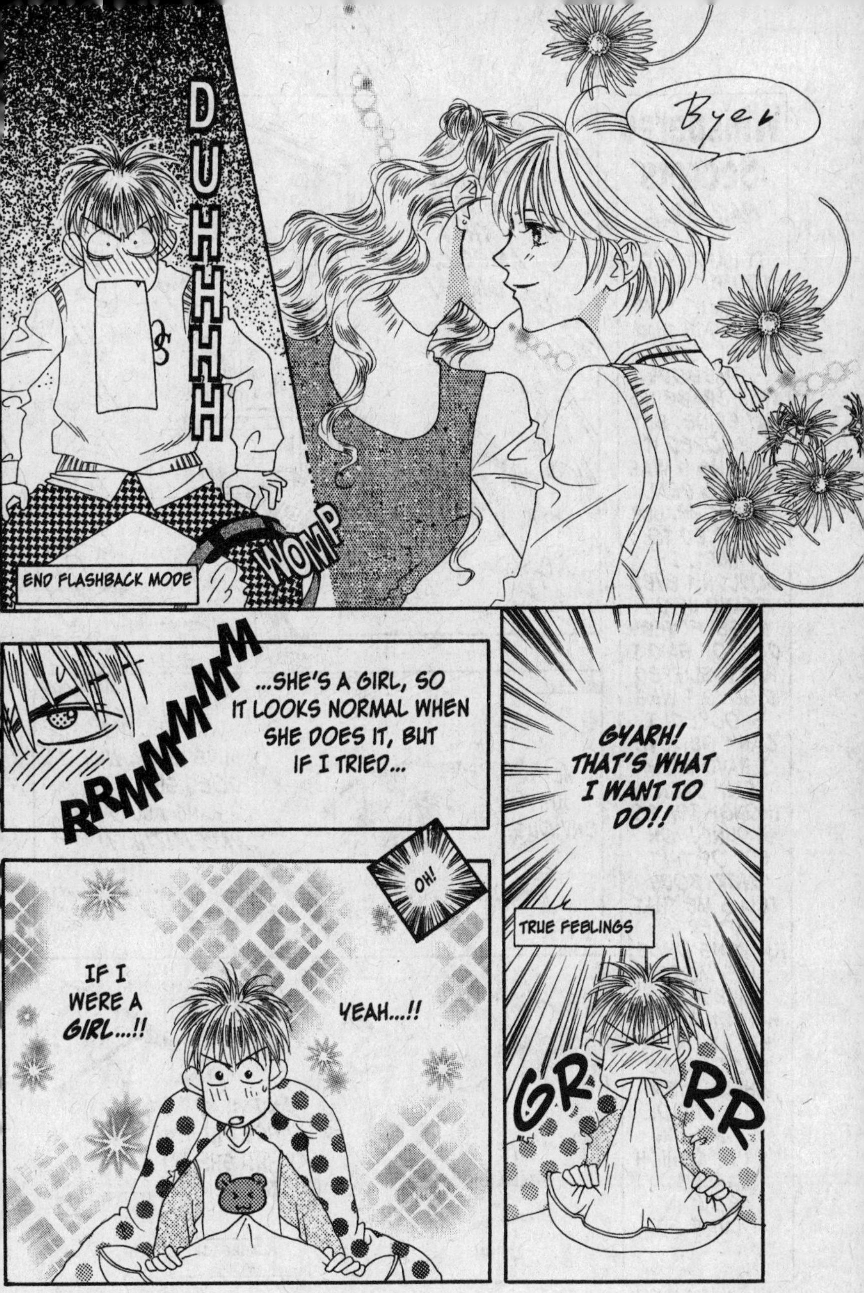
Byee
DUHHHHH
WOMP
END FLASHBACK MODE
GYARH! THAT'S WHAT I WANT TO DO!!
TRUE FEELINGS
GRRR
...SHE'S A GIRL, SO IT LOOKS NORMAL WHEN SHE DOES IT, BUT IF I TRIED...
RRMMMMMM
OH!
YEAH...!!
IF I WERE A GIRL...!!

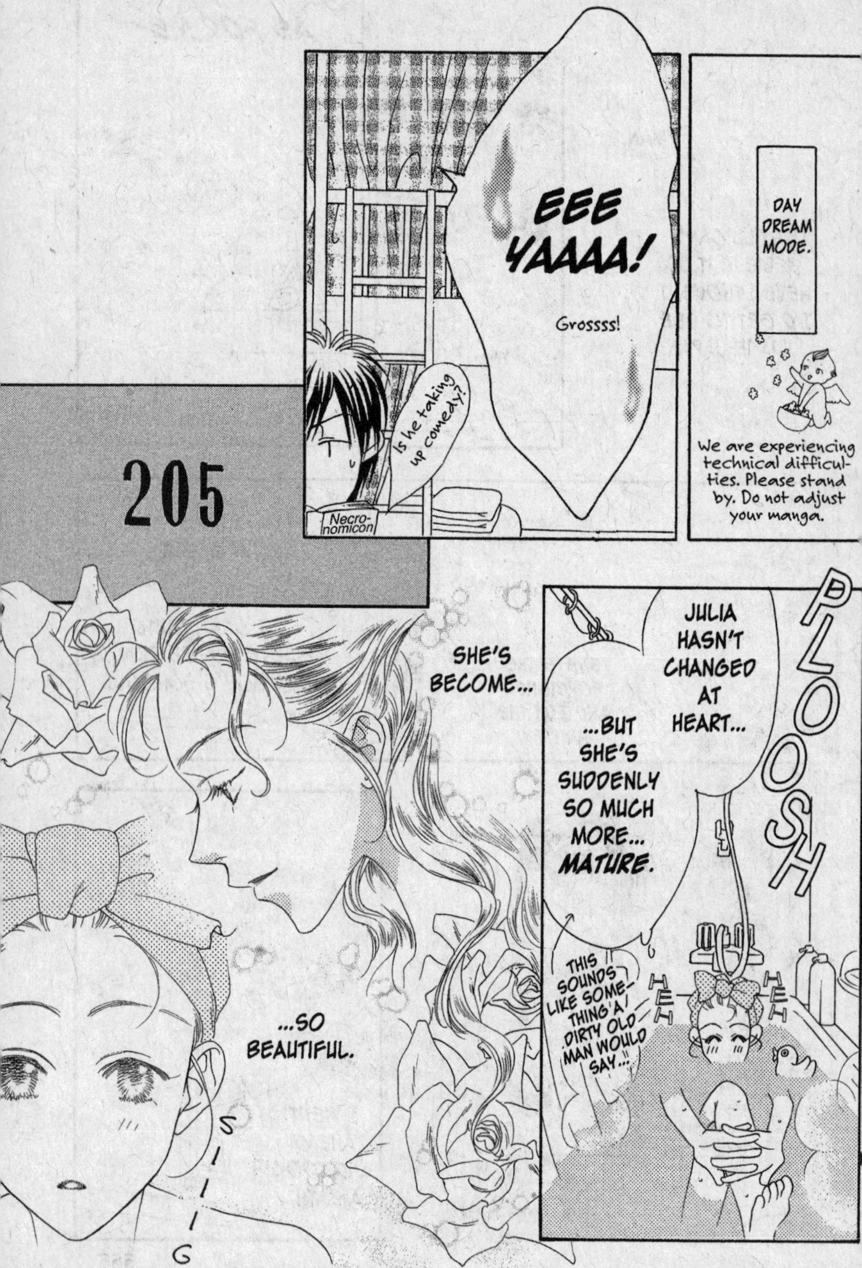
DAY DREAM MODE.
We are experiencing technical difficulties. Please stand by. Do not adjust your manga.
EEE YAAAA!
Grossss!
Is he taking up comedy?
Necro-nomicon
205
PLOOSH
JULIA HASN'T CHANGED AT HEART...
...BUT SHE'S SUDDENLY SO MUCH MORE... MATURE.
HEH HEH
THIS SOUNDS LIKE SOME-THING A DIRTY OLD MAN WOULD SAY...!
SHE'S BECOME...
...SO BEAUTIFUL.
SIIIGH

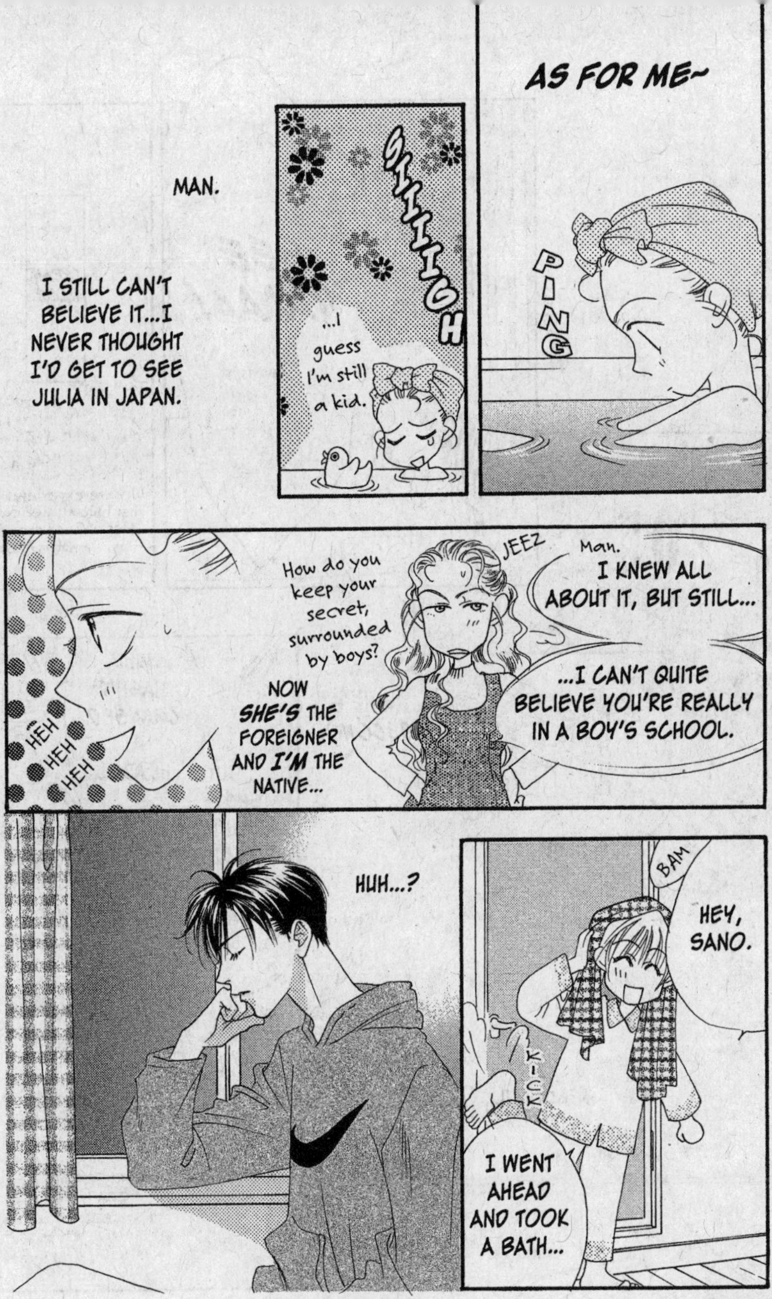
AS FOR ME~
PING
SIIIIGH
...I guess I'm still a kid.
MAN.
I STILL CAN'T BELIEVE IT...I NEVER THOUGHT I'D GET TO SEE JULIA IN JAPAN.
Man.
I KNEW ALL ABOUT IT, BUT STILL...
...I CAN'T QUITE BELIEVE YOU'RE REALLY IN A BOY'S SCHOOL.
JEEZ
How do you keep your secret, surrounded by boys?
NOW *SHE'S* THE FOREIGNER AND *I'M* THE NATIVE...
HEH HEH HEH
BAM
HEY, SANO.
KICK
I WENT AHEAD AND TOOK A BATH...
HUH...?

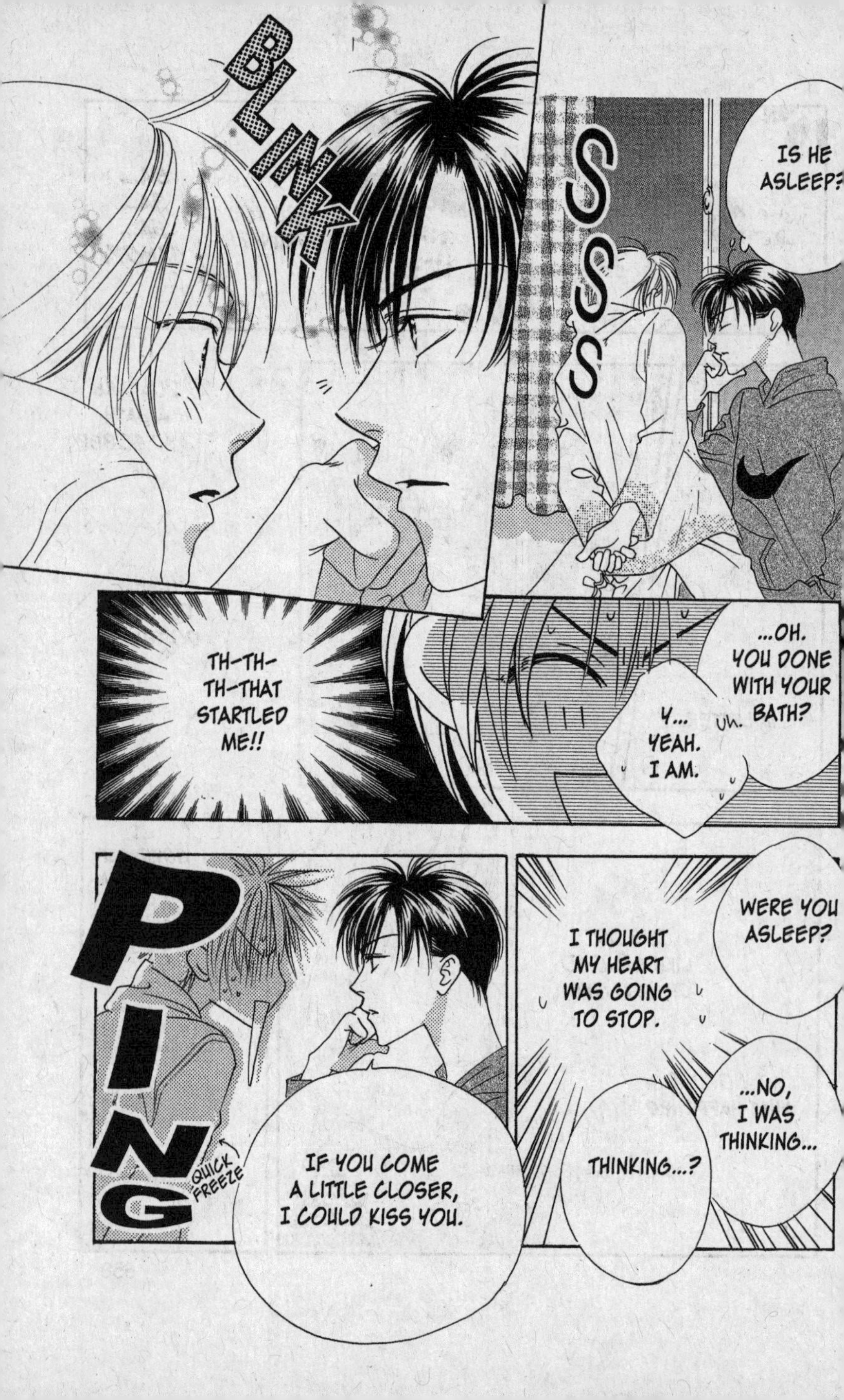
IS HE ASLEEP?
SSS
BLINK
...OH. YOU DONE WITH YOUR BATH?
uh.
Y... YEAH. I AM.
TH-TH-TH-THAT STARTLED ME!!
WERE YOU ASLEEP?
I THOUGHT MY HEART WAS GOING TO STOP.
...NO, I WAS THINKING...
THINKING...?
PING
QUICK FREEZE
IF YOU COME A LITTLE CLOSER, I COULD KISS YOU.

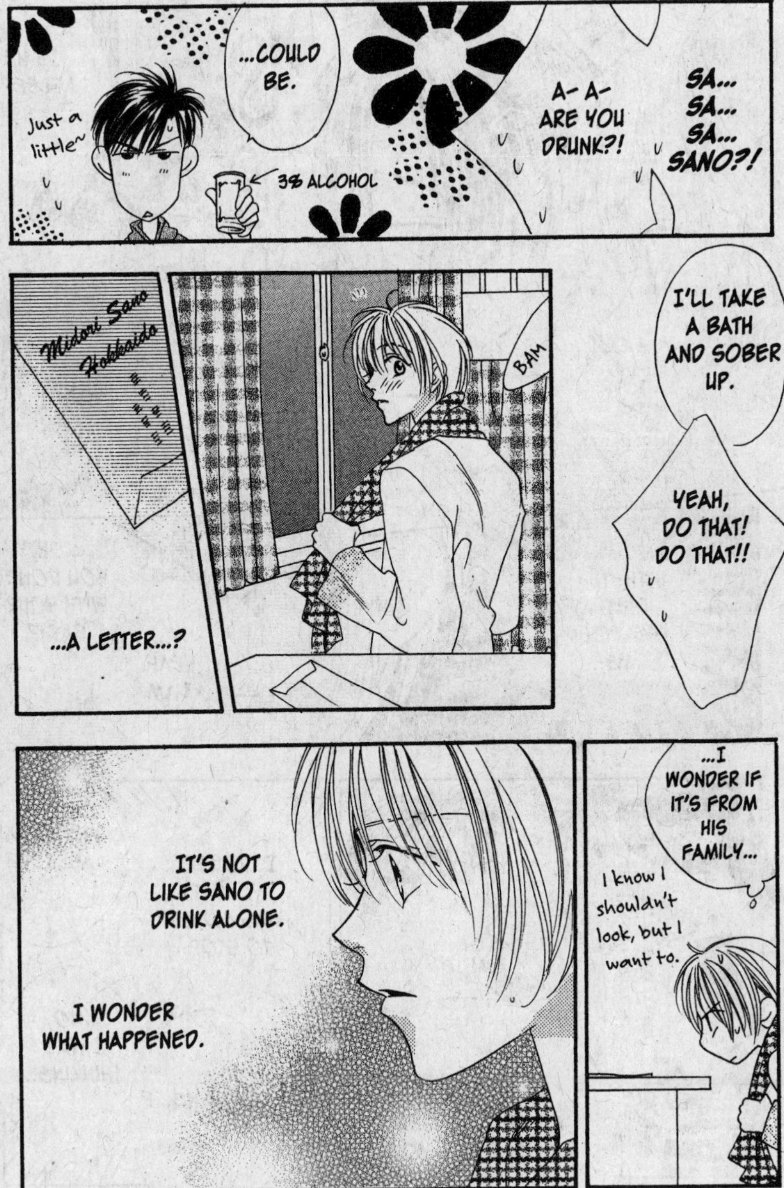

SA... SA... SA... SANO?!
A- A- ARE YOU DRUNK?!
...COULD BE.
3% ALCOHOL
Just a little~
I'LL TAKE A BATH AND SOBER UP.
YEAH, DO THAT! DO THAT!!
BAM
Midori Sano
Hokkaido
...A LETTER...?
...I WONDER IF IT'S FROM HIS FAMILY...
I know I shouldn't look, but I want to.
IT'S NOT LIKE SANO TO DRINK ALONE.
I WONDER WHAT HAPPENED.

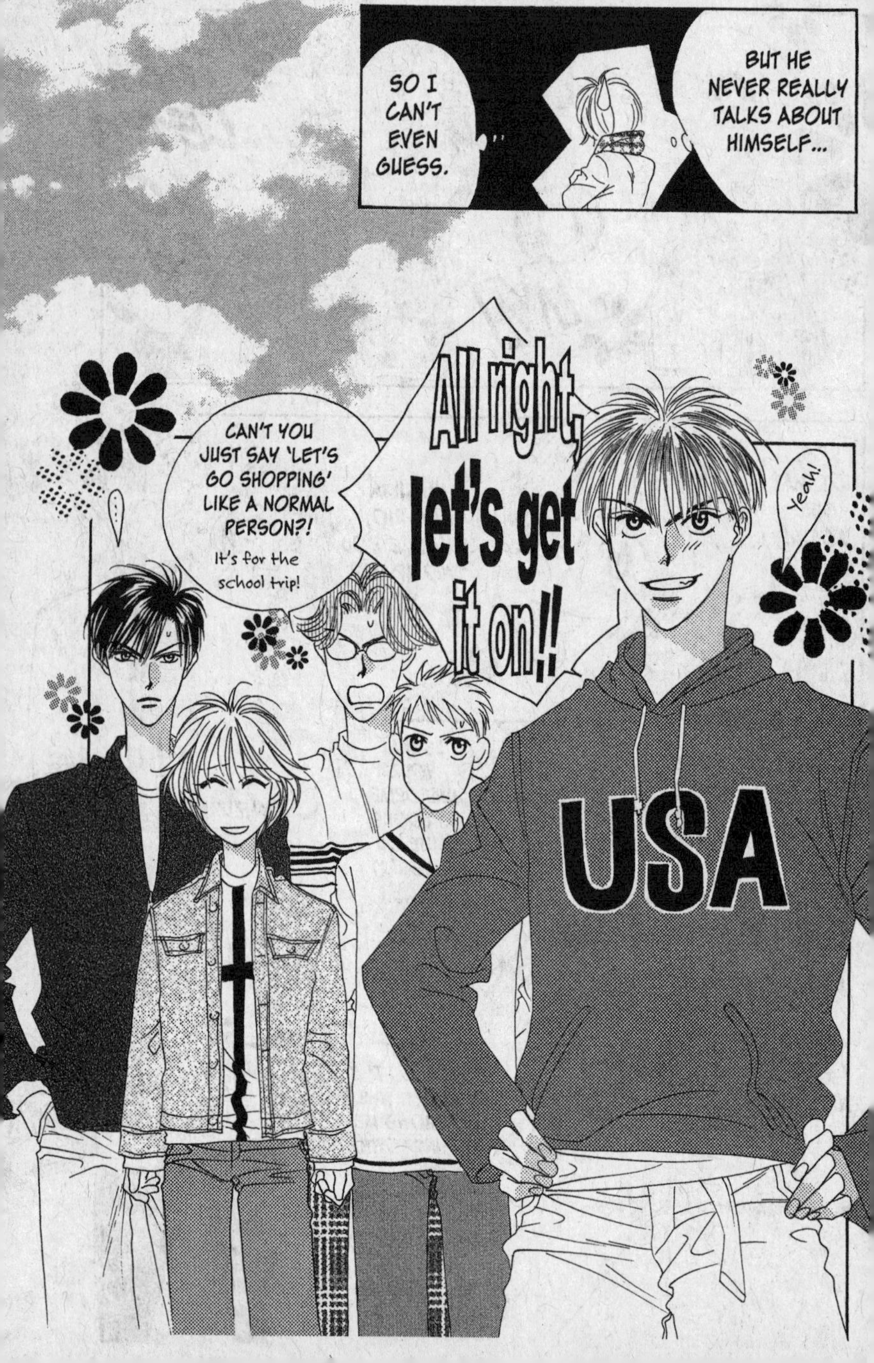
BUT HE NEVER REALLY TALKS ABOUT HIMSELF...
SO I CAN'T EVEN GUESS.
All right, let's get it on!!
Yeah!
CAN'T YOU JUST SAY 'LET'S GO SHOPPING' LIKE A NORMAL PERSON?!
It's for the school trip!

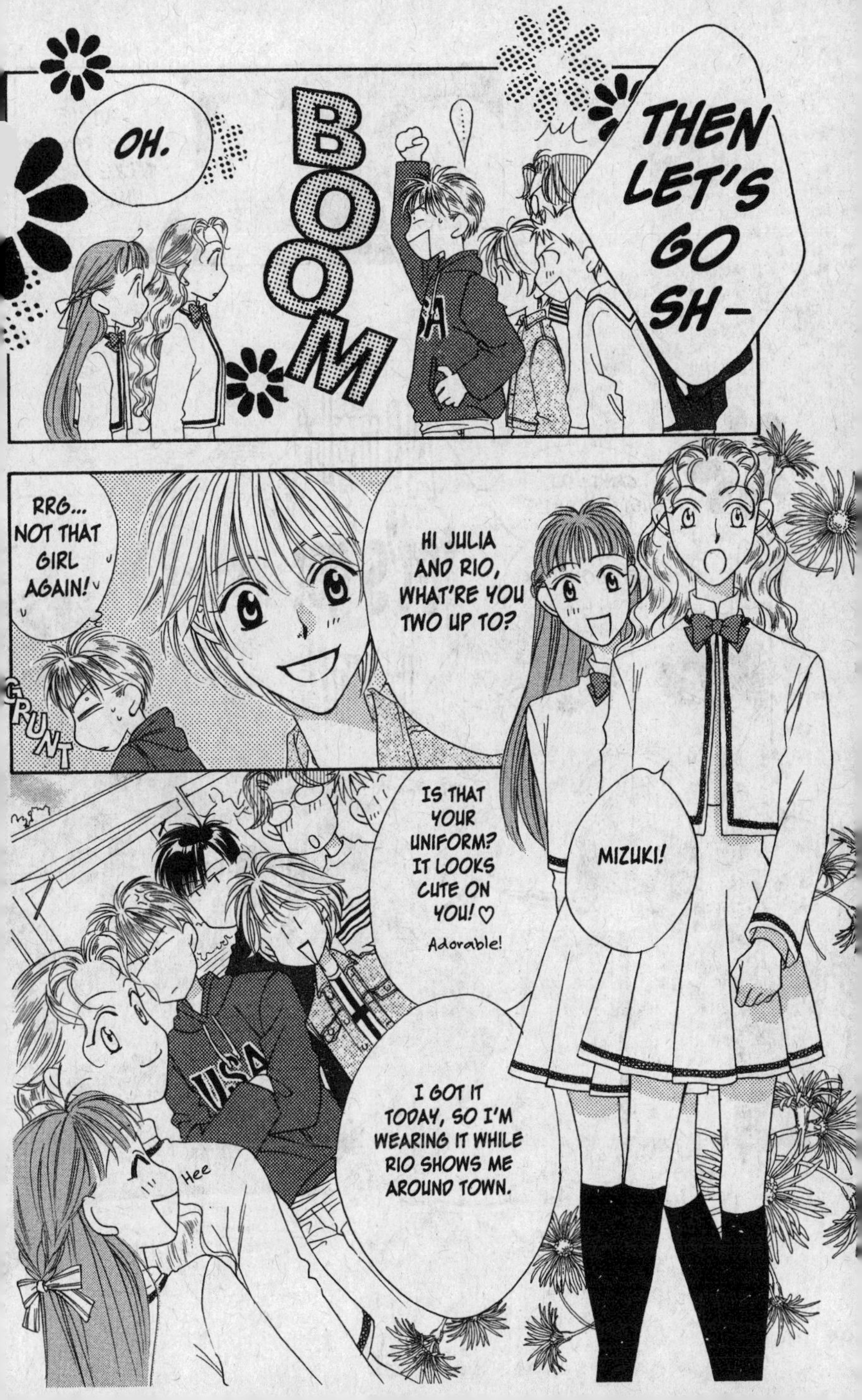
THEN LET'S GO SH–
BOOM
OH.
MIZUKI!
HI JULIA AND RIO, WHAT'RE YOU TWO UP TO?
RRG... NOT THAT GIRL AGAIN!
GRUNT
IS THAT YOUR UNIFORM? IT LOOKS CUTE ON YOU! ♡
Adorable!
I GOT IT TODAY, SO I'M WEARING IT WHILE RIO SHOWS ME AROUND TOWN.
Hee

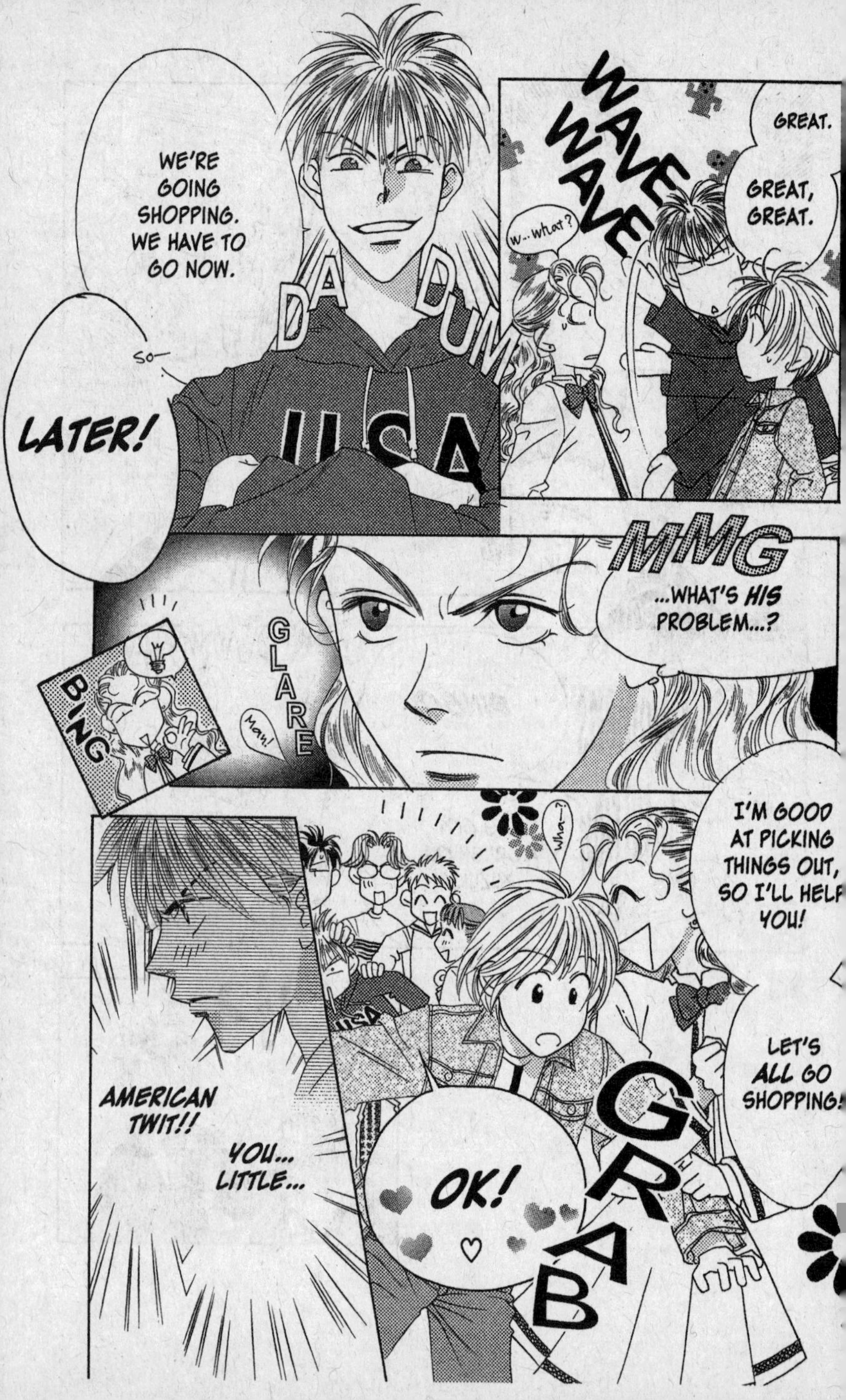
GREAT.
GREAT, GREAT.
WAVE WAVE
W-.. what?
WE'RE GOING SHOPPING. WE HAVE TO GO NOW.
DA DUM
SO—
LATER!
MMG
...WHAT'S HIS PROBLEM...?
GLARE
Man!
BING
I'M GOOD AT PICKING THINGS OUT, SO I'LL HELP YOU!
LET'S ALL GO SHOPPING!
What—?
GRAB
OK!
YOU... LITTLE...
AMERICAN TWIT!!

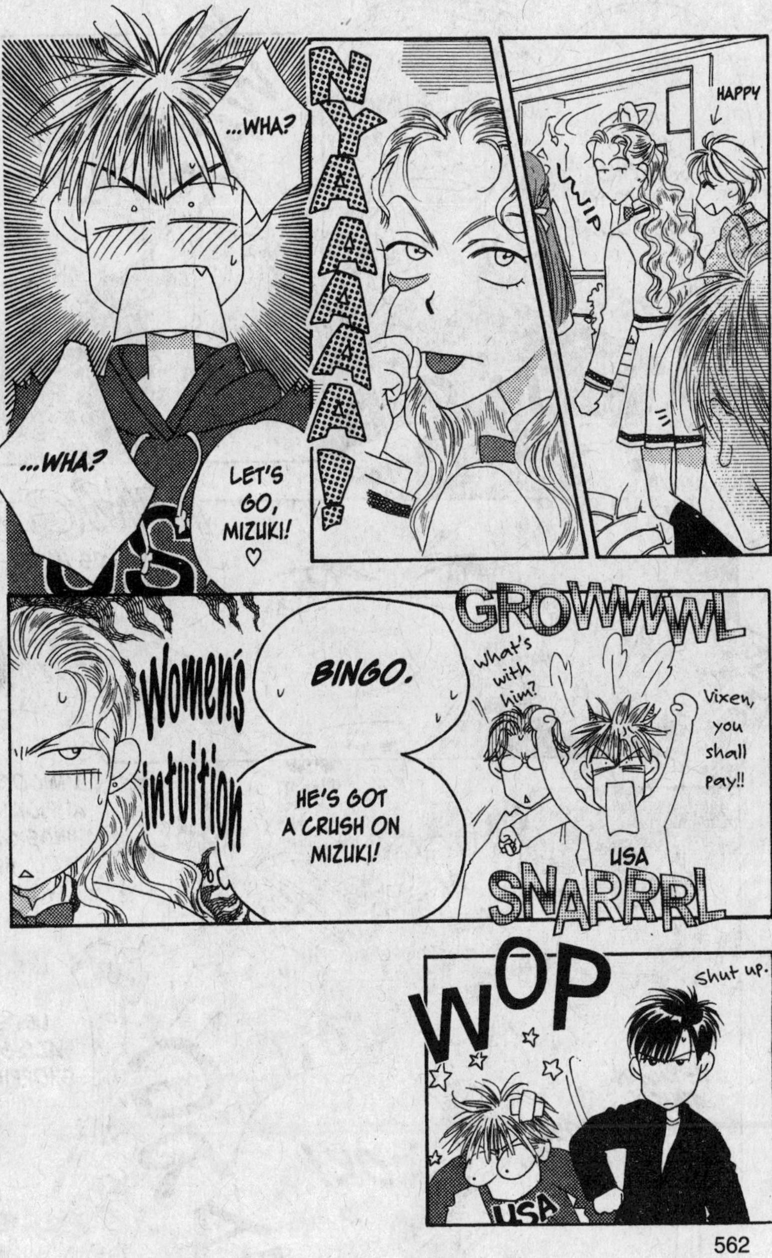
HAPPY
WHIP
NYAAAAA!!
...WHA?
...WHA?
LET'S GO, MIZUKI! ♡
GROWWWWL
Vixen, you shall pay!!
what's with him?
USA
SNARRRL
BINGO.
HE'S GOT A CRUSH ON MIZUKI!
Women's intuition
Shut up.
WOP
USA

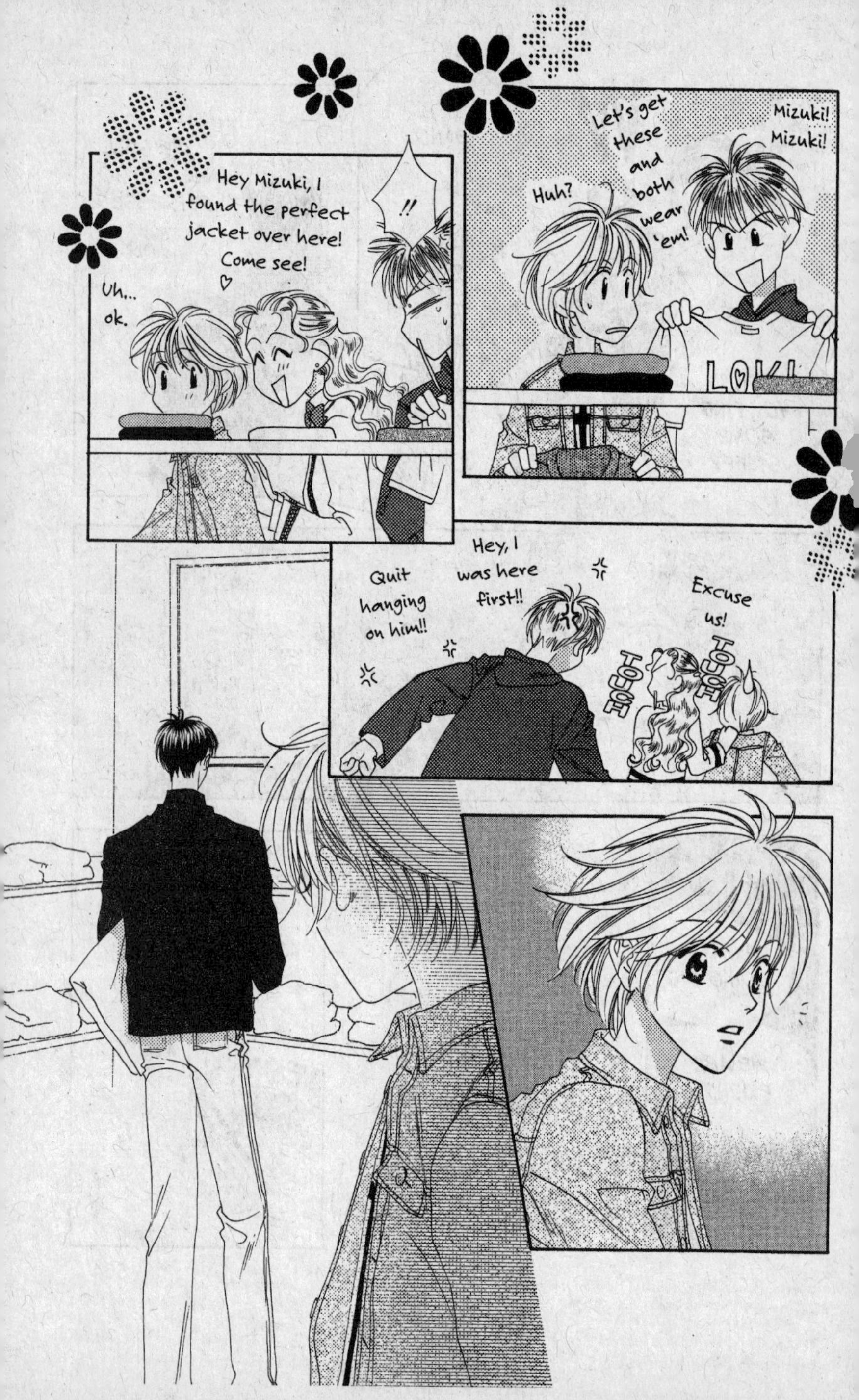
Mizuki! Mizuki!
Let's get these and both wear 'em!
Huh?
!!
Hey Mizuki, I found the perfect jacket over here! Come see! ♡
Uh... ok.
Excuse us!
TOUGH
TOUGH
Hey, I was here first!!
Quit hanging on him!!

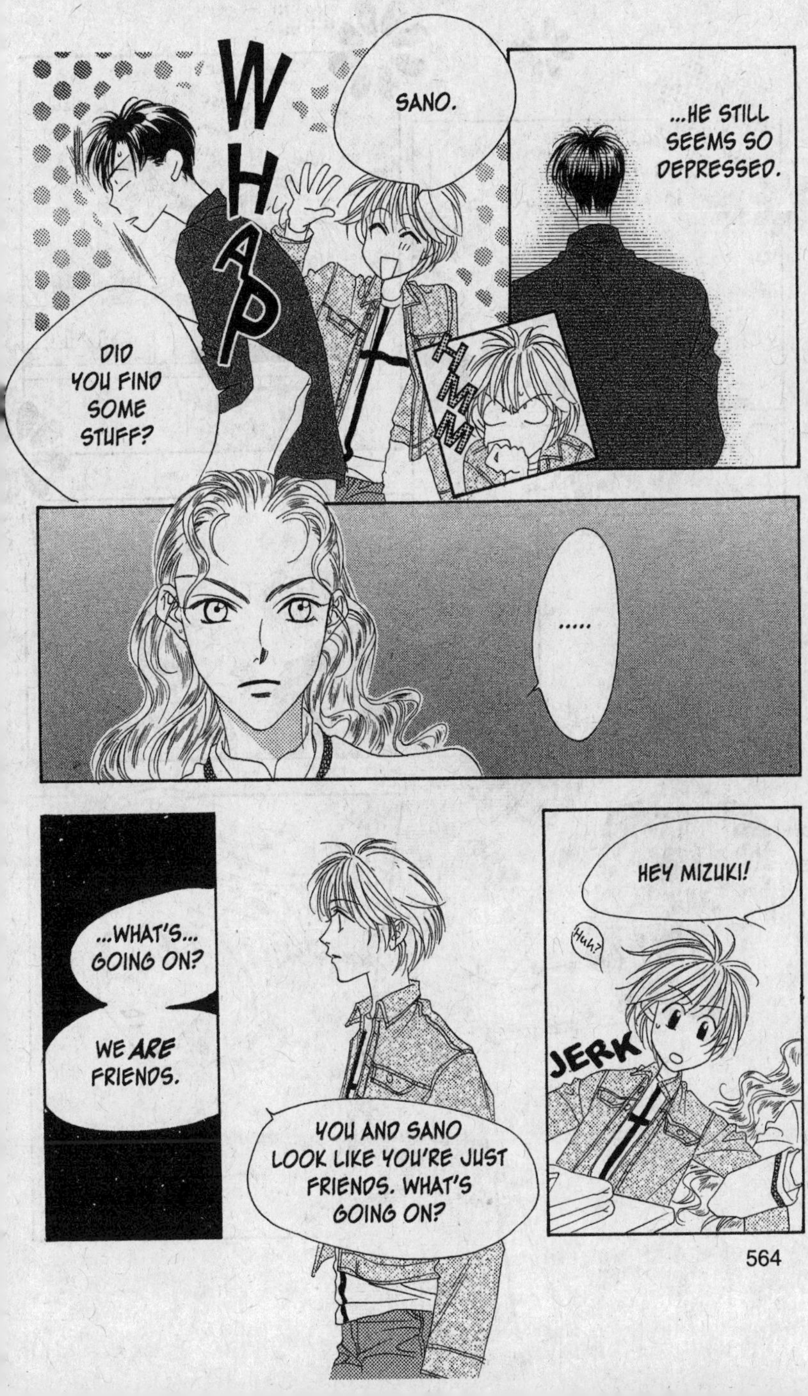
...HE STILL SEEMS SO DEPRESSED.
SANO.
WHAP
DID YOU FIND SOME STUFF?
HMMM
.....
HEY MIZUKI!
Huh?
JERK
YOU AND SANO LOOK LIKE YOU'RE JUST FRIENDS. WHAT'S GOING ON?
...WHAT'S... GOING ON?
WE ARE FRIENDS.

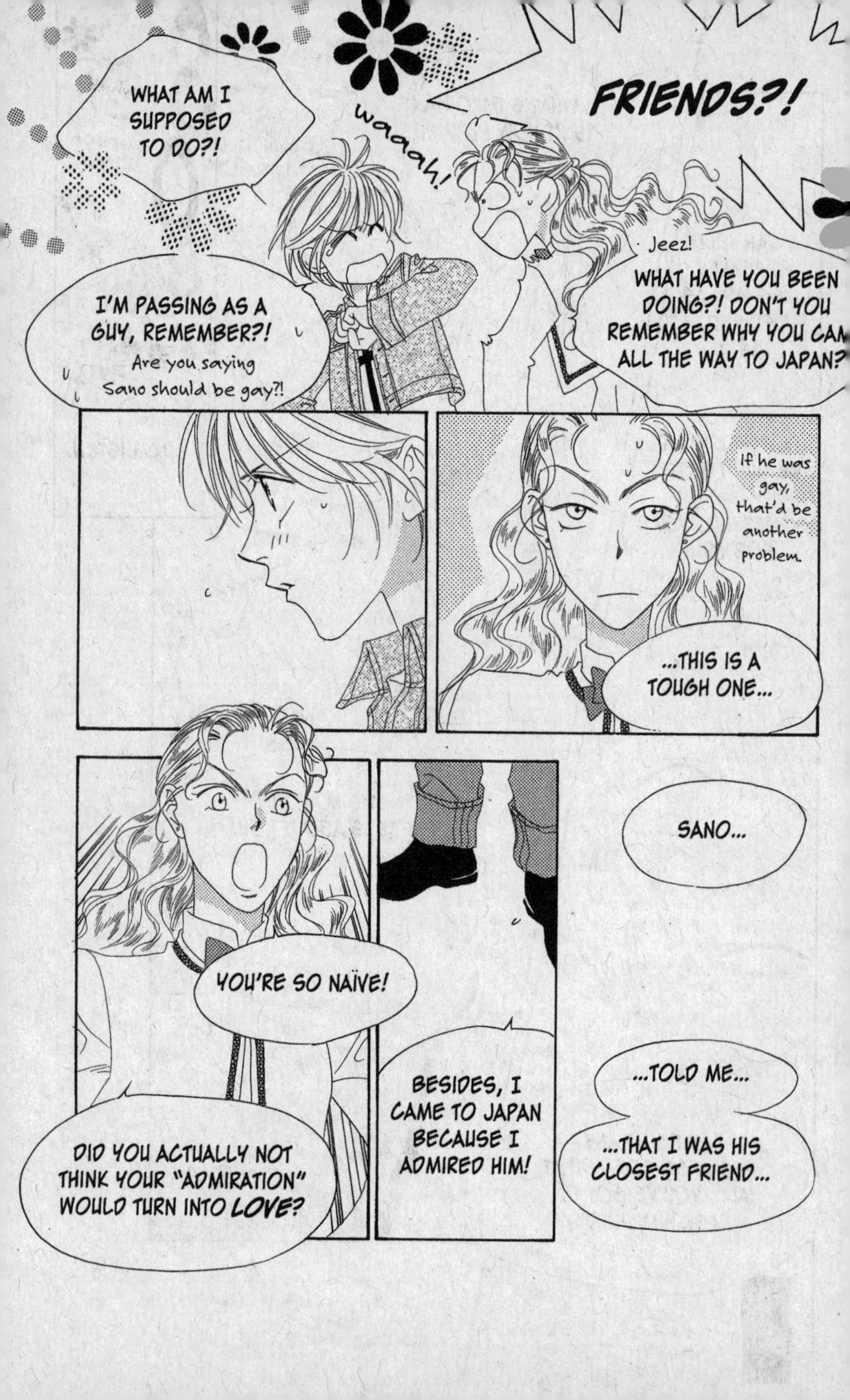
FRIENDS?!
Jeez!
WHAT HAVE YOU BEEN DOING?! DON'T YOU REMEMBER WHY YOU CAM ALL THE WAY TO JAPAN?
waaah!
WHAT AM I SUPPOSED TO DO?!
I'M PASSING AS A GUY, REMEMBER?!
Are you saying Sano should be gay?!
If he was gay, that'd be another problem.
...THIS IS A TOUGH ONE...
SANO...
...TOLD ME...
...THAT I WAS HIS CLOSEST FRIEND...
BESIDES, I CAME TO JAPAN BECAUSE I ADMIRED HIM!
YOU'RE SO NAÏVE!
DID YOU ACTUALLY NOT THINK YOUR "ADMIRATION" WOULD TURN INTO LOVE?

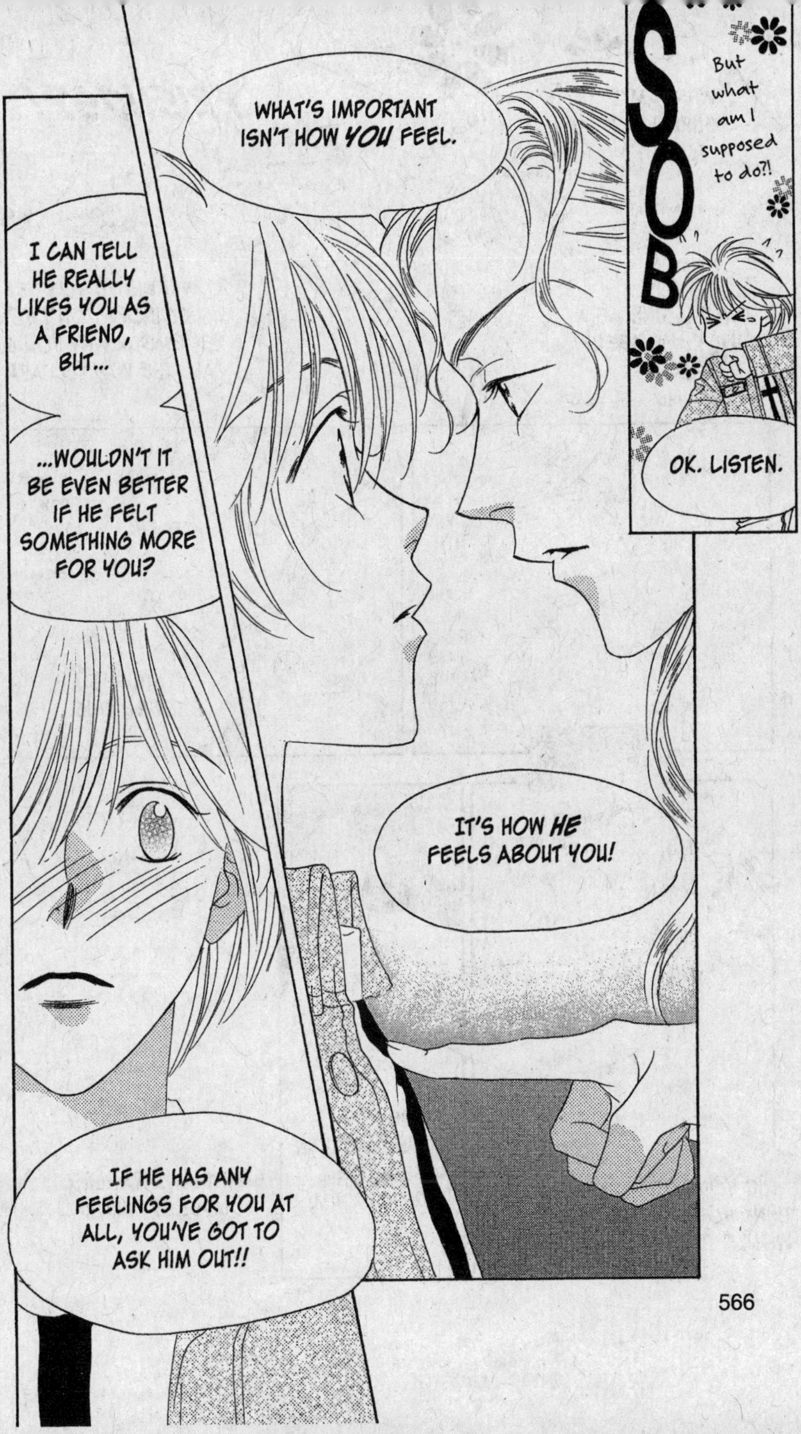
SOB
But what am I supposed to do?!
OK. LISTEN.
WHAT'S IMPORTANT ISN'T HOW *YOU* FEEL.
IT'S HOW *HE* FEELS ABOUT YOU!
I CAN TELL HE REALLY LIKES YOU AS A FRIEND, BUT...
...WOULDN'T IT BE EVEN BETTER IF HE FELT SOMETHING MORE FOR YOU?
IF HE HAS ANY FEELINGS FOR YOU AT ALL, YOU'VE GOT TO ASK HIM OUT!!

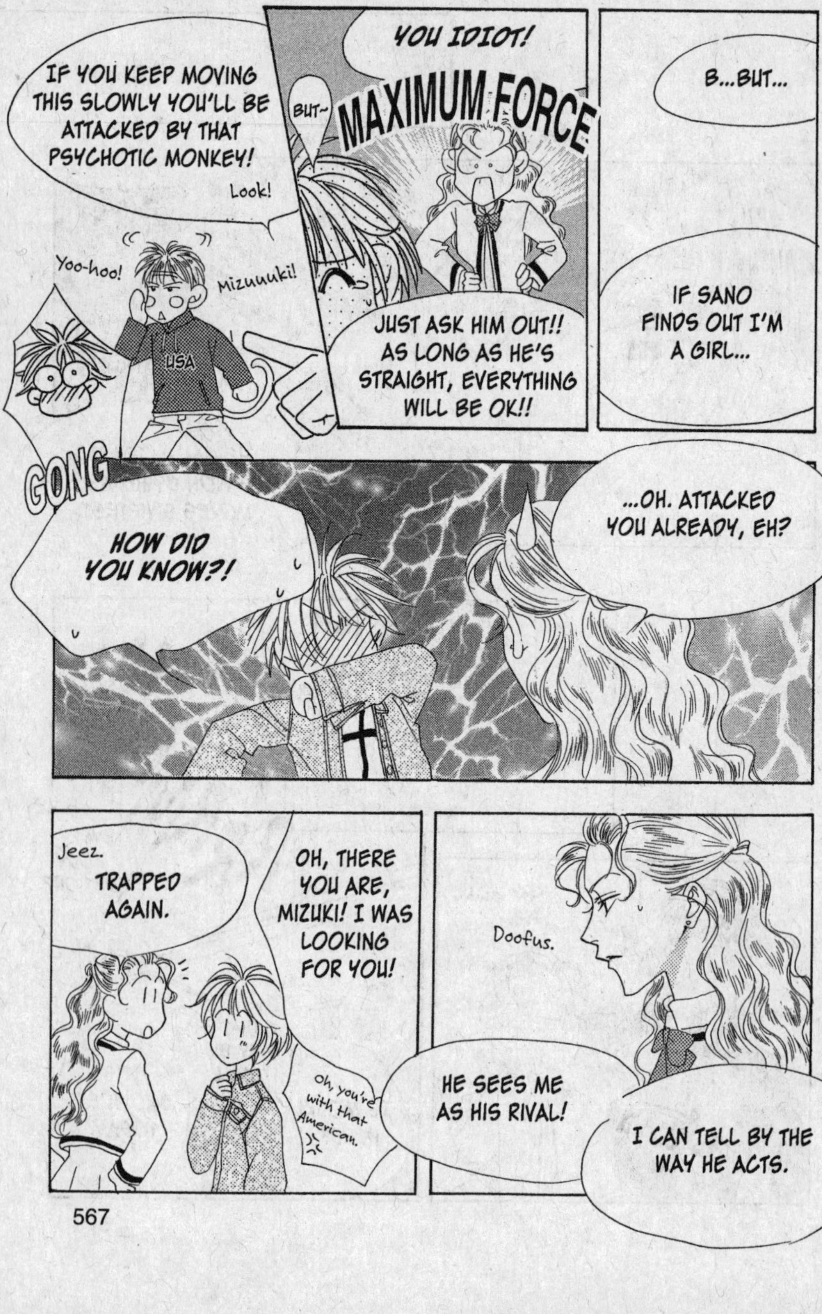
B...BUT...
IF SANO FINDS OUT I'M A GIRL...
YOU IDIOT!
MAXIMUM FORCE
BUT~
JUST ASK HIM OUT!! AS LONG AS HE'S STRAIGHT, EVERYTHING WILL BE OK!!
IF YOU KEEP MOVING THIS SLOWLY YOU'LL BE ATTACKED BY THAT PSYCHOTIC MONKEY!
Look!
Mizuuuki!
Yoo-hoo!
USA
...OH. ATTACKED YOU ALREADY, EH?
GONG
HOW DID YOU KNOW?!
Doofus.
HE SEES ME AS HIS RIVAL!
I CAN TELL BY THE WAY HE ACTS.
OH, THERE YOU ARE, MIZUKI! I WAS LOOKING FOR YOU!
Jeez.
TRAPPED AGAIN.
Oh, you're with that American.

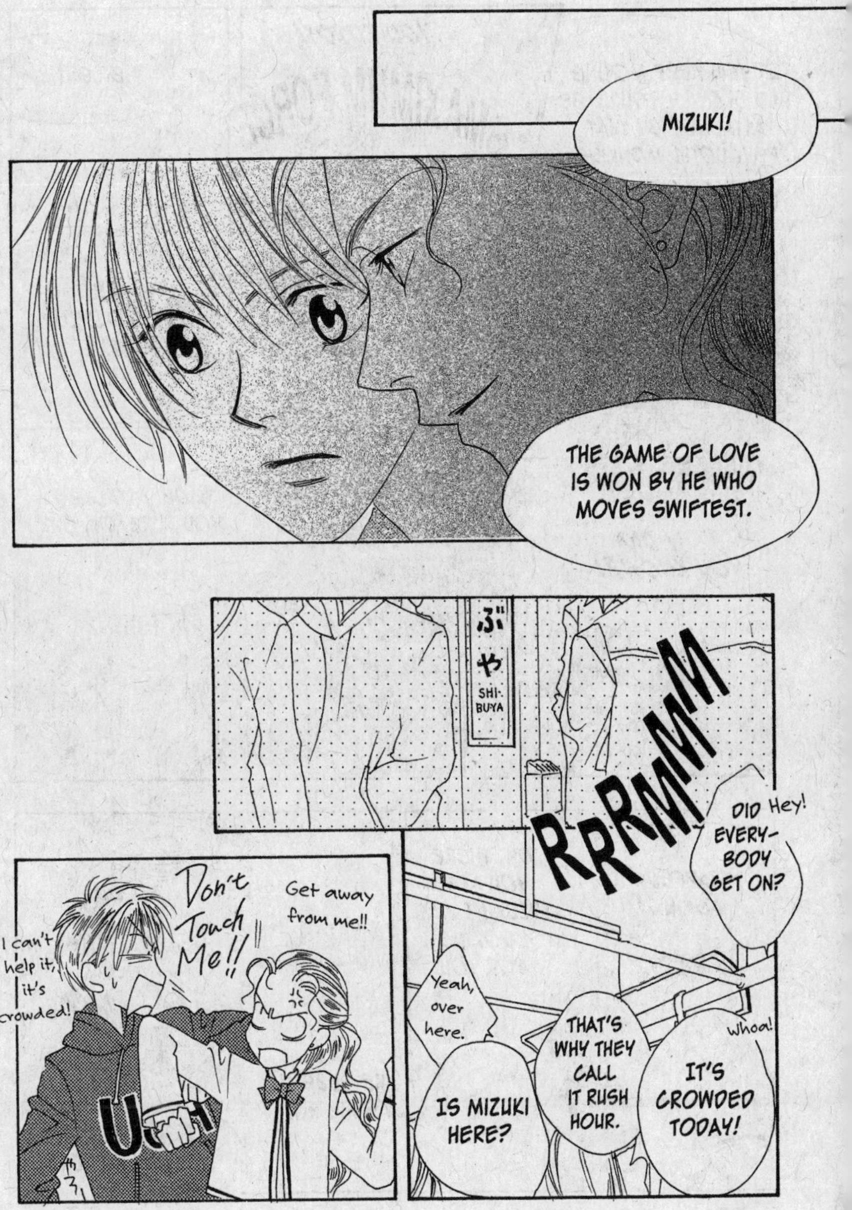
MIZUKI!
THE GAME OF LOVE IS WON BY HE WHO MOVES SWIFTEST.
ぶや
SHI-BUYA
RRRMMM
Hey!
DID EVERY-BODY GET ON?
Whoa!
IT'S CROWDED TODAY!
THAT'S WHY THEY CALL IT RUSH HOUR.
Yeah, over here.
IS MIZUKI HERE?
Get away from me!!
Don't Touch Me!!
I can't help it, it's crowded!

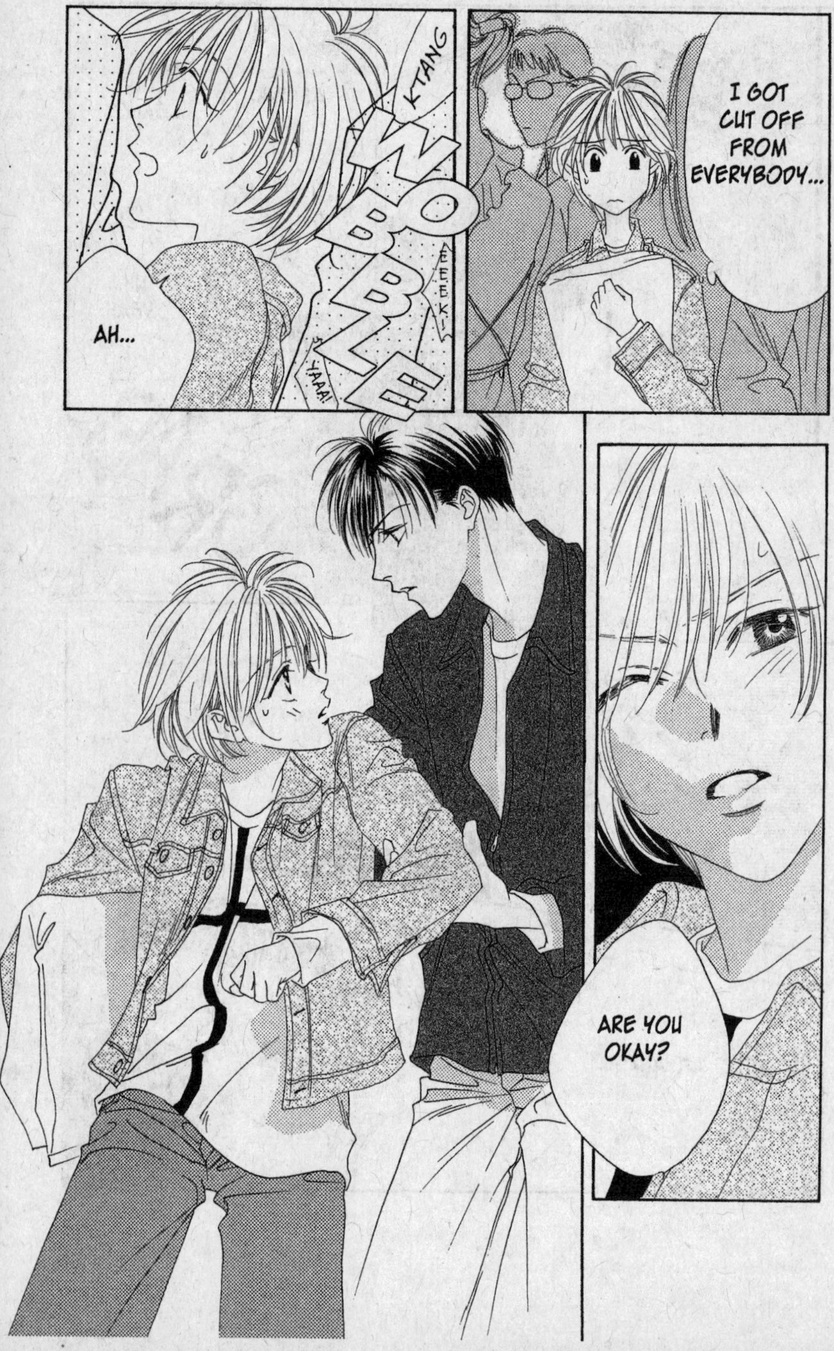
I GOT CUT OFF FROM EVERYBODY...
KTANG
WOBBLE
EEEK!
YAAA!
AH...
ARE YOU OKAY?

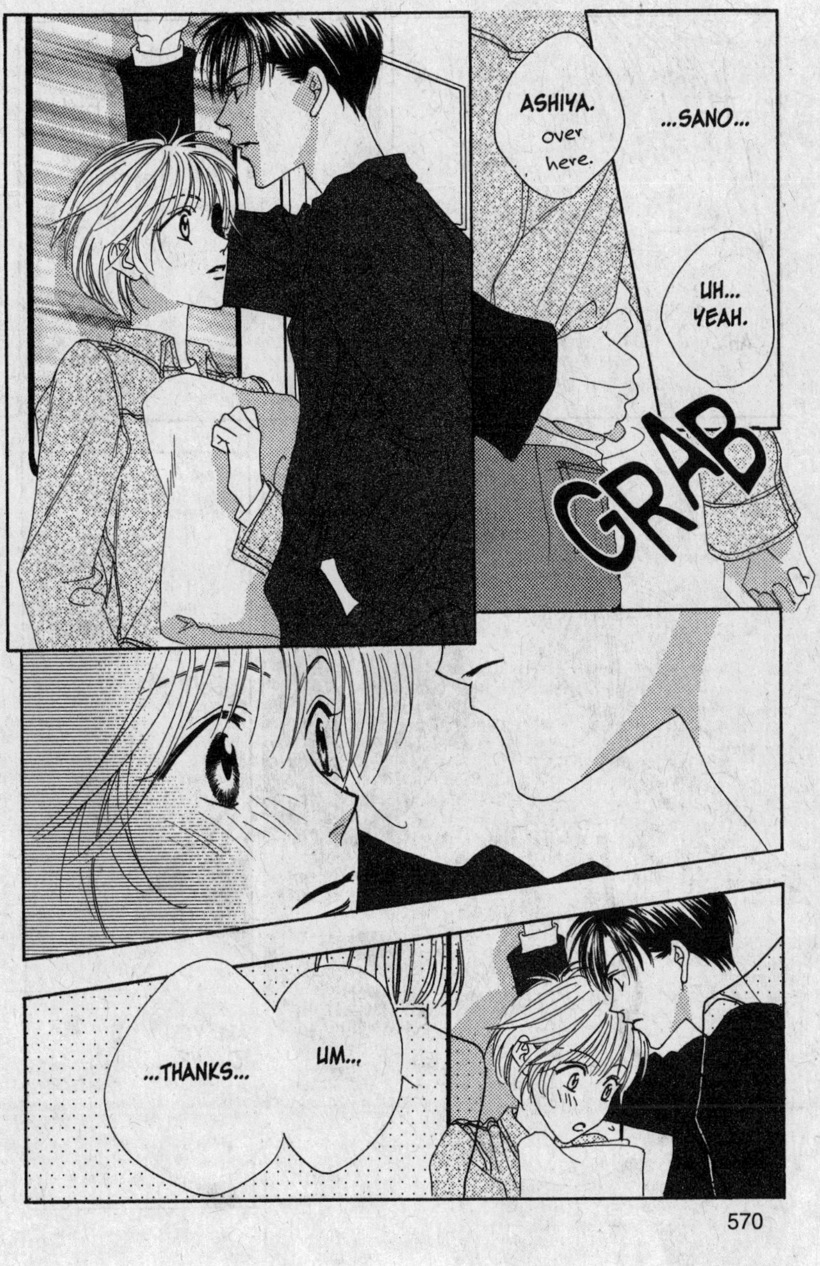
...SANO...
ASHIYA. over here.
UH... YEAH.
GRAB
UM...,
...THANKS...

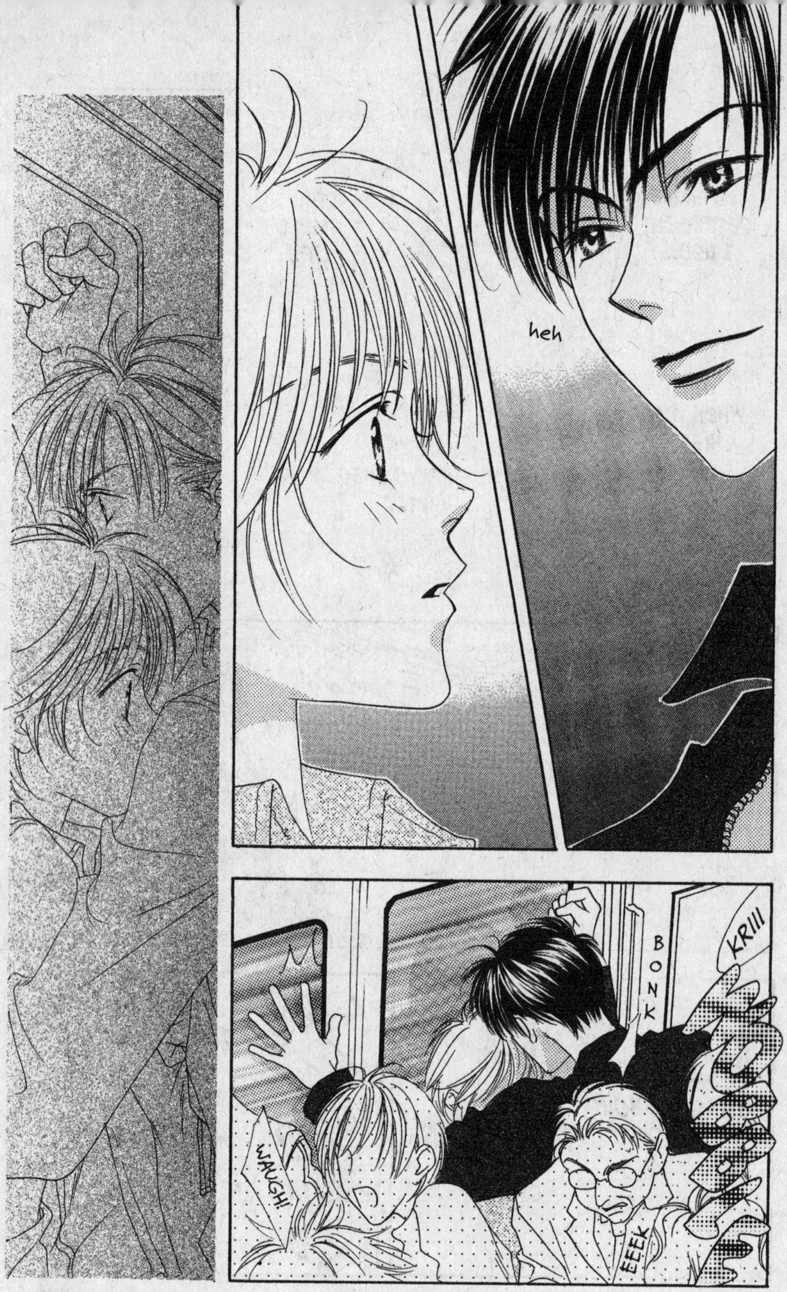
heh
KRIII
BONK
EEEK
WAUGH!

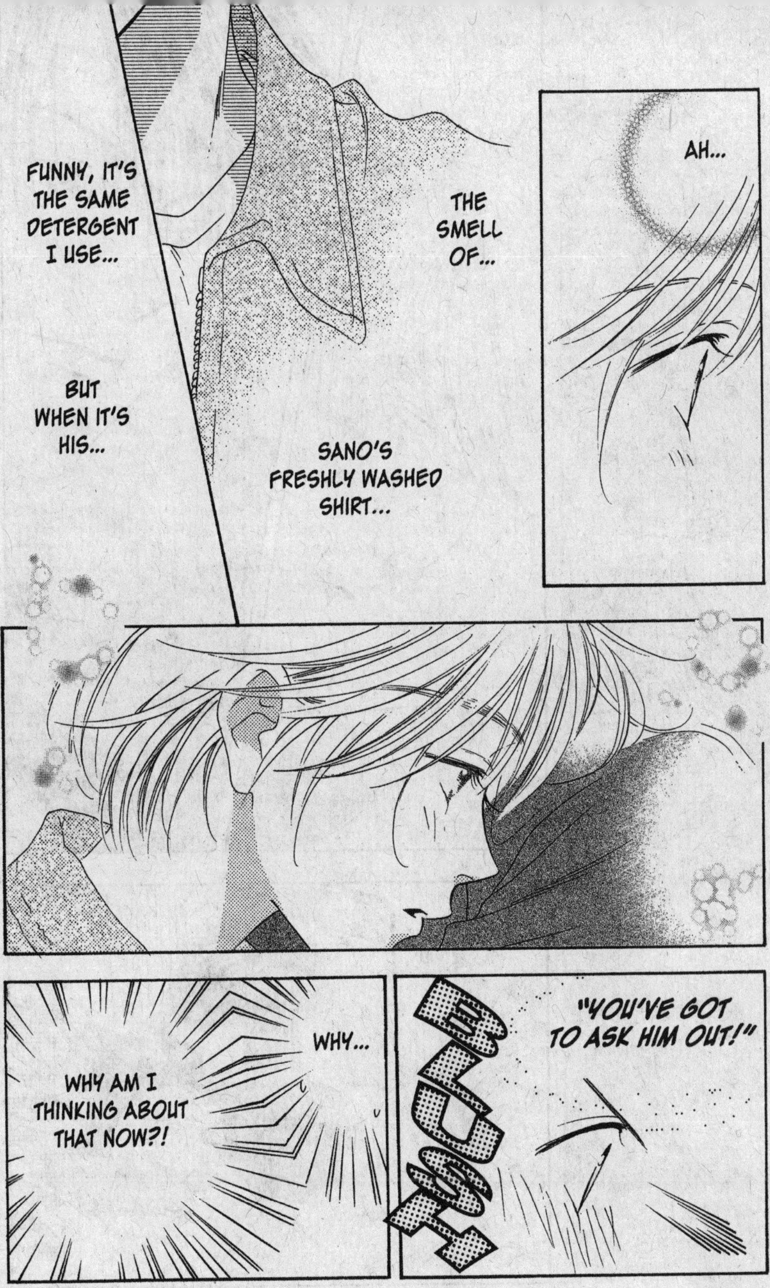
AH...
THE SMELL OF...
SANO'S FRESHLY WASHED SHIRT...
FUNNY, IT'S THE SAME DETERGENT I USE...
BUT WHEN IT'S HIS...
"YOU'VE GOT TO ASK HIM OUT!"
BLUSH
WHY...
WHY AM I THINKING ABOUT THAT NOW?!

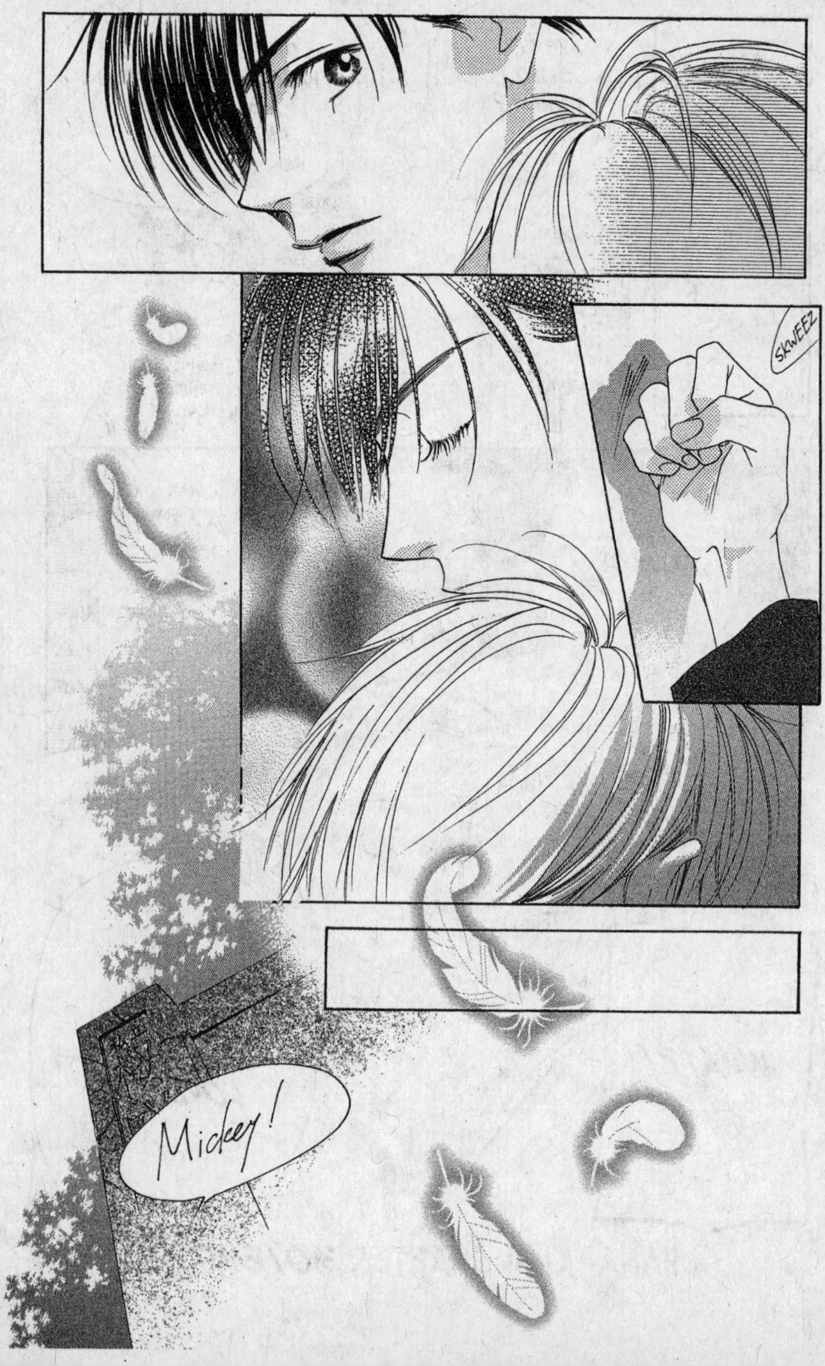
SKWEEZ
Mickey!

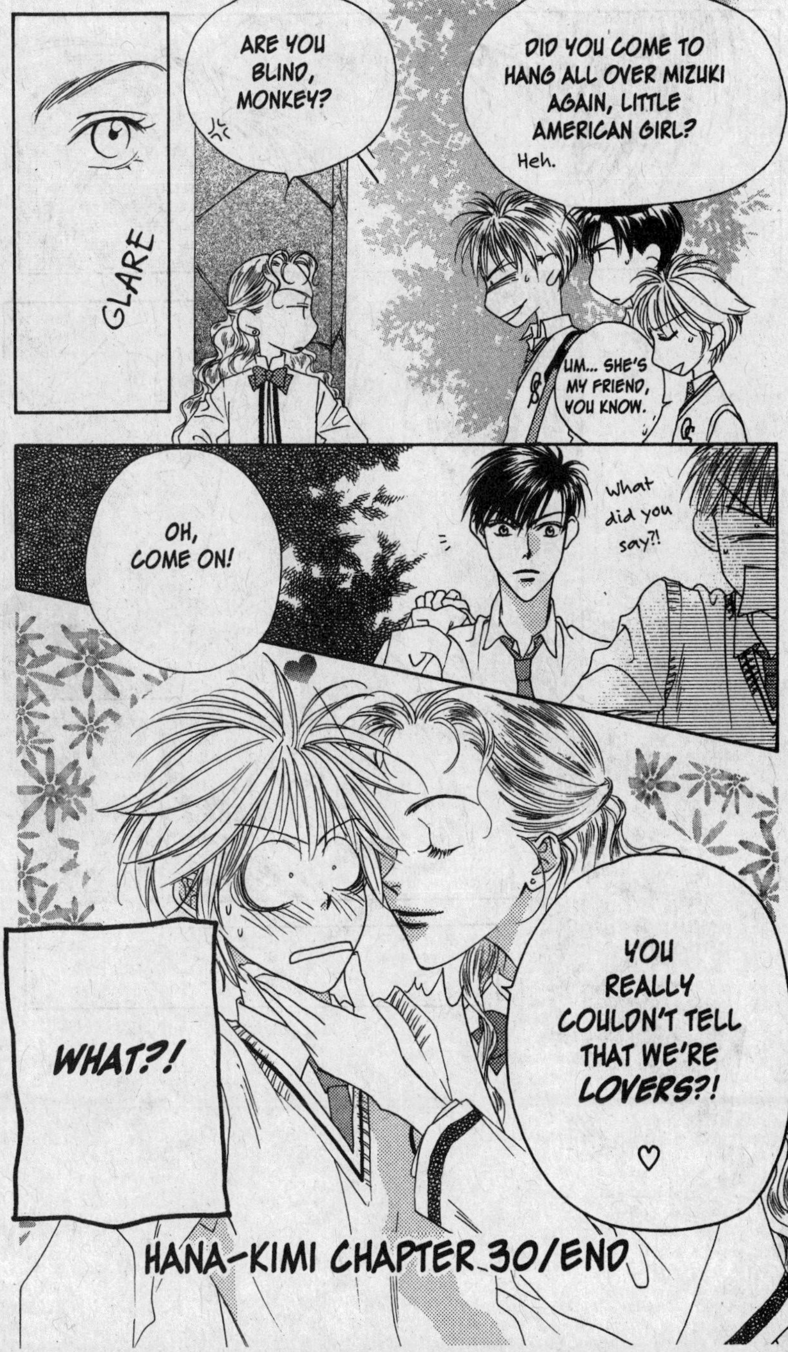
DID YOU COME TO HANG ALL OVER MIZUKI AGAIN, LITTLE AMERICAN GIRL?
Heh.
ARE YOU BLIND, MONKEY?
UM... SHE'S MY FRIEND, YOU KNOW.
GLARE
What did you say?!
OH, COME ON!
YOU REALLY COULDN'T TELL THAT WE'RE LOVERS?!
WHAT?!
HANA-KIMI CHAPTER 30/END

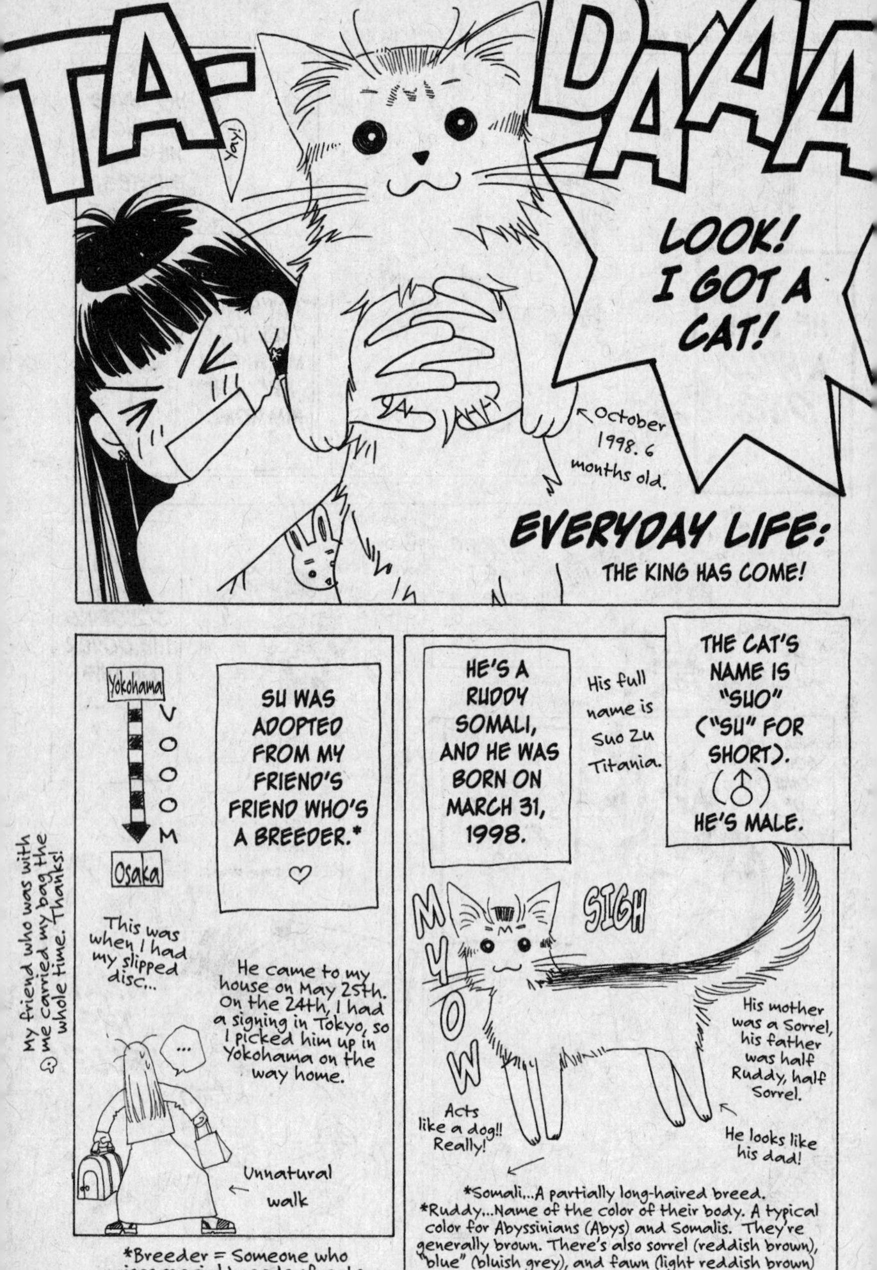
TA-DAAA
Yay!
LOOK! I GOT A CAT!
October 1998. 6 months old.
EVERYDAY LIFE:
THE KING HAS COME!
THE CAT'S NAME IS "SUO" ("SU" FOR SHORT). (♂) HE'S MALE.
His full name is Suo Zu Titania.
HE'S A RUDDY SOMALI, AND HE WAS BORN ON MARCH 31, 1998.
SIGH
MYOW
His mother was a Sorrel, his father was half Ruddy, half Sorrel.
He looks like his dad!
Acts like a dog!! Really!
*Somali...A partially long-haired breed.
*Ruddy...Name of the color of their body. A typical color for Abyssinians (Abys) and Somalis. They're generally brown. There's also sorrel (reddish brown), "blue" (bluish grey), and fawn (light reddish brown)
SU WAS ADOPTED FROM MY FRIEND'S FRIEND WHO'S A BREEDER.* ♡
Yokohama
VOOOOM
Osaka
My friend who was with me carried my bag the whole time. Thanks!
This was when I had my slipped disc...
He came to my house on May 25th. On the 24th, I had a signing in Tokyo, so I picked him up in Yokohama on the way home.
...
Unnatural walk
*Breeder = Someone who raises special breeds of cats.

ON THE FIRST DAY, HE WAS ALREADY USED TO MY HOUSE! (HA HA!)

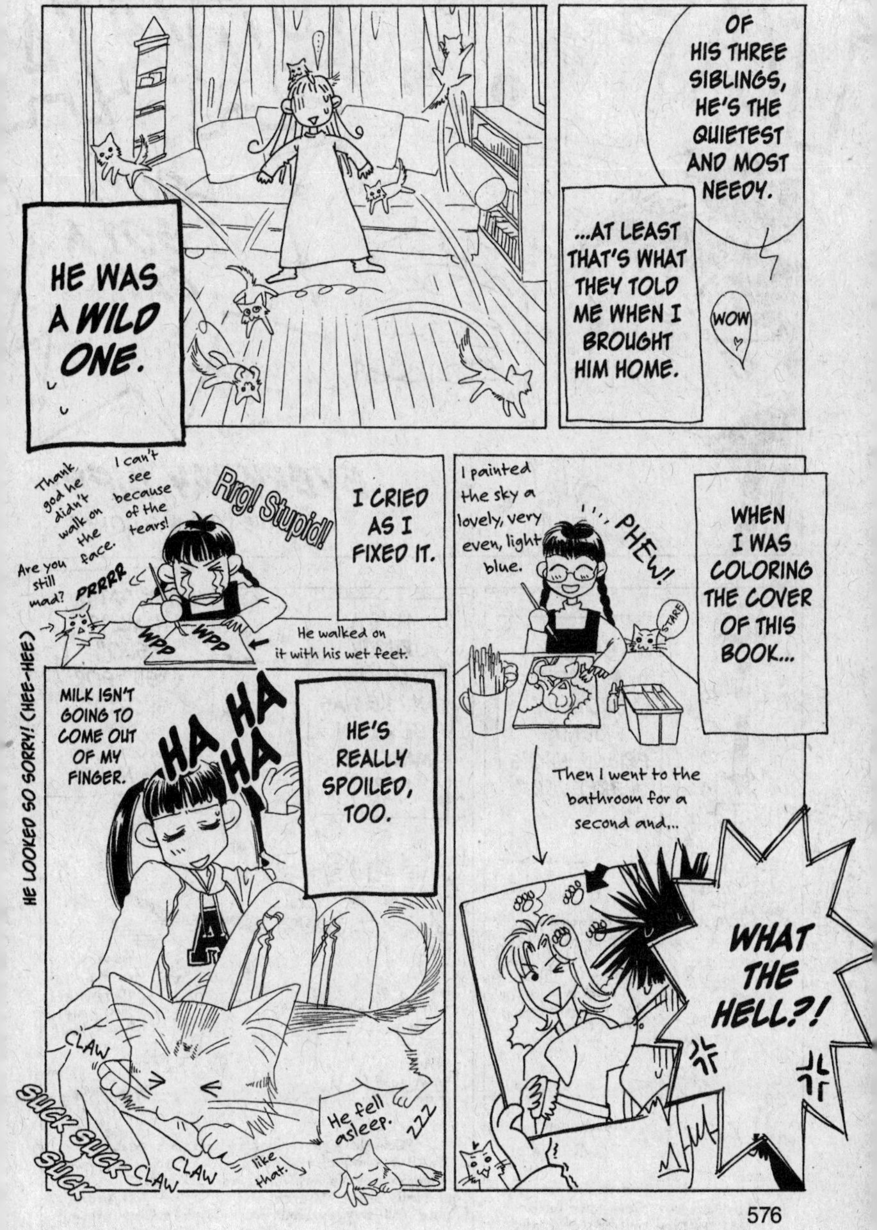

OF HIS THREE SIBLINGS, HE'S THE QUIETEST AND MOST NEEDY.
...AT LEAST THAT'S WHAT THEY TOLD ME WHEN I BROUGHT HIM HOME.
WOW
HE WAS A WILD ONE.
WHEN I WAS COLORING THE COVER OF THIS BOOK...
PHEW!!
I painted the sky a lovely, very even, light blue.
STARE
Then I went to the bathroom for a second and...
WHAT THE HELL?!
I CRIED AS I FIXED IT.
Rrg! Stupid!
I can't see because of the tears!
Thank god he didn't walk on the face.
Are you still mad?
PRRRR
WPP
WPP
He walked on it with his wet feet.
HE'S REALLY SPOILED, TOO.
HA HA HA
MILK ISN'T GOING TO COME OUT OF MY FINGER.
He fell asleep.
ZZZ
like that.
CLAW
CLAW
CLAW
SUCK SUCK SUCK

HE LOOKED SO SORRY! (CHEE-HEE)

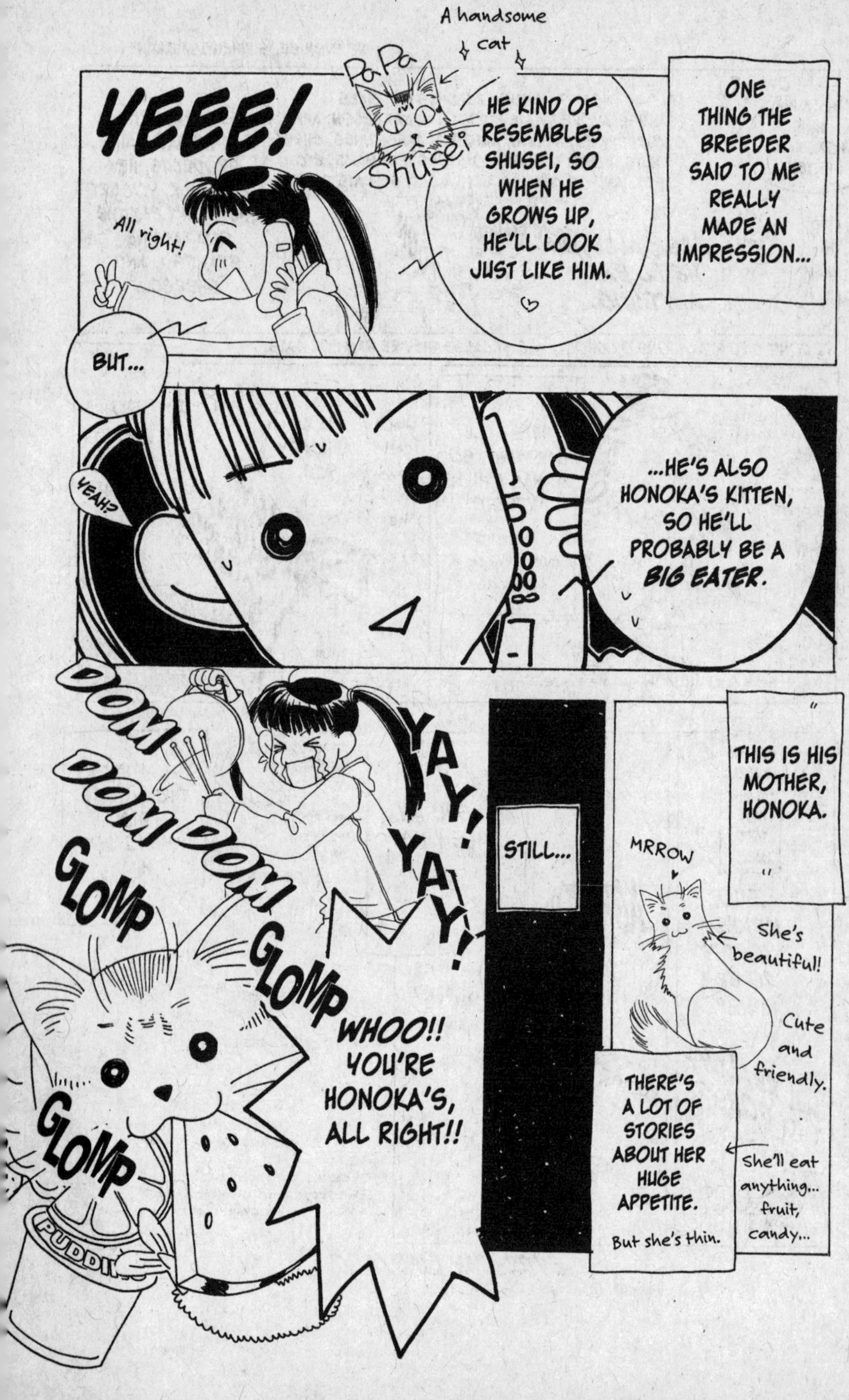
ONE THING THE BREEDER SAID TO ME REALLY MADE AN IMPRESSION...
HE KIND OF RESEMBLES SHUSEI, SO WHEN HE GROWS UP, HE'LL LOOK JUST LIKE HIM.
A handsome cat
PaPa
Shusei
YEEE!
All right!
BUT...
...HE'S ALSO HONOKA'S KITTEN, SO HE'LL PROBABLY BE A BIG EATER.
YEAH?
THIS IS HIS MOTHER, HONOKA.
MRROW
She's beautiful!
Cute and friendly.
THERE'S A LOT OF STORIES ABOUT HER HUGE APPETITE.
But she's thin.
She'll eat anything... fruit, candy...
STILL...
YAY! YAY!
DOM DOM DOM DOM
GLOMP
GLOMP
WHOO!! YOU'RE HONOKA'S, ALL RIGHT!!
GLOMP

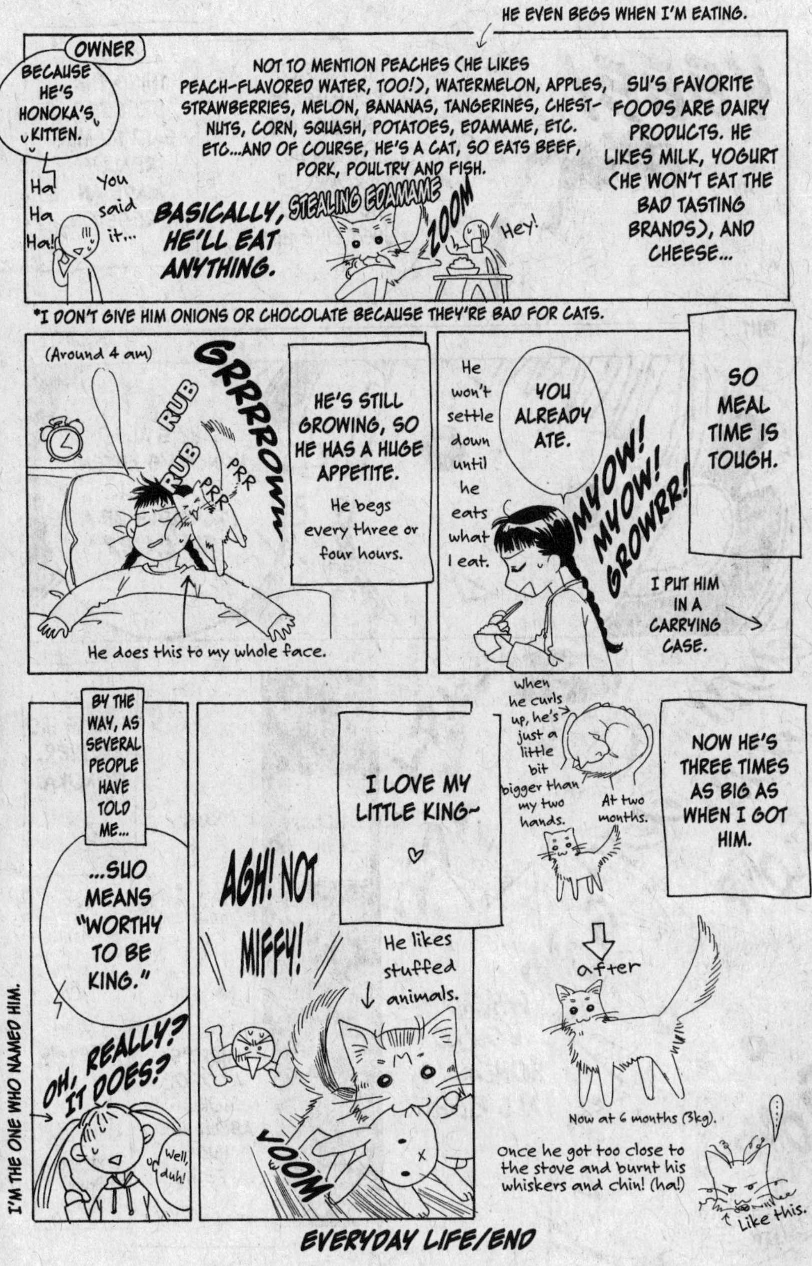
HE EVEN BEGS WHEN I'M EATING.
SU'S FAVORITE FOODS ARE DAIRY PRODUCTS. HE LIKES MILK, YOGURT (HE WON'T EAT THE BAD TASTING BRANDS), AND CHEESE...
NOT TO MENTION PEACHES (HE LIKES PEACH-FLAVORED WATER, TOO!), WATERMELON, APPLES, STRAWBERRIES, MELON, BANANAS, TANGERINES, CHESTNUTS, CORN, SQUASH, POTATOES, EDAMAME, ETC. ETC...AND OF COURSE, HE'S A CAT, SO EATS BEEF, PORK, POULTRY AND FISH.
Hey!
ZOOM
STEALING EDAMAME
BASICALLY, HE'LL EAT ANYTHING.
You said it...
Ha Ha Ha!
BECAUSE HE'S HONOKA'S KITTEN.
OWNER
*I DON'T GIVE HIM ONIONS OR CHOCOLATE BECAUSE THEY'RE BAD FOR CATS.
SO MEAL TIME IS TOUGH.
YOU ALREADY ATE.
He won't settle down until he eats what I eat.
MYOW! MYOW! GROWRR!
I PUT HIM IN A CARRYING CASE.
HE'S STILL GROWING, SO HE HAS A HUGE APPETITE.
He begs every three or four hours.
GRRRROWW
(Around 4 am)
RUB RUB
PRR PRR
He does this to my whole face.
NOW HE'S THREE TIMES AS BIG AS WHEN I GOT HIM.
When he curls up, he's just a little bit bigger than my two hands.
At two months.
after
Now at 6 months (3kg).
Once he got too close to the stove and burnt his whiskers and chin! (ha!)
!
Like this.
I LOVE MY LITTLE KING~ ♡
AGH! NOT MIFFY!
He likes stuffed animals.
ZOOM
BY THE WAY, AS SEVERAL PEOPLE HAVE TOLD ME...
...SUO MEANS "WORTHY TO BE KING."
OH, REALLY? IT DOES?
Well, duh!
I'M THE ONE WHO NAMED HIM.
EVERYDAY LIFE/END

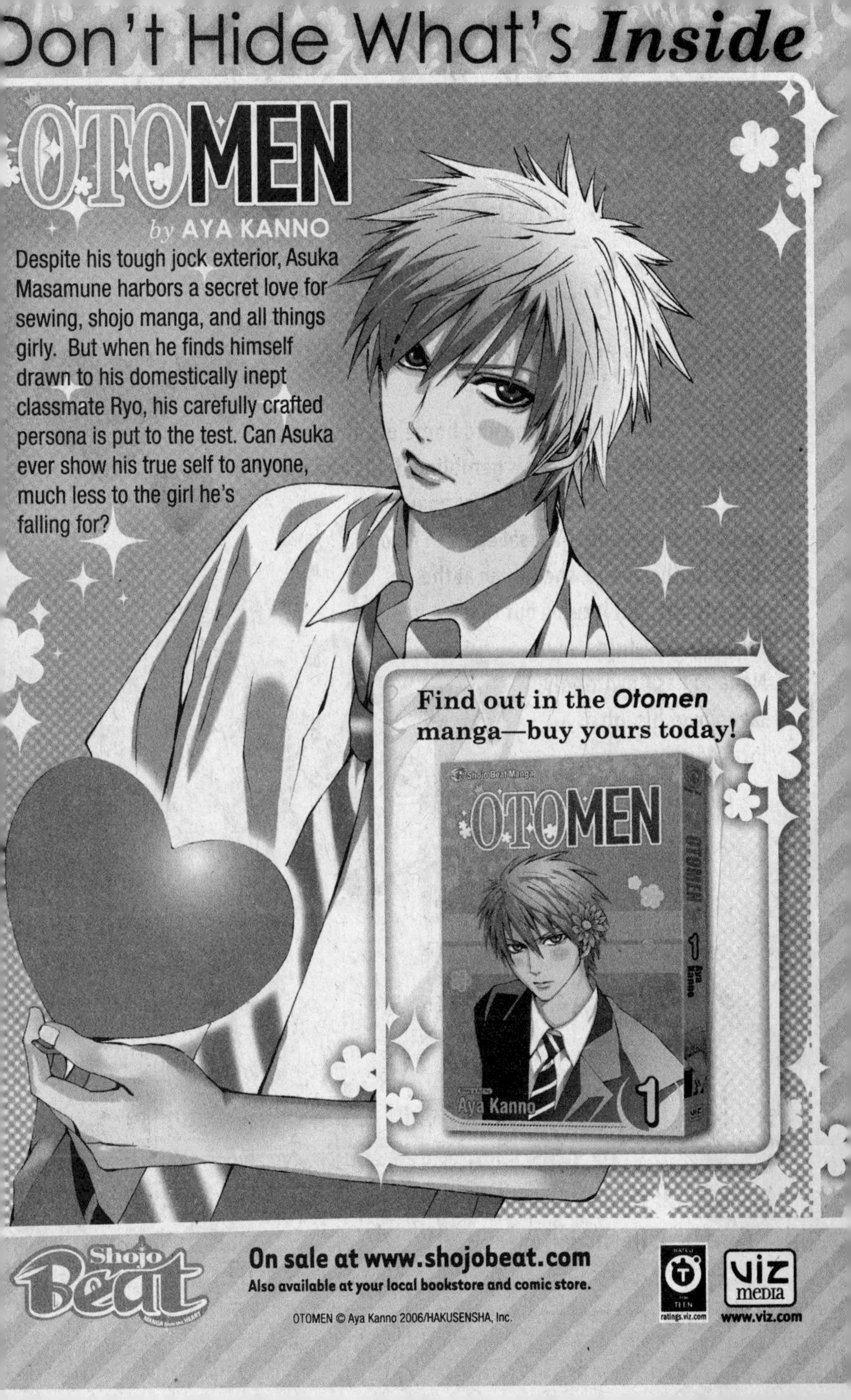
Don't Hide What's Inside
OTOMEN
by AYA KANNO
Despite his tough jock exterior, Asuka Masamune harbors a secret love for sewing, shojo manga, and all things girly. But when he finds himself drawn to his domestically inept classmate Ryo, his carefully crafted persona is put to the test. Can Asuka ever show his true self to anyone, much less to the girl he's falling for?
Find out in the Otomen manga—buy yours today!
Shojo Beat Manga
OTOMEN
Aya Kanno
1
Shojo Beat
On sale at www.shojobeat.com
Also available at your local bookstore and comic store.
OTOMEN © Aya Kanno 2006/HAKUSENSHA, Inc.
T
TEEN
ratings.viz.com
VIZ MEDIA
www.viz.com

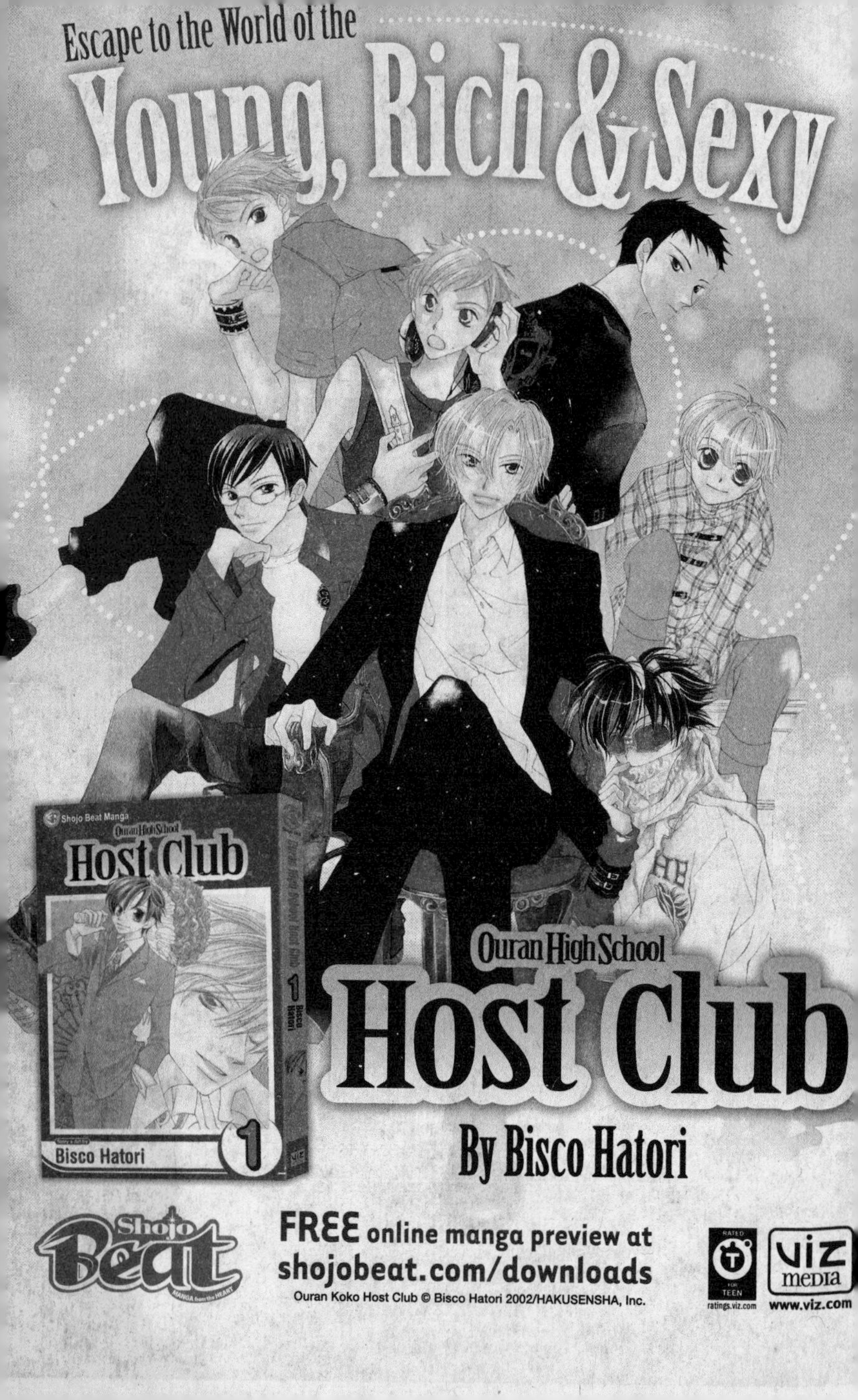
Escape to the World of the
Young, Rich & Sexy
Shojo Beat Manga
Ouran High School
Host Club
1
Bisco Hatori
Ouran High School
Host Club
By Bisco Hatori
Shojo Beat
FREE online manga preview at
shojobeat.com/downloads
Ouran Koko Host Club © Bisco Hatori 2002/HAKUSENSHA, Inc.
RATED T FOR TEEN
ratings.viz.com
VIZ MEDIA
www.viz.com

Hey! You're Reading in the Wrong Direction!

This is the ***end*** of this graphic novel!

To properly enjoy this VIZ graphic novel, please turn it around and begin reading from ***right to left.*** Unlike English, Japanese is read right to left, so Japanese comics are read in reverse order from the way English comics are typically read.

1
1
2
3
4
2
5
6
3
7
8
4
9
5
142

Follow the action this way

This book has been printed in the original Japanese format in order to preserve the orientation of the original artwork. Have fun with it!

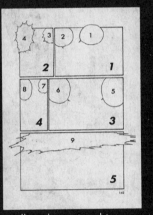